A TO Z OF
ANCIENT GREEK
AND ROMAN
WOMEN

Revised Edition

A TO Z OF WOMEN

A TO Z OF
ANCIENT GREEK
AND ROMAN
WOMEN

REVISED EDITION

MARJORIE LIGHTMAN AND
BENJAMIN LIGHTMAN

Facts On File
An imprint of Infobase Publishing

A to Z of Ancient Greek and Roman Women, Revised Edition

Copyright © 2008, 2000 by Marjorie Lightman and Benjamin Lightman

Facts On File, Inc.
An imprint of Infobase Publishing
132 West 31st Street
New York NY 10001

Library of Congress Cataloging-in-Publication Data

Lightman, Marjorie.
  A to Z of ancient Greek and Roman women / Marjorie Lightman and Benjamin Lightman.—Rev. ed.
    p. cm.—(A to Z of women)
  Rev. ed. of: Biographical dictionary of ancient Greek and Roman women. 2000.
  Includes bibliographical references and index.
  ISBN-13: 978-0-8160-6710-7
  ISBN-10: 0-8160-6710-4
  1. Women—Rome—Biography—Dictionaries. 2. Women—Greece—Biography—Dictionaries. 3. Women—
Biography—To 500—Dictionaries. I. Lightman, Benjamin. II. Title.

  HQ1136.L54 2007
  305.4092'237—dc22   2007011873

Facts On File books are available at special discounts when purchased in bulk quantities for businesses, associations, institutions, or sales promotions. Please call our Special Sales Department in New York at (212) 967-8800 or (800) 322-8755.

You can find Facts On File on the World Wide Web at http://www.factsonfile.com

Text design by Cathy Rincon
Illustrations by Melissa Ericksen

Printed in the United States of America

VB Hermitage 10 9 8 7 6 5 4 3 2 1

This book is printed on acid-free paper.

For our children

CONTENTS

PREFACE

A to Z of Ancient Greek and Roman Women, Revised Edition, was an unexpected intellectual adventure. We have extended the time period to include women of the later Roman Empire. Like many others who have studied the Greco-Roman world, we were less familiar with the fourth through sixth centuries C.E. than with earlier times, although the period had well-known names, such as Theodora and Justinian, and well-documented achievements, such as the codification of Roman statutory law. We were also reasonably well acquainted with the development of Christianity and its spread across the empire, accompanied by doctrinal disputes, political manipulation, and the flowering of early monasticism in the Egyptian desert. Nonetheless, the period remained largely peopled with a dizzying cast of rulers and usurpers, frequently in alliances and misalliances generated by the turmoil and change of repeated Germanic invasions. All of these historical characters and events, moreover, had for a backdrop the growing desperation of the West, as wealth moved to the East and the empire split into halves.

In some ways, researching the later period posed the same challenges as researching women of the Hellenistic era. As in the Hellenistic period, the later Roman Empire was a period of politically powerful women who lived complicated lives in which historical fact sometimes far exceeded the imagination of fiction. The two periods also shared a sense of possibility, change, and instability. After the death of Alexander the Great, Greek rulers spread far and wide. The eastern Mediterranean developed multiple centers of power, and, as in the later Roman Empire, the hegemonic imperative became more cultural than political. In the earlier period, hegemony followed the spread of Greek culture, which, in the later Roman Empire, was supplanted by Christianity grafted on a pervasive pagan Neoplatonism.

The periods also shared a major lack: Neither had a contemporaneous narrator whose work could shape an understanding of the era as compelling as those by Thucydides and Tacitus or as readable as Livy. For both periods, we found ourselves stitching together women's lives from disparate, sometimes hostile, often little-known sources. In the later Roman period, in contrast with the earlier, the sources were more often than not hagiographic. Buried in Christian pietistic writings, however, were Greco-Roman women whose lives had been shaped by the opportunities and limitations of society. Like a puzzle whose full picture only becomes visible when enough of the pieces are already in place, we slowly discovered the extraordinary political, social, economic, and psychological roles these women played in the development of Christianity and the evolution of the Roman state. The Augustae of the later Roman Empire were as numerous, devious, politically astute, smart, and aggressive as their counterparts of centuries ago, including the 15 women named

Cleopatra of Hellenistic Egypt. Like their more ancient sisters, these late Roman women were also interesting.

Educated, and with a degree of legal and psychological independence probably not seen again until the 19th century, they had benefited from centuries of gradual emancipation. The transformation in the Greco-Roman world over the course of centuries had been accompanied first by the spread of Greek culture and later by Roman law. From the early third century C.E. onward, Roman citizenship was widespread. Also by the third century, women's legal and economic independence protected by Roman law were commonplace. One of the unintended consequences resulting from the spread of Christianity within the context of a society organized under Roman law and custom was the extraordinary women of the late empire.

It did not take us very long to settle into a familiar working pattern and again to let ancient women dominate our daily lives and our social conversation. As with the writing of the first edition, it became a rule at dinner that neither of us could discuss the women whose biographies we were currently writing. Not only could we bore everyone with the minutiae of the research, but we often didn't agree. We had many provocative conversations that excluded everyone present except the two of us. Some of the discussions became so heated that one or another of us stormed out of the room and finished dinner from leftovers.

Although our differences tended to disappear as we actually put words to paper, the heated discussions reflected changes in scholarship, events in the larger world, and, we hope, a maturing of our own thinking. Scholarship about women and about the late empire has taken giant steps since the first edition. The contextualizing of women's lives to augment scarce sources with circumstantial probabilities has become a biographical genre. So, too, has thinking about the interpretation of the sources in light of contemporary times. Power, politics, religion, and gender have clothed the historical exploration of Greco-Roman women with modern dress.

Fortunately, we found that our earlier decisions about writing the women's biographies were still valid. All the biographies begin with a heading that provides the subject's name, birth and death dates (or where that information is unknown, the century in which she lived), and the place(s) in which she lived. We have tried to begin each biography by characterizing briefly what the subject did and, in many cases, to imagine from her perspective the situation presented by the (invariably) male sources. We have also augmented the general paucity of information about a specific life with contextual information. Sometimes we created a situational biography that rests on probabilities, but without exceeding the boundaries of the sources or the interpretations offered by modern scholars.

Following each biography we have provided the reader with the sources of our information, both ancient and modern. The Mediterranean may have been the mare nostrum for the centuries of Greco-Roman life, but the boundaries of the city-states and the Roman Empire underwent many changes. This book includes maps to orient the reader and a general bibliography to facilitate understanding of the changing ancient world. There is also an index of the women profiled. Since over the roughly 1,000 years covered by *A to Z of Ancient Greek and Roman Women, Revised Edition,* half the population was female, the more than 500 women included can only be considered representative of the millions who have been left out. These are the women for whom enough significant literary information survives to suggest the course of their lives.

As with the first edition, this new and expanded revision would have been impossible without help. Every one of our friends contributed. Frances Collin, our literary agent, was responsible for our working with Facts On File. William Zeisel, our friend, colleague, and Marjorie's partner in the consulting firm of QED Associates LLC, was at our side throughout the process of research and writing, and Ronald Cluett, a historian of the later Roman Empire, was a loyal supporter, reader, and commentator. We also wish to thank Elena Stolyarik, Robert Hoge, and Rick Schonke at the American Numismatic Society in New York City for their help and patience in finding the coins with images of the women included in this book.

In contrast with the first edition, when we did most of our research at the Library of Congress in Washington, D.C., this time we did a large part of the research on the Web. We could not have worked as efficiently and comfortably with the newly available electronic tools if our children had not been readily available for consultation and advice. However, they provided more than functional support. They kept us focused on the future generations of students who we hope will discover an interest in women of the Greco-Roman world.

—Marjorie Lightman and Benjamin Lightman
Washington, D.C.
March 2007

INTRODUCTION

Overview

When the first edition of this book was published in 2000, it was notable for identifying women's presence in every aspect of public life: not just a few women, or even only elite women, but women across the spectrum of ancient society from the Hellenic period through the high Roman Empire. The biographies confirmed, as scholars had often noted, that the Greco-Roman world was indeed gender segregated, but with women-only institutions as well as institutions that excluded women. Alongside the male-only Roman Senate were the Vestal Virgins and the sorority of the Bona Dea.

Along with gender segregation, the biographies also suggested that there was a gender balancing in which formal and informal, public and private spheres of segregated power worked in tandem to assure the needs of the society. As circumstances demanded, gender distinctions disappeared, and women took their place in all of the society's essential institutions. In the ancient city-state, with its finite resources and population, everyone was important, especially if the community supported an army of men who went to war and did not contribute productive labor, often during the critical growing season. Of necessity, in ancient life there was de facto a wider diffusion of power that included women than was incorporated into law or expressed in literature.

A to Z of Ancient Greek and Roman Women, Revised Edition, includes the formidable pagan and Christian women of the Roman Empire in the fourth through sixth centuries C.E. It extends through the reign of Theodora, who was the last Augusta to hold sway over an empire that stretched from Rome to Constantinople and Alexandria to Carthage. The biographies in this revision inform, enlarge, and, in some cases, alter the interpretation of Greco-Roman women presented in the previous edition. The new biographies emphasize the spaces between literature, law, custom, and the circumstances, personalities, and experiences that shaped the lives of individual women. They include tumultuous periods of time when the gap between socially affirmed expectations of women's behavior and the lives many women lived appears quite wide and biographies from other times when there is a greater congruence.

Not surprisingly, war, natural disasters, political instability, economic crisis, and the character of a woman's father, son, or husband were instrumental in shaping the possibilities of a woman's life. However, just as important was the dominating power of the region. Hellenic, Hellenistic, Roman, and Greco-Roman society offered women different kinds of opportunities and placed them under different limitations. Distinctive codes of law, a wide variety of sacrosanct social traditions, and the transformative religious experience of early Christianity continually reformulated the ways in which women understood themselves, their responsibilities, and their obligations over the course of the millennium.

The Roman Empire

Roman rule provided a political overlay that carried with it a unifying patina of Greco-Roman life, law, and culture. Greco-Roman culture, which was a dynamic mix of Hellenistic traditions and ideas with the institutions and statutory law of the Latin-speaking Roman conquerors, governed for six centuries—more than half the millennium covered by this edition. Greek culture, however, long preceded Roman rule, as the biographies of women from the coast of Asia Minor, the Aegean Islands, and mainland Greece amply demonstrate. Greek culture followed Alexander the Great, his generals, and the extraordinary women around them throughout the eastern half of the Mediterranean in the fourth century B.C.E. After Alexander's death, Egypt fell to Greek domination. The Greek women who ruled and coruled through the Hellenistic period made Egypt a competing power with Rome for control of the Mediterranean until the end of the last century B.C.E.

By the second century B.C.E., Rome controlled the western Mediterranean and, at the end of the first century B.C.E., after civil wars and a final confrontation with Cleopatra VII in Egypt, the entire region. The Roman civil wars opened opportunities for women, and the first two centuries of the empire were a "golden age" for Greco-Roman women, especially those from the propertied classes, who attained a heretofore unknown degree of personal autonomy. Women's increased personal autonomy and economic presence continued to expand, even during the economic chaos that followed and despite the repeated efforts of imperial reform. As imperial rule changed into autocratic power, women began to assume the trappings of imperial authority.

The new biographies focus on the transformative centuries in which the empire was beset with Germanic invasions and declining productivity and population, especially in the West and North Africa. The biographies reveal the degree to which scarcity dominated ancient life. Neither food, labor, or any other necessary goods of consumption had a large enough surplus for society to ever rest secure about its basic needs. The inefficiencies of production and distribution, especially in agriculture, left the cities, even at the height of imperial Rome, always vulnerable to shortages. The dependence on slave labor, moreover, further increased the inefficiency in production. Not only was slave labor expensive to maintain, but the threat of uprisings among the enslaved further diverted limited resources. The combination of economic inefficiencies and a slave culture touched relationships from marriage to inheritance and influenced women's economic independence and political aspirations.

Scarcity also afflicted the invading German tribes, who sometimes needed grain more than gold. No amount of foraging could sufficiently feed the traveling populations and cities could often buy off the threat of siege with food. However, neither Italy nor Greece produced a regular surplus of food. Italy was not fully self-sufficient in grain after the second century B.C.E. The breadbaskets of the ancient world were North Africa and Egypt, which, after having centuries of absentee landlords, rapacious administrators, and natural disasters, were also no longer able to feed the empire by the fifth century C.E. Augustine, who was bishop of Hippo, near Carthage, lamented the dimension and consequence of change in North African agriculture. Where once there had been abundance there was only subsistence farming, and the mighty monuments of Roman urban life, the baths, the roads, the libraries, and the temples, were falling into decay. Even books were no longer easily accessible.

The disruptive presence of large numbers of poor people became a new reality of city life as land collected in the hands of the elite. The ideal of the independent citizen farmer became an increasingly distant mirage, while the urban poor multiplied and landed estates grew larger, embracing whole villages of free, freed, and enslaved workers. By the fifth and sixth centuries, chronic depopulation compounded by repeated invasions resulted in the forced bonding of laborers to the land. Augustine's correspondence with the younger Melania and her mother, Albina, as well as the wealthy poet, Proba, illustrates the vast gulf between rich and poor, especially in the countryside. It also documents the existence of large numbers of women landholders, who were among the wealthiest Romans of the time.

Christianity

Christianity was for women, perhaps far more than for men, a religion accompanied by social revolution. In *A to Z of Ancient Greek and Roman Women, Revised Edition,* the biographies of women who were early converts to Christianity suggest the trajectory of their spiritual journeys, their role in Christianizing the senatorial classes and in providing a financial base for the emerging episcopate. Above all, however, the new biographies detail the relationship between being Greco-Roman and becoming Christian. The choices women made rested on the gender expectations of the Greco-Roman society that nurtured them and the increasing autonomy allowed them. The Christian religious transformation they experienced led to a new kind of individual and personal quest that often proved to be incompatible with the historical, gendered, and corporate culture of the pagan world. Some of the biographies describe women's close relationships with eminent men of the church. Bishops, priests, and monks, who were often financially dependent on the largesse of the wealthy, found their most likely benefactors and friends among celibate and ascetically inclined women. Together, they shared a spiritual and intellectual search for salvation. Many wound up living side-by-side in communal houses and monasteries, which the women often had built and endowed.

At the opening of the third century, the Christian woman Perpetua was martyred in Carthage. Her prison journal is among the earliest and most extensive writing extant by a Christian or pagan woman. In her ecstatic and personal passion she had visions and spoke in tongues. She personified the quest of individual women who, during the subsequent centuries, were attracted to celibacy and an ascetic lifestyle. The pleas of her father and love for her nursing child could not deter her from a willing death. She had turned from her family defined by blood to her new family of fellow Christians joined in their search for a Christian salvation.

The individuality of the Christian pursuit of grace affected the family, which, along with land, were the twin pillars of ancient stability. Pagan Greco-Roman society construed the responsibilities and obligations of the landed family to extend beyond the nuclear core to include a host of dependents, from poorer relatives to slaves, freed slaves, and their respective kin across the generations. Insofar as wealth carried inherited obligations and responsibilities for the larger group, family wealth had a corporate character.

Marriage in propertied families was a functional arrangement intended to produce a new generation and bring in new wealth. Elite marriage was monogamous and divorce was possible. By definition, marriage was a contract that defined property rights and their intergenerational transfer; companionship, caring, and passion were not part of the contract or even necessary conditions for a successful marriage. There was no social role for a never-married woman of a landed family, and at all times and in all places women from propertied families not only married but were expected to bear children, except for the rare woman who became a full-time priestess or spent 30 years as a Vestal Virgin.

Women, however, were not necessarily powerless pawns in the marriage market. Depending on their age, their wealth, and their political position, they could and did bargain on their own behalf. While marital negotiations would seem a familiar part of history among the imperial family or the very rich, less familiar is the routine presence of complicated betrothal agreements among the less powerful or wealthy. Cicero's letters to Atticus, who was a friend and facilitator during Cicero's divorce from his wife, Terentia, provided an unusually intimate glimpse of divorce in accord with the conditions of a betrothal contract agreed upon more than 20 years earlier. The letters offer further insight into the contractual discussions for Cicero's second marriage, to a far younger woman whose dowry he sorely needed. No less interesting are the letters that delineated the limits of his authority over his daughter Tullia and her choice of partners, or the conditions of the betrothal, especially when he, like many Greco-Roman men, was in a distant place of the empire while his wife and agent attended family affairs at home.

The innumerable papyri fragments of marriage contracts affirm the hard negotiations that characterized what each partner contributed to the marriage and expected to take back in case of divorce. By and large, however, under Greek as well as Roman law, noncitizens and the poor had either no right, or only a limited right, for a contractual marital relationship. Nor was a contract necessary. Epitaphs across the Mediterranean provide extensive evidence of long and loving noncontractual marriages. These relationships also evidence pride in women's virtues no different from those celebrated among the elite. Marital relationships that lasted unto death were lauded, and poor as well as rich women were everywhere praised for modesty, fidelity, silence, and fecundity.

However democratic and widespread the virtues of womanhood, it was always better to be a rich woman than a poor man and, better still, a very rich woman. Simply said, for the ancients wealth was evidence of goodness. It isn't that the ancient world was the epitome of market capitalism; rather wealth was evidence of good standing with the gods, whose favor everyone sought. Until the rise of Christianity, preordained fate governed life, and there was neither escape nor forgiveness. The gods were not omniscient beings endowed with mercy of the Judeo-Christian tradition, but rather the uncaring elemental powers of nature—the earth, water, sky, and air. Put another way, the gods did not exercise control over the forces of nature; they were the forces of nature. When the poets spoke of Mars in the arms of Venus they were not speaking metaphorically about love taming war but quite literally about Mars, the god of war who was war, and Venus, both love and the goddess of love.

For the most part, the rich and the poor, those with a marriage contract and those who simply lived together as husband and wife, all regarded children as a gift of the gods. Without a clear vision of an afterlife, the security of the living was best assured by caring for ancestors. Children were their parents' assurance of proper rites for the dead. They could make the dead rest in peace and sustain the honor of the family in life. Children were a woman's crowning glory, and for a woman who

was not an ascetically inclined Christian, fertility always was the central mystery of ancient life.

Women's ability to bear children, however, was an uncertain gift of the gods and a mixed blessing. The reality of medicine and medical knowledge left pregnancy, childbirth, and its aftermath fraught with danger. In the early empire, the state's efforts to encourage families recognized women who bore three children with full and independent control over their property. It was a powerful prod that over time became a status obtainable by purchase. In the centuries of peaceful empire, the death rate for women in childbirth was possibly higher than that of soldiers in battle, and the purchase of independent control over property a safer road to a preeminent symbol of status.

Christianity changed the world for women. Asceticism and monasticism held a particular appeal. Women's engagement with the individual, ecstatic, and spiritual side of Christianity made them among the first adopters of the new asceticism that began to sweep the Christian world in the fourth century. From Syncletica in Egypt to Macrina in Asia Minor, women sought to free themselves from the burdens of secular life in pursuit of a union with God. They founded communal houses for women who never married and for widows who refused to remarry, used their wealth to establish the beginnings of Christian public charitable services, and developed friendships with each other and with male clerics that would have been unlikely in the differently sexualized pagan world.

Christianity offered women their first opportunity to live socially sanctioned lives outside Greco-Roman gendered roles. For poor women, celibacy offered a freedom from sexual abuse that was as common on the streets as water from the fountains of Rome, and for the slave woman, the dream of a better life after death. It also posed a revolutionary threat to the elite. The chronic underpopulation for which women were blamed and imperial policy vainly sought to reverse was heightened by the emergence of an ascetic, celibate lifestyle. Women celibates not only countered imperial efforts to increase families, but also roiled secular politics, divided families, and engaged women in the public life of the empire as never before.

Pagans viewed Christian women who chose celibacy and either gave away their wealth or used it to enhance the church as willfully squandering precious corporate assets that rightfully belonged to the family. Well into the fifth and sixth centuries, mixed families of Christians and pagans were still not unusual. Conflicts within the family over a woman's use of personal wealth are a recurring motif in the biographies of ascetic women who corresponded with Jerome, the noted churchman. The biographies of women like the elder Melania reveal the kind of lengthy negotiations and arrangements within propertied families that accompanied a woman's decision to pursue an ascetic lifestyle.

Women made different decisions about the style of their asceticism. Some women, like Syncletica, simply gave away their wealth and lived as a recluse in the Egyptian desert; others, like Melania, Paula, the Augusta Eudoxia, Olympias, and Egeria, followed a different path. They settled a portion of their wealth on relatives who disagreed with their calling. This was especially evident among the women in Rome, who also sought to avoid court-mandated settlements or the appointment of trustees. In further contrast with Syncletica, these women actively engaged in international debates about the nature of Christ and the position of Mary. Most important, however, they kept under their control a sufficient portion of their wealth to found monasteries and travel widely and often, including trips to Palestine. With surprising frequency, they also supported male religious colleagues whose letters have survived to tell us about them.

The wealthy women who became active Christians before the Council of Chalcedon in 451 C.E. joined a heterodox church in which doctrinal controversy was ongoing. With the Chalcedon compromise, orthodoxy was defined, but not everywhere accepted. The Eastern part of the empire, in particular, remained heavily Monophysite and supported the single and divine nature of Christ. Imperial women were active supporters of the debates over the nature of Christ, and Theodora was in large part responsible for the establishment of a Monophysite

episcopate that led to the final schism with the West. No less controversial was the role of Mary. Her identity as the Mother of God, in contrast to mother of the human Christ child, opened the way for women to claim their place in the church. It erased the "sin" of Eve and was a political position jealously guarded by the imperial women, especially Pulcheria, who rested her imperial authority on her celibacy and devotion to Mary.

Ancient Sources

In *A to Z of Ancient Greek and Roman Women, Revised Edition,* unlike a monograph about a single woman or a group portrait of women during a particular period and place, the entries range across the sweep of Greek and Roman history. This inclusiveness of time and space emphasizes the unending cycles of war, the repeated political uprisings, the democracy of natural disaster, as well as the relatively short intervals of peace and prosperity. The more than 500 biographies of women included in this book also reveal that networks among elite women and between women and men wove a web of relationships through society's public and private affairs. The biographies make clear that affairs of state moved in lockstep with the affairs of the family and religion and together they shaped a social order that was hierarchical in status, wealth, and power, but also gender inclusive.

This edition follows the first edition and draws on information about women from the extant Greek and Latin literature. Some of the ancient authors are more familiar to modern readers than others: the histories of Herodotus; the letters, speeches, and essays of Cicero; the multivolume history of Rome by Livy; the sophisticated commentary of Tacitus; the multitudinous works of Plutarch; and the letters of the younger Pliny. Less-familiar works include the histories written by Polyibus, Sallust, and Dio Cassius, and the women described by Athenaeus or the Greco-Roman women included by Josephus in his history of the Jews. This expanded edition also includes church historians like Eusebius, some of the work by Tertullian, Sozomen, Ambrose, and the ecclesiastical history of Socrates. Also included is information from Gregory of Nyssa, who wrote about his sister Macrina, and the churchmen who maintained extensive correspondences with women, such as John Chryostom with Olympias, Augustine with a number of women, and, above all, Jerome who maintained decades-long correspondences with women in the West and East.

About some centuries and many places we have no literary information. What we have, however, reinforces the sense of a shared body of stories and historical references to places, events, customs, and people that formed a continuous tradition over a very long period of time. Ancient authors, some of whom wrote hundreds of years after the events they narrated, tantalize the modern reader with allusions that assume familiarity with people and events, especially women to whom they may briefly refer. The inference that a woman may have been well known to her contemporaries and far less incidental to the narrated events than would appear highlights both the frustration of limited information and the danger of unexamined modern assumptions and easy generalizations.

The entries in the expanded edition include rich women, poor women, and those in between. Some were illiterate and many were well educated. Some traveled; others never left home. Some were slaves. Others owned slaves, male and female. Everyone faced the immediacy of death from violence, accident, or infection. The classes of society that experienced the greatest insecurities of life in the ancient world, however, are also those who have left the least-informative written records. In the literature, even in the best-informed periods, women from nonelite backgrounds appear most often when they amassed wealth and influenced men and events. The information about these women rarely includes the identity of their blood kin, although they may claim an elite non–Greco-Roman parentage. On occasion there may be mention of a mother's name or a city of origin, but the woman is far more likely to be described by her physical charms and her relationships with important men.

In contrast with the literary sources, thousands of epitaphs and donations to temples and other religious sites document the names of slaves and freedmen and women. They can also be identified in business contracts and court cases, as well as in fragments of personal correspondence that have been found among the papyri, remains from the ancient garbage heaps in the sands of Egypt. This book, however, uses only literary sources since with rare exception the inscriptions are fragmentary and lack the coherence of the traditional literature.

The surviving literature not only reflects the viewpoint of men, and elite men at that, but also of the victor in the rise and fall of ancient city-states and empires. Homer, whose works were the literary fountainhead of the Greeks, wrote the story of the Greek victory over Troy. Virgil, writing in the first century C.E. under Augustus, provided a Latin extension of the Trojan warriors to account for the glory of imperial Rome. Livy's history of Rome, only parts of which survive, was a celebration of Augustus's new empire. The gloss of the victor becomes even more evident with the advent of Christian histories. The church history of Eusebius, the letters of Jerome, the writings of Gregory of Nyssa, John Chrysostom, and Augustine were Christocentric at a time when Neoplatonism still dominated Greco-Roman culture.

The surviving literature has been estimated as about one-tenth of the literature that was generally available in the fourth through sixth centuries. In addition to literature, only a fraction of the records from the state bureaucracy, ranging from tax receipts to correspondence, such as the letters between the younger Pliny and the emperor Trajan, still exist. Also lost has been much of the record-keeping from a millennium of trans-Mediterranean business that involved corporate entities as well as individual merchants. Fortunately, the garbage heaps of Egypt have provided contracts for marriages and wills from at least one place in the empire.

Despite ample evidence in the surviving literature written by men that elite women were as likely to be as literate as men, especially from the Hellenistic period onward, with the exception of some poetry by Sappho and a young Latin poet Sulpicia, no pagan literature written by women has survived. In the early Christian literature, the *Passion of Perpetua* written at the opening of the third century c.e., the sayings of Syncletica, and the poetry by the Augusta Eudocia and Proba in the fifth century c.e. make an only slightly less scanty collection. More available are letters written to women by men which reference the women's part of the correspondence. In the pre-Christian literature of the first century b.c.e., Cicero had a voluminous correspondence that included women. Among Christians, Jerome, Chrysostom, Augustine, Gregory of Nyssa, and numerous men who were bishops of Rome, Antioch, Alexandria, Constantinople, Tyre, and Carthage had similarly lengthy correspondences with Christian women.

The ancient world's diverse literature was more readily available than one would expect. In every city or ancient town there were places where the illiterate could find writers for their personal and business needs. There were also scriptoria, often in the household of wealthy people with literary pretensions, in which the business of publishing was carried out with copyists preparing books for distribution and sale. The buying and selling of literary papyrus rolls was widespread. Augustine lamented the decline in his regular supply of new "books" from Rome as the Germanic invasions increasingly strangled business in the early fifth century. The great library in Alexandria, which prided itself on acquiring a copy of every new book published, had 800,000 papyrus rolls in its collection before it burned in the sixth century c.e. Seven libraries dotted the city of Rome, which was a tribute to its literate population and leadership of the empire. Ancient public and private libraries collected poetry, plays, history, philosophy, letters, journals, travels, medicine, mathematics, astrology, and astronomy. Over the centuries, however, wars, natural disasters, and outbreaks of religious fanaticism destroyed them. The monumental arches that mark the entrance to the ancient libraries of Pergamum and Ephesus, near the coast of modern Turkey, suggest the richness of a lost literature.

Since the publication of the first edition of this book, a new poem by Sappho has been uncovered, and while it provides no startling information, it adds to the body of literature by pagan women. More may appear in the future, especially women's correspondence. It is the absence of women's private correspondence that perhaps most hinders writing the biographies of women. The letters that John Chrysostom, the exiled bishop of Constantinople, wrote Olympias after she had left her life in the capital to wander in Asia Minor beg for the letters she wrote him. How can we definitively know whether or not Macrina was the intellectual muse her brother, Gregory of Nyssa, claimed, if we have none of her letters to him?

This new edition includes more than 500 women. While this is not all the women, or even most of the women we know about from the Greco-Roman world, it is most of the women who appear in literature and about whom we have something meaningful to say. Evenly distributed over time, 500 women would be about 40 women per century. Few would argue the foolhardiness of a general discussion of Western women in the 19th or 20th centuries on the basis of 40 per century. As it happens, ancient sources about women are not equally distributed across time or geography. Information about women tends to cluster. Tacitus, for example, focused on the Julio-Claudian women in the first century c.e. This period was also the high point of Latin poetry, in which Ovid addressed women and love and Horace satirized the life of the upper classes. The historians Suetonius and Livy contribute further information about this period. Similarly, women in the late republic and the civil war years were a part of Cicero's voluminous correspondence, the subjects of the first generation of Latin love poets like Catullus, and were also reported on by Livy and Suetonius.

Modern Scholarship

The challenge to modern scholarship has been not only to understand the lives of ancient women through the lens of our own times, but also to understand the ancients within their times. Since the late 18th and early 19th centuries, when modern scholarship about antiquity began, the task has been complicated by the gendered character of our own society, on one hand, and the ancients' efforts to extract moral instruction from history, on the other hand. In consequence, nuanced discussions about gender, especially about women, have rarely appeared. More often the modern discussion of ancient works has been about what women ought to be and do and how they have conformed to or deviated from prescribed behavior. Until quite recently, even the discussion of prescribed behavior has been rather two-dimensional. Until the last decades, a sense that flesh-and-blood women, who lived through often-difficult times and made painful decisions, were a major part of antiquity has remained largely absent from the scholarship. The general lack of examination of women has been attributed to an absence of information. Ancient history has always suffered from insufficient or incomplete information. In the case of women, the very real lacunae have been accepted as reason enough to largely ignore them. As the discipline of women's history has matured, however, the focus on women has suggested new approaches to the traditional literature and new insights.

Intergenerational time lines that move families from father to son, for example, ignore the importance of alliances between mothers and daughters, both of whom could be married women bearing children at the same time. The mother and grown daughter alliance, which was possibly ancient women's most powerful emotional and frequent political bond, linked families and the next generation of children. Cross-generational alliances could include sisters, cousins, and extended kin to further confuse neat male-based generational descent. Moreover, through death and divorce, women and men often married more than once. Women, however, tended to marry men closer to their own age as they grew older, gaining independence over wealth and bargaining power within their marriage even as their multiple marriages also added other complications to male-centered generational lines.

Previously neglected literature that was considered less interesting, less reliable, and less important by earlier generations has proved to include useful references to lives women led. Scholars have begun to look more closely at the purposeful portrayal of women in the moral instruction through historical example that characterized the works of Greco-Roman historians and led to their often two-dimensional female portraits. They have begun the exploration of powerful female cliques bound into networks of relationships affirmed by kinship, friendship, religious beliefs, and political goals. Often multigenerational and sometimes in opposing political camps, the cliques could be deadly enemies of one another, no less violent than the men around them, and often using the men around them as public ciphers for political power. In the Hellenistic and imperial periods, the groupings of women who surrounded the various claimants to the throne vied for power and wealth that could award them control over a weak emperor or landed estates so large as to equal a semiautonomous satrapy.

Scholars have also begun to reexamine ancient speeches to juries, whose intent to defame and persuade sometimes only confirmed contemporary prejudice. There are also polemical tracts written and circulated for political ends. These include celebrations of patronage as well as vitriolic attacks, both of which suggest that the worthiness of women subjects had some relationship with their power. Finally, the early Christian theologians had a number of women friends. The relationships between these men and women, which possibly would have been less likely among pagans, speak to the change of values for women introduced with Christianity and also for women's use of the new opportunities.

An important aspect of modern scholarship has been to develop authoritative texts and to assess the relative authenticity of information from ancient written sources. Not all ancient authors have been accorded equal status. The scholarship has distinguished between what amounts to ancient historical gossip, repeated by ancient authors often hundreds of years after the event, from reliable observation and commentary. At the extremes, few would confuse Thucydides' work about the war between Athens and Sparta with Procopius's vitriolic attack on the Augusta Theodora. At least in part, however, praise of Thucydides has rested on his subject matter. He, and his most highly regarded fellow ancient commentators, addressed the triad of public honor, wealth, and position that formed the playing field of ancient elite male life. The focus on men, on war, and on politics also framed a vision of ancient life that most comfortably agreed with the European imagination of earlier centuries about what was important to know about the Greeks and Romans.

In no small part, the ancient men and values lauded affirmed the political and gender divisions of European society during the centuries when modern scholarship came into being and elevated the study of Greece and Rome to define the modern, educated man. However familiar the ancient male values appeared to Europeans, it was nonetheless a narrow vision that equated history with the political evolution of the senate, the assembly, and the Areopagus, or in modern terms, Congress and Parliament, and also elevated great men to the status of historical inevitability. Well into the 1960s, scholarship posed little challenge to the ancients' statements, particularly about women. It accepted unexamined the ancient assessment of women as the less important background of a warrior culture. Praise of virtuous women was reiterated and women's immorality and decadence accepted as a causative factor for the failure of public institutions and the breakdown of the family. Impossibly virtuous, and equally impossibly infamous, ancient women continued to dot the scholarly literature and to affirm male virtue or act as the harbingers of dire events to come.

The 21st century, however, is in some ways more like the ancient world than were the late 18th through 19th centuries when modern Greco-Roman scholarship began to assume its privileged position among the educated. It is also critically different. As in the ancient world, we have come to accept a broad sexual palette that includes serial marriage, live-in and live-out relationships of all kinds, and many variations of short-term liaisons. A quick glance at any current magazine demonstrates that in the 21st century a woman can be accepted in the "best" society unashamedly unmarried, pregnant, and with a string of lovers to her credit. So, too, the ancients had a broad sexual palette.

In the West, this broad sexual palette is situated within a nation's civil code of law. In the third

century C.E., the emperor Caracalla declared that, with minor exceptions, all people living under Roman rule were Roman citizens. For the first time in history, there was a uniform civil code in which the same family and personal law defined women's status across the Mediterranean. Between the third and sixth centuries, the statutory law was expanded, modified, and reinterpreted. The emperor Justinian ordered a review and synthesis of the subsequent centuries of conflicting edicts, laws, and decisions. Theodora played a part in the elimination of cross-class prohibitions on contractual marriage, made prostitution illegal in Constantinople, and limited the rights of slave-owners and employers to force women to perform in the theater. The sixth-century compilation affirmed that marriage was a monogamous and consensual contract, albeit a special contract. As with every contract it incorporated the conditions of its own dissolution, not unlike contemporary prenuptial agreements. Marriage without a formal contract was considered equally binding under the law and socially acceptable. In a manner reminiscent of present-day circumstances, people who lived together and presented themselves as a couple were regarded as such, with all the complicated claims on joint property if they separated.

The Greco-Roman world, like the contemporary one, may have had both a multiplicity of legitimate sexual relationships and, after the third century, a uniform code of civil law that governed marriage. In the ancient world, however, class always trumped law. The ancients categorized women by birth, wealth, and family affiliation. At all times and in all places, Greco-Roman society was a slave culture and the sexual behavior of slaves belonged to property law. Women slaves could be used by their owners or by anyone who had the owner's permission, for any sexual purpose. Sex with a slave woman had no legal or moral consequences for the man, providing it was in accord with property law. Children born to slave women increased the numbers of slaves a man owned and enhanced his capital worth. Poor free or freedwomen, on the other hand, probably lived with the perpetual threat of sexual violence, since men often failed to distinguish the exact status of a woman especially when in search of sex. Without wealth or a man to protect them, they may have well suffered more than slaves.

Except when historians like Livy sought to make a moral point of civic virtue and used the behavior of a slave or freedwoman as the object of their case, it was elite women who have appeared in this male-dominated history. It was with elite women that men generally conspired in the endless cycles of political intrigue that engaged every generation. When, however, men were charged with treason, their elite women coconspirators were more often than not charged with the sexual crime of adultery. For the ancients, there appears an equation between an elite woman's sexual behavior and treason to the state. Women's adultery was neither a property violation as with slaves, nor a violation of personal male honor. Adultery among elite married women was a dangerous public act that challenged power and threatened the stability of the state.

Conclusion

Perspective is possibly the foremost issue in shaping ancient biographical information about a woman into a narrative that speaks to modern audiences. Perspective faces the challenge of information from ancient sources that were overwhelmingly male and for whom the questions of the contemporary world were unknown. In *A to Z of Ancient Greek and Roman Women, Revised Edition,* an effort has been made to view events, people, and circumstances from the perspective of the woman who is the subject of the biography. In a situation where a group of women have participated in the same historical events, each biography attempts to shift into the unique perspective of the woman subject.

The effort to speak through the eyes of the woman subject about events in her life from fragmentary sources and at a moment in time she could not have imagined asks the reader to turn an understanding of the past almost on its head. The biographies start with the woman in the story and not with the men around her. The biographies describe what she did and seek to portray the reasonableness of her behavior within the circumstances.

The entries pay less attention to either the vitriolic attacks for licentious behavior or praise for passive virtues. Instead, the focus is on what a woman did, who she was, and what were the consequences of her actions. These questions open the way to understanding the choices she faced and the limitations she suffered. When situated within the broadest possible historical context, the entries invite readers to contemplate the variety and quality of ancient women's lives.

At least as difficult to communicate as perspective are the pervasive and powerful assumptions about a world foreign to the modern mind. Ancient women were no more or less rational than their contemporary sisters. However, the physical, social, economic, and political environment of the ancient world rested on ideas about life and death, the gods, politics, geography, power, and relationships among men and between men and women that bear little similarity with our own. The Hellenistic women rulers, the politically ambitious women of Rome, the imperial women who ruled in the names of their sons, and the women who chose to become ascetics were responding to circumstances and conditions that, even if we have the best available information, would still be strange to contemporary sensibilities.

In many biographies, there also is a very immediate sense of the fragility of life and the pervasive underpopulation that characterized even the wealthiest periods in the ancient world. Women's lives were dominated by this fragility. Women watched children die seemingly almost as frequently as they experienced their births. Nonetheless, women guarded the city walls when the men went to fight. Women organized households on estates in the countryside, which were the center of production for goods and services all though the millennium, and in the cities, Roman matronae proudly assumed responsibility for the multigenerational households that incorporated living and working, poor and rich, free and slave.

In an effort to communicate more clearly, the language used in this book to describe women's status, relationships, and honors may differ slightly from older translations of ancient authors and familiar modern historians. The entries refer to a woman as a "ruler" or "woman ruler" or "coruler" rather than queen which carries historical meanings not necessarily a part of the ancient world. In addition, titles such as Augusta are untranslated because they have no exact modern equivalent and are clear through context. Such relationships as husband, companion, lover, partner, ally, friend, and consort describe specific and unique kinds of relationships. Epithets, such as businesswoman, financial manager, and political actor are the modern terms for activities in which some women engaged.

From the perspective of many women in this book, the public sphere shrinks and the family and religion expand. In religion and in the *oikos* or *domus,* women were present and powerful. Over the millennium, the household changed, from the relatively small landholdings of ancient Greece to the imperial household of Constantinople, but its centrality in ancient life remained constant. The changes in the household reflected transformations in the larger society; they also reflected the shifting power and authority of women.

Unlike the households of modern times, the ancient household was not a part of the private sphere. It was a public space for ancient life as important as the forum. The transmutation of the public ancient household into the private modern home has moved out of the historical eye ancient women's pivotal control over food, healthcare, the bearing and rearing of children, the choosing and arranging for marital partners, clothing, clan finances, and assignment of labor. Along the historical way, women's responsibility for these vital functions became the curiosity of female fertility rites and women became secluded from the public urban fray.

The biographies of the first and the revised edition suggest that the survival, let alone the success, of ancient society involved a far broader definition of power, authority, and gender than has been traditionally acknowledged by ancient authors or modern scholars. The focus of the extant ancient authors has left us more a gendered history of men through the development of important male-dominated public institutions and military power than an exploration of ancient society. Early modern scholarship borrowed from the ancients to implicitly and explicitly explore the singular issue of modernism, which was the emergence of the secular state within a gendered European culture. The attraction to a history of civil institutions and warrior values, however, has clouded the primacy of religion and the corporate household. It isn't that modern scholarship has failed to explore the family and religion, but rather that until quite recently politics and military might have retained their power over the scholarly imagination as the most important aspects of society, placing women in a secondary position, at best.

In these more than 500 biographical entries, no person escaped their fate, and women never escaped their gender. Nor was the past like the present, only in another time. It was radically different, even when it appeared most similar. While the triumphal marches of the military through the city of Rome were a demonstration of power and newly captured wealth, it was the women left behind who secured the city, not only the safety of its walls, but the social order that supported military prowess. For the ancients, women were essential for economic and social survival. Starting from the perspective of a woman, the gods, the state, and the family lived and died together, whether it was the imperial *domus* of Constantinople, the country estates of the high empire, or the households of a Greek city-state. The unusual women who appear in the extant ancient literature were those who extended their sway into the male sphere. The efforts and compromises they made to function in a man's world, whether it was by the adoption of celibacy or the use of sons as ciphers for legitimacy, are our evidence of powerful ancient women who stood with authority and power at the edge of male consciousness. In *A to Z of Ancient Greek and Roman Women, Revised Edition,* are the women that even men could not ignore.

Roman World, ca. Second Century C.E.

Baltic Sea

North Sea

Brigantes
Lindum

Virocunium

BRITANNIA

Isca **Iceni**

London

Cassiterides

Thames R.

English Channel

Batavians

Germania Inferior

Colonia Agrippina

GERMANIA

Augusta Treverorum

Mogontiacum

ATLANTIC OCEAN

Paris

Belgica

Lugdunensis

Vistula R.

Rhine R.

Danube R.

Raetia

Noricum

Lauriacum

Pannonia

Iazyges

DACIA

GAUL

Bay of Biscay

Aquitania

Lugdunum

Vienna

Cisalpine Gaul

Emona

Aquileia

ILLYRICUM

Tergeste

Siscia

Mursa

Sirmium

Taurasia

Cremona

A L P S

Germania Superior

Narbonensis

Nîmes

Rhone R.

Genoa

Po R.

Ariminum

Dalmatia

Upper Moesia

Narbo

Massilia

Pisa

Etruria

A P E N N I N E S

Naissus

Caesaraugusta

Tarraconensis

Celtiberians

Nearer Baetica

Lusitania

HISPANIA

Farther Baetica

BALEARIC ISLANDS

CORSICA

Aleria

SARDINIA

Aemilia

ITALIA

Latium
Rome

Campania

Capua

Naples

Samnium

Corfinium

Canusium

Apulia

Tarentum

Calabria

Brundisium

MACEDONIA

Dyrrachium

Apollonia

Adriatic Sea

Epirus

Tyrrhenian Sea

Mediterranean Sea

Bruttium

Messana

Locri

SICILIA

Agrigentum

Syracuse

Ionian Sea

Mauretania Tingitana

Caesarea

Mauretania Caesariensis

Hippo Regius

Utica

Carthage

Cirta

Zama

Agrigentum

Numidia

Theveste

Thapsus

NORTH AFRICA

Proconsular Africa

Oea

Tripolis

Ptolemaïs

Arsinoë

Berenice

GERMANIA	Region
Pannonia	Subregion or province
Syracuse	City or city-state
Brigantes	Tribe or ethnic group
A L P S	Mountain range

0 ——— 300 miles

0 ——— 300 km

© Infobase Publishing

Christian and Pagan Areas of the Roman Empire by 300 C.E.

Baltic Sea

North Sea

ATLANTIC OCEAN

Virocunium
Lindum
BRITANNIA
Isca
London
Cassiterides
Thames R.

English Channel

Vandals

Frisians

Franks

Germania Inferior
Colonia Agrippina
Mogontiacum

GERMANIA

Augusta Treverorum
Paris
Belgica
Lugdunensis

Burgundians
Vistula R.

Danube R.
Rhine R.

GAUL

Bay of Biscay

Aquitania
Lugdunum
Vienna
Taurasia

Raetia
Noricum
Lauriacum
Pannonia
Visigoths
DACIA

Tarraconensis

Narbonensis
Nîmes
Narbo
Massilia
Rhône R.

Cisalpine Gaul
Aquileia
Emona
Tergeste
Genoa
Po R.
APENNINES
Cremona
Ariminum
Pisa
Etruria

ALPS

ILLYRICUM
Siscia
Mursa
Sirmium

Dalmatia
Adriatic Sea

Upper Moesia
Naissus

Lusitania

Caesaraugusta

Baetica

BALEARIC
ISLANDS

CORSICA
Aleria

SARDINIA

Aemilia
ITALIA
Rome
Campania
Naples
Capua
Canusium
Apulia
Tarentum
Brundisium
Calabria

Corfinium
MACEDONIA
Dyrrhachium
Apollonia
Epirus

Tyrrhenian Sea

Bruttium

Mediterranean Sea

Caesarea

Hippo Regius
Utica
Carthage
Cirta
Zama
Numidia
Theveste
Thapsus

Messana
Locri
SICILIA
Agrigentum
Syracuse

Ionian Sea

Mauretania

NORTH AFRICA

Proconsular Africa

Oea

Tripolis

Ptolemaïs
Arsinoë
Berenice

© Infobase Publishing

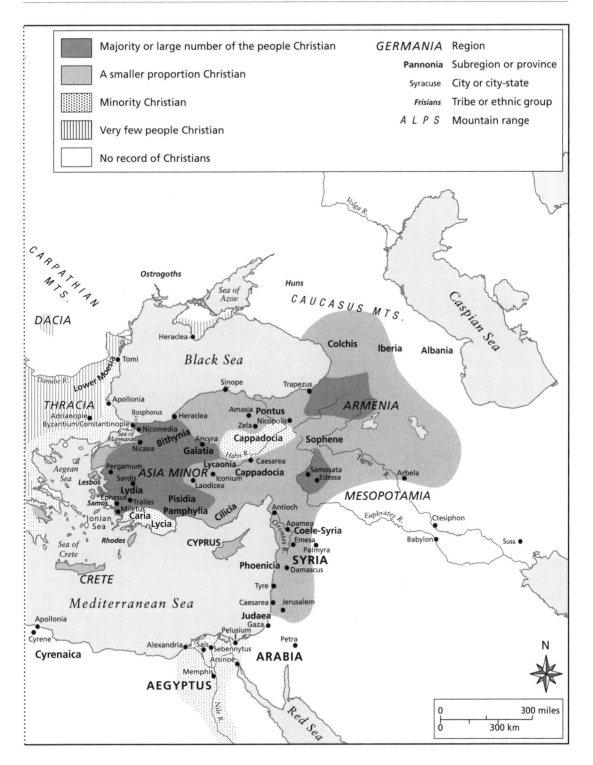

Legend:

- Majority or large number of the people Christian
- A smaller proportion Christian
- Minority Christian
- Very few people Christian
- No record of Christians

GERMANIA — Region
Pannonia — Subregion or province
Syracuse — City or city-state
Frisians — Tribe or ethnic group
A L P S — Mountain range

Volga R.

C A R P A T H I A N M T S.

Ostrogoths

Sea of Azov

Huns

C A U C A S U S   M T S.

Caspian Sea

DACIA

Heraclea

Black Sea

Colchis **Iberia** **Albania**

Tomi

Sinope

Trapezus

Danube R. Lower Moesia

Apollonia

Amasia **Pontus**

ARMENIA

THRACIA

Adrianople
Byzantium/Constantinople

Bosphorus Heraclea

Zela Nicopolis

Adrianople

Nicomedia

Sea of Marmara

Ancyra **Cappadocia**

Sophene

Nicaea **Bithynia**

Galatia

Pergamum

Halys R.

Caesarea

Tigris R.

Arbela

Aegean Sea

Sardis

ASIA MINOR

Lycaonia

Iconium **Cappadocia**

Samosata
Edessa

Lesbos

Ephesus Tralles

Laodicea

MESOPOTAMIA

Samos

Lydia

Miletus

Pisidia

Antioch

Euphrates R.

Ctesiphon

Ionian Sea

Caria

Pamphylia

Cilicia

Apamea **Coele-Syria**

Babylon Susa

Rhodes

Lycia

CYPRUS

Emesa Palmyra

Orontes R.

Sea of Crete

Phoenicia **SYRIA** Damascus

CRETE

Tyre

Mediterranean Sea

Caesarea Jerusalem

Judaea

Apollonia

Gaza

Petra

Cyrene

Pelusium

Alexandria Sais Sebennytus

ARABIA

Cyrenaica

Arsinoe

Memphis

AEGYPTUS

Nile R.

Red Sea

N

0 — 300 miles
0 — 300 km

Roman Empire and Germanic Kingdoms, ca. Fifth Century C.E.

Hibernia

North Sea

BRITANNIA

London

Thames R.

English Channel

Jutes

Saxons

Colonia Agrippina

GERMANIA

Baltic Sea

Vandals

Elbe River

Vistula R.

ATLANTIC OCEAN

Amorica

Remi

Augusta Treverorum

Paris

Andegavum
Turones

Rhine R.

Danube R.

Heruli

Favianae

Lauriacum

Gepids

Bay of Biscay

A L P S

Atilla

Aquileia
Grado

Asturica

Rhone R.

Mediolanum

Vasio

Aug.
Taurinorum

Po R.

Ravenna

Bracara

Arelate

Arausia

Reii

Barcino

HISPANIA

CORSICA

BALEARIC

ISLANDS

SARDINIA

ITALIA

Rome

Tyrrhenian Sea

Adriatic Sea

MACEDONIA

Mediterranean Sea

Hippo
Regius

Milev

Carthage

NORTH AFRICA

Ionian Sea

© Infobase Publishing

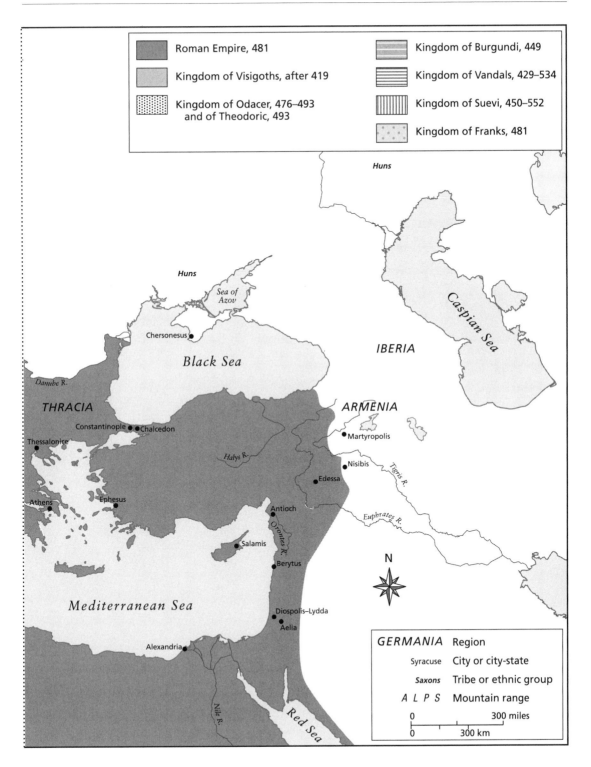

Roman Empire, 481

Kingdom of Visigoths, after 419

Kingdom of Odacer, 476–493
and of Theodoric, 493

Kingdom of Burgundi, 449

Kingdom of Vandals, 429–534

Kingdom of Suevi, 450–552

Kingdom of Franks, 481

Huns

Huns

Sea of Azov

Chersonesus

Black Sea

IBERIA

Caspian Sea

Danube R.

THRACIA

ARMENIA

Constantinople • Chalcedon

Martyropolis

Thessalonice

Halys R.

Nisibis

Tigris R.

Edessa

Athens

Ephesus

Antioch

Euphrates R.

Orontes R.

Salamis

N

Berytus

Mediterranean Sea

Diospolis–Lydda

Aelia

Alexandria

Nile R.

Red Sea

GERMANIA   Region

Syracuse   City or city-state

Saxons   Tribe or ethnic group

A L P S   Mountain range

0   300 miles

0   300 km

Acte, Claudia

(first century C.E.)   Roman: Italy
self-made woman

Acte was born a slave in Asia Minor. She and the handsome young emperor Nero became lovers in 55 C.E. Their passion put her in danger of Nero's disapproving and powerful mother, the younger Julia AGRIPPINA. Nero hid their affair. Nero's tutor and adviser, the philosopher Lucius Annaeus Seneca, and his friend Annaeus Serenus shared the secret. Acte, who claimed descent from the kingly Attalidae and had probably gained her freedom, from the emperor Claudius, pretended that Serenus was her lover.

It was a short-lived deception. Agrippina discovered the relationship; she only inflamed Nero's passion by her attacks on Acte. Shifting tactics, Agrippina offered Nero her rooms for their assignations. Rumors spread that Agrippina sought to seduce her son. Acte, in fear of her life, told Nero that his mother boasted of committing incest and that the troops were grumbling about an incestuous emperor. Alarmed, Nero first avoided Agrippina and later had her killed, in 59 C.E.

Acte could not hold Nero's passion. Even before Agrippina's murder. Acte had been pushed aside. In 68 C.E., however, the extravagant and beautiful Nero came to an inglorious end. He returned from Greece to a corn shortage in Rome, an angry populace, and a senate that opposed him. Events soon escalated, and he was declared a public enemy. Finally, he committed suicide. It was the loyal and loving Acte, along with his old nurses, who dressed him in gold-embroidered white robes and carried his ashes to the Pincian Hill, where he was entombed. Acte, who had grown wealthy with estates in Sardinia and Italy, paid 2,000 gold pieces for the funeral of her lover.

Sources

Dio Cassius. *Roman History* 61.7.1.
Suetonius. *The Lives of the Caesars:* Nero 28.1, 50.
Tacitus. *Annales* 13.12–13, 46; 14.2.
Balsdon, J. P. V. D. *Roman Women.* New York: John Day Comp., 1963, pp. 108, 128.
Bauman, Richard A. *Women and Politics in Ancient Rome.* London: Routledge, 1994, p. 194.
Oxford Classical Dictionary, ed. by Simon Hornblower and Antony Spawforth. 3d. ed. New York: Oxford University Press, 1996, p. 336.
Pauly, A., G. Wissowa, and W. Kroll. *Real-Encyclopadie d. Classischen Altertumswissenschaft 1893–.* (Germany: multiple publishers) 399.

Acutia

(first century C.E.)   Roman: Rome
convicted conspirator

Acutia was convicted of treason in the trials that followed the downfall of Lucius Aelius Sejanus in the last years of the emperor Tiberius. Although her full name remains elusive, Acutia's husband was Publius Vitellius. He committed suicide in 31 C.E. after he had been charged with diverting military funds to support a conspiracy led by Sejanus.

The dour and aging emperor had retired to Capri and left Sejanus in Rome. As prefect of the Praetorian Guard he became the emperor's eyes and ears in the capital. His aspirations grew. He sought to marry his lover Livia Julia Claudia LIVILLA, the emperor's niece, and perhaps even become regent for her young son after the death of Tiberius. His plans had almost succeeded when the aged emperor charged him with treason. A purge followed. Prosecutors grew rich from the trials. In 37 C.E. Laelius Balbus prosecuted Acutia before the Senate for her presumed participation in the conspiracy. Although convicted, she may have escaped death. There is no record of her execution, and the tribune Junius Otho vetoed the usual reward taken by a successful prosecutor.

Sources

Tacitus. *Annales* 6.47.
Levick, Barbara. *Tiberius the Politician.* London: Thames and Hudson, 1976, p. 216.
Marsh, Frank Burr. *The Reign of Tiberius.* New York: Barnes and Noble, 1931, p. 217.
Marshall, A. J. "Women on Trial before the Roman Senate." *Classical Views* 34 (1990): 333–336, 348.

Ada

(fourth century B.C.E)   Greek: Asia Minor
ruler

Ada was the younger daughter of Hecatomnus. She married her brother Idrieus. They ruled Caria, in southwestern Asia Minor, as a virtually independent satrapy within the Persian empire. Ada and Idrieus succeeded their brother and sister Mausolus and ARTEMISIA II, famed for building the first mausoleum and one of the seven wonders of the ancient world, which Artemisia completed to memorialize Mausolus after his death.

Ada was the sole ruler of Caria after Idrieus's death until her brother Pixodarus seized power and expelled her. She retired to Alinda, a Carian fortress that remained under her control. In 334 B.C.E., she allied herself with Alexander the Great when he invaded Caria. She led the troops that captured one of the two forts at Halicarnassus.

With Alexander's aid she defeated Pixodarus and regained control over Caria. She was again the sole ruler. She adopted Alexander, which assured his succession and recognized his suzerainty.

Sources

Arrian. *Anabasis of Alexander* 1.2.3.
Strabo. *Geography* 114.217, C657.
Brill's New Pauly. Encyclopedia of the Ancient World. Vol. 1, *Classical Tradition.* Edited by Manfred Landfester et al. Boston: Brill, 2002, pp. 130–131.

Aelia Iunilla

(?–31 C.E.)   Roman: Rome
political victim

Aelia Iunilla died because she was the daughter of APICATA and Lucius Aelius Sejanus. Her father, head of the Praetorian Guard, had become the most powerful man in Rome when he alone had the ear of the emperor after Tiberius retired to Capri in 27 C.E. He was also the lover of Livia Julia Claudia LIVILLA, widowed daughter-in-law (and niece) of Tiberius and mother of the emperor's infant grandson. Around Livilla and Sejanus a conspiracy grew. The ailing emperor learned of Sejanus's perfidy from the younger ANTONIA, Livilla's mother. Vengence followed quickly. In October of 31 C.E., the Senate voted to execute Sejanus.

Eight days after her father died, her mother killed herself. In December Iunilla and her young brother were seized on Senate orders that there be no descendants of Sejanus. Traditionally, the Romans did not kill virgins, and it was said that Iunilla was raped before she was strangled.

Sources

Dio Cassius. *Roman History* 58.11, 5.
Tacitus. *Annales* 6.5, 9.
Levick, Barbara. *Tiberius the Politician.* London: Thames and Hudson, 1976, p. 178.

Aelia Paetina

(first century C.E.)   Roman: Rome
political victim

Aelia Paetina married the future emperor Claudius during the years when it seemed unlikely he would rule. She had a daughter, ANTONIA (4), born in about 28 C.E. When Claudius's prospects improved in the reign of his nephew Gaius Caligula, he divorced Aelia to marry the better-connected Valeria MESSALLINA.

After Messallina's death in 48 C.E., the powerful freedman Narcissus proposed to the emperor that he remarry Aelia. Aelia, the daughter of Aelius Catus, consul in 4 C.E., posed no threat to the imperial freedmen who controlled the bureaucracy and exercised their influence over Claudius. Claudius, however, married the younger AGRIPPINA and Narcissus soon lost his position and his life.

Sources

Suetonius. *The Lives of the Caesars:* Claudius 26.2, 3.

Tacitus. *Annales* 12.1–2.

Balsdon, J. P. V. D. *Roman Women.* New York: John Day Comp., 1963, p. 122.

Levick, Barbara. *Claudius: The Corruption of Power.* New Haven, Conn.: Yale University Press, 1993, pp. 25, 55, 70.

Syme, Ronald. *The Augustan Aristocracy.* Oxford: Clarendon Press, 1986, index.

◉ Aemilia (1)

(second century B.C.E.)   Roman: Rome
priestess

Aemilia was one of three Vestal Virgins charged with violating the vow of chastity in 114 B.C.E. A daughter of the clan of the Aemilii, she was one of the six virgins dedicated for a period of 30 years to protect the sacred flame of Rome in the temple of Vesta, the goddess of the hearth, and one of the oldest temples in the Forum.

Aemilia had an affair with L. Veturius, a Roman equestrian, and induced two of her sister Vestals, LICINIA (4) and MARCIA (1), similarly to engage Veturius's companions. It was said that Aemilia had several lovers, including Licinia's brother. Tried before the *pontifex maximus,* Lucius Caecilius Metellus, Aemilia was found guilty and condemned to death. Licinia and Marcia, initially declared innocent, were retried and condemned the following year. Evidence against the women came from a slave, Manius, who felt insufficiently rewarded by the women for his role as their go-between.

Romans traditionally regarded violations of chastity by the Vestal Virgins as signs of ill omen. Tales of their promiscuity often accompanied other indications of impending trouble for the city-state and sometimes preceded periods of political instability. In 111 B.C.E. a fire destroyed much of Rome and during these years there was a war against Jugurtha of Numidia in North Africa.

Sources

Dio Cassius. *Roman History* 26.87.

Livy. *From the Founding of the City* 63.

Orosius. *Seven Books of History Against the Pagans* 5.15, 20–22.

Plutarch. *Moralia: Quaestiones Romanae* 83.

Bauman, Richard A. *Women and Politics in Ancient Rome.* London: Routledge, 1994, pp. 52–58.

Pauly, A., G. Wissowa, and W. Kroll. *Real-Encyclopadie d. Classischen Altertumswissenschaft 1893–.* (Germany: multiple publishers) 153.

◉ Aemilia (2)

(first century B.C.E.)   Roman: Rome
political wife

Aemilia was the daughter of CAECILIA METELLA (1) from the rich and powerful Metelli clan. Aemilia's father was Marcus Aemilius Scaurus, consul in 115 B.C.E. After the death of her father, Aemilia's mother married Lucius Cornelius Sulla, the general who later became dictator of Rome. It was considered the match of the season, a great coup for Sulla who gained critical political support and wealth from the Metelli. For Caecilia, it was a chance to play politics using her family's stature and wealth to support a newcomer from an old patrician family that had long been out of the limelight.

Sulla and Caecilia Metella persuaded Gnaeus Pompeius (Pompey the Great) to divorce his wife ANTISTIA (2) and marry Aemilia. At the time, Aemilia was pregnant and living with her husband, Manius Acilius Glabrio, future consul in 67 B.C.E. An alliance with Sulla and the Metelli through Aemilia clearly enhanced and enriched Pompey.

Aemilia's views on her divorce and remarriage are not known. She died during childbirth in 80 B.C.E. shortly after her marriage with Pompey.

Sources

Plutarch. *Vitae Parallelae (Parallel Lives): Pompeius* 9.2.

Plutarch. *Vitae Parallelae (Parallel Lives): Sulla* 33.3

Haley, Shelly P. "The Five Wives of Pompey the Great." In *Women in Antiquity*, ed. by Ian McAuslan and Peter Walcot. Oxford: Oxford University Press, 1996, pp. 103 ff.

Pauly, A., G. Wissowa, and W. Kroll. *Real-Encyclopadie d. Classischen Altertumswissenschaft 1893–*. (Germany: multiple publishers) 154.

Syme, Ronald. *The Roman Revolution*. London: Oxford University Press, 1963, pp. 31–32.

▣ Aemilia Lepida (1)

(first century B.C.E.)   Roman: Rome
political wife

Aemilia Lepida, daughter of Mamercus Lepidus Livianus, consul in 77 B.C.E., was jilted by Quintus Caecilius Metellus Pius Scipio. She then agreed to marry Marcus Porcius Cato Uticensis. The two men could not have been more dissimilar. Cato was a self-righteous, unpleasant ascetic, while Scipio was corrupt and depraved.

On hearing of her engagement, Scipio changed his mind, and they were married about 73 B.C.E. Cato wanted to sue Scipio. Dissuaded by friends, he instead wrote and widely circulated a satiric poem ridiculing his rival. The result was a lasting feud.

Aemilia Lepida's son, Metellus Scipio, died at 18; her daughter, CORNELIA (6), married Publius Licinius Crassus in 55 B.C.E. He died in 53. In 52, Cornelia married Gnaeus Pompeius (Pompey the Great). Aemilia's new son-in-law, one of the most powerful politicians in Rome, supported the election of her husband as consul. Scipio's election made him immune from any law suits. He thereby avoided a bribery charge, and Aemilia Lepida became the wife, as well as the daughter, of a consul.

Sources

Plutarch. *Vitae Parallelae (Parallel Lives): Cato Minor* 7.

Pauly, A., G. Wissowa, and W. Kroll. *Real-Encyclopadie d. Classischen Altertumswissenschaft 1893–*. (Germany: multiple publishers) 166.

Syme, Ronald. *The Augustan Aristocracy*. Oxford: Clarendon Press, 1986, p. 245.

▣ Aemilia Lepida (2)

(first century B.C.E.–first century C.E.)
Roman: Rome
unjustly convicted of adultery

Aemilia Lepida was successfully prosecuted before the Senate by her vindictive ex-husband in a curious case that had political overtones. An aristocratic woman of impeccable lineage, she was the daughter of CORNELIA (7) and the granddaughter of MUCIA TERTIA and Gnaeus Pompeius (Pompey the Great). Her father, Quintus Aemilius Lepidus, was the son of the triumvir Marcus Aemilius Lepidus and JUNIA (1). She had been affianced to Lucius Julius Caesar, the grandson of Augustus, but Lucius died before the marriage could take place.

Around 2 C.E., she contracted a less auspicious marriage with the much older, but wealthy, Publius Sulpicius Quirinus who had been consul in 12 B.C.E. Three years later they were divorced. She then married Mamercus Aemilius Scaurus, a distinguished orator with an unsavory reputation, who was the last living male of the republican Aemilii Scauri clan.

In 20 C.E., her divorced first husband, Quirinus, now an even more ancient relic, charged her with adultery, attempting to poison him, and falsely claiming that he was the father of her child. She was also accused of consulting astrologers about the imperial family, a treasonous offense under recent imperial Roman law. Her brother Manius Aemilius Lepidus defended her.

Aemilia Lepida earned a good deal of sympathy from women. Not only were the charges brought many years after the divorce, but she, the descendant of a great and noble family, was accused by a man of lesser distinction in tiresome old age.

The emperor Tiberius played a role in the affair. Appearing simultaneously magnanimous and condemnatory, he ruled that there was no evidence of treason. Aemilia was, however, convicted of falsely claiming Quirinus as the father of the child she bore during their marriage. By default, therefore, she was guilty of adultery during her marriage with Quirinus.

Aemilia was banished, but a plea by Scaurus, her current husband, waived the confiscation of her property. Tiberius later announced that her slaves confessed under torture that she had attempted to poison her first husband.

Sources

Suetonius. *The Lives of the Caesars:* Tiberius 49.1.

Tacitus. *Annales* 3.22–23.

Balsdon, J. P. V. D. *Roman Women.* New York: John Day Comp., 1963, p. 220.

Marshall, A. J. "Women on Trial before the Roman Senate." *Classical Views* 34 (1990): 333–366, p. 343.

Pauly, A., G. Wissowa, and W. Kroll. *Real-Encyclopadie d. Classischen Altertumswissenschaft 1893–.* (Germany: multiple publishers) 170.

Syme, R., *Augustan Aristocracy.* Oxford: Clarendon Press, 1986, pp. 112, 115.

▣ Aemilia Lepida (3)

(first century B.C.E.–first century C.E.)
Roman: Rome
political victim

Aemilia Lepida was a woman of impeccable lineage. Her mother was JULIA (7), the child of the great general Marcus Vipsanius Agrippa, and JULIA (6), the daughter of Augustus and his first wife, SCRIBONIA. No less illustrious on her father's side, Aemilia Lepida was the daughter of Lucius Aemilius Paullus, the brother of Marcus Aemilius Lepidus, the triumvir.

Her engagement to the future emperor Claudius ended when her father was executed for treason in 8 C.E. and her mother was banished for adultery. She later married Marcus Junius Silanus Torquatus, who had a respectable career, including the consulship in 19 C.E. They had two daughters, JUNIA LEPIDA and JUNIA CALVINA, and three sons, Marcus Junius Silanus, Lucius Junius Silanus Torquatus, and Decimus Junius Silanus Torquatus.

Aemilia Lepida's link to Augustus, however, led to the downfall of her children. Lucius was forced to commit suicide, Marcus was executed, and Junia Calvina was exiled, all through the machinations of the younger AGRIPPINA. Junia Calvina was later allowed to return to Rome by the emperor Nero. Nero, however, was responsible for

the forced suicide of Decimus and the condemnation of Junia Lepida. Aemilia Lepida's own death is not recorded.

Sources

Suetonius. *The Lives of the Caesars:* Augustus 19.1.

——. *The Lives of the Caesars:* Claudius 26.1.

Tacitus. *Annales* 12.4.

Pauly, A., G. Wissowa, and W. Kroll. *Real-Encyclopadie d. Classischen Altertumswissenschaft 1893–.* (Germany: multiple publishers) 169.

Syme, Ronald. *The Augustan Aristocracy.* Oxford: Clarendon Press, 1986, index.

▣ Aemilia Lepida (4)

(first century C.E.)   Roman: Rome
duplicitous wife

Aemilia Lepida and her younger brother, Marcus Aemilius Lepidus, were the last descendants of the great republican family of the Aemilii Lepidi. Aemilia married Drusus Julius Caesar, and Marcus married Drusus's sister, JULIA DRUSILLA (1). Drusus and his brother Nero Julius Caesar were the great-grandsons of Augustus and stood in direct line of succession to the elderly emperor Tiberius.

Aemilia Lepida was a reputed lover of and possible coconspirator with Lucius Aelius Sejanus, commander of the Praetorian Guard. In 30 C.E. while Sejanus still held power over Rome, her husband was imprisoned. Although the nature of the offense is not known he died while still in prison some three years later. In 31 C.E. Sejanus was charged with treason and executed. Aemilia remained safe under the protection of her father, Marcus Aemilius Lepidus, consul in 6 C.E. and a great favorite of Tiberius.

After her father's death, however, Aemilia was charged with adultery. She did not try to defend herself and committed suicide in 36 C.E. Her brother, the last of the Aemilii, died four years later, in 39, after having been accused of participation in a somewhat mysterious conspiracy led by Gnaeus Cornelius Lentulus Gaetulicus.

Sources

Dio Cassius. *Roman History* 58.3.8.

Tacitus. *Annales* 6.40.

Levick, Barbara. *Tiberius the Politician.* London: Thames and Hudson, 1976, pp. 55, 170, 215.

Pauly, A., G. Wissowa, and W. Kroll. *Real-Encyclopadie d. Classischen Altertumswissenschaft 1893–.* (Germany: multiple publishers) 167.

Syme, Ronald. *The Augustan Aristocracy.* Oxford: Clarendon Press, 1986, p. 136.

▣ Aemilia Tertia

(second–first century B.C.E.)   Roman: Rome
power broker

Aemilia Tertia's life was shaped by the wars against Carthage. Her father, Lucius Aemilius Paullus, consul in 219 and 216 B.C.E., died in Hannibal's defeat of the Romans in 216 at Cannae in Canusium. Her husband, Publius Cornelius Scipio Africanus Major, led the Romans to victory over Hannibal at Zama in North Africa in 202.

In 195 B.C.E., Aemilia supported, and possibly participated in, the popular effort to repeal the Oppian law. Passed by the Senate as an austerity measure after the defeat at Cannae, the law barred displays of status and wealth. Specifically the law forbade carriages within a mile of Rome or in Roman towns except for religious festivals, purple trim on women's clothing, or women's possession of more than a half an ounce of gold. Although after Hannibal's defeat, austerity laws directed against men were lifted, until the women protested the law remained in effect against them.

All of Aemilia's children left a mark on Roman history. The eldest, Publius Cornelius Scipio, who suffered ill health, which prevented him for following a military and political career, became an outstanding orator. The second son, Lucius Cornelius Scipio, was praetor in 174. Of her two daughters, the eldest, CORNELIA (1), married her cousin Publius Cornelius Scipio Nasica. The younger, CORNELIA (2), married Tiberius Sempronius Gracchus and was the mother of two of Rome's most famous reformers, Tiberius and Gaius Sempronius Gracchus. In the political battles around the land bills supported by her grandsons, her son-in-law, Scipio Nasica, emerged as a leader of the conservative faction that assassinated Tiberius.

An aprocryphal story about the marriage of the younger Cornelia possibly suggests something of Aemilia's expectations of her husband. Attending a dinner of senators, Scipio was urged by those present to arrange his daughter's marriage with Tiberius Sempronius Gracchus. He agreed, and the contract was concluded on the spot. On returning home he told Aemilia. She was furious because she had not been consulted. She added that it was improper for him to act without having consulted her, even if the bridegroom was the desirable Tiberius Sempronius Gracchus.

Aemilia outlived her husband and faced the political attacks against him that erupted after his death in the early 180s B.C.E. Since her daughter's marriage in fact happened after her husband's death she probably *was* consulted. She also freed her husband's slave/lover and arranged for her marriage. While not without precedent, it nonetheless speaks well for the woman.

Aemilia was independently wealthy, in part, from her dowry, gifts from her husband, and a wide circle of clients. Possibly she also benefited from the spoils of her brother, Lucius Aemilius Paullus Macedonicus, consul in 168 B.C.E., who led the Romans to victory in the Third Macedonian War. She was said to have lived and traveled in comfort, accompanied by a number of retainers. She left her fortune to Publius Cornelius Africanus Numantinus, her adopted grandson. The date of Aemilia's death is unknown.

Sources

Livy. *From the Founding of the City* 38.57.5–8.

Polybius. *Histories* 31.26.1–6; 31.27.1–4.

Valerius Maximus. *Factorum et dictorum memorabilium libri IX* 6.7.1.

Balsdon, J. P. V. D. *Roman Women.* New York: John Day Comp., pp. 47, 215.

Bauman, Richard A. *Women and Politics in Ancient Rome.* London: Routledge, 1994, index.

Pomeroy, Sarah B. *Goddesses, Whores, Wives, and Slaves: Women in Classical Antiquity.* New York: Schocken Books, 1975, *passim.*

Pauly, A., G. Wissowa, and W. Kroll. *Real-Encyclopadie d. Classischen Altertumswissenschaft 1893–.* (Germany: multiple publishers) 180.

▣ Afriana (Carfania)

(?–48 B.C.E.)   Roman: Rome
advocate

Afriana, also called Carfania, represented herself and others in cases brought before the praetor. The wife of Licinius Bucco, a senator of the first century B.C.E., Afriana lived during a time of turmoil and civil war when many men were in flight, in the army, or dead. Families found themselves pulled apart by the passions of the times and sometimes on opposing sides. Afriana, like other women, moved into spheres of activity usually reserved for men: She went into the law courts.

Afriana's success irritated some and provoked others to ridicule, which reflected the Romans' contradictory views of women and the law. On one hand, women were assumed to be unknowing and in need of protection. On the other hand, ignorance of the law, even on the part of a woman, was not an acceptable defense in the courts.

By the later first century B.C.E., however, women owned property in their own name and increasingly both sued and were sued. After Afriana, however, the law was changed so that women could plead for themselves before a magistrate but were prohibited from representing others. Afriana died in 48 B.C.E.

Sources

Ulpian. *The Civil Law* 11.1.232n.30.

Valerius Maximus. *Factorum et dictorum memorabilium libri IX* 8.3.2.

Bauman, Richard A. *Women and Politics in Ancient Rome.* London: Routledge, 1994, pp. 50–51.

Marshall, A. J. "Ladies at Law: The Role of Women in the Roman Civil Courts." In *Studies in Latin Literature and Roman History,* ed. by C. Deroux. Brussels, Belgium: Latomus, 1989, pp. 38–54.

▣ Agariste (1)

(sixth century B.C.E.)
Greek: Sicyon and Athens
mother of Cleisthenes

Agariste was the daughter of Cleisthenes, ruler of Sicyon, a Greek city northwest of Corinth, in the years between 600–570 B.C.E. Cleisthenes determined that Agariste would marry the best man in all of Greece. At the conclusion of the Olympic Games in c. 576 B.C.E., he invited worthy contestants to arrive in Sicyon within the next 60 days and spend a year as his guests. At the end of that time, one among them would marry his daughter.

Thirteen eminent men from 12 cities accepted the challenge. Cleisthenes assessed their families, expectations, and cities of origin. He tested their prowess in wrestling and running. At the end of a year, he gave a banquet and invited everyone in the city.

His favorite appeared to be Hippocleides, described as the wealthiest and the most handsome of the Athenians. Under the influence of too much wine, however, Hippocleides danced on a table and stood on his head waving his legs. Outraged at this behavior, Cleisthenes instead chose Megacles, a member of the aristocratic Alcmaeonidae of Athens.

Agariste gave birth to two children: Cleisthenes, who became the Athenian statesman regarded as the creator of Athenian democracy, and Hippocrates, the father of AGARISTE (2).

Sources

Herodotus. *The Persian Wars* 6.126–31.

Blundell, Sue. *Women in Ancient Greece.* London: British Museum Press, 1995, p. 67.

Hammond, N. G. L. *A History of Greece.* Oxford: Oxford University Press, 1967, p. 148.

Pomeroy, Sarah B. *Goddesses, Whores, Wives, and Slaves: Women in Classical Antiquity.* New York: Schocken Books, 1975, pp. 34–35.

▣ Agariste (2)

(c. 520/510 B.C.E.–?)   Greek: Athens
mother of Pericles

Agariste was born between 520 and 510 B.C.E. She was the daughter of Hippocrates, the son of AGARISTE (1), after whom she was named. Her father was a member of the family of the aristocratic Alcmaeonidae, and her uncle was Cleisthenes, who was one of the founders of Athenian democracy.

She married Xanthippus, an Athenian politician and general who helped defeat the Persians at the battle of Mycale in 479. According to Herodotus, Agariste dreamed that her son was delivered by a lion. The son, born in 494 B.C.E., became the great Athenian statesman Pericles. She had two other children: Ariphron (II), named after her husband's father, and a daughter who died of the plague in 430.

Sources

Herodotus. *The Persian Wars* 6.131.

Plutarch. *Vitae Parallelae (Parallel Lives): Pericles* 3.1–2.

Davies, J. K. *Athenian Propertied Families, 600–300 B.C.* Oxford: Clarendon Press, 1971, pp. 456–457.

▣ Agariste (3)

(fifth century B.C.E.)   Greek: Athens
witness

Agariste testified against the brilliant, dissolute, and popular general Alcibiades at his celebrated trial in Athens (415 B.C.E.). She was a member of the aristocratic Alcmaeonidae family and the wife of Alcmaeonides, a leading Athenian.

Agariste had witnessed Alcibiades and his friends in a drunken revel staging a travesty of the sacred Eleusinian rites for goddesses Demeter and Kore. The episode happened at night in the house of Charmides, a friend of Alcibiades. It is possible, and even probable, that Agariste was visiting kin when the event happened.

Few extant records record women's court testimony in fifth century Athens, nor are there many records of well-born women moving around the city after dark.

Sources

Andocides. *On the Mysteries* 1.16.

Plutarch. *Vitae Parallelae (Parallel Lives): Alcibiades* 19.1–2.

MacDowell, Douglas M., ed. *Andokides, On the Mysteries.* Oxford: Clarendon Press, 1962, p. 75.

Pomeroy, Sarah B. *Goddesses, Whores, Wives, and Slaves: Women in Classical Antiquity.* New York: Schocken Books, 1975, pp. 81, 119.

▣ Agathocleia

(third century B.C.E.)
Greek: Samos and Egypt
adventurer and murderer

Agathocleia came to Egypt from the island of Samos off the coast of Asia Minor with her brother,

Agathocles, and their mother, OENANTHE. The name of their father is unknown. Agathocleia was a dancer, and her mother played the tambourine. Oenanthe became one of Ptolemy III's many lovers and brought her children into the life of the palace. Shortly after Ptolemy IV became ruler in 221 B.C.E., he became wildly infatuated with Agathocleia. It was rumored that through him she controlled Egypt.

In 205 B.C.E. Agathocleia and her brother arranged the murder of Ptolemy IV and his wife, ARSINOË III PHILOPATOR. The conspirators included Oenanthe and Sosibius, guardian of Ptolemy's son. The deaths were kept secret for several days while Agathocles had himself appointed regent. Philammon, a coconspirator and murderer of Arsinoë, left Alexandria, and Agathocleia and Oenanthe took over care of the five-year-old boy-ruler.

The murder of Arsinoë, even more than the death of Ptolemy, aroused the anger of the Greek troops and the Alexandrian populace. A crowd, eager for revenge, collected at the stadium. A naked Agathocleia, along with her mother, brother, sisters, and relatives, were turned over to the mob and torn limb from limb. The women, especially those who had been close to Arsinoë, led the slaughter.

Sources

Athenaeus. *Deipnosophistae* 13.577.

Plutarch. *Moralia: Amatorius* 9.

Polybius. *Histories.* 14.11.2; 15.25.3–33.

Pomeroy, Sarah B. *Women in Hellenistic Egypt.* New York: Schocken, 1984, *passim.*

▣ Agesistrata

(?–241 B.C.E.)   Greek: Sparta
reformer

Agesistrata, and her mother Archidamia, and her daughter-in-law AGIATIS were among the wealthiest women in Sparta during the middle decades of the third century B.C.E. They were committed to reform, especially land reform. Along with their friends, retainers and dependents, they constituted an influential political bloc in support of Agis IV, who led a reformist revolution in 244 B.C.E. to overthrow the reigning ruler, Leonidas II.

Agis IV, who was Agesistrata's son, was deposed and killed in 241. After her son's death, Agesistrata and her mother were executed. She died willingly, her final wish being that her death benefit Sparta.

Sources

Plutarch. *Vitae Parallelae (Parallel Lives): Agesilaus* 4.2; 7.7; 9.5–6; 20.7.

Mosse, Claude. "Women in the Spartan Revolutions of the Third Century B.C." In *Women's History and Ancient History,* ed. by Sarah B. Pomeroy. Chapel Hill: University of North Carolina Press, 1991, pp. 138–153.

▣ Agiatis
(third century B.C.E.)   Greek: Sparta
reformer

Agiatis, the wealthy daughter of Gylippos, a well-respected Spartan, was heir to her father's fortune. Committed to reform, she was part of an aristocratic and wealthy faction that also included her mother-in-law, AGESISTRATA, and the latter's mother, ARCHIDAMIA.

Her first husband, Agis IV, seized power from the ruler Leonidas II in 244 B.C.E. at a time when a small oligarchy controlled large estates, and held mortgages on much of the remaining farmland. It was also a period of declining population, which seriously depleted manpower for the military and labor for agriculture. Agis sponsored a number of reforms and abolished mortgages to relieve debt. A conservative revolt led by the deposed Leonidas in 241 resulted in the death of Agis and left Agiatis a widow with a small son.

Leonidas sought to marry Agiatis to his son Cleomenes, who was quite young. Agiatis who wanted no part of a marriage to Cleomenes or anyone else married under protest. In 235 Cleomenes followed Leonidas as ruler. Influenced by Agiatis and her circle, Cleomenes III pursued the reform policies that had been an anathema to his father, and in 227–226 he canceled debts, redistributed land, and extended citizenship to some of the indigenous population and resident aliens. During the same years he was also successful in war and expanded Spartan territory; however, his policies garnered opposition, and he was overthrown in

222. He fled to Egypt, where he committed suicide in 219. It is not known what happened to Agiatis or her son.

Sources

Plutarch. *Vitae Parallelae (Parallel Lives): Agesilaus* 4.2.

Plutarch. *Vitae Parallelae (Parallel Lives): Cleomenes* 1.1–3.

▣ Aglaonice
(fourth century B.C.E.)   Greek: Thessaly
seer, prophet, astronomer, sorceress

Aglaonice was from Thessaly, which since the time of Alexander the Great in the fourth century B.C.E. had a reputation for circles of women with astrological and astronomical knowledge. Aglaonice was reputed to prophesize the eclipses of the moon. Her skill in prediction was confused with an ability to cause the eclipse and make the moon reappear after an eclipse.

Sources

Plutarch. *Coniugalia praecepta* 48, 145c; de. def., 13, 417a.

Brill's New Pauly: Encyclopedia of the Ancient World: Classical Tradition, Vol. 1, edited by Manfred Landfester et al. Boston: Brill, 2002, p. 343.

Pomeroy, Sarah, ed. *Plutarch's Advice to the Bride and Groom and a Consolation to His Wife.* New York: Oxford University Press, 1999.

▣ Agrippina the Elder, Vipsania
(c. 14 B.C.E.–33 C.E.)
Roman: Germany and Rome
political player and power broker

Vipsania Agrippina was an extraordinarily powerful and ambitious woman fully conscious of her noble heritage and determined to see that she, her husband, and their children received the titles, honors, respect, and positions due them. She was the daughter of JULIA (6), the only child of Augustus and his first wife, SCRIBONIA. Her father was Marcus Vipsanius Agrippa, Augustus's greatest general and closest confidant.

Around 5 C.E., Agrippina married Germanicus Julius Caesar, whose lineage matched hers. He was the son of Nero Claudius Drusus and the younger ANTONIA. His father was the brother of the future

The deified Vipsania Agrippina was commemorated with this coin after her death.
(Date: 37 C.E.–41 C.E. 1952.81.2, Archives, American Numismatic Society)

emperor Tiberius; his mother, the daughter of Mark Antony and the independent-minded sister of Augustus, OCTAVIA (2). In 4 C.E., Augustus adopted Tiberius, who in turn, adopted Germanicus as his son to form a line of fictive kin and ensure the future of the family and state.

Agrippina accompanied her husband on his campaign to lower Germany in 14 C.E. She was generous and popular with the troops, whom she helped with food, clothing, and medical care. Stories about her echo the attributes of courage and strong character that marked the ancient heroines. In 15 C.E., as Roman troops retreated toward a bridge that crossed the Rhine, pursued by the Germans, Agrippina stationed herself at the head of the bridge and stopped the retreat. The troops stood their ground and won the battle.

In 18 C.E., Agrippina, pregnant with her ninth child, accompanied her husband to Syria, after Tiberius made Germanicus consul with responsibility for all the provinces in the East. A military man himself, Tiberius was not comfortable with Germanicus's overly aggressive tactics and sent his friend Gnaeus Calpurnius Piso as governor to encourage a more moderate policy. Piso went to Syria with his wife, MUNATIA PLANCINA, a woman

as strong, outspoken, and arrogant as Agrippina. The two men did not like each other and did not get along. Nor did the two women.

When Munatia criticized Germanicus before the troops, Germanicus ordered Piso and his wife to leave Syria. They went to the island of Cos off the coast of Asia Minor. On October 10, 19 C.E., Germanicus died of a mysterious illness in Antioch. Before he died, he accused Piso and Munatia of poisoning him. Piso and Munatia openly rejoiced at the death of Germanicus and immediately sought to reassert their authority.

Agrippina believed not only that Germanicus had been poisoned by Piso and Munatia, but also that Tiberius was behind the deed. She returned to Rome with her husband's ashes, determined to avenge his death and to promote the interests of her six surviving children: Drusus Julius Caesar, Nero Julius Caesar, Gaius Caligula, the younger AGRIPPINA, JULIA DRUSILLA (1), and JULIA LIVILLA. The population of Rome turned out to pay Germanicus homage. The emperor's mother, LIVIA DRUSILLA; the taciturn Tiberius; and Antonia, Germanicus's own mother, did not attend the ceremonies. People took their absence as confirmation that Tiberius might have had a hand in the death of Germanicus.

Agrippina brought formal charges against Piso and Munatia. Poisoning could not be proved so the main charge was treason. Tiberius presided over the trial in the Senate. Piso killed himself before the end of the trial after having written to Tiberius protesting his loyalty. Munatia's trial had been separated from that of her husband. Livia, her close friend, intervened; Tiberius told the Senate that his mother wanted no action taken against Munatia, and she escaped conviction. Agrippina was furious. She and Livia, who had long disliked each other, were further alienated.

Agrippina spent the years 19–29 c.e. in Rome working to promote her sons as heir to Tiberius. Livia Julia Claudia LIVILLA and Lucius Aelius Sejanus, prefect of the Praetorian Guard, were her opponents. Livilla, the sister of Germanicus, was Agrippina's sister-in-law. She was the grand-niece of Augustus and the widow of Tiberius's son, Drusus Julius Caesar. Sejanus was a military man of equestrian background who had become Tiberius's confidant, and after 27 c.e., when Tiberius retired from Rome to Capri, he controlled access to the emperor. Although an uncle on his mother's side had been a consul suffectus, Sejanus had neither family nor family connections in the senatorial class that allowed him any aspiration to achieve for himself the position of emperor. In the person of Livilla, he found an ally whose sons were possible successors. Sejanus and Livilla became lovers and schemed to make Livilla's son the successor to Tiberius.

Agrippina was at the center of a group of powerful people who hated and resented the enormous influence exercised by Sejanus. They regarded his background with arrogant distaste and his position as an impediment to their own power. The senatorial families who supported Agrippina acted in the belief that tradition was on their side. There may have been an attempted conspiracy to supplant Tiberius with Agrippina's oldest son, Drusus Julius Caesar.

In 24, Sejanus initiated a barrage of legal attacks against Agrippina and her supporters. In the subsequent trials, some were exiled; others committed suicide or were executed. Despite the coolness between Agrippina and Livia, however, so long as Livia remained alive, Sejanus could not directly attack her or her children. Short of the emperor, Livia alone could forestall Sejanus.

In 25, Tiberius refused Sejanus's request to marry Livilla. In 26, Tiberius also refused Agrippina's request to marry. Gaius Asinius Gallus, a widower and no friend of Tiberius, was the man most likely to have been Agrippina's choice. Her intention may well have been to ally herself with a man of suitable background who could and would promote her interests. Gallus was known to be ambitious, and married to Agrippina, he might become the stepfather of an emperor. Tiberius, however, hated Gallus, who had once married his former wife, VIPSANIA AGRIPPINA.

Sejanus harassed Agrippina and fed her belief that the emperor had poisoned her husband. She came to believe that Tiberius intended also to poison her. While dinning with the emperor, she did not eat and when offered some fruit by Tiberius, she instead handed it to her servants. Tiberius remarked to his mother that it would not be surprising if he took action against someone who thought he was trying to poison her.

Tiberius made no immediate move against Agrippina or her sons. Doing so would have caused a confrontation with his mother who was already in her 80s. After the death of Livia in 29, however, Tiberius sent a letter to the Senate in which he accused Agrippina of arrogance and pride and her son Nero of homosexuality. Supporters of Agrippina gathered outside the Senate with signs and shouted that the letter was a fabrication of Sejanus. The Senate did nothing. Sejanus informed Tiberius of the Senate's inaction and the behavior of the mob. Tiberius sent another letter that denounced the actions of the crowd and demanded that the matter be decided by him. Agrippina was exiled to the tiny island of Pandateria off the coast of Campania. Nero was banished to Pontia off the same coast and executed or forced to commit suicide in 31. In 30, Sejanus convinced Tiberius that Agrippina's son Drusus was also a threat and should be imprisoned. He was incarcerated under the palace.

In 31, the end came for Sejanus. Following receipt of information from the younger Antonia, mother-in-law to Agrippina and mother to Livilla, Tiberius ordered Sejanus imprisoned for treason. Sejanus was strangled on October 18. His death did not help Agrippina, who died of starvation in 33, as did her son Drusus.

After her death, Tiberius accused Agrippina of adultery with Gallus. Agrippina's reputation for chastity, however, was only equaled by that of Tiberius's mother, Livia. The very characteristics for which Tiberius hated Agrippina—ambition and determination—were those for which she was also most honored. She would have rejoiced to see that in the end it was her son Caligula who succeeded Tiberius as emperor of Rome.

Sources

Suetonius. *The Lives of the Caesars:* Tiberius 53.
Tacitus. *Annales* 1.33, 69; 2.43, 55, 70, 72, 75; 3.1, 3–4, 17; 4.12, 17, 40, 52–54, 60; 5.3–4; 6.25.
Balsdon, J. P. V. D. *Roman Women.* New York: John Day Comp., 1963, *passim.*
Bauman, Richard A. *Women and Politics in Ancient Rome.* London: Routledge, 1994, *passim.*
Levick, Barbara. *Tiberius the Politician.* London: Thames and Hudson, 1976, *passim.*
Marsh, Frank Burr. *The Reign of Tiberius.* New York: Barnes and Noble, 1931, *passim.*
Oxford Classical Dictionary, ed. by Simon Hornblower and Antony Spawforth. 3d. ed. New York: Oxford University Press, 1996, p. 1,601.
Syme, Ronald. *Tacitus.* 2 vols. Oxford: Clarendon Press, 1958, *passim.*

▣ Agrippina the Younger, Julia
(15–59 C.E.)   Roman: Italy
Augusta; political player

Julia Agrippina grew up under the influence of her formidable mother the elder, Vipsania AGRIPPINA. Like her mother, she was ambitious for herself and her son, and had witnessed the destruction wrought by ambition on members of her family and friends close to the emperor. No more ruthless than those around her, she was exiled and recalled, hated and adored. A brilliant woman, politically astute, charming on occasion, and cultured, she left a now lost memoir that justified her choices during the reigns of three different emperors, one of whom

was her brother; the second, her husband; and the third, her son.

The younger Agrippina was born on November 6, 15 C.E., at Ara Ubiorum (modern Cologne), one of nine children and the eldest daughter of Agrippina and Germanicus Julius Caesar. Her father was Augustus's stepgrandson, and her mother was Augustus's granddaughter by his only child JULIA (6). Agrippina the Younger married Gnaeus Domitius Ahenobarbus in 28, when she was 13. He was described as despicable, cruel, and dishonest. He was also rich.

Only a year later, in 29, Agrippina's mother and brother Nero Julius Caesar were banished by Tiberius for plotting against him. In 31, Nero Julius Caesar died through either murder or suicide, and in 33, her mother died by starvation. Her brother Drusus Julius Caesar, imprisoned in 30, died in prison in 33.

Julia Agrippina's son Nero Claudius Caesar was born in 37, the same year that her one surviving brother, Gaius Caligula, succeeded Tiberius as emperor. Caligula honored Agrippina along with his two other surviving sisters as honorary Vestal

Julia Agrippina
(Date: 51 C.E.–52 C.E. 1001.130042, Archives, American Numismatic Society)

Virgins and raised their status and influence with an honor that was without precedent by adding their names to the annual oaths of allegiance to the emperor. When JULIA DRUSILLA (1), Caligula's favorite, died in 38, he deified her.

After her sister's death, Agrippina had an affair with her brother-in-law, Marcus Aemilius Lepidus, who may have had his eye on succession as perhaps did Agrippina. In 39, Caligula exiled Agrippina for joining a plot to assassinate him, although what actually happened remains a mystery. It is possible that Agrippina and her only surviving sister, JULIA LIVILLA, feared that their increasingly irrational brother might turn on them. Their position was further threatened by MILONIA CAESONIA, whom Caligula married in 40, already pregnant with a child.

Agrippina returned from exile when Claudius became emperor in 41 C.E., a year after her husband Domitius Ahenobarbus died. She set out to protect and promote the interests of her son, the future emperor Nero, and to find a new husband. Possibly, she married Lucius Cornelius Sulla Felix, consul in 33, but if so, the marriage was short-lived. Servius Sulpicius Galba better fit her needs. He was very wealthy and liked by Claudius; however, he had a wife, Aemilia Lepida. Aemilia's mother was said to have slapped Agrippina in public over her forward behavior. Agrippina finally settled on Gaius Passienus Crispus, consul in 44, a very wealthy older man.

The fact that Passienus Crispus was already married to a most formidable woman failed to deter Agrippina. His wife, DOMITIA, Agrippina's former sister-in-law, was not a woman easily thrust aside. She and her sister DOMITIA LEPIDA had hated Agrippina since her earlier marriage to their brother, and they took every opportunity to undermine her. Their hatred was returned in full.

Agrippina was said to have poisoned Passienus Crispus for his wealth, and in 48, with the death of Claudius's wife Valeria MESSALLINA, she focused on her uncle. Never one to leave her affairs with men to chance, she used Marcus Antonius Pallas, one of the powerful freedmen surrounding Claudius, to further her influence. Successful in

her pursuit, she married Claudius in 49, after the Senate removed the prohibition against marriage between uncle and niece. Possibly to her credit, the next years of his reign were marked by increased cooperation with the Senate and a decline in extra-judicial murder.

With Pallas's aid, she persuaded Claudius to adopt Nero. In 50, he became one of the emperor's two sons. The other, Britannicus, son of Valeria Messallina, was younger by several years. Agrippina also arranged to have Nero marry Claudia OCTAVIA, Claudius's daughter. Only nine years old at the time of Agrippina's marriage with Claudius, she had been affianced to Lucius Junius Silanus since infancy. With the help of Lucius Vitellius, Claudius's close confidant and adviser, Silanus was accused of incest with his sister JUNIA CALVINA. He committed suicide in 49, on the day that Agrippina married Claudius, and Junia Calvina was banished by her. Nero and Claudia Octavia married in 53.

Never one for half-measures, Agrippina eliminated real and potential enemies. She had Silanus's brother, the unambitious Marcus Junius Silanus, poisoned so that his connections to Augustus would not imperil her son's claim, as well as to prevent any possibility that he would seek to avenge his brother's death. She arranged the execution of the powerful freedman Narcissus, who had urged Claudius to marry another woman. She also rid herself of possible rivals and arranged to have the beautiful LOLLIA PAULINA, a former wife of her brother Gaius Caligula, and whom Claudius found attractive, charged with using magic, banished, and eventually killed.

With Nero positioned to become emperor, Agrippina would tolerate no rival for her son's affections. In 54 she had her old enemy Domitia Lepida accused of using magic and posing a threat to Italy from the slaves on her vast estates in Calabria. Domitia was the grandmother of Britannicus, Nero's rival for the emperorship, and she had pampered Nero during the three years his mother was in exile. She was put to death.

Agrippina received the title Augusta, only the second woman to be so honored while alive and the first to carry the title during her husband's lifetime. Despite widespread and malicious gossip that she had poisoned Claudius, Nero followed Claudius as emperor in 54. On every count Agrippina had succeeded. She was truly her mother's daughter.

She exercised enormous power during the early years of Nero's reign, generally viewed as Nero's best years. However, her domination of his life came to a predictable end. Nero had an affair with ACTE, a freedwoman, in spite of Agrippina's objections. Agrippina's lover, Pallas, lost his power, and Lucius Annaeus Seneca and Sextus Afranius Burrus, Nero's closest advisers, turned against her. In order to frighten Nero, Agrippina seems to have hinted that she might support efforts to supplant him with his younger stepbrother Britannicus. In 55, Nero had Britannicus murdered.

Nero then fell in love with POPPAEA SABINA (2), a woman whom Agrippina hated and feared for her lowly origins and for her influence over Nero. Poppaea hated Agrippina, no less. She forced Nero to choose between herself and his mother. Nero had long been exasperated over his mother's attempts to dominate him and control his public behavior. The threat alone or in combination with other circumstances marked the end of Agrippina's dominion.

An elaborate plot was developed. A freedman, Anicetus, who hated Agrippina, arranged to have a ship on which Agrippina was to travel sink at sea and drown her. The plot failed. The ship did not completely sink, and Agrippina managed to swim ashore. Anicetus was less inventive the second time. Caught stretched out on her couch, she was repeatedly stabbed by Anicetus's henchmen. She was cremated the same night.

Sources

Dio Cassius. *Roman History* 52.1–14; 59.22.5–9; 60.4.2; 61.31.6, 8; 61.32.
Suetonius. *The Lives of the Caesars: Gaius Caligula* 7.
———. *The Lives of the Caesars: Claudius* 26.3; 39.2; 43.44.
———. *The Lives of the Caesars: Nero* 5.2; 6.1–4; 28.2; 34.1–4.
Tacitus. *Annales* 4.53; 12.1–9, 22, 25–27, 37, 41–42, 56–59, 64–69; 13.1–2, 5, 13–16, 18–21; 14.1–12.

Balsdon, J. P. V. D. *Roman Women.* New York: John Day Comp., 1963.
Barrett, Anthony A. *Agrippina: Sex, Power, and Politics in the Early Empire.* New Haven, Conn.: Yale University Press, 1996.
Bauman, Richard A. *Women and Politics in Ancient Rome.* London: Routledge, 1994.
Ferrill, A. *Caligula: Emperor of Rome.* London: Thames and Hudson, 1991.
Ginsberg, Judith. *Representing Agrippina: Constructions of Female Power in the Early Roman Empire.* New York: Oxford University Press, 2006.
Levick, Barbara. *Claudius: The Corruption of Power.* New Haven, Conn.: Yale University Press, 1993.
Oxford Classical Dictionary, ed. by Simon Hornblower and Antony Spawforth. 3d. ed. New York: Oxford University Press, 1996, p. 777.
Pauly, A., G. Wissowa, and W. Kroll. *Real-Encyclopadie d. Classischen Altertumswissenschaft 1893–.* (Germany: multiple publishers) 556.
Syme, Ronald. *The Augustan Aristocracy.* Oxford: Clarendon Press, 1986, p. 172.
———. *Tacitus.* 2 vols. Oxford: Clarendon Press, 1958, *passim.*

▣ Albina the Elder

(?–388 C.E.)   Roman: Rome
Christian ascetic

Albina lived during the political and religious turmoil of the fourth century that included Goths invading Italy and Christianization of the Roman elite. Her patrician family, the Caeionii, exemplified the process of intermarriage between Christians and pagans that enabled Christianity to permeate the senatorial ranks. Although her husband and mother's names are unknown, her father was Caeionius Rufus Albinus, consul 345 and 346 C.E. Albina's two daughters, MARCELLA and ASELLA, gained renown as ascetics in the early monastic movement of Christianity. After the death of her husband, Albina remained a celibate widow, a Christian *univira,* who married only once and was respected by pagan and Christian alike.

Albina owned vast estates in multiple provinces across the empire that she had inherited from her family and her husband and over which she had the right to bequeath, sell, or donate as she chose.

In senatorial families like hers, there was a tension between maintaining the integrity of family wealth and assuring its transfer to the next generation and the choice of an ascetic lifestyle, especially when it included donations of family property to support monasteries and the church.

The situation was particularly stark for Albina's family since neither of her daughters was likely to bear children. The elder one, Marcella, was widowed only seven months after her marriage and before she had any children. Albina proposed a second marriage to an elderly suitor Naeratius Cerealis. Despite a settlement that would have left Marcella among the wealthiest women in Rome, she refused. Asella, the younger daughter, never married and since youth pursued a monastic life.

Albina compromised with her family to protect the family property and allow her and her daughters to pursue ascetic lives. She gave the greater portion of her wealth to her brother, C. Caeionius Rufus, and to his children, her nieces and nephews. Marcella did the same. Freed from the burden of her wealth, Albina lived with her daughters on the Aventine, a wealthy residential section of the city, in a community of like-minded women who practiced simplicity of person, prayer, and study of the scriptures. They left the house infrequently, most often on errands of mercy.

Albina died in 388 C.E.

Sources

Jerome. Letter 44, 127.

Prosopography of the Later Roman Empire. Vol. I. Edited by A. H. M. Jones, J. R. Martindale, and J. Morris. Cambridge: Cambridge University Press, 1971. Reprinted 1992. p. 32.

Yarbrough, Anne. "Christianization in the Fourth Century: The Example of Roman Women." *Church History* 45, no. 2 (June 1976): 150–155.

◉ Albina the Younger
(c. 370–431 C.E.)
Roman: Italy, North Africa, and Palestine
wealthy, devout Christian

Albina sought a middle way that avoided the rigorous asceticism of her daughter, the younger MELA-NIA, yet acknowledged her attraction to an ascetic life. Fortunate or sagacious, she successfully divested herself of her estates at the very moment the Goths circled Rome. She left Italy for Africa as the Goths sacked Rome, and she never returned.

Albina was the granddaughter of C. Caeionius Rufus, brother of the elder ALBINA, who had successfully maintained the Caeionii family line after his sister and her daughters, MARCELLA and ASELLA, had retreated into an ascetic life. It is unknown if her father, Ceionius Rufius Albinus, prefect of Rome in 389–391 C.E., was pagan. Her grandmother Caecina Lolliana was a priestess of Isis and her uncle Publilius Caeionius Caecina Albinus was a Roman pontifex responsible for official state cults.

Albina married Valerius Publicola—a union she entered reluctantly. Since youth, she had been drawn to the ascetic examples of her great-aunt the elder Albina and her cousins Marcella and Asella. Albina named her daughter after her mother-in-law, the elder MELANIA, a renowned Christian ascetic. It was perhaps no surprise when the younger Melania sought to emulate her older female relatives and live an ascetic life. Albina and her husband, however, acting in a manner reminiscent of her own parents, persuaded Melania to marry Valerius Pinianus, scion of another ancient aristocratic family.

After the death of her two young children, the younger Melania convinced her husband to practice celibacy and distribute their vast fortune to charity. Albina, her husband, and the extended families on both sides opposed the couple's decision. The future of two families rested on Melania and Pinianus. With the exception of Albina's brother who did not marry, they were the only surviving members of their respective families from whom children could come.

The families acted to thwart the couple, at least in their effort to disperse the family property. Albina reluctantly joined her husband in a suit against the younger couple that claimed they were minors and therefore without full authority over their assets. Albina's reluctance may have been further heightened by pressure from her renowned mother-in-law who had returned to Italy after an absence of 27 years, in part to encourage her grandchildren to live celibate lives. The elder Melania stayed with the family on her trip to Italy. She strengthened the young couple's resolve and urged Albina and Publicola to moderate their opposition. She succeeded. Publicola relented. He gave his support to the young couple just before his death sometime in 406 C.E., after his mother's departure.

After Publicola died, and Albina was free to follow her own inclinations, she joined Melania and Pinianus in a modest villa on the Appian Way, and Pinianus put his palatial house on the Aventine up for sale. However, they were still threatened with suits over the family property from members of the extended families whose networks of relationships dominated the Senate. They sought imperial intervention from the emperor in Ravenna through SERENA who was in Rome. She was the right choice. The emperor had grown up in her household, and her husband, Stilicho, had been regent for the emperor during his minority. Serena, herself a Christian, obliged. She secured an edict that allowed Melania and Pinianus not only to dispose of their assets, but to use governors in the provinces in which they owned properties to act as their agents and to remit the proceeds to them directly.

It was none too soon to sell. The Goths were in Italy and heading to Rome. Pinianus was already unable to find a buyer for his large house as political and economic conditions rapidly deteriorated. In 408, Albina went with Melania, Pinianus, and their respective entourages to Sicily. From there Melania, Pinianus, and presumably Albina successfully sold their Italian holdings. Two years later, Alaric and the Goths sacked Rome and the three of them left Sicily for North Africa. Before leaving they managed to liquidate estates in Sicily and everywhere else except Spain and Africa. Although not as wealthy as her daughter and son-in-law, Albina was a large landholder. In addition to her father's wealth, some part of the holdings of her great-aunt, the elder Albina, had become hers. She benefited from divesting her estates just in time as did her daughter and son-in-law.

After the sack of Rome in 410, many wealthy Romans left for Africa, especially those with family or business connections there. Albina and her daughter and son-in-law arrived with significant amounts of liquid capital. They settled on their unsold estates in Tagaste, a region that had once been rich farmland, but a long period of Roman mismanagement and corruption compounded by drought had impoverished the area and eroded the urban infrastructure. It also was an area in which orthodox Christianity, favored by Albina and her family, faced serious competition from the Donatists, a sect that arose during the Diocletian persecutions at the end of the third century. These successors of Christians who had willingly suffered and even died for their faith were now a rigorist community with their own bishops and churches. Efforts at reconciliation with the orthodox church were rebuffed or botched while the Donatists claim of "purity," since only the truly righteous could hold membership, held a strong appeal among the poor, as did their claim of independence from any state authority.

The Donatists were a significant force around Carthage, but it was the orthodox bishop Alypius, known for his knowledge of the scriptures and a friend of the orthodox and illustrious Augustine, bishop in nearby Hippo, who welcomed them.

They were also well received by the local populace, Donatist and orthodox alike, who viewed them as an economic bonanza. Shortly after their arrival, the family visited the famous Augustine. Excited by the appearance of such a wealthy family, locals filled the church. They raised the cry for Augustine to ordain Pinianus and that he serve in Hippo. Some became quite unruly and uttered threats against the family. Violence threatened. Augustine restrained the congregation and insisted he would not ordain Pinianus without the man's consent.

Pinianus had no intention of being ordained. The matter appeared settled when he agreed that should he change his mind and become a cleric, he would serve in Hippo. Albina, however, was not satisfied. During the fracas the congregation had made clear that they wanted the family's money. Augustine responded to Albina in a long letter. Acknowledging that clergy, including bishops, sometimes sought wealthy benefactors, he defended the congregation, himself, and Alypius against the accusation that all they wanted from the family was their wealth.

The family spent approximately four years in Tagaste, not Hippo, and Tagaste benefited. Albina donated hangings and gold to the church under Alypius. Her children built a brother/sister house for religious life on their estates, in which, presumably, they lived with Melania as head of the community of young women, virgins, and widows and Pinianus in charge of the men. On the estates they also installed two bishops, one Donatist and one orthodox, and when they left they donated to the church in Tagaste the whole of the estate including buildings, workers, workshops, and artisans, all of which was greater in area than the city.

In 417, the family left for Palestine by way of Alexandria. They settled in Jerusalem, where they met the ascetic and noted churchman Jerome. Over the next years, Albina and Pinianus were often Melania's only links with the outside world as she lived an increasingly cloistered life. Albina continued to faithfully serve her daughter until her death in 431. Augustine dedicated to her his book *De Gratia Christi et de Peccato Originali* (On the grace of God and original sin).

Sources

Augustine. Letter 124; 125; 126.

Palladius. *The Lausiac History* 62.

Brown, Peter. *Augustine of Hippo: A Biography.* Berkeley: University of California Press, 1967.

Gerontius. *The Life of Melania the Younger.* Introduction, Translation, and Commentary by Elizabeth A. Clark. New York. Edward Mellon Press, 1984, *passim.*

James, A. H. M. *The Later Roman Empire 284–602: A Social, Economic, and Administrative Survey.* 2 vols. Norman: University of Oklahoma Press, 1964.

O'Donnell, James J. *Augustine: A New Biography.* New York: HarperCollins, 2005.

Prosopography of the Later Roman Empire. Vol. I. Edited by A. H. M. Jones, J. R. Martindale, and J. Morris. Cambridge: Cambridge University Press, 1971. Reprinted 1992. p. 33.

Yarbrough, Anne. "Christianization in the Fourth Century: The Example of Roman Women." *Church History* 45, no. 2. (June 1976): 149–165.

Albucilla

(first century C.E.)   Roman: Rome
alleged conspirator; convicted adulterer

Albucilla, notorious for her many lovers, divorced her one and only husband, Satrius Secundus. In 37 C.E., Albucilla and three senators, Lucius Arruntius, Gnaeus Domitius Ahenobarbus, who was the husband of the younger AGRIPPINA, and Vibius Marsus, as well as several lesser men, were accused of adultery and treason against the emperor Tiberius. The charges appear to have been instigated by Quintus Naevius Cordus Suetonius Macro, the prefect of the Praetorian Guard, without the knowledge of the already dying emperor. Macro presided over the questioning of witnesses and the torture of slaves.

The Senate deliberately moved slowly reflecting their sense that Macro had fabricated the charges and that the emperor had not long to live. All except Albucilla and Arruntius managed to escape punishment. Arruntius committed suicide. Albucilla, however, was not so successful. Carried into the Senate after a failed suicide attempt, she was convicted of adultery and died in prison.

Sources

Dio Cassius. *Roman History* 58.27.4.

Tacitus. *Annales* 6.47–48.

Bauman, Richard A. *Women and Politics in Ancient Rome.* London: Routledge, 1994, pp. 116, 164.

Levick, Barbara. *Tiberius the Politician.* London: Thames and Hudson, 1976, pp. 198–199.

Marsh, Frank Burr. *The Reign of Tiberius.* New York: Barnes and Noble, 1931, *passim.*

Marshall, A. J. "Ladies at Law: The Role of Women in the Roman Civil Courts." In *Studies in Latin Literature and Roman History,* ed. by C. Deroux. Brussels, Belgium: Latomus, 1989, p. 348.

Alce

(fourth century B.C.E.)   Greek: Athens
self-made woman

Alce, born a slave, worked as a prostitute and succeeded in gaining freedom, respectability, and citizenship for her eldest son. Working in a brothel owned by Euctemon of Cephsia in Piraeus outside of Athens, she cohabited with another slave, Dion, and had two sons. After some sort of violent fracas, Dion fled to Sicyon. Alce continued to work for Euctemon until she became too old. He freed her, and she took over the management of his tenement in Athens.

In time, Euctemon left his wife and children and moved in with Alce, who persuaded him to have her eldest son by Dion recognized as his own. Philoctemon, the eldest son of Euctemon's first wife, objected to the boy's registration in his father's phratry, which was the prerequisite for citizenship and inheritance. Euctemon threatened Philoctemon that he would marry again and have a second family. Faced with the prospect of an unknown number of future stepsisters and -brothers that could significantly diminish his portion of the estate, Philoctemon capitulated.

Sources

Isaeus. Speeches of Isaeus 6.18–26.
Sealey, R. "On Lawful Concubinage in Athens." *Classical Antiquity* 3 (1984): pp. 111–133.
Walters, K. R. "Women and Power in Classical Athens." In *Woman's Power, Man's Game: Essays on Classical Antiquity in Honor of Joy K. King*, ed. by Mary DeForest. Wauconda, Ill.: Bolchazy-Carducci, 1993, pp. 203–204.

Alexandra

(first century B.C.E.)   Jewish: Judaea
conspirator

Alexandra gained the support of CLEOPATRA VII to oppose her son-in-law, Herod the Great, and died in an attempt to overthrow him. She was the daughter of John Hyrcanus II, the Hasmonaean high priest of Judaea (63–40 B.C.E.). Her daughter, Mariamme I, married Herod the Great after he thwarted an invasion of Judaea by Antigonus, an anti-Roman Hasmonaean leader.

Herod, appointed king of Judaea by Mark Antony and the Roman Senate, made an obscure Jew from Babylonia, Hananel, high priest. Angry that a Hasmonaean was not appointed, Alexandra appealed to Cleopatra, who always engaged in one or another intrigue against Herod in hope of extending her rule over Judaea. Alexandra was suc-

cessful: Herod appointed her 17-year-old son Aristobulus, high priest.

Herod had Aristobulus drowned at a bathing party in Jericho in 36 B.C.E. Alexandra informed Cleopatra of his murder, and Cleopatra pressed Antony to right the wrong. However, Herod charmed Antony, who wanted a strong ruler to carry out his policies. Herod reappointed Hananel high priest. Thus ended Cleopatra VII's dream of acquiring control over Judaea.

Subsequently Herod fell ill, and Alexandra conspired with Herod's sons to seize control over the fortifications of Jerusalem, enabling them to usurp the rule of Herod. The plot failed, and Herod had Alexandra executed in 28 B.C.E.

Sources

Josephus. *Antiquitates Judaicae (Jewish Antiquities)* 15.23–27, 35–40, 53–56, 62–65, 74–76, 247–52.
Grant, Michael. *The Jews in the Roman World.* New York: Charles Scribner's Sons, 1973, p. 69.
Jones, A. H. M. *The Herods of Judaea.* Rev. ed. Oxford: Clarendon Press, 1967, *passim*.

Amalasuntha

(?–535 C.E.)   Goth: Italy
ruler

Amalasuntha was a Goth. She was regent for her son and ruled Italy as a semiautonomous region of the Roman Empire. Her mother was Ausefleda and her father was Theodoric, leader of the Goths who ruled Italy for 36 years as a nominal part of the Roman Empire. Educated as a Roman, Amalasuntha was eloquent in Greek and Latin, as well as the spoken dialects of the Goths. Her education reflected her father's admiration for Roman law and administration, which he had learned as a young man during the 10 years he spent in Constantinople as a hostage to assure Goth compliance with Roman agreements.

In 515, she was betrothed to Eutharic, a Goth of elite lineage from Spain. Three years later she gave birth to a son Athalaric and later a daughter Matasuntha. The emperor Justin appointed her husband consul in 519, which placed him in line to succeed her father, Theodoric. Unfortunately, in 522 Eutharic died, four years before Theodoric.

After her father's death in 526, Amalasuntha became regent for her underage son, Athalaric. She followed the conciliatory policies of her father and continued to merge Goth and Roman civil law. She welcomed collaboration with the Senate and restored confiscated properties to the families of two notable senators who had been executed, the philosophers Boethius and Symmachus. Eloquently, she wrote to the emperor Justin urging that the tomb of her father should also be the burial place of old hatreds.

For six years after assuming the regency there was peace, even though Goths were unaccustomed to rule by a woman. In 532, her control over her son was challenged as too Roman and inappropriate for a future leader of the Goths. She had no choice but to allow her son to come under the care of a faction who resented her pro-Roman policies. Amalasuntha became aware of the plot against her. Although she forestalled the plotters with military assignments that scattered the leaders to posts on the northern frontier, she decided to also act more forcefully.

Amalasuntha made overtures to Justinian, who had become emperor in 527, and requested safe refuge in Constantinople and a stopping place along the way. He complied. She prepared for travel to Epidamnus, on the coast of Illyria opposite the heel of Italy, and, if necessary, on to Constantinople. She sent a ship ahead with treasure amounting to some twice the annual expenditures of the Western empire and instructed the captain not to unload but await further instructions. She was not idle in Italy. She arranged to kill the pro-Goth faction in the court and the army and waited in Ravenna for the outcome. When she learned of their deaths, she recalled the ship and its treasure.

Amalasuntha's problems were far from over. Her son was dying, and a woman alone was not an acceptable ruler to Romans or Goths. In the East, Justinian harbored plans to restore the glory of the empire and regain control over Western territories that included Italy. Her cousin Theodahad, who was as ambitious as she offered an alternative to the imperial power of the East and a male figurehead for her rule in Italy. Theodahad, no respecter of the niceties of law, had accumulated vast tracts of land equal in size to modern Tuscany. Amalasuntha had successfully brought suit against him in the courts and forced him to repudiate some of his land claims. In the flux of the moment Justinian's envoys negotiated separately with these two very different personalities. As an opening bid in the negotiations, Theodahad offered his Tuscan properties in return for a safe haven in Constantinople. Amalasuntha may have offered her loyalty in the rule of Italy. Neither, however, desired escape to the East.

In October 534, Amalasuntha's son died. She reached an agreement with Theodahad that distributed power and authority between them. It was an alternative to the threat posed by Justinian from the East to them both, and also established a male figure in authority over Italy. Treachery was possible, but the threat of an invasion by Justinian was the bulwark against which Amalasuntha gambled. However, Amalasuntha no longer had the support of the Goth or Roman elites. Competing factions filled Italy with plots of ambition and revenge and with conspiracies fed by slights, resentments, and quarrels accumulating over years. Justinian's policy of setting one group against another successfully destabilized the situation.

THEODORA, the Augusta, and Justinian worked in tandem to destabilize Italy. Amalasuntha posed no threat to Theodora. Had she delivered Italy, she might have gained a position as ruler of a semiautonomous region within the larger empire. There has, however, been a tradition that records collusion between Theodora and Theodahad's wife, Gudelina. Possibly, Theodahad had been led to believe that he had Justinian's agreement to rule Italy under the suzerainty of Constantinople, if he surrendered Sicily and removed Amalasuntha. Justinian, abetted by Theodora, may have emboldened Theodahad to betray Amalasuntha.

Theodahad acted. Amalasuntha was imprisoned on an island in Lake Bolsena in Tuscany. Even there, she posed a threat. Theodahad arranged her assassination in April 535. Family members of the plotters whom she had ordered assassinated three years earlier were only too happy to comply. Justinian used Amalasuntha's murder to order an invasion of Italy.

Sources

Cassiodorus. *Variae* 11, 1, 6f.; 8, 1–8; 9–1; 10–1.4, 19–24; 8f.

Procopius. *Gothic Wars* vol. I–V. ii. 1–29; iii. 10–30; iv. 1–31.: *Secret History* xvi. 1, 5; xxiv. 23.

Bury, J. B. *Later Roman Empire from the Death of Theodosius to the Death of Justinian,* vol. 2. New York: Dover Publications Inc., 1958, 159–167.

Frankforter, A. Daniel. "Amalasuntha, Procopius, and a Woman's Place." *Journal of Women's History* 8 (Summer 1996): 41–57.

Prosopography of the Later Roman Empire. Vol. III. Edited by A. H. M. Jones, J. R. Martindale, and J. Morris. Cambridge: Cambridge University Press, 1971. Reprinted 1992, 65.

▣ Amastris

(fourth–third century B.C.E.)
Persian: Asia Minor
ruler

Amastris was a prudent regent who ruled Heraclea Pontica on the Black Sea after the death of her husband. She was the daughter of Oxyartis, the brother of the Persian king Darius III. Her first husband, Craterus, was one of 80 Macedonian officers who had married women of the Persian nobility after Alexander the Great's victory at Guagamela in 331 B.C.E. After the death of Alexander, they divorced, and Amastris married Dionysius, tyrant of Heraclea Pontica (337–305 B.C.E.). She had three children: Clearchus, Oxathres, and Amastris.

After Dionysius died, Amastris became regent. She gained the support of Antigonus, who sought control of Asia Minor after Alexander's death. Later Amastris switched her allegiance to Lysimachus, another of Alexander's former generals, who had become ruler of Thrace and northwest Asia Minor. Lysimachus, who coveted her wealthy city, offered her marriage to seal the alliance. In 302, they married and had a son, Alexandrus.

Lysimachus divorced Amastris to marry ARSINOË II PHILADELPHUS, the daughter of Ptolemy I Soter who ruled Egypt. Amastris resumed her rule over Heraclea, which she enlarged and established a city named after herself.

In 289, Amastris was murdered by her sons. Her former husband, Lysimachus, avenged her death and took control of the city of Amastris.

Sources

Arrian. *Anabasis of Alexander* 7.4.

Diodorus Siculus. *Library of History* 20.109.6–7.

Strabo. *Geography.* 12.3.10.

Cary, M. *A History of the Greek World from 323 to 146 B.C.* London: Methuen, 1951, pp. 55, 98.

Der Kleine Pauly; Lexikon der Antike, ed. by Konrat Julius Furchtegott and Walther Sontheimer. Stuttgart, Germany: A. Druckenmuller, 1984, pp. 289–290.

▣ Anastasia (1)

(?–early fourth century C.E.)   Roman: Italy
political actor

Anastasia was associated with a plot to assassinate Constantine the Great. She was Constantine's half sister. They shared the same father, Constantius I. Constantine's mother, however, was their father's first wife, HELENA, who had inspired her son's adoption of Christianity in 313. Anastasia's mother was the emperor's second wife, FLAVIA MAXIMIA THEODORA.

The marriage of Anastasia's mother Flavia and Constantius was a political arrangement. Flavia was the daughter of the emperor Maximian, who had appointed Constantius Caesar in the West. Marriage with Flavia successfully situated Constantius as next in line to succeed Maximian.

Constantine followed Constantius as emperor, and Anastasia married Bassianus. Constantine appointed him Caesar in the West, in charge of Italy and Illyricum. Bassianus, influenced by his brother Senechio, who supported the Western emperor Licinius, agreed to assassinate Constantine. Constantine discovered the plot and executed Bassianus. Nothing more is known of Anastasia.

Sources

Brill's New Pauly: Encyclopedia of the Ancient World: Classical Tradition, Vol. 1. Edited by Manfred Landfester et al. Boston: Brill, 2002, p. 643.

◉ Anastasia (2)

(?–early sixth century C.E.)
Roman: Constantinople, Jerusalem
political actor

Anastasia was among the wealthy women in Constantinople whose strong religious beliefs and imperial connections affected the politics of the time. Like many others close to imperial power, she died far from Constantinople.

Married to Pompeius, a nephew of the emperor Anastasius I, who reigned between 491 and 518 C.E., she had at least one child, a son. Among her friends was ANICIA JULIANA, whose lineage reached back to Theodosius the Great, who had ruled a century earlier between 383 to 395, and whose husband was a general under Anastasius in his war against the Persians. Both women were orthodox Christians who supported the Chalcedon compromise of 451 which affirmed the two natures of Christ, human and divine, cojoined yet separate. When the Chalcedon compromise came under threat by Monophysites, who supported a single divine nature of Christ, the women's friendship became a political alliance.

The women used their connections with the imperial establishment on behalf of visiting clergy and played a part in the growing estrangement between East and West. In 511 they lobbied for Sabas, one of the founders of Eastern monasticism, when he came to Constantinople to plead with the emperor on behalf of the persecuted orthodox practitioners and bishops in the East. In 518, the emperor granted Anastasia the status of *patricia,* an honor from the emperor for service to the empire, and in 519 she corresponded with the Roman bishop Hermisdas in hope that her explanation of events would contribute to healing a misunderstanding over the actions of Acacius, the bishop of Constantinople. The controversy had begun in 481 when Acacius, a moderate bishop, had helped draft a letter issued by the emperor Zeno to the Egyptian church designed to reconcile East and West. It had the opposite effect, and the Western church excommunicated Acacius, although he retained his position in Constantinople.

Decades later, in January 532, there was a serious threat to the rule of Justinian. Mobs besieged the palace. Anastasia's nephews Pompeius and Hypatius were in the palace, and the mob raised the cry for Hypatius to become emperor. Justinian ordered them out. The rioters surged to Hypatius's house, dragged him out, and proclaimed him emperor. Senators who felt slighted or overlooked or who hated the low-class background and visible power of the Augusta THEODORA joined the fray.

The mob, as well as the disgruntled senators, failed to understand Theodora. She rallied her husband and his supporters with an impassioned speech that effectively ended the revolt. Pompeius and Hypatius were executed. Justinian confiscated the property of the two families, presumably including that of Anastasia, although he later restored much of it along with their honorific titles.

After the revolt, Anastasia went to Jerusalem to live a religious life. She founded a monastery on the Mount of Olives where she spent the rest of her life.

Sources

Procopius. *Persian Wars* I, xxiv; 19–21, 53, 56–58.
Theophanus. *Chronicle* AM 6005.
Prosopography of the Later Roman Empire. Vol. II. Edited by A. H. M. Jones, J. R. Martindale, and J. Morris. Cambridge: Cambridge University Press, 1971. Reprinted 1992, 76–77.

◉ Anastasia (3)

(?–576 C.E.)   Roman: Constantinople, Egypt
religious woman

Anastasia was a well-born woman of religious principle who lived in Constantinople. Her religious vocation followed upon her efforts to escape the attentions of the emperor Justinian and any potential conflict they would have caused with the Augusta THEODORA. From Justinian, Anastasia received the title *patricia,* granted to favored persons. He encouraged her to live in the palace. Noted for her good sense and faced with his attentions, Anastasia left Constantinople for Alexandria.

She either established or joined a monastery in the neighborhood of Ennaton, about five miles distant from Alexandria. She supported herself by weaving cloth, a common occupation for monastic women of the time. After the death of Theodora in 548, Justinian or his agents attempted to find her. She left the monastery, adopted male clothing, and went into the desert.

She met Father Daniel, a monk who became her mentor and protector for the remaining decades of her life. Near Wadi Natrum, a center of monasticism at the time, she entered a cave, where she lived as an anchorite (solitary ascetic) for 28 years, until she died in 576. During all her years in the desert she kept her identity and sex hidden to all except her mentor, Father Daniel.

Sources

Prosopography of the Later Roman Empire. Vol. II. Edited by A. H. M. Jones, J. R. Martindale, and J. Morris. Cambridge: Cambridge University Press, 1971. Reprinted 1992, 77.

▣ Ancharia

(first century B.C.E.) Roman: Rome
mother of Octavia

Ancharia was the first wife of Gaius Octavius and the mother of OCTAVIA (1). Her husband came from a wealthy equestrian family in Velitrae. After she died, her husband married ATIA (1); their only son, Octavian, became the emperor Augustus.

Sources

Plutarch. *Vitae Parallelae (Parallel Lives): Antonius* 31.
Suetonius. *The Lives of the Caesars: Augustus* 4.

▣ Anteia

(first century C.E.) Roman: Rome
stoic

Anteia belonged to the fourth generation of a Roman family noted for literary and philosophical achievements and for principled acts rooted in honor and commitment. She, like all of her predecessors, experienced the wrath of the emperors. Anteia was the wife of Helvidius Priscus the Younger, a well-known Stoic of his day.

When Priscus was executed by the emperor Domitian for presenting a farce that Domitian

interpreted as criticism of his recent divorce, Anteia remained in Rome. Her mother-in-law, FANNIA (2), and her grandmother-in-law, the younger ARRIA, were exiled. After Domitian's death, Anteia collaborated with her husband's friend Pliny the Younger to charge Publicius Certus, whose accusations had led to her husband's death. She arranged for Fannia and Arria to press suit jointly with Pliny and testify. The Senate, after much debate, agreed to let Pliny proceed with the suit. However, the new emperor, Nerva, not wanting to rake up the past, prevented the case from going forward.

Cornutus Tetullius spoke in the Senate on behalf of the women. He explained that even if no legal penalty would be exacted, Certus should be disgraced and stripped of his honors. The women wanted a truthful and accurate rendering of how Publicius Certus had sought the death penalty for Helvidius to curry favor with Domitian. They succeeded at least insofar as Certus failed to become consul.

Anteia had three children, two of whom died in childbirth.

Sources

Pliny the Younger. *Epistulae* 9.13.
Suetonius. *The Lives of the Caesars:* Domitian 10.

▣ Antigone

(third century B.C.E.)
Greek: Macedonia, Egypt, and Epirus
married to a ruler

Antigone married the deposed ruler of Epirus, Pyrrhus (319–272 B.C.E.). The marriage assured aid to Pyrrhus from Antigone's mother, BERENICE I. Berenice had married her own brother, Ptolemy I Soter, to become the second most powerful voice in Egypt. Pyrrhus had ruled Epirus while still a minor, but had been deposed in 302 B.C.E. and had fled to his brother-in-law Demetrius I in Macedonia. After having secured peace with Egypt, Demetrius had sent Pyrrhus to Egypt to cement friendly relations.

Married, Antigone and Pyrrhus returned to Epirus well equipped with men and funds. Rather than war, Pyrrhus offered to rule jointly with

Neoptolemus, the usurper. Antigone learned of a plot by Neoptolemus to poison Pyrrhus from a woman named Phaenarete and informed her husband. Forewarned, Pyrrhus invited Neoptolemus to dinner and killed him. Antigone had a son, named Ptolemy after her father. Her husband built a city and named it Berenicis in her honor.

Sources
Plutarch. *Vitae Parallelae (Parallel Lives): Pyrrhus* 4–6.

◉ Antistia (1)
(second century B.C.E.)   Roman: Rome
reformer

Antistia was the wife of the rich, arrogant, and powerful Appius Claudius Pulcher, who was consul in 143 B.C.E. and part of the reform faction around Tiberius and Gaius Sempronius Gracchus.

She and CORNELIA (2), the mother of the Gracchi, were contemporaries. Antistia's daughter CLAUDIA (2) married Tiberius. The marriage cemented a political alliance between her husband and son-in-law over agrarian reform. Another daughter, CLAUDIA (3), became a Vestal Virgin. She used the power of her office to shield her father from destruction, therby enabling him to celebrate a disputed triumph for the defeat of the Salassi in Cisalpine Gaul. Antistia was the grandmother, through her son, Appius Claudius Pulcher, consul in 79 B.C.E., of the beautiful and infamous CLODIA (2) and the brilliant, brash, amoral Publius Clodius Pulcher.

Sources
Plutarch. *Vitae Parallelae (Parallel Lives): Tiberius Gracchus* 4.1–3.

◉ Antistia (2)
(first century B.C.E.)   Roman: Rome
political victim

Antistia fell victim to an upper-class pattern of using serial marriages to move up the social and political ladder of power. In 86 B.C.E., her father, Publius Antistius, had been prosecutor against Gnaeus Pompeius (Pompey the Great) in a case of misappropriating public funds. He was so taken with Pompey's handling of his own defense that he sought him out as a son-in-law. The young Antistia and Pompey married.

In 82, Antistius was killed in the Senate on orders of the younger Gaius Marius during the armed conflict between the Marian forces and Lucius Cornelius Sulla after the death of the elder Marius. Pompey served under Sulla. Sulla, no less impressed than Antistius had been years earlier, persuaded Pompey to marry AEMILIA (2), the daughter of his wife CAECILIA METELLA (1). Pompey divorced Antistia. After the divorce, Antistia and her mother committed suicide.

Sources
Appian. *Roman History: Bella civilian (Civil Wars)* 1.88.
Plutarch. *Vitae Parallelae (Parallel Lives): Pompeius* 4.2–3; 9.1–2.
Pauly, A., G. Wissowa, and W. Kroll. *Real-Encyclopadie d. Classischen Altertumswissenschaft 1893–*. (Germany: multiple publishers) 60.

◉ Antistia Pollitta
(?–65 C.E.)   Roman: Italy
political victim

Antistia Pollitta and her husband were rumored to have plotted an overthrow of the emperor Nero. She was the daughter of Lucius Antistius Vetus, consul with Nero in 55 C.E. Her husband was the wealthy and philosophically inclined Rubellius Plautus. Both could trace their lineage to the beginning of the empire: she to Mark Antony and the independent-minded OCTAVIA (2), sister of the emperor Augustus, and he to LIVIA DRUSILLA, Augustus's powerful wife and Augusta in her own right.

Rumors of Rubellius Plautus's ambition were circulated by enemies of the younger AGRIPPINA, Nero's mother. It was said that Agrippina planned to remove Nero and install Plautus as emperor. There was hope that the rumors would effect a split between mother and son. Called upon to defend herself, however, Agrippina convinced her son of her unwavering allegiance. Nonetheless, reports of Plautus as a possible alternative to Nero did not cease. Alarmed, the emperor suggested that Rubellius Plautus retire to his family estates in Asia where he could enjoy the life of contemplation. Antistia, along with a few of their friends, accompanied her husband.

Given the situation, Antistia's father urged her husband to take up arms against the emperor. There was discontent on which he could capitalize, and he was about to suffer the consequences of treason regardless of his behavior. Plautus refused. He had no taste for war, even though he understood it was only a matter of time before Nero had him killed. Perhaps he also hoped that if he remained passive, Nero would spare Antistia and their children.

In 62 C.E., Antistia stood by as a centurion beheaded her husband and sent his head to Nero in Rome. Thereafter, Antistia remained in mourning. In 65 Nero ordered the suicide of her father, who had retired with Antistia to his estate in Formiae. Antistia went to Nero in Naples to plead for her father's life. He refused even to receive her. Informed that there was no hope, her father divided his money among his slaves and ordered them to remove all furnishings except for three couches in one room. Antistia, Antistius Vetus, and his mother-in-law SEXTIA (2) severed their veins. Covered with a single cloth, they were carried to the baths, where they died. Antistia was the last to expire. Nero had the Senate indict them after their death.

Sources
Tacitus. *Annales* 14.22, 58–59; 16.10–11.
Marshall, A. J. "Ladies at Law: The Role of Women in the Roman Civil Courts." In *Studies in Latin Literature and Roman History,* ed. by C. Deroux. Brussels, Belgium: Latomus, 1989, pp. 351–352.

Antonia (1)
(first century B.C.E.)   Roman: Rome
captured by pirates

Antonia suffered the dangers of sea travel in the ancient world. She was captured by pirates. More fortunate than many others, she was ransomed by her father Marcus Antonius, a famous orator and consul in 99 B.C.E., who only a year earlier had celebrated a triumph for defeating the Cilician pirates.

Sources
Plutarch. *Vitae Parallelae (Parallel Lives): Pompeius* 24.

Antonia (2)
(first century B.C.E.)   Roman: Rome
divorced wife

Antonia was divorced by Mark Antony, who became convinced that she was having an affair with his friend Publius Cornelius Dolabella. She was Antony's second wife, as well as his cousin. Antonia, the daughter of Gaius Antonius, coconsul with Marcus Tullius Cicero in 63 B.C.E., would not have been the only woman of the late republic to find Dolabella a desirable lover. The third husband of Cicero's daughter TULLIA (2), he was notoriously attractive, considered quite dissolute and, chronically short of funds, a well-known womanizer.

Antonia and Antony had a daughter, ANTONIA (3), who married the wealthy Pythodorus from Tralles.

Sources
Plutarch. *Vitae Parallelae (Parallel Lives): Antonius* 9.

Antonia (3)
(c. 54/49 B.C.E.–?)   Roman: Rome and Tralles
political wife

Antonia, born between 54 and 49 B.C.E., was the daughter of Mark Antony and his second wife ANTONIA (2). It was intended that their daughter marry Marcus Aemilius Lepidus, the son of a fellow triumvir. However, as her father's alliance with CLEOPATRA VII focused his political ambitions in the East, an alliance became Antonia and Pythodorus of Tralles, a wealthy commercial city in Asia Minor, became more desirable. They married in 34 B.C.E.

Antonia and Pythodorus had a daughter, PYTHODORIS, who married the ruler of Pontus, Polemon, and later Archelaus, who ruled Cappadocia. Antonia died quite young, but her daughter ruled Pontus during the reign of Augustus.

Sources

Macurdy, Grace. *Hellenistic Queens*. Reprint. Chicago: Ares Publishers, 1985, pp. 10–11.

Oxford Classical Dictionary, ed. by Simon Hornblower and Antony Spawforth. 3d. ed. New York: Oxford University Press, 1996, p. 113.

Pauly, A., G. Wissowa, and W. Kroll. *Real-Encyclopadie d. Classischen Altertumswissenschaft 1893–.* (Germany: multiple publishers) 113.

▣ Antonia (4)

(28 –66 C.E.)   Roman: Rome
political player; possible conspirator

Antonia, born in 28 C.E., was the only child of the emperor Claudius and his second wife AELIA PAETINA. Her position as the emperor's daughter opened the possibility of succession for her husbands. She could become the emperor's wife, if she survived.

Antonia married Gnaeus Pompeius Magnus, the son of Marcus Licinius Crassus Frugi, consul in 27 C.E., and Scribonia, about whom we only know her name. Antonia's husband belonged to the group of powerful aristocrats who opposed Claudius's wife Valeria MESSALLINA. By virtue of his own lineage cojoined with that of Antonia, Pompeius became a serious contender to succeed Claudius and challenged the primacy of Messallina's son, Britannicus, as the most favored heir. By 46 or early 47, Messallina convinced Claudius that Pompeius was dangerous. Both he and his parents were killed.

The widowed Antonia married Faustus Cornelius Sulla Felix, the lethargic half brother of Messallina, who posed no threat to the latter's ambitions. Sulla and Antonia outlived both Messallina and Claudius and for a time flourished. Sulla became consul in 52. However, in 58 he was banished and later killed by the emperor Nero.

In 66, Antonia was herself killed. Possibly she was a participant in the Pisonian conspiracy (65 C.E.) against Nero. Gaius Calpurnius Piso, the ineffectual figurehead of the conspiracy, supposedly promised to divorce his wife and marry Antonia after Nero's assassination. They were to meet in the temple of Ceres on the day of the planned assassination and proceed to the camp of the Praetorian Guard where Piso would be proclaimed emperor. The marriage would have clothed Piso in Antonia's lineage, and she would at last become the wife of an emperor.

Perhaps, however, she did not seek the role of emperor's wife and was not even among the conspirators. After Nero caused the death of his wife POPPAEA SABINA (2), he was said to have asked Antonia to marry him in an effort to repair his damaged reputation. Only after she refused did he order her death.

Sources

Suetonius. *The Lives of the Caesars:* Claudius 27.1–2.
———. *The Lives of the Caesars:* Nero 35.4.
Tacitus. *Annales* 13.23, 47; 14.57; 15.53.
Balsdon, J. P. V. D. *Roman Women.* New York: John Day Comp., 1963, p. 123.
Bauman, Richard A. *Women and Politics in Ancient Rome.* London: Routledge, 1994, p. 172.
Oxford Classical Dictionary, ed. by Simon Hornblower and Antony Spawforth. 3d. ed. New York: Oxford University Press, 1996, p. 113.
Pauly, A., G. Wissowa, and W. Kroll. *Real-Encyclopadie d. Classischen Altertumswissenschaft 1893–.* (Germany: multiple publishers) 115.
Syme, Ronald. *The Augustan Aristocracy.* Oxford: Clarendon Press, 1986, *passim.*

▣ Antonia the Elder

(39 B.C.E.–?)   Roman: Rome
political player

Antonia, elder daughter of Mark Antony and the independent-minded OCTAVIA (2), sister of the emperor Augustus, grew up in a household filled with children from her parents' multiple marriages. Her parents had married to cement the Pact of Brundisium in 40 B.C.E. that established a Roman state divided between her father and her uncle. The pact failed, leading to a renewal of civil war that pitted Roman against Roman and left many children of the senatorial class orphans and without clear claim or access to family or wealth.

Antonia was born in 39 B.C.E., when her parents were in Greece negotiating with her uncle Octavian. He sought Antony's aid in a campaign against Sextus Pompeius Magnus, the son of Gnaeus Pompeius Magnus (Pompey the Great) and leader of the remaining republican forces. After her parents' divorce in 32, Antonia and her younger sister ANTONIA stayed with their mother in a household that also included the three children from Octavia's previous marriage to Gaius Claudius Marcellus, an opponent of Caesar and supporter of Pompey, who had died in 40 B.C.E. After Antony's defeat at Actium in 31, and his subsequent suicide in 30, Octavia's household grew to include the son of Antony's deceased wife, FULVIA (2), and the son and daughter of Antony and CLEOPATRA VII.

Antonia married Lucius Domitius Ahenobarbus, to whom she had been affianced since about 24 B.C.E. Ahenobarbus, of an old republican family, has been characterized, like many of his ancestors, as arrogant, cruel, addicted to chariot racing, and rich. He held the consulship in 16 B.C.E. and died in old age in 25 C.E.

It was Antonia's only marriage. She had three children, all of whom took a place in the politics of their time: Gnaeus Domitius Ahenobarbus, consul in 32 C.E. and father of the future emperor Nero; and two forceful women, DOMITIA, wife of Gaius Sallustius Crispus Passienus, and DOMITIA LEPIDA, the mother of Valeria MESSALLINA.

Sources

Oxford Classical Dictionary, ed. by Simon Hornblower and Antony Spawforth. 3d. ed. New York: Oxford University Press, 1996, p. 113.

Pauly, A., G. Wissowa, and W. Kroll. *Real-Encyclopadie d. Classischen Altertumswissenschaft 1893–.* (Germany: multiple publishers) 113.

Syme, R. *Augustan Aristocracy.* Oxford: Clarendon Press, 1986, *passim.*

Antonia the Younger

(January 31, 36 B.C.E.–May 1, 37 C.E.)   Roman: Italy
Augusta; power broker

Antonia was an enigmatic woman who made difficult, and sometimes even inexplicable, life choices. In many ways Antonia epitomized the ideal Roman *matrona.* She was a woman of strong character and impeccable morality; she was intelligent and married only once. Twice she was named Augusta. She refused the title offered by her grandson Gaius Caligula when he became emperor 37 C.E. After her death the title was again bestowed, this time by her son, the emperor Claudius.

Antonia was the younger daughter of OCTAVIA (2) and niece of Augustus. She was born January 31, 36 B.C.E., when her father, Mark Antony, was in Egypt with CLEOPATRA VII. After the civil war and Antony's death in 30, Antonia lived in her mother's household with the children of her parents' multiple marriages, including those of her father and Cleopatra.

Antonia married Nero Claudius Drusus, the son of LIVIA DRUSILLA, and the stepson of the emperor Augustus, in 16. Drusus was a popular young leader, and his marriage with Antonia made him a likely successor to Augustus. After Drusus's unexpected death while campaigning in Germany in 9 B.C.E., Antonia remained a widow despite her youth and the urging of Augustus to remarry. She lived with Livia who helped raise her children: Germanicus Julius Caesar, Livia Julia Claudia LIVILLA, and Claudius, the future emperor.

Her eldest son Germanicus became as popular as had been his father and married the elder AGRIPPINA, a granddaughter of Augustus. By then, Tiberius, Antonia's brother-in-law, was emperor. Germanicus, who was the most likely heir to Tiberius, died as had his father before him, campaigning in Germany. Agrippina brought his ashes back to Rome convinced that Tiberius had arranged her husband's death. Inexplicably, Antonia made no appearance at the public honors for her dead son. Nor did Tiberius or Livia. Their absence fed rumors of conspiracy.

Antonia's daughter Livilla married Drusus Julius Caesar, the son of Tiberius and his first wife, VIPSANIA AGRIPPINA, in 4 C.E. Livilla and Drusus had a daughter, JULIA (8), and twin sons, Germanicus and Tiberius Gemellus. Antonia's daughter was later widowed and left with a grown daughter and one living son, Tiberius Gemellus.

Antonia the Younger and her son Claudius
*(For Antonia the Younger: Date: 41 C.E.–45 C.E. 1001.1.22213, Archives, American Numismatic Society.
For Claudius: Date: 51 C.E.–52 C.E. 1001.1.30042, Archives, American Numismatic Society)*

Antonia watched the struggle that developed between her widowed daughter, Livilla, and her widowed daughter-in-law, Agrippina, as each competed to secure her own son as successor to Tiberius. They became the center of factions that gave no quarter. Agrippina surrounded herself with an elite circle of the Senate, and Livilla joined forces with her lover, Lucius Aelius Sejanus, the prefect of the Praetorian Guard and the most powerful man in Rome in the years after the departure of Emperor Tiberius for Capri. Antonia stepped in when catastrophe occurred.

Agrippina was forced into exile and suicide. Two of her grandsons, Nero Julius Caesar and Drusus Julius Caesar, died; the former was executed, and the latter starved himself to death while imprisoned. Antonia took the three remaining children of Germanicus and Agrippina—the future emperor Gaius Caligula and his sisters, Julia Drusilla (1) and Julia Livilla—into her household.

Certainly Antonia must have been affected by the exile of her daughter-in-law and the death of her two grandsons. She must also have known of her daughter's alliance with Sejanus and the harm that would befall her if he fell from power. Nonetheless, Antonia arranged to smuggle a letter to Tiberius in Capri, accusing Sejanus of unknown charges that may have led to his arrest and death by strangulation. Tiberius placed Livilla in the custody of Antonia, and she witnessed Livilla's suicide by starvation.

Although both her daughter and daughter-in-law were dead, her son Claudius and grandson Gaius Caligula lived, and Antonia remained a significant person of influence and wealth. She supported the political career of Lucius Vitellius who came from an equestrian background, gained power in the reign of her grandson Gaius Caligula, and was consul three times. She also fostered the career of the future emperor Tiberius Flavius Vespasian.

Antonia maintained extensive connections in the East and owned a great deal of property in Egypt. Berenice (1), the daughter of Salome and niece of Herod the Great, was one of her clients and friends. Berenice and her young son, Marcus Julius Agrippa, lived in Rome during the reign of

Tiberius, and Agrippa stayed in Antonia's household for a few years. Later Antonia came to his aid and lent him 300,000 drachmas to pay a debt owed to the imperial treasury.

Antonia died on May 1 in 37 c.e., only months after her grandson became emperor. It was just as well. Caligula's behavior became increasingly bizarre, and in 38 he ordered the execution of Antonia's grandson, Tiberius Gemellus. Rumors spread that he had driven Antonia to commit suicide by his ill-treatment or that he had had her poisoned.

Sources

Dio Cassius. *Roman History* 58.3.9.

Josephus. *Antiquitates Judaicae (Jewish Antiquities)* 18.156, 161–67, 181 ff., 204, 237.

Suetonius. *The Lives of the Caesars:* Gaius Caligula 1.1; 10.1; 15.2; 23.2; 24.1.

———. *The Lives of the Caesars:* Claudius 1.6; 3.2; 4.1–4; 11.2.

Tacitus. *Annales* 2.43, 84; 3.3; 4.3; 10, 12, 39–41.

Balsdon, J. P. V. D. *Roman Women.* New York: John Day Comp., 1963, *passim.*

Bauman, Richard A. *Women and Politics in Ancient Rome.* London: Routledge, 1994, pp. 138–139.

Ferrill, A. *Caligula: Emperor of Rome.* London: Thames and Hudson, 1991, *passim.*

Leon, Harry J. *The Jews of Ancient Rome.* Philadelphia: Jewish Publication Society of America, 1960, p. 20.

Levick, Barbara. *Claudius: The Corruption of Power.* New Haven, Conn.: Yale University Press, 1993, *passim.*

———. *Tiberius the Politician.* London: Thames and Hudson, 1976, *passim.*

Marsh, Frank Burr. *The Reign of Tiberius.* New York: Barnes and Noble, 1931, *passim.*

Oxford Classical Dictionary, ed. by Simon Hornblower and Antony Spawforth. 3d. ed. New York: Oxford University Press, 1996, p. 113.

Pauly, A., G. Wissowa, and W. Kroll. *Real-Encyclopadie d. Classischen Altertumswissenschaft 1893–.* (Germany: multiple publishers) 114.

▣ Antonia Tryphaena

(first century c.e.)   Roman: Asia Minor
ruler

Antonia Tryphaena was the daughter of Pythodoris and Polemon I of Pontus, a kingdom in north-

western Asia Minor; she was the great-granddaughter of Mark Antony and his second wife, Antonia (2). Antonia Tryphaena married Cotys, the ruler of Thrace.

When Cotys was murdered, Antonia accused his uncle Rhascuporis of committing the crime in order to annex her husband's territory. Antonia gave testimony at the trial held before the Roman Senate in 18 c.e. Rhascuporis was found guilty and banished.

Antonia left her three sons in Rome to be raised with the future emperor Gaius Caligula, and she went to Cyzicus on the island of Arctonnesus in the Black Sea. Very wealthy she used her money to pay for civic improvements including dredging the channel between the city and the mainland. She also became a priestess of Livia Drusilla in whose household in Rome resided her children.

After her father died, Antonia returned to Pontus and ruled as guardian and regent for her son Polemon II. Her head and name appeared on the obverse of coins in accord with Pontus's status as a client kingdom of Rome.

Sources

Tacitus. *Annales* 2.64–67.

Macurdy, Grace. *Hellenistic Queens.* Reprint. Chicago: Ares Publishers, 1985, pp. 10–11.

Magie, David. *Roman Rule in Asia Minor, to the End of the Third Century after Christ.* 2 vols. Princeton, N.J.: Princeton University Press, 1950, p. 513.

Marshall, A. J. "Ladies at Law: The Role of Women in the Roman Civil Courts." In *Studies in Latin Literature and Roman History,* ed. by C. Deroux. Brussels, Belgium: Latomus, 1989, p. 355.

▣ Antonina

(?–sixth century c.e.)   Roman: Constantinople
political actor

Antonina was clever, and she possessed outstanding organizing abilities that furthered her husband's military campaigns and enhanced their accumulation of personal wealth. Her husband, Belisarius, was Justinian's leading general and she was an ally, possibly a confidant, and, on occasion, an adversary of the Augusta Theodora.

The two couples, Antonina and Belisarius and Theodora and Justinian, made a formidable foursome whose impact shaped the empire during its last reach for territorial *imperium.* Antonina's grandfather and father were charioteers; her mother was an actress, which Romans not only considered déclassé, but synonymous with promiscuity and, especially for women, prostitution. Like Theodora, Antonina's early life probably included a number of liaisons, some of them resulting in children. A son Photius is known. She also had a daughter Joannina who was born after Antonina married Belisarius.

Belisarius was a Goth, born in the Balkans somewhere between Thrace and Illyria. He became a military bodyguard under the reign of Justin, Justinian's predecessor. Belisarius and Antonina encountered the same legal barrier as Justinian and Theodora over forming a contractual marriage. A law enacted under Constantine the Great in the fourth century forbade a marriage contract between a man of senatorial rank and an actress. Since marriage contracts were prenuptial arrangements of property and inheritance was a major means for gaining new wealth, older men were vulnerable, and families needed legal protection against hasty marriages and lost fortunes. Justin, in his waning days, lifted the ban for whomsoever the emperor chose. He had waited until after the death of his wife EUPHEMIA (1), who was herself not well born but who adopted the prejudices of the society to which she gained admission.

Antonina accompanied Belisarius on his military campaigns. She was his closest confident, gifted strategist, and skillful organizer. It was reported that in 533, on a longer-than-expected voyage to Africa, when the lack of wind resulted in a 16-day trip to Sicily, the water carried by the fleet spoiled, except on Belisarius's ship. Antonina had had the foresight to store the water in glass jars and bury them in sand in the dark ship's hold to retard the growth of mold.

Antonina was with Belisarius during the siege of Rome three years later. In Naples she worked with her husband's secretary Procopius to assemble a fleet loaded with grain and soldiers for delivery to Rome through Ostia, its port city. The final lap of the trip proved particularly difficult. Not only were the oxen that were to pull the barges up the shallow Tiber to Rome exhausted, but the road along one side of the river was held by the enemy and the other was too narrow for the animals.

Antonina and the fleet commanders evolved a scheme. They outfitted small boats with fences made of planks to create a holding area for the grain. After loading the grain, archers and sailors boarded. The small boats were able to navigate the river and when the wind failed, the sailors rowed. On the narrow road, another part of the army marched parallel with the flotilla to protect it. Grain and troops arrived safely in Rome.

Antonina remained in Italy until 540 and returned to Constantinople with her husband. She received the title of *patricia* for service to the empire. She also formed a relationship with Theodora, possibly based less on friendship than mutual service. In 536, at the request of Theodora, Antonina and her husband had worked to depose the Roman bishop Silverius who had recently assumed office and refused to reinstate Anthemius, a Monophysite, as bishop of Constantinople. The time was rife with controversy over the nature of Christ, and the Monophysites, who supported the single divine nature of Christ, counted Theodora among their most steadfast allies. Their candidate had been Vigilius and they looked to Theodora and her connections to reverse their defeat.

The women also shared a concern over John the Cappadocian, Praetorian Prefect in the East and second in power only to the emperor. A man without education or manners, he had a genius for efficiently collecting revenue by whatever means necessary to finance Justinian's wars and building programs. Theodora hated his influence and Antonina feared a rival to her husband. In 541, the two women initiated a complicated intrigue. Antonina sought to gain the trust of EUPHEMIA (2), the young daughter of John who he adored. Antonina used their newfound intimacy to share information about her husband's dissatisfaction with the emperor Justinian. Euphemia responded, probing Antonina for details. As Antonina and Theodora had anticipated, Euphemia took the intelligence to her father. Through Euphemia, John arranged a midnight meeting beneath the city wall in April or May 541. Theodora arranged for a group of loyalists to overhear the seditious intent and inform Justinian. John lost his position and was eventually exiled, stripped of his wealth, and imprisoned.

Antonina found support from Theodora at a critical point in her life. When she was about 60 years old, Antonina became passionately attached to a young man named Theodosius, who her husband had adopted as a son. Her passion far exceeded her discretion and she, who had maintained a working relationship with her husband for many years whatever the amatory pursuits of either, forced a public confrontation. Her husband behaved as expected and threatened Theodosius with death. Theodora hid the young lover and, moreover, arranged for Antonina to continue the liaison.

Theodora also fostered the relationship between Antonina and her husband. After Antonina and Belisarius quarreled in 543, Justinian relieved Belisarius of his command and demanded that he deposit in government accounts the very considerable personal wealth he had accumulated as a result of his military campaigns in the East. Justinian and Theodora, always pressed for funds to finance their reign, had long resented the vast fortune that Belisarius had accumulated during his military career. Justinian and Theodora also refused to see him when he came to the palace. Theodora informed him, however, that his command and money would be restored if he mended relations with Antonina, and so he did. However, Justinian also ordered him to finance his next campaign at his own expense.

Nor was that the only effort to gain Belisarius and Antonina's fortune. Photius severed his relationship with his mother over her liaison with Theodosius, and Joannina became sole heir to their immense fortune. Theodora sought to marry Joannina to Anastasius, one of her three grandsons, who were the children of her daughter, born before her marriage with Justinian. The boy may have been the son of Anastasius, the brother of the former emperor Anastasius, and a quite suitable partner for Antonina's daughter. Antonina, however,

opposed the match and, with the agreement of her husband, delayed it rather than openly confront Theodora, although the reasons for the opposition have never been clear. Not to be outmaneuvered, Theodora moved the two young people into the palace where they lived together. They were said to also have fallen in love and when Joannina reached marriageable age, they wed.

Antonina again accompanied Belisarius to Italy in the summer of 544 when Rome was under siege by the Ostrogoths. She remained in Italy for the next four years, during a series of inconclusive campaigns plagued by insufficient troops and supplies. In 548, Belisarius sent her to Constantinople to implore Theodora to send him reinforcements, but she found that Theodora had died. Less than a year after the death of Theodora, in the early part of 549, Antonina removed Joannina from the palace and separated her from her husband. Her reasons have remained elusive.

Antonina outlived her husband and Justinian, both of whom died in 565. Last heard of, in her 80s, she was living with Vigilantia, the sister of Justinian.

Sources

Procopius. *Gothic Wars.* V. v. 5, xviii. 18, 43; VI. iv. 6, 14, 20; vii. 4 ff, 15; VII. xix, 7, 30; xxviii. 4; xxx. 2, 3, 26.
———. *Persian Wars.* I. xxv. 13 ff, 23.
———. *Secret History.* i. 16, 17, 25–29, 31, 34–36, 38–39, 42; ii. 1–5, 14, 16–17; iii. 2, 4, 7, 12, 15–18; iv. 18–19, 23, 38; v. 14, 20, 23–24, 27, 33.
———. *Vandal Wars.* III xii. 2; xiii. 23–24; xix 11; xx. 1.
Bury, J. B. *Later History of the Roman Empire from the Death of Theodosisus to the Death of Justinian.* Vol. II, 233–242, 247–249. New York: Dover Publications, 1938.
Prosopography of the Later Roman Empire. Vol. III. Edited by A. H. M. Jones, J. R. Martindale, and J. Morris. Cambridge: Cambridge University Press, 1971. Reprinted 1992, pp. 91–93.

▣ Antye

(third century B.C.E.)   Greek: Tegea
poet

Antye was a well-known and well-respected poet of the third century B.C.E. Born in Tegea, a city on the southern Greek peninsula, she was said to have written in the traditional form and to have mirrored Homer in her grammar and sentence structure. However, she was attracted to the bucolic themes that were characteristic of the emerging traditions of the period after the death of Alexander the Great.

Although Antye's lyric poems have been lost, 19 Doric epigrams are extant. They are grave in tone and restrained in style. Her quatrains, possibly used as funerary inscriptions, are sensitive without being sentimental.

Sources

Lyra Graeca, v. 2, p. 241.

Der Kleine Pauly; Lexikon der Antike, ed. by Konrat Julius Furchtegott and Walther Sontheimer. Stuttgart, Germany: A. Druckenmuller, 1984, p. 417.

Fantham, Elaine, et al. *Women in the Classical World.* New York: Oxford University Press, 1994, p. 166.

Geoghegan, D. *Antye: A Critical Edition with Commentary.* Rome: Edizioni dell-Ateneo & Bizzarri, 1979, *passim.*

Gow, Andrew S. F., and Denys L. Page. *The Greek Anthology: Hellenistic Epigrams.* 2 vols. Cambridge, England: Cambridge University Press, 1965, pp. 89 ff.

Oxford Classical Dictionary, ed. by Simon Hornblower and Antony Spawforth. 3d. ed. New York: Oxford University Press, 1996, p. 78.

Apama (1)

(fourth–third century B.C.E.)
Persian: Persia and Antioch
progenitor of Seleucid dynasty

Apama was the ancestor of the Seleucids, who ruled over portions of Asia for some 250 years. Her father, the Bactrian Spitamenes, organized a serious revolt in Sogdiana against Alexander the Great. Defeated in 328 B.C.E., he fled into the territory of his allies, the Messagetae. They cut off his head and sent it to Alexander as a token of submission.

Apama, however, survived and became one of the 80 elite Persian women married to Alexander's Macedonian officers at Susa in 324 in an effort to erase the distinction between the conquered and conqueror. Her husband, Seleucus I, was commander of the Silver Shields, which guarded the right flank of Alexander's army. After Alexander's death, Seleucus and Apama were the only couple not to divorce.

Seleucus conquered Babylon, Media, and Susiana to establish the Seleucid Empire. He named a number of cities after Apama. In 298, for strategic reasons, he also married the much younger STRATONICE (2), the daughter of Demetrius I, ruler of Macedonia. According to the ancient sources, Apama's son Antiochus I fell in love with Stratonice. Apama regained her former position in 293, when her husband allowed her son and Stratonice to marry.

Seleucus may have decided that he could no longer govern his eastern provinces from Antioch. He made Antiochus his partner and as coruler, sent him with Stratonice to govern the eastern territories. Antiochus I eventually succeeded his father and with Stratonice secured a dynasty that ruled parts of Asia Minor for over two centuries.

Sources

Appian. *Syrian Wars* 59–62.

Plutarch. *Vitae Parallelae (Parallel Lives): Demetrius* 38.

Cary, M. *A History of the Greek World from 323 to 146 B.C.* London: Methuen, 1951, pp. 43, 54.

Macurdy, Grace. *Hellenistic Queens.* Reprint. Chicago: Ares Publishers, 1985.

Oxford Classical Dictionary, ed. by Simon Hornblower and Antony Spawforth. 3d. ed. New York: Oxford University Press, 1996, p. 118.

Apama (2)

(third century B.C.E.)   Greek: Cyrene
ruler

Apama ruled Cyrene, in North Africa, after the death of her husband. She was overthrown by her daughter. Apama was the daughter of STRATONICE (2) and Antiochus I, ruler of the Seleucid Empire in Asia. In 275 B.C.E., she married Magas, the ruler of Cyrene and the stepbrother of Ptolemy II Philadelphus of Egypt. She had a daughter, BERENICE II OF CYRENE, whom her husband affianced to the future Ptolemy III to secure a union of Egypt and Cyrene. Magas died in 258, and Apama became the ruler of Cyrene. Antigonus Gonatus, ruler of Macedonia and an enemy of Egypt, sent his half brother, the handsome Demetrius, to make an offer of marriage to Berenice and to foil a union with Egypt.

Apama welcomed Demetrius. She favored the house of the Seleucids from which she came, against a union with Egypt which was generally opposed also by the independent-minded Cyrenicians. There is some confusion as to whether Apama married Demetrius or became his lover after he married her daughter. In any case, Berenice, afraid of losing power, led a rebellion in which Demetrius was killed in Apama's bedroom as she tried to shield him with her body.

Apama's life was spared by her daughter, and nothing further is known about her.

Sources

Justin. *Epitome* 26.3.
Cary, M. *A History of the Greek World from 323 to 146 B.C.* London: Methuen, 1951, pp. 84, 138.
Macurdy, Grace. *Hellenistic Queens.* Reprint. Chicago: Ares Publishers, 1985, pp. 131 ff.

▣ Apega

(third–second century B.C.E.) Greek: Sparta
political player

Apega was collaborator, supporter, and agent for the reform policies of her husband, Nabis, ruler of Sparta (207–192 B.C.E.). Nabis canceled debts, redistributed property, and extended citizenship to select indigenous and foreign residents. Apega traveled to Argos to collect gold jewelry and cloth from women to provide funds to support her husband's reforms.

The opposition accused Nabis of prosecuting the wealthy and confiscating land. They also charged Nabis with seizing their wives for the pleasure of his supporters and mercenaries. A curious tale that suggests the determination of Nabis, and perhaps Apega, to extract wealth from the rich has survived. Nabis supposedly constructed a replica of Apega. With the replica at his side, he summoned wealthy men and asked for contributions. Any who refused were required to take the hand of the replica, whose clothing concealed sharp nails. Using a spring mechanism, the replica embraced the recalcitrant donors and drove nails into their flesh. Contributions were usually forthcoming and those who refused were killed by the replica of Apega.

Sources

Polybius. *Histories* 13.6–7; 18.17.

▣ Apicata

(first century C.E.) Roman: Rome
avenger

Apicata took revenge on her husband and his lover. Her lineage is unknown. Her husband was the infamous Lucius Aelius Sejanus, prefect of the Praetorian Guard and confidant to the emperor Tiberius. After Tiberius went to Capri in 27 C.E., Sejanus became the main conduit for information to the emperor and consequently the most powerful man in the city.

Sejanus collected a discontented faction around him and divorced Apicata when it appeared possible that he might marry his lover and coconspirator, Livia Julia Claudia LIVILLA, the widowed daughter-in-law and niece of Tiberius. In October of 31, however, Sejanus fell out of favor and was charged with crimes sufficiently heinous to cause his immediate execution. Apicata's eldest son Strabo was killed six days later, and Apicata committed suicide the next week. The two younger children, AELIA IUNILLA and Capito Aelianus, were strangled in December on orders of the Senate so that Sejanus might leave no heirs.

Before her death, Apicata extracted revenge. She sent a letter to Tiberius accusing her husband and Livilla of poisoning Livilla's husband, Drusus Julius Caesar, eight years earlier in 23. Drusus had been Tiberius's son. His death was a critical turning point in Tiberius's life now compounded by the discovery of the conspiracy led by Sejanus in whom he had placed his trust. He took the accusation seriously enough to extract a confirmation of the murder in confessions gathered under torture from Livilla's doctor and a slave even though it was already some eight years after the event.

Sources

Dio Cassius. *Roman History* 58.11.5–7.
Tacitus. *Annales* 4.3.
Bauman, Richard A. *Women and Politics in Ancient Rome.* London: Routledge, 1994, p. 147.

Levick, Barbara. *Tiberius the Politician.* London: Thames and Hudson, 1976, pp. 161, 201, 274; notes 71, 72.

Syme, Ronald. *Tacitus.* 2 vols. Oxford: Clarendon Press, 1958, p. 402.

▣ Appuleia Varilla

(first century B.C.E.–first century C.E.)
Roman: Rome
convicted adulterer

Appuleia Varilla was indicted on charges of treason and adultery in 17 C.E. She was one of several people also accused of slander against the emperor. Her father was Sextus Appuleius, consul in 29 B.C.E. and proconsul of Asia; her mother was Quinctilla, a niece of OCTAVIA (1), the half sister of Augustus. The name of Appuleia's husband is unknown. The name of her lover, however, was Manlius.

Appuleia was accused of defaming the new emperor Tiberius and his mother LIVIA DRUSILLA as well as Augustus, only recently deified after his death two years earlier in 15 C.E. Tiberius informed the Senate that neither he nor his mother wished to pursue the charges of slander or treason. The apparently less frivolous charge of adultery stood. If convicted Appuleia could have lost half her dowry and a third of her property, and could also have been banished. Tiberius, however, suggested that she simply be handed over to her family and be removed at least 200 milestones from Rome. Her lover was banned from living in Italy or Africa.

Sources

Tacitus. *Annales* 2.50.

Levick, Barbara. *Tiberius the Politician.* London: Thames and Hudson, 1976, p. 197.

Marsh, Frank Burr. *The Reign of Tiberius.* New York: Barnes and Noble, 1931, *passim.*

Marshall, A. J. "Women on Trial before the Roman Senate." *Classical Views* 34 (1990): 333–366, p. 342.

Pauly, A., G. Wissowa, and W. Kroll. *Real-Encyclopadie d. Classischen Altertumswissenschaft 1893–.* (Germany: multiple publishers) 33.

Syme, Ronald. *The Augustan Aristocracy.* Oxford: Clarendon Press, 1986, *passim.*

▣ Apronia

(first century C.E.)   Roman: Rome
murder victim

Apronia was probably murdered by her husband, the praetor Plautius Silvanus, sometime in 24 C.E. for unknown reasons. She died by falling or being thrown out of a window in her husband's house. Her father Lucius Apronius, who had been a legate to the emperor's adopted son Germanicus Julius Caesar, quickly brought Silvanus up on charges before the emperor Tiberius. Silvanus claimed that Apronia must have committed suicide. He had been fast asleep at the crucial time, and moreover, he suffered from spells inflicted upon him by his long-divorced first wife, Fabia NUMANTINA, whom he was in the process of suing.

Tiberius visited the scene of the crime. He examined the room and window where the event had occurred and found evidence that Apronia had been forcefully ejected. He referred the case to the Senate. Before the case was heard, URGULANIA, the grandmother of Silvanus and a close friend of LIVIA DRUSILLA, the mother of Tiberius, sent Silvanus a dagger. Urgulania, a formidable woman whose arrogance was backed by her influence, left Silvanus little choice. After a fruitless attempt at suicide, Silvanus arranged for someone to open his arteries. With his death the charges against his first wife were dismissed.

Sources

Tacitus. *Annales* 4.22.

Pauly, A., G. Wissowa, and W. Kroll. *Real-Encyclopadie d. Classischen Altertumswissenschaft 1893–.* (Germany: multiple publishers) 10.

▣ Arcadia

(400–444 C.E.)   Roman: Constantinople
political actor and celibate Christian

Arcadia was one of three young women, all daughters of Augusta AELIA EUDOXIA and her husband, the Eastern emperor Arcadius, who swore to remain virgins and serve Christ. Led by their older sister, PULCHERIA, Arcadia and MARINA took a vow that freed them from unwanted offers of marriage and pressure to marry and also limited the circle that dominated their brother the emperor Theodosius II, during his long reign from 408–450.

Arcadia's mother died in the autumn of 404 and her father four years later in the spring of 408 when her brother, Theodosius II, was only seven years old. Anthemius, an elderly Praetorian Prefect of the East, assumed the regency. The education of Arcadia and her siblings was in the hands of a young eunuch Antiochus, who also supervised the imperial household.

When Pulcheria was 14 in 413, she assumed control. Leading Arcadia and Marina in a public display, she declared their dedication to virginity and their brother's rule. Their oath, inscribed on the altar in the Great Church in Constantinople, eliminated the possibility that one of them would marry and introduce into the family a husband and new kin that might include a rival to their brother. It also established their place in the religious politics that dominated the day. As virgins above reproach, they aligned with Mary, Mother of God, and claimed a voice in the church.

In July 414, Pulcheria became Augusta and regent for her brother. She set a somber atmosphere in the household. Arcadia, Marina, and the young emperor fasted twice a week, prayed, and read from the scriptures. Their version of a virtuous life contrasted with the more robust lifestyle of their mother, who had enjoyed the pleasures of food and clothing. It also echoed the rhetorical ideals of the republic and early empire. Not only did they dress modestly and eschew cosmetics, but they spent time weaving. In this deeply Christian environment, they also provided aid for the poor and sick and sheltered the homeless.

Arcadia and Marina were devoted to Pulcheria and followed her lead in both religion and politics. Orthodox Christians, they held to the belief that Christ was of two natures, divine and human, cojoined yet separate. They fervently believed that Mary was Mother of God (*Theotokos*) and rejected any suggestion that diminished her status to Mother of Christ (*Christotokos*).

Although Arcadia remained in her sister and brother's shadow, she was not without an independent sphere of influence and power. She was independently wealthy, owning properties in the suburbs and provinces that were inherited from her parents or given to her by her brother, and from which she drew fresh food and income. Since she had access to both Pulcheria and Theodosius, supplicants sought her out, men as well as women, and dignitaries sent to Constantinople on missions from elsewhere in the empire, especially from the East, viewed her as an important personage.

She was a partner in Pulcheria's opposition to Nestorius, the bishop of Constantinople. Nestorius had become bishop on April 10, 428, with the tacit, if not active, endorsement of the imperial clique. He was an impolitic man who, whatever the sincerity of his beliefs, failed to comprehend that in his position, diplomacy was the better part of virtue. From the pulpit he denounced women's engagement with the affairs of state and church and initiated a personal attack against Pulcheria. Inflamed, Pulcheria organized her forces, among whom were her sisters. Arcadia was included in the flurry of letters from worthy people, especially bishops, in the major cities of the empire, who supported or opposed Nestorius. Her support for Pulcheria was never in question.

Arcadia moved out of the palace with Pulcheria after her brother married EUDOXIA. Although she owned houses in the city, she stayed most of the time with Pulcheria in one of her sister's houses.

Arcadia died a virgin.

Sources

Sozomen. *Historia Ecclesiastica* IX. 1. 1–5.
Theophanus. *Chronicle.* AM 5905.
Holum, Kenneth. *Theodosian Empresses: Women and Imperial Dominion in Late Antiquity.* Berkeley: University of California Press, 1982.
Prosopography of the Later Roman Empire. Vol. II. Edited by A. H. M. Jones, J. R. Martindale, and J. Morris. Cambridge: Cambridge University Press, 1971. Reprinted 1992, pp. 129–130.

▣ Archidamia

(third century B.C.E.)   Greek: Sparta
reformer

Archidamia and her daughter AGESISTRATA were the two wealthiest women in Sparta during the middle decades of the third century B.C.E. Respectively the grandmother and mother of the reformist king Agis IV, they used wealth and position to secure political and economic reform.

With friends and kin, including AGIATIS, the king's wife, Archidamia formed a political alliance that supported land redistribution and the reduction and cancellation of debts. The reformers met strong opposition from those who had vastly increased their wealth through inheritance and foreclosure during the preceding decades, when a declining citizen population found it increasingly difficult to pay mortgage installments. In 241 B.C.E., after Agis initiated his land and debt policies, he was overthrown and killed. Archidamia and her daughter Agesistrata were executed.

Sources

Plutarch. *Vitae Parallelae (Parallel Lives): Agesilaus* 4.2; 7.5–7; 9.5–6; 20.7.
Mosse, Claude. "Women in the Spartan Revolutions of the Third Century B.C." In *Women's History and Ancient History,* ed. by Sarah B. Pomeroy. Chapel Hill: University of North Carolina Press, 1991, pp. 138–153.

▣ Archippe (1)

(sixth–fifth century B.C.E.)   Greek: Athens
political wife

Archippe was the wife of Themistocles (528–462 B.C.E.), the famous Athenian politician and military leader who was exiled in the decade after the battle of Salamis in 479 B.C.E. Probably Themistocles first wife, her father was Lysander from the deme of Alopece. Archippe had three sons: Archeptolis, Polyeuctus, and Cleophantes. Plato characterized Cleophantes as good at horseback riding and not much else.

Her exiled husband left Athens for Persia, where he convinced the king of his usefulness, despite having been responsible for the strategy that defeated the Persians at Salamis. He settled in Magnesia, where he appears to have had a second family. Themistocles killed himself when it became clear that he could no longer serve the Persians without endangering the Greeks.

Although Archippe appears not to have lived in Asia, it is unclear if her marriage was ended by divorce or death.

Sources

Plato. *Meno* p. 93d–e.
Plutarch. *Vitae Parallelae (Parallel Lives): Themistocles* 32.1–2.

▣ Archippe (2)

(*c.* 410 B.C.E.–?)   Greek: Athens
self-made woman

Archippe was an Athenian, probably born in 410 B.C.E. or soon after. Although she died a rich woman and a citizen with sons to inherit her wealth, she did not come from a wealthy background nor was she from a family of Athenian citizens.

Archippe married Pasion, who was some 20 years her senior, around 395. An Athenian money changer, Pasion had started life as a slave and he became an Athenian citizen after 391. At the time of their marriage, however, he was already considered the wealthiest banker and manufacturer in Athens. Sources estimate that Pasion earned 100 minae per year through money changing and between 20 and 60 minae from his shield workshop at a time when 60 minae equaled 1 talent, the approximate cost of building an Athenian battleship.

Archippe and Pasion had two sons, Apollodorus and Pascicles. The former was 24 and the latter 10 when their father died. Pasion left real estate worth 20 talents and capital of almost 40 talents. He left his estate to his sons after Archippe had received a large dowry plus property. In his will he appointed Phormion, his business manager, as one of two legal guardians of Archippe's wealth and instructed her to marry him.

Archippe married Phormion, who was not an Athenian citizen. Her son Apollodorus objected to his mother's marriage. The marriage may well have effectively removed Apollodorus from control over his mother's wealth and may also have forced a restructuring of the estate to pay out her dowry. In an effort to annul the marriage, the son charged Phormion with adultery. Since Athenian law prohibited a legal marriage between a citizen woman and a noncitizen, by implication Archippe had gained citizenship through her first husband.

Although the court stipulated that Phormion's sons would have no claim over any of the residual inheritance, the suit failed to annul the marriage or eliminate Archippe's portion under the will. Ten years later, Phormion was granted citizenship. The two sons born to Archippe and Phormion also became citizens. When Archippe died those sons inherited her property.

Sources

Demosthenes. *Private Orations* 45.28, 74; 45.3; 46.21.

Godolphin, Francis B., ed. *The Greek Historians: The Complete and Unabridged Historical Works of the Herodotus translated by George Rawlinson, Thucydides translated by Benjamin Jowett, Xenophon translated by Henry G. Dakyns, Arrian translated by Edgard J. Chinnock.* 2 vols. New York: Random House, 1942, pp. 765–766.

Lacey, W. K. *The Family in Classical Greece.* Ithaca, N.Y.: Cornell University Press, 1968, *passim.*

Pauly, A., G. Wissowa, and W. Kroll. *Real-Encyclopadie d. Classischen Altertumswissenschaft 1893–.* (Germany: multiple publishers) 541–542.

▣ Archo
(second century B.C.E.)   Greek: Thessaly
war victim

Archo's life was inextricably linked with that of her sister THEOXENA. Their father Herodicus, a leading citizen, had died fighting the invasion of Thessaly by Philip V of Macedon in the late second century B.C.E. Archo's husband also died opposing Philip. As part of a policy of consolidation of his sovereignty, Philip forced whole villages and towns to move. Uprooted from her ancestral home, Archo left with a small child. She married Poris, a prominent citizen from Aenea in northeastern Greece and had several more children before she died.

Archo's sister, widowed in the same invasion, also had a son but chose not to remarry. After Archo's death, Theoxena married Poris to consolidate the estate and to be mother to all the children. In 182 B.C.E., the entire family died in new violence unleashed by Philip V.

Sources

Livy. *From the Founding of the City* 40.3–4.

▣ Aretaphila
(first century B.C.E.)   Greek: Cyrene
avenger

Aretaphila retired to her loom after avenging her husband's murder. Born into a distinguished family in Cyrene in North Africa during the first century B.C.E., she married Phaedimus, a well-born Cyrenian. He was murdered by Nicorates, the tyrant of Cyrene.

Nicorates forced Aretaphila to marry him after the murder. Determined to avenge the death of Phaedimus, she tried to poison Nicorates. Caught, she claimed that the draught was a love potion and stood by her story under torture. Despite the misgivings of Nicorates' mother, Calbia, who distrusted Aretaphila, she succeeded not only in saving her life, but also in regaining her position as the tyrant's wife. Fearful of any further direct attack on Nicorates, Aretaphila used her daughter to entice Nicorates' brother Leander into marriage. Her daughter then convinced him that even he, the brother of the tyrant, was not safe. Leander arranged for Nicorates' murder and became tyrant.

Leander proved no better a ruler than Nicorates, and Aretaphila determined that his tyrannical rule over the people of Cyrene must also end. She sought out the African ruler Anabus and encouraged him to attack Cyrene. Then she bribed him to arrange a meeting with Leander on the pretext of making peace. Instead, in accordance with his agreement with Aretaphila, Leander and his mother were turned over to the people of Cyrene. They were both killed.

Aretaphila was asked by the people of Cyrene to rule. She, however, having achieved her goals, retired to private life.

Sources

Plutarch. *Moralia: De mulierum virtutibus* 257d–e.
Polyaenus. *Strategemata* 38.

▣ Arete (1)
(fifth–fourth century B.C.E.)
Greek: Cyrene and Greece
philosopher

Arete was a philosopher in Athens at the end of the fifth century B.C.E. She was a disciple of her father,

Aristippus, a teacher of rhetoric, who was a companion of Socrates. Although Socrates left no written work, Plato portrayed Socrates and his companions in vivid dialogues. The dialogues indicate that Socrates questioned previously unexamined assumptions.

Arete taught philosophy to her son Aristippus, whom she named after her father. He became a founder of the Cyrenaic school, which held that pleasure of the senses was the supreme good, since only sensory impressions are knowable and pleasure preferable to pain.

Sources
Diogenes Laertius. *Lives of the Eminent Philosophers* 2.86.

▣ Arete (2)
(fourth century B.C.E.)   Greek: Syracuse
political player

Arete and her mother, ARISTOMACHE, shared tumultuous turns of fortune. Arete was the daughter of Dionysius I and the wife of Dion, both of whom ruled Syracuse, Sicily, in the third century B.C.E. After the death of Thearides, her first husband and her father's brother, she married Dion, who was her mother's brother.

Dion, who held an influential position under her father, Dionysius I, and his successor, Dionysius II, was attracted to the philosophy of Plato. He persuaded Dionysius II to invite Plato to Syracuse in 366 B.C.E. Fearful that Dion wanted to supplant him and become Plato's ideal philosopher-king, Dionysius II exiled him. Plato left Syracuse soon after. Arete and her mother remained behind.

In 361, Dionysius threatened to seize the exiled Dion's property unless Dion persuaded Plato to return to Syracuse. Arete and her mother convinced of Dionysius' seriousness, urged Dion to act quickly. Plato returned and requested that Dion be brought from exile. Instead, Dionysius sold Dion's property. Plato again left Syracuse.

Dionysius also forced Arete, still in Syracuse, to marry his friend Timocratus. In 357/356 B.C.E., Dion captured Syracuse while Dionysius was in Italy. Fearful of her reception, Arete went with her mother to meet him. Her mother informed Dion that Arete had been forced into a second marriage. Dion embraced Arete as his true wife.

Dion's rule became increasingly authoritarian, and opposition increased. The two women were aware of unrest in city, but Dion would not heed their counsel. Callippus, a former supporter of Dion was one of the leaders of the opposition. He feared Arete and her mother and swore his loyalty to them with a sacred oath. He then treacherously murdered Dion in 354. Arete and her mother were imprisoned. Arete gave birth to boy while incarcerated.

Soon Callippus was killed. Arete and Aristomache were released. They found support from Hicetas, a friend of Dion. However, enemies persuaded him to send Arete and her mother to Greece. Once on board the ship, they were murdered.

Sources
Diodorus Siculus. *Library of History* 14.44.8; 16.6.4.
Plato. *Epistulae* 7.345c–347.
Plutarch. *Dion* 3.3–4; 6.1–2; 21.1–6; 51.1–5; 57.5; 58.8–10.

▣ Ariadne, Aelia
(c. 455/456–515 C.E.)
Roman: Dacia, Constantinople
Augusta

Aelia Ariadne retained her position as Augusta despite the turmoil that left the diadem and scepter of the emperor a prize of violence. The daughter of a powerful mother, the Augusta VERINA, and the emperor Leo, she was born sometime before her father became emperor in February 457. On becoming emperor, Leo formed a strong palace guard under an Isaurian chieftain who took the name of Zeno and brought to Constantinople a sizable force. In 466 or 467, Ariadne, who was about 12 years old, was betrothed to Zeno as his second wife. She gave birth to a son shortly thereafter. In 474, after the death of her father, her seven-year-old son Leo II became emperor and her husband Zeno became regent. The widowed Augusta Verina continued to live in the palace. A year later, the boy died and the Senate elevated Zeno to emperor. Ariadne became Augusta.

Zeno's 17-year reign was never accepted by the elite of Constantinople and suffered from mockery heaped upon the emperor as a country bumpkin. Accused of sustaining his rule by bribery and skillful unprincipled diplomacy, he was not ruthless by standards of the time, nor did he use capital punishment. Among Zeno's problems was a conspiracy led by his mother-in-law, who hated him. Verina instigated a plot to replace Ariadne and Zeno with herself and Patricius, the former Master of the Soldiers and her reputed lover. She solicited her brother Basiliscus who, in turn, recruited two Isaurian officers Illus and Trocundees to join them. Verina revealed the plot by her brother and the Isaurians to Zeno. She urged him to flee with Ariadne. He followed her advice, and in January 475 Zeno and Ariadne left Constantinople with a good part of the state treasury to a stronghold in Isauria. They remained in Asia Minor for more than a year and a half.

Verina suffered a double cross. Her brother Basiliscus took on the role of emperor and elevated his wife ZENONIS to Augusta. He executed Verina's coconspirator Patricius. However, Basiliscus failed to rally popular or elite support. His onetime collaborator Illus turned his support to Zeno and their united forces marched toward the capital. Basiliscus fled. Soon captured, he, his wife, and children were killed. Ariadne and Zeno returned to Constantinople in August 476.

Ariadne and Verina joined forces against Illus, whose influence over Zeno dimmed their own. In 478, Verina instigated a conspiracy to assassinate Illus. However, he was only injured and retreated to Isauria. He demanded that Zeno turn Verina over to him before he would return to Constantinople. Zeno had to choose between Verina and Illus. He chose Illus whose support he needed and Verina was confined to a stronghold in Isauria. By late 479, Verina's imprisonment supplied a pretext for Marcian, the son of Anthemius, who had been emperor in the West between 467 and 474 and to whom Ariadne's younger sister, LEONTIA, had been betrothed, with a reason to attack Zeno. Only the military intervention of Illus saved Zeno.

Despite Illus's success, Ariadne demanded Verina's return to Constantinople. Zeno sent Ariadne to Illus, but he refused to release Verina. Ariadne forced a choice between her and Illus. Zeno chose her. She arranged for Illus's assassination. He was attacked in the city and his right ear severed. However, the assassin was killed instead.

The one-eared Illus requested permission to depart and received the position of Master of Soldiers in the East from Zeno. He, along with many of his supporters, went to Antioch and forged alliances to unseat Zeno. Ariadne and Zeno continued to seek the release of Verina. Leontius, an Isaurian general, went to Antioch to demand her return, only to become a supporter of Illus when the latter offered him the position of emperor. Illus brought Verina to Tarsus to crown Leontius emperor. A proclamation, issued in her name as the reigning Augusta, was spread throughout the empire to establish the legitimacy of Leontius. In the ensuing civil war, Illus was defeated in autumn of 484 with the help of the Ostrogoths. Illus fled with Verina and Leontius to a fortress in the mountains of Isaurus, where Verina died shortly after arrival. Zeno ruled until his death in April 491.

Ariadne, the sole survivor of her generation, became a power broker for the next emperor. Important political leaders and the Senate met and bowed to her choice for a successor to her husband. She selected Anastasius, who was around 60 years old and had not engaged in politics. He was a member of the 30 Silentiaries, a group of imperial guards made up of distinguished men of wealth and property honored with an appointment by the emperor. Unlike Zeno or Leontius in appearance and education, Anastasius was a choice consonant with the ideals and interests of the elite. On May 20, 491, Ariadne married him. Through Ariadne, his reign connected with the past and gained legitimacy.

Ariadne died in 515, after having reigned as Augusta for some 41 years. Among imperial women, only LIVA, the wife of Augustus, lived close to the imperial center for as many decades, although Livia was never formally an Augusta until after her death.

Sources

Theophanes. *Chronicle.* AM 5951, 5965, 5983, 5971, 6008.

Bury, J. B. *Later Roman Empire from the Death of Theodosius to the Death of Justinian.* New York: Dover Publications, 1958.

Prosopography of the Later Roman Empire. Vol. IIIA. Edited by A. H. M. Jones, J. R. Martindale, and J. Morris. Cambridge: Cambridge University Press, 1971. Reprinted 1992, pp. 140–141.

▣ Aristomache

(fourth century B.C.E.)   Greek: Syracuse
political player

Aristomache was at the center of a struggle for control over Syracuse, in Sicily, during the fourth century B.C.E. She, her daughter, and her brother, who was also her daughter's husband, constituted a faction influenced by Plato and his ideal of a philosopher-king. Their struggles began after the death of Dionysius I in 376 B.C.E. and ended with their own murders sometime after 354.

Aristomache, the daughter of Hipparinus, a notable of Syracuse, was the wife of the tyrant Dionysius I. She was a cowife, married on the same day that Dionysius also married DORIS of Locri, the daughter of Xenetus, from a leading family in Locri. Dionysius was said to have dined with both women and then bedded each in turn. Other sources claim that Dionysius feared the women and slept with them only after they were searched.

Aristomache bore no children until Dionysius killed Doris's mother, who allegedly had used drugs to prevent Aristomache from conceiving a child. Of her subsequent two daughters, it is known that Sophrosyne married Dionysius II. The other, ARETE (2), was her mother's lifetime ally. Her first husband was Thearides, the brother of Dionysius I. Her second husband was Dion, Aristomache's brother.

After the death of Dionysius I, Aristomache threw in her lot with Arete and Dion, who held a high position at the court of Dionysius II. Influenced by Plato, Dion sought to make Dionysius II a philosopher-king and in 366, he persuaded Dionysius to invite Plato to Syracuse. However, Dionysius exiled Dion in 365 after he became convinced that Dion intended his overthrow. Dion went to Athens, and Plato soon followed.

Aristomache and her daughter remained in Syracuse, where they lobbied on behalf of Dion and protected his wealth as best they could. Dionysius demanded that Dion persuade Plato to return. It was both promise and threat. If Plato returned, Dion would no longer be threatened, but if he refused to come, Dion's estate in Syracuse would be confiscated. Aristomache and Arete were vulnerable and alarmed. They wrote Dion to urge Plato's return.

Even though Plato returned, Dionysius confiscated Dion's estate. He also forced Arete to marry his friend Timocratus. When Plato had difficulty leaving, Dion had no choice but to raise a mercenary army and wage war against Dionysius. In 357–56, Dion marched on Syracuse while Dionysius was in Italy. Aristomache met him. Since Arete was uncertain of her reception, Aristomache assumed control over the situation and informed her brother of Arete's forced marriage. Dion embraced Arete as his wife.

Aristomache remained close to her daughter and brother during his rule of Syracuse and Dion might well have come to a less bloody end had he listened more closely to her advice. Dion sought to emulate a philosopher-king. He lived modestly with his wife and sister and eschewed the ribald and coarse entertainments of his military companions. He also sought to circumscribe the democratic assembly of citizens. His attempt to establish an aristocratic government bred discontent. In a critical error of judgment he allowed the murder of Heracleides, who had once won a naval victory over Dionysius but had had become Dion's opponent. Filled with remorse over the slaying, Dion failed to listen closely to Aristomache when she and Arete reported a plot against him led by Callippus, a man who Dion believed to be a friend.

Hearing that Aristomache and Arete had become convinced of his treachery, Callippus approached the women. He proclaimed his loyalty. The women demanded a binding oath in the sanctuary of Demeter and Persphone, where the sacred rites were performed. Callippus donned the purple vestments of the goddesses and recite the oath while holding a blazing torch. All to no avail.

Callippus had Dion murdered in 354 B.C.E. Aristomache and Arete were imprisoned. There Arete gave birth to a boy, a posthumous son of Dion. No sooner had Callippus set out on military campaigns, however, than he lost control over Syracuse. In another turn of fortune, Aristomache, Arete, and the baby were released from prison into the friendly care of Hicetas of Syracuse, a friend of Dion. This, however, was the act of treachery that ended their lives.

Hicetas, persuaded by opponents of the Dion faction, sent the women with the baby to Greece. No doubt the women agreed, since their lives and that of Dion's posthumous son hung by a thread in Syracuse. Once on board ship, the three were murdered, either by sword or by drowning.

Sources

Diodorus Siculus. *Library of History* 14.44.8; 16.6.4.

Plato. *Epistulae* 7.345c–347.

Plutarch. *Dion* 3.3–6; 6.1–2; 18.6–9; 19.8; 21.5–6; 51.1–5; 56.1–6; 58.8–10.

Valerius Maximus. *Factorum et dictorum memorabilium libri IX* 9.13–4.

Arrecina Tertulla

(first century C.E.)   Roman: Rome
young wife

Arrecina Tertulla was the daughter of Arrecinus Clemens, one of the two prefects of the Praetorian Guard under the emperor Gaius Caligula. She married the future emperor Titus in the 60s C.E. She died before his father, Vespasian, became emperor. They had no children.

Sources

Suetonius. *The Lives of the Caesars: Titus* 4.2.

Levick, Barbara. *Claudius: The Corruption of Power.* New Haven, Conn.: Yale University Press, 1993, pp. 37–38.

Arria Fadilla

(first–second century C.E.)   Roman: Gaul
mother of Antoninus Pius

Arria Fadilla was from Nemausus (Nimes) in Roman Gaul. She was a member of the new provincial elite that came to power with the emperor Trajan and that formed the dynasty of the Antonines. She was well educated and very wealthy. Like many of the women in these elite families, she successfully managed her own business affairs with properly inherited from her father's as well as her mother's sides of the family.

Her father, Arrius Antoninus, had been consul suffectus in 69 C.E. and proconsul of Asia. He was a friend of the emperor Marcus Cocceius Nerva, under whom he served a second time as consul, and with whom he shared an interest in Greek poetry. His poetry was sufficiently well known for Pliny the Younger to have commented favorably upon it. Arria Fadilla's mother was Boionia Procilla, whose family probably had connections to the emperor Trajan.

Arria Fadilla married Aurelius Fulvus, a man also from a provincial consular family in Nimes. It was a successful marriage. Their son, Titus Aurelius Fulvus Boionus Arrius Antoninus, became the emperor Antoninus Pius (reigned 137–61) after his adoption by Hadrian.

Sources

Pliny the Younger. *Epistulae* 4.3.

Scriptores Historiae Augustae. Antoninus Pius 1.4

Pauly, A., G. Wissowa, and W. Kroll. *Real-Encyclopadie d. Classischen Altertumswissenschaft 1893–.* (Germany: multiple publishers) 44.

Syme, Ronald. *Tacitus.* 2 vols. Oxford: Clarendon Press, 1958, pp. 604–605.

Arria the Elder

(first century C.E.)   Roman: Italy
stoic

Arria lived a life of passionate commitment shared by her daughter, the younger ARRIA, and her granddaughter, FANNIA (2). Living in the most influential political circles of her time, her behavior underscored traditions of character, family loyalty, and honor admired and rarely practiced in the conflicts that racked elite Roman society during the middle decades of the first century C.E.

Educated and articulate, Arria and her husband, Caecina Paetus, followed the teachings of the Stoics. They believed in the dignity of the

Senate and the responsibility of senators to speak out about the affairs of the empire. In 42 C.E. Paetus sided with Lucius Arruntius Camillus Scribonianus, legate in Dalmatia and consul in 32, when Scribonianus led two legions in an ill-conceived and ill-fated revolt against the emperor Claudius. Even though Arria was a friend of Valeria MESSALLINA, the wife of Claudius, she traveled with Paetus to Dalmatia in support of the insurgency. The legions, however, refused to march on Rome, and the revolt was quashed in four days. Scribonianus was killed, and Paetus was taken prisoner.

Arria sought to accompany her husband on board the ship taking him to Rome. She argued that a man of his rank, even though a prisoner, should be accorded several slaves for his toilet and table. Were she present, she would be able to serve him. When the soldiers refused her request, Arria hired a small fishing boat and followed behind her husband's ship to Rome. There, at the emperor's palace, she encountered Vibia, the wife of Scribonianus, also newly returned from Dalmatia, who had testified against her own husband in the resulting inquiry. When the woman approached, Arria turned away, declaring that she would not suffer conversation with a woman who clung to life although her murdered husband had died in her arms.

Arria's strength of character rested on her conviction that marriage bound her with her husband in public as well as in private life. Her husband and their beloved son were both critically ill, and the son died. Arria arranged for the funeral and kept the news from Paetus so that grief would not tip the scales in his own struggle to live.

Her death was as noble as her life. Awaiting her husband's conviction for treason, she refused to appeal to her friend Messallina and made it clear to her family that she planned to die with him. Her son-in-law, Publius Clodius Thrasea Paetus, sought to dissuade her. He asked if she would tell her daughter to die in similar circumstances. Arria responded that she would, if her daughter had as harmonious a shared life with her husband as Arria had with hers. When her family sought to protect her from herself, she beat her head against a wall until she lost consciousness, making plain that they could not force her to live.

When the time came for Paetus to die, Arria was by his side. She took the sword and plunged it into her breast, sealing her immortality by telling him that it did not hurt.

Sources

Dio Cassius. *Roman History* 60.16.5–7.

Pliny the Younger. *Epistulae* 3.16.

Martial. *Epigrammata* 1.13

Oxford Classical Dictionary, ed. by Simon Hornblower and Antony Spawforth. 3d. ed. New York: Oxford University Press, 1996, p. 175.

Pomeroy, Sarah B. *Goddesses, Whores, Wives, and Slaves: Women in Classical Antiquity*. New York: Schocken Books, 1975, p. 161.

◉ Arria the Younger

(first century C.E.)   Roman: Italy

stoic

Arria belonged to a circle of distinguished men and women who shaped the literary and philosophical ideas of the period and who were active in the politics of the day. Often, they risked their fortunes and their lives to oppose the emperors. Her mother, the elder ARRIA, and her father, Caecina Paetus, had committed suicide in 42 C.E. after her father had been convicted of treason against the emperor Claudius.

By marrying Publius Clodius Thrasea Paetus, consul suffectus in 56, Arria, who was related to the Stoic satirist Aulus Persius Flaccus (34–62 C.E.), entered into a senatorial family that reinforced the union of honor, politics and Stoic discourse. Her husband upheld the family tradition when he walked out of the Senate after a self-serving letter was read in which the emperor Nero enumerated the charges that justified the death of his own mother, the younger AGRIPPINA.

The almost inevitable happened in 66. Thrasea Paetus was accused in the Senate of treason. Helvidius Priscus, the husband of Arria and Thrasea Paetus's only child, FANNIA (2), was also accused. Priscus, a fellow student of Stoicism, had married Fannia in about 55. The accusation that he shared Thrasea Paetus's views was no doubt justified.

Arria's husband was condemned to death, and Priscus was banished. Thrasea Paetus learned of his fate while hosting a dinner. He urged his guests to leave so as not to be implicated in his affairs and turned his attention to committing suicide. Arria intended to follow her mother's example and die with her husband, but he convinced her to live for the sake of their daughter. She and Fannia were closely linked thereafter. Since Fannia was already a grown woman and married, Arria may have used her own wealth to augment the losses to her daughter from the confiscation of both Thrasea Paetus's and Priscus's estates.

In 66, Arria and Fannia left Rome voluntarily with the banished Priscus. The three returned in 68, when Galba supplanted Nero as emperor. Priscus immediately began a prosecution of Marcellus Epirus, who had received 5 million sesterces for his earlier successful prosecution of Priscus and Thrasea Paetus. Fortune as well as honor was at stake. Among the senators, more than a few had financially benefited from the late persecutions and were themselves vulnerable to attack from newly returned exiles. The Senate was divided, and Priscus withdrew his case on the advice of friends.

Priscus continued to attack Epirus outside the Senate. Around 75, the emperor Vespasian, angered by Priscus's attacks and claiming that he did the state no service by constantly harping on wrongs from the past, again exiled him. Fannia and Arria left with him. Soon after, Priscus was executed, although sources note that Vespasian had sent a letter that arrived too late to prevent the execution.

Arria and Fannia returned to Rome after the death of Vespasian, and they once more entered on a collision course with the emperor. At the time of Thrasea Paetus's death, Junius Arulenus Rusticus, then plebeian tribune, had offered to veto the Senate's resolution condemning Thrasea Paetus. His offer had been refused, for Thrasea Paetus did not wish to jeopardize the young man at the beginning of his career by causing him to directly oppose the Senate and the emperor. In 93, the emperor Domitian ordered the execution of Rusticus, who had been consul suffectus in 92, for his praise of the dead Thrasea Paetus and the elder Helvidius Priscus.

He also ordered the execution of the younger Helvidius Priscus, Fannia's stepson, and he expelled all philosophers from Rome in an attempt to rid himself of Stoic sympathizers. Arria and Fannia were among those exiled.

More specifically, Arria and Fannia were expelled for commissioning a laudatory memoir of the younger Helvidius Priscus. Fannia attempted to take full blame and to spare her mother another exile, to no avail. The women, however, once more outlived their tormentor and returned to Rome in 96. At the request of the younger Pliny, Arria and Fannia joined with ANTEIA, the widow of the younger Helvidius Priscus, in a suit to clear the latter's name. Pliny brought the matter before the Senate, but no action was taken.

Arria died before Fannia, although the exact date is unknown.

Sources

Pliny the Younger. *Epistulae* 3.11; 9.13.
Tacitus. *Annales* 16.21–29, 33–35.
Tacitus. *Historiae* 4.3–9.
Suetonius. *The Lives of the Caesars:* Domitian 10.
Suetonius. *The Lives of the Caesars:* Vespasian 15.
Balsdon, J. P. V. D. *Roman Women.* New York: John Day Comp., 1963, p. 58.
Oxford Classical Dictionary, ed. by Simon Hornblower and Antony Spawforth. 3d. ed. New York: Oxford University Press, 1996, p. 175.

Arsinoë

(fourth century B.C.E.)   Greek: Macedonia
progenitor of Ptolemaic line

Arsinoë was the mother of the Ptolemaic line of Greek rulers in Egypt that lasted from 323 B.C.E., after the death of Alexander the Great, until Egypt became a Roman province in 30 B.C.E. She was probably a lover of Philip II, ruler of Macedonia (359–336 B.C.E.). She married a Macedonian named Lagus, who was the father of her son Ptolemy. Ptolemy, a general in Alexander's army, became Ptolemy I Soter, ruler of Egypt.

Sources

Oxford Classical Dictionary, ed. by Simon Hornblower and Antony Spawforth. 3d. ed. New York: Oxford University Press, 1996, p. 1,271.

Pauly, A., G. Wissowa, and W. Kroll. *Real-Encyclopadie d. Classischen Altertumswissenschaft 1893–*. (Germany: multiple publishers) 24.

▣ Arsinoë I
(300 B.C.E.–?)   Greek: Greece and Egypt
political player

Arsinoë I and her sister-in-law, Arsinoë II Philadelphus, vied for power in the generation born after the death of Alexander the Great. Born in 300 B.C.E., she was the daughter of Nicaea (1) and Lysimachus, one of Alexander's generals. In 289 or 288 she married Ptolemy II Philadelphus and had three children: Ptolemy III Euergetes, Berenice Syra, who married the Seleucid king Antiochus II, and Lysimachus.

Arsinoë was no match for her sister-in-law. After escaping from her husband/stepbrother Ptolemy Ceraunus, who ruled Macedonia, Arsinoë II persuaded Ptolemy II to become her husband and banish Arsinoë on trumped up charges of conspiracy. The very wealthy Arsinoë went to Coptus in Upper Egypt where she lived in great splendor and exercised considerable power. Her eldest son ruled Egypt after his father's death.

Sources
Polybius. *Histories* 25.5.
Cary, M. *A History of the Greek World from 323 to 146 B.C.* London: Methuen, 1951, *passim.*
Macurdy, Grace. *Hellenistic Queens.* Reprint. Chicago: Ares Publishers, 1985, pp. 109–111.
Oxford Classical Dictionary, ed. by Simon Hornblower and Antony Spawforth. 3d. ed. New York: Oxford University Press, 1996, p. 177.

▣ Arsinoë II Philadelphus
(c. 316–270 B.C.E.)
Greek: Egypt and Macedonia
coruler; deified

Arsinoë II played an important role in the complicated marital and political coalitions formed in the generation born after the death of Alexander the Great in 323 B.C.E. She was the daughter of Ptolemy I Soter of Egypt and Berenice I. In 300

or 299 B.C.E., she married Lysimachus, a companion of her father and of the late Alexander. Her husband had become ruler of Thrace and had gained control of Macedonia and Thessaly in the years since Alexander's death. He shed his second wife to marry Arsinoë and cement relations with her father.

Arsinoë was about 16 when she married; Lysimachus was 60 or 61. She strongly influenced her elderly husband who gave her the towns of Heraclea, Tius, Amastris, and Cassandria. They had three sons. Determined that one of her sons would succeed her husband, she convinced Lysimachus to eliminate Agathocles, his eldest son by a previous marriage. He charged the boy with treason and put him to death in 283.

Lysimachus was killed in battle in 281. Arsinoë, who was in Ephesus, dressed her maid in royal clothing while she darkened her face and dressed in rags. With her three sons, she went to the shore where ships were waiting to take them to Macedonia. She escaped and the maid, whom she left behind, was killed. Settling in Cassandreia, she raised a mercenary army from her own wealth.

Arsinoë II
(Date: 270 B.C.E.–240 B.C.E. 1935.117.1086, Archives, American Numismatic Society)

Arsinoë married Ptolemy Ceraunus, her half brother, who ruled Macedonia and Thrace after having killed Seleucus I to become king. The distrustful Arsinoë forced Ceraunus to marry her in front of the Macedonian troops outside the gates of Cassandreia. Shortly thereafter, Ceraunus killed two of her sons even as she held them. The eldest, who had warned his mother against the marriage, had escaped to Illyria before the wedding. Fearful of Arsinoë's brother, Ptolemy II, Philadelphus, Ceraunus spared Arsinoë. She, however, mindful of her vulnerable position, left for Egypt.

Almost 40 years old, Arsinoë married her brother Ptolemy II after persuading him to banish his wife, ARSINOË I. Theirs was the first sibling marriage among the Greek rulers of Egypt. Prior to the marriage, Ptolemy II had been defeated by Antiochus I, and Egyptian forces had been driven from Syria. After the marriage, Arsinoë energized her new husband to lead the Egyptians to a victory that included the capture of Phoenicia and most of the coast of Asia Minor from Miletus to Calycadnus in Cilicia. She also strengthened Egyptian sea power to expand the sphere of Egypt's influence.

She and her husband ruled for about five years. She was the first Greek woman ruler of Egypt to have her portrait appear along with that of her husband on coins. She and her husband were also the first Ptolemaic rulers to deify themselves during their lifetime. She was considered an incarnation of the Egyptian goddess Isis. Poets composed verses about her, and the court of Alexandria flourished. Arsinoë wanted her son Ptolemy, whose father was Lysimachus, to become king of Macedonia, but she died in 270 B.C.E. before she could succeed.

Sources

Justin. *Epitome* 24.2–3.

Polyaenus. *Strategemata* 18.57.

Burstein, Stanley Mayer. "Arsinoe II Philadelphos: A Revisionist View." In *Philip II, Alexander the Great, and the Macedonian Heritage,* ed. by W. Lindsay Adams and Eugene N. Borza. Washington, D.C.: University Press of America, 1982, pp. 197–212.

Cary, M. *A History of the Greek World from 323 to 146 B.C.* London: Methuen, 1951, *passim.*

Macurdy, Grace. *Hellenistic Queens.* Reprint. Chicago: Ares Publishers, 1985, *passim.*

Oxford Classical Dictionary, ed. by Simon Hornblower and Antony Spawforth. 3d. ed. New York: Oxford University Press, 1996, p. 177.

Pomeroy, Sarah B. *Women in Hellenistic Egypt.* New York: Schocken, 1984, *passim.*

Tarn, William Woodthorpe. *Hellenistic Civilization.* London: Methuen, 1966, *passim.*

▣ Arsinoë III Philopator
(third century B.C.E.)   Greek: Egypt
ruler

Arsinoë III, a brave, beloved, and virtuous ruler, was victimized by her brother/husband and eventually murdered in a conspiracy headed by her husband's lover and brother. Born in 235 B.C.E., she was the daughter of BERENICE II OF CYRENE and Ptolemy III Euergetes. In 217 Arsinoë, who was still a young woman, was present on the battlefield of Raphia in Coele-Syria where she rallied the troops and prevented a defeat by Antiochus III the Great in the Fourth Syrian War. After the battle, she married her brother, Ptolemy IV Philopator. Arsinoë, who was much younger than her brother, gave birth to a boy in 210.

The marriage was not happy. Ptolemy was addicted to drink and debauchery. He became besotted with AGATHOCLEIA, who had come to Egypt from Samos with her mother and brother. Along with her mother, OENANTHE, and her brother, Agothocles, Agathocleia murdered Ptolemy and Arsinoë in 205. Enraged primarily at the death of Arsinoë, whom they admired, the army and the people of Alexandria tore the assassins limb from limb.

Sources

Athenaeus. *Deipnosophistae* 276b.

Polybius. *Histories* 5.83–84; 15.33.

Macurdy, Grace. *Hellenistic Queens.* Reprint. Chicago: Ares Publishers, 1985, pp. 136–141.

Oxford Classical Dictionary, ed. by Simon Hornblower and Antony Spawforth. 3d. ed. New York: Oxford University Press, 1996, pp. 177–178.

Pomeroy, Sarah B. *Women in Hellenistic Egypt.* New York: Schocken, 1984, pp. 50–51.

Arsinoë Auletes

(65 B.C.E.–43/40 B.C.E.)   Greek: Egypt
coruler; insurgent leader

Arsinoë Auletes engaged in a struggle with her older sister CLEOPATRA VII for control over Egypt that cost her life. Her mother was possibly CLEOPATRA VI TRYPHAENA, and her father was Ptolemy XII Auletes. She was born about 65 B.C.E. She seems to have been as strong-willed as Cleopatra VII but without her charm, allure, diplomatic skills, or culture. In 48, when Julius Caesar decreed that Cleopatra VII and her brother Ptolemy XIII, should be joint rulers of Egypt and marry each other, he also made Arsinoë Auletes and her other brother, Ptolemy XIV, joint rulers of Cyprus. Arsinoë was kept under watch by Caesar.

Jealous of Cleopatra VII's more prominent role, she escaped to Alexandria aided by the eunuch Ganymede. She was about 17 when the Egyptian forces in Alexandria, led by their commander-in-chief Achillas, declared her ruler of Egypt. Not satisfied with a secondary role, she soon vied with Achillas over control of the armed forces. She had him killed and took charge. She appointed Ganymede head of the armed forces in the fight against Caesar. The Egyptian forces, unhappy under the control of a woman and a eunuch, asked Caesar to send the young Ptolemy XIII, Arsinoë's brother, to discuss peace terms. Instead, the Egyptian forces rallied around Ptolemy XIII. Arsinoë was defeated after a hard struggle.

Fearful that Arsinoë would again rally the Egyptians, Caesar took her to Rome and paraded her in regal attire and chains in his triumph. In 41, he allowed Arsinoë to go free, and she became a suppliant in the temple of Artemis at Ephesus. After Caesar's death, Mark Antony, at the request of Cleopatra VII, ordered that she be taken from the temple and killed.

Sources

Appian. *Roman History: Bella civilian (Civil Wars)* 5.9.
Dio Cassius. *Roman History* 42.35, 39–40, 42; 43.19.2–4.
Josephus. *Antiquitates Judaicae (Jewish Antiquities)* 15. 89–90.
Macurdy, Grace. *Hellenistic Queens.* Reprint. Chicago: Ares Publishers, 1985, *passim*.

Pauly, A., G. Wissowa, and W. Kroll. *Real-Encyclopadie d. Classischen Altertumswissenschaft 1893–.* (Germany: multiple publishers) 28.

Artacama

(fourth century B.C.E.)   Persian: Persia
political wife

Artacama married Ptolemy, the future ruler of Egypt, when he was still a general in the army of Alexander the Great. Artacama was the daughter of Artabazus (387–325 B.C.E.), who was appointed satrap of Dascylium by Artaxerxes II, king of Persia. After subduing the Persians, Alexander arranged to have 80 of his most distinguished Macedonian officers marry women of the Persian aristocracy in an effort to meld conquerors and conquered.

The marriages, including that of Artacama and Ptolemy, took place in 324 at Susa. After the death of Alexander in 323, the experiment in union through marriage fell apart. Artacama and Ptolemy divorced.

Sources

Arrian. *Anabasis of Alexander* 7.4.
Cary, M. *A History of the Greek World from 323 to 146 B.C.* London: Methuen, 1951, p. 250.

Artemisia I

(fifth century B.C.E.)   Greek: Asia Minor
ruler

Artemisia captained five ships in Xerxes' Persian fleet at the battle of Salamis against the Greeks in 480 B.C.E. Widowed, and with a young son, she ruled Halicarnassus, Cos, Nisyrus, and Calyndus in southwestern Asia Minor. Her father was Lygdamis of Halicarnassus, and her mother was thought to be of Cretan background. She assumed rule over Halicarnassus, whose inhabitants were Greek, after the death of her husband. Although she ruled under Persian suzerainty, it was not necessary for her bring a fleet into battle.

Artemisia provided ships as well as wise and practical counsel for Xerxes. She was the only one of his naval commanders to urge him—correctly—

not to engage the Greek fleet in the straits of Salamis. She escaped after the Persian defeat by sinking an enemy vessel. Later she transported part of Xerxes' family to Ephesus.

A white marble figure was erected in the portico of the temple of Artemis in Sparta to commemorate her actions at Salamis.

Sources

Herodotus. *The Persian Wars* 7.95–100.
Pausanias. *Description of Greece* 3.11, 3.
Hammond, N. G. L. *A History of Greece.* Oxford: Oxford University Press, 1967, p. 239.
Oxford Classical Dictionary, ed. by Simon Hornblower and Antony Spawforth. 3d. ed. New York: Oxford University Press, 1996, p. 184.

Artemisia II

(fourth century B.C.E.)   Greek: Asia Minor
ruler

Artemisia ruled Caria, a virtually independent satrapy of Persia in southwest Asia Minor, after the death of her brother/husband, Mausolus, in 353 or 352 B.C.E. In memory of her husband, she continued to build a mausoleum he had begun in Halicarnassus that would become one of the Seven Wonders of the Ancient World.

The foundation of the Mausoleum was about 100 by 140 feet with a high base upon which stood a colonnade of some 36 Ionic columns supporting a pyramidlike cap that reached a height of about 140 feet. The architect was Pythius, who was said to have sculpted a major chariot group frieze for the structure. Other well-known sculptors of the time, including Scopas, Bryaxis, Timotheus, and Leochares, were also said to have contributed to the project.

Following in her husband's Panhellenic literary, scientific, and artistic path, Artemisia sponsored a competition in oratory attended by the leading figures of the day, including Isocrates. The winner was Theopompus. She also must have had an interest in horticulture and named a plant after herself.

An attack on Rhodes by exiles expecting support from Athens gave Artemisia reason for attacking and conquering Rhodes. She died a short time later in 351 B.C.E.

The Mausoleum, with its sculptured groupings of animals and human figures, was destroyed in an earthquake before the 15th century C.E. In 1857 the site was excavated by C. T. Newton. Among the pieces brought to the British Museum were colossal statutes of Mausolus and Artemisia.

Sources

Aulus Gellius. *Noctes Atticae* 10.18.1–6.
Pliny the Elder. *Naturalis Historia* 25.36; 36.30–32.
Oxford Classical Dictionary, ed. by Simon Hornblower and Antony Spawforth. 3d. ed. New York: Oxford University Press, 1996, p. 184.

Artonis

(fourth century B.C.E.)   Persian: Persia
political wife

Artonis was one of 80 noble Persian women who were married the elite Macedonian officers of Alexander the Great in a mass ceremony in Susa in 324 B.C.E. She was the daughter of Artabazus, who defected to Alexander the Great and was made satrap of Bactria.

Artonis married Eumenes, a Greek from Cardia, who was Alexander's principal secretary. Eumenes divorced Artonis after Alexander died.

Sources

Arrian. *Anabasis of Alexander* 7.4.

Artoria Flaccilla

(first century C.E.)   Roman: Rome
loyal wife

Artoria Flaccilla lived among the rich, the educated, and the imperial elite. Her husband, Novius Priscus, was a close friend of the philosopher Lucius Annaeus Seneca. For some eight years at the beginning of Nero's reign, Seneca and Sextus Afranius Burrus were the emperor's two most important advisers. Burrus died in 62 C.E., and Seneca fell from favor as Nero's behavior became more extreme. In 65, Nero falsely accused Seneca of participating in the Pisonian conspiracy to kill the emperor and forced him to commit suicide. Nero sent Priscus into exile, and Artoria Flaccilla voluntarily went with her husband.

Sources

Tacitus. *Annales* 15.71.

▣ Asella

(c. 334–fifth century C.E.)   Roman: Rome
ascetic

Asella's parents dedicated their newborn daughter to a life of Christian asceticism and virginity. She exceeded her parents' expectations. Asella lived with her sister, MARCELLA, in the first house in Rome devoted to chaste virgins and widows.

Asella's family was extremely wealthy and she came from a patrician line. Her grandfather Caeionius Rufius Albinus had been consul in 345–346. Nonetheless, she was born at a time when there was a sense of foreboding and concern for the future. Christianity was on the rise and asceticism was a new movement. It touched older beliefs. The virginal woman was a Roman pagan tradition. The patrician Roman families had always dedicated daughters to fill the ranks of the Vestal Virgins, a position that contributed to family honor and was regarded as assuring the well-being of Rome. The position had a term of 30 years after which an honorably retired woman was left financially well rewarded, with wealth that would accrue to the family. Dedicating a child at birth to a life of Christian virginity, however, offered no comparable honor to the family or long-term financial benefit. Rather, Asella's parents were drawn to a new view of virginity that allowed their daughter to find Christ for eternity. For such parents, the promise never to seek a husband for a daughter was the greatest gift they could bestow upon their child.

Asella's mother was the elder ALBINA, who chose not to remarry after the death of her husband. A woman who wed only once had the status of *univira,* which also had a long tradition of honor among pagans. Her mother's motivation, however, was clearly Christian, not pagan. Asella's older sister, Marcella, became a notable Christian ascetic, a frequent correspondent with the church father Jerome, and an expert in Christian doctrine who Christians in Rome consulted on disputed points of theology. Marcella, like her mother, chose an ascetic life after having been married and widowed, but never having borne any children. The family was not pleased with either her mother or sister's choice. Peace was kept by an agreement whereby that part of the family fortune held by her mother and Marcella was given to her maternal uncle, nieces, and nephews to secure it within the family line.

Asella, whose financial relationship with the family and its wealth is unknown, adopted a more extreme ascetic lifestyle than her sister and at an earlier age. At age 10, she consecrated herself to Christ. She sold her gold necklace without notifying her parents, although what she did with the proceeds of the sale remains unknown, and she began to dress plainly in dark clothes, although neither of her parents had wished her to assume a monkish garb.

Her mother died in 388 and Asella, her sister, and the women around them who shared their passion for a modest Christian life moved to a smaller residence in a suburb of Rome. In contrast with the other members of the community, Asella lived alone in a small cell. She rarely met with her sister or anyone else.

Jerome's correspondence with Asella and the women around her provides a coda on her life. He wrote a letter to Marcella in 384 in which he praised Asella's devotion to Christ and commented that her holy knees were as hard as a camel's from constant prayer. He asked Marcella not to show his comment to Asella since she would find the praise unwelcome. A year later, Jerome left Rome and wrote Asella as he sailed away. Jerome's leave-taking had been controversial. He was accused by some in the Christian community of hastening the death of BLAESILLA from fasting by his encouragement of excessive asceticism. He also aroused comment for his close relationship with PAULA and EUSTOCHIUM, friends of Asella and her sister Marcella. His letter to Asella, although not apologetic, was a self-serving explanation of his behavior to a woman he evidently admired for her saintliness.

Asella was still alive in 405 according to the historian Palladius.

Sources

Jerome. Letters XXIV, XXV.

Palladius. *The Lausiac History* 41. 4.

Prosopography of the Later Roman Empire. Vol. I. Edited by A. H. M. Jones, J. R. Martindale, and J. Morris. Cambridge: Cambridge University Press, 1971. Reprinted 1992, p. 117.

▣ Aspasia

(fifth century B.C.E.)   Greek: Athens
self-made woman

Aspasia was the most famous woman of Athens during the height of its democracy in the fifth century B.C.E. She was clever, intelligent, sophisticated, cultured, and politically astute. Her father, Axiochus, was from Miletus on the southwest coast of Asia Minor. Aspasia was Pericles' companion and lived with him from 445 B.C.E., some five years after he divorced his wife, HIPPARETE (1), until his death in 429.

Very much a part of the public life of the city, she participated in its intellectual and political ferment. She visited with Socrates and his disciples. There is some indication that several of the men who visited with her may even have been accompanied by their wives or other female companions. She is also said to have educated a group of young women, possibly resident foreigners or freedwomen.

Pericles, always open to political attack, was especially vulnerable in his relationship with Aspasia. Her public presence so close to him and among the elite of the city drew comments, sometimes amusing, other times derisive and biting. In the winter of 441–440 B.C.E., war broke out between Samos and Miletus, Aspasia's birthplace, over possession of the city of Priene. Aspasia was accused of persuading Pericles to make war against the Samians after the Milesians lost and appealed to Athens for help. According to treaty, Athens had no right to intervene; nevertheless, Pericles conquered Samos.

After Pericles died, Aspasia joined forces with Lysicles, a popular leader described as a low-born sheep dealer who became famous through his association with her. He died in 428.

Aspasia had two children, one with Pericles and the other with Lysicles. Pericles had been the author of the Athenian law that restricted citizenship to children born of two citizen parents. However, Aspasia and Pericles' son became a citizen after the death of Pericles' two sons from his earlier marriage. The child took Pericles' name and grew up to become an Athenian general.

The exact date of Aspasia's death is not known.

Sources

Athenaeus. *Deipnosophistae* 5.219b–c.

Plato. *Menexemus* 235e–236d; 249d, e.

Plutarch. *Vitae Parallelae (Parallel Lives): Pericles* 24.2–6; 25.1; 32.1–3.

Blundell, Sue. *Women in Ancient Greece.* London: British Museum Press, 1995, p. 148.

Davies, J. K. *Athenian Propertied Families, 600–300 B.C.* Oxford: Clarendon Press, 1971, p. 458.

Oxford Classical Dictionary, ed. by Simon Hornblower and Antony Spawforth. 3d. ed. New York: Oxford University Press, 1996, p. 192.

Pomeroy, Sarah B. *Goddesses, Whores, Wives, and Slaves: Women in Classical Antiquity.* New York: Schocken Books, 1975, pp. 89–90.

▣ Atia (1)

(first century B.C.E.)   Roman: Italy
mother of Octavia and Augustus

Atia can truly be said to be a woman known by her children. She was the mother of Octavian, who became the emperor Augustus, and OCTAVIA (2) and the stepmother of OCTAVIA (1). Atia was the elder daughter of Marcus Atius Balbus and JULIA (4), the younger sister of Julius Caesar. Her first husband, Gaius Octavius, died in 58 B.C.E., leaving her with two children. She then married Lucius Marcius Philippus, who was consul in 56.

When Caesar was murdered, Octavian was in Apollonia on the Adriatic Sea, where he had been sent by his uncle for experience in campaigning. Atia and Philippus wrote advising him to come to Rome with dispatch, but to keep a low profile and assess the situation. Atia, concerned that the Senate had decreed not to punish the assassins, advised Octavian to use wiles and patience rather than seek confrontation.

Octavian took their advice and first stopped at Brundisium, where he discovered that he was Caesar's heir. Atia supported Octavian's plan to accept his inheritance and avenge Caesar's death. The 19th-year-old Octavian began his march on Rome.

Octavian was 20 years old and serving his first consulship when Atia died in 43. She had a public funeral. Octavian conferred the highest posthumous honors on her.

Sources

Appian. *Roman History: Bella civilian (Civil Wars)* 3.13, 14.
Suetonius. *The Lives of the Caesars:* Augustus 61.
Oxford Classical Dictionary, ed. by Simon Hornblower and Antony Spawforth. 3d. ed. New York: Oxford University Press, 1996, p. 207.
Pauly, A., G. Wissowa, and W. Kroll. *Real-Encyclopadie d. Classischen Altertumswissenschaft 1893–.* (Germany: multiple publishers) 34.

Atia (2)

(first century B.C.E.)   Roman: Italy
niece of Julius Caesar

Atia and her older sister Atia (1), the mother of the emperor Augustus, were the nieces of Julius Caesar through their mother Julia (4), Caesar's sister. Their father was Marcus Atius Balbus.

Atia married Lucius Marcius Philippus, consul suffectus in 38 B.C.E. He was the stepson of her sister, who had married Philippus's father after the death of her first husband. They had a daughter, Marcia (3), who later married Paullus Fabius Maximus, consul suffectus in 45 B.C.E.

Sources

Oxford Classical Dictionary, ed. by Simon Hornblower and Antony Spawforth. 3d. ed. New York: Oxford University Press, 1996, p. 207.
Pauly, A., G. Wissowa, and W. Kroll. *Real-Encyclopadie d. Classischen Altertumswissenschaft 1893–.* (Germany: multiple publishers) 35.

Syme, Ronald. *The Augustan Aristocracy.* Oxford: Clarendon Press, 1986, *passim.*

Atilia

(first century B.C.E.)   Roman: Italy
accused adulterer

Atilia, the daughter of Serranus Gavianus, tribune in 57 B.C.E., married Marcus Porcius Cato Uticensis in 73 B.C.E. He was on the rebound from Aemilia Lepida (1), who had unexpectedly rejected him. Cato, an unpleasant person, was 22 years old. Atilia was about 16. Plutarch wrote that Cato was a virgin; presumably so was Atilia. Although not unusual for a woman, it was indicative of an unusual man.

At first the marriage was sufficiently successful for Atilia to wish to accompany Cato on a political mission for the Senate in the East, and to be concerned for his safety when he went without her. There were several children. Nonetheless, the marriage ended in divorce, with Cato accusing Atilia of infidelity.

Sources

Plutarch. *Vitae Parallelae (Parallel Lives): Cato Minor* 7.3; 9.1–2; 24.1.
Pauly, A., G. Wissowa, and W. Kroll. *Real-Encyclopadie d. Classischen Altertumswissenschaft 1893–.* (Germany: multiple publishers) 79.

Attia Variola

(first century C.E.)   Roman: Rome
litigant

Attia Variola sued her father for her patrimony. She was born into an aristocratic family and married a member of the Praetorian Guard. Her father, a lovesick old man, remarried at the age of 80. Eleven days later, he disinherited Attia. The case was tried before the entire Centumviral Court, consisting of 180 jurors. Attia was represented by Gaius Plinius Caecilius Secundus (Pliny, the Younger), who gave one of his best speeches. The stepmother and her son both lost any right to inherit.

Sources

Pliny the Younger. *Epistulae* 6.33.

Attica, Caecilia

(51 B.C.E.–?)   Roman: Rome
heiress

Caecilia Attica was the beloved only child of Titus Pomponius Atticus, whose lifetime friendship with Marcus Tullius Cicero included a correspondence that provides rare insight into personal and family life during the late republic. Her father came from a wealthy equestrian family and inherited additional wealth from an uncle who had adopted him. He married PILIA in 56 B.C.E., when he was 53. She came from an old family in the city of Cora not far from Rome. It was his first marriage. Their daughter Attica was born in 51.

The extant correspondence from 68 to 43 B.C.E. between Atticus and Cicero covers both personal and professional concerns. As Attica was growing up, the letters traced the seasonal movements from city to country, the trips with her mother to visit friends and family in and out of Rome, and concern with the various illnesses she suffered.

In 37 Attica married Marcus Vipsanius Agrippa, a close friend of Atticus and a lifelong supporter, friend, and leading military commander of Octavian, the future emperor Augustus. The marriage made Agrippa immensely wealthy. Her father gained a relationship with the closest circle around Octavian. One can only guess at the relationship between the lively 14-year-old Attica and the austere Agrippa. In 31, Attica gave birth to a daughter, VIPSANIA AGRIPPINA.

After her father's death in 32, Attica was suspected of having an affair with her tutor, Quintus Caecilius Epirota, a learned freedman. She was either divorced or died young. Agrippa contracted another marriage in 28 B.C.E.

Sources

Cicero. *Epistulae ad Atticum* 12.1, 6, 13, 33; 13.14, 19, 21a, 52; 14.16.11.
Cicero. *Brutus* 17.7.
Suetonius. *The Lives of Illustrious Men: De Grammaticis* 16.
Oxford Classical Dictionary, ed. by Simon Hornblower and Antony Spawforth. 3d. ed. New York: Oxford University Press, 1996, p. 267.
Pauly, A., G. Wissowa, and W. Kroll. *Real-Encyclopadie d. Classischen Altertumswissenschaft 1893–.* (Germany: multiple publishers) 78.

Aurelia (1)

(second–first century B.C.E.)   Roman: Rome
mother of Julius Caesar

Aurelia came from the patrician family of the Aurelii Cottae, whose members included two consuls between the years 76 and 74 B.C.E. She married Gaius Julius Caesar, who died in 85 B.C.E. She never remarried. They had three children: a son, the great Gaius Julius Caesar, who was 16 when his father died, and two daughters, JULIA (3) and JULIA (4).

It was Aurelia who detected the presence of the notorious Publius Clodius Pulcher disguised as a woman in Caesar's house during the Bona Dea rites, a traditional festival restricted to well-born women.

Aurelia died in 54 while Caesar was campaigning in Britain.

Sources

Plutarch. *Vitae Parallelae (Parallel Lives): Caesar* 10.
Balsdon, J. P. V. D. *Roman Women.* New York: John Day Comp., 1963, p. 244.
Oxford Classical Dictionary, ed. by Simon Hornblower and Antony Spawforth. 3d. ed. New York: Oxford University Press, 1996, p. 219.
Pauly, A., G. Wissowa, and W. Kroll. *Real-Encyclopadie d. Classischen Altertumswissenschaft 1893–.* (Germany: multiple publishers) 219.

Aurelia (2)

(first century C.E.)   Roman: Rome
woman of means

Aurelia appears at the moment she was about to sign her will in a vivid and humorous letter written by Pliny the Younger. Even though a *tutor,* functioning in the role of agent, probably was still necessary or customary for some kinds of transactions, Aurelia, like many Roman women of the later first century, controlled her own affairs and could make bequests of her own choosing. The signing of a will moreover, was an occasion when propertied and wealthy women dressed in an elaborate fashion, clothing being itself valuable as well as indicative of wealth.

Marcus Regulus, an advocate, seemingly made it a habit to persuade people to include him in their wills. He was present as one of the witnesses on the festive occasion of the signing. He asked Aurelia to leave him her dress. Aurelia thought he was joking, but he was insistent, and so she wrote the bequest of her dress into her will while he stood by. Pliny concluded his letter with the report that Aurelia was still alive and Regulus still awaited his bequest.

Sources
Pliny the Younger. *Epistulae* 2.20.

▣ Aurelia Orestilla
   (first century B.C.E.)   Roman: Rome
   possible conspirator

Aurelia Orestilla was the wife of Lucius Sergius Catiline when he led an uprising against the senate in 63 B.C.E. Her father was Gnaeus Aufidius Orestes, consul in 71. She married, had a daughter, and was widowed. Left wealthy, she married the impoverished but well-born Catiline in 68. Vicious rumors circulated around the marriage; one accused Catiline of having murdered his son to marry Aurelia because she refused to become the stepmother of a grown son.

Catiline had a varied political career. Increasingly impoverished, however, he rallied a political base among the indebted, both low and high born. The combination of inflation with the rigidity of a land-based economy and the absence of a flexible money supply resulted in indebtedness and mortgaged estates that fed frustration and became politically charged. Catiline became the leader of a conspiracy against the Senate to ease debt. The conspiracy was uncovered and Catiline fled Rome in 62.

Catiline was said to have written his friend Quintus Lutatius Catullus that he had sufficient funds to meet his own obligations. However, Aurelia and her daughter paid some part of the debt incurred by others on his behalf, and he left Aurelia vulnerable to law suits stemming from the conspiracy. Catiline was subsequently put to death without a trial. Whatever her role in the conspiracy, or the resulting law suits, Aurelia remained unharmed, her wealth intact.

Sources
Appian. *Roman History: Bella civilian (Civil Wars)* 2.2.
Cicero. *In Catalinum* 114
Cicero. *Epistulae ad familiares* 8.7.2.
Sallust. *Bellum Catilinae* 15.2; 35.3, 6.
Pauly, A., G. Wissowa, and W. Kroll. *Real-Encyclopadie d. Classischen Altertumswissenschaft 1893–*. (Germany: multiple publishers) 261.

▣ Aurelia Severa
   (?–213 C.E.)   Roman: Rome
   priestess

Aurelia Severa was tried and convicted of violating her vow of chastity. One of four Vestal Virgins convicted in 213 C.E. by the emperor Marcus Aurelius Antoninus, she and her colleagues CANNUTIA CRESCENTINA, CLODIA LAETA, and POMPONIA RUFINA, caused a major scandal. In an earlier age, the conviction of four out of six Vestals would have been regarded as a sign of approaching calamity, but times had changed. Although still regarded as part of ancient tradition, awe had given way to greater skepticism. Nonetheless, Aurelia was buried alive in the ancient tradition.

Sources
Dio Cassius. *Roman History* 78.16, 1–3.

▣ Axiothea (1)
   (fourth century B.C.E.)   Greek: Greece
   philosopher

Axiothea came from the city of Philius on the Peloponnese, the peninsula in southern Greece. She studied philosophy under Plato at the Academy he established in Athens.

Sources
Diogenes Laertius. *Lives of the Eminent Philosophers* 3.46.

▣ Axiothea (2)
   (fourth century B.C.E.)   Greek: Cyprus
   heroine

Axiothea died rather than surrender when the city of Paphos was seized in a war among Alexander the Great's successor generals. She was the wife of

Nicoles of Paphos on the island of Cyprus. Nicoles had sided with Antigonus, who controlled most of Asia Minor after the death of Alexander, against a coalition led by Ptolemy I Soter of Egypt, Cassander of Macedonia, and Lysimachus of Thrace. Nicoles committed suicide in 310 B.C.E. when Ptolemy's army surrounded his palace.

Ptolemy had issued no instructions about the women. As his army stormed the palace, Axiothea killed her daughters so that it would be impossible for the enemy to rape them. She urged her sisters-in-law to join her in committing suicide. After they killed themselves, the brothers of Nicoles set fire to the palace and perished in the blaze.

Axiothea was praised by the ancient historians for her bravery in choosing death for herself and her children over a life of slavery.

Sources

Diodorus Siculus. *Library of History* 20.21.1.
Polyaenus. *Strategemata* 8.48.

B

Balbilla, Julia
(second century C.E.)   Greek: Asia Minor
poet

Julia Balbilla was a poet who accompanied the imperial entourage of Vibia SABINA and her husband, the emperor Hadrian, on a trip to Egypt in 130 C.E. She inscribed five epigrams on the left foot of the Colossus of Memnon in Thebes.

Her epigrams were in Aeolian Greek, the language used by the great poet SAPPHO eight centuries earlier. They juxtapose the mortal and the immortal. They tell the story of Memnon, a mythical king of Ethiopia who was killed by Achilles at Troy and whom Zeus made immortal. Balbilla claimed for herself piety and a royal lineage to Balbillus the Wise and the ruler Antiochus. On the Colossus, she hoped that her words would last forever, and she, a mortal descendant of a king, would become immortal.

Sources
Balsdon, J. P. V. D. *Roman Women.* New York: John Day Comp., 1963, p. 140.
Bowie, E. L. "Greek Poetry in the Antonine Age." In *Antonine Literature,* ed. by D. A. Russell. Oxford: Clarendon Press, 1990, p. 63.
Fantham, Elaine, et al. *Women in the Classical World.* New York: Oxford University Press, 1994, pp. 353–354.

Pauly, A., G. Wissowa, and W. Kroll. *Real-Encyclopadie d. Classischen Altertumswissenschaft 1893–.* (Germany: multiple publishers) 559.

Barsine (1)
(fourth century B.C.E.)
Persian: Asia Minor and Egypt
adventurer

Barsine lived an adventurous life in difficult times. She was the daughter of Artabazus, a Persian, who succeeded his father, Pharnabazus, as satrap of Dascylium, a city on the Black Sea in Asia Minor. She married a Rhodian mercenary leader, Mentor, who along with his brother Memnon had entered the service of Artabazus in a revolt of the satraps (362–360 B.C.E.) quelled by the Persian ruler Artaxerxes III.

In 353 Barsine, Memnon, and Mentor fled. Barsine and Mentor went to Egypt where Mentor assembled an army of Greek mercenaries. In 344, while supposedly guarding the city of Sidon in Phoenicia against an attack by Artaxerxes, he instead helped Artaxerxes capture the city. Artaxerxes rewarded him by appointing him general. In this position Mentor helped Artaxerxes conquer Egypt in 343. He also secured a position for his younger brother, Memnon. After Mentor's death, probably in 342 B.C.E., Barsine married Memnon. Memnon fought successfully against Philip II of Macedon in 336 and became commander-in-chief of the Persian forces under Darius. He died suddenly around 333 B.C.E.

Barsine was captured by Alexander the Great in Damascus after the death of Memnon. Her high birth, beauty, Greek education, and amiable disposition brought her to his personal attention. She was said to be the only woman with whom Alexander had a sexual relationship prior to his marriage. Alexander married the daughter of Barsine and Mentor to his naval commander, Nearchus.

After Alexander's death Barsine lived in Pergamum in Asia Minor and took part in the struggles for power among Alexander's generals. Her pawn in these struggles was Heracles, whom some claimed was her son by Alexander. Although probably not the son of Alexander, and possibly not even the son of Barsine, the 17-year-old boy was taken by Alexander's former general Polyperchon from Pergamum to use as a bargaining chip with Cassander when he sought to gain control over Macedonia. Polyperchon reached an agreement with Cassander to kill Heracles in exchange for land, support, and additional troops. Heracles was murdered in 309 B.C.E. Polyperchon also killed Barsine.

Sources

Diodorus Siculus. *Library of History* 10.20.1–4; 10.28.1–4.
Justin. *Epitome* 11.10; 15.2.
Plutarch. *Vitae Parallelae (Parallel Lives): Alexander* 21.7–11.

◉ Barsine (2)

(fourth century B.C.E.)   Persian: Persia
wife of Alexander the Great; political victim

Barsine, called Stateira by Plutarch, was the eldest daughter of Darius, the ruler of Persia. In 324 B.C.E., after having conquered Persia, Alexander the Great arranged a mass marriage of his most distinguished officers to 80 aristocratic Persian women in a revolutionary effort at ethnic harmony. He married Barsine even though he already had a wife, ROXANE, whom he had married in 327. Barsine's sister DRYPETIS married Hephaestion, Alexander's closest companion.

After the death of Alexander, Barsine was a potential rallying point in the bitter battles for power that erupted among Alexander's generals. To protect the position of her infant son, Roxane had Barsine and her sister murdered and hid their bodies in a well.

Sources

Arrian. *Anabasis of Alexander* 7.4.
Diodorus Siculus. *Library of History* 17.6.
Plutarch. *Vitae Parallelae (Parallel Lives): Alexander* 70.1–3.
Burn, Andrew Robert. *Alexander the Great and the Hellenistic World.* London: English Universities Press, 1964, p. 122, 170, 182.

◉ Bastia

(first century B.C.E.)   Roman: Rome
hard-hearted woman

Bastia lived through the Social War (90–88 B.C.E.) and the proscriptions that followed in the dictatorship of Lucius Cornelius Sulla. She was the wife of Gaius Papius Mutilus, a Samnite from southern Italy and one of the two leading generals in the armies fighting Rome. Despite passage of a law that granted Italians full Roman citizenship, Mutilus refused all Roman offers of peace and led resistance in the last stronghold in 80 B.C.E. in the city of Nola.

His final defeat by Sulla coincided with the onset of the proscriptions, a bloodbath precipitated by the Roman system of rewarding informers for uncovering the whereabouts of people on the lists of those wanted by the state. Papius Mutilus was listed, but Bastia was not. He came in disguise to Bastia's house to seek refuge. She would not admit him. It is unclear if she also threatened to report him. He stabbed himself to death on her doorstep. Her death is not recorded.

Sources

Livy. *From the Founding of the City* 89.

Berenice (1)

(first century B.C.E.–first century
C.E.)   Jewish: Judaea
political client

Berenice, the daughter of SALOME and the niece of
Herod the Great of Judaea, had close ties with the
Roman imperial family through her friend, the
younger ANTONIA. After Berenice's husband, Aristobulus, was executed in 7 B.C.E., she brought
Marcus Julius Agrippa, her young son and future
ruler of Judaea, to Rome and placed him in Antonia's care. He grew up with Tiberius's son Drusus
Julius Caesar, with whom he became a close friend,
and Antonia's son, the future emperor Claudius.
These relationships stood him, his sister HERO-
DIAS, and their kin in good stead over the course of
his political life.

When Berenice died, she left her freedman Protos in the service of Antonia. It was not an unusual
bequest from a client, especially to a patron such as
Antonia, who had business interests in the East. It
was probably also an effort on Berenice's part to
assure security for Protos.

Sources

Josephus. *Antiquitates Judaicae (Jewish Antiquities)* 17.12;
    18.143, 156, 164–165.
Leon, Harry J. *The Jews of Ancient Rome.* Philadelphia: Jew-
    ish Publication Society of America, 1960, p. 20.
Levick, Barbara. *Claudius: The Corruption of Power.* New
    Haven, Conn.: Yale University Press, 1993, p. 12.

Berenice (2)

(first century C.E.)
Jewish: Judaea and Rome
political player

Berenice might have become Augusta had she not
been a foreigner and a Jew. Politically astute,
intelligent, charming, and beautiful, Berenice had
great influence with the emperors Vespasian and
Titus. Born in 29 C.E. she was the oldest daughter
of Marcus Julius Agrippa I, the king of Judaea,
and Cypros, the granddaughter of Herod the
Great. She had a younger sister, DRUSILLA (2)
with whom there was a lifelong sibling rivalry. In

41 she married into a very wealthy Jewish family
in Alexandria. When her husband died she married her uncle Herod, the king of Chalcis in Leb-
anon, with whom she had two sons. After Herod
died she lived with her brother, Agrippa II, who
succeeded her husband as king of Chalcis. To
quiet rumors of incest, Berenice married Polemon, priest-king of Olba in Cilicia, whom she
soon left.

She was responsible for the appointment of her
former brother-in-law, Tiberius Julius Alexander,
to the post of procurator of Judaea in 46. However,
her attempts to persuade Gessius Florus, procurator of Judaea appointed by the emperor Nero in
64, to change his policies toward the Jews failed.
When the Jews revolted against his harsh rule, Berenice barely escaped.

In 67, Vespasian, accompanied by his son Titus,
arrived in Judaea to quell the rebellion. Titus fell in
love with Berenice, who at 39 was some 11 years
his senior, although age had evidently made no
inroads on her beauty, charm, or diplomatic skills.
She and her brother, Agrippa, sided with Vespasian
in his successful attempt to become emperor in
place of Vitellius. Berenice accompanied her
brother to Berytus (Beirut) where Vespasian was
encamped, charmed the emperor, and plied him
with gifts.

After conquering Jerusalem in 70, Titus returned
to Rome in triumph to share the emperorship with
his father. Berenice came to Rome in 75 and lived
with Titus for several years. Widespread criticism
of the liaison forced its end. When Titus became
emperor in 79, Berenice returned to Rome, but
once again criticism ended the relationship. Berenice has been called the "mini-Cleopatra"—
though Titus and Vespasian were no Julius Caesar
and Mark Antony.

Sources

Josephus. *Antiquitates Judaicae (Jewish Antiquities)* 18.132;
    19.267–277, 354; 20.104, 145–146.
Josephus. *Bellum Judaicum (Jewish Wars)* 2.217, 220–222,
    310–314.
Grant, Michael. *The Jews in the Roman World.* New York:
    Charles Scribner's Sons, 1973.

Oxford Classical Dictionary, ed. by Simon Hornblower and Antony Spawforth. 3d. ed. New York: Oxford University Press, 1996, p. 4.

Perowne, Stewart. *Hadrian.* Westport, Conn.: Greenwood Publishing, 1976, *passim.*

Berenice I
(340–281/271 B.C.E.)
Greek: Macedonia and Egypt
political player; deified

Berenice I was the most influential woman in Egypt at the end of the fourth and beginning of the third centuries B.C.E. She supplanted her cousin EURYDICE (3) in the affections of her stepbrother Ptolemy I Soter. Born in 340 B.C.E., Berenice was the granddaughter of Cassander, a general under Alexander the Great, and the great-granddaughter of Antipater, one of Alexander's successors. Her mother was Antigone, and her father, a Macedonian named Lagus.

Berenice married Philippus, a Macedonian, and had several children, among whom were Magas, later king of Cyrene, and ANTIGONE. Widowed,

Ptolemy I Soter and Berenice I
(Date: 270 B.C.E.– 240 B.C.E. 1956.183.28, Archives, American Numismatic Society)

she came to Egypt as a companion to her aunt Eurydice, who had married Ptolemy I Soter as part of a plan by Antipater to secure marital alliances among the successors to Alexander and thereby recreate his empire.

Berenice, some 26 years his junior, became Ptolemy's lover in 317 and persuaded him to reject her aunt. Their love was celebrated in the Seventeenth Idyll of the leading poet of the period Theocratus of Syracuse. She bore two children, ARSINOË II PHILADELPHUS and Ptolemy II Philadelphus. Ptolemy designated their son as heir and appointed Ptolemy Philadelphus joint ruler in 285.

Berenice married her daughter Antigone to Pyrrhus, later ruler of Epirus, who sought a close relationship to secure Ptolemy's support. He returned to Epirus with money and an army. Just as Ptolemy named a town in Berenice's honor in Egypt, so too Pyrrhus named a town in her honor in Epirus.

Berenice died between 281 and 271 and was deified by her son, who built temples to honor his parents.

Sources
Plutarch. *Vitae Parallelae (Parallel Lives): Pyrrhus* 4.4; 6.1.

Macurdy, Grace. *Hellenistic Queens.* Reprint. Chicago: Ares Publishers, 1985, pp. 103–109.

Oxford Classical Dictionary, ed. by Simon Hornblower and Antony Spawforth. 3d. ed. New York: Oxford University Press, 1996, p. 239.

Pomeroy, Sarah B. *Women in Hellenistic Egypt.* New York: Schocken, 1984.

Pauly, A., G. Wissowa, and W. Kroll. *Real-Encyclopadie d. Classischen Altertumswissenschaft 1893–.* (Germany: multiple publishers) 9.

Berenice II of Cyrene
(c. 273–221 B.C.E.)
Greek: Cyrene and Egypt
ruler

Berenice was a woman of courage, great strength of character, and enormous ambition. She overcame the treachery of her mother, APAMA (2), to become ruler of Cyrene, in North Africa, and succeeded in linking Cyrene with Egypt through her marriage to Ptolemy III Euergetes.

Born in 273 B.C.E., Berenice was part of the tangled web of relationships among five generations of successors to Alexander's empire. Her father, Magas, king of Cyrene, was the great-grandson of Cassander, one of the generals in the army of Alexander. Her grandmother BERENICE I had gone to Egypt after her father's birth. Already a widow with several children, her grandmother became the wife of Ptolemy I Soter and mother of Berenice's stepuncle Ptolemy II Philadelphus—and consequently the most influential woman of her day.

Ptolemy II had been responsible for her father's rule over Cyrene. Before her father died, he arranged her marriage to Ptolemy III, the future ruler of Egypt, for the union would extend the alliance between Cyrene and Egypt into the next generation. Berenice's mother, Apama, came from the house of the Seleucids, also successor rulers to Alexander with an empire centered in Asia Minor. She opposed Berenice's marriage, as did Antigonus Gonatus of Macedonia, who had concluded an alliance with the Seleucids. The marriage was also opposed by the home-rule partisans of Cyrene.

After her father's death, Berenice's mother invited the half brother of Antigonus Gonatus, the handsome Demetrius the Fair, to come to Cyrene and marry Berenice. Sources, sometimes unclear about this web of relationships, especially with regard to the women, differ as to whether Apama or Berenice married Demetrius. They agree that he became Apama's lover.

Fearful of the intentions of her mother and Demetrius, Berenice, who was about 18 years old, led a successful revolt in 255. Demetrius was killed in Apama's bedroom, despite Apama's attempt to shield him with her own body. Berenice prevented any harm to her mother.

In 247, shortly after he became ruler, Berenice married Ptolemy III. They had four children. One son, Magas, was scalded to death in his bath by another son, the future Ptolemy IV Philopator, who felt that Berenice favored Magas. A daughter, ARSINOË III PHILOPATOR, married her brother Ptolemy IV, and another daughter, Berenice, died in 238. In all accounts, Berenice's marriage was successful. It has given rise to one of the famous stories

Berenice II of Cyrene
(Date: 246 B.C.E.–221 B.C.E. 1967.152.626, Archives, American Numismatic Society)

of antiquity. When Ptolemy embarked on a campaign to Syria in aid of his sister, BERENICE SYRA, Berenice vowed to dedicate to the gods a lock of her hair if he returned safely. According to a literary tradition that the Roman poet Catullus was said to have borrowed from the earlier poet Callimachus, Berenice deposited her tresses at the temple of Aphrodite in Alexandria. The hair disappeared, and Conon, a Greek astronomer residing in Alexandria in the imperial service, rediscovered the tresses in a constellation of stars he named the Lock of Berenice. It is known today as the Coma Berenices.

After the death of her husband in 221, Berenice ruled jointly with her son Ptolemy IV. Her power was soon challenged by one of the ministers, Sosibius. Rivalry between mother and minister dominated imperial affairs. Chafing under his mother's domination, Ptolemy IV had Sosibius assassinate Berenice in 221 B.C.E. A decade later in 211 or 210 he established an eponymous priesthood and a special cult in her honor.

Sources

Catullus. *Poems* 66.
Justin. *Epitome* 26.3.

Polybius. *Histories* 5.36.1.

Cary, M. *A History of the Greek World from 323 to 146 B.C.* London: Methuen, 1951, *passim.*

Macurdy, Grace. *Hellenistic Queens.* Reprint. Chicago: Ares Publishers, 1985.

Oxford Classical Dictionary, ed. by Simon Hornblower and Antony Spawforth. 3d. ed. New York: Oxford University Press, 1996, p. 239.

Pomeroy, Sarah B. *Women in Hellenistic Egypt.* New York: Schocken, 1984, *passim.*

▣ Berenice III Cleopatra

(second–first century B.C.E.)   Greek: Egypt
ruler

Berenice III Cleopatra ruled Egypt jointly with her father and then for short time independently. Her mother was either Cleopatra IV or Cleopatra V Selene. Her father was Ptolemy IX Soter II, also known as Lathyrus.

She remained in Egypt after her father was driven into exile and in 102 or 101 B.C.E. married her uncle, Ptolemy X Alexander I. In the twisted web of relationships among the Ptolemies, Alexander was the youngest son of Berenice's grandmother. The marriage took place shortly after the death of her grandmother, who had been coruler with Alexander. Berenice fled with Alexander after he was deposed in a popular revolt in 89. They went to Syria, where he was killed the next year. She returned to Egypt, where her father had once again assumed control, and became coruler with him. He died in 80, leaving Berenice his heir.

The women around Berenice were anxious that she marry a male kinsman and appoint him coruler. There was good reason for concern. Rome depended on Egypt for its corn and was positioned to exert its influence over Egyptian affairs. Taking the initiative, Lucius Cornelius Sulla, then dictator of Rome, sent a son of Ptolemy X Alexander to Egypt to marry Berenice and become Ptolemy XI Alexander II.

Neither Berenice nor the people of Alexandria welcomed the new arrival. Nineteen days after he wedded Berenice, in 80 B.C.E., he had her murdered. Angered by the murder of Berenice, whom the admired, the Alexandrians revolted, and Ptol-emy XI Alexander II, the last direct male descendant of Alexander the Great's general Ptolemy I, died in ignominy.

Sources

Appian. *Roman History: Bella civilian (Civil Wars)* 1.102.

Cicero. *De lege agrarian* 2.42.

Macurdy, Grace. *Hellenistic Queens.* Reprint. Chicago: Ares Publishers, 1985, *passim.*

▣ Berenice IV Cleopatra

(first century B.C.E.)   Greek: Egypt
ruler

Berenice ruled Egypt for two to three years before she was murdered in a struggle for power with her father, Ptolemy XII Neos Dionysus Auletes. She was either the daughter or the sister of Cleopatra VI Tryphaena. Auletes was a weak man. He used bribes that depleted his own wealth and placed tax burdens upon the populace to strengthen his claim to rule. In 58 B.C.E. he went to Rome to seek Roman support against a threatened revolt. In his absence Berenice and Cleopatra VI Tryphaena were recognized as joint rulers by the Alexandrians. The latter died after one year, and Berenice ruled for two more years (58/57–56/55 B.C.E.).

The Alexandrians insisted that Berenice marry. They sought to both strengthen Berenice's position and preclude the claims of Auletes. Choices were limited, and two potential matches fell through. A hasty marriage was arranged for Berenice with a Seleucid whose behavior was so crude that the Alexandrians called him "Fish-packer." Berenice had him strangled within a few days. In the meantime, Auletes had journeyed to Ephesus where he hoped to bribe Gabinius, the Roman proconsul of Syria, to secure his position in Alexandria. Gabinius restored Auletes in 55, and her father immediately ordered Berenice's execution.

Sources

Dio Cassius. *Roman History* 39.57.

Josephus. *Antiquitates Judaicae (Jewish Antiquities)* 13.13.1; 15.1.

Strabo. *Geography* 12.3.34.

Macurdy, Grace. *Hellenistic Queens.* Reprint. Chicago: Ares Publishers, 1985, *passim.*

Pomeroy, Sarah B. *Women in Hellenistic Egypt.* New York: Schocken, 1984, p. 24.

Skeat, Theodore Cressy. *The Reigns of the Ptolemies.* Munich: Beck, 1969, pp. 37–39.

▣ Berenice Syra

(c. 280–246 B.C.E.)
Greek: Egypt and Antioch
ruler

Berenice struggled to control the Seleucid Empire and failed. Born about 280 B.C.E. to ARSINOË I and Ptolemy II Philadelphus, in 252, she became the pawn in a dynastic marriage arrangement between Ptolemy and the Seleucid Antiochus II. With a dowry so large that she was referred to as "Dowry Bearer" (Phernophorus), Ptolemy hoped her marriage would neutralize Antiochus as he pursued war against Antigonus Gonatus in Macedonia.

Berenice's dowry probably encompassed the territory Ptolemy had previously captured from Antiochus. Since she was almost 30, it was said that Ptolemy also sent jars of Nile water to encourage her fertility. Despite wealth and the birth of a son, the union was no bargain for Antiochus or the Seleucids. The marriage opened a conflict between Berenice and LAODICE I, Antiochus's first wife, whom he had repudiated as a condition for the alliance with Berenice.

The women's conflict rent the empire. Laodice, with whom Antiochus had had four children, moved herself and her family from Antioch to Ephesus. Henceforth, both cities served as capitals of the empire. In 251, after Antiochus assured Berenice that her infant son would be his heir, he returned to Laodice and declared the latter's 20-year-old son his successor. Antiochus promptly died.

Berenice, who remained in Antioch, charged that Laodice had poisoned Antiochus and pressed the claims of her son. A number of cities in Syria, including Antioch, supported her. She also appealed for aid to her father, Ptolemy II. Her message reached Egypt shortly after her father's death. Her brother, Ptolemy III Euergetes, sent a fleet to aid her.

Laodice bribed the chief magistrate of Antioch to kidnap Berenice's son. Berenice pursued the kidnappers in a chariot, striking the chief magistrate with a spear and killing him with a stone. The child, however, was dead. Berenice appealed to the people. The magistrates who had colluded in the murder became fearful. They produced a child whom they claimed was Berenice's son, but they refused to release him to Berenice.

Berenice moved into a palace in Daphne, a suburb of Antioch, guarded by Galatian soldiers and her women retainers and supporters. In 246, assassins sent by Laodice attacked and murdered Berenice, despite the efforts of the women to shield her with their bodies. As a final note, although her brother's fleet arrived too late to save her, her retainers concealed her death until his arrival and thereby enabled her brother to rally to his side all those in Syria who supported Berenice, precipitating the Third Syrian War (246–241 B.C.E.).

Sources

Appian. *Syrian Wars* 65.

Justin. *Epitome* 27.1, 4.

Polyaenus. *Strategemata* 8.50.

Valerius Maximus. *Factorum et dictorum memorabilium libri IX* 9.10.1.

Bevan, Edwyn B. *The House of Selecus.* 2 vols. London: Edward Arnold, 1902, pp. 181 ff.

Cary, M. *A History of the Greek World from 323 to 146 B.C.* London: Methuen, 1951, pp. 86–88.

Macurdy, Grace. *Hellenistic Queens.* Reprint. Chicago: Ares Publishers, 1985, pp. 87 ff.

Oxford Classical Dictionary, ed. by Simon Hornblower and Antony Spawforth. 3d. ed. New York: Oxford University Press, 1996, p. 239.

Pomeroy, Sarah B. *Women in Hellenistic Egypt.* New York: Schocken, 1984, pp. 14, 17.

Pauly, A., G. Wissowa, and W. Kroll. *Real-Encyclopadie d. Classischen Altertumswissenschaft 1893–.* (Germany: multiple publishers) 10.

▣ Bilistiche

(third century B.C.E.)
Greek or Phoenician: Egypt
self-made woman

Bilistiche's background is uncertain. Her beauty and astuteness, however, are well attested. She had once been a slave brought to Alexandria. Described as an Argive freedwoman much sought after by men, her name suggests she may have been Macedonian or Phoenician in origin or ancestry.

She grew rich and famous as the favored lover of Ptolemy II Philadelphus. She was the First woman of her background to sponsor horses in the Olympic games. Her horses won the four-horse chariot race in 268 B.C.E. and the two-horse race at the next festival. She managed her wealth well. There is a record of her having made a loan in 239 or 238 when she was well into old age.

Among other honors, she was appointed to an eponymous priesthood, and Ptolemy II dedicated shrines and temples to Aphrodite in her honor. The date of her death is not known.

Sources

Athenaeus. *Deipnosophistae* 13.596.

Plutarch. *Moralia: Amatorius* 753f.

Harris, H. A. *Sport in Greece and Rome.* Ithaca, N.Y.: Cornell University Press, 1972, pp. 178–79.

Pomeroy, Sarah B. *Women in Hellenistic Egypt.* New York: Schocken, 1984, pp. 53–55.

▣ Blaesilla
(c. 383–c. 384 C.E.)   Roman: Rome
Christian ascetic

Blaesilla embraced an ascetic regime that killed her. Her mother, PAULA THE ELDER, was a leader in the new movement of Christian monasticism. Blaesilla's family reached back to the esteemed CORNELIA (2) and the famed Scipio in the second century B.C.E. Her father was the Roman senator, Toxotius, from a well-established Greek family. She had three sisters and a brother. Paulina and Rufina died young, and the third, EUSTOCHIUM, followed her mother to Palestine where they founded a monastery and worked with the eminent ascetic Jerome to translate the Bible from Greek to Latin. Her brother remained in Rome, married, and his daughter, the younger PAULA, succeeded her grandmother and aunt as director of the monastery.

Blaesilla's mother was influenced by her friend, MARCELLA, and the spreading news of monastic life in Egypt. The women altered their personal demeanor and urban households to conform to a life of rigorous prayer, study, and chaste widowhood. Paula encouraged her youngest daughter Eustochium to join them and sent her to live with Marcella, who had gained a reputation as a Christian teacher.

Paula discouraged her other children from following her lifestyle. Her daughter Rufina died after she had been betrothed and Paulina married, but died in childbirth. Blaesilla also married. She became a widow less than a year later. Before her marriage, she enjoyed the luxuries afforded the daughter of a very wealthy Roman patrician family. She loved clothing, makeup, and extravagant hairstyles. She surrounded herself with soft silks and pillows. However, she became seriously ill after the death of her husband. When she recovered, she rejected any proposal to remarry, despite the urging of her mother, and began to adopt an increasingly severe and disturbing daily regime.

Blaesilla fasted frequently, ate sparingly, dressed in the simplest coarse dark clothing, eschewed ornaments, and spent most of her time reading religious texts and praying. Her austerity was so severe that it aroused criticism as inappropriate fanaticism from Christians and pagans alike. Her regime also took its toll on her body. Dressed in clothing no better than that of a slave, she was pale and could barely stand upright or walk, but, however weak, she always had a Christian text in her hand.

Her piety won Jerome's praise and increasingly distressed more moderate Christians around her. The personal, as well as social and economic benefits, to the community from marriage, children, and family were of lesser value for Jerome than the individual quest for salvation. He viewed lifelong virginity as women's greatest virtue, followed by a prayerful and celibate widowhood as a poor second. His asceticism, which rejected cleanliness, the comforts and pleasures of well-made clothing, and good food in favor of fasting and uncomfortable drab clothing, elevated the value of bodily suffering and prayer. It was an inversion of good and bad that appeared abnormal and often abhorrent to pagans and many Christians. Even among those

Christians who admired the ascetic self-discipline, few chose to join.

Blaesilla, still in her 20s, died. At the funeral, her mother, Paula, fainted from the taunts of demonstrators blaming her for her daughter's extreme lifestyle. Jerome also received his share of the blame. He wrote a letter to Paula, which expressed his sadness at Blaesilla's death and that ascetics, like him, were not welcome by the larger Roman Christian community. They blamed men like him for misleading women like Blaesilla and for her death from fasting.

In 385, not long after Blaesilla's death, Paula and Eustochium, along with an entourage, left Rome to join Jerome in Jerusalem.

Sources

Jerome. Letters XXXVIII, XXXIX., xxxiv, xxii.
Prosopography of the Later Roman Empire. Vol. I. Edited by A. H. M. Jones, J. R. Martindale, and J. Morris. Cambridge: Cambridge University Press, 1971. Reprinted 1992, p. 162.
McNamara, Jo Anne. "Cornelia's Daughters: Paula and Eustochium," *Women's Studies* (1984), 11.9–27.

Boudicca

(first century C.E.)   Celtic: Britain
ruler

Boudicca led a revolt of the Iceni in East Anglia against the Roman settlements in Britain. She was the wife of Prasutagus, whom the Romans had made a client-king. He died in 59 or 60 C.E., and in his will he named the emperor Nero coheir with Boudicca and her daughters in the hope that this would insure the stability of his lands and his family.

His effort was in vain. Roman imperial agents whipped Boudicca and raped her daughters. They pillaged the lands of the Iceni and confiscated estates of prominent families. Heavy Roman taxation, complicated by the harsh demands of money lenders who supplied the silver and gold against the security of land, caused others to ally themselves with the Iceni.

Led by Boudicca, the Iceni, assisted by the Trinovantes, revolted in 60 C.E. A large woman with long tawny hair flowing down to her hips, a harsh voice, and blazing eyes. She held a spear ready while leading her troops into battle, and she terrified the Romans. Her forces plundered the Roman strongholds at Colchester, Verulamium, and London.

In time, she was defeated by a large and organized Roman force and she committed suicide. Damned with faint praise, the ancients wrote that she possessed greater intelligence than most women.

Sources

Dio Cassius. *Roman History* 62.1–12.
Tacitus. *Agricola* 16.1–2.
Tacitus. *Annales* 14.31–37.
Dudley, Donald R., and Graham Webster. *The Rebellion of Boudicca.* New York: Barnes and Noble, 1962, *passim.*
Oxford Classical Dictionary, ed. by Simon Hornblower and Antony Spawforth. 3d. ed. New York: Oxford University Press, 1996, p. 256.

Busa

(third century B.C.E.)   Roman: Italy
patriot

Busa was a woman of unknown background and great wealth. In 216 B.C.E. she resided in Canusium, the town in Apulia to which the Roman general Publius Cornelius Scipio retreated in disarray with some 10,000 soldiers after their devastating defeat by Hannibal at Cannae.

Townspeople provided shelter for the fleeing soldiers. To regroup, Scipio needed more than shelter; Busa gave him food, clothing, and financial support, providing the means to raise new soldiers and rearm. Busa was honored by the Roman Senate at the end of the war.

Sources

Livy. *From the Founding of the City* 22.52.7; 54.1–3.
Valerius Maximus. *Factorum et dictorum memorabilium libri IX* 4.8.2.
Bauman, Richard A. *Women and Politics in Ancient Rome.* London: Routledge, 1994, p. 23.

C

Caecilia

(first century C.E.)   Roman: Italy
mother of Pliny the Younger

Caecilia was with her son in Misenum on the Bay of Naples when Mount Vesuvius erupted in August 79 C.E. She begged her son to leave her, but the 18-year-old Pliny refused. Together they walked out of the town. Both escaped unharmed.

Caecilia was a member of the Plinii, a provincial family that was wealthy and well connected. Her husband owned estates in Comum (Como). Widowed when her son was still young, there is no indication that she married again. Her son was adopted by his uncle, Pliny the Elder, a famous writer and naturalist. The elder Pliny stayed too long to observe the eruption of Mount Vesuvius and was killed.

Sources

Pliny the Younger. *Epistulae* 6.20.

Caecilia Metella (1)

(second–first century B.C.E.)   Roman: Rome
power broker

Caecilia Metella was a widow already 50 years old when she married Lucius Cornelius Sulla. It was the marriage of the Roman social season. She gained a political husband on the way up; he gained a wife with wealth and connections. The subsequent years may well have been more difficult and bloody than she had anticipated; however, only death ended their relationship.

Sulla was not her first husband. Born into the Metelli clan, her relatives held the office of consul or censor and celebrated triumphs 12 times within a 12-year period. Her father was Lucius Caecilius Metellus Delmaticus, consul in 119 B.C.E. Her first husband, Marcus Aemilius Scaurus, was wealthy, a consul, and a *princeps senatus,* the senior member of the Senate. They had three children, including AEMELIA (2). Caecilia Metella married Sulla in 88 B.C.E., after the death of Scaurus. With the support of the Metelli, the 50-year-old Sulla became consul in the same year. She was his fourth wife, and as with his earlier marriages, he had married her to forge an alliance with her influential and wealthy family. With Sulla she had twins: Faustus Cornelius Sulla and FAUSTA.

When Lucius Cornelius Cinna seized control of Rome in 87 and ordered Sulla removed from his command, Caecilia Metella escaped from Rome with her children and a year later, in 86 joined Sulla in Greece. Although their property in Rome was attacked and their houses burned, Sulla refused to accept Cinna's authority. They returned to Italy, and Sulla's army defeated the opposition forces. He entered Rome victorius. In 82 he was elected dictator.

Caecilia Metella did not live long after his victory. She died from an illness that Sulla may have transmitted to her and that was sufficiently contagious for the priests to have forbidden him to be with her or to have her funeral in the house. To avoid ritual contamination, to observe the strict letter of the law, and perhaps to satisfy his own fears, he transported her to a neutral house and divorced her posthumously. Her funeral, however, allowed no misunderstanding of his feelings. Ignoring his own recent funerary law, he spared no expense on her burial.

Sources
Plutarch. *Vitae Parallelae (Parallel Lives): Sulla* 6.10–12; 22.1; 35.1–2.
Oxford Classical Dictionary, ed. by Simon Hornblower and Antony Spawforth. 3d. ed. New York: Oxford University Press, 1996, p. 267.
Pauly, A., G. Wissowa, and W. Kroll. *Real-Encyclopadie d. Classichen Altertumswissenschaft 1893–*. (Germany: multiple publishers) 134.
Syme, Ronald. *The Roman Revolution*. London: Oxford University Press, 1963, pp. 20, 31.

 Caecilia Metella (2)
(second–first century B.C.E.)   Roman: Rome
political player

Caecilia Metella, born into one of Rome's wealthiest and most illustrious families, died with an unsavory reputation. Her father was Lucius Metellus Calvus, consul in 142 B.C.E., and her husband was Lucius Licinius Lucullus, praetor in 104. Her husband was convicted of bribery, and she was reputed to be promiscuous.

She had two sons. The eldest, Lucius Licinius Lucullus, supported and served under the general Lucius Cornelius Sulla. He was an excellent soldier and administrator and served as consul in 74. The younger son was Marcus Terentius Varro Lucullus, consul in 73.

Sources
Plutarch. *Vitae Parallelae (Parallel Lives): Lucullus* 1.

Caedicia
(first century C.E.)   Roman: Rome
possible conspirator

Caedicia was exiled from Italy without a trial in the aftermath of the Pisonian conspiracy against the emperor Nero in 65 C.E. Her husband, Flavius Scaevinus, was the conspirator designated to stab Nero. Scaevinus was a man of senatorial rank whose mind was said to have been destroyed by debauchery. He was betrayed by a servant. The exact role played by Caedicia in the conspiracy is unclear.

Sources
Tacitus. *Annales* 15.49, 53–55, 70–71.

Caenis Antonia
(?–75 C.E.)   Roman: Rome
self-made woman

Caenis Antonia spanned the decades from Julio-Claudian rule to the Flavians. She was a mature woman when she became the lover of the future emperor Vespasian. Earlier, in 31 C.E., she was a freedwoman secretary of the younger ANTONIA, and it was she who was said to have carried the letter from Antonia to the emperor Tiberius describing the treachery of the emperor's confidant Lucius Aelius Sejanus. When Antonia demanded that Caenis Antonia destroy the message about Sejanus after Tiberius had the information, she was said to have responded that she could not erase her memory.

Caenis Antonia and Vespasian became lovers during the lifetime of his wife, DOMITILLA FLAVIA (I). After her death, they lived as husband and wife. She was a woman reputed to like money and power. During her years with the emperor Vespasian, she acquired vast sums by selling state priesthoods and offices including positions as governor, general, and procurator. She died in 75 C.E.

Sources
Dio Cassius. *Roman History* 64.1–4.
Suetonius. *The Lives of the Caesars:* Vespasian 3.
Balsdon, J. P. V. D. *Roman Women*. New York: John Day Comp., 1963, p. 131.

Pauly, A., G. Wissowa, and W. Kroll. *Real-Encyclopadie d. Classischen Altertumswissenschaft 1893–.* (Germany: multiple publishers) 126.

Caesaria

(?–556 C.E.)   Roman: Syria, Alexandria
devout Christian

After she was widowed, Caesaria founded a monastery where she wanted to live out her life. It was near Alexandria in Egypt. Her husband's name is unknown. However, she had connections with the imperial family in Constantinople, possibly through Anastasius I, emperor in the West, who came from Samosata on the Euphrates. At some point in her life, she received the honorary title *patricia,* usually given by the emperor for services rendered. She evidently was quite wealthy. As was not unusual in the East, she was a Monophysite, which in the debate of the times about the nature of Christ, placed her politically as well as theologically in the camp with the Augusta THEODORA, who actively sought to spread the Monophysite doctrine in the East.

She corresponded with Severus, bishop of Antioch, the leading theologian of the Monophysites. The monastery she founded appeared to have separate quarters for men and women. She lived in the monastery for some 15 years until she died.

Sources

John of Ephesus. *Vitae Sanctorum Orientalium* 54–56.
John of Niku. *The Chronicle of John of Niku* 90.13; 116.6.
Severus of Antioch. *Letters.*
Prosopography of the Later Roman Empire. Vol. II. Edited by A. H. M. Jones, J. R. Martindale, and J. Morris. Cambridge: Cambridge University Press, 1971. Reprinted 1992, pp. 248–249.

Calpurnia (1)

(first century B.C.E.)   Roman: Rome
wife of Julius Caesar

Calpurnia married Gaius Julius Caesar in 59 B.C.E. to cement an alliance between Caesar and her father, Lucius Calpurnius Piso Caesoninus, consul in 58. She was 18 years old and Caesar's third wife.

She remained attached to Caesar even as he contemplated a marriage with the daughter of Mark Antony in 53. She warned him against going to the Senate on the fateful Ides of March 44 B.C.E. After his assassination, she turned his papers over to Mark Antony along with a large sum of money.

Sources

Plutarch. *Vitae Parallelae (Parallel Lives): Caesar* 63.
Suetonius. *The Lives of the Caesars: Caesar* 21; 81.
Oxford Classical Dictionary, ed. by Simon Hornblower and Antony Spawforth. 3d. ed. New York: Oxford University Press, 1996, p. 279.
Pauly, A., G. Wissowa, and W. Kroll. *Real-Encyclopadie d. Classischen Altertumswissenschaft 1893–.* (Germany: multiple publishers) 279.

Calpurnia (2)

(first century C.E.)   Roman: Rome
self-made woman

Calpurnia revealed to the emperor Claudius the scandalous behavior of his wife Valeria MESSALLINA and her lover Gaius Silius. Calpurnia was one of Claudius's two favorite freedwomen. Bribed with promises of gifts and influence by Messallina's political enemy Narcissus, the powerful freedman secretary of the emperor, Calpurnia described the mock marriage that had taken place between Messallina and Silius. Claudius had both Messallina and Silius put to death in 48 C.E.

Sources

Tacitus. *Annales* 11.29–30.
Levick, Barbara. *Claudius: The Corruption of Power.* New Haven, Conn.: Yale University Press, 1993, p. 67.

Calpurnia (3)

(first–second century C.E.)   Roman: Rome
wife of Pliny the Younger

Calpurnia married Pliny the Younger after the death of his second wife in 97 C.E. Her grandfather, Calpurnius Fabatus, and Pliny both came from Comum. Pliny described Calpurnia to her aunt, CALPURNIA HISPULLA, in rapturous terms. He praised Calpurnia's discerning interest in his books and writings. She was supportive when he was involved with a case and glad to have his company when he was free. She was, he claimed, an ideal woman.

Calpurnia had a miscarriage and went to Campania to recover. Pliny waited for her letters and begged her to write as often as twice a day. Her husband attributed her miscarriage to her youthful ignorance of the hazards of pregnancy. Calpurnia accompanied Pliny to Bithynia-Pontus in northwest Asia Minor, where he had been sent by the emperor Trajan in 110 to reorganize the disorderly province. She returned to Italy on news of the death of her grandfather.

Sources

Pliny the Younger. *Epistulae* 4.19; 6.4, 7; 7.5; 8.10, 11, 19; 9.36; 10.120.

Oxford Classical Dictionary, ed. by Simon Hornblower and Antony Spawforth. 3d. ed. New York: Oxford University Press, 1996, p. 279.

Pauly, A., G. Wissowa, and W. Kroll. *Real-Encyclopadie d. Classischen Altertumswissenschaft 1893–*. (Germany: multiple publishers) 130.

▣ Calpurnia Hispulla

(first–second century C.E.)   Roman: Italy
woman of means and character

Calpurnia Hispulla was a close friend of Pliny the Younger and his family, especially his mother, CAECILIA. Although they owned estates in different parts of Italy, her father, Calpurnius Fabatus, had been born in Comum, the same town that was the home of Pliny's family. She raised her niece, CALPURNIA (3), who at a relatively young age became Pliny's third wife. Pliny attributed many of the qualities of his wife's character to the influence of Calpurnia Hispulla.

Sources

Pliny the Younger. *Epistulae* 4.19; 8.11.

▣ Calvia Crispinilla

(first century C.E.)   Roman: Rome
political survivor

Calvia Crispinilla prospered by pandering to the tastes of the times. Her lineage is unknown, but she lived within the imperial circle under Nero, survived the transition to the Flavians, and died a rich old woman. During the reign of Nero, Calvia arranged entertainments, apparently lascivious in nature. Under her care was the young Greek eunuch Sporus, who resembled Nero's wife POPPAEA SABINA (2), whom he had killed in a fit of anger.

Calvia joined the conspiracy against Nero. She encouraged Lucius Clodius Macer, the governor in Africa, to revolt in 68 C.E. and supported his policy of cutting off the corn supply to Rome. Despite her visibility, she avoided retribution after Clodius Macer was killed by orders of Servius Sulpicius Galba, who supplanted Nero. She was said to have used her popularity to secure a husband behind whose propriety she could stand invisible.

Calvia managed to survive the reigns of Galba, Otho, and Vitellius and to become richer with each regime. As time passed, her wealth and the absence of any children as heirs made her very attractive to men whose fortunes had waned or been lost, as well as to all other kinds of adventurers and fortune hunters. She was courted until she died.

Sources

Dio Cassius. *Roman History* 62.12.3–4.

Tacitus. *Historiae* 1.73.

Charles-Picard, Gilbert. *Augustus and Nero: The Secret of the Empire*. Trans. by Len Ortzen. New York: Thomas Y. Crowell Comp., 1965, p. 162.

▣ Calvina

(first–second century C.E.)   Roman: Italy
financial head of household

Calvina settled her father's estate and faced insolvency. Her father was C. Plinius Calvinus, part of the Plinii, a well-known provincial landowning family whose most famous members were the naturalist Pliny the Elder and his letter-writing nephew Pliny the Younger.

Calvina's father had left his estate encumbered and Calvina strapped for cash to meet the outstanding notes. She wrote Pliny the Younger about the situation. Although not fully knowledgeable of the total encumbrances on the estate, Pliny agreed that Calvina might have no choice but to sell land. If, however, he was the only creditor or the principal one, he would surrender his claim and consider the 100,000 sesterces that he had loaned her father a gift. Pliny also surrendered claim to a second 100,000 sesterces raised by her father for her dowry.

Pliny encouraged Calvina to accept his offer and protect her father's memory. As a friend, he would not her father's memory sullied by his having died insolvent. He assured her that the gift would not leave him in straitened circumstances; although his fortune was small, his expenditures were similarly restricted.

Sources

Pliny the Younger. *Epistulae* 2.4.

Pauly, A., G. Wissowa, and W. Kroll. *Real-Encyclopadie d. Classischen Altertumswissenschaft 1893–.* (Germany: multiple publishers) 5.

◉ Cannutia Crescentina

(?–213 C.E.)   Roman: Rome
priestess

Cannutia Crescentina was one of four Vestal Virgins condemned in 213 C.E. for violating the vow of chastity. The Vestal Virgins guarded the flame of Vesta in one of the oldest temples in the Forum.

In earlier times pollution among Vestal Virgins was believed an ill omen for the city. By the third century C.E., these old beliefs had declined or given way to new kinds of religious experience. Nonetheless, the power of tradition and the historical association between the chastity of the Vestal Virgins and the well-being of Rome exceeded the life of the ancient religious belief and maintained a hold over the imagination of Rome.

Crescentina was convicted with AURELIA SEVERA, CLODIA LAETA, and POMPONIA RUFINA and condemned to die in the ancient rite of being buried alive. She, however, committed suicide by jumping off the roof of her house.

Sources

Dio Cassius. *Roman History* 78.16.1–3.

◉ Cartimandua

(first century C.E.)   Brigantian: Britain
ruler

Cartimandua led the Brigantes, the most populous tribe in Britain, for some 26 years, between 43 and 69 C.E. The last surviving member of the family who had traditionally led the tribe, she negotiated a treaty with the emperor Claudius to become a client state. The treaty brought peace to the northern border of Roman Britain and prosperity to the Brigantes for the six years.

Her alliance with the Romans, however, was controversial. Venutius, her husband, favored greater independence. There was a series of political crises. In 51 Cartimandua turned over to the Romans a defeated Welsh leader, Caratacus, who had fled to the Brigantes. A quarrel ensued between Cartimandua and Venutius. Twice between the years 52 and 57 Rome intervened on her behalf, and the two were reconciled.

In 69, when Cartimandua discarded Venutius in favor of his armor-bearer, Vellocatus, whom she made joint ruler, she effectively separated her husband from his most important client-chief and provided herself with male support more favorable for her policy of close ties with Rome. However, in 68–69, while the Roman forces in Britain were otherwise occupied, Venutius and his supporters defeated Cartimandua in battle.

Rome rescued her but did not restore her to her former position, and thereby lost the opportunity to maintain a strong and friendly buffer state on its northern British border.

Sources

Tacitus. *Annales* 12.36.

Tacitus. *Historiae* 3.45.

Oxford Classical Dictionary, ed. by Simon Hornblower and Antony Spawforth. 3d. ed. New York: Oxford University Press, 1996, pp. 296–297.

Richmond, I. A. *Journal of Roman Studies* (1954): pp. 43 ff.

◉ Casta Caecilia

(first–second century C.E.)   Roman: Rome
acquitted of corruption

Caecilia Casta was indicted along with her husband, Caecilius Classicus, her daughter, and her son-in-law on charges of malfeasance for behavior and acts incurred during her husband's tenure as provincial governor in Baetica, Spain. It was quite usual for Roman officials to augment their personal fortunes when serving abroad; it also was not unusual for them to be sued on their return to Rome, particularly if they had been especially avaricious. Only after Rome became an empire, however, did women frequently join their husbands on posts abroad and become subject to suit.

Casta's husband died before the trial began. Pressed by the Baeticians, the Senate voted to allow the prosecution to proceed against Casta, her daughter, her son-in-law, and her husband's estate. Pliny the Younger acted for the Senate as one of two prosecuting counsels.

There was direct evidence against Caecilius Classicus. Letters were found among his papers boasting of the amounts of money he had taken. In one, addressed to a woman in Rome, he claimed that he would return to Rome with 4 million sesterces. To gather evidence against Casta, the Baeticians had secured the services of Norbanus Licinianus, known as the Inquisitor for his style in court. During the trial in 100 C.E., however, one of the witnesses accused Norbanus of conspiring with Casta to upset any case against her.

The disposition of the charges rested with the Senate, and the consequences could be quite dire, ranging from the confiscation of property to death or exile. The Senate found the daughter and son-in-law not guilty. Classicus's estate was stripped of any gains, and the confiscated funds were to be divided among the victims. Any payments made to creditors in the period since the end of his governorship were similarly to be returned. His residual estate, which consisted mostly of his debts, was awarded to his daughter.

Much to Pliny's disgust, Casta was found not guilty. Since her daughter, not she, was the residual legatee, she escaped unscathed, not even responsible for the unpaid debts on her husband's estate. Norbanus, however, was found guilty of colluding with Casta and was exiled.

Sources
Pliny the Younger. *Epistulae* 3.9.

Marshall, A. J. "Women on Trial before the Roman Senate." *Classical Views* 34 (1990): pp. 333–366.

▣ Castricia
(?–fifth century C.E.)   Roman: Constantinople
political player

Castricia was one of Augusta AELIA EUDOXIA's close friends. She was also friends with MARSA and EUGRAPHIA, two women of similar class and wealth. Their friendship became a political alliance on more than one occasion.

Her husband, Saturninus, who held the office of Master of the Soldiers, was one of several officials surrendered by the emperor Arcadius to appease the Goth leader Ganais when he was poised to invade the city in 399. Saturninus awaited execution, when John Chrysostom, bishop of Constantinople, interceded and successfully had his sentence commuted to exile.

Whatever goodwill Castricia held for the bishop was obliterated in 403. Chrysostom, never the most politic of men, attacked rich older women who tried to make themselves look younger and more attractive with makeup and elaborate hairstyles that included paste-on curls. He compared their appearance with streetwalkers. Castricia took the attack personally and regarded it as a covert assault on the power women exercised in the city and at the palace. With her women friends she went to Eudoxia. Persuaded by them that Chrysostom held misogynistic views rooted in the original sin of Eve and that he was dangerous to the collective interests of wealthy and powerful women in the city, she led the attack to have him removed.

Chrysostom was a complicated man who was genuinely troubled by the extraordinary wealth of a few when most were in want. He also had ambivalent views about women. He proclaimed from the pulpit that they did not belong in the public sphere, even though he had close relationships with some women of wealth and power in the city. He maintained a lifetime correspondence with OLYMPIAS (3), who he met while bishop. SALVINA, who was a part of the intimate imperial circle, was also among the few to whom he revealed his intention to leave the city before it was publicly announced. A nuanced appreciation of Chrysostom's attitude and relationships with women, however, was not the way of Constantinople politics. The Augusta and her friends successfully forced him to resign.

Sources

Palladius. *The Lausiac History* p. 25.
Socrates. *Historia Ecclesiastica* 6.6. 8–12.
Sozomen. *Historia Ecclesiastica* 8.4 4–5.
Zosimus. *New History* 5.18 6–8.
Brill's New Pauly: Encyclopedia of the Ancient World: Classical Tradition. Edited by Manfred Landfester, in collaboration with Hubert Conick and Helmut Schneider. Boston: Brill, 2006. Vol. 1.
Prosopography of the Later Roman Empire. Vol. II. Edited by A. H. M. Jones, J. R. Martindale, and J. Morris. Cambridge: Cambridge University Press, 1971. Reprinted 1992, p. 271.

▣ Celerina, Pompeia

(first–second century C.E.)   Roman: Rome
friend and wealthy mother-in-law of Pliny the Younger

Pompeia Celerina, the daughter of Pompeius Celer, was a wealthy woman. She married twice. Her daughter was the second wife of Pliny the Younger. The daughter died about 97 C.E., but Celerina and Pliny remained friends. He was probably closer to her age than that of her daughter.

Celerina owned several villas in Umbria and Perusia. Pliny considered the purchase of a nearby estate. The price was 3 million sesterces. Somewhat strapped for cash since his wealth was chiefly in land, he planned to borrow from Celerina. He felt quite comfortable using her money as if it were his own. Celerina, in turn, used Pliny's connections with the emperor Trajan. She requested the appointment of her kinsman, Caelius Clemens, to a proconsulship.

Sources

Pliny the Younger. *Epistulae* 1.4; 3.19; 10.51.
Pauly, A., G. Wissowa, and W. Kroll. *Real-Encyclopadie d. Classischen Altertumswissenschaft 1893–.* (Germany: multiple publishers) 126.

▣ Chaerestrate

(fourth century B.C.E.)   Greek: Samos
mother of Epicurus

Chaerestrate was the mother of Epicurus, the famous philosopher and founder of one of the great ancient schools of philosophy. Her husband was Neocles, an Athenian schoolmaster, who immigrated to Samos, an island off the west coast of Asia Minor. Possibly, she read charms for people.

Chaerestrate had four sons. Epicurus was born in 341 B.C.E. The others, whose dates are uncertain, were Neocles, Chaeredemus, and Arisobulus.

Sources

Diogenes Laertius. *Lives of the Eminent Philosophers* 10.1–4.

▣ Chelidon

(first century B.C.E.)   Greek: Sicily
office manager

Chelidon was of Greek origin and an associate of Gaius Verres, praetor in 74 B.C.E. and governor of Sicily from 73 to 71. In 70, after his return to Rome, Verres was tried on charges of corruption while holding the office of praetor. Marcus Tullius Cicero, noted orator and statesman, was one of the prosecutors.

Chelidon had already died by the time of the trial; nevertheless, she was very much a part of Cicero's speech to the court. Cicero disparaged her as a *meretrix,* a "street-walking prostitute," and attacked Verres for his relationship with her. Cicero's description of her role in Verres's administration, however, belied his disparagement. She had her own household, and Verres used her household as his headquarters. She was surrounded by people seeking favors, as was the praetor himself. She was a person with whom people transacted their business: She oversaw payments and promissory notes.

In short, Cicero's description suggests she may have been closer to Verres's office manager than a prostitute. Chelidon also may well have had the intelligence for business that the corrupt Verres found useful. In a final irony, Chelidon left Verres a legacy in her will.

Sources
Cicero. *In Verrum* 2.1, 120 ff., 136 ff.; 2.2, 116.
Bauman, Richard A. *Women and Politics in Ancient Rome.* London: Routledge, 1994, pp. 66–67.
Hillard, Tom. "On Stage, Behind the Curtain: Images of Politically Active Women in the Late Roman Republic." In *Stereotypes of Women in Power: Historical Perspectives and Revisionist Views,* ed. by Barbara Garlick, Suzanne Dixon, and Pauline Allen. New York: Greenwood Press, 1992, pp. 42–45.

▣ Chilonis (1)
(seventh century B.C.E.)   Greek: Sparta
heroine

Chilonis allegedly switched places with her husband to allow him to escape from prison. Chilonis married the Spartan ruler Theopompus (720–675 B.C.E.). After Theopompus was captured by the Arcadians, Chilonis traveled to Arcadia. Impressed by her fortitude and audacity in undertaking such a trip, the Arcadians allowed her to visit her husband in prison. Chilonis exchanged clothes with her husband, and he escaped while she remained behind. Theopompus later captured a priestess of Diana in a procession at Pheneus. He exchanged her for Chilonis.

Sources
Polyaenus. *Strategemata* 8.39.
Der Kleine Pauly; Lexikon der Antike, ed. by Konrat Julius Furchtegott and Walther Sontheimer. Stuttgart, Germany: A. Druckenmuller, 1984, p. 1,146.

▣ Chilonis (2)
(third century B.C.E.)   Greek: Sparta
heroine

Chilonis was willing to commit suicide rather than fall into the hands of her ex-husband. She was the granddaughter of a deceased ruler of Sparta and had married Cleonymus, son of the former king of Sparta, Cleomenes II. She was much younger than her husband and beautiful.

After she fell in love with Acrotatus, whose father ruled Sparta, she left her husband. Her

desertion and the politics of succession led Cleonymus to ally himself with Pyrrhus against Sparta in 272 B.C.E. When an attack was imminent, Chilonis was said to have kept a rope around her neck so that she could kill herself rather than suffer capture by her former husband. Through a defense strategy aided by the city's women, the attack on Sparta was repelled. Chilonis was spared.

Sources
Plutarch. *Vitae Parallelae (Parallel Lives): Pyrrhus* 26.8–9; 27.5; 28.1–3.

▣ Chilonis (3)
(third century B.C.E.)   Greek: Sparta
heroine

Chilonis twice chose exile. She was the daughter of the Spartan king Leonidas II, who was a foe of the land and debt reforms initiated under his predecessor, Agis IV. She married Cleombrotus, who supplanted her father as king and forced him into exile. Chilonis went into exile with her father. When her father returned and ordered Cleombrotus exiled in 241 B.C.E., she again went into exile, this time with her husband.

Sources
Plutarch. *Vitae Parallelae (Parallel Lives): Agesilaus* 17 ff.
Plutarch. *Vitae Parallelae (Parallel Lives): Cleomenes* 38.5–12.
Mosse, Claude. "Women in the Spartan Revolutions of the Third Century B.C." In *Women's History and Ancient History,* ed. by Sarah B. Pomeroy. Chapel Hill: University of North Carolina Press, 1991, pp. 146, 147.

▣ Chiomara
(fourth century B.C.E.)   Galatian: Asia Minor
avenger

Chiomara was the wife of Ortiagon, a chief of the Tectosagi Gauls in Asia Minor. They were defeated by the Romans near what is now Ankara, in Turkey. Chiomara was taken prisoner and raped by a centurion, who afterwards arranged for her ransom.

During the exchange, she instructed the Gauls to kill the centurion. His head was cut off, and Chiomara wrapped it in the folds of her dress.

When she returned to her husband, she threw the head at his feet and revealed the rape. Chiomara was admired for her intelligence and spirit.

Sources

Livy. *From the Founding of the City* 38.24.
Plutarch. *Moralia: De mulierum virtutibus* 22.
Polybius. *Histories* 21.38.

▣ Claudia (1)

(third century B.C.E.)   Roman: Rome
possibly tried for treason

Claudia was born into a proud patrician family and is remembered for her arrogance. Her father was Appius Claudius Caecus, the famous censor of 312 B.C.E. who opened the citizen rolls to include a far larger number of Romans and who was responsible for building the Appian Way.

Her brother, Publius Clodius Pulcher, led a Roman naval battle against the Carthaginians at Drepana in 249 B.C.E. during the First Punic War. After disparaging unfavorable omens, he suffered a defeat and lost 93 out of 123 ships. The story is told that before the battle when the sacred chickens would not eat, he threw them into the sea, saying that they could drink instead.

Claudia revealed a similar disregard for tradition. Caught amid the crowds in 246 while attending the games in Rome, she was reputed to have said that she only wished the crowd could be put aboard another fleet and her brother brought back from the dead so that he could drown them all and clear the mobs from Rome.

Romans of the third century B.C.E. did not take such remarks lightly. Claudia was fined and possibly tried for treason.

Sources

Aulus Gellius. *Noctes Atticae* 10.6.1.
Suetonius. *The Lives of the Caesars:* Tiberius 2.2–4.
Valerius Maximus. *Factorum et dictorum memorabilium libri IX* 1.4.3; 8.1.4.
Balsdon, J. P. V. D. *Roman Women.* New York: John Day Comp., 1963, p. 43.
Pauly, A., G. Wissowa, and W. Kroll. *Real-Encyclopadie d. Classischen Altertumswissenschaft 1893–.* (Germany: multiple publishers) 382.

▣ Claudia (2)

(second century B.C.E.)   Roman: Rome
reformer

Claudia was part of the movement for land reform in the politics of Rome during the 130s B.C.E. Her parents were ANTISTIA (1) and Appius Claudius Pulcher, consul in 143 B.C.E. Her sister was CLAUDIA (3). Claudia married the tribune Tiberius Sempronius Gracchus. The union cemented his alliance with her father in a coalition that supported an agrarian law to regulate private usage of public land and to distribute public land to the landless.

The reforms addressed the need for citizens, especially veterans to have sufficient land to support themselves and to disperse the increasing numbers of landless who were collecting in Rome and transforming Roman life. The alliance of Claudia's husband and father deeply divided her husband's family. Although the brothers Gaius and Tiberius Gracchus, cousins of Claudia's husband, were in accord, their sister SEMPRONIA (1) was married to Publius Cornelius Scipio Aemilianus, who bitterly opposed the land commission.

The marriage between Claudia and Tiberius Gracchus was said to have been arranged by their fathers over dinner. Antistia, Claudia's mother, was furious at not being consulted. She was said to have relented, however, since Tiberius was seen as a very desirable "catch." (There was a similar story told about AEMILIA TERTIA and her daughter CORNELIA [2]. Since Tiberius Gracchus was the son of this same Cornelia, a remarkable women in her own right, the story would appear to be a confusion among a group of strong women all of whom were kin, albeit of different generations, and all in search of desirable marital partners for their daughters.)

Tiberius Gracchus was murdered by his cousin Publius Cornelius Scipio Nasica. Hundreds of his supporters were also murdered. Nothing is known about the widowed Claudia.

Sources

Plutarch. *Vitae Parallelae (Parallel Lives): Tiberius Gracchus* 4.
Richardson, Keith. *Daggers in the Forum: The Revolutionary Lives and Violent Deaths of the Gracchus Brothers.* London: Cassell, 1976, pp. 41, 46.

Pauly, A., G. Wissowa, and W. Kroll. *Real-Encyclopadie d. Classischen Altertumswissenschaft 1893–*. (Germany: multiple publishers) 385.

◉ Claudia (3)

(second century B.C.E.)   Roman: Rome
priestess

Claudia was a Vestal Virgin and sister of CLAUDIA (2). Chosen from among the very young women of elite families, the Vestal Virgins maintained the flame that assured the continuity and purity of the city. They served Vesta, the goddess of the hearth. Living in one of the oldest temples in the Forum, their well-being was equated with the well-being of the city. Impropriety by any one of them was an omen of misfortune for Rome.

They were not, however, immune to the calls of honor demanded by family. Claudia was a daughter of ANTISTIA (1) and Appius Claudius Pulcher, consul in 143 B.C.E. He had led an army in Cisalpine Gaul against the Salassi, whom he defeated at the cost of several thousand Roman soldiers. The Senate refused him permission to celebrate so costly a victory with a procession in Rome. He chose to defy the Senate and mount a triumph at his own expense.

According to Roman tradition, a tribune could intervene on behalf of the citizenry. In this case, Claudia learned that a tribune would intervene and prevent her father's triumph. She mounted her father's chariot, threw herself into his arms, and was carried in the procession. The sanctity of her person protected her father from any interference. Claudia appears to have been the first Vestal Virgin to use her power to frustrate the will of the Senate.

Sources

Cicero. *Pro Caelio* 34.
Suetonius. *The Lives of the Caesars:* Tiberius 2.4.
Valerius Maximus. *Factorum et dictorum memorabilium libri IX* 5.4, 6.
Balsdon, J. P. V. D. *Roman Women*. New York: John Day Comp., 1963, pp. 42–43.
Bauman, Richard A. *Women and Politics in Ancient Rome*. London: Routledge, 1994, p. 47.

Pauly, A., G. Wissowa, and W. Kroll. *Real-Encyclopadie d. Classischen Altertumswissenschaft 1893–*. (Germany: multiple publishers) 38.

◉ Claudia (4)

(first century B.C.E.)   Roman: Rome
political player

Claudia was a member of the family who divided between republicans and Caesarians during the Roman civil wars of the late first century B.C.E. Bound together by complicated natal family ties further entangled by marriages, divorces, remarriages, and love affairs, Claudia and the women of her generation had multiple and sometimes conflicting allegiances.

Claudia's mother was a Servilia of the Caepio family. Claudia's father was the unprincipled and arrogant Appius Claudius Pulcher. Her uncle was the notorious tribune Publius Clodius Pulcher, and her aunt was CLODIA (2), the woman Gaius Valerius Catullus portrayed in poetry as his faithless lover Lesbia. Claudia was also a niece of CLODIA (1) and Clodia (2).

Claudia married Marcus Junius Brutus in 54 B.C.E., and SERVILIA (1) became her mother-in-law. Brutus was quaestor to her father in Cilicia in 53 and, like her father, joined the republicans under Gnaeus Pompeius Magnus (Pompey the Great) against Gaius Julius Caesar. In 49, the men went with Pompey to Greece, leaving the women behind. As the city sat poised between Ceasar and the republicans, women such as Claudia sought to protect family assets and to assure their family's future, whoever the victor.

Her father died in Greece. After Caesar's defeat of Pompey at Pharsalus in 48, Brutus accepted the pardon offered by Caesar and assumed control over a provincial command. However, her husband was a complicated, even tortured and brooding, man, who felt conflicted loyalties between his mother, a woman of substantial power in Caesar's camp, and his step-uncle, the republican Marcus Porcius Cato. Brutus, against his mother's wishes, divorced Claudia in 45. After her divorce she disappeared from the historical record.

Sources

Pauly, A., G. Wissowa, and W. Kroll. *Real-Encyclopadie d. Classischen Altertumswissenschaft 1893–.* (Germany: multiple publishers) 389.

Syme, Ronald. *The Augustan Aristocracy.* Oxford: Clarendon Press, 1986, p. 198.

———. *The Roman Revolution.* London: Oxford University Press, 1963, pp. 58–59.

▣ Claudia (5)

(53? B.C.E.–)   Roman: Rome
political pawn

Claudia, or Clodia as she may possibly have been called, was the stepdaughter of Mark Antony and a niece of CLODIA (1), CLODIA (2), and CLODIA (3). In 43 B.C.E., when she was about 10, Antony arranged her marriage with Octavian, the future emperor Augustus, in order to cement the Second Triumvirate, the alliance established that year among himself, Octavian, and Marcus Aemilius Lepidus.

Claudia's father was the notorious Publius Clodius Pulcher, who had been killed in 52 B.C.E. by his hated rival and political enemy Titus Annius Milo when they passed each other on the road. Her mother was FULVIA (2), who in 45 married Antony and unsuccessfully undertook to protect her husband's interests against the other triumvirs while he was in the East. However, the triumvirate lasted only for a five-year period, before the events of the civil war overtook the accord. Octavian formally divorced Claudia, without ever having consummated the marriage, in 41 B.C.E. Although Claudia would have reached a marriageable age anytime after 41 or 40, with her mother dead and her stepfather deeply enmeshed with CLEOPATRA VII and his new family in the East, there is no record of marrying: She may well have died young.

Sources

Suetonius. *The Lives of the Caesars:* Augustus 62.1.

Balsdon, J. P. V. D. *Roman Women.* New York: John Day Comp., 1963, p. 178.

Delia, Diana. "Fulvia Reconsidered." In *Women's History and Ancient History,* ed. by Sarah B. Pomeroy. Chapel Hill: University of North Carolina Press, 1991, p. 202.

Pauly, A., G. Wissowa, and W. Kroll. *Real-Encyclopadie d. Classischen Altertumswissenschaft 1893–.* (Germany: multiple publishers) 390.

▣ Claudia (6)

(first century C.E.)   Roman: Italy
member of artistic circle

Claudia had two husbands, each of whom was an artist. Her fist husband composed poetry to music. After his death, she married Publius Papinius Statius (c. 45–96 C.E.), who came from Naples to settle in Rome where he established a reputation as a poet.

She and Statius mingled in eminent circles and were part of a group associated with the emperor Domitian. Although not wealthy, Statius had sufficient means to live well. His poetry addressed the pleasant possibilities of life. In one poem he urged Claudia to leave Rome and return with him to Naples; in another and he praised her for nursing him through an illness.

Claudia had one daughter with her first husband, but no children with Papinius Statius.

Sources

Statius. *Silvae* 3.5.

Der Kleine Pauly; Lexikon der Antike, ed. by Konrat Julius Furchtegott and Walther Sontheimer. Stuttgart, Germany: A. Druckenmuller, 1984, p. 396.

Oxford Classical Dictionary, ed. by Simon Hornblower and Antony Spawforth. 3d. ed. New York: Oxford University Press, 1996, p. 1,439.

▣ Claudia Pulchra

(first century C.E.)   Roman: Rome
political player; exiled

Claudia Pulchra was a victim in the ceaseless struggles for position and power during the reign of Tiberius. She was a grandniece of Augustus and the daughter of Messalla Appianus, consul in 12 B.C.E., and the younger Claudia MARCELLA, Augustus's niece. She became the third wife of Quinctilius Varus, who owed his career to her connections. A military man, he ultimately suffered an ignominious defeat in Germany and committed suicide. They had a son, also named Quinctilius Varus.

The widow Claudia had wealth and standing. She was a close friend of her second cousin, the elder Agrippina, who had a high profile in the politics of the times. Agrippina opposed Tiberius, who she believed had caused the death of her husband. Her enemies became the enemies of her friends. One of them, Gnaeus Domitius Afer, accused Claudia in 26 C.E. of illicit relations with an otherwise unknown man named Furnius, of engaging in a plot to poison the emperor Tiberius, and of using magic against the emperor. This was a familiar triad of accusations used in political battles of the period.

Agrippina interceded with Tiberius on Claudia's behalf. She met Tiberius as he was sacrificing to a statue of Augustus and demanded to know why he would allow Claudia Pulchra to be convicted. Claudia, she argued, was a living person, more of an image of Augustus than any senseless statue. She was not successful. Claudia Pulchra was convicted of lewdness and probably exiled. The following year, after brought suit against Claudia's son, who had inherited his father's substantial wealth. By that time, Tiberius had left Rome, and the Senate allowed the suit to lapse.

Sources

Tacitus. *Annales* 4.52.

Bauman, Richard A. *Women and Politics in Ancient Rome.* London: Routledge, 1994, pp. 147–149.

Levick, Barbara. *Tiberius the Politician.* London: Thames and Hudson, 1976, pp. 165 ff.

Marshall, A. J. "Women on Trial before the Roman Senate." *Classical Views* 34 (1990): 333–366, p. 344.

Syme, Ronald. *The Augustan Aristocracy.* Oxford: Clarendon Press, 1986, *passim*.

▣ Cleito

(fifth century B.C.E.)   Greek: Greece
mother of Euripides

Cleito was thought to be well born. She was the mother of the great Greek tragedian Euripides, who was born in 485 B.C.E. Her husband was a merchant named Mnesarchus or Mnesarchides.

Sources

Murray, Gilbert. *Euripides and His Age.* London: Oxford University Press, 1965, p. 35.

▣ Cleoboule

(c. 407/400– B.C.E.–?)   Greek: Athens
fraud victim; mother of Demosthenes

Cleoboule was probably an Athenian. She was born between 407 and 400 B.C.E. Her father, Gylon, had committed treason and fled to the Bosporus after being condemned to death in Athens. After 403 B.C.E., his death sentence was commuted to a heavy fine.

Although her father may never have returned to Athens, he provided Cleoboule and her elder sister Philia with substantial dowries of 5,000 drachmas. She married a man named Demosthenes sometime early in the 380s. He was a well-to-do Athenian citizen; his wealth, with the exception of his house, was not in land but in the manufacturing of cutlery, pursued mainly in a home factory with slave labor.

In 358–384 or 384–383, Cleoboule gave birth to a son, also named Demosthenes, who became the greatest orator of Athens. She later gave birth to a daughter. Her husband died in 377, when her son was about seven, and her daughter, about five years old. She was left a large estate worth nearly 14 talents, although its exact amount was kept deliberately unclear since her husband sought to protect his estate from any claims on her absent father. He also left a will in which he appointed his brother Aphobus one of three guardians of his estate along with another brother, Demophon, and a friend, Therippides.

Under the terms of the will, Cleoboule was to have 8,000 drachmas to marry Aphobus. When her daughter came of age, she was to have a dowry of 12,000 drachmas and marry Demophon. Both men failed to fulfill the terms of the will: Aphobus did not marry Cleoboule, and Demophon did not marry her daughter. They did, however, embezzle the inheritances of both women and, in addition, depleted the residual estate, which was to go to Demosthenes.

Cleoboule raised the children without adequate resources. Their finances were so extreme that at one time even the fees of Demosthenes' tutor were unpaid. Her situation was further complicated by her son's constant illnesses.

Cleoboule looked to her son to right the wrong done them. When Demosthenes came of age, he took the executors to court. He sued and finally won his case after some five years of litigation. In the end, however, the family received only a small portion of the original estate.

Sources

Plutarch. *Vitae Parallelae (Parallel Lives): Demosthenes* 3.4.1–5.
Davies, J. K. *Athenian Propertied Families, 600–300 B.C.* Oxford: Clarendon Press, 1971, pp. 113–141.

▣ Cleobuline
(sixth century B.C.E.)   Greek: Rhodes
poet

Cleobuline wrote riddles in verse in imitation of her father, the philosopher Cleobulus of Rhodes. Her father advocated the education of women. Cleobuline was a literate woman in the sixth century B.C.E., a time when few men and fewer women could read or write. She was mentioned by Cratinus, one of the greatest poets of Old Attic comedy, who named one of his plays after her.

Sources

Diogenes Laertius. *Lives of the Eminent Philosophers* 1.89.91.
Pomeroy, Sarah B. *Goddesses, Whores, Wives, and Slaves: Women in Classical Antiquity.* New York: Schocken Books, 1975, p. 56.

▣ Cleodice
(sixth century B.C.E.)   Greek: Greece
mother of Pindar

Cleodice was the mother of the great Greek poet Pindar. She gave birth in Boeotia, in central Greece, in 518 B.C.E. Her husband was Daiphantus. All that is known of her background comes from the extant lines of Pindar's poetry, he claimed to be of the Aegidae tribe of Sparta, which would mean that his parents came from aristocratic families.

Sources

Herodotus. *The Persian Wars* 4.149.

▣ Cleopatra (1)
(fifth century B.C.E.)   Greek: Macedonia
victim of family violence

Cleopatra married Perdiccas II, ruler of Macedonia (c. 450–413 B.C.E.). Widowed with a young son in 413, she married Archelaus, her grown stepson. Although his mother was reputed to have been a slave, Archelaus succeeded Perdiccas and was guardian of Cleopatra's young child—her former husband's heir.

Archelaus was ruthless. Fearing his ward, he pushed him into a well and was said to have claimed that he had fallen and drowned while chasing his pet goose. Cleopatra's fate after the death of her son is unknown.

Sources

Aristotle. *Politics* 5.131b.
Plato. *Gorgias* 471c.
Thucydides. *History of the Peloponnesian War* 2.100.
Macurdy, Grace. *Hellenistic Queens.* Reprint. Chicago: Ares Publishers, 1985, pp. 15–16.

▣ Cleopatra (2)
(fourth century B.C.E.)   Greek: Macedonia
political player

Cleopatra suffered the fury of OLYMPIAS (1) after the death of Philip II. Cleopatra was the niece of Attalos, one of Philip's prominent Macedonian generals. Younger than Olympias, she married Philip II when Olympias's son by Philip, Alexander the Great, was a grown man.

The enmity between the two women and their respective supporters was already evident at Cleopatra's wedding feast, which Alexander attended. Attalos proposed a toast calling upon the Macedonians to ask that the gods grant the bride and groom a son so that there would be a legitimate heir to the throne. Incensed at the implication, Alexander threw a glass of wine in Attalos's face. Philip drew his sword and made for Alexander. Drunk, Philip tripped and fell on his face.

Cleopatra lived in Macedonia, but Olympias and her children, including Alexander, went to Epirus. Philip and Alexander later reconciled, and Cleopatra gave birth to a son. After the murder of Philip II in 336 B.C.E., however, it was Alexander, not Cleopatra's child, who became ruler. After Alexander established his rule, Olympias returned to Macedonia.

While Alexander was campaigning, Olympias killed Cleopatra's infant son and took her revenge on the younger woman. Cleopatra either committed suicide by hanging herself or was dragged over a bronze vessel containing charcoal until she roasted to death. Alexander was said to have felt that the death was too harsh. He, however, ordered her uncle and a number of her kinsmen put to death.

Sources

Justin. *Epitome* 9.7, 12.
Pausanias. *Description of Greece* 8.7.5.
Plutarch. *Vitae Parallelae (Parallel Lives): Alexander* 9.6–11.
Burn, Andrew Robert. *Alexander the Great and the Hellenistic World.* London: English Universities Press, 1964, pp. 44–45, 64.
Macurdy, Grace. *Hellenistic Queens.* Reprint. Chicago: Ares Publishers, 1985, pp. 30, 32.
Tarn, William Woodthorpe. *Alexander the Great.* 2 vols. Boston: Beacon Press, 1956, pp. 2–3.

◉ Cleopatra (3)
(c. 354–308 B.C.E.)
Greek: Macedonia, Epirus, and Asia Minor
coruler

Cleopatra was a daughter molded by a powerful mother. Lifetime allies, Cleopatra and her mother OLYMPIAS (1) fought to rule Macedonia. Born in 354 B.C.E., the child of Olympias and Philip II (359–336 B.C.E.), Cleopatra was the sister of Alexander the Great. In 336, at 18 years of age, she married her uncle Alexander I, ruler of Milossia (c. 342–330 B.C.E.) in Epirus.

Her husband was 28 years old and a notable general. The marriage cemented the alliance between Epirus, the center of her mother's influence, and Macedonia, ruled by her father, Philip II. Although her father was assassinated during the wedding celebration, her brother assumed control over Macedonia and the alliance held. Cleopatra remained in Epirus and gave birth to two children, Neoptolemus and Cadmeia. Six years later, after her husband's death in 330, she ruled in the name of her young children along with her mother.

In 325, Olympias assumed the roles of guardian over Cleopatra's children and regent of Epirus while Cleopatra went to Macedonia. Alexander, already traveling in the East, had appointed the general Antipater ruler of Macedonia in his absence. Olympias and Cleopatra were hostile to Antipater, and Cleopatra sought to raise support against him. Alexander, however, only scoffed at Cleopatra's quest and is said to have remarked that their mother had gotten the best of the deal: Their mother ruled Epirus while Cleopatra was sent on a fool's errand, since Macedonia would never accept a woman ruler.

The death of Alexander in 323 inaugurated a period of political turmoil. Three of Alexander's generals, Antipater, Craterus, and Perdiccas, vied for control of his empire, with Perdiccas in the dominant position and Antipater in control of Greece. Cleopatra could have chosen any one of them as a husband, although each would have objected to her marriage with any of the others.

Instead, she pursued a different path. Pushed by Olympias, and with her eyes still on Macedonia, Cleopatra invited Leonnatus, a handsome Macedonian general in Alexander's army who had distinguished himself in Asia, to become her husband. Related to the ruling house and governor of Phrygia in Asia Minor, Leonnatus modeled himself after Alexander. He was only too happy to accept Cleopatra's offer, recognizing it no doubt as a stepping stone for both of them in pursuit of a larger sphere of power. He died in a battle with Greek insurgents before the marriage could take place.

With Macedonia still the sought-after prize, and a score to settle with Antipater, Olympias and Cleopatra upset plans for a marriage between NICAEA (1), Antipater's daughter, and Perdiccas. Instead, Olympias organized a marriage between Perdiccas and Cleopatra. Cleopatra left for Sardis in Asia Minor in 322 B.C.E.

Perdiccas evidently feared the enmity of Antipater more than he desired the alliance with Cleopatra and Olympias. He decided to marry Nicaea. He also, however, secretly promised Cleopatra that he would later divorce Nicaea and marry her. News of the secret arrangement came to the attention of Antipater and caused a permanent breach between the two men. Cleopatra was kept under watch in Sardis to prevent her from marrying Perdiccas. Sources differ over whether or not Perdiccas married Nicaea before his assassination in 321.

The drama of Perdiccas, and Antipater on the one side, and Olympias and Cleopatra on the other was watched by other generals of the late Alexander's army, all of whom sought their own spheres of power. Eumenes, a Greek general, supported Cleopatra, but she prevented him from attacking Antipater to preserve favor with the Macedonian populace. Eumenes' death in 316 left her without allies.

Tired of her semiconfinement in Sardis, Cleopatra planned to leave for Egypt in 308 to marry Ptolemy I Soter, one of the most successful of Alexander's successors. With orders from Antigonus, who controlled a large portion of Asia Minor, not to allow her to leave, the commander in Sardis arranged for a group of women to murder her. Antigonus quickly put the women to death to hide his involvement, and he gave Cleopatra a splendid funeral.

Sources

Arrian. *Successors* I.24, 40.

Diodorus Siculus. *Library of History* 16.91.3; 18.23.1–3; 20.37.3–6.

Justin. *Epitome* 13.6.

Plutarch. *Vitae Parallelae (Parallel Lives): Alexander* 68.4.

Plutarch. *Vitae Parallelae (Parallel Lives): Eumenes* 3.8.

Carney, Elizabeth D. "What's in a Name?" In *Women's History and Ancient History,* ed. by Sarah B. Pomeroy. Chapel Hill: University of North Carolina Press, 1991, p. 157.

Cary, M. *A History of the Greek World from 323 to 146 B.C.* London: Methuen, 1951, p. 12.

Macurdy, Grace. *Hellenistic Queens.* Reprint. Chicago: Ares Publishers, 1985, index.

▣ Cleopatra (4)

(first century C.E.)   Roman: Rome
self-made woman

Cleopatra belonged to the group of freedmen and women who attained power under the emperor Claudius. She was said to be Claudius's favorite, a position she shared with CALPURNIA (2), another freedwoman. Her access to the emperor made her a useful ally in the intrigues of imperial life. At the same time, access had a price, and Cleopatra expected to retire a rich woman.

When the behavior of Valeria MESSALLINA, the emperor's wife, appeared to open the way for a revival of power for the senatorial elite, the powerful freedmen felt threatened. Narcissus, one of Claudius's two most important secretaries, paid Cleopatra to vouch for Calpurnia's report that Messallina and her lover Gaius Silius had undergone a marriage ceremony. If this was true, it would mean at the least that Messallina had made the emperor appear a fool. Possibly, it was more, and the ceremony was the first move in a conspiracy.

Silius and Messallina died in the wake of the affair, and Cleopatra was all the richer from it.

Sources

Tacitus. *Annales* 9.30.

▣ Cleopatra (5)

(first century C.E.)   Roman: Rome
political client

Cleopatra was a friend and client of the wealthy, smart, and beautiful POPPAEA SABINA (2), one of the many lovers, and later the second wife, of the emperor Nero. Cleopatra married a well-to-do Roman businessman, Gessius Florus, from Clazomenae, a city on a small island off the southern shore of the Gulf of Smyrna. She used her relationship with Poppaea to secure from Nero an appointment for her husband as procurator of Judaea in 64 C.E.

Poppaea, though thought to have Jewish sympathies, did the Jews no service: Cleopatra's husband, Florus, was a ruthless governor.

Sources

Josephus. *Antiquitates Judaicae (Jewish Antiquities)* 20.252.

Jones, A. H. M. *The Herods of Judaea,* Rev. ed. Oxford: Clarendon Press, 1967, p. 235 ff.

Oxford Classical Dictionary, ed. by Simon Hornblower and Antony Spawforth. 3d. ed. New York: Oxford University Press, 1996, p. 635.

⊡ ## Cleopatra I (The Syrian)
(c. 215–176 B.C.E.)
Greek: Asia Minor and Egypt
ruler

Cleopatra I, known as the Syrian, was the first woman of the Ptolemaic line to act as regent for her son and to mint coins in her own name. Born in Syria, the daughter of LAODICE III and Antiochus III, whose ancestor Seleucus I was a general under Alexander the Great, she was one of three daughters strategically married to insure her father's alliances.

Her father had defeated Ptolemy IV Philopator at the battle of Panium in 200 B.C.E. and regained Coele-Syria, which he had previously lost to Ptol-

Cleopatra I (The Syrian)
(Date: 193 B.C.E.–192 B.C.E. 1944.100.70712, Archives, American Numismatic Society)

emy at the battle of Raphia in 217. With the Romans on the horizon, Antiochus sought peace on the Egyptian/Syrian border. The marriage of Cleopatra and the future Ptolemy V Epiphanes was arranged when they were still children.

Cleopatra and Ptolemy married at Raphia in 193. She was 22, and he was about 17. Antiochus gave her Coele-Syria as part of her dowry, no doubt to assuage Egyptian sensibilities. The marriage was successful. Cleopatra was the bolder, more vigorous, more ambitious, and more intelligent of the two, and they shared power. After her husband's death in 180 B.C.E., Cleopatra became sole regent for her young son, who was about six years old at the time. She proved to be an able ruler. Under her rule, Egypt remained peaceful. She discarded her husband's plan to campaign against her brother Seleucus IV in Syria and kept peace with both Syria and Rome.

Her two sons later ruled Egypt as Ptolemy VI Philometor and Ptolemy VIII Euergetes II, and her daughter, CLEOPATRA II PHILOMETOR SOTEIRA, became one of the greatest long-reigning woman rulers of Egypt. She died in 176 B.C.E.

Sources

Josephus. *Antiquitates Judaicae (Jewish Antiquities)* 12.154–55.

Macurdy, Grace. *Hellenistic Queens.* Reprint. Chicago: Ares Publishers, 1985, pp. 141–147.

Pomeroy, Sarah B. *Women in Hellenistic Egypt.* New York: Schocken, 1984, p. 23.

Oxford Classical Dictionary, ed. by Simon Hornblower and Antony Spawforth. 3d. ed. New York: Oxford University Press, 1996, p. 346.

⊡ ## Cleopatra II Philometor Soteira
(c. 185?–115 B.C.E.)   Greek: Egypt
ruler

Cleopatra II was one of the ablest rulers of Hellenistic Egypt, ruling for 57 years. Born between 185 and 180 B.C.E., the daughter of CLEOPATRA I (THE SYRIAN) and Ptolemy V Epiphanes, she overcame extraordinary obstacles in her quest for power.

After the death of her mother, who had been regent for her children, Cleopatra married her younger brother Ptolemy VI Philometor in 175 or 174. Two eunuchs from Coele-Syria, Eulaeus and Lenaeus, assumed the regency for the young household. Their governance was a disaster, and they were defeated in a battle with Cleopatra's uncle, the Seleucid Antiochus IV. The defeated Eulaeus persuaded Cleopatra's brother/husband, the young Ptolemy VI, to withdraw with him to the island of Samothrace. Her youngest brother went to Alexandria, where Cleopatra joined him. They were declared joint rulers by the populace, and he took the title of Ptolemy VIII Euergetes II.

Antiochus continued to meddle in Egyptian affairs in an effort to exercise control. He supported Ptolemy VI, who now resided in Memphis, and launched an attack on Cleopatra and Ptolemy VIII in Alexandria. Cleopatra and Ptolemy VIII sent envoys to Rome to plead for Roman intervention. In the meantime, Ptolemy VI, fearful of Antiochus's intentions, contacted Cleopatra and his brother to arrange a settlement between them. Cleopatra, the eldest of the three, brokered a peace.

Cleopatra ruled along with her two brothers from 170 to 164 B.C.E., after the Romans forced Antiochus to withdraw to Syria. Cleopatra and Ptolemy VI were supported by the powerful Jewish community of Alexandria and put their army under the control of two Jewish generals. A resumption of the quarrel between the brothers, resulted in a victory for Ptolemy VI. Cleopatra and he ruled jointly from 164 onward, while Ptolemy VIII withdrew from Egypt to Cyrene.

Cleopatra had four children with Ptolemy VI, one of whom, Ptolemy Eupator, ruled jointly with his father for a brief time. Another became Ptolemy VII Neos Philapator and became joint ruler with his father in 145 and sole ruler after his father died in battle in the same year. There were also two daughters, Cleopatra III and Cleopatra Thea.

After the death of Ptolemy VI, Ptolemy VIII returned to Alexandria from Cyrene, murdered the 17-year-old Ptolemy VII, and bowed to the demands of the Alexandrians to marry his sister Cleopatra. Cleopatra III also married Ptolemy VIII, her uncle and her mother's second husband, in 142, while her mother was still his wife. Furious

at this slight, Cleopatra bided her time for 10 years. Then in 132, with the support of the Jews, she organized a revolt in Alexandria, and in 130 Ptolemy VIII fled to Cyprus.

Cleopatra III and her children went with Ptolemy. Cleopatra II's four-year-old son with Ptolemy VIII was also taken. Ptolemy murdered the boy and sent pieces of his body packed in a hamper as a birthday present to Cleopatra in Alexandria. A year later, after Ptolemy VII returned to Egypt with Cleopatra III and captured Alexandria, Cleopatra fled to Antioch, bringing with her vast wealth to secure support from her former son-in-law, Demetrius II. Demetrius had been married to her daughter Cleopatra Thea. He rose to her defense but was killed in battle.

Cleopatra eventually returned to Alexandria and reconciled with her brother/husband to reign peacefully with him and with her daughter Cleopatra III. Reforms were issued in the names of the three rulers. Among these were a prohibition against imprisonment without trial, a decrease in taxes, improved judicial proceedings, and reforms in housing and ownership of land.

Cleopatra died in 115 B.C.E., shortly after her husband's death. She was more than 70 years old.

Sources

Diodorus Siculus. *Library of History* 33.13.1; 34.14.1.

Livy. *From the Founding of the City* 44.19.6–14; 45.9–13.1–9.

Polybius. *Histories* 28.1, 20–21.

Cary, M. *A History of the Greek World from 323 to 146 B.C.* London: Methuen, 1951, p. 222.

Macurdy, Grace. *Hellenistic Queens.* Reprint. Chicago: Ares Publishers, 1985, index.

Oxford Classical Dictionary, ed. by Simon Hornblower and Antony Spawforth. 3d. ed. New York: Oxford University Press, 1996, pp. 346–347.

Pomeroy, Sarah B. *Women in Hellenistic Egypt.* New York: Schocken, 1984.

▣ Cleopatra III
(c. 165?–101 B.C.E.)   Greek: Egypt
ruler

Cleopatra III let no one stand in the way of her quest for power. Her life was shaped by struggles with her mother and her children to become the dominant ruler of Egypt. Enormously wealthy, she was the daughter of CLEOPATRA II PHILOMETOR SOTEIRA and her husband/brother, Ptolemy VI Philometor. Born between 165 and 160 B.C.E. in 142, she became the wife of her uncle, Ptolemy VIII Euergetes II, who was simultaneously her mother's second husband. She was the sister of CLEOPATRA THEA.

After 10 years of marriage marked by discord between the women, Cleopatra II led a successful revolt in 132, and Ptolemy VIII was forced to flee Alexandria. Cleopatra III supported her husband and fled with him to Cyprus accompanied by her five children: Ptolemy IX Soter II Lathyrus Ptolemy Alexander, CLEOPATRA TRYPHAENA, CLEOPATRA IV, and CLEOPATRA V SELENE. They also brought to Cyprus Ptolemy VIII's four-year-old son from his marriage with Cleopatra II. The boy was murdered, and parts of the body were sent to the boy's mother in Alexandria.

In 129 Ptolemy VIII reconquered Alexandria, and eventually both Cleopatras reconciled. Over the next 13 years, mother and daughter ruled together with their joint husband. In the name of the three rulers there were reforms in the courts, in debt, in land holdings, and in taxes. At his death in 116, Ptolemy VIII left Cleopatra III, the younger of the two women, in control of Egypt with the right to choose either one of her sons as coruler. Her mother died soon after, and left her the unchallenged ruler.

She was forced by the populace in 116 to name her son Ptolemy IX Soter II as coruler instead of the younger Ptolemy Alexander, whom she found more pliable. She sent her younger son to Cyprus but asserted her position by presenting her name and image before that of her older son on official documents and other iconography. She also made his life miserable.

Ptolemy IX had married his sister, Cleopatra IV, whom he dearly loved. Cleopatra found that this daughter had a mind of her own and was not to be dominated. In a short time, Cleopatra succeeded in securing her son's divorce and a new marriage to his younger sister, Cleopatra V Selene, whom she

more easily controlled. In 110, Cleopatra also secured the agreement of Ptolemy IX to accept her younger son, Ptolemy X Alexander I, as his joint ruler. Soon, however, they quarreled, and Ptolemy Alexander returned to Cyprus.

Ptolemy IX sought to counter his mother's power by siding against the Jews, who were the second most privileged group in Alexandria after the Greeks and were her supporters. He received a request from Antiochus IX Cyzicenus, his cousin and the ruler of Antioch, for help in fighting against the forces of John Hyrcanus, the Jewish high priest, who was attacking the Greeks in Samaria. Ptolemy sent 6,000 troops without telling his mother.

In 108, Cleopatra accused Ptolemy IX of seeking to poison her. She incited a mob and Ptolemy IX was driven into exile. She recalled her younger son, Ptolemy X, from Cyprus as her coruler and sent an army to capture Ptolemy IX. The troops, with the exception of the Jews, revolted, and Ptolemy IX became ruler of Cyprus. Cleopatra put the commander of the troops to death.

Cleopatra and Ptolemy X quarreled. In 102 B.C.E. her older son, Ptolemy IX, invaded Palestine from his base in Cyprus, captured Judaea, and advanced toward Egypt. Cleopatra collected her grandchildren along with her will and a large amount of treasure, which she deposited in the temple of Aesculapius on Cos, an island off the coast of southern Asia Minor. She then led an army into Palestine where she halted Ptolemy's advance. She was only dissuaded from trying to regain Coele-Syria by her Jewish advisers, who threatened to withdraw their support if she captured Alexander Jannaeus, the brother of John Hyrcanus, who controlled the area. Instead, she signed a treaty of alliance and mutual aid with him.

Cleopatra was worshiped as Isis, the great mother of the gods, and cults were established in her honor. She provided funds for an expedition by Eudoxus of Cyzicenus to India for a shipment of precious stones and perfumes. She died at about 60 years old, before Eudoxus's return in 101. She may have been murdered, perhaps by Ptolemy X.

Sources

Josephus. *Antiquitates Judaicae (Jewish Antiquities)* 13.285, 287, 328, 331, 348–55.

Livy. *From the Founding of the City* 14.67.

Cary, M. *A History of the Greek World from 323 to 146 B.C.* London: Methuen, 1951, pp. 222–223.

Macurdy, Grace. *Hellenistic Queens.* Reprint. Chicago: Ares Publishers, 1985, index.

Oxford Classical Dictionary, ed. by Simon Hornblower and Antony Spawforth. 3d. ed. New York: Oxford University Press, 1996, p. 347.

Cleopatra IV

(second century B.C.E.)
Greek: Egypt and Syria
insurgent leader

Cleopatra IV threatened the power of her mother in Egypt and her sister in Syria. She was the daughter of Cleopatra III. Her father, Ptolemy VIII Euergetes II, was also her great-uncle. She married her brother, Ptolemy IX Soter II Lathyrus, who became coruler with her mother after her father's death in 316 B.C.E.

Her mother sought to exercise control over Ptolemy IX, who was her oldest son. In the conflict between mother and wife, her husband reluctantly sided with his mother and agreed to reject Cleopatra in favor of marriage with a younger sister, Cleopatra V Selene, who was more amenable to his mother's influence. Cleopatra left Egypt for Cyprus, where another brother, Ptolemy Alexander, ruled.

Like many of the Cleopatras, Cleopatra IV had enormous wealth. In Cyprus she raised an army and took it to Syria. At this time the half brothers Antiochus IX Cyzicenus and Antiochus VIII Grypus were waging war against each other. Both were first cousins of Cleopatra IV through their mother, Cleopatra Thea, who was the sister of Cleopatra III. Grypus was married to another of Cleopatra's own sisters, Cleopatra Tryphaena. The other half brother was available.

In Antioch, Cleopatra offered her support to Cyzicenus and married him. Grypus captured Antioch and Cleopatra in 112 B.C.E. He might not have murdered Cleopatra, but her sister, fearing

Cleopatra would seduce her husband, had Cleopatra killed even though she had sought santuary in the temple of Artemis. Later, Cleopatra's husband Cyzicenus recaptured Antioch. He had his sister-in-law Cleopatra Tryphaena killed to appease the spirit of his murdered wife.

Sources

Justin. *Epitome* 39.3.

Downey, Glanville. *A History of Antioch in Syria from Seleucus to the Arab Conquest.* Princeton, N.J.: Princeton University Press, 1961, p. 129.

Macurdy, Grace. *Hellenistic Queens.* Reprint. Chicago: Ares Publishers, 1985.

Cleopatra V Selene

(c. 131/130–69 B.C.E.)
Greek: Egypt and Syria
political player

Cleopatra V Selene engaged in a series of matrimonial alliances to secure a sphere of power in the politics of Egypt and Syria. She was the youngest daughter of Cleopatra III and Ptolemy VIII Euergetes II, who was also her great-uncle. In 116 B.C.E., when she was about 14 or 15 years old, her mother arranged her first marriage with her brother Ptolemy IX Soter II Lathyrus, in the belief that she would be more malleable to her mother's machinations than his previous wife, her older sister Cleopatra IV.

In 108, with the support of the Jews of Alexandria, her mother incited a successful revolt to drive Ptolemy IX Soter II from Egypt. Cleopatra remained in Alexandria with her mother. Her deposed husband assembled an army in Cyprus, where he had fled. He defeated the Jewish army in Syria and conquered Judaea. Sometime during this period Cleopatra, who was still in Alexandria, divorced Ptolemy IX. Threatened by his advancing army, she left Alexandria for Syria. With her mother's support, she brought troops with her and carried a large dowry of treasure to Antiochus VIII Grypus in Antioch.

Grypus was kin by a former marriage and was a partner who could offer Cleopatra and her mother an alternative base of power in their war against Ptolemy. At the time, there was almost continuous warfare for control over the Seleucid Empire between two half brothers, Antiochus VIII Grypus and Antiochus IX Cyzicenus. Cyzicenus had been married to Cleopatra IV. She had been murdered by order of her sister CLEOPATRA TRYPHAENA, who was Grypus's wife. To avenge the murder of Cleopatra IV, Cyzicenus murdered Cleopatra Tryphaena.

Cleopatra V married Grypus, but the union was short-lived. He was murdered in 96 B.C.E. by his leading general, Heracleon of Beroea, during an attempted coup. Meanwhile in Egypt, Cleopatra's mother was murdered, possibly by one of her sons. Cleopatra became a free agent, able to choose her allies. She married Cyzicenus, her husband's half-brother and bitterest enemy, who occupied Antioch soon after her husband's death.

She was not his wife for long either. Cyzicenus died in battle along with the eldest son of Grypus in about 95 or 94. Antiochus X Eusebes, the son of Cyzicenus, staked his claim for power. He conquered Antioch and reigned from 94 to 92. Cleopatra married Eusebes, once more negotiating her enormous wealth for political power. Although Eusebes died fighting in 92, Cleopatra survived. She moved to Ptolemais in Phoenicia and lived in great luxury with her children for nearly two decades.

In 75, she sent her two sons by Eusebes to Rome where they contested the legitimacy of Ptolemy XII Neos Dionysus (Auletes), son of Ptolemy IX. The Romans refused to support their claim. Cleopatra also sought to place her son, Antiochus Asiaticus, in power in Syria. Tigranes I the Great of Armenia, who controlled Syria, campaigned against her in Phoenicia. In 69 she was captured in Ptolemais by Tigranes, who brought her to Seleuceia on the Euphrates and had her killed. Her son ruled over Syria from 69 to 68 B.C.E. after Tigranes withdrew from Antioch.

Sources

Appian. *Syrian Wars* 49.69.
Cicero. *In Verrum* 4.27.
Josephus. *Antiquitates Judaicae (Jewish Antiquities)* 13.6.5; 365, 367, 370–371.
Strabo. *Geography* 16.7, 49.
Macurdy, Grace. *Hellenistic Queens.* Reprint. Chicago: Ares Publishers, 1985, index.

▣ Cleopatra VI Tryphaena

(?–57 B.C.E.)   Greek: Egypt
coruler

Cleopatra VI Tryphaena was the daughter of Ptolemy IX Soter II Lathyrus. Her mother was one of his lovers. Cleopatra married her half-brother Ptolemy XII Neos Dionysus (Auletes) in 80 or 79. A weak man, Ptolemy XII's rule was challenged by CLEOPATRA V SELENE, who was living in Ptolemais and looking to settle her sons by Antiochus X Eusebus.

Cleopatra was very young when she married, and her brother/husband was only about 15 when be became ruler. Much of his time and money was spent bribing Romans to support his claims to the throne. The heavy taxes levied to pay for these bribes left him highly unpopular. Rome finally recognized his rule in 59 B.C.E., after Julius Caesar, who was consul in that year, received a large settlement. When the Alexandrians threatened revolt, Ptolemy XII went to Rome to seek support. Cleopatra shared power with BERENICE IV CLEOPATRA in Egypt for about a year until she died in 57.

Cleopatra may have been the mother of ARSINOË AULETES and the most famous Cleopatra, CLEOPATRA VII. She may also have been the mother of sister of Berenice IV Cleopatra. In addition, she had two sons, Ptolemy XIII and Ptolemy XIV.

Sources

Dio Cassius. *Roman History* 39.12.
Macurdy, Grace. *Hellenistic Queens.* Reprint. Chicago: Ares Publishers, 1985, index.
Pomeroy, Sarah B. *Women in Hellenistic Egypt.* New York: Schocken, 1984, p. 24.
Skeat, Theodore Cressy. *The Reigns of the Ptolemies.* Munich: Beck, 1969, p. 35.

▣ Cleopatra VII

(c. 69–30 B.C.E.)
Greek: Egypt, Asia Minor, and Italy
ruler

Cleopatra VII is one of the most famous women of history, the subject of legend and literature. A protagonist in the politics and wars that marked the end of the Roman republic and an independent

Egypt, she was courageous, intelligent, arrogant, clever, and charming. She had a facility for languages and was possibly the only Ptolemaic ruler who spoke fluent Egyptian. She was also extremely rich. The last in the long line of Ptolemaic rulers, many of whom were powerful women, she was born in 69 B.C.E. and ruled Egypt from 51 to 30. Ambitious for Egypt, she used Julius Caesar and Mark Antony to solidify her rule and extend her empire. In turn, she offered them her treasury. She exhibited some of the characteristics of Alexander the Great, and had Antony followed her advice, together they might well have ruled a world empire.

Cleopatra was the daughter of Ptolemy XII Neos Dionysus (Auletes). Her mother's identity has remained uncertain. The most likely candidate is CLEOPATRA VI TRYPHAENA, who married Auletes in 80 or 79 B.C.E. Possibly, she was the daughter of one of Auletes' lovers. However, none of the ancient sources, which were sometimes quite hostile toward Cleopatra, challenged her legitimate right to rule Egypt.

Cleopatra was 14 in 55 B.C.E. when her father returned to power in Egypt with the support of Rome. Ptolemy XII was a weak man who had spent several years and a great deal of money bribing Romans to support him over the objections of the Alexandrians. He had left Egypt for Rome in 58. In his absence, the Alexandrians recognized as joint rulers his wife Cleopatra VI Tryphaena and BERENICE IV CLEOPATRA, who was either the aunt, sister, or stepsister of Cleopatra. Cleopatra VI died a year later. Berenice IV Cleopatra ruled alone until Auletes returned and murdered her.

Before her father died in 51, he named the 17-year-old Cleopatra and her brother, Ptolemy XIII, joint rulers of Egypt. Cleopatra was seven years older than her brother; she married him within the year. The young rulers were surrounded by three men who expected to exercise power: Prothinus, a court eunuch; Theodolltus, a Greek from Chios who was Ptolemy's tutor; and Archillas, who commanded the army in Alexandria. Conflict was not slow in coming. From the beginning, Cleopatra allied herself with the Romans. In 49 she supplied Gnaeus Pompey, the son of the republican general Gnaeus Pompeius (Pompey the Great), with 60 ships in addition to money and supplies of corn. The advisers, fearful that she might achieve an

Cleopatra VII and Mark Antony
(Date: 36 B.C.E. 1977.158.621, Archives, American Numismatic Society)

independent basis of power supported by the Romans, alleged that she sought to rule alone.

With the help of an Alexandrian mob, Cleopatra was expelled from the city in 48 B.C.E. Undeterred, she raised a mercenary army and returned to fight her brother. In 48, Julius Caesar arrived in Egypt in pursuit of Gnaeus Pompeius (Pompey the Great) and found the armies of Cleopatra and her brother arrayed against each other. Caesar sent a message to Cleopatra encamped in Pelusium. To escape assassination, Cleopatra wrapped herself in bedclothes and used a small boat to smuggle herself into Alexandria to meet Caesar. She secured his support.

In an effort to appease the Alexandrians, who were affronted by the Romans marching through the city, and to calm conflict between Cleopatra and her brother, Caesar read to an assembled group of Alexandrians a copy of Auletes' will that had been left in his care. He affirmed Auletes' instructions and made Cleopatra and her brother corulers of Egypt under the protection of Rome.

In a further effort to assure peace within the ruling clique in Alexandria, Caesar proposed that Cleopatra's younger sister, ARSINOË AULETES, and their youngest brother, Ptolemy XIV, leave Egypt and become joint rulers of Cyprus. Arsinoë Auletes, however, jealous of Cleopatra, fled to Alexandria and joined up with the Egyptian army, which declared her ruler. She quarreled with the general Archillas, had him murdered, and assumed control over the army. The mercenary army had no liking for a woman commander and welcomed the young Ptolemy XIII, who came from Alexandria under a ruse of bringing the army to Caesar's side. War followed. In 47 Caesar defeated the army and captured Arsinoë, whom he brought to Rome. Ptolemy drowned in the Nile trying to escape.

By now Caesar had become Cleopatra's lover, and she was pregnant with his child. Born in June 47, the child was named Ptolemy Caesar. He became known as Caesarion. Cleopatra married her younger brother, Ptolemy XIV, who was about 12 years old at the time, and Caesar returned to Rome leaving Alexandria quiet and Cleopatra in power, supported by three Roman legions. In 46 Cleopatra joined Caesar in Rome along with her young son

and her husband, Ptolemy XIV. She lived in one of Caesar's houses and held court. After his assassination in 44, she returned to Egypt. Shortly thereafter, she had her husband poisoned and named her son, the three-year-old Caesarion, joint ruler.

During the ensuing Roman civil war, Cleopatra sided with the Caesarians. She supplied Publius Cornelius Dolabella with four legions and excused herself from helping his opponent Gaius Cassius Longinus the Tyrannicide on the grounds that there was famine in Egypt. After the defeat of Dolabella, she tried to sail with her fleet to join Mark Antony and Octavian, but a storm destroyed many of her ships. An illness prevented her from sailing again, and the victory of the Caesarians made further aid unnecessary.

In 41 Cleopatra was summoned by Antony to Tarsus. Antony's mission was to consolidate power and raise revenues to pay for the war. Cleopatra convinced him that she had supported the Caesarians, probably provided him with immediate material aid, and successfully seduced him. Antony spent the winter of 41–40 with her in Egypt. At her request, he arranged for the murder of her sister Arsinoë Auletes, who was in Ephesus and who Cleopatra felt might be a future threat. In the spring of 40, Antony left Egypt to return to Rome.

Between 40 and 37 B.C.E., Cleopatra remained in Egypt. In 37 Antony was again in the East, and he summoned Cleopatra to meet him in Antioch where they formed an alliance. She agreed to provide him with aid and in return received control over Coele-Syria, Cyprus, and a part of Cilicia. Antony also acknowledged that he was the father of their twins, CLEOPATRA SELENE and Alexander Helios.

In 35 OCTAVIA (2), who had married Antony in 40 to seal the pact of Brundisium and who under Roman law was still his wife, brought Antony reinforcements from her brother, Octavian. She came with far fewer troops than Antony had expected and Octavian had promised. Antony told her to stop at Athens: The alliance with Cleopatra provided for his needs, and Cleopatra had no interest in Octavia's presence. With Cleopatra's resources, Antony mounted a successful eastern campaign against the Armenians in 34. Afterward, Antony and Cleopatra divided power. She and Caesarion continued to be corulers of Egypt, Cyprus, Libya, and Coele-Syria. Alexander Helios was given Armenia, Media, and Parthia, and little Ptolemy Philadelphus, their other son, was named ruler of Phoenicia, Syria and Cilicia. Coins were struck with Antony on one side and Cleopatra on the other.

Cleopatra had succeeded. She was joint ruler with the most powerful Roman in the East and had an empire that extended well beyond her patrimony of Egypt. She crowned her success with marriage to Antony after he divorced Octavia in 32.

Octavian declared war against Cleopatra. He could not leave Antony and Cleopatra in control of the East, the richer and more populous part of the ancient Greco-Roman world. Octavian needed the resources of the East and the corn of Egypt to feed Rome. However, Octavian feared declaring war directly against Antony who remained popular among Romans, especially those in the army. Cleopatra wanted Antony to focus on the East, but she reluctantly supplied Antony with money, men, and ships to fight Octavian. Antony adopted a two-part plan in which he would proceed against Octavian and, only if that failed, would he fall back on extending his rule in the East.

Romans supporting Antony met with him and Cleopatra at Ephesus. They were clear: They wanted Cleopatra to return to Egypt. They adamantly opposed recognizing Caesarion as the legitimate son of Caesar and Cleopatra and as a possible coruler of Rome. However, Cleopatra was furnishing 200 of the 800 ships of the fleet as well as 2,000 talents. She refused to go back to Egypt. She claimed that the Egyptians would be insulted and that her soldiers would not fight. Perhaps she also feared that Antony might be persuaded to abandon her if she was not physically present. Antony stood by Cleopatra, much to the disgust of his Roman army.

In the battle of Actium in 31 B.C.E., Antony's Roman troops wanted the navy to attack Octavian's ships. If they won, Octavian would be forced to send his army into battle. If Octavian's fleet won, the army under Antony would withdraw to the interior, forcing Octavian to follow. Cleopatra's ships were stationed in the rear. Antony put trea-sure aboard fast ships that were also stationed in the rear. This aroused suspicion among the troops, and some of Antony's fleet deserted him at the beginning of the battle. Cleopatra ordered her ships back to Egypt, and Antony, probably thinking that his army might desert him, abandoned the fight, boarded a fast ship, and followed her. The rest of his army surrendered. Antony committed suicide before Octavian arrived in Egypt.

On August 10, 30 B.C.E., Cleopatra killed herself by poison from an asp rather than face being paraded as a captive in Octavian's triumph.

Sources

Appian. *Roman History: Bella civilian (Civil Wars)* 4.61–63, 82; 5.8–9.

Dio Cassius. *Roman History* 42.35 ff; 49.41.

Josephus. *Antiquitates Judaicae (Jewish Antiquities)* 15.4.1.

Plutarch. *Vitae Parallelae (Parallel Lives): Antonius* 25–29; 30; 53–86.

Plutarch. *Vitae Parallelae (Parallel Lives): Caesar* 49.

Plutarch. *Vitae Parallelae (Parallel Lives): Pompeius* 78.

Suetonius. *The Lives of the Caesars: Caesar* 52.

Burnstein, Stanley M. *The Reign of Cleopatra.* Westport, Conn.: Greenwood Press, 2004, *passim.*

Chauveau, Michel. *Cleopatra: Beyond the Myth.* Translated from the French by Lorton. Ithaca, N.Y.: Cornell University Press, 2002.

Jones, Prudence. *Cleopatra: A Sourcebook.* Norman: University of Oklahoma Press, 2006.

Macurdy, Grace. *Hellenistic Queens.* Reprint. Chicago: Ares Publishers, 1985, index.

Oxford Classical Dictionary, ed. by Simon Hornblower and Antony Spawforth. 3d. ed. New York: Oxford University Press, 1996, p. 347.

Pomeroy, Sarah B. *Goddesses, Whores, Wives, and Slaves: Women in Classical Antiquity.* New York: Schocken Books, 1975, pp. 187–188.

———. *Women in Hellenistic Egypt.* New York: Schocken, 1984, index.

Syme, Ronald. *The Roman Revolution.* London: Oxford University Press, 1963, index.

Cleopatra Selene

(40 B.C.E.–? C.E.)
Greek: Egypt, Italy and Mauritania
coruler

Cleopatra Selene ruled the Roman client kingdom of Mauritania with her husband, Juba. She and her twin, Alexander Helios, were born in 40 B.C.E. to CLEOPATRA VII and Mark Antony. After the battle of Actium and the death of her parents when she was about 11 years old, she walked with her brother in Octavian's triumph. Alexander died shortly thereafter, and OCTAVIA (2), the ex-wife of Mark Antony, raised Cleopatra in her own household.

In 20 B.C.E., Octavian, now Augustus, arranged a marriage between Cleopatra Selene and Juba of Mauritania. Juba had been paraded in a triumph of Julius Caesar in 46 B.C.E. and, like his new wife, had been brought up since childhood in Rome. Augustus was fond of him and, before becoming emperor, had granted him Roman citizenship and had taken him on some of his campaigns.

Juba was an extraordinarily cultured man who wrote many books, all now lost. He and Cleopatra brought Roman and Greek culture to Mauritania. They had a son named Ptolemy who succeeded his father as king and ruled until 40 C.E. He was killed on orders of the emperor Gaius Caligula, who wanted his wealth. They also had a daughter, DRUSILLA (1), who married Marcus Antonius Felix, a freedman of the younger ANTONIA, the mother of the emperor Claudius. As procurator of Judaea, Felix was the judge at the trial of St. Paul.

Cleopatra issued coins in her own name with Greek inscriptions. Her husband's coins were in Latin. She was the last Cleopatra, and her son was the last royal Ptolemy. It is not known when she died, but the iconography of her coins suggests she might have been alive as late as 11 C.E.

Sources

Josephus. *Antiquitates Judaicae (Jewish Antiquities)* 13.420.
Josephus. *Bellum Judaicum (Jewish Wars)* 1.116.
Tacitus. *Historiae* 5.9.
Balsdon, J. P. V. D. *Roman Women.* New York: John Day Comp., 1963, index.
Grant, Michael. *The Jews in the Roman World.* New York: Charles Scribner's Sons, 1973, p. 159.
Macurdy, Grace. *Hellenistic Queens.* Reprint. Chicago: Ares Publishers, 1985, index.
Oxford Classical Dictionary, ed. by Simon Hornblower and Antony Spawforth. 3d. ed. New York: Oxford University Press, 1996, p. 347.
Roller, Duane W. *The World of Juba II and Kleopatra Selene: Royal Scholarship on Rome's African Frontier.* New York: Routledge, 2003.

◉ Cleopatra Thea

(second century B.C.E.) Greek: Egypt and Syria
coruler

Cleopatra Thea was used by her father to enhance his power in Syria and then took control of her own destiny and sought to find an able man to rule the Seleucid Empire. She was the daughter of CLEOPATRA II PHILOMETOR SOTEIRA. Her father was her mother's brother and husband Ptolemy VI Philometor.

In 162 B.C.E., Demetrius I Soter gained control over Syria, but he soon became unpopular. Alexander Balas, an impostor who bore a remarkable resemblance to Antiochus IV, the former ruler of Syria, was put forward as the rightful heir. In exchange for influence and possibly even territory, Ptolemy VI arranged for Alexander's marriage with Cleopatra Thea. Alexander Balas defeated Demetrius with support from Egypt, Pergamum, and the Jews. He and Cleopatra Thea had a son, Antiochus.

Alexander proved to be an incompetent ruler who immersed himself in luxurious living and debauchery. In 147, Demetrius II, the eldest son of the defeated Demetrius I, led an army of mercenaries from Crete into Syria. At this point, Ptolemy VI quarreled with Alexander and recalled his daughter. Cleopatra Thea then married Demetrius II, who was several years her junior.

Alexander was defeated. Forced to flee, he took his and Cleopatra Thea's son, whom he left with desert chiefs. Ptolemy persuaded the people of Antioch to recognize Demetrius as ruler. Alexander returned to fight Demetrius. Alexander and Ptolemy VI died in battle.

The young Demetrius was another inept ruler. He too became highly unpopular, blamed for the persecution of Alexander Balas's supporters and the cruelty of his mercenary troops. Diodotus, the governor of Syria, gained possession of Cleopatra Thea's son, drove Demetrius from Antioch and proclaimed little Antiochus ruler. However, Diodotus had the

Cleopatra Thea and her son Antiochus VIII Grypus
(Date: 125 B.C.E.–121 B.C.E. 1977.158.705, Archives, American Numismatic Society)

boy murdered a year or two later since Antiochus was a threat to his power.

Cleopatra Thea, who had two sons with Demetrius, Seleucus V and Antiochus Grypus, accompanied her inept husband to Seleuceia-in-Pieria, a port city in Syria, after his defeat by Diodotus. In 139, her husband was captured by Mithradates and the Parthians. Fearing Demetrius lost and that Diodotus (now renamed Tryphon) might secure his position, she invited her brother-in-law, Antiochus VII Sidetes from Rhodes, to Sleuceia-in-Pieria to marry her and become ruler.

Sidetes accepted Cleopatra Thea's offer, was welcomed by the people, and proved to be an able ruler. In 138 he defeated Tryphon, who committed suicide. The couple returned in triumph to Antioch and order was restored to the rest of the country. Sidetes also reconquered Judaea. Cleopatra Thea gave birth to a son, Antiochus Cyzicenus.

Over the next several years nothing is known about Cleopatra Thea. Her husband, however, campaigned against the Parthians and among them discovered his brother Demetrius II alive. He had become a favorite of Mithradetes, who had

betrothed him to his daughter Rhodogune. Sidetes secured Demetrius's freedom before he died in battle in 129. Demetrius II returned to reign in Syria. It was at this time that Cleopatra Thea's mother Cleopatra II arrived in Antioch. She sought support from Demetrius II in her struggle with her husband/brother Ptolemy VIII Euergetes, who was also Cleopatra Thea's uncle. Cleopatra Thea hated Demetrius and certainly did not welcome her mother. Her mother, Cleopatra II, however, brought with her enough wealth to secure cooperation from Demetrius, who set out with an army to fight for her cause. The people of Antioch revolted as soon as he left.

Taking advantage of the situation in Antioch, and in revenge against Cleopatra II, Ptolemy VIII declared an impostor, Alexander Zebinas, ruler of Antioch in 128. Zebinas defeated Demetrius II. Demetrius fled to Ptolemais and sought refuge with Cleopatra Thea. She refused to receive him. She then arranged for his murder by the governor of Tyre. She also murdered their son Seleucus V

Cleopatra Thea and her first husband,
Alexander I Balas
(Date: 150 B.C.E.–145 B.C.E. 1959.124.2, Archives, American Numismatic Society)

lest he aspire to rule. Given the climate of the times, she might have been seeking to avert her death at Demetrius's hands, as he would no doubt have sought to avenge the earlier death of his father, Demetrius I.

Ptolemy VIII quarreled with Alexander Zebinas and switched his support to Cleopatra Thea, who became joint ruler of Syria with her son Antiochus VIII Grypus in 125. Cleopatra Thea issued silver coins with her head, name, and titles. She was the first Hellenistic woman ruler to strike coins in her own name. On later coins her head appeared with that of Grypus; her head, however, was in front of her son's.

In 123, she believed that she faced a final challenge to her position. CLEOPATRA TRYPHAENA, the daughter of Ptolemy VIII, and Grypus were betrothed. She was said to have offered her son a drink containing poison after he came in from a hunt. He became suspicious and offered her the drink instead. She refused. Afraid of her machinations, Grypus had her killed in 121 or 120 B.C.E.

Without her powerful presence neither of her sons, Grypus nor Antiochus IX Cyzicenus, were able to rule successfully. They waged war against each other, killed each other's wife, and succeeded in destroying the power of the Seleucids.

Sources

Appian. *Syrian Wars* 67–69.
Diodorus Siculus. *Library of History* 28; 32.9c; 33.
Josephus. *Antiquitates Judaicae (Jewish Antiquities)* 13.80–82, 109–110, 137, 221–222.
Justin. *Epitome* 39.2.
Livy. *From the Founding of the City* 60.
Downey, Glanville. *A History of Antioch in Syria from Seleucus to the Arab Conquest.* Princeton, N.J.: Princeton University Press, 1961, pp. 119–129.
Macurdy, Grace. *Hellenistic Queens.* Reprint. Chicago: Ares Publishers, 1985, index.

Cleopatra Tryphaena

(second century B.C.E.)
Greek: Egypt and Asia Minor
military leader

Cleopatra Tryphaena murdered her sister CLEOPATRA IV and was, in turn, murdered by her sister's husband. She was the daughter of CLEOPATRA III. Her father, Ptolemy VIII Euergetes II, was also her uncle. The viciousness of her relationship with her sister reflected their mother's earlier struggle for power.

In 125 B.C.E., her father had installed her aunt CLEOPATRA THEA as joint ruler of Syria with one of her aunt's sons, Antiochus VIII Grypus. Two years later, in 123, he arranged a marriage between Cleopatra Tryphaena and Grypus. Cleopatra Thea perceived the advent of another woman as a threat to her power. She sought to poison her son. He had her murdered in 121 or 120, and the marriage went forward. Cleopatra Tryphaena moved to Antioch.

Her father died in 116, and her mother forced an end to the marriage between Cleopatra Tryphaena's sister Cleopatra IV and her brother Ptolemy IX Soter II Lathyrus. Her sister went to Cyprus, where their mother had previously placed another brother in charge. There she raised a mercenary army, which she led to Antioch and offered to Grypus's half-brother, Antiochus IX Cyzicenus. She also married him. She was now her sister Cleopatra Tryphaena's enemy.

Grypus drove Cyzenicus out of Antioch in 112 and captured Cleopatra IV. Cleopatra Tryphaena could not have had any illusions about her sister or what she could buy with her wealth. She feared that her husband would become her sister's pawn. She insisted that Cleopatra IV be killed.

Cyzicenus later recaptured Antioch and killed Cleopatra Tryphaena to appease the spirit of his murdered wife.

Sources

Justin. *Epitome* 39.3.
Downey, Glanville. *A History of Antioch in Syria from Seleucus to the Arab Conquest.* Princeton, N.J.: Princeton University Press, 1961, pp. 127–128.
Macurdy, Grace. *Hellenistic Queens.* Reprint. Chicago: Ares Publishers, 1985, index.

Cleora

(fifth–fourth century B.C.E.)   Greek: Sparta
wife of ruler

Cleora was the wife of Agesilaus II of Sparta, who came to power in 399 B.C.E. She had two daughters,

Eupolia and Proanga, and a son, Archidamus, who succeeded his father in 360 B.C.E.

Sources

Plutarch. *Vitae Parallelae (Parallel Lives): Agesilaus* 19.5.

▣ Clodia (1)

(first century B.C.E.)   Roman: Rome
political wife

Clodia was the eldest of three sisters, all named Clodia, and the only one of them to lead a life free of notoriety. Her mother was from the powerful and aristocratic Metelli clan, and her father was Appius Claudius Pulcher, consul in 79 B.C.E. When Clodia married Quintus Marcus Rex, consul in 68, her father was still alive and the family intact. However, he died soon after and left debts that far outweighed assets. Even though her oldest brother assumed family responsibility and worked to restore their fortunes, it was a financial disaster for her two sisters, CLODIA (2) and CLODIA (3), and transformed their lives.

Sources

Pauly, A., G. Wissowa, and W. Kroll. *Real-Encyclopadie d. Classischen Altertumswissenschaft 1893–*. (Germany: multiple publishers) 72.

Syme, Ronald. *The Roman Revolution*. London: Oxford University Press, 1963, pp. 20, 23.

▣ Clodia (2)

(95 B.C.E.–?)   Roman: Italy
adventurer

Clodia was well born, smart, and educated. She lived her life with scant regard for tradition amid the rich, famous, and notorious in the last decades of the republic. One of six children, she was born in 95 B.C.E. into the aristocratic Metelli clan. Her mother's name is unknown. Her father was Appius Claudius Pulcher, consul in 79 B.C.E. He died in 76, leaving the family in poverty. Her eldest brother, Appius Claudius Pulcher, sought to restore the family's fortunes and was regarded as corrupt even in an age known for its corruption. Publius Clodius Pulcher, her younger brother, became tri-

bune, curried popular favor, and enforced populist laws with armed mobs.

With little more than her beauty and her brains, Clodia married her first cousin Quintus Metellus Celler by 62 B.C.E. and was widowed in 59, when her husband unexpectedly died before he assumed his proconsulship of Transalpine Gaul. Although it is unclear at what point she became part of the social set that included the well born, the notorious, the rich, and the cultured, she began an affair with the poet Gaius Valerius Catullus toward the end of her husband's life when she was about thirty-five years old, and Catullus, some 6 to 10 years younger.

Her lover was one of Rome's greatest poets, and his life marked the opening of the richest period in Latin poetry. Born around 85 B.C.E. in the vicinity of Verona, he lived his adult life primarily in Rome. He wrote in the years that preceded full-scale civil war, when festering political, social, and economic problems already made a patent mockery of the historical ideals of the republic. His poetry, built on Alexandrine literary traditions that had come into Roman culture from the East, often portrayed the political intrigue and gossip of the clannish Roman elite with a vivid and witty sting. Above all, however, his poetry recorded his love for Lesbia.

Lesbia was his name for Clodia. It was a reference to SAPPHO, the greatest woman poet of the ancient world, and a tribute to Clodia's beauty and intelligence. The Lesbia poems followed the demand of poetic love for a grand passion of a mostly unhappy kind and may or may not reflect a progression that fully matched the reality of their relationship. Catullus largely portrayed himself as an adoring lover who suffered the imperious and unfaithful attentions of his adored. He portrayed Lesbia as the dominant partner in the relationship and as a woman unlikely to surrender herself for very long to idylls of love with a poet.

The Lesbia poems also convey a timeless emotional reality. Catullus's aching love for Clodia/Lesbia stands historically marked by lyrical lines of wanting. The less ardent love of Lesbia/Clodia wraps itself around her demands for gifts of value and her calculated uses of the love-struck poet for her own ends. One of Catullus's repeated laments, and sometimes the subject of his most wickedly funny poems about Lesbia/Clodia, is her unwillingness to be faithful to him alone.

Among her other men was Marcus Caelius Rufus. Some 8 to 10 years her junior, Caelius was a part of the same social set. He had come to Rome as a protégé of Marcus Tallius Cicero and had been on the periphery of the conspirators around Lucius Sergius Catilina in 63 B.C.E. He held several political offices and was aedile under Cicero in Cilicia in 50. An acknowledged orator, he had a caustic wit and charm, and was a brilliant prosecutor.

Clodia began an affair with him after she was widowed, and the younger Caelius rented a house next door to her brother Publius. The relationship lasted about two years. It ended acrimoniously. In 56, Caelius was charged with a five offenses including killing the Egyptian ambassador, robbing Clodia, and attempting to poison her. Clodia was among those who brought the charges.

Both Clodia and her brother Clodius were enemies of the orator and statesman Cicero, consul in 63 B.C.E. Cicero had testified against Clodius after the Bona Dea scandal in 62 (see TERENTIA [1]) and had made clear his dislike for Clodia's lifestyle. Her brother gained revenge when he was tribune in 58 and passed a bill that exiled Cicero. Among Caelius's defenders was Cicero, only recently returned from exile and now presented with an opportunity to attack his enemy Clodia.

Cicero's speech in favor of Caelius was a model courtroom oration. Vivid, clever, and very funny, the speech destroyed Clodia's credibility and her reputation. Cicero addressed her as if he were her most illustrious ancestor, the famous censor Appius Claudius. He instantly reduced her, a woman close to 40 years old, to the status of a child whose behavior was unsuitable for a woman. Cicero accused her of behaving in the manner of a prostitute. He very carefully never accused her of actually being one, only of having a lifestyle associated with immoral women. He pointed to her household, to her travels to the resort town of Baiae, to her collection of jewels, and to her friendships with men. He described her as the Medea of the

Palatine who had led a mere youth astray, although Caelius was hardly an innocent. As a final blow, he insinuated that she and her brother, his sworn enemy, had an incestuous relationship.

Caelius was acquitted, and nothing more was heard of Clodia. However, the information in the speech, when viewed without malice, also makes clear that Clodia had succeeded. She used her beauty and brains to offset her father's financial debacle and lived an independent, rich, and varied life, loved by one of Rome's greatest poets and with close ties to her family, especially her brother Clodius.

Sources

Cicero. *Epistulae ad Atticum* 12.38, 42.

Cicero. *Pro Caelio, passim.*

Plutarch. *Vitae Parallelae (Parallel Lives): Cicero* 29.1–5.

Balsdon, J. P. V. D. *Roman Women.* New York: John Day Comp., 1963, pp. 54–55.

Bauman, Richard A. *Women and Politics in Ancient Rome.* London: Routledge, 1994, pp. 69–73.

Grimal, Pierre. *Love in Ancient Rome.* Trans. by Arthur Train, Jr. New York: Crown Publishers, 1967, pp. 148–156.

Oxford Classical Dictionary, ed. by Simon Hornblower and Antony Spawforth. 3d. ed. New York: Oxford University Press, 1996, p. 350.

Pauly, A., G. Wissowa, and W. Kroll. *Real-Encyclopadie d. Classischen Altertumswissenschaft 1893–.* (Germany: multiple publishers) 66.

Quinn, Kenneth, ed. *Catullus: The Poems.* 2d. ed. New York: St. Martin's Press, 1977, pp. 54–203.

▣ Clodia (3)

(first century B.C.E.)   Roman: Rome
convicted adulterer

Clodia was divorced for adultery after her brother incited rebellion among the troops under her husband's command. Her parents came from aristocratic families. Her mother's name is unknown, but it is certain that she came from the Metelli family. Her father was Appius Claudius Pulcher, consul in 79 B.C.E. Tragedy struck her family when her father died destitute in 76. She was the youngest of three sisters, all named Clodia. CLODIA (1) married Quintus Marcus Rex, consul in 68; CLODIA (2) was the lover of the poet Catullus, among others. Her youngest brother, Publius Clodius Pulcher, was a populist politician whose base of power lay with armed mobs and urban plebs.

Clodia married Lucius Licinius Lucullus, consul in 74. Her husband, a relative on her mother's side, was an able soldier, politician, and provincial administrator, lacking only the gift of evoking loyalty from troops and colleagues. He held military commands in Africa and Asia from which he greatly enhanced his personal wealth. He appears to have been among the few Romans of the time to have understood that strangling the cities with usurious interest rates, tax, or tribute to Rome was economically counterproductive. He successfully reorganized the debts owed Rome with a payment plan at moderate interest rates for the cities in the East.

Clodia's wealthy husband and her populist brother ran on a collision course. In 68 B.C.E., when her husband was in Armenia and his troops were ready to mutiny, her brother incited rebellion. The war had been longer than anticipated, and its end was not in sight. Although the army had gained significant victories, there was a sense that Lucullus had benefited far more than had the soldiers. This was just the kind of situation in which her brother thrived. Gifted with articulating the discontent of Romans, her brother also believed that Lucullus had failed to adequately reward him. Moreover, the leadership in Rome had turned against Lucullus. Led by the equites, whose incomes suffered from his financial reorganization, they successfully clamored for him to be relieved of his command.

Lucullus returned to Rome a frustrated and angry man who had to fight for a triumph. Shortly after he returned, he divorced Clodia for adultery. She had been in Italy for several years alone at a time when women were increasingly able to have independent social lives. Her sister Clodia (2) the lover of the poet Catullus, was part of a literary and social circle regarded by others as dissolute. With whom Clodia engaged in adulterous relationships is not clarified in the sources, which simply assert her immorality. Their hostility toward her probably reflects their conservative nature and is an extension of their view of her brother and sister.

Clodia had a son with Lucullus who died fighting on the side of Marcus Junius Brutus against Octavian and Mark Antony at Philippi in 42 B.C.E.

Sources
Cicero. *Pro Milone* 73.
Plutarch. *Vitae Parallelae (Parallel Lives): Lucullus* 34.1; 38.1.
Balsdon, J. P. V. D. *Roman Women.* New York: John Day Comp., 1963, p. 186.
Pauly, A., G. Wissowa, and W. Kroll. *Real-Encyclopadie d. Classischen Altertumswissenschaft 1893–.* (Germany: multiple publishers) 67.

Clodia (4)
(first century B.C.E.–first century C.E.) Roman: Rome
long-lived woman

Clodia was the wife of an otherwise unknown Claudius Aufilius during the late republic. She survived her husband and her 15 children. She was said to have died at the age of 115.

Sources
Pliny the Elder. *Naturalis Historia* 7.48, 158.
Pauly, A., G. Wissowa, and W. Kroll. *Real-Encyclopadie d. Classischen Altertumswissenschaft 1893–.* (Germany: multiple publishers) 68.

Clodia Laeta
(?–213 C.E.) Roman: Rome
priestess

Clodia Laeta was one of four Vestal Virgins accused of sexual misconduct in 213 C.E. by the emperor Marcus Aurelius Antoninus (Caracalla). Clodia protested, claiming that Antoninus knew her to be a virgin. Still, she and her three sister Vestals, AURELIA SEVERA, CANNUTIA CRESCENTINA, and POMPONIA RUFINA, were condemned. Clodia suffered the traditional punishment of being buried alive. In contrast with earlier times, the improprieties of Clodia and her sister Vestal Virgins raised few fears of omens of disaster for Rome. Nonetheless, loyalty to tradition survived religious faith and an expectation of chastity from the Vestals remained the norm.

Sources
Dio Cassius. *Roman History* 78.16.1–3.

Cloelia (1)
(sixth century B.C.E.)
Roman: Rome and Etruria
heroine

Cloelia led a group of Roman hostages to freedom. A heroine from the sixth century B.C.E., before the union of Etruria and Rome, she was among the hostages sent by Rome to the Etruscans as surety for a peace treaty. In a story that may well be apocryphal, Cloelia successfully organized some of the hostages to swim back to Roman territory across the Tiber. The furious Etruscan ruler, Porsenna, demanded that Cloelia be returned; but in admiration of her daring, he promised her safety.

Cloelia returned. Porsenna allowed her to chose one-half of the hostages to take back to Rome. With the approval of the hostages, she chose the younger boys, because, she argued, they were the most vulnerable. Cloelia was honored by the Romans with a statue on the Via Sacra.

Sources
Livy. *From the Founding of the City* 2.13.6–11.
Polyaenus. *Strategemata* 31.
Oxford Classical Dictionary, ed. by Simon Hornblower and Antony Spawforth. 3d. ed. New York: Oxford University Press, 1996, p. 254.

Cloelia (2)
(first century B.C.E.)   Roman: Rome
faultless wife; divorced

Cloelia suffered divorce from the future dictator Lucius Cornelius Sulla in 88 B.C.E., ostensibly because she was childless. Faultless in marriage, she secured Sulla's praise and gifts of value as part of the divorce. Within a few weeks of the divorce, her ex-husband married his fourth wife, CAECILIA METELLA (1), who was both very wealthy and better connected.

Sources
Plutarch. *Vitae Parallelae (Parallel Lives): Sulla* 6.10, 11.
Syme, Ronald. *The Roman Revolution.* London: Oxford University Press, 1963, p. 20.

Coesyra
(sixth century B.C.E.)   Greek: Athens
political wife

Coesyra was the daughter of Megacles from the aristocratic Athenian clan of the Alcmaeonidae and was ready for marriage at a critical political moment. In 560 B.C.E. her father and his ally Lycurgus had deposed Pisistratus, the tyrant of Athens. When the relationship between Lycurgus and Megacles soured, her father offered the deposed Pisistratus an alliance. Marriage with Coesyra sealed the bargain.

Pisistratus, however, already had grown sons and had neither the need nor the desire for more children—especially with Coesyra, for her family suffered under an ancient curse. An ancestor, also named Megacles, had been an archon in Athens in 632 B.C.E. He had promised to spare the lives of a group of men who had seized the Acropolis. Instead, he induced some of them to leave the sacred precinct of Athena and killed a number of others at the altar of Eumenides. No good would come of any descendants of Megacles, it was said.

Coesyra reported to her mother that her husband's sexual behavior inhibited conception. Her father again changed sides and joined the opposition that drove Pisistratus out of Athens.

Sources
Herodotus. *The Persian Wars* 1.60–61.

Constantia
(361/362–383 C.E.)   Roman: Italy
Augusta

Constantia's youth made becoming Augusta unlikely. She was the daughter of the empress Flavia Maxima FAUSTINA and the emperor Constantine II. She became Augusta after her husband, Gratian, became emperor in 379.

Constantia was born after her father died campaigning in 361. She lived with her mother in Constantinople. A usurper, Procopius, claimed to be emperor. With a few regiments under his control, he captured Constantinople. To gain some legitimacy and to curry favor with the troops, he took the four-year-old Constantia and her mother captive. He displayed them on marches with his troops, sometimes taking them almost into battle. He was soon overthrown by Gratian.

Constantia married Gratian in 374 and died before her husband in 383.

Sources

Ammiamus Marcellinus. *Histories* xxi. 15, 6; xxvi. 7, 10; 9, 3.

Brill's New Pauly: Encyclopedia of the Ancient World: Classical Tradition, Vol. 3, edited by Manfred Landfester et al. Boston: Brill, 2002, 708–709 (names her Constantina).

Prosopography of the Later Roman Empire. Vol. I. Edited by A. H. M. Jones, J. R. Martindale, and J. Morris. Cambridge: Cambridge University Press, 1971. Reprinted 1992, p. 221.

▣ Constantia, Flavia Julia
(?–c. 329 C.E.)
Roman: Italy, eastern Roman Empire, and Rome
Augusta; early Christian

Flavia Julia Constantia, a half sister of the emperor Constantine the Great, was a participant in the political and religious controversies of the early Christian church. She was greatly influenced by the Alexandrian priest Arius, whose teaching that Christ the Son was subordinate to God the Father was the most serious doctrinal controversy of the period. She was one of six children. Her father Constantius I had been appointed Caesar in the West under Maximian by the emperor Diocletian. Her mother was Flavia Maximiana THEODORA. In 313 C.E. Constantia married Valerius Licinius, the emperor of the East, to bolster his alliance with Constantine.

The marriage of Constantia and Licinius in Milan spurred Valerius Maximinus Daia to begin a war. His defeat left her husband and half brother the two supreme rulers of the empire, and Constantia became Augusta in the East. Using her position, she sought to foster a reconciliation in the church. She corresponded with Bishop Eusebius of Caesarea, a leader of the Arian sect and today recognized as the church's first historian, and brought Eusebius to meet with Arius before the Council of Nicaea in 325.

The alliance between her half brother and husband faltered, and Constantine defeated her husband in battle at Chrysopolis in 324. She fled with her husband but intervened with her brother and secured her husband's freedom. Her efforts were short-lived. Her husband, allowed to rule over a much smaller area with its capital at Nicomedia in Asia Minor, was later put to death after being accused of plotting against Constantine.

After the death of her husband, she and her two children, Licinius and Helena, returned to Rome and lived in Constantine's court. She exercised sufficient influence for her half brother to mint coins with her likeness and to name the port city of Gaza after her. Her work with church leaders continued. She was present at the Council of Nicaea in 325 and persuaded her Arian friends to formally recognize the doctrine of the unity of God the Father and Son, and to take confession. She died about 329. Her young son, Licinius, was executed on orders of Constantine for unknown reasons.

Sources

Eutropius. *Breviarium ab urbe condita* 10.5, 6.

Pauly, A., G. Wissowa, and W. Kroll. *Real-Encyclopadie d. Classischen Altertumswissenschaft 1893–.* (Germany: multiple publishers) 13.

▣ Constantina
(?–354 C.E.)
Roman: Italy, Asia Minor, Antioch
Augusta

Constantina, the eldest daughter of the Augusta FLAVIA MAXIMA FAUSTA and the emperor Constantine the Great, was cruel. Perhaps because her father executed her mother for reasons unknown in 326 when she was young.

She married her first cousin King Hanniballianus, who was the son of her father's brother. In 335, her father made her Augusta. Constantine also gave her husband control of Pontus, Armenia Minor, and Cappadocia in Asia Minor. After the death of Constantine in 337, the army mutinied and murdered a number of high-ranking officials including King Hanniballianus.

The three sons of Constantine, Constantine, Constantius, and Constans, fought over the empire. Constans, the youngest, defeated Constantine, the eldest, who died during the battle. Constans now controlled two-thirds of the empire. In 350, he was killed in a palace revolution by Magnentius, one of his senior officers, who offered to marry Constantina. Her remaining brother, Constantius, refused the alliance. Constantina encouraged Vetranio, Master of Soldiers, to take sides against Magnentius, who was eventually defeated. She then married Flavius Claudius Constantius Gallus, another cousin and nephew of her father. Appointed Caesar in 351 by the remaining brother who had become Constantine II, they resided in Antioch where they spied on everyone and executed anyone who they even suspected of slandering them. They caused such chaos that Constantine had Gallus killed.

Constantina went to visit her brother to secure his pardon, but contracted a fever and died in Bythnia, in northwest Asia Minor, in 354. Her remains were buried in Rome. The basilica of St. Agnes was built by her, and she founded a monastery in Rome.

Sources
Ammiamus Marcellinus. xiv. 1, 1; 7, 4; 9, 3; 11, 6, 22.
Philostorgius. *Historia Ecclesiastical* 3, 22.
Valesius. Excerpts 5, 14–15.
Bleckmann, Bruno. "Constantina, Vetranio, and Gallus Caesar." *Chiron* 24 (1994): 30 ff.
Brill's New Pauly: Encyclopedia of the Ancient World: Classical Tradition, Vol. 3, edited by Manfred Landfester et al. Boston: Brill, 2002, p. 709.
Prosopography of the Later Roman Empire. Vol. I. Edited by A. H. M. Jones, J. R. Martindale, and J. Morris. Cambridge: Cambridge University Press, 1971. Reprinted 1992, p. 222.

Corellia Hispulla
(first–second century C.E.)   Roman: Italy
affluent woman; litigant

Corellia Hispulla, the daughter of HISPULLA and Corellius Rufus, enjoyed a lifelong friendship with Pliny the Younger. They engaged in business and shared family successes and concerns. Corellia married their mutual friend Mucinius Justus. Throughout her life she bought and sold shares in property that she had inherited from family and friends. At one time she expressed an interest to Pliny in owning land on Lake Comum (Como). Instead of disposing of a recent legacy of five-twelfths of an estate, he offered it to Corellia at whatever price she wished to pay. She gave him 700,000 sesterces for the land. Later, when she found out that Pliny could have received 200,000 more, she offered him the difference, but he refused.

In the legalistic society of the first century C.E., many if not most propertied people probably found themselves in court at one time or another. Pliny defended Corellia in a suit brought against her by the consul-elect Caecilius. The content of the suit is unknown, but Pliny maintained friendly relations with Caecilius. After her husband's death from painful gout, she assumed responsibility for her children and continued to correspond with Pliny about their education.

Sources
Pliny the Younger. *Epistulae* 1.12; 3.3; 4.17; 7.11, 14.

Corinna
(third century B.C.E.)   Greek: Tanagra
poet

Corinna was a poet from Tanagra, in Greece, who probably lived in the third century B.C.E. Her parents were Procatia and Acheloadorus. She wrote lyric poems in a local Boeotian dialect. Her subjects were the legends of gods and heroes presented in a simple and straightforward narrative without metaphors or similes. Unlike SAPPHO's work, her poetry was neither passionate nor personal.

In the works of Pausanius and Plutarch there are references to her life that place her in the sixth century B.C.E. as a contemporary of the Greek poet Pindar, against whom she was said to have won five competitions. Pausanius wrote that in her tomb at Tanagra there was a painting that portrayed her in the gymnasium at Thebes binding her hair with a fillet in honor of her victory over Pindar. He credited her victory to her beauty and to the Aeolian dialect of her poetry, which he claimed was understood better than the Doric used by Pindar. However, her name first appeared in the first century B.C.E., possibly as a later addition to the compendium of women poets originally collected by the Alexandrians. The third century B.C.E. is now considered a more likely time period for her life.

Knowledge of her poetry has come mainly from papyrus texts written in the first three centuries C.E. Propertius and Ovid, Roman poets of the first century C.E., named their poetic lovers Corinna in celebration of her beauty, gracefulness, and intelligence.

Sources

Ovid, *passim*.

Pausanias. *Description of Greece* 9.22.3.

Propertius. *Elegies passim*.

Campbell, David A. *Greek Lyric*. 5 vols. Cambridge: Harvard University Press, 1982–93, pp. 1–3, 19–23.

Fantham, Elaine, et al. *Women in the Classical World*. New York: Oxford University Press, 1994, pp. 166–167.

Oxford Classical Dictionary, ed. by Simon Hornblower and Antony Spawforth. 3d. ed. New York: Oxford University Press, 1996, p. 290.

Page, Denys L. *Corinna*. London: Society for the Promotion of Hellenic Studies, 1953.

Pomeroy, Sarah B. *Goddesses, Whores, Wives, and Slaves: Women in Classical Antiquity*. New York: Schocken Books, 1975, p. 52.

▣ Cornelia (1)

(second century B.C.E.)   Roman: Rome
political player

Cornelia was widowed after her husband killed her nephew and then committed suicide. She was the elder daughter of AEMILIA TERTIA and the great Publius Cornelius Scipio Africanus Major, the conqueror of Hannibal and sister of CORNELIA (2).

Her father was attracted to Greek philosophy and literature, and educated his children, including his daughters, in the controversial new learning of the period.

Cornelia married a cousin, Publius Cornelius Scipio Nasica, consul in 138 B.C.E. Her husband and her nephew Tiberius Sempronius Gracchus, the son of her sister Cornelia (2), were opponents. Faced with a growing landless population that collected in Rome, Tiberius and his brother Gaius led the effort to reform the use of public land and forgive debts. Their powerful opposition was led by conservative landed interests. Cornelia's conservative husband was in the forefront of the mob that killed Tiberius.

Scipio Nasica left Rome to escape popular anger. Eventually he committed suicide in Pergamum. Cornelia remained in Rome and later lived with her mother on their estates in Southern Italy.

Sources

Plutarch. *Vitae Parallelae (Parallel Lives): Tiberius Gracchus* 19.1–6; 21.3–4.

Pauly, A., G. Wissowa, and W. Kroll. *Real-Encyclopadie d. Classischen Altertumswissenschaft 1893–*. (Germany: multiple publishers) 406.

Richardson, Keith. *Daggers in the Forum: The Revolutionary Lives and Violent Deaths of the Gracchus Brothers*. London: Cassell, 1976, pp. 94–95.

▣ Cornelia (2)

(c. 190s–121 B.C.E.)   Roman: Italy
political player

Cornelia was both formidable and influential. Born in the 190s B.C.E. into one of Rome's most distinguished families, Cornelia was the second daughter of AEMILIA TERTIA and the general who had conquered Hannibal, Publius Cornelius Scipio Africanus Major. Her father was attracted to Greek culture and gave his daughters, Cornelia and her sister CORNELIA (1), an education in Greek literature and philosophy, which was still unusual even for men. She married only once, raised her children as a widow, and bore the death of both her sons with courage and fortitude.

Cornelia was a wealthy woman. She received 25 talents from her mother on her marriage and another 25 talents after her mother's death. She married well, the wealthy and much older Tiberius Sempronius Gracchus who was comfortable with an unusually well-educated wife. He was a fine soldier and an excellent provincial governor, consul twice, in 177 and 163, and censor in 169. Her marriage gave rise to an apocryphal story. As repeated by the historian Livy, Cornelia's father arranged her marriage at the urging of Roman senators without the prior approval of her mother. Her mother, furious at not having been consulted, only forgave her husband when she discovered that the bridegroom was the illustrious Tiberius Sempronius Gracchus.

Her husband died in 154 b.c.e., and Cornelia became a sought-after widow. She remained interested in the East, and Ptolemy VIII Physcon, ruler of Cyrene, offered her marriage in 154. Almost continually at odds with his older brother, Ptolemy VI Philometor, he no doubt rightly believed that his influence in Rome would be greatly enhanced through a marital alliance with Cornelia. So too would his purse. After her husband's death, however, Cornelia devoted herself to her children and managing her estates. She employed Greek tutors for her children to provide an education for them like her own in philosophy and mathematics. In a famous story that is most probably apocryphal, when a visitor, possibly Ptolemy, displayed to her a collection of magnificent jewels, Cornelia pointed to her children and replied that they were her jewels.

Of the 12 children she had borne before her husband's death, only three survived into adulthood. Her two sons, Tiberius and Gaius Gracchus became the most famous men of their day. They led Rome in an effort for land reform and debt forgiveness that would stem the growing problems of a landless urban poor. Both were killed, but not before politics had also rent the family. Her son Tiberius was killed by his political opponent and uncle, the husband of Cornelia's sister. Her only daughter, SEMPRONIA (1), married Scipio Aemilianus in 129, another opponent of the reforms. It was an unhappy marriage, and his sudden death provoked rumors that Sem-

pronia and Cornelia had murdered him. The two women were close and lived together after Sempronia was widowed.

Historians have differed over Cornelia's politics about land reform, which had so dominated the life and death of her sons. On one hand, in a fragment of a letter that she was purported to have written and that had been preserved by the historian Cornelius Nepos, she chastised her son Gaius for policies that were destroying the state. On the other hand, the validity of the letter has been seriously challenged since Nepos wrote at a time when the ruling oligarchy wanted the Gracchi discredited. Plutarch, moreover, reported that Cornelia hired men from abroad to come to Rome disguised as reapers and aid Gaius. What has never been disputed was her influence on the behavior of her children. Although Gaius attacked the tribune Marcus Octavius for his veto of Tiberius's agrarian reforms in 133 b.c.e., he also withdrew the bill that might have meant exile for the same tribune, claiming it was at the request of his mother.

After the assassination of Tiberius, Cornelia retired to her estate in Misenum on the Bay of Naples where she entertained notables of the day. While there, she received news of Gaius's death. Cornelia wrote voluminously, and her letters were published, although only the challenged fragment quoted by Nepos remains. She died in 121. The Romans honored her with a bronze statue.

Sources

Cicero. *Brutus* 104, 211.

Livy. *From the Founding of the City* 38.57.5–8.

Nepos. "Letter of Cornelia," in Horsfall, N., pp. 41–43.

Pliny the Elder. *Naturalis Historia* 34.31.

Plutarch. *Vitae Parallelae (Parallel Lives): Gaius Gracchus* 4.1; 13.2.

Plutarch. *Vitae Parallelae (Parallel Lives): Tiberius Gracchus* 1.4–5; 4.1–3; 19.1–6; 21.3–4.

Polybius. *Histories* 31.27.

Valerius Maximus. *Factorum et dictorum memorabilium libri IX* 4.4.

Bauman, Richard A. *Women and Politics in Ancient Rome.* London: Routledge, 1994.

Oxford Classical Dictionary, ed. by Simon Hornblower and Antony Spawforth. 3d. ed. New York: Oxford University Press, 1996, p. 392.

Pauly, A., G. Wissowa, and W. Kroll. *Real-Encyclopadie d. Classischen Altertumswissenschaft 1893–*. (Germany: multiple publishers) 407.

Stockton, David. *The Gracchi.* Oxford: Clarendon Press, 1986, pp. 24–25.

Cornelia (3)

(second–first century B.C.E.)   Roman: Rome
great-great-grandmother of Tiberius

Cornelia was the great-grandmother of the powerful, independent, and wealthy LIVIA DRUSILLA, the wife of Augustus and mother of the emperor Tiberius. Cornelia married Marcus Livius Drusus, consul in 112 B.C.E., who successfully opposed the election of Gaius Gracchus as tribune. Widowed during her husband's consulship, she also outlived her son, who was tribune in 91. Her son was assassinated after proposing reforms for which the ruling oligarchy would be credited.

Sources
Pauly, A., G. Wissowa, and W. Kroll. *Real-Encyclopadie d. Classischen Altertumswissenschaft 1893–*. (Germany: multiple publishers) 409.

Cornelia (4)

(second–first century B.C.E.)
Roman: Rome and Italy
businesswoman

Cornelia was the daughter of the Roman general and dictator Lucius Cornelius Sulla. In 82–81 B.C.E., her father led a ruthless proscription that solidified his power and eliminated key opposition families. Cornelia benefited from the sudden surplus of properties available on the market and bought for a relatively small sum a beautiful villa at Baiae, one of the most desirable locations on the Bay of Naples, which figured prominently in the lives of the Roman elite during the last century B.C.E. The property she acquired had once belonged to Gaius Marius, the brilliant general and major opponent of Sulla, who died in 86. Cornelia later sold the property to Lucius Licinius Lucullus, the husband of CLODIA (3), for some 33 times the original sum. This is an unusually vivid illustration of the inflation that accompanied life throughout the century and that was the cause of at least some of the political instability.

Cornelia was the wife of Quintus Pompeius Rufus, son of her father's coconsul in 88 B.C.E. With her husband, who was murdered at the end of 88, she had two children: Quintus Pompeius Rufus, tribune in 52, and POMPEIA (1), who became the wife of Julius Caesar and was a suspect in the Bona Dea scandal of 62.

In 51, her son became involved in a public trial and sought from her several farm properties that she held in trust for him. Initially she refused, but an emissary convinced her to change her mind. It remains unclear whether she was rapacious, as reported by the ancient commentator Valerius Maximus, or simply a good businesswoman.

She spent much of her life in Baiae and died there.

Sources
Plutarch. *Vitae Parallelae (Parallel Lives): Marius* 34.2.
Valerius Maximus. *Factorum et dictorum memorabilium libri IX* 4.2.7.
Pauly, A., G. Wissowa, and W. Kroll. *Real-Encyclopadie d. Classischen Altertumswissenschaft 1893–*. (Germany: multiple publishers) 412.

Cornelia (5)

(?–68 B.C.E.)   Roman: Rome
brave woman

Cornelia was the granddaughter of Lucius Cornelius Cinna, consul in 87–84 B.C.E. and political ally of the general Gaius Marius. In 84 she married Julius Caesar, the nephew of JULIA (1) and Marius. For both it was a first marriage. He was 16 years old; she was probably slightly younger. They had one daughter, JULIA (5).

These were difficult years. After Marius's death and Lucius Cornelius Sulla's victory over Cinna, Sulla initiated a proscription against Marian supporters. Cornelia was vulnerable. Caesar could provide little support. He had rejected Sulla's demand that he break with the Marian faction and divorce Cornelia. Stripped of his priesthood and forbidden his inheritance, he went into hiding and left Rome for Asia where over the next decade he studied and honed his military skills. Cornelia, despite her husband's proscription from public life and the loss of her dowry, remained in

Italy, if not Rome. Possibly she was aided by Caesar's aunt Julia.

Several years before Cornelia's death Sulla pardoned Caesar, and he returned to Rome and his wife. She died in 68 B.C.E. Caesar gave the funeral oration.

Sources

Plutarch. *Vitae Parallelae (Parallel Lives): Caesar* 1.1–2.
Suetonius. *The Lives of the Caesars: Caesar* 1.1–3.
Pauly, A., G. Wissowa, and W. Kroll. *Real-Encyclopadie d. Classischen Altertumswissenschaft 1893–*. (Germany: multiple publishers) 413.

Cornelia (6)

(first century B.C.E.)   Roman: Rome
cultured woman

Cornelia was the beautiful and cultured daughter of AEMILIA LEPIDA (1) and the corrupt Quintus Caecilius Metellus Pius Scipio, consul in 52 B.C.E. Said to be educated in mathematics and philosophy, she married Publius Licinius Crassus, the younger son of the triumvir, in 55 B.C.E. He died in 53 fighting the Parthians in Syria. The following year she married Gnaeus Pompeius (Pompey the Great). Her new husband sought an alliance with Cornelia's prominent, rich, and aristocratic family. He also rescued her father from a bribery charge and made him his coconsul.

The marriage was successful. When Pompey left Italy at the head of the republicans in 49, Cornelia and their young son, Sextus, went to the island of Lesbos. After Caesar defeated Pompey at Pharsalus in 48, Cornelia met her husband in Mitylene, the chief city of Lesbos. Together they sailed to Cilicia in southern Asia Minor and then to Egypt, where she witnessed his fatal stabbing as he landed on September 28, 48 B.C.E.

Cornelia left Egypt for Cyprus and then, with Caesar's permission, returned to Italy bearing her husband's ashes.

Sources

Appian. *Roman History: Bella civilian (Civil Wars)* 2.83, 85.
Plutarch. *Vitae Parallelae (Parallel Lives): Pompeius* 55, 66, 74, 76, 78–80.

Oxford Classical Dictionary, ed. by Simon Hornblower and Antony Spawforth. 3d. ed. New York: Oxford University Press, 1996, 392.
Pomeroy, Sarah B. *Goddesses, Whores, Wives, and Slaves: Women in Classical Antiquity*. New York: Schocken Books, 1975, p. 171.
Pauly, A., G. Wissowa, and W. Kroll. *Real-Encyclopadie d. Classischen Altertumswissenschaft 1893–*. (Germany: multiple publishers) 417.
Syme, Ronald. *The Roman Revolution*. London: Oxford University Press, 1963, p. 40.

Cornelia (7)

(c. 46 B.C.E.–?)   Roman: Rome
political wife

Cornelia was the daughter of POMPEIA (2) and Faustus Cornelius Sulla. Her grandfathers were Lucius Cornelius Sulla, the formidable dictator of Rome, and Gnaeus Pompeius (Pompey the Great), consul in 70 and the leader of the republican forces against Caesar.

Born no later than 46 B.C.E., she married Quintus Aemilius Lepidus and joined in the most politically active circle of women in Rome. Her father-in-law was a member of the Second Triumvirate, established in 43 B.C.E., together with Mark Antony and Octavian. Her mother-in-law, JUNIA (1), was the daughter of SERVILIA (1). Servilia, once the lover of Julius Caesar, was the half sister of Cato Uticensis, and the mother of Marcus Junius Brutus.

Cornelia's two children, AEMILIA LEPIDA (2) and Manius Aemilius Lepidus, consul in 11 C.E. survived the civil wars and became public figures in the early empire.

Sources

Tacitus. *Annales* 3.22.1.
Syme, Ronald. *The Augustan Aristocracy*. Oxford: Clarendon Press, 1986, index.

Cornelia (8)

(?–16 B.C.E.)   Roman: Rome
eulogized by Propertius

Cornelia was eulogized by Propertius in a long poem commissioned by her husband after her death in 16 B.C.E., during the consulship of her brother, Publius Cornelius Scipio. Presented in the form of a funeral oration or a long epitaph, Cornelia speaks for herself from the grave. She accounts for her life and measures herself against the highest of traditional Roman ideals. Proudly she describes herself as an *univira,* a woman married only once. She admonishes her two children to know their history and to carry on the noble family tradition, to assure the immortality of her name.

Cornelia gives her lineage on both her mother's and her father's side. She reaches back into Roman history of the second century B.C.E. and to her ancestor the great general Publius Cornelius Scipio Africanus Major, who conquered Hannibal. She identifies her parents as SCRIBONIA and her second husband, Publius Cornelius Scipio, consul suffectus in 35 B.C.E. She speaks movingly of her marriage and her husband, Paullus Aemilius Lepidus, consul suffectus in 34 and censor in 22. She figuratively soothes his sorrow and assures him that it will pass.

Cornelia was the half sister of JULIA (6). Her two sons were Lucius Aemilius Paullus, consul in 1 C.E., and Marcus Aemilius Lepidus, consul in 6 C.E. Lucius Aemilius Paullus married the grandaughter of Augustus, JULIA (7), in 4 B.C.E.

Sources

Propertius. *Elegies* 4.11.36, 61–72.
Pauly, A., G. Wissowa, and W. Kroll. *Real-Encyclopadie d. Classischen Altertumswissenschaft 1893–.* (Germany: multiple publishers) 419.
Syme, Ronald. *The Augustan Aristocracy.* Oxford: Clarendon Press, 1986, index.

▣ Cornelia (9)

(first century B.C.E.–first century
C.E.)   Roman: Rome
loyal wife

Cornelia, a member of the Scipiones family, married Lucius Volusius Saturninus, consul in 3 C.E. In 24 C.E., when her husband was 62, she bore him a son, Quintus Volusius Saturninus, who became consul in 56. Her husband died in the year his son became consul when he was 93 years old.

Sources

Pliny the Elder. *Naturalis Historia* 7.62.
Pauly, A., G. Wissowa, and W. Kroll. *Real-Encyclopadie d. Classischen Altertumswissenschaft 1893–.* (Germany: multiple publishers) 423.
Syme, Ronald. *The Augustan Aristocracy.* Oxford: Clarendon Press, 1986, pp. 252 ff.

▣ Cornelia (10)

(first century C.E.)   Roman: Rome
priestess

Cornelia received a dowry of 2 million sesterces when she became a Vestal Virgin in 23 C.E. The commitment to the priesthood was optional after 30 years. Since Cornelia became a priestess at a young age, she could later marry. Moreover, her wealth would remain intact throughout her priestly years, and she could leave the priesthood a very wealthy woman.

Sources

Tacitus. *Annales* 4.16.
Pauly, A., G. Wissowa, and W. Kroll. *Real-Encyclopadie d. Classischen Altertumswissenschaft 1893–.* (Germany: multiple publishers) 422.

▣ Cornelia (11)

(first century C.E.)   Roman: Rome, Germany
adulterer

Cornelia went to Germany with her husband, Gaius Calvisius Sabinus, consul in 26 C.E. and then governor of Pannonia. Although by this time it was not uncommon for wives accompany their husbands, military camps at night were largely off-limits to women. With the complicity of the tribune Titus Vinius, Cornelia entered the camp after dark disguised as a soldier. She watched the drills and, according to Tacitus, committed adultery in the general's headquarters.

Returning to Rome in 39 C.E., Cornelia was charged with accompanying the sentries on their rounds and watching them drill. Her husband was accused of abetting her. They both committed suicide before the trial.

Sources

Dio Cassius. *Roman History* 59.18.4.
Tacitus. *Historiae* 1.48.

Pauly, A., G. Wissowa, and W. Kroll. *Real-Encyclopadie d. Classischen Altertumswissenschaft 1893–.* (Germany: multiple publishers) 424.

Cornelia (12)

(?–90 C.E.)   Roman: Rome
priestess

Cornelia was the head of the college of Vestal Virgins when the emperor Domitian began a purity campaign in 83 C.E. to improve public morality. He attacked the Vestal Virgins and the temple in the Forum as a sinkhole of immorality that had existed from before his reign. Three of the Vestal Virgins, the two sisters OCULATA and VARRONILLA, were forced to choose how they should die. Cornelia was found innocent of any charges.

Domitian was determined that she be found guilty. He renewed the charges in 90 and convened the pontiffs at his villa in the city of Alba Longa, some 15 miles southeast of Rome, rather than in the pontifical court in Rome. Cornelia was condemned and sentenced to death for incest without being present to rebut the charges. Such was Domitian's hostility to Cornelia that he also decreed that the punishment should be entombment while still alive, instead of allowing her to choose her own manner of death.

Cornelia protested her innocence as she was led to her burial place. Celer, the Roman equestrian accused of consorting with her, protested his innocence as he was whipped to death in a public square.

Sources

Pliny the Younger. *Epistulae* 4.11 ff.
Suetonius. *The Lives of the Caesars:* Domitian 8.
Balsdon, J. P. V. D. *Roman Women.* New York: John Day Comp., 1963, p. 241.
Pauly, A., G. Wissowa, and W. Kroll. *Real-Encyclopadie d. Classischen Altertumswissenschaft 1893–.* (Germany: multiple publishers) 426.

Cornificia

(?–211 C.E.)   Roman: Rome
political victim

Cornificia was the daughter of the younger Anna Galeria FAUSTINA and the emperor Marcus Aure-

lius. A period of unrest followed her father's death in 180 C.E. In 193 Septimius Severus became emperor. He died in 211 leaving two sons who hated each other; the brothers, Marcus Aurelius Antoninus known as Caracalla, and Septimius Geta, quarreled over succession.

Their mother was JULIA DOMNA, with whom Cornificia maintained at least a formal friendship. Julia Domna sought to mediate between her sons. After calling for a meeting with Geta and his mother, Caracalla instead sent centurions who murdered Geta in his mother's arms. Cornificia visited Julia Domna to mourn Geta's death. Caracalla took offense. Geta, he claimed, had committed treason, and anyone who wept for his death also committed treason.

He ordered that Cornificia die. She was allowed to commit suicide. Cornificia opened her veins and went to her death mindful that she was a daughter of the great emperor Marcus Aurelius, and calling upon her spirit that was soon to be free of her body.

Sources

Dio Cassius. *Roman History* 78.16.6a.
Herodian. *History of the Empire* 4.6.3.
Balsdon, J. P. V. D. *Roman Women.* New York: John Day Comp., 1963, p. 154.

Cratesicleia

(third century B.C.E.)
Greek: Sparta and Egypt
reformer

Cratesicleia was a Spartan aristocrat who gambled her life and fortune in support of reform during the third century B.C.E. She was the wife of the Spartan ruler Leonidas II, who led a conservative faction that opposed debt relief or land and citizenship reform. Her son Cleomenes III (260–219 B.C.E.), who followed his father in 235, pursued reformist policies. To support him, Cratesicleia pooled her property with that of other family members and allowed a redistribution of the land to ease the burden of debt that was driving many into poverty.

Although she did not seek a second husband, a marital alliance with Aristonous X assured her son support from one of the most prominent citizens of Sparta. When Cleomenes sought the aid of Ptolemy III Euergetes of Egypt in a war against Antigonus III, ruler of Macedonia, Ptolemy demanded Cratesicleia and Cleomenes' children as hostages. Willingly she went.

After Cleomenes' defeat in 222 B.C.E., he went to Egypt where Ptolemy III promised ships and money. Ptolemy III died in 221, and his successor, Ptolemy IV Philopator, was no friend. Cleomenes led a group of Spartans in an attack to free the hostages. They killed a number of Egyptians but failed to ignite a revolt in Alexandria. Rather than face capture, Cleomenes and his soldiers killed themselves.

Ptolemy IV ordered Cratesicleia, her women attendants, and her grandsons killed. Although she requested that she die first, she was the last to be killed.

Sources

Plutarch. *Vitae Parallelae (Parallel Lives): Cleomenes* 6.1–2; 11.1–2; 22.3–7; 38.3–6.
Mosse, Claude. "Women in the Spartan Revolutions of the Third Century B.C." In *Women's History and Ancient History,* ed. by Sarah B. Pomeroy. Chapel Hill: University of North Carolina Press, 1991, pp. 145–146, 148.

▣ Cratesipolis

(fourth century B.C.E.)   Greek: Sicyon
ruler

Cratesipolis became ruler of the Greek city of Sicyon in 314 B.C.E. after the death of her husband, Alexander, the son of Polyperchon—a general under Alexander the Great. On her husband's death, she was welcomed by the soldiers, who esteemed her highly for her acts of kindness, her practical skills, and her daring.

When the people of Sicyon revolted, she crushed the rebellion. The name Cratesipolis, meaning conqueror of the city, was conferred on her after her victory. She also ruled Corinth until she was defeated by Ptolemy I Soter in 308.

Sources

Diodorus Siculus. *Library of History* 19.67.1–2; 22.37.1.
Macurdy, Grace. *Hellenistic Queens.* Reprint. Chicago: Ares Publishers, 1985, pp. 106, 233.

▣ Crispina

(first century C.E.)   Roman: Rome
brave woman

Crispina ransomed her father's body after his death. Her father, Titus Vinius, consul in 69 C.E., was a close adviser of the emperor Servius Sulpicius Galba. He was murdered by the soldiers of Marcus Salvius Otho when they assassinated Galba in 69. Taking responsibility for the burial rites, she negotiated payment with the slayers and retrieved his body.

Sources

Tacitus. *Historiae* 1.47.

▣ Crispina Bruttia

(second century C.E.)   Roman: Rome
political player

Crispina Bruttia lived and died by intrigue. Her father was Gaius Bruttius Praesens, consul in 180 C.E., and her husband, Lucius Aelius Aurelius Commodus, was the elder son of the emperor Marcus Aurelius. She married in 177, the same year that her husband became joint ruler with his father. Three years later, after the death of her father-in-law, her husband became emperor.

Her sister-in-law Annia Aurelia Galeria LUCILLA vied with Crispina for position and influence. About 182, Lucilla organized a plot to assassinate her brother. It failed. She was exiled and then executed. In 187, Crispina suffered a similar fate. She was found guilty of adultery and banished to Capri, where she was killed.

Sources

Dio Cassius. *Roman History* 72.33.1; 73.6.
Herodian. *History of the Empire* 1.8.4.
Scriptores Historiae Augustae. Commodus 5.11.
*Scriptores Historiae Augustae.*Marcus Aurelius Antoninus (Caracalla) 27.8.
Balsdon, J. P. V. D. *Roman Women.* New York: John Day Comp., 1963, pp. 147–148.

Pauly, A., G. Wissowa, and W. Kroll. *Real-Encyclopadie d. Classischen Altertumswissenschaft 1893–*. (Germany: multiple publishers) 17.

◫ Cynane
(?–322 B.C.E.)
Greek: Macedonia and Asia Minor
political player

Cynane vied with OLYMPIAS (1) to rule Macedonia after the death of Alexander the Great. She and Alexander were half-siblings through their father, Philip II. Her mother was Audata from Illyria along the Adriatic Sea opposite Italy. Cynane was said to have fought by the side of her father when he campaigned in Illyria, and she killed Caeria, an Illyrian woman ruler, in combat. She married Amyntas, Philip's nephew, and had a daughter, EURYDICE (ADEA) (2). Alexander had Amyntas killed, probably to solidify his claim to Macedonia after his father's death. Cynane did not marry again.

Cynane was independently wealthy and after Alexander's death determined to use her daughter to lay claim to Macedonia. Her plan was simple: The generals had declared two children, Philip Arrhidaeus and Alexander IV, joint rulers of Macedonia in 323. Alexander was the son of Alexander the Great and ROXANE. He was an infant and fiercely protected by his mother. Philip Arrhidaeus, however, was the son of Philip II and PHILINNA, less protected and not fully competent. Cynane decided to marry her daughter Eurydice to Philip. In 322, she organized an army and took her daughter to Asia where Philip resided under the control of Alexander's general Antipater, who had been appointed regent for the two heirs.

Antipater failed to stop Cynane and her army from crossing the Strymon River. She came face to face with the Macedonian forces under Alcestas, who ordered her to withdraw or be killed. Cynane declared herself ready to die unless Alcestas met her demand that Philip Arrhidaeus marry Eurydice. On orders of Alcestas, she was killed before her own daughter and the Macedonian troops.

Shocked by what had happened, the troops threatened to revolt unless the marriage took place.

Perdiccas, who held the chief executive authority after the death of Alexander, acquiesced, even though he had hoped to marry CLEOPATRA (3), the daughter of Olympias and full sister of Alexander, and claim the Macedonian throne for himself.

Sources
Polyaenus. *Strategemata* 8.16.
Carney, Elizabeth D. "The Career of Adea-Eurydice," pp. 496–498.
Macurdy, Grace. *Hellenistic Queens*. Reprint. Chicago: Ares Publishers, 1985, pp. 48–52.
Pomeroy, Sarah B. *Women in Hellenistic Egypt*. New York: Schocken, 1984, pp. 6–7.

◫ Cynisca
(fourth century B.C.E.)   Greek: Sparta
self-made woman

Cynisca, a wealthy woman, was the daughter of the Spartan ruler Archidamus and the sister of Agis II, who succeeded her father. She was among the first women to breed horses and the first to gain an Olympic victory.

At the beginning of the fourth century B.C.E., when the owner of the horses and the racing driver no longer needed to be the same person, the races opened to women. Cynisca's horses won the four-horse chariot race and two other victories. Her name was inscribed on the victor lists. She erected a memorial of bronze horses at Olympia to celebrate her victory, as well a statue of herself in Elis sculpted by Apelles.

Sources
Pausanias. *Description of Greece* 3.8.1–2; 3.15.1; 6.1.6.
Harris, H. A. *Sport in Greece and Rome*. Ithaca, N.Y.: Cornell University Press, 1972, p. 178.
Pomeroy, Sarah B. *Goddesses, Whores, Wives, and Slaves: Women in Classical Antiquity*. New York: Schocken Books, 1975, p. 130.

◫ Cytheris Volumnia
(first century B.C.E.)   Roman: Rome
self-made woman

Cytheris Volumnia was a famous, beautiful, and wealthy freedwoman of the late Roman republic. A talented mime, she was the lover of several politically important men including Mark Antony and Marcus Junius Brutus. In a letter to his friend Lucius Papirius Paetus, written in 46 B.C.E., Marcus Tullius Cicero mentioned her presence at a dinner party he had attended. Years later, the poet Virgil composed his Tenth Eclogue on the theme of Cornelius Gallus's obsession with Cytheris.

Sources

Plutarch. *Vitae Parallelae (Parallel Lives): Antonius* 9.5.

Cicero. *De amicitia* 9.26.2.

Pomeroy, Sarah B. *Goddesses, Whores, Wives, and Slaves: Women in Classical Antiquity.* New York: Schocken Books, 1975, pp. 198–199.

D

Danae

(third century B.C.E.)   Greek: Athens and Syria
political player

Danae saved her lover and died a traitor. Her mother, LEONTION, rivaled Theophrastus, Aristotle's successor, as the leading philosopher in Athens. Her father, Metodorus, was the most important disciple of Epicurus. Her father died several years before his teacher, who took responsibility for Danae's future. In his will, Metodorus left Danae a dowry and instructions to his executors to arrange a marriage for her with another member of the Epicurean school when she came of age.

Nothing is known of the intervening years before Danae became the favored attendant of the powerful LAODICE I in Antioch. The very wealthy Laodice had established her own household after her husband, Antiochus II, had married a younger woman. Later reconciled with him, he mysteriously died before he could renege on his promise to appoint her son his heir.

Among the cities under Laodice's control was Ephesus. She appointed a man named Sophron to govern the city. He and Danae were lovers. For unknown reasons, Laodice became suspicious of Sophron and summoned him to Antioch, intending to kill him. Danae signaled him a warning during his audience with Laodice. Sophron grasped the situation and requested that Laodice give him two days to contemplate their discussion. He escaped. Later he helped the Egyptians take Ephesus and became a commander in the Egyptian navy.

Laodice discovered Danae's treachery and ordered her thrown off a cliff. While she was being led to her death, Danae was reputed to have said that it was no wonder the gods were despised. She had saved her lover and was to be killed, while Laodice had murdered her husband and was rewarded with glory and a kingdom.

Sources

Athenaeus. *Deipnosophistae* 593c–d.
Diogenes Laertius. *Lives of the Eminent Philosophers* 10.19–20.
Macurdy, Grace. *Hellenistic Queens.* Reprint. Chicago: Ares Publishers, 1985, pp. 85–86.

Deinomache

(fifth century B.C.E.)   Greek: Athens
mother of Alcibiades

Deinomache was the daughter of Megacles of the aristocratic family of the Alcmaeonidae. She married Cleinias, who outfitted a trireme and fought against the Persians at Artemisium in 480 B.C.E. Widowed in 447 when her husband was killed in a battle with the Boeotians, she had a son, Alcibiades, known for his beauty, his treachery, and his leadership of the Athenians.

Sources

Plutarch. *Vitae Parallelae (Parallel Lives): Alcibiades* 1.1.

◉ Demarete
(fifth century B.C.E.)   Greek: Syracuse
political player

Demarete was immortalized on coins issued by her husband, Gelon, who ruled Gela and Syracuse, two of the greatest Hellenic cities in Sicily during the fifth century B.C.E. Demarete was the daughter of Theron (488–472 B.C.E.), who ruled Acragas located in southwest Sicily. After she married Gelon, he conquered Syracuse in 485 and made it his seat of power.

An alliance between Demarete's father and husband defeated the invading Carthaginians under Hamilcar at Himera. The victory was celebrated throughout the Greek world. Her husband issued celebratory coins in gratitude to the gods. The large silver decadrachms called Demareteia depicted Demarete on the reverse.

She and her husband were buried on her estate. A costly tomb, erected by the people, was destroyed by the Carthaginians in 396 B.C.E.

Sources

Herodotus. *The Persian Wars* 7.153–66.
Diodorus Siculus. *Library of History* 11.38.3–4.
Hammond, N. G. L. *A History of Greece.* Oxford: Oxford University Press, 1967, p. 270.

◉ Domitia
(?–59 C.E.)   Roman: Rome
political player

Domitia was contentious, proud, and unforgiving. She was the eldest daughter of ANTONIA THE ELDER and the arrogant Lucius Domitius Ahenobarbus, consul in 16 B.C.E. Augustus was her great-uncle and her grandparents were Mark Antony and OCTAVIA (2). She may have had two early marriages: to Decimus Haterius Agrippa, consul in 22 C.E., and to Quintus Junius Blaesus, consul suffec-

tus in 26 C.E. In a contentious suit against her brother, Gnaeus Domitius Ahenobarbus, consul in 32 C.E., she was defended by her third and last husband, the famous orator Gnaeus Passienus Crispus, consul in 44 C.E.

Domitia and her sister, DOMITIA LEPIDA, had opposed the marriage of their brother and the younger Julia AGRIPPINA. After her brother's death, Agrippina settled on Domitia's husband, Passienus Crispus, as a likely replacement. Dislike between the two women turned into enmity when Domitia and Crispus who divorced largely on account of Agrippina's interference.

In 54 Domitia Lepida was put to death by Agrippina. A year later, Domitia joined with an enemy of Agrippina, JUNIA SILANA, in a plot to turn Agrippina's son, the emperor Nero, against his mother. They planned to convince the emperor that his mother was conspiring with Rubellius Platus to supplant him. A freedman of Domitia, the actor Paris, carried the damning report about Agrippina to Nero. Nero ordered that his mother be killed. However, the prefect of the Praetorian Guard, Sextus Afranius Burrus, persuaded Nero that Agrippina be given a hearing. She managed to convince Nero of her innocence.

Although Domitia succeeded in outliving Agrippina, Nero had her poisoned in 59 C.E., when she was more than 60 years old, so that he could acquire her property.

Sources

Dio Cassius. *Roman History* 62.17.1–2.
Suetonius. *The Lives of the Caesars: Nero* 34.5.
Tacitus. *Annales* 13.19–21.
Balsdon, J. P. V. D. *Roman Women.* New York: John Day Comp., 1963, index.
Pauly, A., G. Wissowa, and W. Kroll. *Real-Encyclopadie d. Classischen Altertumswissenchaft 1893–.* (Germany: multiple publishers) 90.
Syme, Ronald. *The Augustan Aristocracy.* Oxford: Clarendon Press, 1986, index.

◉ Domitia Lepida
(?–54 C.E.)   Roman: Rome
political player

Domitia Lepida was the beautiful younger daughter of ANTONIA THE ELDER and the arrogant Lucius

Domitius Ahenobarbus, consul in 16 B.C.E. Her lineage was of the highest order. Her grandmother was OCTAVIA (2) and her great-uncle was Augustus. She inherited the traits of her father's family—pride in ancestry, arrogance, ambition, and an implacable hatred for enemies—which shaped a lifetime of conflict in the most intimate circles of imperial power. She vied with her daughter, the strong-willed Valeria MESSALLINA, and her sister-in-law, the younger Julia AGRIPPINA, for influence over the emperor Claudius.

Domitia Lepida, before she was 20 and sometime after the birth of Messallina, had been left a widow by Marcus Valerius Messalla Barbatus. Her second husband was Faustus Cornelius Sulla. They had a son, Faustus Sulla, consul in 52 C.E., and their marriage ended either by death or divorce.

The marriage of the emperor Claudius and her daughter Messallina placed Domitia in the privileged position of mother-in-law to the emperor and subsequently as grandmother to Britannicus, the heir apparent. In 41 Claudius arranged a third marriage for his widowed or divorced mother-in-law with his friend Gaius Appius Junius Silanus, consul in 28 C.E. The marriage may well have aroused Messallina's fears. Silanus, a good friend of Claudius and now the husband of her powerful and manipulative mother, posed a clear threat to her dominant position of influence over the aging emperor. A year after the marriage, in 42, Silanus was charged with treason and executed. Messallina and Narcissus, one of Claudius's powerful freedmen secretaries, had orchestrated his removal.

The resulting estrangement between mother and daughter was never healed. Although Domitia hurried to Messallina's side when her daughter was accused of treason for enacting a marriage ceremony with her lover, Gaius Silius, she simply advised her daughter to kill herself. Finally killed by one of the soldiers in 48 Domitia took her body for burial.

Years before her daughter's death, Domitia Lepida and her sister, DOMITIA, had opposed the marriage of their brother with the younger Agrippina. After her brother's death in 39, the widowed Agrippina was herself exiled by her own brother, the emperor Gaius Caligula. During her exile, Domitia had cared for her nephew, the future emperor Nero. Agrippina was recalled by Claudius in 41. She never forgave Domitia for opposing her marriage and now further resented any influence she might have acquired over Nero. When Agrippina married Claudius, her dislike for Domitia was further exacerbated by Domitia's relationship with Britannicus, Claudius and Messallina's son.

Agrippina, desirous of enhancing the position of her son Nero at the expense of Britannicus, and fearful that Domitia's influence with the elderly Claudius would favor Britannicus at the expense of Nero, arranged to have her old enemy found guilty of using magic and posing a threat to the peace in Italy by failing to curb the slaves on her estates in Calabria. She was put to death in 54 C.E.

Sources

Suetonius. *The Lives of the Caesars: Nero* 6.3; 7.1.

Tacitus. *Annales* 12.64–65.

Bauman, Richard A. *Women and Politics in Ancient Rome.* London: Routledge, 1994, index.

Levick, Barbara. *Claudius: The Corruption of Power.* New Haven, Conn.: Yale University Press, 1993, p. 76.

Pauly, A., G. Wissowa, and W. Kroll. *Real-Encyclopadie d. Classischen Altertumswissenschaft 1893–.* (Germany: multiple publishers) 102.

Syme, Ronald. *The Augustan Aristocracy.* Oxford: Clarendon Press, 1986, index.

Domitia Longina

(?–c. 140 C.E.)   Roman: Rome
Augusta

Domitia Longina lived a long life and was successful at imperial intrigues, including murder. She was the daughter of a distinguished general, Gnaeus Domitius Corbulo, whom the emperor Nero ordered to commit suicide in 66 C.E. She divorced her first husband, the patrician Lucius Aelius Lamia Aemilianus, at the insistence of the future emperor Domitian. She married Domitian in 70 C.E., and they had a son and a daughter, both of whom died. Domitian awarded her the title Augusta and divorced her. There were rumors that

Titus, the brother of Domitian, had been her lover. She appears to have taken as a lover the freedman actor Paris, who was the rage of Rome and a very desirable lover. Around 84, Domitian had Paris executed and remarried Domitia, claiming that it was the will of the people.

Domitia feared that Domitian would kill her. She joined a conspiracy that murdered her husband in 96. Domitia lived another 40 years and died shortly before 140. A temple in her honor was built in Gabii with a donation of 10,000 sesterces by one of her freedmen on the condition that a celebration would be held annually on her birthday.

Sources

Dio Cassius. *Roman History* 65.4; 67.3.1–2; 67.15.2.

Suetonius. *The Lives of the Caesars:* Domitian 1.3; 3.1; 14.1.

Suetonius. *The Lives of the Caesars:* Titus 10.2; 67.15.2–4.

Balsdon, J. P. V. D. *Roman Women.* New York: John Day Comp., 1963, pp. 131–132.

Pauly, A., G. Wissowa, and W. Kroll. *Real-Encyclopadie d. Classischen Altertumswissenschaft 1893–.* (Germany: multiple publishers) 103.

▣ Domitia Lucilla
(?–155/161 C.E.)   Roman: Rome
political player

Domitia Lucilla was a very rich woman at the center of a network of connected families that came to the fore under the emperor Trajan. According to her son, she was educated and also fluent in written Greek. She corresponded with Fronto, her son's teacher, and was a friend of his wife, Gratia, whom she invited in 143 C.E. to celebrate her birthday in Naples where she was staying with her son.

She had only one husband, Marcus Annius Verus, whose father, also named Marcus Annius Verus, was consul in 126 C.E. They had two children: a daughter, Annia Cornificia Faustina, and a son, Marcus Annius, born in 121. Marcus became the emperor Marcus Aurelius (161–180 C.E.) after he had been adopted by his aunt Annia Galeria, the elder FAUSTINA and her husband, the emperor Antoninus Pius.

Domitia Lucilla managed her own business affairs, especially after the death of her husband around 124. She had inherited her wealth from her mother, also named Domitia Lucilla, who had been adopted by her great-uncle Publius Calvius Tullus, consul in 109. The family's fortune had originated with her great-grandfather, Gnaeus Domitius Afer, an orator and businessman who had a large tile factory outside Rome.

She remained on good terms with both her children and gave advice on family affairs. When her daughter Faustina married, she asked her son to give his sister as a dowry the inheritance left to him by his father, since he would have his grandfather's fortune. Marcus agreed, noting that his sister should not be poorer than her husband.

Domitia Lucilla evidently was an influential woman. The future emperor Marcus Didius Julianus was brought up in her house, and she helped to secure his appointment to the Board of Twenty, a court that decided cases of inheritance. He later became a wealthy senator, and then emperor for a brief period. Domitia Lucilla died between 155 and 161 C.E.

Sources

Scriptores Historiae Augustae. Didius Julianus 1.3–4.

Scriptores Historiae Augustae. Marcus Aurelius Antoninus (Marcus Aurelius) 1.3.

Birley, Anthony Richard. *Marcus Aurelius: Emperor of Rome.* Boston: Little, Brown, 1966, index.

Oxford Classical Dictionary, ed. by Simon Hornblower and Antony Spawforth. 3d. ed. New York: Oxford University Press, 1996, p. 152.

▣ Domitia Paulina (1)
(first century C.E.)   Roman: Spain
political player

Domitia Paulina came from Cádiz in Spain; nothing is known of her parentage. She was the wife of Publius Aelius Hadrianus Afer. They had a daughter, DOMITIA PAULINA (2), and a son who became the emperor Hadrian. Domitia Paulina died when Hadrian was 10 years old, and Hadrian became a ward of the future emperor Trajan.

Sources

Scriptores Historiae Augustae. Hadrian 1.1–2.

Pauly, A., G. Wissowa, and W. Kroll. *Real-Encyclopadie d. Classischen Altertumswissenschaft 1893–.* (Germany: multiple publishers) 107.

▣ Domitia Paulina (2)

(?–130 C.E.)   Roman: Rome
political player

Domitia Paulina was the sister of the future emperor Hadrian and the daughter of Publius Aelius Hadrianus Afer and DOMITIA PAULINA (1). She married Lucius Iulius Ursus Servianus, who was about 30 years her senior. Trajan considered her husband a possible successor. Her husband, consul in 102, sought to further his prospects at the expense of his brother-in-law Hadrian, whom he accused of extravagance and debt. This turned out to be a serious error of judgment, especially once his brother-in-law became emperor.

When Paulina died in 130, Hadrian paid her no public honor. He also showed no favor to her grandson, Gnaeus Pedianus Fuscus, born to her daughter Julia. When he adopted Lucius Aelius as his successor, he had the already 90-year-old Servianus and his 18-year-old grandson Fuscus put to death for challenging the adoption.

Sources

Dio Cassius. *Roman History* 69.17.1–2.
Scriptores Historiae Augustae. Hadrian 1.1–2; 2.6; 15.8; 23.8.
Balsdon, J. P. V. D. *Roman Women.* New York: John Day Comp., 1963, p. 139.
Oxford Classical Dictionary, ed. by Simon Hornblower and Antony Spawforth. 3d. ed. New York: Oxford University Press, 1996, pp. 786–787.
Pauly, A., G. Wissowa, and W. Kroll. *Real-Encyclopadie d. Classischen Altertumswissenschaft 1893–.* (Germany: multiple publishers) 108.

▣ Domitilla, Flavia (1)

(first century C.E.)
Roman: Italy and North Africa
mother of two emperors

Flavia Domitilla was born in Ferulium, Italy. Her father, Flavius Liberalis, was a scribe or law clerk in a praetor's court. He went before a board of arbitration and successfully gained for her full Roman citizenship.

Before she married the future emperor Vespasian, Domitilla had a de facto marriage with Statilius Capella, a Roman equestrian from Africa. When she married Vespasian, he was an army officer. She had two sons, Titus and Domitian, and a daughter, Flavia Domitilla. Domitilla and her daughter both died before Vespasian became emperor in 69 C.E. Her sons, Titus and Domitian, succeeded their father.

Sources

Suetonius. *The Lives of the Caesars:* Vespasian 3.

▣ Domitilla, Flavia (2)

(first century C.E.)
Roman: Italy and Pandateria
political player, exiled

Flavia Domitilla was the niece of the emperor Titus Flavius Domitian. She married Flavius Clemens, the emperor's cousin. They had two young sons whom Domitian favored as successors. Shortly after her husband's consulship in 95 C.E., the couple was accused of denying the traditional gods in favor of Jewish or Christian rites. Her husband was executed, and she was exiled to Pandateria. Nothing more is heard of the children.

Sources

Dio Cassius. *Roman History* 67.14.1–3.
Grant, Michael. *The Jews in the Roman World.* New York: Charles Scribner's Sons, 1973, pp. 225–256.
Oxford Classical Dictionary, ed. by Simon Hornblower and Antony Spawforth. 3d. ed. New York: Oxford University Press, 1996, p. 600.
Pauly, A., G. Wissowa, and W. Kroll. *Real-Encyclopadie d. Classischen Altertumswissenschaft 1893–.* (Germany: multiple publishers) 227.

▣ Domnica

(c. fourth century C.E.)
Roman: Pannonia, Constantinople
Augusta

Domnica was in Constantinople on that fateful ninth of August in 378 when Valens, her husband and emperor, lost one of history's decisive battles and his life. Although the Eastern Roman Empire never fully recovered from the defeat at Adrianople, Domnica kept the victorious Goths from invading Constantinople. With the city under siege, Domnica withdrew from the treasury the money allocated for the army and distributed it among residents willing to defend the walls. She became the spirit of the city as the defenders piled rocks into huge barricades and mounted rock-throwing artillery on the perimeter walls. Relief finally came with Theodosius in the winter of 379 after Gratian, the emperor in the West, appointed him the new emperor of the East.

Domnica had exercised influence on her husband Valens throughout his reign. Appointed emperor in the East in 364 by his brother Valentinian I, Valens was never considered a skilled soldier. However, Domnica's father, Petronius, who Valens raised to the rank of patrician, was a military man who commanded the Martensian legion, named after the Babylonians who filled its ranks. According to sources he was also considered ugly in spirit and appearance and was extraordinarily avaricious, but loyal.

Domnica had already given birth to three children, Dominica, Anastasia, and Galates, by the time her husband became emperor. It was probably she who saw to the education of her children and also convinced Valens to be baptized an Arian Christian. His faith, which was apparently sincere, was tested while visiting Caesarea in 369 or 370, when their young son Galates fell critically ill. Valens summoned Basil, the bishop of Caesaria, to pray for his son's survival. Basil, an orthodox Christian, demanded that Valens renounce his Arian views. The emperor refused, and the boy died shortly after being baptized an Arian Christian.

Nothing more is known of Domnica.

Sources

Ammiamus Marcellinus. XXXI. 15, 1–12.
Socrates. *Historia Ecclesiastica* V, 1.3.
Sozimus. *Historia Ecclesiastica* VII, 1. 2.
Theodoret. *Historia Ecclesiastica* IV, 12. 3–4; 19. 8–9.

◉ Doris
(fifth–fourth century B.C.E.) Greek: Syracuse
political player

Doris married Dionysius I, the tyrant of Syracuse, in Sicily (c. 430–367 B.C.E.). She was the daughter of Xenetus, from the leading family of Locri in Greece. On the same day that she married Dionysius, he also married ARISTOMACHE, who came from Syracuse. Gossip circulated that Doris's mother gave Aristomache potions to prevent pregnancy and that Aristomache only became pregnant after Dionysius had Doris's mother killed.

Dionysius was said to have been devoted to his wives. He dined with them both and slept with each in turn. It was also said that Dionysius was so fearful of the women that he had each wife searched before going to bed with her.

Despite the great support for Aristomache among the people of Syracuse, on Dionysius's death, Doris's son Dionysius II succeeded his father.

Sources

Diodorus Siculus. *Library of History* 16.6.
Plutarch. *Vitae Parallelae: Dion* 6.3.
Valerius Maximus. *Factorum et dictorum memorabilium libri* IX 9.13.4.

◉ Drusilla (1)
(39 C.E.–?) Roman: Mauritania and Judaea
political wife

Drusilla was the granddaughter of CLEOPATRA VII and Mark Antony, the daughter of CLEOPATRA SELENE and Juba II, who ruled the Roman client state of Mauritania in North Africa. Born in 39 C.E., she married Marcus Antonius Felix, a freedman of the younger ANTONIA. Her husband was appointed procurator of Judaea sometime after 52.

After her death her husband married DRUSILLA (2), the daughter of Agrippa I, king of Judaea.

Sources

Josephus. *Antiquitates Judaicae (Jewish Antiquities)* 20.7.2.
Tacitus. *Historiae* 5.9.
Pauly, A., G. Wissowa, and W. Kroll. *Real-Encyclopadie d. Classischen Altertumswissenschaft 1893–*. (Germany: multiple publishers) 2.
Perowne, Stewart. *The Later Herods,* p. 59.

◉ Drusilla (2)
(first century C.E.) Jewish: Judaea and Rome
political player

Drusilla competed with her older sister, BERENICE (2), for influence, wealth, and power. A member of a great Jewish dynasty, she was the daughter of Cypros and Agrippa I, king of Judaea (41–44 C.E.), and the granddaughter of Mariamme and Herod the Great. Her brother, Agrippa II, ruled the territories north of Judaea and often was the focus of the sisters' conflict, especially after the twice-widowed Berenice went to live with him.

Drusilla married Azizus, ruler of Emesa, after he agreed to be circumcised and follow the Jewish faith. She left her husband to become the second wife of Marcus Antonius Felix, a freedman of the younger ANTONIA. Felix had been appointed procurator of Judaea by the emperor Claudius in 52 C.E. He remained procurator for eight years, and toward the end of his tenure, he presided over the preliminary hearing of Paul on charges of creating disturbances and profaning the Jewish Temple. Felix sought Drusilla's advice. Both listened to Paul testify.

Drusilla left Judaea for Rome with Felix at the end of his procuratorship and did not return. Felix's brother Pallas, an ally of the younger Agrippina, was Claudius's financial secretary and was among the richest, most powerful men in Rome. Drusilla used her influence to shield Felix when Pallas fell from power in Rome after the death of Agrippina.

Drusilla gave birth to a son named Antonius Agrippa, who died during the eruption of Vesuvius in 79.

Sources

Josephus. *Antiquitates Judaicae (Jewish Antiquities)* 19.354–55; 20.139, 141.
Tacitus. *Historiae* 5.9.
Grant, Michael. *The Jews in the Roman World.* New York: Charles Scribner's Sons, 1973, index.
Perowne, Stewart. *The Later Herods*, index.

▣ Drypetis

(fourth century B.C.E.)   Persian: Persia
political player

Drypetis was one of the daughters of Darius III, ruler of Persia, who was defeated by Alexander the Great. She was among some 80 women of the Persian aristocracy married to Macedonian officers of Alexander's army at Susa in 324 B.C.E. Drypetis married Hephaestion, Alexander's childhood friend and closest companion, while Alexander married her sister BARSINE (2).

After the deaths of Hephaestion later that year and Alexander in 323 B.C.E. Drypetis and her sister were murdered by ROXANE, the wife of Alexander, to eliminate any rivals to Roxane's infant son.

Sources

Arrian. *Anabasis of Alexander* 7.4.
Diodorus Siculus. *Library of History* 17.6.
Burn, Andrew Robert. *Alexander the Great and the Hellenistic World.* London: English Universities Press, 1964, p. 182.

▣ Duronia

(second century B.C.E.)   Roman: Rome
accomplice to embezzlement

Duronia was infatuated with her second husband, Titus Sempronius Rutilus, and abetted him in fraud. Rutilus was guardian for the estate of Publius Aebutius, Duronia's son by her first husband. He had misused the funds, and her son was about to come of age.

Duronia set about discrediting Aebutius so as to prolong Rutilus's guardianship and thereby avoid an accounting of the estate. She told her son that some while ago when he was seriously ill, she had taken a vow that if he recovered she would have him initiated into the rites of the Bacchae. In 186 B.C.E. Romans feared the Bacchic rites, which were secret, restricted to the young and virile, and generally regarded as licentious, even dangerous to the well-being of the state. Aebutius's initiation into the cult may well have been judged as leaving him unfit to assume responsibility over his own estate.

Aebutius, who appears to have been a somewhat naive young man, told his freedwoman lover HISPALA FAECENIA of his mother's vow. Before Hispala had gained her freedom, she had accompanied her mistress to the rites and knew the ceremonies to be not only licentious or dangerous but also violent. She convinced Aebutius to refuse his mother's request. Together they went to Aebutius's aunt, who in turn went to the consul. Aided by the testimony of Hispala Faecenia to the consul Postumius, a scandal with serious political implications was uncovered, and a number of people were executed. Exactly what happened to Duronia and her second husband, however, remains unknown.

Sources

Livy. *From the Founding of the City* 39.9.2–12.

Balsdon, J. P. V. D. *Roman Women.* New York: John Day Comp., 1963, pp. 37–41.

E

Egeria
(c. fourth–early fifth century C.E.)
Roman: Spain, Gaul
traveler, devout Christian pilgrim, writer

Egeria spent more than three years visiting biblical sites. She was intrepid. Her journal of the trip is largely extant, except for the opening sections, but provides no personal information or reasons for her trip. She was sufficiently well off not to have appeared concerned about money. She knew no Greek and her written Latin had errors in cases and tenses typical of provincial dialects. She probably came from Spain or possibly Gaul. Egeria's trip began in the 380s, although her journal was written after 394. Using evidence from her journal, her home has been attributed to places that range from Arles to close to Mont-Saint-Michel in Normandy.

Egeria traveled to the Christian holy sites in search of information and to experience them first-hand. Unlike many religious women of the period, she never intended to settle in Palestine. However, she was a devout woman. Possibly, she was part of a formal women's community or a less institution-alized circle of devout Christian women. Whatever the exact character of her home community, her descriptions suggest that her information and experiences were meant to be shared. She appears to have been the community's eyes and ears and her journal relayed to them a living sense of the places where great events happened in the Old and New Testaments.

Visiting the Holy sites was increasingly popular for Christians, even during these centuries of polit-ical uncertainty and economic problems. Travelers from across the empire frequently converged at the same place. Egeria appears to have traveled alone, although, in a manner reminiscent of the pilgrims en route to Canterbury in a later period, she joined guided groups to many of the sites. She also joined groups to traverse significant distances, with or without the support of a contingent of soldiers to keep them safe. Most often, donkeys were available or camels in the desert, but mountains often had narrow hardscrabble paths that had to be climbed on foot. Egeria climbed Mount Sinai and traced the route of the Israelites from Egypt to the Red Sea, which included a four-day trip across the des-ert. She also climbed Mount Nebo where Moses supposedly died. She was always welcomed by the clergy and monks who lived at or near places she visited and who often guided her to sites that were difficult to reach.

Egeria's knowledge of biblical events came from sources that predated Jerome's translation of the bible into Latin when he was in Palestine at the monastery built by PAULA and EUSTOCHIUM. She used Jerome's earlier translation from Greek to Latin of the *Onomasticon* by the church historian Eusebius, as a road map for her journey. This book linked events in both the Old and New Testaments, along with geographical descriptions, locations of the actual sites, the proper names of cities and villages, roads, mountains, deserts, and the people who inhabited the area.

In Jerusalem and Bethlehem, Egeria not only visited the sacred places mentioned in the Gospels, but devoted some 25 chapters in her journal to the ordinary and special liturgical rites that formed the annual calendar practiced in Jerusalem. She described the churches in which the rituals took place, the people who participated, the times of day for the various rites, and the special prayers for days of feasting and fasting. Also, she paid particular attention to rites which took place in Bethlehem.

Her route home was through Constantinople where she made a side trip to visit the holy monks and the tomb of the Apostle Saint Thomas in Edessa, Mesopotamia.

This journey took 25 days. From Antioch, she crossed the Euphrates, which she compared with the fierce current of the Rhone, but much larger. She visited the various shrines of martyrs and some of the numerous anchorite cells occupied by reclusive ascetics. She went to Carrhae, where Abraham had lived. She arrived on a saint's feast day and wrote that she was able to speak to anchorite ascetics who descended on the city and vanished when the celebration was over.

After returning to Antioch, she left for Selucia in what is now southern Turkey to visit the shrine of Saint Thecla. There she visited the deaconess Marthana, whom she had met while the latter was visiting Jerusalem, and who led a group of ascetic women living near the shrine. She then resumed her journey to Constantinople.

She ended this part of the chronicle with the information that she was going to make a final excursion to Ephesus to visit the shrine of Saint John. Her audience would hear from her in letters or in person if she returned alive. She asked them to remember her. Nothing more is known.

Sources

Egeria. *Egeria: Diary of a Pilgrimage.* Translated and annotated by George E. Gingras. New York: The Newman Press, 1970.

Sivan, Hagith. "Who Was Egeria? Piety and Pilgrimage in the Age of Gratian." *The Harvard Theological Review,* vol. 81, 1 (January 1988): 59–72.

———. "Holy Land Pilgrimage and Western Audiences: Some Reflections on Egeria and Her Circle." *Classical Quarterly* 38(ii): 528–535.

Weber, Clifford. "Egeria's Norman Homeland." *Harvard Studies in Classical Philology,* 92 (1989): 437–456.

▣ Egnatia Maximilla

(first century C.E.)   Roman: Rome
loyal wife

Egnatia Maximilla, the wealthy wife of Glitius Gallus, accompanied her husband into exile after he was implicated in a failed conspiracy to assassinate the emperor Nero. She and her husband settled on the island of Andros in the Aegean Sea. An inscription found on the island indicates that they were held in high esteem by the island community despite the fact that her wealth had been confiscated.

Sources

Tacitus. *Annales* 15.71.

▣ Elpinice

(c. 510? B.C.E.–)   Greek: Athens
well-known Athenian

Elpinice was born around 510 B.C.E. Her father was Miltiades, the Athenian politician and general responsible for the great Greek victory over the Persians at Marathon in 490. Her mother, HEGESIPYLE, was the daughter of Olorus, ruler of Thrace.

Shortly after Marathon, her father led the naval forces in an unsuccessful attack on the island of Paros. Seriously wounded and too ill to testify on his own behalf, he was fined 50 talents in a trial prompted by political rivals after his defeat. He died in prison in 489 B.C.E. with the fine unpaid. The family was left in poverty. Without a dowry, Elpinice had no choice but to live with her brother, Cimon, a leader in Athenian politics and also a renowned general. His political rivals linked their names in scandalous gossip that was only heightened by her beauty. It was rumored that the painter Polygnotus, a friend of her brother, used her face for the portrait of Laodice in his painting of the Trojan women. In time, her brother paid off his father's fine, and Elpinice married one of Athens's wealthiest men, Callias, who waived a dowry for an alliance with the illustrious Phileidae.

Elpinice remained very much a visible woman after her marriage. Twice she lobbied Pericles. In 463, she sought to protect her brother after he was charged with taking bribes from Alexander I. After Pericles defeated the Samians, she upbraided him for spending Greek lives against Greek allies and not, like her brother, against a foreign foe.

Elpinice and Callias may have divorced. They had one son, Hipponicus. On his father's death, Hipponicus inherited his estate and became the richest man in Greece.

Sources

Nepos. *Cimon* 1.2.
Plutarch. *Vitae Parallelae (Parallel Lives): Cimon* 4.1, 3, 5–7; 14.4.
Davies, J. K. *Athenian Propertied Families, 600–300 B.C.* Oxford: Clarendon Press, 1971, pp. 302–303.
Walters, K. R. "Women and Power in Classical Athens." In *Woman's Power, Man's Game: Essays on Classical Antiquity in Honor of Joy K. King,* ed. by Mary DeForest. Wauconda, Ill.: Bolchazy-Carducci, 1993, pp. 194–214.

Ennia Thrasylla
(? B.C.E./C.E.–38 C.E.)   Roman: Rome
political player

Ennia Thrasylla was the granddaughter of Tiberius Claudius Thrasyllus, a famous astrologer from Alexandria. Her grandfather gained Roman citizenship from the emperor Tiberius, whom he had originally met on the island of Rhodes. When Tiberius retired to Capri, Thrasyllus followed. Ennia married Quintus Naevius Cordus Suetonius Macro, prefect of the *vigiles,* the large fire and police force stationed in Rome. Tiberius used Macro to capture Lucius Aelius Sejanus, the former prefect of the Praetorian Guard, whom Tiberius had come to suspect of treacherous designs.

Macro then became prefect of the Praetorian Guard. He was close to Gaius Caligula, Tiberius's most likely successor. Macro and Ennia worked as a husband-and-wife team to assure their future position. It was rumored that Ennia seduced the young Caligula after the death of the latter's wife, JUNIA CLAUDILLA, and even promised him marriage as part of a plan to expand her and her husband's sphere of influence. Alternatively, Caligula might have seduced Ennia in order to secure her husband's support and may even have agreed in writing to marry her if he became emperor.

Caligula appointed Macro prefect of Egypt. In 38 C.E. Caligula rid himself of the powerful couple by forcing them to commit suicide.

Sources

Suetonius. *The Lives of the Caesars:* Gaius Caligula 12; 26.
Tacitus. *Annales* 6.45.
Levick, Barbara. *Tiberius the Politician.* London: Thames and Hudson, 1976, pp. 174, 215.

Epicharis
(?–65 C.E.)   Roman: Rome
conspirator

Epicharis was an imperial freedwoman who participated in a failed conspiracy to kill the emperor Nero in 65 C.E. Impatient at delays by the assassins, she approached Volusius Proculus, one of the men used by Nero to kill his mother, the younger AGRIPPINA. Although Proculus had been made an officer of the fleet, he was known to be dissatisfied with the emperor's reward. Epicharis solicited his participation in the plot without revealing the names of her coconspirators.

Proculus reported his conversation with Epicharis to Nero. She denied any wrongdoing, and there was no apparent corroborating evidence. Nero ordered her taken into custody. Soon, however, several of the conspirators confessed and began to implicate others. Nero ordered Epicharis tortured. She refused to speak. On the second day, no longer able to stand, she was dragged in a chair before her inquisitors. She managed to strip the strap band from her chest and put it around her neck, and then tipped the chair and killed herself.

She is remembered for her courage in keeping silent when well-born men were betraying those close to them.

Sources

Tacitus. *Annales* 15.51, 57.

Erinna
(fourth century B.C.E.)   Greek: Telos
poet

Erinna was an esteemed poet who lived on the Greek island of Telos, off the coast of western Asia Minor. She wrote about her personal life and feelings. Her most famous poem, "Distaff," consisted of 300 hexameters. It was written before she was 19 years old. Only a few fragments have survived. They movingly relate childhood experiences with her friend Baucis and lament Baucis's death shortly after her marriage. She also wrote two funeral epigrams to Baucis.

Erinna died young and never married.

Sources

Fantham, Elaine, et al. *Women in the Classical World.* New York: Oxford University Press, 1994, pp. 164–165.

Gow, Andrew S. F., and Denys L. Page. *The Greek Anthology: Hellenistic Epigrams.* 2 vols. Cambridge, England: Cambridge University Press, 1965, pp. 281 ff.

Oxford Classical Dictionary, ed. by Simon Hornblower and Antony Spawforth. 3d. ed. New York: Oxford University Press, 1996, p. 556.

Pomeroy, Sarah B. *Goddesses, Whores, Wives, and Slaves: Women in Classical Antiquity.* New York: Schocken Books, 1975, pp. 137–139.

Euboea
(third–second century B.C.E.)
Greek: Euboea
political player

Euboea, the daughter of Cleoptolemus of Chalcis, located on the island of Euboea off the coast of Greece, was well born and beautiful. In 192–191 B.C.E. Antiochus III the Great of Syria occupied the island prior to invading Greece. Euboea charmed him. At the age of 50, he married her and spent the whole of the winter with her in Chalcis.

After his defeat by the Romans, he retreated to Ephesus with Euboea.

Sources

Athenaeus. *Deipnosophistae* 10.439e, f.
Polybius. *Histories* 20.8.

Eudocia
(438/439–471/472 C.E.)
Roman: Italy, Carthage
political player

Eudocia, the eldest daughter of the Augusta LICINIA EUDOXIA and Valentinian III, emperor in the West, was only four or five years old when she was betrothed to Huneric, the son of Gaiseric, ruler of the Vandals. Although Roman marriage law forbade a legal marriage contract between a Roman and a non-Roman, the betrothal was spurred by the Vandal threat to invade Italy. The invasion was averted.

When Eudocia's father was assassinated in 455, Petronius Maximus became Roman emperor in the West. He forced her mother Eudoxia to marry him. He also insisted that Eudocia should marry his son, Palladius, who he appointed Caesar. Her mother hated Maximus and was rumored to have asked the Vandal ruler Gaiseric for help.

Less than three months later, in June 455, the Vandals led by Gaiseric captured Rome and sacked the city. Gaiseric took Eudocia, her mother, and her younger sister, PLACIDIA, back to Carthage, along with a great deal of gold and numerous slaves. In 456, Eudocia married Gaiseric's son Huneric, to whom she had earlier been betrothed. Within a few years, and at the request of Leo I, emperor in the East, her mother and sister were sent to Constantinople. Eudocia, however, remained in Carthage, perhaps involuntarily, and Gaiseric may have received some part of Eudocia's dowry paid by Leo to facilitate her mother and sister's return.

Eudocia was Huneric's second wife. Sometime between their earlier betrothal and marriage in 456, Huneric had married another woman. However, when Eudocia arrived in Carthage, Gaiseric accused the woman of trying to kill him, ended the marriage, and sent the woman back to her family.

Eudocia remain in Carthage for 16 years and gave birth to a son, Hilderic, who later ruled the Vandals. In 471 or 472, Eudocia went to Jerusalem and died shortly thereafter.

Some six years later, in 478, ambassadors returning to Constantinople from Carthage reported that Eudocia's son Hilderic admired the Romans and had allowed the orthodox Church at Carthage to ordain a bishop, despite his staunch adherence to Arian Christianity. Hilderic wanted Leo to know, furthermore, that he no longer made any claim for his mother's wealth under the original betrothal agreement or through her line of descent for inheritance.

Sources

Procopius. *Vandelic War* III. v. 3–7.

Theophanes. *Chronicle* AM 5947, 5949, 5957, 5964.

Bury, J. B. *History of the Later Roman Empire from the Death of Theodosius I to the Death of Justinian.* Vol. 1. New York: Dover Publications, 1958.

Prosopography of the Later Roman Empire. Vol. II. Edited by A. H. M. Jones, J. R. Martindale, and J. Morris. Cambridge: Cambridge University Press, 1971. Reprinted 1992, pp. 407–408.

▣ Eudocia, Aelia (Athenais)
(c. 400–October 20, 460 C.E.
Greek: Athens, Antioch, Constantinople, Jerusalem
Augusta

Aelia Eudocia, a resolute and educated woman, married the emperor Theodosius II and engaged in the politics of religion, wealth, and power. She succeeded in living life on her own terms, even as she and the formidable Pulcheria vied for dominion over the interpretation of Christian doctrine and influence over the emperor. Her final years mark the best that the early centuries of Christianity offered women of position, independent authority, and wealth. She died honored and revered.

Athenais was born in either Antioch or Athens, the daughter of Leontius, a prominent sophist and teacher of rhetoric, and a woman about whom we only know that she was Roman. Her father, a pagan at a time when Christianity was spreading rapidly, provided her with a classical education

from which she developed a lifelong passion for reading and writing poetry. At some point in her youth she moved to Constantinople and lived with her maternal uncle, Asclepiodotus, a minor government official, and his wife. It was through them that she met her future husband.

On June 7, 421, she married Theodosius II. She and her husband were both about 20 years old. Shortly before her marriage, she had been baptized by the bishop of Constantinople and took the name of Aelia Eudocia, which allied her to the Theodosian women of the imperial line.

With marriage Eudocia gained an empire. The studious and mild-mannered Theodosius may also have been personally more appealing than has been generally thought, especially in view of the violence which often dominated women's sexual experience. The emperor gained a beautiful wife who was well educated and loved literature. Theodosius, shy with women with the exception of his sisters, may have found her pagan education and literary interests a stimulating contrast to a focused diet of Christian virtue, modesty, and doctrinal controversies. Also, his powerful and overbearing sister, Pulcheria, approved the union.

Some 100 years later, John Malalas, a Syrian from Antioch who lived between 480 and 570, composed a chronology of world history with a romanticized version of the courtship between Eudocia and Theodosius. According to Malalas, Eudocia's father had died and left a large estate to his two sons, who refused to provide for their sister. She went to live with her aunt, who introduced her to Pulcheria. Taken with Eudocia's intelligence and beauty, Pulcheria informed her brother that she had found the perfect woman for him to marry. Theodosius and his boyhood friend Paulinus invited her to the palace, where they remained concealed behind a curtain. Immediately upon seeing her, Theodosius decided she would become his wife.

Malalas incorporated many classic tropes of ancient literature, some of which, such as hiding behind the curtain, extended into Shakespeare's times and beyond. A more calculating historical assessment has focused on the role of Pulcheria.

From the beginning, the relationship between the sisters-in-law bore directly on the affairs of church and state. Eudocia, whose conversion has always been assumed perfectly sincere, was far more tolerant of diverse points of view and behavior among Christians than was Pulcheria. Although they had different interpretations of Christianity, Pulcheria may well have been comfortable that her position would dominate. Eudocia's modest family with its pagan background may have further forestalled any misgivings that Eudocia would become a competing power in politics or religion. Another and less-often-examined possibility might focus on Eudocia's own calculated aggressiveness in wooing the emperor. She was adept at securing her own ends and meeting all expectations. A year after her marriage in 422, Eudocia gave birth to a daughter, LICINIA EUDOXIA. On January 2, 423, Eudocia became Augusta. Coins were issued with her image.

For the first time, two women of the same generation who were associated with the same emperor held the title of Augusta. During this period, conflict was minimized since Pulcheria spent most of her time in her own establishments on the outskirts of the city. Not unexpectedly, Eudocia used her position to attend to the well-being of her family. Her uncle and brothers were appointed to important positions in the government. Asclepiodotus became Praetorian Prefect of the East and consul for 423. One brother Gesius became governor of Illyricum and another Valerius became the governor of Thrace, consul for 432, and Master of Offices in 435.

Doubtless, Eudocia supported her husband in his efforts to improve education by reorganizing and strengthening the schools of literature and rhetoric in Constantinople. In religious matters, orthodoxy prevailed, but Eudocia and her uncle had a hand in sponsoring measures that, at least temporarily, ended the persecution of Jews and pagans. Earlier, Theodosius I had issued edicts penalizing Christian heretics, pagans, and Jews so severely that most pagans converted to Christianity, at least nominally. In contrast, Theodosius II proclaimed that Christians were not to use violence against Jews and pagans if they lived quietly and created no disorder. Moreover, the penalties for violations were severe. Those who attacked Jews or pagans and their property were subject to triple or quadruple damages and government officials up to the office of governor would suffer the same penalties if they failed to effect a policy of toleration. Between 422 and 423, the edict was under the authority of Eudocia's uncle, Asclepiodotus. However, a letter from St. Simeon the Stylite, whose holiness carried great weight, threatened Theodosius with divine punishment unless he ended tolerance. Asclepiodotus was removed from his position.

Perhaps it was inevitable that Eudocia's more tolerant Christianity would conflict with Pulcheria's uncompromising views. Possibly it was not religion at all, but too little space in the emotional vortex of the imperial family for each woman's sphere of influence to find sufficient room. The first public conflict between the two was over the bishop Nestorius, who should have united, not divided, them. In 428, Nestorius, who had a reputation for rhetoric and learning, was appointed

Aelia Eudocia
(Date: 408 C.E.–450 C.E. 1967.153.187, Archives, American Numismatic Society)

bishop of Constantinople with the imperial stamp of approval. It soon became apparent that he was opinionated, tactless, lacked political skills, and offended key laypeople as well as some prominent clergy and monks. He also alienated women, rich and poor, by refusing to allow them to participate in evening services since their comings and going in the city after dark might result in opportunities for promiscuity. In 431, Eudocia allied herself with her husband and firmly supported Nestorius. Since it is unlikely that she supported Nestorius's views, she probably seized the opportunity to join Theodosius in one of the few instances in which he disagreed with his sister. Whether she sought to drive a wedge between them or to make a statement of her public political power (possibly both or neither), it was a public fight that stretched across the empire.

The conflict reached a crisis when Anastasius, chaplain to Nestorius, delivered a sermon in the Great Church in which he referred to Mary as *Christotokos* (Mother of Christ) instead of *Theotokos* (Mother of God). The distinction was far from arcane. Christian doctrine was still in flux, and a contentious issue was the relationship between the human and divine within Christ. Mary as *Theotokos*, Mother of God, rather than *Christotokos*, Mother of the human Christ, was enormously popular among the people and many of the clergy. Through Mary as the Mother of God, women could stand with the disciples at the very core of Christian doctrine, since a woman had borne, not a human named Jesus, but the divine Jesus son of God. All women who chose virginity gained from Mary *Theotokos*, a refracted holiness that erased the curse of Eve, which men claimed made women responsible for the loss of Eden.

Mary *Theotokos* opened the door for women to claim full participation in the church. Pulcheria, who at 13 or 14 years old, had pledged her virginity, staked her power on her holiness and her right to participate in the church. She had a strong ally in Cyril, the bishop of Alexandria. Insofar as the religious and political were coextensive, the bishops were the world court of the time. It was, nonetheless, a case of politics and strange bedfellows. Eudocia's sympathies might have reasonably led her to oppose Nestorius; Cyril ought to have been a supporter. He was an unscrupulous man who manipulated the Alexandrians for his own political gain. It was he who excited the mob to burn the great library and museum of Alexandria with its more than 800,000 papyrus rolls. The same mob killed the philosopher HYPATIA, who was the first woman and last head of the most prestigious center of learning in the entire Mediterranean.

Nestorius suffered less from the kind of unscrupulousness that characterized Cyril than from an unbounded misogyny, which was always a particular danger to women in the formative centuries of Christian doctrine. His misogyny led him into a confrontation with Pulcheria when he refused to honor her as the bride of Christ in his prayers for the imperial household as his predecessors had done. When, as was her custom, she arrived at the Great Church of Constantinople to take communion with her brother and the participating priests, Nestorius refused her entry. He rejected her claim that since a woman had borne Jesus son of God, she, through her vow of virginity, had risen above the sin of Eve. Instead, he told her that as a woman she only had given birth to Satan.

The conflict over Nestorius gave Cyril an opportunity to raise the status of Alexandria over Constantinople, one of his long-term political objectives. He sent to Theodosius, Eudocia, Pulcheria, and her two sisters, ARCADIA and MARINA, sets of documents, ostensibly to prove with historical evidence that Mary was the Mother of God. He also implied that Nestorius's views were heretical. Somewhat inaccurately, he attributed to Nestorius the doctrine that the human and divine natures in Christ were separate and not conjoined.

The emperor authorized a council at Ephesus in Asia Minor in 431. The supporters of Cyril and Memnon, who was the bishop of Ephesus, intimidated the opposition. Cyril gave lavish bribes and sent MARCELLA and Droseria, two women close to Eudocia, 2,250 pounds of gold each, in hopes they might influence the Augusta. Cyril and Memnon succeeded in discrediting Nestorius. In response, a smaller group held a separate council that upheld Nestorius and deposed Cyril and

Memnon. However, Cyril and Memnon, who had popular support, were reinstated. Nestorius, tired of the controversy, asked the emperor to be sent back to his old monastery near Antioch. An angry emperor gave up the fight. Pulcheria was acclaimed by the people while Eudocia and Theodosius were the losers.

Eudocia had another child, Flacilla, who died at an early age in 431. In the fall of 437, Eudocia's daughter, LICINIA EUDOXIA, married the Roman emperor of the West, Valentinian III, in Constantinople. At about this time, Eudocia met the renowned younger MELANIA, who had arrived from Jerusalem where she and Eudocia had previously met. It was a crucial meeting for Eudocia, who was apparently ready for a change in life. Her daughter lived in Ravenna, the administrative capital of Italy. Her sister-in-law, Pulcheria, was a source of tension, and possibly, her marital relationship was no longer interesting or the emperor attentive. Eudocia looked to other pursuits. With Melania's help, she convinced her husband to allow her to make a pilgrimage to Palestine.

On her way to Jerusalem in February or March 438, she stopped at Antioch, which may have been the city of her birth. She won acclaim with a speech before the local council that ended with an allusion to a Homeric line that boasted a shared heredity of race and blood. In Jerusalem, she spent time with Melania, visited holy places, and prayed at the empty tomb of Christ. When she returned to Constantinople early in 439, she brought the bones of Saint Stephen and was greeted in a public celebration by her husband and the people of the city.

Bringing back saintly relics from Palestine enhanced her public position. She and Pulcheria were viewed as sisters in power as well as in law. Cyrus, Prefect of the City, whose poems Eudocia admired, became Prefect of the East, undoubtedly her doing. The emperor, at her behest, extended the walls of Antioch and erected a new basilica. In the succeeding years, however, conflict between Eudocia and Pulcheria seems to have easily ignited, although they both appeared to respect a set of boundaries: Neither exercised complete domination over the weak emperor. His passivity may

have allowed them each to go her own way; he largely ignored them and they him.

A third person successfully entered the heretofore closed circle, however, and altered the existing dynamics. An imperial eunuch, Chrysaphius, encouraged discord between the women. In 441, he aroused Eudocia's anger by harping on the presence of a chamberlain in Pulcheria's household and absent from hers. Theodosius refused Eudocia when she requested that he assign her a chamberlain. Chrysaphius urged Eudocia to press Theodosius that Pulcheria withdraw from public life and become a deaconess, since she was a virgin and an ascetic. The emperor acquiesced, perhaps thinking it would diminish his sister's influence or perhaps desiring not to become involved in any dispute between these two high-powered women. Possibly, he was clever enough to gauge Pulcheria's reaction. Proclus, the bishop of Constantinople and Pulcheria's friend, reminded her that as a deaconess she would be a member of the clergy and subject to the authority of the bishop. Pulcheria was skilled at picking her battles and withdrawing from the fray when she thought it prudent. She was also uninterested in the bishop exercising authority over her. She withdrew to her own establishment in Hebdomon. She also turned her chamberlain over to Eudocia.

Chrysaphius conspired to eliminate Eudocia. John Malalas, writing some 100 years later, related the events in a tale that mixed biblical and classical motifs of treason and adultery. According to the account, Theodosius gave his wife the gift of a rare large apple, which in the ancient world was the fruit of desire and carnal love. She in turn gave it to Paulinus, a favorite of hers and a childhood friend of the emperor, who had injured his foot. He in turn presented it to Theodosius. When the latter asked Eudocia what she had done with the apple, she replied that she had eaten it. The archetypal elements of the tale—the apple, the woman, and sexual desire—make it suspect. The further suggestion of impropriety or adultery between Paulinus and Eudocia echoes stories of the Julio-Claudian women, who were accused of adultery when the men around them were accused of treason. That Eudocia was guilty of adultery or treason, however, seems unlikely. The only ancient corroboration of Malalas's story comes from Nestorius, writing from afar and years later in 451, which has all the characteristics of a similarly unfounded accusation of adultery against Pulcheria and Paulinus.

What is certain is that relations between Eudocia and Theodosius had deteriorated. Eudocia may have welcomed time and distance away from him and his sisters. She planned another trip to the Holy Land. The palace issued a statement that Eudocia was embarking on a pilgrimage to Palestine. She left with all her imperial honors in place, including the scepter, a symbol of her public power. She also had her immense fortune, a large retinue of servants and retainers, and two close religious confidants, John the Deacon and Severus a priest. After she left, Theodosius lashed out at the people she left behind.

Sometime between 440 and 443, Theodosius exiled and then killed Paulinus, an echo of behavior from an earlier time when Augustus first exiled his daughter JULIA and then killed or exiled the men around her, although their innocence or guilt was unproven. Another favorite, Cyrus, who had angered Theodosius because the people acclaimed him, not the emperor, for improvements to the city, lost his position and was sent to an undesirable bishopric. Shortly thereafter, Theodosius sent his general Saturninus to Jerusalem. He ordered the execution of John the Deacon and Severus. Ancient sources reported that Eudocia killed Saturninus. Finally, Theodosius deprived Eudocia of her imperial ministers and stopped issuing coins with her image.

Eudocia's wealth and other titles remained untouched and gave her enormous influence in Palestine, where she owned extensive land. In effect, she created her own dominion, issuing edicts and securing obedience. She repaired the walls of Jerusalem, erected shelters for the indigent, the aged, and pilgrims who visited the city, and built and decorated churches. She disbursed an immense amount of gold, including sums given to the clergy, monks, and the poor.

She also ordered religious tolerance and protected the Jews who she permitted to pray at the ruins of Solomon's Temple. Tolerance was neither desired nor accepted by those whose beliefs offered no space for others. A group of monks, at the instigation of their leader Barsauma, killed some Jews as they prayed. Eudocia ordered that they be put to death without a trial. A large mob gathered in front of her establishment to protest her decision to kill the monks, and the governor of the province intervened. A mild earthquake that occurred as the governor was questioning Basauma was taken as a sign of God's disapproval. The monks were released with no further disorder. Her defense of the Jews would appear to have been a principled act, even though it resulted in her opposing the same monk whose holiness had impressed her on her first visit to Palestine.

Eudocia did not live as an ascetic in Palestine anymore than she had in Constantinople. Her circle of friends included poets, writers, and philosophers, as well as clergy with humanistic tastes. Eudocia also continued to compose poems about religious and secular subjects, several of which have survived. Although her poetic efforts have not won acclaim from critics, her work was important. It marked a transition between the classical and the Christian. One poem from this later period of her life, the *Martyrdom of St. Stephen,* confirmed her long-time attraction to the saint. She had brought his bones to Constantinople and restored his church in Jerusalem. Another was *Homerocentoes,* in which she inserted into Bible stories words and lines borrowed from the *Iliad* and the *Odyssey.*

In a world still saturated with the pagan, especially in education, the replacement of Christian content for pagan within the respected classical texts was of critical importance. These were transitional cultural expressions. They were used for teaching and learning Greek in a way that reflected the growing dominance of Christianity and at the same time denied any sharp break with the Greco-Roman literary tradition. The mere survival of these poems has to be recognized and applauded, given the filters of transmission from antiquity, even late antiquity, that has so systematically erased women's written work. In this case, moreover, not only has the work survived but it speaks to a woman's role in the transformation of Greco-Roman to Christian literary tradition.

Eudocia's wealth and status made her an important person and assured that she was kept abreast of affairs in the capital. It also made her a participant in the eddies of empire that reached Palestine. Neither the death of Theodosius nor the successful machinations of Pulcheria and Marcian to rule affected her personal life and dominion as much as their convening of a new Council at Chalcedon in 451. Eudocia, along with many in Jerusalem, Alexandria, and Syria, was Monophysite and believed that the divine nature in Christ had absorbed the human after Incarnation. When Juvenal, the bishop of Jerusalem, returned from Chalcedon, where he had reversed his former position and accepted the new orthodoxy, he was driven from the city. Rioting and looting by rampaging monks broke out and a number of people were killed. The monks replaced Juvenal with Theodosius, one of their own leaders. Eudocia strongly supported their cause and approved of their closing the doors of the city against a possible attack by imperial forces. She also provided them with means to defend themselves. Despite the involvement of Constantinople in the purposeful enforcement of the Council's decisions, however, Eudocia suffered no diminution of her independence or loss of wealth for her opposition. Possibly she was too far from Constantinople or simply no longer important enough to matter. Perhaps her lifelong opponent Pulcheria was no longer interested in competition.

Eudocia outlived Pulcheria, but she did not have happy years. Political upheaval and economic woes shook the larger empire. She was besieged on all sides. Finally, she accepted the decisions of Chalcedon. She died on October 20, 460, her standing as Augusta undimmed and her sway of power diminished but unchallenged.

Sources

Evagrius, H. E. *Ecclesiastical History* i. 20.
Gerontius. *The Life of Melania the Younger.* Translation, Introduction, and Commentary by Elizabeth A. Clark, New York: Edwin Mellon Press, 1984.
John Malalas. *Chronicle.* 353, 355 ff.
Socrates. *Historia Ecclesiatica* VII. 21. 8–9; 42. 2; 44.
Theophanes. *Theophanes, Chronographia,* AM 5911, 5937, 5940, 5947.
Bury, J. B. *History of the Late Roman Empire from the Death of Theodosius I to the Death of Justinian.* Vol. I, New York: Dover Publications Inc. 1938, 220–231.
Cameron, Alan. "The Empress and the Poet: Paganism and Politics at the Court Of Theodosius II." *Yale Classical Studies* 27 (1981): 217–289.
Holum, Kenneth G. *Theodosian Empresses: Women and Imperial Dominion in Late Antiquity.* Berkeley: University of California Press, 1982.
Prosopography of the Later Roman Empire. Vol. II. Edited by A. H. M. Jones, J. R. Martindale, and J. Morris. Cambridge: Cambridge University Press, 1971. Reprinted 1992, pp. 408–409.
Usher, Mark David. "Prolegomenon to the Homeric Centos." *American Journal of Philology* 8 (1997): 305–332.

◉ Eudoxia, Aelia

(380–404 C.E.)   Roman: Constantinople
Augusta

Eudoxia was a spirited and determined woman with a temper. Although only 15 or 16 at the time of her marriage to the emperor Arcadius, she knew the importance of her position, what was due her, and opposed anyone or anything that threatened her status or the status of her family. Her attitude, which was characteristic of a wealthy Roman *matrona,* may have come from her Roman mother. Her father, Flavius Bauto, was of Frankish descent. He became Master of Soldiers in the West under the emperor Valentinian II, sometime after 383. In 385 he was consul with the two-year old Arcadius, son of Theodosius the Great and the future husband of Eudoxia. Probably a Christian, he died in 388.

Eudoxia was sent to Constantinople as a child, although it is unclear if she went before or after her parents' deaths. She was raised in the household of MARSA and her husband, Promotus, a Roman who held the same high office in the East as did her father in the West. Marsa's household attracted the most elite circle of the next generation of Roman imperial leaders. Eudoxia met a friend of Marsa's two sons, her future husband Arcadius, who had remained in Constantinople while his father, the

Aelia Eudoxia
(Date: 395 C.E.–404 C.E. 1977.158.968, Archives, American Numismatic Society)

emperor Theodosius I, led Roman armies in the troubled West. In the same household, Eudoxia had the opportunity to become part of a circle of women that included Marsa as well as CASTRICIA and EUPHEMIA (2).

These were difficult political times, with Goths at the borders around the empire and usurpers vying for imperial power in the West. After Theodosius I died one son, Arcadius, became emperor of the East and another, Honorius, emperor of the West. Arcadius was young and inexperienced. The Praetorian Prefect of the East, Flavius Rufinus dominated the inept emperor. Rufinus was by birth a Gaul, not a Roman, and his greatest achievement would be a marriage between his daughter and the emperor. Eutropius, chamberlain of the royal household, who also exercised influence over the emperor, opposed any such union. Most opposition came from supporters of Promotus, since Rufinus had been responsible for Promotus's exile and indirectly responsible for his later death at the hands of the barbarians.

Eudoxia and Arcadius were married on April 27, 395, shortly after Rufinus returned to Con-stantinople from a trip to Antioch. Rufinus's absence from the city appears to have provided an opportunity to arrange and sign the legal contracts for a betrothal. The subsequent ceremonies of the wedding, which Rufinus witnessed on his return, presented him with a fait accompli. The organization of the events speaks to the networks of relationships that effectively tied together multi-generational families of wealth and influence across the empire. It also suggests the power these families exercised when they closed ranks and acted according to class interests. Eudoxia, ethnically half Roman and half Frankish and at most one generation Christian, entered into marriage with the political agenda of an establishment that styled itself as the elite inheritors of ancient Rome.

After her marriage, there was little Eudoxia or her backers could do to prevent Rufinus from following a disastrous military policy in the West. It was possible, however, to address the power of the chamberlain Eutropius, no friend of Rufinus, who had nonetheless overstepped his status as a eunuch when he was named consul in 398.

Eudoxia precipitated Eutropius's downfall using virtue and fertility as her sword. Her children came quickly and were healthy. Her daughter Flacilla was born on June 10, 397; a second, Pulcheria, on January 19, 399; and a third, ARCADIA, on April 13, 400. In 399, Eudoxia appeared before her husband accompanied by two wailing daughters, Flacilla and Pulcheria, and pregnant with the third. She claimed that Eutropius had insulted her and he should be dismissed immediately. What chance had he against the evidence of fecundity, the most potent of all female virtues? Eutropius was exiled and his property confiscated.

Eudoxia played a prominent role in the selection of Aurelian, a Roman and Prefect of Constantinople, who, as Praetorian Prefect of the East and consul in 400, presided over the trial of Eutropius. The political tensions of the period, however, assured that every victory brought a counterattack. Gainas led his Ostrogoths toward Constantinople along with the Gothic forces of Tribigild. They demanded that Arcadius dismiss Aurelian and hand him over to them along with Saturninus, the husband of Eudoxia's friend Castricia, and the enigmatic Count John, about whom little is known except that he was a frequent visitor to the palace and a special favorite of Eudoxia. Acadius agreed, and only the intervention of John Chrysostom, the bishop of Constantinople, whose own interests on behalf of the orthodox Church made it desirable to oblige Eudoxia, prevented their death. Instead they were exiled. Their exile, however, deprived Eudoxia of important allies.

Arcadius proclaimed Eudoxia Augusta on January 9, 400, even though she had not yet borne the much desired son and heir. Bronze, silver, and gold coins were issued with her image as Augusta on one side and the right hand of God reaching down from heaven to crown her with a wreath on the other side. Five months later, Aurelian regained his former position after a revolt against Gainas. On April 1, 401, amid great rejoicing, Eudoxia gave birth to a son, the future emperor Theodosius II, amid rumors that the child's father was the also-returned Count John. Her daughter Flacilla died, and Eudoxia gave birth to a fifth child, MARINA, on February 10, 403.

Eudoxia, not her husband, played the dominant role in state religious affairs. A fervent orthodox Christian willing to use her position to combat paganism and Arianism, both of which remained popular in the Eastern empire, her religious authority was accepted by the clergy and the populace. Her dogmatism, however, was modified by her admiration for pious clergy. Four monks called the Tall Brothers, who were widely known and renowned for their height and their piety, appealed to her after being charged with heresy and their monastic settlement in the desert of Upper Egypt ransacked. She summoned their accuser Theophilus, the bishop of Alexandria, to a synod she arranged to account for his actions, even though the monks were followers of Origin, whose doctrine the orthodox considered heretical.

In 400, a delegation led by Porphyry, bishop of Gaza, asked Eudoxia to intervene with her husband to suppress what he considered rampant paganism in Gaza and to destroy the sites of pagan worship, especially the temple of Zeus Marnas.

Eudoxia was pregnant and susceptible to the bishop's offer of prayers for a male child. However, she failed. The people of Gaza, her husband noted, paid their taxes promptly and did not cause any trouble. Eudoxia promised to try again. On January 6, 402, at the baptism of her son, she arranged to slip a petition into the infant's hand and to have his hand raised with a request that the petition be granted by the emperor. Arcadius, unaware of the ruse, agreed to honor the petition. Subsequently bound by his promise, Eudoxia oversaw the destruction of pagan temples, including the temple of Zeus, upon whose site Eudoxia paid for the construction of a church. Completed after her death, the church was dedicated to her.

Eudoxia had a theatrical sense which she used to political advantage. Wearing a simple shift to suggest her piety and humility, she carried a chest with the bones of Christian martyrs to their final resting place. She led a nighttime procession nine miles across the city from the Great Church of Constantinople to the newly completed martyrs' chapel in the church of Saint Thomas. She theatrically manipulated circumstances to reconcile the estranged bishops of Constantinople and Gabala, using a tactic that again depended on her son. Severian, bishop of Gabala, had ingratiated himself with Eudoxia and other influential persons in the city in hopes of increasing his influence and fortune. His crass behavior soon aroused the anger of John Chrysostom, bishop of Constantinople, whose authority he threatened. He expelled Severian. Eudoxia ordered his return. She forced Chrysostom to reconcile with Severian by unrepentantly placing her infant son on Chrysostom's knee and imploring the bishop to extend himself if he cared about the well-being of her child.

Eudoxia often exercised de facto public authority since her torpid husband rarely left the palace grounds. Her personal power, however, also invited conflict with the bishops who were flexing their moral *imperium* and extending their authority. On February 26, 398, John Chrysostom, an austere, uncompromising, blunt, and self-righteous cleric with a reputation for delivering eloquent sermons, became bishop of Constantinople. Initially, the imperial family concurred, believing that he would support their prerogatives. Chrysostom's tenure opened with cordiality and he praised Eudoxia extravagantly when she led the procession carrying relics of the saints. However, he was deeply misogynist and believed that women carried Eve's sin. According to him, women were vain, as men were not, and women were morally handicapped, as men were not. Women lacked the prerequisites of spiritual leadership, and men must be ever vigilant against the insinuation of themselves into positions of power. A bishop holding these views would inevitably conflict with the independent women of Constantinople.

Chrysostom may well have been genuinely appalled by the extravagant expenditures of the wealthy on huge palaces, costly furnishings, expensive clothing, and jewels, while the bulk of the population lived on a subsistence level, if not in outright deprivation. He condemned the rich and the renowned, and he was a charismatic preacher. The masses flocked to hear him. He also attracted a devoted coterie of wealthy women, often widows, who responded to his power and authority and who contributed money to the causes, people, and churches he favored. His relationship with these women was often double-edged. On one hand, he shielded the women from some of the demands of male relatives who pressured widows to remarry or who sought control over their fortunes. However, the women he appointed deaconesses, the lowest order of the Church, became subject to him as their bishop. He, not their male relatives, gained authority to receive their wealth on behalf of the church and to oversee their behavior.

Chrysostom soon alienated a number of his fellow clergy. Some envied his visibility and importance. His strictness rubbed the rich lifestyle of others. He instituted reforms and ended the practice of clerics using young women who took vows of virginity as live-in housekeepers. He removed church officials, including bishops, for selling church offices. He attacked those who embraced an unsuitably luxurious lifestyle and forced monks to withdraw to monasteries and cease to live among the people.

In 403, Chrysostom delivered a scathing sermon against the extravagant wealthy women in which he used the word *Jezebel.* The congregation took the reference to mean Eudoxia. Her three closest friends, Marsa, Eugraphia, and Euphemia, also considered themselves insulted and reinforced Eudoxia's fury. She demanded that her husband take action. Arcadius convened a council of clerics to investigate Chrysostom, but Chysostom refused to attend. The council condemned him, not because of the charges, but because he failed to appear. Arcadius decided to banish Chrysostom, but mobs rallied around the Great Church and prevented his seizure. He delivered two sermons in which he again referred to Eudoxia as Jezebel and compared her to Salome, Eve's sister who demanded the head of John the Baptist.

On the third day, Chrysostom secretly left the city. Eudoxia changed her mind. No more or less superstitious or credulous than those around her, she sought the signs of heavenly favor and disfavor. Perhaps she interpreted the death of her daughter Flacilla or the illness of one of her other children as a sign of God's displeasure. Possibly, she changed her mind for the more mundane reason that Chrysostom's departure had too high a political cost.

Eudoxia sent members of her own guard to find Chrysostom with messages that denied responsibility for his exile and implored him to return. Chrysostom was found in Bithynia and brought back, but he refused to resume his position until a council overturned the earlier findings. Eudoxia housed him in one of her palaces until popular acclaim brought him to the pulpit. However, the reconciliation was brief. The Prefect of the City erected a silver statue of Eudoxia close to the Great Church. Customary music for its dedication heard during church services enraged Chrysostom who complained bitterly to the prefect. Eudoxia again felt attacked and threatened to convene a synod. Chrysostum delivered a sermon again linking her behavior with that of Salome. Arcadius confined Chrysostom to his residence and in June 404 exiled him to Armenia.

That night the Great Church of Constantinople caught fire, which then spread to the senate building and parts of the palace. Rioting spread to other cities and threatened the rule of the imperial family, but the uprisings were forcibly suppressed. On October 6, 404, Eudoxia, pregnant once again, died leaving behind four young children.

Sources

Palladius. *Dialogue* 8, 9.

Socrates. *Historia Ecclesiastica* VI. 18, VIII. 27.

Sozomen. *Historia Ecclesiastica* VIII. 6, 10, 13, 15–16, 18, 20, 27; IX. 1.

Zosimus. *New History/Zosimus.* A translation with commentary by Ronald T. Ridley. Canberra: Australian Association of Byzantine Studies, 1982.

Bury, J. B. *History of the Later Roman Empire: From the Death of Theodosius to the Death of Justinian.* Vol. I. New York: Dover Publications, 1958.

Holum, Kenneth. *Theodosian Empresses: Women and Imperial Dominion in Late Antiquity.* Berkeley: University of California Press, 1982.

Prosopography of the Later Roman Empire. Vol. II. Edited by A. H. M. Jones, J. R. Martindale, and J. Morris. Cambridge: Cambridge University Press, 1971. Reprinted 1992, p. 410.

▣ Eudoxia, Licinia
(422–493? C.E.)

Roman: Constantinople, Italy, Carthage

Augusta

Licinia Eudoxia played an important role in the debate over the nature of Christ, which dominated religious controversy during the period and split the empire. She was born in 422, the daughter of Augusta AELIA EUDOCIA, and the Eastern Roman emperor, Theodosius II. Brought up and educated in Constantinople, she was betrothed as an infant to Valentinian III, also a child and next in line to become emperor of the West. The marriage took place in Constantinople on October 29, 437, when Licina Eudoxia was 15 or 16. Her mother-in-law, GALLA PLACIDIA, continued to exercise a great influence on her son, even after her regency ended. On the new coins, Licinia Eudoxia and Valentinian were depicted with Theodosius II between them to signify the harmony of both the marriage and the two Roman empires. Licinia Eudoxia solidified her position with the birth of two girls, EUDOCIA in 438/39 and PLACIDIA in 440. Eudoxia became Augusta in Ravenna in 439.

Licinia Eudoxia
(Date: 437 C.E.–455 C.E. 1970.201.1, Archives, American Numismatic Society)

In 449, Licinia Eudoxia played a part in a series of critical religious councils. A council, convened in Ephesus against the will of the bishop of Rome, Leo I, adopted the Monophysite position of Eutyches, bishop of Constantinople, and affirmed the single nature of Christ. Eudoxia was an orthodox Christian, and in 450, the following year, at the request of Leo, she wrote to her father, Theodosius II, asking him to intervene and uphold the orthodox position that Christ had two natures, divine and human cojoined yet distinct. Her father died that year, and the Monophysite position was overturned by a second council in 451.

Her oldest daughter, Eudocia, was four or five years old when she was betrothed to Huneric, the son of the Vandal leader Gaiseric. Although Roman law forbade intermarriage with barbarians, Gaiseric threatened to invade Italy and marriage was an attractive alternative to war. The betrothal, however, had unforeseen consequences. Eudoxia's husband, Valentinian, was murdered at the instigation of Petronius Maximus, who became emperor on March 17, 455. Although Licinia Eudoxia hated Maximus, she was forced her to marry him and Eudocia was forced to marry his son Palladius.

Rumors began to circulate that Eudoxia had asked Gaiseric to avenge her. In May 455, Gaiseric arrived outside Rome. Maximus was killed while he was fleeing the city and on June 3, Gaiseric entered Rome. He spent about two weeks ransacking the city and returned to Carthage with immense booty and thousands of captives, including Licinia Eudoxia and her two daughters. Eudocia, perhaps against her will, married Huneric, fulfilling the terms of the earlier betrothal.

After the marriage, perhaps in 460, Gaiseric allowed Licinia Eudoxia to go to Constantinople, where she spent her remaining years and was responsible for the construction of the church of St. Euphemia. She died around 493 C.E.

Sources
Procopius. *Vandelic War* III. iv. 15, 20, 36–39; V. 3, 6.
Socrates. *Historia Ecclesiastica* VII. 4.
Theophanes. *Chronicle* AM 5926, 5947, 5949.
Zonaris. *Historia Nova* xxiii. 25.19, 22, 23, 26, 27.
Prosopography of the Later Roman Empire. Vol. II. Edited by A. H. M. Jones, J. R. Martindale, and J. Morris. Cambridge: Cambridge University Press, 1971. Reprinted 1992, pp. 410–412.

Eugraphia
(?–early fifth century C.E.)
Roman: Constantinople
political player

Eugraphia belonged to the set of interconnected wealthy Roman families whose landholdings extended across empires and who sought control over the emperor. Educated and independent, she was friends with MARSA, CASTRICIA, and the Augusta Aelia EUDOXIA, wife of the emperor Arcadius. Eugraphia was part of the group in Constantinople that arranged the betrothal and marriage of Aelia Eudoxia and Arcadius while Flavius Rufinus, the most powerful man in the empire and a political opponent, was temporarily absent from Constantinople. She was also among the women, led by the Augusta, who confronted John Chrysostom, bishop of Constantinople.

Ostensibly the confrontation was about wealth, which had become concentrated in fewer and fewer

hands as land became aggregated into estates that included whole towns. The population drift from the countryside to the cities swelled the urban underclass, while trade increased and further enriched the well off. Most of the population lived at a subsistence level or even in dire poverty. Chrysostom railed against the uncaring wealthy in charismatic sermons that entranced the poor and beguiled many of the rich. However, he was not a diplomatic man. In 403, he attacked rich old widows who adorned themselves as if they were young with face paint and elaborate hairstyles. He compared them to common prostitutes. Eugraphia and her wealthy friends considered his remarks a personal attack. They had the ear of the Augusta and turned her against the bishop. Eugraphia also provided her house for meetings of clerics who opposed the very visible and righteous bishop, including Theophilus, bishop of Alexandria, and Severian, bishop of Gabala, whose stars were dimmed by Chrysostom.

Eugraphia disappears from the records, but the battle between the women and Chrysostom succeeded. Chrysostom lost his position and left the city.

Sources
Palladius. *Dialogue.* 4, 8.
Zosimus. *New History/Zosimus.* Translation with commentary by Ronald T. Ridley. Canberra: Australian Association for Byzantine Studies, 1982. 5. 23. 2; 8. 16. 1–2.
Prosopography of the Later Roman Empire. Vol. II. Edited by A. H. M. Jones, J. R. Martindale, and J. Morris. Cambridge: Cambridge University Press, 1971. Reprinted 1992, p. 417.

Euphemia (1) (Lupicina)
(?–524 C.E.)   Roman: Balkans
Augusta

Euphemia was born Lupicina, a barbarian, a slave, and possibly a prostitute. She died an Augusta, wife of the emperor. Her husband, Justin, an Illyrian peasant who purchased her from her owner, rose through the armed forces and had received Senatorial rank. Her status grew with his, as did their wealth. In time they were able to contract a marriage.

The Senate declared her husband emperor in 518, following the death of the elderly emperor Anastasius. She changed her name from Lupicina to Euphemia, after Saint Euphemia of Chalcedon. Her name was not only more suitable for the wife of an emperor, but also declared the couple's support for orthodox Christianity. In a society ridden with strife over the nature of Christ, Euphemia and Justin supported the Council of Chalcedon, which had rejected the Monophysite position and established as orthodoxy that Christ embodied within himself two natures, human and divine, cojoined yet separate.

Euphemia and Justin were quite elderly when he became emperor. Having no children of their own, Justin followed custom and adopted his favorite nephew Justinian. Euphemia favored Justinian but was adamant against his marriage with THEODORA. She had assumed the airs of the elite and scorned Theodora's disreputable background. She succeeded in preventing their marriage of cohabitation from becoming a formal contractual marriage. Only after her death did Justin allow passage of the law permitting marriage between a man of Senatorial rank and an actress at the emperor's discretion.

Euphemia provided the funds for the construction of a church of St. Euphemia and a monastery. She was entombed in the church she built. Her husband was buried beside her several years later.

Sources

Procopius. *Secret History* vi. 17 (under Lupicina); ix. 47, 48, 49 (under Euphemia).

Prosopography of the Later Roman Empire. Vol. II. Edited by A. H. M. Jones, J. R. Martindale, and J. Morris. Cambridge: Cambridge University Press, 1971. Reprinted 1992, p. 423.

◉ Euphemia (2)

(c. sixth century C.E.)
Roman: Constantinople
political pawn

Euphemia, the daughter of John the Cappadocian, became the unwitting instrument of her father's downfall. John was Praetorian Prefect and highly regarded by the emperor Justinian for his efficiency in tax collection. John's cruelty and greediness endeared him to few but made him invaluable to Justinian who needed money to finance his grand plans. He was, however, especially hated by the Augusta THEODORA, who felt that he had too much influence over her husband. John also was suspected to harbor an ambition to become emperor, which roused Theodora's ally ANTONINA on behalf of her husband Belisarius who was Justinian's leading general. The two women hatched a plan.

Antonina sought out Euphemia. She lamented that the emperor failed to appreciate her husband's accomplishments. Asked by Euphemia, innocently or otherwise, why her husband did not use the troops under his command to change things, Antonina replied that her husband was engaged in campaigns far from Constantinople. He needed a partner. She suggested that Euphemia arrange a meeting with her father. Euphemia informed her father. In the meantime, Antonina informed Theodora of the meeting, which was to be held at night under the walls in a suburb of Constantinople. Theodora told her husband and also arranged for two trusted officials and a contingent of soldiers to hide behind a wall. The officials overheard the plans for a coup. John escaped the officers who came to arrest him. He fled into the city where he was apprehended and banished.

Nothing more is known of Euphemia.

Sources

Procopius. *Persian Wars* I, xxv. 13–30.

Bury, J. B. *Later Roman Empire from the Death of Theodosius to the Death of Justinian.* Vol. II. New York: Dover Publications Inc., 1958, pp. 57–58.

◉ Eurydice (1)

(fourth century B.C.E.)
Illyrian: Illyricum and Macedonia
political player

Eurydice used her intelligence, prestige, and wealth to protect herself and her children in the struggles over succession in Macedonia. The grandmother of CLEOPATRA (3) and Alexander the Great through her son Philip, she probably was from Illyria, northwest of Macedonia. The daughter of Sirrhas, she may have been descended from a branch of the Bacchiadae clan, originally of Corinth, some of whom migrated to Illyria and founded the royal family of Lyncestis. As an adult Eurydice learned to read and write, a rare accomplishment, especially for a woman, and one for which she justly was both grateful and proud.

She married twice. Her first husband was Amyntas III, ruler of Macedonia (393–70 B.C.E.). Their marriage strengthened the relationship between Illyria and Macedonia. She had three sons, Alexander, Perdiccas, and Philip, each of whom would in turn rule. She also had a daughter, Eurynoë.

She was widowed in 370, and her son Alexander succeeded his father. She married her daughter's husband, Ptolemy of Alorus, for dynastic reasons. It is not known what happened to Eurynoë, but it is known that Ptolemy killed Eurydice's son Alexander in 368 B.C.E. Never declared ruler, Ptolemy governed as regent over her other two sons for the next three years.

During Ptolemy's regency, a usurper named Pausanius attempted to claim the throne of Macedonia. Eurydice called on the Athenian general Iphicrates, whom her first husband had adopted as a son, to support the claim of her two remaining sons as the legitimate rulers of Macedonia. She put her two surviving children in his arms and pleaded their case. He drove out the usurper.

Later, when her son Perdiccas became old enough to rule, he had the regent Ptolemy killed. Perdiccas died in battle and was succeeded by her third son, Philip II, in 359. It remains unclear when Eurydice died.

Sources

Diodorus Siculus. *Library of History* 15.71.1; 77.5.
Justin. *Epitome* 7.4–5.
Plutarch. *De liberis educandis* 20.14.
Strabo. *Geography* 7.7, 8.
Macurdy, Grace. *Hellenistic Queens*. Reprint. Chicago: Ares Publishers, 1985, index.

▣ Eurydice (2) (Adea)
(c. 337–317 B.C.E.)   Greek: Macedonia
political player

Eurydice fought to rule Macedonia. She allied herself with Cassander during the turmoil in the decade after the death of Alexander the Great.

Eurydice, originally called Adea, was the granddaughter of Philip II of Macedon and an Illyrian princess, Audata. Her mother was CYNANE, and her father, Amyntas, was Philip's nephew. She learned the skills of hunting and fighting from her mother, who had hunted and fought at the side of her grandfather.

In 322 B.C.E., Eurydice and her mother joined the complicated struggle for power that resulted from the unexpected death of Alexander a year earlier. Their interest was Macedonia. The generals of Alexander's army had already carved up his empire, and Philip Arrhidaeus, the son of Philip II and PHILINNA, and the infant son of Alexander the Great and Roxane, had been declared the joint rulers of Macedonia. The general Antipater, who had represented Alexander in Europe during the Asia campaign, was declared regent and the effective ruler of Macedonia.

Cynane raised an army and went to Asia. To further Eurydice's claim over Macedonia, Cynane was determined that Eurydice marry the weak Philip. Cynane was killed in front of the troops on orders of Alcestas, the brother of Perdiccas, who had been the second in command of Alexander's army. Outraged by the murder, the army demanded that Eurydice and Philip Arrhidaeus be allowed to wed. Once married, Eurydice followed her mother's footsteps. She inflamed the troops against Antipater. By the time Antipater returned to Triparadessus, he found the troops unpaid and close to revolt. Somehow he turned the situation around and persuaded Eurydice and her husband, as well as Roxane and her infant son, to return with him to Macedonia.

Antipater died in 319, and Eurydice, now in Macedonia, found herself allied with his heir Polyperchon. Disagreements between them led to her offering an alliance to Cassander, who was seeking to overthrow Polyperchon. She arranged for her weak husband to proclaim Cassander regent. At the same time her stepgrandmother OLYMPIAS (1), who ruled in Epirus and who had unsuccessfully sought to control Macedonia for decades, allied herself with Polyperchon and raised an army against Eurydice.

At the border of Macedonia Eurydice met the army of Olympias. The soldiers regarded Olympias as sacred. They refused to fight. Olympias imprisoned Eurydice and tortured her. She sent her a sword, a noose, and hemlock and ordered her to commit suicide. Eurydice damned Olympias with the same fate befell her and hanged herself with the straps of her gown. She had not yet reached 20 when she died in 317.

In 316, Cassander defeated Olympias and had her murdered. He gave Eurydice a royal burial at Aegae.

Sources

Arrian. *Successors* 1.30–33, 42, 44.

Diodorus Siculus. *Library of History* 18.39.2–4; 18.49; 19.11, 1–8.

Justin. *Epitome* 14.5.1–4, 8–10.

Carney, Elizabeth D. "The Career of Adea-Eurydice." *Historia* 36 (1897): pp. 496–502.

Macurdy, Grace. *Hellenistic Queens.* Reprint. Chicago: Ares Publishers, 1985, pp. 40 ff, 48–52.

Oxford Classical Dictionary, ed. by Simon Hornblower and Antony Spawforth. 3d. ed. New York: Oxford University Press, 1996, p. 575.

▣ Eurydice (3)
(fourth–third century B.C.E.)
Greek: Macedonia, Egypt, and Miletus
political player; military leader

Eurydice experienced several turns of fortune during her life. Her father, Antipater, claimed Greece and Macedonia after the death of Alexander the Great in 323 B.C.E. Antipater cemented alliances with marriages for his three daughters. Eurydice married Ptolemy I Soter in 322 or 321 B.C.E. Her sister NICAEA (1) married Lysimachus, who governed Thrace; PHILA (1) married Demetrius, who later ruled Macedonia.

Eurydice was probably the third or fourth wife of Ptolemy I and bore four children: a son, Ptolemy Ceraunus, and three daughters, LYSANDRA, Ptolemais, and Theoxena. Eurydice had brought with her to Egypt her younger cousin BERENICE I. Her elderly husband fell in love with Berenice, who in 317 persuaded Ptolemy to make her son his successor.

Supplanted by the younger woman, the wealthy Eurydice never remarried. She went to live in Miletus, a city in Asia Minor, where she had considerable influence. In 286 she arranged the marriage of her daughter, Ptolemais, with Demetrius I, the widower of her sister Phila and the sometime ruler of Macedonia. The alliance enhanced the position of her ambitious son, who was said to have been violent and cruel. For a short while Ceraunus ruled Macedonia. Eurydice moved to Cassandreia in Macedonia. She controlled the city with her army and was honored with a festival called Eurydicaea.

Sources

Polyaenus. *Strategemata* 6.72.

Cary, M. *A History of the Greek World from 323 to 146 B.C.* London: Methuen, 1951, pp. 13, 43, 55, 58.

Macurdy, Grace. *Hellenistic Queens.* Reprint. Chicago: Ares Publishers, 1985, pp. 102–104.

▣ Eurydice (4)
(fourth–third century B.C.E.)
Greek: Thrace and Macedonia
political player

Eurydice was a participant in the unending conflict for control over Macedonia in the generations after the death of Alexander the Great. She was the daughter of NICAEA (1) and the granddaughter of Antipater, the general Alexander had assigned to rule Europe when he went to Asia on his last campaign. Her father, Lysimachus, ruled Thrace and married her mother to enhance the ties between Antipater and himself. Her sister was ARSINOË I. Eurydice married her cousin, also named Antipater who was the son of THESSALONICE and Cassander, ruler of Macedonia. Her marriage thereby extended into the next generation the historical link between Thrace and Macedonia.

On the death of her father-in-law, her mother-in-law divided Macedonia between Eurydice's husband, Antipater, and his brother, Alexander. Her husband, the elder brother, felt that he should have inherited all of Macedonia. He killed his mother and fought with his younger brother. Alexander appealed for help to the general Demetrius, who had his own ideas as to who should rule Macedonia. He arrived with his troops, murdered Alexander, drove Antipater and Eurydice out of the country, and made himself ruler.

Eurydice and Antipater fled to her father in Thrace. Lysimachus eventually made peace with Demetrius, which resulted in a quarrel with his son-in-law, Antipater. He had Antipater killed and then imprisoned Eurydice for siding with her husband. She probably died there, since she ceased to be an actor in the Macedonian drama.

Sources
Justin. *Epitome* 16.1, 2.
Macurdy, Grace. *Hellenistic Queens.* Reprint. Chicago: Ares Publishers, 1985, pp. 55–58.

◉ Euryleonis
(fourth century B.C.E.)   Greek: Sparta
self-made woman

Euryleonis was a wealthy Spartan woman. She was one of the first three women whose horses won races at the Olympic Games. Her name was inscribed on the lists of victors and on inscriptions that she erected. A statue of Euryleonis commemorating her victory in a two-horse chariot race stood in the temple of Aphrodite in Sparta.

Sources
Pausanias. *Description of Greece* 3.17.6.
Pomeroy, Sarah B. *Goddesses, Whores, Wives, and Slaves: Women in Classical Antiquity.* New York: Schocken Books, 1975, p. 130.

◉ Eusebia
(?–360 C.E.)   Greco-Roman: Constantinople
Augusta

Eusebia played an influential role in the policies of her husband, the emperor Constantius II, third son of Constantine the Great. A noted beauty whose father was probably Flavius Eusebius, a former consul, she became the emperor's second wife in 353/54.

Eusebia interceded to prevent the execution of the young future emperor Julian, cousin of the emperor, on spurious charges. In 355, despite opposition by some of his advisors, she convinced

her husband to appoint Julian Caesar for the West on the grounds that it was better to appoint a relative than anyone else. She was also responsible for the appointment of her brothers Flavius and Hypatius as consuls in the same year, and she arranged that no taxes be paid by her family.

Eusebia's great misfortune was her, or her husband's, inability to have children. Malicious gossip about Eusebia that circulated widely accused her of injuring Helen, her husband's sister and the wife of Julian, to avoid Helen's bearing a child. Eusebia died early in 360, supposedly from a fertility drug.

Sources
Ammiamus Marcellinus. XV. 2.8; 8.3; XVI. 10. 18.
Prosopography of the Later Roman Empire. Vol. I. Edited by A. H. M. Jones, J. R. Martindale, and J. Morris. Cambridge: Cambridge University Press, 1971. Reprinted 1992, pp. 300–301.

◉ Eustochium
(c. 368–c. 419/420)
Roman: Rome, Palestine
ascetic and Christian scholar

Eustochium chose to remain a virgin, devote herself to Christ, and live an ascetic life in a community with other like-minded women. She and her mother, the elder PAULA, founded monasteries in Palestine where they lived with the famed churchman Jerome and worked with him on a translation of the complete Bible from Greek to Latin. After the death of her mother, she restored the heavily indebted monasteries to financial stability and left them secure in the hands of her niece, the younger PAULA.

Eustochium mingled with leaders of the state and the educated elite who were attracted to Christianity. She was one of five children from a wealthy patrician family. Her mother Paula traced her lineage to the renowned CORNELIA (2). Her father, a senator, was descended from an old Greek family. Her sisters, BLAESILLA, Paulina, Rufina, and brother, Toxotius, named after his father, were all well educated and expected to continue the family tradition.

The fourth century was a period of political and economic disarray. The debasement of imperial coinage reflected economic dislocations that reduced agricultural production and income for the poor, the rich, and the state. The century also witnessed the development of Christian monasticism, among both women and men. In Rome, MARCELLA, a friend of the family and one of the early renowned Christian scholars and ascetics, used her house as a haven for chaste virgins and celibate widows who chose to live a simple and contemplative life. Eustochium's mother became a part of Marcella's Christian circle. After her husband died, she chose not to remarry and to initiate a monastic lifestyle for her children and her household. She sent Eustochium to live with Marcella, who was increasingly a teacher and scholar of Christianity as well as an ascetic role model. Eustochium mastered Greek and Hebrew which enabled her to read the ancient religious texts in their original languages.

The renowned ascetic and churchman Jerome arrived in Rome in 382 and changed the lives of Eustochium and her mother. Paula met him at Marcella's house where he would read aloud from the scriptures. He became a spiritual mentor for both Paula and Eustochium. Eustochium, however, was still young, and family members, other than her mother, tried to dissuade her from intensifying her devotion to Christ. Despite family pressure, in 384, when she was about 16, Eustochium took a vow of perpetual virginity. Jerome took the occasion to write her one of his longest letters, in which he outlined the motives for adopting a life of virginity and the rules to be followed. In Eustochium, Jerome found a woman with whom his own complicated ambivalences about women and sexuality could be safely explored. However, Eustochium had chosen the ascetic life after reflection and study with Marcella. Jerome's letters to her were more a polemic addressed to the unconvinced than a contribution to her spiritual path. The letters say nothing of her views, except that she had chosen never to marry.

Jerome came under criticism in Rome for his close relationship with Paula and for the death of Blaesilla, who had fallen ill after stringent fasting. The Roman bishop Damascus, a strong supporter, died in 384. His successor Siricius disliked Jerome and Jerome reluctantly left the city for Palestine in 385. Eustochium, her mother, and an entourage of young women, former servants, and perhaps eunuchs soon followed. On a 10-day stopover in Cyprus they met with bishop Epiphaneus and visited monasteries. They continued to Antioch and met Jerome. Together, they began a leisurely trip to Jerusalem, stopping to visit the important holy sites in Egypt, including the monasteries in the Nitrea Mountains. In Jerusalem, they visited the male and female monasteries that the elder MELANIA had built. They decided to build their own monasteries.

The group settled in Bethlehem, where they lived for some three years while their permanent quarters were being constructed. Paula was Eustochium's teacher as she built monasteries for women and for men as well as a hostelry for travelers. The men's monastery was administered by a male ascetic under Jerome's direction. The women, who came from different provinces and social strata, were divided into three groups and housed in separate buildings, each led by a woman responsible to Paula. All wore coarse clothing, took part in the household tasks, and made clothes for themselves and others. Each ascetic worked and ate separately, but came together several times a day in small groups for prayers, reading from the psalter, and the singing of hymns. Men and women came together on Sundays to worship at the Church of the Holy Sepulchre.

Eustochium and Paula were instrumental in Jerome's work to create an authoritative translation of the Greek Bible into Latin. A Latin edition of the Bible was seriously needed. What had been a bilingual empire, joined by the multilingual education of the elite, was separating according to language. Even an admired scholar and church father like Augustine knew no Greek. Paula and Eustochium reached back to the older pagan tradition, having mastered not only Latin and Greek but also Hebrew. They were the perfect foils for Jerome as he attempted the arduous task of translation. In the almost daily meetings with Jerome, they addressed questions about the interpretation of the text, uncertainties about the sense of one language expressed in another, and felicities of words and phrases. Some of the commentaries that he wrote came from their suggestions, and he dedicated a number of his works to them.

Eustochium faced a perilous situation in 404 when her mother died. After liberally providing for the children she left behind in Italy, Paula had spent all that she possessed and all she could borrow. Jerome did not think that Eustochium could ever repay her mother's debts. Eustochium, however, was a gifted administrator who confounded Jerome and not only paid off the debt but put the monasteries on a sound financial basis. Possibly, Eustochium turned to her family in Italy for help, particularly to her brother Toxotius who had been well endowed by her mother before she encountered financial difficulties.

Paula and Eustochium had remained in close contact with their family in Italy. Her brother Toxotius and his wife Laeta also felt the pull of asceticism and decided that their daughter, the younger Paula, should follow her grandmother's and aunt's footsteps, and that they would not arrange a marriage for her. Laeta wrote to Jerome in Bethlehem requesting advice on raising her. He urged her to send the child to Paula and Eustochium. The elder Paula died before the younger Paula left for Palestine when she was about 13 or 14 years old.

The Roman world changed forever when the city of Rome fell to the Goths in 410. Palestine, however, was at the outer reaches of the empire, and the eddies of change were slower. Business continued in the traditional fashion. Eustochium confronted the ever-present need for money to support the monasteries. In 416, the younger Paula was already in Palestine and working with Eustochium when Jerome wrote to Augustine with greetings from them and noted that in 415 the two women had sent a presbyter named Firmus on business, first to Ravenna and afterward to Africa and Sicily, but had not heard from him. Jerome enclosed a letter to be given to Firmus by Augustine if he could be located. The business most likely had to do with estates that the women, most probably the younger Paula, had inherited and may have wanted sold.

As a comment on the changes in society that were taking place, Jerome also apologized to Augustine for not sending the Latin translations that Augustine had requested, since there was a severe shortage of clerks who knew the written Latin language. However, religious controversies continued. Also in Palestine in 415, a council met at Diospolis and acquitted Pelegius of heresy. Pelegius developed an attractive fusion of Neoplatonism and Christianity in which he resolved the vexing issue of the presence of evil in a world created by God without evil. He posited that there was no original sin, that men and women had free will to choose good or evil, and that over the long course of time they would choose good. His acquittal was an occasion for rejoicing among his followers, which became a riot. Some of the buildings in the monastic compounds of Eustochium and Paula were burned.

In 417, Eustochium and Paula sent a letter to Innocent, the bishop in Rome, complaining of the murders, fires, and other outrages in their district consequent to the findings of the council. Innocent wrote to John, bishop of Jerusalem, demanding to know why he had not protected the victims and not seized the perpetrators. Before anything was done, however, Innocent and John died, and Eustochium followed in 419/20, soon after.

Sources

Jerome. Letter XXII. 2
————. Letter XXII. 2, 20.
————. Letter X, XXII, CXXXIV, CXXXVII.
McNamara, Jo Anne. "Cornelia's Daughters: Paula and Eustochium." *Women's Studies* (1984): 9–27.
Yarbrough, Anne. "Christianization in the Fourth Century: The Example of Roman Women." *Church History* 45, no. 2 (June 1976): 149–165.

Euthydice (Eurydice)

(fourth–third century B.C.E.)
Greek: Athens, Cyrene, and Macedonia
political player

Euthydice (also called Eurydice) fared well in the turbulent Greek political world of the late fourth century B.C.E. She came from a prominent Athenian clan, the Philaidaes. Her father, Miltiades, traced his ancestry to the general of the same name who had won the decisive victory over the Persians at Marathon in 490 B.C.E. She married Ophellas, a Macedonian officer in the army of Alexander the Great and who had joined Ptolemy when he became ruler of Egypt after Alexander's death. She went with her husband when Ptolemy sent Ophellas to Cyrene in North Africa where he subdued a revolt and became a virtually independent ruler, albeit under the suzerainty of Ptolemy.

Her husband and Agathocles, the tyrant of Syracuse, joined in a campaign to conquer Carthage. Her name was well known in Athens, and therefore many Athenians joined Ophellas's force. The expedition was not a success. The troops marched through the desert, and in 309 Agathocles murdered her husband.

After her husband's death, Euthydice returned to Athens. She married the handsome Demetrius I, who ruled Macedonia, had collected three wives, and was at a high point in his turbulent career. She gave birth to a son, Corrhagus.

Sources

Plutarch. *Vitae Parallelae (Parallel Lives): Demetrius* 14.2; 20.40; 53.4.

Oxford Classical Dictionary, ed. by Simon Hornblower and Antony Spawforth. 3d. ed. New York: Oxford University Press, 1996, p. 1,068.

▣ Eutropia, Galeria Valeria
(third–fourth century C.E.)
Roman: Syria, Italy, and Judaea
wife of the co-emperor, early Christian

Galeria Valeria Eutropia outlived her husband Maximian, coruler of the Roman Empire with Diocletian, and died a devout Christian. She was part of a circle of strong, independent, and wealthy women that included two Augusta—her daughter Flavia Maxima FAUSTA, and HELENA FLAVIA JULIA (I), who was the mother of Constantine—and Constantine's half sister, Flavia Julia CONSTANTIA. All of them influenced the political events and religious controversies of the day.

Eutropia was born in Syria. Her husband, a general under the emperor Diocletian, was appointed Caesar in the West and then co-Augustus. In addition to her daughter Fausta, she had a son Maxentius. On May 1, 305 C.E., the emperor Diocletian retired. Her husband reluctantly followed, and she settled with him in the court of Constantine. Maxentius, passed over for succession in favor of Galarius and Constantine, immediately took up arms and within the year persuaded his father to support him. The following years were filled with unsuccessful reconciliations and wars over succession. In 307, her daughter Fausta married the future emperor Constantine as part of her husband's effort to form an alliance between himself and Maxentius. The effort failed, and Eutropia found her children on opposite sides of the struggles for control over the empire, or some part of it.

Five years later, in 310 Maximian attempted to seize power and assassinate his son-in-law Constantine. Fausta revealed the plot to her husband. It failed, and soon after Maximian committed suicide. In 311, Eutropia's son, Maxentius, engaged in an armed struggle with her son-in-law. A year later, in 312, Constantine defeated him at the Milvian Bridge in one of the most famous battles of the later Roman Empire. It was not much of a battle; Maxentius died by drowning in the Tiber. However, this was the military encounter in which Constantine was said to have successfully tested the power of Christianity to bring him victory. Thereafter, Christianity, despite setbacks, was on the rise.

All during these conflicts among her kin, before and after her husband's death, Eutropia appears to have remained at Constantine's court. She, her daughter, Constantine's half sister, and his mother formed a nucleus of Christian women around whom probably gathered women of lesser rank and clerics. Constantia and Helena were close to the priests Arrius and Eusebius, and Helena has long been credited by some with bringing Christianity to her son.

After the death of her husband, Eutropia traveled to visit Christian holy places. Her life becomes less well documented although she is known to have visited the site of Mambre, revered by Jews and Christians. Constantine arranged for shrines to be erected after she reported that the site was being defiled by Jews and pagans with their markets and fairs. She probably died soon after.

Sources

Barnes, Timothy. *The New Empire of Diocletian and Constantine*. Cambridge: Harvard University Press, 1982, pp. 33, 34.

Lane Fox, Robin. *Pagans and Christians*. New York: Alfred A. Knopf, 1987, p. 674.

F

Fabia

(first century B.C.E.)   Roman: Rome
priestess

Fabia was a Vestal Virgin at the temple of Vesta in the Forum. In 73 B.C.E. she was accused of licentious behavior with Lucius Sergius Catiline, a young Roman patrician who led a conspiracy against the Senate that was successfully squelched by Fabia's brother-in-law Marcus Tullius Cicero, consul in 63 B.C.E. Fabia was exonerated.

In 58 she gave her half sister TERENTIA (1), Cicero's wife, sanctuary during the turbulent year of her husband's exile. She and Terentia were well-to-do women, and Fabia may have provided Terentia with cash until she could raise money from her own estates.

Sources

Asconius. Commentary on Cicero's *Pro Milone* 91c.
Cicero. *In Catalinum* 3, 9.
Balsdon, J. P. V. D. *Roman Women.* New York: John Day Comp., 1963, p. 239.

Fabiola

(?–c. 399 C.E.)   Roman: Rome, Palestine
founder of the first charity hospital in Europe

Fabiola lived with conflict and passion. Her life ricocheted between extremes of violence and repentance, celibacy and marriage, and wealth and poverty. She walked in sackcloth to ask forgiveness for her sins, founded Europe's first public hospital for the poor, and studied with the eminent ascetic Jerome. Fabiola lived as a wealthy and worldly Roman matron through two marriages. Although she gave her money to the poor, like many other wealthy women, she retained enough to support herself, her travels, and her projects. Unlike women who founded monasteries, however, Fabiola had an innovative vision of Christian charity, rooted in social action.

Fabiola came from a Roman patrician clan, the Fabia, converted to Christianity at a young age, and made an unfortunate first marriage. Her husband was violent and unfaithful. She obtained a divorce under civil law which recognized a woman's right to initiate divorce proceedings and to claim compensation for cause. She remarried, which was legal and desirable in upper-class Roman society where there was no clear role for an unmarried young man or woman. However, divorce and remarriage, even with cause, was not the Christian way in the fourth and fifth centuries. In addition, the growing ascetic movement elevated the value of lifelong celibacy, and, for the first time in the Greco-Roman world, never having married was more admired than being married. While it remained acceptable for a widow to remarry, it was the celibate widow and never-married virgin who were the more celebrated.

After the death of her second husband, Fabiola changed. Jerome, who wrote a warm and loving letter about her after her death, claimed that she saw the light of God. Dressed in sackcloth, Fabiola paraded back and forth in front of the Lateran Basilica, the largest church in Rome and home to the bishop, to seek forgiveness for her divorce and remarriage outside the church and to atone for her sins with public penance. Her intensity and perhaps theatricality impressed the bishop and she was allowed to take communion.

Fabiola sold her extensive properties and began to support monasteries and the poor throughout Italy. In Rome, she established the first public hospital, open to anyone in need. The application of the Christian principle of nondiscrimination for those in need was so unusual at the time that she had to walk the streets to find sick people and according to Jerome she would sometimes carry them to the hospital on her back. Fabiola tended to the sick herself, bathing, feeding, and cleansing their wounds, undeterred by unsightly injuries or infectious diseases. She also founded a nursing home adjacent to the hospital for anyone who needed additional time to recover and had no one to care for them, another application of Christian principles revolutionary to the period.

Fabiola's hospital and nursing home were very much needed. During the third and fourth centuries, the cities had ever-larger numbers of people on the streets and uncared for as economic dislocations upset historical networks of private patronage that had provided a basic social net. The very rich became more dependent on imperial favor and largesse than on the numbers of clients who waited outside their door for their attention, and too many landless poor had drifted into the city without work or family. An always harsh world had become harsher. Christian charity was welcome news. Fabiola provided a model for charity hospitals throughout Christendom, which extends to the present day.

Fabiola visited Jerome, the elder PAULA, and EUSTOCHIUM in Bethlehem in 394. As with most women of her time and class, she had a fine education which enabled her to read and write Greek and Hebrew as well as Latin. She also had an inquiring mind that found a mentor in Jerome, who liked smart, educated women and the role of intellectual guide. A threatened attack by the Germans was on the horizon and Fabiola returned to Rome, having visited for less than a year. Her innovative social reforms, however, were not over. Once back, she established a hospice for travelers, as well as a resting place for the poor and sick at Portus, two miles north of Ostia. The need must have been in the air. Pammachus, son-in-law of the elder Paula and the widower of her daughter Paulina, had a similar plan. After his wife's death, he became a monk, an urban ascetic, who dressed in rough robes and sought to use his wealth for the poor. They established independent hospices until it became apparent to Fabiola that collaboration would enhance both their efforts. The collaboration lasted until Fabiola died not long after in 399/400.

Sources

Jerome. Letter LXIV, LXXVII.

Prosopography of the Later Roman Empire. Vol. I. Edited by A. H. M. Jones, J. R. Martindale, and J. Morris. Cambridge: Cambridge University Press, 1971. Reprinted 1992, p. 323.

Fadia

(first century B.C.E.)
Roman: Italy and Greece
ignored wife

Fadia was the de facto wife of Mark Antony during the period when he studied in Athens. They had at least one child, and their relationship was sufficiently well acknowledged for Marcus Tullius Cicero to attack Antony in the second Philippic as the son-in-law of a lowborn freedman. Fadia's father was the freedman Quintus Fadius.

Sources

Cicero. *Orationes Philippicae* 2.2, 4.

Pauly, A., G. Wissowa, and W. Kroll. *Real-Encyclopadie d. Classischen Altertumswissenschaft 1893–.* (Germany: multiple publishers) 3.

Fannia (1)

(first century B.C.E.)   Roman: Rome
litigant

Fannia married Gaius Titinius from the city of Minturnae, located on the coast southeast of Rome. He divorced her and in 100 B.C.E., applied to retain her dowry on account of her immoral character. Fannia argued that Titinius had known her character before they married. The adjudicator was the consul Gaius Marius, the famous general.

Marius established that Titinius had married Fannia fully aware of her reputation and with the intention of divorcing her and keeping the dowry. He advised him to drop the case. Titinius refused. Marius fined Fannia a small sum and fined Titinius an amount equal to the value of the dowry to be paid to Fannia.

In 88 Fannia returned the favor by hiding Gaius Marius in her house when he was fleeing after his defeat by Lucius Cornelius Sulla.

Sources

Valerius Maximus. *Factorum et dictorum memorabilium libri IX* 8.2.3.

Balsdon, J. P. V. D. *Roman Women*. New York: John Day Comp., 1963, p. 220.

Bauman, Richard A. *Women and Politics in Ancient Rome*. London: Routledge, 1994, pp. 49–51.

Fannia (2)

(?–107 C.E.)   Roman: Italy
stoic; exiled

Fannia was an educated, cultured, and determined woman who lived a principled life. She was the daughter of the younger ARRIA and Publius Claudius Thrasea Paetus, as well as the granddaughter of the elder ARRIA and Caecina Paetus. Like her parents and grandparents, she was a follower of the Stoics.

Fannia married the elder Helvidius Priscus, who was already 55 years old and had a son, Helvidius Priscus, and a daughter-in-law, ANTEIA. Fannia and her mother voluntarily accompanied her husband into exile in 66 C.E. after the death of her father, Thrasea Paetus. They returned after the accession of the emperor Galba in 69. Her husband became praetor in 70 while still a supporter of Vespasian, who had become emperor after Galba's assassination in 69. Vespasian became increasingly angered with Priscus's persistent efforts to prosecute and discredit those whose false charges had brought about his own exile and the death of his fatherin-law during the previous regime. On Vespasian's orders, Priscus was again exiled, and Fannia and her mother again left with him. He was killed while in exile.

Fannia and Arria returned after the death of Vespasian. The new emperor, Domitian, was no friend of art, philosophy or dissent, principled or otherwise. In relatively short order, Fannia's stepson, the younger Helvidius Priscus, was condemned for writing a farce that Domitian believed to be a reflection on his own divorce. In 93 Domitian executed Priscus and in an effort to rid himself of dissenters, ordered all philosophers out of Rome.

A laudatory memoir of Priscus began to circulate in Rome. Fannia and her mother were tried for their support of the memoir written by Herennius Senecio. At the trial, Senecio declared that he had written the work at the behest of Fannia, which she corroborated and added that she had not only commissioned the work but had made private material available to Senecio. In her testimony Fannia sought to exonerate her mother from any responsibility; both were nonetheless exiled. Fannia retained a copy of the memoir, despite the Senate's order that all copies be destroyed.

In 96, after Nerva succeeded Domitian, Fannia and Arria returned to Rome. At the request of Pliny the Younger, a family friend, Fannia and Arria joined Anteia in a suit to restore Priscus's name and recover damages. The case was controversial, and the Senate was split. Pliny was pressed to drop the charges. Many among the elite felt that, should he succeed, they too would then be exposed to similar prosecution.

Fannia probably died in 107. She had contracted tuberculosis from nursing her relative JUNIA (3), who was a Vestal Virgin.

Sources

Tacitus. *Annales* 16.34–35.

Pliny the Younger. *Epistulae* 3.II.16; 7.19.

Balsdon, J. P. V. D. *Roman Women.* New York: John Day Comp., 1963, pp. 58–59.

Pauly, A., G. Wissowa, and W. Kroll. *Real-Encyclopadie d. Classischen Altertumswissenschaft 1893–.* (Germany: multiple publishers) 6.

▣ Fausta
(first century B.C.E.)   Roman: Rome
political player

Fausta and her twin brother, Faustus Cornelius Sulla, were children of the general and dictator Lucius Cornelius Sulla and CAECILIA METELLA (1) of the wealthy and prominent Metelli family, who bankrolled part of her husband's rise to power. She was a half sister of AEMILIA (2). Fausta's first husband was Gaius Memmius, who served as tribune and later as praetor. They were divorced in 55 B.C.E.

In 54 Fausta married Titus Annius Milo. Her husband's fiercest political opponent, Publius Clodius Pulcher, campaigned to become tribune while her husband sought election as consul. In January 52, Fausta was with her husband when the two men and their entourages met accidentally on the street. A fight ensued, and Milo had Clodius killed. Milo was charged, tried, and exiled.

Fausta remained in Rome while Milo went into exile. Milo asked his colleague, Marcus Tullius Cicero, to take care of his confiscated estate and provide that Fausta would secure the portion of the property that was reserved for her. Cicero fulfilled his obligations and left Fausta with modest means to support herself.

Rumors swirled around Fausta. It was whispered that she had not been true to either of her husbands and that Milo had found her in bed with the historian Sallust. However, she and Milo never divorced, despite stories about her sexual exploits that continued into the last days of the republic, some even attributed to her twin brother.

Sources

Asconius. Commentary on Cicero's *Pro Milone* 28.55

Aulus Gellius. *Noctes Atticae* 17, 18.

Cicero. *Epistulae ad Atticum* 5.8, 2f.

———. *Pro Milone* 28.55.

Macrobius. *Saturnalia* 2.2, 9.

Balsdon, J. P. V. D. *Roman Women.* New York: John Day Comp., 1963, p. 55.

Pauly, A., G. Wissowa, and W. Kroll. *Real-Encyclopadie d. Classischen Altertumswissenschaft 1893–.* (Germany: multiple publishers) 436.

▣ Fausta, Flavia Maxima
(289/290–324/325 C.E.)
Roman: Italy, Gaul, Asia, and North Africa
Augusta

Flavia Maxima Fausta died on orders of her husband, the emperor Constantine, for reasons that are obscure. Born in 289 or 290 C.E., she was the daughter of the co-emperor Maximian and his wife, Galeria Valeria EUTROPIA. Fausta and the future emperor Constantine signed a marriage contract in 293 when her father sought to strengthen relations with Constantine after his elevation to the status of Caesar. Fausta was 3 or 4 years old at the time of the contract signing, and Constantine, 19. They married 14 years later in 307, by which time her father had once retired and then re-entered the fray of armed conflict in support of his son who had been passed over for succession. A closer union with Constantine, however, remained desirable. In 311, Fausta warned Constantine that her father plotted to murder him while her slept. Maximian was seized and allowed to commit suicide. Her mother remained at Constantine's court.

Around 324, after Constantine became sole emperor, Fausta and her mother-in-law, HELENA FLAVIA JULIA (1), assumed the title of Augusta. Fausta, Eutropia, Helena, and Constantine's half sister Flavia Julia CONSTANTIA formed a powerful group of independentminded and wealthy women around Constantine. Although nothing has been recorded of Fausta's religious persuasion, the other three women were active Christians and very much a part of the evolving church.

The events of the subsequent years are unclear. In 326 when Fausta was 36 or 37 years old something sparked her death. Possibly at the urging of her mother-in-law Helena, Fausta died, scalded to death in the baths, either by accident, suicide, or intention. Constantine also poisoned his popular son, the 20-year-old Crispus, whose dead mother had been Constantine's longstanding lover before he married Fausta. At the same time, Licinius, the 12-year-old son of his half sister Constantia, was killed. Later commentators have speculated that Fausta had been involved in the death of Crispus and Licinius to protect her own sons. Alternatively, conflict between Fausta and her powerful mother-in-law may have erupted into conspiracy or confrontation with Constantine.

Fausta had three sons—Constantine II, Constantius, and Constans—and two daughters—Constantia, who married Gallus Caesar (351–354), and Helena, who married the emperor Julian (361–363).

Sources

Epitome de Caesaribus, 41.11 ff.

Eutropius. *Breviarium ab urbe condita* 6.10

Zosimus. *New History/Zosimus.* A translation with commentary by Ronald T. Ridley. Canberra: Australian Association of Byzantine Studies, 1982, 2.29

Balsdon, J. P. V. D. *Roman Women.* New York: John Day Comp., 1963, pp. 167, 169–170.

Barnes, Timothy. *The New Empire of Diocletian and Constantine.* Cambridge: Harvard University Press, 1982.

▣ Faustina, Aelia Flavia Maxima
(fourth century C.E.)
Roman: Constantinople
Augusta

Flavia Maxima Faustina married Constantine II in 360. He was the son of Constantine the Great and she was his third wife. Her husband died a year later in 361 while campaigning. After his death, her daughter CONSTANTIA (2) was born. Mother and daughter lived in Constantinople. A usurper, Procopius, led a revolt among the troops and claimed the title of emperor. Whether Faustina was or was not a part of the plot remains unknown. However, Procopius induced Faustina, along with her four-year-old daughter, to accompany him as he led his troops into battle. Despite his effort to establish legitimacy through the visible presence of mother and daughter, the revolt soon crumbled.

Nothing more is known about Faustina, although her daughter Constantia later married the emperor Gratian.

Sources

Ammiamus Marcellinus. xxi. 6, 4; (15, 6); xxvi. 7, 10; 9, 3.6.

Prosopography of the Later Roman Empire. Vol. I. Edited by A. H. M. Jones, J. R. Martindale, and J. Morris. Cambridge: Cambridge University Press, 1971. Reprinted 1992, p. 326.

▣ Faustina the Elder, Annia Galeria
(c. 94–140/141 C.E.)
Roman: Baetica/Narbonensis, Italy, and Asia
Augusta

Annia Galeria Faustina lived a privileged life that brought her honor, influence, and wealth during a period without any wars of succession or civil strife. Educated and intelligent, she came from the new elite of distinguished provincial families that emerged with the emperor Trajan and became the Antonine dynasty. She was the daughter of Marcus Annius Verus, consul in 126 C.E. Her mother, Rupilia Faustina, was descended from republican nobility. At about 16 years old, around 110, she married the future emperor Antoninus Pius. They had four children, two sons and two daughters, one of whom was the younger FAUSTINA, the future wife of the emperor Marcus Aurelius.

Faustina's husband was twice her age and very wealthy. They lived primarily on their estates in Italy and in the oldest settled parts of Spain and Gaul. They traveled together, and she accompanied her husband to Asia for his proconsulship. Some 18 years after her marriage, her husband was chosen by Hadrian as his successor. Hadrian adopted her husband, and her husband, in turn, adopted both the later emperor Marcus Aurelius and Lucius Verus to establish a line of succession. When it became obvious that Verus would not become the next emperor, her husband left to her the delicate negotiation that arranged for their daughter Faustina's marriage to Marcus Aurelius, instead of to Verus as had been originally planned.

Becoming the imperial couple dramatically transformed their lives. Although always wealthy, there nonetheless was a significant difference between the lifestyle of a private couple and that of an imperial couple. The household now included the feeding and housing of all those closely associated with the emperor. Moreover, the entire household moved with the emperor. Immediately after he assumed the role of emperor, it was reported that Faustina approached her husband about insufficient funds for household expenses, to which he was said to have replied that now that he was emperor there would never be sufficient funds.

The couple was always in the spotlight and faced with malicious court gossip. Her husband consistently ignored what he heard that suggested Faustina's sexual or other kinds of moral deficiencies.

In 138 Faustina was honored by the Senate with the title of Augusta and accorded the right to have coins struck in her name. She died shortly thereafter in 140 or 141 C.E. A temple was built and dedicated to her with suitable endowments and a priesthood. In 145, her husband named a new charity after her, Puellae Faustinianae, for destitute girls. Gold and silver statues of her voted by the Senate were paid for by her husband, who did not remarry. She left her personal fortune to her daughter, Faustina.

Sources

Scriptores Historiae Augustae. Antoninus Pius 1.7; 3.8; 5.2; 6.7–8.

Balsdon, J. P. V. D. *Roman Women.* New York: John Day Comp., 1963, pp. 142, 144, 145.

Oxford Classical Dictionary, ed. by Simon Hornblower and Antony Spawforth. 3d. ed. New York: Oxford University Press, 1996, p. 99.

Syme, Ronald. *Tacitus,* 2 vols. Oxford: Clarendon Press, 1958, p. 605.

▣ Faustina the Younger, Annia Galeria
(125/130–175 C.E.)
Roman: Italy, Asia, Gaul, and Germany
Augusta

Faustina was born between 125 and 130 C.E. to the emperor Antoninus Pius and the elder FAUSTINA.

On both sides of her family she came from provincial nobility, and her parents intended that she be the wife of her father's successor. She was originally affianced to Lucius Verus, but her mother arranged, after her father became emperor, that she instead wed her cousin Marcus Aurelius. The agreement took place in 139. They married in 145. One of their daughters was Annia Aurelia Galeria LUCILLA.

Faustina was intelligent, well educated, and independently wealthy since childhood, with an inheritance from her mother who had unexpectedly died in 140 or 141 C.E. An active woman, she traveled widely with the emperor despite regular pregnancies and the birth of 12 children. Faustina was granted the title of Augusta and the right to mint coins in 147. During her lifetime she accrued additional titles from cities around the empire. Her presence, with one of her young daughters, at the German front in Sirmium where her husband was campaigning near the Danube between 170 and 174, led to her title "Mother of the Camp."

From fragments of Faustina's letters to her husband reported in the ancient sources, it is clear that they regularly discussed the affairs of state, even

Annia Galeria Faustina the Younger
(Date: 161 C.E.–175 C.E. 1944.100.49230, Archives, American Numismatic Society)

military affairs. They sometimes disagreed. She urged Aurelius to impose the fullest possible extent of punishment on Gaius Avidius Cassius, the supreme military commander in the East who raised a revolt. Her husband, however, granted clemency to Cassius's family.

She was the most visible woman in the empire and always subject to gossip. On more than one occasion she was denounced to the emperor for treason or adultery. When faced with one such accusation, the emperor was said to have responded that if he were to divorce Faustina, she could reclaim her dowry, and since his position as emperor rested on his adoption by her father, he wondered whether he would have to return to her the empire.

Faustina died suddenly in 175 far from home in Cappadocia near the Taurus Mountains. Marcus Aurelius had her consecrated by the Roman Senate and established an endowment for poor girls in her name, as one had been endowed in the name of her mother.

Sources

Scriptores Historiae Augustae. Aurelian. 6.2.6; 19.2–9; 26.5–9; 29.1–3.

Balsdon, J. P. V. D. *Roman Women.* New York: John Day Comp., 1963, pp. 141–147.

Oxford Classical Dictionary, ed. By Simon Hornblower and Antony Spawforth. 3d. ed. New York: Oxford University Press, 1966, p. 99.

▣ Flaccilla, Aelia Flavia

(?–386 C.E.)   Roman: Spain, Constantinople
Augusta

Aelia Flavia Flaccilla, first wife of Theodosius the Great, had gold, silver, and bronze coins issued with her portrait wearing the diadem (royal purple headband) and the imperial fibula (brooch) that signified the power and authority to rule. She was the first woman raised to the rank of Augusta since the reign of Constantine the Great early in the century, and never before had the iconography of the coins suggested the public assimilation of imperial power into the status of Augusta.

Flaccilla's portrayal on the coinage reflected a conscious imperial policy to promote a family dynasty. Flaccilla came from an elite Spanish family and married Theodosius in 376, during his temporary retirement from the army and imperial service. She became Augusta about 384, after Honorius was born. He was her third child. Her son Arcadius later became emperor in the East. Her daughter Pulcheria died when she was only nine or ten years old.

Flaccilla was a devout and orthodox Christian and, amid the splintered and competing Christian factions of the times, never hesitated to use her position on behalf of the orthodox agenda. She dissuaded her husband from meeting the respected Arian bishop Eunomlius of Cyzicus, fearful that he would influence the emperor. She followed the new Christian path of women's piety and provided aid for the poor and sick, as well as widows and orphans. Modeling her behavior on scripture and on the efforts of women across the empire to give substance to Christianity, she deviated radically from her elite upbringing and visited hospitals, personally feeding the patients. Her humanitarian efforts gained her popular favor and contributed to the reorienting of women's virtuous behavior by moderating Roman imperiousness based on birth and class with the new orthodoxy of Christian classless rhetoric. Her daughter-in-law Aelia Eudoxia and her granddaughter PULCHERIA effectively combined the new piety to expand the power and authority of imperial women encapsulated in the images of Flavia on the imperial coinage.

Flavia died in Thrace in 386. Gregory of Nyssa, bishop of Constantinople, delivered an eulogy that claimed the empire felt her death more than earthquakes, floods, or wars. A statue in her honor was erected in the house of the Senate.

Sources

Gregory of Nyssa. *Oratorio funebris in Flaccillam Imperatricem.*

Sozomen. *Historia Ecclesiastica.* 7.6.3.

Theodoret. *Historia Ecclesiastica.* 5.18, 2–3; 19.

Brill's New Pauly: Encyclopedia of the Ancient World: Classical Tradition, Vol. 5, edited by Manfred Landfester et al. Boston: Brill, 2002, p. 448.

Holum, Kenneth G. *Theodosian Empresses: Women and Imperial Dominion in Late Antiquity.* Berkeley: University of California Press, 1982, index.

Prosopography of the Later Roman Empire. Vol. I. Edited by A. H. M. Jones, J. R. Martindale, and J. Morris. Cambridge: Cambridge University Press, 1971. Reprinted 1992, pp. 341–342.

Pauly, A., G. Wissowa, and W. Kroll. *Real-Encyclopadie d. Classischen Altertumswissenschaff 1893* (Germany: multiple publishers) VI. (1909) 2,431–2,433.

Flora

(first century B.C.E.)   Roman: Rome
self-made woman

Flora, whose origins, status, and family remain unknown, was so beautiful that the rich and illustrious Caecilius Metellus included a portrait of her among the decorations in the Forum's ancient temple of Castor and Pollux, with which his family was associated.

She was the lover of Gnaeus Pompeius Magnus (Pompey the Great), an often-married man whose appeal to women was well attested by the caring and devotion of his wives. Flora was reputed to have said that she never left the embraces of Pompey without the marks of his teeth to evidence his passion. She refused the advances of Pompey's friend Geminus, claiming devotion to Pompey. Geminus went to Pompey, who offered no opposition. To her great distress, he also ended his affair with her.

Sources
Plutarch. *Vitae Parallelae (Parallel Lives): Pompeius* 2.3.

Floronia

(?–216 B.C.E.)   Roman: Rome
priestess

Floronia was one of the six Vestal Virgins serving in 216 B.C.E. in the temple of Vesta, one of the oldest temples in the Forum. She and a sister priestess, OPIMIA, were convicted for licentious behavior. Floronia's lover, Lucius Cantilius, a scribe and a member of a minor order of the priestly college, was beaten to death. She was either buried alive or committed suicide before she could be entombed.

The improper behavior of the Vestals was considered a harbinger of ill omen for the city. The devastating defeat of the Romans by Hannibal and the Carthaginians at Cannae in the same year was perceived as retribution for Floronia and Opimia's misdeeds.

Sources
Livy. *From the Founding of the City* 22.57.2–5.

Fulvia (1)

(first century B.C.E.)   Roman: Italy
political player

Fulvia was a member of a prominent Roman family and socialized with the political elite of her day. Her lover was Quintus Curius, also from a prominent family. Curius had financial problems, and it was rumored that Fulvia needed more money than he could provide. After he was ejected from the Senate, Curius joined the conspiracy led by the thwarted patrician Lucius Sergius Catiline in 63 B.C.E. From his boastful and threatening behavior, Fulvia drew from Curius information about the developing conspiracy.

Catiline was in debt and had failed in his attempts to win high office. He began to organize discontented veterans and small landowners. He was joined by a group of men and women from respectable and even elite families who also suffered from the effects of inflation on fixed incomes. They planned to take over Rome.

Fulvia arranged with Marcus Tullius Cicero, consul in 63, to act as a conduit of information about the conspiracy. Cicero promised Fulvia that her lover Curius would be rewarded for his role as informant. As their situation became more desperate, Catiline and his conspirators decided to set fire to Rome and murder Cicero. The plot failed. Fulvia informed Cicero of the planned attempt on his life. Catiline left Rome, and he and his followers were declared public enemies by the Senate. Julius Caesar convinced the Senate that Curius should not receive the large reward that had been promised by Cicero.

Catiline was killed in battle, and five of his ringleaders were executed in Rome after Cicero obtained written evidence of their plot. Nothing more is heard of Fulvia.

Sources

Sallust. *Bellum Catilinae* 23.3 ff.; 26.3; 28 2.

Balsdon, J. P. V. D. *Roman Women.* New York: John Day Comp., 1963, p. 49.

Bauman, Richard A. *Women and Politics in Ancient Rome.* London: Routledge, 1994, pp. 67–69.

Pauly, A., G. Wissowa, and W. Kroll. *Real-Encyclopadie d. Klassischen Altertumswissenschaft 1893.* (Germany:multiple publishers) 113.

◙ Fulvia (2)

(?–40 B.C.E.)   Roman: Italy and Greece
political player

Fulvia was indomitable and fearless. She had an implacable determination and possessed a spirit and strength of character unmatched by any of her three husbands. Among the many strong and independent women of the late republic, Fulvia holds a unique position. She alone among these Roman women crossed the gender boundary and stepped into the male preserve of military action during civil war.

Fulvia was the wealthy daughter of Marcus Fulvius Bambalio and Sempronia, both from atrophying ancient families. Her mother was the sister of SEMPRONIA (2), who was said to have had a part in the conspiracy of Lucius Sergius Cataline in 63 B.C.E. Fulvia's first husband was the brash, tempestuous, and sometimes brilliant aristocrat Publius Clodius Pulcher. His oratory in favor of populist positions was supported by armed bands in his tribuneship of 58 B.C.E.

Clodius again campaigned for tribune while a bitter enemy, Titus Annius Milo, campaigned for consul. They accidentally met on the road in January 52. Fulvia was with her husband surrounded by their retinue. A dispute ensued, and Milo had Clodius killed. Fulvia brought Clodius's body back to Rome, where she placed it in the courtyard of their house and incited the crowd with a display of his wounds. The body was carried into the Senate and burned as the Senate house itself caught fire.

Milo was tried. He was defended by Marcus Tullius Cicero, consul in 63 and the man responsible for thwarting the earlier conspiracy led by Cat-

iline in which Fulvia's aunt may have had some part. There was a history of enmity, however, between the opposing sides in the trial. Nearly a decade earlier, Cicero had spoken on behalf of the prosecution against Clodius, who had been caught in the house of Julius Caesar disguised as a woman during the women-only rites of the Bona Dea. Rumor had it that Clodius was there for an assignation with Caesar's wife, POMPEIA (1). He was declared innocent by a heavily bribed jury. Clodius became Cicero's sworn enemy; as tribune in 58, he secured Cicero's exile. At the trial, Fulvia testified. She also arranged the public lamentations of her mother, among others, that aroused the sympathies of the onlookers. Milo was convicted and sent into exile. Cicero transferred his enmity from Fulvia's husband to her.

With Clodius, Fulvia had a daughter, CLAUDIA (5), and a son, Publius Claudius, who later became praetor. Her second husband was Gaius Scribonius Curio, tribune in 50 B.C.E. and another brilliant orator. He became an ally of Julius Caesar from whom he received a large monetary gift. He served under Caesar in 49 and was killed in a military campaign in Africa. Their son, Scribonius Curio, was executed by Octavian after his victory at Actium in 31 B.C.E.

After her second husband's death, Fulvia married Mark Antony by 45 B.C.E. A year later, in 44, Cicero accused Fulvia and Mark Antony of taking bribes and selling properties and favors for vast sums of money. The attack was directed against Fulvia. Cicero claimed that Fulvia conducted property auctions in the women's quarters of Antony's house and that Antony preferred an avaricious Fulvia to the Roman Senate and people. In January 43, enemies of Antony, led by Cicero, attempted to have the Senate declare Antony a public enemy. Fulvia, her mother-in-law, JULIA (2), and their supporters visited the houses of key senators during the night to secure their vote against the motion. The next morning, dressed in mourning clothes, they buttonholed senators on their way to the Senate with lamentations and cries. Their claim that it was contrary to Roman law to declare a citizen a public enemy without a trial, no doubt persuaded some. All in all the women enabled Antony's supporters to defeat the bill.

After Antony's defeat at Mutina in April 43, however, he left Italy and was declared an outlaw by the Senate. In Rome, Antony's enemies instituted a series of lawsuits against Fulvia to deprive her of her property. Titus Pomponius Atticus Cicero's closest friend and one of the wealthiest and most generally respected men in Rome, aided Fulvia. He accompanied her to court, provided the necessary surety to assure her future legal appearances, and lent her money without interest or security to enable her to make the payments due on the estate that she had purchased before Antony's exile.

Fulvia worked to enhance Antony's position in relation to the two other members of the ruling Second Triumvirate, Octavian and Lepidus. In 43, when the triumvirate was formed, Claudia, Fulvia's daughter with Clodius, was to become the first wife of Octavian and cement the alliance. The triumvirs proscribed Cicero, and he was killed on December 7, 43. It was said that his head was sent to Fulvia and Antony. The ancient sources are uniformly hostile to Fulvia and embroidered her response to Cicero's death in gruesome detail. They depict her as avaricious and cruel. Her avarice was specifically blamed for the death of Quintus Salvidienus Rufus. After his name appeared on the lists, he offered her his house, said to be the reason she had had him proscribed. It was to no avail. He was killed.

Proscriptions raised needed money as well as rid the triumvirs of real and imagined enemies. Still, money was a problem. At one point, the triumvirs ordered the 1,400 richest women in Rome to provide an evaluation of their property preparatory to a special tax. The women protested. The women's arguments, as articulated by HORTENSIA, spoke to their unique position. They argued that this was not a war against an outside enemy, as had been the war against Hannibal when women willingly surrendered their personal wealth. This was a civil war in which husbands and sons fought against brothers and cousins. This was not *their* war, according to the women. They were supported by

Antony's mother, Julia, and by the independent-minded OCTAVIA (2), who was Octavian's sister, but not by Fulvia.

Lucius Antonius, the brother of Antony, became consul, along with Publius Servilius, in 41, while Antony went to the East. Fulvia and Lucius worked together closely in Antony's interests. They largely dominated the political scene in Rome. They especially sought to assure Antony honor for the distributions to the troops, since he, not Octavian, had been responsible for the defeat of Brutus and Cassius at the battle of Philippi in 42. Their anti-Octavian policy extended into the prosperous regions of Umbria, Etruria, and the Sabine country north of Rome. They attempted to form a coalition there of soldiers and property owners against Octavian after protests against Octavian's confiscations for the resettlement of veterans.

Furious at Fulvia's opposition, Octavian officially divorced Claudia in 41, after a two-year marriage that was never consummated. She had been a child at the time of the union, which was primarily a politically symbolic act, as was the divorce. Octavian also publically read a copy of the pact Antony had made with the soldiers in Rome who were against war and demanded a settlement. With Antony still in the East, however, Fulvia backed Lucius Antonius in support of the Italian cities against Octavian. The Perusine War ensued. Lucius Antonius marched into Rome without opposition and then left to advance north in order to link up with Antony's generals, who controlled the Gallic provinces.

Fulvia and Lucius Antonius sent messages to Antony. They urged his generals in Italy and Gaul to assist them. Octavian was in a precarious position both on land and at sea. If Antony's cohorts had united against him, Octavian could not have received reinforcements and most probably would have been defeated. However, without direct instructions from Mark Antony, most of the generals did not act. Lucius Antonius went to the ancient city of Perusia north of Rome, where he was surrounded by the forces of Octavian. Fulvia, who was not in Perusia, persuaded some of Antony's forces to aid Lucius.

Octavian launched a vitriolic and obscene attack on Fulvia as the main instigator in the Perusine War since she was the most vulnerable. Octavian feared to offend Antony, and Lucius Antonius's republican principles made an attack on him equally undesirable. Lucius Antonius surrendered early in 40, and Octavian appointed him governor of Spain in order to maintain good relations with Antony. Fulvia fled to Greece with her children. Antony blamed her no less than had Octavian. He left her in the city of Sicyon, where she became ill and died.

Fulvia and Antony had two sons. The eldest, Antyllus, was executed on Octavian's orders after Antony's defeat at Actium. The other, Iullus Antonius, was brought up in the household of Octavia, the emperor's sister and Antony's wife after divorcing Fulvia.

Sources

Appian. *Roman History: Bella civilian (Civil Wars)* 3.51; 4.29.32; 5.14, 19, 21, 33, 43, 50, 52, 55, 59.

Asconius. Commentary on Cicero's *Pro Milone*

Cicero. *Orationes Philippicae* 2.44, 113; 5.4, 11; 6.2, 4.

Dio Cassius. *Roman History* 46.56.4; 47.8.2–5; 48.4.1–6; 5.1–5; 6.1–4; 10.2–4; 12.4; 15.2; 28.3–4.

Martial. *Epigrammata* 20.

Plutarch. *Vitae Parallelae (Parallel Lives): Antonius* 10.3–5.

Babcock, Charles L. "The Early Career of Fulvia." *American Journal of Philology* 86 (1965), pp. 1–32.

Bauman, Richard A. *Women and Politics in Ancient Rome.* London: Routledge, 1994, index.

Delia, Diana. "Fulvia Reconsidered." In *Womens History and Ancient History,* ed. by Sarah B. Pomeroy. Chapel Hill: University of North Carolina Press, 1991, pp. 197–217.

Oxford Classical Dictionary, ed. by Simon Hornblower and Antony Spawforth. 3d. ed. New York: Oxford University Press, 1996, p. 614.

Pauly, A., G. Wissowa, and W. Kroll. *Real-Encyclopadie d. Klassischen Altertumswissenschaft 1893.* (Germany:multiple publishers) 113.

Syme, Ronald. *The Roman Revolution.* London: Oxford University Press, 1963, index.

G

Galeria Fundana

(first century C.E.)   Roman: Rome
political player

Galeria Fundana both suffered poverty and enjoyed imperial wealth over the decades of a tumultus marriage with Aulus Vitellius, emperor for nine months before Vespasian in 69 C.E. She has been lauded in the sources for her probity and modesty in the face of both adversity and excess. Galeria's father had been a praetor, but little else is known of her family. She married Vitellius after he divorced his first wife, PETRONIA. They had two children, a girl and a boy.

By all accounts her husband was a spendthrift. By the time of their marriage, he had already gone through the money accumulated from an African command and had divorced his first wife when she refused to give him access to her fortune. His casualness with money was combined with lusty appetites. He was well known in Rome for his overindulgence in drink and food. The emperor Servius Sulpicius Galba offered him the command of troops in Lower Germany at a moment when he had no other apparent future and was hounded by debt collectors.

Vitellius raised the funds to equip himself with a mortgage on his house. He also took from his mother, SEXTILIA, some pearls to pawn or sell.

Galeria and their children remained in Rome in straitened circumstances living in the rather poor rented quarters of a tenement. She faced his unhappy creditors.

Vitellius was declared emperor by his forces in Lower Germany while Marcus Salvius Otho was declared emperor by the Praetorian Guard in Rome. Galeria and her mother-in-law were in danger as the opposing forces prepared to meet each other. Vitellius sought to protect them with a letter to the brother of Otho threatening to kill him and his children if his family was harmed. After a tense period in which Galeria and Sextilia remained unharmed, Vitellius's army defeated Otho outside of Rome.

No happier in splendor than in poverty, Galeria moved into Nero's palace with Vitellius. Over the next months, Vitellius spent huge amounts on food, drink, and entertainment in which Galeria took as little part as possible. She, was not, however, without influence. As emperors go, Vitellius was far from among the most bloodthirsty, though he did kill some of Otho's supporters. The sources credit Galeria for protecting Trachalus, an adviser to Otho who may well have been her earlier protector.

The weaknesses of Vitellius were eventually his undoing, and the armed forces in varying parts of the empire revolted and rallied around Vespasian. Vitellius was killed in December 69. Galeria's young son was also killed, but Galeria and her daughter were unharmed. Vespasian made a fine match for her daughter and even provided her with a dowry.

Sources

Suetonius. *The Lives of the Caesars:* Vespasian 14.
Suetonius. *The Lives of the Caesars:* Vitellius 6.
Tacitus. *Historiae* 2.60, 64.

▣ Galla

(?–394 C.E.)   Roman: Italy, Constantinople
political player

Galla was young and very beautiful when she became the second wife of Theodosius the Great after his first wife, FLACCILLA, died. Galla offered the middle-aged emperor an opportunity to cement a dynastic relationship between the Eastern and Western parts of the empire through her deceased father, the Western emperor Valentinian I.

However, JUSTINA, Galla's mother, had her own political plans for which her desirable daughter was the perfect bargaining chip. Galla had fled with her mother and her brother, Valentinian II, to Thessalonica in northern Greece after the usurper, Maximus, invaded Italy. The price of her marriage was the support of Theodosius against Maximus and in favor of the restoration of Valentinian II in Italy and as emperor of the West. Since both Theodosius and Galla desired similar ends, the marriage was never in doubt.

Like her mother, Galla was most likely an Arian Christian. Her relationship with her stepson, the future emperor Arcadius, was, on at least one occasion, stormy. After an argument, she was forced to leave the palace.

She bore three children, but only one survived—GALLA PLACIDIA born in 388/389. Galla died from a miscarriage in 394.

Sources

Cassiodorus. *Variarum x.* 21.24 (a. 535; letters sent to Theodora by Gudeliva).
Procopius. *Gothic Wars* V. iv. 1–31.
———. *Secret History.*

Brill's New Pauly. Encyclopedia of the Ancient World. Vol. V. *Classical Tradition.* Edited by Manfred Landfester, in collaboration with Hubert Canick and Helmut Schneider. Boston: Brill, 2006, p. 667.
Bury, J. B. *History of the Later Roman Empire: From the Death of Thodosius I to the Death of Justinian.* Vol. I. New York: Dover Publications, Inc., 1958, p. 198.
Holum, Kenneth G. *Theodosian Empresses: Women and Imperial Dominion in Late Antiquity.* Berkeley: University of California Press, 1982, pp. 45–46.
Prosopography of the Later Roman Empire. Vol. I. Edited by A. H. M. Jones, J. R. Martindale, and J. Morris. Cambridge: Cambridge University Press, 1971. Reprinted 1992, p. 382.

▣ Gallitta

(first century B.C.E.–first century C.E.)
Roman: Rome and Germany
adulterer

Gallitta was caught in the paradox of the Julian laws. Intended to uphold traditional values, the *leges Juliae,* passed in 18 B.C.E. and expanded in 9 C.E., all but forced a husband to prosecute his wife, for adultery, since he would otherwise open himself to the charge of procuring.

Gallitta, the wife of a military tribune, had an affair with a centurion. Her husband had reported this to the legate of the consul, who in turn told the emperor Trajan. The centurion lover was banished. The husband, now satisfied and still in love with his wife, did not bring any charges against her. But in Roman legal logic, no husband could condone adultery by his wife unless he gained a financial return from her sexual activities. In that case he would be not her husband but her pimp and could be prosecuted by a third person under the charge of procuring. Gallitta's husband, therefore, faced a serious threat of prosecution.

Instead, Trajan punished Gallitta. The emperor ruled that she should be banished to an island and forfeit half her dowry and one-third of her property. Her fate could have been worse. She could have been condemned to death and all of her property confiscated.

Sources

Pliny the Younger. *Epistulae* 6.31.

Berger, Adolf. *Encyclopedic Dictionary of Roman Law.* Philadelphia: American Philosophical Society, 1953, p. 352.

Gardner, Jane F. *Women in Roman Law and Society.* London: Routledge, 1995, pp. 127–131.

▣ Glaphyra (1)

(first century B.C.E.)   Greek: Asia Minor
political player

Glaphyra from Cappadocia, in Asia Minor, met the Roman general Mark Antony in 41 B.C.E. when she was in the court of the ruler of Commona. They had an affair. Sources credit her with his decision to appoint her son, Archelaus, ruler of Cappadocia in 36. She was the grandmother of GLAPHYRA (2).

Sources

Appian. *Roman History: Bella civilian (Civil Wars)* 5.7.
Dio Cassius. *Roman History* 49.32.3–4.
Martial. *Epigrammata* 11.20.

▣ Glaphyra (2)

(first century B.C.E.–first century C.E.)
Greek (probable Roman citizen): Cappadocia
and Judaea
adventurer

Glaphyra married three times into ruling families. She was a beautiful and smart woman, the daughter of Archelaus, ruler of Cappadocia, and the granddaughter of GLAPHYRA (1), who was said to have had an affair with the Roman general and triumvir Mark Antony. Her first husband was Alexander, the son of Mariamme I and Herod the Great. Her father-in-law was the ruler of Judaea and closely associated with the Roman Julio-Claudians. Glaphyra and Alexander had two sons, Alexander and Tigranes. The latter became ruler of Armenia (6–12 C.E.).

Glaphyra was not popular among the Jews. Proud of her elite birth, she flaunted her higher status in relation with the other women of the court. In 6 B.C.E., her father-in-law, Herod, executed her husband for conspiring against him. Herod returned Glaphyra's dowry and made clear that she was no longer welcome in Judaea. She

returned to Cappadocia and married the learned king Juba II of Mauritania after the death of his wife, CLEOPATRA SELENE. They divorced, and she returned again to Cappadocia.

Her third husband was Archelaus II, the son of Malthace and Herod and the half brother of her first husband. They met after the death of Herod, when Archelaus visited her father in Cappadocia. He had inherited and ruled part of his father's kingdom. He divorced his wife in order to marry Glaphyra. The marriage created political problems for her new husband. He was a Jew, and it was considered an offense against the Torah for him to marry a woman who had been the wife of his half-brother and with whom she had had children. Glaphyra died soon after the marriage. Before her death, she was said to have dreamed that her first husband forgave her.

Sources

Josephus. *Antiquitates Judaicae (Jewish Antiquities)* 7.341, 345–53.
———. *Bellum Judaicum (Jewish Wars)* 1.476, 552–53; 2.114.
Jones, A. H. M. *The Herods of Judaea.* Rev. ed. Oxford: Clarendon Press, 1967, index.
Perowne, Stewart. *The Later Herods*, pp. 22–23, 58.

▣ Glycera

(fourth century B.C.E.)
Greek: Athens and Babylon
self-made woman

Glycera was acknowledged as the most beautiful woman of Athens. She went to Babylon at the behest of Harpalus, a Macedonian, who was a lifelong friend of Alexander the Great. Harpalus was physically handicapped and could not serve as a foot soldier. Alexander appointed him as treasurer headquartered in Babylon when he left to campaign in India. Harpalus, who was said to have believed that Alexander would never return, he embezzled large sums of money to support an extravagant lifestyle. Prior to Glycera, he had lived with PYTHONICE, another Greek woman of great beauty, whom he treated well and for whom he gave a splendid funeral and erected a monument when she died. He did no less for Glycera who also lived in great splendor until Alexander returned and discovered Harpalus's misuse of funds. Harpalus fled with money and some soldiers. He bribed the Athenians, including Demosthenes, in an attempt to gain asylum in Athens. Refused, he fled to Crete, where he was murdered. Glycera's death is unrecorded.

Sources
Athenaeus. *Deipnosophistae* 13.586c.
Diodorus Siculus. *Library of History* 17.108.4–8.

Gorgo
(fifth century B.C.E.)   Greek: Sparta
patriot

Gorgo has been portrayed in the sources as smarter and wiser than the men around her. She was the only child of Cleomenes I, ruler of Sparta (520–490 B.C.E.). After the death of her father, perhaps by suicide, she married Leonidas, a stepbrother of her father, who succeeded him as ruler in 490.

Gorgo was an astute and steadfast advocate of the Greek cause against the Persians at a time when their conflict dominated the future of the West. She was only eight years old when Aristagorus, tyrant of Meletus, came to Sparta in 499–98 to obtain Cleomenes' support, ostensibly to free the Greek settlements in western Asia Minor from Persian rule. In their final meeting, Aristagorus came to the house of Cleomenes, and found him in a room with Gorgo. He asked to speak to Cleomenes privately, but Cleomenes told him to speak in front of his daughter. Aristagorus offered Cleomenes a bribe of 10 talents to betray his fellow Greeks and raised the offer as Cleomenes remained firm. Gorgo turned to her father and urged him to leave the room or he would certainly be corrupted by the everincreasing amount of money. Cleomenes left the room.

Later prior to the invasion by the Persian king Xerxes, Demaratus, a Greek exile living in the Persian city of Susa, discovered the Persian plan to invade Greece and sent a message of warning. He inscribed his message on wood and then laid it over with wax. When the tablet arrived in Sparta, Gorgo suggested removing the wax to see if a message lay beneath it. The Spartans sent word of the plan to the other cities in Greece.

It was Gorgo's husband, Leonidas, who held the pass at Thermopylae in one of history's most famous battles. He secured the retreat of the main body of his troops while he fiercely counterattacked with his small remaining force. He held off the Persians for two critical days before he was killed.

Sources
Herodotus. *The Persian Wars* 5.51; 6.75; 7.205, 239.
Burn, Andrew Robert. *Persia and the Greeks: The Defense of the West, c. 546–478 B.C.* New York: St. Martin's Press, 1962, pp. 199, 394.

Gratilla
(first century C.E.)   Roman: Rome
stoic

Gratilla followed the Stoic philosophy. Her husband, Junius Arulenus Rusticus, a well-known disciple of Stoicism, was executed by the emperor Titis Flavius Domitian in 93 C.E. after he had written in praise of two earlier Stoics: Thrasea Paetus, who had been condemned by the emperor Nero, and Helvidius Priscus, who had been executed by the emperor Titus Flavius Vespasian. Gratilla went into exile, following in the footsteps of the two praised Stoics' women: the younger ARRIA and FANNIA (2).

Sources
Pliny the Younger. *Epistulae* 3.11; 5.1.

Gygaea
(fifth century B.C.E.)   Greek: Macedonia
political pawn

Gygaea was the daughter of Amyntas, ruler of Macedonia, and the sister of Alexander I (495–50 B.C.E.), with whom she lived. Bubares, a Persian, arrived to investigate the deaths of several Persian envoys said to have been murdered by the Macedonians on orders from Alexander for insulting Macedonian women at a banquet. Her brother sidetracked the investigation by arranging a marriage between Gygaea and Bubares, accompanied by a substantial dowry. Gygaea had a son, Amyntas, who governed the city of Alabanda in southwest Asia Minor.

Sources

Herodotus. *The Persian Wars* 5.21; 8.136.

Burn, Andrew Robert. *Persia and the Greeks: The Defense of the West, c. 546–478 B.C.* New York: St. Martin's Press, 1962, p. 134.

Macurdy, Grace. *Hellenistic Queens.* Reprint. Chicago: Ares Publishers, 1985, p. 15.

H

Hagesichora

(seventh century B.C.E.)   Greek: Sparta
choral leader

Hagesichora led a women's chorus in Sparta during the second half of the seventh century B.C.E. Described in the sources as beautiful with golden hair, she probably came from an elite family whose daughters took leadership positions in the religious festivals that marked the Spartan calendar.

Traditionally Spartan choruses of 10 women, accompanied by the flute and divided into 2 parts, sang poetic hymns to the gods. Hagesichora led one of the five-voice sections. It remains unclear if she sang or only performed other tasks of direction and production. Also uncertain were the relationships among the women. They appear to have been loving, sensual, and possibly erotic.

Sources

Bing, Peter. *Games of Venus: An Anthology of Greek and Roman Erotic Verse from Sappho to Ovid.* New York: Routledge, Chapman and Hall, 1993, (Alcman, frag. 1.39–101).

Bowra, C. M. *Greek Lyric Poetry from Alcman to Simonides* 2d. ed. Oxford: Clarendon Press, 1967, pp. 30–65.

Fantham, Elaine, et al. *Women in the Classical World.* New York: Oxford University Press, 1994, pp. 12–15.

Page, Denys L. *Alcman: The Partheneion.* Oxford: Clarendon Press, 1951.

Pomeroy, Sarah B. *Goddesses, Whores, Wives, and Slaves: Women in Classical Antiquity.* New York: Schocken Books, 1975, p. 55.

Hedyto

(fifth century B.C.E.)   Greek: Athens
mother of Isocrates

Hedyto married Theodorus, a very rich man living in Athens during the 430s and 420s B.C.E. Her husband owned a workshop in which slaves made flutes. She had five children, one of whom, Isocrates, became a famous philosopher and rhetorician. His system of teaching rhetoric profoundly influenced education in writing and speaking.

Sources

Davies, J. K. *Athenian Propertied Families, 600–300 B.C.* Oxford: Clarendon Press, 1971, p. 246.

Hegesipyle

(sixth–fifth century B.C.E.)
Thracian: Thrace and Athens
mother of Cimon

Hegesipyle, the daughter of Olorus, a wealthy Thracian ruler, married Miltiades (c. 550–489 B.C.E.), a member of the aristocratic Athenian family in the Philaidae. Their marriage strengthened the family links between Athens and Thrace. Her husband's father and grandfather had ruled over Chersonesus (Gallipoli), on the Thracian peninsula, under the suzerainty of Athens. In 524, Hippias, the tyrant of Athens, sent her husband to rule in his family's tradition. Hegesipyle gave birth to Cimon, who became a famous Athenian statesman and soldier, and to ELPINICE.

Sources
Plutarch. *Vitae Parallelae (Parallel Lives): Cimon* 4.1.

▣ Helena
(c. late fourth century B.C.E.)
Roman: Egypt, Alexandria
painter

Helena was a painter who learned her craft from her painter father, Timon. She worked in the period after the death of Alexander in 323 B.C.E. Helena painted a scene of Alexander the Great defeating the Persian ruler, Darius, at the Battle of Issus in southern Asia Minor. The painting, exhibited in Rome, has not survived. Possibly, she created a mosaic copy of the painting that has been found in Pompeii. However, the attribution remains disputed, primarily on the grounds of gender, since other mosaic work by women has not been uncovered.

Sources
Prosopography of the Later Roman Empire. Vol. III. Edited by A. H. M. Jones, J. R. Martindale, and J. Morris. Cambridge: Cambridge University Press, 1971. Reprinted 1992, pp. 63–66

▣ Helena Flavia Julia (1)
(?–327 C.E.)
Roman: Italy, Germany, Judaea, Asia, and Syria
Augusta; early Christian

Helena lived during a period of significant religious change. The daughter of an innkeeper from Drepanum in Bithynia, an area in northwest Asia Minor, she was a convert to Christianity, a supporter of the Arian cause, and an influential actor at the court of her son Constantine. She has been credited with introducing her son to Christianity, influencing him to end Christian persecution, and acting as a mediator to achieve compromise at the Council of Nicaea.

The lover or perhaps an early wife of Constantius, she gave birth to the future emperor Constantine in the military city of Naissus on the Danube in 285 C.E. Constantius either divorced or simply left Helena to marry Flavia Maximiana THEODORA, the daughter or stepdaughter of Maximian. Constantius's new father-in-law became co-Augustus at the behest of the emperor Diocletian in 293 and appointed Constantius as his second-in-command with the title of Caesar in the West.

Thirteen years later, in 306 C.E., her son Constantine became emperor. She and her son had remained close as he followed his father to power. She grew wealthy with extensive properties in Rome. Over the course of decades, she generously supported the troops and friends around her son and helped finance the construction of Constantine's new capital, Constantinople. She assumed the title of Augusta along with Flavia Maxima FAUSTA, Constantine's wife, in 324.

She also became a devout Christian. At the time of Constantine's rise to power, the position of Christianity in the empire was still uncertain, and its adherents were subject to periodic persecution. Some tradition has ascribed to Helena the conversion of her son, who was said to have marked his

Helena Flavia Julia (1)
(Archives, American Numismatic Society)

151

soldiers' armor with a cross to test the power of the new God at the battle of Milvian Bridge in 312. His victory was also the victory of Christianity. Helena, however, was influenced by the bishop Eusebius, as was Flavia Julia CONSTANTIA, Constantine's half sister, and both were Arians at a moment when the Arian movement posed the greatest threat to the unity of the church. Helena not only used her wealth to support the Arian cause, but it was said that she played a critical role in the agreement at the Council of Nicaea, which averted a schism.

In 326 a scandal occurred, the details of which are obscured. Constantine authorized the execution of his 20-year old son, Crispus, who was the child of his lover, MINERVINA, born prior to his marriage with Fausta. He also had Fausta killed or compelled her to commit suicide. Tradition has implicated Helena in the deaths. There is no evidence that Fausta shared Helena's devotion to Christianity, and she may have challenged Helena's Christian coalition. Possibly, Helena suspected Fausta of trying to gather a basis of support to assure the succession of one of her own sons.

Immediately after the tragedy, Helena, probably now in her late 70s, made a pilgrimage to Jerusalem where she supported the building of churches and shrines. She died in 327 in Constantinople. She was buried in Rome.

Sources

Eusebius. *Vita Constantini.*

Balsdon, J. P. V. D. *Roman Women.* New York: John Day Comp., 1963, pp. 165–170.

Barnes, Timothy. *Constantine and Eusebius.* Cambridge: Harvard University Press, 1981, pp. 220–221.

Barnes, Timothy. *The New Empire of Diocletian and Constantine.* Cambridge: Harvard University Press, 1982.

Lane Fox, Robin. *Pagans and Christians.* New York: Alfred A. Knopf, 1987, pp. 309–311, 670–671.

Pauly, A., G. Wissowa, and W. Kroll. *Real-Encyclopadie D. Classischen Altertumswissenschaft 1893–.* (Germany: multiple publishers) 7.

▣ Helena, Flavia Julia (2)

(?–360 C.E.)

Roman: Italy, Constantinople, Gaul

Augusta

Helena, the daughter of FLAVIA MAXIMA FAUSTA and Constantine the Great, married Julian in 355, soon after he became Caesar with authority over Britain and Gaul. Her husband, who had been raised an Arian Christian, had spent time in Athens studying Neoplatonism and had personally rejected Christianity. It remains unclear whether or not Helena was aware of her husband's religious and philosophical positions; she was, however, likely to have been fully cognizant of the political reasons for her marriage.

EUSEBIA, Augusta and wife of Constantius II, promoted the marriage to a reluctant Constantius. The office of Caesar and marriage with Helena provided an opportunity for Julian to prove himself in wars against the Alamanni and the Franks, far from Constantinople. Failure in battle would probably lead to his death and remove a potential rival, while success would provide a husband for Helena and an effective general for Constantius.

Constantius was Julian's stepuncle. His father, Julius Constantius, was a half brother to Constantius's father, Constantine I. Constantius was also the brother of Helena. Named after her famous grandmother, HELENA, she was born in Constantinople and was several years older than Julian. She had a tempestuous youth. Her mother, Fausta, had been killed by her father in 326, for unknown reasons. Her sister CONSTANTINA married Hanniballianus from Asia Minor, who died violently. After her father's death, her three brothers warred with one another until only Constantius was left to rule.

Eusebia promoted Helena's marriage, but grew increasingly fearful that Helena's children would pose a threat to Constantius. After their marriage Helena accompanied her husband on campaigns into Gaul, and ancient gossip has attributed to Eusebia a part in Helena's subsequent miscarriage and stillbirth. Julian, however, was an able general and realized Constantiuis's greatest fear of becoming a potential rival. He was declared emperor by his troops shortly before Helena's death in 360.

Sources

Ammiamus Marcellinus. XV. 8, 1; XVI. 10, 18.

Prosopography of the Later Roman Empire. Vol. I. Edited by A. H. M. Jones, J. R. Martindale, and J. Morris. Cambridge: Cambridge University Press, 1971. Reprinted 1992, pp. 409–410.

Helvia

(second–first century B.C.E.)   Roman: Italy
mother of Cicero

Helvia's famous child, Marcus Tullius Cicero, was an orator, a statesman, and consul in 63 B.C.E. Although he was a prolific letter writer who had no hesitation in praising those he admired, he never referred to his mother and only sparingly to his father. The reasons remain unclear. She came from a respectable family that had social and economic connections in Rome. She married Marcus Cicero, the son of Marcus Cicero and Gratidia. Her husband came from a well-to-do family based near the town of Arpinum about 70 miles from Rome. Marcus was not a well man, and he spent a great amount of his time in study.

In addition to Marcus, born on January 3, 106, their second son, Quintus, was born about two years later. The family moved to Rome while the children were still young with the intention of providing them the best possible education.

Sources

Plutarch. *Vitae Parallelae (Parallel Lives): Cicero* 1.1.
Shackleton Bailey, D. R. *Cicero.* New York: Charles Scribner's Sons, 1971, p. 4.

Herodias

(first century C.E.)
Jewish: Judaea, Italy, and Gaul
loyal wife

Herodias was the sister of Agrippa I, ruler of Judaea. Her brother's friendship with the emperor Gaius Caligula saved her life and fortune. Her brother had grown up in Rome as a close friend of Drusus Julius Caesar, the son of the emperor Tiberius. He was also a friend and client of the future emperor Gaius Caligula, who made him ruler over part of the territory once ruled by his grandfather Herod the Great.

Herodias was the daughter of BERENICE (1) and Aristobulus IV, and the grandniece of Herod the Great. Herodias's first husband was her stepuncle Hero. Their daughter was named Salome. Widowed, she married Antipas, the stepbrother of her first husband and another of her stepuncles. She was his second wife. Her husband was attacked by John the Baptist, who claimed the marriage violated the Torah's kinship law for legal marriage. Antipas feared a revolt and had John killed. At Salome's request, he gave her John's head as a reward for dancing at a party.

Antipas ruled Galilee and Peraea (Transjordan) from 4 B.C.E. to 39 C.E. Herodias became furious that her brother, Agrippa, had received a higher status than her husband, who had served Rome longer. In 39 she persuaded her reluctant husband to go with her to Italy where he sought the same status as her brother from the emperor Caligula. Her brother sent a letter to Caligula accusing Antipas of plotting against the life of the former emperor Tiberius, among other treasonable actions. Caligula banished Antipas to Gaul but offered to allow Herodias to keep her property and avoid banishment when he found out that she was Agrippa's sister. Herodias, however, rejected the offer and went into exile with her husband.

Sources

Josephus. *Antiquitates Judaicae (Jewish Antiquities)* 18.109–11; 136.240–55.
Grant, Michael. *The Jews in the Roman World.* New York: Charles Scribner's Sons, 1973, p. 125.
Perowne, Stewart. *The Later Herods,* index.

Herpyllis

(fourth century B.C.E.)   Greek: Greece
companion of Aristotle

Herpyllis became the companion of the great philosopher Aristotle after the death of his wife, PYTHIAS. One of their sons was named Nichomachus after Aristotle's father. Aristotle named his greatest work, the *Nichomachean Ethics,* after their son.

When Aristotle died, he left his property to Herpyllis and the two children. He appointed Nicanor, who served under Alexander the Great, executor. The executor was instructed to care for Herpyllis and, should she choose, to help her find a suitable husband. The will offered her a choice of one of the two houses that Aristotle owned plus a sum of money and five servants.

Sources

Athenaeus. *Deipnosophistae* 13.589c.
Diogenes Laertius. *Lives of the Eminent Philosophers* 5.1, 12–14.

Flaceliere, Robert. *Love in Ancient Greece.* Trans. by James Cleugh. New York: Crown Publishers, 1962, p. 125.

◉ **Hipparchia**
(fourth–third century B.C.E.)   Greek: Greece
philosopher

Hipparchia was born in Maroneia, in the northeastern part of Greece. She and her brother, Metrocles, adopted the philosophy of the Cynics. She threatened suicide unless her parents allowed her to marry Crates of Thebes (c. 365–285 B.C.E.), the leading proponent of Cynicism. Her parents asked Crates to dissuade her. Crates was said to have removed his clothes and stood before her to ask her if she was prepared to choose a helpmate naked in body and without any worldly possessions. She married him. They traveled together and lived a life of Cynic poverty, exhorting others to renounce their possessions for a simple life free of entanglements. Only this way, they claimed, could one achieve independence, peace, happiness, and reconciliation in midst of troubled times, wars, and social chaos.

Hipparchia matched her wits with challengers. Theodorus, an atheist, challenged her in an argument at a banquet. She asserted that any act not considered wrong when undertaken by Theodorus, would also not be wrong when done by her. Thus, if Theodorus struck himself, then she did no wrong if she too struck him. When he asked whether she was a woman who gave up the loom, she was said to have replied that time spent weaving the threads of her mind and educating herself was more important than time spent weaving cloth.

Sources

Diogenes Laertius. *Lives of the Eminent Philosophers* 6.96–98.
Pomeroy, Sarah B. *Goddesses, Whores, Wives, and Slaves: Women in Classical Antiquity.* New York: Schocken Books, 1975, p. 136.

◉ **Hipparete (1)**
(sixth–fifth century B.C.E.)   Greek: Athens
independent wife

Hipparete divorced the famous Athenian statesman Pericles by mutual consent after five years of marriage. Hipparete had two sons with Pericles, Xanthippus and Paralus. Her second husband, Hipponicus, was the son of the beautiful and maligned ELPINICE and the nephew of the renowned Cimon. Hipponicus was enormously wealthy after he inherited his father's silver mines. They had two children, HIPPARETE (2), and a son, Callias. The daughter married the general Alcibiades.

Contrary to some reports, Hipparete's divorce from Pericles had nothing to do with ASPASIA, who only became a part of Pericles' life five years later.

Sources

Plutarch. *Vitae Parallelae (Parallel Lives): Pericles* 24.5.
Davies, J. K. *Athenian Propertied Families, 600–300 B.C.* Oxford: Clarendon Press, 1971, pp. 260–263.

◉ **Hipparete (2)**
(?–417/416 B.C.E.)   Greek: Athens
rich Athenian

Hipparete sought unsuccessfully to end her marriage with the Athenian statesman Alcibiades. Her father, Hipponicus, was the wealthiest man in Athens. After her grandfather died, her father inherited the family property, including silver mines. Hipparete's mother, HIPPARETE (1), was the divorced wife of Pericles, Athens's most famous ruler.

Hipparete married Alcibiades sometime in the late 420s B.C.E. and was said to have been a proper and affectionate wife to her brilliant and mercurial husband, who led the Athenian navy to victory at Cyzicus in 421. Both charming and handsome, her husband was notorious for his sexual exploits and pranks, some of which were incorporated into several of Plato's Socratic dialogues. Nonetheless, Hipparete had every reason to expect from her husband the respect due to a well-born wife and adherence to the expected social proprieties. After he repeatedly brought prostitutes into their home, she fled to her brother's house. On her own, in a show of public independence, she went to register her divorce. Alcibiades intercepted her en route and forcibly carried her across the public market back into his house.

Alcibiades's interest in maintaining his marriage may have had more to do with money than affection. Hipparete had a dowry of 20 talents. The sum was huge when one considers that the total revenue of Athens in 431 B.C.E. was estimated at 1,000 talents. Under Athenian law, Alcibiades would have been forced to return the money had they divorced. Half of the dowry had been given at their marriage, and the second half would come due upon the birth of a son. Hipparete died shortly after the birth of that son in 417 or 416 B.C.E.

Sources

Andocides. *On the Mysteries* 4.14.

Plutarch. *Vitae Parallelae (Parallel Lives): Alcibiades* 8.2–6.

Davies, J. K. *Athenian Propertied Families, 600–300 B.C.* Oxford: Clarendon Press, 1971, pp. 19, 259–261.

Pomeroy, Sarah B. *Goddesses, Whores, Wives, and Slaves: Women in Classical Antiquity.* New York: Schocken Books, 1975, p. 90.

▣ Hispala Faecenia

(second century B.C.E.)   Roman: Rome
patriot

Hispala Faecenia was a celebrated hero of Rome who provided the information that uncovered a major religious scandal in 186 B.C.E. She had taken a young man of means, Publius Aebutius, for a lover. He was the only son of DURONIA and ward of his stepfather, Titus Sempronius Rutilus, whom his mother adored. Duronia conspired to avoid the discovery of Rutilius's misuse of her son's inheritance.

Aebutius revealed to Hispala that his mother planned to have him become an initiate of the Bacchic cult. Hispala was horrified. While still a slave, Hispala had attended Bacchic rites with her mistress. The secret cult, in which membership was said to be limited to those under 20 years old who had sworn to engage in unusual sex, robbery, and even murder, was believed to include some 7,000 people in Italy. She warned Aebutius that his mother and stepfather were out to destroy his reputation and made him promise not to be initiated into the rites. When he told his parents that he refused to be initiated, they threw him out of their house.

Aebutius related the story to his aunt, who advised him to go to the consul. Taken seriously by the authorities, they turned to Hispala for details. Finally persuaded to reveal information about the rituals in exchange for protection from retributory violence, she moved into a safe space above the household of the consul's own mother-in-law.

When presented with the facts, the Senate voted to execute the men found guilty of participation in the rites. The women implicated in the scandal were turned over to their families for punishment. The Senate voted 100,000 sesterces as a reward to Hispala and Aebutius. In addition, she was given the right to alienate her property and to marry any man of free birth. Moreover, it was decreed that the consuls and other officials should protect her. She left her property to Aebutius when she died.

Sources

Livy. *From the Founding of the City* 39.8–14, 19.

Balsdon, J. P. V. D. *Roman Women.* New York: John Day Comp., 1963, pp. 37–43.

Bauman, Richard A. *Women and Politics in Ancient Rome.* London: Routledge, 1994, pp. 35–37.

▣ Hispulla

(first century C.E.)   Roman: Italy
affluent woman

Hispulla was part of the well-to-do and educated circle of men and women who lived primarily on their estates as they struggled with the political uncertainties of the late Julio-Claudian period. She was the wife of Corellius Rufus, a close friend of Pliny the Younger. Her husband was afflicted with a progressively painful gout, evidently inherited from his father. He told Pliny that the only reason he chose to continue to live in great agony was to outlive the emperor Domitian, whose reign of terror lasted from until 96 C.E. and left many of his friends dead or in exile.

In his 67th year, with Domitian dead, her husband could no longer endure the pain and decided to end his life by fasting. Hispulla and her daughter, CORELLIA HISPULLA, tried to dissuade him but to no avail. Hispulla then sent for Pliny as their last hope. As he ran to her house, a messenger met him with the news that Rufus could not be deterred, and his friend died shortly thereafter.

Sources

Pliny the Younger. *Epistulae* 1.12.

▣ Honoria, Justa Grata

(c. 417/418 C.E.–c. 452 C.E.)
Roman: Italy, Constantinople
Augusta

Strong-willed and intelligent, Justa Grata Honoria followed in the footsteps of her mother, AELIA GALLA PLACIDA. She refused to play a secondary rule to her younger, incompetent brother, the emperor Valentinian III, and her intent to rule threatened the empire.

After her father, Constantius III, died on September 2, 421, Honoria and her siblings remained in Ravenna, Italy, with her mother the widowed Augusta Placidia, who exercised great influence over her ineffectual half brother, Honorius, the new emperor. Rumors of a plot by Placidia to replace Honorius caused conflicts that threatened violence and in 423 Honoria fled with her mother to the emperor Theodosius II and his powerful sister, PULCHERIA, in Constantinople.

Honorius died on August 14, 423. A usurper named John seized power in the West. Theodosius and Pulcheria found it in their interest to strike an agreement with their aunt Placidia. They recognized Valentinian, who was Honoria's younger brother, as the legitimate emperor of the West. Theodosius also recognized Placidia's title of Augusta. Theodosius gained authority over Dalmatia and a part of Pannonia previously held by the Western emperor. To seal the agreement, the infant child of Theodosius and AELIA EUDOCIA, LICINIA EUDOXIA, was betrothed to the child-emperor Valentinian, with the marriage to take place when both came of age.

Honoria left with her mother and brother Valentinian for Italy accompanied by an army sent by Theodosius to overthrow the usurper. Although temporarily shipwrecked in the Adriatic Sea off the coast of Dalmatia, they successfully reached Italy. The army defeated and executed the usurper emperor John and on October 23, 425, in Rome, Valentinian became Augustus. Shortly thereafter, Honoria received the title Augusta, and gold coins were issued in her honor. For the first time on a coin a female child wore the diadem of a royal headband with a scepter of purple representing royal authority. Possibly it was done to assure she would become regent for her younger brother in case her mother died while he was still a minor. As she grew older, she also received her own estate on the grounds of the palace in Ravenna and a personal fortune. However, the long-planned marriage of her brother on October 29, 437, to Licinia Eudoxia, the daughter of Aelia Eudocia and Theodosius II, came to fruition and introduced another woman into the Western imperial circle. Eudoxia, moreover, bore two daughters over the next few years further distancing the ambitious Honoria from a dynastic and political role in the empire.

Honoria took a lover, Eugenius, a low-born manager of her estate. Possibly, she was pregnant. More probably, the story of a lover and the inference of a pregnancy was part of an ancient literary trope for a conspiracy to unseat her brother. The tale has elements that reach back to JULIA, the daughter of Augustus, and LIVILLA, during the reign of Tiberius, when lovers were part of elite women's participation in imperial conspiracies.

In 449, Eugenius was executed and Honoria was exiled from the palace and betrothed, against her will, to Flavius Bassus Herculanus, a very wealthy Roman senator, who had no designs on the throne. Honoria, however, was not deterred. In 450, she secretly requested support from Attila, king of the Huns, through Hyacinthus, a trusted eunuch, to whom she also entrusted a ring to guarantee the authenticity of her message. Attila claimed the ring was an offer of marriage. He responded with a letter to Theodosius II in Constantinople that demanded Honoria as a bride and half of the Western empire as her dowry. Theodosius instructed his half brother Valentinian to hand Honoria over to Attila, ostensibly to prevent an attack by the Huns. Instead, Valentinian tortured and killed Hyacinthus. He would have also executed Honoria but for the intervention of her mother. She instead lost only her symbol of power, the diadem.

In 451, Attila invaded and was barely repulsed at Châlons. In 452 he again invaded to claim Honoria as his bride. He captured cities in his path and destroyed Aquileia, but he could not overcome plague and food shortages, which sent him into retreat. He died the following year without having claimed Honoria, and Honoria disappears from history.

Sources

Jordanes. *Getica.* 223, 224.
Olympiodorus. *Fragments.* 34.
Priscus. *Fragments.* 2, 7, 8, 15.
Sozomen. *Historia Ecclesiastica* X. 16. 2.
Theophanes. *Chronicle.* AM 5943.
Bury, J. B. "Justa Grata Honoria," *Journal of Roman Studies* 9 (1919): pp. 1–13.
Prosopography of the Later Roman Empire. Vol. II. Edited by A. H. M. Jones, J. R. Martindale, and J. Morris. Cambridge: Cambridge University Press, 1971. Reprinted 1992, pp. 568–569.

◙ Horatia

(seventh century B.C.E.)   Roman: Rome
war victim

Horatia's story comes from the period of early Roman history when fact and myth are inexorably intertwined. As it is told, marriage between Horatia and a son of the Curiatii family from nearby Alba Longa, southwest of Rome, had been arranged. In a battle with the Curiatii, two of her three brothers died. Her remaining brother killed her fiancé. Horatia met her brother as he returned from battle and recognized the cloak he carried from the body of his slain opponent. She had made that cloak for her soon-to-be husband. She cried. Her brother drew his sword and killed her.

When her brother was brought to trial, her father, Publius Horatius, justified his son's actions and declared he would have killed Horatia had his son not already done so. No Roman woman who mourned for an enemy of Rome deserved to live. Her brother was acquitted but was forced to do penance.

Sources

Livy. *From the Founding of the City.* 1.26.
Valerius Maximus. *Factorum et dictorum memorabilium libri IX* 6.3, 6.
Pomeroy, Sarah B. *Goddesses, Whores, Wives, and Slaves: Women in Classical Antiquity.* New York: Schocken Books, 1975, pp. 152–153.

◙ Hortensia

(first century B.C.E.)   Roman: Rome
orator

Hortensia was an orator. She was well educated and articulate. Her father was the famous Roman orator Quintus Hortensius (114–50 B.C.E.). She was also a wealthy woman and was the chosen spokesperson to argue against a special tax levied against women in 42 B.C.E.

The triumvirs Antony, Octavian, and Lepidus were hard-pressed for cash. Needing to overcome a shortfall of some 200 million drachmas for war preparations, they published an edict requiring 1,400 of the wealthiest women to make an evaluation of their property and to donate a portion to the triumvirs. In usual fashion, anyone found to be concealing information would be fined, and informers, whether free or slave, would be rewarded.

The women objected and successfully enlisted support from LIVIA DRUSILLA and OCTAVIA (2), respectively, the wealthy and independent wife and the stepsister of Octavian. They were repulsed, however, by FULVIA (2), the wife of Mark Antony and the woman most directly engaged by the military aspects of war. United, they marched into the Forum where Hortensia spoke for all of them.

She declared that the women had not been involved in any actions against the triumvirs and should therefore not be penalized. Why, she asked, should women pay taxes, since they could not be involved in politics or the military and therefore could not share in the honors and wealth that men acquired? If Rome were fighting a foreign enemy, the women would have no hesitation in supporting the government with all means in their power. But this was a civil war, and women should not be required to give aid in a conflict between Roman citizens that men had fomented. Hortensia pointed out that such an assessment had never before been demanded in the whole history of Rome.

The crowd supported them. Despite their evident anger, the triumvirs eliminated the tax for all but 400 of the women and in addition levied a tax on all men who owned more than 100,000 drachmas.

Sources

Appian. *Roman History: Bella civilian (Civil Wars)* 4.32–34.

Valerius Maximus. *Factorum et dictorum memorabilium libri IX* 8.3.3.

Bauman, Richard A. *Women and Politics in Ancient Rome.* London: Routledge, 1994, pp. 81–83.

Pomeroy, Sarah B. *Goddesses, Whores, Wives, and Slaves: Women in Classical Antiquity.* New York: Schocken Books, 1975, pp. 175–176.

◉ Hydna

(fifth century B.C.E.)   Greek: Scione

patriot

Hydna was a Greek heroine in the war against the Persians in 480 B.C.E. She was the daughter of Scyllis, from Scione, a city on a peninsula in the Thracian Sea controlled by Athens. She learned to swim and dive as a child alongside her father. When the Persians attacked the Greeks, Xerxes anchored the Persian fleet off Mount Oelion. During a storm, Hydna and her father swam to the fleet and, diving underwater, cut a number of the ships' anchor ropes. Many of the ships drifted and were tossed on the rocks and sank.

Statues of Hydna and her father were dedicated at Delphi. Her statue may have been plundered by the emperor Nero and carried off to Rome in the first century C.E.

Sources

Pausanias. *Description of Greece* 10.19.1–2.

Harris, H. A. *Sport in Greece and Rome.* Ithaca, N.Y.: Cornell University Press, 1972, pp. 112–113, 124–125.

◉ Hypatia

(370 C.E.– 415 C.E.)

Greek: Alexandria, Egypt

philosopher

Hypatia is the best-known woman mathematician and philosopher from the Greco-Roman world. Born in 370 C.E., she followed in the footsteps of her father, Theon, to direct the Mouseion and library in Alexandria. Hypatia was a Platonist, although her most notable work was most likely in mathematics, not philosophy.

She probably collaborated with her father on his commentary of Ptolemy's *Almagest* and possibly composed commentaries on Ptolemy's astronomy. Also with her father she produced a new version of Euclid's *Elements*, which became the standard edition of Euclid into contemporary times. Hypatia wrote commentaries on *Arithmetica*, composed by the earlier philosopher Diophantus, and on the *Conics* written by Appollonius. Extant letters from the bishop Synesius of Cyrene, Hypatia's former student, suggest that she developed a new or better astrolabe (an ancient astronomical instrument used to determine measurements in relation with the Sun) and a hydroscope (a device designed to allow for the study of objects underwater).

Hypatia was part of the pagan elite around the Roman prefect Orestes in his conflict with the bishop Cyril. In many ways she personified the complicated role of sexuality in early Christianity that simultaneously allowed women previously unimagined alternatives and damned the pagan idealism and rationality of platonic thought. Her public visibility incensed the Christian fanatical fringes for whom female sexuality was the cause of man's fall from God's grace. In 415, either with Cyril's encouragement or as a result of the atmosphere he nurtured, Hypatia was dragged from her chariot and attacked by a band of Christians, probably monks, who literally tore her limb from limb.

Sources

John Malalas. *Chronicle* 359.

Suda. 166.

Theophanes. *AM* 5906.

Deakin, Michael. *Hypatia of Alexandria: Mathematician and Martyr.* Amherst, Mass: Prometheus Books, 2007, *passim.*

Dzielska, Maria. *Hypatia of Alexandria.* Translated by F. Lyra. Cambridge, Mass.: Harvard University Press, 1995, *passim.*

Jones, A. H. M., ed. *Prosopography of the Later Roman Empire.* Vol. II. Cambridge: Cambridge University Press, pp. 575–576.

O'Connor, J. J., and E. F. Robertson. *Hypatia of Alexandria.* Printonly/Hypatia.html, pp. 1–3.

Rist, J. M. "Hypatia," *Phoenix.* Vol. 19.3. Toronto: Trinity College Press (Autumn 1965) pp. 214–225.

Wider, Kathleen. "Women Philosophers in the Ancient Greek World," *Hyaptia.* Vol. 1. Bloomington: Indiana University Press (Spring 1986) pp. 21–57.

Ilia

(second–first century B.C.E.)   Roman: Rome
victim

Ilia was the first wife of the young Lucius Cornelius Sulla, the future dictator of Rome. Her husband married increasingly rich and well-connected women as his career soared. Ilia probably died after the birth of their only child, CORNELIA (4).

Sources
Plutarch. *Vitae Parallelae (Parallel Lives): Sulla* 6.10.

Ismenodora

(first century C.E.?)   Greek: Thespiae
self-made woman

Ismenodora snatched a much younger man for her husband. A wealthy and beautiful young widow who lived in Thespiae, a city in central Greece, she fell in love with Bacchon, the son of a relative and friend. The friend had asked Ismenodora to arrange a suitable marriage for the boy, but she was not enthusiastic about the idea of the much older and richer Ismenodora becoming the boy's wife.

Bacchon, shy and still a minor, sought advice. He found no consensus. Ismenodora, convinced that his hesitation was primarily embarrassment, took matters into her own hands. She invited to her house some of her women and men friends who favored the marriage. When Bacchon walked by, which he invariably did, they dragged him in, locked the doors, put on wedding garments, and the couple were married.

Sources
Plutarch. *Moralia: Amatorius* 749d–750a; 745h–755b.

Isodice

(fifth century B.C.E.)   Greek: Athens
loyal wife

Isodice was probably the second wife of Cimon, an Athenian statesman and soldier of renown. She came from the aristocratic Athenian family of the Alcmaeonidae. Her father was Euryptolemus, a son of Megacles. Isodice's husband was grief-stricken at her death. She had for certain one son, Callias, and possibly bore an additional three children, all boys.

Sources
Diodorus Siculus. *Library of History* 10.31.
Plutarch. *Vitae Parallelae (Parallel Lives): Cimon* 4.8–9; 16.1–2.

Julia (1)

(?–68 B.C.E.)   Roman: Rome
brave woman

Julia was descended from a patrician family. When she died, her nephew Julius Caesar used the occasion to glorify himself by tracing her ancestry to the gods. Her mother was a Marcia from the family of the Marcii Reges, the ancient kings of Rome. Julia married Gaius Marius, a noted general and statesman. Her husband held seven consulships before he died in 86 B.C.E. She had one son, also named Gaius Marius, born in 110 B.C.E.

Julia's life was worthy of her lineage. She supported her husband in the tense and sometimes violent confrontations of his political career. She was often alone, honored by some and despised by others. She managed the difficult time of her husband's illness, and after Marius's death, she remained a symbol for the Marians. Julia opposed her son's consulship of 82 B.C.E. She was convinced he was being used for his name by the Marian forces. Events proved her fears well founded. Her son led an army against Lucius Cornelius Sulla and was defeated. He committed suicide.

After Sulla's victory Julia remained in Rome, both vulnerable and proud. She may have supported Caesar as he left the city after he refused Sulla's terms, which included that he divorce his young and even more vulnerable wife CORNELIA (5). It is also possible that she aided Cornelia, whose family had close ties to Marius. She survived Sulla's proscriptions of 81–80 and lived to see her nephew Caesar return from the East. She died in 68 B.C.E.

Sources

Suetonius. *The Lives of the Caesars:* Caesar 6.1.

Balsdon, J. P. V. D. *Roman Women.* New York: John Day Comp., 1963, p. 46.

Oxford Classical Dictionary, ed. by Simon Hornblower and Antony Spawforth. 3d. ed. New York: Oxford University Press, 1996, p. 776.

Pauly, A., G. Wissowa, and W. Kroll. *Real-Encyclopadie D. Classischen Altertumswissenschaft 1893–.* (Germany: multiple publishers) 541.

Julia (2)

(first century B.C.E.)   Roman: Rome
power broker

Julia lived amidst the maelstrom of civil war politics after Caesar's assassination and played a part in the diplomacy of the Second Triumvirate. Her father was Lucius Julius Caesar, consul in 90 B.C.E. and censor in 89. Her aunt was JULIA (1), wife and widow of Gaius Marius, and Julius Caesar was her cousin. Her mother was a Fulvia whose family had supported reform since the Gracchi. She married

Marcus Antonius Creticus, praetor in 74 B.C.E., whom she dominated. Their eldest son, born in 83, grew up to become the famous triumvir Mark Antony. A younger son, Lucius Antonius, became his brother's ally. After the death of her husband in 72, Julia married Publius Cornelius Lentulus Sura, consul in 71. Her second husband was implicated in the conspiracy of Lucius Sergius Catiline and executed on the orders of Marcus Tullius Cicero in 63.

In November 43 the triumvirs undertook a proscription and issued death warrants for some 300 senators and 2,000 equestrians. Among them was Julia's brother, Lucius Julius Caesar, consul in 64 B.C.E. and the uncle of Antony, whom he had opposed after Caesar's murder. Faced with proscription, he took refuge in Julia's house. She secured his pardon from Antony and the restitution of his citizenship. Antony was said to have observed that Julia was a fine sister but a very difficult mother.

Julia remained a widow. She lived in Rome when Antony was in the East with Cleopatra VII. Her younger son, Lucius, consul in 41, and her daughter-in-law Fulvia (2) were defeated in Italy by Octavian in the Perusine War of 40 B.C.E. Fearing retribution, Julia left Rome and took refuge in Sicily where she was kindly treated by Sextus Pompeius, who controlled the island. Pompeius, who sought an alliance with Antony against Octavian, sent Julia with two of his envoys to Athens to meet Antony as he returned to Italy from the East.

With the alliance secured, Julia accompanied Antony from Athens to Brundisium in Italy in 39. He laid siege to the city when he was refused admittance. War with Octavian appeared imminent. However, the troops on both sides demanded a settlement. Julia took part in the subsequent negotiations. The result was the pact of Brundisium, sealed with the marriage of Antony and Octavian's sister, Octavia (2). Julia was mollified with a letter from Octavian assuring her that she need not have fled Rome since she was his kinswoman, and that he would have seen to her safety.

Sources
Appian. *Roman History: Bella civilian (Civil Wars)* 2.143; 4.37; 5.52, 63.
Dio Cassius. *Roman History* 48.15.2; 48.27.4; 51.2, 5.
Plutarch. *Vitae Parallelae (Parallel Lives): Antonius* 1.1–3; 2.1–2; 22.3.
Balsdon, J. P. V. D. *Roman Women.* New York: John Day Comp., 1963, pp. 52–53.
Pauly, A., G. Wissowa, and W. Kroll. *Real-Encyclopadie D. Classischen Altertumswissenschaft 1893–.* (Germany: multiple publishers) 543.

Julia (3)
(first century B.C.E.)   Roman: Rome
politically well connected

Julia was the daughter of Aurelia (1), who came from the family of the Aurelii Cottae, and Gaius Julius Caesar, who died in 85 B.C.E. She was the elder sister of Julius Caesar and Julia (4). Her first husband was Lucius Pinarius of whom little is known except that they had a son, Lucius Pinarius Scarpus. She later married the equestrian Quintus Pedius and had another son, Quintus Pedius, consul in 43 B.C.E. In his will, Julius Caesar left a share of his fortune to her two sons. They gave their inheritance to Octavian, who had inherited three-quarters of the estate.

Sources
Suetonius. *The Lives of the Caesars:* Caesar 83.2.
Pauly, A., G. Wissowa, and W. Kroll. *Real-Encyclopadie D. Classischen Altertumswissenschaft 1893–.* (Germany: multiple publishers) 545.
Syme, Ronald. *The Augustan Aristocracy.* Oxford: Clarendon Press, 1986.
Syme, Ronald. *The Roman Revolution.* London: Oxford University Press, 1963, p. 128.

Julia (4)
(?–51 B.C.E.)   Roman: Rome
witness

Julia, along with her mother Aurelia (1), gave testimony against Publius Clodius in the notorious Bona Dea scandal of 62 B.C.E. Julia was the daughter of Gaius Julius Caesar, who died in 85 B.C.E. Her mother came from the illustrious Aurelii Cottae. Julia was the younger sister of Julius Caesar, with whom she remained close throughout her life. She married Marcus Atius Balbus from Aricia and had two daughters. The eldest, ATIA (1), married Gaius Octavius, and Julia became the grandmother of Octavian, the future emperor Augustus and the independent OCTAVIA (2).

In 62, Caesar was *pontifex maximus,* and his household was the site of the celebration of the Bona Dea rituals presided over by Julia and Aurelia. The religious rites, restricted to elite women, were a traditional part of the Roman *pax deorum,* which joined the well-being of the state with the proper performance of an annual cycle of religious ritual. Publius Clodius Pulcher, an aristocrat of the finest lineage, violated the sanctity of the female-only rite. He entered the household disguised as a woman. It was alleged that he had an assignation with Caesar's wife POMPEIA (1). Discovered and tried with testimony from Julia and her mother, he was acquitted with the help of large bribes. Caesar was said not to have taken the matter seriously, although he did divorce his wife in its wake.

After the death of her son-in-law Gaius Octavius, Julia's grandson Octavian lived with her for eight years from 58 B.C.E. until her death in 51. The 12-year-old Octavian delivered her funeral oration.

Sources

Suetonius. *The Lives of the Caesars*: Augustus 4; 8.
Suetonius. *The Lives of the Caesars:* Caesar 74.2.
Pauly, A., G. Wissowa, and W. Kroll. *Real-Encyclopadie D. Classischen Altertumswissenschaft 1893–.* (Germany: multiple publishers) 546.
Syme, Ronald. *The Roman Revolution.* London: Oxford University Press, 1963, p. 112.

▣ Julia (5)

(83–54 B.C.E.)   Roman: Rome
political wife

Julia, born in 83 B.C.E., was the only child of Julius Caesar. Her mother was CORNELIA (5), the young first wife of Caesar. Julia was to marry Quintus Servilius Caepio until her father and Gnaeus Pompeius (Pompey the Great) established a political alliance (along with Marcus Licinius Crassus) in April 59 for which her marriage with Pompey formed the symbolic center.

The union did not appear promising. Julia was Pompey's fourth wife. He was some 23 years her senior and already had adolescent sons plus a daughter of marriageable age. Nonetheless it worked. Not only did Pompey and Caesar draw closer together, but the sources claim that Pompey handed over his provinces and armies to friendly legates so that he and Julia could spend time on his estates in Italy. The sources did not approve of what they considered to be this dereliction of his duty.

Julia had a miscarriage in 55, precipitated by the arrival of servants carrying her husband's clothes splattered with blood from an altercation to which she later learned he was a witness, not a participant. She died a year later in childbirth. Her child died a few days later. Her death in 54 distressed her husband, her father, and their followers, who felt that she was the bond that kept their alliance alive. Indeed, that alliance dissolved within a few years. At the demand of the populace her body was carried to the Campus Martius for final rites.

Sources

Plutarch. *Vitae Parallelae (Parallel Lives): Caesar* 23.5–7.
Plutarch. *Vitae Parallelae (Parallel Lives): Pompeius* 47.6; 53.1–5.
Valerius Maximus. *Factorum et dictorum memorabilium libri IX* 4.6.4.
Oxford Classical Dictionary, ed. by Simon Hornblower and Antony Spawforth. 3d. ed. New York: Oxford University Press, 1996, p. 776.
Pauly, A., G. Wissowa, and W. Kroll. *Real-Encyclopadie D. Classischen Altertumswissenschaft 1893–.* (Germany: multiple publishers) 547.

▣ Julia (6)

(39 B.C.E.–15 C.E.)
Roman: Italy, Gaul, and Pandateria
political player

Julia held a unique position in the Augustan empire: She was the only child of the emperor. Born in 39 B.C.E., her mother was SCRIBONIA, whom her father divorced to marry LIVIA DRUSILLA. Her father ignored his own record of notorious divorce and second marriage to insist that Julia live with rules and strictures from an idealized vision of Rome's past. Brought up in the household of her stepmother, she was to be an example of women who lived lives dutifully devoted to father, children, husband, and kin. Her father insisted she be taught the ancient arts of spinning and weaving and discouraged friendships without his permission and approval.

Julia, however, was her father's daughter in more ways than Augustus may have foreseen, and the place she sought for herself was more than as a model and docile wife bringing forth strong sons. Educated and well read, she had a sharp and witty tongue that challenged her father's restrictive vision for her life. Julia, and possibly Augustus, suffered the unintended consequences of their different expectations. Beguiled by Julia's charm and wit, her father underestimated her determination to use fully her position as Caesar's daughter. She, on the other hand, may have lost sight of her father's ruthlessness.

Julia married Marcus Claudius Marcellus, the son of Augustus's independent-minded sister OCTAVIA (2), in 25 B.C.E. The marriage might have provided Augustus with a solution to his dynastic problems had Marcellus not died two years later. In 21 Julia married Marcus Vipsanius Agrippa, Augustus's confidant, supporter, and adviser. Some 21 years older than Julia, this was his third marriage. Moreover, to marry Julia, Agrippa divorced the elder MARCELLA, who was Julia's cousin and with whom he had had a harmonius marriage. Despite the inauspicious circumstances, Julia had five children over the next eight years: Gaius Caesar; Lucius Caesar; Agrippa Postumus, who was born after the death of his father; and two daughters, JULIA (7) and the elder AGRIPPINA. Augustus adopted her three sons and brought them up as members of his household to prepare for succession.

Again widowed in 12 B.C.E., Julia married her father's grown stepson, Tiberius. As with Agrippa, to marry Julia Tiberius divorced his wife, VIPSANIA AGRIPPINA, with whom he had had an agreeable relationship. The new marriage initially promised success, and Julia traveled with Tiberius to northern Italy when he campaigned in the Balkans, but the relationship quickly deteriorated. The witty and outgoing Julia thrived in a world distasteful to her husband. He was stern and disciplined, little given to the hothouse of gossip, intrigue, and power politics that was the lifeblood of imperial Rome. Primarily a military man, he appeared most comfortable with more retiring women like his first wife. During her husband's self-imposed exile in 6 B.C.E., Julia remained in Rome. Secure in her position as Caesar's daughter, she surrounded herself with a set of friends more her own age and more in tune with her tastes.

She was alleged to have engaged in a series of love affairs, and in 2 B.C.E., her father created a public scandal with a letter to the Senate in which he described her transgressions and named her lovers. They made up a formidable group and included the poet Sempronius Gracchus; the consul of 9 B.C.E. Quinctius Crispinus; the patrician Appius Claudius Pulcher, and Cornelius Scipio, who was her stepbrother. Their names resonated with republican glory, and their probable leader was Iullus Antonius, the son of Mark Antony and FULVIA (2), who had married Julia's cousin, the elder Claudia MARCELLA, in 21 B.C.E. after her divorce from Agrippa.

Growing up in the households of Octavia, Livia, and the other elite women who raised the motherless or fatherless children left in the wake of civil wars, this first postwar generation of men and women had probably known one another since childhood. By 2 B.C.E. Julia and her circle were in their late 30s and early 40s. Like Julia, most had been married more than once. Many already had nearly grown children and honorable political careers. By then Julia's father was an old man. His power was unchallenged, and his plans for succession repeatedly frustrated. The viciousness with which he attacked Julia and her friends would possibly suggest a political motive hiding behind the cloak of sexual misbehavior.

The descriptions of Julia that have come down over time—soliciting in the Forum, indiscriminate lewdness, and multiple simultaneous relationships—strain credulity when compared with the evidence of an educated, proud, and witty 40-year old Roman woman who had had three marriages, was twice widowed, and had borne five children in eight years. The punishments meted out by her father were equally contradictory. He issued a decree divorcing Julia from Tiberius, who was still on Rhodes. When Tiberius wrote to ask that Julia be allowed to keep her personal property, Augustus refused and instead allowed her only a modest allowance. She was banished to the island of Pandateria off the coast of Naples. Her mother, Scribonia, a woman renowned for her virtue, accompanied her. No man was allowed to visit her unless he was screened to determine that he was politically safe and physically unattractive. Her father further decreed that any illicit association with her, or for that matter with any woman of the Julian house, was henceforth high treason.

The banishment was not popular, and eventually Augustus allowed Julia to move to Reggio in southern Italy. The men said to have been involved with her were also exiled, with the exception of Antonius, who was executed. Of the other women in the circle, Augustus issued an edict that they should not be punished for indiscretions more than five years old.

Julia's father died without ending her exile. His will specified that she should not be buried in his tomb. Tiberius showed no pity or kindness to her when he became emperor. He stopped the allowance granted her by Augustus, since the emperor had made no provision for it in his will. He also restricted her to her house and allowed no visitors. She died in 15 c.e. at the age of 53.

Sources

Dio Cassius. *Roman History* 54.6.5; 55.10.12–16, 13.1; 56.32.4; 57.18.1a.
Macrobius. *Saturnalia* 2, 5.
Pliny the Elder. *Naturalis Historia* 21.9.
Seneca. *De beneficiis* 6.32.1–2.
Suetonius. *The Lives of the Caesars*: Augustus 63.1–2; 64.1–3; 65.1–4.
———. *The Lives of the Caesars*: Tiberius 7.2–3; 11.4; 50.1.
Tacitus. *Annales* 1.53.
Balsdon, J. P. V. D. *Roman Women*. New York: John Day Comp., 1963, pp. 81–87.
Bauman, Richard A. *Women and Politics in Ancient Rome.* London: Routledge, 1994, index.
Fantham, Elaine. *Julia Augusti.* New York: Routledge, 2006.
Ferrill, A., "Augustus and His Daughters," pp. 332–346.
Hallett, Judith. "Perusinae Glandes and the Changing Image of Augustus." *American Journal of Ancient History* 2 (1977): 151–171.
Levick, Barbara. *Tiberius the Politician.* London: Thames and Hudson, 1976, index.
Oxford Classical Dictionary, ed. by Simon Hornblower and Antony Spawforth. 3d. ed. New York: Oxford University Press, 1996, pp. 776–777.
Pauly, A., G. Wissowa, and W. Kroll. *Real-Encyclopadie D. Classischen Altertumswissenschaft 1893–.* (Germany: multiple publishers) 550.
Richlin, A. "Julia's Jokes, Galla Placidia, and the Roman Use of Women as Political Icons." In *Stereotypes of Women in Power: Historical Perspectives and Revisionist Views,* ed. by B. Garlick, S. Dixon, and P. Allen. New York: Greenwood Press, 1992, pp. 65–91.
Syme, Ronald. *History in Ovid.* New York: Oxford University Press, 1978, pp. 193ff.
———. *The Roman Revolution.* London: Oxford University Press, 1963, index.

◉ Julia (7)

(19 B.C.E.–28 C.E.)   Roman: Italy
political victim

Julia suffered the same tragic fate as her mother. Born in 19 B.C.E., the granddaughter of Augustus, her birth was heralded with the promise of lifelong splendor. She was one of five children; her mother JULIA (6), was the only daughter of Augustus, and her father, Marcus Vipsanius Agrippa, was the famous general, statesman, and confidant of the emperor. At her father's death, when she about seven years old, she and her younger siblings— Gaius Caesar, Lucius Caesar, Agrippa Postumus, and the elder AGRIPPINA—came under the authority of her grandfather. He imposed on them traditions of virtue contradicted by the realities of the new empire. In the face of imperial wealth and status, the girls were taught spinning and weaving; their relationships were closely controlled; and their future was managed.

Augustus almost succeeded in his efforts to mold his granddaughter. In 4 B.C.E. Julia married

Lucius Aemilius Paullus, consul in 1 C.E. and a distant relation through their respective grandmothers. Julia's mother-in-law, CORNELIA (8), whose virtue and glory was eulogized in the poetry of Propertius, came from a family that embodied the greatness of the Roman republic. Over the next decade, however, tragedies followed one after another. In 2 B.C.E. Julia's mother became part of a public scandal that resulted in her exile for adultery and conspiracy. Four years later her brother Lucius died, followed two years later by her brother Gaius. Her third brother, Agrippa Postumus, was accused of brutal rebellious behavior by the emperor and sent to Surrentum. The Senate later voted to exile him on the island of Planasia.

In 8 C.E., exactly 10 years after her mother's exile, Julia too was exiled. The nature of her crime remains unclear. She was sent to the island of Trimerus off the Apulian coast on grounds of adultery with Decimus Junius Silanus, a Roman aristocrat. At the same time, her husband, Aemilius Paullus, was accused of conspiracy against the aged emperor and executed. The poet Ovid also exiled was sent to Tomis on the Black Sea, a far outpost of the empire where he remained until his death. After the exile of her mother, Augustus had issued an edict that illicit behavior with any woman of the Julian clan would be considered high treason, yet to punish Silanus Augustus merely revoked his friendship with him. Silanus went into voluntary exile and was later allowed to return to Rome by the emperor Tiberius through the intervention of his influential brother Marcus Silanus.

In exile, Julia gave birth, but Augustus refused to allow the father to acknowledge the child, and it was exposed on the emperor's orders. After 20 years in exile, Julia died in 28 C.E.

Sources

Suetonius. *The Lives of the Caesars*: Augustus 64.1–3; 65.1, 4. Tacitus. *Annales* 3.24; 4.71.

Bauman, Richard A. *Women and Politics in Ancient Rome.* London: Routledge, 1994, pp. 120–121.

Fantham, Elaine. *Julia Augusti.* New York: Routledge, 2006.

Levick, Barbara. *Tiberius the Politician.* London: Thames and Hudson, 1976, index.

Oxford Classical Dictionary, ed. by Simon Hornblower and Antony Spawforth. 3d. ed. New York: Oxford University Press, 1996, p. 777.

Pauly, A., G. Wissowa, and W. Kroll. *Real-Encyclopadie D. Classischen Altertumswissenschaft 1893–.* (Germany: multiple publishers) 551.

Syme, Ronald. *The Augustan Aristocracy.* Oxford: Clarendon Press, 1986, index.

———. *History in Ovid.* New York: Oxford University Press, 1978, pp. 206ff.

———. *The Roman Revolution.* London: Oxford University Press, 1963, index.

▣ Julia (8)

(?–43 C.E.)   Roman: Rome
political victim

Julia shared the tragic fate of many women born with her name. She was both pawn and actor in the drama of succession to the emperor Tiberius who was her grandfather on her father's side. Through her mother, Livia Julia Claudia Livilla, she was directly descended from OCTAVIA (2), the independent-minded sister of the emperor Augustus. She married Nero Julius Caesar, the older son of the elder AGRIPPINA. The marriage joined the direct descendants of Augustus and of his wife LIVIA DRUSILLA in a line of succession through Julia's father Drusus Julius Caesar.

When her father died in 23 C.E., succession became an open hunting ground among the probable heirs. The battle for succession was dominated by women. Julia's mother, LIVILLA, was a willing player. Her opponent was the wily and ruthless Agrippina. Each sought to secure the place of emperor for her son. Livilla had one son, Julia's young brother, Tiberius Gemellus, the survivor of twin sons born in 19 C.E. Agrippina had, in addition to Julia's husband, two other sons waiting in the wings.

The married Julia was apparently close to Livilla, but her husband was not Agrippina's favorite child. In addition, neither one of the couple appears to have been politically adroit. Julia's husband was brash and indiscreet, outspokenly looking forward to his own time of power. Julia rashly disclosed her husband's intemperate remarks to her mother.

Were not the wealth and power of the empire the prize, the couple's behavior would have been less noteworthy. However, Julia's mother had become the accomplice of Lucius Aelius Sejanus, the prefect of the Praetorian Guard. With Tiberius relatively secluded in Capri, Sejanus became the emperor's eyes and ears in Rome. His aspirations possibly expanded to include marriage with Julia's mother and even a regency over her small son.

The tales brought by Julia to her mother were used as evidence by Sejanus to convince Tiberius that Julia's husband Nero Julius Caesar was treacherous. In a letter to the Senate in 29 C.E., Tiberius denounced him and his mother, Agrippina, for plotting against the emperor. Agrippina was exiled to Pandateria, and Nero, to Pontia. He was put to death the following year.

Shortly thereafter, Tiberius turned on Sejanus and accused him before the Senate of treason. He was executed. Julia's mother was accused and convicted of being Sejanus's lover and of conspiring with him to poison her husband, Tiberius's son, eight years earlier. Released into the care of Julia's grandmother the younger ANTONIA her mother starved herself to death.

Still a widow in 33, Tiberius arranged that Julia marry Gaius Rubellius Blandus, consul suffectus in 18 C.E. He came from an equestrian background, which limited the threat any child of their marriage would pose to the existing aspirants for succession. Although Rubellius Blandus was close to 60, and Julia, about 30, they soon had a son, Rubellius Plautus. Julia however was still not safe. By 43 Julia's uncle Claudius had succeeded Tiberius. Valeria MESSALLINA was his wife, and Julia posed a possible obstacle to her plans for the succession. Fearing a rival in anyone connected to the imperial family, even Julia's equestrian son, Messallina accused Julia of immoral conduct. She was put to death.

Sources

Dio Cassius. *Roman History* 58.8, 9; 21.1; 60.18.4.
Tacitus. *Annales* 3.29.4; 6.27.1; 13.32.5; 13.43.4.
Bauman, Richard A. *Women and Politics in Ancient Rome.* London: Routledge, 1994, index.
Levick, Barbara. *Claudius: The Corruption of Power.* New Haven, Conn.: Yale University Press 1993, pp. 56–57.
Levick, Barbara. *Tiberius the Politician.* London: Thames and Hudson, 1976, index.
Marsh, Frank Burr. *The Reign of Tiberius.* New York: Barnes and Noble, 1931, pp. 182, 192.
Pauly, A., G. Wissowa, and W. Kroll. *Real-Encyclopadie D. Classischen Altertumswissenschaft 1893–.* (Germany: multiple publishers) 552.
Syme, Ronald. *The Augustan Aristocracy.* Oxford: Clarendon Press, 1986, index.
———. *Tacitus.* 2 vols. Oxford: Clarendon Press, 1958, index.

Julia Aquilia Severa

(third century C.E.)   Roman: Rome
Vestal Virgin married to emperor

Julia Aquilia Severa was a Vestal Virgin pressed into marriage by the increasingly unstable emperor Elagabalus in 219 or 220 C.E. after he divorced JULIA CORNELIA PAULA. In a letter to the Senate, Elagabalus wrote that not only had he fallen in love with Julia, but it was fitting that he, the high priest, should marry a Vestal Virgin, a high priestess, to create godlike children. Subsequently, he divorced Julia Severa, married and divorced other women, and then again married her in 221. Elagabalus was murdered the following year.

Sources

Dio Cassius. *Roman History* 80.9.3–4.
Herodian. *History of the Empire* 5.6.2.
Balsdon, J. P. V. D. *Roman Women.* New York: John Day Comp., 1963, p. 159.
Pauly, A., G. Wissowa, and W. Kroll. *Real-Encyclopadie D. Classischen Altertumswissenschaft 1893–.* (Germany: multiple publishers) 557.

Julia Avita Mamaea

(?–235 C.E.)   Roman: Syria and Italy
power broker

Julia Avita Mamaea successfully wielded power during difficult times in the third century C.E. Born the younger daughter of JULIA MAESA and the consul Julius Avitus, she married Gessius Marcianus, a knight from Arca Caesarea in Syria. She was widowed after the birth of her son, Alexianus, who would become the emperor Severus Alexan-

Julia Avita Mamaea
*(Date: 232 C.E. 1944.100.53321, Archives,
American Numismatic Society)*

der. All sources agree that Julia ruled her son and through him the empire.

Like her mother and her aunt, JULIA DOMNA, Julia Mamaea was intelligent, strong willed, courageous, pragmatic, and power-loving. Interested in Christianity, she provided the theologian Origen with a military escort to come to Alexandria and deliver to her a sermon. Not surprisingly, her son, after he assumed power, kept statutes of Christ and Abraham along with the deified emperors of Rome in his private chapel.

Julia Mamaea's position as the dominant imperial force in the empire was won with blood. Her mother had successfully plotted with Julia's older sister, JULIA SOAEMIAS BASSIANA, to make Julia's nephew Elagabalus emperor of Rome. Once emperor, Elagabalus's behavior became increasingly scandalous and bizarre. Julia Soaemias not only failed to curb her son but appeared to revel in his extravagances. Julia Maesa feared that Elagabalus would be overthrown, bringing to an end her own position of power and influence. She then conspired with her younger daughter, Julia Mamaea, to replace Elagabalus with Alexianus.

Julia Maesa persuaded the 16-year-old Elagabalus to adopt the 12-year-old Alexianus. His name became Marcus Aurelius Alexander Caesar. Julia Mamaea declared to the army that late emperor Caracalla was the father of her son, just as her sister had earlier claimed the late emperor father of Elagabalus. Keeping her nephew appeased and the troops well bribed, she had the younger boy tutored in Latin and Greek and trained to behave as an emperor. Within the year Julia Mamaea and her mother arranged for the Praetorian Guard to kill Elagabalus and Julia Soaemias. Alexianus assumed the name Marcus Aurelius Severus Alexander and became emperor in 222 C.E.

Julia Mamaea and her mother took up the reins of government in the boy's name. They gained the support of the Senate, establishing an advisory council of 16 distinguished senators. They neither sought the right to sit in the Senate nor to sign decrees and they did not object when the Senate abolished the right that had been granted Julia Soaemias. They appointed Domitius Ulpian, a distinguished jurist, head of the Praetorian Guard and charged him to restore order and discipline in the army which had become lax and unruly under Elagabalus. With Ulpian's advice, they instituted financial reforms that increased the treasury and allowed them to ease the burden of taxation that had escalated under Caracalla and Elagabalus. Expenditures for the imperial household were modified. The corn supply was assured, and loans at low interest were made available from the treasury. In 223 the Praetorian Guard, angered at the strict discipline imposed by Ulpian, mutinied and pursued him into the palace. Ulpian was killed in spite of Severus's attempt to save him. The leader of the revolt was later executed.

After the death of her mother in 224, Julia Mamaea alone directed Severus Alexander. She instituted additional needed reforms and pushed her son to ward behavior that was judicious and fair, avoiding mass executions or deportations. For 12 years, between 222 and 235, the empire was largely peaceful. During this period she may have ended a marriage between her son and Gnaea Seia Herennia Sallustia Barbia ORBIANA, whose name appeared on coins and inscriptions between 225 and 227. The daughter of Sallustius Macrinus,

167

whom Severus Alexander had appointed Caesar, her father was executed for treason and Orbiana was sent back to Africa.

In 233 the Persian king Artaxerxes invaded Mesopotamia. Julia went with her son to Antioch to oversee the troops. The campaign was not a great success, but the Persians suffered enough casualties to allow the Romans to regain Mesopotamia. A greater threat now took place on the Rhine, were German tribes invaded. Severus again went to the front accompanied by Julia Mamaea. She tried to placate the Germans rather than fight. The Roman army regarded her behavior as cowardly. In addition, they coveted for themselves the bribe money that she used to buy off the Germans. In 235 they revolted under the leadership of Maximinus and murdered both Julia Mamaea and her son.

Sources

Dio Cassius. *Roman History* 79.30.2–4; 38.4; 80 (fragment)

Herodian. *History of the Empire.* 5.3.3, 7.1–5, 8.2–3, 10; 6.1–9.

Scriptores Historiae Augustae. Alexander Severus 3.1; 14.7; 26.9–11; 59.8; 60.1–2; 63.5.

Balsdon, J. P. V. D. *Roman Women.* New York: John Day Comp., 1963, pp. 156–164.

Oxford Classical Dictionary, ed. by Simon Hornblower and Antony Spawforth. 3d. ed. New York: Oxford University Press, 1996, p. 777.

▣ Julia Cornelia Paula

(third century C.E.)   Roman: Italy
Augusta

Julia Cornelia Paula was the unfortunate first wife of the emperor Marcus Aurelius Antoninus Elagabalus. He was the son of Julia Soaemias Bassiana and took his name from the sun-god of Emesa in Syria, for whom he was the hereditary priest. Julia Paula came from an aristocratic family in Rome. She married Elagabalus probably in the summer of 219 C.E., when he was about 16. Her marriage to the young emperor may well have been an effort to improve relations between the emperor and the Senate. The nuptials were accompanied by an expensive celebration with elaborate banquets, gladiatorial contests, and the slaughter of some 51 tigers.

Julia Paula was given the title Augusta, and her name appeared on coins. Elagabalus, whose behavior became increasingly bizarre, divorced her within a year. He claimed that she had a blemish of some sort on her body. She returned to private life; her successor, Julia Aquilia Severa, would be hardly more successful as the emperor's wife.

Sources

Dio Cassius. *Roman History* 80.9.1–4.

Herodian. *History of the Empire* 5.6.1.

Pauly, A., G. Wissowa, and W. Kroll. *Real-Encyclopadie D. Classischen Altertumswissenschaft 1893–.* (Germany: multiple publishers) 564.

▣ Julia Domna

(second century–218 C.E.)
Roman: Syria and Italy
Augusta

Julia Domna was ambitious, indomitable, and handsome. She came from Emesa in Syria, where her father, Julius Bassianus, was the priest in the Temple of the Sun. In 187 C.E. she married Lucius Septimius Severus, whom she had met earlier while he commanded a legion in Syria. He was said to have remembered that her horoscope matched his and sought her out after his wife died. North African, from an equestrian family, he was consul in 190 and became emperor in 193. They had two sons: Marcus Aurelius Antoninus Caracalla was born in 188, Septimius Geta, in 189.

After Septimius Severus became emperor, Julia, her sister Julia Maesa, and the latter's two daughters, Julia Soaemias Bassiana and Julia Avita Mamaea, collected around them an interesting circle that included the Greek philosopher Philostratus, from whom Julia commissioned a biography of Apollonius; the physician and medical writer Galen; and possibly the historians Appian and Dio.

Early in her husband's reign, Julia traveled with him. She rebuilt the temple of Vesta in Rome and restored a meeting hall for women erected by Vibia SABINA in the Forum of Trajan. Her influence on her husband diminished after 197 when he appointed Plautianus, a fellow countryman from Africa, as prefect of the Praetorian Guard. A cruel and avaricious man, he perceived Julia as his enemy. In 201 he threatened her with the charge of adultery. The accusation, either dismissed or never pursued, nevertheless curtailed her power. In 202, Plautianus's daughter PLAUTILLA married her son Caracalla. Her son hated Plautilla as much as Julia hated Plautilla's father.

Julia Domna regained her former position when Caracalla convinced his father that Plautianus was traitor. After Plautianus was murdered on January 22, 205, Caracalla divorced Plautilla and banished her to the island of Lipara. Once more secure, Julia Domna and her whole family accompanied her husband to Britain during his campaign of 208–11. She was named Augusta and was also given the title of Mater Castrorum (Mother of the Encampment).

After the death of her husband in 211, Julia Domna successfully opposed dividing the empire between her two sons. She worked to bridge their mutual hatred. In February 212, Caracalla requested a meeting with his brother with Julia present to resolve their differences. Caracalla, instead, sent centurions to murder Geta, who died in Julia's arms.

Julia Domna handled her unstable son Caracalla carefully, and as a result, her relationship with him remained excellent. She focused him on his responsibilities as emperor and sought to curb his excessive expenditures. She spent a great deal of time in Nicomedea on the Black Sea in Asia Minor in 214–15 while her son was in the East on military campaigns. There she received petitions and answered most of the official correspondence. Dispatches to the Senate were sent in her name as well as his. She held public receptions attended by prominent men who sought from her the services and benefits of an emperor. When Caracalla became disabled by venereal disease, which increasingly affected his temper, she effectively governed in his name.

In April 217 Caracalla was murdered at the instigation of the Praetorian prefect Macrianus, who feared for his own life. Julia Domna received the news in Antioch where she was conducting the business of government. Initially, Macrianus allowed Julia to retain her guards and other honors. She began to lay plans to overthrow Macrianus and rule in his stead. He became suspicious and ordered her out of Antioch. Ill with breast cancer but unwilling to surrender power, she committed suicide by starvation in Antioch in 218.

Sources

Dio Cassius. *Roman History* 76.15.6–7; 78.2.1–6; 18.2–3; 79.23–24.

Herodian. *History of the Empire* 3.15.6; 4.3, 4–5.

Scriptores Historiae Augustae. Alexander Severus 18.8.

Balsdon, J. P. V. D. *Roman Women.* New York: John Day Comp., 1963, pp. 150–156.

Birley, Anthony Richard. *Septimius Severus: The African Emperor.* New Haven, Conn.: Yale University Press, 1989, index.

Levick, Barbara. *Julia Domna: Syrian Empress.* New York: Routledge, 2007.

Oxford Classical Dictionary, ed. by Simon Hornblower and Antony Spawforth. 3d. ed. New York: Oxford University Press, 1996, p. 777.

Pauly, A., G. Wissowa, and W. Kroll. *Real-Encyclopadie D. Classischen Altertumswissenschaft 1893–.* (Germany: multiple publishers) 566.

Julia Drusilla (1)
(16–38 C.E.)   Roman: Rome
deified

Julia Drusilla was born in 16 C.E. into a family plagued by misfortune. Her mother, the elder AGRIPPINA, and her father, Germanicus Julius Caesar, were a popular couple and leading contenders in the politics of succession to Tiberius. Disaster struck when her father died suddenly at Antioch in 19 C.E. Convinced that he had been poisoned under orders from Tiberius, her mother returned to Rome and entered the fray of imperial politics. A decade later her mother and elder brother, Nero Julius Caesar, were accused of treason. Both exiled in 29, Nero was executed in 31, and her mother died by starvation in 33. Another brother, Drusus Julius Caesar, imprisoned in 30, died in 33.

In 33, as the reign of the ailing Tiberius was drawing to an end, Julia Drusilla married Lucius Cassius Longinus, consul in 30 C.E. After her brother, Gaius Caligula succeeded Tiberius, he dissolved her marriage. Her second husband was Marcus Aemilius Lepidus, the son of Marcus Aemilius Lepidus, consul in 6 C.E. Still clearly close with her brother, rumors of an incestuous relationship were fueled when Caligula named her his heir during an illness in 37. In the malicious gossip of the time, it was also rumored that her husband was her brother's lover.

When Julia Drusilla died in 38, Caligula could hardly contain his grief. He enforced public mourning throughout the empire. Although there was no precedent, Julia Drusilla was deified as Panthea, and the emperor had her statue placed alongside the temple statues of the traditional female deities.

Sources

Dio Cassius. *Roman History* 59.11.1–6.
Suetonius. *The Lives of the Caesars:* Gaius Caligula 7; 24.1–2.
Tacitus. *Annales* 6.15.4.
Balsdon, J. P. V. D. *Roman Women.* New York: John Day Comp., 1963, p. 250.
Bauman, Richard A. *Women and Politics in Ancient Rome.* London: Routledge, 1994, pp. 159–163.
Ferrill, A. *Caligula: Emperor of Rome.* London: Thames and Hudson, 1991, index.
Oxford Classical Dictionary, ed. by Simon Hornblower and Antony Spawforth. 3d. ed. New York: Oxford University Press, 1996, p. 777.
Pauly, A., G. Wissowa, and W. Kroll. *Real-Encyclopadie D. Classischen Altertumswissenschaft 1893–.* (Germany: multiple publishers) 567.
Syme, Ronald. *The Augustan Aristocracy.* Oxford: Clarendon Press, 1986, index.

◉ Julia Drusilla (2)

(c. 40–January 24, 41 C.E.)   Roman: Rome
political victim

Julia Drusilla was born in 40 C.E., either on the day of her parents' marriage or a month before they wed. She was the daughter of the emperor Gaius Caligula and his fourth wife, MILONIA CAE-SONIA. Her father, who was probably mad, claimed that her birth was sudden and therefore supernatural. Supposedly, when she displayed her temper by scratching the faces of playmates, her father proudly claimed that by her temper he knew her to be his daughter.

Drusilla died after her head was dashed against a wall on January 24, 41, the same day on which her mother and father were murdered.

Sources

Dio Cassius. *Roman History* 59.28.8.
Suetonius. *The Lives of the Caesars:* Gaius Caligula 25.3–4; 58.
Pauly, A., G. Wissowa, and W. Kroll. *Real-Encyclopadie D. Classischen Altertumswissenschaft 1893–.* (Germany: multiple publishers) 568.

◉ Julia Flavia

(65–91 C.E.)   Roman: Rome
Augusta; deified

Born in 65 C.E., Julia was the daughter of the future emperor Titus Flavius Vespasianus by his second wife, MARCIA FURNILLA. Her parents divorced in 64. She was declared Augusta by her father during his short reign, 79–81.

Her father unsuccessfully sought to marry her with his brother, the future emperor Titus Flavius Domitian. Julia instead married her cousin Titus Flavius Sabinus, who was consul with Domitian in 82 and whom Domitian executed in 84. After her husband's death, Julia lived openly with Domitian. She died in 91, and Domitian deified her. Her death has been attributed to an abortion.

Sources

Dio Cassius. *Roman History* 67.3.2.
Pliny the Younger. *Epistulae* 4.11
Suetonius. *The Lives of the Caesars:* Domitian 22.1.
Suetonius. *The Lives of the Caesars:* Titus 4.2–4.
Balsdon, J. P. V. D. *Roman Women.* New York: John Day Comp., 1963, p. 133.
Oxford Classical Dictionary, ed. by Simon Hornblower and Antony Spawforth. 3d. ed. New York: Oxford University Press, 1996, p. 600.
Pauly, A., G. Wissowa, and W. Kroll. *Real-Encyclopadie D. Classischen Altertumswissenschaft 1893–.* (Germany: multiple publishers) 552.

Julia Livilla

(18–41 C.E.)
Roman: Italy, Germany, and Gaul
political player

Julia Livilla came from a family plagued by misfortune. She was the youngest daughter of the popular elder Vipsania AGRIPPINA and Germanicus Julius Caesar. Born in 18 C.E., one year before her father's unexpected death, her life was burdened with her mother's suspicions. Bringing her husband's ashes back from Antioch where he had died, Agrippina was convinced that her husband's death had been orchestrated by the emperor Tiberius. Scarcely a decade later, her mother and brother, Nero Julius Caesar, were charged with treason by Tiberius and exiled to islands off the coast. The next year, he imprisoned another brother, Drusus Julius Caesar.

In 33, the same year in which her exiled mother starved herself to death and her brother Drusus died in prison, she married Marcus Vinicius, consul in 30 and 45. It was not a brilliant match, but it may have been a peaceful one. Her husband, a gentle person and a fine orator, came from an equestrian background outside the eternal imperial fray.

In 37 her brother Gaius Caligula became emperor. He honored all his living siblings. Although their sister JULIA DRUSILLA was Caligula's favorite, all the siblings were subject to malicious gossip about incestuous relations. In 39, Julia Livilla joined other family members and accompanied the emperor and the army to Mainz in Germany. On arrival, Caligula accused them of conspiracy, treason, and adultery in a plot that included Julia Livilla, the younger AGRIPPINA, Marcus Aemilius Lepidus, and the governor of Upper Germany Gnaeus Cornelius Lentulus Gaetulicus. Julia Livilla and her sister were banished to the Pontian islands. Lepidus was executed.

When her uncle Claudius became emperor in 41, he recalled both Julia Livilla and Agrippina from exile and restored their property. However, Valeria MESSALLINA, her uncle's wife, was fearful of Julia Livilla's beauty and jealous of both sisters' influence over Claudius. Julia Livilla was soon accused of adultery with Lucius Annaeus Seneca, a brilliant orator and philosopher. Again exiled, this time to the island of Pandateria, she was killed soon after.

Sources

Dio Cassius. *Roman History* 60.4.1; 8.4–5.
Suetonius. *The Lives of the Caesars:* Gaius Caligula 24.3.
Tacitus. *Annales* 6.15.
Ferrill, A. *Caligula: Emperor of Rome.* London: Thames and Hudson, 1991, index.
Levick, Barbara. *Tiberius the Politician.* London: Thames and Hudson, 1976, index.
Oxford Classical Dictionary, ed. by Simon Hornblower and Antony Spawforth. 3d. ed. New York: Oxford University Press, 1996, p. 777.
Pauly, A., G. Wissowa, and W. Kroll. *Real-Encyclopadie D. Classischen Altertumswissenschaft 1893–.* (Germany: multiple publishers) 575.
Syme, Ronald. *The Augustan Aristocracy.* Oxford: Clarendon Press, 1986, index.

Julia Maesa

(second century–224 C.E.)
Roman: Syria, Asia, and Rome
power broker

Julia Maesa was ambitious and thrived in a world of intrigue populated by strong women and weak men. She was the daughter of Julius Bassianus of Emesa in Syria and the sister of JULIA DOMNA. She married a Syrian, Julius Avitus, consul suffectus and proconsul of Asia under her brother-in-law, the emperor Lucius Septimius Severus. Avitus died during the reign of Marcus Aurelius Antoninus Caracalla, Julia Maesa's nephew. She had two daughters, JULIA SOAEMIAS BASSIANA and JULIA AVITA MAMAEA. After the murder of Caracalla and the suicide of his mother, Julia Domna in 218 C.E., the emperor Marcus Opellius Macrinus ordered Julia Maesa to leave Rome and return to Emesa. She left with a great deal of wealth, amassed during the previous reigns.

Julia Maesa plotted with her daughter Julia Soaemias, a widow with a son, to have the boy declared the child of Caracalla and thereby challenge the legitimacy of the emperor Macrinus. The boy, Varius Avitus Bassianus, a very handsome 14-year-old, was priest of the sun-god at Emesa, a position that he inherited from his great-grandfather.

Julia Maesa
(Date: 218 C.E.–222 C.E. 1970.77.1, Archives,
American Numismatic Society)

Smuggled into the army camp along with enough of Julia Maesa's gold to smooth the way, the soldiers proclaimed him emperor.

When Macrinus attacked, she and her daughter leaped from their chariots and rallied the retreating troops. With the young boy leading the forces, they defeated Macrinus on June 8, 218. Macrinus was killed as he fled to Rome in disguise. The boy immediately assumed all of the titles and honors of the emperor without waiting for confirmation by the Senate and took the name Elagabalus, after the sun-god of Emesa.

The 15-year-old emperor, along with Julia Maesa, her daughters Julia Soaemias and Julia Mamaea, and their entourage, began the trip to Rome. Over a year later, in July 219, they arrived.

Elagabalus's behavior became increasingly erratic and bizarre. Julia Soaemias, who enjoyed the luxurious life, failed to restrain him. Concerned that his foolishness would result in the loss of her own power and position, Julia Maesa conspired with her second daughter, Julia Mamaea, to replace Elagabalus with her other grandson. They convinced Elagabalus to adopt his 12-year-old cousin Julia Mamaea's son Alexianus, and let it be

known to the army that Alexianus was also a son of Caracalla. The plot succeeded. Elagabalus and his mother were killed by the Praetorian Guard in 222, and Alexianus was declared emperor as Marcus Aurelius Severus Alexander.

His mother, Julia Mamaea, now received the title of Augusta and carefully supervised the education and upbringing of her son. Since he was only 13, Julia Maesa and Julia Mamaea were unimpeded. No action was taken without the approval of the two women. They ruled well. They improved relations with the Senate by establishing an advisory council of 16 senators. Julia Maesa died two years later in 224 and was deified by her grandson.

Sources

Dio Cassius. *Roman History* 79.30.2–4, 38.4.
Herodian. *History of the Empire* 5.3.2–3, 9–12; 5.5–6; 6.1, 4; 7.1–3; 8.3–4.
Scriptores Historiae Augustae. Marcus Aurelius Antoninus (Marcus Aurelius) 9.
Balsdon, J. P. V. D. *Roman Women.* New York: John Day Comp., 1963, index.
Oxford Classical Dictionary, ed. by Simon Hornblower and Antony Spawforth. 3d. ed. New York: Oxford University Press, 1996, pp. 777–787.

▣ Juliana, Anicia
(c. 461–527/528 C.E.)
Roman: Constantinople
political player

Anicia Juliana's bloodline reached back to Theodosius the Great, which in the rapidly changing fortunes of the time was a currency of legitimacy with incalculable value; her blood relationship with the Vandals, moreover, only made her more desirable.

Juliana was the grandaughter of the Augusta LICINIA EUDOXIA and Valentinian III, emperor in the West. Her father, Anicius Olybrius, a member of an illustrious and powerful Italian family, was in the East when Gaiseric led the Vandals into Rome in 455. Her mother, PLACIDIA, however, was in Rome. Her mother, grandmother, and her aunt EUDOCIA either accompanied or were taken by Gaiseric back to Carthage after he sacked the city. Gaiseric insisted that Eudocia marry his son

Huneric in accordance with a betrothal that he had arranged with Valentinian III years earlier before the latter's death. Within a few years, and no doubt having received a substantial payment from her father and, possibly, Emperor Leo I, Gaiseric released her grandmother and mother, who returned to Constantinople.

Juliana's mother reached Constantinople in 460 and Juliana was born in 461. In August 461, Gaiseric demanded that her father become emperor in the West. It was a self-serving, but not altogether impossible, demand made at a moment of political disarray. Majorian, emperor since 457, had died. Through his wife Placidia, Olybrius had a connection to Valentinian and the Theodosian line in the West. He was at least as likely a legitimate successor as anyone else, and, from Gaiseric's perspective, a most desirable successor, since Olybrius's wife Placidia and Eudocia were sisters. It didn't happen.

In 472, however, Juliana's father briefly was emperor of the West. The sequence of events was another variation of the potential for exploiting his wife and daughter's kinship with Eudocia and Valentinian. Leo I, the emperor of the East, sent Olybrius to settle a dispute between Anthemius, the emperor in the West, and Anthemius's son-in-law Ricimer. Leo also dispatched a secret emissary to Anthemius ordering Olybrius's assassination, since he feared the association with Gaiseric. The plan, discovered by Ricimer and revealed to Olybrius, resulted in a vote of the Senate, in April 472, to make Olybrius emperor in the West. Anthemius was killed in July 472. Olybrius died, the unchallenged emperor of the West, on November 2, 472.

Juliana and her mother remained in Constantinople all during this period. However, even after her father's death, she could not escape imperial politics. In 478, still unmarried, the emperor Zeno offered her, along with a huge amount of money, to Theoderic, leader of the Goths. The offer was rebuffed. Soon after, she married Flavius Areobindas. Son of a consular family, he became consul in 506 and served as a general under the emperor Anastasius I in the campaign against Persia.

Juliana and her husband were orthodox Christians. They both supported the Chalcedon doctrine which upheld the two natures of Christ, human and divine, conjoined yet separate. In 481, Zeno issued a decree to reconcile the orthodox position with the more moderate Monophysites, who never accepted the Chalcedon compromise and adhered to the single divine nature of Christ. Zeno's adviser was Acacius, the Patriarch of Constantinople, and when Zeno failed, Acacius was excommunicated by Felix II, bishop of Rome. The Acacian Schism began, lasting until 519, with Alexandria a stronghold of Monophytism and Constantinople favoring orthodoxy. During this period and despite imperial and church pressure, Juliana resisted any change in her position.

In 512, when the prelate Timothy attempted to use a Monophysite text in St. Sophia, a mob rioted and marched to Juliana's house proclaiming her husband as emperor. He refused and the elderly emperor Anastasius dispersed the crowd by offering to resign. In 519, she corresponded with Hormisdas, bishop of Rome, to facilitate legates from the Roman bishop in Constantinople in another attempt to end the schism.

Juliana was aware of her public position. She built a number of churches, including one dedicated to the Mother of God, and improved and enlarged the Church of Saint Euphemia, built by her grandmother Licinia Eudoxia and improved by her own parents. The oldest and most famous copy of *Materia Medica* of Dioscorides, an illuminated Byzantine manuscript now in the Austrian National Library, was given to her as a gift in appreciation of her support for the construction of a church in about 512.

Juliana died in 527/528 C.E.

Sources

John Malalas. *Chronicle* XIV vi., XVI. i, iii.

Malchus. *Fragments* 13, 16.

Priscus. *Fragments* 29, 204, 209. 1–2.

Theophanes. *Chronicle* AM 6005.

Prosopography of the Later Roman Empire. Vol. II. Edited By A. H. M. Jones, J. R. Martindale, and J. Morris. Cambridge: Cambridge University Press, 1971. Reprinted 1992, pp. 635–636.

◉ Julia Phoebe

(first century B.C.E.–first century C.E.)
Roman: Rome
loyal attendant

Julia Phoebe was a freedwoman of JULIA (6), the only child of the emperor Augustus and SCRIBONIA. When Julia was banished by Augustus in 2 B.C.E., Julia Phoebe, who was close to Julia, committed suicide.

Sources

Suetonius. *The Lives of the Caesars: Augustus* 65.2–3.

◉ Julia Procilla

(?–69 C.E.)
Roman: Gallia Narbonensis and Rome
honorable woman; murder victim

Julia Procilla died violently at the hands of marauding soldiers in 69 C.E. She had lived a principled life that sought to balance study and political engagement. Born in Narbonese Gaul, her father was an imperial official named Julius Proculus. She married Julius Graecinus, an equestrian and student of philosophy. Her husband became a senator under the emperor Tiberius and attained the office of praetor. In 40 C.E., already irritated with him because of his interest in philosophy, the emperor Gaius Caligula had Graecinus executed when he refused to accuse Marcus Junius Silanus of treason.

In the same year, Julia Procilla gave birth to a son, Gnaeus Julius Agricola. After the death of her husband, she returned with her son to Massilia (Marseilles), where she attended to his education. Later, Agricola's son-in-law, the great Roman historian Cornelius Tacitus, would write that Agricola would have immersed himself in philosophy had his mother not wisely tempered this inclination and arranged that he also study more practical arts.

Her son became quaestor of Asia, tribune, praetor, consul, and later legate of Britain. In 69 Julia Procilla was murdered on her estate by plundering sailors of the insurgent emperor Otho. The estate itself was looted and a good part of Agricola's inheritance was lost.

Sources

Tacitus. *Agricola* 4.7.

◉ Julia Soaemias Bassiana

(second century–222 C.E.)
Roman: Syria and Italy
Augusta

Julia Soaemias Bassiana successfully plotted to make her son emperor. She was the elder of JULIA MAESA's two daughters. Her father was Julius Avitus and her grandfather was Julius Bassianus, priest of the sun-god at Emesa in Syria. She married Sextus Varius Marcellus, an equestrian from Apamea in Syria who died leaving her with a son, Varius Avitus.

Julia Soaemias conspired with her mother to have her young son challenge the rule of Macrinus, who had supplanted Marcus Aurelius Antoninus Caracalla as emperor. Caracalla had been her cousin; his mother was her aunt, JULIA DOMNA. Julia Soaemias and her mother had lived with them in Rome. After Caracalla's death the women were expelled. Using the large fortune her mother had accumulated during the reigns of Septimius Severus and Caracalla, she gained support from the troops in Syria after she declared that her son was the child of Caracalla and the legitimate heir. Gannys, who was her lover and her son's tutor, and an army soldier named Comazon were her coconspirators in the army camp who rallied the troops to her cause. The defeated Macrinus fled and was murdered on the way to Rome.

Avitus, the hereditary priest of the sun-god Elagabalus at Emesa in Syria, became Emperor Elagabalus in 218 C.E. He was 15 years old. Immediately he assumed all the titles of the office without regard for custom, which assigned to the Roman Senate the right to bestow the offices and titles of the emperor. Julia Soaemias, her son, her mother, her sister JULIA AVITA MAMAEA, Gannys and Comazon, and their supporters traveled to Rome Elagabalus carried with him the black conical stone image of the sun-god. In Nicomedea, Elagabalus murdered Gannys after he attempted to temper the young emperor's behavior.

When the party reached Rome a year later, in July 219, Elagabalus heaped honors on his mother.

She was named Augusta and called Mater Augustorum (Mother of Augustus) and Mater Castorum (Mother of the Encampment). Elagabalus reputedly brought her into the Senate chamber. She also presided over a female senate that issued a set of rules of etiquette for women, including clothing to be worn in public and proper means of conveyance. Elagabalus's behavior became increasingly erratic and scandalous as he married and divorced a number of women including JULIA CORNELIA PAULA and the Vestal Virgin JULIA AQUILIA SEVERA Julia Soaemias, who enjoyed her lifestyle, made no attempt to curb her son.

Her mother, Julia Maesa, determined that Elagabalus and her daughter must be removed before his troops revolted. She hatched a plot with her younger daughter, Julia Mamaea, to replace Elagabalus with Alexianus, Julia Mamaea's son. Julia Maesa first persuaded Elagabalus, who was 16, to adopt Alexianus, who was 12. When Elagabalus began to suspect a plot, Julia Maesa and Julia Mamaea had soldiers of the Praetorian Guard murder him and Julia Soaemias in Rome in 222. Their bodies were stripped naked and dragged all over Rome. Alexianus, who was 13, was proclaimed the new emperor, but power remained in the hands of the women, Julia Mamaea and her mother.

Sources

Dio Cassius. *Roman History* 79.30.2–4, 38.4; 80.3–6, 20.2.

Herodian. *History of the Empire* 5.3.3, 8.8–10.

Balsdon, J. P. V. D. *Roman Women.* New York: John Day Comp., 1963, pp. 156–162.

Oxford Classical Dictionary, ed. by Simon Hornblower and Antony Spawforth. 3d. ed. New York: Oxford University Press, 1996, p. 778.

Pauly, A., G. Wissowa, and W. Kroll. *Real-Encyclopadie D. Classischen Altertumswissenschaft 1893–.* (Germany: multiple publishers) 596.

Junia (1)

(first century B.C.E.)   Roman: Rome
conspirator

Junia was one of three daughters born to SERVILIA (1) and Decimus Junius Silanus, consul in 63 and 62 B.C.E. Her sisters were JUNIA (2) and JUNIA TERTIA. Her mother had been the lover of Julius Caesar, and her uncle was the republican Marcus Porcius Cato Uticensis. Her half brother was Marcus Junius Brutus, one of Caesar's assassins. Her father was dead by 57 B.C.E. her forceful mother who wielded power by virtue of her personality and connections, arranged marriages for all three sisters. Shortly after 61, Junia married Marcus Aemilius Lepidus, consul in 46 and, along with Antony and Octavian, a member of the Second Triumvirate. She had two sons, Marcus and Quintus.

Her husband was removed from office by Octavian, and Octavian's general, Gaius Maecenas, prosecuted her son Marcus for plotting to assassinate Octavian on his return to Rome in 30 B.C.E. He sent Marcus to Octavian in Actium, where he was executed. Maecenas also charged Junia, claiming that she was aware of the plot. To spare her the trip to Actium, Maecenas demanded surety that she would appear before Octavian when he came to Rome. Her husband went to the consul suffectus, Lucius Saenius, to put himself up as security for his wife or else be allowed to accompany her to Actium. The consul released Junia. Whether she subsequently made peace with Octavian or died is unrecorded.

Sources

Appian. *Roman History: Bella civilian (Civil Wars)* 4.50.

Pauly, A., G. Wissowa, and W. Kroll. *Real-Encyclopadie D. Classischen Altertumswissenschaft 1893–.* (Germany: multiple publishers) 193.

Syme, Ronald. *The Augustan Aristocracy.* Oxford: Clarendon Press, 1986, pp. 19, 35.

Junia (2)

(first century B.C.E.)   Roman: Rome
political player

Junia was one of three daughters born to SERVILIA (1) and her second husband, Decimus Junius Silanus, consul in 63–62 B.C.E. The other two were JUNIA (1) and JUNIA TERTIA. Marcus Junius Brutus, the tyrannicide, was her half brother, and the republican Marcus Porcius Cato Uticensis, her uncle. Although her father died in 57, her mother was well able to care for her. One of the most politically astute women of her day, Servilia and Julius Caesar had been lovers, remained friends, and traded favors.

Junia married Publius Servilius Isauricus, consul in 48 B.C.E. and a supporter of Julius Caesar. He was a good choice. A careful man, he navigated a narrow course through the political conflicts after the death of Caesar. Marcus Tullius Cicero, who did not trust him, tried to win him over, but he claimed family obligations. Related to the tyrannicides not only through Junia's half brother Brutus but also through two brothers-in-law, Gaius Cassius Longinus and Marcus Aemilius Lepidus, he sought a conciliatory role. He might even have entertained the idea of serving as a mediator between Caesarians and the republicans, which his mother-in-law, Servilia, would have welcomed.

Junia gave birth to a son and a daughter. Her daughter, SERVILIA (3), was to have married the young Octavian in 43 B.C.E. when her uncle, Marcus Aemilius Lepidus, was part of the Second Triumvirate with Octavian and Antony. Octavian instead married CLAUDIA (5), the daughter of FULVIA (2) and the stepdaughter of Antony. To placate Junia's husband, Octavian supported him in his successful bid for the consulship for 41. Junia's daughter, Servilia, later married her cousin Marcus Aemilius Lepidus, the son of her sister Junia. Junia's son-in-law was prosecuted by Octavian's intimate friend and supporter Gaius Maecenas for plotting to kill Octavian in 30 B.C.E. and was sent to Actium, where he was executed.

Sources
Suetonius. *The Lives of the Caesars:* Augustus 62.1.

Pauly, A., G. Wissowa, and W. Kroll. *Real-Encyclopadie D. Classischen Altertumswissenschaft 1893–.* (Germany: multiple publishers) 192.

Syme, Ronald. *The Augustan Aristocracy.* Oxford: Clarendon Press, 1986, pp. 19, 35.

▣ Junia (3)
(first–second century C.E.)   Roman: Rome
priestess

Junia, a Vestal Virgin, became seriously ill with tuberculosis and had to be removed from the house of the Vestals. The Stoic FANNIA (2), was related to Junia and nursed her. Junia died of the disease. Fannia, who had suffered exile three times, became infected and also died.

Sources
Pliny the Younger. *Epistulae* 7.19.

▣ Junia Calvina
(?–79 C.E.)   Roman: Italy
long-lived woman

Junia Calvina was the only one of five siblings to die a natural death. Unconventional and beautiful, she was the last direct descendant of the emperor Augustus. Her great-grandmother was Augustus's only daughter, JULIA (6). Her mother was AEMILIA LEPIDA (3) and her father, Marcus Junius Silanus Torquatus, was consul in 19 C.E.

Junia's clear claim on succession by virtue of her ancestry simultaneously made her a desirable marriage partner and left her vulnerable. She married Lucius Vitellius, consul suffectus in 48 C.E., the younger son of a close ally of the emperor Claudius. Divorced for unknown reasons the same year, she was accused by her former father-in-law, Vitellius, of incest with her brother Lucius Junius Silanus Torquatus. The sources attributed the charge to the younger Julia AGRIPPINA, the emperor Claudius's niece, who would become his wife a year later, and who was assiduous in clearing the way for the succession of her son, Nero. Julia Calvina was sent into exile in 49, and her brother committed suicide on the day that Agrippina married Claudius.

Agrippina prevailed, and Nero became emperor. After his mother's death, Nero ended Junia's exile, and she returned to Rome. Her other siblings were not as fortunate. Nero forced her brother Decimus Junius Silanus to commit suicide. Her sister JUNIA LEPIDA was falsely accused of engaging in magical practices and having sexual relations with her nephew, Lucius Junius Silanus. In 79, when the emperor Vespasian was informed on his deathbed that a huge crevice had appeared in the mausoleum of Augustus, he was said to have quipped that it was for Julia Calvina, Augustus's long-lived last descendant.

Sources

Suetonius. *The Lives of the Caesars:* Vespasian 23.

Tacitus. *Annales* 12.4.8; 14.12.

Balsdon, J. P. V. D. *Roman Women.* New York: John Day Comp., 1963, pp. 129–130.

Oxford Classical Dictionary, ed. by Simon Hornblower and Antony Spawforth. 3d. ed. New York: Oxford University Press, 1996, p. 787.

Pauly, A., G. Wissowa, and W. Kroll. *Real-Encyclopadie D. Classischen Altertumswissenschaft 1893–.* (Germany: multiple publishers) 198.

Syme, Ronald. *The Augustan Aristocracy.* Oxford: Clarendon Press, 1986, index.

◉ Junia Claudilla

(first century C.E.)   Roman: Rome
political wife

Junia Claudilla was the daughter of Marcus Junius Silanus, a noted orator and consul suffectus in 15 C.E., and the sister of Junia Silana. Her mother is unknown. The emperor Tiberius arranged her marriage to Gaius Caligula in 33. She died in childbirth a few years later, before her husband became emperor. In 38, Caligula forced her father to commit suicide.

Sources

Suetonius. *The Lives of the Caesars:* Gaius Caligula 6.20.1; 12.1–2.

Levick, Barbara. *Tiberius the Politician.* London: Thames and Hudson, 1976, pp. 207, 215.

Pauly, A., G. Wissowa, and W. Kroll. *Real-Encyclopadie D. Classischen Altertumswissenschaft 1893–.* (Germany: multiple publishers) 199.

◉ Junia Lepida

(first century C.E.)   Roman: Italy
political player

Junia Lepida, one of five siblings, including Junia Calvina, who were the last generation of direct descendants of the emperor Augustus, was a victim of the struggle for succession to the emperor Claudius. Her mother, Aemilia Lepida (3), was the great-granddaughter of Augustus, and her father, Marcus Julius Silanus Torquatus, was an orator of note and consul in 19 C.E.

She married the eminent jurist Cassius Longinus, consul suffectus in 30 C.E. In 65 the emperor Nero accused her of engaging in magical practices and having sexual relations with her nephew Lucius Junius Silanus. He also charged her nephew and husband with treason.

Silanus was murdered before his exile took place, and her husband was exiled to Sardinia. He was later recalled by the emperor Vespasian. Nothing more is known about Junia.

Sources

Tacitus. *Annales* 16.8.

Pauly, A., G. Wissowa, and W. Kroll. *Real-Encyclopadie D. Classischen Altertumswissenschaft 1893–.* (Germany: multiple publishers) 203.

Syme, Ronald. *The Augustan Aristocracy.* Oxford: Clarendon Press, 1986, index.

◉ Junia Silana

(?–59 C.E.)   Roman: Italy
political player

Junia Silana was both beautiful and of noble lineage. Under three different emperors she took part in the battles waged among the elite over power, prestige, and succession. She was the daughter of Marcus Junius Silanus, consul suffectus in 15 C.E. Her sister, Junia Claudilla, married the young Gaius Caligula probably in 30 or 31 and died in childbirth a few years later. Caligula forced her father to commit suicide in 38. After Claudius became emperor in 48, she married Gaius Silius, consul designate and considered one of the handsomest men in Rome.

Her marriage was destroyed by the relationship between her husband and Valeria Messallina, wife of the emperor. Messallina and Silius may have been allies in a conspiracy to supplant Claudius. The powerful freedmen around Claudius, led by Narcissus, convinced the emperor of their nefarious intent, and the lovers were seized and executed.

Junia was a close friend of the younger Julia Agrippina who followed Messallina as the wife of Claudius and who was intent upon her son Nero's succession to the emperor. She broke with Agrippina, however, when the latter told the young

Sextius Africanus, whom the widowed Junia wanted to marry, that Junia was both immoral and too old. Gossip had it that Agrippina was not interested in Africanus but hope to keep Junia a widow so that she might inherit her estate.

Junia found an opportunity for revenge. In 55, when Nero began to tire of his mother's domination, Junia arranged for Nero to suspect Agrippina of conspiracy. She had two of her clients tell Atimetus, a freedman of Nero's aunt DOMITIA, that Agrippina was plotting with Rubellius Plautus against Nero. Domitia had ample cause to share Junia's hated of Agrippina. Agrippina, the widow of Domitia's brother, had persuaded Domitia's husband, consul in 44 C.E., to divorce his wife so that he could marry her. She was also responsible for the execution of Domitia's sister, DOMITIA LEPIDA.

Junia's revenge failed. Nero was prepared to order his mother's death but was persuaded to allow Agrippina to defend herself. A delegation was sent to Agrippina, who convinced them of her innocence. The accusers, including Junia Silana, were exiled in 55. In 59 Nero lifted her exile, but she died in Tarentum (modern Taranto) before she could return to Rome.

Sources

Suetonius. *The Lives of the Caesars:* Gaius Caligula 12.

Tacitus. *Annales* 11.12; 13.19–21.

Balsdon, J. P. V. D. *Roman Women.* New York: John Day Comp., 1963, pp. 120–121.

Bauman, Richard A. *Women and Politics in Ancient Rome.* London: Routledge, 1994, pp. 196–198.

Pauly, A., G. Wissowa, and W. Kroll. *Real-Encyclopadie D. Classischen Altertumswissenschaft 1893–.* (Germany: multiple publishers) 205.

Syme, Ronald. *The Augustan Aristocracy.* Oxford: Clarendon Press, 1986, index.

▣ Junia Tertia

(73 B.C.E.–22 C.E.)   Roman: Italy
political player

Junia Tertia outlived her enemies and supporters alike, dying at age 95 in the reign of the emperor Tiberius. The youngest of three sisters, her parents were SERVILIA (1) and Decimus Junius Silanus, consul in 62 B.C.E. Her father died by 57, but her mother played a significant part in the politics before and after the assassination of Julius Caesar. Her mother arranged her marriage with Gaius Cassius Longinus, later one of Caesar's assassins. They had a son who assumed the *toga virilis* on the Ides of March in 44 B.C.E.

Despite a recent miscarriage, Junia Tertia was present at a meeting at Antium on June 8, 44 B.C.E., called and presided over by her mother, who was acknowledged to have once been the lover and still a friend of the recently slain Caesar. Also present were Junia's husband, Cassius; Marcus Tullius Cicero; her half brother Brutus; and his wife PORCIA, the daughter of Marcus Porcius Cato Uticensis and a cousin of Junia. The meeting was called to decide on a response to the Senate's offer to appoint Brutus and Cassius supervisors for the collection of corn taxes in the provinces of Asia and Sicily. It provided an honorable way for them to escape the city in the aftermath of Caesar's assassination. Cicero argued that the offer should be accepted; Brutus was undecided and Cassius contemptuous. No decision was taken, but Servilia declared that she would see to it that the offer was withdrawn.

Junia's husband, Cassius, committed suicide in 42 B.C.E. after his camp was captured at Philippi by the troops of Antony and Octavian. She never remarried and died a very wealthy widow in 22 C.E. She left legacies to almost every important patrician. Although she did not mention the emperor Tiberius, he allowed a splendid celebration of her funeral. Emblems of 20 great republican houses were carried in the funeral procession.

Sources

Cicero. *Epistulae ad Atticum* 14.20.2; 15.11.1.

Macrobius. *Saturnalia* 2.2; 5.

Tacitus. *Annales* 3.76.

Pauly, A., G. Wissowa, and W. Kroll. *Real-Encyclopadie D. Classischen Altertumswissenschaft 1893–.* (Germany: multiple publishers) 206.

Syme, Ronald. *The Augustan Aristocracy.* Oxford: Clarendon Press, 1986, index.

———. *The Roman Revolution.* London: Oxford University Press, 1963, pp. 69, 116, 492.

Junia Torquata

(first century B.C.E.–first century C.E.)
Roman: Rome
priestess

Junia Torquata was a Vestal Virgin for 64 years and served as the head of the Vestal college for much of that time. Considered a woman of exemplary virtue, she lived a more fortunate life than did her siblings. She was born into a noble family, probably the daughter of Appia Claudia and Junius Silanus, about whom little is known.

In 8 C.E., her brother Junius Silanus was charged with an adulterous relationship with JULIA (7), the granddaughter of the aging emperor Augustus. He went into voluntary exile. In 20, her brother Marcus used his influence with the emperor Tiberius to allow Junius's return to Rome. Two years later, her brother Gaius Silanus was accused of extortion and treason. Found guilty, he was exiled.

Junia intervened with the emperor. Tiberius requested of the Senate that Gaius Silanus be sent to the island of Cythnus rather than the bleak and uninhabited island of Gyaruss. The Senate acquiesced and also approved a motion supported by Tiberius that any property of Silanus that came from his mother should not be confiscated but given to his son.

Sources

Tacitus. *Annales* 3.69.
Syme, Ronald. *The Augustan Aristocracy.* Oxford: Clarendon Press, 1986, pp. 193, 196.

Justina

(?–c. 391 C.E.)   Roman: Gaul, Italy
regent

Justina ruled as regent for her son Valentinian II (who was co-emperor in the West with his stepbrother Gratian) after the death of her husband, Valentinian I. Justina was beautiful, and Valentinian divorced his first wife to marry her. She traveled with her husband and had four children, before he had a stroke and died on maneuvers in 375. Justina, with the support of her husband's ministers, especially the military leaders in Illyricum, and her uncle, friend, and longtime confidant, Cerealis, led the troops to declare her four-year-old son Emperor Valentinian II, with *imperium* over Italy, Africa, and Illyricum. The threat of insurrection from the Illyricum army led Justina's stepson and emperor in the West, Gratian, to accept the *imperium* of Valentinian II and Justina's regency.

Justina was the daughter of Lustus and the sister of Cerealis, a tribune of the imperial stables. At an early age she was betrothed to Magnentius, a senior military general in the short-lived reign of Constans. One of the three sons of Constantine the Great, Constans died in battle with his brother following Constantine's death. In January 350, Magnentius led a coup in Gaul. He was proclaimed Augustus and the western provinces quickly accepted his rule, but in September 351, Constantius II, the most successful son of Constantine, defeated him in battle. Two years later, in 353, he committed suicide in Gaul. Justina's life during the period is unknown.

On August 25, 383 C.E., Justina's stepson, Gratian, died in Britain in an army revolt led by Magnus Maximus. The troops declared Maximus emperor. However, he made no effort to invade Italy, and Theodosius, who recognized Maximus, compensated Justina for the loss of Britain with rule over Dacia and Macedonia.

Politics and religion were never far apart. Justina was an Arian Christian as had been the Augusta HELENA, the mother of Constantine the Great, and his half sister CONSTANTIA, as well as the Augusta EUSEBIA and DOMNICA. Arianism had less support in the East than the West where it was especially popular among the Germans. In Milan, which was the western seat of power, the Arian bishop, Auxentius, asked Ambrose, the orthodox bishop of Milan, to provide an Arian church. Ambrose refused. In 386, Justina issued an edict through her son that granted freedom of assembly to those who had that right by a church council under the emperor Constantius II and an order to exile Ambrose. It failed. Thousands of Ambrose's followers flocked to the church. Ambrose kept up the spirits of the collected thousands blockaded in the church by singing hymns. Justina gave up and withdrew her troops.

In 387, Maximus invaded Italy, and Justinia fled with Valentinian and her daughter Galla to Thessalonica in Macedonia. Theodosius came to Thessalonica and was entranced by the beauty of Galla, whom Justina had knowingly used as bait to secure her return to Rome. A marriage was agreed upon and Theodosius sent Justina and her children to Rome by ship. Maximus was defeated. Valentinian regained control over Italy in 388. Justina disappears from the historical record and probably died within the year.

Sources

Ambrose. *Letter* XX.

Ammiamus Marcellinus XXVIII. 2, 10. XXX. 10. 4.

Socrates. *Historia Ecclesiastica* IV. 31. 10–17.

Sozomen. *Historia Ecclesiastica* VII. 13. 2, 11; 14. 7.

Zosimus. *New History/Zosimus.* A translation with commentary by Ronald T. Ridley. Canberra: Australian Association of Byzantine Studies, 1982.

Jones, A. H. M. *The Later Roman Empire 284–602: A Social Economic and Administrative Survey.* 2 vols. Norman: University of Oklahoma Press, 1964.

Prosopography of the Later Roman Empire. Vol. I. Edited by A. H. M. Jones, J. R. Martindale, and J. Morris. Cambridge: Cambridge University Press, 1971. Reprinted 1992, pp. 488–489.

L

Labda

(seventh century B.C.E.)   Greek: Corinth
heroine

Labda was said to have lived during the seventh century B.C.E. in Corinth, which had been captured by Dorian Greeks invading from the north during the previous century. Her father was Amphion from the clan of the Bacchiadae, the first Dorian rulers. She married Eetion, one of the conquered Lapithi.

Her husband consulted the oracle at Delphi since he had not yet fathered a son. The priestess foretold that Labda would have a son who would conquer Corinth. Her family saw the prophecy as a message of their downfall. They sent 10 men to kill the son Labda had delivered. Labda allowed them into the house to admire the child, who beguiled them. They returned with the intention of kidnapping the boy. Labda overheard their plans. She successfully hid the baby in a bin. The would-be assassins returned to Corinth and claimed that the child had been killed.

Her son Cypselus overthrew the Bacchiadae and became tyrant of Corinth (c.657–25 B.C.E.).

Sources

Herodotus. *The Persian Wars* 5.92.

Oxford Classical Dictionary, ed. by Simon Hornblower and Antony Spawforth. 3d. ed. New York: Oxford University Press, 1996, p. 420–421.

Laelia

(second–first century B.C.E.)   Roman: Rome
orator

Laelia was an elegant speaker. Her father was Gaius Laelius, consul in 140 B.C.E. and one of the greatest orators of his time. After the Punic Wars, the study of Greek literature and philosophy spread among the educated elite of Rome. Laelia's family became patrons of literature and art. Her father taught her rhetoric. Laelia married Quintus Mucius Scaevola, an outstanding orator and consul in 117 B.C.E. He taught Marcus Tullius Cicero, who compared Laelia favorably with her father. Years later, the great rhetorician Quintilian also praised her.

Laelia's daughter Mucia and her granddaughters Licinia (1) and Licinia (2) were also elegant rhetoricians.

Sources

Cicero. *Epistulae ad Brutum* 58.211–12.
Quintilian. *Institutio Oratoria* 1.1, 6.
Bauman, Richard A. *Women and Politics in Ancient Rome.* London: Routledge, 1994, pp. 47–48.

Laïs

(fifth–fourth century B.C.E.)
Greek: Sicily, Corinth, and Thessaly
self-made woman

Laïs was beautiful. Her mother was Lysandra, a lover of Alcibiades, the Athenian statesman and general. When she was seven years old, she and her mother were brought to Corinth, Greece, as prisoners after the fortified town of Hycarra in Sicily fell during the Peloponnesian Wars.

Laïs was said to have been the lover of the famous painter Apelles, although her dates make the claim improbable. More likely, she followed a lover to Thessaly, in northern Greece, where she was said to have died at the hands of women who feared her beauty. The women were said to have stoned her after they lured her into the temple of Aphrodite.

Her tomb beside the river Peneus was said to have an epitaph that recorded her power to enslave the invicible Greeks with her godlike beauty.

Sources

Athenaeus. *Deipnosophistae* 13.588c–89b.
Plutarch. *Vitae Parallelae (Parallel Lives): Alcibiades* 39.4–5.
Plutarch. *Moralia: Amatorius* 767f–68b.
Plutarch. *Nicias* 15.4.
Licht, Hans. *Sexual Life in Ancient Greece.* Trans. by J. H. Freese. London: Abbey Library, 1971, p. 347.

Lamia

(fourth–third century B.C.E.)
Cyprian: Cyprus and Egypt
flute player

Lamia, a noted flute player, captivated the handsome Macedonian general Demetrius I when she was taken prisoner in 306 B.C.E., after he defeated Ptolemy I in a naval battle. No longer young herself, she was said to have been older than Demetrius.

Sources

Plutarch. *Vitae Parallelae (Parallel Lives): Demetrius* 16.3–4; 20.4; 27.2–6.

Lanassa

(fourth–third century B.C.E.)
Greek: Syracuse, Corcyra, and Greece
political player

Lanassa left her husband, took back her dowry, and then offered herself in marriage to the ruler of Macedonia. She was the daughter of Agathocles, the tyrant of Syracuse, on the island of Sicily. She married Pyrrhus, the great general and ruler of Epirus in northwestern Greece. As her dowry, she had been given the large island of Corcyra (modern Corfu) off the coast of Greece in the Ionian Sea.

She became disenchanted with Pyrrhus, who had taken another wife, and left Epirus for Corcyra. In 292 or 291 B.C.E. she offered to marry the handsome Demetrius I, ruler of Macedonia, and to bring him Corcyra as a dowry. The offer was too good to refuse. She became one of Demetrius's wives. In 288, her new husband was defeated by her former husband and the general Lysimachus. Demetrius fled to Asia. He died five years later, in 283 B.C.E.

Lanassa had a son, Alexander, by her first husband.

Sources

Plutarch. *Vitae Parallelae (Parallel Lives): Pyrrhus* 9.1; 10.5.
Macurdy, Grace. *Hellenistic Queens.* Reprint. Chicago: Ares Publishers, 1985, pp. 66–67.

Laodice I

(third century B.C.E.)
Greek: Syria and Asia Minor
ruler

Laodice fought for power for herself and her sons in the tumultuous generations following the death of Alexander the Great in 323 B.C.E. Her grandfather Seleucus founded the Seleucid Empire, encompassing Asia Minor and western Asia. Her father was Achaeus, Seleucus's younger son. The older son, Antiochus I, became ruler after her grandfather's death. She married his son and her cousin, Antiochus II. She had two sons, Seleucus Callinicus and Antiochus Hierax, and two daughters, Stratonice and Laodice.

Her husband repudiated her in 252 B.C.E. to marry BERENICE SYRA, the daughter of Ptolemy II Philadelphus of Egypt. The match secured for him the friendship of Ptolemy, the return of previously lost territories, and Berenice's dower wealth. He named Berenice's son his heir. To appease Laodice, Antiochus gave her estates near the cities of Babylon and Borsippa. Laodice, who was very wealthy even before her former husband's settlement, moved herself and her children to Ephesus, which became a second royal center. In time, Laodice enticed Antiochus to Ephesus and persuaded him to abandon Berenice. The elderly Antiochus died in 246, possibly poisoned by Laodice, soon after he had named her son his successor.

Laodice and Berenice fought to control the empire. Berenice had supporters in Antioch and some of the towns of Syria. She requested aid from her father in Egypt. Laodice arranged to have Berenice's son kidnapped. Berenice pursued the kidnappers on a chariot and killed one with a stone. Faced with a hostile crowd, the kidnappers produced a child. Without relinquishing him, they claimed he was the son of Berenice. Berenice withdrew to a palace in Daphne, a suburb of Antioch, with a guard of Galatian troops. Laodice, afraid of the arrival of Egyptian forces, had her murdered despite the efforts of Berenice's women retainers to shield her with their bodies.

Ptolemy III Euergetes I, Berenice's brother, had in the meantime succeeded their father in Egypt. He arrived too late to save his sister, but the events precipitated the Third Syrian War (246–41). At this point, Laodice and her son moved their court to Sardis away from the coast of Asia Minor. They left Ephesus governed by Sophron, the lover of DANAE, Laodice's favorite woman retainer. For an unknown reason, Laodice became disenchanted with Sophron and summoned him to Sardis. Danae warned him, and he succeeded in winning enough time to escape. He offered himself to Ptolemy and became a commander in the Egyptian fleet. Laodice killed Danae for her treachery.

Although Ptolemy made some important gains in Asia Minor, Laodice and her son Seleucus II successfully organized resistance to the invasion. While Seleucus fought to regain his territories in 245 B.C.E., he left his brother Antiochus Hierax, who was still a minor, in Sardis in Asia Minor. When Seleucus requested reinforcements, Laodice, who favored her younger son, had the troops sent on condition that Hierax became the coruler of the Seleucid Empire in Asia Minor.

Laodice's end is not recorded. Her two sons, however, became so weakened by fighting each other that they lost control of most of their territory.

Sources

Appian. *Syrian Wars* 65.
Athenaeus. *Deipnosophistae* 13.593c.
Justin. *Epitome* 27.
Pliny the Elder. *Naturalis Historia* 7.53.
Polyaenus. *Strategemata* 8.50.
Valerius Maximus. *Factorum et dictorum memorabilium libri IX* 9.10.1.
Bevan, Edwyn B. *The House of Selecus.* 2 vols. London: Edward Arnold, 1902, pp. 181 ff.
Cary, M. *A History of the Greek World from 323 to 146 B.C.* London: Methuen, 1951, pp. 86–88, 109, 369, 395–399.
Downey, Glanville. *A History of Antioch in Syria from Seleucus to the Arab Conquest.* Princeton, N.J.: Princeton University Press, 1961, pp. 87ff.
Macurdy, Grace. *Hellenistic Queens.* Reprint. Chicago: Ares Publishers, 1985, pp. 82–90.
Oxford Classical Dictionary, ed. by Simon Hornblower and Antony Spawforth. 3d. ed. New York: Oxford University Press, 1996, p. 814.
Tarn, W. W. *The Cambridge Ancient History 7.* New York: Cambridge University Press, p. 715ff.

Laodice III

(third–second century B.C.E.)
Persian: Asia Minor and Asia
philanthropist

Laodice III was generous and supported worthy causes throughout the Seleucid Empire. Born the daughter of Mithradates II, the king of Pontus in northern Asia Minor, she was married with great pomp and ceremony in 221 B.C.E. to Antioch III. Her husband, a descendant of Seleucus I, who had fought under Alexander the Great, reigned over territory from Anatolia, Syria, and Babylonia into central Asia.

Laodice established dowries for the daughters of the poor. After her husband conquered the city of Caria in Asia Minor, she granted 10 years of corn to its inhabitants at a fixed price, which prevented profiteering. Her husband established a priesthood in her honor, and civic cults honoring her were founded in several cities. Her two sons were Seleucus IV and Antiochus IV, and her daughter, CLEOPATRA I (THE SYRIAN), married Ptolemy V Epiphanes of Egypt.

Sources

Polybius. *Histories* 5.43, 1–4.
Macurdy, Grace. *Hellenistic Queens.* Reprint. Chicago: Ares Publishers, 1985, pp. 91–93.
Oxford Classical Dictionary, ed. by Simon Hornblower and Antony Spawforth. 3d. ed. New York: Oxford University Press, 1996, pp. 814–815.
Pomeroy, Sarah B. *Women in Hellenistic Egypt.* New York: Schocken, 1984, pp. 15–16.

▣ Lastheneia

(fourth century B.C.E.)   Greek: Greece
philosopher

Lastheneia came from the city of Mantinea in the Peloponnese, the peninsula in southern Greece. She studied philosophy with Plato and his successor, Speusippus, at the Academy in Athens. She was reputed to have sometimes dressed like a man.

Sources

Diogenes Laertius. *Lives of the Eminent Philosophers* 3.46.
Hawley, Richard. "The Problem of Women Philosophers in Ancient Greece." In *Women in Ancient Societies: An Illusion of the Night,* ed. by Leonie J. Archer, Susan Fischler, and Maria Wyke. New York: Routledge, 1994, pp. 74, 81–82.

▣ Leaena

(sixth century B.C.E.)   Greek: Athens
brave woman

Leaena was the lover of Aristogeiton. In 514 B.C.E. Aristogeiton and Harmodius, both members of an ancient Athenian clan, attempted to murder Hippias, the tyrant of Athens, and his younger brother Hipparchus. Harmodius and Hipparchus were killed in the struggle. Hippias was unharmed, and his guards seized Aristogeiton.

Hippias tortured Leaena, but she refused to betray her lover. She died. Aristogeiton, also tortured, was executed. A bronze lioness was later erected in Leaena's honor at the entrance to the Acropolis.

Sources

Pausanias. *Description of Greece* 23.1–2.
Pliny the Elder. *Naturalis Historia* 7.23, 87.

▣ Leontia

(c. 457 C.E.–?)   Roman: Constantinople
political actor

Leontia was determined to become Augusta like her mother, VERINA, and sister, ARIADNE. She was the younger daughter of Verina and the emperor Leo I, born sometime after her father became emperor in 457. Briefly betrothed to another, she married Marcian, whose father, Anthemius, had been the Roman emperor in the West from 467 to 472. They had at least two daughters.

Leontia lived in the West while her family engaged in an internecine struggle for the imperial mantle. After her father died in 474, her sister and her sister's husband, Zeno, came to the fore. Zeno, who had been second in power under Leo, became regent for his seven-year-old son, Leo II. The child died within a year. Zeno assumed the title of emperor and Ariadne became Augusta.

Verina was alive and living in the palace. She loathed Zeno and plotted his downfall. She elicited the support of her brother Basiliscus and, in winter 475, Zeno fled with Ariadne and a goodly part of the treasury to Isauria, whence he originally had come and where he had allies and kin.

Verina's brother double-crossed her and became emperor. Verina, ever inventive, plotted anew and helped Zeno and Ariadne return to the city in summer 476. Basiliscus and his wife and children were killed. Verina still was not content. She attempted to assassinate Illus, an earlier ally who had become a general close to Zeno. She failed. Illus demanded from Zeno that Verina be handed over to him. He imprisoned her in a castle in Isauria.

From her castle-prison in Isauria, Verina reached out to Leontia and Marcian. Marcian had been watching the situation in the East with covetous eyes. Verina offered him an opportunity to interfere and Leontia was the excuse. Toward the end of 479, Marcian laid claim to rule the East. Leontia, he argued, had been born after her father Leo had become emperor and thereby was a more legitimate heir than Ariadne. He, not Zeno, ought to be emperor. The populace, never any friend of Zeno, rallied around Marcian, and he had almost captured Zeno when Illus arrived with an Isaurian force and defeated him.

Leontia fled to the safety of a monastery and Marcian became a priest. He was banished to Cappadocia. Marcian escaped and attacked Ancyra (modern Ankara) but was defeated. Leontia and Marcian were confined together in a fortress in Isauria. Nothing more is heard of them.

Sources

John Malalas. *Chronicle* XIV, viii.
Theophanes. *Chronicle* AM 5971, 5972.
Bury, J. B. *History of the Later Roman Empire from the Death of Theodosius to the Death of Justinian.* New York: Dover Publications Inc., 1958.
Prosopography of the Later Roman Empire. Vol. II. Edited by A. H. M. Jones, J. R. Martindale, and J. Morris. Cambridge: Cambridge University Press, 1971. Reprinted 1992. p. 667.

▣ Leontion

(fourth–third century B.C.E.)   Greek: Athens
philosopher

Leontion was a philosopher and companion of the philosopher Epicurus at his school in Athens. Leontion's philosophical writings rivaled those of Theophrastus, the student, collaborator, and ultimately successor to Aristotle. She and Metrodorus (330–277 B.C.E.), another disciple of Epicurus, became lovers. They had a son named after Epicurus and a daughter, DANAE.

In his will, Epicurus ordered his trustees to provide for the children's maintenance, to give Danae a dowry, and when she came of age to find a member of the Epicurean school for her to marry.

Sources

Athenaeus. *Deipnosophistae* 593c–d.
Diogenes Laertius. *Lives of the Eminent Philosophers* 10.19–21, 23.
Seneca. *Epistulae* 52.3.
Hawley, Richard. "The Problem of Women Philosophers in Ancient Greece." In *Women in Ancient Societies: An Illusion of the Night,* ed. by Leonie J. Archer, Susan Fischler, and Maria Wyke. New York: Routledge, 1994, pp. 74, 80–81.
Pomeroy, Sarah B. *Goddesses, Whores, Wives, and Slaves: Women in Classical Antiquity.* New York: Schocken Books, 1975, p. 141.

▣ Licinia (1)

(?–154 B.C.E.)   Roman: Rome
convicted murderer

Licinia and PUBLILIA (1) were convicted in 154 B.C.E. of poisoning their husbands, both of whom were ex-consuls. Licinia's husband was Claudius Asellus. Licinia assigned the property she owned to the praetor as surety for her presence in the city after she was charged. After her conviction, she was turned over to her family and put to death.

Sources

Livy. *From the Founding of the City* 48.
Valerius Maximus. *Factorum et dictorum memorabilium libri IX* 6.3, 7.
Bauman, Richard A. *Women and Politics in Ancient Rome.* London: Routledge, 1994, p. 39.
Pauly, A., G. Wissowa, and W. Kroll. *Real-Encyclopadie D. Classischen Altertumswissenschaft 1893–.* (Germany: multiple publishers) 178.

▣ Licinia (2)

(second century B.C.E.)   Roman: Rome
reformer

Licinia was the elder daughter of Publius Licinius Crassus Dives Mucianus, a wealthy expert in Roman law, a noted orator, and consul in 131 B.C.E. Her family was part of the circle around the

Gracchi that demanded tax and land reform. Her sister LICINIA (3) married Gaius Sempronius Gracchus, strengthening the families' political ties.

Licinia married quite young in 143 B.C.E. Her husband was Gaius Sulpicius Galba, also a supporter of the Gracchi. From 121 to 119 he served on the land commission that Gaius Gracchus had established at Carthage. In 110 he was condemned for corruption during the Jugurthine War in Numidia, North Africa. Nothing more is known of Licinia.

Sources

Cicero. *Brutus* 82, 85–90.

Oxford Classical Dictionary, ed. by Simon Hornblower and Antony Spawforth. 3d. ed. New York: Oxford University Press, 1996, p. 1,454.

Pauly, A., G. Wissowa, and W. Kroll. *Real-Encyclopadie D. Classischen Altertumswissenschaft 1893–.* (Germany: multiple publishers) 179.

Richardson, Keith. *Daggers in the Forum: The Revolutionary Lives and Violent Deaths of the Gracchus Brothers.* London: Cassell, 1976, pp. 41, 180.

◉ Licinia (3)

(second century B.C.E.)   Roman: Rome
reformer

Licinia, the younger daughter of Publius Licinius Crassus Dives Mucianus, a noted legal expert, orator, and consul in 131 B.C.E., participated in the violent struggle for land and tax reform. Her family was a political ally of the Gracchi, and her marriage with Gaius Sempronius Gracchus had probably been arranged since her childhood. Married to him in 133 B.C.E., she brought to the union a significant dowry from her wealthy family. She had an older sister, LICINIA (2).

Determined to carry forward the reforms of his brother Tiberius, her husband was elected tribune in 123 and 122. He passed a series of measures that included land distribution, subsidies for wheat, the establishment of new colonies for citizens, and public works. The measures reflected efforts to address the simultaneous problems of an increasing class of landless citizens and the inflation that accompanied their settling in the city. Opposition

to him and to the reforms he represented, however, was strong. His proposal to grant citizenship to people of Italy outside Rome was defeated, and he lost the election for tribune in 121.

As his opponents moved to overturn the most objectionable of the reforms, skirmish occurred in which one person was killed. The Senate summoned Gaius to the Forum. Licinia was fearful he would be assassinated, as had been his brother before him. Her fears were well founded: Gaius was murdered in the Forum.

After Gaius's murder in 121, his enemies sought to destroy his allies. They pursued Licinia through attacks on her property. Her wealth was saved by the efforts of her uncle the eminent jurist Publius Mucius Scaevola. However, to recover her dowry, her uncle was forced to publicly disavow her husband and lay responsibility on him for the riot in which he was killed.

Sources

Plutarch. *Vitae Parallelae (Parallel Lives): Gaius Gracchus* 21.1–2; 15.2, 5; 17.5.

Pauly, A., G. Wissowa, and W. Kroll. *Real-Encyclopadie D. Classischen Altertumswissenschaft 1893–.* (Germany: multiple publishers) 180.

Richardson, Keith. *Daggers in the Forum: The Revolutionary Lives and Violent Deaths of the Gracchus Brothers.* London: Cassell, 1976, pp. 114, 187–189.

◉ Licinia (4)

(?–113 B.C.E.)   Roman: Rome
priestess

Licinia, Vestal Virgin and daughter of Gaius Crassus, tribune in 145 B.C.E., challenged authority. In 123 she dedicated an altar, oratory, and sacred couch at the temple of the Bona Dea. The praetor, Sextus Julius Caesar, protested that she had no prior authorization to do such a thing. The Senate sent the case to the pontifices, who ruled the donations unsanctified and ordered them removed.

In 114, a slave charged three Vestal Virgins with illicit behavior. AEMILIA (1) was accused of having an affair with an equestrian, L. Veturius. Licinia and MARCIA (1) were said to have had relationships at Aemilia's instigation with her lover's friends.

Aemilia was condemned, but the *pontifex maximus* Lucius Caecilius Metellus found the two others innocent. Then a special *quaestio* (investigation) was called, over which Lucius Cassius Longinus Ravilla presided. Licinia's cousin Lucius Licinius Crassus, an outstanding orator, defended them, but to no avail. Both were condemned to death.

Sources

Cicero. *Brutus* 43.160.
Cicero. *De domo sua* 53.136.
Dio Cassius. *Roman History* 26.fr.87.
Livy. *From the Founding of the City* 43.
Orosius. *Seven Books of History Against the Pagans* 5.15, 20–22.
Plutarch. *Moralia: De fortunata Romanorum* 83.
Bauman, Richard A. *Women and Politics in Ancient Rome.* London: Routledge, 1994, pp. 52 ff.

 ## Licinia (5)

(first century B.C.E.)   Roman: Rome
elegant conversationalist

Licinia was noted for the elegance of her speech. She was part of a family for whom conversation was a practiced art. Her mother, MUCIA, and her grandmother LAELIA had also been regarded as elegant conversationalists. Her grandfather was the famous orator Gaius Laelius, and she was the elder daughter of Lucius Licinius Crassus, a well-known orator and consul in 95 B.C.E.

Licinia married Publius Scipio Nasica, praetor in 93. Her sister LICINIA (6) married the son of the general Gaius Marius. Cicero praised both women for the beauty and precision of their conversation.

Sources

Cicero. *Brutus* 211–212.
Pauly, A., G. Wissowa, and W. Kroll. *Real-Encyclopadie D. Classischen Altertumswissenschaft 1893–.* (Germany: multiple publishers) 183.

Licinia (6)

(first century B.C.E.)   Roman: Rome
elegant conversationalist

Licinia, the younger daughter of MUCIA and the famous orator Lucius Licinius Crassus, consul in 95 B.C.E., was born into a family whose members were famous for their elegant conversation. Licinia and her sister LICINIA (5) were admired for their speaking abilities. They both took after their mother and grandmother LAELIA.

Licinia married Gaius Marius, the son of the great general Gaius Marius, consul seven times. Her husband was offered the consulship of 82 after his father's death. His mother, JULIA (1), urged him to reject the office. She feared he was being used by the Marians against the dictator Lucius Cornelius Sulla. Her fears were well founded. After a defeat by Sulla, he committed suicide.

Sources

Cicero. *Epistulae ad Atticum* 12.49.1.
Cicero. *Brutus* 211–12.
Pauly, A., G. Wissowa, and W. Kroll. *Real-Encyclopadie D. Classischen Altertumswissenschaft 1893–.* (Germany: multiple publishers) 184.

Licinia (7)

(first century B.C.E.)   Roman: Rome
priestess

Licinia, a Vestal Virgin and a member of the aristocratic Licinii, was accused in 73 B.C.E. of immoral behavior with her cousin Marcus Licinius Crassus. Both were subsequently found innocent.

Crassus had spent time with Licinia in private to persuade her to sell him a villa she owned in the suburbs of Rome at a price less than its true value. The immensely wealthy Crassus, who had made a fortune buying property cheaply during the Sullan proscriptions, was renowned for his eagerness to acquire more. He eventually bought the land. The attack on Licinia was probably led by Crassus's enemies.

Sources

Plutarch. *Vitae Parallelae (Parallel Lives): Crassus* 1.4ff.
Balsdon, J. P. V. D. *Roman Women.* New York: John Day Comp., 1963, p. 239.
Pauly, A., G. Wissowa, and W. Kroll. *Real-Encyclopadie D. Classischen Altertumswissenschaft 1893–.* (Germany: multiple publishers) 185.

Livia

(?–92 B.C.E.) Roman: Rome
political wife

Livia married twice, and each marriage produced a child important in the history of the Roman revolution. She was the daughter of Marcus Livius Drusus, consul in 112 B.C.E. In 104, she married Quintus Servilius Caepio, praetor in 91, and gave birth to two daughters, SERVILIA (1), who became the lover and friend of Julius Caesar, and SERVILIA (2), and a son, Gnaeus Servilius Caepio. Divorced around 98 B.C.E. because of a quarrel between her brother and her husband, she married Marcus Porcius Cato in 96. They had a daughter, Porcia, and a son, Marcus Porcius Cato Uticensis, who became one of the republican leaders against Caesar. Livia's second husband died just before the wars in Italy, and she died shortly thereafter in 92 B.C.E.

Sources

Oxford Classical Dictionary, ed. by Simon Hornblower and Antony Spawforth. 3d. ed. New York: Oxford University Press, 1996, p. 1,394.

Pauly, A., G. Wissowa, and W. Kroll. *Real-Encyclopadie D. Classischen Altertumswissenschaft 1893–*. (Germany: multiple publishers) 35.

Syme, Ronald. *The Augustan Aristocracy.* Oxford: Clarendon Press, 1986, p. 25.

Livia Drusilla

(January 30, 58 B.C.E.–29 C.E.)
Roman: Italy
power broker

Livia was the most important woman of her time. Her character, discretion, and intellect complemented her strategic skills and were enhanced by the advantage of a long life. She spanned the period before the onset of civil war, through the reign of her husband Augustus and much of that of her son Tiberius. In her household were nurtured many of the enmities and alliances that shaped the first 50 years of the empire, and her travels and correspondence with friends and clients spread her reach across the Roman world. Her reception rooms were always filled with visitors and petitioners. Her household, which sometimes encompassed 1,000 people or more, included multiple generations of children, grandchildren, nieces and nephews, more distant kin and clients of the extended Julio-Claudian families.

Born on January 30, 58 B.C.E., she was the daughter of Marcus Livius Drusus Claudianus, from the illustrius Claudian clan, and Alfidia, the daughter of a rich councillor from the Italian city of Fundi. Livia's father lived well into the years of the civil war and fought against Mark Antony and Octavian. He killed himself after the defeat of Marcus Brutus and Gaius Cassius at Philippi in 42 B.C.E.

Livia married twice. Her first husband, whom she married at the age of 15 or 16, in 43 or 42 B.C.E., was Tiberius Claudius Nero, quaestor in 48 and a distant relative. She gave birth on November 16, 42 B.C.E. to Tiberius, the future emperor. Her husband's political allegiance followed a not-too-unusual course for the times. A republican and a supporter of Caesar, he commanded Caesar's fleet in the Alexandrian War in 47 B.C.E. After Caesar's death, however, he called for special honors for the assassins. In 41, he sided with Antony against Octavian. In 40, as part of the Perusine war, he attempted to ignite a slave revolt in Campania. When the war failed, he fled from Rome and Octavian with Livia and their infant son. In Sicily he joined the friendly Sextus Pompeius. After a falling-out with Pompeius, he rejoined Antony in Achaea. He, along with Livia and their young son, returned to Rome in 39 after the Pact of Misenum secured peace under the Second Triumvirate. In that same year, Livia became pregnant with her second child.

She also began an affair with Octavian. How it started remains unclear. That it quickly became notorius, however, is well attested. In a society reeling with the social dislocations of civil war, it was still a flagrant violation of tradition for the pregnant Livia to live openly with Octavian while both were divorcing their respective spouses. Octavian divorced SCRIBONIA on the day she gave birth to his only child, JULIA (6). He sought an opinion from the college of pontifices about contracting a marriage with the still-pregnant Livia. They ruled in his favor. Perhaps there was little else they could do except to accept the new marriage but to establish that Tiberius Claudius Nero was the legitimate father of the unborn child. Gossip about the behavior of both Octavian and Livia reached epic proportions. On January 28, 38 B.C.E. Livia's first husband presided over the wedding feast.

After the birth of Livia's second son, Nero Claudius Drusus, both boys went to live with their father to avoid further scandal. Shortly thereafter, their father died and left Octavian guardian. The boys moved back into Livia's household. The three months between the birth, death, and the return of the boys to their mother kept tongues wagging. Again in 36 during a food shortage in Rome, the couple caused scandalous gossip when they tastelessly hosted a banquet for the gods. Subsequently they changed their image: Livia adopted a modest persona and her unconventional move from one husband to another faded into history while Octavian's future sexual exploits never exceeded what was considered acceptable among the aristocracy. The two became a model Roman husband and wife and remained married for 50 years, until the death of the emperor in 14 C.E. Over the course of the next decades the memory of their union's notorious beginning so faded that years later, when Augustus meted out harsh punishments to his daughter and granddaughter for their adulterous behavior, nary an eyebrow was raised in remembrance of the past.

After their marriage, even before Octavian became Augustus, Livia's elevated status was clear. In 35 B.C.E., Livia and Octavian's independent-minded sister OCTAVIA (2) were accorded the status of *tribunica sanctissima,* which made any assault upon their person as if an attack on the state. Never previously held by a woman nor ever again, it was probably Octavian's intention to protect Octavia from her husband Antony, and it would not have been politic to exclude Livia. The office also gave the women independent authority over property and wealth. Then in 18 and 9 B.C.E., with the passage of the Julian laws, which Livia supported, she was granted rights that released her from any form of even token male guardianship. In one of those ironies of history, had those same laws been in effect at the onset of their affair, both Livia and Octavian would have been sent into exile on different islands for adultery and much of their wealth confiscated. Moreover, instead of hosting their wedding, her first husband could have been prosecuted for pandering. No less ironic, these same laws were the basis for Augustus's later exile of his daughter and granddaughter.

A wealthy woman to begin with, Livia managed people and property well. Her alliances with other women, many of whom were also influential in the public and private affairs of the period, constituted a circle within which she did business and traded favors. Some were her peers, like her sister-in-law Octavia. Some were clients from abroad like SALOME, the sister of Herod the Great, who bequeathed to Livia the towns of Jamnia, Phasaelis, and Archelais. Still others were well-born women who sought her influence. She was instrumental in having the son of her close friend URGULANIA made consul in 2 B.C.E. She probably had a hand in the marriage of the future emperor Claudius to PLAUTIA URGULANILLA, granddaughter of Urgulania. In 16 C.E., when the senator Lucius Piso obtained a summons against Urgulania for money owed him and Urgulania refused to pay, it was to Livia's house she went and put herself under her friend's protection.

Livia invited into her house her extended family and clients from abroad. In addition to her own children, Tiberius and Drusus, there were Augustus's daughter Julia and Julia's chidren—twin sons, Gaius Caesar and Lucius Caesar, and two daughters, JULIA (7) and the elder Vipsania AGRIPPINA. After Livia's youngest son, Drusus, died in 9 B.C.E., her daughter-in-law, the younger ANTONIA and her three children, Germanicus, Claudius, and Livia Julia LIVILLA Claudia, moved into the household. Gaius Caligula and two of his sisters, JULIA DRUSILLA and JULIA LIVILLA, also lived with Livia for a short time after their mother, the elder Agrippina, was exiled. Marcus Salvius Otho, grandfather of the later emperor Otho, was yet another later political figure who grew up in Livia's household.

Livia and Augustus's relationship joined both family and the affairs of state, and sometimes the two were indistinguishable. The events and arrangements in which she was central ranged from macro state decisions to micro private affairs. Augustus regularly asked her advice. Often he took it. After a plot was uncovered against him led by Gnaeus Cornelius, a descendant of Pompey the Great, she argued that he could coop the conspirators. It was Livia who persuaded Augustus and Tiberius to implement the arrangements for Claudius, the future emperor who was afflicted with some kind of palsy. In addition there was a steady stream of senators and other officials who came to consult and curry favor. Livia arranged for Marcus Salvius Otho to be made a senator. When Quintus Haterius, whose remarks offended the emperor and who had accidentally knocked down Tiberius, came to apologize, Livia saved him from being executed. She sometimes went beyond the bounds of Augustus's decisions. During his daughter Julia's 20 years of exile she helped Julia.

In all Livia worked unceasingly, especially, to enhance the interests of her family and particularly the future of her own sons. Although Augustus had adopted her children, she faced arrogant opposition from Augustus's Julian relatives who felt their family without peer, and succession to Augustus their birthright. Along with Livia, Octavia and Marcus Vipsanius Agrippa completed Augustus's most intimate circle. Her sister-in-law Octavia, whose household rivaled Livia's in its size and influence, had married her daughter the elder MARCELLA to Agrippa. The links by marriage were further extended through the marriage in 25 B.C.E. of Octavia's son Marcus Claudius Marcellus and Julia, Augustus's daughter.

Succession seemed assured with Agrippa as regent should anything happen too soon for the next generation to assume control. Barely two years later, in 23, Marcellus, the most likely heir, died. Agrippa then divorced Marcella and married Julia, and they had three sons in rapid succession: Lucius Caesar, Gaius Caesar, and Agrippa Postumus, all of them possible heirs to Augustus. Once more the line of succession seemed secure. Years earlier, Livia

and Titus Pomponius Atticus, the very wealthy father-in-law of Agrippa's first wife Caecilia ATTICA, had arranged for the marriage of Livia's son Tiberius with Attica and Agrippa's daughter VIPSANIA AGRIPPINA. They married in 20 or 19 B.C.E. At the time it appeared a desirous union. All during the civil war years there were problems with money, and Atticus had enormous wealth. Agrippa was in his prime, and clearly a family link between Livia and Agrippa could only be advantageous in strengthening both of their positions in the intimate circle around Augustus.

Agrippa died unexpectedly in 12 B.C.E. The three sons born of his second marriage with Julia were adopted by Augustus. The line of succession through the Julians still appeared in place. However, marriage to Julia appeared to be the way to succession, so Tiberius divorced Vipsania and married his stepsister Julia in 11 B.C.E. It seems likely that Livia and Augustus had both agreed to the arrangement, even though it was said that Augustus favored Livia's younger son, Nero Claudius Drusus. In 9 B.C.E. the younger son died from an infection after a fall off his horse.

Livia had successfully used unexpected deaths in the Julian family to place Tiberius in the most advantageous position for succession as regent over her husband's young grandsons, if not as emperor. In 6 B.C.E. Augustus granted Tiberius *tribunicia potestas* (powers of a tribune) for five years and asked him to go to the East on a diplomatic mission. Tiberius, however, had his own views and was not necessarily amenable to the plans of his mother and adoptive father.

Much to Livia's consternation and Augustus's anger, Tiberius insisted that he be allowed to retire to the island of Rhodes. For four days he refused food, and threatened to kill himself if they failed to agree. They agreed, and he left Rome. He walked away from his parents, his wife, and an empire. Tiberius's behavior was outside the bounds of acceptability. In 2 B.C.E., he changed his mind and asked to return to Rome. Augustus refused. Livia persuaded him to appoint Tiberius legate to Rhodes in an attempt to paint over his own involuntary stay on the island. It was, however, another four years, in 2 C.E., before she finally secured Augustus's agreement for Tiberius to return to Rome.

Fate took a hand. In the same year, the cherished grandson of Augustus, Lucius Caesar, died on his way to Spain. A second grandson, Gaius, was wounded and died two years later in 4 C.E. Augustus banished the third grandson, Agrippa Postumus, in the same year. Although a fine physical specimen, his cruelty and ungovernable temper made him clearly unfit to rule. Tiberius alone remained among the possible successors.

Livia's good fortune in her son Tiberius did not pass unnoticed among the elite whose lives were lived in the arena of imperial power. Rumors abounded that Livia was responsible for the deaths of the grandsons and later, even for the death of her partner and husband, Augustus. Augustus fell gravely ill during August 14 C.E. in Nola some 20 miles east of Naples. Livia sent an urgent message to Tiberius, who was on his way to Illyricum (the Balkans), to come to Nola. In the meantime, Livia admitted only a trusted few to Augustus's side. Optimistic bulletins were issued. It is not clear whether Tiberius arrived before or after Augustus's death, but only after his arrival was public notice given that Augustus was dead. His death occurred on August 19, just shy of his 76th birthday. Livia's son and Augustus's adopted son, Tiberius, was named successor.

Agrippa Postumus, the difficult grandson in exile on the island of Planasia, was immediately put to death. It is not known whether Augustus had given prior orders to his close adviser, Gaius Sullustius Crispus, or whether Livia had issued orders for the execution under Augustus's name. Tiberius knew nothing about the execution and decided that the Senate should look into it, but Crispus and Livia persuaded him to drop the matter. In her husband's will, Livia was named Julia Augusta and was adopted into the Julian gens. She was granted exemption from the *lex Voconia*, which limited women's rights to inheritance. Augustus left her one-third of his estate, and her son, Tiberius, two-thirds. She also became the priestess of her husband's cult after his deification.

Livia had succeeded. She had lived to see her son succeed her husband, and he, anxious perhaps to demonstrate his independence from a mother who had herself become symbolic of the new imperial Rome, was embarrassed by the role she played. Livia assiduously coveted honors that Tiberius foiled. He refused to allow an altar to celebrate her adoption into the Julian clan. Members of the Senate proposed a number of possible titles for Livia, such as *parens patriae* (Parent of her Country) or *mater patriae* (Mother of her Country). Others wanted to add *Iuliae filius* (Son of Julia [Augusta]) to Tiberius's name. Tiberius claimed history had no such honors for women and added that he would also refuse similarly nontraditional honors for himself. He also refused requests that she be granted *lictores,* the traditional attendants who carried fasces, symbols of the legitimacy and inviolability of Roman magistrates.

In public Tiberius and Livia maintained correct relations. Gossip circulated, however, that their private relations were more difficulty. Tiberius retired to Capri. Livia remained in Rome. In the next three years, he only visited her once and then only for a few hours. Still, her influence remained significant. She intervened and brought about the acquittal of her friend MUNATIA PLANCINA, who, along with her husband Gnaeus Calpurnius Piso, had been accused of treason after the death of Germanicus Julius Caesar, husband of the elder Agrippina. She also was responsible for advancing the career of Gaius Fufius Geminus, consul in 29 C.E. and the husband of her friend MUTILIA PRISCA, in spite of Tiberius dislike for him. After Livia's death the two women and Fufius were forced to commit suicide.

Livia died in 29 at the age of 86. Tiberius did not attend her funeral and would not allow her to be deified. He also refused to execute her will in which her largest bequest was to the future emperor Galba, whom she had befriended. Her reach into the future, however, was long. Her eulogy was delivered by her grandson and future emperor, the young Gaius Caligula, who had lived for a short time in his grandmother's house. He called her *Ulixes stolatus,* "Ulysses in skirts." When he became emperor, he executed her will, and when Claudius, who also had lived in her household, became emperor, he deified her.

Sources

Dio Cassius. *Roman History* 48.15.3–4, 34.3, 44; 49.38.1; 53.33.4; 54.19.3–4; 55.2.5–6, 10a, 10, 14, 1 seq., 32.1–2; 56.30.5–32.1–2, 46.1–3, 47.1; 57.3, 5–6; 57.12; 58.2.1–6; 59.2.3; 60.5.2.

Suetonius. *The Lives of the Caesars:* Augustus 62.2; 63.1; 84.2; 101.2.

———. *The Lives of the Caesars:* Gaius Caligula 10.1; 16.3; 23.2.

———. *The Lives of the Caesars:* Claudius 1.1; 4; 11.2.

———. *The Lives of the Caesars:* Galba 5.2

———. *The Lives of the Caesars:* Tiberius 4.3; 6.1–3; 10.2; 12.1; 13.2; 50.2–3; 51.

Tacitus. *Annales* 1.3–7, 8, 10, 13–14, 33; 2.14, 34, 43, 77, 82; 3.15, 17, 34, 64, 71; 4.8, 12, 16, 21–22, 57, 71; 5.13; 6.5, 26, 29; 12.69.

Barrett, Anthony. *Livia: First Lady of Imperial Rome.* New Haven, Conn.: Yale University Press, 2002.

Bauman, Richard A. *Women and Politics in Ancient Rome.* London: Routledge, 1994, index.

Levick, Barbara. *Tiberius the Politician.* London: Thames and Hudson, 1976, index.

Marsh, Frank Burr. *The Reign of Tiberius.* New York: Barnes and Noble, 1931, index.

Oxford Classical Dictionary, ed. by Simon Hornblower and Antony Spawforth. 3d. ed. New York: Oxford University Press, 1996, p. 876.

Pauly, A., G. Wissowa, and W. Kroll. *Real-Encyclopadie D. Classischen Altertumswissenschaft 1893–.* (Germany: multiple publishers) 37.

Syme, Ronald. *The Augustan Aristocracy.* Oxford: Clarendon Press, 1986, index.

———. *The Roman Revolution.* London: Oxford University Press, 1963, index.

▣ Livia Ocellina
(first century C.E.)   Roman: Rome
political player

Livia Ocellina, a wealthy and beautiful woman, married Gaius Sulpicius Galba, consul suffectus in 5 B.C.E. She ignored his short stature and hunchback: After he removed his robe and displayed his body so that she should have no illusions about him, she was said to be even more anxious for the union.

Her husband had previously been married to MUMMIA ACHAICA, the mother of his two children, Gaius and Servius Sulpicius Galba. Livia Ocellina adopted Servius, who took her name and the surname Ocella. Her adopted son grew up to become a favorite of both Augustus and Tiberius. He ruled for a short while during the troubled year of the four emperors then was assassinated in January 69 C.E.

Sources

Suetonius. *The Lives of the Caesars:* Galba 3.4; 5.1.

▣ Livia Orestilla
(first century C.E.)   Roman: Rome
political victim

Livia Orestilla suffered the consequences of her beauty. She attracted the attention of the emperor Gaius Caligula when she was the wife of the handsome, popular Gaius Calpurnius Piso, a member of a prominent family and an excellent orator. Caligula attended their wedding in 37 C.E., and the sources report that he had the bride taken to his own home. The next day he announced that he had taken a wife in the ancient way. The relationship ended within two months.

In 40, Caligula accused the reunited Livia and Piso of adultery and exiled them. Although there is no further mention of Livia, Piso returned to Rome during the reign of the emperor Claudius.

Sources

Dio Cassius. *Roman History* 59.8.7–8.

Suetonius. *The Lives of the Caesars:* Gaius Caligula 25.1.

Ferrill, A. *Caligula: Emperor of Rome.* London: Thames and Hudson, 1991, p. 108.

Pauly, A., G. Wissowa, and W. Kroll. *Real-Encyclopadie D. Classischen Altertumswissenschaft 1893–.* (Germany: multiple publishers) 42.

▣ Livilla, Livia Julia Claudia
(c. 13 B.C.E.–31 C.E.)   Roman: Rome
conspirator

Livilla, sometimes called Livia Julia, died in the struggle to secure succession of her son. Twice widowed by men who were the emperor Tiberius's likely successors, she was the daughter of the younger ANTONIA and Tiberius's brother Nero Claudius Drusus, consul in 9 B.C.E. Born in 13 B.C.E., her great-uncle was the emperor Augustus. One grandmother was the independent-minded OCTAVIA (2), Augustus's sister, and the other, LIVIA DRUSILLA, his wife.

After her father's death in 9, she lived with her mother and brothers in her grandmother Livia's household. In 1 B.C.E. she married Gaius Julius Caesar, the oldest grandson of Augustus, who also had spent part of his youth in Livia's household. Gaius died of battle wounds in 4 C.E. Livilla remarried. Her second husband was Drusus Julius Caesar, the son of Tiberius. The marriage, which united the Julian and Claudian family lines, provided her husband with a privileged position for succession.

Livilla and Drusus had a daughter, JULIA (8), and years later twin sons, Germanicus and Tiberius Gemellus, born in 19 C.E. Despite her husband's vicious personality and dissolute lifestyle, Livilla expected him to succeed his 65-year-old father. Drusus, however, died in 23 C.E. In the same year one of the twins, Germanicus, also died, leaving Livilla with a grown daughter and a young son—and the issue of succession to Tiberius again unsettled.

Livilla set about to protect her own interests and especially those of her son. Two women opposed her: Her mother, Antonia, sided with Livilla's sister-in-law Agrippina in promoting Gaius Caligula, Agrippina's youngest son, as successor. Although Antonia was well regarded, Tiberius had no love for Agrippina, who was convinced that Tiberius had murdered her husband Germanicus, despite the absence of clear evidence. Devoted to the interest of her children and fearful of Agrippina, Livilla allied herself with Lucius Aelius Sejanus, prefect of the Praetorian Guard in Rome. Tiberius was a military man who had never liked the urban life of Rome. He may also have been tired of dynastic infighting, possibly distressed at his increasingly displeasing appearance, and ready to enjoy other pursuits. He retired to Capri in 26 C.E. and left Sejanus as his eyes and ears in the capital.

Livilla and Sejanus had good reason to join forces. Sejanus could not aspire to the position of emperor—it would be some decades more before a man born outside the charmed circle of the elite could rule. Livilla offered Sejanus the link with the imperial family that only birth could secure. While Tiberius did not view him as a threat, Sejanus already had control over the Praetorian Guard and unique access to the emperor. If not emperor, he could possibly aspire to become regent for the young Tiberius Gemellus, provided the way was clear of other contenders.

In 20 C.E. Livilla's daughter, Julia, had married Nero Julius Caesar, the eldest surviving son of her sister-in-law Agrippina. In 23 C.E., with the death of Livilla's husband, her grown son-in-law was a more likely successor than her still young child. Already quaestor, probably in 26, Nero was intemperate, made rash statements, and openly staked his claim to the empire. Whether with conscious intent to harm or simply the loose tongue of a lover, Livilla passed on to Sejanus information from conversations with her daughter about Nero, whom both mother and daughter disliked.

Sejanus convinced Tiberius that Nero and his mother, Agrippina, were conspiring against the emperor. Tiberius exiled them both. Deported in 29, Nero was executed in 31. Drusus Julius Caesar, Nero's brother and a second son of Agrippina, supported Sejanus's accusation. While Drusus's position had been enhanced with the banishment of his brother, it proved a short-lived advantage. Only a year later, he too was imprisoned.

Gaius Caligula, the remaining son of Agrippina, and Gemellus, the young son of Livilla, were now the two most probable heirs of Tiberius. Caligula was more favorably positioned since he was much older. In 30, however, Sejanus appears to have gained Tiberius's consent for his marriage. It is possible that the planned marriage was not with Livilla, who was about 43 years old, but with her widowed daughter Julia, now around 25. In any case, through either of the unions, he would have moved closer to the imperial family and perhaps Livilla's son would also have moved closer to becoming the heir.

Good fortune ended abruptly; Livilla's downfall followed that of Sejanus. Possibly Caligula convinced Livilla's mother, Antonia, that Sejanus was engaged in a conspiracy. Surely not a conspiracy aimed directly against Tiberius, since the latter's immediate death would only have endangered Sejanus's own position. Most likely it was a conspiracy aimed at Caligula, who was the last impediment to the son of Livilla. It remains unclear why Antonia supported Caligula when she must have been aware that the downfall of Sejanus would also bring down her daughter and probably her granddaughter Julia and her grandson Gemellus. Whatever the reasons, she informed Tiberius, and Sejanus was killed, as were his two children. APICATA, the divorced wife of Sejanus, killed herself two days after Sejanus's execution and left a letter for Tiberius in which she accused Sejanus and Livilla of eight years earlier having poisoned Drusus, Livilla's husband and Tiberius's son.

The slaves and attendants of Livilla and Sejanus were tortured. Their "confessions" allowed Tiberius to declare that Sejanus and Livilla had engaged in a conspiracy against the children of Agrippina and Germanicus. After Tiberius heard the case, Livilla was turned over to the custody of her mother, Antonia. She starved herself to death.

Sources

Dio Cassius. *Roman History* 57.22.1–2; 58.11.6–7.

Suetonius. *The Lives of the Caesars:* Tiberius 62.1.

Tacitus. *Annales* 2.43, 84; 4.3, 12, 39–40, 60.

Bauman, Richard A. *Women and Politics in Ancient Rome.* London: Routledge, 1994, p. 147.

Levick, Barbara. *Tiberius the Politician.* London: Thames and Hudson, 1976, index.

Marsh, Frank Burr. *The Reign of Tiberius.* New York: Barnes and Noble, 1931, index.

Oxford Classical Dictionary, ed. by Simon Hornblower and Antony Spawforth. 3d. ed. New York: Oxford University Press, 1996, p. 876.

Pauly, A., G. Wissowa, and W. Kroll. *Real-Encyclopädie D. Classischen Altertumswissenschaft 1893–.* (Germany: multiple publishers) 38.

Syme, Ronald. *The Augustan Aristocracy.* Oxford: Clarendon Press, 1986, index.

▣ Lollia Paulina

(first century C.E.)   Roman: Italy
political player

Lollia Paulina was rich, smart, and beautiful. All three attributes shaped her life. Her father possibly was consul suffectus in 13 C.E., although the family enmity with Tiberius leaves his career open to question. Her mother was Volusia, also of a consular family. Lollia inherited enormous wealth from her grandfather Marcus Lollius, consul in 21 B.C.E., who made the family fortune in spoils from the provinces.

The emperor Caligula was determined to marry Lollia. Her husband, Memmius Regulus, consul in 31 C.E. was in Greece as governor of Moesia and was agreeable to a divorce. She and Caligula married in 38. Lollia had emeralds and pearls of enormous value and beautifully worked to cover her head, hair, ears, neck, and fingers. She adorned the emperor with her beauty and her jewels, but her wealth and beauty were not sufficient. Caligula divorced her a year later in 39 and forbade her to remarry.

Ten years later, in 48, Lollia was again in the running to become the wife of an emperor. This time it was Claudius. She was supported by Gaius Julius Callistus, one of the influential freedmen of the emperor, on the grounds that she was childless, would remain so, and was therefore a possible stepmother for Claudius's offspring free of any competing claims.

The younger AGRIPPINA's success over Lollia in the competition for Claudius apparently did not sufficiently eliminate the threat Agrippina felt she posed. Moreover, she wanted Lollia's property and jewels. Agrippina charged her with consulting astrologers. Claudius condemned Lollia without a hearing. She was stripped of her vast wealth, except for 5 million sesterces to enable her to live, and was banished in 49 C.E. Agrippina sent a tribune to force Lollia to suicide. As a rebuke to his mother, Agrippina's son, the next emperor Nero, allowed Lollia Paulina's ashes to be brought back to Rome and erected a tomb to house her remains.

Sources

Dio Cassius. *Roman History* 59.12.1, 23.7; 61.32.4.

Pliny the Elder. *Naturalis Historia* 9.57, 117–19.

Suetonius. *The Lives of the Caesars:* Gaius Caligula 25.

Tacitus. *Annales* 12.1–2; 14.12.

Bauman, Richard A. *Women and Politics in Ancient Rome.* London: Routledge, 1994, pp. 181–182.

Levick, Barbara. *Claudius: The Corruption of Power.* New Haven, Conn.: Yale University Press, 1993, pp. 70–71.

Oxford Classical Dictionary, ed. by Simon Hornblower and Antony Spawforth. 3d. ed. New York: Oxford University Press, 1996, p. 883.

Pauly, A., G. Wissowa, and W. Kroll. *Real-Encyclopadie D. Classischen Altertumswissenschaft 1893–.* (Germany: multiple publishers) 30.

Syme, Ronald. *The Augustan Aristocracy.* Oxford: Clarendon Press, 1986, index.

▣ Lucilia

(second–first century B.C.E.)   Roman: Rome
mother of Gnaeus Pompeius (Pompey the Great)

Lucilia came from a rich aristocratic family. Her father was a senator, and her uncle Gaius Lucilius, a famous poet and satirist. She married Gnaeus Pompeius Strabo, consul in 89 B.C.E. He was a successful general but had a reputation for cruelty and corruption. He died in an epidemic, and his body was dragged through the streets by the people, who hated him. He and Lucilia had a son, Gnaeus Pompeius (Pompey the Great).

Sources

Valleius Paterculus. *Historiae Romanae libri II* 2.29.1 ff.

Syme, Ronald. *The Roman Revolution.* London: Oxford University Press, 1963, p. 28.

▣ Lucilla, Annia Aurelia Galeria

(148–182 C.E.)
Roman: Asia, Africa, Germany, and Rome
Augusta

Annia Aurelia Galeria Lucilla, the daughter of the emperor Marcus Aurelius, organized an unsuccessful conspiracy against her brother, the emperor Commodus. She was born in 148 C.E., the daughter of the younger Annia Galeria FAUSTINA and Marcus Aurelius. Had she been born a son rather than a daughter, she may well have been a worthy successor to her father. Her father became emperor in 161, succeeding Antoninus Pius. In 164 her father arranged her marriage with Lucius Verus, whom he had made co-emperor in 161. The marriage took place in Ephesus, and she was given the title Augusta. She was some 18 years younger then her weak and ineffectual husband who died in 169 on his way back to Rome from the Danube.

Against her will and the wishes of Faustina, Marcus Aurelius immediately had Lucilla marry the much older Tiberius Claudius Pompeianus, a native of Antioch. She was 21, and he was probably over 50. Her new husband was her father's trusted friend and had been a commander in all of his campaigns. His father had been prefect of Egypt, and the family was descended from rulers in the East. Lucilla undoubtedly considered the marriage beneath her and detested the sedentary country life that suited her ailing husband.

Marcus Aurelius died in 180, and was succeeded his son Commodus, whom he had appointed joint ruler in 177. Commodus treated his sister Lucilla

Annia Aurelia Galeria Lucilla
(Date: 164 C.E.–169 C.E. 1959.228.28, Archives, American Numismatic Society)

respectfully. She sat on the imperial seat at the theater and retained other privileges. However, she hated her sister-in-law, CRISPINA BRUTTIA, and recognized her brother's limitations. In 182 Lucilla had uncovered sufficient discontent with her brother's rule to organize a conspiracy for his overthrow. Members of the group included her cousin Ummidius Quadratus; Paternus, who was head of the imperial guard; and, Claudius Pompeianus Quintianus, who was to do the actual stabbing. Pompeianus turned out to be an inept murderer. He was arrested while announcing to Commodus his intention to stab him. Lucilla was banished to Capri and soon afterward killed. Her son, Claudius Pompeianus, was later murdered by the emperor Caracalla.

Sources

Dio Cassius. *Roman History* 71.1, 3; 73.4.4–5.
Herodian. *History of the Empire* 1.8.3–6, 8; 4.6.3.
Scriptores Historiae Augustae. Commodus 4.1, 4; 5.7.
———. Marcus Aurelius Antoninus (Marcus Aurelius) 7.7; 9.4; 20.6.–7.6.
Balsdon, J. P. V. D. *Roman Women.* New York: John Day Comp., 1963, index.
Oxford Classical Dictionary, ed. by Simon Hornblower and Antony Spawforth. 3d. ed. New York: Oxford University Press, 1996, p. 99.
Pauly, A., G. Wissowa, and W. Kroll. *Real-Encyclopadie D. Classischen Altertumswissenschaft 1893–.* (Germany: multiple publishers) 123.

▣ Lucretia

(sixth century B.C.E.)   Roman: Rome
heroine

Lucretia was a Roman heroine from the early years of the city-state when myth and history were inexorably intertwined. She was the wife of Lucius Tarquinius Collatinus. As the story goes, her husband was present at a dinner in which the men boasted about the virtue of their wives. Among them was Sextus, the son of Tarquinius Superbus, the last king of Rome. After Tarquinius Collatinus claimed no other wife could compare with his, the men agreed to go together to each of their houses to see what the women were doing. The wives were all found to be socializing until they came to Lucretia's residence. She was busily engaged in working with wool, and her servants were busy doing useful tasks, all signs of a virtuous Roman matron. The men agreed that she was the winner.

Sextus returned a few days later while Lucretia's husband was away. He raped her after she refused his advances. Afterward he demanded her silence by threatening to ruin her reputation. He promised he would kill her and place a naked dead slave in bed by her side.

Lucretia summoned her husband, her father, and her uncle Lucius Junius Brutus. She told them that her heart was pure, but her body had been desecrated. She made them swear that they would avenge her. Lucretia then stabbed herself and set an example for all future women of Rome.

According to Roman tradition, Tarquinius Collatius and Junius Brutus led a revolution in 510 B.C.E. that established the Roman republic. They became the first consuls. While the story may be apocryphal, Lucretia was revered, and Romans credited her for the end of the monarchy and the creation of the republic.

Sources

Livy. *From the Founding of the City* 1.57.6–11, 58–60.
Oxford Classical Dictionary, ed. by Simon Hornblower and Antony Spawforth. 3d. ed. New York: Oxford University Press, 1996, p. 888.
Pomeroy, Sarah B. *Goddesses, Whores, Wives, and Slaves: Women in Classical Antiquity.* New York: Schocken Books, 1975, pp. 160–161.

▣ Lysandra

(fourth–third century B.C.E.)
Greek: Egypt, Macedonia, and Syria
power broker

Lysandra was a fighting woman. She was the daughter of two Macedonian rulers of Egypt, EURYDICE (3) and Ptolemy I Soter. In 298 B.C.E. her father-in-law, Cassander I, ruler of Macedonia, died, and her sister-in-law THESSALONICE became regent. She divided rule between Alexander V, her younger favored son, and his brother Antipater. Lysandra married Alexander.

Enraged that Thessalonice had deprived him of rule over all of Macedonia, Antipater murdered his mother. Alexander asked the general Demetrius, called the Besieger, for help in avenging her death. Instead, Demetrius murdered Alexander, ousted Antipater, and made himself king of Macedonia in 295 B.C.E. Lysandra fled with her children to her father's court in Egypt.

Two years later, Lysandra married Agathocles, the son of Lysimachus of Thrace. Her father-in-law became ruler of Macedonia in 285 after defeating Demetrius. He married Lysandra's half sister ARSINOË II PHILADELPHUS. Arsinoë persuaded her elderly husband to have Lysandra's husband Agathocles murdered on suspicion of treason in 283. Lysandra fled with her children to Antioch seeking the protection of Seleucus, an enemy of her father-in-law. In 281, Lysimachus was defeated and killed in a battle with Seleucus.

Lysandra was so angry over the murder of Agathocles that it was difficult for members of her father-in-law's family to retrieve his body. Nothing more is known of Lysandra's saga.

Sources

Pausanias. *Description of Greece* 1.9, 10.3–5.

Plutarch. *Vitae Parallelae (Parallel Lives): Demetrius* 36.1–5.

Macurdy, Grace. *Hellenistic Queens.* Reprint. Chicago: Ares Publishers, 1985, pp. 55–58.

M

Macrina

(c. 270–340 C.E.)   Roman: Pontus
early Christian

Macrina was a matriarch whose grandchildren shaped early Christian asceticism. As a child, she and her family were influenced by Gregory of Thaumaurgus, the first bishop in the city of Neocaesarea, in Pontus, the region of modern Turkey north of Cappadocia. It was an area noted as a center of early Christianity. In 112, two centuries before the conversion of Constantine, the younger Pliny had written to the emperor Trajan from Asia Minor, where he was governor of the province of Bithynia, to request guidance about the Christians.

Persecutions against Christians persisted with more or less vigor in different parts of the empire including Asia Minor until the early fourth century. Macrina and her family were affected in 306, a scant six years before the battle at the Mulvian bridge and the conversion of Constantine. Her estates were confiscated but she escaped with her husband and children into the countryside where they stayed hidden for several years. After 312, she and her family returned to the city. They were honored for their steadfastness and their property was reinstated.

Macrina educated her daughter Emmelia as a Christian and lived long enough to take part in the religious upbringing of her grandchildren, Peter, Basil, and Gregory, each of whom became a notable bishop. Her granddaughter, the younger Macrina, became a famous ascetic and founded a monastery.

Her children and grandchildren remembered her as a model of piety and of maternal caring. The exact date of her death is unknown.

Sources
Basil. *Epistle* 204, 6; 223: 3.
Catholic Encyclopedia, Vol. IX, 1990.

Macrina the Younger

(c. 327–379/380 C.E.)   Roman: Pontus
religious leader

Macrina was the dominant personality in a family of extraordinary achievement, renown, and piety. According to her brother Gregory, the bishop of Nyssa, her principles became those of the people around her and the imprint of her personality shaped them all. Companion to her three notable brothers, the bishops Peter, Basil, and Gregory, she founded and led a monastery for women on the family's estate in Annisa, in Pontus, not far from the Black Sea. Her asceticism rested on a simple life, work, study, and prayer. Gregory credited her in a eulogy written after her death with inspiring their brother Basil to develop a monastic rule for men.

According to Gregory, their mother, Emmelia, educated Macrina in the scriptures and the psalter, which she recited daily. Her brothers had a more traditional education, which included pagan literature and philosophy. However, in writing about Macrina, Gregory noted that his sister was familiar with classical literature. Possibly, she learned from her brothers as much as she taught them. Alternatively, she may have discovered the Greek literature that was available in the family household through her own initiative.

Macrina's younger life followed a traditional path for well-born girls, albeit within a family of strong women and devoted Christians. She was 12 years old when her father arranged for her betrothal and, as was frequently the situation, the marriage was postponed until Macrina was older. However, her prospective husband died and Macrina refused to consider another marriage partner. She argued that her betrothal remained valid since she and her prospective husband would be reunited by the coming Resurrection. In her Christian family the argument held weight.

After the death of her father in 340, Macrina, her mother, and her grandmother, the elder MACRINA, raised Macrina's eight younger siblings. Macrina waited on her mother, baked bread, and performed the other manifold chores for a household of children, adults, and dependents, including other kin and slaves, all living together in a compound of buildings, stables, and gardens. For her younger brother Peter, who later became bishop of Sabaste, she became mother, father, and teacher. Affluent and educated, Macrina's engagement with the busy household also discouraged further pressure for marriage.

Although her later fame has highlighted the spiritual, Macrina was an eminently practical woman. She shared with her mother oversight of the family's holdings. In addition to the household and its gardens, they together managed four income-producing estates in three provinces on which they paid taxes to three rulers.

Gradually, however, she and her mother lived a more monastic life. Macrina's experiences with ascetic living echoed and influenced adherents in other parts of the empire. During these decades, asceticism was a new and expanding phenomenon that was probably, at least in part, a spiritual response to the deteriorating conditions of life in the empire. Not only was there the familiar threat of violence among contenders for the imperial purple, but there was a loss of security as wars with the tribes that had previously remained on the borders of the empire came ever closer. The century was also a period of widespread economic deterioration, which accelerated a decline in urban infrastructure. Fewer new roads, baths, arenas, and aqueducts were built or kept in repair. The transport of goods was more difficult, and agricultural productivity declined. A life of private contemplation that struggled to erase the power of externalities held an appeal, especially when it was reinforced by the Christian promise of Resurrection.

Macrina, along with Basil's colleagues among churchmen like Eustathius of Sebaste, also in Asia Minor, influenced Basil's development of communal monastic rules for men. Gregory wrote that when their brother Basil returned from schooling in Athens, skilled in rhetoric and disdainful of the local residents, it was Macrina who convinced him through example and argument to embrace an ascetic life.

Basil's presence, and the marriage of Macrina's sisters in 357, changed the household. Macrina persuaded her mother to organize their life in an even more overtly monastic fashion. Unlike other monasteries and houses for widows and virgin women in which wealthy members still had the services of slaves or attendants, Macrina insisted that their household eliminate all earthly distinctions of birth or wealth. All of the women in the household were expected to undertake household chores, eat the same food together, and enjoy similarly simple sleeping arrangements. They lived without luxury, worked, studied religious texts, prayed, and sang hymns.

After her mother's death in 370/371, Macrina and her brothers inherited the family assets equally. Basil built a monastery for men on the family property in Annisa. Across a small stream, Macrina built a house for virgin women and widows. The two monasteries were separate and distinct, although on occasion they shared services and food. The siblings, Basil, Peter, Gregory, and Macrina, however, remained in continuous communication through visits and letters. In contrast with Basil, Macrina chose not to direct the women's house; instead she became its spiritual mother, setting an example for sisters to emulate. She donated her portion of the inheritance from her mother to the local church for charitable purposes and probably expected that the donation would also assure care for the future for her monastery.

Macrina also insisted that the women's community be as self-sufficient as possible. Her emphasis on self-sufficiency, like her donation to the local church, became a common practice in the later monastic movement. Possibly, however, self-sufficiency was for her as much a necessity as a virtue: If the monastery were to survive, there was little choice but for it to provide for itself. The practical aspect of Macrina may have considered self-sufficiency an investment in the uncertain future no less than the donation of land secured the relatively fragile local church.

Gregory was with Macrina as she lay dying. He described her room, the pallet she used for a bed, the simplicity of her cloak, and the modesty of her physical needs. Gregory did not dwell on her philosophical ideas. However, in his work, *On the Soul and the Resurrection,* he created a dialogue in which Macrina was his teacher and she discoursed on philosophical questions that interwove Christian and pagan thought. Possibly, she was only Gregory's Diotoma. Neither her learning nor her persona were representative of a real woman, but rather an inspiration. Alternatively, her insights may have had all the sophistication and clarity Gregory attributed to her.

Macrina died in 379/380 with Gregory at her bedside.

Sources

Corrigan, Kevin. "Syncletica and Macrina: Two Early Lives of Women Saints." Available online. URL: http://www.peregrina.com/voxbenedictina. Accessed June 19, 2007.

Gregory of Nyssa. *Ascetic Works, On the Soul and Resurrection, passim. Life of Macrina,* in *Handmaids of the Lord: Contemporary Descriptions of Feminine Asceticism in the First Six Christian Centuries.* Translated and edited by Joan M. Peterson. Kalamazoo: Cistercian Publication, Inc., 1996.

Roth, Catherine. "Platonic and Pauline Elements in the Ascent of the Soul in Gregory of Nyssa's Dialogue on the Soul and the Resurrection." *Vigiliae Christianae* 46, no. 1 (March 1992): 20–30.

◉ Maecia Faustina
(third century C.E.)
Roman: Italy and North Africa
ruler for son

Maecia Faustina was able, wealthy, noble and lived during difficult times in the third century C.E. Her family was old and honored. Her mother, Fabia Orestilla, was the daughter of the consul Annius Severus. Her father, Marcus Antonius Gordianus, was a man of culture and wealth. A follower of the Epicurian school, he traced his lineage back to the Gracchi on his father's side and to the emperor Trajan on his mother's. Maecia Faustina spent her childhood in a house built by the great republican general Pompey whose previous owners also included the triumvir Mark Antony and the emperor Tiberius. She married Junius Balbus, a man of consular rank, and gave birth to a son, Antonius, who became emperor at the age of 13.

Her father, while proconsul of Africa, was asked to become emperor of Rome by a young group of aristocrats in revolt against the emperor Maximinus, whom they considered hostile to the Senate. Reluctantly, he accepted. In 238 C.E., at the age of 79, he was recognized by the Senate. He took the title Gordian I and made Maecia Faustina's brother, Gordian II, his colleague. Her brother died soon after in battle, and her father committed suicide, having ruled for only 22 days.

After the deaths of the two Gordians, the Senate appointed Decius Caelius Balbinus and Pupienus Maximus joint emperors. They were a part of a senatorial board of 20 that had led the earlier opposition to Maximinus. To satisfy the poplar demand for imperial continuity, they elevated Maecia's son to Caesar. Three months later, the two emperors were murdered by the Praetorian Guard. Maecia Faustina and her husband had probably bribed the Praetorian Guard to act quickly. The 13-year-old Antonius was declared emperor on July 9, 238.

The new emperor, who took the name Gordian III, followed a political course favored by the Senate. Maecia Faustina directed the affairs of state, supported by the faction that had supported her father and opposed Maximinus. Reform policies were initiated in administration, fiscal affairs, and the army. Efforts were taken to limit frivolous charges against the rich and notable. Attention was paid to strengthening defenses at the frontiers, and gross abuses of power in the provinces were prosecuted. Despite efforts of reform, however, it was a period of financial difficulty and political instability.

In 241, Gaius Furius Timesitheus was appointed prefect of the Praetorian Guard and assumed effective control over the young emperor. Gordian III married Timesitheus's daughter, Furia Sabina Tranquillina in the same year. The able Timesitheus died in 243. Gordian appointed Philippus from Arabia to take his place. Gordian III died of battle wounds in 244, and Philippus took the title of emperor.

Nothing is known of the final fate of Maecia Faustina.

Sources

Scriptores Historiae Augustae. Gordian 22.4; 23.6–7; 25.3–4.

Townsend, Prescott W. "The Administration of Gordian III." *Yale Classical Studies* 15 (1955): 59–132.

Townsend, Prescott W. "The Revolution of A.D. 238: The Leaders and Their Aims." *Yale Classical Studies* 14 (1955): 49–97.

◉ Maesia

(first century B.C.E.)
Roman: Umbria and Rome
lawyer

Maesia was a native of Sentium from Umbria, in Italy. Tried on a criminal charge, she conducted her own defense before the praetor Lucius Titus. She was acquitted by the jury. Praised for her skill in successfully pleading her case, she was also denigrated with the epithet "androgyne" for stepping beyond the traditional female role.

Sources

Valerius Maximus. *Factorum et dictorum memorabilium libri IX* 8.3.1.

Bauman, Richard A. *Women and Politics in Ancient Rome.* London: Routledge, 1994, p. 50.

Marshall, A. J. "Ladies at Law: The Role of Women in the Roman Civil Courts." In *Studies in Latin Literature and Roman History,* ed. by C. Deroux. Brussels, Belgium: Latomus, 1989, pp. 41, 47.

◉ Magia

(first century B.C.E.)   Roman: Italy
mother of Virgil

Magia was the mother of Virgil, Rome's greatest poet. She lived near Mantua in northern Italy and was married to a man who may have begun his career as a potter. Her husband may have been employed by her father as an assistant to the magistrates before their fortunes improved, and he became a landowner able to provide Virgil with a good education.

Virgil was probably born on October 15, 70 B.C.E. According to legend, Magia gave birth in a ditch on the side of the road while traveling with her husband in the country.

Sources

Suetonius. *The Lives of Illustrious Men: De grammaticis (Grammarians), Virgil* 1–3.

Oxford Classical Dictionary, ed. by Simon Hornblower and Antony Spawforth. 3d. ed. New York: Oxford University Press, 1996, p. 1,602.

◉ Mallonia

(first century C.E.)   Roman: Rome
political victim

Mallonia is the only name we know of a woman reputed to be of high rank. She was said to have attracted the attentions of the emperor Tiberius around 26 C.E. The emperor was already old, emaciated and bald with a face disfigured by blotches. He repelled Mallonia, who may have been a good deal younger, and she refused his advances. Tiberius supposedly gathered derogatory information about her, which resulted in a trial. Tiberius pressed her to regret her behavior toward him. After leaving the court, she returned home and stabbed herself. A rude joke about Tiberius and Mallonia became current in the next street-corner Atellan farce, a popular entertainment of the day.

Sources

Suetonius. *The Lives of the Caesars:* Tiberius 45.

Marcella

(?–410 C.E.)   Roman: Rome
Christian ascetic and scholar

Marcella was the descendant of an illustrious family of consuls and praetorian prefects. Although she had all the arrogance, wealth, self-assurance, and confidence of an elite Roman, she chose to become an ascetic Christian who struggled with humility, charity, and prayer.

Marcella's mother was the elder ALBINA, a Christian who was lauded as *univira,* a widowed woman who never remarried. No information survives about Marcella's youth, but she was probably brought up Christian. She was well educated in both the classical and Christian texts and in Latin and Greek.

She married and was widowed seven months later. Her family assumed that she would remarry. There was no reason for her to remain alone, although at any one time in the cities and villas of large landed estates across the empire there were probably a significant number of households headed by women who chose to be unmarried. Roman history had a number of women who made lives for themselves alone after the death of their husbands. The renowned CORNELIA (2) retreated to the country and her estate became a gathering place for the elite of the second century B.C.E. Moreover, she lived with her widowed and childless daughter, SEMPRONIA. Some 400 years later, in the second century C.E. the younger Pliny regularly corresponded with his widowed aunt who lived alone and managed her own estates. Exiled men, like Cicero in the late Republic, left women, like his wife TERENTIA,

behind to salvage family property and lobby for their return. All during the centuries, the time and distance routinely traveled on business or as part of civil and military assignments further contributed to many women at home managing family life and business affairs for months and years at a time.

However, widowhood was not a sought-after status. Aside from the emotional loss, families of position and wealth needed legitimate heirs. Historically, the elite families were the linchpin of social and economic life. Great families like that to which Marcella belonged were at the apex of a pyramid that spread out to include slaves, freedmen and women, and less wealthy friends, families, and kin. Their relationships, like the properties they owned, extended across the empire and over generations. Continuity not only provided a living generation to celebrate their ancestors (which also meant celebrating the greatness of Rome), but it also insured the network of obligations and responsibilities that bound together disparate groups into a functioning social system.

As Marcella was young and attractive, her mother had no difficulty finding a wealthy, though much older, suitor, Naeratius Cerealis, whose family had the consular credentials that admitted him to the inner circle of Roman high society. His offer to Marcella was generous. Although women controlled their own wealth and had personal legal rights, there were liabilities to being a woman alone, and a powerful male protector was never unimportant. Acknowledging the difference in their ages, Cerealis also offered her his fortune upon his death.

Marcella refused. She claimed that had she sought to remarry, she would have been more interested in a husband than a fortune. For her family, however, the more disturbing decision was that she would live out her life dedicated to Christ. Her decision may not have been wholly unexpected, since her parents had decided that Marcella's younger sister, ASELLA, would remain an unmarried virgin and dedicate her life to God.

Marcella's mother accepted Marcella's decision with a caveat. She, possibly after a family council, requested that Marcella assign her portion of the family wealth to her uncle, C. Caeionius Rufus, and his four children. Marcella agreed, perhaps with some reluctance, since she may have had other plans. However, as in many other cases when wealthy women gave away their wealth, whether to churches or relatives, she retained sufficient income and property to support her new life. It was sufficient for her to travel, make donations, and support several houses around the city with day-to-day household expenses for a resident population that included numbers of short- and long-term visitors, dependents, disciples, slaves, freedmen and women, and sundry others.

According to Jerome, Marcella led the first generation of well-born woman in Rome who publicly embraced celibacy and established Christian houses for like-minded women. She already lived with her mother and her sister when she invited virgin women and chaste widows to join them in her palatial house on the Aventine in a wealthy residential section of Rome. The women prayed together, fasted, and studied religious texts and the Bible, primarily in Greek, thereby using their sophisticated upper-class bilingual educations to ascetic ends. Their simple lifestyle also did not lack for attendants to serve them. Jerome, writing Marcella with advice, urged her to leave the house as infrequently as possible, except on Christian missions and reminded her to treat the lowliest of slave women as she would treat her social peer.

Marcella's household became a center for the visiting elite of Christendom. Visiting priests and bishops from the East met their Western and African counterparts. The bishop of Rome, Athanasius, brought information to Marcella about the growing monastic movement. Priests from Alexandria informed her about the rules of Saint Anthony, one of the originators of monastic life, who was still living in the desert of Lower Egypt. Marcella became acknowledged as a teacher. The elder PAULA sent her daughter EUSTOCHIUM to live and study with her before they left Rome in 385. Christians asked her to settle disputes over the interpretation of texts. She modestly never took credit for herself, however, and always noted the authority from whom she had gained insight.

All during her life Marcella also maintained an extensive correspondence. The letters of Jerome mention her years of corresponding with Paula, the elder MELANIA, and Eustochium, to name only a few. After the exchange of many letters, Marcella met Jerome in 382 when he came to Rome. They discussed the scriptures and, subsequently over the years, exchanged letters on points of interpretation. It was at a scripture reading in Marcella's house that the elder Paula had met Jerome. Three or four years later, in 386 C.E., a year after Jerome left Rome and soon after Paula and Eustochium joined him, he wrote Marcella on behalf of the three of them urging her to join them in Palestine. She chose to remain in Rome. After the death of her mother in 388, Marcella and her young disciple, PRINCIPIA, moved to a smaller house in a suburb of Rome, which she shared with other women who followed her lifestyle. Her sister, Asella, also lived in the house, in a small cell of her own.

Marcella's retiring public posture contrasted with her engagement in the Christian debates of the day. A contretemps involving Jerome had even sent her lobbying to the bishop of Rome. In 397, Tyrannius Rufinus, who translated a number of works by Origen and had been a close colleague of the elder Melania for many years in the East, arrived in Rome. During his stay, he published a translation of a work of Origen, whose theology was now considered suspect by some of the orthodox. In the preface, Rufinus included praise of Origen from an early work translated into Latin by Jerome. Jerome, who had since distanced himself from Origen, was furious at the implication that he still held his earlier views. The normally retiring Marcella, siding with Jerome, wrote letters, produced witnesses, and demanded that the bishop Anastasius condemn Origen as a heretic. The bishop bowed to her demands, much to the gratification of Jerome.

On August 24, 410, the Goths under Alaric invaded Rome. The inhabitants were starving. The conquerors looted, burned buildings, and killed. Soldiers broke into Marcella's house, demanded money, and beat her with clubs when they discovered she had none. She pleaded with them to spare her young disciple Principia. They did and took both of them to the Basilica of Paul, which was safe. A few days later Marcella died with Principia at her side.

Sources

Jerome. Letter XXIII, XXVII, XXXII, XXXVIII, XLI, XLVI, LIX, XLVII, CXXVII.

Prosopography of the Later Roman Empire. Vol. I. Edited by A. H. M. Jones, J. R. Martindale, and J. Morris. Cambridge: Cambridge University Press, 1971. Reprinted 1992, pp. 542–543.

▣ Marcella the Elder, Claudia

(43 B.C.E.–? B.C.E./C.E.)   Roman: Rome
political player

The elder Claudia Marcella belonged to the generation whose childhood was marred by the violence of civil wars. Born in 43 B.C.E., Marcella was one of three siblings: a brother, Marcus Claudius Marcellus, born in 42, and a sister, the younger Claudia MARCELLA, born in 39. Her father, Gaius Claudius Marcellus, consul in 50 B.C.E., died by the time she was three years old and she grew up under the care of her mother, OCTAVIA (2). As intermittent civil war took its toll, her mother collected in her household children from her own two marriages and the orphaned children from the marriages of her ex-husband Mark Antony with FULVIA (2) and with CLEOPATRA VII. Octavia educated, dowered, and married the children of this extended family, assuring republican family lines into the next generation.

Marcella married Marcus Vipsanius Agrippa in 28 B.C.E. She was about 15; he was 36 years old. She was his second wife. Agrippa was a military man loyal to Octavian throughout the civil war. She brought Agrippa a tie to an elite republican house and to Octavian himself since not only was Octavian Marcella's uncle but her great-grandmother was JULIA (4), the favorite sister of Julius Caesar.

Although austere and older, Agrippa appears to have been a good husband. A daughter may have been born to them. Seven years later, however, the

marriage succumbed to new political realities. Marcella's brother had died two years earlier. He had been the husband of JULIA (6), Augustus's only child, and favored for succession. In 21 B.C.E., when there was unrest in Rome and Augustus was obliged to leave the city, he sought someone of unquestioned loyalty. Who better qualified than Agrippa, and how better to assure his already tested loyalty than a marriage with his daughter Julia. Marcella was divorced with Octavia's concurrence.

Marcella almost immediately married again. Her new husband was her childhood playmate, Iullus Antonius, consul in 10 B.C.E. He was the handsome, cultured second son of Fulvia and Mark Antony, and he was some 20 years Agrippa's junior. With Antonius she became part of the most visible group of post-civil war aristocrats in public life with ties to the republican past. They were a part of the group around the emperor's daughter, Julia.

Augustus had made clear on many occasions that his daughter and her friends lived a lifestyle he found objectionable. In 2 B.C.E. Augustus provoked a public scandal with a letter to the Senate detailing the adulterous behavior of his daughter and her friends. It seems probable that more than illicit sex was involved. Julia was exiled. We have no evidence to what part, if any, Marcella played in the scandal. However, her husband was identified as the group's ringleader and condemned to death for adultery and conspiracy against Augustus. He was either executed or forced to commit suicide.

Marcella and Antonius had a son, Lucius, and perhaps a daughter. Nothing is known of the end Marcella's life.

Sources

Dio Cassius. *Roman History* 54.6.5.

Plutarch. *Vitae Parallelae (Parallel Lives): Antonius* 87.2–3.

Seneca. *Ad Marciam de consolatione* 2.3–4.

Suetonius. *The Lives of the Caesars:* Augustus 63.1.

Balsdon, J. P. V. D. *Roman Women.* New York: John Day Comp., 1963, p. 208.

Pauly, A., G. Wissowa, and W. Kroll. *Real-Encyclopadie D. Classischen Altertumswissenschaft 1893–.* (Germany: multiple publishers) 422.

Syme, Ronald. *The Augustan Aristocracy.* Oxford: Clarendon Press, 1986, index.

Marcella the Younger, Claudia

(39 B.C.E.–? C.E.)   Roman: Rome
political wife

Claudia Marcella was born in 39 B.C.E. and grew up part of the first post-Actium generation. Her father, Claudius Marcellus, was consul in 50 B.C.E. and died in 40. She spent her youth in the household of her mother, OCTAVIA (2), with her siblings, the children of her mother's marriage with Mark Antony, and the orphaned children of Mark Antony and his two wives, FULVIA (1) and CLEOPATRA VII. Marcella, the descendant of a great republican house, was the great-granddaughter of JULIA (4), the favorite sister of Julius Caesar. She and her siblings provided a critical link between the republican past and the new empire.

About 15 B.C.E. when she was 24, she married Paullus Aemilius Lepidus, consul suffectus in 34 B.C.E. and censor in 22. Possibly there had been an earlier marriage. The marriage linked two honored republican houses and tied them closely to the imperial circle. Before her husband died, Marcella gave birth to a son, Paullus Aemilius Regulus.

After her husband's death she married Marcus Valerius Messalla Barbatus Appianus, consul in 12 B.C. She outlived him. They had a daughter, CLAUDIA PULCHRA, and a son, Messalla Barbatus. Her son married DOMITIA LEPIDA, and their child, Valeria MESSALLINA, would become the wife of the emperor Claudius. Marcella would have been about 64 when Messallina was born; it is not known if she was still alive.

Sources

Balsdon, J. P. V. D. *Roman Women.* New York: John Day Comp., 1963, pp. 71, 73, 74.
Pauly, A., G. Wissowa, and W. Kroll. *Real-Encyclopadie D. Classischen Altertumswissenschaft 1893–.* (Germany: multiple publishers) 423.
Syme, Ronald. *The Augustan Aristocracy.* Oxford: Clarendon Press, 1986, index.

Marcellina

(c. 330–335–c. 398 C.E.)   Roman: Trier, Rome
Christian ascetic

Marcellina lived in Rome and provided her younger brother Ambrose, bishop of Milan, with a trusted Roman base. When Ambrose was ill, she traveled to Milan to nurse him. In Milan and Rome she was part of the elite circle of women who lived ascetic lives but remained active in religious politics.

Marcellina had another younger brother Satyrus. Her father was also named Ambrose and was Prefect of Gaul, which included jurisdiction over Spain, Britain, and part of Africa. Her mother, a native of Rome, remains otherwise unknown. The family had long been Christian. Sometime around 533, Marcellina publicly vowed to live her life a virgin and an ascetic, after she had spent five years studying with Liberius, the bishop of Rome. Ambrose described the ceremony of her dedication to asceticism in his writing on virginity.

Marcellina remained at home in Rome with her mother to educate her brothers until she felt the need for a more contemplative life. With a group of like-minded women she established a communal house in a family residence on the outskirts of the city. When Ambrose became bishop of Milan, he turned over his estates to the church but left Marcellina a life interest from the revenue.

They were contrasting personalities. Ambrose was an electric leader and a committed Christian proselytizer. He dominated the Christian community in Milan. Marcellina, most of the time living in Rome, was always in the background, even when she visited Milan. Nonetheless, she influenced him, and he admired her. He was also concerned with her tendency to extreme asceticism, which he feared could affect her health.

Marcellina and Ambrose frequently exchanged letters. In a long letter, Ambrose described his conflict with JUSTINA, who wanted a basilica in Milan reserved for Arian believers. Marcellina worried about the political unrest that the conflict might engender. Despite the presence of soldiers, however, the populace rallied behind Ambrose. Justina did not prevail, and his sister's fears were allayed.

The death of Satyrus in 379 saddened Marcellina and Ambrose. Nineteen years later, Ambrose died, in 397, and Marcellina followed not long after, in about 398.

Sources

Ambrose. Letters XX, XXII, XLI.

Prosopography of the Later Roman Empire. Vol. I. Edited by A. H. M. Jones, J. R. Martindale, and J. Morris. Cambridge: Cambridge University Press, 1971. Reprinted 1992, p. 544.

◉ **Marcia (1)**

(?–113 B.C.E.)   Roman: Rome
priestess

Marcia was one of three Vestal Virgins charged with illicit relations in 114 B.C.E. It was believed an ill omen for Rome for three out of the six Vestals, who protected the sacred flame in one of the city's oldest temples on the Forum, to be charged with the most serious crime they could commit.

Of the three, only one, AEMILIA (1), was found guilty and condemned. Her partner was identified as L. Veturius, an equestrian. Although Marcia and the third Vestal, LICINIA (4), were declared innocent by the *pontifex maximus,* popular protest resulted in the establishment of a special tribunal to reexamine the case. Lucius Cassius Longinus Ravilla conducted the investigation. Both Marcia and Licinia were found guilty and condemned to death in 113.

Marcia was accused of having had only one man, a companion of Veturius. Her sister Vestal, Aemilia, was said to have made the arrangements. The evidence was given by a slave.

Sources

Dio Cassius. *Roman History* 26, 87.
Livy. *From the Founding of the City* 43.
Orosius. *Seven Books of History Against the Pagans* 5.15, 20–22.
Plutarch. *Moralia: Quaestiones Romanae* 83 (284).
Bauman, Richard A. *Women and Politics in Ancient Rome.* London: Routledge, 1994, pp. 53–55, 57–58.

◉ **Marcia (2)**

(first century B.C.E.)   Roman: Rome
political wife

Marcia divorced her husband to marry another man, who died and left her a wealthy widow. She then remarried her first husband. Other than the obvious financial benefit, any reason for her remarriage remains obscure. Marcia was one of three siblings. Her father was Lucius Marcius Philippus, consul in 56 B.C.E., and her stepmother was ATIA (1), the mother of the future emperor Augustus and his sister OCTAVIA (2) by her first husband. Her father's marriage, probably sometime around 58 B.C.E., was followed by her brother's marriage to her stepmother's sister, ATIA (2). In consequence, there was a double relationship between Marcia and her siblings and Augustus and his sister.

Marcia became the second wife of the younger Marcus Porcius Cato. Her husband, attracted to the Stoic philosophy, was a stubborn man of rigid principles and somewhat unpleasant personality. He believed that he alone lived in accordance with the traditions of the ancients. He also believed that one should only engage in sex to produce children. He had two children by his first wife and three daughters with Marcia.

A close friend of her husband, Quintus Hortensius, consul in 69 B.C.E., was a famous orator and, like Cato, one of the leaders of the conservative oligarchy. When he was in his early 60s and already had grown children, he sought to marry PORCIA, Cato's eldest daughter by his first wife, ATILIA. Porcia was already married and had two sons. Undeterred, Hortensius asked Cato to divorce Marcia so that he could marry her. Cato agreed if it was amenable all around. Neither Marcia nor her father objected. The divorce and new marriage took place in 56 B.C.E. Cato hosted the wedding. No children resulted, and Hortensius died leaving Marcia a much richer woman. She then remarried Cato.

During the five remaining years of Cato's life, he was said to have refrained from sex with Marcia since he felt that they already had enough children and Marcia had experienced a sufficient burden in bearing them. Marcia might well have concurred with their abstinence, given the high death rate for women bearing children. Abstinence was abetted by Cato's absence. He spent of these years fighting with Gnaeus Pompeius (Pompey the Great) against Caesar. In 46, he died by his own hand in Africa after Caesar defeated the remaining core of senatorial opposition. Her stepdaughter Porcia also killed herself a year before the defeat of Brutus and Cassius at the battle of Philippi in 42. Marcia's life after Cato is unrecorded.

Sources

Lucan. *Pharsalia* 2.326–89.
Plutarch. *Vitae Parallelae (Parallel Lives): Cato Minor* 25.1–5; 52.
Balsdon, J. P. V. D. *Roman Women.* New York: John Day Comp., 1963, p. 190.
Pomeroy, Sarah B. *Goddesses, Whores, Wives, and Slaves: Women in Classical Antiquity.* New York: Schocken Books, 1975, pp. 158, 160–161.
Gordon, Hattie. "The Eternal Triangle, First Century B.C." *Classical Journal* 28 (1933): 574–578.
Pauly, A., G. Wissowa, and W. Kroll. *Real-Encyclopadie D. Classischen Altertumswissenschaft 1893–.* (Germany: multiple publishers) 115.

◉ Marcia (3)

(first century B.C.E.–first century C.E.)   Roman: Italy, Cyprus, Asia, Spain
patron of the arts

Marcia was born into an ancient and honored republican family with close ties to the nascent empire through Octavian, later the emperor Augustus, and his sister OCTAVIA (2). Part of the circle that included some of the greatest of the Latin poets, and she was on the periphery of the scandals in 8 C.E. that rocked the Roman elite and resulted in the banishment by Augustus of his granddaughter JULIA (7) and the exile of the poet Ovid.

Marcia's immediate family relationships were complicated. Her father was Lucius Marcius Philippus, tribune in 49 B.C.E., consul suffectus in 38 and governor of Spain in 34–33?; her mother, ATIA (2), was the younger sister of her grandfather's second wife. The older ATIA (1) had already been married once before she married Marcia's grandfather. During her earlier marriage the older Atia had had two children, Octavian and Octavia. Marcia, therefore, had Augustus and Octavia as a stepuncle and aunt. Their children were her stepcousins.

To further complicate the relationships, after Marcia's father died, her mother married Quintus Fabius Maximus, the father of Paullus Fabius Maximus, whom Marcia married in 16 B.C.E. Her husband had an illustrious career. A close associate of Augustus, he was appointed quaestor in 22 or 21, elected consul in 11, was proconsul in Asia in 10–9, and then governor in northwest Spain in 3–2 B.C.E.

Her husband was also known as an orator and a patron of poets. Horace, whose principal benefactor was Gaius Maecenas, wrote an ode in honor of her marriage in 16 B.C.E. Marcia followed her husband and was honored by a dedication at Paphos in Cyprus. A close friend of Marcia and her mother was Ovid's third wife, whose name remains unknown. Marcia appears in Ovid's poetry. He composed a wedding ode to Marcia and her husband in 12 or 13 C.E. In a poem of 4 C.E., he wrote that her beauty matched her noble birth.

In 8 C.E., Augustus banished Ovid to Tomis on the Black Sea for reasons that are still obscure. Ovid used his poetry and the friendship of Marcia and his wife in an attempt to have the banishment rescinded. In a poem written about 13 C.E., he admonished his wife to affirm her devotion to Marcia. Whatever may have been Marcia's efforts on Ovid's behalf, however, they were unsuccessful.

Her husband died in 14. Rumors arose that Fabius Maximus had committed suicide and that at the funeral Marcia had blamed her indiscretion for his death. Her husband had supposedly accompanied Augustus on a secret trip to Planasia where Agrippa Postumus, the third son of the great general Marcus Vipsanius Agrippa and Augustus's daughter JULIA (6), had been exiled. Still without a firm designation of his heir, Augustus was exploring the possibility that the boy's personality disorders had mitigated, and perhaps of pardoning him. Marcia, a friend of Augustus's wife LIVIA DRUSILLA, purportedly told her of the trip, and the resulting anger of the emperor caused her husband to kill himself.

Marcia and Maximus had a son, Paullus Fabius Persicus, consul in 34 C.E., and a daughter, Fabia NUMANTINA.

Sources

Dio Cassius. *Roman History* 56.30, 1–2.
Tacitus. *Annales* 1.5.1 ff.
Levick, Barbara. *Tiberius the Politician.* London: Thames and Hudson, 1976, p. 64.

Oxford Classical Dictionary, ed. by Simon Hornblower and Antony Spawforth. 3d. ed. New York: Oxford University Press, 1996, p. 582.

Pauly, A., G. Wissowa, and W. Kroll. *Real-Encyclopadie D. Classischen Altertumswissenschaft 1893–.* (Germany: multiple publishers) 120.

Syme, Ronald. *The Augustan Aristocracy.* Oxford: Clarendon Press, 1986, index.

———. *History in Ovid.* New York: Oxford University Press, 1978, index.

◉ Marcia (4)

(?–193 C.E.)   Roman: Rome
conspirator

Marcia, probably a freedwoman of the co-emperor Lucius Verus, protected herself and her own interests at a time when imperial power, always arbitrary, had become increasingly unbounded. As a young woman and the lover of Ummidius Quadratus, she was persuaded by Annia Aurelia Galeria LUCILLA, sister of the emperor Commodus, to join in a plot to kill the emperor. The plot was discovered. Quadratus and Lucilla were executed in 182 C.E. Marcia, however, escaped charges and punishment and became companion and lover of Commodus, whom she greatly influenced. She favored Christianity and persuaded Commodus to adopt a benign policy toward Christians. She asked Victor, the bishop of Rome, for a list of Christians who had been deported to Sardinia and persuaded Commodus to allow them to return to Rome.

Commodus's behavior became increasingly bizarre until in 192, he decided to present himself to the Roman people on the first day of the new year in a gladiator's costume instead of the traditional purple worn by Romans with the power of *imperium.* Marcia could not dissuade him, nor could his servant Eclectus or Aemilius Laetus, the prefect of the Praetorian Guard. In fact, their efforts to control the emperor almost led to their execution: A slave boy of the emperor found a list of proscribed names. Marcia discovered that the list contained the names of many prominent senators and that her name, as well as Eclectus and Laetus, headed the list.

Marcia, Eclectus, and Laetus decided to kill Commodus. Marcia poisoned a cup of wine. Commodus, already made very ill, was strangled. They sent the body to the edge of the city and spread a rumor that Commodus had died of apoplexy. They chose a distinguished senator, Publius Helvius Pertinax, to replace Commoodus and revealed their plot to him. He was declared emperor by the Praetorian Guard on January 1, 193. Marcia married Eclectus. Six months later, Pertinax was executed by members of the Praetorian Guard who were angered by his strict discipline, and Marcia and her husband were also killed.

Sources

Dio Cassius. *Roman History* 73.4, 6–7, 22.4–6; 74.16.5.

Herodian. *History of the Empire* 1.8.4–5, 8, 16.4, 17.4–11; 2.1.3.

Scriptores Historiae Augustae. Commodus 11.9; 17.1–2.

———. Didius Julianus 6.2.

———. Pertinax 4.5–2.

Balsdon, J. P. V. D. *Roman Women.* New York: John Day Comp., 1963, pp. 148–150.

Oxford Classical Dictionary, ed. by Simon Hornblower and Antony Spawforth. 3d. ed. New York: Oxford University Press, 1996, p. 922.

◉ Marcia Furnilla

(first century C.E.)   Roman: Rome
political wife

Marcia Furnilla, the daughter of Antonia Furnilla and the senator Marcius Barea Sura, married Titus Flavius Vespasianus after his first wife, ARRECINA TERTULLA, died. They had one child, JULIA FLAVIA. Titus divorced Marcia Furnilla in 64 C.E., before he became emperor.

Sources

Suetonius. *The Lives of the Caesars:* Titus 4.2–3.

◉ Marciana, Ulpia

(?–112 C.E.)
Roman: Spain, Germany, Italy, and Asia
Augusta; deified

Ulpia Marciana lived with her brother, the emperor Trajan, most of her adult life. Their parents were

Marcus Ulpius Traianus and a woman named Marcia who probably came from Spain. Before she moved in with her brother, she had married Matidius, a little-known senator from Vicetia in northern Italy. Her husband came from the heartland of Antonine support that flourished with her brother's rise to imperial power. After being widowed, Marciana joined Trajan and his wife Pompeia PLOTINA in Cologne, where Trajan commanded the troops on the Rhine before he became emperor. It was a large household and also included MATIDIA (1), Marciana's daughter and a favorite of Trajan and his wife, and Matidia's two daughters, the half-sisters Vibia SABINA and MATIDIA (2).

In 99 C.E. Marciana and her family settled in Rome with Trajan and Plotina. Trajan spent much of the early years of his reign away campaigning, leaving Plotina and Marciana in Rome sometimes for as long as three years at a time. In his absence they patronized the leading figures of the day to encourage the arts and the study of literature and philosophy. The future emperor Hadrian, adopted by Trajan, was brought up by the women and married Marciana's granddaughter Vibia Sabina in 100.

Ulpia Marciana
(Date: 113 C.E. 1967.153.140, Archives, American Numismatic Society)

Marciana and Plotina initially refused the Senate's request to honor them with the title Augusta. Both, however, accepted in 105. Marciana was the first woman to receive this honor who was not either the wife or the daughter of an emperor. In 112 Marciana and Plotina were given the right of coinage. Marciana died that same year. When Plotina died in 122, Hadrian consecrated both of them.

Sources

Pliny the Younger. *Panegyricus* 84.
Balsdon, J. P. V. D. *Roman Women.* New York: John Day Comp., 1963, pp. 133–136.
Oxford Classical Dictionary, ed. by Simon Hornblower and Antony Spawforth. 3d. ed. New York: Oxford University Press, 1996, p. 1,570.
Syme, Ronald. *Tacitus.* 2 vols. Oxford: Clarendon Press, 1958, pp. 231, 233, 246, 603.

◉ Maria

(c. 385–407/408 C.E.)
Roman: Rome, Ravenna
political pawn

Maria married the emperor of the West, Honorius, to assure her parents' political future. Her mother, SERENA, was the favorite niece of Honorius's father, Theodosius the Great, and her father, Stilicho, was the emperor's greatest general. She was their oldest daughter, born in 385; one year earlier than her future husband, Honorius.

When Theodosius died in 395, he left Stilicho regent for Honorius, and both the young emperor and his sister, GALLA PLACIDIA, in the care of Serena. Although Stilicho was regent, it was a position that would end with Honorius's majority and leave him dependent on a young and weak emperor. Serena, who had always been a favorite of Theodosius and treated as a daughter, also had no assured future with Honorius. Marriage between the cousins, Maria and Honorius, however, provided Stilicho and Serena a place within the intimate family, even after Honorius came of age. There was also the possibility of a dynasty. If Stilicho's non-Roman birth excluded him from becoming emperor, than he could still become the founder of an imperial line. Maria's betrothal, in 398 at about 13 years old, provided for her parents and, potentially, for the continuity of the empire into the next generation with children from the young couple.

Maria's education included a thorough grounding in orthodox Christianity as well as Greek and Latin language and literature. Claudian, a leading poet of the day and a protégé of her mother, praised Maria's competence in classical Greek at her wedding celebration. No doubt she was also taught the rules of deportment for diplomatic life and to manage complicated households of slaves, dependents, extended family, and a constant round of visitors. Possibly, she also was taught the rudiments of business that would allow her to manage distant estates and income-producing properties.

At the time of their marriage, the Western empire was in serious peril from the invading Goths under Alaric. The tried generalship of Stilicho was invaluable, and his loyalty, assured by Maria, should have satisfied the fears of the young emperor surrounded by spies, sycophants, and assassins. However, Honorius was neither a soldier nor talented in his choice of advisors. Possibly, he was also not a very good husband. Although no details are known of Maria's life as a wife, there is some evidence that Honorius was impotent or uninterested and the marriage was never consummated.

Maria died childless toward the end of 407 or early 408; shortly thereafter her father was assassinated.

Sources

Zosimus. *New History/Zosimus.* A translation with commentary by Ronald T. Ridley. Canberra: Australian Association of Byzantine Studies, 1982.

Oost, Stewart Irwin. *Galla Placidia Augusta: a Biographical Essay.* Chicago: University of Chicago Press.

Prosopography of the Later Roman Empire. Vol. II. Edited by A. H. M. Jones, J. R. Martindale, and J. Morris. Cambridge: Cambridge University Press, 1971. Reprinted 1992, p. 720.

▣ Marina

(403–449 C.E.)   Roman: Constantinople
ascetic and political actor

Marina and ARCADIA supported their oldest sister, PULCHERIA, and brother, Theodosius II. Orphaned young, they followed Pulcheria's lead and offered a public vow of virginity that removed the obligation to marry. Marina became a significant landowner in Constantinople and used her resources to further the interests of her family.

Marina's father, Arcadius, was the eastern Roman emperor. Her mother, Augusta AELIA EUDOXIA, was a formidable woman who vigorously defended her dominion. After the death of Aelia Eudoxia in 404, followed by that of Arcadius four years later in 408, the Praetorian Prefect administered the government as regent for the underage emperor. In 413, the 14-year-old Pulcheria made a public declaration of virginity with Marina and Arcadia while dedicating an altar in the Great Church at Constantinople. A year later, Pulcheria was elevated to Augusta by her younger brother, and she became regent and guardian for him, Marina, and Arcadia.

Pulcheria introduced an ascetic lifestyle into the palace. The family fasted twice weekly, prayed, and read from the scriptures. Marina and her sisters wore modest clothing, eschewed cosmetics, and spent time in traditional women's arts. Like previous Christian imperial women, they helped the poor and sick and provided shelter for the homeless.

Although the outward trappings of their lives were modest, Marina and Arcadia were satellite centers of power within the imperial circle. They entertained visitors from abroad and brought petitions to the attention of Pulcheria and Theodosius. Marina acquired palatial dwellings in the city and the suburbs. Her property holdings in one part of the city were so extensive that the district became known by her name. Cash rental income from artisans and tradesmen, as well as income in kind and produce from farms outside the city, filled her coffers and kitchens. She also owned income-producing estates in the provinces; some of them inherited from her father and others gifts from her brother.

Marina lived with Pulcheria for most of her life, even after both left the imperial palace. The household formed a political as well as economic unit. The sisters were highly visible in the city and the positions they held represented an imperial statement. They were orthodox Christians who adhered to the Chalcedonian creed that the divine and human nature of Christ was cojoined yet separate and leaders in the conflict to unseat Nestorius, the bishop of Constantinople, who challenged their interpretation of Mary as Mother of God. In the controversy with Nestorius, Marina, like her sisters, received letters and calls from both sides entreating support. Marina and Arcadia were unwavering. They followed their sister and maintained that Nestorius's position of Mary as Mother of Christ was heretical and demeaned the status of women. Nestorius, whose appointment had not been opposed by the imperial circle, turned the doctrinal dispute argument into a political contest. Marina helped Pulcheria successfully maintain her imperial authority.

Marina died on August 3, 449.

Sources

Sozomen. *Historia Ecclesiastica* IX. 1, 3.

Theophanes. *Chronicle* AM 5901, 5905, 6053, 6054, 6057.

Holum, Kenneth. *Theodosian Empresses: Women and Imperial Dominion in Late Antiquity.* Berkeley: University of California Press, 1982.

▣ Marsa

(?–early fifth century C.E.)
Roman: Constantinople
political player

Marsa, along with EUGRAPHIA and CASTRICIA, were intimates of Augusta AELIA EUDOXIA, wife of the emperor Arcadius. Marsa's husband Flavius Promotus held the post of Master of Soldiers in the East and was consul in 389. Eudoxia, whose father held the position comparable to Marsa's husband in the West, had been sent to Constantinople as a girl to live with Marsa and her family. She grew up with Marsa's two sons and met her future husband Arcadius through them.

Marsa's husband quarreled with Flavius Rufinus, who was the Praetorian Prefect of the East and who dominated the weak emperor Arcadius. At one point, it came to blows, and Flavius Promotus struck Rufinus in the face. Rufinus persuaded Arcadius to transfer Promotus to Thrace, where he was killed in 391 by barbarians, perhaps at the instigation of Rufinus. Marsa remained in Constantinople, a political ally of Eudoxia. She played a supporting role in Eudoxia's opposition to John Chrysostom, bishop of Constantinople.

John Chrysostom had been appointed bishop of the city in 398. Faced with widespread poverty and the extraordinary wealth of the privileged few, he began to preach against the ostentatious life. In 403, Chrysostom lashed out against wealthy older widows, claiming their fancy hair made them look more like streetwalkers than proper women. Marsa and her circle considered this a direct attack and determined to end Chrysostom's tenure. They enlisted Eudoxia, whom he also had offended by suggesting that women had no place in public life, and allied themselves with bishops and monks to whom Chrysostom had been no more gracious. Chrysostom went into exile in 404.

The exact dates of Marsa's birth and death remain unknown.

Sources

Palladius. *Dialogue* 4. 8.

Socrates. *Historia Ecclesiastica* VI. 15. 1–3.

Zosimus. *New History/Zosimus.* Translation and commentary by Ronald T. Ridley. Canberra: Australian Association for Byzantine Studies, 1982, 5, 23, 2; 8.16. 1–2.

Prosopography of the Later Roman Empire. Vol. II. Edited by A. H. M. Jones, J. R. Martindale, and J. Morris. Cambridge: Cambridge University Press, 1971. Reprinted 1992, p. 72.

▣ Martina

(? B.C.E.–19/20 C.E.)   Syrian: Syria and Italy
poisoner

Martina, well known for her skill with poisons, became a suspect in 19 C.E. after the sudden death of Germanicus Julius Caesar, the popular general and probable heir to Tiberius. Martina was a client and possibly even a friend of MUNATIA PLANCINA, the wife of Gnaeus Calpurnius Piso, consul in 7 B.C.E. and political opponent of Germanicus. She appears to have been with Munatia, who had accompanied her husband to the East, when he was sent by Tiberius to temper Germanicus's aggressive policies. Piso and Germanicus were soon at odds. So too were Munatia and the elder AGRIPPINA, Germanicus's wife. After Germanicus's death, Agrippina carried his ashes back to Rome convinced that her husband had died from poison in a plot supported, if not arranged, by the emperor.

In Rome charges were brought against Munatia and Piso, who returned under guard after soldiers friendly to Germanicus had seized them in the East. Martina was also sent back to Rome to testify at the trial. She died on her arrival in Italy. Her death further inflamed passions on both sides. Although no poison was found on her body, some claimed that she had hidden the poison in her hair.

Sources

Dio Cassius. *Roman History* 57.18.6–10.
Tacitus. *Annales* 2.74; 3.7.
Levick, Barbara. *Tiberius the Politician.* London: Thames and Hudson, 1976, pp. 96–97, 103–104.

▣ Matidia (1)
(68–119 C.E.)
Roman: Italy, Asia, and Germany
Augusta; deified

Matidia lived in the multigenerational household of the emperor Trajan. Born no later than 68 C.E., she was the only child of Trajan's older sister Ulpia MARCIANA and Matidius, an obscure senator from northern Italy. Her first marriage seems to have been to a man named Mindius of whom nothing is known. She gave birth to a daughter named MATIDIA (2). She then married Lucius Vibius Sabinus, consul in 97 C.E., and they had a daughter, Vibia SABINA. Her husband died shortly after his consulship, and she moved with her daughters and her mother into the household of Trajan and Pompeia PLOTINA.

Matidia was honored with the title Augusta by Trajan. While her daughter Sabina, who had married the future emperor Hadrian in 100 C.E., remained in Rome, Matidia and Hadrian accompanied Trajan and Plotina on the campaign to the East in 114. Three years later, in 117, Trajan became ill and died in Syria. A letter of Trajan's named Hadrian his adopted son and heir. Rumors circulated about the authenticity of the letter. Plo-

Matidia (1)
(Date: 115 C.E.–117 C.E. 1001.112738, Archives, American Numismatic Society)

tina and Matidia, however, supported the soldiers' acclamation of Hadrian as the new emperor. Hadrian, who was campaigning in Syria, met them in Antioch and sent Plotina and Matidia to Rome with Trajan's ashes.

Although Hadrian's marriage was difficult, he remained close with his mother-in-law. When she died in 119, Hadrian gave the funeral oration and deified her. He also issued coins in her honor with the epithet "Diva Augusta Matidia." She was probably the first woman deified by the emperors to have a temple in Rome.

Sources

Dio Cassius. *Roman History* 69.1.
Scriptores Historiae Augustae. Hadrian 5.9; 9.9; 19.5.
Balsdon, J. P. V. D. *Roman Women.* New York: John Day Comp., 1963, pp. 133–139.
Birley, Anthony Richard. *Marcus Aurelius: Emperor of Rome.* Boston: Little, Brown, 1966, p. 241.
Oxford Classical Dictionary, ed. by Simon Hornblower and Antony Spawforth. 3d. ed. New York: Oxford University Press, 1996, p. 937.
Pauly, A., G. Wissowa, and W. Kroll. *Real-Encyclopadie D. Classischen Altertumswissenschaft 1893–.* (Germany: multiple publishers) 28.

Matidia (2)

(first–second century C.E.)
Roman: Italy, Asia, Germany, and Egypt
never married

Matidia was an extremely unusual woman in a society where nearly everyone, man and woman, married at least once. She never married. Matidia grew up with her mother, half sister, and grandmother in the household of Pompeia PLOTINA and the emperor Marcus Ulpius Trajan. Her mother was the only child of Ulpia MARCIANA, the eldest sister of the Trajan. Matidia's half sister, Vibia SABINA, became the wife of the emperor Hadrian.

Matidia shared a taste for cultured life with her mother, Marciana, and Plotina. In latter life she was close to her great-nephew Marcus Aurelius and when he was emperor, his daughters sometimes stayed with her. At her death, she left bequests of a million sesterces to some members of her family and associates. The money was to be administered by the younger Annia Galeria FAUSTINA, the wife of the emperor, and distributed at the rate of 50,000 sesterces a year.

Like many wealthy women who remained childless, she attracted a number of hangers-on who hoped to be remembered in her will. They persuaded her to include a number of codicils. As she lay unconscious, on her deathbed some took the opportunity to seal the codicils, thereby assuring their validity. Over half of her estate became encumbered and was assigned to nonfamily members, an illegal condition under the provisions of *Lex Falcidia.*

The bequests grew into a contentious issue. Marcus Cornelius Fronto, orator, former tutor, and close friend of Marcus Aurelius, sought a solution. He expressed particular concern about the jewels, especially Matidia's valuable pearls. Faustina, the emperor's wife, refused to buy the pearls or any of the other jewelry. Fronto surmised that she feared being accused of buying them cheaply. Finally, Aurelius washed his hands of the matter and turned over the problem of the will and jewels to his co-emperor, Lucius Verus.

Sources

Fronto. *Epistulae* pp. 95–99.
Birley, Anthony Richard. *Marcus Aurelius: Emperor of Rome.* Boston: Little, Brown, 1966, pp. 132, 241.

Melania the Elder

(c. 340–c. 410 C.E.)
Roman: Spain, Italy, Egypt, Palestine
ascetic

Melania lived a varied and rich life. She was an intellectually and physically fearless woman who risked her life and her honor for what she believed. Fully engaged, she left her mark on everyone she met. Melania lived at the forefront of the emerging Christian ascetic movement in the fourth century. She embraced the ascetic life with enormous gusto, relishing the deprivation of bathing and the luxurious living she abandoned. She also eschewed a life of solitary confinement or a communal life with only virgin women and widows and traveled widely, mingling with leading thinkers and religious figures. Although she was a great admirer of Origen, she did not attack those who held orthodox opinions contrary to her own. Melania was more interested in converting pagans to Christianity than splitting the church with heresies.

Melania was the granddaughter of Antonius Marcellinus, consul in 341. The name of her husband remains unknown. Born in Spain, at 14 years old she married and soon moved to Rome. Eight years later when she was 22, her husband and two of her three sons died of the same illness. In November 372, she left her remaining son, Valerius Publicola, in Rome, took all her movable goods, and sailed to Alexandria where she sold everything and became an ascetic.

Not unexpectedly her relatives, possibly on both sides of the family, were furious. She had carried away a part of the family wealth, while they were probably jockeying for position to gain control over the young widow and the money. In a social and economic environment where inheritance was one of the principal roads to wealth, her usurpation of the movable goods and their subsequent sale diminished the total wealth available to everyone connected with her. Nor was the fourth century a time when new assets were easily created. The Goths were threatening Italy and the Vandals Spain. Scarcely a generation later, Rome fell to Alaric and Spain to the Vandals.

Leaving aside some suspicion that Melania left Rome precipitously to avoid the family using their influence either to stop her or establish claim to her wealth, she was possibly a cannier woman of business than has been thought. Alexandria was a good destination. It was a major trading center and well equipped for buying and selling objects, including gold or silver. Alexandria had another attraction. It was at the edge of the desert, where the new ascetic movement was burgeoning. From the perspective of economics as well as her future religious life, Melania may have seen more advantage in sailing for Egypt than defending her wealth in court against her family in Italy.

Melania possessed vast income-producing estates in Italy, Spain, Africa, Gaul, and Britain. As a widow, she probably had absolute control over the portion of her family's properties that she inherited or that had been her dowry. If she was regent for her son, she also probably held legal control over the inheritance that would be his on attaining his majority. Her annual income would be the sum of these properties, including the profit from slave workshops, whatever monies she had that were loaned out, or in modern terms, invested in operations she did not necessarily own but financed, as well as income from urban properties with rentals for shops and apartments. If she were more speculative, she might also have had an interest in mines and even the risk capital pools established for shipping.

Before and after arriving in Alexandria, Melania provided amply for her son. She also sold estates in Italy, Spain, Africa, and Gaul and used the income for charitable and religious purposes. Her distribution of funds to the poor may have further encouraged some of her family to seek control over her inheritance. From their perspective, simply to give money away outside of the family or to those distantly connected with the family would be evidence of an inability to manage affairs.

Melania saw a different world. Wealth was the weight that held her earthbound when she wanted to soar. She adopted a personally severe lifestyle. She wore the coarsest clothing, ate the simplest food sparingly, fasted, and eschewed all other comforts. When she was 60, she boasted that over the past decades she had washed only her fingertips and had never been transported in a litter or slept in a bed. The chronicler Palladius and her cousin, Paulinus of Nola, praised her masculine qualities; they found it difficult to believe a woman could endure such an ascetic life. However, her asceticism was neither male nor female, it rested on the irrelevance of bodily comfort to the joy of her discovery of the spiritual self.

Melania traveled from Alexandria to Mount Nitria in the Egyptian desert where she spent about six months. She met with monks of renown, including Dioscorus, bishop of Hermopolis, Isidore the Confessor, and four monks known as the Tall Brothers. Many of those she met had been banished for their orthodoxy by the Arian bishop of Alexandria. Melania used her own money to supply their needs, and since they were without serving women, in the evenings she served them herself. The Roman consul of Palestine unknowingly imprisoned her, finding her in the company of the banished man, and sought a bribe for her release. Indignant, Melania reverted to her posture of proud and arrogant Roman and informed him of her illustrious background. He apologized and released her.

In 375, many of the orthodox in exile were allowed to return and Melania went to Jerusalem where she lived for 27 years. She still had enough funds for building projects and charity. When her funds were unavailable or insufficient, however, she had no hesitation about soliciting more from family and friends, including the son she left behind. In 379, she built a monastery that brought 50 widows and young women virgins together in communal life. It became a stopping place for innumerable bishops, monks, other church officials, and male and female visitors who came on pilgrimage to Jerusalem. The elder PAULA and Jerome, who were among her visitors, received information that helped them establish their own communities on the Mount of Olives.

Melania read widely and was attracted to the works of the Christian thinker Origen. Nor did she read casually: She studied the texts and was committed to the distribution of Christian ideas and learning through the written word. Tyranius Rufinus of Aquileia, a translator of the works of Origen, whom she had met in the Egyptian desert, joined her Jerusalem. They distributed money to churches, monasteries, prisoners, and refugees, as well as providing shelters for travelers for some 18 years. Melania also built him a monastery for men on the Mount of Olives in which he trained monks as copyists.

Melania's religious beliefs were tinged with Origenism, which deviated from strict orthodoxy. Her generosity of spirit found an echo in Origen. Not only did he offer everyone the promise of ultimate salvation, but his position also promised women an end of the burden of Eve's sin. Not surprisingly, Melania also sought to moderate conflicts over doctrine among the bishops, although on more than one occasion she participated in the defense of her beliefs and of those in whom she believed. In 394, bitter controversy broke out when Epiphanius, the bishop of Salamis in Cyprus, attacked Origen in a sermon that he preached while visiting Jerusalem. The contretemps, related by Jerome, lasted at least three years and grew increasingly complicated. It became almost farcelike, with an unwilling ordination and a secret intercepted letter. After several appeals to authority, Melania and Rufinus helped smooth both sides, and a peaceful compromise became possible.

The late fourth century was followed by even more difficult times. Word reached Melania in Jerusalem that the writings of Origen were under attack in Rome and that her granddaughter and husband, the younger MELANIA and Pinianus, were faced with family opposition about adopting an ascetic life and selling their estates. She hastened to Rome, traveling as far as Italy with her friend Rufinus who later met up with her in Rome. It was sometime in 402 when Melania landed in Naples where her family waited, including her son Public-

ola and his wife, the younger ALBINA, and the younger Melania and Pinianus. They visited Paulinus of Nola, who lived nearby, before proceeding on to Rome. He remarked on the sight of Melania wearing simple garments and sitting on a tiny thin horse smaller than a donkey, accompanied by the decorated horses and litters with gilded side-cloths shielding wealthy women dressed in silk clothing.

She lived with her family in Rome for several years during which she encouraged the younger Melania and her husband toward an increasingly ascetic lifestyle. She also acted as an intermediary with their parents and extended families in discussions about their life choices.

The interpretation of the works of Origen reached a critical eruption during this period that turned Jerome, who had long been a friend, visitor, and admirer of Melania, into a lifelong enemy. Origen had developed a Christian Neoplatonism which integrated the pagan philosophy with Christian faith. The doctrine presented many with an appealing union. He also established a hierarchy that had a satisfying clarity. God was supreme. Christ the son was a second God, ranked below the father and embodying *logos* (wisdom). The Holy Spirit was within the Saints, which ranked below Christ but a cut above everyone else. Eventually everyone created by God would be redeemed, including the devil. Free will allowed choice but it precluded the permanent choice of evil.

Some began to call Origenism a heresy. Jerome, who once had been an admirer and had translated some of Origen's work from Greek into Latin, now distanced himself from his earlier praise. When Rufinus published a translation of one of Origen's works in which he repeated in the preface some admiring words that Jerome had once written, Jerome became incensed and broke off relations with Rufinus and Melania, who strongly supported her partner. He never forgave her, and, after her death, Jerome referred to her as perfidious and would not even mention her name.

His attack on Melania was a sophistic exercise and disproportionate to the circumstances. Over many years Melania had freely given of herself and her wealth. Jerome had accepted her largesse and praised her goodness. In a letter to ASELLA, written in 385, he praised her behavior after the tragic deaths of her husband and two children. In another letter he again praised her, this time for her moderation, since she neither had rent her clothes nor cried out and unbound her hair, but tearless when faced with tragedy, vowed to serve Christ. To some degree, however, Melania prevailed. The younger Melania and Pinianus retained their friendship with Rufinus, Palladius, and Paulinus of Nola, all of whom were Origenists in Jerome's eyes.

It is not clear when Melania left Rome, although it was probably before 406 since her son was still alive and he was known to have died by the end of the year. Possibly her business acumen once more served her well. At some point she went to Sicily, where she sold her remaining property. It was none too soon, since by 408 Alaric and his Goths were at the gates of Rome. She was in Africa when she received word of her son's death in 406. She returned to Jerusalem, disbursed the rest of her money, and died in 410.

Sources

Jerome. Letter XXX 9; XLV 4, CXXXIII 3.

Palladius. *The Lausiac History* XLVI, LIV 54.

Paulinus of Nola. *Letter* 29.

Clark, Elizabeth A. "The Lady Vanishes: Dilemmas of a Feminist Historian after the Linguistic Turn." *Church History* 67, no. 1 (March 1998): 14–31.

Prosopography of the Later Roman Empire. Vol. I. Edited by A. H. M. Jones, J. R. Martindale, and J. Morris. Cambridge: Cambridge University Press, 1971. Reprinted 1992, pp. 592–593.

▣ Melania the Younger

(c. 383–December 31, 439 C.E.)
Roman: Rome, Sicily, Africa, Palestine
ascetic

Melania admired her grandmother, the elder MELANIA, and at very early age determined to live a life patterned on hers. Her grandmother was not an easy woman to emulate. She lived life with gusto, although a Christian ascetic. She flaunted custom, although when necessary she behaved as an arrogant Roman aristocrat, and she used her

wealth to fund her causes, despite the pleas of her family. The younger Melania, however, was successful in her quest. Using tragedy and opportunity to her advantage, she lived in a chaste marriage, confounded custom, traveled widely, studied Christian texts, and played an active role in the extraordinary happenings of her times.

Melania came from a mixed Christian/pagan family, which was not uncommon among the Roman aristocracy of the time. Melania's father was Valerius Publicola, the sole surviving child of the elder Melania. Her mother, the younger ALBINA, was a devout Christian and member of the patrician Caeionii clan that was a political and economic force in Rome. Melania's grandfather, Ceionius Rufinus Albinus, had been prefect of Rome from 389–391. He may have been pagan, and her uncle, the eminent Rufius Volusianus, converted to Christianity on his deathbed.

In 397, at age 14, Melania married the 17-year-old Pinianus. His views on the marriage are unknown, but she was not happy. Although an extremely suitable match that brought together two young people from similar backgrounds, Melania did not want to marry. It was unlikely that her parents forced her into marriage and in fact was not legally possible. Rather, she was young, and, it was probable that, despite her pleas to remain unmarried and live an ascetic life, her family offered many reasonable arguments about the suitability of the match, the importance of the union for the future of both families, and the assurance that she would find her life as a married woman and mother rich and fulfilling.

Melania gave birth to a girl and then a boy. Both died. There must have been enormous anticipation and great sadness. The children's deaths confirmed Melania's belief that her destiny was to follow in the path of her grandmother. She implored her husband to allow her to live the chaste life that she so ardently desired. She offered to honor and follow him if he would choose an ascetic life and practice chastity in their marriage. If this was not his choice, however, she offered him his freedom and the dowry she had brought with her. She argued with her resistant husband passionately that had God wished them to have children, the children would not have died. Pinianus could not long withstand the despair that affected her health.

Melania's parents, especially her father, argued against their adoption of celibacy. Nor was the young couple's decision approved by other relatives, friends, and associated peers. Melania was an only child, and their decision effectively ended the family line, which had an illustrious history of consuls and praetorian prefects. Pinianus's brother Valerius was incensed at their intention to devote their wealth to the poor. The times were not good, and perhaps he viewed the couple's generosity as a wanton dissipation of the family assets to people they neither knew nor for whom they held any obligations or responsibilities. Insofar as family wealth was corporate, regardless of who held the legal title in any one generation, the wealth could be understood as belonging as much to Valerius and Valerius's children as to Pinianus and his.

As it happened, Melania and Pinianus were not yet 25. They could choose celibacy, but they were below the minimum age to divest family property under their own authority. Her father, and reluctantly her mother, instituted a suit to stop attempts to liquidate or donate family property. They had the support of the extended families, whose conflicting loyalties and contentious relationships were subsumed to the collective interest in maintaining the combined families' wealth.

Melania and Pinianus were not deterred. They evolved a gradualist approach. Melania wore plain coarse garments. She transformed her silk robes into coverings for church altars and adapted other garments for use as religious ornamentation. She also increased her periods of fasting. Her husband, who found it more difficult to adopt an ascetic life, adopted coarse garments following Melania's lead and pressure. Together they visited the sick and poor, as well as prisoners and those working in mines. They also welcomed travelers into their house.

Melania's grandmother, who had lived in Jerusalem for the past 27 years, heard about the couple's efforts to lead an ascetic life and to withstand family opposition. The news came at about the same time as controversy over the possibly hereti-

cal nature of the Christian thinker Origen's work surfaced in Rome. The elder Melania had long been attracted to Origen's work, and her close companion in Jerusalem was Tyrannius Rufinus of Aquileia, the foremost translator of Origen from Greek to Latin. The elder Melania decided the time had come to return to Rome. In Italy she was welcomed by the whole family—her son, Publicola, and daughter-in-law, the younger Albina, and her granddaughter, the younger Melania and her granddaughter's husband, Pinianus. They traveled to Rome where the elder Melania stayed with the family until her return to Africa sometime before Publicola's death in 406. While in Rome, the elder Melania strengthened the young couple's resolve and also urged her son and daughter-in-law to moderate their opposition. Publicola relented just before his death and gave his support to the young couple. After his death, the widowed Albina, who was always a reluctant opponent, joined her daughter in a celibate life.

Melania, Pinianus, and Albina moved out of their palatial residence to a more modest villa on the Appian Way. However, they were still threatened with suits from their extended families. The Roman elite were relatively few in number and the city small. The networks of relationship among the two extended families dominated the Senate and the courts in the city. The couple appealed directly to the emperor through SERENA in whose household the young emperor Honorius had grown up. No doubt Melania and her husband, as well as Albina, had on occasion found themselves in the same company as Serena. She too was a Christian and, even though the politics of the senatorial elite were often in opposition, sometimes deadly opposition, with the emperor, in many instances they shared class interests. In fact, Pinianus had offered to sell Serena the palatial house from which he had only recently moved with Melania and his mother-in-law.

Serena secured from the emperor the necessary authority to liquidate family estates. The emperor allowed them to dispose of their property throughout the empire and also ordered the governors and prefects of the provinces in which they held estates to sell the properties for them and remit the proceeds directly to them. It was all that the couple needed. It not only gave them full authority, but also eliminated the possibility that they or an agent would have to personally travel to the provinces, finalize the transfers, and arrange for the payment transfers. They began the liquidation of their discretionary assets and the sale of estates immediately. It was a complicated task. The two together were probably among the richest Romans with an annual income estimated by the ancient author and contemporary Gerontius as approximately 120,000 pieces of gold, which would have a probable equivalency of about 1,666 pounds of gold in modern terms. One estate, near Rome, included a palatial villa and 62 settlements, each inhabited by some 400 slaves. In all, Melania freed 8,000 slaves in Rome. Others threatened revolt and refused to be sold. Those she gave to Pinianus's brother for three coins. In addition to Italian estates in Campania, they also had properties in Sicily, Africa, Spain, Britain, Gaul, and North Africa, all of which were income producing and mostly profitable.

They distributed their movable goods to the poor. They gave some 100,000 coins through various emissaries to be spent on charitable enterprises. Additionally, Melania sent 10,000 pieces of gold and silver to Egypt and adjacent provinces, 10,000 pieces of gold to churches on various islands, 10,000 to Antioch and vicinity, and 15,000 to Palestine. She also made large donations to a variety of places in the West.

Melania was perhaps as astute a businesswoman as her grandmother. In 408–409, along with her husband and mother, she left for Sicily, having held on to their properties in Sicily, Spain, and Africa. They had sold out as the Italian political situation rapidly deteriorated. Alaric and his army of Goths were en route to Rome, Stilicho had been executed by Honorius, and their protector, Serena, had been strangled by orders of the Roman Senate. The pagan prefect of Rome, with the approval of the Senate, decided to confiscate Melania and Pinianus's remaining property in the city. Although the prefect was killed before he could execute the order, destruction by the Goths two years later resulted in the loss of any unsold property.

Their trip to Sicily was eventful. Blown off course to an island where the inhabitants of the city were being held for ransom, they paid 2,500 gold coins toward the sum demanded by the attackers, along with an extra 500 gold coins and provisions to relieve the dire situation within the city. In Sicily, Melania and Albina lived with some 60 free or freedwomen, of whom some were her own former slaves. Pinianus lived with 30 men. He spent his time reading, gardening, and holding conferences with visiting holy men. They also continued to liquidate property and sold most of their estates in Numidia and Mauritania but retained those in Spain, where invasions had temporarily overwhelmed the land market.

In 410, as Alaric invaded Rome, the couple left Sicily for North Africa and their estates at Thagaste, not far from Carthage, in the bishopric of Alypius, renowned for his knowledge of the scriptures. Nearby was Hippo and the bishop Augustine whom they were also eager to meet. As with many of their properties, the estate at Thagaste was larger than the nearby city. In addition to the central villa and outbuildings, it housed a resident population of freed and enslaved workers, including craftsmen expert in working gold, silver, and copper. Soon after their arrival, Melania, Pinianus, and Albina visited Hippo. Their wealth and generosity excited the community who filled the church. The congregation demanded that Augustine ordain Pinianus, which they believed would commit him to a donation. Augustine refused unless Pinianus consented and added that he would leave his post of bishop rather than engage in a forced ordination. When the congregation became unruly, Melania and her mother felt physically threatened. The three returned to Thagaste unhappy and angry.

Pinianus sent a message to Augustine threatening to leave Africa if he were ordained against his will. A compromise was reached. Pinianus agreed to reside in Hippo, should he decide to be ordained. Alypius, who had the interests of his own bishopric to contend with, refused to join Augustine in the compromise. There was further negotiation, and in the end Melania demanded that Augustine not sign the compromise agreement. Augustine, however, wrote Albina a long letter in which he explained, if not justified, the behavior of the congregation as well as his own ambiguities about the need to seek support from wealthy Christians for the benefit of the church and the poor.

Poverty and heresy consumed Augustine's time. The area of Thagaste and Hippo were poor. Although still untouched by the Goths, the agricultural and urban infrastructure had been declining for several generations. Independent landowners had all but disappeared, and land had devolved into estates like that owned by Melania and Pinianus, who, until the capture of Rome in 410, had largely been absentee landlords. Not only was poverty rife, but there was no Christian unity. The Donatist church was everywhere. Donatism arose in the Diocletian persecutions at the end of the third century when passionate Christians willingly suffered and even died for their faith. The successors of these passionate Christians became a sect with ordained bishops and churches. Their adherents maintained a strong appeal among the poor and championed independence from imperial authority. Efforts at reconciliation with the mainstream orthodox community were rebuffed or botched. Donatists dominated in many of the places around Carthage, and Augustine's opposition notwithstanding, they were sufficiently forceful that before Melania and Pinianus donated their estate at Thagaste to the traditional orthodox church, they also established two bishops on the property, one orthodox and the second Donatist.

Melania, Pinianus, and Albina remained at Thagaste for approximately four years. They built two large monasteries, one for women and the other for men. Urged by Alypius, Augustine, and the bishop of Carthage, they also endowed them. In the women's monastery Melania and Albina lived with 130 virgin women and widows, and Pinianus lived with 80 men. During their stay, Melania became more rigorous in her asceticism and began longer fasts accompanied with repeated readings of the Latin and Greek scriptures. She also directed the women residents, who followed a strict regimen of deportment and prayers.

In 414, disregarding the compromise oath by Pinianus, they left Thagaste, never to return. On their way to Jerusalem, they stopped in Alexandria, where they were welcomed by Cyril, the bishop of the city. After their arrival in Jerusalem in 417, Melania and Albina lived together in cells for pilgrims attached to the Church of the Holy Sepulcher. They sold their remaining property in Spain and used the money to travel back to Egypt and visit the ascetics who lived in the desert. Following in the footsteps of her grandmother, they went into the mountains of Nitria and distributed money everywhere.

Upon return to Jerusalem, Melania shut herself away in a small cell made of wood on the Mount of Olives that she had earlier asked her mother to prepare. There she stayed each year from January through Easter for 14 years, rarely seeing anyone except her mother and husband. The rest of the year, she lived in Jerusalem with her mother, until she had a monastery constructed where she stayed for some 11 years with women selected by Pinianus. The monastery had its own cistern and oratory for prayers. Reminiscent of the younger MACRINA, Melania chose not to direct the institution but devoted herself to teaching and providing the example of a holy life.

In 432, Pinianus died and Melania retreated to a solitary life. After some four years, she built a monastery for ascetic men by securing funds from an anonymous donor. In 436, her uncle Rufius Volusianus notified her by letter that he was going to Constantinople to assist in the marriage arrangements of LICINIA EUDOXIA, the daughter of the Augusta AELIA EUDOCIA, to the emperor in the West, Valentinian III. Melania set off for Constantinople ostensibly to convert her pagan uncle to Christianity. The overland trip of some 1,200 miles on animals provided by the state took approximately 40 days.

On her arrival, she found Volusianus seriously ill. Fearful he would die unbaptized, she threatened to tell the emperor about his condition. She also sent for Proclus, the bishop of Constantinople, who convinced him to accept baptism. Volusianus died in January 437, with Melania at his bedside.

Melania remained in Constantinople and mourned her uncle's death for 40 days. She became an intimate of Aelia Eudocia, who was delighted with her renowned holy visitor. Eudocia expressed her desire to make a pilgrimage to Palestine. Eudocia's daughter had married and left to live in Ravenna, and she felt a growing estrangement from Theodosius. Melania convinced the emperor that a trip for Eudocia was an ideal arrangement for everyone.

Melania left for Jerusalem in February 437, on an arduous journey in which the travelers encountered heavy snow and extreme cold but reached the city in time to celebrate Easter. She had a small martyrion built on the Mount of Olives to house the bones of Saint Stephen. Word arrived that Eudocia was arriving in Palestine, and Melania went to meet her at Sidon on the coast. Eudocia announced that she had come to pray at the Holy Places and to see her "mother" Melania. When Eudocia left the city, Melania escorted her as far as Caeserea. Melania knew her death was near and went to celebrate the Nativity in Bethlehem, after bidding farewell to the women and men in her monastery. She died on December 31, 439.

Sources

Augustine. *Letters* CXXIV, CXXV, CXXVI.

Gerontius. *The Life of Melania the Younger.* Introduction, translation and commentary by Elizabeth A. Clark. New York: The Edwin Mellon Press, 1984.

Palladius. *The Lausiac History* 54, 61.

Socrates. *Historia Ecclesiastica* VII. 47.

Brown, Peter. *Augustine of Hippo: A Biography.* Berkeley: University of California Press, 1967, 2000, index.

Clark, Elizabeth A. "The Lady Vanishes: Dilemmas," pp. 14–31.

Jones, A. H. M. *The Later Roman Empire,* 284–602 Vol. II, p. 787.

O'Donnell, James J. *Augustine: a New Biography.* New York: HarperCollins, 2005, index.

▣ Melinno

(second century B.C.E.)   Greek: Italy
poet

Melinno was a Greek poet who wrote in a Doric dialect most probably during the first half of the second century B.C.E. Possibly she lived in one of the Greek cities in southern Italy, all of which came under Roman control after the defeat of Pyrrhus in the middle of the third century.

She composed a hymn to the power of Rome in five Sapphic stanzas. In it she depicted warlike Rome, the conqueror of the world, as a goddess who was the daughter of Ares, father of the Amazons. Nothing is known about her personal life.

Sources

Bowra, C. M. "Melinno's Hymn to Rome," *Journal of Roman History* 47 (1957) pp. 21–28.

Oxford Classical Dictionary, ed. by Simon Hornblower and Antony Spawforth. 3d. ed. New York: Oxford University Press, 1996, p. 953.

▣ Melissa

(late seventh century B.C.E.)   Greek: Greece
murder victim

Melissa was the daughter of Proclus, the ruler of Epidaurus in Greece. She married Periander, the tyrant of Corinth. He fell in love with her after seeing her body revealed through her dress while she was pouring wine for workmen in a field. He murdered her in a fit of jealously and in despair made love to her dead body.

Periander sent a messenger to Thesprotia to consult the oracle of the dead on Acheron, presumed to be the entrance to Hades. He sought the whereabouts of a pledge given to him by a stranger. Melissa was said to have appeared and refused to reveal information about the pledge. She claimed to be cold in the clothing with which she was buried that had not been burned. As proof of who she was, she sent a message to Periander revealing knowledge that he had had sex with her dead body.

Periander ordered all the married women of Corinth, including slaves, to go to the temple of Hera and remove their clothing. The garments were then burned in a pit while he called out the name of Melissa. He then sent a second messenger to the oracle, and Melissa's ghost was assuaged.

Sources

Athenaeus. *Deipnosophistae* 589 ff.

Herodotus. *The Persian Wars* 3.50; 5.92.

Blundell, Sue. *Women in Ancient Greece*. London: British Museum Press, 1995, p. 68.

Pomeroy, Sarah B. *Goddesses, Whores, Wives, and Slaves: Women in Classical Antiquity*. New York: Schocken Books, 1975, p. 35.

▣ Messallina, Valeria

(c. 20–48 C.E.)   Roman: Rome
power broker

Valeria Messallina died condemned and notorious. Smart, beautiful, arrogant, ruthless, even cruel, and certainly seductive, she sought to secure her position in the face of a disapproving Senate and a powerful group of imperial freedmen who dominated the reign of her husband, the emperor Claudius. Her parents DOMITIA LEPIDA and Messalla Barbatus linked her with the greatest houses of the old republic, and on both sides she was a Julian, a descendant of OCTAVIA (2) and a descendant of the emperor Augustus. Messallina was somewhere between 14 and 20 years old in 38 or 39 C.E. when she married the 48-year-old Claudius, after he divorced his second wife, AELIA PAETINA. In a society that prized above all men's military prowess and idealized the male body, the young and beautiful Messallina's future was linked with her far-from-ideal second cousin who since birth had suffered from a form of palsy that affected his walk and caused a speech impairment.

Claudius had not been expected to become emperor. The many legitimate candidates seemed to assure that there would be no problems of succession after the death of his uncle Tiberius. Claudius's physical condition was perceived as an unalterable barrier by Augustus, his grandmother LIVIA DRUSILLA, and Tiberius. Livia persuaded her husband to consult with Tiberius as to the part Claudius should play in public life. A decision was made to carefully circumscribe his public appearances so as to protect Claudius and themselves from possible ridicule. One by one, however, possible successors to Tiberius died, leaving only the young Gaius Caligula and the infant Nero. Caligula succeeded Tiberius, but after Caligula was murdered, the unanticipated happened. Amid the general disorder and looting, Claudius was found by a soldier hiding in the palace in fear for his life. He was taken to the praetorian camp and declared emperor by the Praetorian Guard, even as the Senate sat in debate over the restoration of the republic.

Claudius became emperor in January 41, three years after his marriage with Messallina. They already had a daughter, Claudia OCTAVIA, and Messallina was some seven or eight months' pregnant with a son, Britannicus. In an uncertain world, the less-than-perfect Claudius and Messallina were raised to power by the troops and the myths of their lineage, but without the support of many, if not most, of the Senate. Claudius ruled through a small and increasingly powerful clique of freedmen—Narcissus, Polybius, Pallas, and Callistus. In concert with her husband and alone, Messallina used these men to rid herself of real or perceived threats to herself, her son, and her husband. To this end she also used the skillful politician Lucius Vitellius, a man from the equestrian order and a close confidant of Claudius, and Publius Suillius Rufus, a senator with a reputation as a ruthless prosecutor.

Danger to Claudius and Messallina came from many sides, most especially from those who could also claim the legitimate mantle of the Julio-Claudian family. JULIA LIVILLA was the sister of the murdered Caligula, a child of the elder AGRIPPINA. Like Messallina, she could claim descent from Octavia. She had been exiled by her brother Caligula for adultery. Julia Livilla's husband Marcus Vinicius had offered himself as a possible candidate to succeed Caligula after the latter's murder. One of his claims was the lineage of his wife. Although Claudius allowed her to return to Rome in 41 C.E., Julia Livilla was accused of adultery and again exiled. This time, she was also killed. Her alleged lover, Lucius Annaeus Seneca, a well-known orator and writer, was also exiled.

Gaius Appius Junius Silanus, consul in 28 C.E., was the descendant of several august republican houses, a popular leader of soldiers, and a favorite with the Senate. He was governor of Hispania Tarraconensis when Claudius recalled him to Rome in

41. Removed from immediate access to an army and the rights of *imperium,* he appeared less of a direct threat. Claudius honored him and arranged that he and Domitia Lepida marry. Domitia, Messallina's mother, was no less a contender for power than her daughter. Widowed, her marriage to Silanus was mutually advantageous. He gained a direct connection to the imperial family, and she, a husband of high repute.

By the following year, the effort to integrate Silanus into the imperial family and regime had failed. Charged with plotting to kill the emperor, he was executed without trial on Claudius's orders. The tale of his condemnation reads like a French farce and reflects poorly on Claudius, Narcissus, and Messallina. Supposedly, Narcissus broke into Claudius's bedroom before daybreak to inform the emperor that he had had a dream in which Silanus had attacked Claudius. Messallina appeared immediately and told Claudius that she had had a similar dream. The two of them had previously arranged for Silanus to come to the emperor's bedchamber. When he arrived, Claudius thought he was forcing his way into his room to assassinate him and ordered him executed. Whatever the reasons—Messallina may well have suspected Silanus's loyalty—by siding with the freedman she violated the code of kin and class, angering her mother. Like her daughter, Domitia Lepida was beautiful, arrogant, wealthy, and accustomed to power. She was also more politically astute than Messallina. Her mother was an ally Messallina could ill afford to lose, both for her political connections and for the advice she might have given over the years that followed.

The death of Silanus sparked an abortive revolution by the Senate in 42. Since the death of Tiberius, tension between the emperor and the Senate had heightened. The senators were led in Rome by Lucius Annius Vinicianus, who had been involved in a plot against Caligula, and Lucius Arruntius Camillus Scribonianus, consul in 32 and now the governor of Dalmatia with an army under his command. Arruntius called on Claudius to resign. The soldiers, however, did not back him, and the revolt ended four days later. The leaders committed suicide. Messallina, Claudius, and his loyal freedmen had others executed. The sources claim that the victors were merciless and included men and women among the condemned. The numbers of condemned, however, suggest no more bloody an end than was traditional, and in fact less extreme than some earlier proscriptions.

For the already suspicious Claudius and Messallina, the revolt strengthened their focus on possible plots. They found evidence of intrigue everywhere. In 43 Suillius Rufus accused JULIA (8), the wife of Rubelius Blandus and the daughter of Livia Julia Claudia LIVILLA and Tiberius's son Drusus Julius Caesar, of immoral conduct. She was found guilty and killed. The climate of suspicion increased the imperial reliance on freedmen, further infuriated the elite, and fed popular gossip with tales of imperial excess, especially about Messallina.

As in all of Roman history, the gossip about women focused on sexual promiscuity, and Messallina was a perfect subject. Beautiful, young, and seductive, she had no hesitation in using her charms for her own interests. It was not hard for whispers to suggest that she had had sex with 25 men in 24 hours and that she had used false names to entertain men in brothels. The tales about Messallina's sexual misconduct steadily expanded in number and outrageousness. There were accounts of her forcing innocent wives and daughters into sex games in the imperial household while being watched by their loving and distraught husbands and brothers.

Nor was Claudius exempt from sexual attacks. Messallina was accused of supplying him with women and of assuring her own safety from his anger by exciting his appetites. The link between sex and blood, never far separated in Roman prurient literature, placed a long list of killings at the door of Messallina, with and without the aid of Claudius and the imperial freedmen. Messallina was said to have had the prefect of the Praetorian Guard, Catonius Justus, killed before he could reveal her sexual misconduct to Claudius. In 46 C. E., when Marcus Vinicius, the husband of Agrippina's daughter Julia Livilla, died and was given a state funeral, Messallina was said to have poisoned him because he refused to succumb to her charms and might have sought vengeance for the earlier death of his wife.

Later in 46 or early 47, the death of Gnaeus Pompeius Magnus, bearer of a great republican name, had serious political overtones. He was the husband of ANTONIA (4), the daughter of Claudius and his divorced second wife AELIA PAETINA. Messallina was said to have wanted him killed to prevent any possible future son who would present an alternative in succession to her son Britannicus. The sources attributed his death, however, to Claudius, not Messallina, and add that Claudius also killed some 35 senators and more than 300 equestrians. Among these were Pompeius's parents, Marcus Lucinius Crassus Frugi and Scribonia. Their two younger sons were exiled. After the bloodbath, Antonia was married to an unthreatening husband, Faustus Cornelius Sulla Felix, the half brother of Messallina.

Messallina was said to have arranged the death of Claudius's freedman Polybius for his opposition to further purges by Messallina, particularly that of Decimus Valerius Asiaticus. Polybius's death in 46 marked the first break in solidarity between Messallina and the powerful freedmen clique. Without the support of the senators, and handicapped by her image of sexual promiscuity, sowing uncertainty among the freedmen would prove a fatal error for Messallina, but not before the successful prosecution of Decimus Valerius Asiaticus.

In 47 Asiaticus was accused of adultery with POPPAEA SABINA (1) and of bribery of the troops. Asiaticus, consul in 35 and 46 C.E., was a native of Vienne, a city on the Rhone in Gaul. He was immensely wealthy and proud and lived in great splendor. He owned the famous gardens of Lucullus, which had belonged to Lucius Licinius Lucullus in the republican era. The package of accusations against him, attributed to Messallina, mixed the trivial and banal with the threat of revolt. Messallina was said to have wanted Asiaticus's gardens. She implicated Poppaea, an extremely beautiful, wealthy, and independent-minded woman whom she believed to be his lover and knew to be a rival for the attention of Mnester, a well-known actor of the day. Messallina used Publius Suillius Rufus to

lodge the charge of adultery while her son's tutor, Sosibius, told Claudius that Asiaticus was about to travel to Germany where he planned to foment trouble among the troops.

In a tale reminiscent of the earlier condemnation of Silanus, on orders of Claudius, Asiaticus was brought to the palace in chains from the city of Baiae, a fashionable resort on an inlet of the Bay of Naples. At an informal hearing in the emperor's bedchamber with Messallina present, Suillius presented the charges that Asiaticus had corrupted the military and committed adultery with Poppaea. The sources record that Asiaticus's defense moved the listeners to tears. Nonetheless, Messallina instructed Lucius Vitellius, consul in 34, 43, and 47, that Asiaticus was to be indicted. When Claudius asked Vitellius whether Asiaticus should be acquitted, Vitellius, after praising the latter's past service, proposed suicide. Asiaticus committed suicide, and Messallina forced Poppaea Sabina to kill herself rather than face imprisonment.

Asiaticus had been among the key instigators in the destruction of Caligula, and he had put his name forward as a possible replacement. His enormous wealth and influence in Gaul could well have been used to influence and aid forces opposed to Claudius. Desire for the gardens of Lucullus or jealousy over Mnester, even if true, could in this case have covered the ongoing fear of conspiracy that marked Claudius's and Messallina's reign. However, the death of an exconsul without a trial aroused further resentment among senators and others opposed to Messallina and Claudius. Conversely, it further pushed Messallina's and Claudius' dependence on the imperial freedmen.

In 48 Messallina fatally mistook the degree of support she had among the clique of freedmen. She fell in love with Gaius Silius, a senator and one of the most handsome men in Rome. Silius was already married to JUNIA SILANA. Messallina persuaded him to divorce her. She appeared everywhere in public with Silius, openly showed her infatuation, and showered him with gifts from the imperial household. It was a dangerous situation, in part because Claudius was rapidly aging, and once more talk of succession was in the air.

Silius personified the kind of senator that Claudius and the imperial freedmen had most often feared and killed. Possibly, he may have already begun to array the forces in the Senate that needed only support from Messallina to change the advisers around the emperor and the tone of his reign. The powerful freedmen probably sensed the potential of Silius and Messallina's partnership. For Messalina's part, in the face of an increasingly debilitated Claudius, whose health and susceptibility to youthful female charms were an apparent danger, there was more to be said for an alliance with Silius, who was her contemporary, than with Claudius and the freedmen, especially after Silius promised to adopt her son Britannicus. Ardor overbalanced caution. With Claudius in Ostia, she and Silius sealed their bargain and acted out a marriage ceremony, without any attempt at concealment.

Her allies among the freedmen deserted her. Narcissus persuaded Callistus and Pallas that action had to be taken to destroy Messallina. Silius, consul designate in 48, was young, ambitious, well connected, and a danger to all of them. He would use his influence with Messallina to undermine their positions under Claudius, and if something happened to the emperor, their lives would be in danger. Narcissus took the lead. His position was the most precarious. Lucius Vitellius took a more ambivalent position so that he would emerge unscathed no matter what happened.

The scenario was analogous to one that had been played before. Narcissus had CALPURNIA (2) and CLEOPATRA (4), lovers of Claudius, tell the emperor about the marriage. Narcissus then told him that all of Rome was aware of the wedding and urged Claudius to act before he was deposed by Silius. Claudius gave orders for the couple's apprehension. Narcissus took Claudius to Silius's house to see the valuables Messallina had given him. Fearing that Claudius would still forgive Messallina if she confronted him, Narcissus kept Messallina and their children away from Claudius. He turned aside the Vestal Virgin VIBIDIA, who demanded that Messallina be allowed to defend herself.

On word of what happened, Silius went to the Forum, and Messallina retired to the garden that once had belonged to Asiaticus. Silius offered no defense and was executed along with a number of senators and knights. Domitia Lepida hurried to her daughter's side and told her the only honorable way out was to kill herself. Messallina still felt that she could persuade Claudius to forgive her if she could only see him alone. Narcissus had made it impossible. Messallina tried to stab herself but failed, and she was killed by one of the men sent by Narcissus. Her body was turned over to her mother.

The ultimate irony was that Claudius replaced his wife Messallina with the younger AGRIPPINA, a more ruthless and devious woman than Messallina and surely as intelligent. Agrippina succeeded where Messallina has failed and skillfully maneuvered the elevation of her son Nero to become emperor, perhaps poisoning Claudius to make it possible.

Sources

Dio Cassius. *Roman History* 60.8.4–5, 12.5, 14.1–4, 18.1–4; 61.30.8, 31.1–5.

Juvenal. *Satires* 6.115–32; 10.329–45.

Suetonius. *The Lives of the Caesars:* Claudius 26.2; 27.1; 29.3; 36; 37.2; 39.1.

Tacitus. *Annales* 11.1–5; 12.26–38.

Balsdon, J. P. V. D. *Roman Women.* New York: John Day Comp., 1963, pp. 97–107.

Bauman, Richard A. *Women and Politics in Ancient Rome.* London: Routledge, 1994, index.

Grimal, Pierre. *Love in Ancient Rome.* Trans. by Arthur Train, Jr. New York: Crown Publishers, 1967, pp. 277–288.

Levick, Barbara. *Claudius: The Corruption of Power.* New Haven, Conn.: Yale University Press, 1993, index.

Oxford Classical Dictionary, ed. by Simon Hornblower and Antony Spawforth. 3d. ed. New York: Oxford University Press, 1996, pp. 1,576–1,577.

Pauly, A., G. Wissowa, and W. Kroll. *Real-Encyclopadie D. Classischen Altertumswissenschaft 1893–.* (Germany: multiple publishers) 403.

Syme, Ronald. *The Augustan Aristocracy.* Oxford: Clarendon Press, 1986, index.

▣ Milonia Caesonia

(c. 5–41 C.E.)   Roman: Rome
political player

Milonia Caesonia, born about 5 C.E., joined with her husband, the emperor Gaius Caligula, in the imaginative and extravagant productions that characterized the emperor's last years. Condemned in the sources as promiscuous, she was murdered at the same time as the emperor.

Milonia was the youngest child of VISTILIA, a woman from Umbria, who was notable for having married six men and having borne children with all of them. By the time Milonia married Caligula, she already had three children from a previous marriage. Neither young nor beautiful, she was Caligula's fourth wife. They married about the time she gave birth to a daughter, JULIA DRUSILLA (2). Caligula loved her and was more faithful to her than to any other woman with whom he consorted.

Milonia, dressed in helmet, cloak, and shield, was reputed to have accompanied her husband to review the troops and was said to have sometimes paraded nude among friends. She probably became very wealthy. Caligula appointed her, along with other wealthy individuals, to priesthoods and collected 10 million sesterces from each of them for the honor. On January 24, 41, Caligula, Milonia Caesonia, and their daughter were murdered.

Sources
Dio Cassius. *Roman History* 59.23.7–8; 28.5–7.
Pliny the Elder. *Naturalis Historia* 7.39.
Suetonius. *The Lives of the Caesars:* Gaius Caligula 25.3–4; 59.
Syme, Ronald. "Domitius Corbulo." *Journal of Roman Studies* 60 (1970): p. 31.

▣ Minervina
(third–fourth century C.E.)   Roman: Asia
lover of Constantine

Minervina was the lover of the future emperor Constantine. Their relationship ended when Constantine married Flavia Maxima FAUSTA in 307 C.E. Minervina had a son, Crispus, who grew up in the palace. In a scandal whose details are obscure, Constantine had the 20-year-old Crispus poisoned and his own wife, Fausta, killed in 326.

Sources
Balsdon, J. P. V. D. *Roman Women.* New York: John Day Comp., 1963, p. 167.

▣ Minucia
(?–337 B.C.E.)   Roman: Rome
priestess

Minucia came from a plebeian family that had once been patrician. She was the first plebeian Vestal Virgin, one of the guardians of the sacred flame of Rome in the temple of Vesta in the Forum. In 337 B.C.E. she was convicted of adultery on the testimony of her slave. She suffered the traditional punishment of being buried alive.

Sources
Livy. *From the Founding of the City* 8.15.8.
Bauman, Richard A. *Women and Politics in Ancient Rome.* London: Routledge, 1994, pp. 17, 223, footnote 18.

▣ Monica
(c. 333–387 C.E.)   Roman: Africa, Italy
devout Christian

Monica was a fiercely determined woman. Remembered in history through her son Augustine's portrayal in his *Confessions,* she was a major figure in his life and responsible for his conversion to Christianity. A largely self-educated woman, she moved from her rural upbringing into the elite Christian circles around Ambrose, bishop of Milan.

Monica was born in Thagaste, a North African town on a high plateau some 200 miles from the sea. Even in Monica's childhood the area was in decline. From the third century onward, a combination of rapacious Roman administrators, insurrections, insufficient capital, and, in some years, poor weather conditions had converted an earlier agricultural breadbasket into a land of subsistence farming and borderline poverty. The decline in productivity also spurred the devolution of land ownership into the hands of a few families, who, until after the sack of Rome, largely lived in Italy. When the younger MELANIA, her husband, and mother, ALBINA, left Italy around 410, they went to their estates in Thagaste, which was not far from Hippo, where Augustine had returned from Italy to spend his mature years as bishop.

Monica married Patricius, a small landowner of the kind rapidly disappearing in the province. It was a mixed marriage: Monica was a Christian, her husband a pagan, not an uncommon phenomenon in the mid-fourth century. In addition to Augustine, born when she was 23 in the mid-350s, she may have had two daughters. She also had a second son, Navigius, who was with her and Augustine years later in Italy.

Although neither Monica nor her husband had received more than a rudimentary education, both believed that only education could provide their children with a way out of the agricultural decline they witnessed around them. Education was expensive and it strained the family's finances. At one point, Augustine had to return from Madara, a nearby town, because the family could not cover his school fees. A wealthier relative, Romanianus, took a particular interest in Augustine and provided help. Only the academies in major cities, however, could provide the polished finish to an education. Carthage, the city second to Rome in the western Mediterranean, was the nearest major center to Thagaste and money was found to send Augustine. The neighbors praised Patricius for the sacrifices he made. After her husband's death, Monica provided the funds to finish Augustine's education, and it was arguably Monica who had made the years in Carthage a reality from the beginning.

Her husband was the less sophisticated of the two. And while he was master of the household, Monica was the force that shaped it. She lived with the tension of a hotheaded man whose flaring temper always threatened violence. According to her son, she avoided a confrontation and waited until he was calm to explain her position as reasonable and advantageous in the circumstances. However, in a world where beating women was as common as bread, he never beat her. When asked by other women her secret, she sarcastically replied that marriage was a contract that obliged women to behave like slave girls. She noted that sharp tongues often paid a high price. Raised as a devout orthodox Christian in the rural African tradition that included family meals eaten together at tombs of dead-but-not-forgotten family members and feasts on the Sabbath, she also believed in marital fidelity, although her husband was often unfaithful.

She suffered his infidelities, and at the end of his life, when he became a Christian, he begged her forgiveness, which she gave.

When Augustine returned to Thagaste in 375 to teach literature, Monica forbade him to enter her house. He had embraced Manichaeanism, considered heretical, and hated by both pagans and Christians. A small secret sect that had a burst of popularity in Africa during Augustine's years at Carthage, its doctrine obviated personal guilt and adapted the popular Neoplatonic belief in an incorruptible soul. The doctrine focused on the leading issue of debate at the time—the resolution of the presence of evil with a God that was good. It proposed that the soul, a small portion of a human, was good. All else—desires, rage, sexual impulses, etc.—was evil. The good was essentially passive, while the bad was active. Therefore, acts of goodness had no part in combating evil. However, the incorruptible soul would eventually reject evil, but only through internal struggle. The focus on internal struggle attracted Augustine. For Monica, however, a dream sufficed. She allowed Augustine back into her house after she had dreamed that he would eventually return to orthodox Christianity.

To Monica's great sorrow and consternation, Augustine left Africa for Rome in 382, following the tradition of promising provincials seeking to test themselves at the center of the empire. Monica accompanied him to the port and begged him to return home or else allow her to go with him. Unable to confront her and unwilling to have her accompany him, he sailed secretly. A distraught Monica returned home. After a year, in 384, Augustine was appointed teacher of rhetoric in Milan and shortly thereafter Monica appeared, having traveled first to Rome and then to Milan to find him.

Monica was not only a firm believer in dreams, but had no doubt she knew which ones were the bearer of critical omens. She warned Augustine against entanglements with women, especially married ones. Believing in his glorious future, she also discouraged him from engaging in a contractual marriage too early least he not aim high enough in society for his choice of wife. In 385/386 in Milan, she arranged a betrothal with a Christian heiress. The betrothal included a two-year waiting period after Augustine separated from his longtime companion who had accompanied him from Africa and who Monica must have known intimately. The couple had lived as husband and wife for some 15 years and had a child, Adeodatus, who Monica treated as a grandson.

Monica became a fervent admirer of bishop Ambrose of Milan, specially since he had some influence on Augustine's rejection of Manichaeanism. While in Milan, Augustine had become ill. In autumn 386, Monica, her second son, Navigius, her grandson, Adeodatus, and a few close friends, including Alypius, later bishop of Thagaste, accompanied him to recuperate in a friend's villa in the foothills of the Alps near Lake Como. It was during the retreat and recovery that Augustine had a conversion experience. After they returned to Milan, in April 387, Monica's dream came true as she watched the baptism of Augustine and Adeodatus at the hands of Ambrose.

Augustine had decided that he wanted to return to Thagaste and live a quiet life with his son, mother, and brother. There he could gather some close friends around him, and Monica and Navigius would look after the small estate. The entourage went to Ostia, the port for Rome and the point of embarkation to Africa. Monica fell ill. She told her sons that she no longer desired to be buried beside her husband in Thagaste, and that she should be buried in Ostia. She told Augustine that her one wish that he should become an orthodox Christian before she died had come true. After nine days of illness, Monica died at the age of 56.

Sources

Augustine, *Confessions* IX.ix, 19, 21; II. iii, 7; IX. 10–11.
Brown, Peter. *Augustine of Hippo, A Biography.* Berkeley: University of California Press, 2000.
O'Donnell, James J. *Augustine: A New Biography.* New York: HarperCollins, 2005.

▣ Mucia
(second–first century B.C.E.)   Roman: Italy
elegant speaker

Mucia was born into a family renowned for rhetorical skill. She was the daughter of LAELIA, well known for her elegant speaking. Her father, Quintus Mucius Scaevola, consul in 117 B.C.E., was admired as an orator, as was her grandfather, Gaius Laelius.

Mucia married Lucius Licinius Crassus, consul in 95 B.C.E., who was himself a remarkable orator. Mucia had two daughters, LICINIA (5) and LICINIA (6), who carried on the family tradition of eloquence.

Sources

Cicero. *Brutus* 211–212.
Quintilian. *Institutio Oratoria* 1.1, 6.
Bauman, Richard A. *Women and Politics in Ancient Rome.* London: Routledge, 1994, pp. 47–48.

▣ Mucia Tertia
(first century B.C.E.)   Roman: Italy
power/broker

Mucia Tertia helped mediate the pact of Misenum in 39 B.C.E. between her son, Sextus Pompeius Magnus, and Mark Antony and Octavian. A woman of independent spirit, she was one of several Roman women who negotiated among the warring factions on several occasion during the civil wars.

Daughter of Quintus Mucius Scaevola, consul in 95 B.C.E., she was the third wife of Gnaeus Pompeius (Pompey the Great), Roman general and leader of the republicans at the outbreak of civil war in 49 B.C.E. She married him after the death of his second wife, AEMILIA (2). They had two sons, Gnaeus Pompeius Magnus and Sextus Pompeius, and a daughter, POMPEIA (2). She and Pompey divorced in 62. There were rumors of lovers and tales of salacious propositions, common for all divorces among the elite, who were always subject to insistent gossip, both true and false. Mucia's second husband was Marcus Aemilius Scaurus, a quaestor under Pompey and praetor in 56. They had a son, Marcus Aemilius Scaurus. Her husband was charged with bribery during the consular elections in 53. Her former husband contributed to his conviction and exile. Mucia did not accompany her husband out of Italy.

After Pompey's defeat at Pharsalus in 48 and his murder in Egypt, Sextus took up his father's mantle.

Sextus controlled the sea and made Sicily a friendly retreat for the Roman elite escaping the proscriptions. Mucia had been in Rome, at least for much of this period. When Octavian became alarmed at Sextus's overtures to Antony, he sent Mucia to placate Sextus. In a further gesture of reconciliation, Octavian also married SCRIBONIA, the sister of Sextus's father-in-law, Lucius Scribonius Libo. These efforts failed. In 40 B.C.E. Antony and Octavian were reconciled with the signing of the Treaty of Brundisium, and Antony married the latter's sister, OCTAVIA (2). Sextus, however, still controlled the sea lanes and cut off the corn supply to Italy. Faced with possible famine, the people demanded a settlement between the triumvirs and Sextus. A mob sent Mucia, who strongly favored an agreement, to her son in search of peace after threatening to burn her and her house. The protagonists met on the coast at Puteoli, north of Naples. The troops on both sides demanded an accord. The result was the Treaty of Misenum in which Sextus became reconciled with the triumvirate. The agreement soon fell apart, and Sextus was defeated and executed in 36 B.C.E. In consideration of Mucia's efforts, Octavian spared her other son, Marcus Aemilius Scaurus, who had faced the death penalty after the battle of Actium.

Sources

Appian. *Roman History: Bella civilian (Civil Wars)* 5.69, 72.
Cicero. *Epistulae ad Atticum* 1.12.
Dio Cassius. *Roman History* 51.5.
Suetonius. *The Lives of the Caesars:* Caesar 50.
———. *The Lives of Illustrious Men: De Grammaticis* (Grammarians), 14.
Balsdon, J. P. V. D. *Roman Women.* New York: John Day Comp., 1963, p. 53.
Oxford Classical Dictionary, ed. by Simon Hornblower and Antony Spawforth. 3d. ed. New York: Oxford University Press, 1996, p. 999.
Pauly, A., G. Wissowa, and W. Kroll. *Real-Encyclopadie D. Classischen Altertumswissenschaft 1893–.* (Germany: multiple publishers) 28.
Syme, Ronald. *The Augustan Aristocracy.* Oxford: Clarendon Press, 1986, pp. 255, 264.
———. *The Roman Revolution.* London: Oxford University Press, 1963, pp. 32, 33.

Mummia Achaica

(first century B.C.E.–first century C.E.)   Roman: Rome
mother of emperor Servius Sulpicius Galba

Mummia Achaica was the great-great-granddaughter of Lucius Mummius, consul in 146 B.C.E. Her father's probable name was Lucius Mummius Achaica. Her mother was Lutatia, the daughter of Lutatius Catullus, consul in 78 B.C.E. She married Gaius Sulpicius Galba, a squat ugly man who had a hunchback. They had two sons: Gaius, who later committed suicide, and Servius Sulpicius Galba, born December 24, 3 B.C.E., who later succeeded Nero as emperor.

Sources

Suetonius. *The Lives of the Caesars:* Galba 3–4.
Syme, Ronald. *The Augustan Aristocracy.* Oxford: Clarendon Press, 1986, pp. 75, 77.

Munatia Plancina

(?–33 C.E.)   Roman: Italy, Asia, and Syria
political player

Munatia Plancina was the aristocratic, wealthy, arrogant daughter or possibly granddaughter of Lucius Munatius Plancus, consul in 42 B.C.E. and censor in 22. Her paternal family was on the winning side of the civil wars. Plancus had served under Julius Caesar, supported Marcus Junius Brutus, and switched first to Mark Antony and then to Octavian. It was he who proposed the name Augustus for Octavian.

Munatia, a friend of LIVIA DRUSILLA, married Gnaeus Calpurnius Piso, a friend of the emperor Tiberius. In 17 C.E. she accompanied her husband to the East after Tiberius appointed him governor of Syria at least in part to restrain the impetuous adventurism of Germanicus Julius Caesar headquartered in Syria and accompanied by his wife, the elder AGRIPPINA.

Germanicus, the favored heir of Tiberius, and Agrippina were well regarded by the troops. Munatia and Piso curried favor with the troops to counter the popular couple. Munatia attended military exercises and maneuvers, as did Agrippina. Conflicts soon arose between Germanicus and Piso, and they came to dislike each other, as did their wives. Munatia made disparaging remarks about Germanicus and Agrippina before the troops, and Agrippina, every bit her match, did the same to support Germanicus.

Tensions escalated after Piso refused Germanicus's request for troops to take to Armenia. Germanicus ordered Piso to leave Syria. Munatia and her husband went to the island of Cos off the southern coast of Asia Minor. Germanicus suddenly fell seriously ill in Antioch and died on October 10, 19 C.E. Before dying, he declared himself poisoned by Piso and Munatia. Munatia and Piso made no secret that they regarded the death as good news. Piso set out to take Syria by force from Gnaeus Sentius Saturninus, who had become temporary governor appointed by the officers until Tiberius could send a new appointment. However, the troops failed to support Piso. Defeated, Piso and Munatia were taken to Rome to be tried on charges of treason.

In Rome neither Tiberius nor Livia nor Germanicus's own mother, the younger ANTONIA, attended the ceremony when Agrippina returned with her husband's ashes in 19 C.E. Rumors were rife that Tiberius and Livia had colluded in Germanicus's death so that Tiberius's son, Drusus Julius Caesar would succeed his father. Agrippina formally accused Munatia and Piso of poisoning her husband. Piso was tried in the Senate with Tiberius presiding. Munatia first supported her husband, but she soon distanced herself, and Livia intervened on her behalf to separate her trial from that of her husband. Unable to prove that Piso poisoned Germanicus, he was convicted of trying to regain Syria by force. He killed himself before the trial ended and sent a letter to Tiberius protesting his loyalty and asking that his two sons be spared. He made no mention of Munatia.

Tiberius sought support for Munatia from her sons, who refused. Munatia was freed when Tiberius told the Senate that Livia asked that the charges against her be dropped. The death of Livia in 29 deprived Munatia of her protector, but no harm immediately followed. In 33, however, she was again accused and convicted, and she killed herself. The charges are not clear, but it is known that her death quickly followed on the heels of that of her chief enemy, Agrippina.

Sources

Dio Cassius. *Roman History* 57.18.9–10; 58.22.5.

Tacitus. *Annales* 2.43, 55, 57, 71, 74, 82; 3.9, 13, 15–18; 6.26.

Balsdon, J. P. V. D. *Roman Women.* New York: John Day Comp., 1963, p. 95.

Bauman, Richard A. *Women and Politics in Ancient Rome.* London: Routledge, 1994, pp. 140–143.

Levick, Barbara. *Tiberius the Politician.* London: Thames and Hudson, 1976, pp. 157, 210.

Marsh, Frank Burr. *The Reign of Tiberius.* New York: Barnes and Noble, 1931, pp. 85–104.

Oxford Classical Dictionary, ed. by Simon Hornblower and Antony Spawforth. 3d. ed. New York: Oxford University Press, 1996, p. 1,000.

Pauly, A., G. Wissowa, and W. Kroll. *Real-Encyclopadie D. Classischen Altertumswissenschaft 1893–.* (Germany: multiple publishers) 44.

Syme, Ronald. *The Augustan Aristocracy.* Oxford: Clarendon Press, 1986, pp. 369, 374.

▣ Musa, Thea Urania

(first century B.C.E.–first century C.E.)
Italian: Italy and Parthia
ruler

Musa was a slave woman from Italy who became the wife of the ruler of Parthia. In 20 B.C.E. Musa was part of a gift Augustus gave to the king of Parthia, which lay south of the Caspian Sea in Asia. It was a client kingdom of Rome ruled by Phraates IV from 38 to 2 B.C.E. Phraates married Musa and gave her the name Thea Urania Musa after she had borne him a son.

Musa persuaded her husband to send his older sons, along with their wives and children, to Rome. In 10 or 9 B.C.E. Phraates IV turned them over to the Roman governor of Syria, Marcus Titius, who arranged their trip. In 2 B.C.E. Musa and her son, also named Phraates, poisoned her husband. Her son took control of the kingdom and married Musa in the same year. Despite the notoriety of the marriage, Phraates V reached an accord with

Thea Urania Musa and Phraates V
(Date: 2 B.C.E.–4 C.E. 1977.158.794, Archives, American Numismatic Society)

Augustus, and the heads of Musa and Phraates V appeared on coins. In 4 C.E. Phraates V was either overthrown or killed in a revolt. Nothing more is known about Musa.

Sources

Debevoise, Nielson Carel. *A Political History of Parthia.* Chicago: University of Chicago Press, 1938, pp. 143, 147–149, 151–152.

Oxford Classical Dictionary, ed. by Simon Hornblower and Antony Spawforth. 3d. ed. New York: Oxford University Press, 1996, p. 1,175.

Mutilia Prisca

(? B.C.E.–30 C.E.)   Roman: Rome
political victim

Mutilia Prisca and her husband, Gaius Fufius Geminus, consul in 29 C.E., were both favorites of the powerful and influential LIVIA DRUSILLA. Livia was instrumental in advancing the career of Geminus, who became an ally of the powerful Lucius Aelius Sejanus in the political battles of the late 20s.

Geminus used his stinging wit against Tiberius. In 30, a year after Livia died, Tiberius forced both Mutilia Prisca and Geminus to commit suicide, after he charged Geminus with treason for being impious and disrespectful. Before he died Geminus went to the Senate and read his will in which he left his estate in equal amounts to his children and the emperor. Mutilia Prisca, furious about the charges and distraught over her husband and his behavior, went to the Senate armed with a dagger and stabbed herself.

Sources

Dio Cassius. *Roman History* 58.5–6.

Tacitus. *Annales* 4.12; 5.2.

Levick, Barbara. *Tiberius the Politician.* London: Thames and Hudson, 1976, pp. 176–177.

Myrrhine

(sixth–fifth century B.C.E.)   Greek: Athens and Asia Minor
loyal wife

Myrrhine was the daughter of the well-born Athenian Callias and the granddaughter of Hyperochides. She married Hippias, the eldest son of Pisistratus, tyrant of Athens (546–527 B.C.E.). Hippias succeeded his father and ruled from 527 to 510 B.C.E. Initially, he was an enlightened ruler like his father, but threats from Persia and later Sparta resulted in a harsher rule. During these years Myrrhine had five sons and a daughter, Archedice. Her daughter married Aeantides, the son of Hippoclus, tyrant of Lampsacus at the eastern entrance to the Hellespont. Hippocles was favored by the Persian king Darius, and Hippias sought to gain Persian support against his domestic enemies.

In 510, Hippias surrendered to a Spartan force supported by Athenians who wanted to free the city. Myrrhine went with her husband and family to Sigeum near Troy in Asia Minor and then to her son-in-law in Lampsacus. Her husband later went to the court of Darius and fought alongside the Persians at the battle of Marathon in 490 in a vain attempt to regain control of Athens. Nothing is known of Myrrhine's death.

Sources

Thucydides. *History of the Peloponnesian War* 6.55, 59.

◙ Myrtis

(fifth?–century B.C.E.)   Greek: Greece
poet

Myrtis was a Greek lyric poet from Anthedon in Boeotia, in central Greece. She was said to have composed a poem about the tragic hero Eunostus, who was killed after a false accusation by a woman he rejected. None of her work survives. Some sources claim that she was also the teacher of the poets Pindar and CORINNA, a lyric poet from Tanagra in Boeotia. In one fragment by Corinna she appears to criticize Myrtis for competing against Pindar. However, Corinna most probably lived in

the third century B.C.E., some 200 years after Pindar and Myrtis.

Sources

Plutarch. *Moralia: Quaestiones Graecae* 40.
Campbell, David A. *Greek Lyric.* 5 vols. Cambridge: Harvard University Press, 1982–93, pp. 2, 15–17.
Edmonds, J. M., ed. and trans. *Lyra Graeca: Being the Remains of All the Greek Lyric Poets from Eumelus to Timotheus, Excepting Pindar.* Rev. ed. 3 vols. Cambridge: Harvard University Press, 1959, pp. 3, 15.
Oxford Classical Dictionary, ed. by Simon Hornblower and Antony Spawforth. 3d. ed. New York: Oxford University Press, 1996, p. 1,017.
Page, Dennys L. *Corinna.* London: Society for the Promotion of Hellenic Studies, 1953, p. 31.

◙ Myrto

(fifth–fourth century B.C.E.)   Greek: Athens
wife of Socrates

Myrto was the first wife of Socrates and with him had two sons, Sophroniscus and Menexenus. The children were still young in 399 B.C.E. when Socrates committed suicide after being found guilty of corrupting youth and introducing strange gods. Although there is no record that Myrto and Socrates divorced, at some point Socrates had a second wife, XANTHIPPE.

Sources

Athenaeus. *Deipnosophistae* 13.555d–56.
Aulus Gellius. *Noctes Atticae* 15.20.6.
Diogenes Laertius. *Lives of the Eminent Philosophers* 2.26.
Fitton, J. W. "That Was No Lady, That Was. . . ." *Classical Quarterly* 64 (1970): 56–66.

N

Neaera

(fourth century B.C.E.)
Greek: Corinth, Athens
self-made woman

Neaera began life as a slave in a Corinthian brothel. Her struggle to move across the social and legal boundaries from slave to free and gain the position of legal wife dominated her life. That her daughter and her grandson may have become Athenian citizens was her crowning achievement. She first gained her freedom after two wealthy young men purchased her from the brothel. The young men allowed her to buy her way out of slavery on the condition that she leave and never return to Corinth. There is no record of what influence she brought to bear for them to agree to free her.

Neaera raised the money she needed from her admirers. One of them, Phrynion, an Athenian citizen, took Neaera and her three children, all born during her time of slavery, to Athens. Dissatisfied with her treatment by Phrynion, Neaera joined with Stephanus, another admirer and an Athenian citizen. She claimed to be Stephanus's wife. At the same time, her relationships with other men provided sufficient income for her to care for her family.

Stephanus claimed Neaera's daughter, Phano, as his legitimate child and arranged marriage for her with a man named Phraestor. She had a respectable dowry of one-half talent. After the marriage, when Phano was already pregnant, Phraestor discovered her background. He threw her out of the house. Phano moved back into her mother's house. Phraestor also refused to return her dowry, claiming to have been deceived.

The ensuing scandal opened the way for Stephanus's enemies to attack him. Two men, Appolodorus and his brother-in-law Theomnestus, brought suit against Neaera for not being a citizen and claiming to be legally wed to a citizen. Although the suit was against Neaera, the attack was directed against Stephanus in revenge for an earlier injury. If convicted, Neaera could have been sold back into slavery, and Stephanus fined 1,000 drachmas.

Whatever the decision, no harm came to Neaera, who continued to live as before. When the angry Phraestor became seriously ill, Neaera and Phano moved into his house and nursed him. He agreed to acknowledge his paternity of Phano's son, especially since he was otherwise childless and at odds with his family. Property was now at stake; serious business in ancient Athens. Phraestor's clansmen challenged Phano's citizenship on the basis that her mother was not an Athenian citizen. Phraestor countersued. However, he refused to testify under oath that Phano was an Athenian citizen and that they had been married under the Athenian law.

Neaera and Phano did not give up. Some time later, Phraestor married Phano to Theogenes of Erchia, again without revealing her origins in order to try to obtain Athenian citizenship for Phano's son. Eventually, Phano married a highly placed religious magistrate, and it is possible that she finally gained the citizenship so dearly sought by her mother for her and her son.

Sources

Demosthenes. *Private Orations* 59.30–32.

Fantham, Elaine, et al. *Women in the Classical World.* New York: Oxford University Press, 1994, pp. 114–115.

Pomeroy, Sarah B. *Goddesses, Whores, Wives, and Slaves: Women in Classical Antiquity.* New York: Schocken Books, 1975, pp. 67–68.

Walters, K. R. "Women and Power in Classical Athens." In *Woman's Power, Man's Game: Essays on Classical Antiquity in Honor of Joy K. King,* ed. by Mary DeForest. Wauconda, Ill.: Bolchazy-Carducci, 1993, pp. 204–205.

◉ Nicaea (1)

(fourth century B.C.E.)
Greek: Macedonia and Thrace
political pawn

Nicaea was the daughter of Alexander the Great's trusted general Antipater. When Alexander departed for his last expedition to the East, he left Antipater behind to govern Macedonia and the cities of Greece. After Alexander's unexpected death in 323 B.C.E., Antipater was one of three generals who jockeyed to rule Alexander's empire. It became advantageous for Nicaea to marry one or another of her father's colleagues. Perdiccas sought her out, and a match was agreed upon. However, in the fluid world of post-Alexander politics, OLYMPIAS (1), the mother of Alexander the Great, was a force to reckon with, and she hated Antipater, who had denied her authority in Macedonia while Alexander was alive and in the East.

To thwart Antipater, Olympias offered Perdiccas the hand of her daughter, CLEOPATRA (3). Marriage with Cleopatra offered Perdiccas an alliance with the Macedonian ruling house. Caught between the two choices, he promised Cleopatra to marry her, although he would first marry Nicaea

and later divorce her. It is not clear whether he married Nicaea, but the sources agree that Antipater discovered the plan and broke with Perdiccas. Cleopatra also turned him down. The only victor was Olympias, who had succeeded in creating a breech between Antipater and Perdiccas.

Antipater instead formed an alliance with Craterus and Ptolemy I Soter of Egypt, also Macedonian colleagues under Alexander. To assure these alliances, Antipater used his three daughters as surety. PHILA (1) and Craterus married, as did EURYDICE (3) and Ptolemy. Nicaea married Lysimachus, a close companion of Alexander who governed Thrace, to ensure his continued neutrality. Lysimachus named a city in Bithynia in Asia Minor after his wife, who had three children. One daughter, ARSINOË I, became for a time coruler of Egypt. Another daughter, EURYDICE (4), married her cousin Antipater. She was killed in the wars over Macedonia. Her son, Agathocles, should have succeeded his father, but he was killed to eliminate any chance of his succession through the machination of Lysimachus's later wife, ARSINOË II PHILADELPHUS.

Sources

Diodorus Siculus. *Library of History* 18.23.1–3.

Cary, M. *A History of the Greek World from 323 to 146 B.C.* London: Methuen, 1951, pp. 12–13, 55–57.

Macurdy, Grace. *Hellenistic Queens.* Reprint. Chicago: Ares Publishers, 1985, pp. 37, 59, 102, 109, 113.

◉ Nicaea (2)

(third century B.C.E.)   Greek: Corinth
ruler

Nicaea ruled Corinth for a short time after the death of her husband, Alexander (290–245 B.C.E.). He had succeeded his father, who had ruled Corinth and the surrounding areas under the suzerainty of Demetrius I. He repudiated Demetrius and left Nicaea as his heir.

Nicaea set about finding another husband amid the quicksands of Greek political alliances during the third century B.C.E. Antigonus Gonatus, the son of Demetrius I and PHILA (1) who had once controlled Corinth, sought to reassert his control. He offered her marriage with his son, Demetrius II, and arranged to celebrate the wedding in Corinth. On arrival, he immediately sent a group of soldiers to the fort and bluffed the troops there into surrendering. Nothing more is heard of Nicaea.

Sources

Justin. *Epitome* 28.

Plutarch. *Vitae Parallelae (Parallel Lives): Aratus* 17.1–3.

Cary, M. *A History of the Greek World from 323 to 146 B.C.* London: Methuen, 1951, p. 140.

▣ Nicopolis

(second century B.C.E.)   Roman: Rome
self-made woman

Nicopolis was a wealthy woman who took the relatively impoverished, young, and nobly born Lucius Cornelius Sulla for her lover. She appointed Sulla her heir before she died. It was not the only time that Sulla, future dictator of Rome, would financially benefit from his relationships with women.

Sources

Plutarch. *Vitae Parallelae (Parallel Lives): Sulla* 2.4.

▣ Nossis

(third century B.C.E.)   Greek: Locri
poet

Nossis was a Greek poet from Locri, a city in southern Italy. Influenced by the poetry of SAPPHO, she wrote dedications, mostly to the gods, and epigrams, only 12 of which survive. Nossis was probably well born. She was the daughter of Theophilis, and she paid tribute to her mother and grandmother in the dedication of a valuable linen wrap to the goddess Hera.

Nossis explored new possibilities in the very formulaic and conventional form of a dedication. She added a personal voice that spoke to women and about women. She praised the beauty of women's bodies and celebrated the sweetness of desire as the greatest of all pleasures, even sweeter than the sweetest honey. Speaking as if from the grave, Nossis asked any passing stranger to remember her. The conceit and the lament were characteristic of the ancients, but her language carried the passion that raises poetry above the trite and sentimental.

Sources

Fantham, Elaine, et al. *Women in the Classical World.* New York: Oxford University Press, 1994, pp. 165–166.

Gow, Andrew S. F., and Denys L. Page. *The Greek Anthology: Hellenistic Epigrams.* 2 vols. Cambridge, England: Cambridge University Press, 1965, pp. 434 ff.

Oxford Classical Dictionary, ed. by Simon Hornblower and Antony Spawforth. 3d. ed. New York: Oxford University Press, 1996, p. 1,049.

Skinner, Marilyn B. "Nossis Thelyglossos: The Private Text and the Public Book." In *Women's History and Ancient History,* ed. by Sarah B. Pomeroy. Chapel Hill: University of North Carolina Press, 1991, pp. 20–47.

▣ Numantina, Fabia

(first century C.E.)   Roman: Rome
litigant

Fabia Numantina successfully withstood a trial on charges brought by her not-completely-sane second husband. She had family ties with the emperor Augustus. Her grandmother ATIA (2) and the emperor's mother, ATIA (1), were sisters. Her mother, MARCIA (3), was Augustus's young stepcousin, and her father, Paullus Fabius Maximus, consul in 11 B.C.E., was his friend. Numantina's first husband was Sextus Appuleius, consul in 14 C.E. They had a son who died while young. She noted on his gravestone that he was the last of the illustrious house of the Appuleii.

Widowed, Numantina remarried. Her second husband was Plautius Silvanus, praetor in 24 C.E. Silvanus may have been a fortune hunter who married the rich Numantina in order to divorce her after securing some part of her wealth and a settlement.

He may have succeeded, at least in part. After they were divorced, Silvanus married APRONIA, the daughter of Lucius Apronius, and brought a suit against Numantina. He charged her with the use of spells and drugs to drive him insane while they had been married. Before the conclusion of the suit, Silvanus threw Apronia out of a window and killed her. He was forced to take his own life. Numantina was acquitted of all charges.

Sources

Tacitus. *Annales* 4.22.

Syme, Ronald. *The Augustan Aristocracy.* Oxford: Clarendon Press, 1986, pp. 59, 418.

Occia

(? B.C.E.–19 C.E.)   Roman: Rome
priestess

Occia was a Vestal Virgin with an unblemished record of dedication for 57 years, from 38 B.C.E. until her death in 19 C.E. One of six women devoted to the protection of the sacred flame in the temple of Vesta in the Forum, the purity of the Vestals was associated with the well-being of the city. Usually the women served for a term of 30 years and retired well endowed. Occia's length of service was unusually long and successful through difficult decades of civil war.

Sources

Tacitus. *Annales* 2.86.1.
Balsdon, J. P. V. D. *Roman Women.* New York: John Day Comp., 1963, p. 236.

Octavia (1)

(first century B.C.E.)   Roman: Rome
half sister to Augustus and Octavia

Octavia was the half sister of the emperor Augustus and OCTAVIA (2). They all shared the same father, Gaius Octavius, who came from a wealthy equestrian family. Her mother was ANCHARIA, her father's first wife. Octavia married Sextus Appuleius and bore him two sons: Sextus Appuleius, consul in 29 B.C.E., and Marcus Appuleius, consul in 20 B.C.E.

Sources

Suetonius. *The Lives of the Caesars:* Augustus 4.1.
Oxford Classical Dictionary, ed. by Simon Hornblower and Antony Spawforth. 3d. ed. New York: Oxford University Press, 1996, p. 1,059.
Pauly, A., G. Wissowa, and W. Kroll. *Real-Encyclopadie D. Classischen Altertumswissenschaft 1893–.* (Germany: multiple publishers) 95.
Singer, Mary. "The Problem of Octavia Minor and Octavia Major." *Transactions of the American Philogical Association* (1948): 268–274.
Syme, Ronald. *The Augustan Aristocracy.* Oxford: Clarendon Press, 1986, index.
———. *The Roman Revolution.* London: Oxford University Press, 1963, pp. 112, 378, 421.

Octavia (2)

(69–11 B.C.E.)   Roman: Italy and Greece
power broker

Octavia was dignified, intelligent, and attractive; she was held in high regard as a woman of virtue and principle. She played an important role in the shifting political realities of the civil war and the early empire. She acted to promote the best interests of her husbands and of her brother, the emperor Augustus. In the aftermath of civil war, she led the way in nurturing the children of the republican elite to assure the continuity of the great houses of the past.

Born in 60 B.C.E., she died in 11 B.C.E., having married twice, borne five children and been a close adviser to her husbands and her brother. She was the daughter of Gaius Octavius, praetor in 61 B.C.E., and the niece of Gaius Julius Caesar on the side of her mother, ATIA (1). Around 54 B.C.E., Octavia married Gaius Claudius Marcellus, who was more than 20 years her senior. Consul in 50 B.C.E., he initially supported Gnaeus Pompeius (Pompey the Great) and tried to bring about Caesar's recall, for which Caesar later forgave him.

Marcellus died in 40 B.C.E. With him Octavia had three children: the elder Claudia MARCELLA, born in 43; Marcus Claudius Marcellus, born in 42; and the younger Claudia MARCELLA, born in 39, after her father's death. Octavia married Mark Antony in the autumn of 40, so quickly after her first husband's death that she needed a special dispensation from the Senate. The new marriage sealed the treaty of Brundisium, which divided the empire between her brother Octavian, her husband Antony, and Marcus Aemilius Lepidus.

Octavia and Antony settled in Athens during the winters of 39–38 and 38–37. In 37, she brokered the treaty of Tarentum, in which Antony agreed not to support Sextus Pompeius Magnus, the younger son of Pompey the Great and to turn over two squadrons, consisting of 120 ships, to Octavian for use against Sextus. In return Octavian promised him four legions. Octavia persuaded Antony to furnish her brother with an additional 10 ships. She also persuaded her brother to supply Antony with a bodyguard of 1,000 soldiers of his choosing. Antony then went east to deal with the client states and to fight the Parthians. Octavia, who had just given birth to a second daughter by Antony, the younger ANTONIA, accompanied him as far as Corcyra in the Ionian Sea. Her health deteriorated, and she returned to Rome.

Antony summoned CLEOPATRA VII to Antioch and resumed their relationship. They agreed that she would rule over Coele-Syria, Cyprus, and a part of Cilicia, and he acknowledged her twins,

CLEOPATRA SELENE and Alexander Helios as his sons. She provided him with significant material and financial support. In the face of Antony's alliance with Cleopatra, Octavia persuaded Octavian in 35 B.C.E. to allow her to bring Antony additional troops and equipment. Octavian, however, only sent one-tenth of the promised troops and a furious Antony told Octavia she need go no further than Athens. Sadly Octavia returned to Rome. Despite the urging of her brother, Octavia refused to leave Antony's house and claimed that under Roman law she was his wife.

In 35 Octavia and Octavian's wife, LIVIA DRUSILLA, were accorded the privilege of *tribunica sanctissima,* a status neither previously nor ever again held by a woman. The office made any assault on their persons an attack on the state. It also gave the women independent authority over their property and wealth. It was probably Octavian's intention to protect his sister from Antony, and given the context, impossible to exclude his wife in the honor. So long as Octavia remained Antony's putative wife, she was the visible symbol of the Treaty of Brundisium, and Octavian was constrained in his behavior toward Antony, who remained in the East. In 32, however, Antony officially divorced Octavia and thereby removed for Octavian his major impediment to war. Even so, Octavian was careful to declare war against Cleopatra, rather than Antony. Antony not only had support among the troops, but few found palatable the prospect of yet another openly declared war between two Roman generals.

After Cleopatra's and Antony's death in 30 B.C.E., Octavia brought up the children of her first and second marriages, as well as Iullus Antonius, Antony's son with FULVIA (1), and Cleopatra Selene, Antony's daughter with Cleopatra. She brought in Nestor of Tarsus, a philosopher and teacher, for Marcellus. She had her brother assign money from Antony's estate to the two Antonias, and probably for his son, to ensure that they were well educated.

She married them all well. The elder Marcella married Marcus Vipsanius Agrippa, the great general and close confidant of Augustus, in 28 B.C.E. The younger Marcella married Marcus Valerius

Messalla Appianus, consul in 12 B.C.E. The elder ANTONIA was betrothed to Lucius Domitius Ahenobarbus, consul in 16 B.C.E., the younger Antonia, to Livia's son Nero Claudius Drusus, consul in 9 B.C.E. Octavia's son Claudius Marcellus and Livia's son Tiberius were regarded as Augustus's most likely successors, and he took both of them when he went campaigning in Spain in 27 B.C.E. In 25, Augustus and Octavia arranged a marriage between Augustus's only child, JULIA (6), and her son Marcellus, which marked him as the most probable heir apparent.

Two years later Marcellus fell ill and died. Octavia never completely recovered from the loss. She spent a good deal of time alone, dressed in mourning clothes, and for the remaining 12 years of her life did not allow her son's name mentioned in her presence. Her relationship with her sister-in-law, Livia, deteriorated. Livia's son Tiberius remained alive and healthy, a constant reminder of Octavia's loss. Her sadness, however, did not prevent her from continuing to oversee the marriages of the children of her household: In 20 B.C.E. Cleopatra Selene married Juba II, king of Mauritania, a man of culture, who had been granted Roman citizenship by Augustus.

In the same year, Augustus had a crisis. He needed someone trustworthy in Rome, which faced food shortages, while he traveled to the provinces. Octavia convinced her brother that Agrippa, his closest military ally and friend, should marry his daughter Julia, who was also Octavia's widowed daughter-in-law. The two men would then be linked through the living symbol of Julia, as Octavian and Antony had been joined through Octavia decades before. The new marriage required Agrippa to divorce Octavia's daughter the elder Marcella. Octavia immediately married Marcella to the handsome, young, and dashing Iullus Antonius, who also had grown up in her household. Everyone seemed to benefit. Marcella exchanged Agrippa, who all concur was a good husband, for a much more handsome man with a seemingly bright future, who was her contemporary and childhood mate. The widowed Julia had a new husband with a standing at least equal to that of her first husband, and

Augustus had a reliable man in Rome. Finally, the intimate threesome surrounding Augustus of Livia, Octavia, and Agrippa was strengthened.

In 15 Octavia became a grandmother when the younger Antonia and Nero Claudius Drusus, the younger son of Livia, gave birth to Germanicus Julius Caesar. Octavia died in 11 B.C.E. and was given a state funeral. Augustus and the popular Nero Claudius Drusus, at that moment the more likely heir to the emperor, delivered funeral orations. She was widely esteemed by the people for her virtue, nobility, loyalty, and humanity. In her honor, Augustus erected the Porticus Octaviae, which contained a building housing a fine library.

Sources

Appian. *Roman History: Bella civilian (Civil Wars)* 5.64, 76, 93, 95.

Dio Cassius. *Roman History* 48.31.3; 49.43.8; 54.6.4–5, 35.4–5.

Plutarch. *Vitae Parallelae (Parallel Lives): Antonius* 31.1–5; 53.1–5; 54.1–2; 87.1–3.

Suetonius. *The Lives of the Caesars:* Augustus 61.2; 63.1.

Balsdon, J. P. V. D. *Roman Women.* New York: John Day Comp., 1963, index.

Bauman, Richard A. *Women and Politics in Ancient Rome.* London: Routledge, 1994, index.

Oxford Classical Dictionary, ed. by Simon Hornblower and Antony Spawforth. 3d. ed. New York: Oxford University Press, 1996, p. 1,059.

Pauly, A., G. Wissowa, and W. Kroll. *Real-Encyclopadie D. Classischen Altertumswissenschaft 1893–.* (Germany: multiple publishers) 96.

Syme, Ronald. *The Augustan Aristocracy.* Oxford: Clarendon Press, 1986, index.

———. *The Roman Revolution.* London: Oxford University Press, 1963, index.

▣ Octavia, Claudia

(39/40–62 C.E.)   Roman: Italy
faultless wife; banished

Claudia Octavia was an emperor's daughter and subject to the dangerous intrigues of those closest to imperial power. Born in 39 or 40 C.E., her mother was Valeria MESSALLINA, and her father, the emperor Claudius. Her life was transformed when her father ordered the death of her mother and chose the younger AGRIPPINA for his next wife. Even before her own marriage to Claudius, Agrippina sought to marry Octavia and her son, Nero. There was, however, a standing arrangement between Octavia and Lucius Junius Silanus, praetor in 48 C.E. This obstacle was overcome when Lucius Vitellius, consul in 47 C.E., one of the emperor's closest advisers, and an ally of Agrippina, charged JUNIA CALVINA, who was his former daughter-in-law, of incest with her brother, Silanus. The engagement was dissolved, and Silanus committed suicide on the day that Agrippina married Claudius. Junia Calvina was exiled.

In 53 C.E. Octavia, who was 13 or 14, married the 16-year-old Nero. The next year, her husband became emperor. His affections were soon transferred to a freewoman, ACTE, despite Agrippina's strong disapproval. He then fell in love with the beautiful and wealthy POPPAEA SABINA (2). In 59 Nero arranged to have his mother murdered, and three years later, he divorced Octavia, claiming her sterile after he failed to prove her adultery with a slave. He exiled her to Campania, where she was kept under military guard.

Octavia kept her dowry, and her popularity was undiminished. She received the house of the deceased Burrus, a freedman of Claudius and Nero, and the estate of Rubellius Plautus, who had been forced to suicide by Nero. But rumors of her return led to demonstrations of approval, and her statues were hung with flowers while those of Poppaea were destroyed. Nero and Poppaea became alarmed. He bribed Anicetus, prefect of the fleet at Misenum and the murderer of his mother Agrippina, to testify that Octavia had committed adultery with him. Octavia was banished to the island of Pandateria where she was murdered on June 9, 62 C.E.

Sources

Dio Cassius. *Roman History* 61.7.1–3, 31.7–8; 62.13.1–2.
Suetonius. *The Lives of the Caesars:* Claudius 27.1–2.
———. *The Lives of the Caesars:* Nero 7.2; 35.1–3.
Tacitus. *Annales* 11.32, 34; 12.1–5, 8, 9, 58; 13.18; 14.1, 59–64.
Balsdon, J. P. V. D. *Roman Women.* New York: John Day Comp., 1963, pp. 124, 126–127.
Bauman, Richard A. *Women and Politics in Ancient Rome.* London: Routledge, 1994, pp. 205–208.

Oxford Classical Dictionary, ed. by Simon Hornblower and Antony Spawforth. 3d. ed. New York: Oxford University Press, 1996, pp. 336.
Pauly, A., G. Wissowa, and W. Kroll. *Real-Encyclopadie D. Classischen Altertumswissenschaft 1893–.* (Germany: multiple publishers) 428.

Oculata

(first century C.E.)   Roman: Rome
priestesses

Oculata and her sister, also named Oculata, were Vestal Virgins. In 83 C.E. the sisters and a third colleague, VARRONILLA, were convicted of incest by the pontifical college as part of a campaign against immorality launched by the emperor Domitian. The Vestal Virgins, six in number, served to protect the eternal flame of Rome in one of the oldest temple in the Forum. Historically, any kind of illicit behavior was considered an ill omen for the city and was punished by entombment. In this case, however, the three women were allowed to commit suicide. Their supposed lovers were sent into exile.

Sources

Dio Cassius. *Roman History* 67.3.3(2)–4(1).
Suetonius. *The Lives of the Caesars:* Domitian 8.4.
Balsdon, J. P. V. D. *Roman Women.* New York: John Day Comp., 1963, p. 241.

Oenanthe

(third century B.C.E.)
Greek: Samos and Egypt
conspirator; murderer

Oenanthe left the island of Samos and went to Egypt with her two children, AGATHOCLEIA and Agathocles. She was a tambourine player and her daughter was a dancer. Oenanthe and her son became lovers of Ptolemy III Euergetes. Her daughter, Agathocleia, became the lover of Eugertes' son, Ptolemy IV Philopator.

Oenanthe joined the conspiracy to overthrow Ptolemy IV and ARSINOË III PHILOPATOR in 205 B.C.E. Her son proclaimed himself regent of the murdered rulers' five-year-old boy, and he placed the child under the guardianship of Oenanthe and Agathocleia. However, Arsinoë III, more than her husband, had been widely admired, and her murder aroused the anger of the army and the populace. The conspirators were seized. Oenanthe and her daughter were driven through the streets naked before being killed by the mob.

Sources

Athenaeus. *Deipnosophistae* 13.577.
Polybius. *Histories* 14.11.1; 15.25.3–33.
Pomeroy, Sarah B. *Women in Hellenistic Egypt.* New York: Schocken, 1984, index.

◉ Olympias (1)
(fourth century B.C.E.)
Greek: Epirus and Macedonia
ruler

Olympias was probably the most remarkable woman of her day. Both revered and feared, she was proud, imperious, and passionate, as well as beautiful, tempestuous, and ruthless. She sought and used political power fearlessly with the charisma of a seductress and the skill of a sorcerer. Born into a family that traced its ancestry back to Archilles, her father, Neoptolemus, was ruler of Molossia in Epirus, a part of northwestern Greece. From youth onward Olympias zealously practiced mystery rites (later identified with Demeter and Dionysius) that used snakes, with which she became expert and terrorized friend and foe. She met her husband, Philip, the future king of Macedonia, when she was quite young and he was about 20 years old and they had both traveled to the island of Samothrace in the northeast Aegean to be initiated into religious rites for the worship of the Cabiri gods, who promoted fertility in women and the land, and also protected seafarers.

Olympias married Philip II in 357 B.C.E. She gave birth to a son, the future Alexander the Great, in 356, and to a daughter, CLEOPATRA (3), two years later. Philip had already been married probably more than once. With her husband away on military campaigns, Olympias solidified her position of leadership in his household and developed close relations with her children that lasted over the course of her lifetime. She supervised the children's education and made sure that her daughter followed her example and learned to hunt, ride, and use weapons.

Olympias had a ready wit as well as a sharp tongue and a violent temper. When Philip claimed that a young and beautiful woman had cast a spell over him, Olympias looked at the woman and noted that witchcraft was not necessary. When Alexander claimed that his father was Zeus, Olympias laughed and responded that her son slandered her if he compared her with Zeus's wife, Hera.

After almost 20 years of marriage, Philip unexpectedly married a much younger woman, CLEOPATRA (2), the niece of Attalos, one of his most prominent generals. The reasons may have been passion or demands of his supporters that he marry a Macedonian woman. Olympias and Alexander withdrew to Epirus. In 336 Philip was murdered during a celebration of their daughter Cleopatra's marriage. Ancient rumors implied that Olympias had a hand in the murder. There is no question that her husband's death and the ascendency of her son, Alexander, vastly improved her position. No woman was her peer.

Murder was a feature of Macedonian politics, and Olympias had no hesitation in using it to protect her position. She was responsible for the death of the widowed Cleopatra and her small son, killed while Alexander was away campaigning. Alexander was said to have felt that the punishment too harsh, but to preclude any future threat, he had Attalos and all of his kinsmen killed as well.

When Alexander set out in 334, Olympias presided over the court of Macedonia and vied for power with Antipater, the general whom Alexander left behind as overseer of Greece and Macedonia. Olympias and Antipater wrote many letters to Alexander complaining bitterly about each other's conduct. In 331, furious, she left Macedonia for her inherited lands in Epirus, which she ruled along with her daughter Cleopatra after the death of the letter's husband in 330. As was her way, she ruled despotically with little regard for popular support and in 325 Olympias sent Cleopatra back to Macedonia to stir up trouble against Antipater. Alexander expressed little fear of his mother's plans, since he believed the Macedonians would never accept rule by a woman. Alexander's unexpected death in 323, however, altered the political realities and posed new possibilities for Olympias's unceasing struggle to gain control over Macedonia. Cognizant of Alexander's view about female rule, Olympias invited the young and handsome Leonnatus, a general under Alexander and distant kin, to marry her daughter Cleopatra and become titular ruler over Macedonia. He accepted but was soon killed in battle.

At the same time other claimants came forth. EURYDICE (2), a granddaughter of Philip II and the Illyrian princess Audata, married her cousin Philip Arrhidaeus, the feeble son of Philip II and PHILINNA. The rival generals agreed to recognize as joint kings Philip Arrhidaeus and Alexander IV, the infant son of ROXANE and Alexander the Great. In 322, Olympias, whose hatred for Antipater was unappeased, sent her daughter Cleopatra to Asia to offer marriage to Perdiccas, one of his two major opponents. Marriage into the family of Alexander with its ties to the rulers of Macedonia was a prize that Perdiccas could not turn down. When Antipater discovered the possible liaison he and his allies put Cleopatra under guard in Sardis.

In 319 Antipater died, and the dissolution of Alexander's empire accelerated. Polyperchon, whom Antipater had named as his successor, Antigonus, and Antipater's son Cassander engaged in a three-way struggle that opened space for Olympias to maneuver for power. Polyperchon invited Olympias to return to Macedonia from Epirus and take charge of her grandson Alexander IV. Olympias hesitated and was advised by her closest ally, the general Eumenes, to wait until the struggle between Polyperchon and Cassander produced a clear victor. In 317 Cassander landed in Macedonia. Eurydice, pulling the strings behind her husband and always opposed to Olympias, had her husband recognize Cassander. With the legitimacy accorded by Philip Arrhidaeus, Cassander was acknowledged the strongest contender for rule over Macedonia.

Polyperchon fled to Epirus with Roxane and her son, Alexander IV, and begged help from Olympias. With Polyperchon's support Olympias had found the moment to confront Eurydice and Philip Arrhidaeus, regain the throne for the young Alexander

IV, and make herself regent. She led her army into Macedonia in 317. Instead of waiting for the return to Cassander, who was in southern Greece, Eurydice and her husband met Olympias at the border. At the appearance of Olympias, whom they regarded as sacred, the Macedonian army refused to fight, and Olympias won the day without any bloodshed.

Olympias executed the weak Philip Arrhidaeus and had Eurydice commit suicide. She ordered the execution of 100 of Cassander's closest Macedonian supporters, including his brother. She had achieved her long-sought goal—rule over Macedon through her barely six-year-old grandson, Alexander IV. Cassander, however, was still very much alive. Moving north, he slipped his army into Macedonia, catching Olympias by surprise. She withdrew with a small force to Pydna, the capital, where she was besieged. With her were Roxane and Alexander IV. Her collaborator Polyperchon failed to break the siege. The city faced starvation. She allowed some soldiers to leave the city, possibly to ease the pressure on diminishing supplies. They fled to Cassander, who directed them to various parts of Macedonia to undermine support for Olympias. In 316 Olympias surrendered to Cassander after he promised to spare her life.

Cassander sought to honor his pledge and succeed in killing Olympias simultaneously. He sent friends who offered her a ship to Athens. Olympias refused, recognizing a ruse. Since she refused to leave the country, Cassander arranged for the relatives of those she killed to accuse her in the assembly. No one was allowed to speak on her behalf. She was condemned. Cassander refused her request to appear before the assembly, fearing her power. He sent 200 soldiers to murder her. When they came into her presence, however, they did not kill her. Cassander then sent relatives of her victims, who did kill her. Olympias faced death as she had lived and asked no mercy. For generations, the Macedonians continued to revere her grave at Pydna.

Sources

Dio Cassius. *Roman History* 16.91.4; 18.57.2, 58.2–3, 65.1–2; 19.11.1–9; 35–36; 49–51.

Pausanias. *Description of Greece* 1.9.1–4; 8.7.5.

Plutarch. *Vitae Parallelae (Parallel Lives): Alexander* 2.1–9; 31–34; 5.7; 9.5–11; 10.6–8; 39.7–8; 68.4–5; 77.8.

Carney, Elizabeth D. "The Career of Adea-Eurydice." *Historia* 36 (1987): 496–502.

———. "Olympias." *Ancient Society* 18 (1987): 35–62.

———. "What's in a Name?" In *Women's History and Ancient History*, ed. by Sarah B. Pomeroy. Chapel Hill: University of North Carolina Press, 1991, pp. 154–157, 163.

Heckel, Waldemar. "Philip and Olympias." In *Classical Contributions: Studies in Honor of Malcolm Francis McGregor*, ed. by G. S. Shrimpton and D. J. McCargar. Locust Valley, N.Y.: J. J. Augustin, 1981, pp. 51–57.

Macurdy, Grace. *Hellenistic Queens*. Reprint. Chicago: Ares Publishers, 1985, pp. 22 ff.

Oxford Classical Dictionary, ed. by Simon Hornblower and Antony Spawforth. 3d. ed. New York: Oxford University Press, 1996, p. 1,066.

Pauly, A., G. Wissowa, and W. Kroll. *Real-Encyclopadie D. Classischen Altertumswissenschaft 1893–*. (Germany: multiple publishers) 5.

◉ Olympias (2)

(third century B.C.E.)   Greek: Epirus
ruler

Olympias ruled Epirus in northwestern Greece after the death of her husband. She was the daughter of Pyrrhus, the general and ruler of Epirus. Her father was succeeded by his son Alexander II, who married Olympias. They were probably stepsiblings. They had two sons, Pyrrhus and Ptolemy, and three daughters, PHTHIA (nicknamed Chryseis), Nereis, and Deidamia.

After the death of her husband in 240 or 239 B.C.E., Olympias became regent for her son Pyrrhus II. When the Aetolians threatened to annex the northern half of Acarnania, which had been assigned by treaty to Epirus, Olympias offered her daughter Phthia in marriage to Demetrius II, who in 239, had just become ruler of Macedonia. Demetrius accepted the alliance and divorced his wife STRATONICE (3). In the war that followed, Demetrius saved Acarnania. However, Olympias's son Pyrrhus died. She relinquished rule to her second son, Ptolemy, who also died. Shortly thereafter, she too died.

Sources

Justin. *Epitome* 28.1, 3.

Macurdy, Grace. *Hellenistic Queens*. Reprint. Chicago: Ares Publishers, 1985, p. 79.

Walbank, Frank. *Philip V of Macedon*. Cambridge, England: Cambridge University Press, 1940, p. 9.

◉ Olympias (3)

(c. 361–fifth century C.E.)
Roman: Constantinople, Asia Minor
religious leader

Olympias embraced an ascetic lifestyle and organized a community of women whose monastic lives were never far from the political and religious conflicts of Constantinople. Her deep and abiding relationship with John Chrysostom during and after his tenure as bishop of Constantinople has been memorialized in his letters to her written after he left Constantinople in 420. The letters suggest the complex and complicated politics of the imperial city in which she lived, the difficulties of exile, and the intersection of doctrinal disputes, Christian theology, and personal loyalty that marked life amid the violence of the early fifth century.

Olympias was very wealthy. Her father, Seleucus, held a post in the court of the emperor Julian and had been elevated by him to the position of count. Her grandfather, Ablabius, had exercised great influence over Constantine the Great, under whom he served. It was Ablabius who established the family, acquired a huge fortune, and became a leader in the senate in Constantinople. He was appointed Praetorian Prefect of the East, but later executed for designs on the emperorship. Olympias's mother was Alexandra, who is little known, except that like Olympias's grandfather, she was a Christian, whereas Olympias's father was pagan.

Olympias was orphaned young and Procopius, the Prefect of Constantinople, became her guardian. Theodosia, the sister of Amphilocius, bishop of Iconium, oversaw her education in the city. In late 384 or early 385, Olympias married Nebredius, a much older man, who became Prefect of the City in 386. She was his second wife, his first having been the sister of FLACCILLA, Augusta and first wife of the emperor Theodosius. Although the sources agree that her husband died soon after their marriage, they vary over how long he lived, ranging from a few days to 20 months. However long, the marriage left Olympias the stepmother of a son close to her own age. She developed a close lifelong relationship with her stepson's wife, Salvina. Possibly, she also mingled with members of the imperial household. Aelia Eudoxia, Theodosius's second wife, was fond of Olympias's stepchildren and grandchildren who played with Eudoxia's children at the palace even after the premature death of Olympias's stepson.

Widowed, wealthy, and still young, Olympias attracted attention. Theodosius sought to arrange a second marriage for her with one of his relatives, Helpidius. She refused. She argued that if Christ had wanted her married, he would not have so precipitously removed her husband. It was a variation of the argument used by Marcella, another late fourth-century rich and young widow but to less avail. The emperor provoked exactly the situation that had sent the elder Melania, yet a third rich young widow of the period, racing from Rome away from her extended families, when he charged Olympias with irresponsible spending and put her property in the care of Clementius, the prefect of Constantinople until she was 30. In addition, she was prohibited from meeting with bishops or entering the Great Church of Constantinople. Possibly, she had not only refused to remarry, but also indicated that she was interested in an ascetic life and would make a gift to the church.

Theodosius restored Olympias's control over her property in 391, on his return from defeating the usurper Maximus in the West and Nectarius, the bishop of Constantinople, ordained her a deaconess before she was 30, no doubt realizing the suspicions of the emperor, and clearly an exception to the usual prerequisite age of 60. Ordination limited Olympias's personal autonomy, since she was now officially under the authority of the bishop, who also gained, at the least, the power of moral suasion over the use of her wealth and ownership over whatever property and gold or silver she gave to the church. There is some suggestion that the bishop also may have welcomed her views on religious matters. Olympias, however, could well afford whatever she donated to the church, especially if she gained a formal position in the clergy that ended the pressure from the emperor for her to remarry.

Nectarius was succeeded by John Chrysostom as bishop of Constantinople. Unlike his predecessor, Chrysostom lived simply and plainly. He was a charismatic orator drawn to the humanity of the crucifixion story. His sermons attracted crowds who adored him, not only for his theological clarity, but also for his compassion. Chrysostom responded to Olympias's quest for an ascetic life, her energy, and her wealth. She offered a contrast with women whose wealth fueled an arrogance that demeaned those around them and who seemed indifferent to widespread suffering and poverty.

Their relationship evolved into a personal friendship. He was a complex man whose relationships with women had unresolved issues. He was a misogynist who believed that all women carried the original sin of Eve. He condemned wealthy women for using arts that seduced and deceived men and also for exercising inappropriate power in the public sphere. Yet, he sought the approval of educated women and engaged with them in serious debate. His letters to Olympias, written years after both of them had left Constantinople, conveyed their caring for each other and the pleasure of companionship.

While Chrysostom was still bishop of the city, Olympias built a monastery adjacent to St. Sophia, the great church of the city, and connected the two with a private passageway. She brought together a community which included the female members of her household, although there is no indication that they collectively or individually were in search of an ascetic life: the households of three wealthy sisters who were also relatives, Elisanthia, Martyria, and Palladia; Olympia, her niece; and an additional group of young women from senatorial families. Eventually, some 250 women dwelled in the monastery. A few of the women took orders and became deaconesses, no doubt with suitable donations to the church and to the new monastery. To establish an endowment for the monastery and the church, Olympias donated 10,000 pounds of gold, 20,000 ponds of silver, and estates in Cappadocia, Gaul, Thrace, Bithynia, and other provinces, along with residences and other real estate in the capital itself and the surrounding suburbs.

Olympias, who was an only child and close to the center of imperial largesse, had inherited a family fortune that had been growing for two generations. Over time, the value of her land and capital in the form of gold, silver, and other movable goods, including slaves, animals, and clothing, had compounded beyond her ability to spend the income. Despite the size of her donations, she remained a very rich woman. Over the years, she donated additional funds to high church officials in the provinces and she regularly provided shelter, food, and other amenities to a steady stream of visiting church dignitaries who came to Constantinople. She also supported Chrysostom throughout the years of his exile.

There is no evidence that Olympias chose to eliminate earthly distinctions of status among slaves, freedwomen, and the well born as had the younger MACRINA when she established her house for virgins and widows at the beginning of the fourth century in Asia Minor, nor that she chose a rigorous style of self-denial as had the elder MELANIA or her granddaughter, the younger MELANIA. Life in the monastery promoted simplicity and devotion to the Christian precepts of prayer and helping the poor, but the degree of asceticism practiced left the inhabitants quite comfortable by the standards of the times. To live simply meant wearing coarse cloth and plain garments, avoiding personal ornamentation, and following a regular lifestyle of plain food, assigned time for prayer and contemplation, attendance at church, and service to the poor, widows, and orphans.

Nonetheless, the simplicity of her lifestyle stood in sharp contrast to that of her peers. The concentration of wealth that made it possible for some women to give substantial gifts to churches and monasteries also enabled others to live in extraordinary luxury. Roman society had long regarded wealth as evidence of worthiness and correlative with power. Every wealthy family was surrounded by eddies of dependent kin, freed people, friends of friends, political associates and allies, and a host of hangers-on. However, for the poor or unfortunate, or the deserving and talented who were outside the circles of the great families and their dependents, no obligation existed. Christianity altered the historical dynamic. Olympias and her sisters demonstrated that for some rich women austerity and serving the poor was a new way.

Chrysostom confronted the ruling elite from the perspective of an ascetic Christian comfortable with sisters like Olympias. He attacked the blatant display of wealth amid widespread poverty at a time of serious economic disarray. Although his quarry included high-living churchmen and corrupt civil servants, he specifically attacked women. He may have regarded women as more malleable or less dangerous than men. However, the elite women of Constantinople wielded enormous power within imperial circles. They heard Chrysostom's criticism of curls, clothes, and adornment as an attack on their prominence and power. His equation of women's efforts to appear youthful and alluring with streetwalkers insulted both their sense of style and their rightful position in society. The women turned to the Augusta AELIA EUDOXIA, who was their social leader.

What role did Olympias play in the subsequent political confrontation between Chrysostom and the Augusta? She had connections with the imperial family. Aelia Eudoxia regarded her stepson and his children as intimates. After her stepson died, Salvina, her stepdaughter-in-law, remained unmarried and was a regular visitor to both Olympias at the monastery and Eudoxia at the palace. Despite these ties, Olympias was unable to arrange a détente between Chrysostom and the Augusta nor able to dissuade Chrysostom from pursuing a course that could only lead to his downfall.

Chrysostom had widespread support among the populace, but that was insufficient. Through the connecting passageway that the women traveled to reach the church for services and to meet daily with Chrysostom, they unknowingly went to meet with him for the last time. On his final day, he called together four women, including Olympias and Salvina, the only one not domiciled in the monastery, to inform them of his departure, before he made his announcement from the pulpit. He urged them to obey his successor. They refused.

He left Constantinople on June 20, 404. That night a fire destroyed both St. Sophia, Constantinople's great church, and the senate house. It was not known who was responsible. The city was uneasy. Without imperial opposition, Arsacius, the brother of Nectarius, was appointed bishop in Chrysostom's place. Olympias and the supporters of Chrysostom refused to attend his services, and Olympias refused to take communion from him. The emperor was not pleased.

Olympias tried but failed to restore Chrysostom to his former position. The prefect of the city charged her with contributing to the fires, but, lacking proof, then charged her and other women with refusing to take communion from the new bishop. He offered to dismiss the charges if they agreed to take communion. All agreed, except Olympias who incurred a heavy fine.

Olympias left Constantinople and went to either Cyzicus or Nicomedia in Asia Minor. She continued to correspond with Chrysostom and to provide him and his entourage with funds that enabled him to aid the poor and even ransom people kidnapped by Isuarian bandits. The date of her death is not known.

Sources

John Chrysostom. *Letters to Olympias.*
Palladius. *Dialogues* X, XVI, XVII.
———. *The Lausiac History* 56.
"The Life of Olympias." In Clark, Elizabeth A. *Jerome, Chrysostom and Friends: Essays and Translations.* New York: The Edward Mellon Press, 1979, pp. 107–144.
Sozomen. *Historia Ecclesiastica* VIII. ix, xxiv, xxvii.
Meyer, Wendy, "Constantinopolitan Women in Chrysostom's Circle." *Vigiliae Christianae* 53, no. 3 (August 1999) pp. 265–288.
Prosopography of the Later Roman Empire. Vol. I. Edited by A. H. M. Jones, J. R. Martindale, and J. Morris. Cambridge: Cambridge University Press, 1971. Reprinted 1992, pp. 642–643.

Opimia

(?–216 B.C.E.)   Roman: Rome
priestess

Opimia was a Vestal Virgin accused of violating her vow of chastity in 216 B.C.E. One of six Vestals,

she was responsible for maintaining the eternal flame in the temple of Vesta, one of the oldest temples in the Forum. She was charged together with a colleague, FLORONIA. It was considered an extremely serious ill omen for the state when the Vestal Virgins trangressed. Opimia was either entombed or committed suicide.

Sources

Livy. *From the Founding of the City* 22.57.2–5.
Bauman, Richard A. *Women and Politics in Ancient Rome.* London: Routledge, 1994, pp. 23–24.

Orbiana

(third century C.E.)   Roman: Italy
possible Augusta

Gnaea Seia Herennia Sallustia Barbia Orbiana was 15 years old when she married the 17-year-old emperor Severus Alexander in 225 C.E. She may have immediately been declared Augusta. The marriage was recorded with a run of celebratory coins struck in gold, silver, and bronze. Orbiana was on the obverse and, with probably unintentional irony, *Concordia* (harmonious agreement) on the reverse.

Orbiana's new mother-in-law, JULIA AVITA MAMAEA, who had dominated the reign since her son had become emperor at 13, did not welcome the intrusion of Orbiana or her father, Sallustius Macrinus, or Macrinianus. Possibly, the father was elevated to the position of Caesar, and the marriage may have been part of plot to overthrow the emperor or to eliminate Julia Mamaea. Whatever the intention, it failed. Julia Mamaea emerged unscathed. Orbiana's father was executed; Orbiana was divorced and exiled to Libya in 227 C.E.

Sources

Herodian. *History of the Empire* 6.1, 9–10.
Scriptores Historiae Augustae. Alexander Severus 20.3; 49.4–5.
Balsdon, J. P. V. D. *Roman Women.* New York: John Day Comp., 1963, p. 163.
Gibbon, Edward. *The Decline and Fall of the Roman Empire.* New York: Heritage Press, 1946, p. 117.

P

Papiria

(third–second century B.C.E.)
Roman: Rome
financially strapped well-born woman

Papiria was divorced and left financially strapped. She was the daughter of Caius Papirius Maso, consul in 231 B.C.E. She married Lucius Aemilius Paullus Macedonius, general and statesman, who was twice consul. She had two sons, Quintus Fabius and Publius Cornelius. When her husband divorced her, he was criticized in the Senate. Her virtues were enumerated: She was beautiful and virtuous and had borne sons. It is said that her husband held his shoe high and commented that it too was new and good-looking, but that only he knew where it pinched.

Papiria ceased to participate in women's rites to which her birth and status admitted her since her divorce left her poor. Publius Cornelius however was adopted by Publius Cornelius Scipio, son of the Publius Cornelius Scipio Africanus Major who conquered Hannibal. He inherited a large fortune from his adoptive grandmother AEMILIA TERTIA, who was the wife of Scipio Africanus. Papiria's son gave her all of his grandmother's servants, ornaments, and utensils used in religious ceremonies. Her son's generosity was noted, and many women offered prayers for such a son. It was observed that the son's gift was exceptional, especially in Rome, few ever willingly parted with anything they had gained.

Sources

Plutarch. *Vitae Parallelae (Parallel Lives): Aemilius Paulus* 5.2–3.
Balsdon, J. P. V. D. *Roman Women.* New York: John Day Comp., 1963, pp. 43, 211–212.
Pauly, A., G. Wissowa, and W. Kroll. *Real-Encyclopadie D. Classischen Altertumswissenschaft 1893–.* (Germany: multiple publishers) 78.

Paula the Elder

(347–January 26, 404 C.E.)
Roman: Rome, Bethlehem
ascetic, Christian scholar

Paula had the virtues of her ancestor, the fabled CORNELIA (2), mother of the famed Gracchi brothers of the early Republic, and the independence that allowed her to choose an ascetic life and follow the churchman and ascetic Jerome to Palestine. A daughter of patrician parents, Blaesilla and Rogatus, her mother's ancient Roman bloodlines were matched by her father's illustrious Greek ancestry. Paula married Toxotius, a senator, and bore four daughters, BLAESILLA, Paulina, EUSTOCHIUM, and Rufina, as well as a son, Toxotius, before she left Italy and founded a complex of monasteries, where she lived with Jerome and was editor and supporter for his translation of the Greek Bible into Latin.

After the birth of her son, Paula and her husband embraced celibacy. Her husband died in 379, when Paula was in her early 30s, and her son was still a baby. It was a close relationship and she mourned his loss. Paula arranged for the marriages of Blaesilla, Paulina, and Rufina, although Rufina died before her marriage took place. Paula's fourth daughter, Eustochium, chose celibacy and was steadfast in her decision despite family pressure to marry.

Paula's decision to live a celibate life mirrored the ideals of the early Christians and made sense for her own life. Although Paula was insulated by wealth, her senatorial ties exposed her to political instabilities. The Roman Senate was weak but prominent. Although the Senate had long since dissipated its political power in an increasingly autocratic environment, its authority of tradition and concentration of wealthy men made it a target for each new emperor and a scapegoat for each new imperial disaster. Paula's friends and family suffered show trials and defended themselves against political vendettas disguised as lawsuits. Personal feuds moved across generations as the larger political winds of empire shifted. The larger instabilities mixed with private disappointments and sorrow. Her husband and her daughter died young and her daughter Blaesilla's husband died soon after their marriage. Her daughter Paulina died in childbirth. In the face of so many losses in a short time, unmarried celibacy may not have been a hard choice.

It was also in the air. Christianity offered a consolation for the sorrow and pain of loss and personal salvation through an ascetic life. The message was powerful. In Rome, MARCELLA, a social peer and part of the same small elite, had already organized a house for celibate young women and widows. They eschewed luxury, wore simple dress, prayed, read the Christian texts, did household tasks, fasted, and lived according to the precepts of the new religion as it had first been practiced. Paula became part of Marcella's circle. She sent Eustochium to live in her house and learn from her.

Paula soon organized her own household for widows and young women who chose a celibate life. The residents included her daughters, Eustochium, before she went to Marcella, and the widowed Blaesilla. They studied Greek and learned Hebrew, which enabled them to read ancient religious texts not yet translated into Latin. Unlike Marcella, Paula was not a scholar interested in textual analysis or the historical meaning of texts. Her correspondence with Jerome reflected her search for more mystical, spiritual, and moral sustenance.

The arrival of Jerome in Rome in 382 marked a turning point in Paula's life. Paula first heard Jerome at a reading of the scriptures organized for women by Marcella. He had come to Rome with Paulinus, bishop of Antioch, and Epiphanius, bishop of Salamis, from whom she also heard stories of women who had embraced ascetic lives in the East. Paula and Eustochium developed a close mentor relationship with Jerome. As was the custom among Christians, men and women could work, study, and pray together or separately. They visited each other's houses and shared food.

The cross-gender friendships that evolved among celibate men and women were not, however, a usual part of traditional Greco-Roman social mores. And as Paul had warned the Christians centuries earlier, it was wont to be misunderstood. Paula's close relationship with Jerome subjected them to gossip, no doubt with sexual overtones, as well as insinuations that he was angling to become her beneficiary, a not unheard of situation in a society where inheritance was a major means of acquiring wealth.

Paula's widowed daughter Blaesilla died sometime after 383 and before Jerome's departure from Rome in 385. Her death intensified the disapproval that surrounded Jerome and his friendship with Paula, her daughters, and friends. Blaesilla died just three months after she adopted a lifestyle of prayer and severe fasting. Ironically, Paula had encouraged Blaesilla to remarry. With her daughters Rufina and Paulina already dead and Eustochium committed to asceticism, Blaesilla was the only remaining daughter from whom she could hope to have grandchildren. Possibly, not grandchildren or celibacy, but concern for Blaesilla was Paula's primary motivation. Blaesilla had already been ill before her husband died and Paula may have feared that an ascetic regime would upset her delicate health and even lead to death.

Many Christians and pagans criticized Jerome after Blaesilla's death for encouraging women to pursue a rigorous asceticism. Although unfair, insofar as Jerome never approved or encouraged extreme fasting, the criticism reflected a more pervasive Christian distaste of the ascetic life as an antisocial choice. Women were needed and, if they turned inward and away from family, worldly pursuits, and goods, that posed a challenge to an already unstable society.

The balance between collective good and personal salvation, however, was sometimes modified by the politics of church affairs. In 384, the bishop of Rome, Damascus, a strong supporter of Jerome, died and was succeeded by Siricius, who disliked Jerome. Public disapproval following the death of Blaesilla compounded by the hostility of Siricius, left Jerome with little choice but to leave Rome.

Paula was soon ready to follow him. Overcome with grief, she fainted during Blaesilla's funeral procession. In a letter from Jerome praising Blaesilla and consoling Paula, he warned against excessive grief and cited the example of the elder MELANIA who simultaneously buried a husband and two sons. Paula followed Melania's example, in action, if not in her stoic behavior at the graveside. She too left Rome with her daughter Eustochium, but left her son behind, as Melania had.

Paula had a different relationship with her daughters and her son. Her daughters were closer to her in age and, as women, in experience. A life of celibacy offered a freedom that men had always enjoyed. A woman ascetic looked to her own salvation through her own efforts without needing to serve her husband, family, and children. Marriage to the Lord was a commitment that allowed Paula to leave her son in the care of her husband's family, to which, technically, under Roman law he, but not she, belonged. Like Melania, she attended to the practical and left him well endowed. She never saw him again, nor did he visit her, as she pursued a life bordered by the Christian world community, not bloodlines.

Paula, 38 years old, accompanied by Eustochium and an entourage of many young women, some of whom were probably her former slaves, freedwomen, and servants, left to join Jerome. She and her entourage followed a well-trod pilgrims' path. They stopped at Cyprus for 10 days during which Paula saw bishop Epiphanius and visited monasteries to which she contributed funds. Then they traveled to Antioch, where they met with Jerome and paid a visit to Paulinus.

With Jerome, they set out for Jerusalem. They stopped to visit the important religious sites in Egypt and Palestine. Paula's stamina was amazing to Jerome, although it was just the same kind of stamina that was exhibited by EGERIA as well as the elder and younger MELANIAS, and the myriad other women who made the pilgrimage to Christian sites during these centuries.

Paula decided to build a monastery. They visited the monasteries of the elder Melania on the Mount of Olives to gather ideas about construction and the organization of the community. They settled in Bethlehem. For the next several years Paula and Eustochium supervised construction of a monastic compound that contained a chapel, separate residences for women and men, administrative quarters, and a library. Paula directed the compound and the women. Jerome supervised the men's section. Eustochium worked as their second.

Paula gathered young women—well born, modest, or poor. Unlike the younger MACRINA and like OLYMPIAS, her monastery allowed upper-class women attendants. The only condition was that they not be the same women who served them in Rome, lest they simply recreate their former lifestyle. Paula divided the women into three groups, each in a separate building and each with its own supervisor. The groups worked and ate separately but came together for prayer and the singing of psalms. They studied the scriptures and read from the psalter several times during the day. Everyone wore the same simple, coarse clothing and had almost no contact with men. Collectively, they were self-sufficient and made clothing for themselves as well as for sale and donation. Aside from food and clothing, the women had no personal possessions. On Sundays, the men and women met to worship at the Church of the Nativity.

Jerome wrote that Paula dressed like the other women and only bathed when she was ill. Her bed was the ground and her blanket was made of coarse goat's hair. Paula, however, was so profligate in disbursing money to the poor and other charitable causes that Jerome warned her that she would not have enough for her own needs. She refused to listen and borrowed money. Eustochium was faced with a large deficit when she took over the monasteries after her mother's death.

Paula now began her greatest work. She and Eustochium aided Jerome in the translation of the Bible from Greek into Latin. Both of them were fluent in Greek and Hebrew. They met daily, and Jerome reviewed his work for them. He wrote that when he was stuck between competing problems about the translation, Paula would question him about which he thought was most probable until he made a decision. At her request, Jerome translated Origen's *Homilies on Saint Luke's Gospels* and revised his first psalter. He dedicated many of his works to Paula and Eustochium.

Paula died on January 26, 404, a year before the translation was complete. She had lived many lives: as a Roman *matrona,* honored for her fecundity and her lineage; as a religious ascetic in search of her own path; as a traveler and founder of a monastic compound; and as a collaborator in one of the period's great literary efforts. Many bishops, priests, monks, young women, celibates, and laypeople came to her funeral. The psalms were chanted in Latin, Greek, and Syriac by the diverse mourners. She was buried beneath the Church of the Nativity.

Sources

Jerome. *Letters* XXX, XXXIII, XXXIV, XXXIX, XLVI.

McNamara, Jo Ann. *"Cornelia's Daughters: Paula and Eustochium." Women's Studies* 11 (1984): 9–27.

Peterson, Joan M. *Handmaids of the Lord: Contemporary Descriptions of Feminine Asceticism in the First Six Christian Centuries.* Kalamazoo, Mich.: Cistercian Publications Inc., 1996. pp. 123–167.

Prosopography of the Later Roman Empire. Vol. I. Edited by A. H. M. Jones, J. R. Martindale, and J. Morris. Cambridge: Cambridge University Press, 1971. Reprinted 1992, pp. 674–675.

Yarbrough, Anne. "Christianization in the Fourth Century: The Example of Roman Women." *Church History* 45, no. 2 (June 1976): 149–165.

Paula the Younger

(c. 402–? C.E.)   Roman: Rome, Bethlehem
ascetic, head of a monastery

Paula directed a monastic compound in Bethlehem that included three residences for women, one for men, a chapel or church, working areas, administrative quarters, and probably a library and scriptorium. Her mother, Laeta, was a well-born Christian from a mixed Christian pagan family. Her father, Toxotius, was the son of the elder PAULA, who had founded the monastic compound with her daughter, EUSTOCHIUM, and the churchman and ascetic Jerome. Through her grandmother, Paula, the young Paula could trace her lineage back to the fabled CORNELIA (2), mother of the Gracchi brothers in the second century B.C.E., and to the Scipios.

Paula's father, Toxotius, was a child when his father died, his mother chose to become an ascetic, and he went to live with his paternal relatives. His mother arranged for his financial future and went off with her daughter Eustochium to join Jerome in Africa. He never again saw her again. Toxotius's wife Laeta felt the pull of asceticism that had absorbed his mother. When their daughter Paula was born, he and Laeta agreed that they would not seek a husband for her and she would be allowed to live a Christian celibate life.

In 403, Laeta wrote to Jerome in Bethlehem asking his advice on bringing up their daughter Paula to lead an ascetic life. Jerome sent back a lengthy letter that outlined an educational program beginning with blocks shaped like letters and extending to a Greek tutor. The proposed program was rigorous and supportive, practical and theoretical. Jerome made clear that the attitudes to knowledge and learning developed in young years molded mature minds. The program blended classical tradition and Christian learning into something new but imbued with a respect and love of learning and language.

Jerome included the visual arts as well as reading, writing, and speaking Latin and Greek (without an accent). Jerome urged Paula's parents to praise her well for learning and to keep her away from boys, although an older male tutor was of no concern. He then went on to outline rules of deportment that included very moderate eating, fasting, in-depth reading, and understanding of the scriptures with memorization of much of their content. Only after she had completed her basic education was she to read the *Song of Songs,* then, no doubt, sufficiently formed and instructed to hold a Christian appreciation of its content.

In addition, Jerome urged that she learn to spin wool and make clothing, both of which were the archetypical occupations of ancient women, and the practical arts of self-sufficiency practiced in the monastery. Finally, Jerome urged Laeta to send Paula to her grandmother and Eustochium in Bethlehem where they could serve as her role models. Her parents waited until she was about 14 or 15 years old to follow his advice. Her grandmother, the elder Paula, had died by then, but she went to live with her aunt Eustochium who had become leader of the monastery and who trained the younger Paula to succeed her.

The monastery's finances occupied Eustochium's attention in the years following her mother's death and probably provided the younger Paula with a thorough education in the business aspects of administering a monastic complex responsible for the lives of hundreds of people. The elder Paula had left the monastery in debt. She had used all of her own fortune and had borrowed as well. Jerome feared that Eustochium would not free the monastery from debt in her lifetime. Eustochium, however, proved a talented administrator who restored the monastery's finances while Paula lived with her.

The two women tapped resources throughout the empire. In 415 they sent a presbyter Firmus to Ravenna and Sicily and then back to Africa, possibly Carthage. The business probably involved properties they had inherited. Jerome wrote to Augustine in Hippo in 416, included greetings from Paula and Eustochium and an inquiry about Firmus, with whom they had lost touch but who might be detained in Africa. He also enclosed a letter for Firmus which he asked Augustine to deliver, should he be nearby.

The women also had to address doctrinal issues. A troublesome situation had arisen in 415, after a church council at Diospolis in Palestine acquitted a cleric who followed Pelagius of heresy. Pelagius preached an appealing popular doctrine that denied Original Sin and assured men and women of their free will to choose between good and evil. Celebrations became riots and the opposing groups fought each other. Paula and Eustochium sent a letter to Innocent, bishop in Rome, complaining about the murders, looting, and burning of buildings, some of them within their monastic compound. Innocent responded with a sharp letter to John, bishop of Jerusalem. However, both men died sometime in 419/420, as did Eustochium.

Paula, who was 19 or 20 years old, stepped into Eustochium's place and became head of the women's monasteries and overall director of the compound.

Sources

Jerome. *Letters* CXXXIV, CXXXVI, CXXXVII.

McNamara, Jo Ann. "Cornelia's Daughters: Paula and Eustochium." *Women's Studies* 11 (1984): 9–27.

Yarbrough, Anne. "Christianization in the Fourth Century: The Example of Roman Women." *Church History* 45, no. 2 (June 1976): 149–165.

Paulina

(first century C.E.)   Roman: Rome
victim of deception

Paulina was a devotee of Isis. Isis worship had been brought from Egypt to Rome, where it attracted a wide following. The underlying sensuality and sexuality in the worship of a figure who was simultaneously wife, mother, and prostitute affirmed female sexual potency and was especially attractive to women. Paulina became the center of a scandal that rested on the naïveté of some Isis followers and that had serious political consequences.

She had rejected the advances of one Decius Mundus. Undeterred, he was said to have bribed a priest in the temple of Isis to inform Paulina that she was desired by the Egyptian god Anubis. Paulina made no secret of her appointment in the temple with the god, even telling her husband of the assignation. Later Mundus bragged of his deception. Paulina learned of his duplicity and her husband went to the authorities. After an inquiry Mundus was exiled.

The emperor Tiberius had the priests of Isis crucified and deported thousands of worshipers to Sardinia.

Sources
Josephus. *Antiquitates Judaicae (Jewish Antiquities)* 18.65–80.
Tacitus. *Annales* 2.85.5.
Balsdon, J. P. V. D. *Roman Women.* New York: John Day Comp., 1963, p. 247.

 Paxaea
(first century C.E.)
Roman: Italy and the Balkans
charged with treason and extortion

Paxaea and her husband, Pomponius Labeo, the former governor of the Roman province of Moesia in what is now Serbia, were tried in the Senate on charges that probably included treason and extortion. The emperor Tiberius had turned against Labeo in 34 C.E., the same year as the trial. The precise nature of the treason of which Labeo was accused is not known. It is also uncertain if Paxaea was charged with both crimes or just one.

Paxaea and her husband committed suicide before the Senate reached a verdict. After her death, the emperor Tiberius declared that Paxaea had been in no danger despite the fact that she was guilty.

Sources
Tacitus. *Annales* 6.29.
Levick, Barbara. *Tiberius the Politician.* London: Thames and Hudson, 1976, pp. 197, 213 ff.
Marshall, A. J. "Women on Trial before the Roman Senate." *Classical Views* 34 (1990): 331–366.

Perictione
(fifth century B.C.E.)   Greek: Athens
mother of Plato

Perictione, an Athenian from a distinguished family that traced its ancestry back to Solon, was nota-ble for being the mother of the great philosopher Plato. She was born in the early 440s. Her father was Glaucon, and her brother Charmides was the protagonist in a Socratic dialogue named after him. Perictione married Ariston, a man from a similar background, and in addition to Plato, they had two other sons, Adeimantus and Glaucon, and a daughter, POTONE. After the death of her husband, she married her maternal uncle, Pyrilampes. He served as an ambassador in Persia and was noted for his breeding of Persian peacocks.

Sources
Diogenes Laertius. *Lives of the Eminent Philosophers* 3.1.3–4.
Plato. *Charmides* 158a.
Davies, J. K. *Athenian Propertied Families, 600–300 B.C.* Oxford: Clarendon Press, 1971, pp. 330, 332–333.

Perpetua, Vibia
(181–203 C.E.)
Roman: Carthage, North Africa
martyr

Perpetua successfully sought and found martyrdom. She died in Carthage on March 7, 203, after having been mauled by wild animals during games to celebrate the birthday of the emperor's son Geta. When she died, she was 22 years old, married, and had recently given birth to her first child, a son.

The narrative of her martyrdom is among the few lengthy surviving works written by a woman from the Greco-Roman world, and one of the earliest written by a Christian woman. After she and a small band of coreligionists had been imprisoned, Perpetua recorded three visions, each of which strengthened her faith and affirmed her death. Her narrative ended on the night before the group was to enter the arena. A fellow Christian who witnessed their death added an introduction and conclusion. The narrative circulated after her death, then disappeared. Her name and martyrdom, however, remained a part of tradition. A manuscript was uncovered in the 17th century and published. Since then additional copies in both Latin and Greek have been found.

During Perpetua's lifetime, North Africa was an important trading and agricultural region in a largely peaceful empire. In the western Mediterranean, Carthage was second only to Rome in size and importance. Punic in tradition and Roman in culture, spoken and written Latin were widespread among men and women. Perpetua wrote in a vernacular rather than literary Latin, which was even more readily understood and easily copied for distribution.

Carthage was also a center of Montanism, a thread of Christianity that emerged in the mid-second century in Asia Minor. Led by a wandering priest Montanus and two women Prisca and Maximilla, it emphasized the immediacy of redemption through the direct intercession of the Holy Spirit. At the time of Perpetua's martyrdom, the church father and most famous Montanist, Tertullian, was alive and writing in Carthage. Declared a heresy by the church of the West, Montanism may have had a particular attraction for women like Perpetua who even before she was arrested had already experienced visions, prophesized, and spoke in tongues.

Perpetua expected visions while in prison. Her public admission of faith before hostile Roman administrators who condemned her to death gave her standing, authority, and authenticity to prophesize for the community of faithful Christians she would leave behind. Her visions were seamless and holistic dreamlike sequences which mingled past, present, and future with metaphors and similes from the Bible stories as she knew them. The visions successfully tied her death to salvation. The Holy Spirit visited her and strengthened her personal Christian commitment. She saw her younger brother, a pagan who had died from cancer, brought into the Christian fold and God's presence. Her visions were powerful intoxicants that protected her, even while in the arena.

The narrative provides some historical information about her and her coreligionists. She was clearly the leader of the small imprisoned band. She also appears to have been the only one who was born into a family of some wealth and property. She was the best educated among the group, which included Saturninus and Secundulus, about whom not a great deal is known, and Revocatus and Felicity, who were servants, if not slaves or freed slaves. Felicity was also her friend, although not her equal by birth or education. She shared Perpetua's devotion to Christ and fierce determination to die for her beliefs.

Perpetua and Felicity were new Christians. Catechumens, they had not yet been baptized when they entered prison. After Perpetua's first vision, which assured the group of their martyrdom, she and Felicity underwent baptism. Felicity was also eight months pregnant and feared she might not give birth in time to enter the arena with Perpetua. Her delivery of a healthy girl came earlier than expected, and she gave the baby to her sister, who was not imprisoned although presumably a Christian. Felicity and Perpetua went into the arena together.

The narrative opens before the arrest, when the group lived together in the house of Perpetua's father, although he was absent. By the time he arrived the group was under surveillance, probably for practicing Christian rites. In Carthage at this time, it was a crime simply to admit to being a Christian. No evidence of other wrongdoing was necessary, and death was the usual punishment. Enforcement of the law was in the hands of the proconsuls or governor, who were directly responsible to Rome. The law was unevenly applied, affected by class and citizenship, as well as bribes, personal relationships, and the inclination of the presiding officers.

Perpetua's father begged her not to identify herself as a Christian. Possibly, she had only to assert that she was a Roman and loyal to the emperor. Although the genus of the emperor demanded a religious sacrifice, educated Romans were intellectually sophisticated in a range of philosophical positions from Stoicism to Neoplatonism. Few would have confused the guiding spirits or God of the universe with the emperor's genus. Those who were Christian, moreover, had already received instruction from the bishop to avoid voluntary martyrdom. Perpetua's declaration before the proconsul was an assertion of belief tinged with a desire for martyrdom.

Throughout the narrative Perpetua portrayed her father as a caring man, the epitome of pagan rationality. He attempted to dissuade her by reason. There was no harm to the tradition of offering sacrifices to the spirits, since the gods were unknowable and not to sacrifice might upset the age-old pact between the gods and the community. When reason alone failed to dissuade her, he spoke of his love for her, as well as her responsibilities to him, her family, and her child. He became increasingly distraught as Perpetua became increasingly certain. Finally, he pleaded with her: She was his favored child and he needed her. As Perpetua moved through her visions, however, her father's growing anguish gained a distant, almost muted, quality and once she declared herself a Christian to the court, the gulf between them became unbridgeable. His Punic-Roman universe of assumptions ceased to be hers. She had changed her allegiance from the family of blood kin to the Christian community that was her family of choice. Her freedom was in her faith. She raced to the death that he wanted her to avoid. What on his part was a deathwatch, she and her coreligionists eagerly awaited as the precursor of Resurrection.

The narrative also offers a glimpse of the limits of *patria potestas* over a daughter among the propertied in North Africa at the opening of the third century. By the late Republic, women had secured a functional independence, especially after marriage or widowhood, and also with motherhood, under Julian laws of Augustus in 23 and 27 C.E. As the empire matured, women's personal independence became increasingly a functioning reality, and by the time of Perpetua, adult women suffered few legal restrictions in private affairs. They also held priesthoods in some state religions and in many of the mystery religions and were the patronesses of good deeds and city improvements across the empire. Shortly after Perpetua's death, in 212 C.E., the emperor extended Roman citizenship, with some exceptions, to all residents within the empire and assured the personal legal rights of women.

Rights over property, claims in court, inheritance, guardianship, and contracts, however, were not necessarily consonant with proscribed roles within the family in which women still were expected to be subservient to the authority of the father. Perpetua's father was either unwilling or unable to compel his daughter to abandon Christianity. He did not threaten her or attempt forcibly to separate her from her Christian community. Throughout the narrative he respected her decisions and actions, even though they led to her death and his despair.

The narrative also raises many unanswerable questions. Her son appears to have still been an infant. Had she come to her father's house for her confinement? Was Felicity a new acquaintance or was she a member of the household who had known Perpetua since both were children? Above all, there is no information about Perpetua's husband. Any girl of her social and economic class, especially a favored daughter, would have been betrothed with a civil contract that assured her future. While it is possible she was widowed or divorced, it must have happened only recently given that she had an infant child. It is hard to understand why her husband is never mentioned.

Perpetua offered no special reason for the attention the authorities paid her and her coreligionists among the larger Christian community, although the narrative suggests that those arrested worshiped in her father's house. Not all members of the larger Carthage Christian community were arrested or were even threatened with arrest. Fellow Christians outside the prison watched over the group. An opening invocation and a conclusion to the narrative by a fellow Christian who visited with her, witnessed her death, and cared for a written copy of her visions highlights the selectivity and the freedom of others to come and go in the prison. Bribes paid to the soldiers gained the prisoners better conditions. Perpetua's brother and father brought her child to stay with her.

The group speculated about the animals they might encounter in the arena. Although there were different kinds of games, the games to honor the birthday of the emperor's son Geta pitted the prisoners against wild animals. These bloody and violent spectacles mostly used bears or lions, which often had first been excited and tantalized with the promise of blood. Since the prisoners in the contest were already condemned to death through the processes of law, the crowds had no more moral compunction about their death than did later crowds gathered for hangings. It was a sport.

Perpetua's narrative ended the night before she and her coreligionists entered the arena. A fellow Christian described her last day. Perpetua did not die in the arena. Barely injured, she was sent from the arena by the calls of the crowds which had been sated. In a side room, she came out of a self-induced trance unaware that she had already been in the arena until she saw the bruises on her body. However, her survival did not alter her death sentence. She was killed by the sword of a young army man. Unsure of himself, he first sent the sword into her clavicle. She cried out in pain and took his hand to direct his thrust deep into her chest.

Sources

Perpetua. *The Passion of SS. Perpetua and Felicity,* translated by W. H. Shewring. New York: Kuboaa, 2000.

Klawiter, Fredrick. "The Role of Martrydom and Persecution in Developing the Priestly Authority of Women in Early Christianity." *Church History* 49.3 (Sept. 1980): 251–261.

Salisbury, Joyce, E. *Perpetua's Passion: The Death and Memory of a Young Roman Woman.* New York: Rutledge, 1997.

Wypustek, Andrzej. "Magic, Montanism, Perpetua and the Severan Persecution." *Vigilae Christlanae* 51.3 (1997): 276–297.

◉ Petronia
(first century C.E.) Roman: Rome
political player

Petronia was the daughter of a wealthy consul and had a large personal fortune. She married Aulus Vitellius, the future emperor. She made a will naming their son, Petronianus, her heir on condition that Vitellius renounce his paternal rights. Vitellius agreed, but their son died. Vitellius said the young man had had suicidal leanings and had mistakenly taken poison that was intended for him. It was generally believed that Vitellius had murdered his son to obtain the inheritance.

Petronia divorced Vitellius. She married Cornelius Dolabella. Dolabella supported the emperor Servius Sulpicius Galba and was banished by the emperor Marcus Salvius Otho, who supplanted Galba in 69 C.E. After Otho's death, Dolabella returned. When Vitellius became emperor later in 69, he ordered Dolabella killed. Nothing more is known of Petronia.

Sources

Suetonius. *The Lives of the Caesars:* Vitellius 6.
Tacitus. *Historiae* 2.64.

◉ Phaenarete
(fifth century B.C.E.) Greek: Athens
mother of Socrates

Phaenarete was the mother of the great philosopher Socrates. Her husband, Sophroniscus, was an Athenian sculptor or stonemason. Phaenarete was a midwife. She belonged to the Alopece clan.

Sources

Diogenes Laertius. *Lives of the Eminent Philosophers* 2.18.

◉ Phila (1)
(c. 351–283 B.C.E.) Greek: Macedonia
wise, loyal and influential wife

Phila was a woman of exceptional character who used the circumstances in which she found herself to exert influence and exercise power. She was said to have been close to her father and his confidant since her childhood. Her father, Antipater, the Macedonian general whom Alexander the Great left with oversight of the Greek city-states and Macedonia when he went east on campaign, was generally regarded as a wise ruler, and Phila learned well. Her mother was Stratonice, daughter of a Macedonian named Corrhagus.

After Alexander's unexpected death, his generals divided the empire. Antipater and Craterus became convinced that a third general, Perdiccas, was plotting to make himself dominant. They formed an alliance with Ptolemy I Soter, the Macedonian general who had made himself ruler of Egypt. To cement the alliance, Phila married Craterus in 322 B.C.E., and another daughter of Antipater, EURYDICE (3), married Ptolemy I Soter. A third daughter, NICAEA (1), married Lysimachus, the former companion and bodyguard of Alexander who ruled Thrace, to assure his neutrality to the pact. Phila

253

had a son also named Craterus. Her husband was killed leading his troops in 321.

Before she was even able to bury her husband, her father arranged a marriage with the 18-year-old Demetrius who was the son of his longtime fighting companion, Antigonus. He was some 12 years her junior and an extraordinarily handsome man. A notorious womanizer, he was frequently engaged in multiple sexual adventures and married several women. Once his wife, however, Phila remained steadfastly loyal. Demetrius recognized her political sagacity, and she was undoubtedly the most important and influential woman in his life.

In 319, Antipater died and Antigonus, with the aid of Demetrius, attempted to reunite Alexander's empire. Left behind, Phila sent a ship filled with letters, bedding, and clothing to Demetrius when he besieged Rhodes in 305. Unfortunately for her husband, it was intercepted by the Rhodians. She also quelled troublemakers on the home front. She was said to have arranged marriages and given dowries to settle many women and to have protected many suffering from false allegations. She also resolved disputes among the soldiers whose camps she visited and was regarded by them as a fair arbitrator.

In 298, Phila accompanied Demetrius when he set sail for Syria to marry their daughter, STRATONICE (2), to Seleucus I. They stopped at Cilicia, in southern Asia Minor, which was ruled by Pleistarchus, a brother of Phila. Pleistarchus was furious at the landing and further angered by any alliance with Seleucus, for Demetrius had been the common enemy of both Pleistarchus and Seleucus. After the wedding, Demetrius seized Cilicia. Phila went to Macedonia where her other brother, Cassander, was king to convince him not to side with Pleistarchus.

In 294 the Macedonian army invited Demetrius I to become king because he was related to Antipater through his marriage to Phila. For Phila it was a great moment of success that was short-lived. The alliance with Seleucus I fell apart. Demetrius was defeated and captured by Seleucus in 285. Seleucus kept him in luxurious confinement, and he drank himself to death in 283. Phila committed suicide by taking poison. In addition to Stratonice, Phila and Demetrius had a son, Antigonus Gonatus, who reestablished control over Macedonia.

Sources

Plutarch. *Vitae Parallelae (Parallel Lives): Demetrius* 14.2–3; 22.1; 31.3; 32.1–3; 37.3; 45.1; 53.3.

Diodorus Siculus. *Library of History* 18.18.7; 19.59.3–6; 20.93.4.

Cary, M. *A History of the Greek World from 323 to 146 B.C.* London: Methuen, 1951.

Macurdy, Grace. *Hellenistic Queens.* Reprint. Chicago: Ares Publishers, 1985, pp. 58–69.

Phila (2)

(third century B.C.E.)

Greek: Asia, Asia Minor and Macedonia

power broker

Phila grew up living with her father, Seleucus I, whose rule extended from Asia Minor into central Asia. Her mother, STRATONICE (2), had gone to the eastern part of the empire as the wife of Antiochus I, her father's son by APAMA (1) and coruler. When Antiochus succeeded her father, Phila was about 21. Her mother arranged for her to marry her uncle Antigonus Gonatus, who had become ruler of Macedonia. The marriage sealed a compact in which Antiochus I surrendered any claim to Macedonia and renounced his claim to what is now called the Gallipoli Peninsula.

Phila's husband was a fine man, a sound general, and a prudent ruler. He was educated in philosophy and had philosophers, poets, and historians as friends. Among the guests at Phila's elaborate wedding was the noted poet Aratus, who wrote a hymn and poems for the occasion. Her marriage appears to have been successful and was remarkable for its longevity. She had been married for 37 years when her husband died in 239 B.C.E.

Phila's son Demetrius II succeeded his father as ruler of Macedonia. He married STRATONICE (3), who was both a half sister and niece of his mother, but later divorced her.

Sources

Plutarch. *Vitae Parallelae (Parallel Lives): Demetrius* 31.3; 38.

Bevan, Edwyn R. *The House of Seleucus.* 2 vols. London: Edward Arnold, 1902, v. 1, pp. 145, 173.

Macurdy, Grace. *Hellenistic Queens.* Reprint. Chicago: Ares Publishers, 1985, pp. 69–70.

Philesia

(fifth–fourth century B.C.E.)
Greek: Athens and Sparta
wife of Xenophon

Philesia, an Athenian woman, married Xenophon, who came from a wealthy family and was a follower of Socrates. Xenophon, known for his work on household management, asserted that a man should marry a woman sufficiently young and pliable to bend to his ways.

Xenophon, however, was rarely at home. He spent most of his life in the military. In 401 B.C.E. he left Athens and joined Greek mercenaries in Asia Minor under Cyrus II to gain control over Persia. The expedition was a failure, and Xenophon, with the rank of general, led the Greek forces to safety. In 399 he enlisted his troops in the services of Sparta in Asia Minor and was exiled by Athens. From 396 to 394 he served with Agesilaus, ruler of Sparta, campaigning in Asia Minor. When the Agesilaus returned to Sparta, Xenophon went with him and fought against Athens. In honor of his service, the Spartans gave him an estate at Scillus near the city of Olympia. Philesia and their two sons went there with him. Later, the area came under attack, and the family moved to Corinth.

Athens rescinded his exile in 366 after relations with Sparta improved. Xenophon returned to Athens in that year and lived there until his death in 354. Philesia, if still living, would have returned with him. Both their sons served with the Athenians against Sparta. One son was killed in battle in 362 B.C.E.

Sources

Diogenes Laertius. *Lives of the Eminent Philosophers* 2.48–59.

Philinna

(fourth century B.C.E.)
Greek: Thessaly and Macedonia
cowife of Phillip II

Philinna was especially vulnerable in the household of Philip II, ruler of Macedonia. With the exception of OLYMPIAS (1), she was the only wife of Philip II to have a son. She came from Larissa in northwest Thessaly. Larissa had called on Philip to help overthrow the tyrant of Phaere who threatened them. Philip complied and married Philinna in 356 B.C.E. to solidify his ties with the aristocratic families of Larissa. Their son Philip Arrhidaeus was born in the 350s. The child was born with some impairment, which could have been epilepsy or a limited mental capacity. Alternatively, as one of the sources contends, he may have been debilitated with poison fed him by Olympias.

Philip had married Olympias the year before his marriage with Philinna, and she bore him the future Alexander the Great and CLEOPATRA (3) thereafter. Olympias was formidable, and determined that Alexander would be her husband's heir. She succeeded, and Alexander became king after the death of his father. After the unexpected death of Alexander in 323, however, Alexander's infant son was declared joint ruler with Philinna's son, Philip Arrhidaeus. There is no mention of Philinna in the subsequent struggles for power. Possibly, even probably, she was already dead.

Philinna had another son, Amphimachus Triparadeisus, who was born before she married Philip and not a part of the post-Alexander struggles.

Sources

Diodorus Siculus. *Library of History* 16.14.2.
Justin. *Epitome* 13.2, 11.
Greenwalt, W. S. "The Search for Philip Arrhideaus." *Ancient World* 10 (1984): 69–77.
Hammond, N. G. L. *A History of Greece.* Oxford: Oxford University Press, 1967, pp. 539, 573.
Macurdy, Grace. *Hellenistic Queens.* Reprint. Chicago: Ares Publishers, 1985, pp. 26–27.

Phryne

(fifth century B.C.E.)   Greek: Greece
self-made woman

Phryne, renowned for her beauty, lived in Athens and became very wealthy. Her father was Epicles from Thespiae in southern Greece. Phryne modeled for the great sculptor Praxiteles who inscribed an epigram on the nude Cnidian Aphrodite expressing his passion for her. She also modeled for the painter Apelles who portrayed her as Aphrodite rising from the sea.

Praxiteles was said to have offered her the gift of one of his works. Desiring the piece he most valued, she was said to have told a slave to run and tell Praxiteles that his studio was on fire. Praxiteles ran to his studio crying that all of his work was in vain if he lost his sculptures of Eros and Satyr. Phryne chose Eros which she donated to the temple of Eros at Thespiae. It is also said that a group of friends paid Praxiteles to sculpt a golden statue of Phryne, which she dedicated at Delphi.

In contentious Athens, it was not surprising that a suit was brought against Phryne, who chose her friends, lovers, and patrons from among the artistic and public men of the day. She was charged by Euthius with corrupting young women by organizing them to worship the Thracian god Isodaetes. If convicted, she could have been put to death. One of her presumed lovers, the orator Hyperides, successfully defended her. To counter the prejudice against her on the part of the judge, he was said to have torn off Phryne's clothes and exposed her breasts. The judge, it was said, feared that Phryne was a ministrant of the goddess Aphrodite and declared her innocent. It was also reported that the Athenians later passed a law prohibiting women from removing their clothes during a trial.

Sources

Athenaeus. *Deipnosophistae* 13.567d–e, 590e–591f.

Pausanias. *Description of Greece* 1.20.1–2; 9.27.5; 10.15.1.

Plutarch. *Moralia: Amatorius* 753.

Fantham, Elaine, et al. *Women in the Classical World.* New York: Oxford University Press, 1994, pp. 175–176.

Licht, Hans. *Sexual Life in Ancient Greece.* Trans. by J. H. Freese. London: Abbey Library, 1971, pp. 311, 348 ff.

Pomeroy, Sarah B. *Goddesses, Whores, Wives, and Slaves: Women in Classical Antiquity.* New York: Schocken Books, 1975, p. 141.

▣ Phthia

(third century B.C.E.)   Greek: Epirus and Macedonia
coruler

Phthia, who was often called Chryseis, no doubt in reference to her golden hair, lived with her mother, OLYMPIAS (2), who ruled Epirus as regent for her young son after the death of her husband, Alexander

II. To prevent the Aetolian League from annexing the northern half of Acarnania, which by treaty had been assigned to Epirus, Olympias established an alliance with Demetrius II, who became ruler of Macedonia in 239 B.C.E. Phthia and Demetrius married to solidify the relationship after he divorced his wife, STRATONICE (3), who had borne him no male heirs. Demetrius prevented the takeover of Acarnania and won territory from the Aetolian League.

Demetrius, however, was a rather weak ruler. He suffered a series of defeats and died in 229. Phthia's son Philip, who was born in 238 B.C.E., succeeded his father. Since he was only nine years old at the time, his uncle Antigonus Doson was regent. Antigonus Doson took full control, married Phthia, and adopted Philip.

During the earthquake of 227 in Rhodes, Phthia sent corn and lead to help the inhabitants. In 221 her son became Philip V, ruler of Macedonia.

Sources

Justin. *Epitome* 28.1.

Polybius. *Histories* 5.89.7.

Tarn, William Woodthorpe. "Phthia-Chryseis." In *Athenian Studies Presented to William Scott Ferguson.* Cambridge: Harvard University Press, 1940, pp. 483 ff.

Walbank, Frank. *Philip V of Macedon.* Cambridge, England: Cambridge University Press, 1940, pp. 5, 9–10, 258.

▣ Pilia

(?–c. 44/43 B.C.E.)   Roman: Rome and Italy
loyal wife and friend

Pilia lived a protected life during the tumultuous decades that led to civil war in the second half of the first century B.C.E. Her husband, Titus Pomponius Atticus, was one of the wealthiest men of Rome. In a period when fortunes were lost through confiscation, wantonness, and inflation, Atticus's wealth only increased. Careful to maintain good relations all across the political spectrum, Atticus was banker to many, including Marcus Tullius Cicero and Octavian. He and Pilia, however, always had time for their private life. From the time they married in February 56 B.C.E. until her probable death in 44 or 43 B.C.E., Atticus loved her, and she would seem to have returned the feeling. They often traveled together and entertained on estates spread through southern and central Italy. They had one child, Caecilia ATTICA, who was born in 51 and was cherished by both of them.

Atticus was already 53 when he married the much younger Pilia. It appeared to be a first marriage for both of them. Atticus was Cicero's closest friend and ally, and in their frequent correspondence, there is no indication that either Atticus or Pilia had extended families. The demands on Atticus called him to Rome and sometimes left Pilia free to travel in Italy to visit friends in resort towns or to attend weddings and funerals. The close friendship with Cicero was strengthened by the marriage of Atticus's sister and Cicero's brother. An unhappy marriage, it provided all the members of the family with a constant source of comment, gossip, and advice. Atticus and Pilia were frequent visitors with Cicero and his wife TERENTIA (1). It was TULLIA (2), Cicero's daughter, with whom Pilia was friends, and they were probably close in age. Tullia stayed with Pilia a number of times when she was at a crossroads in her own life.

Illness loomed large in ancient life. On August 19, 44 B.C.E., a greatly perturbed Cicero was on his way to Pompeii by ship when he wrote Atticus about the news from Marcus Junius Brutus that Pilia had suffered some form of paralysis. That was the last letter between the men that mentioned Pilia.

In 37 their daughter Attica was betrothed to Marcus Vipsanius Agrippa, the great general and supporter of Octavian, the new emperor Augustus. She brought with her a huge dowry.

Sources
Cicero. *Epistulae ad Atticum* 4.16; 5.11; 8.7; 10.13.47a, 15; 14.17, 19; 15.1a; 16.7, 11.

◉ Pipa (Pipara)
(third century C.E.)
German: Germany and Italy
young lover

Pipa, who was also called Pipara, was the daughter of Attalus Publius Licinius, leader of the Marcomani, a west German tribe. In 253 C.E. Publius Licinius Egnatius Gallienus, who was co-Augustus with his father the emperor Valerian, fell in love with Pipa while he was married to Cornelia SALONINA, a highly cultured Greek woman from Bithynia in Asia Minor. Although Pipa's feelings are unrecorded, she became his lover. Her father received a large portion of Pannonia, territory lying west of the Danube, either in return for his daughter or for his help in repelling Germanic invasions, or perhaps for both. It is not known what happened to Pipa, but Salonina remained Augusta and accompanied Gallienus on his campaigns.

Sources
Scriptores Historiae Augustae. Gallienus 21.3.

◉ Placidia
(c. 439/443–? C.E.)
Roman: Rome, Carthage, Constantinople
political actor

Placidia lived her life in the shadow of imperial power and politics. Born a year or so after her sister EUDOCIA, between 439 and 443, she was the daughter of LICINA EUDOXIA and Valentinian III and the granddaughter of AELIA EUDOCIA and Theodosius II. Placidia married Aninius Olybrius, son of a patrician Roman family around 454. She was in Rome without her husband in 455, when Gaiseric led a Vandal invasion and sacked the city. He took Placidia, her sister, and her mother to Carthage as hostages.

Placidia's sister, who had earlier been betrothed to Gaiseric's son Huneric, was either forced or agreed to marry him. It then took until 460 to conclude successful negotiations for the release of Placidia and her mother. They returned to Constantinople where her husband Olybrius had been throughout the ordeal. Placidia gave birth to a daughter, ANICIA JULIANA, in 461. After the emperor in the West, Majorian, died on August 2, 461, Gaiseric demanded that Placidia's husband Olybrius become the new emperor. The elevation of Olybrius would have made Huneric the brother-in-law of the emperor through his marriage with Placidia's sister. For the wily Gaiseric, this relationship would also establish a claim of legitimate succession. Gaiseric's plan did not succeed.

The political threat posed by Olybrius and Placidia was sufficiently potent that in 472 Leo I sent

Olybrius on a diplomatic mission to Italy, ostensibly to settle a dispute between the emperor of the West, Anthemius, and his son-in-law, Ricimer. Olybrius was then to journey to Carthage and meet with Gaiseric. Leo also sent a secret emissary instructing Anthemius to have Olybrius assassinated. The messenger was intercepted, and the contents conveyed to Ricimer, who informed Olybrius. Ricimer, with the Senate's approval, declared Olybrius emperor in the West in April 472. It was a short-lived reign. Olybrius died of dropsy seven months later in November 472. Placidia and her daughter remained in Constantinople during her husband's reign.

Placidia and her husband were orthodox Christians and renovated the church of Saint Euphemia in Constantinople, which had been built with funds provided by her mother, Eudoxia. In 478, the emperor Zeno, with the approval of Placidia, sent ambassadors to Huneric, who was still her brother-in-law and an Arian Christian, to seek approval to install an orthodox bishop in Carthage. Huneric, who had prosecuted orthodox Christians, not only agreed, but released the emperor from any residual obligations of unpaid dowry or promises from his betrothal with Placidia's sister some 20 years earlier. Finally, he thanked Zeno for honoring Placidia.

Nothing more is known of Placidia. Her daughter Anicia Juliana had a notable career of her own.

Sources

John Malalas. *Chronicle* XIV. v., vi., viii.

Procopius. *Vandelic Wars* III. v. 3, 6; vi. 6.

Bury, J. B. *History of the Later Roman Empire: From the Death of Theodosius I to the Death of Justinian.* 2 vols. New York: Dover Publications, Inc., 1958.

Clover, Frank M. "The Family and Early Career of Ancinius Olybrius." *Historia* 27 (1978): 169–196.

Prosopography of the Later Roman Empire. Vol. II. Edited by A. H. M. Jones, J. R. Martindale, and J. Morris. Cambridge: Cambridge University Press, 1971. Reprinted 1992, p. 887.

▣ Placidia, Aelia Galla

(388/390–November 27, 450 C.E.)
Roman: Constantinople, Spain, Gaul, Italy
Augusta

Aelia Galla Placidia lived a life of high adventure and daring at the center of imperial power. For 12 years, she ruled the Roman Empire in the West as regent for her son. She was the half sister of two weak emperors, Honorius and Arcadius, over whom she exercised significant influence. Captured by the Goths under Alaric during the sack of Rome in 410, she married Alaric's brother Athaulf and for five years traveled with him and his army throughout Spain and Gaul. Athaulf died during this time and Placidia returned to Italy and married the emperor, Constantius III.

Placidia was the daughter of GALLA, the second wife of the emperor Theodosius I. Born in Constantinople while her father was campaigning in the West, she lived with her mother until her death in 394. Her father, who died the following year, provided her with her own household and independent wealth. He also arranged that she and her 10-year-old half brother Honorius, who became emperor in the West, would live in Rome in the household of his favorite niece, SERENA, the wife of his trusted general Stilicho. The choice of Serena, who was a devout orthodox Christian, probably was a political decision about the children's future that included their religious orientation and education as well as likely marriage partners.

Placidia was betrothed to Eucherius, the son of Serena and Stilicho, but when Placidia came of age, she refused the match for reasons unknown. Instead, Honorius married their 14-year-old daughter, MARIA, and after her death, the youngest daughter, THERMANTIA. Stilicho had amassed enemies, including the weak Honorius, who feared his power. On August 22, 408, Honorius's assassins killed Stilicho. Thermantia, still a virgin, returned to her mother's household. Placidia remained unmarried and living in her own establishment in Rome, as did the widowed Serena and her daughter.

Led by Alaric, the Goths blockaded Rome in October 408. Rumors circulated that Serena and Alaric were colluding to capture the city. There may have been no basis to the rumors, but the Senate harbored years of accumulated frustration and rage toward Serena, fueled by hatred of the power held by her husband, and voted an order for her death. Fearful still of her power, they appealed to Placidia to authorize their action since with Honorius in Ravenna, she was the highest imperial personage in the city. Placidia supported the Senate.

Why? One can only speculate. Their relationship may have deteriorated after Placidia refused to marry Eucherius. Once Placidia had an independent household, the two women were competing for influence in almost every sphere of public affairs, and their competition may have fueled their hostility toward one another. It is even possible that Placidia believed the rumors. Clearly, with Serena's death Placidia became the preeminent woman in the empire of the West.

Alaric withdrew his forces, but two years later, on August 24, 410, he captured and sacked Rome. Placidia was taken captive. Alaric died toward the end of the year 410 and his brother-in-law Athaulf took control. Athaulf and possibly Placidia saw an opportunity. Their union opened the vista of a legitimate claim of power in the West through her Theodosian bloodline. Placidia, then in her 20s, agreed to marry Athaulf, despite the objections of Honorius.

They married in Narbonne, in January 414. Among Athaulf's gifts to his bride were 50 handsome youths each carrying two containers, one with gold and the other with gems. Athaulf also issued a statement that he had once believed Gothic values should replace Roman values in the territories he controlled. However, he had come to realize that it was impossible to have a republic without laws. He wanted Roman law restored and to prevail, but Gothic spirit to invigorate his empire. Possibly, Roman law was a precondition for her consent, especially since it enhanced the legitimacy of her marriage.

Honorius sought the return of his half sister. Athaulf had other ideas. He concluded an agreement with the emperor Honorius to serve as an agent for Rome to protect the borders against additional invasions in return for supplies of grain and the province of Gaul. In 412, he led his forces into Gaul bringing Placidia with him. He conquered Narbonne, Bordeaux, and Toulouse. An insurrection against Honorius in North Africa, however, cut off Italy's grain supply and the pact was cancelled. The Goths continually faced the problem of finding sufficient food. Foraging was rarely enough for an army that included three or four people to support each soldier. One of Honorius's generals, Constantius, an Illyrian by birth, captured Arles and cut its food supplies to Athaulf's forces. Athaulf retreated to Barcelona. There Placidia gave birth to a son, Theodosius, who died soon after.

In September 415, Athaulf was fatally stabbed while visiting his stable. Before dying, he requested that his brother, who was to succeed him, promise that Placidia could return to Italy. However, a usurper, Singeric, seized control, killed Athaulf's children by a former wife, and forced Placidia to march on foot with other captives for 12 miles. Seven days later, he was killed. The new leader Wallia treated Placidia well and reached an agreement with Honorius and Constantius that echoed the earlier agreement with Athaulf. In return for 600,000 measures of grain, he agreed to enter into Roman service, attack the Vandals, Alans, and Sueves who had invaded Spain, and return Placidia.

Placidia returned to Italy five years after being taken prisoner by Alaric. She was well into her 20s and by Roman standards no longer young. She was also a widow who had lost a child. She had no reason to marry again. However, if she were to marry, Constantius was the best political choice. Honorius was inept as a military leader, and military leadership was all that stood between the Romans and the various barbarian groups wandering around Italy. Constantius, all acknowledged, was an effective general and also the de facto ruler in the West. Moreover, Placidia, all the sources insist, was quite beautiful, and Constantius had long been attracted to her.

Placidia married Constantius on January 1, 417, the same day he became consul for the second time. She bore two more children, Justa Grata Honoria, in 417/418 and Placidius Valentinius on July 3, 419, both of whom played important roles in her future political life. On February 8, 421, her husband became Constantius III. His de facto position, recognized with the approval of Honorius, made him a second Augustus in the West.

Placidia became Augusta and coins were issued in her honor.

The eastern Roman emperor Theodosius II and his sister the Augusta PULCHERIA, however, refused to recognize Placidia's title. Their opposition reflected a widespread view that Honorius had lost the West to the Germans. Under his reign, Rome had been captured for the first time in over 1,000 years. That Placidia had been seized and become the wife of a Goth only added insult to injury.

Constantius's reign was brief. He died on September 2, 421. Honorius, who seems to have been enthralled with his half sister, began to demonstrate his affections in public. Rumors flew that an unhappy Placidia was conspiring with the opponents of Honorius. Her allies, composed of Athaulf's kin in her service and other supporters, clashed with those of Honorius. In 423, Honorius banished her, and she fled with her children from Ravenna to Constantinople.

Honorius died in August 423 and an obscure pretender, John, seized control. From the perspective of Constantinople, Placidia and her children carried the Theodosian bloodline. Pulcheria and

Theodosius II formally recognized Placidia's title of Augusta, issued coins with her portrait, and affirmed her son Valentinian's claim to the West, giving him the title of Caesar. In return, Placidia ceded rule over some of Valentinian's western territories to Theodosius.

Pulcheria and Theodosius sent an army to Italy, accompanied by Placidia and her children. When Placidia's ship was wrecked off the Dalmatian coast, she vowed to build a church to Saint John the Divine to whom she had prayed for deliverance. The imperial army captured the usurper John and took him to Aquiliea where Placidia ordered his execution. Soon after, a large force of Huns under the command of a Roman, Flavius Aetius, who supported John, arrived in Italy. Placidia pardoned Aetius and accepted his services. Sufficient bribes induced the Huns to leave. She restored some privileges to the church that John had abolished and journeyed to Rome, where Valentinian III was declared Augustus on October 23, 425. Her daughter Justa Grata Honoria became Augusta at about the same time. In Ravenna, she built the church she had vowed to build with an inscription, *"Galla Placidia, along with her son Placidius Valentinian Augustus and her daughter Justa Grata Honoria Augusta, fulfilled their vow for their liberation from the danger of the sea."*

Since Valentinian was only six, Placidia was the de facto ruler of the Roman Empire in the West for the next 12 years. Her relations with Theodosius II remained cordial, but the years were troubled with disturbances on almost all the borders. The Franks threatened northeastern Gaul and the Goths the south. Insurrections among previously loyal allies and generals led to a constant round of shifting alliances. Placidia appointed as Master of Both Services (supreme military command) a man named Felix, who had no interest in political influence which might threaten her. Aetius, who had been sent to Gaul and had support among the Huns, since he had spent many years among them, was sufficiently successful against Rome's enemies that he could pressure Placidia to appoint him coequal with Felix. He later replaced Felix as supreme commander after the latter was assassinated.

Galla Placidia
(Date: 421 C.E. 1950.57.6, Archives, American Numismatic Society)

There was also unrest in Africa. Boniface, an able soldier and general who had aided Placidia (including financial support), when she fled from Honorius, began to consolidate his own power. Although he made protestations of orthodoxy to Augustine, who was bishop at Hippo, he married an Arian Christian who may have had ties to the Vandals. When Placidia ordered Boniface to return to Italy, he refused. The sources are unclear about subsequent events but in 428 an army led by a Goth, Sigisvault, with the title Count of Africa, conquered Carthage and Hippo. Facing defeat, Boniface formed a pact with Gaiseric, leader of the Vandals, to reconquer Africa and divide the spoils. Augustine's letters suggest that the military operations caused an extraordinary degree of devastation to people and property.

Placidia quickly realized that to avoid civil war she had to persuade Boniface to support her and join forces with an army sent by the emperor Theodosius from Constantinople. He agreed, but Gaiseric easily defeated the Romans, and Boniface returned to Italy where Placidia appointed him to replace Aetius. Civil war resulted when Aetius refused to step down. Boniface defeated Aetius but died of wounds a short time later. Aetius escaped to Dalmatia and with the help of Rugila, leader of the Huns, returned to Italy where Placidia was forced to reappoint him to his old position.

Aetius succeeded in clearing Italy of raiding armies and established himself in Ravenna as de facto ruler. The position of Aetius, coupled with the marriage of her son Valentinian III in October 437 to Licinia Eudoxia, the daughter of Aelia Eudocia and Theodosius III, effectively ended her regency.

Always an orthodox Christian, she built, restored, and beautified several churches including the church of the Holy Cross in Ravenna, St. Stephan's at Rimini, the Church of the Holy Cross in Jerusalem, and the Basilica of St. Paul Outside the Walls in Rome. On a visit to Rome with Valentinian in 450, a group of bishops, including Leo the Great, bishop of Rome, complained bitterly about the decisions of the "Robber Council" held at Ephesus in August 449, which had rejected the orthodox position of the two natures in Christ and instead supported the

Monophysite doctrine that the divine nature in Christ had absorbed the human. Placidia sent a letter to Theodosius II urging him to intervene and uphold orthodoxy. She also wrote to Pulcheria whose views matched her own.

Placidia died on November 27, 450. The site of her burial is unknown.

Sources

Corpus Inscriptionum Latinarum. xi. 276.

Placidia. Letter, 56.

Procopius. *Vandelic Wars* III. iii. 4, 10, 16–18, 27–29, 36; III. iv. 15.

Socrates. *Historia Ecclesiastica* VII, 24, 2–3.

Sozomen. *Historia Ecclesiastica* IX, 16.2.

Theophanes. *Chronicle* AM. 5895, 5911–5912, 5913, 5962.

Zosimus. *New History/Zosimus.* A translation with commentary by Ronald T. Ridley. Canberra: Australian Association of Byzantine Studies, 1982.

Ost, Stewart I. *Galla Placidia Augusta: a Biographical Essay.* Chicago: University of Chicago Press, 1968.

———. "Galla Placidia and the Law." *Classical Philology* 63 (1968): 114–121.

———. "Some Problems in the History of Galla Placidia." Classical Philology 60 (1965): 1–10.

Prosopography of the Later Roman Empire. Vol. II. Edited by A. H. M. Jones, J. R. Martindale, and J. Morris. Cambridge: Cambridge University Press, 1971. Reprinted 1992, pp. 888–889.

Plangon

(404–? B.C.E.)   Greek: Athens
self-made woman

Plangon's life was made difficult by the perfidious behavior of her husband and the criminal behavior of her father. Her father was Pamphilus, a wealthy and prominent citizen of Athens. Born around 404 B.C.E., shortly before the end of the Peloponnesian War, she married Mantias with a substantial dowry of 100 minas.

In 388 her father, who held the rank of general, was dismissed from service, convicted of embezzlement, and his property confiscated. The family was ruined. Her husband promptly divorced her, while she either was still pregnant or had just given birth to a son. Plangon did not succeed in recovering her dowry from Mantias, or possibly her dowry had also been confiscated as part of her father's estate. In any event, she was without the means to arrange another marriage. In addition, Mantias refused to acknowledge her child, named Boiotus, and introduce him into his phratry.

Mantias later married another woman with a dowry. Plangon, however, was beautiful, and Mantias remained sexually attracted to her. They continued a relationship, even after he remarried. She had another son, this one named after Pamphilus, whom Mantias also refused to acknowledge. With two sons who were without the legal recognition that would entitle them to citizenship and the right to inherit from their father, Plangon initiated a suit against Mantias.

Plangon was very clear on her goals and offered her ex-husband a settlement. If he would give her 30 minas, a reasonably substantial sum at the time, her brother would adopt the two boys. She assured him if the arbiter in the suit asked her to swear to the fact that Mantias was the father of the boys, she would refuse. Mantias accepted Plangon's offer. When the arbiter asked her if Mantias was the father of the boys, however, she answered in the affirmative. Mantias, fearing attack by his political foes if he engaged in a protracted suit, gave in and agreed that he was the father. He then enrolled both sons in his phratry. Her sons assumed their rightful citizenship and became heirs of a wealthy estate.

Sources
Demosthenes. *Private Orations* 39.40.
Walters, K. R. "Women and Power in Classical Athens." In *Woman's Power, Man's Game: Essays on Classical Antiquity in Honor of Joy K. King,* ed. by Mary DeForest. Wauconda, Ill.: Bolchazy-Carducci, 1993, pp. 205–208.

Plathane
(fifth–fourth century B.C.E.)   Greek: Athens
wife of Isocrates

Plathane lived during the Pelopennesian Wars between Athens and Sparta. Her first husband was Hippias, an obscure Athenian. She had three sons before she was widowed. Her second husband was the famous sophist Isocrates. His family lost their

wealth during the war. In the contentious and litigious society of Athens, however, Isocrates successfully supported them through teaching and speechwriting.

Isocrates adopted her youngest son, who became a poet and also a speechwriter.

Sources
Plutarch. *Moralia, Vitae decem Oratorum.* 838a, c; 839b.
Davies, J. K. *Athenian Propertied Families, 600–300 B.C.* Oxford: Clarendon Press, 1971, p. 247.

Plautia Urgulanilla
(first century B.C.E.–first century C.E.)
Roman: Italy
political player

Plautia Urgulanilla was the first wife of the future emperor Claudius. They married in about 10 C.E. She was the daughter Marcus Plautius Silvanus, consul in 2 B.C.E., and the granddaughter of URGULANIA, a close friend of the powerful LIVIA DRUSILLA. No doubt the two older women had a central role in arranging the marriage. On the one hand, Claudius, while of the finest ancestry, suffered from an impairment that affected his speech and walk. Plautia, on the other hand, had some odd relatives. For example, her only brother, Marcus Plautius Silvanus, praetor in 24 C.E., murdered his wife, APRONIA, by throwing her from a window. He committed suicide before he could be tried.

Plautia and Claudius had two children, a boy, Drusus, who choked to death when he tossed a pear and caught it in his mouth, and a daughter, Claudia. Claudius divorced Plautia and rejected Claudia as his daughter. He claimed that his freedman Bota was Plautia's lover and the father of the child.

Sources
Suetonius. *The Lives of the Caesars:* Claudius 26–27.
Balsdon, J. P. V. D. *Roman Women.* New York: John Day Comp., 1963, p. 122.
Levick, Barbara. *Claudius: The Corruption of Power.* New Haven, Conn.: Yale University Press, 1993, pp. 16, 23–25.
Pauly, A., G. Wissowa, and W. Kroll. *Real-Encyclopadie D. Classischen Altertumswissenschaft 1893–.* (Germany: multiple publishers) 66.

Plautilla

(second–third century C.E.)   Roman: Rome
Augusta

Plautilla was her father's ally in a bitter struggle for power during the reign of Septimius Severus. Her father was Gaius Fulvius Plautianus, the prefect of the Praetorian Guard under Severus. Between 197 and 205 C.E., Plautianus exercised de facto power. During these years he worked to secure Plautilla's future. Hostile stories about him during this period claim that he was obsessed with Plautilla and that he had grown men castrated so only eunuchs would attend and instruct her. In 202 Plautilla married Marcus Aurelius Antoninus Caracalla, the son of the emperor. She received the title Augusta at the time of her marriage. Her dowry was said to be equal to the wealth of 50 elite women.

JULIA DOMNA, the powerful wife of Severus and mother of Caracalla, opposed the marriage. She was an impacable enemy of Plautianus, whose authority had diminished hers and who had attacked her with charges of adultery. Her strong influence on her son, not surprisingly, led him to hate Plautilla. He refused to eat or sleep with her and swore to kill her and her father when he became emperor. Despite the formal marriage, Plautilla lived in her father's house.

In 205, Caracalla orchestrated the downfall of Plautianus by convincing his father that the latter was about to assassinate him. Caracalla formally divorced Plautilla, and Severus banished her to Lipara, an island north of Sicily. She was killed by Caracalla after he became emperor, as he had promised.

Sources

Dio Cassius. *Roman History* 76.14.4–5, 15.2; 77.1.2, 2.4–5, 3.1, 4.4, 6.3.

Herodian. *History of the Empire* 3.10.5–7, 13.2–3; 4.6.3.

Balsdon, J. P. V. D. *Roman Women.* New York: John Day Comp., 1963, pp. 152–153.

Oxford Classical Dictionary, ed. by Simon Hornblower and Antony Spawforth. 3d. ed. New York: Oxford University Press, 1996, p. 614.

Pauly, A., G. Wissowa, and W. Kroll. *Real-Encyclopadie D. Classischen Altertumswissenschaft 1893–.* (Germany: multiple publishers) 117.

Plotina, Pompeia

(first–second century C.E.)
Roman: Gaul, Italy, Asia, Egypt, Germany, Syria, and Greece
Augusta

Pompeia Plotina has been depicted as a plain and virtuous woman with high moral standards and sound judgment. The portrayal does not do her justice. She was a close adviser on policy to her husband, the emperor Trajan, and her views shaped his policies in such diverse areas as provincial taxes and political appointments. In contrast with her husband, she was interested in the arts and was attracted to philosophy, especially Epicureanism. The future emperor Hadrian, who had been left fatherless, lived with her as a child and was part of a family circle that also included Trajan's sisters and nieces. Plotina arranged for Hadrian to marry Vibia SABINA. When Trajan's life ended, Plotina saw to it that there was a peaceful transition to the new regime.

Plotina came from the new aristocracy that dominated the Antonine period. Her father was

Pompeia Plotina
(Date: 117 C.E. 1001.1.22178, Archives, American Numismatic Society)

Lucius Pompeius from Nemausus (Nimes) in the Roman province of Narbonensis. She married Marcus Ulpius Trajan before he became emperor. She had no children with her husband, who was born in Spain of an Italian father and Spanish mother. All his life a military man, in 88 C.E. Trajan went to stem a revolt in Upper Germany. He was appointed governor of the province 10 years later in 97. Plotina accompanied him. Living with them in Cologne were Ulpia MARCIANA, Trajan's widowed sister, and her daughter, MATIDIA (1), as well as her two granddaughters, Vibia Sabina and MATIDIA (2).

Trajan was adopted by the emperor Nerva and succeeded him at the end of January 98. Plotina accompanied her husband to Rome early in 99. Her multigenerational household followed. With her husband away for long periods of time campaigning, she assumed responsibility for the running of the household and the affairs of the emperor in Rome. The Senate sought to honor Plotina and Marciana with the title of Augusta in 100 C.E., but both women refused. It was her proud boast that the woman she was before her husband became emperor, was the woman she remained. Five years later, in 105, they relented. In 112, coins were issued depicting Plotina on the obverse and the goddess Vesta on the reverse.

In 113 Plotina, Matidia, and Hadrian accompanied Trajan to the East where he was to begin a military campaign against the Parthians. It was an ill-fated trip. First they barely escaped death from a terrible earthquake in Antioch in 115, and then Trajan suffered a stroke. August 9, 117, Hadrian received a dispatch that he had been adopted by Trajan. Two days later, he learned that Trajan had died in Selinus in southern Asia Minor and that the army had declared him emperor. Plotina and Matidia were with Trajan in his final days, and rumors arose that Plotina had signed the adoption decree after Trajan's death. Certainly, she would have chosen Hadrian as the successor to her husband.

Plotina remained close with Hadrian after he became emperor. She became a patron to the Epicurean school in Athens and urged Hadrian to open the selection of the school's head beyond the limit of those who held Roman citizenship. Hadrian honored Plotina on coins with Divus Trajan on the obverse and her portrait as Diva Plotina on the reverse. When she died sometime between 121 and 123, he had her consecrated and built two temples, one in the Campus Marius in Rome and the other in Nimes. In his funeral oration, he praised Plotina for her modesty and reasonableness.

Sources

Dio Cassius. *Roman History* 68.5.5; 69.1.3–4, 10.3–3a.

Pliny the Younger. *Panegyricus* 83; 84.

Scriptores Historiae Augustae. Hadrian 2.10; 4.1, 4, 10; 5.9; 12.2.

Balsdon, J. P. V. D. *Roman Women.* New York: John Day Comp., 1963, pp. 133–139.

Fantham, Elaine, et al. *Women in the Classical World.* New York: Oxford University Press, 1994, pp. 349–53.

Oxford Classical Dictionary, ed. by Simon Hornblower and Antony Spawforth. 3d. ed. New York: Oxford University Press, 1996, p. 1,214.

Pauly, A., G. Wissowa, and W. Kroll. *Real-Encyclopadie D. Classischen Altertumswissenschaft 1893–.* (Germany: multiple publishers) 131.

Syme, Ronald. *Tacitus.* 2 vols. Oxford: Clarendon Press, 1958.

Pompeia (I)

(first century B.C.E.)   Roman: Rome
political wife

Pompeia is remembered for her divorce from Gaius Julius Caesar in the aftermath of a scandal during celebration of the rites of the Bona Dea. She was the granddaughter of Lucius Cornelius Sulla, the Roman general and dictator, and ILIA, one of his early wives, through her mother CORNELIA (4). Her father, Quintus Pompeius Rufus was the son of Quintus Pompeius Rufus, consul in 88 B.C.E. She married Julius Caesar in 67 B.C.E. after the death of his first wife, CORNELIA (5). Five years later, in December of 62 when her husband was *pontifex maximus* and head of the priestly college, his house was the setting for the annual Bona Dea celebration. Restricted to elite women, the celebration of the goddess was an annual nocturnal event held under the supervision of the wife of the *pontifex maximus* with the assistance of the Vestal Virgins.

During the ceremony in 62, Publius Clodius Pulcher, a brash young aristocrat, disguised himself as a woman slave lute player and gained admittance to the house. Rumor had it that he had an assignation with Pompeia. Caesar's mother, AURELIA (1), recognized the culprit, and he was ousted. Caesar divorced Pompeia without the accusation of adultery but with the assertion that the wife of the *pontifex maximus* must be above suspicion. Clodius was accused of sacrilege and put on trial in 61. He was acquitted when Marcus Licinius Crassus bribed the jury. Crassus probably hoped to use Clodius's popularity with the masses for his own ends. Caesar was not perturbed by what had happened, remained on friendly terms with Clodius, and refused to give a deposition against him. Nothing more is heard of Pompeia.

Sources

Balsdon, J. P. V. D. *Roman Women.* New York: John Day Comp., 1963, pp. 244 ff.
Cicero. *Epistulae ad Atticum* 1.12; 13.16.
Plutarch. *Vitae Parallelae (Parallel Lives): Caesar* 9.1–8; 10.1–10.
———. *Vitae Parallelae (Parallel Lives): Cicero* 28.1–4; 29.9.
Oxford Classical Dictionary, ed. by Simon Hornblower and Antony Spawforth. 3d. ed. New York: Oxford University Press, 1996, p. 1,214.
Pauly, A., G. Wissowa, and W. Kroll. *Real-Encyclopadie D. Classischen Altertumswissenschaft 1893–.* (Germany: multiple publishers) 52.

Pompeia (2)

(first century B.C.E.)   Roman: Rome
political wife

Pompeia was the daughter of Gnaeus Pompeius Magnus (Pompey the Great). Her father was three times consul, a much-loved general, and leader of the republicans during the civil war of 49–48 B.C.E. He was also a man who married well and often. Her mother, MUCIA TERTIA, was from a consular family and had been her father's third wife.

Pompeia and Faustus Cornelius Sulla, quaestor in 54, were to marry. He was the son of Lucius Cornelius Sulla, who had been dictator of Rome in 81 B.C.E. and was a former father-in-law to Pompey. The planned marriage was temporarily derailed when Gaius Julius Caesar formed an alliance with Pompey in 59 B.C.E. Caesar also had a daughter, JULIA (5). She was to have married Servilius Caepio but instead married Pompey to cement the alliance between the two men. It was proposed that Pompeia marry Caepio.

Nothing came of the planned marriage with Caepio, and Pompeia married Faustus Sulla as originally planned. Her husband inherited substantial wealth from his father. He spent a great portion of it on living lavishly. He served under Pompey in the East and was killed in 46 fighting with Pompey in the civil war. Pompeia gave birth to CORNELIA (7), whose son became consul in 11 C.E. Pompeia married a second time to Lucius Cornelius Cinna, consul suffectus in 32 B.C.E. They had two children: Gnaeus Cornelius Cinna, consul in 5 C.E., and Pompeia Magna.

Sources

Plutarch. *Vitae Parallelae (Parallel Lives): Caesar* 14.7.
Syme, Ronald. *The Augustan Aristocracy.* Oxford: Clarendon Press, 1986, index.

Pompeia Macrina

(first century C.E.)
Roman Greek: Lesbos and Sparta
conspirator

Pompeia Macrina was exiled, and the members of her family were killed in a conflict with the emperor Tiberius for reasons that remain obscure but are probably related to the exercise of power in Greece. Her father, Pompeius Macer, a friend of both Augustus and Tiberius, was a member of an important Greek family from Mytilene on the island of Lesbos. He became a high-ranking Roman equestrian, and Augustus appointed him procurator of Asia. Pompeia Macrina's brother, Quintus Pompeius Macer, praetor in 15 C.E., was the first senator from the eastern part of the empire and one of the few provincials Augustus admitted to the Senate.

Pompeia Macrina married Iulius Argolicus, a member of the Euryclad dynasty of Sparta. Her husband and his father, Iulius Laco, the most prominent men in Sparta, had held Roman citizenship since her husband's grandfather had been made ruler of Sparta by the future emperor Augustus as a reward for participating in the battle of Actium against Mark Antony 31 B.C.E. Shortly before 2 B.C.E., however, the same grandfather had been banished by Augustus for fomenting discord in Greece. After Tiberius became emperor, the dynasty was restored and her husband appointed ruler. In 33 C.E. her husband and his father were removed and punished on orders of Tiberius. Perhaps their reach had begun again to upset the balance of power.

Shortly thereafter, the ire of the emperor shifted from Pompeia Macrina's husband to herself, her father, and her brother. They were accused of supporting the cult of Theophanes of Mytilene, the great-grandfather of Pompeia Macrina. Theophanes had been very close to Pompey the Great, to whom he owed his Roman citizenship; he had served as his secretary and written a life of the general. As a favor to Theophanes, Pompey declared Mytilene a free city, and after Theophanes died he was deified at Mytilene. Pompeia's father and brother committed suicide, rather than wait to be condemned. Pompeia Macrina was exiled.

Sources

Tacitus. *Annales* 6.18.
Levick, Barbara. *Tiberius the Politician.* London: Thames and Hudson, 1976, pp. 211–212.
Marsh, Frank Burr. *The Reign of Tiberius.* New York: Barnes and Noble, 1931, pp. 207, 294.
Pauly, A., G. Wissowa, and W. Kroll. *Real-Encyclopadie D. Classischen Altertumswissenschaft 1893–.* (Germany: multiple publishers) 128.

▣ Pompeia Paulina

(first century C.E.)   Roman: Rome
political victim

Pompeia Paulina exhibited the classic virtue of a true Roman woman: a willingness to die with her husband. The wife of the philosopher, orator, and statesman Lucius Annaeus Seneca, she was part of a circle of educated Romans who sought to lead a principled life under the emperor Nero. Her husband was the tutor of the emperor and later became his political adviser and minister. In 65 C.E. Nero demanded that he commit suicide. He accused Seneca of taking part in the Pisonian conspiracy against him.

Pompeia planned to kill herself at the same time. Both cut veins in their arms, but Seneca also cut arteries in his legs. In the meantime, fearing that he would be attacked for cruelty, Nero ordered that Pompeia not die and sent soldiers to be sure that her slaves and freedmen bandaged her. She lived, but from that point on she was said to have been very frail, her face unusually pale. She died a few years later.

Sources

Tacitus. *Annales* 15.63, 64.
Balsdon, J. P. V. D. *Roman Women.* New York: John Day Comp., 1963, p. 57.
Pauly, A., G. Wissowa, and W. Kroll. *Real-Encyclopadie D. Classischen Altertumswissenschaft 1893–.* (Germany: multiple publishers) 130.

▣ Pomponia (1)

(third–second century B.C.E.)
Roman: Rome
mother of Publius Cornelius Scipio Africanus

Pomponia was honored as the mother of Publius Cornelius Scipio Africanus, the general who conquered Hannibal. Born of an ancient family, she married Publius Cornelius Scipio, consul in 218 B.C.E. She had two sons. The eldest, Publius Cornelius Scipio Africanus, was victorious over Hannibal at Zama in 202 B.C.E. and successfully ended the Punic Wars. Her younger son, Lucius Cornelius Scipio Asiageus, served as consul in 190 B.C.E. The legend that Pomponia died in childbirth when Scipio Africanus was born is false.

Sources

Polybius. *Histories* 10.4.3–9; 5.1–5.
Pauly, A., G. Wissowa, and W. Kroll. *Real-Encyclopadie D. Classischen Altertumswissenschaft 1893–.* (Germany: multiple publishers) 28.
Scullard, H. H. *Scipio Africanus: Soldier and Politician.* Ithaca, N.Y.: Cornell University Press, 1970, pp. 28, 30.

Pomponia (2)

(first century B.C.E.)   Roman: Italy
angry wife

Pomponia suffered life with a hot-tempered and irritable husband with whom she was often angry. She and her brother Titus Pomponius Atticus had been friends since childhood with the brothers Marcus Tullius and Quintus Tullius Cicero. In 70 B.C.E. when she and Quintus married, the alliance strengthened friendship with kinship, and the best wishes of all accompanied the marriage.

The marriage was a failure, although it lasted for some 25 years. Pomponia was several years older than her husband and much wealthier. Quintus was neither an insightful nor an especially talented man. He lived in the shadows of his brother's fame and his wife's money. Moreover, both her brother, Atticus, and her brother-in-law, Marcus, interfered in the relationship.

The letters between Cicero and Atticus provide an unusually intimate look at the marriage. They also record the annual cycles of visiting and traveling that included Cicero's wife, TERENTIA (I), and later Atticus's wife, PILIA, as well as the childhoods of their respective children, Quintus, Marcus, TULLIA (2) and Caecilia ATTICA. Time and again Pomponia demanded that Quintus recognize her position and her authority over the household, and he, either from insensitivity, ignorance, or perversity, chose to make household arrangements through his freedmen and slaves, instead of his wife. She was not a silent sufferer and railed against him to her brother and her brother-in law. Marcus Cicero, whose pomposity slips through many of his letters, regarded her as a shrew. Angered still more by her brother-in-law's support for her inept husband, she would refuse to sleep with her husband or to be his hostess, which led to further estrangement and fury all around.

The marriage finally ended in divorce in 44 B.C.E. They had one son, Quintus Cicero, whom each parent tried to turn against the other. Quintus and his son were killed in the proscriptions in 43. Pomponia outlived both of them.

Sources

Cicero. *Epistulae ad Atticum* 5.I.3 ff.; 14.13.5.
Balsdon, J. P. V. D. *Roman Women.* New York: John Day Comp., 1963, pp. 46, 212.
Johnson, W. H. *"The Sister-in-Law of Cicero." Classical Journal* 8 (1913): 160–165.
Shackleton Bailey, D. R. *Cicero.* New York: Charles Scribner's Sons, 1971, index.

Pomponia Galla

(first century C.E.)   Roman: Italy
friend of Pliny the Younger; disinherited her son

Pomponia Galla, a Roman matron and friend of Pliny the Younger, had disinherited her worthless son Asudius Curianus and made Pliny, along with several other eminent Romans, her coheirs. Although it remains unclear what exactly constituted "worthlessness" in Pomponia's eyes, her assessment of her son was largely affirmed after her death.

After her death, Curianus asked Pliny to agree to give him Pliny's share of the inheritance, which he would secretly return. The son hoped that this would set a precedent for the other coheirs to renounce their shares in his favor. Pliny proposed an alternative. He would waive his share if, Curianus could prove that his mother should not have disinherited him. Curianus asked Pliny to investigate the case himself. Pliny held a hearing with two eminent advisers who listened to Curianus. They ruled in favor of Pomponia's decision to disinherit.

Despite the ruling, the son brought suit in the Centumviral court against all the coheirs except Pliny. Since the outcome of a suit was never certain, Pliny acted as a mediator and settled the suit with the assignment of a fourth part of the estate to Curianus. Pliny voluntarily added his portion.

Sources

Pliny the Younger. *Epistulae* 5.1.

Pomponia Graecina

(?–c. 83 C.E.)   Roman: Italy
political player

The aristocratic Pomponia Graecina was the wife of Aulus Plautius, who was consul suffectus in 29 c.e. and led the successful Roman attack to secure southern Britain in 43. Pomponia was devoted to JULIA (8), to whom she was related. When Julia, who had once been the daughter-in-law of the elder AGRIPPINA, was executed on orders of Valeria MESSALLINA in 43, Pomponia put on mourning clothes, which she wore until her death around 83. In 57, Pomponia was charged with immorality for becoming a believer in an alien superstition, possibly one of the monotheistic religions. She was turned over to the jurisdiction of her husband, and a family council declared her innocent.

Sources

Tacitus. *Annales* 13.32.3–5.
Balsdon, J. P. V. D. *Roman Women.* New York: John Day Comp., 1963, p. 248.
Pauly, A., G. Wissowa, and W. Kroll. *Real-Encyclopadie D. Classischen Altertumswissenschaft 1893–.* (Germany: multiple publishers) 83.
Syme, Ronald. *Tacitus.* 2 vols. Oxford: Clarendon Press, 1958, p. 532.

Pomponia Rufina

(?–213 C.E.)   Roman: Rome
condemned priestess

Pomponia Rufina was one of four Vestal Virgins accused in 213 C.E. by the emperor Marcus Aurelius Antoninus Caracalla of unchaste behavior. Pomponia, along with AURELIA SEVERA and CLODIA LAETA, were buried alive. The fourth Vestal, CANNUTIA CRESCENTINA, killed herself.

Vestals served the goddess Vesta and were responsible for keeping the sacred flame burning. In an earlier age, the condemnation of four of the six Vestals would have been taken as an omen of calamitous times for Rome, but by the third century C.E. few appeared to have feared such a consequence.

Sources

Dio Cassius. *Roman History* 78.16.1–3k.
Herodian. *History of the Empire* 4.6.4.
Pauly, A., G. Wissowa, and W. Kroll. *Real-Encyclopadie D. Classischen Altertumswissenschaft 1893–.* (Germany: multiple publishers) 86.

Popilia

(?–102 B.C.E.)   Roman: Rome
loyal wife

Popilia was said to have been the first Roman woman honored with a public funeral oration. Her son Quintus Lutatius Catullus delivered the oration in her honor in 102 B.C.E., the year he became consul.

Sources

Cicero. *De oratores* 2.44.
Balsdon, J. P. V. D. *Roman Women.* New York: John Day Comp., 1963, p. 46.

Poppaea Sabina (1)

(?–47 C.E.)   Roman: Italy
political player

Poppaea Sabina was beautiful, rich, and arrogant. Born during the early empire when many women competed for power and wealth, she was forced to suicide by her opponent, Valeria MESSALLINA. Her father was Poppaeus Sabinus, consul in 9 C.E., who was said to have gained his position more through friendship than merit. She married Titus Ollius from Picenum, a relative unknown in imperial politics. Her daughter, POPPAEA SABINA (2), later became the wife of the emperor Nero. In 31 her husband died, probably in Tiberius's purge of Lucius Aelius Sejanus and his supporters. Poppaea emerged unscathed from the debacle. She remarried; her new husband was Publius Lentulus Scipio, consul suffectus in 24 C.E. Their son, Publius Scipio Asiaticus, became consul suffectus in 68.

Her conflict with Valeria Messallina began over the attractive Mnester, the leading pantomimist and pop culture idol in Rome, who became lover to both women. Although both were beautiful and very rich, Messalina was not only younger and more powerful, she was the emperor's wife. In 47 Messallina attacked Poppaea through Decimus Valerius Asiaticus, one of the leading political figures of the day and an opponent of Messallina's marriage with Claudius.

Asiaticus and Poppaea were accused of adultery, and in addition, he was charged with plotting against the emperor. Consul in 46 and a native of the city of Vienne on the Rhone, Asiaticus was an impressive man with a following. He was not only wealthy but owner of a house and gardens in Rome that were the envy of many, including Messallina. Although Claudius may not have thought Asiaticus was himself a threat, Asiaticus had voiced approval of the earlier assassination of the emperor Gaius Caligula. It was certainly possible to imagine that should there be a conspiracy, Asiaticus would throw his political weight and wealth on the side of the conspirators.

Claudius ordered Asiaticus's arrest, and he was brought to Rome in chains. Publius Suillius and Lucius Vitellius were the prosecutors. Suillius owed Claudius for his recall after having been banished for corruption by Tiberius and he had again become a notorious prosecutor, growing richer every day on the percentage of property gained with each conviction. Vitellius, one of the most successful politicians of the day and easily moved by Messallina, was another of Claudius's sycophants. With Messallina present, Asiaticus was judged at a mock trial in a bedroom of the emperor. Vitellius recommended that Asiaticus commit suicide. Without any official verdict, Asiaticus took his own life.

Poppaea was not tried but also committed suicide after being threatened with prison by supporters of Messallina. Claudius may not have known of her death since he was reputed to have asked her husband about her whereabouts at a dinner soon after.

Sources

Tacitus. *Annales* 11.1–4.
Balsdon, J. P. V. D. *Roman Women.* New York: John Day Comp., 1963, pp. 124 ff.
Bauman, Richard A. *Women and Politics in Ancient Rome.* London: Routledge, 1994, pp. 172 ff.
Levick, Barbara. *Claudius: The Corruption of Power.* New Haven, Conn.: Yale University Press, 1993, pp. 62, 64.
Pauly, A., G. Wissowa, and W. Kroll. *Real-Encyclopadie D. Classischen Altertumswissenschaft 1893–.* (Germany: multiple publishers) 3.
Syme, Ronald. *The Augustan Aristocracy.* Oxford: Clarendon Press, 1986, pp. 178, 184, 299.

Poppaea Sabina (2)

(31?–65 C.E.)   Roman: Italy
Augusta

Poppaea Sabina followed in the footsteps of her mother, POPPAEA SABINA (1), and she avenged her downfall at the hands of Valeria MESSALLINA. She has been accused of duplicity, promiscuity, and sundry other vile acts as she moved through two marriages prior to her marriage with the emperor, which occurred after the death of his powerful mother, the younger Julia AGRIPPINA, and his divorce from his popular wife. Endowed with wit, beauty, and intelligence, she successfully usurped Messallina's daughter, Claudia OCTAVIA, as the wife of Nero and became Augusta. Along the way, she made fool of her first husband, Rufius Crispinus, the man who had accused her mother of adultery.

Poppaea's father, Titus Ollius, came from Picenum, was relatively unknown, and probably died in 31 C.E., the same year she was born. Possibly her father's death was tied to the downfall of Lucius Aelius Sejanus, the prefect of the Praetorian Guard accused of treason in the same year. In any case, Poppaea was not given his name, but that of her maternal grandfather, the more illustrious Poppaeus Sabinus, consul in 9 C.E.

Her first marriage, around 44, was with Rufius Crispinus, prefect of the Praetorian Guard under the emperor Claudius. Her husband had grown rich and gained the office of praetor through Messallina. Among the services he performed for her was to bring a charge of adultery against Poppaea's mother, which had led to her suicide. The younger Poppaea repaid him in kind. After she gave birth to a son, she became the lover of the young senator Marcus Salvius Otho, whose reputation as a spendthrift is better remembered than his rule as emperor for a few months in 69. For seven years after her husband lost his position of influence in 51 when the younger Agrippina supplanted Messallina as the wife of Claudius, she remained married. She also continued her open liaison with Otho.

In 58 Poppaea and Crispinus divorced, and she married Otho. She was one year older than her 27-year-old second husband who was a friend of the new emperor, the young Nero. A boastful and not very subtle man, Poppaea's beauty and accomplishments were often her husband's chosen subject. Nero's appetites were whetted. The emperor sent Otho to govern the province of Lusitania in western Spain and became her lover before the year was out.

Poppaea, six years Nero's senior, threatened to end their relationship unless he divorced his wife, Octavia and married her. Not only was Nero faced with the prospect of divorce from a popular and loyal wife, but his mother, the powerful Agrippina, was also against the new marriage. There is no clear evidence that Poppaea urged Nero to murder his mother or knew of his plans to do so. Nonetheless, it was to Poppaea's advantage that Nero had her killed in 59. Poppaea, however, still had three years to wait before Nero divorced Octavia. Between 59 and 62, Nero eliminated several potential rivals, around whom a conspiracy could gather in support of Octavia. Finally with the death in 62 of Sextus Afranius Burrus, who was the head of the Praetorian Guard, Octavia lost her last serious political supporter. Nero appointed Gaius Tigellinus the new head of the guard. It was reported that Poppaea, abetted by Tigellinus, tried unsuccessfully to use Octavia's slaves and charge her with adultery. In the end, Nero divorced her on grounds of sterility. He returned her dowry in the form of the confiscated house of Burrus and the estates of Rebellius Plautus, whom he had exiled and murdered. Octavia was soon banished under an armed guard to the Campania region of Italy.

Poppaea married Nero 12 days after his divorce despite public protests. A false rumor that Nero had repented and recalled Octavia led joyous crowds to surge into the streets, destroying statues of Poppaea and carrying likenesses of Octavia covered with flowers. Some even came to the palace but were repelled by the guards. The statues of Poppaea were replaced, and the fear that Octavia could be the center of an uprising sealed her doom. Octavia was exiled to the island of Pandateria and executed. In 63 Poppaea gave birth to a daughter named Claudia. Although the daughter died after a few months, the title of Augusta was bestowed

upon them both. Poppaea had reached the pinnacle of her ambitions.

There is evidence that Poppaea was religious and interested in some of the mysticism of the East. She also showed some sympathy for the Jews. In 64, the Jewish priest Josephus came to Rome as part of a delegation to secure the release of some Jewish priests who had been sent to Rome in chains by the Roman governor of Judaea. Josephus became friends with Aliturus, an actor who was a favorite of the emperor. Through him, he was introduced to Poppaea, who not only obtained the release of the priests but sent Josephus home laden with gifts. She later persuaded Nero to accede to a Jewish request to prevent the tearing down of a wall that had been erected in the Jewish temple in Jerusalem.

Poppaea's remedies to preserve her beauty became fashionable among the women in Rome. They adopted her practice of washing her face with ass's milk several times a day as a way of whitening the skin and keeping it free of wrinkles. Nero wrote a poem praising Poppaea's amber-colored hair, and it became a popular hair dye color for women. Poppaea had once expressed a desire to die before her beauty started to fade. Her wish was granted. In 65 she was again pregnant when a kick from Nero whom she had angered for some unknown reason killed her. In remorse, he did not cremate the body but had it embalmed and stuffed with spices. She was then placed in a mausoleum of the Julian clan and deified. A public funeral was held, and Nero eulogized her beauty. After her death he ordered that her son by her first husband be drowned and, in 68, her ex-husband executed.

Sources

Dio Cassius. *Roman History* 62.11.2–3, 12.1, 13.1–2, 28.1–2; 63.26.4.
Josephus. *Antiquitates Judaicae (Jewish Antiquities)* 20.195.
———. *Vitae* 13–16.
Juvenal. *Satires* 6.462.
Pliny the Elder. *Naturalis Historia* 28.183; 33.140; 37.50.
Plutarch. *Vitae Parallelae, Galba.* 19.2–5.
Suetonius. *The Lives of the Caesars:* Nero 35.1–3.
———. *The Lives of the Caesars:* Otho 3.1–2.
Tacitus. *Annales* 13.45–46; 14.1–2, 59–65; 15.23; 16.6, 7.

———. *Historiae* 1.13, 22, 78.

Balsdon, J. P. V. D. *Roman Women.* New York: John Day Comp., 1963, index.

Bauman, Richard A. *Women and Politics in Ancient Rome.* London: Routledge, 1994, pp. 199–209.

Griffin, Marian T. *Nero: The End of a Dynasty.* New Haven, Conn.: Yale University Press, 1985, pp. 75–76, 98–104.

Oxford Classical Dictionary, ed. by Simon Hornblower and Antony Spawforth. 3d. ed. New York: Oxford University Press, 1996, p. 1,221.

Pauly, A., G. Wissowa, and W. Kroll. *Real-Encyclopadie d. Classischen Altertumswissenschaft 1893–.* (Germany: multiple publishers) 4.

Smallwood, E. Mary. "The Alleged Jewish Tendencies of Poppaea Sabina." *Journal of Theological Studies* (1959): 29–35, pp. 329–335.

Syme, Ronald. *Tacitus.* 2 vols. Oxford: Clarendon Press, 1958, v. 1, pp. 290, 316–317, 353, 376.

Townsend, G. B. "Traces in Dio Cassius of Cluvius, Aufidius and Pliny." *Hermes* 89 (1961) 227–248.

Walter, Gerard. *Nero.* Trans. by Emma Craufurd. Westport, Conn.: Greenwood Press, 1976, pp. 109–127.

Warmington, B. H. *Nero: Reality and Legend.* New York: W. W. Norton, 1969, pp. 47, 50, 139–140.

◉ Porcia

(?–43 B.C.E.)   Roman: Italy
political player and victim

Porcia was a passionate woman as devoted to the cause of republican Rome as her father, Marcus Porcius Cato Uticensis, a leader among the optimates opposing Gaius Julius Caesar. She lived and died by her father's code of honor. Her mother, ATILIA, and her father were divorced. Porcia's first husband was Marcus Calpurnius Bibulus, coconsul with Caesar in 59 B.C.E. His election had been arranged by her father with large scale bribes. Bibulus opposed the agrarian law supported by Caesar and Gnacus Pompeius (Pompey the Great). Prevented from using his consular veto, he withdrew to his home, and tried to prevent a meeting of the Senate. On each day there was to be a meeting for the rest of the year, he observed the heavens for omens and declared the day inauspicious.

Porcia gave birth to two sons during her marriage with Bibulus. They accompanied her husband in 51 B.C.E. when she remained in Rome and went as proconsul to Syria. She never saw any of them again. After the outbreak of civil war her husband sided with the optimates and died in 48 as he attempted to prevent Caesar from reaching Epirus. By 45, her father, her brother, and one of her sons were also dead.

Also in 45, she married Marcus Junius Brutus. It was a strange union. She bore the mantle of her father, who in many ways, both good and bad, was the last great voice of the republic and at the same time she was a victim of the war. Brutus was a complex man and no less a victim. He admired Porcia's father and had fought on the side of Pompey against Caesar, even though Pompey had earlier been responsible for the death of his own father. Caesar pardoned Brutus after the battle of Pharsalus in 48 and appointed him praetor. Again in Rome, holding office and beholden to Caesar, Brutus divorced his wife to marry Porcia. Brutus's mother, SERVILIA (1), who was Cato's half sister, had once been the lover of Caesar, remained his friend, and opposed Brutus and Porcia's marriage.

Porcia was said to have sensed that Brutus was engaged in a secret undertaking. She sought to convince him that whatever he might plan, she was a worthy confidant. She made a deep gash in her thigh that bled freely. Violent pains, chills, and fever followed. Brutus was distressed. She claimed that her ability to inflict the cut and withstand the pain was evidence of her ability to keep confidences. She was her father's daughter and her husband's partner. Brutus revealed to her the plot against Caesar. After Brutus left for the Forum, Porcia fainted and for a while lost the power of speech. A messenger ran to tell Brutus that his wife was dead, and even as Porcia regained consciousness, Brutus participated in the assassination of Caesar.

Porcia attended meetings after the assassination to assess her husband's future. She was present at a meeting at Antium on June 8, 44, that included JUNIA TERTIA, the wife of Gaius Cassius Longinus; Marcus Favonius, an admirer of Cato; Brutus; Cassius; and Marcus Tullius Cicero. Her mother-in-law, Servilia, presided over the discussion to consider an offer made by the Senate at the instigation of Mark Antony for Brutus and Cassius to supervise the collection of corn taxes in the provinces of Sicily and Asia until the end of the year. In reality, it was an honorable way for them to leave Rome in the wake of the passions raised by the assassination. Brutus and Cassius were uncertain whether or not to accept. Finally, Servilia took it upon herself to try to arrange for the Senate to rescind the offer.

Brutus did leave Italy for the East in August 44. Porcia, who had been with him outside Rome, returned to Rome. Porcia was ill and despondent, and her friends were worried that she might kill herself. Despite their efforts, Porcia took her own life in the summer of 43. Brutus committed suicide in October 42 after his defeat at Philippi.

Sources

Cicero. *Epistulae ad Atticum* 13.9.2; 15.11, 22.4.
Cicero. *Brutus* 17.7.
Dio Cassius. *Roman History* 44.13.2–14.1; 47.49.4.
Plutarch. *Vitae Parallelae (Parallel Lives): Brutus* 13.1–11; 15.5–9; 53.5–6.
Valerius Maximus. *Factorum et dictorum memorabilium libri IX* 4.6.5.
Balsdon, J. P. V. D. *Roman Women.* New York: John Day Comp., 1963, pp. 50–51.
Bauman, Richard A. *Women and Politics in Ancient Rome.* London: Routledge, 1994, p. 75.
Oxford Classical Dictionary, ed. by Simon Hornblower and Antony Spawforth. 3d. ed. New York: Oxford University Press, 1996, p. 1,224.
Pauly, A., G. Wissowa, and W. Kroll. *Real-Encyclopadie d. Classischen Altertumswissenschaft 1893–.* (Germany: multiple publishers) 28.
Syme, Ronald. *The Roman Revolution.* London: Oxford University Press, 1963, pp. 22, 58, 116.

Potone

(fifth–fourth century B.C.E.)   Greek: Athens
sister of Plato

Potone was the sister of the philosopher Plato and mother of Speusippus, his successor. The daughter of PERICTIONE and Ariston, she came from distinguished Athenian families. She married Eurymedon, and their son became a famous philosopher

who succeeded Plato as head of the Academy, the school in Athens that Plato had founded.

Sources

Diogenes Laertius. *Lives of the Eminent Philosophers* 4.4.
Oxford Classical Dictionary, ed. by Simon Hornblower and Antony Spawforth. 3d. ed. New York: Oxford University Press, 1996, p. 1,434.

Praecia

(first century B.C.E.)   Roman: Rome
self-made woman; political player

Praecia was of obscure origin but beautiful, witty, and engaging. Her lover was Publius Cornelius Cethegus, a patrician and master of political intrigue, who was said to have wielded as much power as a consul during the 70s B.C.E. He was regularly accused of taking his orders from Praecia, and the evidence offered was the successful advancement of those who curried her favor.

She was specifically associated with the advancement of Lucius Licinius Lucullus, consul in 74, and his brothers Marcus Licinius Lucullus and Marcus Antonius Creticus. Lucius Lucullus, an able soldier and fine administrator, was beholden to Praecia for his appointment as governor of the province of Cilicia in Asia Minor and, later, to the command of the campaign against Mithridates the Great.

Sources

Plutarch. *Vitae Parallelae (Parallel Lives): Lucullus* 6.2.2–4.
Balsdon, J. P. V. D. *Roman Women.* New York: John Day Comp., 1963, p. 53.
Bauman, Richard A. *Women and Politics in Ancient Rome.* London: Routledge, 1994, pp. 65–66.

Praxilla

(fifth century B.C.E.)   Greek: Sicyon
poet

Praxilla, a poet from Sicyon in Greece, wrote short poems, drinking songs, and hymns of which only a few fragments survive. Her innovation in meter, the praxilleion, was named in her honor. She juxtaposed the conventional and the unconventional, a characteristic that was mocked by some critics. In one poem, Adonis is asked on his arrival in Hades what he will miss most. His list is headed with sunlight, followed by the shining stars and the moon, and then ripe cucumbers, apples, and pears. In another fragment, she linked the parts of the body with two different stages of life. The viewer was described as the possessor of a virgin's head and a married woman's body. Lysippus of Sicyon, a famous sculptor, caste a bronze statue of her.

Sources

Campbell, David A. *Greek Lyric.* 5 vols. Cambridge: Harvard University Press, 1982–1993, pp. 371–381.

Edmonds, J. M., ed. and trans. *Lyra Graeca: Being the Remains of All the Greek Lyric Poets from Eumelus to Timotheus, Excepting Pindar.* Rev. ed. 3 vols. Cambridge: Harvard University Press, 1959, pp. 73–79.

Oxford Classical Dictionary, ed. by Simon Hornblower and Antony Spawforth. 3d. ed. New York: Oxford University Press, 1996, p. 1,242.

Prisca

(third century–c. 316 C.E.)   Roman:
Balkans, Syria, Italy, Asia and Greece
politically influential wife of the emperor; early Christian sympathizer

Prisca's life was intertwined with that of her daughter, VALERIA (2), and both suffered the same tragic fate. Prisca and her husband, the future emperor Diocletian, came from Dalmatia on the Adriatic coast. Both were of lowly birth. Diocletian, commander of the guard, was chosen emperor by the army after the death of the emperor Numerian in 284 C.E. Embattled in the East, he did not reach Rome until 303. Prisca traveled with him.

After Diocletian resigned on May 1, 306, Prisca appears to have gone to live with her daughter. Both she and her daughter sympathized with Christianity, although they were probably not converts. Her son-in-law, Galerius, who followed Diocletian as emperor and initially persecuted Christians, issued the Edict of Toleration before his death in 311, which may have reflected the women's influence.

After his death, Galerius was succeeded by Valerius Licinius, whom the women mistrusted. Prisca and Valeria went to live under the protection of

Maximin Daia, who was then Augustus of the East. Valeria rejected his proposal of marriage.

He put to death some of their friends and banished both of them to a remote area of Syria. Prisca wrote Diocletian for help, but he no longer had the power or physical stamina to come to her aid. When Maximin was killed in 313, Prisca and her daughter spent some 15 months in disguise trying to return to Dalmatia and Diocletian. His death in 316 put an end to their hopes. They were recognized in the Macedonian city of Thessalonica. Their heads were cut off, and their bodies thrown into the sea. Why the two women were so vigorously pursued remains a mystery.

Sources

Lactantius. *De Mortibus Persecutorum* 15, 39, 50–51.

Balsdon, J. P. V. D. *Roman Women.* New York: John Day Comp., 1963, pp. 165–169.

Gibbon, Edward. *The Decline and Fall of the Roman Empire.* New York: Heritage Press, 1946, pp. 333–334.

Proba, Anicia Faltonia

(?–c. 432 C.E.)   Roman: Rome, Carthage
founder of a monastery

Anicia Faltonia Proba, one of the wealthiest women in Rome, was a devout Christian who founded a monastery in North Africa after fleeing Rome and the Goths in 410. Many fled earlier during the siege in 408 when the younger MELANIA and her mother-in-law the younger ALBINA sold their property and left. During the tense days before the city fell in 410, there were whispers that Proba, who was a member of the Anicii family, ordered the gates of the Porta Salaria, which were near several of her extensive estates, opened to admit the Goths. The more sympathetic claimed she could not stand the suffering of the populace under siege. However, she also managed to liquidate many of her estates that were under threat. Jerome criticized the avarice of the clergy, the church, and the monks who bought some of the properties, undoubtedly at fire-sale prices.

There is some uncertainty about whether Proba's father was Quintus Clodius Hermogenianus Olybrius, who was consul in 379, or Clodius Celsinus Adelphius. The former would mean that her grandmother was the poet FALTONIA BETITIA PROBA, and the latter would make the poet her mother, with which most historians agree. Proba married Sextus Petronius Probus, consul in 371, whose rapacity as Praetorian Prefect in Illyricum, Gaul, and Italy accounted for his huge fortune. Her family was also accused of cornering the gold market in Rome. She bore three sons, Anicius Hermogenianus Olybrius and Anicius Probinus, consuls in 395, and Anicius Probus, consul in 406. Her husband, a Christian, was baptized shortly before he died around 395. She remained a widow.

She left the city as soon as possible after her husband's death and sailed to Africa with her daughter-in-law Juliana, the widow of Anicius Olybrius, who had recently died, and a large retinue of widows and young women including slaves, dependents, freedwomen, and probably eunuchs. Like many other refugees from Rome, the group settled in Carthage. It was not difficult for the refugees to adjust. In stature and size Carthage was the city second only to Rome in the western Mediterranean.

Proba established a monastery, bribing Heraclian, the count of Africa and the military authority for the region, to assure its safety. She also corresponded with Augustine in nearby Hippo, who treated her with deference, appreciating her wealth and influence. Proba requested guidance from Augustine on prayers. Augustine's reply was ambiguous. He wrote that she was already noble, wealthy, and mother of an illustrious family and while he praised her interest in prayer, he also noted Christ's admonition that a camel could more easily pass through the eye of a needle than a rich man enter the kingdom of heaven. His indirect attack on her wealth was softened with a conclusion that noted what was impossible for man was possible for God, after all, Zacharius, a rich man, entered heaven.

Augustine's letter probably captured a more general frustration among Africans who were witnessing the rich escapees. Africa was not a wealthy place and could hardly have viewed the new rich women's monasteries as substitutes for investment in the crumbling infrastructure of the towns and cities or, in the case of bishops like Augustine,

funds to support the poor and to endow the churches. When Albina, Melania, and Pinianus had visited Augustine in Hippo, which was within a year or so of his correspondence with Proba, the women had felt threatened by the force of the congregation's desire for their money. Augustine wrote a long letter to Albina explaining, if not justifying, the need for clerics to court wealthy benefactors for their churches and communities.

About this time, the doctrine of Pelagianism began to spread among Christians. It was an appealing doctrine that posited a synergistic union of Neoplatonism and Christianity. Neoplatonic thought still permeated the world of the fifth century in which Christianity, although the official religion of the state for two centuries, had not yet overcome classical pagan traditions. Pelagius asserted that God, the ultimate source of good, would not have created evil and therefore there could be no Original Sin. A powerful dark force of evil, intent on corrupting nature and the human race, could not corrupt the soul, which was, by definition, incorruptible. Moreover, humans had the free will to wage an arduous battle within themselves to defeat evil. It was each one's individual responsibility.

The absence of Original Sin was a great attraction, especially to women who suffered the taint of Eve. The reliance on a doctrine of individual responsibility and a rigorous reflective life also absolved the wealthy from consideration of the consequences of their rapacious behavior. The wealthy women who were ready to adopt ascetic lifestyles and even distribute some of their wealth to the poor and the sick had no need to acknowledge that their families bore a significant degree of responsibility for the century's economic disasters and raging Goths.

Women like Proba and the younger Melania who were attracted by the doctrine never felt the force of Augustine's anti-Pelagius pen, instead he congratulated Proba and Juliana for the decision by Juliana's daughter to forgo marriage and remain a virgin dedicated to Christ. He declared that a life dedicated to Christ and virtue bestowed a greater glory on the family than a consulship.

Proba died in Carthage before 432.

Sources

Ammiamus Marcellinus. XXX. v, 1–10.

Augustine. Letters CXXX, CXXXI, CL.

Jerome. Letter CXXX. 7

Procopius. *Vandelic Wars* III. ii. 27.

Brown, Peter. *Augustine of Hippo; a Biography.* Berkeley: University of California Press, 1967. pp. 340, 351.

Brown, P. R. L. "Aspects of Christianization of the Roman Aristocracy." *The Journal of Early Christian Studies* 51 (1961): 1–11.

Prosopography of the Later Roman Empire. Vol. I. Edited by A. H. M. Jones, J. R. Martindale, and J. Morris. Cambridge: Cambridge University Press, 1971. Reprinted 1992, p. 732.

◉ Proba, Faltonia Betitia
(c. 320–c. 370 C.E.)   Roman: Rome
Christian poet

Faltonia Betitia Proba was an early Christian poet whose works were read into the medieval era. Writing in the fourth century, her poetry was a syncretistic effort to blend pagan form and Christian content. She used the structure and language of Virgil to tell new Christian tales. The adaptation of classical poetry to Christian motifs appealed to a society whose education and mentality remained rooted in classical literature, even as its politics and public religion became Christian. It was a genre practiced across the empire in Latin and Greek, although the pagan poets chosen differed in the East and West. In addition to work by Proba, there is poetry extant from AELIA EUDOCIA, an Augusta who retired to Jerusalem, wrote in Greek, and used Homer as her basic text.

Proba was born into an elite family, the Petronii, which intermarried with the Anicii, said to be the richest family in Rome. Her father may have been Petronius Probianus, who was consul in 322, and her mother Demetrias. She was either the mother or grandmother of ANICIA FALTONIA PROBA, who fled Rome in 410 and established a monastery in Carthage. She married Claudius Celcinus Adelphius, Prefect of Rome in 351. In 352, her husband was charged with treason, but seems to have escaped conviction. They had two sons, Q. Clodius Hermogenianus Olybrius, who was consul in 379, and Faltonius Alypius Probus.

The extant poem was composed between 353–370 C.E. The poem, comprised of some 694 lines of Virgil, was divided about equally between stories from the Old and New Testaments. Except for the introduction, she substituted her own words while holding to Virgil's outline and meter. After some lines devoted to creation, Adam and Eve, their departure from Eden, and the flood, she tells the story of Christ's birth, her own conversion to Christianity, the Resurrection, and Christ's ascension to heaven. The poem concludes with a call to Christians, including her husband and children, to solemnize their faith. Although Jerome, in a letter to a fellow bishop Paulinus, deprecated Proba's poetry, it remained popular until medieval times and was possibly an example of the kind of poetry that became a teaching text with a new Christian focus.

Sources

Jerome. Letter LIII. 7.

Clark, Elizabeth A. and Diane F. Hatch. *The Golden Bough, the Oaken Cross; the Vergilian Cento of Faltonia Betita Proba.* Chico, Calif.: Scholars Press, 1981.

Green, R. P. H. "Proba's Cento: Its Date, Purpose and Reception." *Classical Quarterly* 45 (1995): 55d1–563.

Prosopography of the Later Roman Empire. Vol. I. Edited by A. H. M. Jones, J. R. Martindale, and J. Morris. Cambridge: Cambridge University Press, 1971. Reprinted 1992, p. 732.

Sivan, Hagith. "Anician Women, the Cento of Proba, and Aristocratic Conversion in the Fourth Century." *Vigiliae Christianae* 47 (1993): 140–157.

◉ Publilia (1)
(second century B.C.E.)   Roman: Rome
convicted murderer

Publilia (or Publicia) and LICINIA (1) were accused of poisoning their respective husbands for reasons that are obscure. Both of the men were ex-consuls. Publilia's husband was Postumius Albinus. Publilia used her property as surety for her person. Found guilty, she was strangled by decree of her own family.

Sources

Livy. *From the Founding of the City* 48.

Valerius Maximus. *Factorum et dictorum memorabilium libri IX* 6.3.8.

Bauman, Richard A. *Women and Politics in Ancient Rome.* London: Routledge, 1994, p. 39.

▣ Publilia (2)

(first century B.C.E.)   Roman: Italy
ill-used young heiress

Publilia was a young and wealthy heiress, ill used by the orator and statesman Marcus Tullius Cicero, who was a trustee of her estate. They married shortly after Cicero divorced TERENTIA (1), his wife of long standing, in 46 B.C.E. It could not have been an easy situation for Publilia. The marriage caused a good deal of gossip. He was a 60-year-old man, and she, a young woman of means. Some claimed he had been seduced by her beauty, but his freedman made no bones about what he wanted: her money. Cicero was in dire need of funds, including the next payment on the dowry of his daughter TULLIA (2).

As it happened, Cicero's unhappy daughter Tullia divorced her husband around the same time and died in childbirth only months later, in February 45 B.C.E. Cicero was inconsolable and retreated to his estate in Astura on the coast south of Rome. He also no longer needed Publilia's money. He claimed Publilia had not concealed her feeling of relief over Tullia's death. In the spring of 45, Cicero avoided Publilia and members of her family by escaping to the estate of his friend, Titus Pomponius Atticus. A divorce soon followed. After the divorce, Publilia's family sent an emissary to Cicero to explore the possibility of a remarriage. Cicero wrote Atticus that he found the offer repugnant.

Publilia then married her guardian, Gaius Vibius Rufus. It was a more successful relationship. Her husband, who had acquired the chair on which Julius Caesar used to sit, quipped that with Caesar's chair and Cicero's wife, he might become either a Caesar or a Cicero. He did become consul suffectus in 16 C.E.

Sources

Cicero. *Epistulae ad Atticum* 12.32.1.
Dio Cassius. *Roman History* 57.15.6–7.
Plutarch. *Vitae Parallelae (Parallel Lives): Cicero* 41.3–4.
Shackleton Bailey, D. R. *Cicero.* New York: Charles Scribner's Sons, 1971: pp. 202–203, 210–211.

Syme, Ronald. *The Augustan Aristocracy.* Oxford: Clarendon Press, 1986, p. 225.

▣ Pudentilla, Aemilia

(second century C.E.)   Roman: North Africa
independent woman

Aemilia Pudentilla of Oea (Tripoli) used all her intelligence and skill to maintain a life over which she could exercise control and so chose her own husband. Widowed by Sicinius Amieus while still young and attractive, she had two sons, Sicinius Pontianus and Sicinius Pudens. Threatening to withhold her husband's estate from her if she refused, her father-in-law pressed her to marry her brother-in-law Sicinius Clarus. Pudentilla agreed to an engagement but successfully postponed the marriage for some 13 years until the old man died.

Then, at age 40 she announced to her sons that a husband would improve her failing health. Her son Sicinius Pontianus waited anxious lest a new husband deprive him and his brother of their inheritance. In 156 C.E. the author of the *Golden Ass,* Apuleius, who was a rhetorician and poet from a wealthy family in Madaura, North Africa, with whom Pontianus had become friends earlier in Athens, fell ill in Oea. Pontianus invited him to recover in his mother's house. Some 15 years younger than Pudentilla, Apuleius enjoyed her intelligence and admired her character. With the sons' approval, they married.

Sicinius Aemilianus, the brother of the suitor she had held off for 13 years, and Herennius Rufinus, the father-in-law of Pontianus, opened a suit against Apuleius on the grounds that he had used magic to win Pudentilla. Initially the sons backed the suit. Pontianus later recanted, although he died before the trial took place in late 158 or early 159. Apuleius spoke in his own defense and easily discredited his accusers. He pointed out that Pudentilla, despite her wealth, had made over a small dowry to him, which was put in trust. If she died without having any children, the dowry would revert to her sons. If she gave birth to a son or daughter, half would go to the children of the second marriage, and half to those of the first. He later published his defense, entitled *The Apologia*. After the trial, Pudentilla and her husband moved to Carthage where her health improved and he enhanced his reputation as rhetorician, philosopher, and poet.

Sources

Apuleius. *Apologia.*

Oxford Classical Dictionary, ed. by Simon Hornblower and Antony Spawforth. 3d. ed. New York: Oxford University Press, 1996, p. 131.

▣ Pulcheria, Aelia

(January 19, 399–July 453 C.E.)   Roman:
Constantinople
Augusta

Pulcheria made her mark in the political and religious history of the empire. From her youth onward, she was a major force on a world stage, as regent for her younger brother Theodosius II and, after 414, as Augusta.

Pulcheria's mother died in childbirth in 404 leaving five children. Four years later, in May 408, her father, the emperor Arcadius, died. Over the next six years, Antiochus, a eunuch in the imperial service, cared for the orphaned children and shaped their education, which included both Greek and Latin. Pulcheria was an able student, later praised for her writing and elocution in both languages. Both domestic and foreign affairs during these years were in the hands of Anthemius, the Praetorian Prefect of the East, who was regent for the young emperor Theodosius II.

Pulcheria took the first, and perhaps her most critical, public step in assuming control over her siblings, the household, and the empire before July in 413 when she was 14 years old. She dedicated an altar in the Great Church at Constantinople, inscribed with her commitment to virginity and her brother's rule. It ended any discussions of betrothal and marriage and immediately enhanced her status within the church. She convinced her sisters to undertake similar vows, sealing the boundaries of the imperial household from agnate relations with their own agenda for power.

It was a politically astute move and possibly a heartfelt one as well. Pulcheria clothed herself with the holy mantle of Mary, *Theotokos* (Mother of God), which, in the religious debates of the time, allowed her to rise above the denigrating stigma of Eve's transgression and assured her a place of influence in Christian discourse. Insofar as religion and politics overlapped, her elevated position in the church enhanced her political effectiveness. It also eliminated two of the handicaps suffered by women in power: a husband and the specter of death like that of her mother from childbirth.

As regent for her brother, coins were issued in Pulcheria's honor. She named the elderly Auralean, who had ties with her mother, AELIA EUDOXIA, as Praetorian Prefect of the East. Pulcheria's lifestyle conformed to her religious declaration. She instituted prayers and regular fasting for herself and her siblings, studied the scriptures, and dressed modestly, which eliminated any contention between herself and the clergy over a woman's proper deportment. She even engaged in weaving, an ancient symbol of womanhood with echoes from Homer to Augustus. She also aided the poor and provided shelters and places for worship out of her personal income.

Pulcheria
(Date: 414 C.E.–453 C.E. 1948.19.1947, Archives, American Numismatic Society)

Propriety and modesty, however, did not preclude the exercise of power. She was forceful in decision-making and efficient in implementation, although careful to attribute authority to her brother. She supported Cyril, bishop of Alexandria, in an outrage against civil authority that has reverberated across the centuries. Cyril launched a campaign against Arians and other heretics and against the Jews, who had long been allowed to live in the city, work, and follow their own religious dictates, providing they paid taxes. Cyril urged his fanatical Christian followers to drive out the Jews and to seize their property. The mobs he incited also killed HYPATIA, a renowned pagan philosopher and teacher, and burned the Alexandrian library and museum with its more than 800,000 papyrus scrolls. Orestes, the civil governor of the city, protested to Pulcheria and Theodosius that Cyril had exceeded his authority. His delegation received scant attention in Constantinople.

Pulcheria's orthodoxy, however, was malleable, especially with regard to military policy. Since her brother was not a military man and the empire needed an efficient fighting machine, Pulcheria revived a practice of Theodosius the Great and appointed Germans, who were Arian Christians, to high military positions. Her policy depended on the historical antipathy between Goths and Huns, Arians and orthodox Christians, to assure the loyalty of both and to act as counterweights to any Roman generals who might aspire to become emperor.

In 421 a Roman army invaded Persia to protect Christians. Possibly, Pulcheria considered the invasion a relatively low-risk war to strengthen the image of her studious and gentle brother. Although it ended in a stalemate, Theodosius and Pulcheria claimed victory and issued coins with a new iconography that for the first time depicted the Augusta and the emperor on both sides. The coins signified that the victory was as much Pulcheria's as it was that of the emperor and the army.

Theodosius married AELIA EUDOCIA in 421 and altered the character of the imperial household as well as the relative positions of power and influence within it. In a highly romanticized version of the courtship, written some 100 years after the

event, John Malalas credited Pulcheria with choosing the bride. If she was not the agent, she must have been asked for her approval of the match. From Pulcheria's perspective there was much to be said in favor of Eudocia. She was agreeable without being an apparent political threat. She was interesting and well educated but came from a modest family and had been raised a pagan, which meant she and her family had no relatives in high position or standing in religious affairs. No doubt there also were other, and perhaps more obvious choices among Pulcheria's circle of women friends. However, Theodosius may have had a more active role in the choice than has been generally thought and so may have Eudocia.

Eudocia gave birth to a daughter LICINIA EUDOXIA in 422 and was elevated to Augusta on January 2, 423. Coins were issued in her honor similar to those struck for Pulcheria. There were now two Augustae in the East, and both were in the imperial household in Constantinople. The next years of Pulcheria's life would have to take account of Eudocia, who had an independent agenda that included the appointment of her relatives to important positions and her influence with the emperor for a more inclusive Christianity.

After a decade of good relations, discord erupted in 431 over Cyril, the bishop of Alexandria, and Nestorius, who had become bishop of Constantinople in 428. There had been no dissent from the imperial family about the elevation of Nestorius as bishop. Noted for his rhetoric and knowledge, he unfortunately soon also revealed a tactless, highly opinionated, misogynistic, and impolitic side to his personality. In addition to attacks against pagans and heretics in general, his attacks on Arian Christians angered many of the high-ranking German members of the military.

He also alienated elite women, refusing them participation in evening services, claiming that their nighttime excursions might result in promiscuity. The women regarded his statement as a challenge to their personal autonomy and a slur on their virtue, as well as an abridgement of their religious duties. Finally, he insulted Pulcheria. He refused to honor her as the bride of Christ in his prayers for the imperial household, as his predecessor had done. When she arrived at the Great Church to take communion with her brother, Nestorius refused to allow her to enter. She demanded to know why, since she had pledged her virginity to Mary, who was the mother of God. He replied that women only gave birth to evil and Satan.

Pulcheria rested her public image and political base on her vow of virginity and her position in the affairs of the church was inseparable from Mary *Theotokos,* Mother of God. She had many supporters for her theological position within the Church and among wealthy aristocrats, both men and women. Mary *Theotokos* was also popular among the masses, especially women whose status was elevated in her reflected glory. Cyril of Alexandria quickly rose to her defense, his support fed by his resentment of the greater prestige and importance accorded Constantinople over Alexandria. The conflict reached a crisis when Anastasius, chaplain to Nestorius, delivered a sermon in the Great Church and identified Mary as *Christotokos,* Mother of the Christ, not God. Without naming Nestorius, Cyril intimated that the latter held heretical opinions about the divine and human nature of Christ and sent elaborate documents to Pulcheria, her sisters, Eudocia, and Theodosius in which he offered historical evidence that Mary was properly *Theotokos,* not *Christotokos.*

Theodosius and Eudocia continued their firm support for Nestorius, although his misogyny would not appear to be consonant with Eudocia's tastes, interests, or learning. However, she may have taken advantage of the controversy to join her husband in one of the few instances in which he disagreed with his sister. To quiet the uproar, Theodosius authorized the convening of a church council at Ephesus in 431. Memnon, bishop of Ephesus, and Cyril organized mobs that intimidated the supporters of Nestorius, who, not unexpectedly, was condemned. A smaller council made up of late-arriving supporters of Nestorius held a counter-meeting and deposed Cyril and Memnon. The emperor accepted the verdict of the second council, but Nestorius had lost support in Constantino-

ple and protests erupted in the streets. Theodosius decided to depose Nestorius and reinstate Cyril and Memnon. After protests continued, Nestorius indicated that he was tired of the battle and requested that the emperor send him back to his former monastery near Antioch. In disgust, the emperor, undoubtedly with advice from Pulcheria, deposed Nestorius and allowed Cyril and Memnon to resume their offices. Pulcheria's approval soared among the people of the city.

If the first round went to Pulcheria, the next collision was a victory for her opponent. In 438, about a year after the marriage of Eudocia's daughter Licinia Eudoxia and Valentinian III, emperor in the West and son of PLACIDIA, Eudocia left Constantinople on a pilgrimage to Palestine. On her return around 439, she brought the bones of Saint Stephen and the public greeted her with euphoria. For the first time, Pulcheria had to contend with a woman peer. It must have been a bitter moment when Eudocia gained the appointment of Cyrus, a poet she admired, to the important position of Praetorian Prefect of the East. Even more so, when he won public acclaim for the renovation of buildings, the construction of a protective seawall, and better city lighting.

While Pulcheria's influence over her brother declined, she still had available to her enormous resources across the empire. She was responsible for the construction of three churches dedicated to Mary as the Mother of God: the church of Theotokos near Saint Sophia, Theotokos Hodegretia (Our Lady Who Leads to Victory), and the most famous, Blachernae, which later housed a robe of the Virgin Mary that came to be regarded as a protector of the city. She also constructed churches to house the relics of saints including Stephen and Lawrence among others.

She had a large personal staff, free and slave, plus a military contingent provided by the government. She owned two palaces, Hebdomon and Rufinianai, as well as a number of dwellings in and around the city. Within the city she also owned properties rented to artisans, which provided a stream of regular income. She had farms in the suburbs of the city that produced food and other crops that served the household and also earned income. Around her were men and women who also had large numbers of slaves, estates, and dependents. Her sisters, who were often in her household, owned their own houses and properties in the city and its environs. Women from well-connected families served as her attendants, and a select group of women pledged to virginity lived in her household. Their personal wealth further augmented her own.

Power, not wealth per se, was often the stake in imperial politics, where one day's victor might become the next day's exile. Pulcheria, at the apex of the webs of influence and power that wrapped themselves around imperial life, was a master of strategic withdrawal, which she amply demonstrated over the next several years.

Amid the continuing tensions between Pulcheria and her sister-in-law, the eunuch Chrysaphius gained influence over Theodosius. He sought to remove Pulcheria from the palace. Playing on the rivalry between the two women, he aroused Eudocia's suspicions by pointing to an inequality with Pulcheria, a chamberlain in Pulcheria's household who officially should have been in the service of the emperor's wife. Theodosius refused Eudocia's request that another chamberlain be assigned to her. Chrysaphius suggested that in light of Pulcheria's vow of virginity and asceticism she should withdraw from political affairs and become a deaconess. Pulcheria was reminded by her friend Proclus, the Patriarch of Constantinople, that as a deaconess she would be under his authority. Pulcheria, who was not about to be under anyone's control, withdrew to her own household on the outskirts of the city and turned the chamberlain over to Eudocia. Coins continued to be issued with her portrait.

Time was on Pulcheria's side. Eudocia was not happy in Constantinople and her marriage was in difficulty. An official announcement from the imperial palace stated that Eudocia was going on another pilgrimage to Jerusalem. Eudocia left with her honors in place and established herself as an almost independent ruler over her extensive lands in Palestine. She never returned to Constantinople

and from her position at the edge of the empire was later forced to accept the decision of the Council of Chalcedon in 451, which was Pulcheria's great achievement.

Her rival had departed but Chrysaphius still exercised influence that thwarted Pulcheria's return to her previous position of power. His days were limited, and it was the politics of religion that would be his downfall. Chrysaphius became embroiled in the unraveling of a compromise adopted in 443 over the perennially divisive issue of the human and divine natures of Christ. The 443 compromise had also affirmed that Mary was *Theotokos,* the Mother of God, which was critical from Pulcheria's perspective and allowed her to support the compromise. The unraveling was occasioned by contentious relationships among the leading bishops as much as by doctrinal disputes, although the disputes and the contentiousness were also often indistinguishable from the jockeying for secular power and authority.

Dioscorus, bishop of Alexandria, was contentious and jealous of the famous clergy in Antioch and opposed Nestorianism. He favored a doctrine that emphasized Christ's divinity as espoused by Eutyches, a monk who was also Chrysaphius's godson, and which was also the doctrine Theodosius supported. However, Eusebius, bishop of Dorylaeum in Asia Minor, and Flavian, bishop of Constantinople, accused Eutyches of heresy at a synod in Constantinople in November 448. Eutyches was excommunicated, a move supported by Leo I, bishop of Rome.

Theodosius, at the request of the Alexandrian bishop Dioscorus, convened a second council at Ephesus in August 449 where Eutyches was reinstated under pressure from the emperor, and the bishops Flavian, Eusebius, and others who had supported the excommunication were deposed. Leo wrote to Pulcheria and urged her to intervene and call a third council to nullify the second and affirm the first. Letters from Emperor Valentinian III, Augusta Licinia Eudoxia, and Valentinian's powerful mother, GALLA PLACIDIA, maintained a solid front from the West. Galla Placidia, who also wrote directly to her niece Pulcheria, highlighted the political/religious alignment of the ostensible religious controversy with the emperor and his bishops on one side and Pulcheria with hers on the other.

Pulcheria, an ardent supporter of the compromise of 443, remained stymied by Chrysaphius until sometime between March and July of 450, when he finally fell from favor, lost his fortune, and was exiled. Pulcheria resumed her preeminent position as counselor to her brother. On July 28, however, Theodosius fell from his horse in a hunting accident and died.

Pulcheria and Aspar, Master of Soldiers, faced the urgent issue of succession. It was still several centuries before a woman or a non-Roman would be emperor. Neither Pulcheria nor Aspar, a non-Roman, could rule alone. They arranged that Marcian, a formerly undistinguished Roman military officer, be declared emperor. Pulcheria married Marcian to solidify control over him and confer legitimacy on his reign. It was to be an unconsummated marriage, which allowed Pulcheria to remain physically a virgin, politically the Augusta, and unquestionably true to her vows to the church. The coronation took place at her Hebdomon palace, and it was she who invested Marcian with imperial authority. Coins were struck in which an image of Christ was placed between the couple.

Pulcheria turned Chrysaphius over to one of his enemies and exchanged letters with Leo in Rome preparatory to a council to reverse the decisions of Ephesus. There was to be no repeat of the rowdiness and violence that had marked 449. The new council was to be held near Chalcedon, across the Bosporus from Constantinople. She warned the governor of the province, on pain of dire punishment, to insure a peaceful environment.

The council met from the eighth of October until the first of November 451. In addition to 520 bishops, Pulcheria, and Marcian, a number of prominent laymen attended. The results were never in doubt. The bishops overturned the decisions of the earlier council and deposed Dioscorus. They adopted Leo's definition of the two natures of Christ, human and divine, each nature preserved in union in Christ.

The bishops affirmed the doctrine of *Theotokos,* Mary the Mother of God, under pressure from Pulcheria and Marcian and over the objections of some bishops who favored a more nuanced statement. Pulcheria also had an agenda that prepared for the future. Over the objections of Leo, she and the emperor persuaded the council to elevate Constantinople to the level of Rome and to accord both the power to establish new sees in Asia, Thrace, and Pontus. The assembled bishops repeatedly acclaimed Pulcheria and compared her with Helena, the mother of Constantine the Great. The council crowned Pulcheria's lifelong devotion to religion and political power.

While the Chalcedon Council's doctrine is still the official position of the Roman Catholic Church, it aroused strong opposition among the monks in Palestine and Alexandria. In Jerusalem riots occurred in 452, with some monks retreating to the walled palace of Eudocia, who supported them. However, Pulcheria and the emperor prevailed and the new orthodoxy withstood the riots. Pulcheria died in July 453 and was entombed in the mausoleum of Constantine the Great. She bequeathed all of her wealth to the poor.

Sources

John Malalas. *Chronicle* XIV. v, vi.

Pope Leo. *Letters* 79, 95, 105.

Sozomen. *Historia Ecclesiastica* IX. 1, 3.

Theophanes. *Chronicle* AM 5901, 5905, 5940, 5942, 5945.

Bury, J. B. *History of the Roman Empire from the Death of Theodosius I to the Death of Justinian.* 2 vols. New York: Dover Publications, Inc., 1958. pp. 349–355.

Holum, Kenneth. "Pulcheria's Crusade and the Ideology of Imperial Victory." *Greek Roman and Byzantine Studies* 18 (1977): 153–172.

———. *Theodosian Empresses: Women and Imperial Dominion in Late Antiquity.* Berkeley: University of California Press, 1982.

Prosopography of the Later Roman Empire. Vol. II. Edited by A. H. M. Jones, J. R. Martindale, and J. Morris. Cambridge: Cambridge University Press, 1971. Reprinted 1992, pp. 929–930.

▣ Pythias

(?–c. 335 B.C.E.)   Greek: Asia Minor
wife of Aristotle

Pythias was the wife of Aristotle. They met in Atarneus on the west coast of Asia Minor opposite the island of Lesbos. Her uncle and adopted father who ruled Atarneus had an interest in philosophy. He had gone to Athens and studied at the famous Academy. After Plato died, he invited Aristotle to teach in Atarneus.

Aristotle and Pythias had one daughter before she died sometime after 335 B.C.E. Aristotle requested that his executor, Nicanor, who had served under Alexander the Great, marry his daughter when she came of age. He did.

Sources

Diogenes Laertius. *Lives of the Eminent Philosophers* 5.1, 12.

Oxford Classical Dictionary, ed. by Simon Hornblower and Antony Spawforth. 3d. ed. New York: Oxford University Press, 1996, p. 166.

▣ Pythodoris

(first century B.C.E.–first century C.E.)   Roman: Asia Minor and Pontus
Roman client ruler

Pythodoris married Polemon, and after his death she ruled Pontus. The granddaughter of Mark Antony, in about 34 B.C.E., her mother ANTONIA (3) had married Pythodorus from Tralles in Caria, Asia Minor. Her father, an ally of her grandfather, was immensely wealthy and influential throughout Asia at a time when Antony had extended his rule in the East.

Polemon was much older than Pythodoris. He too had fought with Antony against the Parthians. The son of the wealthy rhetorician Zeno, from Laodicea in Asia Minor, he and his father were rewarded by Antony with Roman citizenship and control over Pontus and lesser Armenia. Her husband stood between the Romans and the Parthians. Subsequently, Augustus confirmed his rule over Pontus but removed Lesser Armenia from his control.

In 15 B.C.E. Polemon fought alongside Marcus Vipsanius Agrippa in support of Augustus and Rome. He was rewarded with rule over Bosporus. In 8 B.C.E. he was killed fighting. Although Polemon and Pythodoris had a son, the young man was uninterested in ruling, and Rome recognized Pythodoris as her husband's successor. She pursued her husband's policy of support for Rome in eastern Asia Minor. The coins she issued bearing the heads of LIVIA DRUSILLA and other members of the imperial family make clear her client status.

Pythodoris married Archelaus, the ruler of Cappadocia, with the approval of Rome since the marriage established a powerful bulwark against invasions. Her husband, however, fell out of favor with Augustus's successor Tiberius, and was lured to Rome with a letter from Livia Drusilla. On Archelaus's arrival, Tiberius requested the Senate to try him for treason. Old and infirm, Archelaus died before a decision was reached.

Pythodoris was allowed to retain rule over Pontus, but the other portions of her domain became a Roman province. It is not known how long she reigned or when she died. Two of her children by her first husband, however, were very successful. Her daughter ANTONIA TRYPHAENA married Cotys of Thrace and ruled Pontus as regent for her son after the death of her mother. Her youngest son, Zeno, ruled Armenia for 17 years.

Sources

Strabo. *Geography* 12.29.

Macurdy, Grace. *Hellenistic Queens.* Reprint. Chicago: Ares Publishers, 1985, pp. 10–11.

Magie, David. *Roman Rule in Asia Minor, to the End of the Third Century after Christ.* 2 vols. Princeton, N.J.: Princeton University Press, 1950, pp. 486–487.

Oxford Classical Dictionary, ed. by Simon Hornblower and Antony Spawforth. 3d. ed. New York: Oxford University Press, 1996, p. 113.

▣ Pythonice

(fourth century B.C.E.)   Greek: Greece, Asia Minor, and Babylon
self-made woman

Pythonice became the companion of Harpalus, a friend of Alexander the Great. Originally from

Corinth, Pythonice had moved to Athens where she met Harpalus, a Macedonian of high birth. She accompanied him to Babylon.

Although Harpalus had a deformity that made him unable to fight in Alexander's army, his skill with accounts led Alexander to assign him charge of the treasury deposited in Babylon in 331 B.C.E. Harpalus, like many others, believed that Alexander would never return from India. He raided the treasury to support a luxurious lifestyle that he enjoyed with Pythonice. During this period she bore a girl, whom Harpalus acknowledged as his daughter.

Pythonice died, probably before Alexander confounded expectations, returned alive and discovered Harpalus's embezzlement. Harpalus not only privately mourned her, but provided a magnificent funeral accompanied by songs and music. He built a tomb to her memory in Babylon and commissioned Charicles, the son-in-law of Phocion, a great Athenian general and statesman, to erect a costly monument over her grave in Hermus on the road from Athens to Eleusis, which later sources still noted as well worth a visit.

Harpalus made his escape from Alexander and Babylon with a fleet of ships and troops, but he was killed in Crete in 323 B.C.E. The Athenians Phocion and Charicles, provided for the education of Pythonice's daughter.

Sources

Athenaeus. *Deipnosophistae* 13.586c.
Diodorus Siculus. *Library of History* 17.108.4–6.
Pausanias. *Description of Greece* 1.37.5.
Plutarch. *Vitae Parallelae (Parallel Lives): Phocion* 22.1–3.
Licht, Hans. *Sexual Life in Ancient Greece.* Trans. by J. H. Freese. London: Abbey Library, 1971, pp. 401–402.

Quarta Hostilia

(?–c. 179 B.C.E.)   Roman: Rome
convicted murderer

Quarta Hostilia's second husband, the consul Gaius Calpurnius Piso, died in 180 B.C.E. and rumors circulated that Hostilia had poisoned him. Her motive was said to have been a desire for the advancement of Quintus Fulvius Flaccus, the son of her first husband, also Quintus Fulvius Flaccus, who had been consul four times. Twice the younger Quintus Fulvius Flaccus had failed to be elected consul. Witnesses came forward to testify that Hostilia had upbraided him for his failure and pressed him to try again. She assured him that the next time he would succeed. Her son became consul in 179, succeeding his deceased stepfather. Hostilia was convicted of poisoning her husband.

Sources

Livy. *From the Founding of the City* 40.37.1–7.

R

Rhea

(second–first century B.C.E.)   Roman: Italy
devoted mother

Rhea was a devoted mother and she had an equally devoted son. Her family was from Nursia, northeast of Rome. Widowed, alone she raised her son, Quintus Sertorius who became a successful army commander and led one of the divisions when Lucius Cornelius Cinna captured Rome in 87 B.C.E. Along with Cinna, Sertorius became praetor in 83 B.C.E. The following year he took command of Spain. He opposed Lucius Cornelius Sulla and fought successfully to maintain his authority over the province.

Sertorius received news of Rhea's death while in Spain. His pain was obvious. He withdrew into his tent and for several days refused to see anyone. His fellow officers finally forced him to emerge.

Sources
Plutarch. *Vitae Parallelae (Parallel Lives): Sertorius* 2; 22.6–7.

Rhodopis

(sixth century B.C.E.)
Thracian: Samos and Egypt
self-made woman

Rhodopis successfully used her beauty to achieve fame and wealth. Said to be of Thracian back-

ground, she and Aesop, the famous writer of fables, were fellow slaves of Iadmon on the island of Samos. She was brought to Egypt by Xantheus, also of Samos, during the time of the pharaoh Amasis (569–525 B.C.E.).

Charaxus of Lesbos, the brother of the poet SAPPHO, purchased her freedom. She remained in Egypt and amassed a considerable fortune. As a memorial to herself, in the temple at Delphi, she spent 10 percent of her wealth to purchase a number of iron spits used for roasting whole oxen. Sappho satirized Charaxus and Rhodopis in a poem, and thus Rhodopis's name became familiar throughout Greece.

Sources
Herodian. *History of the Empire* 2.134–36.

Roxane

(?–313 B.C.E.)
Persian: Asia Minor and Greece
political player

Roxane's fate was determined by her father, her husband, and finally her son. A Persian by birth, she married Alexander the Great and was mother of his only son. For six war-filled years after Alexander's death, she successfully maneuvered to protect the child's future. In the end, she and her son

285

were victims of the power that the very name of Alexander evoked.

Her father, Oxyartes, was a nobleman from Bactria who led the Sogdians against the invasion of Alexander in the eastern provinces of Persia after Alexander's defeat of Darius, the Persian king. Roxane, her mother, and her sisters had been sent for safety to the Sogdian Rock, which had so precipitous a drop that it was considered impregnable. In heavy snows, some 300 volunteers, promised significant rewards from Alexander, scaled the heights and conquered the citadel. Roxane was among the daughters of Oxyartes captured. She was immediately acknowledged the most beautiful woman in Persia, with the exception of the wife of the ruler Darius. Alexander married her in 327 B.C.E., and her father became his ally.

Roxane gave birth to Alexander IV in August 323, soon after her husband's unexpected death. Alexander's senior generals agreed that the new born son and the weak Philip Arrhidaeus, the last living son of Alexander's father Philip II, were Alexander's legitimate heirs. Roxane and her son became both actors and hostages in the subsequent struggle for control over the disintegrating empire. Conflict intensified after 319 and the death of Antipater, whose authority in Greece and Macedonia had assured a degree of stability. In the struggle that ensued among the next generation of leaders, possession of Roxane and her son became one of the critical conditions asserting legitimacy.

Roxane was not the only woman with a stake in the future of Macedonia and a claim to rule. OLYMPIAS (1), Roxane's mother-in-law and the mother of Alexander the Great, was equally determined that only the son of Alexander should rule; EURYDICE (2), wife and regent for the impaired Philip Arrhidaeus, was no less determined that her candidate maintain control over Macedonia. With Eurydice in Macedonia under the protection of Antipater, Olympias had made a strategic retreat to Epirus, where she ruled. After Antipater's death, one of the major claimants, Polyperchon, fled to Epirus with Roxane and her son and sought support from Olympias to help regain Macedonia from Eurydice and Polyperchon's opponent, Cassander.

Olympias, regarded as sacred by the people of Macedonia, seized the opportunity to ally herself with Roxane and her grandson. She marched into Macedonia in 317 to eliminate Eurydice and Philip Arrhidaeus and their supporters. At the sight of Olympias, the army joined her ranks en masse. Olympias won without a fight. She executed Philip and forced Eurydice to commit suicide. Olympias ruled Macedonia with Roxane and Alexander IV, who was barely six years old.

However, Cassander, Polyperchon's opponent, returned from the Peloponnesus and slipped his forces into Macedonia, catching Olympias by surprise. Unable to raise more troops in Macedonia, Olympias withdrew to Pydna. Although Polyperchon tried to free her, he failed, and in 316 Olympias surrendered to Cassander and delivered to him Roxane and Alexander IV. Cassander killed Olympias, despite a promise to spare her life. Roxane and Alexander IV remained alive for some six years during which Alexander was nominally ruler, but in reality a captive. He and Roxane were killed when the boy was 12 years old, just about the time he might have become an independent political force.

Sources

Arrian. *Anabasis of Alexander* 4.19.5, 20.4; 7.4.4.

Diodorus Siculus. *Library of History* 18.3.3; 19.35.5, 52.4, 61.1, 105.1–4.

Cary, M. *A History of the Greek World from 323 to 146 B.C.* London: Methuen, 1951, pp. 2, 20, 29.

Oxford Classical Dictionary, ed. by Simon Hornblower and Antony Spawforth. 3d. ed. New York: Oxford University Press, 1996, p. 1,336.

▣ Rubria

(first century C.E.)   Roman: Rome
priestess

Rubria was a Vestal Virgin, dedicated to chastity. According to the sources, she was raped by the emperor Nero.

Sources

Suetonius. *The Lives of the Caesars: Nero* 28.1.

S

Sabina, Vibia

(c. 87/88–136 C.E.)   Roman: Rome, Greece,
Italy, Britain, Asia, Syria, Palestine, and Egypt
Augusta

Vibia Sabina was a cultured woman who traveled
extensively. She married the future emperor
Hadrian, whom she had known since childhood.
Their marital relationship appears to have been
distant and formal. She was childless and spent her
time largely separated from her husband among a
circle of women. Her mother, MATIDIA (1), was the
daughter of Ulpia MARCIANA, the sister of the
emperor Trajan. Her father, Matidia's second husband, was Lucius Vibius Sabinus, consul in 97 C.E.,
who died shortly after his consulship. Her mother
and grandmother accompanied Trajan and his
wife, Pompeia PLOTINA, to Rome after he became
emperor and lived with them during Sabina's
childhood.

Plotina, along with Sabina's grandmother and
mother, shaped the intellectual life of imperial
Rome during Trajan's reign. It was Plotina who
instigated Sabina's marriage with Hadrian. Sabina
married the future emperor in 100 C.E., when she
was 12 or 13 years old and he was 25.

Sabina probably remained in Rome when
Hadrian campaigned against the Dacians between

Vibia Sabina
*(Date: 128 C.E.–136 C.E. 1967.153.145, Archives,
American Numismatic Society)*

101 and 106. She was not with her husband in
Syria when he received word from Plotina and
Matidia at Selinus in Cilicia, on August 8, 117
that Trajan had died. The women clearly controlled the always delicate transition between
emperors, and Hadrian, adopted by Trajan immediately before his death, was successfully acclaimed

the new emperor. Sabina, however, did accompany her husband to Britain when he campaigned there in 122.

It was not until 128 that Hadrian proclaimed Sabina Augusta. Differences in temperament and Hadrian's decided preference for boys may have hindered the marriage. However, the marriage, although childless, endured. In 121 and 122 Hadrian dismissed several men from his service—including one of his secretaries, the historian Gaius Suetonius, and Septicius Clarus, the prefect of the Praetorian Guard—for being too close with Sabina, although there was no evidence of anything more than friendship.

In 128 Sabina accompanied Hadrian on his trip to the Near East and visited Athens, Corinth, and other cities in Greece. They traveled to Ephesus, Smyrna, and Antioch and through Syria, Palestine, and Egypt. They returned to Rome sometime in 132. It was on this journey that Sabina was accompanied by the Greek poet Julia BALBILLA, who carved five epigrams on the foot of the Colossus of Memnon in Thebes. Sabina died some four years later in 136 or 137. Hadrian consecrated her, and she was commemorated on posthumous coins.

Sources

Scriptores Historiae Augustae. Hadrian 1.2; 2.10; 11.3; 23.9.

Balsdon, J. P. V. D. *Roman Women.* New York: John Day Comp., 1963, pp. 139–140.

Oxford Classical Dictionary, ed. by Simon Hornblower and Antony Spawforth. 3d. ed. New York: Oxford University Press, 1996, pp. 1,341–1,342.

Perowne, Stewart. *Hadrian.* Reprint. Westport, Conn.: Greenwood Publishing, 1976.

◉ Salome

(first century B.C.E.–first century C.E.) Jewish: Judaea
client of Livia Drusilla

Salome was a client and friend of LIVIA DRUSILLA. The daughter of Antipater, an Idumaean from the area south of Judaea, her father had received Roman citizenship and became procurator in Judaea as a reward for aid to Julius Caesar. Her brother was the future Herod the Great, king of Judaea, over whom she exercised a great deal of influence. Salome corresponded with Livia and on occasion sought her intervention. Salome wanted Livia to support her marriage with Syllaeus, an influential Nabataean Arab who governed Arabia under the indolent ruler Obades. The sources differ as to Livia's response, and in the end Salome did not marry him. On her brother's death Salome inherited three towns, Jamnia, Azotus, and Phasaelis. When she died, she bequeathed the three towns to Livia.

She had a daughter, BERENICE (1), and a grandson Agrippa I who grew up in Livia's household in Rome together with the future emperor Gaius Caligula. Caligula later appointed him king of Judaea.

Sources

Josephus. *Antiquitates Judaicae (Jewish Antiquities)* 17.10.

Josephus. *Bellum Judaicum (Jewish Wars)* 1.566.

Perowne, Stewart. *The Later Herods: The Political Background of the New Testament.* New York: Abingdon Press, 1950, p. 41.

◉ Salonina, Cornelia

(third century C.E.)
Greek: Asia Minor, Italy and Rome
Augusta

Cornelia Salonina, a cultured neo-Platonist, was Augusta during the troubled decades of the mid-third century C.E. She was the wife of the emperor Publius Licinius Gallienus. Her husband became sole ruler after his father was captured by the Persians in 260 C.E. Salonina was Greek speaking and came from Bithynia, in northwest Asia Minor.

Neoplatonic idealism stood in sharp contrast with the steadily deteriorating economic situation of the period and the unending struggle to maintain the integrity of the empire's borders. Salonina accompanied Gallienus on his campaigns and was with him in the military camp when he was assassinated in 268. Salonina and Gallienus had two sons. The eldest, Valerian, died in 258, and the younger son, Publius Licinius Cornelius Saloninus Valerianus, became Caesar after the death of his brother and died shortly thereafter in 260 or 261.

When Salonina died, a coin celebrating peace was issued in her honor.

Sources

Scriptores Historiae Augustae. Gallienus 21.3–5.

Salvina (Silvina)

(?–c. 404 C.E.)   Moor/Roman: Africa,
Constantinople
Christian woman

Salvina, sometimes called Silvina, was part of a wealthy and well-connected coterie of women in Constantinople who supported the charismatic, popular, and controversial bishop John Chrysostom. Salvina came from Africa, her father was named Gildo, and he was the son of the Mauretanian king Nubal. Nubal had accumulated vast estates in Africa through war and the judicious support of Roman interests. After he sided with Theodosius the Great against an insurrection by his brother, he became Count of Africa and Master of Soldiers. To cement his allegiance, around 388, Theodosius negotiated a betrothal between the emperor's nephew, Nebredius, and Salvina.

Nebredius was a nephew to Theodosius through his first wife, FLACCILLA. Unlike Salvina, he had been brought up in Constantinople at the imperial palace along with his cousins, Theodosius's much younger sons and future emperors Arcadius and Honorius. Well-educated, independently wealthy, and urbane, he and Salvina lived in or near the imperial palace in Constantinople. After the death of Flaccilla, they and their children remained on intimate terms with the emperor and his second wife, AELIA EUDOXIA.

Gildo died in an abortive attempt to seize power after the death of Theodosius in 398. His properties were confiscated. However, Salvina's marriage and the lives of her son and daughter were unaffected. She and her children remained at the imperial palace, intimate with the emperor and Eudoxia. Two years later in 400, she received a letter from the erudite and ascetic church father Jerome that, making no mention of her father, consoled her on the recent loss of her husband, who must have died in the intervening years.

The religion of Salvina's youth is unknown. However, after her marriage she became a fervent orthodox Christian. She found a congenial spirit and possibly a friend in late 384 or early 385 when she became the stepdaughter of OLYMPIAS (3). The orphaned Olympias, heiress of a huge fortune, was the young second wife of a much older widower who was Salvina's father-in-law, also called Nebredius. Closer in age to Salvina than to her husband, they became intimates.

They also both became young widows. Olympias's husband died about 20 months after their marriage, and some three years later Salvina was widowed. Neither woman chose to remarry, despite the availability of suitable partners and pressure from the emperor who was concerned that their fortunes and their futures be secured within his orbit of power. Olympias resolved the pressure to remarry by taking church orders and becoming a deaconess. Jerome, who had never met Salvina and was writing at the behest of a friend of her husband's family, praised her recently deceased husband's virtues and counseled her on the modesty, celibacy, and decorum suitable to a Christian widow. She followed his advice. Unlike Olympias who had no children, Salvina had a son and daughter which probably also diminished the imperial pressure to remarry.

Both women became devotees of John Chrysostom, who succeeded Nectorius as bishop of the city in 398. Chrysostom was a charismatic speaker and a man of great personal modesty who exemplified Christian asceticism. The populace adored him. Women like Salvina and Olympias also responded to his intellect and modesty. Although his views of women in general were firmly rooted in a misogynist reading of the scriptures, beginning with the sin of Eve, he accepted individual or small groups of women who adopted an ascetic and celibate life as fellow seekers after Christ and spiritual sisters. Around him grew a circle of women led by Olympias, who built a monastery adjacent to the Great Church of Constantinople and connected to the church with a private passageway. Some 250 women joined her in a communal ascetic life, including Salvina's daughter

Olympia, named after her stepgrandmother. Salvina, however, remained outside the monastery, although a close confidante of Olympias and a frequent visitor.

For neither Salvina, who continued to live on the grounds of the imperial compound, or Olympias, who lived within her monastery, were celibacy and modesty equal to the loss of worldly position. Olympias had serving women in the monastery and Salvina a household of slaves, eunuchs, freedmen and women, and dependents. Nonetheless their personal demeanor stood in contrast with the extravagance practiced by other women of their economic and social class.

Chrysostom railed against elite women who used the arts of hairdressing and makeup to look young. He preached increasingly acerbic and vitriolic sermons that compared the appearance of painted women and their curls with streetwalkers. Not unexpectedly, he alienated a group of very powerful women who believed that his religious language cloaked an attack on their public roles and power. Eudoxia, the Augusta, was among them. Chrysostom's distress at the contrast between profligate wealth and pervasive poverty in the city, however, was not restricted to women. He also lashed out at men, as well as the lifestyles of some bishops and monks. The women rallied the men and the result was an imperial order from Arcadius for Chrysostom to leave Constantinople.

In the morning on the day he left, June 20, 404, he met with a small group who entered the church unobserved through the connecting passage from the monastery. They were Olympias, Pentadia, and Procla who were deaconesses, and one woman not resident in the monastery, Salvina. That night fires destroyed the Great Church of Constantinople and the Senate House. Opponents and supporters of Chrysostom each blamed the other. Arsacius, a brother of Nectarius, was named bishop of Constantinople, but Chrysostom's supporters, including Olympias and possibly Salvina, refused to take communion from him. They were threatened with heavy fines. The nuances of Salvina's response are not known, but Olympias was said to have been

the only woman to pay the fine. Nothing more is known of Salvina's life.

Sources

Jerome. Letter LXXIX.
Palladius. *Dialogues* X, XVI, XVII.
Meyer, Wendy. "Constantinopolitan Women in Chrysostom's Circle." *Vigiliae Christianae* 53, no. 3 (1999): 269–270.
Prosopography of the Later Roman Empire. Vol. I. Edited by A. H. M. Jones, J. R. Martindale, and J. Morris. Cambridge: Cambridge University Press, 1971. Reprinted 1992. pp. 620, 799.

▣ Sancia

(?B.C.E.–33 C.E.)   Roman: Rome
convicted of treason

Sancia was either an innocent victim of a vendetta against her brother, or his accomplice. Her brother, Considius Proculus, had risen to the rank of praetor. He accused Publius Pomponius Secundus of treason in 31 C.E. The accusation against Pomponius was one of a spate of charges for conspiracy and treason pressed against alleged accomplices of Lucius Aelius Sejanus, treasonous former head of the Praetorian Guard. Pomponius was not brought to trial but was kept under house arrest until after the death of Tiberius in 37 C.E.

Two years after Considius's charge and while Pomponius was under house arrest, in 33 Quintus Pomponius Secundus, a brother of the accused, entered a countercharge against Considius. Sancia's brother was seized while celebrating his birthday, brought to the Senate, tried for treason, and executed on the same day. Sancia was also charged, convicted, and exiled without delay. The charges and countercharges were matters of life and death, frequently driven by financial reward: a successful prosecution generally resulted in the prosecutor receiving a portion of the confiscated estate. There is a suggestion in the sources that Sancia might have been an innocent victim of greed.

Sources

Tacitus. *Annales* 6.18.
Levick, Barbara. *Tiberius the Politician.* London: Thames and Hudson, 1976, p. 205.

Marsh, Frank Burr. *The Reign of Tiberius.* New York: Barnes and Noble, 1931, pp. 206–207.

Marshall, A. J. "Women on Trial before the Roman Senate." *Classical Views* 34 (1990): p. 346.

Sappho

(c. 612 B.C.E.–?)   Greek: Lesbos
poet

Sappho was ranked with the greatest poets of antiquity. Called "the tenth muse" by the philosopher Plato, her poetry was read and recited by Greeks and Romans across the Mediterranean. She composed nine books of lyric poetry. Some were love poems addressed to individual women; others were women's wedding songs. Still others address the goddesses of music, poetry, literature, and dance. Only one complete poem, "Hymn to Aphrodite," and a number of fragments have survived. There is enough extant, however, to suggest her union of the spiritual and the physically passionate, always with women as her subject.

Sappho taught a group of young women music and poetry and probably led rites in celebration of Aphrodite. Possibly she belonged to a formal school where women lived together until marriage. Alternatively the arrangements may have been a less formal sharing of poetry, music, and mutual affection.

Born about 612 B.C.E. in Eresus, on the west coast of the island of Lesbos, her parents, Cleis and Scamandronymus, were well-to-do landowners. She was orphaned at about age 6, and about 14, exiled to Sicily. She later returned to Mytilene, on the east coast of Lesbos, where she lived for the remainder of her life.

Saphho married Cercylas, a wealthy man from Andrus. She had a daughter named Cleis. One of her brothers, Charaxus, sold wine from Lesbos to the Egyptians. From an extant lampoon in her poetry, we know that in Egypt her brother met RHODOPIS, a famous beauty of her day, and was sufficiently enthralled to purchase her freedom.

Sources

"A New Sappho Poem," Martin West. *Times Literary Supplement.* November 9, 2005.

Sappho: Poems and Fragments. Translated by Stanley Lombardo. Introduction by Pamela Gordon. Indianapolis, Ind.: Hacket Publishing Company, 2002.

If Not, Winter: Fragments of Sappho. Translated by Anne Carson. New York: Alfred A. Knopf, 2002.

Blundell, Sue. *Women in Ancient Greece.* London: British Museum Press, 1995, pp. 82–91.

Bowra, C. M. *Greek Lyric Poetry from Alcman to Simonides* 2d. ed. Oxford: Clarendon Press, 1967, pp. 176 ff.

Edmonds, J. M., ed. and trans. *Lyra Graeca: Being the Remains of All the Greek Lyric Poets from Eumelus to Timotheus, Excepting Pindar.* Vol. 2. Cambridge: Harvard University Press, 1959, pp. 140–307.

Oxford Classical Dictionary, ed. by Simon Hornblower and Antony Spawforth. 3d. ed. New York: Oxford University Press, 1996, p. 1,355.

Snyder, Jane McIntosh. "Public Occasion and Private Passion in the Lyrics of Sappho of Lesbos." In *Women's History and Ancient History,* ed. by Sarah B. Pomeroy. Chapel Hill: University of North Carolina Press, 1991, pp. 1–19.

Sassia

(first century B.C.E.)   Roman: Italy
victim in a celebrated trial

Sassia was caught up in a vicious family quarrel that resulted in charges and countercharges of murder and attempted murder. She had three husbands. With the first she had a son, Cluentius Habitus, and a daughter, Cluentia. Widowed, she married Aulus Aurieus Melinus and gave birth to a daughter. He was killed in the proscriptions following the victory of Lucius Cornelius Sulla in 81 B.C.E. Her third husband was Statius Albius Oppianicus, who was said to have been responsible for her second husband's death. Oppianicus had three children from a previous marriage. His son, named Oppianicus, married Sassia's daughter by her second husband. The children of the first and third marriage did not get along, and therein lies the tangled tale of two trials.

In 74 B.C.E. Sassia's son Cluentius charged his stepfather, Statius Albius Oppianicus, with attempted murder. The elder Oppianicus was convicted of an attempt to poison his stepson. Subsequently, the presiding arbiter of the court and some members of the jury were themselves convicted of various offenses, including bribery. A consensus emerged that the elder Oppianicus had been a victim of corrupt testimony. Subsequently, the elder Oppianicus died, and the younger Oppianicus charged Cluentius with murder. At the trial in 66 B.C.E., Marcus Tullius Cicero was one of Cluentius's defenders. In his statement, Cicero painted Sassia and the younger Oppianicus as the villains, not Sassia's son Cluentius. He portrayed Sassia as an odious person who controlled those around her and would stop at nothing, not even murder, to have her own way. It was she, not her stepson, who was the true instigator of the trial.

He alleged that Sassia, a wealthy widow after the death of her first husband, had fallen in love with Melinus when he was married to her daughter Cluentia. After her daughter and Melinus divorced, Sassia married him. Her son Cluentius disapproved. Sassia hated him for his disapproval. Her new husband, Melinus, was about to charge the elder Oppianicus with the murder of a kinsman, when Oppianicus left Larinum, a city on the Adriatic side of Italy where they all lived, to join the victorious forces of Sulla. Appointed the chief magistrate at Larinum, he arranged to have Melinus proscribed and killed.

The elder Oppianicus then asked Sassia to marry him, but she refused unless he agreed to kill two of his three sons, because she did not want to be the stepmother of his three sons. The elder Oppianicus complied, and she married him. Cicero charged that Oppianicus later left Sassia after she had an affair with a plebeian, Sextus Albius, and that Oppianicus died from a fever contracted after being thrown from a horse. Cicero made no effort to support this gruesome tale with independent evidence or witnesses. He did, however, succeed in securing the acquittal of Cluentius and later boasted that he had won the case with dust thrown into the eyes of the jury.

Cluentius was most likely guilty of bribery and the murder of his stepfather in an attempt to secure his inheritance. The younger Oppianicus, on the other hand, was also motivated by a desire to reinstate his inheritance, which had probably disappeared with his father's conviction. Sassia, the ostensible villain of Cicero's defense, lost her reputation, no small factor in Roman life, but held tight to her money and her freedom.

Sources

Cicero. *Pro Cluentio* 175–90.
Hoenigswald, Gabriele S. "The Murder Charges in Cicero's Pro Cluentio." *Transactions and Proceedings of the American Philological Association* 93 (1962): pp. 109–123.

Satria Galla
(first century C.E.)   Roman: Rome
political player

Satria Galla had no family of note, but she was very beautiful. Her first husband was Domitius Silius, whom she divorced to marry his close friend, the eminent Gaius Calpurnius Piso. Piso was well born and very rich. In Rome of the mid-first century C.E., newly adorned with imperial munificence, he lived in a grand style. They were a popular couple. In 65 he was accused of leading a plot to overthrow the emperor Nero. Urged to rally his supporters, he instead, chose suicide, possibly to protect Satria and his estate.

Sources

Tacitus. *Annales* 15.59.

Scribonia
(70 B.C.E.–? C.E.)   Roman: Italy and Pandateria
political player

Scribonia valiantly stood her ground and fought against forces far stronger than her own in political battles that stretched from the end of the republic into the reign of Tiberius. She married three times, watched her sons die, and voluntarily accompanied her daughter into exile. Until the end of her life she stood ready to use her voice on behalf of her kin and possibly, to support conspiracies against the emperor.

Born about 70 B.C.E., her mother was Sentia, and her father, Lucius Scribonius Libo. She had a brother, Lucius, who was consul in 34 B.C.E. Her first husband was Gnaeus Cornelius Lentulus Marcellinus, consul in 56 B.C.E. She was either widowed or divorced, and their son, Cornelius Marcellinus, probably died before he reached manhood. Her second husband, a man of about her own age, was Publius Cornelius Scipio, consul suffectus in 35 B.C.E. They had two children: Publius Cornelius, consul in 16 B.C.E., and CORNELIA (8). Her daughter died after she had married and borne children. She was eulogized in a poem by Propertius in which she spoke as if from the grave, praising her mother's lineage and addressing her with tender and affectionate words.

Probably divorced from her second husband in 40 B.C.E., Scribonia married Octavian, who was about seven years her junior. She was the aunt of Sextus Pompeius Magnus, the younger son of Gnaeus Pompeius Magnus (Pompey the Great), and his closest unmarried female relative. The marriage was part of an effort to strengthen relations between Octavian and Sextus Pompeius. Octavian, however, was a problematic husband. Intent on securing control over Italy, the future of the marriage was inseparable from the fortunes of the civil war. Octavian's forces had been victorious in the Perusine War, but Sextus's fleet controlled the seas, and Antony was about to invade Italy. The demands of the army, facilitated by a small group of influential women, led the opposing leaders to forge the Treaty of Brundisium in 40. The treaty affirmed the Second Triumvirate and recognized Sextus.

Although the marriage between Scribonia and Octavian had been politically useful, at least for Scribonia it was never satisfactory and quickly outlived its initial purpose. It ended in divorce in 39 on the very day Scribonia gave birth to JULIA (6). It was anything but a friendly parting. Octavian gave as his reason for divorce Scribonia's continuous opposition and arguments. He had, in fact, flagrantly insulted her by publicly flaunting his affair with LIVIA DRUSILLA. He made no attempt to conceal his passion for the 18-year-old Livia, who was married, the mother of one child, and pregnant with another.

Scribonia's daughter Julia was the only child Octavian ever fathered. Although divorced, Scribonia's link with her daughter remained strong during the years that Julia grew up primarily in her stepmother's household. Thirty-seven years later, in 2 B.C.E., Julia, now the wife of the future emperor Tiberius and the mother of JULIA (7), was exiled to Pandateria, charged by her father, now emperor Augustus, with multiple adulteries. Scribonia voluntarily went with her daughter into a bleak exile. Five years later, the two women were allowed to go to Rhegium at the tip of Italy, where they remained for 10 more years until Julia died. While Scribonia was in voluntary exile, her granddaughter was also banished by Augustus for adultery. Her granddaughter had married a first cousin, Lucius Aemilius Paullus. He was the son of Scribonia's daughter Cornelia, and was executed for conspiring against the emperor.

In 16 C.E. her great-nephew Marcus Scribonius Libo Drusus, praetor in that year, was accused of plotting against Tiberius. The charge was based on a list he had compiled with mysterious marks against names of the members of the imperial family and a number of senators. Many viewed Libo as a ridiculous and rather stupid young man; nonetheless, Tiberius took the charges seriously. He may have considered Libo's connection to Scribonia a potential threat. Libo, accompanied by a number of aristocratic women, went to his wife's relatives to plead with them to intervene on his behalf. Most feared to do so. Scribonia was possibly among his supporters. If there was truth to the conspiracy charged, it was possible that she played a part since she surely had no love for the emperor. She urged Libo to face execution rather than commit suicide. Despite Scribonia's plea, Libo committed suicide. Nothing more is heard of Scribonia.

Sources

Propertius. *Elegies* 55–57.

Seneca. *Epistulae* 70.10

Suetonius. *The Lives of the Caesars:* Augustus 62.2; 63.1.

———. *The Lives of the Caesars:* Tiberius 25.1–3.

Tacitus. *Annales* 2.27–31.

Leon, E. F. "Scribonia and Her Daughters." *Transactions of the American Philosophical Association.* Vol. 82. Atlanta, Ga., pp. 168–172.

Levick, Barbara. *Tiberius the Politician.* London: Thames and Hudson, 1976.

Oxford Classical Dictionary, ed. by Simon Hornblower and Antony Spawforth. 3d. ed. New York: Oxford University Press, 1996, p. 1,370.

Pauly, A., G. Wissowa, and W. Kroll. *Real-Encyclopadie d. Classischen Altertumswissenschaft 1893–.* (Germany: multiple publishers) 32.

Syme, Ronald. *The Augustan Aristocracy.* Oxford: Clarendon Press, 1986, index.

———. *The Roman Revolution.* London: Oxford University Press, 1974, pp. 213, 229.

▣ Sempronia (1)

(second century B.C.E.)   Roman: Italy
political player

Sempronia was rich in family and unfortunate in marriage. She was the granddaughter of Publius Scipio Aemilianus Africanus, who defeated Hannibal in 202 B.C.E. Her grandfather had been attracted to Greek learning and had educated his daughters as well as his sons. Her mother, CORNELIA (2), married the upstanding but much older Tiberius Sempronius Gracchus, twice consul and once censor, who valued an educated wife. He died when Sempronia was young. Widowed her mother raised her and her two famous brothers, Tiberius and Gaius, with the same education in Greek philosophy, the arts, rhetoric, and mathematics that she had received.

Between 152 and 147, Sempronia married her cousin Publius Cornelius Scipio Aemilianus, a distinguished soldier and cultured statesman, consul in 147 and 134. Their relationship was not harmonious. Sempronia may have had some kind of deformity that inhibited her from bearing children, and in addition, her husband was politically opposed to her brothers. Tiberius and Gaius championed proposals for reform in the use of public lands for the benefit of the growing landless, especially veterans. They were opposed by a wealthy conservative faction to which her husband belonged. When he returned to Rome after a victorious campaign in Spain, he led the fight to prevent the organization of an agrarian commission for distributing public land in accordance with the new Gracchi laws. In the explosive atmosphere generated by the Gracchi proposals, living with a husband who was her brother's political opponent must have been both taxing and

wrenching for Sempronia. Unpopular with the urban mob, her husband died unexpectedly in bed in 129 B.C.E. after the assassination of Tiberius in 133 and before that of Gaius. In the heated political situation, rumors circulated that Sempronia and her mother were responsible for Aemillianus's death.

Sempronia may have joined her mother in the country outside Rome after the deaths of both her brothers and husband. The women lived a cultured life and welcomed visitors. They also remained very much current with affairs in Rome. In 101 Sempronia testified in a criminal trial when tribune, Lucius Appuleius Saturninus, brought action against the censor Metellus Numidicus, who had refused to inscribe Lucius Equitius as a citizen. Equitius claimed that he was the illegitimate son of Sempronia's brother Tiberius Gracchus. He sought to use his claim to win popular support for election to the office of tribune. Despite the hostile questioning of Saturninus and the demands of Equitius's supporters, Sempronia adamantly denied that Equitius was her brother's son. The suit against Numidicus was dismissed. We hear no more of Sempronia after trial.

Sources

Appian. *Roman History: Bella civilian (Civil Wars)* 1.20.

Valerius Maximus. *Factorum et dictorum memorabilium libri IX* 3.8.6; 9.7.1, 15.1.

Balsdon, J. P. V. D. *Roman Women.* New York: John Day Comp., 1963, pp. 194, 214.

Bauman, Richard A. *Women and Politics in Ancient Rome.* London: Routledge, 1994, pp. 48–49.

Pauly, A., G. Wissowa, and W. Kroll. *Real-Encyclopadie d. Classischen Altertumswissenschaft 1893–.* (Germany: multiple publishers) 99.

Richardson, Keith. *Daggers in the Forum: The Revolutionary Lives and Violent Deaths of the Gracchus Brothers.* London: Cassell, 1976, pp. 26, 29, 115.

Stockton, David. *The Gracchi.* Oxford: Clarendon Press, 1979, pp. 24–26.

▣ Sempronia (2)

(first century B.C.E.)   Roman: Rome
possible conspirator

Sempronia chose her lovers and squandered her fortune. She was smart, fun, fearless, and dangerous to be around. Her father was probably Sempronius Tuditanus, consul in 129 B.C.E. Accomplished in Greek and Latin, she was said to have been adept at the seductive use of the lyre and dance. Sempronia was accused of supporting Lucius Sergius Catiline, who had incurred large debts and organized a conspiracy that included destitute soldiers and the impoverished well-born, both men and women.

The conspirators, who intended to enact relief from debt, planned a coup against the elected officials. The women were supposed to render slaves impotent to protect their masters, to set fires, and to persuade husbands to join the conspirators or to kill them. The conspirators allegedly met in Sempronia's house while her husband, an opponent of any such movement, was away.

The conspiracy failed, and Catiline was killed. Nothing happened to Sempronia. It is possible that she never had any association with the conspiracy. Marcus Tullius Cicero, who rarely missed an opportunity to denigrate the women involved with the men he attacked, never mentioned Sempronia in his speech against Catiline. The accusations against her could well be yet another attack on any woman who was smart, somewhat unconventional, and visible.

Sources

Sallust. *Bellum Catilinae* 25.1–5; 40.5.

Balsdon, J. P. V. D. *Roman Women.* New York: John Day Comp., 1963, pp. 47–49.

Bauman, Richard A. *Women and Politics in Ancient Rome.* London: Routledge, 1994, pp. 67–68.

Hillard, Tom. "On Stage, Behind the Curtain: Images of Politically Active Women in the Late Roman Republic." In *Stereotypes of Women in Power: Historical Perspectives and Revisionist Views,* ed. by Barbara Garlick, Suzanne Dixon, and Pauline Allen. New York: Greenwood Press, 1992, pp. 47–49.

Pauly, A., G. Wissowa, and W. Kroll. *Real-Encyclopadie d. Classischen Altertumswissenschaft 1893–.* (Germany: multiple publishers) 103.

Syme, Ronald. *The Augustan Aristocracy.* Oxford: Clarendon Press, 1986, pp. 26, 198 ff.

———. *Sallust.* Berkeley: University of California Press, 1974, pp. 25–26, 135.

Serena

(?–December 408 C.E.)   Roman: Rome, Constantinople
political player

Serena wielded power, amassed wealth, and died a victim of political intrigue. She was the daughter of Honorius, the brother of Theodosius the Great, and Maria, a Spanish woman from an elite family. She was the emperor's favorite niece and, after the death of her parents, lived with him in Constantinople. She was smart, well educated, attractive, and embraced orthodox Christianity. In 384, she was betrothed to Flavius Stilicho, a Vandal, and her uncle's most trusted general, second only to the emperor in power and authority. Over the next years, they had a son Eucharius and two daughters MARIA and THERMANTIA. Ten years later, in 394, when Theodosius was in Milan, his health failed. His youngest children, Honorius and GALLA PLACIDIA arrived from Constantinople accompanied by Serena. Theodosius had already appointed the 10-year-old boy emperor in the West. He gave Stilicho charge of military forces in the empire of the West and appointed him regent during the boy's minority. The children were to live with Serena.

After his death in January 395, Serena and the children, her own and her new charges, escorted the emperor's body to Constantinople where it was interred in the same church as Constantine the Great. The symbolism made a statement about the just-buried emperor and, no doubt, the presence of Serena was the blood tie to Theodosius that the deceased emperor hoped would protect his children under Stilicho's regency.

For the next eight years, Stilicho was de facto ruler of the West. Serena and Stilicho planned for Honorius's majority. It was a complicated political environment. In the East, Arcadius was a weak emperor and he had an aggressive Praetorian Prefect, Flavius Rufinus. Stilicho had under his command the forces of the West plus the mobile forces of the East that Theodosius had brought with him to Italy before his death. He brought the combined army to Illyrium to confront a force of Goths under the leadership of Alaric. With victory assured, Rufinus made one of history's great tactical errors. He persuaded Arcadius to order Stilicho to halt his assault and return to Constantinople with the troops brought west by Theodosius.

Serena was in Constantinople with the children. She alerted Stilicho that Rufinus's probable plan was to circumscribe Stilicho's authority, and marry his daughter to Arcadius, which would place him in a position to be declared co-emperor. For reasons that remain unclear, Stilicho complied with the emperor's wish to abandon battle with Alaric. However, he also successfully arranged the assassination of Rufinus. Whatever the exigencies of the moment that shaped Stilicho's decision, it was an opportunity lost. Alaric later sacked Rome, and his marauding presence in Italy led directly to Serena's death some 12 years later.

Serena returned to Rome in 396. Possibly, marriage was the path to power that Serena and Stilicho planned. Their children were of comparable age with their charges, the young emperor and his sister. Their son, Eucharius, was betrothed to GALLA PLACIDIA while both were children, and their oldest daughter, Maria, was a match for the young emperor, Honorius. However, children were as chancy as military battles in the ancient world. The marriage between Placidia and Eucharius never took place. Whatever the reason, it appears that Placidia refused to marry Eucharius, and in light of subsequent events, Placidia's refusal demonstrated her independence and a surprising degree of dislike for her aunt, uncle, and cousin. In the spring of 398, Maria, who was then 13, married Honorius. Six years later in 404, Maria died and left no children.

In 407–408 the Goths were in Italy. Stilicho forced the Senate to pay the Goth leader Alaric a large sum, ostensibly for services to the empire. The fighting in Italy and the tax on senators exacerbated political infighting between the Senate, Stilicho, and Serena. Always opposed to imperial power, especially when wielded by imperious women like Serena, they were increasingly suspicious of her husband's loyalties in light of his Vandal origins. Not insignificantly, they also resented Serena's promotion of Christianity.

Although it had been nearly 100 years since Constantine adopted Christianity, the well-born and the educated still were largely pagan. When the youger MELANIA and Pinianus, a young Christian couple from among the oldest and wealthiest families in Rome, encountered family opposition to their proposed life of celibacy and the distribution of their assets to the church and the poor, they went to Serena. The network of relationships among the senators would have predisposed them to reinforce the families' efforts to gain control over the young couple. Despite the pending legal case begun by their families, Serena, possibly influenced by her own Christian beliefs, persuaded Honorius to circumvent the Senate and the courts by fiat.

Rumors circulated that Stilicho was in league with Alaric and that he aimed to secure the throne for his son. In addition, since he controlled the military, he was blamed for the attacks and lootings by the Goths. In late 407 or early 408, Serena convinced Honorius to marry her younger daughter, Thermantia, a plan her husband opposed since the marriage provided their enemies evidence of imperial ambitions. And so it did. Events cascaded to catastrophe in May of 408 with the death of the eastern emperor, Arcadius, who left a seven-year-old son and three daughters. Stilicho and Honorius saw a power vacuum and an opportunity, as well as danger. They decided to go East and extend their influence. Serena opposed them. The West was in disarray. Alaric was a threat. In addition, the move East realized the fears of their political enemies that the empire would fall into the hands of Serena and Stilicho.

Stilicho convinced Honorius to stay in Italy. Honorius was beset by conspiratorial factions. On his way to Ravenna, Olympius, an official of the palace, persuaded him that Stilicho intended to kill the seven-year-old son of Arcadius and have his own son declared emperor. He and his coconspirators spread the same rumor among the troops where dissatisfaction was already widespread. Some took up arms and killed a number of officials. News reached Stilicho. After he learned that Honorius was safe, he left for Ravenna. Stilicho allowed himself to be imprisoned on orders of Honorius.

He was beheaded on August 22, 408. His son was later killed in Rome. Honorius sent Serena's daughter, Thermantia, still a virgin, back to her mother.

Stilicho probably had the support of the troops and could have saved himself and even become emperor instead of Honorius. His choices, like those he made at Illyrium a decade earlier, support the hypothesis that despite his effective leadership of the army he was a man of peace who believed in the authority of the emperor over the military. He may well have been a better Roman than the Romans around him, including his wife.

Without Stilicho, the Goths faced no significant opposition. In late 408, Alaric established a blockade around Rome. Many fled, including Pinianus, the younger Melania, and her mother, ALBINA. They left behind a city with civil unrest, an uncertain food supply, and disrupted services. Wild rumors circulated, including that Serena was in league with Alaric to betray the city. The rumors had a life of their own: Accurate information often had less authority than whispered hearsay.

Now widowed, Serena, her daughter, and Placidia remained in the distraught city. The Senate tried to assert leadership. Serena and her husband not only had many enemies among the senators, but she was the symbol of imperial inadequacy and, perhaps, their own failure. The choices in the situation were few. The Senate voted to kill Serena. But what if her death opened the way to a purge when the emperor returned from Ravenna? The Senate sent a delegation to Placidia. She gave consent. Serena was strangled.

Sources

Gerontius. *The Life of Melania the Younger.* Introduction, translation, and commentary by Elizabeth A. Clark. New York: The Edwin Mellon Press, 1984.

Zosimus. *New History/Zosimus.* A translation with commentary by Ronald T. Ridley. Canberra: Australian Association of Byzantine Studies, 1982, iv 1, iv. 57.2; v. 4. 1, 12.1, v 28. 1–3, v 32, v 38. 1–5.

Oost, S. I. *Galla Placidia Augusta: A Biographical Essay.* Chicago: University of Chicago Press, 1968.

———. "Some Problems in the History of Galla Placidia." *Classical Philology* 60 (1965), 1–10.

Prosopography of the Later Roman Empire. Vol. I. Edited by A. H. M. Jones, J. R. Martindale, and J. Morris. Cambridge: Cambridge University Press, 1971. Reprinted 1992, p. 824.

▣ Servilia (1)

(first century B.C.E.)   Roman: Rome
power broker

Servilia worked to enhance the position and fortunes of herself and her kin. A formidable woman with personal charm and intelligence, she influenced powerful men, including her friend and lover, Gaius Julius Caesar. With a wide range of friends, clients, and family connections, she participated openly and covertly in the traffic in favors that was the political medium of exchange among the elite of the late republic. In the complicated and tense times after the death of Caesar in 44 B.C.E. she proved more realistic and practical than her son Marcus Junius Brutus, her half brother Marcus Porcius Cato Uticensis, and her son-in-law Gaius Cassius Longinus.

Servilia was the daughter of Quintus Servilius Caepio, quaestor in 100 B.C.E., and LIVIA, the sister of Marcus Livius Drusus, tribune in 91 B.C.E. Servilia's father quarreled with his brother-in-law, Marcus Drusus, and divorced her mother about 96 B.C.E. Her mother then married Marcus Porcius Cato; their son Cato, born in 95, was Servilia's half brother. Servilia's father died in battle in 89, and her mother and stepfather died shortly before the outbreak of civil war. Servilia, some six years older than her half brother, looked after her siblings from the two marriages and had enormous influence over them.

She married Marcus Junius Brutus, tribune in 83 B.C.E. Her husband was executed by Gnaeus Pompeius Magnus (Pompey the Great) in 77. They had a son, the tyrannicide Marcus Junius Brutus. She then married Decimus Junius Silanus, consul in 62 B.C.E. and had three daughters whose advantageous marriages she later arranged. JUNIA (1) married Marcus Aemilius Lepidus, the triumvir. JUNIA (2) married Publius Servilius Isauricus, consul in 48 B.C.E. JUNIA TERTIA married Cassius, praetor in 44 B.C.E.

Servilla and Julius Caesar became lovers before 64 B.C.E., during Caesar's first consulship when he was said to have given her a pearl costing 6 million sesterces. She sent Caesar an intimate letter during the debate in the Senate over Sergius Catiline in 63. Cato and Caesar were on opposing sides in the debate; Cato demanded to see the letter, claiming it was from enemies of the Senate. Caesar handed it to him. The liaison between Caesar and Servilia was among the reasons Cato hated Caesar with a passion that only war could assuage. Servilia, occasionally restrained Cato. In 62 Caesar supported Servilia's husband Silanus in his successful bid for the consulship. Cato brought a suit of bribery against the second consul, but refrained from similar action against Silanus.

In 59 B.C.E., when Servilia's husband was already dead, Caesar divorced POMPEIA (1), and marriage with Caesar became possible for Servilia. However, she was as practical in love as in her life in general. An alliance between Caesar and Pompey was clearly more desirable and of greater importance at the moment. JULIA (5), Caesar's daughter, married Pompey, and rather than marry Servilia, Caesar married CALPURNIA (1), the daughter of Lucius Calpurnius Piso, whose election to consul in 58 B.C.E. Caesar and Pompey jointly supported. No doubt the young Calpurnia was also more likely than Servilia to have the son Caesar so dearly sought. Servilia's friendship with Caesar continued over the next decade and through the outbreak of hostilities. She purchased several confiscated estates at very low prices after Caesar's defeat of Pompey in 48. Gossip in Rome recognized the relationship between the two and maliciously speculated that Caesar's liaison with Servilia's daughter Junia Tertia was part payment for the estates.

The unforeseen consequence of their passion and friendship contributed to Caesar's death. Despite Servilia's alliance with Caesar, her son Brutus and her half brother Cato sided with Pompey against Caesar once war became unavoidable. For Brutus, his uncle's rhetoric of republican rectitude overcame Pompey's earlier treachery toward his father. Fortunately for Brutus, Servilia's own relationship with Caesar also protected him after Pompey's defeat at Pharsalus in 48 B.C.E. Caesar not only issued orders to spare Brutus's life but spared

many of the latter's friends and appointed Brutus praetor. As he was about to leave for Africa in pursuit of Cato, he put Brutus in charge of Cisalpine Gaul.

Brutus was unable to accept the fortunes of war and the benefits of his mother's friendship with Caesar. He was tortured by feelings of betrayal to the republican cause and all that his uncle Cato claimed as good. Possibly, shame over public knowledge of his mother and Caesar's affair also violated his romantic vision of a virtuous republic. To Servilia's dismay, Brutus divorced his wife in 45 in order to marry PORCIA, the no less tortured daughter of Cato.

After Caesar's murder Servilia concentrated her efforts on doing everything in her power to protect the interests of her family and to support the assassins, including Brutus and her son-in-law Cassius. Servilia presided in a meeting at Antium on the coast south of Rome on June 8, 44. Those present included Brutus and his wife, Porcia, Cassius and his wife, Junia Tertia, Marcus Tullius Cicero, and Marcus Favonius, an admirer of Cato. The family conference was to consider an offer made by the Senate at the instigation of Mark Antony to appoint Brutus and Cassius to supervise the collection of corn taxes in the provinces of Sicily and Asia until the end of the year. It offered them an honorary exile in the face of unrest in Rome after the assassination. Brutus and Cassius were uncertain whether or not to accept. When Cicero went into a long-winded speech of opportunities lost, Servilia cut him short and took it upon herself to try to have the corn commission removed from the senate decree.

By 43 events were moving quickly, and the breakup of the old order was increasingly evident. On May 29, 43, Marcus Aemilius Lepidus, the husband of Servilia's daughter Junia, defeated to Mark Antony and was declared a public enemy by the Senate. Servilia, worried about her daughter and her two grandsons, appealed to Cicero to protect the boys. Brutus supported her with a letter to Cicero. Cicero, after some ambivalence, said he would do what he could.

On July 25, 43 B.C.E., Servilia called another meeting in Rome. Present were Cicero, Publius

Servilius Casca and Antistius Labeo, both participants in the assassination of Caesar, and Brutus's agent Marcus Scaptius. Servilia asked whether it would be advisable for Brutus to bring his forces to Italy or better that he remain away for the time being. Cicero gave his opinion that Brutus should return. In the end, however, Brutus and Cassius were too busy consolidating their gains in the East. After Brutus was killed, Antony sent his ashes back to Servilia in Rome as a mark of respect. Little more is known of Servilia, except that the astute Titus Pomponius Atticus, who maintained good relations with the powerful people on both sides of the civil war, continued his friendship with her and aided her after Brutus's death.

Sources

Cicero. *Epistulae ad Atticum* 13.9.2, 22.4; 14.13; 15.11, 17.

———. *Brutus* 22.12.1–2; 26.18.

Nepos. *Atticus* 11.

Plutarch. *Vitae Parallelae (Parallel Lives): Brutus* 1.5; 2.1; 5.1–4; 6.10

———. *Vitae Parallelae (Parallel Lives): Caesar* 62.3–6.

———. *Vitae Parallelae (Parallel Lives): Cato Minor* 21.2–3; 24.1–2.

Suetonius. *The Lives of the Caesars:* Caesar 50.2.

Balsdon, J. P. V. D. *Roman Women.* New York: John Day Comp., 1963, pp. 51–52, 216–217.

Bauman, Richard A. *Women and Politics in Ancient Rome.* London: Routledge, 1994, pp. 73–76.

Hillard, Tom. "On Stage, Behind the Curtain: Images of Politically Active Women in the Late Roman Republic." In *Stereotypes of Women in Power: Historical Perspectives and Revisionist Views,* ed. by Barbara Garlick, Suzanne Dixon, and Pauline Allen. New York: Greenwood Press, 1992, pp. 53–55.

Oxford Classical Dictionary, ed. by Simon Hornblower and Antony Spawforth. 3d. ed. New York: Oxford University Press, 1996, p. 1,394.

Pauly, A., G. Wissowa, and W. Kroll. *Real-Encyclopadie d. Classischen Altertumswissenschaft 1893–.* (Germany: multiple publishers) 1,394.

Shackleton Bailey, D. R. *Cicero.* New York: Charles Scribner's Sons, 1971, pp. 242–23.

Syme, Ronald. *The Augustan Aristocracy.* Oxford: Clarendon Press, 1986, p. 25.

———. *The Roman Revolution.* London: Oxford University Press, 1963, index.

Servilia (2)

(first century B.C.E.)   Roman: Italy and Asia
political wife

Servilia was the daughter of Quintus Servilius Caepio, praetor in 91 B.C.E., and LIVIA. Her grandfather was Marcus Livius Drusus, consul in 112 B.C.E. Her parents divorced in about 96, after a quarrel between her father and grandfather. Her mother married Marcus Porcius Cato; both of them died before the civil war.

Servilia made an apparently advantageous marriage with the wealthy soldier and administrator, Lucius Licinius Lucullus, consul in 74. Lucullus, a man of culture and an Epicurian, was a member of the powerful Metelli family. He had divorced his first wife, CLODIA (3), after her brother had led a rebellion among his troops while in Asia. Servilia had a son with Lucullus; the marriage ended in divorce. Lucullus always a difficult man, later died insane.

Servilia took her son and went to live with her half brother, Marcus Porcius Cato Uticensis. She traveled with him to Asia. He left her in Rhodes when he went to join Gnaeus Pompeius Magnus (Pompey the Great). Her son, Marcus Licinius Lucullus, fought with his cousin Marcus Junius Brutus against Octavian and Mark Antony. He killed himself, along with Brutus, in 42 B.C.E., after the defeat at Philippi. Servilia's death is unrecorded.

Sources

Plutarch. *Vitae Parallelae (Parallel Lives): Cato Minor* 54.1–2.

Plutarch. *Vitae Parallelae (Parallel Lives): Lucullus* 38.1.

Servilia (3)

(first century B.C.E.)   Roman: Italy
political wife

Servilia was the last member of an ancient republican family with roots in Alba Longa, southeast of Rome, and said to have been founded by Aeneas. Her father was Publius Servilius Isauricus, consul in 48 B.C.E. and an ally of Gaius Julius Caesar. Her mother was JUNIA (2). In 43, she was to marry

Octavian, the future emperor Augustus. The engagement ended when Octavian married the stepdaughter of Mark Antony, to cement the Second Triumvirate. Servilia married instead the son and namesake of the triumvir Marcus Aemilius Lepidus. Her husband became part of a plot to assassinate Octavian. The plot was discovered, and in 30 B.C.E. he was executed for treason. Servilia committed suicide by swallowing burning coals.

Sources
Appian. *Roman History: Bella civilian (Civil Wars)* 4.50.
Livy. *From the Founding of the City* 133.
Suetonius. *The Lives of the Caesars:* Augustus 62,1.
Valleius Paterculus. *Historiae Romanae libri II* 2.88.4.
Syme, Ronald. *The Roman Revolution.* London: Oxford University Press, 1974, pp. 182, 189, 230, 298.

▣ Servilia (4)
(c. 46–66 C.E.)   Roman: Rome
victim

Servilia was young and condemned unreasonably in 66 C.E. She died bravely with her father, Quintus Marcus Barea Soranus, consul suffectus in 52. Her husband, Annius Pollio, had been forced into exile by the emperor Nero for his participation in Pisonian conspiracy in 65. In 66 her father was accused of conspiring with Rubellius Plautus, the philosophically inclined senator who had refused to take up arms against the emperor, even though he knew it was only time until he too would be killed by Nero. It was assumed that the charge against her father, who was an honorable man, was retribution for his having refused to allow the emperor's freedmen to loot the city of Pergamum of its statues and paintings when he was proconsul in Asia.

Servilia, who was not yet 20 years old, was called before the Senate with her father. She was accused of selling her bridal ornaments, including a necklace, to pay magicians. She explained that she had not asked the magicians to cast any spells against the emperor Nero but to preserve the safety of her father. Servilia declared that her father had known nothing of what she had done, and if there was any fault, it was hers alone. Her father interrupted to add that in addition, she had not gone

with him to Asia and had not been implicated in the charges against her husband. His plea that she be tried separately from him was refused. However, the harshness of the sentence was mitigated to allow Barea Soranus and Servilia the choice as to the manner of their death.

Sources
Tacitus. *Annales* 16.30–33.

▣ Sextia (1)
(? B.C.E.–34 C.E.)   Roman: Rome
committed suicide; political victim

Sextia urged her husband to kill himself rather than be executed for treason. She came from a distinguished family. Her first husband, who died in 21 C.E., was Cornelius Sulla, a descendant of Lucius Cornelius Sulla, the dictator of Rome in 81 B.C.E. With him she had two sons, Faustus Sulla, consul suffectus in 31 C.E., and Lucius Sulla Felix, consul in 33. Sextia's second husband was Mamercus Aemilius Scaurus, consul suffectus in 21 C.E. He was a cultured man and a noted orator and advocate, disliked by the emperor Tiberius. In 32, he was accused of treason. The trial was adjourned.

In 34, he was again charged with treason at the instigation of Quintus Naevius Cordus Sutorius Macro, prefect of the Praetorian Guard. Scaurus was alleged to be the lover of Livia Julia Claudia, Livilla, a relative of Tiberius. Livilla had been condemned for her close association with the treasonous Lucius Aelius Sejanus and starved herself to death in 31. As evidence against Scaurus, the prosecution put forth lines extracted from a tragedy written by Scaurus that could suggest references to Tiberius. Sextia urged her husband to commit suicide and both killed themselves before a trial took place. Their suicide gave an honorable end to their lives since they could be buried with due respect, their estates would not be confiscated, and their wills would remain valid.

Sources
Tacitus. *Annales* 6.29.
Levick, Barbara. *Tiberius the Politician.* London: Thames and Hudson, 1976, p. 213.

Sextia (2)

(?–65 c.e.)   Roman: Italy
political victim

Sextia died bravely. She was confronted with unanswerable charges by the emperor Nero. Sextia had watched helplessly as Rubellius Plautus, the husband of her granddaughter ANTISTIA POLLITTA, was pushed to suicide in 62 c.e. Plautus had refused to take up arms against the emperor, although there was some indication that he would have found support had he chosen to do so.

Nero was still not satisfied. Three years later, in 65, Sextia, her granddaughter Antistia, and her son-in-law Lucius Antistius Vetus, consul with Nero 10 years earlier in 55, again were threatened. The three withdrew to Vetus's estate in Formiae. They then severed their veins and had themselves transported to the baths, where they died.

Sources

Tacitus. *Annales* 16.10–11.

Sextilia

(?–c. 69 c.e.)   Roman: Rome
independent woman, Augusta

Sextilia rightly feared that disaster would follow after her son became emperor. A woman of fine character and from a distinguished family, she lived intimately with imperial intrigue. Sextilia married the successful politician and friend of the emperor Claudius, Lucius Vitellius. Her husband supported the younger Julia AGRIPPINA after her marriage with the emperor and was partner in her cleansing of enemies. Placed in charge of Rome while Claudius traveled to Britain, Vitellius died in 52 c.e., leaving Sextilia with two sons, Aulus Vitellius and the younger Lucius Vitellius.

Her eldest son, Aulus, also a friend of Claudius and his successor Gaius Caligula, amassed a considerable fortune as proconsul in Africa. He married a wealthy woman, PETRONIA, divorced her, and married GALERIA FUNDANA, the daughter of a former praetor. He lived extravagantly, gambled, and drank. When the emperor Servius Sulpicius Galba gave him command of the troops in Lower Germany, he was broke. To raise funds and finance his trip, he mortgaged his house, and Sextilia sold some jewels.

Sextilia and Galeria Fundana remained in Rome after Aulus Vitellius went to Germany. Although he left Galeria in straitened financial circumstances with creditors at her door, Sextilia retained a firm control over her own wealth and distanced herself from her son's financial debacle. After the death of Galba, on January 2, 69 c.e., the troops in Lower Germany declared Vitellius emperor. Probably more in response to Vitellius's loose regard for discipline than as a measure of his leadership qualities, the troops hailed him a second Germanicus, in reference to the able soldier and son of the younger ANTONIA who was Tiberius's probable heir. When Sextilia first learned of her son's rise to power, she was said to have responded that she had borne a libertine Vitellius, not a Germanicus.

In Rome Sextilia and Galeria Fundana were in some danger as Marcus Salvius Otho challenged Vitellius. Vitellius wrote Otho's brother and threatened to kill him and his family if the women were harmed. As it turned out, Sextilia may have had her own avenues of access to the camp of Otho, and neither of them were injured. Vitellius defeated Otho, and on his arrival in Rome, he embraced Sextilia and declared her Augusta. He also spent huge sums of money on food, drink, and entertainment. Troops in other parts of the empire deserted to Titus Flavius Vespasian. Vitellius was defeated in battle. Sextilia died shortly before both her sons were killed in December 69.

Sources

Suetonius. *The Lives of the Caesars:* Vitellius 3.1.
Tacitus. *Historiae* 1.75; 2.64, 89.3.

Silia

(first century c.e.)   Roman: Rome and Italy
exile

Silia, the wife of a senator, was involved in a scandal with the emperor Nero. A close friend of Titus Petronius, the probable author of the *Satyricon,* she most likely took part in the notorious entertainments he arranged for the emperor. When Nero turned against Petronius and Petronius committed suicide, a letter attached to his will described the orgies. Nero decided that Silia was guilty of spreading rumors, and he banished her.

Sources

Tacitus. *Annales* 16.18, 20.

Sosia Gallia

(? B.C.E.–c. 24 C.E.)
Roman: Italy, Asia, and Germany (?)
exile

Sosia Galla was a friend and ally of the elder Vipsania AGRIPPINA and was exiled for her allegiance to her. Sosia's husband, Gaius Silius, consul in 13 C.E., had served under Germanicus Julius Caesar, Agrippina's popular husband. Bad blood between the emperor Tiberius and Agrippina reached back to at least 19 C.E. when Germanicus unexpectedly died in Syria and Agrippina became convinced that Tiberius had arranged to have him poisoned.

Subsequently, Agrippina became the center of a powerful anti-Tiberius faction of which Sosia was a part. Lucius Aelius Sejanus, prefect of the Praetorian Guard and confidant of the emperor, launched a series of treason trials against those close to Agrippina, and in 24 Sosia and Silius were charged with treason and extortion. Silius committed suicide before he was condemned. Sosia was exiled and half of her estate was to be confiscated. Marcus Aemilius Lepidus, a friend of Tiberius, intervened and the confiscated amount was reduced to one-quarter, with the rest left for her children.

Sources

Tacitus. *Annales* IV 18–20.

Bauman, Richard A. *Women and Politics in Ancient Rome.* London: Routledge, 1994, pp. 145–146.

Levick, Barbara. *Tiberius the Politician.* London: Thames and Hudson, 1976, p. 163.

Marsh, Frank Burr. *The Reign of Tiberius.* New York: Barnes and Noble, 1931, pp. 169–170.

Marshall, A. J. "Women on Trial before the Roman Senate." *Classical Views* 34 (1990): 333–366.

Sosipatra

(c. late fourth century C.E.)
Roman: Ephesus, Pergamum
philosopher

Sosipatra was a clairvoyant, a magician, and a notable philosopher. Born into a wealthy pagan family near Ephesus, stories of her youth include the fanciful foretelling of her future that suggests she rooted her knowledge of astronomy and astrology in Neoplatonism and the ancient writings of the Chaldeans.

She married Eustathius, a philosopher who had succeeded a renowned sophist, Aedesius, in the school of philosophy at Pergamum. According to a biography by her contemporary, Eunapius, Sosipatra correctly predicted that she would give birth to three sons and that her husband would die within five years. Both came true. Her husband's death was sometime after 358, since he was mentioned as a delegate and master rhetorician sent as part of an unsuccessful mission by the emperor Constantius II to settle disputes with the Persian ruler Sapor.

After the death of her husband, Sosipatra took her husband's place in the academy. She was a successful teacher of philosophy and her reputation grew to exceed his. Her skill as a rhetorician rivaled that of her husband's teacher Aedesius, who after her husband's death helped to raise her children. Her son, Antoninus, also became a philosopher.

Sources

Eunapius. *Lives of the Sophists* V. vi 6.5–10. 5.

Pack, Roger. "A Romantic Narrative in Eunapius." *Transactions and Proceedings of the American Philological Association* 83 (1952): 198–204.

Statilia

(26 B.C.E.–? C.E.)
Roman: Rome, Italy, Asia, and Samos
political survivor

Statilia was very wealthy, widely traveled, and successfully avoided the politics that forced many of her contemporaries to exile or suicide. Her father was Titus Statilius Taurus, a noted military man, a general under Augustus, and twice consul. He died around 16 B.C.E., some 10 years after Statilia's birth in 26 B.C.E. She married Lucius Calpurnius Piso, consul in 1 B.C.E. Inscriptions honoring Statilia and Piso found in Pergamum and on the island of Samos suggest that she accompanied him to Asia Minor where he was proconsul.

Piso was a cantankerous man who spoke his mind regardless of the circumstances or people involved. Not surprisingly, in 24 C.E. he was accused of treason for private conversations against the emperor. There may also have been charges stemming from his tenure in Asia Minor. However, he died before the trial began. A year later, in 25, Statilia's son died. Statilia not only survived but thrived. She was said to have established a second family. Very wealthy in her own right, she was the great-grandmother of STATILIA MESSALLINA, the last wife of the emperor Nero and the only one who managed to survive him.

Sources

Tacitus. *Annales,* IV 21.

Marsh, Frank Burr. *The Reign of Tiberius.* New York: Barnes and Noble, 1931, pp. 172–73.

Syme, Ronald. *The Augustan Aristocracy.* Oxford: Clarendon Press, 1986, pp. 376–77.

◉ Statilia Messallina

(first century C.E.)   Roman: Italy
political player

Statilia Messallina managed her life well. She was renowned for her intelligence, beauty, charm, wealth, and culture. On both her mother's and her father's side, she was descended from consular families affiliated closely with Augustus. The fourth wife of the emperor Nero, she outlived him.

In her father's family were military men whose loyalty to Augustus was well rewarded. They also married well. Her grandfather married Valeria, the daughter of Marcus Valerius Messalla Corvinus, who was the patron of the poet Tibullus. In the literary circle around her grandmother was also the poet SULPICIA (1), whose poems are among the few extant writings by a Roman woman. Statilia's father was either Titus Statilius Taurus, consul in 44 C.E., or Taurus Statilius Corvinus, consul in 45, with the former the more likely candidate.

Her family knew the dangers of great wealth and imperial greed. When the younger Julia AGRIPPINA was the wife of the emperor Claudius, Agrippina persuaded Tarquitius Priscus, a legate of Statilia's father, to charge him with addiction to magical superstitions, among other things, as a means to force his beautiful gardens onto the market. Statilia's father committed suicide before the charges were heard by the Senate. The senators expelled the legate Priscus, despite Agrippina's efforts to save him.

After Statilia became the lover of the emperor Nero, she married Marcus Vestinus Atticus, consul in 65. He was her fourth husband and was aware of her liaison with Nero. Acquiescence was not sufficient, however, to save his life. Perhaps his tongue had been too quick. Nero accused him of mockery and sent soldiers to Vestinus's house while the latter was giving a dinner party. Vestinus had a doctor cut his arteries, and he bled to death.

After the death of Nero's wife POPPAEA SABINA (2), Statilia became the emperor's fourth wife. In 69, the year following Nero's suicide, she was in communication with Marcus Salvius Otho, who hoped to succeed Galba as emperor and evidently had some thoughts of marrying her. One of his last two letters was written to Statilia to bury him and preserve his memory. Her death is not recorded.

Sources

Suetonius. *The Lives of the Caesars: Nero* 35.1.

———. *The Lives of the Caesars: Otho* 10.2.

Tacitus. *Annales* 15.68, 69.

Oxford Classical Dictionary, ed. by Simon Hornblower and Antony Spawforth. 3d. ed. New York: Oxford University Press, 1996, p. 1,438.

Pauly, A., G. Wissowa, and W. Kroll. *Real-Encyclopadie d. Classischen Altertumswissenschaft* 1893–. (Germany: multiple publishers) 45.

Syme, Ronald. *The Augustan Aristocracy.* Oxford: Clarendon Press, 1986, index.

◉ Stratonice (1)

(fifth century B.C.E.)
Greek: Macedonia and Thrace
political wife

Stratonice, from the Macedonian ruling house, married Sitacles, nephew and heir of his uncle the ruler of Thrace, in 429 B.C.E. Her brother Perdiccas II, who succeeded their father Alexander I as ruler of Macedonia, secretly made arrangements with Sitacles to marry Stratonice with a substantial dowry, if he convinced his uncle to withdraw from Macedonia. Sitacles persuaded his uncle to withdraw, and the marriage took place.

Sources

Thucydides. *History of the Peloponnesian War* 2.100–101.

Macurdy, Grace. *Hellenistic Queens.* Reprint. Chicago: Ares Publishers, 1985, p. 14.

▣ Stratonice (2)

(?–254 B.C.E.)   Greek: Macedonia and Asia
political wife and player

Stratonice was the much younger second wife of Seleucus I, who founded the Seleucid Empire after the death of the Alexander the Great. Her marriage in 298 B.C.E. was advantageous for all concerned. Stratonice was the granddaughter of Antipater, whom Alexander had left to govern Greece and Macedonia when he embarked on his final campaign. Her father, Demetrius I, became ruler of Macedonia in 294, in some measure because her mother, PHILA (1), gave Demetrius the legitimacy of Antipater's lineage. Stratonice carried the same gift to Seleucus. Since her father had lost most of his territory, his position was enhanced by an alliance with the powerful Seleucus, even as Seleucus gained a new claim on Macedonia.

Although Seleucus took his new bride back to his capital, Antioch, he did not divorce his first wife, APAMA (1). He founded a city in Asia Minor that he named after Stratonice, and she was worshiped as Aphrodite in the city of Smyrna. She gave birth to a daughter, PHILA (2). Her father and Seleucus later became enemies when Demetrius refused to sell Cilicia to Seleucus or give him Tyre and Sidon. In 293 Seleucus married Stratonice to his son Antiochus. There is a tale that Antiochus fell madly in love with her and was pining away. Seleucus's physician, Arasistratus, revealed his son's passion, and Seleucus arranged for the marriage. More likely, Seleucus was growing old and found it difficult to administer his vast empire, which now include Asia Minor. He made his son Antiochus I coregent of his eastern empire in Asia, married him to Statonice, and sent them off to rule.

There is some indication that Stratonice resisted the arrangement. Nonetheless, Stratonice had two sons with Antiochus. Seleucus, the eldest, became coregent in the East in 280 but was not successful and may have been executed for treason. The younger son, Antiochus II, succeeded his father. Stratonice outlived her husband by seven years and died in 254 B.C.E.

Sources

Appian. *Syrian Wars* 59–61.

Plutarch. *Vitae Parallelae (Parallel Lives): Demetrius* 38.1–8.

Bevan, Edwyn R. *The House of Seleucus.* Vol 1. London: Edward Arnold, 1902, pp. 62–64, 69, 121.

Cary, M. *A History of the Greek World from 323 to 146 B.C.* London: Methuen, 1951, pp. 43, 54.

Macurdy, Grace. *Hellenistic Queens.* Reprint. Chicago: Ares Publishers, 1985.

Oxford Classical Dictionary, ed. by Simon Hornblower and Antony Spawforth. 3d. ed. New York: Oxford University Press, 1996, p. 1,449.

▣ Stratonice (3)

(third century B.C.E.)
Greek: Asia and Macedonia
political leader

Stratonice was willing to face death in defense of the status and honors that she believed were her due. Her father was Antiochus I, who ruled the Seleucid Empire in Asia after 281 B.C.E., and her mother was STRATONICE (2). Around 225 Stratonice married Demetrius II of Macedonia, who was younger than she. Stratonice left him in 239, before he divorced her, obstensibly on account of infertility; however, his immediate marriage to PHTHIA—which cemented an alliance with OLYMPIAS (2) and strengthened his claim over Macedonia—suggests a stronger reason.

Stratonice approached her nephew Seleucus II, who succeeded her father as ruler of the Seleucid Empire, with an offer of marriage, which he rebuffed. She joined forces with another nephew, Antiochus Hierax, to overthrow his older brother, Seleucus. Stratonice led the revolt in Antioch, while Hierax launched an attack in Mesopotamia when Antiochus was campaigning against the Parthians. Antiochus hurried back, defeated Hierax, and captured Antioch. Stratonice, who had taken refuge at Seleuceia Pieria, a port city on the Mediterranean Sea west of Antioch, was executed.

Sources

Appian. *Syrian Wars* XI 59, 1.22.

Bevan, Edwyn R. *The House of Seleucus.* London: Edward Arnold, 1902, vol. 1, pp. 173–174.

Cary, M. *A History of the Greek World from 323 to 146 B.C.* London: Methuen, 1951, pp. 111–12, 147.

Downey, Glanville. *A History of Antioch in Syria from Seleucus to the Arab Conquest.* Princeton, N.J.: Princeton University Press, 1961, p. 91.

Macurdy, Grace. *Hellenistic Queens.* Reprint. Chicago: Ares Publishers, 1985, pp. 71–72.

◉ Sulpicia (1)

(first century B.C.E.)   Roman: Italy
poet

Sulpicia is the only Roman woman whose poetry has survived from the tumultuous years at the end of the republic and the beginning of the empire. Although little is known of her life other than what appears in the poems, she fits the description of a *docta puella,* a well-born and well-educated woman who participated in the most elite intellectual and literary social circles.

She was the daughter or granddaughter of Servius Sulpicius Rufus, a renowned jurist and friend of Marcus Tullius Cicero, and a ward of Valerius Messalla Corvinus, a close political ally and friend of the emperor Augustus since Philippi in 42 B.C.E. Messalla had an illustrious military record, was a historian and orator, and was a patron of the arts. The poet Albius Tibullus was among his circle. At the end of the collected works of Tibullus are some 40 lines organized into 6 short elegiac poems that tradition has ascribed to Sulpicia.

Sometimes called the Garland of Sulpicia, the poems describe Sulpicia's love for Cerinthus, a man whose historical identity remains unknown but who seems to have been part of her social circle. The poems are quite conventional in form, and

they have a youthful feel, more like that of a first infatuation than of experienced passion. However, many of the poems succeed in reconfiguring the coventional motifs to project a woman's own voice. Whether she impatiently speaks about Messalla taking her into the country away from Cerinthus, or speaks directly about her longing for Cerinthus, she is the subject of her poem, and Cerinthus, the object of her desire.

Some of the poems use stronger images of passion. They also take a more conventional perspective. Losing the ingenuous and personal qualities of her writing, they describe her love and her lover sympathetically, but from outside the actual experience. In those verses, Sulpicia and Cerinthus assume more of the character of idealized lovers conventional in Latin love poetry.

Sources

Tibullus. 3.13–18.

Creekmore, Hubert, trans. *The Erotic Elegies of Albius Tibullus.* New York: Washington Square Press, 1966, pp. 105–125.

Fantham, Elaine, et al. *Women in the Classical World.* New York: Oxford University Press, 1994, pp. 323–325.

Luck, George. *The Latin Love Elegy.* London: Methuen, 1959, pp. 100–102.

Oxford Classical Dictionary, ed. by Simon Hornblower and Antony Spawforth. 3d. ed. New York: Oxford University Press, 1996, p. 1,454.

Pomeroy, Sarah B. *Goddesses, Whores, Wives, and Slaves: Women in Classical Antiquity.* New York: Schocken Books, 1975, pp. 173–174.

Pauly, A., G. Wissowa, and W. Kroll. *Real-Encyclopadie d. Classischen Altertumswissenschaft 1893–.* (Germany: multiple publishers) 114.

◉ Sulpicia (2)

(?–c. 94/98 C.E.)   Roman: Rome
poet

Sulpicia wrote love poems to her husband, Calenus. Of these poems only one fragment still exists. She was happily married for more than 15 years, and the text of her poetry seems to have combined fidelity and sensuality with a frankness unusual in the Latin poetry that lauded marriage. She probably died between 94 and 98 C.E.

Sources

Martial. *Epigrammata* 10.35, 38.12–14.

Oxford Classical Dictionary, ed. by Simon Hornblower and Antony Spawforth. 3d. ed. New York: Oxford University Press, 1996, p. 1,454.

Pauly, A., G. Wissowa, and W. Kroll. *Real-Encyclopadie d. Classischen Altertumswissenschaft 1893–.* (Germany: multiple publishers) 4A.

———. *Real-Encyclopadie d. Classischen Altertumswissenschaft 1893–.* (Germany: multiple publishers) supplement p. 9.

▣ Syncletica

(c. fourth century C.E.)   Roman: Egypt
ascetic

Syncletica was an early Christian ascetic. She followed the path of Christians going into the Egyptian desert for a spiritual journey that rejected bodily comforts and earthly wealth. From the famous churchman and ascetic Jerome to the writings of Antony and Pacomius who developed rules for monastic life, the desert fathers were at the forefront of an expanding movement that spread across the empire in the fourth and fifth centuries. Less well recognized were the women who went into the desert. Among the most notable was Syncletica.

Syncletica was an Egyptian Christian of Greek origin. Her biography is meager. Probably born into a propertied Macedonian family that moved to Alexandria, after her parents died she gave her inheritance to the poor and with her blind brother or sister went into the desert. Tradition says that she lived 83 years, was well known in her time, and that acolytes and visitors alike sought her out for her wisdom.

She provided a guide for spiritual growth, especially applicable to women, in which she had a vision of the Christian soul that led to a state of grace. She focused on the struggles for the purity of the soul in relation to the demands of the earthly world. She accepted many paths to grace. The best was a solitary life as an anchorite, for others a cenobitic (or communal) monastic life, and, if neither, then a life in the world that consciously engaged in struggle with temptation, greed, passion, and delusion between the apparently real and true goodness.

Syncletica's writings became a part of the *Apothegms of the Fathers* and, in the Armenian tradition, she was accorded the appellation of a "desert father."

Until this century, only her name remained a part of western tradition, and even that was in dispute.

Sources

Pseudo-Athanasius. *The Life and Regimen of the Blessed and Holy Syncletica.* Translated by Elizabeth Bongie. Toronto: Peregrina Publishing, 1995.

Schaffer, Mary. *The Life of the Blessed & Holy Syncletica by Pseudo-Athanasius, Part II: Study of the Life.* Toronto: Peregrina Publishing, 2001.

Swan, Laura. *The Forgotten Desert Mothers: Sayings, Lives, and Stories of Early Christian Women.* New York: Paulist Press, 2001. 1–71.

T

Tanaquil

(seventh–sixth century B.C.E.)   Etruscan:
Rome
heroine

Tanaquil's story forms part of the earliest history of
Rome, in which fact and legend are inextricably
interwoven. She was said to have been Etruscan
and to have come from a noble family of the Tarquinii. She married Lucius Tarquinius Priscus, who
had an Etruscan mother and whose father was
Demaratus from Corinth. Her husband's mixed
birth limited his opportunities in Tarquinii, and
Tanaquil was said to have persuaded him to move
to Rome.

In Rome, he became influential and established
close relations with King Ancus. When the latter
died, Priscus was elected king by the Comitia, the
assembly of the Roman people. According to
Roman tradition, he became the fifth king of
Rome, reigning from 616 to 579 B.C.E. It was during his reign that the Circus Maximus was laid out,
and the Forum drained.

Tanaquil took great interest in the career of Servius Tullius, who was brought up and educated in
her household. Possibly, the boy's mother had been
captured after the death of his father, who was a
prominent citizen of Corniculum, a city northeast
of Rome. He married Tanaquil's daughter.

Tanaquil was instrument in making Servius
Tullius her husband's successor. After her husband
was killed, she leaned out of her window and
assured the concerned crowd below that her husband had designated Servius Tullius to carry out
the affairs of state while he recuperated. When Servius Tullius had acted as king for a short time and
seemed to be accepted by the people, Tanaquil and
Servius Tullius announced that Priscus was dead.
Tanaquil had two sons, Lucius Tarquinius and
Arruns Tarquinius. They both married daughters
of Servius Tullius.

Sources

Dio Cassius. *Roman History* 2, 7, 9.
Livy. *From the Founding of the City* 1.34.1–12, 39.3–4,
    41.1–7.
Zonaras. *Annales* 7.8, 9.
Oxford Classical Dictionary, ed. by Simon Hornblower and
    Antony Spawforth. 3d. ed. New York: Oxford Univer-
    sity Press, 1996, p. 1,473.

Telesilla

(fifth century B.C.E.)   Greek: Greece
poet and military leader

Telesilla was a renowned poet. She also organized
and led a successful defense of her native city,
Argos, against an invading army of Spartans. She
was honored for both service to the muses and

military victory. Sickly as a youth, her passion for poetry was a source of strength. Nine fragments from larger hymns survive. Her poetry was said to have been addressed to women, and women were her greatest admirers. The Greek meter telesilleion, or acephalous glyconic, was named after her.

At one point in her life, Cleomenes of Sparta defeated the Argive army, which suffered an unusually large number of causalities. He then attacked the city, which was filled with noncombatants. Telesilla organized a defense of the city's walls by the male slaves and any other available men, some too old and some too young to have been a part of the army. She also armed the women with weapons that had been left in the city. She led the women to a confined area through which the Spartans would have to travel. The women fought fiercely, and the Spartans retreated. The sources excuse the Spartan withdrawal with the observation that the Spartans feared the odium of either defeat or victory over an army of women.

The women who fell in battle against the Spartans were buried along the Argive Way. In a temple of Aphrodite in Argos, in front of a seated statue of the goddess, was a slab engraved with the figure of Telesilla holding a helmet. The victory was celebrated once a year by the people of Argos in the Hybristica, or Feast of Outrage. For hundreds of years after the event, on that day women dressed in the shirts and cloaks of men, and men, in the robes of women.

Sources

Pausanias. *Description of Greece* 2.20

Plutarch. *Moralia* 245–246.

Polyaenus. *Strategemata* 8.33.

Edmonds, J. M., ed. and trans. *Lyra Graeca: Being the Remains of All the Greek Lyric Poets from Eumelus to Timotheus, Excepting Pindar.* Rev. ed. 3 vols. Cambridge: Harvard University Press, 1959, vol. 2, pp. 237–245.

Oxford Classical Dictionary, ed. by Simon Hornblower and Antony Spawforth. 3d. ed. New York: Oxford University Press, 1996, p. 1,480.

▣ Terentia (1)

(first century B.C.E.–? C.E.)   Roman: Italy
financial manager; occasional head of household

Terentia was strong, even courageous in the face of adversity. She was ambitious and thought herself a partner with her husband during times of great political danger. As her 30-year marriage disintegrated under the stresses of civil war, she assumed responsibilities for the financial welfare of her children that extended beyond the law or the expectations of traditional Roman society. Terentia came from a Roman family of ancient lineage and noble status, the Fabii. Her only known relative, however, was her half sister FABIA, a Vestal Virgin. Although her age and the date of their marriage are unknown, Terentia married Marcus Tullius Cicero when both were relatively young. Terentia had two children: TULLIA (2), born in 79 B.C.E. shortly after their marriage began, and Marcus, born in 65. She was close to her daughter, and as her daughter grew into adulthood, they were friends and allies in the stressful period of civil war.

Her husband Cicero, who came from Arpinum, was a gifted orator and set on a public career. Terentia's family named enhanced his status as a newcomer in the most elite circles of Roman politics. Her substantial dowry of 400,000 denarii was no less critical for his career. In 63 her husband was elected consul. Her position as wife of a consul assured her place in the social hierarchy. Moreover, her husband's consulship was crowned with the successful defense of the state against a conspiracy led by Lucius Sergius Catiline. Her husband was hailed as a savior of the republic and the acclaim reflected upon Terentia.

Despite the opportunities of his position, Terentia remained wealthier than Cicero and was far more interested than he in the management and growth of her estate. She oversaw her own financial affairs and often managed her husband's finances as well. She was a close friend of the very wealthy Titus Pomponius Atticus, her husband's closest adviser, supporter, and boyhood friend. Their mutual interest in finance and his tie with Cicero were a source of solace and a lifeline in the difficult years when Cicero was exiled and in the negotiations that ended her marriage.

What little is known suggests that Terentia was a generally conservative woman with regard to both economics and religion. During the period of her husband's consulship, there was a serious problem of liquidity compounded by inflation. The roots of the Catiline conspiracy rested in some part on the lack of cash suffered by the rich. Among the issues was a tax on the use of public lands. Terentia was on the side of the conservatives, who sought to preserve free use of the public land and refused to pay the tax. Similarly conservative in religion, her sister was a Vestal Virgin, and with women of her own class, Terentia shared religious ceremonies that marked the annual calendar of Roman life. As the wife of a consul, Terentia participated in the rites of the Bona Dea traditionally restricted to women from families of high officials.

In December 62 B.C.E. the celebration of the rites at the house of Gaius Julius Caesar, the *pontifex maximus,* was disrupted when a man was found to have infiltrated the household disguised as a female flute player. Cicero became a key witness against the brash, brilliant, and dissolute Publius Clodius Pulcher, who was accused of the sacrilegious act. Clodius claimed that he had not been in Rome that day. Cicero, however, testified that Clodius had visited him in Rome on the day in question. The jurors were bribed. Clodius was not convicted, and Cicero made a bitter enemy. Speculation has assigned Terentia a role in Cicero's decision to go forward with his testimony. She was said to have been jealous of CLODIA (2), Clodius's sister, who may have at one time approached Cicero as a possible lover and even a husband. Possibly, Terentia simply regarded Clodius and Clodia as unacceptable by virtue of their lifestyle. Women, no less than men, had divisions and cliques, and Terentia's circle may well have held conservative social, as well as economic, and religious views.

Whatever Terentia's role, the consequences of alienating Clodius became evident within a few years. In 58 Clodius became a tribune and forced Cicero into exile. Clodius's weapon was handed him by Cicero himself. Clodius called for the banishment of anyone who had been responsible for having a Roman citizen killed without trial. Cicero had executed the ringleaders of the Catiline conspiracy without a full trial before the Senate, a clear violation of Roman tradition and against the advice of Julius Caesar. Cicero chose again to ignore the

advice of Caesar and to heed that of Gnaeus Pompeius Magnus (Pompey the Great) and fled to Greece. Clodius won the day. Once the decision to flee was made, Terentia sought to accompany Cicero. He was adamant, however, that she remain behind to look after their daughter, Tullia, and work on his behalf.

Although Terentia was invisible in the political struggle that preceded her husband's decision to flee to Greece, the consequences affected the remaining years of her marriage. She faced a difficult situation on all sides. Clodius succeeded in having passed a decree of exile that confiscated Cicero's property and specified penalties for those who came to his aid. A mob burned his house. She was forced to seek refuge in the temple of Vesta in the Forum with her half sister Fabia, whose position as a Vestal Virgin probably protected her from the mob and from the immediate pursuit of officialdom. Nonetheless, she suffered the public humiliation of being taken before the tribunes and possibly the moneylenders on account of her husband's business affairs.

Cicero's advice to Terentia about money was largely gratuitous. Terentia successfully safeguarded her own wealth and possibly her dowry, which was comingled with Cicero's own funds, even as he was still writing to his friend Atticus that she might well have her estates confiscated. It was she in Rome who arranged for the salvage of Cicero's assets and saw to the well-being of Tullia and Marcus. She took counsel and possibly loans from her sister and Atticus, and had developed some plans for raising more cash through the sale of her own properties. Meanwhile Cicero, not one to hide his sufferings, bemoaned his fate, expressed his devotion, and wallowed in his despair at the state of affairs in which he had left her.

In the political sphere Terentia and Tullia did what they could with support from Tullia's husband, Gaius Calpurnius Piso, who had become quaestor. The situation, however, changed only with the successful election of the new consuls and tribunes, and a break between Cicero's sometime friend Pompey and inimical enemy Clodius. Finally, in 57, Cicero's exile was lifted, and he returned to Rome in triumph. Although Terentia undertook all of her husband's commissions and clearly worked on his behalf, she had also distanced herself from him during his exile. On his return, Cicero was neither grateful nor even understanding of the difficulties with which she successfully coped. His immediate concern was to restore his prestige and public standing, which entailed rebuilding the house that had been burned by the mob, as well as reconstructing and repairing his other properties.

Cicero needed a great deal of money to carry out his plans, and Terentia may have been unhappy with his expenditures, especially since they outstripped the compensation he received from the state. Cicero acknowledged to his friend Atticus that he was spending far more than he had before his exile and challenged Terentia's management of the finances.

Nothing is known about Terentia over the next several years, although her absence from Cicero's letters suggests that their estrangement intensified. However, in 51 Cicero went to Cilicia as proconsul, and Terentia was once more on her own in Rome with Tullia. The two women appear to have been close and allied in Tullia's choice of a third husband.

Tullia's first husband had died in 57 B.C.E. She next had married Furius Crassipes, whom she was in the process of divorcing. While Cicero pondered who would be his next son-in-law, Terentia and Tullia selected Publius Cornelius Dolabella. Recently divorced from a much older woman whom he had married for money, Dolabella was charming, sexy, and a scoundrel with regard to women. He was also rich and a supporter of Caesar.

The smoldering estrangement between Terentia and Cicero flared in 50, when Cicero accused her of falsified accounts. He claimed that the goods of his estate had sold for far more than Terentia reported: Terentia had shortchanged him by more than half. Atticus, not Terentia, was henceforth to care for his finances.

The year of Cicero's return, 49 B.C.E., marked the outbreak of civil war. At first events moved slowly, and Terentia remained in Rome while Cicero went to his estate in Formiae on the coast southeast of Rome to decide with whom to cast his lot. Once more it fell to Terentia to organize their finances, since cash was again a problem and the promise of war a further complication. Terentia conferred with Atticus and used her land as surety with the moneylenders to obtain cash. Terentia, Tullia, and other members of his family joined Cicero at Formiae, and Tullia gave birth to a boy who evidently died shortly thereafter. After Terentia and her daughter returned to Rome, Cicero, a fervent supporter of the republic, arranged to leave Italy for Macedonia where for the third critical time in his life he would not side with Caesar.

With Caesar's army approaching, Terentia and Tullia faced the issue of their own safety. Cicero suggested by letter that they consult other women, and if others were staying in Rome, it might be improper for them to leave. More concrete support came from Terentia's son-in-law Dolabella, who was with Caesar and who would be able to protect them provided that fighting did not erupt in the city. They decided to remain in Rome.

Terentia's marriage was approaching its end. The distance, the uncertainties, and Cicero's penchant for misunderstanding the financial realities of Rome under Caesar's rule contributed to his growing certainty that Terentia had defrauded him. A crisis came with a payment of Tullia's dowry to Dolabella. Cicero simultaneously learned that Tullia was without income, despite the arrangements he had made before he left Italy, and that 60,000 sesterces had been deducted without his authorization from the payment of Tullia's dowry.

Cicero had reached the point in a failing relationship when only his understanding of the situation could possibly be true. He simply asserted that Terentia handled his funds fraudulently, on evidence from her freedman business manager Philotimus. The accusation made no obvious sense nor was the accuser fully creditable (he was the same person whom Cicero had accused of dishonesty two and a half years earlier) and Philotimus may have had a recent falling-out with Terentia.

Terentia was the richer one of the couple when they wed and remained so. Although Cicero was responsible for the children, he was not responsible for her nor she for him. In the nature of Roman marital finances, she lived off her money, not his. Her dowry was the only part of her estate comingled with his, and her claim on those funds was only valid in the case of divorce. That she handled his finances and contributed to the children from her personal wealth was a mark of the emotional unit they formed as a family and not any expectation of law or custom.

Their mutual friend Atticus maintained a delicate balance respecting his friendship, admiration, and support of Cicero and at the same time maintaining sufficiently cordial relations with Terentia to remain an effective go-between. As Cicero requested and as would be quite proper under Roman law and social mores, Atticus took up the responsibility for Tullia's affairs. Terentia, however, still bore the burden of securing all the necessary funds to pay Tullia's dowry installment even after she had reported to Cicero that the war and his position made it impossible at the moment to sell any of his properties.

Despite the dispute over money with Terentia and Tullia's deteriorating relationship with Dolabella, all three worked to secure Cicero a pardon from Caesar. Dolabella succeeded in arranging that Cicero be allowed to return to Italy as far as Brundisium. While in Brundisium and the limbo between pardon and nonpardon, Cicero discovered what he believed to be additional evidence of Terentia's perfidiousness. He also considered ending Tullia's marriage. He refrained from acting against Dolabella for fear Dolabella would turn the mobs against Tullia. He also expressed his concern that Terentia might face the confiscation of her property. However, in Rome Terentia and Tullia appeared to have the situation as well in hand as was possible. Terentia secured her estate. Tullia and she were harmonious collaborators, and they remained in close touch with Atticus, who was always their supporter.

Cicero was pardoned in 47. Aside from the necessary formal relationships, Terentia had no more to do with him. In 46 they divorced. Atticus became the intermediary who fashioned their financial separation. With no more grace than he had shown in his treatment of Terentia when in exile or later waiting for a pardon from Caesar, he accused her of shortchanging the children in her will. After Tullia died in 45 B.C.E. only two issues remained: their son, Marcus, and the return of Terentia's dowry. Cicero was killed in 43, and he may never have repaid all that was due her.

Terentia outlived Cicero by many years. She was said to have been 103 when she died. A wealthy widow, she may well have again married. However, reports that she married Marcus Valerius Messalla or the historian Sallust are false.

Sources

Cicero. *Epistulae ad Atticum* 2.4, 15.3; 4.1.5, 2.5; 7.1.6, 3.12; 11.1.2, 2.16, 5.24.2–3; 12.19.3, 37.3; 16.15.4.
———. *Epistulae ad familiares* 14.1–24.
Pliny the Elder. *Naturalis Historia* 7.158.
Plutarch. *Vitae Parallelae (Parallel Lives): Cicero* 20.3; 29.2–4.
Dixon, Suzanne. "Family Finances: Terentia and Tullia." In *The Family in Ancient Rome: New Perspectives,* ed. by Beryl Rawson. Ithaca, N.Y.: Cornell University Press, 1986, pp. 93–120.
Oxford Classical Dictionary, ed. by Simon Hornblower and Antony Spawforth. 3d. ed. New York: Oxford University Press, 1996, pp. 1,484–1,485.
Pauly, A., G. Wissowa, and W. Kroll. *Real-Encyclopadie d. Classischen Altertumswissenschaft 1893–.* (Germany: multiple publishers) 95.
Shackleton Bailey, D. R. *Cicero.* New York: Charles Scribner's Sons, 1971, index.

Terentia (2)

(first century B.C.E.–? C.E.)   Roman: Rome
literary patron

Terentia was part of the most exciting literary era in the history of Rome. At a moment when the republic was becoming an empire, Roman artists were writing the greatest works of Latin poetry. From Catullus through Virgil and Ovid, Roman civil wars produced two generations of literary genius. During part of this time Gaius Maecenas was one of the two most important patrons who encouraged and supported the literary outburst. Terentia was his spirited wife. She was smart, fun, and beautiful. The poet Horace, a client of Maecenas, who wrote wicked satire with observations about women that were sometimes dour, other times misogynistic, and always amusing, once even praised Terentia. He called her Licymnia, possibly a reference to the third-century B.C.E. poet and rhetorician, and praised her singing and dancing with other women at a religious celebration for the goddess Diana.

Terentia came from the family of the Terenti Varrones and was the sister of Aulus Terentius Varro Murena, who was consul with Augustus in 23 B.C.E. She married Maecenas, a descendant of ancient Etruscan aristocracy. Despite their quarrels, they remained married until his death. Along with Marcus Vipsanius Agrippa, Maecenas was the emperor's key military adviser. For some period of time beginning before the end of civil war, Octavian was Terentia's lover.

Their affair was far from secret. Mark Antony, well away from Rome in Egypt, was said to have written to Octavian that he married CLEOPATRA VII while Octavian played around with a number of women including Terentilla (Terentia), despite his marriage to the pregnant LIVIA DRUSILLA. Gossip about Terentia and Augustus was said to have peaked in 16 B.C.E., when it was rumored that his trip to Gaul on military matters was in some part motivated by his relationship with Terentia. The rumors, however, were contradictory. Either the trip was meant to end the affair or Terentia was to join Augustus.

If the gossip is to be believed, Terentia's affair with Augustus outlived his friendship with her husband. Terentia's brother Varro Murena, became involved in a conspiracy with Fannius Caepio against Augustus around 23 B.C.E. The conspirators were captured and killed. Not much is known about the conspiracy, and Murena may have died simply because of his outspoken views. The times were still unsettled, and Augustus was far from certain that the Senate could be fully controlled. Maecenas, however, had angered Augustus when he revealed to Terentia that her brother was in danger. It was an unacceptable breach of confidence. Although Maecenas was not brought to trial, he lost his power and influence.

Maecenas died in 8 B.C.E., when gossip about Terentia and Augustus had long ended. Maecenas left his vast property to Augustus. Nothing more is heard of Terentia.

Sources
Dio Cassius. *Roman History* 54.19.3.
Horace. *Odes* 2, 12.
Seneca. *Epistulae* 114.6.
Suetonius. *The Lives of the Caesars:* Augustus 66.3; 69.2.
Balsdon, J. P. V. D. *Roman Women.* New York: John Day Comp., 1963, pp. 91, 272, 273.
Syme, Ronald. *The Roman Revolution.* London: Oxford University Press, 1963, pp. 277, 334, 342, 452.

▣ Tettia Etrusc
(?–c. 60 C.E.)   Roman: Italy and Asia (?)
virtuous wife

Tettia Etrusc was praised for her virtue and beauty by the poet Publius Papinius Statius. Probably of senatorial rank, her mother's name and status were unrecorded. Tettia most likely married between 48 and 50 C.E. and had two children, one of whom, Claudius Etruscus, became a patron of the poets Martial and Statius.

Her husband, Tiberius Claudius, was an ambitious and talented freedman originally from Smyrna on the west coast of Asia Minor. He gained his freedom from the emperor Tiberius and lived a long and honored life. He served as a senior administrator to emperors from Tiberius to Domitian. Appointed procurator by Claudius, he was in charge of imperial finances under Vespasian, who elevated him to equestrian status. Tettia may well have accompanied her husband when he served as procurator in an eastern province. However, Tettia did not live as long as her husband. She probably died around 60 C.E. at no more than 30 years old.

Sources
Statius. *Silvae* 3.3, 111–37.
Pomeroy, Sarah B. *Goddesses, Whores, Wives, and Slaves: Women in Classical Antiquity.* New York: Schocken Books, 1975, p. 195.
Weaver, P. R. C. *Familia Caesaris: A Social History of the Emperor's Freedmen and Slaves.* Cambridge, England: Cambridge University Press, 1972, pp. 284–294.

Teuta

(third century B.C.E.)   Greek: Illyricum
ruler

Teuta established an empire in the northern reaches of Greece. She gained control over the sea lanes used by Greek and Italian trading ships and grew rich on booty. An Illyrian by birth, she served as regent for her young stepson, Pinnes, after the death of her husband, Agron, in 231 B.C.E. Eager to build upon her husband's successful expansion of his empire, she sent a large armada of ships and men to Elis and Messenia on the Peloponnesus in southern Greece. En route her troops occupied Epirus in the northwest. Faced with an insurrection in Illyria, Teuta recalled the troops in exchange for a large ransom and a great deal of booty.

Epirus and Acarnania, situated south of Epirus, abandoned their alliances with Aetolia and Achaea to ally themselves with Teuta. She gained control over Atintania and the passes of Antigoneia through which forces could attack central Greece. She further extended her control and plundered Italian as well as Greek trading vessels. When her Illyrian forces killed Italian traders and took others as prisoners, an outraged Roman Senate sent envoys to end her disruption of trade. Teuta received the envoys in autumn of 230. She claimed that she could restrain her own forces but could not prevent others from attacking Italian traders. Her response left open the question of whether she intentionally had challenged the Romans or simply had insufficient authority to control the pirates that plagued the Adriatic.

The Romans, however, chose to view her response as a deliberate provocation, to which they responded with the threat of force. Enraged, Teuta broke off negotiations. Illyrian pirates attacked the envoys on their return voyage, and one or more of the Romans died. Teuta sent no regrets to the Senate, which convinced them that she had authorized the attack. She continued her expansionist policy and led an expedition that besieged the island of Issa off the Dalmatian coast in the Adriatic Sea, where she captured the island of Corcyra (Corfu) off the coast of Illyricum in the spring of 229.

Teuta was close to controlling the mouth of the Adriatic and the Ionian Gulf, which would endanger all Italian shipping from the south of Italy.

The Roman Senate could not countenance this threat, and a surprise attack was launched with a fleet of 200 ships and a force of 20,000 infantry with 2,000 cavalry. Demetrius, Teuta's commander in Corcyra, treacherously turned the island over to the Romans. The Roman forces attacked Illyricum, and Teuta fled with a small force to the inland fortress of Rhizon. She capitulated early in 228 B.C.E., having surrendered most of her territory and, agreed to pay an annual indemnity and to restrict the operations of her ships so that they no longer threatened trade between Italy and Greece.

Sources

Dio Cassius. *Roman History* 12.49.3–7.

Polybius. *Histories* 2.4.7, 6.4, 9; 8.4; 11.4, 16; 12.3.

Hammond, N. G. L. "Illyris, Rome and Macedon in 229–205 B.C." *Journal of Roman Studies* (1968): 1–21.

Oxford Classical Dictionary, ed. by Simon Hornblower and Antony Spawforth. 3d. ed. New York: Oxford University Press, 1996, pp. 1,488–1,489.

Thaïs

(fourth century B.C.E.)
Greek: Athens, Asia, and Egypt
self-made woman

Thaïs was renowned in the ancient world for her beauty, her wit, and her good fortune. Born in Athens, she was the lover of Ptolemy, a friend of Alexander the Great and a general in his army. She was part of the inner circle around Alexander and accompanied Ptolemy and Alexander in the conquest of Persia. There was even some rumor, probably incorrect, that she and Alexander were lovers. Thaïs was also said to have been a part of Alexander's single act of wanton revenge, which was to set fire to Xerxes' palace after the capture of Persepolis in return for Xerxes' desecration of the Acropolis at Athens decades earlier.

Thaïs was with Ptolemy after Alexander's unexpected death. She was at his side when he went to Egypt and became Ptolemy I Soter, the first Greek ruler. They had three children, one of whom was Lagos after Ptolemy's father.

So widespread was her renown that the fourth-century comic playwright Menander named one of his plays after her. The Roman poet Propertius made reference to the play some three centuries later, at the end of the first century B.C.E. when he held up Thaïs as the model of a successful lover.

Sources

Arrian. *Anabasis of Alexander* 3.18.11.
Athenaeus. *Deipnosophistae* 11.484d; 13.566e, 576e.
Diodorus Siculus. *Library of History* 8.17.1–6.
Plutarch. *Vitae Parallelae (Parallel Lives): Alexander* 7.38.1–8.
Propertius. *Elegies* 2.6.3; 4.5, 43–4.
Pomeroy, Sarah B. *Women in Hellenistic Egypt.* New York: Schocken, 1984, pp. 13, 53, 99.
Tarn, William Woodthorpe. *Alexander the Great.* 2 vols. Boston: Beacon Press, 1956, p. 54.

Thebe
(fourth century B.C.E.)
Greek: Pherae and Thessaly
avenger

Thebe hated her husband. She convinced her brothers to kill him and arranged for the deed. Her father was Jason, who ruled Pherae, a city in the northern Greek area of Thessaly. He was assassinated in 370 B.C.E. after 15 years of rule. Thebe married Alexander, her father's successor. Alexander was cruel and faithless, and he abused boys. Her brother may have been one of those he abused. Alexander also may have threatened to marry Thebe's mother, since Thebe had not borne him children.

In 358 or 357, Alexander was murdered by Thebe and her brothers Lycophron, Tisiphonus, and Peitholaus (or Pytholaus). Thebe instigated the assassination and made the arrangements. Telling her brothers that Alexander planned to murder them, she hid them in her house to wait for her husband's return. Alexander returned drunk and feel asleep. She brought out his sword, and when the brothers hesitated, she threatened to wake Alexander unless they did the deed. Some say that Thebe was the one who held the door shut until

her husband was dead. The eldest brother, Tisiphonus, succeeded Alexander as tyrant of Pherae. Nothing more is heard of Thebe.

Sources

Plutarch. *Vitae Parallelae (Parallel Lives): Pelopidas* 28.4–5; 35.3–7.
Diodorus Siculus. *Library of History* 16.14.1.
Xenophon. 6.4, 25–37.

Themista
(fourth–third century B.C.E.)   Greek: Athens
philosopher

Themista was a philosopher. She and her husband Leontius were disciples of the philosopher Epicurus. At age 34, Epicurus returned to Athens and bought a house and garden on the outskirts of the city. Themista and her husband lived with him and his other disciples, who valued a rather austere, simple life and took no part in the public affairs of Athens. They pursued an ideal of self-containment and engagement that was the essential center of the Epicurean philosophy.

Sources

Diogenes Laertius. *Lives of the Eminent Philosophers* 10.5.

Theodora
(?–June 28, 548 C.E.)   Roman: Cyprus, Constantinople
Augusta

Theodora has stirred the imagination of generations. Beautiful, brilliant, and successful, she was Augusta with Emperor Justinian at the last great moment of the ancient Roman Empire. Her marriage was a political partnership that echoed the marriage of Augustus and LIVIA. In contrast with them, however, Justinian was born poor, the son of a provincial military man, and Theodora was an actress born on the streets of Constantinople. Her marriage was a paean to Christian fidelity. The ties between Theodora and Justinian withstood the pressures of court intrigue and political rivalry. She enhanced Justinian, was absolutely loyal to him, and accrued for herself immense influence, wealth, and power. Her politics, however, were in the tradition of empire: stealth, bribery, manipulation, and religious controversy, in which she played a role critical to the development of the independent eastern churches and a permanent split with Rome.

Theodora was born into a city that still had the trappings of chariot racing, circuses, and theater integral to historical Greco-Roman urban life. Her father, Arcacius, who died when she was a child, looked after the animals in the circus for the Green faction; her mother, whose name remains unknown, was a dancer and actress. In Constanti-

nople, the Blues and Greens dominated public competitions. Organized by birth and association, these factions competed for popular favor in the arena, curried political favor with street mobs, and, if all else failed, fought each other.

Theodora had two sisters, Comito and Anastasia. As soon as possible the three of them became performers, probably as a part of the Blues, who employed her mother after her father's death. Accompanying her lover, Hecebolus, governor of Libya, the young Theodora left Constantinople and the arena to travel. They quarreled and she was

A 547 C.E. mosaic from a church in Ravenna with images of Theodora (third from left), her friend Antonina (fourth from left), and Antonina's daughter Joannina (fifth from left)
(Cameraphoto Arte, Venice/Art Resource, NY)

left penniless in North Africa. She worked her way back to Constantinople via Alexandria, where she became a Christian. It was there also that she met Justinian.

Justinian was a military man and nephew of the emperor Justin, who was childless. He adopted Justinian after he became emperor to ensure a line of succession. After the death of his wife and Augusta, EUPHEMIA (1), who supported Justinian and opposed his relationship with the low-born Theodora, Justin altered the law which forbade a contractual marriage between men of senatorial rank and actresses or former actresses. Theodora and Justinian married, and on April 1, 427, Justinian became co-emperor with Justin. On August 1, he became sole emperor after Justin's death.

Theodora was attractive, probably very attractive, since even her most severe critic, the contemporary Procopius, thought her face well shaped and pleasing. Mosaic images of Theodora and Justinian, with their respective retinue, face each other in the apse of the Church of St. Vitale, an octagonal church in Ravenna built in 526–548, when that city was the western seat of the Roman Empire. Attending Theodora are two men and seven women, two of whom, standing to her left, may be her close friend and ally, ANTONINA with her daughter Joannina. Theodora, at the center of the group, has a delicate oval face with a pensive expression and large eyes. A halo encompasses her head and neck and she wears a crown and gown bedecked with jewels and strings of pearls.

Everyone agreed that Theodora was smart, fiercely competitive, loyal to her husband and his interests, and shrewd, with an ironic sense of humor. Although Theodora's formal education was probably picked up along with her rise to power, she was nonetheless able to argue theology and was competent to conduct both personal and public business that required a reasonably sophisticated literacy. She became very wealthy. Justinian gave her gold, jewels, and estates. After he became emperor, he gave her income-producing properties in Asia Minor to pay her expenses and that of her extensive household. In the city he enlarged the Hormisdas palace, adjoining the imperial palace,

to accommodate her household. During their rule she also maintained an independent vacation estate at Hieron, on the Asiatic side of the Bosphorus.

She and the emperor used each other as counterweights, balancing the conflicting stresses of divisive political and religious controversies. She influenced the reform of family law that eliminated prohibitions against women acting as guardians of their children, ended the death penalty for women guilty of adultery, and altered divorce laws to require written notification and cause. She addressed the status of actresses, including a prohibition on the use of force to make free or slave women work in the theater against their will, the prohibition of contracts that bound women to the acting profession, and the affirmation of women's right to leave the stage. She also shaped a reaffirmation and extension of Justin's law that allowed former actresses or their daughters, who were freeborn or freed slaves, to marry men of high rank. She was responsible for an edict passed in 535 that prohibited prostitution in Constantinople and banished all procurers from the city. The antiprostitution law provided that procurers receive compensation based on the average cost of the women they owned or controlled. Theodora paid the cost of some 500 women from her own funds. She moved the women approximately four miles from the city to the Asiatic side of the Bosphorus into a palace that she and Justinian renamed the Convent of Repentance. She and Justinian expanded and endowed the palace for women to receive religious instruction, clothing, maintenance, and education for work necessary to make the institution self-sufficient.

Theodora supported Justinian's ambitious foreign policy that sought to expand the eastern and western borders. She soon became involved in Italian affairs. Although still a part of the empire, Italy had been ruled by the Goths as a semiautonomous region under Theodoric from 496 until 526. He was succeeded by his grandson Athalaric who was a minor with his mother AMALASUNTHA as regent. Six years later, the boy died and his mother and uncle vied for control. Each sought support from Constantinople.

Theodora may have favored the uncle, Theodahad, and possibly, she conspired with his wife,

Gudeliva. Her choice between the two claimants may have represented the one she believed the weaker link, in support of Justinian's goal to reclaim control. Theodahad arranged for the assassination of Amalasuntha. Any agreement he may have thought he had with Justinian, however, was quickly repudiated, and Justinian used the assassination as an excuse to invade Italy. The Goths were confused by the murder and split in their allegiance, which resulted in a Roman occupation of southern Italy for the first time in close to half a century.

Theodora's personal courage and her skill at political brinksmanship were tried by the Nika revolt in Constantinople during January 532. The usual and mutual hostility between the Blue and Green temporarily evaporated when faced with the death penalty for a number of their comrades. They rioted, set fires in the city, stormed the prison, and freed their mates. The initial group of rioters was joined by large numbers of drifters from the provinces who had come to the city impoverished, angered, and frustrated by the high taxes necessary to finance reconquering the western empire. The insurgents demanded the removal of three high officials, especially the Praetorian Prefect, John the Cappadocian, whose office raised imperial revenue with marked efficacy. However, as their number expanded with the addition of senators and other members of the wealthy classes who were angered by the emperor's consolidation of power, their demands grew until Justinian was no longer able to assuage them. The mobs destroyed numerous buildings, including churches, and surrounded the palace. The rebellious senators raised a reluctant Hypatius, nephew of the deceased Anastasius, as the new emperor. Justinian, believing flight by sea was imminent, dismissed all except some 1,500 troops and two of his trusted generals, Belisarius and Mundus.

Theodora intervened. Speaking to the inner council of war, she argued that for the emperor, death was preferable to flight. The alternative, life of a refugee, was unthinkable. The imperial purple was the only shroud she would ever need, and she would stand firm and fight, even if it meant a sure death. The council listened. She persuaded the men

to reverse their position and quell the revolt with military force, leaving Justinian all the stronger.

Theodora and Antonina, wife of Belisarius, had a working relationship. Like Theodora, Antonina had come from lowly origins. She too had been an actress. And she too was a strategic and political partner with her husband. She traveled with her husband on military campaigns, and she held critical posts, some of which determined his success. Over the years, the two women provided each other with mutually useful services. Theodora saved Antonina's marriage. Unlike Theodora, Antonina had lovers. Although usually discrete, she became infatuated with a young man, Theodosius, and her passion overrode discretion. Theodora aided and abetted her desire for time together with him. When Belisarius discovered the relationship, Theodora threatened him with loss of his command and Justinian, delighted at some access to the fortune Belisarius had accumulated, supported her. Belisarius, sufficiently concerned, mended his relationship with Antonina.

More often, however, the two women found common cause against anyone who threatened the delicate balances of imperial power, especially their own or that of their respective husbands. Antonina and Theodora attacked the notorious Praetorian Prefect, John the Cappadocian. Lacking education, courtly manners, or saintliness, John was a lightning rod of popular discontent for his corruption and oppressive system of tax collection. John's abilities were too useful for Justinian to dismiss him, since Justinian was always in need, sometimes in dire need, of funds. John, however, hated and feared Theodora. He also considered Antonina's husband, the popular Belisarius, a key obstacle to his future advancement.

Theodora and Antonina were a devious and fearsome duo to have as enemies. In 541, Antonina contrived to ingratiate herself with EUPHEMIA (2), John's much-loved daughter. Antonina told her that Belisarius was dissatisfied with Justinian. She intimated that her husband had not taken any action but could be prevailed upon to join with others. Euphemia, who shared both her father's fear of Theodora and his dream of advancement, relayed Antonina's conversation to John. A clandestine meeting was arranged in April or May 541. Men loyal to Justinian and dispatched by Theodora were hidden and listened as the plotters made plans. John was promptly revealed to the emperor as a traitor. He lost his position, was stripped of his wealth, imprisoned, and then exiled.

Theodora was as ruthless as her husband when she felt her power threatened, especially by those with whom she was most closely allied. In 543, the plague reached Constantinople, arriving from the east where it had already killed thousands. Justinian became ill and rumors circulated that he was dying. Theodora learned that the generals, including Belisarius, were discussing succession. Since no children had been born to Theodora and Justinian, succession was open to a number of contenders, none of whom would result in Theodora maintaining her position as the foremost woman in the empire, let alone a center of imperial power in her own right. Theodora separated the would-be cabal of generals and, when Justinian recovered, had Belisarius removed from his command. Although in the end Belisarius was reinstated and resumed his campaign in Italy, it was at a high personal cost. He was not only humiliated but also fined. The envy that the royal couple felt for the fortune he had amassed became the price for reinstatement. Belisarius was forced to finance the next Italian campaign out of his own funds.

Throughout the period and the empire, politics and religious doctrine were inseparable. The question of the nature of Christ embroiled all during the centuries of the late empire, and Theodora's most lasting influence may have derived from her identity as a Monophysite. The Chalcedon Compromise of 451 was the position of the orthodox Church supported by Justinian. However, the Monophysites, who held to a single divine nature of Christ at incarnation, remained popular in many areas in the East including Egypt, Constantinople, Palestine, Syria, and Antioch.

Theodora supported the Monophysites with funds, protection, and active encouragement. She befriended Severus, a leading theologian and former bishop of Antioch, and in 535, she arranged the election of Anthimus, a secret Monophysite, as bishop of Constantinople. However, the bishop in Rome, Agapetus I, protested and Justinian removed Anthimus. His removal also led to the resumption of persecutions, which had occurred intermittently over the past hundred years throughout the East. Many Monophysites were tortured, imprisoned, or killed. Theodora established a refuge in her palace for some 500 Monophysites, including Anthimus, Theodosius, the bishop of Alexandria, and other displaced clergy and monks. Justinian sometimes visited them in his search for reconciliation. They were still protected and living in the palace when Theodora, on her deathbed, extracted a promise from Justinian to assure their safety.

In the West, religious controversy became entangled with Justinian's plans to regain control of Italy from the Goths. The death of the Roman bishop Agapetus in April 536 provided Theodora with an opportunity to install a more accommodating candidate. Her choice was Vigilius, the Roman legate in Constantinople who agreed to restore Anthimus and seek an agreement with the Monophysites. She gave him 200 pounds in gold with letters of introduction to Antonina and Belisarius, who were on campaign in Italy, but before he reached Rome, Silverius had been installed by the Goth leader Theodahad.

When Silverius refused to reinstate Anthimus, Theodora conspired with Antonina to remove him in favor of Vigilius. At a meeting with Antonina and Belisarius, Antonina accused Silverius of conspiring with the Goths. He was deposed and exiled. Vigilius became bishop but he failed to fulfill his agreement with Theodora. The western clergy were fervent Chalcedonians and would not countenance a Monophysite bishop in Constantinople.

Justinian and Theodora appeared to accept each other's different beliefs about the nature of Christ, even though the Christians around them warred over the same dispute. Justinian also sought a public accommodation between the two interpretations. As early as 529, he rescinded the exile of Monophysite monks and bishops. Later he convened a conference in Constantinople. At her own expense, Theodora dispatched Monophysite clergy to Nubia to spread the doctrine, and Justinian did not prevent the mission. Instead, he sent a second, orthodox mission along the same route. Theodora managed to delay its arrival.

Their sparring over missions and Justinian's efforts for compromise clouded the more imperative need of the Monophysite community to appoint bishops who could preside over ordinations and secure a faithful clergy. Two former Monophysite bishops had previously ordained priests, without the approval of Theodora or Justinian. None had ordained bishops. New bishops that carried legitimacy were the sine qua non of a separate hierarchy and were essential to sustaining the Monophysite church. In 541, with no resolution of the controversy in sight, Theodora allowed Theodosius, the former bishop of Constantinople, who had taken refuge in her palace, to ordain two Monophysite bishops.

John Baradaeus, as bishop of Edessa, was historically the more significant of the two. Named for the clothes he wore, which were stitched from the hides of asses, he was a Monophysite monk who had come to Constantinople and lived under Theodora's protection. Ordained and disguised as a beggar, he wandered throughout the East, including Syria, Mesopotamia, Asia Minor, and Egypt, where he ordained countless bishops and priests and encouraged Monophysite worshipers. The separate and legitimate church hierarchies he established remain the core of the Jacobite and Coptic churches that survive to this day, despite Arab rule and Muslim dominance. In those churches, Theodora remains venerated as a supporter and protector.

Like all powerful Romans, Theodora advanced the interests of her family. She had a daughter from a relationship before Justinian. Her daughter had three sons: Anastasius, John, and Athanasius. Their father was probably a member of the family of the emperor Anastasius, perhaps his brother. Anastasius was betrothed to Joannina, the daughter of Antonina and Belisarius and heir to her father's fortune. John and Athanasius were both Monophysites. The former married into a wealthy patrician family of consular rank and became consul and patrician in his own name. The latter became a

cleric. Among her more extended family, Theodora favored Justin, the eldest son of her husband's sister Vigilantia, whom she betrothed to her niece Sophia. Sophia was most likely the daughter of Theodora's sister, Comito, who married Sittas, Master of Soldiers, and one of Justinian's most trusted generals. Sophia later became an Augusta in the eastern Roman Empire.

Unlike other Augustas, no coins were struck with her image. The reason is unknown, especially since she demanded honor in ways not previously Roman. All senators and patricians who approached her prostrated themselves to the floor, flat on their faces, and touched the imperial foot with their lips. Perhaps it was her revenge for the utter disdain that Roman society had exhibited to a young actress in the arena without wealth or family connections.

After some 20 years of marriage, Theodora died on June 28, 548.

Sources

Procopius. *Buildings* I. xi. 8–9.
———. *Gothic Wars* VII. xxx. 4; xxxi. 14.
———. *Persian Wars* I. xxiv. 33ff; xxv. 22, 30; II. xxx. 49.
———. *Vandal Wars* IV. ix, 13.
———. *Secret History passim.*
Theophanes. *Chronicle* AM 6016, 6040, 6057.
Bury, J. B., *History of the Later Roman Empire: From the Death of Theodosius I to the Death of Justinian.* 2 vols. New York: Dover Publications Inc., 1958.
Cameron, Avril. *Procopius and the Sixth Century.* Berkeley: University of California Press, 1985.
Evans, James Allan. *The Empress Theodora, Partner of Justinian.* Austin: University of Texas Press, 2002.
Frankforter, A. Daniel. "Amalasuntha, Procopius, and a Women's Place." *Journal of Women's History* 8 (Summer 1996): 41–57.

◉ Theodora, Flavia Maximiana
(third–fourth century C.E.)
Roman: Italy and the western Roman Empire
Augusta

Flavia Maximiana Theodora disappeared from the historical record in 306 C.E. when her husband, the emperor Constantius, died. At the time of his death they were both at York in Britain to suppress a rebellion. Theodora may have been the daughter of Galeria Valeria EUTROPIA, before her mother married Maximian, Caesar in the West under Diocletian. Alternatively, she may have been the daughter of Maximian and an early unknown wife. She married Flavius Valerius Constantius sometime before 289. Her husband became Caesar in the West under Maximian in 293 and became emperor after Maximian abdicated in 305. The couple traveled throughout the empire. She had three sons and three daughters, including Flavia Julia CONSTANTIA.

Sources

Balsdon, J. P. V. D. *Roman Women.* New York: John Day Comp., 1963, pp. 165–66.

Barnes, Timothy. *The New Empire of Diocletian and Constantine.* Cambridge: Harvard University Press, 1982, pp. 33, 37.

Der Kleine Pauly; Lexikon der Antike, ed. by Konrat Julius Furchtegott and Walther Sontheimer. Stuttgart, Germany: A. Druckenmuller, 1984–, v. 5, p. 687.

Theoxena

(third–second century B.C.E.
Greek: Thessaly
heroine

Theoxena's life was linked with that of her sister ARCHO. It was filled with hard choices. They were the daughters of Herodicus, a leading citizen of Thessaly, a region in northern Greece. Their father was killed during an invasion by King Philip V of Macedonia. The husbands of both sisters died opposing him. Widowed, each with a small child, Theoxena and Archo were forced to move in response to Philip's efforts of consolidation over his newly won territory. Her sister remarried. Theoxena, however, remained a widow. After having several children with her second husband, Poris, a well-respected man from Aenea in northeastern Greece, Archo died. Theoxena, concerned about the children, married her former brother-in-law. At this time Philip, who was increasingly convinced that his safety would be threatened by the children of the men he had killed, issued a proclamation for their arrest.

Theoxena was determined that the children not fall into the hands of Philip's soldiers. She believed that they would not only suffer death, but their deaths would be preceded by abuse and sexual assault. She had the full support of Poris who arranged for the family to flee to Athens, where he had friends. They traveled from Thessalonica, stopping in Anea to take part in the annual sacrificial festival to Aeneas, the founder of the city, and boarded a ship under cover of darkness. Winds came up and the ship was pushed back into the harbor. Observed by the army, a ship was sent to capture them. When it became obvious that the family could not outrun the pursuing ship, Theoxena offered the children a choice of death by poison or the sword. The sources capture the frenzied final minutes when Theoxena urged the family on to death, while Poris cried out to the gods. When Philip's men finally boarded the ship, they found no one.

Sources

Livy. *From the Founding of the City* 40.3–4.

Thermantia, Aemilia Materna

(c. ?–July 30, 415 C.E.)   Roman: Rome, Italy
political pawn

Thermantia was the second wife of the emperor Honorius. She was the daughter of SERENA and of Stilicho, the regent for Honorius during his minority. A substitute wife, she replaced her older sister who had died after several years of marriage with the young emperor. Serena overcame her husband's objections and arranged the betrothal of Thermantia to Honorius in 408.

The marriage was never consummated, possibly less a consequence of politics than of the emperor's sexual disinterest. Honorius divorced her when her parents fell from favor in 408. Her father, Stilicho, was murdered on August 22, 408. She left the emperor in Ravenna for Rome, where the Goths led by Alaric threatened the city. She joined her mother shortly before her mother was strangled on orders of the Senate. Thermantia was spared.

She died on July 30, 415.

Sources

Zosimus. *New History/Zosimus.* A translation with commentary by Ronald T. Ridley. Canberra: Australian Association of Byzantine Studies, 1982, 28.1,3; 35. 3; 37.5.

Oost, Stewart I. *Galla Placidia Augusta: A Biographical Essay.* Chicago: University of Chicago Press, 1968.

Prosopography of the Later Roman Empire. Vol. II. Edited by A. H. M. Jones, J. R. Martindale, and J. Morris. Cambridge: Cambridge University Press, 1971. Reprinted 1992. pp. 1,111–1,112.

▣ Thessalonice
(c. 346/340–298/294 B.C.E.)
Greek: Thessaly and Macedonia
ruler

Thessalonice made the mistake of dividing rule over Macedonia between her two sons. War ensued. She and both sons died. Thessalonice was probably the daughter of Nicesipolis, who came from Thessaly, and Philip II, ruler of Macedonia. Her mother died when she was about three weeks old, and she probably grew up with her half brother, Alexander the Great, under the care of his mother OLYMPIAS (1). Thessalonice retreated with Olympias to Pydna when Olympias was besieged by Cassander in 317 B.C.E. As soon as possible after his final victory, Cassander had Olympias killed, followed by the wife and 12-year-old son of Alexander the Great. He spared Thessalonice and married her in 316, thereby establishing a link to the family of Philip II and legitimacy for his claim to rule Macedonia.

In 305, Cassander took the title of king. Cassander named Thessalonica, a city he built at the head of the Thermaic Gulf, in his wife's honor. They had three sons, Philip, Antipater, and Alexander. Cassander died in 298. After the death of her husband, her son Philip ruled for a brief time before he died of consumption. Antipater, the next eldest, should have succeeded Philip, but Alexander, the younger of the two boys, was Thessalonice's favorite. She assigned western Macedonia and Thessaly to Antipater and the rest to Alexander. Antipater murdered Thessalonice and launched a campaign against Alexander. The latter asked Pyrrhus, ruler of nearby Epirus, and the general

Demetrius for aid. Pyrrhus came to his aid, but Alexander was later murdered by Demetrius, who became ruler of all Macedonia in 294 B.C.E.

Sources

Diodorus Siculus. *Library of History* 21.7.

Justin. *Epitome* 16.1.1.

Plutarch. *Vitae Parallelae (Parallel Lives): Demetrius* 36.1–5.

Cary, M. *A History of the Greek World from 323 to 146 B.C.* London: Methuen, 1951, p. 46.

Macurdy, Grace. *Hellenistic Queens.* Reprint. Chicago: Ares Publishers, 1985, pp. 52–54.

▣ Timaea
(fifth century B.C.E.)   Greek: Sparta
lover of Alcibiades

Timaea took the notorious Athenian general and statesman Alcibiades for a lover when he visited Sparta while her husband, the ruler Agis II (427–399 B.C.E.), was away on a military campaign. She conceived a child, Leotychides, whom her husband recognized only when he lay dying.

Leotychides failed to succeed Agis as ruler. He was banished by the successor Agesilaus who seized Agis's estate, kept one-half, and returned the other half to Timaea's family. She may well have died before her husband.

Sources

Plutarch. *Vitae Parallelae (Parallel Lives): Agesilaus* 3.1–2; 4.1.

———. *Vitae Parallelae (Parallel Lives): Alcibiades* 23.7–8.

▣ Timandra
(fifth–fourth century B.C.E.)
Greek: Sicily and Greece
faithful lover

Timandra was taken prisoner in the capture of Hyccara, a fortified town in Sicily, during the Peloponnesian War. She went to Corinth as a slave of the Cytheran poet Philoxenos, who had been in Sicily at the court of the tyrant Dionysius I in Syracuse. She became the lover of Alcibiades, the noted Athenian general and politician who had many lovers and was faithful to none. It was Timandra who arranged his funeral after he was murdered in 404 or 403 B.C.E., while in exile in Phrygia, in Asia Minor. She covered his body with her own garments and gave him the finest funeral she could afford.

Timandra was the mother of Laïs, called the Corinthian, who was one of the most famous beauties of her day.

Sources

Plutarch. *Vitae Parallelae (Parallel Lives): Alcibiades* 39.2–5.

Plutarch. *Nicias* 15.4.

Der Kleine Pauly; Lexikon der Antike, ed. by Konrat Julius Furchtegott and Walther Sontheimer. Stuttgart, Germany: A. Druckenmuller, 1984–, p. 837.

Pomeroy, Sarah B. *Goddesses, Whores, Wives, and Slaves: Women in Classical Antiquity.* New York: Schocken Books, 1975, p. 90.

◙ Timo
(sixth–fifth century B.C.E.)   Greek: Greek Islands
heroine

Timo held a modest position in the temple of Demeter during the 490s B.C.E. Located near Paros on the second largest island of the Cyclades off the southeast coast of Greece, the temple was a well-known center of worship for the goddess of the underworld, Demeter. Timo was captured by the Athenians led by Miltiades in the spring of 489. After the Greeks had won a decisive victory at Marathon and were on the offensive, they laid siege to Paros. The high walls held firm and Timo offered a plan to Miltiades for access to the city.

She told him to jump over the wall enclosing the sacred precinct of Demeter on the hill in front of the city. He approached the sanctuary and suddenly was overcome with horror. He quickly retreated. As he jumped back over the outer wall he injured himself so severely that he was forced to return to Athens, where he was assessed a large fine. He was charged with deception, since he had brought back none of the wealth he had promised. Soon after he died from a gangrene infection as a result of his fall.

Meanwhile the Parians discovered the treachery of Timo. They sought to punish her and sent a messenger to Delphi to query the oracle about a suitable punishment. The priestess at Delphi ruled that gods had decreed that Miltiades would die and Timo had simply been the instrument they used.

Sources

Herodotus. *The Persian Wars* 6.134–35.

◙ Timocleia
(fourth century B.C.E.)   Greek: Thebes
avenger

Timocleia was from Thebes in southeastern Greece. When the forces of Alexander the Great attacked the city in 335 B.C.E., a group of Thracians invaded and plundered her property. She was raped by Hipparchus, the leader of the group, who demanded any gold or silver hidden on the premises. Timocleia claimed that she had hidden her valuables in her well. She led him there. He looked over the edge, and she pushed him in. She threw stones down on his head until he was dead.

The Thracians bound her hands and took her to Alexander. He asked her who she was, and she replied that she was the sister of Theagenes, a Theban general who had led Greek forces against Alexander's father Philip II and died in the battle of Chaeroneia in 338 B.C.E. Alexander, impressed by her demeanor and what she had done, freed her and her children.

Sources

Plutarch. *Vitae Parallelae (Parallel Lives): Alexander* 121–6.

Polyaenus. *Strategemata* 8.40.

◙ Triaria
(first century C.E.)   Roman: Italy
political player

Triaria was ruthless. In 69 C.E., when Rome had four emperors in one year, Triaria was the wife of Lucius Vitellius, whose brother Aulus Vitellius became emperor for a short while. She curried favor, and unlike her sister-in-law or her mother-in-law she encouraged the emperor in his excesses. As Vespasian's forces were advancing on Rome to challenge him, the emperor sent Triaria's husband to capture Tarracina some 65 miles south of Rome. Triaria accompanied him. Some accused her of engaging in the battle and participating in the massacre of soldiers and townspeople.

Soldiers of Vespasian murdered Aulus Vitellius in Rome on December 20, 69. Triaria's husband surrendered in return for his life; however, he was killed. Nothing is heard of Triaria's end.

Sources

Tacitus. *Historiae* 2.63–64; 3.77.

◉ Tullia (1)

(sixth century B.C.E.)   Roman: Rome
political player

In early Rome, where history and legend join in narratives of good and evil, Tullia was the utterly ruthless daughter of Servius Tullius, the sixth king of Rome, traditionally dated 578–535 B.C.E. She married Arruns Tarquinius, the younger son of TANAQUIL and Lucius Tarquinius Priscus, the fifth king of Rome. Tullia's husband lacked ambition and failed to heed her advice. She conspired with her brother-in-law Lucius Tarquinius to murder her husband and Lucius's wife. They succeeded, and they married each other. She badgered her new husband to kill her father and ordered her charioteer to drive over her father's body to show support for her husband.

Her second husband, Lucius Tarquinius Superbus, ruled for five years. While his rule was oppressive, he did build the temples of Jupiter Capitolinus and the Cloaca Maxima and the sewage system of Rome, and extended Roman influence in neighboring Latium. In 510 he was driven from the throne. He was the last king of Rome, and his fall marked the end of Etruscan rule and the birth of the republic. Tullia fled Rome with her husband. He died around 495 B.C.E. The date of her death is unrecorded.

Sources

Livy. *From the Founding of the City* 1.46.3–9, 47–48.7, 59.13.

Alfoldi, A. *Early Rome and the Latins.* Ann Arbor: University of Michigan Press, 1965, pp. 152 ff.

Balsdon, J. P. V. D. *Roman Women.* New York: John Day Comp., 1963, pp. 26–27.

Oxford Classical Dictionary, ed. by Simon Hornblower and Antony Spawforth. 3d. ed. New York: Oxford University Press, 1996, pp. 1,557–1,558.

Scullard, H. H. *A History of the Roman World, 753 to 146 B.C.* London: Routledge, 1980, pp. 55, 76.

◉ Tullia (2)

(c. 79–45 B.C.E.)   Roman: Italy
victim

Tullia lived a sad life: three unsatisfactory marriages, a child who died soon after birth, and a second child whose birth resulted in her own death. As an adult, she had constant money problems, and her parents' divorce after 30 years of marriage left her father emotionally dependent on her. Tullia was born soon after her parents' marriage in about 79 B.C.E. She was the daughter of TERENTIA (1) and Marcus Tullius Cicero. Her childhood promised so much. Her father was a rising political star, praetor in 66 B.C.E. and consul in 63. Her mother was an independently wealthy woman proud of her husband and child. She was surrounded in childhood with loving relationships, especially her parents' friend Titus Pomponius Atticus and his young wife PILIA, to whom she was close. Her aunt, uncle, and cousin on her father's side, and a younger brother, Marcus, completed her immediate family circle.

She married young. Affianced when she was 12 years old, she was 16 in 63 B.C.E., about the time she married her first husband, Gaius Calpurnius Piso Frugi. He was the son of Lucius Calpurnius Frugi, praetor in 74, and his great-grandfather had been consul in 133. While married she maintained close relations with her parents and friends. She traveled with her father to his estates in Italy and regularly visited with Atticus, Pilia, and her other relations.

Politics had always been the leitmotif of her family life, but it was in 58 that the violent side of Roman politics invaded her intimate family. A mob incited by the tribune Publius Clodius Pulcher, who was her father's sworn enemy, attacked her father. Faced with an enmity that was all but implacable, Cicero left for Greece shortly before Clodius succeeded in having passed a formal decree of exile. Her mother sought to accompany him, but he insisted that she remain in Rome to be with Tullia and to work on his behalf.

Although Tullia was a married woman, she faced a sharp change in her status and in her finances after her father's departure. She no longer was the daughter of an honored consul who had been acclaimed a savior of the republic. Their family house in the city was burned, and her mother fled to her sister in the Temple of Vesta. The final exile decree confiscated all her father's property, including the properties he had assigned for her support and the next payments of her dowry. Since in Roman law and custom a woman's father, not her husband or even her mother, was responsible for her dowry and upkeep, Tullia faced seriously straitened circumstances.

Her father suffered a severe depression after his arrival in Greece. As he mulled over the most dire possibilities, it fell to Tullia and her mother to listen to his posted lamentations and to encourage him about a better future. He beseeched Terentia to look after his dearest Tullia and do all she could to settle the latter's dowry and preserve her reputation. The responsibility for what was best, was, of necessity, always left to Terentia and Tullia with counsel from the unfailingly attentive Atticus.

Tullia and Terentia did what they could in the political sphere, aided by Tullia's husband, who had become quaestor. The election of new consuls and tribunes, and Gnaeus Pompeius's (Pompey the Great) break with Cicero's nemesis Clodius, however, radically changed the situation. In the same year as her husband's early death, Cicero's exile was lifted, and Tullia greeted him on her birthday, August 5, 57, as he disembarked at Brundisium. Only recently widowed, she shared his triumphant return.

On her father's return, he became suspicious of her mother's handling of their finances. As he became disenchanted with his wife, it was Tullia who increasingly was his emotional mainstay. Although he had always been an affectionate father, his closer relationship in these later years provided Tullia with the opportunity to influence his behav-

ior. She was especially valuable when his friend Atticus was absent. They discussed political events, and as he reported to Atticus, on occasion he followed her advice.

In December 54, Tullia, who was almost 23, married Furius Crassipes from a minor patrician family. The marriage lasted only two or three years. The reasons for the divorce are not known. Cicero was again away, this time serving as proconsul in Cilicia, when in 50 Tullia and her mother chose Publius Cornelius Dolabella for her third husband. He was an extravagant and dissolute young patrician who had recently divorced his elderly wife Fabia, whom he had married for her money. He was also handsome, charming, and attractive. Cicero was not thrilled with the marriage. Reluctantly he assented even though embarrassed by the fact that Dolabella was prosecuting for bribery Appius Claudius Pulcher, the brother of Publius Clodius Pulcher, at a time when he, Cicero, was making every effort to establish better relations. To smooth troubled feelings, Cicero assured Claudius that Terentia and Tullia, not he, had chosen Dolabella.

Not long after her marriage, her father returned from Asia. Shortly after, in 49, civil war erupted. Her husband, a Caesarian, joined Caesar's army with the onset of hostilities. She gave her father the good advice to wait for developments to unfold. Possibly, she had gained information about Caesar from her husband. It was advice also echoed by Atticus, who was a model of caution about burning bridges with either side.

Cicero, who after much thought had sided with Pompey and the republicans, recognized Tullia's caring and concern for him at a time when she too was burdened with personal concerns. In May of 49, Tullia gave birth to a boy. The baby was premature, born in the seventh month. Her delivery was safe, but the infant died soon after. She was with her mother and father at her father's estate in Formiae. Her husband was not present. Not only had her child died, but she, like Cicero, was having marital problems. Dolabella's philandering and extravagant ways had not changed.

In June, a month or so after Tullia's delivery, Cicero left Italy to join Pompey in Thessalonica.

He asked Tullia and Terentia to forgive him for causing them so much unhappiness and to take care of their health. With husband and father on opposite sides, Tullia and her mother were once again alone in Rome. Safety was always an issue. The question of whether or not they should leave the city and if so, where they should go engaged father, daughter, mother, and son-in-law. As earlier when her father was exiled or abroad as a proconsul, the distance and the difficulties in communication simply made it impossible for anyone other than Tullia and Terentia to decide on their own course of action. Cicero offered any of his villas that were furthest from possible conflict. If prices went up in Rome because of the war, he suggested his farm in Arpinum, in the interior southeast of Italy, where inflation would be less severe.

Despite increasing marital difficulties, Terentia still handled much of the family's money. Ready cash was a problem throughout the period, and the war added even further complications, as the threat of confiscation by whoever was the victor was always in the background. Terentia, on at least one occasion, had to resort to the services of moneylenders. At the same time, Tullia's relations with her husband continued to deteriorate as the second installment of her dowry was coming due. Before her father left, he had made careful arrangements for Tullia's income and her next dowry payment. However her mother had deducted some 60,000 sesterces from the sum that he had set aside and the income from the properties her father had assigned to her was not being paid. Without adequate funds from her father Tullia borrowed money from her mother.

Cicero expressed astonishment at the turn in her affairs and arranged for aid from Atticus. He became convinced that in some fashion Terentia had defrauded him of the money that was to have gone to Tullia. He also questioned the wisdom of payment for the second installment of Tullia's dowry. Tullia, however, decided not to divorce Dolabella at this time and the dowry payment went ahead. It was a sensible decision on her part since whatever Dolabella's faults, he did obtain Caesar's permission for Cicero to return to Italy after Pompey's defeat in Greece. Tullia with Atticus and her friend Pilia met Cicero when he landed at Brundisium in October. Tullia was also again short of money, and again requested help from Atticus.

In June 47 Tullia visited her father in Brundisium where he still waited for Caesar's pardon. The visit was not a happy one. Tullia showered him with affection, but they were both downcast by their respective problems. Tullia left to go to her mother. There was another family discussion about a divorce between Tullia and Dolabella. Again nothing happened. In September 47, Caesar landed at Brundisium; Cicero went to meet him and received a friendly reception. The restoration of his rights followed. With his citizenship no longer in question and his properties secured, her father divorced her mother not a year later, in August 46. He was probably even firmer in his pressure on Tullia to divorce Dolabella. Tullia divorced in the autumn or early winter of the same year.

She was, however, pregnant. In January 45 B.C.E. Cicero wrote Atticus both that he was trying to get Dolabella to return the first installment of Tullia's dowry and that Tullia was about to give birth. Tullia and the baby went to Tusculum with Cicero, where she died of childbirth complications in February. Her infant son died shortly thereafter.

Sources

Cicero. *Epistulae ad Atticum* 1.3; 1.8.2; 1.10.5; 2.8.3; 3.19.2; 4.1.3, 5; 4.2.5; 4.4a; 4.15.4; 7.3.8; 7.13.2; 9.6.4; 10.18.1; 11.1.2; 11.2.2; 11.6.2; 11.7.4; 11.9.2; 11.1; 11.17a.1; 11.23.3; 11.24.2–3; 12.3; 12.5c.

Cicero. *Epistulae ad familiares* 3.12.2–4; 5.6.2; 6.18.5; 14.1.5; 14.4; 14.6; 14.8; 14.13; 14.14.

Cicero. *Epistulae ad Quintum fratem* 2.4.3–4; 2.5.1.

Balsdon, J. P. V. D. *Roman Women.* New York: John Day Comp., 1963, pp. 179, 187–188.

Dixon, Suzanne. "Family Finances: Terentia and Tullia." In *The Family in Ancient Rome: New Perspectives,* ed. by Beryl Rawson. Ithaca, N.Y.: Cornell University Press, 1986, pp. 93–120.

Fantham, Elaine, et al. *Women in the Classical World.* New York: Oxford University Press, 1994, pp. 275–276.

Oxford Classical Dictionary, ed. by Simon Hornblower and Antony Spawforth. 3d. ed. New York: Oxford University Press, 1996, p. 1,558.

Shackleton Bailey, D. R. *Cicero.* New York: Charles Scribner's Sons, 1971, index.

U

Urgulania

(first century B.C.E.–first century
C.E.)   Roman: Italy
political player

Urgulania who was of Etruscan descent was a close
friend of the powerful Livia Drusilla. She supported Livia and, in turn, enhanced her own power
and promoted the position of her family members.
Her husband Marcus Plautius was also of Etruscan
background, and it was due in large measure to her
influence that their son, Marcus Plautius Silvanus,
became consul along with Augustus in 2 C.E. Urgulania was the grandmother of Plautia Urgulanilla, the first wife of the future emperor Claudius.
The marriage was probably arranged by Livia and
Urgulania.

Urgulania was not an easy woman. It might
even be said that she used her position to behave in
a manner others thought outrageous. In 16 C.E. the
augur Lucius Piso, an outspoken member of the
aristocracy who had been consul in 1 B.C.E., brought
suit against Urgulania to recover money that she
owed him. When she was ordered to appear before
the praetor, she went instead to Livia's house pursued by Piso. Livia, furious, persuaded Tiberius to
intervene as Urgulania's advocate. Tiberius's journey to the tribunal was so deliberately slow that
Livia paid the money owed Piso and the case was
dismissed. Urgulania also refused to appear as a
witness in another case before the Senate and a
praetor had to be sent to her house to take evidence, although Roman custom had always been
that even Vestal Virgins had to give evidence in the
Forum or the courts.

In 24 Urgulania's grandson, the praetor Plautius
Silvanus, threw his wife Apronia out of the window of their house. Before the trial in the Senate
opened, Urgulania sent him a dagger. Coming
from a close friend of Livia, it meant that Silvanus
should commit suicide, which he did.

Sources

Tacitus. *Annales* 2.34.1; 4.22.1.
Bauman, Richard A. *Women and Politics in Ancient Rome.*
London: Routledge, 1994, p. 135.
Der Kleine Pauly; Lexikon der Antike, ed. by Konrat Julius
Furchtegott and Walther Sontheimer. Stuttgart, Ger-
many: A. Druckenmuller, 1984–, p. 1,036.
Levick, Barbara. *Tiberius the Politician.* London: Thames
and Hudson, 1976, p. 182.
Oxford Classical Dictionary, ed. by Simon Hornblower and
Antony Spawforth. 3d. ed. New York: Oxford Univer-
sity Press, 1996, p. 1,574.
Syme, Ronald. *The Augustan Aristocracy.* Oxford: Claren-
don Press, 1986, pp. 88, 376, 430.

V

Valeria (1)

(first century B.C.E.)   Roman: Rome
self-made woman

Valeria enhanced the fortunes of her family through marriage with Lucius Cornelius Sulla when he was dictator of Rome. She was the niece of the famous orator Quintus Hortensius Hortales, consul in 69 B.C.E., who supported Sulla.

It is reported that the recently divorced Valeria deliberately leaned over and picked off a piece of lint from Sulla's cloak during a gladatorial game. Having drawn his attention, she noted her desire to secure for herself a piece of his good luck. Subsequently, Sulla was widowed and Valeria became his fifth wife.

Sources

Plutarch. *Vitae Parallelae (Parallel Lives): Sulla* 35.
Balsdon, J. P. V. D. *Roman Women.* New York: John Day Comp., 1963, p. 279.
Pomeroy, Sarah B. *Goddesses, Whores, Wives, and Slaves: Women in Classical Antiquity.* New York: Schocken Books, 1975, p. 157.

Valeria (2)

(third–fourth century C.E.)   Roman:
Germany, Dalmatia, Syria, Asia(?), and Italy
Augusta

Valeria came to a tragic end. Her parents were PRISCA and the emperor Diocletian. She married Galerius after her father had established a system of shared power in 293 C.E. and appointed her husband Caesar to control the Danube region. Although the marriage lasted until her husband's death, she had no children. She evidently was a good mother to her husband's son Candidianus.

Valeria and her mother, Prisca, were sympathetic to the Christians, although there is no evidence that they were members of the church. Diocletian tolerated the followers of Christianity for some 19 years while he expended his energies restoring and shoring up the Roman Empire; however, he was a firm believer that the old Roman traditions of religion, order, and discipline were the foundations for preserving the unity of the empire. Christianity, which had become a growing and unsettling force, undermined this sense of order. Valeria and her mother conformed and burned incense to Jupiter as part of a program to promote ancient religious practices.

In 303 Diocletian allowed Galerius to issue edicts authorizing the persecution of Christians, including the destruction of their buildings. In 304 Diocletian suffered an almost fatal illness and retired the following year. He persuaded Maximian, the Augustus of the East, to step down at the same time and Constantius became the Augustus of the West. Valeria's husband Galerius, became Augustus of the East and Valeria was named Augusta. She lived with her mother in the palace at Nicomedia in Asia Minor. For the remainder of Galerius's life, Valeria and her mother were honored.

Galerius suffered a fatal illness in 311 but before he died, he issued the Edict of Toleration toward the Christians. It is unknown what, if any, part Valeria played in this, but she undoubtedly approved.

Galerius also committed his wife and son to the care of Licinius, who had been co-Augustus with him since 308. For unknown reasons, Valeria mistrusted Licinius. She and her mother took refuge with Maximin Daia, who had become Caesar in 305 and who was a son of her husband's sister. Daia saw political advantage in a marriage with Valeria. The marriage would link him closely with the aged Diocletian and also give him access to her extensive properties and other wealth.

Valeria refused and offered several reasons: She was still in deep mourning for her husband; moreover, her husband had adopted Daia and he was her son as much as he was the son of her husband, therefore marriage with him would be incestuous; and last but not least, it would be shameful for him to divorce his own faithful wife. His response was to put to death many friends of Valeria and Prisca, and he exiled them to a remote area of Syria.

Valeria sought her father's help. Diocletian sent some letters from his retirement palace protesting the treatment of Valeria and her mother, but he was too old and lacked the energy to do more. Valeria's position did not improve after Daia was defeated and killed by Licinius in 313. Licinius regarded the two women as enemies. They escaped Licinius and wandered in disguise for some 15 months in an effort to reach the Dalmatian coast and Diocletian. During that period Diocletian died. His death ended their hopes of finding a protected situation. They were recognized in Thessalonica, in Macedonia. Their heads were cut off in public, and their bodies were thrown into the sea as part of Licinius's purge of all relatives of Galerius and Daia.

Sources

Lactantius. *De Mortibus Persecutorum* 15, 39, 50–51.
Balsdon, J. P. V. D. *Roman Women*. New York: John Day Comp., 1963, pp. 165–169.

Gibbon, Edward. *The Decline and Fall of the Roman Empire.* New York: Heritage Press, 1946, pp. 333–334.
Pauly, A., G. Wissowa, and W. Kroll. *Real-Encyclopadie d. Classischen Altertumswissenschaft 1893–.* (Germany: multiple publishers) 7.
Williams, Stephen. *Diocletian and the Roman Recovery.* New York: Routledge, 1996, pp. 173, 199–200.

◉ Varronilla

(?–83 C.E.)   Roman: Rome
priestess

Varronilla, with the two sisters OCULATA, was one of three Vestal Virgins condemned in 83 C.E. for committing incest. (A fourth Vestal, CORNELIA (12), head of the college, was accused but found innocent.) They were accused in the campaign by the emperor Domitian against immorality in Rome. He claimed that the Vestal Virgins and the temple of Vesta had been a hotbed of sexual immorality since the reigns of his father and his brother. The usual punishment was being buried alive, but Domitian, in what he regarded as a magnanimous gesture, allowed them to commit suicide. Their alleged lovers were sent into exile.

Sources

Suetonius. *The Lives of the Caesars:* Domitian 8.14.
Balsdon, J. P. V. D. *Roman Women.* New York: John Day Comp., 1963, pp. 239, 241.

◉ Verania

(first century C.E.)   Roman: Italy
credulous victim

Verania was swindled. She was a wealthy woman, the daughter of Quintus Veranius, consul in 49 C.E. She married Lucius Calpurnius Piso, whom the emperor Servius Sulpicius Galba adopted as his successor on January 10, 69. Both men were killed five days later. Verania ransomed her husband's head from his killers.

At about 60 years old, she became seriously ill, and Marcus Regulus, whom she disliked as he was an old enemy of her husband, had the audacity to visit. He inquired the date and hour of her birth and then informed her that she would survive her illness. To confirm his assertion he consulted with an expert in the examination of entrails, who was skilled in divining their meaning.

He returned to again reassure her. She rewrote her will and left him a handsome legacy. Shortly thereafter, she took a turn for the worse and cursed him before she died. The sources accuse Regulus of habitually insinuating himself with the seriously ill to secure a legacy.

Sources

Pliny the Younger. *Epistulae* 2.20.

Tacitus. *Historiae* 1.47.

Pauly, A., G. Wissowa, and W. Kroll. *Real-Encyclopadie d. Classischen Altertumswissenschaft 1893–*. (Germany: multiple publishers) 19.

▣ Verginia (1)

(fifth century B.C.E.)   Roman: Rome
heroine

Verginia was the daughter of Lucius Verginius, a plebeian who served as a centurion of the first rank. She was to marry a former tribune, Lucius Icilius. In 449 B.C.E. Appius Claudius tried to seduce her. He was a patrician and leader of the *decemviri,* the magistrates selected to decide on a code of laws to replace the suspended constitution. Despite his offers of money and gifts, she resisted.

While her father was away, Appius Claudius arranged for his client, Marcus Claudius, to seize Verginia in the Forum. Claudius claimed that she was a slave who had been born in his house and secreted away by her father as a small child. A crowd gathered who knew her father, and Claudius agreed to take her case to court. The judge was the same Appius Claudius who lusted after Verginia. He allowed that Claudius could take Verginia to his house and produce her in court when her father returned. At this point, Verginia's fiancé and uncle arrived and demanded that she be allowed to return to her home until the trial. The crowd supported them. Appius Claudius gave way.

When her father returned, Appius Claudius ruled that Verginia was the slave of Marcus Claudius. Her father, fearing that efforts to keep Verginia out the clutches of Appius Claudius were

futile, killed her. For him, her death was preferable to her enslavement.

Sources

Diodorus Siculus. *Library of History* 12.24.

Livy. *From the Founding of the City* 3.44–58.

Valerius Maximus. *Factorum et dictorum memorabilium libri IX* 6.1.2.

Balsdon, J. P. V. D. *Roman Women.* New York: John Day Comp., 1963, pp. 28–29.

Oxford Classical Dictionary, ed. by Simon Hornblower and Antony Spawforth. 3d. ed. New York: Oxford University Press, 1996, p. 1,588.

Pomeroy, Sarah B. *Goddesses, Whores, Wives, and Slaves: Women in Classical Antiquity.* New York: Schocken Books, 1975, p. 153.

▣ Verginia (2)

(fourth–third century B.C.E.)   Roman: Rome
reformer

Verginia challenged the historical division between patrician and plebeian in the practice of religious rites among women. Born a patrician, Verginia married a plebeian, Lucius Volumnius, who became a consul. In 296 B.C.E. omens portending possible troubles for Rome led the Senate to request special attention to religious rites that would assure Rome's safety.

Verginia had always been a member of the patrician women's community and had participated in the rites restricted to patrician women. Despite the high office held by her husband, however, his plebeian birth barred her from further participation and the women would not admit her to the rites. She argued that her marriage did not alter her birth and that she fulfilled the second criterion of having only married once, but to no avail. Not to be silenced or excluded, Verginia sought out a group of plebeian women who had been married only once. She enclosed a portion of her large house and erected an altar. She invited the women to practice the rites that celebrated chaste married women and the well-being of Rome.

Sources

Livy. *From the Founding of the City* 10.23.1–10.

Bauman, Richard A. *Women and Politics in Ancient Rome.* London: Routledge, 1994, pp. 15–16.

Fantham, Elaine, et al. *Women in the Classical World.* New York: Oxford University Press, 1994, pp. 231–232.

▣ Verina (Aelia)

(?–484 C.E.)   Roman: Constantinople
Augusta

Verina lusted after power. Manipulative, clever, determined, and unlucky, she almost wrested rule from the successors to her husband, Emperor Leo I. Her husband, born in Dacia, around the area of contemporary Transylvania, was a soldier who served under Aspar, Master of Soldiers, for the eastern emperor Marcian. In the winter of 457, the emperor died without a clear heir. Aspar, his leading general, was not a contender, since he was both Goth and an Arian Christian. He was, however, the power broker, and he chose Leo. Verina and Leo had two daughters: ARIADNE, born before 457, and LEONTIA, born after Leo became emperor.

Leo had little formal education but was a shrewd and experienced soldier. Faced with the demands of his powerful backer Aspar and German supporters, he assembled a counterforce as a palace guard made of up of fierce fighters from Isauria in Asia Minor. Their leader was Zeno. Sometime before 466, Verina became Augusta and adopted the name Aelia Verina, and in 466/467, Zeno married Ariadne, Leo and Aelia Verina's oldest daughter. They had a son, Leo, soon after.

Leo I died in 474. He had named his grandson Augustus in 473 and the seven-year-old boy became Leo II with his father, Zeno, as regent. The boy died within the year, and the Senate, with the consent of Aelia Verina, selected Zeno as emperor. Verina, however, loathed Zeno, who was physically unattractive, uneducated, slothful, and indolent. He was also disliked by the populace and the elite who mocked his barbarian and country bumpkin manner. Nonetheless, he ruled for 17 years, relying on Isaurian troops, unprincipled diplomacy, and bribery.

Earlier, in 468, Verina had persuaded her husband to appoint her brother, Basiliscus, commander of a large force sent to Africa to subdue the Vandals. He was incompetent and the campaign ended in disaster. However, he survived and became a key member of the group around Verina that hated Zeno and plotted his downfall. Her brother recruited two Isaurian officers, Trocundes and Illus, as additional partners in the plot. Verina planned for her lover, Patricius, formerly Master of Offices, to replace Zeno, which would allow her to resume her former position as foremost Augusta, replacing her daughter, Ariadne, who had become a competing center for power.

Verina convinced Zeno that his life was in danger. He fled with Ariadne and a large treasure to Isauria. There was a bloodbath in Constantinople as the populace murdered many of Zeno's Isaurian supporters. However, Basiliscus double-crossed Verina, and the Senate made him emperor. His wife, ZENONIS, became Augusta and he assassinated Patricius. Verina, undeterred, negotiated with Zeno. Her plot was discovered, and she survived with the help of her nephew, Armatus, Master of Soldiers, who hid her until she could escape.

Basiliscus and Zenonis were Monophysites, who supported the single divine nature of Christ. The emperor issued an edict to outlaw the orthodox compromise of the Council of Chalcedon, that in 451 had affirmed the nature of Christ as human and divine, cojoined yet separate. Doctrinal distinctions had powerful political implications with the Goths, especially the largely Arian army. Significant parts of the East were Monophysite and the West firmly supported the Chalcedon Compromise. Although all the positions were represented in the population of Constantinople, outlawing the orthodox position, which was probably dominant at the time, fueled insurrection. The Isaurian Illus switched allegiance and joined Zeno, who returned to power in August 476. Basiliscus and his family were killed.

Verina, however, was not satisfied when Illus became a patrician and consul in 478 and appointed Master of Offices by Zeno for services to the empire. Verina turned to her daughter, Ariadne, the Augusta, who competed with her for power. They joined forces to attack Illus, whose authority over the weak emperor threatened both of them. Verina used the prefect Epinicius to arrange an assassination. The plot failed, and Illus, initially unaware of Verina's role, sent Epinicius to prison in Isaura. Zeno needed Illus in Constantinople, which was unstable. Illus refused, unless Verina also became his prisoner. Zeno complied and toward the end of 479, Illus sent Verina to Tarsus, in what is now southeastern Turkey on the Mediterranean coast, where she was forced to adopt an ascetic life and live in a monastery. Later, she was transferred to a fortress in Isauria.

Even from a distance, Verina caused upheaval. Her younger daughter, Leontia, had married Marcian, the son of Anthimus, who had reigned in the West from 467 to 472. Marcian was in search of an excuse to invade the East. Verina provided it, in exchange for the recovery of her position of power. Marcian argued that his wife had been born after her father Leo had become emperor and her mother Augusta, and therefore, through his wife he had a greater claim to succession than Zeno, whose wife Ariadne had been born much earlier. Joined by his two brothers and supported by the inhabitants of Constantinople, he was barely defeated by Illus at the end of 479.

Shortly thereafter, Ariadne demanded that Zeno bring her mother back to Constantinople. Illus refused. She arranged to have Illus killed. Illus escaped the assassination, losing his right ear. Illus also felt it prudent to withdraw from the city. Appointed by Zeno Master of Soldiers in the East, he went to Antioch with a large contingent of supporters. It was clear war was planned, and that Illus was inventive and flexible. Initially Illus declared Marcian emperor and then changed his mind. He had Verina brought from Isauria to Tarsus and, dressed in the robes of Augusta, she crowned Leontius, the patrician supporter of Illus, emperor. She issued a proclamation distributed throughout the empire that the pious Leontius was the legitimate emperor. Probably she acted under duress. However, she had changed sides many times.

With the help of the Ostrogoths, Zeno defeated Illus in 484. Illus fled with Verina and Leontius to the fortress of Cherris in the mountains of Isaurius where Verina died a few days later. She was later buried in Constantinople.

Sources

John Malalas. *Chronographia* XV. I, iii.
Procopius. *Vandelic Wars* III. vi. 2, 26.
Theophanes. *Chronicle* AM 5956, 5961, 5965, 5967, 5969, 5971, 5975.
Prosopography of the Later Roman Empire. Vol. II. Edited by A. H. M. Jones, J. R. Martindale, and J. Morris. Cambridge: Cambridge University Press, 1971. Reprinted 1992, p. 1,156.

Vespasia Polla

(first century B.C.E.–first century C.E.)
Roman: Italy
mother of the emperor Vespasian

Vespasia Polla came from an honorable equestrian family in Nursia, some 80 miles northeast of Rome. Her father Vespasius Pollo, an officer, was three times tribune of the soldiers and a prefect of the camp. Her brother became praetor and senator. She married Flavius Sabinas, whose father, Titus Flavius Petro, was a native of Reate in the Sabine country and had fought on the side of Gnaeus Pompeius Magnus (Pompey the Great) in the civil war. He later became a tax collector. Her husband was not a military man and became a collector of import and export taxes in Asia. He later went into banking in what is now Switzerland, where he died. Vespasia was left with two children, Sabinus and the future emperor Titus Flavius Vespasian, who was born on November 17, 9 C.E.

Vespasian was brought up in Cosa on the coast northwest of Rome by his paternal grandmother, Tertulla, about whom we only know her name. Unlike his brother who became a prefect in Rome, Vespasian appeared in no hurry to enter political life. The sources claim that Vespasia pushed him. She was said to have used her sharp tongue and to have unfairly compared him with his brother in an effort to stir his ambition. She was successful; Vespasian became emperor in 69.

Sources

Suetonius. *The Lives of the Caesars:* Vespasian 1–2.2.

Pauly, A., G. Wissowa, and W. Kroll. *Real-Encyclopadie d. Classischen Altertumswissenschaft 1893–.* (Germany: multiple publishers) 1,710–1,711.

Vibidia

(first century C.E.)   Roman: Rome
priestess

Vibidia was senior Vestal Virgin when Valeria MES-SALLINA, the wife of the emperor Claudius, was accused of marrying her lover Gaius Silius. Messallina appealed to Vibidia to ask for mercy from the emperor and to be allowed to plead her case. Narcissus, the powerful freedman secretary of the emperor, was determined to prevent an appeal, but he could not refuse to see Vibidia.

Vibidia argued that under Roman law a wife could not be killed without an opportunity to defend herself. Narcissus promised that Messallina would be allowed to state her case and dismissed Vibidia, but when he saw Claudius wavering, he gave the order for Messallina's execution.

Sources
Tacitus. *Annales* 11.34, 37.
Balsdon, J. P. V. D. *Roman Women.* New York: John Day Comp., 1963, pp. 100–101.
Bauman, Richard A. *Women and Politics in Ancient Rome.* London: Routledge, 1994, pp. 176–177.

Victoria (Vitruvia)

(third century C.E.)   Roman: Gaul
Augusta; governor of Gaul

Victoria's family supported Marcus Cassianius Latinus Postumus, appointed by the future emperor Gallienus to protect the Rhine border of the empire during a period of general unrest, characterized by invasions, economic disruptions, and declining population. Postumus was killed by his own troops when he prohibited the sacking of what is now Mainz.

Victoria's son Victorinus served under Postumus and under Marcus Aurelius Claudius Augustus. He held de facto power for about two years, probably from 269 to 270 C.E. During the two-year period, Victoria took the title Mother of the Camp and Augusta. Coins were issued in her name. After her son died, Victoria supported a general known by the name of Tetricus to become the commander of Gaul. When he led troops in Spain, he was said to have left her in charge of Gaul.

Sources
Scriptores Historiae Augustae. Tyranni Triginta (Thirty Tyrants) v. 3–4, 6.3; 24.1; 25.1; 31.2–3.

Vipsania Agrippina

(33 B.C.E.–20 C.E.)   Roman: Italy
very wealthy woman

Vipsania Agrippina stayed clear of direct engagement in the politics of succession, just as two generations earlier her grandfather had stayed clear of choosing sides in the politics of civil war. Vipsania's grandfather, Titus Pomponius Atticus, was an Epicurean and cultured collector of art as well as shrewd businessman who lived his life outside the deadly high stakes of late republican senatorial politics. Caecilia ATTICA, his only daughter and mother of Vipsania, was reputed to be one of the wealthiest women in Rome. She married Marcus Vipsanius Agrippa, Augustus's loyal friend and greatest general. Vipsania, their only child, was little more than a year old in 32 B.C.E. when her grandfather, already incurably ill, arranged with LIVIA her future marriage with Tiberius. Tiberius was Livia's 10-year-old son and the stepson of Octavian, proclaimed Augustus in 27 B.C.E.

The marriage arrangement was made nine years before the battle of Actium and the first settlement of 23 B.C.E. between a victorious Augustus and the Senate. With the Roman civil war far from over, Atticus's step to establish an alliance with the soon-to-be powerful Livia Drusilla was a bold move. The astute Livia recognized that the alliance strengthened her ties with her husband's confidant and general, Vipsania's father Agrippa, and probably eased very real financial pressures that were a leitmotiv of those years.

Vispania married Tiberius in 20 or 19 B.C.E., after her mother had probably died and her father had remarried, divorced, and married again, this time with JULIA (6), the only child of his friend

Augustus in 27 B.C.E. With the civil war over and Augustus the victor, her widowed father's successive round robin of marriages reflected the new political circumstances. Tiberius and Vipsania were perilously close to these shifts of political fortune. At the time of their marriage there still appeared to be an ample number of heirs to Augustus from the Julian line. Vipsania gave birth to a son, Drusus Julius Caesar, in 13 B.C.E. who like his father, was a Claudian. They would come to the fore in the battles over succession only after others had died. However, in 12 B.C.E., even before Tiberius's own rise to emperor appeared imminent, Vipsania's father, Agrippa, died leaving his wife, Augustus's daughter Julia, a widow with five children. Ever practical, Augustus and Livia pressured Tiberius to divorce Vipsania and marry Julia in 11 B.C.E., thereby neatly conjoining their progeny in one couple and uniting the Julian and Claudian clans.

Vipsania did not stay unmarried long, nor did she choose another Julian or Claudian for a husband. In 11 B.C.E. she married Gaius Asinius Gallus, consul in 8 C.E. and son of the noted republican orator and writer Gaius Asinius Pollio, consul in 40 B.C.E. Vipsania and Gallus had five sons, some of whom were notable in public life of the post-Tiberius generation. Gallus, however, was no friend of Tiberius, even though he was linked to him through his stepson Drusus. Moreover, for reasons that are either illogical or obscure, Tiberius deeply resented the marriage of Vipsania and Gallus: Possibly, Gallus was too tied to the senatorial elite at a time when the Senate could still pose a problem to the emperor, or alternatively, the divorce with Vipsania did not free Tiberius from his feelings about her. Vipsania died in 20 C.E. the only one of Agrippa's children to die peacefully. Ten years later in 30, Tiberius had the Senate indict Gallus who was imprisoned in his own house and after three years, died of starvation.

Sources

Dio Cassius. *Roman History* 14.31.2; 57.2.7; 58.3.1–6.
Nepos. *Atticus* 19.4
Suetonius. *The Lives of the Caesars:* Tiberius 7.2–3.
Tacitus. *Annales* 1.12–13; 3.19.

Balsdon, J. P. V. D. *Roman Women.* New York: John Day Comp., 1963, index.
Levick, Barbara. *Tiberius the Politician.* London: Thames and Hudson, 1976, index.
Oxford Classical Dictionary, ed. by Simon Hornblower and Antony Spawforth. 3d. ed. New York: Oxford University Press, 1996, p. 1,601.
Syme, Ronald. *The Augustan Aristocracy.* Oxford: Clarendon Press, 1986, index.
———. *The Roman Revolution.* London: Oxford University Press, 1963, index.

Vistilia

(first century B.C.E.–? C.E.)   Roman: Italy
much married woman

Vistilia came from Umbrian Iguvium in Italy. She was said to have had six husbands over a period of about 20 years and to have had children with each of them. One of her sons was the general Gnaeus Domitius Corbulo. Her daughter MILONIA CAESONIA married the emperor Gaius Caligula had one child, a daughter, and died with them.

Sources

Pliny the Elder. *Naturalis Historia* 7.39.
Syme, Ronald. *The Augustan Aristocracy.* Oxford: Clarendon Press, 1986, pp. 74, 305.
———. "Domitius Corbulo." *Journal of Roman Studies* 60 (1970): 27–39, pp. 27 ff.

Vitia

(? B.C.E.–32 C.E.)   Roman: Rome
convicted of treason

Vitia was the mother of Fufius Geminus, consul in 29 C.E. He was a client of the powerful LIVIA DRUSILLA, the widow of Augustus and the emperor Tiberius's mother. Livia was instrumental in Geminus's advancement. His wife, MUTILIA PRISCA, was also protected by Livia. Tiberius, however, often held opinions that differed from those of his mother, and he disliked the sharp-tongued Geminus, especially since he was sometimes the object of Geminus's wit. Both Geminus and his wife supported Lucius Aelius Sejanus, the head of the Praetorian Guard who had Tiberius's ear and in the years after Tiberius retreated to Capri, was the conduit of information from Rome to the emperor.

After Livia's death, Tiberius accused Geminus of lacking respect and casting aspersions upon the emperor, which was treason under imperial law. Sejanus either could not or would not come to their aid. Geminus and Mutilia were forced to commit suicide. In 32, after the fall of Sejanus when the Senate was rife with treason trials, Vitia was tried for weeping over her son's death. Her tears were evidence enough of her treason, and she was convicted.

Sources

Tacitus. *Annales* 6.10.

Xanthippe

(fifth century B.C.E.)   Greek: Athens
wife of Socrates

Xanthippe married Socrates in the latter part of his life. She supposedly had a temper, and Socrates may well have been a difficult husband. He was said to have quipped to one of his more brilliant and erratic students that his wife's temper had prepared him to cope with other impudent and unreasonable people.

Xanthippe had one son, Lamprocles. There was, however, another woman in Socrates' life, MYRTO, with whom he had two additional children. The relationship among the three remains unclear.

Sources

Aulus Gellius. *Noctes Atticae* 1.17.1.
Diogenes Laertius. *Lives of the Eminent Philosophers* 2.26.
Pomeroy, Sarah B. *Goddesses, Whores, Wives, and Slaves: Women in Classical Antiquity.* New York: Schocken Books, 1975, p. 67.

Z

Zenobia, Septimia
(third century C.E.)
Syrian: Syria and Asia Minor
great general and ruler

Septimia Zenobia was a military leader with a talent for strategy, a student of philosophy, and a just ruler. She conquered much of Asia Minor and Egypt before Rome brought an end to her rule. Reported to have been incredibly beautiful, she was dark-complexioned with gleaming white teeth that were said to be like a strand of pearls. Stern in her demeanor, she was an accomplished horsewoman, walked miles with her troops, and enjoyed hunting. She drank with the Persians and the Armenians and often bettered them. She was greatly feared in the East; none dared oppose her.

There is some indication that Zenobia was attracted to Judaism, but she certainly was not a convert. She studied Greek language and literature with the philosopher and rhetorician Cassius Longinus, who became her principal adviser. Never accused of licentiousness, she was said to have had sex with her husband once a month for the purposes of procreation.

Her husband was Septimus Odenathus, who seized power and became ruler of Palmyra. He cleverly exploited Rome's weakness by becoming the main protector of their eastern territories against the Persians, whom he defeated. The emperor Gallienus put him in charge of the Roman army of the East with the title of *imperator*. In 267 C.E. he was assassinated in a dynastic quarrel. It is unclear whether or not Zenobia was implicated in his death; however, she immediately assumed power as guardian for their infant son, Septimus Vaballathus.

In an effort to limit her son's power, the Roman emperor restricted the boy's rule to Palmyra, but Zenobia was regent and continued to exercise control over Syria. As she successfully protected Rome's eastern frontiers, successive emperors bestowed his father's former titles of king of kings, consul, and *imperator* on the young boy. Unlike her husband, Zenobia was not content to act under the authority of Rome. She wanted an independent Palmyra. She exploited Roman disorder after the death of the emperor Claudius Gothicus in 270 by assuming control over Egypt and much of Asia Minor.

In September 271 the emperor Aurelian dispatched an army that retook Egypt. With the war raging, she took a final step toward independent rule. Zenobia declared her son Augustus and herself Augusta. Coins were struck with her image and new title. The war, however, did not go well.

In the early part of 272, Aurelian reconquered Asia Minor and launched an attack on Antioch. Zenobia took part in the battle. Her forces were defeated. She escaped with the remnants of her army to Emesa and then fled to Palmyra. She was captured as she was trying to cross the Euphrates after the city fell. Her life was spared, and she probably was paraded in Aurelian's triumph in Rome.

Sources

Scriptores Historiae Augustae. Aurelian 22.1; 25.1–6; 26.1–6; 27.1–6; 28.1–5; 30.1–4.
———. Gallienus 13.2–3.
———. Tyranni Triginta (Thirty Tyrants) 15.8; 30.1–27.
Downey, Glanville. *A History of Antioch in Syria from Seleucus to the Arab Conquest.* Princeton, N.J.: Princeton University Press, 1961, pp. 263 ff.
Miller, Fergus. "Paul of Samosata, Zenobia and Aurelian: The Church, Local Culture and Political Allegiance in Third-Century Syria." *Journal of Roman Studies* 61 (1971): 1–17.

▣ Zenonis

(?–476 C.E.)   Roman: Constantinople

Augusta

Zenonis supported her husband, Basiliscus, and died with him. Like him, she was of non-Roman background. Married to the brother of the Augusta VERINA, she was also at the center of the treacherous imperial circle around Leo I.

After the death of Leo I, in 474, and his grandson a year later, Zeno became emperor. Verina loathed Zeno. She plotted with Basiliscus to replace him with her lover, Patricius. The plot succeeded. Ariadne and Zeno fled to Isauria in Asia Minor. Basiliscus, however, outmaneuvered Verina and became emperor. He made Zenonis Augusta. He and his wife soon alienated support in the city. They were Monophysites, who believed in the single divine nature of Christ. Basiliscus issued an edict outlawing the orthodox compromise of the Council of Chalcedon, that Christ had two natures, human and divine, separate yet united. Religion and politics were intertwined and, although Monophysites were plentiful in the city, the Compromise of Chalcedon was very popular.

Zenonis took a lover, Armatas, a young dandy and a relative of her husband and persuaded the emperor to appoint him to a high position as Master of Soldiers even though he had no military ability. Former allies turned against Basiliscus. Verina stirred the pot of discontent and funded the return of Zeno and Ariadne. In August 476, as a military force neared the city, Basiliscus fled with Zenonis and their children. They were apprehended, sent to Cappadocia, and killed.

Sources

John Malalas. *Chronicle* XV.
Theophanes. *Chronicle* AM 5967, 5969.
Bury, J. B. *History of the Later Roman Empire: From the Death of Theodosius I to the Death of Justinian.* New York: Dover Publications, Inc., 1958.
Prosopography of the Later Roman Empire. Vol. II. Edited by A. H. M. Jones, J. R. Martindale, and J. Morris. Cambridge: Cambridge University Press, 1971. Reprinted 1992, p. 1,156.

REGISTRY

Acte, Claudia, self-made woman	Roman: Italy	first cent. C.E.
Acutia, convicted conspirator	Roman: Rome	first cent. C.E.
Ada, ruler	Greek: Asia Minor	fourth cent. B.C.E.
Aelia Iunilla, political victim; daughter of **Apicata**	Roman: Rome	?–31 C.E.
Aelia Paetina, political victim; mother of **Antonia (4)**	Roman: Rome	first cent. C.E.
Aemilia (1), condemned priestess; colleagues: **Licinia (4)** and **Marcia (1)**	Roman: Rome	second cent. B.C.E.
Aemilia (2), political wife; daughter of **Caecilia Metella (1);** half sister of **Fausta**	Roman: Rome	first cent. B.C.E.
Aemilia Lepida (1), political wife; mother of **Cornelia (6)**	Roman: Rome	first cent. B.C.E.
Aemilia Lepida (2), unjustly convicted of adultery; daughter of **Cornelia (7);** granddaughter of **Mucia Tertia** and **Junia (1)**	Roman: Rome	first cent. B.C.E.– first cent. C.E.
Aemilia Lepida (3), political victim; daughter of **Julia (7);** mother of **Junia Lepida** and **Junia Calvina;** granddaughter of **Julia (6);** great-granddaughter of **Scribonia**	Roman: Rome	first cent. B.C.E.– first cent. C.E.
Aemilia Lepida (4), duplicitous wife; sister-in-law of **Julia Drusilla (1)**	Roman: Rome	first cent. C.E.
Aemilia Tertia, power broker; mother of **Cornelia (1)** and **Cornelia (2)**	Roman: Rome	second– first cent. B.C.E.
Afriana (Carfania), lawyer	Roman: Rome	?–48 B.C.E.
Agariste (1), mother of the Athenian statesman Cleisthenes	Greek: Sicyon and Athens	sixth cent. B.C.E.

Agariste (2), mother of the Athenian statesman Pericles; granddaughter of **Agariste (1)**	Greek: Athens	c. 520/510 B.C.E.–?
Agariste (3), witness	Greek: Athens	fifth cent. B.C.E.
Agathocleia, adventurer and murderer; daughter of **Oenanthe**	Greek: Samos and Egypt	third cent. B.C.E.
Agesistrata, reformer; daughter of **Archidamia;** mother-in-law of **Agiatis**	Greek: Sparta	?–241 B.C.E.
Agiatis, reformer; daughter-in-law of **Agesistrata**	Greek: Sparta	third cent. B.C.E.
Aglaonice, seer, prophet, astronomer, sorceress	Greek: Thessaly	fourth cent. B.C.E.
Agrippina the Elder, Vipsania, political player and power broker; daughter of **Julia (6);** daughter-in-law of **Antonia the Younger** mother of Julia **Agrippina the Younger, Julia Drusilla,** and **Julia Livilla;** granddaughter of **Scribonia**	Roman: Germany and Rome	c. 14 B.C.E.–33 C.E.
Agrippina the Younger, Julia, Augusta; political player; daughter of **Agrippina the Elder;** sister of **Julia Drusilla** and **Julia Livilla;** great-granddaughter of **Julia (6)**	Roman: Italy	c. 15–59 C.E.
Albina the Elder, Christian ascetic	Roman: Rome	?–338 C.E.
Albina the Younger, wealthy, devout Christian	Roman: Italy, North Africa, Palestine	c. 370s–431 C.E.
Albucilla, alleged conspirator; convicted adulterer	Roman: Italy	first cent. C.E.
Alce, self-made woman	Greek: Athens	fourth cent. B.C.E.
Alexandra, conspirator	Jewish: Judaea	first cent. B.C.E.
Amalasuntha, ruler	Goth: Italy	?–535 C.E.
Amastris, ruler	Persian: Asia Minor	fourth–third cent. B.C.E.
Anastasia (1), political actor	Roman: Italy	?–early fourth cent. C.E.
Anastasia (2), political actor	Roman: Constantinople, Jerusalem	?–early sixth cent. C.E.
Anastasia (3), religious woman	Roman: Constantinople, Egypt	?– 576 C.E.
Ancharia, mother of **Octavia (1)**	Roman: Rome	first cent. B.C.E.

Anteia, Stoic	Roman: Rome	first cent. C.E.
Antigone, political wife; daughter of **Berenice I**	Greek: Macedonia, Egypt, and Epirus	third cent. B.C.E.
Antistia (1), reformer; mother of **Claudia (2)** and **Claudia (3);** grandmother of **Clodia (2)**	Roman: Rome	second cent. B.C.E.
Antistia (2), political victim	Roman: Rome	first cent. B.C.E.
Antistia Pollitta, political victim	Roman: Italy	?–65 C.E.
Antonia (1), captured by pirates	Roman: Rome	first cent. B.C.E.
Antonia (2), adulterer; mother of **Antonia (3)**	Roman: Rome	first cent. B.C.E.
Antonia (3), political wife; daughter of **Antonia (2);** mother of **Pythodoris**	Roman: Rome and Tralles	c. 54/49 B.C.E.–?
Antonia (4), possible conspirator; daughter of **Aelia Paetina**	Roman: Rome	28–66 C.E.
Antonia the Elder, political player; daughter of **Octavia (2);** sister of **Antonia the Younger;** mother of **Domitia (1)** and **Domitia Lepida;** grandmother of Valeria **Messallina**	Roman: Rome	39 B.C.E.–?
Antonia the Younger, Augusta; political player; daughter of **Octavia (2);** mother of Livia Julia Claudia **Livilla;** mother-in-law of **Agrippina the Elder;** grandmother of **Agrippina the Younger;** daughter-in-law of **Livia Drusilla**	Roman: Italy	c. January 31, 36 B.C.E.–May 1, 37 C.E.
Antonia Tryphaena, ruler; daughter of **Pythodoris;** great-granddaughter of **Antonia (2)**	Roman: Asia Minor	first cent. C.E.
Antonina, political actor	Roman: Constantinople	?–sixth cent.
Antye, lyric poet	Greek: Tege	third cent. B.C.E.
Apama (1), progenitor of the Seleucid dynasty	Persian: Persia and Antioch	fourth– third cent. B.C.E.
Apama (2), ruler; daughter of **Stratonice (2);** half sister of Phila (2); sister of **Stratonice (3);** mother of **Berenice II of Cyrene**	Greek: Cyrene	third cent. B.C.E.
Apega, political player	Greek: Sparta	third– second cent. B.C.E.
Apicata, avenger; mother of **Aelia Iunilla**	Roman: Rome	first cent. C.E.

Appuleia Varilla, convicted adulterer; grandniece of **Octavia (2)**	Roman: Rome	first cent. B.C.E.–first cent. C.E.
Apronia, murder victim	Roman: Rome	first cent. C.E.
Arcadia, political actor and celibate Christian	Roman: Constantinople	400–444 C.E.
Archidamia, reformer; mother of **Agesistrata**	Greek: Sparta	third cent. B.C.E.
Archippe (1), political wife	Greek: Athens	sixth–fifth cent. B.C.E.
Archippe (2), self-made woman	Greek: Athens	c. 410 B.C.E.–?
Archo, war victim; sister of **Theoxena**	Greek: Thessaly	second cent. B.C.E.
Aretaphila, avenger	Greek: Cyrene	first cent. B.C.E.
Arete (1), philosopher	Greek: Cyrene and Greece	fifth–fourth cent. B.C.E.
Arete (2), political player; daughter of **Aristomache**	Greek: Syracuse	fourth cent. B.C.E.
Ariadne, Aelia, Augusta	Roman: Dacia, Constantinople	c. 455/456–515 C.E.
Aristomache, political player; mother of **Arete (2)**	Greek: Syracuse	fourth cent. B.C.E.
Arrecina Tertulla, young wife	Roman: Rome	first cent. C.E.
Arria the Elder, Stoic; mother of **Arria the Younger;** grandmother of **Fannia (2)**	Roman: Italy	first cent. C.E.
Arria the Younger, Stoic; daughter of **Arria the Elder;** mother of **Fannia (2)**	Roman: Italy	first cent. C.E.
Arria Fadilla, mother of Antoninus Pius	Roman: Gaul	first–second cent. C.E.
Arsinoë, progenitor of the Ptolemaic line	Greek: Macedonia	fourth cent. B.C.E.
Arsinoë I, political player; daughter of **Nicaea (1);** mother of **Berenice Syra;** sister-in-law of **Arsinoë II Philadelphus**	Greek: Greece and Egypt	300 B.C.E.–?
Arsinoë II Philadelphus, coruler; deified; daughter of **Berenice I;** half sister of **Lysandra** and **Antigone**	Greek: Egypt and Macedonia	c. 316–270 B.C.E.
Arsinoë III Philopator, ruler; daughter of **Berenice II of Cyrene;** killed by **Agathocleia**	third cent. B.C.E.	
Arsinoë Auletes, coruler; insurgent leader; sister of **Cleopatra VII**	Greek: Egypt	65–43/40 B.C.E.
Artacama, political wife	Persian: Persia	fourth cent. B.C.E.

Artemisia I, ruler	Greek: Asia Minor	fifth cent. B.C.E.
Artemisia II, ruler	Greek: Asia Minor	fourth cent. B.C.E.
Artonis, political wife; sister of **Artacama**	Persian: Persia	fourth cent. B.C.E.
Artoria Flaccilla, loyal wife	Roman: Rome	first cent. C.E.
Asella, ascetic	Roman: Rome	c. 334–fifth cent. C.E.
Aspasia, self-made woman	Greek: Athens	fifth cent. B.C.E.
Atia (1), daughter of **Julia (4)**; mother of **Octavia (2)** and the emperor Augustus; stepmother of **Octavia (1)**; sister of **Atia (2)**	Roman: Italy	first cent. B.C.E.
Atia (2), daughter of **Julia 4**; younger sister of **Atia (1)**; mother of **Marcia (3)**	Roman: Italy	first cent. B.C.E.
Atilia, accused adulterer	Roman: Italy	first cent. B.C.E.
Attia Variola, litigant	Roman: Rome	first cent. C.E.
Attica, Caecilia, heiress; daughter of **Pilia;** mother of **Vipsania Agrippina**	Roman: Rome	51 B.C.E.–?
Aurelia (1), mother of **Julia (3), Julia (4),** and Gaius Julius Caesar	Roman: Rome	second–first cent. B.C.E.
Aurelia (2), woman of means	Roman: Rome	first cent. C.E.
Aurelia Orestilla, possible conspirator	Roman: Rome	first cent. B.C.E.
Aurelia Severa, condemned priestess; colleagues **Cannutia Crescentina, Clodia Laeta,** and **Pomponia Rufina**	Roman: Rome	?–213 C.E.
Axiothea (1), philosopher	Greek: Greece	fourth cent. B.C.E.
Axiothea (2), heroine	Greek: Cyprus	fourth cent. B.C.E.
Balbilla, Julia, poet	Greek: Asia Minor	second cent. C.E.
Barsine (1), adventurer	Persian: Asia Minor and Egypt	fourth cent. B.C.E.
Barsine (2), political victim; wife of Alexander the Great; sister of **Drypetis**	Persian: Persia	fourth cent. B.C.E.
Bastia, hard-hearted woman	Roman: Rome	first cent. B.C.E.
Berenice (1), political client; patron of **Antonia the Younger;** daughter of **Salome**	Jewish: Judaea	first cent. B.C.E.– first cent. C.E.

Berenice (2), political player; sister and rival of **Drusilla (2)**	Jewish: Judaea and Rome	first cent. C.E.
Berenice I, political player; deified; mother of **Antigone** and **Arsinoë II Philadelphus**	Greek: Macedonia and Egypt	340–281/271 B.C.E.
Berenice II of Cyrene, ruler; daughter of **Apama (2);** mother of **Arsinoë III Philopator;** granddaughter of **Berenice I**	Greek: Cyrene and Egypt	c. 273–221 B.C.E.
Berenice III Cleopatra, ruler; daughter of **Cleopatra IV** or **Cleopatra V Selene**	Greek: Egypt	second–first cent. B.C.E.
Berenice IV Cleopatra, coruler with **Cleopatra VI Tryphaena**	Greek: Egypt	first cent. B.C.E.
Berenice Syra, ruler; daughter of **Arsinoë I**	Greek: Egypt and Antioch	c. 280–246 B.C.E.
Bilistiche, self-made woman	Greek or Phonecian: Egypt	third cent. B.C.E.
Blaesilla, Christian ascetic	Roman: Rome	c. 383–c. 384 C.E.
Boudicca, ruler of the Iceni	Celtic: Britain	first cent. C.E.
Busa, patriot	Roman: Italy	third cent. B.C.E.
Caecilia, mother of Pliny the Younger	Roman: Italy	first cent. C.E.
Caecilia Metella (1), power broker; mother of **Aemilia (2)** and **Fausta**	Roman: Rome	second–first cent. B.C.E.
Caecilia Metella (2), political player; mother of two consular sons	Roman: Rome	second–first cent. B.C.E.
Caedicia, possible conspirator	Roman: Rome	first cent. C.E.
Caenis Antonia, self-made woman; freedwoman of **Antonia the Younger**	Roman: Rome	?–75 C.E.
Caesaria, devout Christian	Roman: Syria, Alexandria	?–556 C.E.
Calpurnia (1), wife of Julius Caesar	Roman: Rome	first cent. B.C.E.
Calpurnia (2), self-made woman	Roman: Rome	first cent. C.E.
Calpurnia (3), wife of Pliny the Younger	Roman: Rome	first–second cent. C.E.
Calpurnia Hispulla, woman of means; aunt of **Calpurnia (3)**	Roman: Italy	first–second cent. C.E.

Calvia Crispinilla, political survivor	Roman: Rome	first cent. C.E.
Calvina, financial manager	Roman: Italy	first–second cent. C.E.
Cannutia Crescentina, condemned priestess; colleagues; **Aurelia Severa, Clodia Laeta,** and **Pomponia Rufina**	Roman: Rome	?–213 C.E.
Cartimandua, ruler	Brigantian: Britain	first cent. C.E.
Casta Caecilia, acquitted of corruption charge	Roman: Rome	first–second cent. C.E.
Castricia, political player	Roman: Constantinople	?–fifth cent. C.E.
Celerina, Pompeia, wealthy woman; mother-in-law of Pliny the Younger	Roman: Rome	first–second cent. C.E.
Chaerestrate, mother of philosopher Epicurus	Greek: Samos	fourth cent. B.C.E.
Chelidon, office manager	Greek: Sicily	first cent. B.C.E.
Chilonis (1), heroine	Greek: Sparta	seventh cent. B.C.E.
Chilonis (2), heroine	Greek: Sparta	third cent. B.C.E.
Chilonis (3), heroine	Greek: Sparta	third cent. B.C.E.
Chiomara, avenger	Galatian: Asia Minor	fourth cent. B.C.E.
Claudia (1), possibly tried for treason	Roman: Rome	third cent. B.C.E.
Claudia (2), reformer; daughter of **Antistia (1);** sister of **Claudia (3)**	Roman: Rome	second cent. B.C.E.
Claudia (3), priestess; sister of **Claudia (2)**	Roman: Rome	second cent. B.C.E.
Claudia (4), political player; niece of **Clodia (1), Clodia (2),** and **Clodia (3)**	Roman: Rome	first cent. B.C.E.
Claudia (5), political pawn; daughter of **Fulvia (2);** niece of **Clodia (1), Clodia (2),** and **Clodia (3)**	Roman: Rome	53 B.C.E.–?
Claudia (6), member of artistic circle	Roman: Italy	first cent. C.E.
Claudia Pulchra, political player; daughter of Claudia **Marcella the Younger**	Roman: Rome	first cent. C.E.
Cleito, mother of playwright Euripides	Greek: Greece	fifth cent. B.C.E.
Cleoboule, fraud victim; mother of orator Demosthenes	Greek: Athens	c. 407/400 B.C.E.–?
Cleobuline, poet	Greek: Rhodes	sixth cent. B.C.E.
Cleodice, mother of poet Pindar	Greek: Greece	sixth cent. B.C.E.

345

Cleopatra (1), wife of two rulers	Greek: Macedonia	fifth cent. B.C.E.
Cleopatra (2), political player	Greek: Macedonia	fourth cent. B.C.E.
Cleopatra (3), coruler; daughter of **Olympias (1);** sister of Alexander the Great	Greek: Macedonia, Epirus, and Asia Minor	c. 354–308 B.C.E.
Cleopatra (4), self-made woman	Roman: Rome	first cent. C.E.
Cleopatra (5), political client; friend of **Poppaea Sabina (2)**	Roman: Rome	first cent. C.E.
Cleopatra I (the Syrian), ruler; daughter of **Laodice III;** mother of **Cleopatra II Philometor Soteira**	Greek: Asia Minor and Egypt	c. 215–176 B.C.E.
Cleopatra II Philometor Soteira, ruler; daughter of **Cleopatra I (the Syrian);** mother of **Cleopatra III** and **Cleopatra Thea**	Greek: Egypt	c. 185?–115 B.C.E.
Cleopatra III, ruler; daughter of **Cleopatra II Philometor Soteira;** sister of **Cleopatra Thea;** mother of **Cleopatra IV, Cleopatra Tryphaena,** and **Cleopatra V Selene**	Greek: Egypt	c. 165?–101 B.C.E.
Cleopatra IV, insurgent leader; daughter of **Cleopatra III;** sister of **Cleopatra Tryphaena** and **Cleopatra V Selene**	Greek: Egypt and Syria	second cent. B.C.E.
Cleopatra V Selene, political player; daughter of **Cleopatra III;** sister of **Cleopatra IV** and **Cleopatra Tryphaena**	Greek: Egypt and Syria	c. 131/130–69 B.C.E.
Cleopatra VI Tryphaena, coruler with **Berenice IV Cleopatra;** possibly mother of **Cleopatra VII,** and **Arsinoë Auletes**	Greek: Egypt	?–57 B.C.E.
Cleopatra VII, ruler; sister of **Arsinoë Auletes;** mother of **Cleopatra Selene**	Greek: Egypt, Asia Minor, and Italy	c. 69–30 B.C.E.
Cleopatra Selene, coruler; daughter of **Cleopatra VII;** mother of **Drusilla (1)**	Greek: Egypt, Italy, and Mauritania	40 B.C.E.–? C.E.
Cleopatra Thea, coruler; daughter of **Cleopatra II Philometor Soteira**	Greek: Egypt and Syria	second cent. B.C.E.
Cleopatra Tryphaena, military leader; daughter of **Cleopatra III;** sister of **Cleopatra IV** and **Cleopatra V Selene;** niece of **Cleopatra Thea**	Greek: Egypt and Syria	second cent. B.C.E.
Cleora, wife of ruler	Greek: Sparta	fifth–fourth cent. B.C.E.
Clodia (1), political wife; sister of **Clodia (2)** and **Clodia (3)**	Roman: Rome	first cent. B.C.E.

Clodia (2), adventurer; sister of **Clodia (1)** and **Clodia (3)**	Roman: Italy	95–? B.C.E.
Clodia (3), convicted adulterer; sister of **Clodia (1)** and **Clodia (2)**	Roman: Rome	first cent. B.C.E.
Clodia (4), long-lived woman	Roman: Rome	first cent. B.C.E.–first cent. C.E.
Clodia Laeta, condemned priestess; colleagues: **Aurelia Severa, Cannutia Crescentina,** and **Pomponia Rufina**	Roman: Rome	?–213 C.E.
Cloelia (1), heroine	Roman: Rome and Etruria	sixth cent. B.C.E.
Cloelia (2), faultless wife; divorced	Roman: Rome	first cent. B.C.E.
Coesyra, political wife	Greek: Athens	sixth cent. B.C.E.
Constantia	Roman: Italy	361/362–383 C.E.
Constantia, Flavia Julia, Augusta; early Christian; daughter of Flavia Maximiana **Theodora**	Rome: Italy	?–329 C.E.
Constantina, Augusta	Roman: Italy, Asia Minor, Antioch	?–354 C.E.
Corellia Hispulla, litigant	Roman: Italy	first–second cent. C.E.
Corinna, poet	Greek: Tanagra	third cent. B.C.E.
Cornelia (1), political player; elder daughter of **Aemilia Tertia;** sister of **Cornelia (2)**	Roman: Rome	second cent. B.C.E.
Cornelia (2), political player; younger daughter of **Aemilia Tertia;** sister of **Cornelia (1);** mother of **Sempronia (1)**	Roman: Italy	c. 190s–121 B.C.E.
Cornelia (3), great-grandmother of **Livia Drusilla** and great-great-grandmother of Tiberius	Roman: Rome	second–first cent. B.C.E.
Cornelia (4), businesswoman; daughter of **Ilia;** mother of **Pompeia (1)**	Roman: Rome and Italy	second–first cent. B.C.E.
Cornelia (5), brave woman; mother of **Julia (5)**	Roman: Rome	?–68 B.C.E.
Cornelia (6), cultured woman; daughter of **Aemilia Lepida (1)**	Roman: Rome	first cent. B.C.E.
Cornelia (7), political wife; daughter of **Pompeia (2);** daughter-in-law of **Junia (1);** mother of **Aemilia Lepida (2)**	Roman: Rome	c. 46 B.C.E.–?
Cornelia (8), eulogized by poet Propertius; daughter of **Scribonia;** half sister of **Julia (6)**	Roman: Rome	?–16 B.C.E.

Cornelia (9), loyal wife	Roman: Rome	first cent. B.C.E.–first cent. C.E.
Cornelia (10), priestess	Roman: Rome	first cent. C.E.
Cornelia (11), adulterer	Roman: Rome and Germany	first cent. C.E.
Cornelia (12), condemned priestess	Roman: Rome	?–90 C.E.
Cornificia, political victim; daughter of **Annia Galeria Faustina the Younger**	Roman: Rome	?–211 C.E.
Cratesicleia, reformer	Greek: Sparta and Egypt	third cent. B.C.E.
Cratesipolis, ruler	Greek: Sicyon	fourth cent. B.C.E.
Crispina, brave woman	Roman: Rome	first cent. C.E.
Crispina Bruttia, political player; sister-in-law of **Annia Aurelia Galeria Lucilla**	Roman: Rome	second cent. C.E.
Cynane, political player; mother of **Eurydice (2)**	Greek: Macedonia and Asia Minor	?–322 B.C.E.
Cynisca, self-made woman	Greek: Sparta	fourth cent. B.C.E.
Cytheris Volumnia, self-made woman	Roman: Rome	first cent. B.C.E.
Danae, political player; daughter of **Leontion**	Greek: Athens and Syria	third cent. B.C.E.
Deinomache, mother of the Greek general **Alcibiades**	Greek: Athens	fifth cent. B.C.E.
Demarete, political player	Greek: Syracuse	fifth cent. B.C.E.
Domitia, political player; daughter of **Antonia the Elder;** granddaughter of **Octavia (2);** sister of **Domitia Lepida;** aunt of **Valeria Messallina**	Roman: Rome	?–59 C.E.
Domitia Lepida, political player; younger daughter of **Antonia the Elder;** granddaughter of **Octavia (2);** sister of **Domitia;** mother of **Valeria Messallina;** sister-in-law of Julia **Agrippina the Younger**	Roman: Rome	?–54 C.E.
Domitia Longina, Augusta	Roman: Rome	?–c. 140 C.E.
Domitia Lucilla, political player	Roman: Rome	?–155/161 C.E.
Domitia Paulina (1), political player; mother of **Domitia Paulina (2)**	Roman: Spain	first cent. C.E.

Domitia Paulina (2), political player; daughter of **Domitia Paulina (1)** | Roman: Rome | ?–130 C.E.

Domitilla, Flavia (1), mother of emperors | Roman: Italy and North Africa | first cent. C.E.

Domitilla, Flavia (2), political exile; niece of the emperor Domitian | Roman: Italy and Pandateria | first cent. C.E.

Domnica, Augusta | Roman: Pannonia, Constantinople | c. fourth cent. C.E.

Doris, political player; wife, along with **Aristomache,** of Dionysius I | Greek: Syracuse | fifth–fourth cent. B.C.E.

Drusilla (1), political wife; daughter of **Cleopatra Selene;** granddaughter of **Cleopatra VII** | Roman: Mauritania and Judaea | 39 C.E.–?

Drusilla (2), political player; sister and rival of **Berenice (2)** | Jewish: Judaea and Rome | first cent. C.E.

Drypetis, political player; sister of **Barsine (2)** | Persian: Persia | fourth cent. B.C.E.

Duronia, criminal | Roman: Rome | second cent. B.C.E.

Egeria, traveler, devout Christian pilgrim, writer | Roman: Spain, Gaul | c. fourth–early fifth cent. C.E.

Egnatia Maximilla, loyal wife | Roman: Rome | first cent. C.E.

Elpinice, well-known Athenian; daughter of **Hegesipyle** | Greek: Athens | c. 510 B.C.E.–?

Ennia Thrasylla, political player; reputed lover of Gaius Caligula | Roman: Rome | ? B.C.E./C.E.–38 C.E.

Epicharis, conspirator | Roman: Rome | ?–65 C.E.

Erinna, poet | Greek: Telos | fourth cent. B.C.E.

Euboea, political player | Greek: Euboea | third–second cent. B.C.E.

Eudocia, political player | Roman: Italy, Carthage | 438/439–471/472 C.E.

Eudocia, Aelia (Athenais), Augusta | Greek: Athens, Antioch, Constantinople, Jerusalem | c. 400–October 20, 460 C.E.

Eudoxia, Aelia, Augusta | Roman: Constantinople | 380–404 C.E.

Eudoxia, Licinia, Augusta	Roman: Constantinople, Italy, Carthage	422–493? C.E.
Eugraphia, political player	Roman: Constantinople	?–early fifth cent. C.E.
Euphemia (1) (Lupicina), Augusta	Roman: Balkans	?–542 C.E.
Euphemia (2), political pawn	Roman: Constantinople	c. sixth cent. C.E.
Eurydice (1), political player; grandmother of **Cleopatra (3)** and Alexander the Great	Illyrian: Illyria and Macedonia	fourth cent. B.C.E.
Eurydice (2) (Adea), political player; military leader; daughter of **Cynane**	Greek: Macedonia	c. 337–317 B.C.E.
Eurydice (3), political player; military leader; sister of **Nicaea (1)** and **Phila (1);** mother of **Lysandra**	Greek: Macedonia, Egypt, and Miletus	fourth–third cent. B.C.E.
Eurydice (4), political player; daughter of **Nicaea (1);** sister of **Arsinoë I**	Greek: Thrace and Macedonia	fourth–third cent. B.C.E.
Euryleonis, self-made woman	Greek: Sparta	fourth cent. B.C.E.
Eusebia, Augusta	Greco–Roman: Constantinople	?–360 C.E.
Eustochium, ascetic and Christian scholar	Roman: Rome, Bethlehem	c. 396–c. 419/420
Euthydice (Eurydice), political player	Greek: Athens, Cyrene, and Macedonia	fourth–third cent. B.C.E.
Eutropia, Galeria Valeria, wife of co-emperor; early Christian; mother of Flavia Maxima **Fausta**	Roman: Syria, Italy, and Judaea	third–fourth cent. C.E.
Fabia, priestess; half sister of **Terentia (1)**	Roman: Rome	first cent. B.C.E.
Fabiola, founder of the first charity hospital in Europe	Roman: Rome, Palestine	?–c. 399 C.E.
Fadia, ignored wife	Roman: Italy and Greece	first cent. B.C.E.
Fannia (1), litigant	Roman: Rome	first cent. B.C.E.
Fannia (2), Stoic; exiled daughter of **Arria the Younger;** granddaughter of **Arria the Elder**	Roman: Italy	?–107 C.E.

Fausta, political player; daughter of **Caecilia Metella (1);** half sister of **Aemilia (2)**	Roman: Rome	first cent. B.C.E.
Fausta, Flavia Maxima, Augusta; younger daughter of **Eutropia;** daughter-in-law of **Helena Flavia Julia**	Roman: Italy, Gaul, Asia, and North Africa	289/290–324/325 C.E.
Faustina, Aelia Flavia Maxima, Augusta	Roman: Constantinople	fourth cent. C.E.
Faustina the Elder, Annia Galeria, Augusta; mother of Annia Galeria **Faustina the Younger**	Roman: Baetica/ Narbonensis, Italy, and Asia	c. 94–140/141 C.E.
Faustina the Younger, Annia Galeria, Augusta; daughter of Annia Galeria, **Faustina the Elder** mother of Annia Auvelia Galeria **Lucilla**	Roman: Italy, Asia, Gaul, and Germany	125/130–175 C.E.
Flaccilla, Aelia Flavia, Augusta	Roman: Spain, Constantinople	?–386 C.E.
Flora, self-made woman	Roman: Rome	first cent. B.C.E.
Floronia, condemned priestess; colleague: **Opimia**	Roman: Rome	?–216 B.C.E.
Fulvia (1), political player	Roman: Italy	first cent. B.C.E.
Fulvia (2), political player; niece of **Sempronia (2);** mother of **Claudia (5)**	Roman: Italy and Greece	?–40 B.C.E.
Galeria Fundana, political player	Roman: Rome	first cent. C.E.
Galla, political player	Roman: Italy, Constantinople	?–394 C.E.
Gallitta, adulterer	Roman: Rome and Germany	first cent. B.C.E.–first cent. C.E.
Glaphyra (1), political player; grandmother of **Glaphyra (2)**	Greek: Asia Minor	first cent. B.C.E.
Glaphyra (2), adventurer; granddaughter of **Glaphyra (1)**	Greek (probably Roman citizen): Cappadocia and Judaea	first cent. B.C.E.–first cent. C.E.
Glycera, self-made woman	Greek: Athens and Babylon	fourth cent. B.C.E.
Gorgo, patriot	Greek: Sparta	fifth cent. B.C.E.
Gratilla, Stoic	Roman: Rome	first cent. C.E.

Gygaea, political pawn	Greek: Macedonia	fifth cent. B.C.E.
Hagesichora, choral leader	Greek: Sparta	seventh cent. B.C.E.
Hedyto, mother of rhetorican Isocrates	Greek: Athens	fifth cent. B.C.E.
Hegesipyle, mother of **Elpinice** and Athenian statesman Cimon	Thracian: Thrace and Athens	sixth–fifth cent. B.C.E.
Helena, painter	Roman: Egypt, Alexandria	c. late fourth century B.C.E.
Helena Flavia Julia Augusta; early Christian	Roman: Italy, Germany, Judaea, Asia, and Syria	?–327 C.E.
Helena, Flavia Julia (2), Augusta	Roman: Italy, Constantinople, Gaul	?–360 C.E.
Helvia, mother of Marcus Tullius Cicero	Roman: Italy	second–first cent. B.C.E.
Herodias, loyal wife; daughter of **Berenice (1)**	Jewish: Judaea, Italy, and Gaul	first cent. C.E.
Herpyllis, companion of Aristotle	Greek: Greece	fourth cent. B.C.E.
Hipparchia, philosopher	Greek: Greece	fourth–third cent. B.C.E.
Hipparete (1), independent woman; mother of **Hipparete (2);** daughter-in-law of **Elpinice**	Greek: Athens	sixth–fifth cent. B.C.E.
Hipparete (2), rich Athenian; daughter of **Hipparete (1)**	Greek: Athens	?–417/416 B.C.E.
Hispala Faecenia, patriot	Roman: Rome	second cent. B.C.E.
Hispulla, family manager; mother of **Corellia Hispulla**	Roman: Italy	first cent. C.E.
Honoria, Justa Grata, Augusta	Roman: Italy, Constantinople	c. 417/418 C.E.– c. 452 C.E.
Horatia, war victim	Roman: Rome	seventh cent. B.C.E.
Hortensia, orator	Roman: Rome	first cent. B.C.E.
Hydna, patriot	Greek: Scione	fifth cent. B.C.E.
Ilia, mother of **Cornelia (4)**	Roman: Rome	second–first cent. B.C.E.
Ismenodora, self-made woman	Greek: Thespiae	first cent. C.E.

Isodice, loyal wife	Greek: Athens	fifth cent. B.C.E.
Julia (1), brave woman; aunt of Julius Caesar	Roman: Rome	?–68 B.C.E.
Julia (2), power broker; mother of Mark Antony; mother-in-law of **Fulvia (2)** and **Octavia (2)**	Roman: Rome	first cent. B.C.E.
Julia (3), politically well connected; elder sister of **Julia (4);** daughter of **Aurelia (1)**	Roman: Rome	first cent. B.C.E.
Julia (4), witness; daughter of **Aurelia (1);** sister of **Julia (3);** mother of **Atia (1)** and **Atia (2);** grandmother of **Octavia (2)**	Roman: Rome	?–51 B.C.E.
Julia (5), political wife; daughter of **Cornelia (5)**	Roman: Rome	83–54 B.C.E.
Julia (6), political player; daughter of **Scribonia;** mother of Vipsania **Agrippina the Elder** and **Julia (7)**	Roman: Italy, Gaul, and Pandateria	39 B.C.E.–15 C.E.
Julia (7), political victim; daughter of **Julia (6);** elder sister of Vipsania **Agrippina the Elder;** mother of **Aemilia Lepida (3);** daughter-in-law of **Cornelia (8)**	Roman: Italy	19 B.C.E.–28 C.E.
Julia (8), political victim; daughter of Livia Julia Claudia **Livilla;** daughter-in-law of Vipsania **Agrippina the Elder;** granddaughter of **Octavia (2)** and **Livia Drusilla**	Roman: Rome	?–43 C.E.
Julia Aquilia Severa, married priestess	Roman: Rome	third cent. C.E.
Julia Avita Mamaea, power broker; younger daughter of **Julia Maesa;** sister of **Julia Soaemias Bassiana;** niece of **Julia Domna**	Roman: Syria and Italy	?–235 C.E.
Julia Cornelia Paula, Augusta; daughter-in-law of **Julia Soaemias Bassiana**	Roman: Italy	third cent. C.E.
Julia Domna, Augusta; sister of **Julia Maesa;** aunt of **Julia Soaemias Bassiana** and **Julia Avita Mamaea**	Roman: Syria and Italy	second cent.–218 C.E.
Julia Drusilla (1), deified; daughter of Vipsania **Agrippina the Elder;** sister of Julia **Agrippina the Younger** and **Julia Livilla**	Roman: Rome	16–38 C.E.
Julia Drusilla (2), political victim; daughter of **Milonia Caesonia**	Roman: Rome	40–January 24, 41 C.E.
Julia Flavia, Augusta; deified; daughter of **Marcia Furnilla**	Roman: Rome	65–91 C.E.
Julia Livilla, political player; daughter of Vipsania **Agrippina the Elder;** sister of Julia **Agrippina the Younger** and **Julia Drusilla (1)**	Roman: Italy, Germany, and Gaul	18–41 C.E.

Julia Maesa, power broker; sister of **Julia Domna;** mother of **Julia Avita Mamaea** and **Julia Soaemias Bassiana**	Roman: Syria, Asia, and Rome	second cent.–224 C.E.
Julia Phoebe, loyal attendant, freedwoman of **Julia (6)**	Roman: Rome	first cent. B.C.E.–first cent. C.E.
Julia Procilla, murder victim	Roman: Gallia Narbonensis and Rome	?–69 C.E.
Julia Soaemias Bassiana, Augusta; elder daughter of **Julia Maesa;** sister of **Julia Avita Mamaea;** niece of **Julia Domna**	Roman: Syria and Italy	second cent.–222 C.E.
Juliana, Anicia, political player	Roman: Constantinople	c.461–527/528 C.E.
Junia (1), conspirator; daughter of **Servilia (1);** sister of **Junia (2)** and **Junia Tertia**	Roman: Rome	first cent. B.C.E.
Junia (2), political player; daughter of **Servilia (1);** sister of **Junia (1)** and **Junia Tertia;** mother of **Servilia (3)**	Roman: Rome	first cent. B.C.E.
Junia (3), priestess	Roman: Rome	first–second cent. C.E.
Junia Calvina, long-lived woman; daughter of **Aemilia Lepida (3);** sister of **Junia Lepida;** last descendant of Augustus	Roman: Italy	?–79 C.E.
Junia Claudilla, political wife; sister of **Junia Silana**	Roman: Rome	first cent. C.E.
Junia Lepida, political player; daughter of **Aemilia Lepida (3);** sister of **Junia Calvina**	Roman: Italy	first cent. C.E.
Junia Silana, political player; sister of **Junia Claudilla**	Roman: Italy	?–c. 59 C.E.
Junia Tertia, political player; youngest daughter of **Servilia (1);** sister of **Junia (1)** and **Junia (2)**	Roman: Italy	73 B.C.E.–22 C.E.
Junia Torquata, priestess	Roman: Rome	first cent. B.C.E.–first cent. C.E.
Justina, regent	Roman: Gaul, Italy	?–c.391 C.E.
Labda, heroine	Greek: Corinth	seventh cent. B.C.E.
Laelia, orator; mother of two daughters named **Mucia;** grandmother of **Licinia (1)** and **Licinia (2)**	Roman: Rome	second–first cent. B.C.E.
Laïs self-made woman	Greek: Sicily, Corinth, and Thessaly	fifth–fourth cent. B.C.E.

Lamia, flutist	Cyprian: Cyprus and Egypt	fourth–third cent. B.C.E.
Lanassa, political player	Greek: Syracuse, Corcyra, and Greece	fourth–third cent. B.C.E.
Laodice I, ruler	Greek: Syria and Asia Minor	third cent. B.C.E.
Laodice III, philanthropist; mother of **Cleopatra I** (the Syrian)	Persian: Asia Minor and Asia	third–second cent. B.C.E.
Lastheneia, philosopher	Greek: Greece	fourth cent. B.C.E.
Leaena, brave woman	Greek: Athens	sixth cent. B.C.E.
Leontia, political actor	Roman: Constantinople	c. 457 C.E.–?
Leontion, philosopher; mother of **Danae**	Greek: Athens	fourth–third cent. B.C.E.
Licinia (1), convicted murderer along with **Publilia (1)**	Roman: Rome	?–154 B.C.E.
Licinia (2), reformer; elder sister of **Licinia (3)**	Roman: Rome	second cent. B.C.E.
Licinia (3), reformer; younger sister of **Licinia (2)**	Roman: Rome	second cent. B.C.E.
Licinia (4), condemned priestess; colleagues: **Aemilia (1)** and **Marcia (1)**	Roman: Rome	?–113 B.C.E.
Licinia (5), elegant conversationalist; daughter of **Mucia;** sister of **Licinia (6)**	Roman: Rome	first cent. B.C.E.
Licinia (6), elegant conversationalist; daughter of **Mucia;** sister of **Licinia (5)**	Roman: Rome	first cent. B.C.E.
Licinia (7), priestess	Roman: Rome	first cent. B.C.E.
Livia, political wife; mother of **Servilia (1)** and **Servilia (2)**	Roman: Rome	?–92 B.C.E.
Livia Drusilla, power broker; rival of **Octavia (2);** mother-in-law of **Antonia the Younger;** close friend of **Munatia Plancina** and **Urgulania;** friend and patron of **Salome**	Roman: Italy	January 30, 58 B.C.E.–29 C.E.
Livia Ocellina, political player	Roman: Rome	first cent. C.E.
Livia Orestilla, political victim	Roman: Rome	first cent. C.E.
Livilla, Livia Julia Claudia, conspirator; daughter of **Antonia the Younger;** granddaughter of **Octavia (2)** and **Livia Drusilla;** mother of **Julia (8)**	Roman: Rome	c. 13 B.C.E.–31 C.E.

Lollia Paulina, political player	Roman: Italy	first cent. C.E.
Lucilia, mother of Gnaeus Pompeius (Pompey the Great)	Roman: Rome	second–first cent. B.C.E.
Lucilla, Annia Aurelia Galeria, Augusta; daughter of Annia Galeria **Faustina the Younger**	Roman: Asia, Africa, Germany, and Rome	148–182 C.E.
Lucretia, heroine	Roman: Rome	sixth cent. B.C.E.
Lysandra, power broker; daughter of **Eurydice (3);** daughter-in-law of **Thessalonice;** half sister of **Arsinoë II Philadelphus**	Greek: Egypt, Macedonia, and Syria	fourth–third cent. B.C.E.
Marcrina (the Elder), Christian ascetic	Roman: Pontus	c. 270–340 C.E.
Macrina (the Younger), religious leader	Roman: Pontus	c. 327–379/380 C.E.
Maecia Faustina, ruler for son	Roman: Italy and North Africa	third cent. C.E.
Maesia, lawyer	Roman: Umbria and Rome	first cent. B.C.E.
Magia, mother of Virgil	Roman: Italy	first cent. B.C.E.
Mallonia, political victim	Roman: Rome	first cent. C.E.
Marcella, Christian ascetic and scholar	Roman: Rome	?–410 C.E.
Marcella the Elder, Claudia political player; daughter of **Octavia (2);** sister of Claudia **Marcella the Younger**	Roman: Italy	43 B.C.E.–? B.C.E./C.E.
Marcella the Younger, Claudia political wife; daughter of **Octavia (2);** sister of **Marcella the Elder;** mother of **Claudia Pulchra;** mother-in-law of **Domitia Lepida;** grandmother of Valeria **Messallina**	Roman: Rome	39 B.C.E.–? C.E.
Marcellina, Christian, ascetic	Roman: Trier, Rome	c. 330–335–c. 398 C.E.
Marcia (1), condemned priestess; colleagues: **Aemilia (1)** and **Licinia (4)**	Roman: Rome	?–113 B.C.E.
Marcia (2), political wife; stepdaughter of **Atia (1)**	Roman: Rome	first cent. B.C.E.
Marcia (3), patron of the arts; daughter of **Atia (2);** stepniece of **Octavia (2);** mother of Fabia **Numantina;** friend of **Livia Drusilla**	Roman: Italy, Cyprus, Asia, and Spain	first cent. B.C.E.–first cent. C.E.
Marcia (4), conspirator	Roman: Rome	?–193 C.E.
Marcia Furnilla, political wife; mother of **Julia Flavia**	Roman: Rome	first cent. C.E.

Marciana, Ulpia, Augusta; deified; sister-in-law of Pompeia **Plotina;** mother of **Matidia (1)**	Roman: Spain, Germany, Italy, and Asia	?–112 C.E.
Maria, political pawn	Roman: Rome, Ravenna	c. 385–404 C.E.
Marina, ascetic and political actor	Roman: Constantinople	403–449 C.E.
Marsa, political player	Roman: Constantinople	?–early fifth cent. C.E.
Martina, poisoner; friend of **Munatia Plancina**	Syrian: Syria and Italy	? B.C.E.–19/20 C.E.
Matidia (1), Augusta; deified; daughter of Ulpia **Marciana;** mother of Vibia **Sabina** and **Matidia (2)**	Roman: Italy, Asia, and Germany	68–119 C.E.
Matidia (2), never married; wealthy daughter of **Matidia (1);** half sister of Vibia **Sabina**	Roman: Italy, Asia, Germany, and Egypt	first–second cent. C.E.
Melania the Elder, ascetic	Roman: Spain, Italy, Egypt, Palestine	c. 340–c. 410 C.E.
Melania the Younger, ascetic	Roman: Rome, Sicily, Africa, Palestine	c. 383–December 31, 439 C.E.
Melinno, poet	Greek: Italy	second cent. B.C.E.
Melissa, murder victim	Greek: Greece	seventh cent. B.C.E.
Messallina, Valeria, power broker; daughter of **Domitia Lepida;** mother of Claudia **Octavia**	Roman: Rome	c. 20–48 C.E.
Milonia Caesonia, political player; mother of **Julia Drusilla (2);** daughter of **Vistilia**	Roman: Rome	c. 5–41 C.E.
Minervina, lover of Constantine	Roman: Asia	third–fourth cent. C.E.
Minucia, convicted priestess	Roman: Rome	?–337 B.C.E.
Monica, devout Christian	Roman: Africa, Italy	c. 333–387 C.E.
Mucia, elegant speaker; daughter of **Laelia;** mother of **Licinia (5)** and **Licinia (6)**	Roman: Italy	second–first cent. B.C.E.
Mucia Tertia, power broker; mother of **Pompeia (2)**	Roman: Italy	first cent. B.C.E.
Mummia Achaica, mother of emperor Servius Sulpicius Galba	Roman: Rome	first cent. B.C.E.–first cent. C.E.

Munatia Plancina, political player; close friend of **Livia Drusilla**	Roman: Italy, Asia, and Syria	?–33 C.E.
Musa, Thea Urania, ruler	Italian: Italy and Parthia	first cent. B.C.E.– first cent. C.E.
Mutilia Prisca, political victim; friend of **Livia Drusilla**	Roman: Rome	? B.C.E.–30 C.E.
Myrrhine, loyal wife	Greek: Athens and Asia Minor	sixth–fifth cent. B.C.E.
Myrtis, poet	Greek: Greece	fifth cent. B.C.E.?
Myrto, wife of philosopher Socrates	Greek: Athens	fifth– fourth cent. B.C.E.
Neaera, self-made woman; mother of Phano	Greek: Corinth and Athens	fourth cent. B.C.E.
Nicaea (1), political pawn; sister of **Phila (1)** and **Eurydice (3);** mother of **Arsinoë I**	Greek: Macedonia and Thrace	fourth cent. B.C.E.
Nicaea (2), ruler	Greek: Corinth	third cent. B.C.E.
Nicopolis, self-made woman	Roman: Rome	second cent. B.C.E.
Nossis, poet	Greek: Locri	third cent. B.C.E.
Numantina, Fabia, litigant; daughter of **Marcia (3);** granddaughter of **Atia (2)**	Roman: Rome	first cent. C.E.
Occia, priestess	Roman: Rome	? B.C.E.–19 C.E.
Octavia (1), half sister of **Octavia (2)** and Augustus; daughter of **Ancharia;** grandmother of **Appuleia Varilla**	Roman: Rome	first cent. B.C.E.
Octavia (2), power broker; daughter of **Atia (1);** mother of Claudia **Marcella the Elder, Marcella the Younger, Antonia the Elder,** and **Antonia the Younger**	Roman: Italy and Greece	69–11 B.C.E.
Octavia, Claudia, faultless wife; banished; daughter of Valeria **Messallina**	Roman: Italy	39/40–62 C.E.
Oculata and her sister of the same name, convicted priestesses; colleague: **Varronilla**	Roman: Rome	first cent. C.E.
Oenanthe, conspirator and murderer; mother of **Agathocleia**	Greek: Samos and Egypt	third cent. B.C.E.
Olympias (1), ruler; mother of **Cleopatra (3)** and Alexander the Great	Greek: Epirus and Macedonia	fourth cent. B.C.E.

Olympias (2), ruler; mother of **Phthia**	Greek: Epirus	third cent. B.C.E.
Olympias (3), religious leader	Roman: Constantinople, Asia Minor	c. 361–fifth cent. C.E.
Opimia, condemned priestess; colleague: **Floronia**	Roman: Rome	?–216 B.C.E.
Orbiana, Augusta; exiled and murdered	Roman: Italy and Libya	third cent. C.E.
Papiria, divorced, financially strapped noblewoman	Roman: Rome	third–second cent. B.C.E.
Paula the Elder, ascetic, Christian scholar	Roman: Rome, Bethlehem	347–January 26, 404 C.E.
Paula the Younger, ascetic, head of a monastery	Roman: Rome, Bethlehem	c. 402–? C.E.
Paulina, victim of deception	Roman: Rome	first cent. C.E.
Paxaea, charged with treason and extortion	Roman: Italy and the Balkans	first cent. C.E.
Perictione, mother of **Potone** and Plato	Greek: Athens	fifth cent. B.C.E.
Perpetua, Vibia, martyr	Roman: Carthage, North Africa	181–203 C.E.
Petronia, political player	Roman: Rome	first cent. C.E.
Phaenarete, mother of Socrates	Greek: Athens	fifth cent. B.C.E.
Phila (1), wise and loyal wife; sister of **Nicaea (1)** and **Eurydice (3);** mother of **Stratonice (2)**	Greek: Macedonia	c. 351–283 B.C.E.
Phila (2), power broker; daughter of **Stratonice (2);** half sister of **Stratonice (3)** and **Apama (2)**	Greek: Asia, Asia Minor, and Macedonia	third cent. B.C.E.
Philesia, wife of philosopher Xenophon	Greek: Athens, Sparta, and Corinth	fifth–fourth cent. B.C.E.
Philinna, cowife of Philip II; **Olympias (1)**	Greek: Thessaly and Macedonia	fourth cent. B.C.E.
Phryne, self-made woman	Greek: Greece	fifth cent. B.C.E.
Phthia, coruler; daughter of **Olympias (2)**	Greek: Epirus and Macedonia	third cent. B.C.E.

Pilia, loyal wife and friend; mother of Caecilia **Attica**	Roman: Rome and Italy	first cent. B.C.E.
Pipa (Pipara), young lover	German: Germany and Italy	third cent. C.E.
Placidia, politial actor	Roman: Rome, Carthage, Constantinople	c. 439/443–? C.E.
Placidia, Aelia Galla, Augusta	Roman: Constantinople, Spain, Gaul, Italy	388/390–November 27, 450 C.E.
Plangon, independent woman	Greek: Athens	404 B.C.E.–?
Plathane, wife of rhetorician Isocrates	Greek: Athens	fifth–fourth cent. B.C.E.
Plautia Urgulanilla, political player; granddaughter of **Urgulania**	Roman: Italy	first cent. B.C.E.–first cent. C.E.
Plautilla, Augusta; banished and executed	Roman: Italy and Lipara	second–third cent. C.E.
Plotina, Pompeia, Augusta; sister-in-law of Ulpia **Marciana;** aunt of **Matidia (1);** great-aunt of Vibia **Sabina** and **Matidia (2)**	Roman: Gaul, Italy, Asia, Egypt, Germany, Syria, and Greece	first–second cent. C.E.
Pompeia (1), political wife; daughter of **Cornelia (4)**	Roman: Rome	first cent. B.C.E.
Pompeia (2), political wife; daughter of **Mucia Tertia;** mother of **Cornelia (7)**	Roman: Italy	first cent. B.C.E.
Pompeia Macrina, conspirator	Roman Greek: Lesbos and Sparta	first cent. C.E.
Pompeia Paulina, political victim	Roman: Italy	first cent. C.E.
Pomponia (1), mother of Publius Cornelius Scipio Africanus	Roman: Rome	third–second cent. B.C.E.
Pomponia (2), angry wife	Roman: Italy	first cent. B.C.E.
Pomponia Galla, disinherited her son	Roman: Italy	first cent. C.E.
Pomponia Graecina, political player; friend of **Julia (8)**	Roman: Italy	?–c. 83 C.E.
Pomponia Rufina, convicted priestess; colleagues: **Aurelia Severa, Cannutia Crescentina,** and **Clodia Laeta**	Roman: Rome	?–213 C.E.

Popilia, loyal wife; honored in public	Roman: Rome	?–102 B.C.E.
Poppaea Sabina (1), political player; mother of **Poppaea Sabina (2)**	Roman: Italy	?–47 C.E.
Poppaea Sabina (2); Augusta; daughter of **Poppaea Sabina (1)**	Roman: Italy	31?–65 C.E.
Porcia, political player; daughter of **Atilia**	Roman: Italy	?–43 B.C.E.
Potone, sister of philosopher Plato, daughter of **Perictione**	Greek: Athens	fifth–fourth cent. B.C.E.
Praecia, self-made woman; political player	Roman: Rome	first cent. B.C.E.
Praxilla, poet	Greek: Sicyon	fifth cent. B.C.E.
Prisca, politically influential wife of emperor; early Christian sympathizer; mother of **Valeria (2)**	Roman: Balkans, Syria, Italy, Asia, and Greece	third cent.–c. 316 C.E.
Proba, Anicia Faltonia, founder of a monastery	Roman: Rome, Carthage	?–c. 432 C.E.
Proba, Faltonia Betitia, Christian poet	Roman: Rome	c. 320–c. 370 C.E.
Publilia (1), convicted murderer along with **Licinia (1)**	Roman: Italy	second cent. B.C.E.
Publilia (2), ill-used second wife of Marcus Tullius Cicero	Roman: Italy	first cent. B.C.E.
Pudentilla, Aemilia, independent woman	Roman: North Africa	second cent. C.E.
Pulcheria, Aelia, Augusta	Roman: Constantinople	January 19, 399–July 453 C.E.
Pythias, wife of Aristotle	Greek: Asia Minor	?–c. 335 B.C.E.
Pythodoris, Roman client ruler; daughter of **Antonia (3);** granddaughter of **Antonia (2);** mother of **Antonia Tryphaena**	Roman: Asia	first cent. B.C.E.–first cent. C.E.
Pythonice, self-made woman	Greek: Greece, Asia Minor, and Babylon	fourth cent. B.C.E.
Quarta Hostilia, convicted murderer	Roman: Rome	?–c. 179 B.C.E.
Rhea, devoted mother	Roman: Italy	second–first cent. B.C.E.
Rhodopis, self-made woman	Thracian: Samos and Egypt	sixth cent. B.C.E.

Roxane, political player; wife of Alexander the Great; daughter-in-law of **Olympias (1)**; sister-in-law of **Cleopatra (3)**	Persian: Asia Minor and Greece	?–313 B.C.E.
Rubria, priestess	Roman: Rome	first cent. C.E.
Sabina, Vibia, Augusta; daughter of **Matidia (1)**; half sister of **Matidia (2)**	Roman: Greece, Italy, Britain, Asia, Syria, Palestine, and Egypt	c. 87/88–136 C.E.
Salome, client and friend of **Livia Drusilla;** mother of **Berenice (1)**	Jewish: Judaea	first cent. B.C.E.– first cent. C.E.
Salonina, Cornelia, Augusta	Greek: Asia Minor and Italy	third cent. C.E.
Salvina (Silvina), Christian woman	Moor/Roman; Africa, Constantinople	?–c. 404 C.E.
Sancia, convicted of treason	Roman: Rome	? B.C.E.–33 C.E.
Sappho, poet	Greek: Lesbos, Sicily	c. 612 B.C.E.–?
Sassia, victim	Roman: Italy	first cent. B.C.E.
Satria Galla, political player	Roman: Rome	first cent. C.E.
Scribonia, political player; mother of **Cornelia (8)** and **Julia (6)**; grandmother of **Julia (7)** and Vipsania **Agrippina the Elder**	Roman: Italy	70 B.C.E.–? C.E.
Sempronia (1), political player; daughter of **Cornelia (2)**; granddaughter of **Aemilia Tertia**	Roman: Italy	second cent. B.C.E.
Sempronia (2), possible conspirator	Roman: Rome	first cent. B.C.E.
Serena, political player	Roman: Rome, Constantinople	?–December 408 C.E.
Servilia (1), power broker; daughter of **Livia;** mother of **Junia (1)**, **Junia (2)**, **Junia Tertia,** and Marcus Junius Brutus	Roman: Italy	first cent. B.C.E.
Servilia (2), political wife; sister of **Servilia (1)**; aunt of **Junia (1)**, **Junia (2)**, and **Junia Tertia**	Roman: Italy, Asia, Rhodes	first cent. B.C.E.
Servilia (3), political wife; daughter of **Junia (2)**; granddaughter of **Servilia (1)**; niece of **Junia (1)** and **Junia Tertia**	Roman: Italy	first cent. B.C.E.

Servilia (4), victim	Roman: Rome	c. 46–66 C.E.
Sextia (1), committed suicide; political victim	Roman: Rome	? B.C.E.–34 C.E.
Sextia (2), political victim; grandmother of **Antistia Pollita**	Roman: Italy	?–65 C.E.
Sextilia, independent woman; Augusta	Roman: Italy	?–c. 69 C.E.
Silia, exile	Roman: Italy	first cent. C.E.
Sosia Gallia, exile	Roman: Italy, Asia, Germany (?)	? B.C.E.–c. 24 C.E.
Sosipatra, philosopher	Roman: Ephesus, Pergamum	c. late fourth cent. C.E.
Statilia, political survivor	Roman: Italy, Asia, Samos	26 B.C.E.–? C.E.
Statilia Messallina, political player	Roman: Italy	first cent. C.E.
Stratonice (1), political wife	Greek: Macedonia and Thrace	fifth cent. B.C.E.
Stratonice (2), political wife and player; daughter of **Phila (1)**; mother of **Phila (2), Stratonice (3),** and **Apama (2)**	Greek: Macedonia and Asia	?–254 B.C.E.
Stratonice (3), political leader; daughter of **Stratonice (2)**; sister of **Apama (2)**; half sister of **Phila (2)**	Greek: Asia and Macedonia	third cent. B.C.E.
Sulpicia (1), poet	Roman: Rome	first cent. B.C.E.
Sulpicia (2), poet	Roman: Italy	?–94/98 C.E.
Syncletica, ascetic	Roman: Egypt	c. fourth cent. C.E.
Tanaquil, heroine	Etruscan: Rome	seventh–sixth cent. B.C.E.
Telesilla, poet and military leader	Greek: Greece	fifth cent. B.C.E.
Terentia (1), financial manager; mother of **Tullia (2)**; half sister of **Fabia**	Roman: Italy	first cent. B.C.E.
Terentia (2), literary patron; reputed lover of Augustus	Roman: Rome	first cent. B.C.E.–? C.E.
Tettia Etrusc, virtuous wife	Roman: Italy and Asia (?)	?–60 C.E.
Teuta, ruler	Greek: Illyricum	third cent. B.C.E.
Thaïs, self-made woman; wife of Ptolemy I Soter	Greek: Athens, Asia, and Egypt	fourth cent. B.C.E.

Thebe, avenger	Greek: Pherae and Thessaly	fourth cent. B.C.E.
Themista, philosopher	Greek: Athens	fourth– third cent. B.C.E.
Theodora, Augusta	Roman: Cyprus, Constantinople	?–June 28, 548 C.E.
Theodora, Flavia Maximiana, Augusta; possible daughter of Galeria Valeria **Eutropia; mother of Flavia Julia Constantia**	Roman: Italy, Britain, Gaul, Spain, and Germany	third–fourth cent. C.E.
Theoxena, heroine; sister of Archo	Greek: Thessaly and Macedonia	third– second cent. B.C.E.
Thermantia, Aemilia Materna, political pawn	Roman: Rome, Italy	?–July 30, 415 C.E.
Thessalonice, ruler; stepdaughter of **Olympias (1);** half sister of **Cleopatra (3)** and Alexander the Great	Greek: Thessaly and Macedonia	c. 346/340– 298/294 B.C.E.
Timaea, wife of Agis II; lover of Alcibiades	Greek: Sparta	fifth cent. B.C.E.
Timandra, faithful lover of Alcibiades; mother of **Laïs**	Greek: Sicily and Greece	fifth– fourth cent. B.C.E.
Timo, heroine	Greek: Greek Islands	sixth–fifth cent. B.C.E.
Timocleia, avenger	Greek: Thebes	fourth cent. B.C.E.
Triaria, political player	Roman: Italy	first cent. C.E.
Tullia (1), political player	Roman: Rome	sixth cent. B.C.E.
Tullia (2), victim; daughter of **Terentia (1)** and Marcus Tullius Cicero	Roman: Italy	c. 79–49 B.C.E.
Urgulania, political player; close friend of **Livia Drusilla;** grandmother of **Plautia Urgulanilla**	Roman: Italy	first cent. B.C.E.– first cent. C.E.
Valeria (1), self-made woman	Roman: Rome	first cent. B.C.E.
Valeria (2), Augusta; exiled and murdered along with her mother **Prisca**	Roman: Germany, Dalmatia, Syria, Asia (?), and Italy	third– fourth cent. B.C.E.
Varronilla, condemned priestess; colleagues: **Oculata** sisters	Roman: Rome	?–83 C.E.
Verania, credulous victim	Roman: Italy	first cent. C.E.
Verginia (1), heroine	Roman: Rome	fifth cent. B.C.E.

Verginia (2), reformer	Roman: Rome	fourth–third cent. B.C.E.
Verina (Aelia), Augusta	Roman: Constantinople	?–484 C.E.
Vespasia Polla, mother of the emperor Vespasian	Roman: Italy	first cent. B.C.E.–first cent. C.E.
Vibidia, priestess	Roman: Rome	first cent. C.E.
Victoria (Vitruvia), Augusta; governor of Gaul	Roman: Gaul	third cent. C.E.
Vipsania Agrippina, wealthy woman; daughter of Caecilia **Attica**	Roman: Rome	33 B.C.E.–20 C.E.
Vistilia, much married woman; mother of **Milonia Caesonia**	Roman: Italy	first cent. B.C.E.–? C.E.
Vitia, convicted of treason; mother-in-law of **Mutilia Prisca**	Roman: Rome	? B.C.E.–32 C.E.
Xanthippe, wife of Socrates	Greek: Athens	fifth cent. B.C.E.
Zenobia, Septimia, great general and ruler	Syrian: Syria and Asia Minor	third cent. C.E.
Zenonis, Augusta	Roman: Constantinople	?–476 C.E.

GLOSSARY

aedile   Roman magistrate responsible for overseeing public order, the food supply, the markets, and public games

Aeneas   Mythological Trojan leader whom the Augustan poet Virgil credited with the founding of Rome in the *Aeneid*

archon   a chief magistrate in a Greek city-state

Atellan farce   Latin bawdy comedy performed in the country and on the streets

augur   Roman priest who interpreted omens

Augusta   Highest imperial title for a woman during the Roman Empire

Augustus   Title conferred on the leader of the Roman Empire after 27 B.C.E.

Bona Dea   Roman goddess of chastity and fertility, whose rites were restricted to well-born Roman women

censor   Roman official who registered citizens

Centumviral Court   Roman board of judges that decided civil suits, especially inheritance

centurion   Professional officer in the Roman army

civic tribune   Official or military commander who administered civil affairs in large cities in the later Roman Empire

client   Free person allied with some more powerful man, woman, or family in a relationship with mutual responsibilities and obligations

client-king   Independent ruler under the authority of a more powerful ruler

Concordia   Goddess of peace and harmony

consuls   Either of two highest civil and judicial magistrates of Rome, elected annually

consul designate   Consul-elect during period between election in August and assumption of office on January 1

consul suffectus   Consul chosen to complete another consul's term

Cynic   Follower of a Greek philosophy that preached a life of virtue lived with few material possessions

decemviri   Early Roman court of noblemen

deme   Main local political unit in Attica; membership was hereditary

dictator   Roman magistrate given unlimited but temporary emergency powers

diva/divus   Goddess or god

docta puella   Well-educated and well-spoken woman, in Latin

drachma   Greek monetary unit or coin

Epicureanism   Greek philosophy that emphasized the physical and sense-based aspects of the world

eques, equites   Wealthy landowning and commercial families that constituted the highest Roman order after the senators

fasces   Bundle of elm or beechwood rods bound together with an ax that symbolized Roman magisterial authority

Flavians   Roman emperors of the Flavian family, from Titus through Domitian, 69–96 C.E.

freedman, freedwoman   Emancipated slave

Ides of March   March 15

imperator   Originally a Roman title for military commander, bestowed by troops after victory; came to denote the emperor's supreme military power

imperium   Power vested in Roman magistrates

Julio-Claudians   Members of the Julian and Claudian families, who ruled Rome from the time of Livia and Augustus, 27 B.C.E., until the death of Nero in 68 C.E.

legate   Deputy or staff member of a military commander, provincial governor, or emperor

legion   Roman army unit consisting of 4,200–6,000 troops, in 10 cohorts of foot soldiers and 300 cavalrymen

lex Falcidia   Roman law of 40 B.C.E. limiting the amount of an estate that could be willed to nonheirs through legacies; stipulated that the heir must receive at least one-quarter of the estate

lictors   Attendant of Roman magistrates

magistrate   General designation for all elected Roman officials except tribunes

military tribune   Any one of six most senior officers of a Roman legion, each assumed command for a two-month period

mina   Greek monetary unit equal to 100 drachmas

Neoplatonism   Reinterpretation of Platonic philosophy begun by Plotinus during third century C.E.

noble   Roman who had consul(s) in the family

obverse/reverse   Front/back of coins; the obverse usually bears a portrait

optimates   Roman faction that favored conservative, aristocratic interests

patrician   Member of one of the original aristocratic families of Rome

pax deorum   Literally, "Peace of the gods": Roman concept of harmonious relations between humans and divinities

phratry   Hereditary Greek social group with jurisdiction over various matters including citizenship and inheritance

plebeian/pleb   Free-born Roman who was not a patrician

pontifex maximus   Leading priestly official during the Roman republic; became the equivalent of high priest during the reign of Augustus; afterward was routinely included among imperial offices and titles

praetor   High Roman magistrate whose duties included presiding over criminal courts, administering provinces, and leading armies

Praetorian Guard   Military bodyguard of the emperor and his family

prefect of Egypt   Roman governor of Egypt beginning with the reign of Augustus

proconsul/propraetor   Former consul or praetor who was appointed as provincial governor or military commander; as imperial agent, duties included collecting taxes, civil administration, paying and provisioning troops, and administering justice

proscription   Process of publicly declaring certain Roman citizens outlaws and making their property liable to confiscation

quaestio   Roman court established to investigate and try criminal cases; a praetor presided over a panel of 30 or more jurors

quaestor   Magistrate who oversaw finances in Rome and the provinces

satrap   Persian title for governor of a territory called a satrapy

sestertium, sesterces   Small Roman silver coin

sophist   Traveling lecturer or teacher who expressed many of the most advanced and controversial ideas in the Greek world during the fifth and fourth centuries B.C.E.

Stoic Practitioner of a philosophy that stressed the importance of virtue and reason

talent Greek monetary unit equal to 60 minas

toga virilis White garment worn by free-born Roman males

tribune of the plebs Any one of 10 representatives of the Roman people elected annually to defend against illegal and abusive acts by patricians; office and person of the tribunes were sacrosanct

tribunicia potestas Public power exercised by a tribune

triumph Roman military commander's public celebration of victory, including a parade to the temple of Jupiter on the Capitol

triumvir Literally, "One of the three men": denoting member of a personal alliance aimed at gaining political supremacy in Rome during the Republic

tutor Roman citizen acting as guardian and financial administrator for a minor, a woman, or another person who lacked right to transact legal and business affairs

tyrant Usurper of rule in a Greek city-state, often with support of the people against the aristocracy

Vesta Roman goddess of the hearth

Vestal Virgin Priestess of Vesta charged with keeping Rome's sacred hearth flame burning; usually selected from senatorial families; had to remain virgin during her 30 or more years of service on pain of death

vigiles Police and fire brigade of city of Rome

BIBLIOGRAPHY

A. Ancient Authors

Ammiamus Marcellinus	
Andocides	*On the Mysteries*
Appian	*Roman History: Bella civilia (Civil Wars), Syrian Wars*
Apuleius	*Apologia*
	Metamorphoses (The Golden Ass)
Aristotle	*Politics*
Arrian	*Anabasis of Alexander*
	Successors
Asconius	Commentary on Cicero's *Pro Milone*
Athenaeus	*Deipnosophistae*
Augustine	*Confessions*
	Letters
Aulus Gellius	*Noctes Atticae*
Cassiodorus	*Variae*
Catullus	Poems
Cicero	*Brutus, De amicitia, De domo sua, De lege agraria, De oratores, Epistulae ad Atticum, Epistulae ad Brutum, Epistulae ad familiares, Epistulae ad Quintum fratrem, In Catalinum, In Verrum, Orationes Philippicae, Pro Caelio, Pro Cluentio, Pro Milone*
Demosthenes	*In Neaeram*
	Private Orations
Dio Cassius	*Roman History*
Diodorus Siculus	*Library of History*
Diogenes Laertius	*Lives of the Eminent Philosophers*
	Epitome Caesaris
Egeria	*Diary of a Pilgrimage*
Eunapius	*Lives of the Sophists*
Eusebius	*Vita Constantini*
Eutropius	*Breviarium ab urbe condita*
Fronto	*Epistulae*

Gerontius	*The Life of Melania the Younger*
Herodian	*History of the Empire*
Herodotus	*The Persian Wars*
Horace	*Odes*
Isaeus	Speeches of Isaeus
Jerome	*Letters*
John Malalas	*Chronicle*
Jordanes	*Getica (Gothic History)*
Josephus	*Antiquitates Judaicae (Jewish Antiquities)*
	Bellum Judaicum (Jewish Wars)
	Vitae
Justin	*Epitome*
Juvenal	*Satires*
Lactantius	*De Mortibus Persecutorum*
Livy	*From the Founding of the City* (vols. 1–14), including the *Epitomae* and *Periochae*
Lucan	*Pharsalia*
Macrobius	*Saturnalia*
Malchus	*Fragments*
Martial	*Epigrammata*
Nepos	*Atticus*
	Cimon
	Letter of Cornelia
Olympiodorus	*Fragments*
Orosius	*Seven Books of History Against the Pagans*
Ovid	*Amores*
Palladius	*The Lausiac History*
	Dialogue
Pausanias	*Description of Greece*
Perpetua	*Passion of SS. Perpetua and Felicity*
Plato	*Alcibiades*
	Charmides
	Epistulae
	Gorgias
	Menexemus
	Meno
Pliny the Elder	*Naturalis Historia*
Pliny the Younger	*Epistulae*
	Panegyricus
Plutarch	*Moralia: Amatorius, De fortunata Romanorum, De liberis educandis, De mulierum virtutibus, Quaestiones Graecae, Quaestions Romanae, Vitae Parallelae (Parallel Lives): Aemilius Paulus, Agesilaus, Agis, Alcibiades, Alexander, Antonius, Aratus, Brutus, Caesar, Cato Minor, Cicero, Cimon, Cleomenes, Crassus, Demetrius, Demosthenes, Dion, Eumenes, Gaius Gracchus, Lucullus, Marius, Nicias, Pelopidas, Pericles, Phocion, Pompeius, Pyrrhus, Sertorius, Sulla, Themistocles, Tiberius Gracchus*
Polyaenus	*Strategemata*

Polybius	*Histories*
Priscus	*Fragments*
Procopius	*Buildings*
	Gothic Wars
	Persian Wars
	Vandal Wars
	Secret History
Propertius	*Elegies*
Pseudo-Athanasius	*Life of the Blessed and Holy Syncletica*
Quintilian	*Institutio Oratoria*
Sallust	*Bellum Catilinae*
Scriptores Historiae Augustae	Alexander Severus, Antoninus Pius, Aurelian, Commodus, Didius Julianus, Gallienus, Gordian, Hadrian, Marcus Aurelius Antoninus (Caracalla), Marcus Aurelius Antoninus (Marcus Aurelius), Maximinus, Pertinax, Tyranni Triginta (Thirty Tyrants)
Seneca	*Ad Marciam de consolatione*
	De beneficiis
	Epistulae
Severus of Antioch	*Letters*
Socrates	*Historia Ecclesiastica*
Sozomen	*Historia Ecclesiastica*
Statius	*Silvae*
Strabo	*Geography*
Suetonius	*The Lives of the Caesars: Augustus, Caesar, Claudius, Domitian, Gaius Caligula, Galba, Nero, Otho, Tiberius, Titus, Vespasian, Vitellius*
	The Lives of Illustrious Men: De grammaticis (Grammarians), Virgil
Tacitus	*Agricola*
	Annales
	Historiae
Theophanes	*Chronicle*
Thucydides	*History of the Peloponnesian War*
Ulpian	*The Civil Law*
Valerius Maximus	*Factorum ac dictorum memorabilium libri IX*
Valleius Paterculus	*Historiae Romanae libri II*
Xenophon	*The Hellenica*
	The Anabasis of Cyrus
Zonaras	*Annales*
Zosimus	*New History (Historia Nova)*

B. Modern Authors

Alfoldi, Andros. *Early Rome and the Latins.* Ann Arbor: University of Michigan Press, 1965.

Babcock, Charles L. "The Early Career of Fulvia." *American Journal of Philology* 86 (1965): 1–32.

Balsdon, J. P. V. D. *Roman Women.* New York: John Day Comp., 1963.

Barnes, Timothy. *Constantine and Eusebius.* Cambridge: Harvard University Press, 1981.

———. *The New Empire of Diocletian and Constantine.* Cambridge: Harvard University Press, 1982.

Barrett, Anthony. *Livia: First Lady of Imperial Rome.* New Haven, Conn.: Yale University Press, 2002.

————. *Agrippina: Sex, Power, and Politics in the Early Empire.* New Haven, Conn.: Yale University Press, 1996.

Bauman, Richard A. *Women and Politics in Ancient Rome.* London: Routledge, 1994.

Berger, Adolf. *Encyclopedic Dictionary of Roman Law.* Philadelphia: American Philosophical Society, 1953.

Best, E. E. "Cicero, Livy and Educated Roman Women." *Classical Journal* 65 (1970): 199–204.

Bevan, Edwyn B. *The House of Selecus.* 2 vols. London: Edward Arnold, 1902.

Bing, Peter. *Games of Venus: An Anthology of Greek and Roman Erotic Verse from Sappho to Ovid.* New York: Routledge, Chapman and Hall, 1993.

Birley, Anthony Richard. *Marcus Aurelius: Emperor of Rome.* Boston: Little Brown, 1966.

————. *Septimius Severus: The African Emperor.* New Haven, Conn.: Yale University Press, 1989.

Blundell, Sue. *Women in Ancient Greece.* London: British Museum Press, 1995.

Bowie, E. L. "Greek Poetry in the Antonine Age." In *Antonine Literature,* ed. by D. A. Russell. Oxford: Clarendon Press, 1990.

Bowra, C. M. *Greek Lyric Poetry from Alcman to Simonides.* 2d ed. Oxford: Clarendon Press, 1967.

————. "Melinno's Hymn to Rome." *Journal of Roman History* 47 (1957): 21–28.

Brill's New Pauly: Encyclopedia of the Ancient World: Classical Tradition. Edited by Manfred Landfester, in collaboration with Hubert Canick and Helmut Schneider. Leiden, Boston: Brill, 2006.

Brown, Peter. *Augustine of Hippo: A Biography.* Berkeley: University of California Press, 2000.

Brown, P. R. L. "Aspects of Christianization of the Roman Aristocracy." *The Journal of Early Christian Studies* 51, parts 1 and 2 (1961): 1–11.

Burn, Andrew Robert. *Alexander the Great and the Hellenistic World.* London: English Universities Press, 1964.

————. *Persia and the Greeks: The Defense of the West, c. 546–478 B.C.* New York: St. Martin's Press, 1962.

Burstein, Stanley Mayer. "Arsinoe II Philadelphos: A Revisionist View." In *Philip II, Alexander the Great, and the Macedonian Heritage,* ed. by W. Lindsay Adams and Eugene N. Borza. Washington, D.C.: University Press of America, 1982.

————. *The Reign of Cleopatra.* Westport, Conn.: Greenwood Press, 2004.

Bury, J. B. *History of the Later Roman Empire: From the Death of Theodosius I to the Death of Justinian.* 2 vols. New York: Dover Publications Inc., 1958.

————. "Justa Grata Honoria." *Journal of Roman Studies* 9 (1919): 1–13.

————. *The Cambridge Ancient History.* 3d. ed. New York: Cambridge University Press, 1970– .

Cameron, Alan. "The Empress and the Poet: Paganism and Politics at the Court of Theodosius II." *Yale Classical Studies.* Vol. XXVII, 1982, pp. 217–289.

————. "Theodosius the Great and the Regency of Stilicho." *Harvard Studies in Classical Philology* 73 (1969), pp. 247–280.

Cameron, Averil. *Procopius and the Sixth Century.* Berkeley: Univeristy of Cambridge, 1985.

————. *The Later Roman Empire,* AD 284–430. Cambridge: Harvard University Press, 1993.

————, and Aemlie Kuhrt, eds. *Images of Women in Antiquity.* Detroit, Mich.: Wayne University Press, 1983.

Campbell, David A. *Greek Lyric.* 5 vols. Cambridge: Harvard University Press, 1982–93.

Carney, Elizabeth D. "The Career of Adea-Eurydice." *Historia* 36 (1987): 496–502.

————. "Olympias." *Ancient Society* 18 (1987): 496–502.

————. "The Sisters of Alexander the Great: Royal Relics." *Historia* 37 (1988): 385–404.

————. "What's in a Name?" In *Women's History and Ancient History,* ed. by Sarah B. Pomeroy. Chapel Hill: University of North Carolina Press, 1991.

Cartledge, Paul. "Spartan Wives: Liberation or License." *Classical Quarterly* 31 (1981): 84–109.

Cary, M. *A History of the Greek World from 323 to 146 B.C.* London: Methuen, 1951.

Chauveneau, Michel. *Cleopatra Beyond the Myth.* Translated from the French by David Lorton. Ithaca, N.Y.: Cornell University Press, 2002.

Charles-Picard, Gilbert. *Augustus and Nero: The Secret of the Empire.* Trans. by Len Ortzen. New York: Thomas Y. Crowell Comp., 1965.

Clark, Elizabeth A. "The Lady Vanishes: Dilemmas of a Feminist History after the Linguistic Turn." *Church History* 67, no. 1 (March 1998): 1–31.

———. *Women in the Early Church.* Collegeville, Minn.: The Liturgical Press, 1983.

Cluett, Ronald. "Roman Women and Triumviral Politics, 43–37 B.C." *Classical Views* (1998).

Cohen, G. M. "The Marriage of Lysimachus and Nicaea." *Historia* 22 (1973): 354–56.

Creekmore, Hubert, trans. *The Erotic Elegies of Albius Tibullus.* New York: Washington Square Press, 1966.

Davies, J. K. *Athenian Propertied Families, 600–300 B.C.* Oxford: Clarendon Press, 1971.

D'Avino, Michele. *The Women of Pompei.* Naples, Italy: Loffredo, 1967.

Debevoise, Nielson Carel. *A Political History of Parthia.* Chicago: University of Chicago Press, 1938.

DeForest, Mary, ed. *Woman's Power, Man's Game: Essays on Classical Antiquity in Honor of Joy K. King.* Wauconda, Ill.: Bolchazy-Carducci, 1993.

Delia, Diana. "Fulvia Reconsidered." In *Women's History and Ancient History,* ed. by Sarah B. Pomeroy. Chapel Hill: University of North Carolina Press, 1991.

Der Kleine Pauly; Lexikon der Antike, ed. by Konrat Julius Furchtegott and Walther Sontheimer. Stuttgart, Germany: A. Druckenmuller, 1984–.

Dixon, Suzanne. "Family Finances: Terentia and Tullia." In *The Family in Ancient Rome: New Perspectives,* ed. by Beryl Rawson. Ithaca, N.Y.: Cornell University Press, 1986.

Downey, Glanville. *A History of Antioch in Syria from Seleucus to the Arab Conquest.* Princeton, N.J.: Princeton University Press, 1961.

Drake, H. A. *In Praise of Constantine: A Historical Study and New Translation of Eusebius' Tricennial Orations.* Berkeley: University of California Press, 1976.

Dudley, Donald R., and Graham Webster. *The Rebellion of Boudicca.* New York: Barnes and Noble, 1962.

Edmonds, J. M., ed. and trans. *Lyra Graeca: Being the Remains of All the Greek Lyric Poets from Eumelus to Timotheus, Excepting Pindar.* Rev. ed. 3 vols. Cambridge: Harvard University Press, 1959.

Evans, James Allan. *The Empress Theodora: Partner of Justinian.* Austin, Tex.: University of Austin Press, 2002.

Everitt, Anthony. *Augustus: The Life of Rome's First Emperor.* New York: Random House, 2006.

Fantham, Elaine. *Julia Augusti.* New York: Routledge, 2006.

———, et al. *Women in the Classical World.* New York: Oxford University Press, 1994.

Ferrill, A. "Augustus and His Daughters: A Modern Myth." In *Studies in Latin Literature and Roman History,* ed. by C. Deroux. Brussels, Belgium: Latomus, 1986.

———. *Caligula: Emperor of Rome.* London: Thames and Hudson, 1991.

Fischler, Susan. "Social Stereotypes and Historical Analysis: The Case of the Imperial Women in Rome." In *Women in Ancient Societies: An Illusion of the Night,* ed. by Leonie J. Archer, Susan Fischler, and Maria Wyke. New York: Routledge, 1994.

Fitton, J. W. "That Was No Lady, That Was. . . ." *Classical Quarterly* 64 (1970): 56–66.

Flaceliere, Robert. *Love in Ancient Greece.* Trans. by James Cleugh. New York: Crown Publishers, 1962.

Forrest, W. G. A. *A History of Sparta.* London: Hutchinson, 1968.

Frankforter, A. Daniel. "Amalasuntha, Procopius, and a Women's Place." *Journal of Women's History* 8 (Summer 1996): 41–57.

Gardner, Jane F. *Women in Roman Law and Society.* London: Routledge, 1995.

Geoghegan, D. *Antye: A Critical Edition with Commentary.* Rome: Edizioni dell'Ateneo & Bizzarri, 1979.

Gibbon, Edward. *The Decline and Fall of the Roman Empire.* New York: Heritage Press, 1946.

Ginsberg, Judith. *Representing Agrippina: Constructions of Female Power in the Early Roman Empire.* New York: Oxford University Press, 2006.

Godolphin, Francis B., ed. *The Greek Historians: The Complete and Unabridged Historical Works of Herodotus translated by George Rawlinson, Thucydides translated by Benjamin Jowett, Xenophon translated by Henry G. Dakyns, Arrian translated by*

Edward J. Chinnock. 2 vols. New York: Random House, 1942.

Gordon, Hattie. "The Eternal Triangle, First Century B.C." *Classical Journal* 28 (1933): 574–78.

Gow, Andrew S. F., and Denys L. Page. *The Greek Anthology: Hellenistic Epigrams.* 2 vols. Cambridge, England: Cambridge University Press, 1965.

Grant, Michael. *The Jews in the Roman World.* New York: Charles Scribner's Sons, 1973.

Green, Peter. *Alexander to Actium.* Berkeley: University of California Press, 1990.

———. *Alexander of Macedon, 356–323 B.C.* Berkeley: University of California Press, 1991.

Greenwalt, W. S. "The Search for Philip Arrhideaus." *Ancient World* 10 (1984): 69–77.

Griffin, Marian T. *Nero: The End of a Dynasty.* New Haven, Conn.: Yale University Press, 1985.

Grimal, Pierre. *Love in Ancient Rome.* Trans. by Arthur Train, Jr. New York: Crown Publishers, 1967.

Haley, Shelly P. "The Five Wives of Pompey the Great." In *Women in Antiquity,* ed. by Ian McAuslan and Peter Walcot. Oxford: Oxford University Press, 1996.

Hallett, Judith. *Fathers and Daughters in Roman Society: Women and the Elite Family.* Princeton, N.J.: Princeton University Press, 1984.

———. "Perusinae Glandes and the Changing Image of Augustus." *American Journal of Ancient History* 2 (1977): 151–171.

Hammond, N. G. L. *A History of Greece.* Oxford: Oxford University Press, 1967.

———. "Illyris, Rome and Macedon in 229–205 B.C." *Journal of Roman Studies* (1968): 1–21.

———, and G. T. Griffith. *A History of Macedonia.* 2 vols. Oxford: Oxford University Press, 1972–79.

———, and H. H. Scullard, eds. *The Oxford Classical Dictionary.* 2d ed. Oxford: Clarendon Press, 1996.

Harris, H. A. *Sport in Greece and Rome.* Ithaca, N.Y.: Cornell University Press, 1972.

Hawley, Richard. "The Problem of Women Philosophers in Ancient Greece." In *Women in Ancient Societies: An Illusion of the Night,* ed. by Leonie J. Archer, Susan Fischler, and Maria Wyke. New York: Routledge, 1994.

———, and Barbara Levick, eds. *Women in Antiquity: New Assessments.* New York: Routledge, 1995.

Heckel, Waldemar. "Philip and Olympias." In *Classical Contributions: Studies in Honor of Malcolm Francis McGregor,* ed. by G. S. Shrimpton and D. J. McCargar. Locust Valley, N.Y.: J. J. Augustin, 1981.

Hemelrijk, Emily A. "Women's Demonstrations in Republican Rome." In *Sexual Asymmetry: Studies in Ancient Societies,* ed. by Josine Blok and Peter Mason. Amsterdam: J. C. Giebon, 1987.

Hillard, Tom. "On Stage, Behind the Curtain: Images of Politically Active Women in the Late Roman Republic." In *Stereotypes of Women in Power: Historical Perspectives and Revisionist Views,* ed. by Barbara Garlick, Suzanne Dixon, and Pauline Allen. New York: Greenwood Press, 1992.

Hoenigswald, Gabriele S. "The Murder Charges in Cicero's Pro Cluentio." *Transactions and Proceedings of the American Philological Association* 93 (1962): 109–23.

Holum, Kenneth G. *Theodosian Empresses: Women and Imperial Dominion in Late Antiquity.* Berkeley: University of California Press, 1982.

———. "Pulcharia's Crusade A.D. 421–422 and the Ideology of Imperial Victory." *Greek, Roman and Byzantine Studies* 18 (1977), pp. 153–172.

Horsfall, Nicholas. *Cornelius Nepos: A Selection Including the Lives of Cato and Atticus.* New York: Oxford University Press, 1989.

Huzar, Eleanor G. "Mark Antony: Marriages vs. Careers." *Classical Journal* 81 (1986): 86–111.

Johnson, W. H. "The Sister-in-Law of Cicero." *Classical Journal* 8 (1913): 160–65.

Jones, A. H. M. *The Herods of Judaea.* Rev. ed. Oxford: Clarendon Press, 1967.

———. *The Later Roman Empire 284–602: A Social Economic and Administrative Survey.* 2 vols. Norman: University of Oklahoma Press, 1964.

Juneau, J. "Pietas and Politics: Eusebia and Constantius at Court." *The Classical Quarterly,* New Series 49, no. 2 (1999): 641–644.

Katz, Marilyn. "Sappho and Her Sisters: Women in Ancient Greece." *Signs* 25, 2 (Winter 2000): 505–531.

Kraemer, Ross Shepard. *Women's Religion in the Greco-Roman World: A Sourcebook.* New York: Oxford University Press, 2004.

Lacey, W. K. *The Family in Classical Greece.* Ithaca, N.Y.: Cornell University Press, 1968.

Lane Fox, Robin. *Pagans and Christians.* New York: Alfred A. Knopf, 1987.

Leon, Harry J. *The Jews of Ancient Rome.* Philadelphia: Jewish Publication Society of America, 1960.

Levick, Barbara. *Claudius: The Corruption of Power.* New Haven, Conn.: Yale University Press, 1993.

———. *Tiberius the Politician.* London: Thames and Hudson, 1976.

———. *Vespasian.* New York: Routledge, 1999.

———. *Julia Domna, Syrian Empress.* New York: Routledge, 2007.

Licht, Hans. *Sexual Life in Ancient Greece.* Trans. by J. H. Freese. London: Abbey Library, 1971.

Luck, Georg. *The Latin Love Elegy.* London: Methuen, 1959.

McAuslan, Ian, and Peter Walcot, eds. *Women in Antiquity.* Oxford: Oxford University Press, 1996.

McCabe, Joseph. *The Empresses of Rome.* New York: Henry Holt, 1911.

McNamara, Jo Anne. "Sexual Equality and the Cult of Virginity in Early Christian Thought." *Feminist Studies* 3, no. 3–4. (Spring–Summer 1976): 145–158.

Macdowell, Doulas M., ed. *Audokides on the Mysteries.* Oxford: Clarendon Press, 1962.

MacMullen, Ramsey. "Women in Public in the Roman Empire." *Historia* 29 (1980): 208–218.

Macurdy, Grace. *Hellenistic Queens.* Reprint. Chicago: Ares Publishers, 1985.

Magie, David. *Roman Rule in Asia Minor, to the End of the Third Century after Christ.* 2 vols. Princeton, N.J.: Princeton University Press, 1950.

Marsh, Frank Burr. *The Reign of Tiberius.* New York: Barnes and Noble, 1931.

Marshall, A. J. "Ladies at Law: The Role of Women in the Roman Civil Courts." In *Studies in Latin Literature and Roman History,* ed. by C. Deroux. Brussels, Belgium: Latomus, 1989.

———. "Women on Trial before the Roman Senate." *Classical Views* 34 (1990): 333–366.

Miller, Fergus. "Paul of Samosata, Zenobia and Aurelian: The Church, Local Culture and Political Allegience in Third-Century Syria." *Journal of Roman Studies* 61 (1971): 1–17.

Mosse, Claude. "Women in the Spartan Revolutions of the Third Century B.C." In *Women's History and Ancient History,* ed. by Sarah B. Pomeroy. Chapel Hill: University of North Carolina Press, 1991.

Munzer, Friedrich. *Romische Adelsparteien und Adelsfamilien.* Stuttgart, Germany: J. B. Metzler, 1920.

Murray, Gilbert. *Euripides and His Age.* London: Oxford University Press, 1965.

O'Donnell, James J. *Augustine: A New Biography.* New York: HarperCollins, 2005.

Oost, Stewart Irvin. "Galla Placidia and the Law." *Classical Philology* 63, no. 2. (1968) 114–121.

Osiek, Carolyn, and David Balch. *Early Christian Families in Context.* Grand Rapids, Mich.: Erdman's, 2003.

Osiek, Carolyn, and Kevin Madigan. *Ordained Women in the Early Church: A Documentary History.* Baltimore: Johns Hopkins, 2005.

Oxford Classical Dictionary, ed. by Simon Hornblower and Antony Spawforth. 3d. ed. New York: Oxford University Press, 1996.

Page, Dennys L. *Alcman: The Partheneion.* Oxford: Clarendon Press, 1951.

———. *Corinna.* London: Society for the Promotion of Hellenic Studies, 1953.

Pauly, A., G. Wissowa, and W. Kroll. *Real-Encyclopadie d. Classischen Altertumswissenschaft 1893– .* (Germany: multiple publishers).

Perowne, Stewart. *Hadrian.* Reprint. Westport, Conn.: Greenwood Publishing, 1976.

———. *The Later Herods: The Political Background of the New Testament.* New York: Abingdon Press, 1950.

Peterson, Joan M. *Handmaid of the Lord: Contemporary Descriptions of Feminine Asceticism in the First Six Christian Centuries.* Kalamazoo, Mich.: Cistercians Publications Inc., 1996.

Pomeroy, Sarah, et al. *Ancient Greece, A Political, Social, and Cultural History.* New York: Oxford University Press, 1999.

————. *Families in Classical and Hellenistic Greece: Representations and Realities.* New York: Oxford University Press, 1998.

————. *Spartan Women.* New York: Oxford University Press, 2002.

————. *Goddesses, Whores, Wives, and Slaves: Women in Classical Antiquity.* New York: Schocken Books, 1975.

————. *Women in Hellenistic Egypt.* New York: Schocken, 1984.

————, ed. *Women's History and Ancient History.* Chapel Hill: University of North Carolina Press, 1991.

————. *Prosopography of the Later Roman Empire.* Vol. 1–3 of 4. Edited by A. H. M. Jones, J. R. Martindale, and J. Morris. Cambridge: Cambridge University Press, 1971. Reprinted, 1992.

Quinn, Kenneth, ed. *Catullus: The Poems.* 2d. ed. New York: St. Martin's Press, 1977.

Rabinowitz, Nancy Sorkin, and Amy Richlin, eds. *Feminist Theory and the Classics.* New York: Routledge, 1993.

Rawson, Beryl. *Marriage, Divorce, and Children in Ancient Rome.* Canberra, Australia: Clarendon Press, 1991.

Rawson, Beryl, ed. *The Family in Ancient Rome.* Ithaca, N.Y.: Cornell University Press, 1986.

Richardson, Keith. *Daggers in the Forum: The Revolutionary Lives and Violent Deaths of the Gracchus Brothers.* London: Cassell, 1976.

Richlin, A. "Julia's Jokes. Galla Placidia and the Roman Use of Women as Political Icons." In *Stereotypes of Women in Power: Historical Perspectives and Revisionist Views,* ed. by B. Garlick, S. Dixon, and P. Allen. New York: Greenwood Press, 1992.

Richmond, I. A. "Queen Cartimandua." *Journal of Roman Studies* (1954): 43 ff.

Roller, Duane W. *The World of Juba II and Kleopatra Selene: Royal Scholarship on Rome's African Frontier.* New York: Routledge, 2003.

Sappho's Lyre: Archaic Lyric and Women Poets of Ancient Greece. Translations with Introduction and Notes by Diane J. Rayor. Forward by W. R. Johnson. Berkeley: University of California Press, 1991.

Schaffer, Mary. *The Life of the Blessed and Holy Syncletica, by Pseudo-Athanasius, Part II: Study of the Life.* Toronto: Peregrina Publishing Company, 2001.

Schultz, Celia E. *Women's Religious Activity in the Roman Republic.* Chapel Hill: University of North Carolina Press, 2006.

Schulz, Fritz. *Classical Roman Law.* Oxford: Clarendon Press, 1969.

Scullard, H. H. *From the Gracchi to Nero: A History of Rome from 133 B.C. to A.D. 68.* New York: Frederick Praeger, 1963.

————. *A History of the Roman World, 753 to 146 B.C.* London: Routledge, 1980.

————. *Scipio Africanus: Soldier and Politician.* Ithaca, N.Y.: Cornell University Press, 1970.

Sealey, R. "On Lawful Concubinage in Athens." *Classical Antiquity* 3 (1984): 111–133.

Seltman, Charles. *Women in Antiquity.* Westport, Conn.: Hyperion Press, 1979.

Shackleton Bailey, D. R. *Cicero.* New York: Charles Scribner's Sons, 1971.

Singer, Mary White. "The Problem of Octavia Minor and Octavia Maior." *Transactions of the American Philological Association* (1948): 268–274.

Sivan, Hagith. "Ancian Women, the Cento of Proba, and Aristocratic Conversion in the Fourth Century." *Vigiliae Christianae* 47, no. 2 (June 1993): 140–157.

Skeat, Theodore Cressy. *The Reigns of the Ptolemies.* Munich: Beck, 1969.

Skinner, Marilyn B. "Clodia Metelli." *Transactions of the American Philological Associaton* 113 (1983): 273–87.

————. "Nossis Thelyglossos: The Private Text and the Public Book." In *Women's History and Ancient History,* ed. by Sarah B. Pomeroy. Chapel Hill: University of North Carolina Press, 1991.

————, ed. "Rescuing Creusa: New Methodological Approaches to Women in Antiquity." *Helios* 13, no. 2 (1986).

Smallwood, E. Mary. "The Alleged Jewish Tendencies of Poppaea Sabina." *Journal of Theological Studies* (1959): 29–35.

Snyder, Jane McIntosh. "Public Occasion and Private Passion in the Lyrics of Sappho of Lesbos." In *Women's History and Ancient History,* ed. by Sarah B. Pomeroy. Chapel Hill: University of North Carolina Press, 1991.

———. *The Women and the Lyre: Women Writers in Classical Greece and Rome.* Carbondale: Southern Illinois University Press, 1989.

Stockton, David. *The Gracchi.* Oxford: Clarendon Press, 1979.

Swan, Laura. *The Forgotten Desert Mothers: Sayings, Lives, and Stories of Early Christian Women.* New York: Paulist Press, 2001.

Syme, Ronald. *The Augustan Aristocracy.* Oxford: Clarendon Press, 1986.

———. "Domitius Corbulo." *Journal of Roman Studies* 60 (1970): 27–39.

———. *History in Ovid.* New York: Oxford University Press, 1978.

———. *The Roman Revolution.* London: Oxford University Press, 1963.

———. *Sallust.* Berkeley: University of California Press, 1974.

———. *Tacitus.* 2 vols. Oxford: Clarendon Press, 1958.

Tarn, William Woodthorpe. *Alexander the Great.* 2 vols. Boston: Beacon Press, 1956.

———. *Hellenistic Civilization.* London: Methuen, 1966.

———. "Phthia-Chryseis." In *Athenian Studies Presented to William Scott Ferguson.* Cambridge: Harvard University Press, 1940.

Townsend, G. B. "Traces in Dio Cassius of Cluvius, Aufidius and Pliny." *Hermes* 89 (1961) 227–48.

Townsend, Prescott W. "The Administration of Gordian III." *Yale Classical Studies* 15 (1955): 59–132.

———. "The Revolution of A.D. 238: The Leaders and Their Aims." *Yale Classical Studies* 14 (1955): 49–97.

Walbank, Frank. *Philip V of Macedon.* Cambridge, England: Cambridge University Press, 1940.

Walcot, Peter. "Plato's Mother and Other Terrible Women." In *Women in Antiquity,* ed. by Ian McAuslan and Peter Walcot. Oxford: Oxford University Press, 1996.

Walker, Susan, and Sally-Ann Ashton, eds. *Cleopatra Reassessed.* London: British Museum, 2003.

Walter, Gerard. *Nero.* Trans. by Emma Craufurd. Westport, Conn.: Greenwood Press, 1976.

Walters, K. R. "Women and Power in Classical Athens." In *Woman's Power, Man's Game: Essays on Classical Antiquity in Honor of Joy K. King,* ed. by Mary DeForest. Wauconda, Ill.: Bolchazy-Carducci, 1993.

Warmington, B. H. *Nero: Reality and Legend.* New York: W. W. Norton and Comp., 1969.

Weaver, P. R. C. *Familia Caesaris: A Social History of the Emperor's Freedmen and Slaves.* Cambridge, England: Cambridge University Press, 1972.

Weimar, W. *Quintus Tullius Cicero.*

Williams, Stephen. *Diocletian and the Roman Recovery.* New York: Routledge, 1996.

Williamson, Margaret. *Sappho's Immortal Daughters.* Cambridge: Harvard University Press, 1995.

Women Poets in Ancient Greece and Rome. Edited by Ellen Greene. Norman: University of Oklahoma Press, 2005.

Wood, Susan E. *Imperial Women: A Study in Public Images, 40 B.C.–A.D. 68.* Leiden: E. J. Brill, 1999.

Yarbrough, Anne. "Christianization in the Fourth Century: The Example of Roman Women." *Church History* 45, no. 2 (June 1976): 149–165.

INDEX

Boldface page numbers indicate extensive treatment of a topic.
Page numbers in *italic* indicate illustrations.

KEN HOM
TRAVELS WITH A HOT WOK

Ken Hom

Travels with a Hot Wok

蟹

PHOTOGRAPHS BY SANDRA LANE

London, New York, Sydney, Dehli, Paris,
Munich, and Johannesburg

Publisher Sean Moore
Editorial director LaVonne Carlson
Project editor Barbara Minton
Jacket design Gus Yoo
Production director David Proffit

US edition ISBN 0-7894-6810-7
First US edition published in 2000 by
Dorling Kindersley, Inc.
95 Madison Avenue
New York, New York, 10016

This is a companion book to the PBS TV television series Great Food
Presented by

Sponsored by

www.looksmart.com

Produced by

●●●● **west 175** productions   🍷 **wine.com** *The best of wine™*

First published 1997 by BBC Books,
an imprint of BBC Worldwide Publishing
80 Wood Lane, London W12 0TT

Edited by Deborah Savage
Designed by Isobel Gillan
Home economist for photography: Sarah Ramsbottom
Stylist for photography: Mary Norton
BBC Executive Producer for Independent Image Ltd: Tom Kinninmont
Series Producer for Independent Image Ltd: Kate Kinninmont

© Promo Group Limited 1998
The moral right of the author has been asserted.
Photographs by Sandra Lane, © BBC Books 1998

Set in Futura by BBC Books
Printed and bound in Great Britain by Butler & Tanner Ltd, Frome and London
Color separations by Radstock Reproductions Ltd, Midsomer Norton
Jacket printed by Lawrence Allen Ltd, Weston-super-Mare

Author's Acknowledgements

I have always been fortunate to have a solid team assisting me in my cookbooks. Their work is reflected in this book. I appreciated their constant questioning and prodding and, under intense pressure, they also remained cool and calm. First I must thank Gordon Wing, my right hand in the kitchen and a keen observer of every step in each recipe; Gerry Cavanaugh, for his insightful editing of my rough words and suggestions; and Andrew Walton Smith (Drew), who checks every detail of the manuscript for inconsistency – to them I am truly indebted. We were assisted superbly by Eric Litzky and Storm Thomas.

Of course, my thanks must also go to all the hardworking team at BBC Books, including my publisher, Chris Weller; the project editor who supervised the book, Khadija Manjlai; the copy-editor, Deborah Savage; Vivien Bowler, the senior commissioning editor; Jane Parsons, her assistant; and the imaginative art director, Frank Phillips, and designer Isobel Gillan for their masterful design. To them I make a deep bow.

For the enticing and mouthwatering photographs, only humble gratitude can be offered to Sandra Lane and her stylist Mary Norton, and her home economist Sarah Ramsbottom.

Both my producer, Kate Kinninmont, and executive producer, Tom Kinninmont, were a source of inspiration; as were Carole Blake and Julian Friedmann, my indispensable advisers. Thank you all.

In Memory of My Chinese Grandparents

CONTENTS

Introduction

The global village is upon us and with it has come the global kitchen and the emergence of a global cuisine. It has been called "East meets West cuisine," "Pacific Rim cuisine," and more recently, "fusion cooking." We need only look at the menus of popular and upscale restaurants throughout the world to discover the extensive and marvellous blending of foods, ingredients, and techniques from the many different cultures at the heart of this new cuisine.

Moreover, in home kitchens worldwide, the new spices, seasonings, foods, and techniques are becoming staple items. Contemporary home-cooked meals quite often reflect an easy, eclectic cosmopolitanism that was impossible, even unthinkable, just twenty years ago. Today, formerly exotic eastern ingredients – such as bok choy, five-spice powder, or soy sauce – are to be found in supermarkets and at home in the pantry, nestling comfortably and familiarly alongside traditional western staples.

Throughout history, every culture has, of course, assimilated foreign influences and every cuisine adopted new techniques and exotic ingredients into its cooking repertoire. The venerable Chinese culinary traditions, for example, are notable for their readiness to assimilate new and appropriate foods and ideas. French cuisine, in all its glory, owes much to Italian cooking traditions and other influences. And these cuisines have reciprocally and profoundly influenced their neighbors.

Historically, though, foods from one culture moved only gradually to another. For example, the tomato, a New World plant, was first introduced into southern France over four hundred years ago, and its integration into the French countryside moved initially at a rate of about one mile every ten years. Potatoes, too, were very slow to become a part of the European diet. This assimilation process worked the same way, East and West: corn, peanuts, and sweet potatoes (again, New World plants) were introduced into China in the sixteenth century and spread very slowly, although much more rapidly than ten miles every century!

What is new about 'fusion' cooking is the speed with which its tenets and techniques have spread. This, of course, is primarily due to the remarkable advances in transport and communication that have characterized modern times. We have moved from horseback to jet planes and from letters delivered by postmen to Internet communication in the past one hundred and fifty years; cultures are linked as never before. "Fusion cuisine" is a natural accompaniment to this process.

Another effect of the transport and communication revolutions is that global travel has rocketed, while vicarious experience and awareness of other cultures has deepened. Insularity, parochialism and ignorance of those other cultures are becoming things of the past. Travel has always been mind-broadening, but today it also widens one's culinary horizons.

Among the blessings of this new global mobility – of people and of products is the proliferation, in metropolitan districts throughout the world, of restaurants serving ethnic cuisines. They have become especially prominent in western cities. Japanese, Thai, Vietnamese, Mexican, Latin American, Korean, and other cuisines are now generally available in most urban centers. The already familiar Chinese restaurants, which once offered only westernized pseudo-Cantonese fare, now serve authentic Sichuan, Hunan, Shanghai, Taiwanese, and other regional cuisines, along with truly authentic Cantonese cooking. The popularity of these ethnic restaurants, along with cook books and television programs on ethnic foods, has led many supermarkets to stock the basic ingredients of these cuisines. Consumers have led the way in developing their own fusion recipes.

Another factor that encourages the adoption of fusion cuisine is a heightened awareness of how a person's general health is based on diet. Today, medical and health experts are warning us about a global epidemic in the so-called 'diseases of affluence,' primarily in the West. These illnesses, especially cardiovascular disease and cancer, appear to stem from relatively recent changes in people's diets. There is irony here because these diseases are most closely linked to greater consumption of meat and dairy products, foods which had come to symbolize prosperity and health.

As westerners have discovered the dangers of consuming too much fatty meat, butter, and cream, they have found at hand eastern substitutes to satisfy and delight their beleaguered palates. Asian cuisines have never been based primarily on meat and dairy products, and they compensate for the absence or reduction of those rich western foods. They lighten the diet but also add refreshing and satisfying flavors, thus making the new fusion tastes appealing as well as wholesome. As the eastern nations 'modernize' and begin to emulate certain aspects of the western lifestyle (I am thinking here of the over-consumption of fatty hamburgers and other 'junk' foods), it is to be hoped that fusion cooking will at least lessen the impact of such unhealthy diets in both the East and West.

Finally, the economic benefits of a global food market allowed a greater selection of foods to be available than ever before. The expansion of trade, improvements in the preservation of ingredients, rapid transport, and innovative marketing and advertising have all come together to create consumer awareness and the possibilities, the needs, and the capabilities required to sustain a global cuisine. The availability and the variety of the earth's bounty combined with a natural tendency to experiment and to try something new and pleasing, has contributed to the rise of fusion cooking.

Although fusion cuisine appears to have caught on relatively quickly, in retrospect one may see the first stirring of the fusion approach about thirty years ago. The introduction of the French *nouvelle cuisine* may possibly be the earliest manifestation of the new, cosmopolitan, and thoughtfully eclectic spirit at work in the kitchen. One of its essentials included shortened cooking times, which the food writers Henri Gault and Christian Millau perceived as a Chinese technique. The great *nouvelle cuisine* chef, Paul Bocuse, noted a Japanese influence, drawn from the work of the many Japanese apprentice cooks then learning their craft in France. This new way of cooking emphasized fresh foods, lightness, inventiveness, and an eager acceptance of whatever produced nutritious, imaginative, and palate-pleasing menus.

Gault and Millau summed up the accomplishments of *nouvelle cuisine* and presciently described the coming emergence of fusion cooking: "There are still thousands of dishes to be invented – and probably one hundred of them will be memorable. [The new cooks] don't disdain special condiments, products, and recipes from the East. Bocuse brings saffron from Iran for his mussel soup; Oliver is learning to lacquer ducks; Guerard mixes together duck and grapefruit." Inventiveness was a crucial factor. As Craig Claiborne, the doyen of American food writers, put it: "The soul of the new cuisine depends upon the inspiration and improvisations of a cook or chef. *Nouvelle cuisine* is not doctrinaire."

Today, Asian ingredients are at home in French cooking, having achieved what Florence Fabricant, a food writer for the *New York Times*, calls "a tantalizing revolution that is transforming the formal bastions of French cuisine." And this is not limited to France itself. Hubert Keller, the chef at the Fleur de Lys restaurant in San Francisco, notes that, "Ten years ago, with our reputation as a traditional French restaurant, we might have been criticized for blending cuisines if we added ingredients like ginger and coconut milk. Now, times have changed."

From France this trend moved to California. During the 1960s, partially as a result of the influence of *nouvelle cuisine* and partially because California is so bountifully supplied with both fresh foods and vibrant ethnic cultures, a "new California cuisine" sprouted and flowered profusely; it soon became the "new American cuisine." Along with inventiveness, innovation, and imagination, this approach to the preparation of nutritious and tasty food incorporates the essence of *nouvelle cuisine*: freshness of ingredients, the avoidance of overcooking, and respect for tradition without slavish adulation. California cuisine added its own virtues to this splendid list: a purposeful, thoughtful introduction of 'exotic' foods and flavorings from Latin America and Asia, an openness to innovation, a receptivity to different tastes and textures, and an almost unprecedented readiness to assimilate aspects of other culinary cultures. With its multicultural population and strategic location on the Pacific Rim, California was destined to become a leader in the new, global fusion style of cooking.

I must mention one of the great chefs who has been a leader of this transformation, Alice Waters, whose now famous restaurant, Chez Panisse, is deservedly renowned as a showcase of all the finest in California cuisine. As her restaurant's name indicates, she reveres French cooking traditions. Keeping the best of the old and adding the best of the new and different sums up excellent fusion cooking. Alice Waters has enticed, beguiled, and trained an entire generation of people who care about fresh and delicious foods - "fusion cooking" before that term was coined.

Alice Waters was a pioneer and Chez Panisse became a model that has been emulated throughout the world. Or, rather, I should say that many chefs and cooks everywhere were thinking and acting along the same lines and reacting imaginatively to the globalization of the world economy and the interpenetration of cultures and cuisines. In Hong Kong, for example, chefs were aware of the cosmopolitan nature both of their patrons and of the foodstuffs that passed through the bustling port city. They seized upon the opportunities before them and imaginatively 'invented' a new Hong Kong cuisine, a fusion of

Chinese and other cultures' foods and techniques, all the while emphasizing the same virtues to be found in *nouvelle* and California cuisine. It was inspired by the spirit of the age (and of the communication/transport revolution).

This happened, of course, not only in Hong Kong, California, and France. Chefs and food writers in the cosmopolitan centers of Australia, Britain, Germany, Thailand, Singapore — even (or especially) those who had been trained in their native classical cuisines — eagerly and innovatively adopted the flexible and imaginative approaches inherent in fusion cooking. So today, from Adelaide and Sydney to London and Paris, and from Bangkok and Hong Kong to San Francisco, Los Angeles, Chicago, and New York — and back again, with many worthwhile detours north and south — fusion restaurants and fusion home-cooking have come to stay, to our benefit and pleasure.

I have been a most fortunate beneficiary of (and participant in) the culinary revolution or reformation over the past quarter of a century. My Chinese–American heritage, with the grand traditions of its glorious cuisine; my childhood in ethnically diverse Chicago; my youthful experience working in the family restaurant; my coming of age in San Francisco and Berkeley, in France and Italy — all of these contributed to my natural tendency towards, and advocacy of, fusion cuisine. For

example, I have always believed that butter worked better than Chinese lard (in small amounts), and that, for many purposes, white potatoes can serve as well as rice.

But the fundamentals have always been the same: freshness, clarity, and balance of tastes and textures, lightness, simplicity, a reliance upon grains, vegetables, fruits, and seafood, with other animal products mainly as a garnish or in a sauce. (A note on freshness: until the jet age, this always meant local or regional supplies, but today the term may include practically every popular food in the world.) And taste, of course, with spices, condiments, and seasonings to enhance, to accentuate, and never to overwhelm the natural tastes of good food. Such are the characteristics of all fine cuisines and, therefore, of fusion cooking.

The goal of fusion cooking, as with all forms of the art, is to provide delicious, wholesome food that is enjoyable to eat. It is a goal attainable with a minimal amount of care, concern, and application. During the past two decades, I have been practicing the fusion style, both professionally and in my home for family and friends. This book is filled with ideas and recipes drawn from that practice, tested in the kitchen, and refined over many years. Remember, fusion cooking is not doctrinaire. It is an approach to cooking whose distinguishing characteristics are flexibility, experimentation, innovation, and imagination — all informed, of course, by proper regard for what is necessary and appropriate in the matter of taste and appearance.

A recipe is not a rigid formula — *you* can determine what is necessary and appropriate. Cooking is an art more than a science; it is creative as well as imitative and is, or should be, more play than work. Follow the few simple, basic rules and then experiment. Discover the tastes and virtues of the various ingredients, some subtle, some assertive, and observe how they mix and match to mutually enhance your foods. Use your imagination, listen to your palate. You will be rewarded with dishes that are both familiar and exotic and deliciously satisfying as well. You will discover your own fusion cooking.

EQUIPMENT

A wonderful aspect of fusion cooking is that it can easily be done in a well-stocked kitchen. Traditional Asian and Chinese cooking equipment is not essential for the preparation of fusion food, but there are some tools which will make it much easier. Moreover, there is an advantage to relying on implements that have been tested over many centuries.

WOK

The most useful and versatile piece of equipment popular with fusion cooks and chefs – the wok – may be used for stir-frying, blanching, deep-frying, steaming, and even smoking foods. Its shape, with deep sides and either a tapered or a slightly flattened but still round bottom, allows for fuel-efficient, quick, and even heating and cooking. In the stir-frying technique, the deep sides prevent the food and oils from spilling over. By using the wok for deep-frying, much less oil is required because of the concentration of the heat and ingredients at the wok's base. You can even use a well-seasoned wok for simple omelettes or bacon and eggs.

There are two basic wok types: the traditional Cantonese version, with short, rounded handles on either side of the edge or lip of the wok; and the *pau* or Peking wok, which has one handle about 12–14 in (30–35 cm) long. The long-handled wok keeps you at a safe distance from the possible splashing of hot oils or water.

You should know that the round-bottomed wok can be used only on gas burners. Woks are now available with flatter bottoms, designed especially for electric stovetops. Although this shape really defeats the purpose of the traditional design, which is to concentrate intense heat at the center, it does have the advantage over ordinary frying-pans in that it has deeper sides to prevent spillage while deep-frying.

Choosing a Wok

Choose a large wok – preferably about 12–14 in (30–35 cm) in diameter, with deep sides. It is easier, and safer, to cook a small batch of food in a large wok than a large quantity in a small one. Be aware that some woks on the market are too shallow or too flat-bottomed and thus no better than a frying-pan. A heavier wok, preferably made of carbon steel, is superior to the lighter stainless steel or aluminium types, which cannot take very high heat and tend to blacken, and possibly scorch the food. There are now on the market good, non-stick, carbon-steel woks that maintain the heat without sticking. However, these need special care to prevent scratching. In recent years, the non-stick technology has improved vastly, so that now they can be safely recommended. They are especially useful when cooking foods that have a high acid level, such as lemons.

Seasoning a Wok

All woks (except non-stick ones) need to be seasoned. Many need to be cleaned especially well before being used for the first time to remove the machine oil which is applied to the surface by the manufacturer to protect the wok in transit. This is the only time you will ever scrub your wok – unless you let it become rusted. Scrub it with a cream cleanser and water to remove as much of the machine oil as possible. Then dry it and put it on the burner over a low heat. Add 2 tablespoons of cooking oil and using paper towels, rub it over the inside of the wok until the entire surface is lightly coated with oil. Heat the wok slowly for about 10–15 minutes and then wipe it thoroughly with more paper towels. The paper will become blackened. Repeat this process of coating, heating and wiping until the paper towel comes away clean. Your wok will darken and become well seasoned with use, which is a good sign.

Cleaning a Wok

Once your wok has been seasoned, it should never be washed with dish detergent. Plain, clear water is all that is needed. The wok should be thoroughly dried after each use. Putting the cleaned wok over low heat for a minute or two should do the trick. If it does happen to become rusted a bit, then it must be scrubbed with a cream cleanser again and re-seasoned.

Wok Accessories

Wok Stand This is a metal ring or frame, designed to keep a conventionally shaped wok steady on the burner, and it is essential if you want to use your wok for steaming, deep-frying, or braising. Stands come in two designs. One is a solid metal ring perforated with about six ventilation holes. The other is a circular, thin wire frame. If you have a gas stove, use only the latter type since the more solid design does not allow for ventilation and might lead to a build-up of gas which could put the flame out completely.

Wok Lid This light and inexpensive domed cover, usually made from aluminium, is used for steaming. The lid normally comes with the wok but, if not, it may be purchased from Asian markets, or you may use any domed pot lid that fits snugly.

Spatula A long-handled metal spatula, shaped rather like a small shovel, is ideal for scooping and tossing food in a wok. Alternatively, any large, long-handled spoon can be used.

Rack When steaming foods in your wok, you will need a wooden or metal rack or trivet, to raise the food to be cooked above the water level. Wok sets usually include a rack, but, if not, Asian markets sell them separately. Department and hardware stores also sell wooden and metal stands, which serve the same purpose. Any rack, improvised or not, that keeps the food above the water so that it is steamed and not boiled, will suffice. You will also find the wire rack very practical for smoking food in the wok.

Bamboo Brush This bundle of stiff, split bamboo is used for cleaning a wok without scrubbing off the seasoned surface. It is an attractive, inexpensive implement, but not essential. A soft sponge or a dishwashing brush will do just as well.

DEEP-FAT FRYERS

These are very useful and you may find them safer and easier to use for deep-frying than a wok. The quantities of oil given in the recipes are based on the amount required for deep-frying in a wok. If you are using a deep-fat fryer instead, you will need about double the amount of oil, but never fill the deep-fryer more than half-full with oil.

CLEAVERS

To Asian cooks, the cleaver is an all-purpose cutting instrument that makes all other knives unnecessary. Once you gain facility with a cleaver, you will see how ito use it on all types of food, to slice, dice, chop, fillet, shred, or crush. In practice, most chefs rely upon three different sizes of cleavers – light, medium, and heavy – to be used appropriately. Of course, you may use your own kitchen knives, but if you decide to invest in a cleaver, choose a good-quality stainless steel model and keep it sharpened.

CHOPPING BOARD

One decided improvement over the traditional implements of Asian and Chinese cooking is the modern chopping board made of hardwood or white acrylic. The typical Asian and Chinese chopping board is of soft wood, which is not only difficult to maintain but, being soft, also provides a fertile surface for bacteria. A hardwood or acrylic board is easy to clean, resists bacterial accumulation, and lasts much longer. Fusion cookery entails much chopping, slicing, and dicing, so it is essential to have a large, dependable, steady chopping board. For reasons of hygiene, never place cooked meat on a board on which raw meat or poultry has been prepared. For raw meats, always use a separate board and clean it thoroughly after each use.

STEAMERS

Steaming is not a very popular cooking method in the West. This is unfortunate because it is the best method for preparing many foods of delicate taste and texture, such as fish and vegetables. Steaming is a method well worth learning. In Asia, bamboo steamers have been in use for thousands of years. Bamboo steamers come in several sizes, of which the 10 in (25 cm) one is the most suitable for home use. The food is placed in the steamer and that, in turn, is placed above boiling water in a wok or pan. To prevent the food from sticking to the steamer as it cooks, clean damp muslin may be used under the food itself. A tight-fitting bamboo lid prevents the steam from escaping; several steamers, stacked one above the other, may be used at the same time. Of course, any kind of wide metal steamer can be used, if you prefer. Before using a bamboo steamer for the first time, wash it and then steam it, empty, for about 5 minutes.

RICE COOKERS

Electric rice cookers are increasing in popularity. They cook rice perfectly and keep it warm throughout a meal. A rice cooker also has the advantage of freeing a burner or element, making for a less cluttered stovetop. They are relatively expensive, however, so unless you eat rice frequently, I do not think they are worth the expense.

MISCELLANEOUS

Stainless steel bowls of different sizes, along with strainers and colanders, round out the list of basic implements. They will be very useful because you will be mixing a lot of wonderful foods, and you will often have to drain or strain oils and juices. It is better to have one too many tools than one too few.

BARBECUE

This is a convenient cooking tool to have for fusion cooks since many recipes can be cooked on a barbecue. Nothing beats the outdoor, smoky flavors of cooking over coals.

Barbecues come in all sizes and prices. However, I highly recommend a good solid one which can last for years. It needs to be cleaned and covered during the wet season. This is, of course, an optional piece of cooking equipment and you can always use your oven grill as a substitute.

INGREDIENTS

Asian ingredients have become an integral part of eating at home and in restaurants. This is not only a trendy dining fashion; these ingredients are now part of home cooks' and chefs' repertoires. This has been driven partly by heath consciousness – most Asian cooking is light and fresh, with very little added animal fat (such as cream, cheese, or butter). Also, as Asian emigration expands throughout the West, cooking becomes ever more cross-pollinated. Greater exposure to Asian cooking techniques through magazines, books, and television programs has broadened the appeal of Asian culture. Formerly exotic Asian ingredients are becoming familiar and widely available.

The following is a brief guide to authentic ingredients which I have used in this book. I have added a few comments on common European ingredients which I have fused with Asian techniques and flavors. In the recipes themselves, I have added page references to the less familiar items.

BEANCURD (see Tofu, page 24)

BEAN SPROUTS

Now widely available, these are the sprouts of the green mung bean, although some Chinese stores also stock yellow soy bean sprouts, which are much larger. Bean sprouts should always be very fresh and crunchy. They will keep for several days when loosely wrapped in paper towels inside a plastic bag in the vegetable compartment of a refrigerator. It is ironic that bean sprouts, now so common in the West, have become a luxury in China, where keeping the bean sprouts fresh is difficult because they are so perishable and refrigeration is so expensive. However, this refreshing, nutritious food has enjoyed a revival in China's more highly priced restaurants.

BLACK BEANS

These small black soy beans, also known as salted black beans, are preserved by being fermented with salt and spices. They have a distinctive, slightly salty taste and a rich pleasant smell. Thus prepared, they are a tasty seasoning, especially when used in conjunction with garlic or fresh ginger. They are inexpensive and can be obtained from Asian grocers, usually in cans labelled 'Black Beans in Salted Sauce', but you may also see them packed in plastic bags. You can rinse them before use, though this is an optional step; I prefer to chop them slightly, to help release their pungent flavor. If you store any unused beans and liquid in a sealed jar in the refrigerator, they will keep indefinitely .

CHINESE CHIVES

The taste of Chinese chives is much stronger and more garlic-like than western chives; their flowers can be used as well as the blades. They have an earthy, onion taste and are delicious by themselves or cooked with other foods. They can be substituted for regular chives but adjust the quantity to allow for their stronger flavor. Rinse and dry the chives, wrap them in slightly damp paper towels and store them in a plastic bag in the refrigerator. Use as soon as possible.

Chinese yellow chives are Chinese chives which have been grown in the dark and are pale yellow in color – like endive – and have a more subtle flavor than the green Chinese chives. Select the freshest leaves possible. Trim any decaying parts. Wash and dry thoroughly and store between paper towels in the lower part of your refrigerator; since they are highly perishable, they will keep for only one or two days. They possess a rich, earthy taste and yet are delicate and fragile at the same time.

CHINESE GREENS

They are available all year and can be treated like cabbage and kept for a week or so in the vegetable crisper of the refrigerator.

Chinese Flowering Cabbage

Chinese flowering cabbage, or *choi sum*, is part of the wide mustard-green cabbage family. This cabbage has green leaves and may have small yellow flowers, which are eaten along with the leaves and stems. In China, this is one of the most common and popular leafy vegetables, and it is delicious as a stir-fry dish. When buying, look for bright leaves and firm, moist-looking stalks.

Chinese Leaves

Chinese leaves, also known as Peking Cabbage, comes in various sizes, from long, compact, barrel-shaped to short, squat-looking types. They are also tightly packed with firm, pale green (or sometimes slightly yellow), crinkled leaves. This versatile vegetable is used for soups and added to stir-fried meat dishes. Its sponge-like ability to absorb flavors and its sweet pleasant taste and texture make it a favorite for chefs, who match it with rich foods. This is a delicious crunchy vegetable with a mild but

distinctive taste. Store it as you would ordinary cabbage.

Chinese White Cabbage

There are many varieties of this. The most common, bok choy, is the one with a long, smooth, milky-white stem and large, crinkly, dark green leaves. The size of the plant indicates how tender it is; the smaller, the better. Bok choy has a light, fresh, slightly mustardy taste and requires little cooking. It is now widely available in supermarkets. Look for firm, crisp stalks and unblemished leaves. Store bok choy in the vegetable crisper of your refrigerator.

CHINESE WHITE RADISH

Also known as *daikon*, *mooli*, or Chinese icicle radish, it is long and white and like a large carrot in shape. It is a winter radish or root and can withstand long cooking without disintegrating. It thus absorbs the flavors of other foods while retaining its distinctive radish taste and texture. Look for firm, heavy, solid, unblemished ones. They should be slightly translucent inside, solid and not fibrous. Always peel before use. Store the radishes in a plastic bag in the vegetable crisper of your refridgerator where they will keep for over a week.

CHILIES

Chilies are used extensively in western China and, somewhat less frequently, in other regions. They are the seed pods of the capsicum plant and can be obtained fresh, dried, or ground. One must differentiate between the various types because, for one thing, they vary greatly in how hot they taste.

Chili-Bean Sauce (see Sauces and Pastes, page 22)

Chili Oil/Chili Dipping Sauce

Chili oil is sometimes used as a dipping condiment

as well as a seasoning in China. Of course, as chilies vary, so do the oils vary in strength and flavor. You can purchase chili oil from Asian grocers. The Thai and Malaysian versions are especially hot; the Taiwanese and Chinese versions are more subtle. These commercial oils are quite acceptable, but I include the following recipe because the home-made version is the best. Remember that chili oil is too dramatic to be used directly for cooking; it is best used as part of a dipping sauce or as a condiment, or combined with other milder oils. I include pepper and black beans in this recipe for additional flavors so that I can also use it as a dipping sauce.

Once made, put the chili oil in a tightly sealed glass jar and store in a cool, dark place, where it will keep for months.

Chili Oil/Chili Dipping Sauce

2 tablespoons chopped dried red chilies
1 tablespoon whole unroasted Sichuan
    peppercorns (page 20)
2 tablespoons whole black beans (page 14)
½ cup (150 ml) peanut oil

Heat a wok over a high heat and add the oil and the rest of the ingredients. Continue to cook over a low heat for about 10 minutes. Allow the mixture to cool undisturbed and then pour it into a jar. Let the mixture stand for two days and then strain the oil. It will keep indefinitely.

Chili Powder

Chili powder is made from dried red chilies. Pungent and aromatic, it ranges from mild to very hot. You will be able to buy it in any supermarket. With chilies in general, your own preference to determine how much 'hotness' to add to each dish.

Dried Red Chilies

Dried red chilies are small, thin, and about ½ in (1 cm) long. They are commonly employed to season the oil used in stir-fried dishes, in sauces, and in braising. They are left whole or cut in half lengthwize with the seeds left in. The Chinese like to blacken them and leave them in the dish during cooking, but because they are extremely hot and spicy, you may choose to remove them immediately after using them to flavor the cooking oil. They can be found in Asian markets as well as in most supermarkets and will keep indefinitely in a tightly closed jar. When eating out, most diners move the chilies to one side of their plates.

Fresh Chilies

Fresh chilies can be distinguished by their small size and elongated shape. They should look fresh and bright with no brown patches or black spots. There are several varieties. Red chilies are generally milder than green ones because they sweeten as they ripen.

To prepare fresh chilies, first rinse them in cold water. Then, using a small sharp knife, slit them lengthwize. Remove and discard the seeds. Rinse the chilies well under cold running water and then prepare them according to the recipe's instructions. Wash your hands, knife, and chopping board before preparing other foods, and be careful not to touch your eyes until you have washed your hands thoroughly with soap and water. The seeds are especially pungent and 'hot' to a fault.

Thai Chilies

They are small, pointed and very hot and they come in orange, red, green, and white.

CILANTRO

Cilantro (also known as Chinese parsley) is the fresh form of coriander and one of the most popular herbs used in fusion cookery. It looks like flat parsley but its pungent, musky, citrus-like flavor gives it a distinctive character that is unmistakable. That is to say, it is an acquired taste for many people. Its feathery leaves are often used as a garnish or they can be chopped and mixed into sauces and stuffings.

Most supermarkets stock it, as do many Asian markets and some vegetable markets. When buying cilantro, look for deep green, fresh-looking leaves. Yellow and limp leaves indicate age and should be avoided.

To store cilantro, wash it in cold water, drain it thoroughly (use a salad spinner to spin the cilantro dry), and wrap it in paper towels. Store it in the vegetable compartment of your refrigerator where it should keep for several days.

CINNAMON STICKS OR BARK

Cinnamon sticks are curled, paper-thin pieces of the bark of the cinnamon tree. Chinese cinnamon comes as thicker sticks of this bark. The latter is highly aromatic and more pungent than the cinnamon sticks commonly found in the West. Try to obtain the Chinese version but, if you cannot find it, the western sticks are an adequate substitute. They add a refreshing taste to braised dishes and are an important ingredient of five-spice powder. Store cinnamon bark or sticks in a tightly sealed jar to preserve their aroma and flavor. Ground cinnamon is not a satisfactory substitute.

COCONUT MILK

Coconut milk is widely usedIn Southeast Asia. It has has similarities to cow's milk: the 'cream'(fatty globules) rises to the top when the milk sits; it must be stirred as it comes to a boil; and its fat is closer in chemical composition to butterfat than to vegetable fat. The milk itself is the liquid wrung from the grated and pressed coconut meat, combined with water.

Coconut milk is not unknown in southern China, a region that has for centuries been open to the influences emanating from Southeast Asia where curries and stews made with coconut milk are common. The milk is used as a popular cooling beverage and in puddings and candies. In Hong Kong and parts of southern China today, one will find many coconut-milk dishes and desserts, directly inspired by Thai and other Southeast Asian cuisines.

In Asian markets, it may be possible to find freshly made coconut milk, especially near areas where there is a large Southeast Asian population. Fortunately, however, an inexpensive canned version can be bought in supermarkets. Many of the available brands are of high quality and can be recommended. Look for the ones from Thailand or Malaysia. You can find them at Asian markets. They are usually sold in cans of 14 fl oz to 15 fl oz (400 ml - 425 ml). Be sure to shake the can well before opening.

CORIANDER, GROUND

Ground coriander has a fresh, lemon-like sweet flavor. Widely used in curry mixes, it can be purchased already ground. However, the best method is to dry-roast whole coriander seeds and then finely grind the seeds. The leafy part of the coriander plant is known cilantro.

CUMIN, GROUND

This common spice adds a touch of fragrance to many fusion recipes. I prefer to oven-roast whole cumin seeds and grind them as I need them.

CURRY POWDER, MADRAS

Although this western-style powder is quite different from those used by the Indian community, there are many reliable commercial brands used by fusion cooks for their exotic and subtle aroma and flavor.

EGGPLANT

These pleasing, purple-skinned vegetables range in size from the larger plump ones, easy to find in all produce stores, to the small thin variety which the Chinese prefer for their more delicate flavor. Look for those with smooth, unblemished skin.

Chinese people normally do not peel eggplant, since the skin preserves texture, taste, and shape. Large western-variety eggplant should be cut according to the recipe, sprinkled with a little salt, and allowed to drain for 20 minutes. They should then be rinsed and blotted dry with paper towels. This process extracts bitter juices and excess moisture from the vegetable before it is cooked, giving a truer taste to a dish. The eggplant also absorb less fat if you do this. If you are using Chinese or Japanese eggplant, the process isn't necessary.

FISH SAUCE (see Sauces and Pastes, page 22)

FIVE-SPICE POWDER

Five-spice powder is less commonly known as five-flavored powder or five-fragrance spice powder, and it is becoming a staple in the spice section of supermarkets. Chinese grocers always keep it in stock. This brown powder is a mixture of star anise, Sichuan peppercorns, fennel seeds, cloves, and cinnamon. A good blend is pungent, fragrant, spicy and slightly sweet at the same time. The exotic fragrance it gives to a dish makes the search for a good mixture well worth the effort. It keeps indefinitely in a well-sealed jar.

GINGER

Fresh ginger root is an indispensable ingredient in authentic Chinese cooking and is one of the most common ingredients adopted by fusion cooks. Its pungent, spicy, and fresh taste adds a subtle but distinctive flavor to soups, meats, and vegetables. It is also an important seasoning for fish and seafood since it neutralizes fishy smells. Fresh ginger looks rather like a gnarled Jerusalem artichoke and can range in size from 3 in (7.5 cm) to 6 in (15 cm) long. It has pale brown, dry skin which is usually peeled away before use. Select fresh ginger which is firm with no signs of shrivelling. It will keep in the refrigerator, well wrapped in plastic wrap, for up to two weeks. Fresh ginger can now be bought at most Asian markets as well as at supermarkets. Dried powdered ginger has a quite different flavor and

should not be substituted for fresh root ginger.

GINGER JUICE

Ginger juice is made from fresh ginger and is used in marinades to give a subtle ginger taste without the bite of fresh chopped pieces. Here is a simple method of extracting ginger juice: cut unpeeled fresh ginger into 1 in (2.5 cm) chunks and drop them into a running food processor. When the ginger is finely chopped, squeeze out the juice by hand through a cotton or linen towel. Alternatively, mash some fresh ginger with a kitchen mallet or the side of a cleaver or knife until most of the fibers are exposed. Then simply squeeze out the juice by hand through a cotton or linen towel.

HOISIN SAUCE (see Sauces and Pastes, page 22)

LEMON GRASS

Originally from Southeast Asia, this plant is little used in China and then usually in dried form for making tea. Its subtle, lemony fragrance and flavor impart a very special cachet to delicate foods and it is a standard ingredient in Thai and Vietnamese dishes. Typical in Asian cuisine, the herb is considered a medicinal agent as well as a spice and is often prescribed for digestive disorders. Lemon grass is closely related to citronella grass. The latter plant has a stronger oil content and is more likely to be used commercially in perfumes and as a mosquito repellent. The two plants should not be confused.

Fresh lemon grass is sold in stalks that can be 2 ft (60 cm) long – it looks like a very long scallion. It is a fibrous plant but this is no problem because what is wanted is its fragrance and taste. The lemon grass pieces are always removed after the dish is cooked. Some recipes may call for lemon grass to be finely chopped or pounded into a paste, causing it to become an integral aspect of the dish.

You can buy lemon grass in Asian markets and in some supermarkets. Get the freshest possible Avoid the dried from for cooking; it is more suited to herbal tea. Keep it loosely wrapped in the bottom part of your refrigerator for up to one week.

Lemon is not a substitute for the unique flavor of lemon grass.

LIME

This small, green, citrus fruit has a delicate, tart taste that is widely used in Asia to impart a zing to food or as a base for sauces. The refreshing juice and the peel have been used by fusion cooks and chefs to impart a unique taste to many dishes.

LOTUS ROOT

This well-known, perennial aquatic plant with its beautiful white and pink water-lily flowers is a native of Asia. Although all the lotus plant is edible, the root or stems are the parts most commonly available. They are buff-colored, wooden-looking and quite long, divided into sausage-like segments each up to 5 in (12 cm). Air passages run the length of the root, giving them a beautiful, paper-chain cross-section. They have a crisp fibrous texture with a mild, distinctive flavor (some say they resemble artichokes). They may be cooked in many ways: stir-fried, mixed with other vegetables, used in vegetarian dishes, dried, steamed in soup, fried, or candied. Used raw in salads cut into slices, they make a most attractive appearance. Look for lotus roots that are firm and free of bruises. Uncut, they can be kept in the bottom part of your refrigerator for up to three weeks.

Fusion chefs love to deep-fry lotus roots because they make a wonderful-looking garnish.

MIRIN

This is a heavy, sweet Japanese rice wine with a light, syrupy texture. It is used only in cooking to add a mild sweetness to sauces or foods. It is especially delicious with broiled foods since, once the alcohol is burned off, only the sweet essence of the mirin remains. There is no fully satisfactory substitute for this unique item but in this book I have suggested dry sherry as an alternative. Mirin can be found in many Asian markets or Japanese speciality food shops. One bottle will last quite a long time and is well worth the search.

MUSHROOMS, CHINESE DRIED

There are many varieties of these, which add a particular flavor and aroma to Chinese dishes. They can be black or brown in color. The very large ones with a lighter color and a cracked surface are the best. They are usually the most expensive, so use them with a light touch. They can be bought in plastic cartons or by the ounce from Asian markets. Store them in an air-tight jar. They have a rich, smoky aroma that fusion cooks prize.

To use Chinese dried mushrooms: soak the mushrooms in a bowl of warm water for about 20 minutes, or until they are soft and pliable. Squeeze out the excess water and cut off and discard the woody stems. Only the caps are used.

The soaking water can be saved and used in soups and as rice water. Strain the liquid through a fine sieve to separate any sand or residue from the dried mushrooms.

MUSTARD GREENS, PICKLED (see Sichuan Preserved Vegetables, page 23)

NOODLES/PASTA

Noodles provide a nutritious, quick, light snack. Several types Chinese noodle have now made their way to the West, including the fresh, thin, egg noodles which are browned on both sides, and the popular thin rice noodles. Both kinds can be bought fresh and dried in Asian markets. Below is a listing of the major types of noodles which are used by fusion cooks and chefs.

Bean Thread (Transparent) Noodles

These noodles, also called cellophane noodles, are made from ground mung beans and not from a grain flour. They are available dried and are very fine and white. Easy to recognize, packed in their neat, plastic-wrapped bundles, they are stocked by Asian markets and supermarkets. They are never served on their own, instead being added to soups or braised dishes or being deep-fried and used as a garnish. They must be soaked in warm water for about 5 minutes before use. Since they are rather long, you might find it easier to cut them into shorter lengths after soaking. If you are frying them, they do not need soaking beforehand, but they do need to be separated. A good technique for separating the strands is to pull them apart in a large paper bag, which stops them from flying all over the place.

Chinese Wheat Noodles and Egg Noodles

These are made from hard or soft wheat flour and water. If egg has been added, the noodles are usually labelled as egg noodles. Supermarkets and delicatessens also stock both the dried and fresh varieties. Flat noodles are usually used in soups, while rounded noodles are best for stir-frying or pan-frying. The fresh ones freeze nicely if they are well wrapped. Thaw them thoroughly before cooking.

To Cook Wheat and Egg Noodles Noodles are very good blanched and served with main dishes, instead of plain rice. I think dried wheat or fresh egg noodles are best for this. If you are using fresh noodles, immerse them in a pan of boiling water and cook them for 3–5 minutes or until you find their texture to your taste. If you are using dried noodles, either cook them according to the instructions on the package or cook them in boiling water for 4–5 minutes. Drain and serve.

If you are cooking noodles ahead of time, or before stir-frying them, toss the cooked and drained noodles in 2 teaspoons of sesame oil and put them into a bowl. Cover this with plastic wrap and refrigerate. The cooked noodles will remain usable for about 2 hours.

Rice Noodles

These dried noodles are opaque white and come in a variety of shapes. One of the most common examples is rice-stick noodles, which are flat and about the length of a chopstick. They can also vary in thickness. Use the type called for in each recipe. Rice noodles are very easy to prepare. Simply soak them in warm water for 20 minutes until they are soft. Drain them in a colander or a sieve, and then they are ready to be used in soups or to be stir-fried.

Somyun noodles

These Korean wheat noodles are different from egg noodles in that they are whiter and contain no egg. The noodles are made of wheat flour, salt, and water (or sometimes mixed with rice flour), kneaded into a dough, and then rolled and cut. In the West, they are usually available dried.

OILS

Oil is the most commonly used cooking medium in China as well as many other parts of Asia. The favorite is peanut oil. Animal fats, usually lard and chicken fat, are also used in some areas, particularly in northern China. I always use groundnut oil, since I find animal fats too heavy.

Throughout this book I have indicated where oils can be re-used. Where this is possible, simply cool the oil after use and filter it through muslin or a fine strainer into a jar. Cover it tightly and keep in a cool, dry place. If you keep it in the refrigerator, it will become cloudy, but it will clarify again when the oil returns to room temperature. I find oils are best re-used just one time more, and this is healthier, since constantly re-used oils increase in saturated fat.

Corn Oil

Corn or maize oil is also quite suitable for Chinese cooking. It has a high heating point although I find it to be rather bland and with a slightly disagreeable smell. It is high in polyunsaturates and is, therefore, one of the healthier oils.

Peanut Oil

I prefer to use peanut for Chinese cooking because it has a pleasant, unobtrusive taste. Although it has a higher saturated fat content than some oils, its ability to be heated to a high temperature without burning makes it perfect for stir-frying and deep-frying. Most supermarkets stock it, but if you cannot find it, use corn oil instead.

OTHER VEGETABLE OILS

Some of the cheaper vegetable oils available include soy bean, safflower, and sunflower oils. They are light in color and taste, and can also be used in Chinese cooking, but they smoke and burn at lower temperatures than peanut oil, so care must be used when cooking with them.

Sesame Oil

This thick, rich, golden brown oil made from sesame seeds has a distinctive, nutty flavor and aroma. It is widely used in Chinese cooking as a seasoning but is not normally used as a cooking oil because it heats rapidly and burns easily. Therefore, think of it more as a flavoring than as a cooking oil. It is often added at the last moment to finish a dish. Sold in bottles, it can be obtained in Asian markets and many supermarkets.

OYSTER SAUCE (see Sauces and Pastes, page 22)

PEPPERCORNS

Black Peppercorns

Black peppercorns are unripe berries from a vine of the Piperaceae family, which are picked, fermented, and dried until they are hard and black. They are best when freshly ground.

Sichuan Peppercorns

Sichuan peppercorns are known throughout China as 'flower peppers' because they look like flower buds opening. They are reddish-brown in color and have a strong, pungent odor, which distinguishes them from the hotter black peppercorns. They are actually not from peppers at all; they are the dried berries of a shrub which is a member of the citrus family. Their smell reminds me of lavender, while their taste is sharp and mildly spicy. They can be ground in a conventional peppermill and are very often roasted before they are ground to bring out their full flavor. They are inexpensive and sold wrapped in cellophane or in plastic bags in Asian markets. They will keep indefinitely if stored in a well-sealed container.

To Roast Sichuan Peppercorns Heat a wok or heavy frying-pan to a medium heat. Add the peppercorns (you can cook about 5 oz (150 g) at a time) and stir-fry them for about 5 minutes, until they brown slightly and start to smoke. Remove the pan from the heat and let them cool. Grind the peppercorns in a pepper mill, clean coffee grinder, or with a mortar and pestle. Seal the mixture tightly in a screw-topped jar until you need some. Alternatively, keep the whole roasted peppercorns in a well-sealed container and grind them when required.

White Peppercorns

White peppercorns are made from the largest of the ripe berries, which are suspended in running water for several days. The berries swell, making the removal of the outer skin easier; the pale-colored inner seeds are sun-dried, which turns them a pale beige color.

Five-pepper Mixture

Five-pepper or five-peppercorn mixture is a fragrant aromatic mixture of whole black, white, pink, and green peppercorns, and allspice berries. Available in supermarkets, this mix, freshly ground, gives food a wonderful tasty touch. It is popular with fusion cooks and chefs because it bestows an added dimension to recipes.

SHRIMP

The most common varieties of shrimp available are farm-raised. Almost all shrimp have been frozen before being offered for sale. What is called fresh shrimp have actually been flash-frozen, shipped, and then thawed for immediate use. These are sized as jumbo, large, medium, and very small ones and are available in supermarkets, fish markets, and in many Asian markets. The jumbo or large sizes are most suitable for recipes used in this book. Fresh shrimp are occasionly available. In any case, avoid buying cooked shrimp, which in most cases, are already overcooked. Thus, any sauce you cook them in will not permeate to flavor the shrimp.

To Peel Shrimp First twist off the head and pull off the tail. It should then be quite easy to peel off the shell and with it the tiny legs. If you are using large or jumbo uncooked shrimp, make a shallow cut down the back of each one and remove the fine digestive cord, which runs the length of each shrimp. Wash the shrimp before you use them.

Chinese Trick for Frozen Uncooked Shrimp After peeling and preparing the uncooked shrimp as instructed above, rinse them twice in 1 tablespoon of salt and 5 cups (1.2 liters) cold water, changing the mixture of salt and water each time. This process helps to firm the shrimp and gives them a crystalline clean taste as well as a crisp texture.

RICE, BASMATI

This fragrant rice from the subcontinent of India and Pakistan is prized for its aromatic and nutty flavor. Widely available in supermarkets, this popular rice is much favored by fusion cooks and chefs.

RICE FLOUR

This flour is made from raw rice and is used to make fresh rice noodles. Store it as you would wheat flour.

RICE PAPER

Made from a mixture of rice flour, water, and salt and rolled out by a machine to paper thinness, rice paper, or *bánh tráng* as is it known, is then dried on bamboo mats in the sun, giving it a beautiful cross-hatch pattern. It is available only in dry form, in a round or triangular shape that is semi-transparent, thin, and hard. It is used extensively for wrapping Vietnamese spring rolls of pork and seafood, which are then fried and wrapped with crisp fresh lettuce and herbs and, finally, dipped in a sweet and sour hot sauce. Although more identified with Vietnamese cooking, rice paper has nevertheless become quite popular and is often used by restaurants in Hong Kong, Taiwan and parts of southern China.

Available from many Chinese grocers and supermarkets, it is inexpensive and comes in packages of 50–100 sheets. All brands are good, especially the ones from Vietnam and Thailand. Choose white-looking rice paper; a yellowish color may be a sign of age. Broken pieces in the packet may also indicate age.

Store rice paper in a dry cool place. After use, wrap the remaining rice papers carefully in the package they came in and put this in another plastic bag and seal well before storing.

RICE WINE, SHAOXING

An important component in Chinese cooking, rice wine is used extensively for cooking and drinking throughout China, but I believe the finest of its many varieties to be from Shaoxing in Zhejiang Province in eastern China. It is made from glutinous rice, yeast and spring water. Chefs use it for cooking as well as in marinades and sauces. Now readily available in Asian markets and in some wine shops in the West, it should be kept tightly corked at room temperature. A good-quality, dry pale sherry can be substituted but cannot equal its rich, mellow taste. Do not confuse this wine with sake, which is the Japanese version of rice wine and quite different. Western grape wines are not an adequate substitute, either.

SAUCES AND PASTES

Chinese and Asian cooking involves a number of thick, tasty sauces and pastes. They are essential to the authentic taste of Chinese cooking, and it is well worth making the effort to obtain them. Most are sold in bottles or tins by Chinese grocers and some supermarkets. Canned sauces, once opened, should be transferred to screw-topped glass jars and kept in the refrigerator where they will last indefinitely.

Chili-bean Sauce

This thick, dark sauce or paste, which is made from soy beans, chilies and other seasonings, is very hot and spicy. It is usually available in jars from Asian markets. Be sure to seal the jar tightly after use and store in the refrigerator. Do not confuse it with chili sauce (see page 15) which is a hotter, redder, thinner sauce made without beans and used mainly as a dipping sauce for cooked dishes.

Fish Sauce

Fish sauce is also known as fish gravy or *nam pla* and is a thin brown sauce made from fermented, salted, fresh fish. It is sold bottled and has a very fishy odor and salty taste. However, cooking greatly diminishes the 'fishy' flavor, and the sauce simply adds a special richness and quality to dishes. The Thai brands are especially good.

Hoisin Sauce

This is a thick, dark, brownish-red sauce, which is made from soy beans, vinegar, sugar, spices, and other flavorings. It is sweet and spicy. Hoisin sauce (sometimes called barbecue sauce) is sold in tins and jars and is available from Asian markets and supermarkets. If refrigerated, it can keep indefinitely.

Oyster Sauce

This thick, brown sauce is made from a concentrate of oysters cooked in soy sauce and brine. Despite its name, oyster sauce does not taste fishy. It has a rich flavor and is used in cooking and as a condiment, diluted with a little oil, for vegetables, poultry and meats. It is usually sold in bottles and can be bought in Chinese grocers and supermarkets. Best kept refrigerated. There is also an oyster-flavored version for vegetarians.

Sesame Paste

This rich, thick, creamy, light or dark brown paste is made from sesame seeds. It is sold in jars by Chinese grocers and is used in both hot and cold dishes. If you cannot obtain it, use peanut butter which resembles it in texture. Avoid using the Middle Eastern sesame paste, which is less flavorful.

Soy Sauce

Soy sauce is an essential ingredient in Chinese cooking. It is made from a mixture of soy beans, flour, and water, which is then fermented naturally and aged for some months. The liquid finally distilled is soy sauce. There are two main types.

Light Soy Sauce

As the name implies, this is light in color, but it is full of flavor and is the better one to use for cooking. It is saltier than dark soy sauce and is known in Chinese grocers as 'Superior Soy'.

Dark Soy Sauce

This sauce is aged for much longer than light soy sauce, hence its darker, almost black color. It is slightly thicker, stronger, and less salty than light soy sauce and is more suitable for stews. I prefer it to light soy as a dipping sauce. It is known in Chinese grocers as 'Soy Superior Sauce'.

Most soy sauces sold in supermarkets are dark soy. Chinese grocers sell both types and the quality is excellent. Be sure you buy the correct one, as the names are very similar.

Thai curry paste

An intensely flavored paste of herbs and spices, this is used to flavor coconut curries and soups as well as other dishes. The red curry paste is made with red dried chilies and the green curry paste with fresh green chilies. Home-made curry paste is time-consuming to prepare; however, ready-made curry pastes of high quality are available in supermarkets.

Whole Yellow-bean Sauce

This thick, spicy, aromatic sauce is made of yellow beans, flour, and salt which are fermented together. It is quite salty, but it adds a distinctive flavor to Chinese sauces. There are two forms: whole beans in a thick sauce and mashed or puréed beans (sold as 'crushed yellow bean sauce'). I prefer the whole-bean variety because it is slightly less salty and has a better texture.

SESAME SEEDS

These are dried seeds of the sesame herb. Unhulled, the seeds range from grayish-white to black in color but, once the hull is removed, the sesame seeds are found to be tiny, somewhat flattened, cream-colored and pointed at one end. Keep them in a glass jar in a cool, dry place; they will last indefinitely.

To Make Toasted Sesame Seeds Heat a frying-pan or skillet until hot. Add the sesame seeds and stir occasionally. Watch them closely and when they begin to brown lightly (about 3–5 minutes), stir them again and pour them onto a plate. When cold, store them in a glass jar in a cool, dark place.

Alternatively, you could pre-heat the oven to 325°F/160°C. Spread the sesame seeds on a baking sheet and roast them in the oven for about 10–15 minutes until they are nicely toasted and lightly browned. Allow them to cool and place in a glass jar until you are ready to use them.

SICHUAN PRESERVED VEGETABLES

The root of the mustard green, pickled in salt and hot chilies. Sold in cans in Asian markets, it gives a pleasantly crunchy texture and spicy taste to dishes. Before using it, rinse in cold water and then slice or chop as required. Any unused vegetable should be transferred to a covered jar and stored in the refrigerator where it will keep indefinitely.

STAR ANISE

The star anise is a hard, star-shaped spice and is the seed-pod of a bush. It is similar in flavor and fragrance to common anise, but is more robust and liquorice-like. Star anise is an essential ingredient of five-spice powder and is widely used in braised dishes, to which it imparts a rich taste and fragrance. It is sold in plastic packs in Asian markets and should be stored in a tightly covered jar in a cool, dry place.

SUGAR

Sugar has been used sparingly in preparing savory dishes in China for a thousand years. Properly employed, it helps balance the flavors of sauces and other dishes. Chinese sugar comes in several forms: as rock or yellow lump sugar, as brown sugar blocks, and as maltose or malt sugar. I particularly like to use rock sugar, which is rich with a more subtle flavor than that of refined granulated sugar. It also gives a good luster or glaze to braised dishes and sauces. You may need to break the lumps into smaller pieces with a wooden mallet or rolling pin. If you cannot find it, use white sugar or turbino sugar (the amber, chunky kind) instead.

TARO ROOT

An ancient food cultivated for a long time, taro was a starch used in China and south-east Asia, long before rice. These tubers vary in shape, but they are roughly spherical, anything from tennis-ball size to about 9 in (23 cm) in diameter, and often covered with a rough skin and brownish hairs. They are starchy, with a sweet flavor, a doughy texture, and a whitish flesh, often with purple streaks. They can be cooked like potatoes and are sometimes used to make flour. They are often combined with meats in braised dishes. However, they are versatile enough to be used in desserts and as a paste for *dim sum*, as well as deep-fried. They must be peeled before using. Buy firm-looking taro without bruises.

Store in a dark, cool place (like potatoes or onions) and use within a week.

TEA, CHINESE BLACK

Chinese black tea is a full-bodied, fragrant and smooth tea, with a rich aroma and a superb bouquet. There are various kinds, of which Keemun is one of the most well known. Tea is used in smoked dishes or in sauces. You can purchase Chinese black teas in Asian markets, delicatessens, and in many supermarkets. I prefer to store tea in canisters, since these keep the tea in the freshest possible condition.

TOFU

Tofu is the Japanese name for beancurd, also known by its Chinese name *doufu*. It has played a crucial role in Chinese cooking for over a thousand years, since it is highly nutritious and rich in protein. Tofu has a distinctive texture but a bland taste. It is made from yellow soy beans, which are soaked, ground, mixed with water, and then cooked briefly before being solidified. In the West, it is usually sold in two forms: firm in cheese-like cakes or soft in a thick yogurt-like texture. It is also available in several dried forms and in a fermented version. The soft, yogurt-like variety (sometimes called silken tofu) is used for soups, while the solid type is used for stir-frying, braising, and poaching. Solid beancurd 'cakes' are white in color and are sold in supermarkets, Asian markets, and in many health-food shops. They are packed in water in plastic containers and may be kept refrigerated in this state for up to five days

provided the water is changed daily. To use this firm tofu, cut the amount required into cubes or shreds using a sharp knife. Do this with care because it is delicate. It also needs to be cooked carefully; too much stirring can cause it to crumble. Whatever its shape or texture, tofu remains highly nutritious.

VINEGAR

Vinegars are widely used in Chinese cooking. Unlike western vinegars, they are usually made from rice. There are many varieties, ranging in flavor from the spicy and slightly tart to the sweet and pungent. The following vinegars can be bought in Asian markets and supermarkets. They are sold in bottles and will keep indefinitely. If you cannot get Chinese vinegars, I suggest you use cider vinegar. Malt vinegar can be used, but its taste is stronger and more acidic.

White Rice Vinegar

White rice vinegar is clear and mild in flavor. It has a faint taste of glutinous rice and is used for sweet and sour dishes. The Japanese white rice vinegar is milder in flavor than its Chinese counterpart.

Black Rice Vinegar

Black rice vinegar is very dark in colur and rich, though mild, in taste. It is used for braised dishes, sauces and sometimes as a dipping sauce for crab.

Red Rice Vinegar

Red rice vinegar is sweet and spicy in taste and is usually used as a dipping sauce for seafood.

WATER CHESTNUTS

Water chestnuts are a sweet root vegetable or bulb, about the size of a walnut. They are white and crunchy. In China, they are eaten as a snack, having first been boiled in their skins, or peeled and then simmered in rock sugar. They are also used in cooked dishes, especially in southern China.

In the West, fresh water chestnuts can sometimes be obtained from Asian markets or gourmet supermarkets. They are tastier than canned ones and will keep, unpeeled, in a paper bag in the refrigerator for up to two weeks. Peel them before use, and, if you have any left over, put them back in the refrigerator, covered with cold water. Canned water chestnuts are sold in supermarkets and Asian markets. They have a good texture but little taste. Rinse them well in cold water before you use them, and store any unused ones in a jar of cold water. They will keep for several weeks in the refrigerator if you change the water daily.

WONTON SKINS

Wonton skins, made from egg and flour, can be bought, fresh or frozen, from Asian markets. They are thin, pastry-like wrappers, which can be stuffed with ground meat and fried, steamed, or cooked in soups. They are sold in little piles of 3¼ in (8 cm) yellowish squares, wrapped in plastic. The number of squares or skins in a packet varies from about 30 to 36, depending upon the supplier. Fresh wonton skins will keep for about five days if stored in plastic wrap or a plastic bag in the refrigerator. If you are using frozen wonton skins, just peel off the number you require and thaw them thoroughly before you use them.

WESTERN INGREDIENTS USED IN FUSION COOKING

BUTTER

Although butter is rarely used by Asian cooks or chefs, in fusion recipes good-quality unsalted butter adds a delicate, slightly rich flavor and sheen to sauces. Unlike in western cooking, the butter is used sparsely in fusion recipes.

CAUL FAT

Caul fat (or *crépine*) is a lacy membrane, often used by European and Chinese cooks to encase stuffings and to keep food moist while cooking. Actually the lower stomach of a pig or cow, caul fat melts during cooking and keeps meats and fillings moist and delicious. It is highly perishable, so buy it in small quantities and use quickly. For longer storage, wrap the caul fat carefully and freeze it. To defrost, rinse in cold water. I find that soaking caul fat in cold water helps to separate the fat, without tearing its lacy and fragile webs. You can order caul fat from your butcher.

CREAM

Like butter, cream is not normally used in Asia. However, in fusion recipes it adds an overtone of richness to the sharp taste of spices, rounding out and uniting the overall flavor of the dish.

CRÈME FRAÎCHE

This sour cream is prized for its wonderful tangy taste and, like cream, adds another dimension of flavors to sauces.

GARLIC

This common flavoring is used by fusion cooks in numerous ways: whole, finely chopped, crushed, and pickled. It is used to flavor oils as well as spicy sauces, and it is often paired with other, equally pungent ingredients, such as sun-dried tomatoes, scallions, black beans, or fresh ginger.

Select fresh garlic that is firm and, preferably, pinkish in color. It should be stored in a cool, dry place but not in the refrigerator, where it can easily become mildewed or begin sprouting.

HERBS: basil, chives, rosemary, thyme, marjoram, sage

These herbs, common in European cooking but relatively unknown in Asia, give fusion dishes a liveliness that is delicate at the same time.

HONEY

Used in fusion cookery to give food a rich, deep-color sheen.

LEMON

Both the zest and juice of this common fruit are used to give fusion dishes a tart accent. Lemon is usually used to balance rich tastes and flavors.

MUSTARD, DIJON

This delectable condiment combines well with Asian flavors such as soy sauce to create a union of aromatic fragrances that gives meat a special fusion taste.

OIL, EXTRA VIRGIN OLIVE

Use the best quality extra virgin olive oil to cook fusion dishes. Its rich, fruity seasoning combines well with the exotic spices of the East.

ORANGE

Like lemon, this tangy fruit is used to balance the sharp spices of Asia.

PEPPERS

Used by many fusion cooks and chefs for their bright colors as well as their delicate taste.

RICE (ARBORIO)

This is the Italian rice that is perfect for making risotto. It is a round, plump rice that absorbs large quantities of liquid without the rice turning into a mush. The starch in the rice makes the dish creamy.

SHALLOTS

Shallots are mild-flavored members of the onion family. They are small – about the size of pickling onions – with copper-red skins. They have a distinctive onion taste, without being as strong or as overpowering as ordinary onions. Readily available, they make an excellent substitute for Chinese shallots, which are difficult to find even in Asian markets. In China, you will find them fresh or pickled, and they are paired with preserved eggs as a snack. They are expensive, but their sweet flavor permeates food; a few go a long way. Keep them in a cool, dry place (not the refrigerator), and peel, slice or chop them as you would an onion.

SPINACH

Western varieties of spinach are quite different from those used in China. Nevertheless, they make satisfactory substitutes for the Chinese variety. Spinach is most commonly stir-fried, so frozen spinach is, obviously, unsuitable, since it is so moist. Chinese water spinach is the type most frequently cooked in China and is available in Asian markets in the West. It has hollow stems and delicate, green, pointed leaves; it is also lighter in color than common spinach and has a milder taste. It should be cooked when it is very fresh, preferably on the day it is bought.

TOMATOES: fresh, canned, sun-dried, puréed

Fresh tomatoes are prized by fusion cooks for their refreshing taste as well as flavor. Canned tomatoes are a convenience and perfectly acceptable. Sun-dried tomatoes are pungent, tangy, dried tomatoes preserved in olive oil. Their intense flavors are a perfect foil for strong Asian spices. Puréed tomatoes are used to enrich sauces.

VANILLA

This common, sweet, fragrant spice marries well with other fusion flavors. Used in desserts, the vanilla pod is split in half and the small dark seeds are scraped out and used.

COOKING TECHNIQUES

A number of cooking techniques are referred to in this book. Here is a short explanation for your reference.

BLANCHING

Putting food into a pan filled with hot water or into moderately hot oil for a few minutes will cook it briefly but not entirely. It is a sort of softening-up process to prepare the food for final cooking. Chicken is often blanched in oil or water after being velveted (that is, coated in egg white and cornstarch). Meat is sometimes blanched to rid it of unwanted gristle and fat and in order to ensure a clean taste and appearance. Blanching in water is common with hard vegetables such as broccoli or carrots. The vegetable is plunged into boiling water for several minutes; it is then drained and plunged into cold water to arrest the cooking process. In such cases blanching usually precedes stir-frying.

BRAISING AND RED-BRAISING

This technique is most often applied to tougher cuts of meat and certain vegetables. The food is usually browned and then put into flavored stock and brought to a boil. It is then simmered gently until cooked. Red-braising is simply the technique by which food is braised in a dark liquid, such as soy sauce. This gives food a reddish-brown color, hence the name. This type of braising sauce can be saved and frozen for re-use. It can be re-used many times and becomes richer in flavor.

BROILING

Next to stir-frying, perhaps the most popular method of cooking fusion foods is barbequing or oven broiling. High heat from charcoals is used to seal juices in and give foods a rich, smoky flavor, and a crisp coating

over a moist- inside. Allow broiled meats and chicken to rest for at least 15 minutes before carving.

DEEP-FRYING

Deep-frying is also popular. The trick is to regulate the heat so that the surface of the food is sealed but does not brown so fast that the food remains raw inside. As with any technique, mastery comes with practice. Because deep-fried food must not be greasy, the process requires a lot of oil. Using a wok for deep-frying makes a great deal of sense since it requires less oil to achieve the depth needed for properly deep-fried foods.

Some points to bear in mind when deep-frying are:

• Wait for the oil to get hot enough before adding the food to be fried. The oil should give off a haze and almost produce little wisps of smoke when it is the right temperature, but you can test it by dropping in a small piece of food. If it bubbles all over then the oil is sufficiently hot. Adjust the heat as necessary to prevent the oil from actually smoking or overheating. You should use only peanut oil for deep-frying because it is relatively odorless.
• To prevent splattering, use paper towels to thoroughly dry the food to be deep-fried. If the food is in a marinade, remove it with a slotted spoon and let it drain before putting it into the oil. If you are using batter, make sure all the excess batter drips off before adding the food to the hot oil.
• Oil used for deep-frying can be re-used. Cool it and then strain it into a jar through several layers of muslin or through a fine mesh to remove any particles of food which might otherwise burn if re-heated and give the oil a bitter taste. Label the jar according to what food you have cooked in the oil and only re-use it for the same thing. Oil can be used up to two more times before it begins to lose its effectiveness.

POACHING

This is a method of simmering food gently in a pan until it is partially cooked. It is then put into soup or combined with a sauce and the cooking process continued. Delicately flavored and textured foods such as eggs and chicken are often poached.

SHALLOW-FRYING

This wok technique is similar to sautéing in a frying-pan and is just as effective. It involves more oil than stir-frying but less than deep-frying. Food is fried first on one side and then on the other. Sometimes, the excess oil is drained off and a sauce added to complete the dish.

SLOW SIMMERING AND STEEPING

These processes are similar. In slow simmering, food is immersed in liquid, which is brought almost to a boil, and then the temperature is reduced so that it simmers, cooking the food to the desired degree. This is the technique used for making stock. In steeping, food is similarly immersed in liquid (usually stock) and simmered for a time. The heat is then turned off and the remaining heat of the liquid finishes off the cooking process.

SMOKING

Smoked foods are popular with fusion cooks. The wok is useful for this process. Simply line the inside of the wok and its lid with aluminium foil. Add the smoking ingredients (usually black tea leaves, sugar, and spices). Place the food, which has first been marinated, on an oiled rack. Slowly heat the ingredients and, when they begin to burn and smoke, cover the wok tightly. Turn the heat to low and slowly smoke according to the instructions in the recipe.

STEAMING

Steaming has been used by the Chinese for thousands of years. Along with stir-frying and deep-

frying it is the most widely used technique. Steamed foods are cooked by a gentle, moist heat which must circulate freely in order to cook the food. It is an excellent method for bringing out subtle flavors and, therefore, is particularly appropriate for fish. Bamboo steamers are used by the Chinese but you can use any one of several utensils.

• *Using a bamboo steamer in a wok* For this, you need a large bamboo steamer about 10 in (25 cm) wide. Put about 2 in (5 cm) of water in a wok. Bring it to a simmer. Put the bamboo steamer containing the food into the wok, where it should rest safely perched on the sloping sides. Cover the steamer with its matching lid and steam the food until it is cooked. Replenish the water as required.

• *Using a wok as a steamer* Put about 2 in (5 cm) of water into a wok. Then put a metal or wooden rack into the wok. Bring the water to a simmer and put the food to be steamed on to a heatproof plate. Lower the plate on to the rack and cover the wok tightly with a wok lid. Check the water level from time to time and replenish it with hot water, ifnecessary. The water should never make direct contact with the food.

• *Using a large roasting pan as a steamer* (if your wok is not large enough to be used). Put a metal or wooden rack into the pan and pour in water to a depth of about 2 in (5 cm). Bring it to a simmer and place the food to be steamed onto a heatproof plate. Lower the plate onto the rack and cover the pan with a lid or aluminium foil. Replenish the water as necessary.

• *Using a steamer* If you have a metal steamer which is wide enough to take a rack of food, this will give you very satisfactory results. Make sure of the level of the water in the bottom: it must not all evaporate or be so deep that it touches the food.

If you do not have a metal or wooden rack, you can use a small, empty can to support the plate of food. Remember that the food needs to remain above the water level and must not get wet. The water level should always be at least 1 in (2.5 cm) below the food. Be sure to use a heatproof plate.

STIR-FRYING

This is the most famous of all Chinese cooking techniques and is a favorite with fusion cooks and chefs around the world. It is possibly the trickiest, since success depends on having all the required ingredients prepared, measured out, and immediately at hand, and on having a good source of strong heat. Its advantage is that, if stir-frying is properly executed, the stir-fried foods can be cooked in minutes in very little oil so they retain their natural flavors and textures. It is very important that stir-fried foods are not overcooked or made greasy. Using a wok is definitely an advantage when stir-frying; its shape conducts the heat well and its high sides enable you to toss the contents rapidly, keeping them constantly moving while cooking. Having prepared all the ingredients for stir-frying, the steps are:

• Heat the wok or frying-pan until it is very hot before adding the oil. This prevents food from sticking and ensures an even heat. Peanut oil and olive oil are my favorites. Add the oil and, using a metal spatula or long-handled spoon, distribute it evenly over the surface. It should be very hot indeed – almost smoking – before you add the next ingredients, unless you are going on to flavor the oil (see next step).
• If you are flavoring the oil with garlic, scallions, ginger, dried red chili, or salt, make sure you wait for the oil to get so hot that it is almost smoking; however, you will need to work very quickly so that these ingredients do not burn and become bitter. Toss them quickly in the oil for a few seconds. In some recipes, these flavorings will then be removed and discarded before cooking proceeds.

• Now add the food to be cooked, and stir-fry by tossing it around the wok or pan with the metal spatula or long-handled spoon. If you are stir-frying meat, let each side rest for just a few seconds before continuing to stir. Keep moving the food from the center of the wok to the sides. Stir-frying is a noisy business and is usually accompanied by quite a lot of splattering because of the high temperature at which the food must be cooked, hence my preference for the long-handled wok.

• Some stir-fried dishes are thickened with a mixture of cornstarch and cold water. To avoid getting a lumpy sauce, be sure to remove the wok or pan from the heat for a minute before you add the cornstarch mixture, which must be thoroughly blended before it is added. The sauces can then be returned to the heat and thickened.

Stir-frying Vegetables

It is easy to use the wok to cook vegetables; however, you need to remember these few hints:

• Never add all the vegetables at once: you must sort them out according to their proper cooking time. Hard vegetables must go in first; then in go softer vegetables, and, lastly, the leafy ones.
• Hard vegetables, such as carrots, baby corn, broccoli, and fennel have very little moisture. They need to be cooked first and require a longer cooking time. You can either blanch them in salted, boiling water for a few minutes to soften them, or you can cook them longer in the wok with a little liquid. Cover the wok to speed up the cooking.
• Softer vegetables, such as red or green peppers, asparagus, or mushrooms, should be added after the hard vegetables have cooked for a few minutes. These vegetables do not need as much cooking as the hard ones.
• Leafy vegetables, such as Chinese bok choy, spinach, and lettuce, are full of moisture and should be added at the last moment and cooked only briefly.
• If, when stir-frying vegetables, the wok becomes dry, do NOT add oil because this will make the vegetables greasy and fatty; add a tablespoon or so of either water or Shaoxing rice wine instead.
• Covering the wok can speed the cooking; however, be careful not to overcook.

Although these are just some of the many techniques used with the wok, you will find the wok is just as useful for cooking any type of food. In other words, use your wok and you will find what an essential tool it can become in your kitchen.

BASICS

基本食譜

Basics ≈

Basic or 'foundation' recipes refer to those combinations of ingredients that recur frequently throughout this book. They include stocks which provide the basis for many different fusion dishes. Good stocks support the flavors of the other ingredients and enhance the overall taste and aromas of the completed ensemble. They can also be used as clear soups.

These stocks are best when homemade, and every kitchen should keep a supply of frozen stock on hand. Of course, reliable good commercial stocks may be used for convenience.

I have given recipes for three types of stock: chicken, fish, and vegetable. The chicken stock is an all-purpose one: I find that the richer stocks – made with ham or pork bones – are heavier and do not quite fit my eating preferences. This simple recipe reflects what I believe works best for any dish, fusion or otherwise.

The vegetables and the herbs in the fish stock help boost its flavor without overwhelming the natural taste of the fish dish.

The vegetable stock solves the problem presented by vegetarian cooking when it comes to stocks: in the absence of poultry, fish, or meat, it is difficult to prepare a truly rich stock, the foundation of any cuisine, but having a greater vegetable-to-water ratio will help give the stock a certain robustness.

Stocks do take time to prepare but it is easy to make your own. Since many recipes in this book rely on them for just the right finish, your first step on the path to success with fusion cooking must be to prepare and maintain an ample supply on hand. I prefer to make large quantities at a time and freeze them. (They keep their flavor for at least three months.) Once you have a supply available, you will be able to prepare any number of soups or sauces very quickly.

Here are several important points to keep in mind when making stock:

● The stock should never boil. If it does, it will turn cloudy and any fat will be incorporated into the liquid. Flavors and digestibility come with a clear stock and clarity is essential for inviting soups and sauces.

● Use a deep, heavy pan so the liquid covers all the solids and evaporation is slow.

● Simmer slowly and skim the stock regularly, helping to keep the stock clear and the flavor clean. Be patient: you will reap the rewards each time you prepare one of these tasty fusion dishes. Do not cover the pan.

● Strain the finished stock well through several layers of muslin or a fine-meshed strainer.

● Let the stock cool thoroughly, refrigerate it, and remove any fat before freezing it.

I have included steamed rice in this chapter since it goes well with many other dishes. Rice is so subtle and congenial that it is perfect for fusion cooking, and it stores well. Experiment with as many different types of rice as you can.

Infused flavored oils are other basics that are frequently used in fusion cooking. Their use was pioneered by Jean-Georges Vongerichten, a young and very talented chef who first made his mark in New York and who has since opened a very successful restaurant, Vong, in London. Jean-Georges came into his own while working at the Oriental Hotel in Bangkok, where he discovered and created his personal fusion cooking. Infused oils are like flavor bridges that bring together subtle and apparently disparate flavors while at the same time enhancing in surprising ways the entire spectrum of tastes. A splash of these aromatic oils provides fragrance with a minimum of fat – an important factor for fusion cooks and chefs. These oils keep well in the refrigerator.

HOMEMADE CHICKEN STOCK ≈

4½ lb (2 kg) uncooked
   chicken bones, such as
   backs, feet, wings
1½ lb (750 g) chicken
   pieces, such as wings,
   thighs, drumsticks, etc.
4 quarts (3.4 liters) cold
   water
6 diagonal 2 x ½ in (5 x 1
   cm) slices of fresh ginger
   (page 17)
9 scallions, green tops
   removed
1 whole head garlic, cloves
   separated but unpeeled
2 teaspoons salt
1 teaspoon whole black
   peppercorns

CHICKEN STOCK IS THE ALL-PURPOSE BASE FOR SOUPS AND SAUCES. ITS CHIEF INGREDIENT IS INEXPENSIVE, IT IS LIGHT AND DELICIOUS, AND IT COMBINES WELL WITH OTHER FOODS, ENHANCING AND SUSTAINING THEM. I HAVE FOUND THIS BASIC, HOMEMADE, CHINESE-INSPIRED CHICKEN STOCK IS PRECISELY THAT: THE ESSENCE OF CHICKEN WITH FUSION COMPLEMENTS OF GINGER AND SCALLIONS. COMBINED WITH FRESH HERBS, BUTTER, INFUSED OILS, OR OLIVE OIL, THIS STOCK GIVES FUSION DISHES THEIR DISTINCTIVE FLAVOR. GOOD STOCK CAPTURES THE ESSENTIAL TASTE OF EAST AND WEST.

GOOD STOCK GENERALLY REQUIRES MEAT TO GIVE IT RICHNESS AND FLAVOR. IT IS THEREFORE NECESSARY TO USE AT LEAST SOME CHICKEN MEAT, IF NOT A WHOLE BIRD, ALONG WITH THE CARCASS. REMEMBER TO SAVE ALL YOUR UNCOOKED CHICKEN BONES AND CARCASSES FOR STOCK. THEY CAN BE FROZEN UNTIL YOU ARE READY TO MAKE IT.

IF YOU FIND THIS RECIPE MAKES TOO MUCH STOCK FOR YOUR NEEDS, MAKE HALF THE RECIPE.

Put the chicken bones and chicken pieces into a very large pan. (The bones can be put in either frozen or defrosted.) Cover them with the cold water and bring to a simmer, uncovered.

Using a large, flat spoon, skim off the foam as it rises from the bones. Watch the heat, so that the stock never boils. Keep skimming until the stock looks clear. This can take 20–40 minutes. Do not stir or disturb the stock.

Now turn the heat down to a low simmer. Add the ginger, scallions, garlic cloves, salt, and peppercorns. Simmer the stock on a very low heat for between 2 and 4 hours, skimming any fat off the top at least twice during this time. The stock should be rich and full-bodied, which is why it needs to be simmered for such a long time. This way the stock (and any soup you make with it) will have plenty of taste.

Strain the stock through several layers of dampened cheesecloth or through a very fine-meshed strainer; then let it cool thoroughly. Remove any fat that has risen to the top. It is now ready to be used or transferred to containers and frozen for future use.

℣Homemade Vegetable Stock ≈

One of the best vegetarian stocks I have ever sampled was one made by Chef Norbert Kostner, the Executive Chef of the famed Oriental Hotel in Bangkok. He kindly shared with me some of his ideas for this superb stock which I adapted in a simpler version suitable for home kitchens. To get assertive flavors, a ratio of 3 ½ quarts (3 liters) of water to at least 11 lb (5 k) of vegetables is needed. (Although such a quantity of vegetables may sound extravagant, remember - we are distilling essences here, and the cost is a fraction of what it would be to make a meat stock.) Browning the vegetables in the oven *before* simmering helps to impart flavor to the stock.

Experiment with different vegetable combinations and always choose what suits your own taste. If you find this recipe makes too much stock for your needs, cut the quantities in half or freeze some. It keeps, frozen, for up to three months.

Soak the dried mushrooms in warm water for 20 minutes. Drain them, saving the liquid. Then squeeze out any excess liquid and save it, also. Now coarsely chop the caps and stems. Strain the mushroom liquid through a fine sieve and set aside.

Coarsely chop the carrots, celery, onions, and radish. Discard the green part of the leeks and wash and coarsely chop the white. Peel the shallots but leave them whole. Coarsely chop the cucumber and tomatoes.

Pre-heat the oven to 450°F/220°C. On a baking sheet, put the scallions, ginger, garlic, shallots, mushrooms, carrots, celery, onions, mooli, and leeks, and brown for 20 minutes. Add the cucumber and tomatoes and brown for another 8 minutes. Place the contents of the baking sheet into a large pan; add the peppercorns, salt, water, and light soy sauce. Cover and bring the mixture to a simmer.

Using a large, flat spoon, skim off any foam as it rises to the top; this will take about 10–20 minutes. Bring the stock to a fast simmer. Now turn the heat down to a moderate simmer and cook for about 2 hours.

Strain the stock through a large colander and then through a very fine-meshed strainer; let it cool thoroughly. It is now ready to be used or transferred to containers and frozen for future use.

Makes about 3 quarts (2.75 liters)

- 2 oz (50 g (2) dried Chinese black mushrooms (page 19)
- 2¼ lb (1 kg) carrots, peeled
- 4 celery sticks
- 2¼ lb (1 kg) onions
- 2¼ lb (1 kg) Chinese white radish (page 15), peeled
- 4 leeks
- 8 oz (225 g) shallots
- 8 oz (225 g) cucumber, peeled and seeded
- 1 kg (2¼ lb) tomatoes, halved
- 6 scallions
- 6 slices of fresh ginger (page 17)
- 10 unpeeled garlic cloves, crushed
- 2 tablespoons black peppercorns
- 1 tablespoon Sichuan peppercorns (page 21) (optional)
- 2 tablespoons salt
- 3 quarts (2.75 liters) water
- 3 tablespoons light soy sauce (page 23)

Homemade Fish Stock ≈

Makes about 4 quarts (3.4 liters)

6 lb (2.75 kg) fish bones from any firm-fleshed, white fish, such as halibut, sea bass, sole, monkfish, or cod

3 ¾ quarts (3.4 liters) cold water

8 oz (225 g) leeks

8 oz (225 g) onions, coarsely chopped

1 lb (450 g) carrots, coarsely chopped

4 oz (100 g) shallots, coarsely chopped

8 sprigs of fresh parsley

4 sprigs of fresh thyme or 2 teaspoons dried thyme

2 bay leaves

5 garlic cloves, unpeeled, crushed

2 teaspoons salt

1 tablespoon whole black peppercorns

Fish stock exists in Oriental cooking mainly for light fish soups, rather than as a basic kitchen ingredient. However, I have discovered the virtues of fish stock while working and living in France. It is easier to make than chicken stock and gives an intense flavor to fish and seafood dishes as well as to sauces that accompany those dishes. Once made, it keeps well, frozen, for at least three months. If you find the recipe makes too muich stock for your needs, however, cut the quantities in half.

Rinse the fish bones under running cold water until the water runs clear. Put the fish bones in a very large pan. Cover them with the cold water and bring it to a simmer.

Meanwhile, trim the leeks and discard any yellow parts. Cut the leeks at the point where they begin to turn green and discard the green parts. Then split the white parts in half and rinse them well in cold running water until there is no trace of dirt. Coarsely chop the leeks.

Using a large, flat spoon, skim off the foam as it rises from the bones. Watch the heat, so that the stock never boils. Keep skimming, until the stock looks clear. This can take 20–30 minutes. Do not stir or disturb the stock.

Now turn the heat down to a low simmer. Add the rest of the ingredients and simmer, uncovered, for 1 hour.

Remove the bones and other ingredients with a large, slotted spoon and strain the stock through several layers of dampened cheesecloth or through a very fine-meshed strainer; then let it cool thoroughly. It is now ready to be used or transferred to containers and frozen for future use.

ⓋSteamed Rice ≈

Steaming is the simple, direct, and efficient technique for cooking rice. I prefer to use Indian basmati rice. It is a superior, long-grain white rice which is dry and fluffy when cooked. Don't use pre-cooked or 'instant' rice for fusion cookery, since it lacks flavor and texture and has a starchy taste.

The secret of preparing rice without it being sticky is to cook it first in an uncovered pan at high heat until most of the water has evaporated. Then turn the heat very low, cover the pan, and finish cooking the rice slowly in the remaining steam.

Here is a good trick to remember: if you make sure that you cover the rice with about 1 in (2.5 cm) of water, it will always cook properly, without sticking. Many recipes on the packages of rice use too much water and the result is a gluey mess. Follow my method and your rice will be perfectly steamed.

For the rice recipes in this book, the best kind to use is a simple, long-grain rice, of which there are many varieties. Along with Basmati, I particularly like Thai fragrant rice, which is widely available. Here are the rules with regard to successfully cooking long-grain rice.

- Use volume, rather than weight, to measure the rice: pour it into a clear measuring cup to the required level.
- The water should be at a level 1 in (2.5 cm) above the surface of the rice; too much water means gummy rice.
- Never uncover the pan once the simmering process has begun; time the process and wait.

Put the rice into a large bowl and wash it in several changes of water until the water becomes clear. Drain the rice, put it in a heavy pan with the right depth of water, and bring it to a boil. Continue boiling until most of the surface liquid has evaporated; this should take about 15 minutes. The surface of the rice should have small indentations, like pitted craters. At this point, cover the pan with a very tight-fitting lid, turn the heat as low as possible, and let the rice cook, undisturbed, for 15 minutes. There is no need to 'fluff' the rice. Let it rest for 5 minutes before serving it.

Serves 4

2 cups (400 ml) long-grain
    white rice
2 ½ cups (600 ml) water

ⓋBasil-flavored Olive Oil ≈

Makes 1 ½ cups (300 ml)

Bunches of fresh basil, including stems, weighing about 4 oz (100 g)

1 ¼ cups (300 ml) extra virgin olive oil

Blanch the basil in a large pan of boiling water for 15 seconds. Remove immediately and plunge into icy-cold water. Drain well and pat dry with paper towels.

Combine the blanched basil with the olive oil in a blender or food processor and purée them. Remove and let stand overnight.

Strain the oil through a fine sieve. Use at once or store, tightly covered, in the refrigerator for up to two weeks. Bring to room temperature and shake before using.

ⓋCilantro-flavored Olive Oil ≈

Makes 1 ½ cups (300 ml)

Bunches of fresh cilantro, including stems, weighing about 4 oz (100 g)

1 ¼ cups (300 ml) extra virgin olive oil

Blanch the cilantro in a large pan of boiling water for 15 seconds. Remove immediately and plunge into icy-cold water. Drain well and pat dry with paper towels.

Combine the blanched cilantro with the olive oil in a blender or food processor and purée them. Remove and let stand overnight.

Strain the oil through a fine sieve. Use at once or store, tightly covered, in the refrigerator for up to two weeks. Bring to room temperature and shake before using.

Ⓥ CHIVE-FLAVORED OLIVE OIL ≈

Put the chives in a juice extractor, blender, or food processor, with the water, and extract the juice. Strain though a fine sieve, if using a blender or processor. You should have a little more than ½ cup (135 ml) of juice.

Combine the chive juice with the olive oil in a blender and mix well. Use at once or store, tightly covered, in the refrigerator for up to three days. Bring to room temperature and shake before using.

MAKES 1 ¾ CUPS (400 ML)

Bunches of fresh chives, weighing about 4 oz (100 g)
2 tablespoons water
1 ¼ cups (300 ml) extra virgin olive oil

Ⓥ WATERCRESS-FLAVORED OLIVE OIL ≈

Put the watercress in a juice extractor, food processor, or blender, with the water, and extract the juice. If using a processor or blender, strain the juice. You should have a little more than ½ cup (135 ml) of juice.

Combine the watercress juice with the olive oil in a blender and blend well. Use immediately or store, tightly covered, in the refrigerator for up to three weeks. Bring to room temperature and shake well before using.

MAKES 1 ¾ CUPS (400 ML)

Bunches of fresh watercress, including stems, weighing about 4 oz (100 g)
2 tablespoons water
1 ¼ cups (300 ml) extra virgin olive oil

ⓥ ORANGE-FLAVORED OIL ≈

MAKES ALMOST 1 CUP (200 ML)

6 tablespoons grated orange zest (4 small oranges)
Almost 1 cup (200 ml) peanut or vegetable oil

Combine the orange zest and oil in a blender or food processor and process for 1 minute. Let stand for two days.

Strain the mixture through a fine sieve. Use at once or store, tightly covered, in the refrigerator for up to six months. Bring to room temperature and shake before using.

ⓥ LEMON-FLAVORED OIL ≈

MAKES ALMOST 1 CUP (200 ML)

3 tablespoons grated lemon zest (2 small lemons)
Almost 1 cup (200 ml) peanut or vegetable oil

Combine the lemon zest and oil in a blender or food processor and mix for 1 minute. Let stand for two days.

Strain the mixture through a fine sieve. Use at once or store, tightly covered, in the refrigerator for up to six months. Bring to room temperature and shake before using.

ⓥ CURRY-FLAVORED OIL ≈

MAKES 1 ¼ CUPS (300 ML)

Almost 1 ¼ cups (300 ml) groundnut or vegetable oil
6 tablespoons Madras curry powder (page 17)

Heat a wok or large frying-pan over high heat. Add the oil, and when it is very hot and slightly smoking, remove from the heat. Then add the curry powder. Stir to mix well. Allow the mixture to cool thoroughly. Let it stand overnight.

Strain the mixture through a fine sieve. Use at once or store, tightly covered, in the refrigerator for up to six months. Bring to room temperature before using.

Garlic, Ginger, and Scallion Oil ≈

Heat a wok or large frying-pan over a high heat. Add the oil, and when it is very hot and slightly smoking, add the garlic, ginger, and scallions. Cook in the hot wok until the vegetables turn brown. Remove immediately from the heat and allow to cool thoroughly. Let stand overnight.

   Strain the mixture through a fine sieve. Use at once or store, tightly covered, in the refrigerator, for up to six months. Bring to room temperature before using.

MAKES 1 ¼ CUPS (300 ML)

1 ¼ cups (300 ml) groundnut or vegetable oil
6 tablespoons peeled, thinly sliced garlic
12 slices of fresh ginger (page 17), 2 x ½ in (5 x 1 cm)
6 scallions

Sesame and Chili Oil ≈

Heat a wok over a high heat, add the peanut or vegetable oil, and when the oil is moderately hot, add the chilies and Sichuan peppercorns. Lower the heat and continue to cook over a low heat for about 10 minutes. Stir in the sesame oil and allow the mixture to cool thoroughly.

   Strain the mixture through a fine sieve. Use at once or store, tightly covered, in the refrigerator for up to six months. Bring to room temperature before using.

MAKES ⅔ CUP (150 ML)

⅔ cup (150 ml) peanut or vegetable oil
3 tablespoons chopped dried red chilies (page 15)
2 tablespoons whole unroasted Sichuan peppercorns (page 21)
3 tablespoons sesame oil

⒱Tomato-Flavored Olive Oil ≈

Makes 1 ¼ cups (300 ml)

2 tablespoons plus 1 ¼ cups
   (300 ml) extra virgin olive oil
3 tablespoons chopped garlic
1 tablespoon finely chopped
   fresh ginger (page 17)
4 oz (100 g) onions, chopped
4 oz (100 g) celery, finely
   chopped
3 tablespoons coarsely
   chopped fresh basil
1 tablespoon chopped fresh
   oregano or 2 teaspoons
   dried oregano
2 bay leaves
6 tablespoons tomato purée
8 tablespoons finely chopped
   canned tomatoes

Heat a non-stick wok or large non-stick frying-pan until it is hot, then add the 2 tablespoons of olive oil. Add the garlic, ginger, onions, celery, basil, oregano, and bay leaves and stir-fry for 5 minutes. Then add the tomato purée and chopped tomatoes. Lower the heat and simmer for 15 minutes.

Now add the remaining olive oil and simmer for another 20 minutes. Remove from the heat and allow to cool thoroughly. Let stand overnight.

Strain the mixture through a fine sieve (the vegetable mixture can be saved and used with pasta). Use at once or store, tightly covered, in the refrigerator for up to two weeks. Bring to room temperature before using.

Homemade Oven-dried Tomatoes ≈

Makes 1 ½ cups (350 g)

1 lb (450 g) tomatoes,
   preferably Roma
2 teaspoons salt
1 teaspoon freshly ground five-
   pepper mixture (page 21)
   or black pepper
1 teaspoon sugar
1 tablespoon extra virgin olive
   oil, plus extra for storing

ALTHOUGH SUN-DRIED TOMATOES IN OLIVE OIL ARE WIDELY AVAILABLE IN SUPERMARKETS, IT IS JUST AS EASY TO MAKE YOUR OWN. YOU CAN ALSO FLAVOR THEM WITH 1 TABLESPOON EACH OF MIXED CHOPPED FRESH HERBS, CHOPPED GARLIC AND OLIVE OIL BEFORE THEY ARE PLACED IN THE OVEN.

Pre-heat the oven to 225°F/110°C.

Slice the tomatoes in half lengthwize. Place them sliced side up on a baking sheet and sprinkle with salt, pepper, sugar, and olive oil. Put them in the oven and leave overnight. The tomatoes should be dry, but not crisp or hard. You can use them immediately or place them in a clean, sterilized, cover them with olive oil, and store in the refrigerator, where they will keep for up to two weeks.

APPETIZERS

開胃品

ⓥ CRISP RICE-PAPER SHRIMP ROLLS ≈

SERVES 4–6 (MAKES 8–9 SHRIMP ROLLS)

For the Filling:

1 oz (25 g) dried bean-thread (transparent) noodles (page 19)

½ lb (225 g) raw shrimp

2 tablespoons plus 1½ teaspoons salt

½ teaspoon freshly ground five-pepper mixture (page 21)

1½ tablespoons extra virgin olive oil

3 tablespoons finely chopped fresh chives

2 tablespoons finely chopped scallions

1 tablespoon finely chopped cilantro

3 tablespoons finely chopped sun-dried tomatoes

For the Sealing Mixture:

5 tablespoons all-purpose flour

5 tablespoons water

One package dried rice paper in 8½ in (22 cm) rounds (page 21)

2 cups (450 ml) oil, preferably peanut, for deep-frying

THESE CRACKLING, PAPER-THIN WRAPPERS, ASSERTIVELY FLAVORED WITH PIQUANT SUN-DRIED TOMATOES, ARE A PERFECT CONTRAST IN TEXTURE TO THE EXPLOSIVE FUSION FILLING OF CHINESE NOODLES WITH WESTERN, AS WELL AS ASIAN, HERBS; THEY NEED NO DIP AND MAKE A PERFECT APPETIZER.

Soak the noodles in a large bowl of warm water for 15 minutes. When soft, drain, and discard the water. Cut the noodles in 3 in (7.5 cm) lengths, using scissors or a knife.

Peel the shrimp and discard the shells. Using a small, sharp knife, remove the fine digestive cords. Wash the shrimp in cold water with a tablespoon of salt. Drain and repeat. Rinse well and pat dry with paper towels.

Combine the shrimp with the remaining salt, pepper, olive oil, chives, scallions, cilantro, sun-dried tomatoes, and the noodles. Mix well and let the mixture sit in the refrigerator for about 1 hour, covered with plastic wrap.

Make the sealing mixture by mixing the flour and water together.

When you are ready to make the shrimp rolls, fill a large bowl with warm water. Dip a round of rice paper in the water and let it soften for a few seconds. Remove and drain on a clean dish towel.

Place one shrimp, with about 1 teaspoon of noodles, on the edge of the rice paper. Roll the edge over the shrimp and noodles immediately, fold up both ends of the rice paper, and continue to roll to the end. Seal the end with a little of the flour-paste mixture. The roll should be compact and tight, like a short, thick cigar, about 3 in (7.5 cm) long. Place the roll on a clean plate and continue the process until you have used up all the mixture. The shrimp rolls can be made ahead to this point; cover loosely with a dry dish towel and refrigerate for up to 4 hours.

Heat a wok or large frying-pan over a high heat. Add the oil, and when it is slightly smoking, turn the heat to medium and deep-fry the shrimp rolls until golden brown. Fry only a few at a time, and if they stick together, do not break them apart until they have been removed from the oil. Drain them on paper towels and serve immediately.

Broiled Shrimp with Spicy Southeast Asian Pesto ≈

This is an easy but spectacular shrimp appetizer that is very tasty. The shrimp are simply broiled, cooked in a matter of minutes, and then drizzled with a sauce made from garlic, chili, basil, ginger, and cilantro, giving them a rich green color as well as a delectable bite. The inspiration is from both Asia and Europe; the combination is what makes fusion cooking so exciting and new.

Soak some bamboo skewers in water for a quarter of an hour or so to prevent them from burning during cooking.

Peel the shrimp and discard the shells. Using a small, sharp knife, remove the fine digestive cords. Wash the shrimp in cold water with a tablespoon of salt. Drain and repeat. Rinse well and pat dry with paper towels. Mix the shrimp with the remaining salt, pepper, and olive oil and skewer them on the bamboo.

Combine the pesto ingredients in a food processor or blender and mix until smooth, like a paste. Set this aside.

Pre-heat the oven broiler to high or make a charcoal fire in the barbecue grill. When the broiler is very hot or the charcoal is ash-white, broil the shrimp on each side for about 2 minutes. Arrange on a warm platter. Drizzle with the pesto and serve immediately.

Serves 4

1 lb (450 g) raw shrimp
2 tablespoons plus
 1 teaspoon salt
½ teaspoon freshly ground
 five-pepper mixture (page
 21) or black pepper
1½ tablespoons extra virgin
 olive oil

For the Pesto Sauce:

3 tablespoons coarsely
 chopped fresh basil
2 tablespoons coarsely
 chopped cilantro
1 tablespoon coarsely
 chopped fresh mint
2 tablespoons coarsely
 chopped garlic
1 tablespoon finely chopped
 fresh ginger (page 17)
1 tablespoon seeded and
 finely chopped fresh red
 chilies (page 16)
2 teaspoons salt
½ teaspoon freshly ground
 five-pepper mixture (page
 21) or black pepper
3 tablespoons extra virgin
 olive oil
1 teaspoon sesame oil
3 tablespoons mirin
 (Japanese sweet rice wine)
 (page 18)
2 tablespoons lemon juice

TWO-MINUTE COCONUT SHRIMP APPETIZER ≈

SERVES 4

½ lb (225 g) large raw
   shrimp (about 8)
2 tablespoons plus
   1 teaspoon salt
2 teaspoons sugar
Freshly ground five-pepper
   mixture (page 21) or black
   pepper
3 tablespoons lime juice
4 tablespoons canned
   coconut milk (page 16)

To Garnish:
3 tablespoons finely sliced
   shallots
2 small fresh red Thai chilies
   (page 16), coarsely
   chopped

MY FIRST EXPERIENCE WITH THIS DELECTABLE APPETIZER WAS AT THE LEMONGRASS RESTAURANT IN BANGKOK. I WAS DETERMINED TO FIND OUT HOW IT WAS MADE AND WAS PLEASED TO LEARN HOW QUICK AND EASY IT IS. THE CHEFS USED COCONUT MILK MADE FROM FRESH COCONUT, BUT I HAVE FOUND CANNED COCONUT MILK PERFECTLY ACCEPTABLE. IMAGINE MY SURPRISE WHEN I WAS TOLD THE SHRIMP WAS COOKED IN THE MICROWAVE! TRULY AN EAST-MEETS-WEST DISH.

Peel the shrimp and discard the shells. Using a small, sharp knife, remove the fine digestive cords. Rinse the shrimp in cold water with a tablespoon of salt. Drain and repeat. Rinse well and pat dry with paper towels.

   Combine the shrimp with the remaining salt, sugar, pepper, and lime juice. Mix well. Arrange the shrimp on a small platter. Pour the coconut milk over the shrimp. Microwave at full power for 2 minutes. If you don't have a microwave, set up a steamer or put a rack into a wok or deep pan and pour in 2 in (5 cm) of water. Bring the water to a boil and lower the shrimp into the steamer or onto the rack. Steam the shrimp for 3–4 minutes, meanwhile heating the coconut milk in a separate pan.

   Remove the shrimp, pour the coconut milk over them, garnish with shallots and chilies, and serve immediately.

PEAR WITH SCALLOPS TREAT ≈

SERVES 4–6

½ lb (225 g) shrimp

2 tablespoons plus
½ teaspoon salt

½ lb (225 g) large sea
scallops, without corals

2 oz (50 g) Italian pancetta
or bacon

1 large Asian pear, or if not
available, a comice,
bosch or anjou pear

cilantro leaves, rinsed and
dried

All-purpose flour,
for dusting

3 egg yolks, beaten with
1 tablespoon water

1 ¼ cups (75 g) dried
breadcrumbs

1 ¼ cups (300 ml) peanut oil

AMONG THE MOST INNOVATIVE FUSION-STYLE CHINESE RESTAURANTS IS THE LAI CHING HEEN, LOCATED IN HONG KONG'S REGENT HOTEL. THE FOUNDATION OF ITS MENU IS CLASSICAL CHINESE CUISINE, BUT THE CHEFS THERE HAVE IMAGINATIVELY REWORKED AND ADAPTED THE TRADITIONAL CANON, TO PRODUCE A FUSION OR COSMOPOLITAN CUISINE WHICH ITS DISCRIMINATING LOCAL AND INTERNATIONAL PATRONS FIND QUITE DELECTABLE.

I HAVE ENJOYED MANY TREATS AT THAT RESTAURANT AND THIS RECIPE EXEMPLIFIES THE VIRTUES OF FUSION COOKING. WE SEE AND TASTE INNOVATIONS THAT ENHANCE TRADITIONAL AND CLASSICAL CUISINES, RETAINING ALL THEIR EXCELLENCE WHILE ADDING EVEN GREATER DIMENSIONS TO THEM.

HERE, THE CHEF HAS CLEVERLY COMBINED CRUNCHY, SLIGHTLY SWEET ASIAN PEAR WITH SOFT, SUCCULENT SCALLOPS. WITHIN THE SCALLOPS, ONE DISCOVERS A FILLING OF FRESHLY MADE SHRIMP PURÉE, AND THE ENSEMBLE IS CROWNED WITH HAM AND CILANTRO, RESTING ON A SLICE OF THE ASIAN PEAR. THE COMBINATION IS DELICIOUS WITH ALL THE TASTES AND CONTRASTING TEXTURES COMING TOGETHER IN A DELIGHTFUL AND UNEXPECTED FASHION.

YOU COULD MODIFY THE RECIPE BY USING HAM INSTEAD OF PANCETTA OR BACON AND PLACING IT WITH THE CILANTRO, SLICED ASIAN PEAR, AND THE SHRIMP PURÉE INSIDE THE SPLIT SCALLOP. THE WONDERFUL TASTE OF THE TREAT IS UNALTERED.

Peel the shrimp and discard the shells. Using a small, sharp knife, remove the fine digestive cords. Wash the shrimp in cold water with a tablespoon of salt. Drain and repeat. Rinse well and pat dry with paper towels. Put the shrimp in a food processor with the remaining salt, and chop finely until it is a firm but sticky paste.

Cut the scallops in half. Finely slice the pancetta or bacon into eight pieces about the size of the scallops. Peel and core the pear and slice lengthwize into discs about the size of the scallops. I find using a 1½ in (4 cm) biscuit cutter helpful for getting neat circular slices. Spoon about 1 tablespoon of the shrimp mixture on eight scallop halves, then cover with a pear slice, one slice of pancetta or bacon, and two cilantro leaves. Finish by placing the other half of the split scallop on top so that it resembles a sandwich. Continue until you have used up the scallops and the shrimp mixture.

Dust each scallop 'sandwich' in all-purpose flour, dip them in the egg mixture, and finally, roll them in the breadcrumbs.

Heat a wok or deep frying-pan until it is hot, add the oil, and when it is hot, add four of the scallop sandwiches; cook them for 3 minutes or until they are golden brown. Drain on paper towels. Now fry the remaining scallop sandwiches. Arrange on a warm platter and serve immediately with the lemon juice and salt and pepper mixture.

To serve:
2 tablespoons (25 ml) fresh lemon juice
1 tablespoon roasted and ground Sichuan peppercorns (page 21), mixed with
1½ tablespoons salt

CRACKLING RICE-PAPER-WRAPPED FISH ≈

SERVES 4

1 lb (450 g) boneless, skinless cod, halibut or sea bass

1 teaspoon salt

½ teaspoon freshly ground five-pepper mixture (page 21)

2 teaspoons Madras curry powder (page 17)

2 tablespoons all-purpose flour

2 tablespoons water

1 packet dried rice paper (page 21) in 8½ in (22 cm) rounds

8 cilantro leaves

3 tablespoons chopped fresh chives

2 tablespoons peanut oil

Tomato-flavored Olive Oil (page 40) and Chive-flavored Olive Oil (page 37), to serve

THIS DISH IS A TYPICAL EXAMPLE OF FUSION COOKING. I USE RICE PAPER (A VERY ASIAN INGREDIENT) TO WRAP COD (A VERY EUROPEAN FISH), AND SEASON IT AT THE SAME TIME WITH FRESH ASIAN AND WESTERN HERBS WITH A TOUCH OF MADRAS CURRY POWDER. IT IS SURPRISINGLY EASY TO MAKE AND THE RESULTS ARE A DELIGHTFUL CRACKLING AND STUNNING-LOOKING APPETIZER THAT WILL SURELY IMPRESS YOUR FAMILY, FRIENDS, AND GUESTS. YOU CAN USE HALIBUT OR SEA BASS INSTEAD OF COD.

Divide the cod into four equal pieces, about 3 x 3 in (7.5 x 7.5 cm). Combine the salt, pepper, and curry powder. Sprinkle the mixture evenly over the fish pieces.

Make the sealing mixture by mixing the flour and water together. Fill a large bowl with hot water and dip one of the rice paper rounds in the water to soften; this will only take a few seconds. Remove and drain on a clean dish towel. In the center of the round, layer two cilantro leaves, a piece of fish, and 2 teaspoons of chives on top. Fold the first edge over the ingredients; then fold in the sides. Fold the remaining side over and seal with a little flour-paste mixture to secure the package. Repeat for the other three rounds to form four packages.

Heat a large, heavy frying-pan over a high heat; then add the oil. When the oil is hot, add the four packages and pan-fry on the seamless side for about 3 minutes or until golden brown. Turn over to the other side and continue to cook until golden brown.

Now arrange the packages on a platter. Drizzle with the tomato-flavored and chive-flavored olive oils and serve immediately.

Steamed Scallops in Spiced Butter Sauce ≈

Serves 4

1 lb (450 g) fresh scallops,
  including corals
2 fresh red chilies (page 16),
  seeded and chopped
1 tablespoon finely chopped
  orange zest
2 teaspoons finely chopped
  fresh ginger (page 17)
1 tablespoon Shaoxing rice
  wine (page 22) or dry
  sherry
1 teaspoon five-spice
  powder (page 17)
½ teaspoon roasted and
  ground Sichuan
  peppercorns (page 20)
1 teaspoon salt
¼ cup (50 ml) homemade
  Fish (page 34) or Chicken
  (page 32) Stock
2 tablespoons unsalted
  butter, cut in small pieces
1 tablespoon finely chopped
  fresh chives, to garnish

Fresh scallops are best cooked by the simple Chinese technique of steaming. Using hot wet vapors, this method brings out the succulent texture of scallops without overcooking them. I combine their natural juices with fish stock to make a tasty dish that is both simple and elegant. The small amount of butter adds a touch of richness. This recipe is ideal for a quick and easy snack, and I think it makes a perfect appetizer for any dinner party.

Place the scallops on a heatproof platter. Then sprinkle evenly the chilies, orange zest, ginger, rice wine or sherry, five-spice powder, Sichuan peppercorns, and salt.

Next, set up a steamer or put a rack into a wok or deep pan and pour in 2 in (5 cm) of water. Bring the water to a boil over a high heat. Carefully lower the scallops into the steamer or onto the rack. Turn the heat to low and cover the wok or pan tightly. Steam gently for 5 minutes.

Remove the platter and pour any scallop juices into a saucepan. Add the stock and reduce by three-quarters. Slowly mix in the butter.

Return the scallops to the sauce to warm, garnish with the chives and serve immediately.

Lemon Grass and Shrimp Quiche ≈

Although quiche has fallen out of fashion, it is a simple and delicious dish. The conception is brilliant: rich egg and cream baked in pastry. It lends itself to any type of food you wish to add to it. Here, I have used two eastern spices to give a new twist to a traditional theme. This quiche makes a perfect appetizer or a delightful light lunch treat.

Put all the pastry ingredients in a food processor and mix to a dough. Roll the dough into a ball on a lightly floured board. Cover with plastic wrap and refrigerate for 30 minutes.

Pre-heat the oven to 350°F/180°C.

Roll out the pastry to ⅛ in (3 mm) thick and press the pastry into a 8 in (20 cm) tart pan. Place a sheet of foil over the surface of the pastry and put about 2 cups (350 g) of dried beans on the foil to weigh it down. Bake the pastry in the oven for 12 minutes. Remove the beans and foil. Lightly mark tiny holes in the pastry surface with a fork. Return the pastry to the oven and continue to bake for 10 minutes. Remove and allow to cool thoroughly.

Pour the cream into a small saucepan, add the lemon grass and ginger, and simmer for about 15 minutes over a very low heat. Strain through a fine sieve, discard the lemon grass and ginger and allow the infused cream to cool.

Pre-heat the oven to 400°F/200°C.

Peel the shrimp and discard the shells. Using a small, sharp knife, remove the fine digestive cords. Wash the shrimp in cold water with a tablespoon of salt. Drain and repeat. Rinse well and pat dry with paper towels.

Coarsely chop the shrimp and combine them with the cream, eggs, remaining salt, and the pepper, scallions and chives. Pour this mixture into the cooked pastry.

Bake the quiche for 25 minutes or until the egg has set. Serve warm or at room temperature.

Serves 4–6

For the Pastry:
1 ¼ cups (150 g) all-purpose flour
4 tablespoons butter
½ teaspoon salt
2 tablespoons cold water
2 tablespoons light cream

For the Filling:
1 ½ cups (350 ml) light cream
3 tablespoons finely chopped lemon grass (page 18)
1 tablespoon finely chopped fresh ginger (page 17)
½ lb (250 g) raw shrimp
2 tablespoons plus 1 teaspoon salt
3 eggs, beaten
¼ teaspoon freshly ground five-pepper mixture (page 21) or black pepper
2 tablespoons finely chopped scallions
2 tablespoons finely chopped fresh chives

SALMON DUMPLINGS ≈

MAKES 30–32

DUMPLINGS

1 package wonton skins
(about 40 skins) (page 25)
Curry-flavored Oil (page 38)
and Tomato-flavored Olive
Oil (page 40),
to serve

For the Stuffing:

1 lb (450 g) boneless,
skinless salmon fillets

2 tablespoons finely
chopped Prosciutto or lean
bacon

3 tablespoons cream cheese

3 tablespoons finely
chopped scallions

2 tablespoons finely
chopped fresh chives

2 teaspoons finely chopped
fresh ginger (page 17)

1 teaspoon salt

½ teaspoon freshly ground
five-pepper mixture (page
21) or black pepper

2 teaspoons paprika

1 teaspoon finely chopped
lemon zest

1 egg

THIS IS A FUSION VERSION OF THE POPULAR SOUTHERN CHINESE DUMPLING SNACK. FRESH SALMON IS COMBINED WITH MILD CREAM CHEESE, WRAPPED IN WONTON SKINS, AND THEN STEAMED FOR A SUBTLE APPETIZER. THIS MAKES A DELIGHTFUL APPETIZER FOR ANY MEAL. I LIKE TO SERVE IT DRIZZLED WITH CURRY-FLAVORED OIL AND TOMATO-FLAVORED OLIVE OIL.

Start by preparing the stuffing. Finely chop the salmon and combine it with the ham or bacon, cream cheese, scallions, chives, ginger, salt, pepper, paprika, lemon zest, and egg.

Place a portion of filling on each wonton skin. Bring up the sides and press them around the filling mixture. Tap the dumpling on the bottom to make a flat base. The top should be wide open, exposing the fish filling.

Set up a steamer or put a rack inside a wok or large, deep pan. Pour in about 2 in (5 cm) of water and bring it to a boil. Put the dumplings on a heatproof plate and carefully place this in the steamer or on the rack.

Cover the pan tightly, turn the heat low, and steam gently for about 5–6 minutes. (You may have to do this in several batches. Keep the first batches warm by covering the dumplings with foil and placing them in a warm but switched-off oven.) Serve the dumplings hot, with the curry and tomato oils drizzled over them.

Tuna Carpaccio ≈

Named after a Venetian Renaissance painter, *carpaccio* is an Italian first course of thin, pounded slices of raw beef which are then drizzled with a creamy vinaigrette sauce, made with olive oil. It is said to have originated at the famed Harry's Bar in Venice. Here is a lighter version, with fusion flavors from East and West. Get the best quality tuna you can afford; it is worth it. This appetizer is easy to make and can be made hours in advance if kept refrigerated. Simply drizzle the dressing over the fillets when you're ready to serve. It is especially refreshing during warm weather.

Divide the tuna into four equal fillets. Place one fillet between two sheets of plastic wrap and, with a mallet or empty bottle, lightly pound the tuna until it is thin. It should be transparent enough to see through. Put the fillet on a large serving plate. Do the same to the remaining fillets. You should now have four thin tuna sheets on four plates.

In a small bowl, combine the scallions, cilantro, and ginger. Sprinkle this mixture evenly over the tuna sheets.

In another bowl, combine the salt, pepper, and lemon zest with the vinegar. Then add the mustard and slowly beat in the olive oil. Drizzle the dressing over the tuna and serve immediately.

Serves 4

- 1 lb (450 g) boneless tuna fillet
- 3 tablespoons finely chopped scallions
- 1 tablespoon finely chopped cilantro
- 2 teaspoons finely chopped fresh ginger (page 17)

For the Dressing:
- 1 teaspoon salt
- ½ teaspoon freshly ground five-pepper mixture (page 21) or black pepper
- 1 teaspoon finely chopped lemon zest
- 2 tablespoons Chinese white rice vinegar (page 24) or cider vinegar
- 1 tablespoon Dijon mustard
- 6 tablespoons extra virgin olive oil

ⓥ Spring Salad with Sesame Oil and Shallot Dressing ≈

Serves 4–6

For the Caramelized Pecans:

½ lb (225 g) pecans, shelled
1 cup (100 g) caster sugar
2 cups (450 ml) oil,
    preferably peanut

For the Salad:

¾ lb (350 g) tender salad
    greens
3 tablespoons finely
    chopped shallots,
    squeezed dry
2 tablespoons Chinese white
    rice vinegar (page 24) or
    cider vinegar
salt and freshly ground black
    pepper
2 teaspoons sesame oil
2 tablespoons oil, preferably
    peanut

Green salads, so popular these days, are not something I grew up with. The Chinese never eat raw greens as such. I discovered salads when I went out into the western culinary world, and I have learned to love them. Nothing beats the crisp flavors of young, tender salad greens. A salad is a refreshing appetizer or can be a clean ending to any meal. Here, I have combined the greens with caramelized pecans, American nuts that are a delicious snack on their own. The caramelized nuts can be made days ahead. The dressing is Asian with a touch of sesame oil. If you are in a rush, you can bypass the caramelized pecans and just make the salad.

Bring a pan of water to a boil. Add the pecans and blanch them for about 5 minutes. Drain the nuts in a colander or sieve, then pat dry with paper towels and spread them on a baking tray. Let the pecans dry for 40 minutes.

Sprinkle the sugar over the pecans and roll them around in it to cover them completely. Place the tray of sugared pecans in a cool, draughty place. Let them dry overnight. (The recipe can be done ahead to this point.)

Heat a wok or large frying-pan over a high heat until it is hot. Add the oil and, when it is hot, turn the heat to medium and deep-fry a batch of the pecans for about 2 minutes, or until the sugar melts and the pecans turn golden. (Watch the heat to prevent burning.) Remove the pecans from the oil with a slotted spoon or strainer. Lay them on a cake rack to cool. (Do not drain them on paper towels or the sugar will stick to it when it dries.) Deep-fry and drain the rest of the pecans in the same way. Once cooled, the caramelized pecans can be kept in a sealed glass jar for about two weeks.

Wash and thoroughly spin-dry the salad greens. In a large salad bowl, combine the shallots with the vinegar and salt and pepper to taste. Slowly beat in the sesame and peanut oils. Add the greens and toss thoroughly. Add the pecans, mix, and serve immediately.

Refreshing Watercress Salad with Japanese Sesame Dressing ≈

Watercress is an ancient and venerable plant and has been a favorite in Europe and Asia for centuries, prized for its piquant, pungent, mustard-like taste. Watercress quickly stir-fried with an array of spices and condiments was a familiar and much-favored aromatic treat in my mother's kitchen as I grew up. However, when I lived in Europe, I discovered the refreshing, tart flavor of this plant eaten fresh from the garden and uncooked in a salad. I include here a suggested Asian dressing as an alternative to the usual European style.

Wash the watercress thoroughly and remove any tough stems. Then spin-dry it in a salad spinner or drain it well in a colander and dry thoroughly with a clean dish towel.

Combine all the dressing ingredients in a small bowl and mix thoroughly. Combine the watercress and dressing, sprinkle the toasted sesame seeds on top, and serve immediately.

Serves 4

1 lb (450 g) watercress
2 teaspoons sesame seeds, toasted (page 23), to serve

For the Dressing:

½ teaspoon salt
A pinch of freshly ground five-pepper mixture (page 21) or black pepper
1 tablespoon light soy sauce (page 23)
1 teaspoon sugar
2 teaspoons Chinese white rice vinegar (page 24) or cider vinegar
2 teaspoons oil, preferably peanut
2 teaspoons sesame oil

ⓥ BILL MEGALOS' TOFU SALAD ≈

SERVES 4

1 lb (450 g) silky Japanese tofu (page 13)
6 tablespoons chopped cilantro
6 tablespoons chopped scallion tops
1 teaspoon salt
½ teaspoon freshly ground black pepper
3 tablespoons extra virgin olive oil

WHILE WE WERE FILMING THE *HOT WOK* BBC TV SERIES, OUR CAMERAMAN, BILL MEGALOS, CONTRIBUTED THIS DELICIOUS AND SIMPLE TOFU DISH. ('TOFU' AND 'TOFU' MEAN THE SAME THING.) THE WEATHER WAS HOT AND DUSTY AND THIS COLD DISH WAS THE PERFECT LUNCHEON FARE.

HE SIMPLY CHOPPED CILANTRO AND COMBINED IT WITH AN EQUAL AMOUNT OF SCALLION TOPS, SALT, AND PEPPER, AND THEN ADDED OLIVE OIL INSTEAD OF THE USUAL SESAME OIL. THE RESULT WAS DELECTABLE, A NUTRITIOUS AND TASTY VEGETARIAN DISH THAT LITERALLY TOOK ONLY MINUTES TO PREPARE.

THE SECRET, I DISCOVERED, WAS THE USE OF SOFT, SILKY JAPANESE TOFU, AN INGREDIENT THAT GUARANTEES SUCCESS. THIS DELICATE VERSION OF TOFU IS AKIN TO A SEMI-SOFT PUDDING, BUT WHAT MAKES IT WORK IS ITS CONGENIALITY, ITS ABILITY TO TAKE ON AMBIENT AROMAS AND FLAVORS. DEFINITELY A FUSION RECIPE TO TRY.

Allow the tofu to drain for 10 minutes. Place it on a platter and sprinkle evenly with the cilantro, scallions, salt, and pepper. Drizzle with olive oil and serve immediately.

ⓥ Alice Chen's Ginger Green Bean Salad ≈

Serves 4

1 lb (450 g) Chinese long
  beans, runner beans or
  French beans, trimmed
3 tablespoons finely
  chopped fresh ginger
  (page 17)
1 teaspoon salt
2 tablespoons oil, preferably
  peanut
2 teaspoons sesame oil
2 tablespoons light soy
  sauce (page 23)

One of the best cooks I know is Alice Chen. Originally from Chengdu, the capital of Sichuan province in western China, Alice now makes her home in California.

Sichuan is a region famous for its spicy cuisine. When Alice made this tasty ginger green bean salad for me one Sunday, I was not surprised at how spicy and stimulating it was to the palate. What did surprise me was how simple and easy it is to make. Alice told me that it was a dish typical of popular 'small eats' snacks in Sichuan.

Although Alice used Chinese long beans (which are also known as yard-long beans because they grow to such a long length), I have found that runner, or French beans, work just as well. The sauce is an excellent alternative to the European oil and vinegar dressing.

If you are using Chinese long beans or runner beans, cut them into 2 in (5 cm) pieces. If you are using French beans, leave them whole. Blanch the beans in a large pan of salted, boiling water for 2 minutes and then immerse them in cold water. Drain thoroughly and set aside.

Combine the ginger and salt and put in a heatproof bowl.

Heat a wok or large frying-pan over a high heat. Add the peanut and sesame oils and, when very hot and slightly smoking, pour the oils over the ginger mixture. Mix in the soy sauce.

Add the beans to the mixture and toss well. Serve the salad immediately or refrigerate it and serve the next day.

PICKLED YOUNG GINGER ≈

FEW FOODS ARE MORE REFRESHING TO THE PALATE THAN PICKLED YOUNG GINGER. ONCE MADE, IT CAN BE EATEN RAW AS A SNACK OR APPETIZER, OR STIR-FRIED WITH OTHER VEGETABLES. AS ITS NAME SUGGESTS, IT ADDS A PIQUANT, SPICY TASTE TO DISHES.

PICKLED GINGER IS EASY TO MAKE. BECAUSE THE ROOT IS YOUNG, IT IS LESS FIBROUS AND HAS A MILDER TANG THAN MATURE GINGER ROOT. BUT IT HAS THE AUTHENTIC FRESH AND FRAGRANT GINGER APPEAL AND IT CAN BE SLICED AND EATEN AS A VEGETABLE.

WITH IT, YOU CAN TURN A SALAD INTO SOMETHING SPECIAL. IF NECESSARY, YOU CAN USE ORDINARY FRESH GINGER BUT THE YOUNG GINGER IS PREFERABLE. RUBBING THE GINGER WITH SALT DRAWS OUT ITS EXCESS MOISTURE, GIVING IT MORE TEXTURE.

THIS SIMPLE DISH CAN BE MADE WELL IN ADVANCE AND IT WILL KEEP FOR AS LONG AS THREE MONTHS IN THE REFRIGERATOR. THE PICKLING PROCESS NEEDS ABOUT A WEEK, AND THEN THE GINGER IS READY TO EAT AS A REFRESHING APPETIZER OR TO USE AS AN ACCOMPANIMENT TO BROILED FOODS.

Wash the ginger well under cold running water. Trim and peel the ginger. Cut the ginger into large 3–4 in (7.5–10 cm) chunks. Blanch the ginger in boiling water for 2 minutes. Remove and rub with the salt and set aside for 1 hour.

Rinse well in cold running water. Dry thoroughly with paper towels and set aside.

Bring the vinegar, salt, garlic, and sugar to a boil in a large enamel or stainless steel saucepan. Put the ginger into a heatproof bowl. Pour the vinegar mixture over, making sure that the liquid completely covers the ginger. When cool, pack the ginger and the liquid into a glass jar and refrigerate.

The ginger will turn slightly pink in about a week, ready to be used.

MAKES 1 LB (450 G)

1 lb (450 g) fresh young
    ginger (page 17)
2 tablespoons salt

For the Pickling Liquid:
2 ½ cups (600 ml) Chinese
    white rice vinegar
    (page 24) or cider vinegar
1 teaspoon salt
6 large garlic cloves, peeled
    and lightly crushed
1 lb (450 g) sugar

Ⓥ Asian-flavored Eggplant Crostini ≈

Serves 4–6

2 lb (900 g) Chinese or
  ordinary eggplant
  (page 13)
3 garlic cloves
½ lb (225 g) fresh tomatoes
1½ tablespoons peanut oil
1 onion, finely chopped
1 tablespoon finely chopped
  fresh ginger (page 17)
2 tablespoons finely
  chopped cilantro
2 tablespoons finely
  chopped scallions
2 teaspoons finely chopped
  orange zest
2 teaspoons chili-bean sauce
  (page 22)
1 teaspoon light soy sauce
  (page 23)
2 tablespoons black rice
  vinegar (page 24)
1 teaspoon sesame oil
¼ teaspoon salt
¼ teaspoon freshly ground
  black pepper
1 tablespoon sesame seeds,
  toasted (page 23)
1 teaspoon sugar
French bread, thinly sliced
  diagonally and toasted,
  to serve

Eggplant dips are popular in Mediterranean countries. During one of my many East–West vegetarian cooking promotions at the famed Oriental Hotel in Bangkok, I offered this spicy dip. We served it on toasted bread, and it proved to be quite popular. The eggplant is first roasted in the oven and then combined with tasty Asian spices to create an unusual East–West treat. You will note that eggplant can work congenially with many robust spices. Since the dip is served at room temperature, it can easily be made in advance.

Pre-heat the oven to 475°F/240°C.

If you are using Chinese eggplant, roast for 20 minutes; if you are using ordinary large eggplant, roast for about 30–40 minutes, or until it is soft and cooked through. Halfway through the roasting, add the garlic and tomatoes. Allow the eggplant to cool and then peel it as well as the tomatoes and garlic. Put them in a colander and drain them for 30 minutes. This procedure can be done hours in advance.

Combine the eggplant, tomatoes, and garlic in a food processor with the rest of the ingredients and process until well blended. Serve with toasted bread slices.

ⓋStir-fried Peanuts with Chilies ≈

SERVES 4–6

½ lb (225 g) raw peanuts
1½ tablespoons oil,
  preferably peanut
2 small fresh red chilies
  (page 16), seeded and
  finely chopped
2 tablespoons coarsely
  chopped garlic
2 teaspoons sugar
1 teaspoon salt

FULL OF FLAVOR AND TEXTURE, THE HUMBLE PEANUT IS A VALUABLE SOURCE OF NUTRITION IN A VEGETARIAN DIET. HERE WE HAVE AN UNUSUAL WAY TO PAY OUR RESPECTS TO PEANUTS, AND STIR-FRYING THEM WITH CHILIES GIVES THEM A WONDERFUL PIQUANT KICK. SERVE THIS DISH AS A SNACK WITH DRINKS OR AS A NOTABLE ADDITION TO ANY MEAL.

Pick over and remove any loose skins from the peanuts.

Heat a wok or large frying-pan over a high heat until it is hot; then add the oil. When the oil is hot and slightly smoking, stir-fry the peanuts for 2 minutes, until they are lightly brown. Then add the chilies and garlic and stir-fry for 2 minutes. Sprinkle in the sugar and salt. Continue to stir-fry for 2 minutes, mixing well. Turn out onto a serving dish and serve warm.

Fresh *Foie Gras* with Ginger and Five-spice Apples ≈

Foie gras is as French or western as can be, while ginger and five-spice seasoning are distinctly Chinese or eastern. As for apples or apple relatives, surely they are universally appreciated? Put them nicely together, as in this fusion recipe, and you have a delightfully cosmopolitan appetizer, combining the unique taste and texture of *foie gras* with the zesty flavors of apple and Chinese spices.

The apples may be prepared well ahead of time and reheated; the *foie gras* cooks very quickly. This is an elegant and impressive appetizer for any special occasion.

Pre-heat the oven to 475°F/240°C.

Cut the *foie gras* into ½ in (1 cm) slices.

Slice the apples into ½ in (1 cm) slices and put in cold water with the lemon juice. This will prevent the apples from turning brown.

Heat a wok or large frying-pan. Drain and dry the apples and add to the pan with the butter and ginger. Stir-fry gently for 2 minutes. Then sprinkle on the five-spice powder, sugar, salt, and pepper and add the chicken stock. Cook for 1 minute. Remove with a slotted spoon and keep warm on a platter. Reserve the juices.

Season the *foie gras* generously with salt and pepper. In a heavy roasting pan, arrange the *foie gras* slices in one layer. Place in the oven and roast for 4 minutes on one side; then turn and roast for another 4 minutes until the *foie gras* is golden and almost caramelized on the outside.

Remove the roasting pan from the oven and drain off *all* the fat. Place the pan with the *foie gras* still in it over a moderate heat, add the apple liquid and reduce to a glaze.

Put the apples on the warm platter, place the *foie gras* slices on top, garnish with salt, pepper, chives, and scallions and serve immediately.

Serves 4–6

¾ lb (350 g) fresh duck *foie gras*

1 lb (450 g) apples, cored and peeled

Juice of 1 lemon

3 tablespoons (35 g) unsalted butter

2 tablespoons finely chopped fresh ginger (page 17)

1 teaspoon five-spice powder (page 17)

1 teaspoon sugar

Salt and freshly ground black pepper

3 tablespoons Homemade Chicken Stock (page 32)

To Garnish:

Coarse sea salt and coarse freshly ground white pepper

2 tablespoons finely chopped fresh chives

1 tablespoon finely chopped scallions

SOUPS

湯

Mussel and Lemon Grass Soup ≈

This is my fusion version of a classic French mussel soup which is made from the broth in which the mussels have been cooked. The briny sea flavor, combined with zesty lemon grass, makes this easy-to-make soup an elegant start to any meal.

Peel the lemon grass stalks to the tender, whitish centers and crush them with the flat of a knife. Then cut them into 3 in (7.5 cm) pieces.

Put the lemon grass, mussels, onions, shallots, ginger, fish stock, rice wine or sherry, parsley, cilantro, butter, bay leaf, thyme, salt, and pepper in a large pan and cook over high heat for 8 minutes or until all the mussels have opened. Discard any that do not open.

Strain the liquid through muslin or a fine-meshed sieve and discard the solids. Remove the mussels from their shells and set aside.

Bring the strained liquid to a simmer and slowly drizzle in the cream, stirring constantly. Adjust the seasoning, if necessary. Return the mussels to the liquid to warm, sprinkle with chives, and serve immediately.

Serves 4–6

3 lemon grass stalks (page 18)

3 lb (1.5 kg) fresh live mussels, well scrubbed

2 small onions, quartered

3 tablespoons coarsely chopped shallots

2 teaspoons finely chopped fresh ginger (page 17)

1 cup (250 ml) homemade Fish Stock (page 34)

3 tablespoons Shaoxing rice wine (page 22) or dry sherry

3 sprigs of flatleaf parsley

3 sprigs of cilantro

2 tablespoons (25 g) butter

1 bay leaf

3 sprigs of fresh thyme or 1 teaspoon dried thyme

1 teaspoon salt

¼ teaspoon freshly ground five-pepper mixture (page 21) or white pepper

1 cup (250 ml) heavy cream

1 tablespoon finely chopped fresh chives, to garnish

Ginger Fish Soup ≈

1 lb (450 g) fresh, flat,
white fish fillets, such as
plaice or sole

½ lb (225 g) tomatoes, peeled
and seeded if fresh, drained
if canned

2 ½ cups (1.2 liters)
homemade Fish (page 34) or
Chicken (page 32) Stock

2 teaspoons salt

1 teaspoon freshly ground five-
pepper mixture (page 21)
or black pepper

2 teaspoons Shaoxing rice wine
(page 22) or dry sherry

2 teaspoons finely shredded
fresh ginger (page 17)

2 tablespoons finely chopped
scallions

1 tablespoon finely chopped
cilantro

1 tablespoon finely chopped
fresh chives

1 tablespoon extra virgin
olive oil

ONE OF THE BEST CHINESE TECHNIQUES FOR COOKING DELICATE FOODS SUCH AS FISH IS TO STEEP THEM (THAT IS, TO ADD THE FISH PIECES TO HOT BROTH AND TURN THE HEAT OFF). THE GENTLE HEAT OF THE BROTH COOKS THE FISH PERFECTLY — RESULTING IN MOIST AND FLAVORFUL FISH — WITHOUT OVERCOOKING IT OR DRYING IT OUT. IN THIS RECIPE, I USE THE TECHNIQUE TO MAKE A LOVELY, ELEGANT FISH SOUP. THIS TYPE OF SOUP IS POPULAR IN FUSION COOKING BECAUSE ONE CAN COMBINE TASTES FROM MANY CULTURES TO CREATE A DELECTABLE, AROMATIC DISH. INFUSED WITH GINGER WHICH IS WIDELY USED IN ASIAN FISH DISHES, THIS EASY SOUP IS SURE TO BECOME ONE OF YOUR FAVORITES.

Remove the skins from the fish and then cut the fillets into pieces about 2 in (5 cm) square and set aside. If you are using fresh tomatoes, cut them into 1 in (2.5 cm) cubes. If you are using canned tomatoes, chop them into small chunks.

Pour the stock into a wok or large pan and bring it to a simmer. Add the salt, pepper, rice wine or sherry, and ginger and simmer for 5 minutes. Then add the fish, remove the pan from the heat and let it sit for 5 minutes or just until the fish turns white. Using a slotted spoon, transfer the fish to individual bowls or a soup tureen. Stir the scallions, coriander, tomatoes, chives, and olive oil into the soup. Ladle the soup over the fish and serve immediately.

THAI CONSOMMÉ WITH SEAFOOD AND SPICES ≈

SERVES 4

6 oz (175 g) raw shrimp

2 tablespoons plus
   1 teaspoon salt

6 oz (175 g) salmon fillets,
   skinned

2 lemon grass stalks
   (page 18)

2 ½ cups (1.2 liters)
   homemade Fish
   (page 34) or Chicken
   (page 32) Stock

1 fresh red chili (page 16),
   seeded and finely
   shredded

¼ teaspoon freshly ground
   five-pepper mixture
   (page 21) or black pepper

2 scallions, finely shredded

2 tablespoons lime juice

5 sprigs of cilantro

THAI SPICES AND HERBS ARE SO FRAGRANT AND AROMATIC THAT THEY CAN EASILY TRANSFORM ANY DISH INTO AN EXPLOSION OF TASTES. IN THIS SAVORY SOUP, I USE THE CHINESE STEEPING TECHNIQUE TO COOK THE SEAFOOD, WHILE SEASONING THE BROTH WITH THAI ESSENCE. I THINK IT MAKES A SENSATIONAL BEGINNING FOR ANY MEAL.

Peel the shrimp and discard the shells. Using a small, sharp knife, remove the fine digestive cords. Wash the shrimp in cold water with a tablespoon of salt. Drain and repeat. Rinse well and pat dry with paper towels. Cut the salmon into 1 in (2.5 cm) cubes.

Peel the lemon grass stalks to the tender, whitish centres and crush them with the flat of a knife. Then cut them into 3 in (7.5 cm) pieces.

In a large pan, bring the stock to a simmer and add the lemon grass. Turn the heat to low, cover, and cook for 10 minutes. Remove the lemon grass with a slotted spoon and discard. Then add the chili, the remaining salt, and the pepper, shrimp, and salmon to the liquid. Cover the pan and remove from the heat. Let it rest for 10 minutes.

Finally, stir in the scallions, lime juice, and cilantro sprigs. Ladle into a large soup tureen or individual bowls and serve immediately.

CRAB WONTONS IN AROMATIC BROTH ≈

WONTON SKINS ARE SUCH A GREAT CONVENIENCE: THEY ARE INEXPENSIVE, BECOMING EASIER TO FIND AND ARE WELL MADE. THIS RECIPE TAKES ADVANTAGE OF THESE VERSATILE, FLEXIBLE PASTRY SHEETS — POPULAR AMONG FUSION CHEFS. TASTY WONTONS ARE FILLED WITH CRAB AND WESTERN AS WELL AS EASTERN HERBS, AND THEN MATCHED WITH A THAI-FLAVORED, INFUSED BROTH. AN EAST–WEST DISH THAT IS EASY TO MAKE, THIS IS A WONDERFUL LIGHT APPETIZER FOR ANY ELEGANT MEAL.

Peel the lemon grass stalks to the tender, whitish centers and crush them with the flat of a knife. Then cut them into 3 in (7.5 cm) pieces.

Bring the stock to a simmer in a large pan, add the lemon grass pieces, lime zest, salt, and pepper and let it simmer for 25 minutes. Remove and discard the lemon grass stalks.

Meanwhile, put the crabmeat in a large bowl, add the olive oil, chives, chervil, shallots, cilantro, scallions, lemon zest, salt, and pepper and mix well.

When you are ready to stuff the wontons, put 1 tablespoon of the filling in the center of the first wonton skin. Dampen the edges with a little water and bring up the sides of the skin around the filling. Pinch the edges together at the top so that the wonton is sealed. It should look like a small drawstring bag. Repeat the process until all the filling has been used.

In another pan, bring salted water to the boil and poach the wontons for 1 minute, or until they float to the top (you may have to do this in batches – there is no need to keep the wontons warm because you will warm them later in the soup). Remove them immediately and transfer them to individual, flat soup plates. Ladle a small amount of the stock into each soup plate, garnish with chives, and serve immediately.

SERVES 6 (MAKES 30–35 WONTONS)

For the Broth:
3 lemon grass stalks (page 18)
10 cups (2.25 liters) homemade Fish (page 34) or Chicken (page 32) Stock
1 teaspoon finely chopped lime zest
Salt and freshly ground pepper

For the Wontons:
¾ lb (350 g) cooked fresh crabmeat
2 teaspoons extra virgin olive oil
3 tablespoons finely chopped fresh chives
2 tablespoons finely chopped fresh chervil
2 tablespoons finely chopped shallots, squeezed dry
1½ tablespoons finely chopped cilantro
2 tablespoons finely chopped scallions
1 teaspoon finely chopped lemon zest
1 teaspoon salt
¼ teaspoon freshly ground five-pepper mixture (page 21) or black pepper
1/2 lb (225 g) wonton skins (page 25)
1½ tablespoons finely chopped fresh chives, to garnish

Oxtail Wonton Soup ≈

Serves 4–6 (makes about 30 wontons)

1 ½ lb (750 g) oxtail, jointed

4 quarts (2.75 liters) homemade Chicken Stock (page 32)

1 teaspoon sesame oil

1½ tablespoons capers, rinsed and chopped

1 tablespoon Dijon mustard

½ teaspoon salt

¼ teaspoon freshly ground five-pepper mixture (page 21) or black pepper

1 teaspoon finely chopped lemon zest

1½ teaspoons dark soy sauce (page 23)

1½ tablespoons finely chopped fresh chives

1 tablespoon finely chopped fresh chervil

2 tablespoons finely chopped shallots, squeezed dry

1 tablespoon finely chopped cilantro

1 tablespoon finely chopped scallions

9 oz (250 g) wonton skins (page 25)

Salt and freshly ground black pepper

1½ tablespoons finely chopped chives, to garnish

Fusion chefs have discovered the convenience and silky texture of wonton skins. Any one of a wide range of tasty fillings may be used to create a special dish by simply wrapping them in these pastry sheets.

For an East–West cookery demonstration at the Regent Restaurant in Sydney, I wanted to offer something that featured these wontons. In collaboration with Serge Dansereau, a very talented Australian chef, I came up with this oxtail wonton soup recipe. Oxtail meat has a rich flavor and works very congenially with these zesty Asian and western spices and seasonings. Together, they make a splendid filling for wontons, and the ensemble transforms a prosaic soup into an exceptional treat.

Cook the oxtail pieces in boiling water for 15 minutes. Remove and drain well. Bring 2 ½ quarts (2.25 liters) of the stock to a simmer in a very large pan, add the oxtail, cover, and simmer for 3 hours or until the oxtail is very tender. Skim the surface from time to time, skimming any foam from the top. Cool thoroughly and remove all surface fat. Keep the stock for the soup – you should have about 1 ¼ quarts (1.2 liters) left.

To make the wonton filling, remove all the meat from the bones and discard the bones. Finely chop the meat and combine it with the sesame oil, capers, mustard, salt, pepper, lemon zest, soy sauce, chives, chervil, shallots, cilantro, and scallions; mix well.

When you are ready to stuff the wontons, put 1 tablespoon of the filling in the center of the first wonton skin. Dampen the edges with a little water, and bring up the sides of the skin around the filling. Pinch the edges together at the top so that the wonton is sealed. It should look like a small, filled bag. Repeat the process until all the filling has been used.

Reheat the soup stock and add the remainder of the chicken stock. Season with salt and pepper to taste.

In another pan, bring salted water to a boil and poach the wontons for 1 minute, or until they float to the top (you may have to do this in batches). Remove them immediately and transfer them to individual flat soup plates. Ladle a small amount of the stock into each soup plate, garnish with chopped chives, and serve immediately.

ⓥGINGER PEA SOUP ≈

SERVES 4

2 tablespoons extra virgin
   olive oil
1 small onion, coarsely
   chopped
1½ tablespoons finely
   chopped fresh ginger
   (page 17)
1 teaspoon salt
¼ teaspoon freshly ground
   white pepper
1 x 10oz package (350 g)
   frozen peas or 1¼ lb (550
   g) fresh peas, shelled
2 ½ cups (1.2 liters)
   homemade Vegetable
   Stock (page 33)
¼ lb (100 g) potatoes,
   peeled and cut in
   small cubes

FRESH, SWEET PEAS IN SEASON ARE A REAL TREAT, WITH THEIR EARTHY FLAVOR AND PLEASANT TEXTURE. AS LEGUMES, THEY ARE QUITE NUTRITIOUS IN TERMS OF THE PROTEIN, IRON, AND B VITAMINS THEY PROVIDE.

HERE, A TOUCH OF FRESH GINGER ADDS ZESTY SPICE TO THIS LUSCIOUS SOUP. I USE POTATOES RATHER THAN CREAM OR BUTTER TO THICKEN THE SOUP SLIGHTLY. THE BONUS IS THAT IT REHEATS VERY WELL, MAKING IT IDEAL FOR EASY SERVING AT YOUR CONVENIENCE.

Heat a wok or large frying-pan over high heat. Add the olive oil, and when it is very hot and slightly smoking, add the onion and ginger and stir-fry for 1 minute. Sprinkle on the salt and pepper to taste. Continue to stir-fry for 3 minutes or until the onion is soft and translucent.

Now add the peas and stir-fry for 1 minute. Pour in the stock and bring the mixture to a simmer. Add the potatoes, cover, and simmer for 20 minutes.

Remove from the heat and allow to cool slightly. When it is cool enough, blend the entire soup mixture in a food processor or blender. Reheat the soup, ladle it into a soup tureen, and serve immediately.

East-West Mushroom Soup ≈

Mushrooms – from the East and West – unite here in a delectable soup. Simple to make, this soup can also be made up to the puréeing stage the day before since it reheats nicely. It makes a lovely appetizer or, served with bread and a light salad, a meal in itself. I use homemade vegetable stock which makes this soup ideal for vegetarians.

Soak the Chinese mushrooms in warm water for 20 minutes. Drain them and squeeze out the excess liquid. Remove and discard the stems and finely shred the caps into thin strips. Wash and slice the button mushrooms.

Heat a wok or large frying-pan with the butter and olive oil over a high heat. Add the garlic and scallions, onion, and shallots and stir-fry for 3 minutes. Then add all the mushrooms and stir-fry for 5 minutes, mixing them well. Add the sugar, salt, pepper, and stock. Turn the heat down and cook for 5 minutes, stirring continuously. Remove the soup from the heat and allow to cool enough to handle. Purée the mixture in a blender and return to the wok or pan. Reheat to a simmer and stir in the crème fraîche, mixing well. Garnish with chives and serve immediately.

Serves 4–6

2 oz (50 g) dried Chinese black mushrooms (page 18)

1 lb (450 g) button mushrooms

2 tablespoons (25 g) unsalted butter

1 tablespoon extra virgin olive oil

1 tablespoon coarsely chopped garlic

3 tablespoons finely chopped scallions

1 small onion, finely chopped

3 tablespoons finely chopped shallots

2 teaspoons sugar

2 teaspoons salt

½ teaspoon freshly ground five-pepper mixture (page 21) or black pepper

5 cups (1.2 liters) homemade Vegetable Stock (page 33)

3 tablespoons crème fraîche

2 tablespoons finely chopped fresh chives, to garnish

Ⓥ SPICY LEMON GRASS, COCONUT AND TOMATO SOUP ≈

SERVES 4–6

3 tablespoons extra virgin olive oil

4 oz (100 g) lemon grass (page 18), coarsely chopped

4 oz (100 g) onions, coarsely chopped

4 oz (100 g) scallions, coarsely chopped

2 tablespoons finely chopped fresh ginger (page 17)

1 tablespoon coarsely chopped garlic

1 fresh red or green chili (page 16), seeded and coarsely chopped

5 cups (1.2 liters) homemade Vegetable (page 33) or Chicken (page 32) Stock

1 lb (450 g) tomatoes, peeled and seeded if fresh or drained if canned, chopped

1 tablespoon sugar

1½ teaspoons salt

1 teaspoon freshly ground five-pepper mixture (page 21) or black pepper

3 tablespoons canned coconut milk (page 16)

2 tablespoons light cream

To Garnish:

2 tablespoons finely chopped fresh chives

1 tablespoon finely chopped cilantro

Basil-flavored Olive Oil (page 36) and Curry-flavored Oil (page 38), (optional)

IN THIS RECIPE, I HAVE MODIFIED THE TRADITIONAL TOMATO SOUP BY ADDING HINTS OF THAILAND – LEMON GRASS AND COCONUT – TO MAKE A SUBTLE AND FRAGRANT ALTERNATIVE TO THIS POPULAR SOUP. IT CAN BE MADE AHEAD OF TIME BECAUSE IT REHEATS EXTREMELY WELL.

Heat a large, heavy pan until it is hot and add the olive oil. When the oil is hot, add the lemon grass, onions, scallions, ginger, garlic, and chili. Stir-fry the mixture for 5 minutes or until the onions are cooked through. Now add the stock, tomatoes, sugar, salt, and pepper. Bring the mixture to the boil, turn the heat down and simmer for 20 minutes.

Remove from the heat and, when it is cool enough, purée the soup in a blender. Strain the soup through a fine sieve.

When you are ready to serve the soup, re-heat it and add the coconut milk and cream. Finally, garnish it with chives and cilantro, and a drizzle of the basil and curry oils if you wish.

Light and Savory Tomato and Ginger Soup ≈

THIS IS SIMPLY A LOVELY SOUP THAT COMBINES EASTERN AND WESTERN INGREDIENTS FOR A UNIQUE AND TASTY FIRST COURSE.

Heat the olive oil in a wok or large frying-pan. Stir-fry the scallions, ginger and shallots gently, without browning, for about 8 minutes. Transfer the mixture to a large pan and add the tomatoes, ground coriander, sugar, stock, salt and pepper. Mix well, bring the mixture to a simmer and cook for 10 minutes. Remove from the heat and allow to cool.

Stir in the cream, cilantro, and chives. Ladle the soup into a blender in small batches and process until completely smooth. Slowly re-heat the soup, adding the butter, and stir well. Ladle the mixture into a soup tureen or individual bowls, garnish with coriander leaves and serve immediately.

Serves 4–6

3 tablespoons extra virgin olive oil
6 tablespoons finely chopped scallions
2 tablespoons finely chopped fresh ginger (page 17)
4 oz (100 g) shallots, finely chopped
½ lb (225 g) tomatoes, peeled and seeded if fresh or drained if canned, chopped
2 teaspoons ground coriander
1 tablespoon sugar
5 cups (1.2 liters) homemade Vegetable (page 33) or Chicken (page 32) Stock
2 teaspoons salt
Freshly ground five-pepper mixture (page 21) or black pepper
½ cup (125 ml) heavy cream
6 tablespoons finely chopped cilantro
4 tablespoons finely chopped fresh chives
2 tablespoons (25 g) unsalted butter, cut in small pieces
cilantro leaves, to garnish

ⓥVEGETARIAN BEAN-THREAD SOUP ≈

SERVES 4

2 oz (50 g) dried bean thread (transparent) noodles (page 19)

5 cups (1.2 liters) homemade Vegetable (page 33) or Chicken (page 32) Stock

1 tablespoon light soy sauce (page 23)

2 teaspoons dark soy sauce (page 23)

1 tablespoon Shaoxing rice wine (page 22) or dry sherry

2 teaspoons sugar

1 teaspoon salt

¼ teaspoon freshly ground five-pepper mixture (page 21) or black pepper

2 teaspoons cornstarch, mixed with 1 tablespoon water

2 teaspoons sesame oil

FOR CENTURIES, CHINESE VEGETARIANS HAVE CLEVERLY USED TEXTURES SIMILAR TO MEATS OR FISH IN THEIR VEGETARIAN DISHES. BUDDHISTS ARE ESPECIALLY TALENTED IN SUCH CULINARY MASQUERADES, WORKING ON THE THEORY THAT ONE MAY HAVE ONE'S CAKE AND EAT IT TOO. THAT IS, IF THE ARTIFICE IS WELL AND DELICIOUSLY DONE.

SHARK'S FIN HAS ALWAYS BEEN PRIZED IN CHINA, BUT IT IS AN EXPENSIVE TREAT, AND BESIDES, IT IS OF ANIMAL ORIGIN. SO, THIS DISH WAS CREATED TO PLEASE VEGETARIANS WHO WISH TO SWIM WITH THE EATERS OF SHARK'S FIN WITHOUT GUILT. BEAN-THREAD NOODLES, WHICH HAVE A TOOTHSOME BITE AND ARE RATHER LONG AND CHEWY, PROVIDE THE ILLUSION OF THE SIMILARLY CHEWY, AND ON ITS OWN, RATHER TASTELESS, SHARK'S FIN. THIS SOUP IS A REAL TREAT AND MUCH BETTER FOR EVERYONE, INCLUDING THE SHARK.

Soak the noodles in warm water for 15 minutes. Drain well.

Heat the stock in a medium-sized pan, turn the heat down to a simmer, add the bean thread noodles, soy sauces, rice wine or sherry, sugar, salt, and pepper. Gently simmer for about 4 minutes. Add the cornstarch mixture and continue to cook for another 3 minutes or until the soup has slightly thickened. Now add the sesame oil and give the soup several good stirs. Pour the soup into a tureen and serve immediately.

ⓋCREAM OF SPINACH AND TOFU SOUP ≈

Serving food on airlines is perhaps one of the most challenging tasks in the food service business. This is especially the case on long-haul flights, in which several meals are served. Research shows that the passenger is better off with light foods since heavier meals are difficult to digest at higher altitudes. Asian airlines are especially good at meeting this challenge by offering satisfying soups. Here is a brilliantly conceived soup that I enjoyed on a Singapore Airlines flight; it is a true fusion of East and West. A savory mix of silky-soft tofu and spinach is puréed with good stock so that it is creamy but without any of the fat that comes with real cream. Bits of chopped tofu and fresh spinach leaves add a textured garnish to this most satisfying soup.

Serves 4

1½ lb (750 g) fresh spinach
½ cup (225 g) silky Japanese
   tofu (page 13)
5 cups (1.2 liters)
   homemade Vegetable
   (page 33) or Chicken
   (page 32) Stock
1 tablespoon light soy sauce
   (page 23)
2 teaspoons sugar
1 teaspoon salt
½ teaspoon freshly ground
   white pepper

To Garnish:
2 oz (50 g) silky Japanese
   tofu (page 13) chopped
Small spinach leaves

Remove the stems of the spinach and wash the leaves well. Gently cut the tofu into 1 in (2.5 cm) cubes. Drain well.

Put the stock into a pan and bring it to a simmer. Add the spinach, tofu, soy sauce, sugar, salt, and pepper and simmer for 4 minutes. Remove from the heat and allow to cool.

When it is cool enough, purée the entire mixture in a blender. Reheat the puréed soup in a clean pan, add the garnish of chopped tofu and spinach leaves, and continue to simmer the soup until they are heated through. Serve immediately.

FISH AND SHELLFISH

蝦蟹

Shrimp in Tea Butter Sauce ≈

THIS RECIPE WAS INSPIRED BY A CLASSIC CHINESE DISH IN WHICH GREEN TEA IS PAIRED WITH SHRIMP. THE STRINGENT, TART TASTE OF THE TEA IS A GOOD FOIL FOR THE RICH SHRIMP. IN THIS FUSION RECIPE, I HAVE TRANSFORMED THE DISH BY ADDING WESTERN ELEMENTS. YOU CAN SERVE THIS DISH WITH STEAMED RICE (PAGE 35).

Peel the shrimp and discard the shells. Using a small, sharp knife, remove the fine digestive cords. Wash the shrimp in cold water with a tablespoon of salt. Drain and repeat. Rinse well and pat dry with paper towels.

Put the tea leaves in a heatproof measuring jug or bowl and pour in the boiling water. Let the tea steep for 15 minutes.

Heat a wok or large frying-pan until it is hot and add the olive oil. Now add the shrimp and stir-fry for 30 seconds. Strain the tea and pour in the liquid. Add half the leaves, discarding the rest. Cook for another minute. Remove the shrimp with a slotted spoon. Add the rice wine or sherry, the shallots, ginger, and fish stock, and over high heat reduce the liquid in the wok or pan by three-quarters. Season the remaining sauce with the salt and pepper. Whisk in the butter, a few pieces at a time. Return the shrimp to the wok or pan and warm briefly. Garnish with scallions and serve at once.

Serves 2–4

1 lb (450 g) raw shrimp
2 tablespoons salt

For the Sauce:
1 tablespoon Chinese green tea leaves
1 cup (250 ml) boiling water
1½ tablespoons extra virgin olive oil
1 tablespoon Shaoxing rice wine (page 22) or dry sherry
2 tablespoons finely chopped shallots
1 teaspoon finely chopped fresh ginger (page 17)
⅔ cup (150 ml) Homemade Fish Stock (page 34)
1 teaspoon salt
½ teaspoon freshly ground five-pepper mixture (page 21) or black pepper
2 tablespoons (25 g) cold unsalted butter, cut in very small pieces
2 tablespoons finely chopped scallions, to garnish

BROILED SHRIMP WITH JAPANESE VINAIGRETTE ≈

SERVING BROILED SHRIMP IS ONE OF THE FASTEST WAYS TO GIVE A SPECIAL TOUCH TO A QUICK MENU. SHRIMP ARE QUICK TO PREPARE AND ALWAYS IMPRESSIVE AS AN APPETIZER OR AS A MAIN COURSE. ALSO, BROILING GIVES THE SHRIMP A SMOKY FRAGRANCE AND THIS JAPANESE-INSPIRED SAUCE PROVIDES THE RIGHT BALANCE OF FLAVORS.

SERVES 2–4

1 lb (450 g) raw shrimp
2 tablespoons salt

For the Marinade:

1 tablespoon light soy sauce (page 23)
1 teaspoon Shaoxing rice wine (page 22) or dry sherry
½ teaspoon salt
¼ teaspoon freshly ground five-pepper mixture (page 21) or black pepper
2 teaspoons sesame oil

For the Sauce:

1 tablespoon light soy sauce (page 23)
2 tablespoons Chinese white rice vinegar (page 24)
1 teaspoon mirin (Japanese sweet rice wine) (page 18) or dry sherry
2 tablespoons finely chopped cilantro
1 tablespoon finely chopped fresh chives
1 teaspoon finely chopped fresh ginger (page 17)

Soak bamboo skewers in cold water for 15 minutes or more. Peel the shrimp and discard the shells. Using a small, sharp knife, remove the fine digestive cords. Wash the shrimp in cold water with a tablespoon of salt. Drain and repeat. Rinse well and pat dry with paper towels. Combine the marinade ingredients and mix with the shrimp. Allow to marinate for 30 minutes. Skewer the shrimp.

Pre-heat the oven broiler to high or make a charcoal fire in the barbecue. When the broiler is very hot or the charcoal is ash-white, broil the shrimp for 3 minutes on each side or until they are cooked. Put the cooked shrimp on a warm platter.

In a small bowl, combine the soy sauce, vinegar, and rice wine or sherry. Then add the cilantro, chives, and ginger. Pour into a serving bowl. Drizzle some of the sauce over the shrimp and serve immediately with the remaining sauce.

Mussels in Lemon Grass and Coconut Butter Sauce ≈

The high demand for seafood has caused a several-fold increase in the price. Fortunately, mussels remain economical and are an ideal fusion food. They cook rapidly and combine well with almost any flavor. Their briny taste is an ideal foil for the citrus zest of lemon grass and the richness of coconut milk. The only hard work is the scrubbing; once that is done, the rest takes literally minutes. This recipe also makes an elegant appetizer for any meal.

Drizzle with Orange-flavored Oil for an extra special touch.

Peel the lemon grass stalks to the tender, whitish centers and crush them with the flat of a knife. Then cut them into 3 in (7.5 cm) pieces.

In a large wok or pan, combine the mussels with the rice wine or sherry and the stock. Bring to a boil and cook for 3–4 minutes or until the mussels are barely opened. Remove them immediately with a slotted spoon and allow to cool. Discard any that do not open. Add the lemon grass, shallots, ginger, turmeric, saffron threads, salt and pepper to the stock and simmer for 5 minutes. Then remove the lemon grass stalks and discard them.

Meanwhile, remove the mussels from their shells and discard the shells. Set aside.

Now add the coconut milk to the stock, stir, then add the butter a piece at a time. Stir in the coriander, scallions, and chives and, finally, return the mussels to the sauce. Give the mixture a final stir, drizzle with the orange-flavored oil, if using, and serve at once.

Serves 2–4

- 3 lemon grass stalks (page 18)
- 3 lb (1.5 kg) fresh mussels, well scrubbed
- 2 tablespoons mirin (Japanese sweet rice wine) (page 18) or Shaoxing rice wine (page 22) or dry sherry
- 1 cup (250 ml) homemade Fish (page 34) or Chicken (page 32) Stock
- 3 tablespoons finely chopped shallots
- 1 tablespoon finely chopped fresh ginger (page 17)
- 1 teaspoon ground turmeric
- A pinch of saffron threads
- Salt and freshly ground five-pepper mixture (page 21) or white pepper
- ⅔ cup (150 ml) canned coconut milk (page 16)
- 2 tablespoons (25 g/1 oz) cold unsalted butter, cut in small pieces
- 1 tablespoon finely chopped cilantro
- 2 tablespoons finely chopped scallions
- 1 tablespoon finely chopped fresh chives
- Orange-flavored Oil (page 38), to serve (optional)

Scallop Pancakes with Chinese Greens ≈

Serves 4
(makes 8 pancakes)

For the Pancakes:

1 lb (450 g) scallops,
   including corals, coarsely
   chopped
2 tablespoons rice flour
2 tablespoons finely
   chopped shallots
2 tablespoons finely
   chopped chives
1 teaspoon salt
½ teaspoon freshly ground
   five-pepper mixture
   (page 21) or black pepper
2 tablespoons extra virgin
   olive oil plus extra if
   needed

For the Greens:

1 lb (450 g) Chinese greens,
   such as Chinese flowering
   cabbage or bok choy
   (page 14)
2 tablespoons extra virgin
   olive oil
3 tablespoons finely sliced
   garlic
1 teaspoon salt
1 teaspoon light soy sauce
   (page 23)
2 teaspoons lemon juice
1 tablespoon finely chopped
   cilantro, to garnish

In this delectable recipe, sweet scallops are made into tasty pancakes and paired with fresh, slightly bitter Chinese greens. It is a classic Chinese combination which I have altered slightly to create a fusion recipe that serves as an appetizer for eight or a main course for four.

Combine the scallops with the rice flour, shallots, chives, salt, and pepper. Set aside.

Cut the Chinese greens into 3 in (7.5 cm) pieces.

Heat the 2 tablespoons of olive oil in a non-stick frying-pan. Form the scallop mixture into eight pancakes in the pan (you may have to do this in batches) and brown lightly on both sides. Add more olive oil, if necessary. Remove and keep warm on a baking pan in a low oven.

To prepare the Chinese greens, heat a wok or large frying-pan over a high heat. Add the olive oil, and when it is hot, add the garlic and stir-fry for 20 seconds until the garlic has browned. Then quickly add the Chinese greens and stir-fry for 3 minutes, or until the greens have wilted a little. Now add the salt, soy sauce, and lemon juice and continue to stir-fry for 1 minute.

Arrange the greens and scallop pancakes on a platter, garnish with chopped cilantro and serve immediately.

CRISPY-FRIED SHRIMP WITH CURRY SPICES ≈

SERVES 4 AS A MAIN
COURSE

1 lb (450 g) raw shrimp
2 tablespoons plus
   1 teaspoon salt
½ teaspoon freshly ground
   five-pepper mixture
   (page 21) or black pepper
1 tablespoon Madras curry
   powder (page 17)
All-purpose flour, for dusting
2 eggs, beaten
2 cups (100 g) dried
   breadcrumbs
2 ½ cups (600 ml) peanut
   or vegetable oil, for
   deep-frying
Lemon juice, to serve

THE AVAILABILITY OF CURRY SPICES IN CONVENIENT CURRY POWDER MIXTURES HAS BEEN A BOON TO BOTH CHEFS AND HOME COOKS. A DASH CAN TRANSFORM ORDINARY DISHES INTO A SPECIAL TREAT. HERE, I HAVE USED THEM TO ENHANCE AN EASY CRISPY SHRIMP DISH, WHICH IS ENCHANTINGLY SPICY AS EITHER AN APPETIZER OR A MAIN COURSE, SERVED WITH STEAMED RICE (PAGE 35).

Peel the shrimp and discard the shells. Using a small, sharp knife, remove the fine digestive cords. Wash the shrimp in cold water with a tablespoon of salt. Drain and repeat. Rinse well and pat dry with paper towels.

In a bowl, combine the shrimp with the remaining salt and the pepper and curry powder and mix well.

Flour the shrimp, shaking off any excess flour. Then dip them in the beaten egg and, finally, in the breadcrumbs.

Heat a wok or large frying-pan over a high heat. Add the oil, and when it is very hot and slightly smoking, add a handful of shrimp and deep-fry for 3 minutes, until golden and crisp. If the oil gets too hot, turn the heat down slightly. Drain the shrimp well on paper towels. Continue to fry the shrimp until you have finished all of them. Serve immediately, with fresh lemon juice for a dipping sauce.

STIR-FRIED SHRIMP WITH MUSTARD HERB SAUCE ≈

THERE ARE VERY FEW FOODS EASIER TO PREPARE THAN SHRIMP. THEY COOK QUICKLY AND ARE ALSO SUCCULENT AND COLORFUL AND ALWAYS POPULAR. IN THIS QUICK RECIPE, SHRIMP ARE STIR-FRIED WITH CHINESE FLAVORS AND THEN RAPIDLY FINISHED OFF WITH A TOUCH OF WESTERN MUSTARD AND HERBS FOR AN UNUSUALLY SUMPTUOUS, QUICKY PREPARED DISH. FOR AN EVEN SPICIER FLAVOR, DRIZZLE WITH SESAME AND CHILI OIL. SERVE WITH PASTA, NOODLES OR RICE.

Peel the shrimp and discard the shells. Using a small, sharp knife, remove the fine digestive cords. Wash the shrimp in cold water with a tablespoon of salt. Drain and repeat. Rinse well and pat dry with paper towels.

Heat a wok or large frying-pan until it is very hot and then add the olive oil. Immediately add the shrimp and garlic and stir-fry for 1 minute. Then add the rice wine or sherry, salt, pepper, sugar, stock, and mustard. Cook for 2 minutes; then add the butter, a piece at a time, and stir for 1 minute. Add the scallions and the fresh herbs. Give the mixture several good stirs and drizzle over the sesame and chili oil, if using.

Turn onto a platter and serve immediately.

SERVES 4

- 1 lb (450 g) raw shrimp
- 2 tablespoons salt
- 1 tablespoon extra virgin olive oil
- 1 tablespoon coarsely chopped garlic
- 1 tablespoon Shaoxing rice wine (page 22) or dry sherry
- 1 teaspoon salt
- ½ teaspoon freshly ground five-pepper mixture (page 21) or black pepper
- ½ teaspoon sugar
- 3 tablespoons homemade Fish Stock (page 34)
- 2 tablespoons Dijon mustard
- 2 tablespoons (25 g) cold unsalted butter, cut in small pieces
- 1 tablespoon finely chopped scallions
- 1 tablespoon finely chopped cilantro
- 1 tablespoon finely chopped fresh flatleaf or curly parsley
- 1 tablespoon finely chopped fresh chives
- Sesame and Chili Oil (page 39), to serve (optional)

CRISP COCONUT SHRIMP FROM THE JERSEY POTTERY RESTAURANT ≈

SERVES 4 AS A SIDE DISH

1 lb (450 g) raw shrimp
2 tablespoons salt
2 oz (50 g) grated coconut
2 cups (100 g) dried
   breadcrumbs
2 tablespoons finely
   chopped fresh flatleaf
   parsley
2 tablespoons finely
   chopped cilantro
1 tablespoon finely chopped
   chervil
All-purpose flour, for dusting
2 eggs, beaten
2 ½ cups (600 ml) peanut
   or vegetable oil, for
   deep-frying

For the Sweet and Spicy Dipping Sauce:
⅔ cup (150 ml) water
3 tablespoons sugar
3 tablespoons Chinese white
   rice vinegar (page 24) or
   cider vinegar
3 tablespoons tomato purée
   or ketchup
2 teaspoons chili-bean sauce
   (page 22)
1 teaspoon salt
½ teaspoon freshly ground
   white pepper
1 teaspoon cornstarch,
   mixed with 2 teaspoons
   water

DURING A VISIT TO JERSEY IN THE CHANNEL ISLANDS, I VISITED A CHARMING RESTAURANT CALLED THE JERSEY POTTERY RESTAURANT, WHICH WAS A CERAMIC FACTORY, STUDIO, AND SHOWROOM AS WELL AS A RESTAURANT WITH CHARMING GARDENS — ALL IN ONE COMPLEX. AMONG THE MANY DELICIOUS DISHES WAS AN OUTSTANDING SHRIMP ENTRÉE, SERVED WITH A SWEET AND SPICY SAUCE WHICH I SAW IMMEDIATELY AS A FUSION-INFLUENCED DISH. THE HEAD CHEF, TONY DORRIS, GAVE ME THE RECIPE, AND I'VE ADAPTED HERE. IT'S EASY TO MAKE AND JUST AS EASY TO EAT.

Peel the shrimp and discard the shells. Using a small, sharp knife, remove the fine digestive cords. Wash the shrimp in cold water with a tablespoon of salt. Drain and repeat. Rinse well and pat dry with paper towels.

In a small pan, combine all the ingredients for the sweet and spicy dipping sauce, except the cornstarch mixture. Bring them to a boil, stir in the cornstarch mixture, and cook for 1 minute. Set aside and allow to cool.

In a bowl, combine the coconut, breadcrumbs, and herbs together, mixing well.

Flour the shrimp, shaking off any excess flour. Then dip them in the beaten egg and finally in the breadcrumb mixture.

Heat a wok or large frying-pan over a high heat until it is hot. Add the oil, and when it is very hot and slightly smoking, add a handful of shrimp, and deep-fry for 3 minutes until golden and crisp. If the oil gets too hot, turn the heat down slightly. Drain the shrimp well on paper towels. Continue to fry the shrimp until you have finished all of them. Serve immediately with the sweet and spicy dipping sauce.

STIR-FRIED SHRIMP AND SCALLOPS IN BLACK BEAN AND TOMATO BUTTER SAUCE ≈

SERVES 4

1 lb (450 g) raw shrimp

2 tablespoons salt

1 lb (450 g) fresh scallops, including the corals

1½ tablespoons olive oil

1½ tablespoons coarsely chopped garlic

1 tablespoon finely chopped fresh ginger (page 17)

2 tablespoons finely chopped shallots

1 tablespoon coarsely chopped black beans (page 14)

1 tablespoon Shaoxing rice wine (page 22) or dry sherry

1 tablespoon light soy sauce (page 23)

½ cup (120 ml) homemade Fish (page 34) or Chicken (page 32) Stock

1 large (6oz) (175 g) tomato, peeled and seeded if fresh, drained if canned, coarsely chopped

2 tablespoons (25 g) cold unsalted butter, cut in small pieces

Chive-flavored Olive Oil (page 37), to serve (optional)

A small handful of fresh basil leaves, cut in strips, to garnish

IT IS NOT SURPRISING FOR ME TO SEE FUSION COOKS AND CHEFS ALL OVER THE WORLD USING CHINESE BLACK BEANS. THESE ARE SMALL BLACK SOY BEANS THAT ARE PRESERVED WITH SALT AND SPICES. THEIR DISTINCTIVE, SALTY, PUNGENT AROMA IMPARTS A RICH FLAVOR TO FOODS THEY ARE COOKED WITH. NOW WIDELY AVAILABLE, THESE BLACK BEANS TRANSFORM ORDINARY DISHES INTO SPECIAL TREATS. IN THIS RECIPE, I HAVE STIR-FRIED SHRIMP AND SCALLOPS WITH THE BLACK BEANS AND FINISHED THEM OFF WITH A EUROPEAN TOUCH. THIS DISH MAKES AN ELEGANT DINNER PARTY MAIN COURSE, SERVED WITH VEGETABLES. DRIZZLE WITH CHIVE-FLAVORED OLIVE OIL FOR A SPECIAL TOUCH.

Peel the shrimp and discard the shells. Using a small, sharp knife, remove the fine digestive cords. Wash the shrimp in cold water with a tablespoon of salt. Drain and repeat. Rinse well and pat dry with paper towels. Clean the scallops and pull off the tough muscles.

Heat a wok or large frying-pan over a high heat. Add the olive oil, then shrimp and scallops and stir-fry for 2 minutes. Remove them with a slotted spoon and set aside. Now add the garlic, ginger, and shallots and stir-fry for 30 seconds. Then add the black beans and continue to stir-fry for another 30 seconds. Add the rice wine or sherry, light soy sauce, and stock. Cook over a high heat for 1 minute. Return the scallops and shrimp to the wok or pan and continue to cook for another 3 minutes until just done and tender.

Finally, add the chopped tomatoes, and when the mixture is hot, slowly whisk in the butter a piece at a time. Turn onto a warm serving platter, drizzle with chive-flavored olive oil, if using, garnish with basil, and serve immediately.

Stir-fried *Persillade* Shrimp ≈

Persillade IS A FRENCH CULINARY TERM WHICH IMPLIES A MIXTURE OF CHOPPED PARSLEY AND GARLIC THAT IS USUALLY ADDED TO DISHES AT THE END OF THE COOKING PROCESS. THIS ROBUST SEASONING GIVES ANY DISH A DISTINCTLY ASSERTIVE FLAVOR. IN THIS RECIPE, I HAVE ADDED TO THE *PERSILLADE* AN EASTERN TOUCH OF CILANTRO TO GIVE A REFRESHING NEW DIMENSION TO A CLASSIC SEASONING. *PERSILLADE* GOES PARTICULARLY WELL WITH A DISH SUCH AS SHRIMP. DRIZZLE WITH GARLIC, GINGER, AND SCALLION OIL AND SERVE WITH STEAMED RICE (PAGE 35).

Peel the shrimp and discard the shells. Using a small, sharp knife, remove the fine digestive cords. Wash the shrimp in a bowl of cold water to which you've added a tablespoon of salt. Drain and repeat. Rinse well and pat dry with paper towels. Combine the shrimp with the egg white, cornstarch, 1 teaspoon salt, sesame oil and pepper. Mix well and place them in the refrigerator for 20 minutes.

Combine all the *persillade* ingredients together in a food processor or blender and process until finely chopped. If you are using a blender, be careful not to overblend the mixture to a purée.

If you are using the peanut oil, heat a wok or large frying-pan over high heat, then add the oil. When the oil is very hot, remove the wok or pan from the heat and immediately add the shrimp, stirring vigorously to keep them from sticking. When the shrimp become opaque, after about 2 minutes, quickly drain them in a stainless steel colander set in a bowl. Discard the oil.

If you choose to use water instead of oil, bring it to a boil in a pan. Remove the pan from the heat and immediately add the shrimp, stirring vigorously to keep them from sticking. When the shrimp become opaque, after about 2 minutes, quickly drain them in a colander set in a bowl. Discard the water.

Clean and reheat the wok or frying-pan over a high heat. Add the olive oil, and when it is hot, return the shrimp to the wok and stir-fry for 20 seconds.

Quickly stir in the *persillade* mixture and mix well.

Turn onto a platter, drizzle with the garlic, ginger and scallion oil, and serve immediately.

SERVES 4

1 lb (450 g) raw shrimp
2 tablespoons plus
  1 teaspoon salt
1 egg white
2 teaspoons cornstarch
1 teaspoon sesame oil
½ teaspoon freshly ground
  white pepper
2 cups (400 ml) peanut oil
  or water
1 tablespoon extra virgin
  olive oil
Garlic, Ginger and scallion
  Oil (page 39), to serve
  (optional)

For the *Persillade*:

2 tablespoons extra virgin
  olive oil
1½ teaspoons finely chopped
  fresh ginger (page 17)
2 tablespoons finely
  chopped garlic
1 teaspoon salt
½ teaspoon freshly ground
  five-pepper mixture
  (page 21) or black pepper
½ teaspoon sugar
1 tablespoon finely chopped
  scallions
1 tablespoon finely chopped
  cilantro
3 tablespoons finely
  chopped fresh flatleaf or
  curly parsley

CRISP-FRIED SQUID WITH BLACK BEAN AÏOLI ≈

SERVES 4

1½ lb (750 g) squid, fresh or frozen

2 oz (50 g) rice flour

2 oz (50 g) potato flour

2 teaspoons salt

1 teaspoon freshly ground five-pepper mixture (page 21) or black pepper

2 ½ cups (600 ml) peanut or vegetable oil, for deep-frying

For the Black Bean Aïoli:

2 egg yolks

1 tablespoon finely chopped garlic

2 tablespoons lemon juice

1 teaspoon salt

½ teaspoon freshly ground five-pepper mixture (page 21) or black pepper

½ cup (120 ml) extra virgin olive oil

½ cup (120 ml) peanut or vegetable oil

1 tablespoon black beans (page 14), rinsed and finely chopped

2 tablespoons finely chopped scallions

About 2 tablespoons water

FRIED SQUID SEEMS TO BE ON EVERY FUSION MENU THROUGHOUT THE WORLD, AND NO WONDER SINCE IT IS DELICIOUSLY ADDICTIVE. CHEFS CAN FRY SQUID QUICKLY SO THAT IT IS TENDER AND TASTY — INSTANT SATISFACTION FOR HUNGRY DINERS, ESPECIALLY WHEN SERVED WITH CHIPS. I MATCHED THIS POPULAR SQUID DISH WITH A TRADITIONAL FRENCH MAYONNAISE GARLIC SAUCE TO WHICH I ADDED AN ASIAN TOUCH OF BLACK BEANS. THIS DISH ALSO MAKES A WONDERFUL APPETIZER FOR SIX TO EIGHT.

Make the black bean aïoli by combining the egg yolks, garlic, lemon juice, salt, and pepper in a bowl, food processor, or blender. Slowly drizzle in the olive oil and the peanut or vegetable oil, until the oil is fully incorporated and emulsified. If you are using a food processor or blender, transfer the aïoli to a bowl. Fold in the black beans and scallions. Refrigerate until you are ready to use the aïoli. If it is too thick, add some or all of the water.

The edible parts of the squid are the tentacles and the body. Ask for it to be cleaned at the fish market, or you can do it yourself: pull the head and tentacles away from the body. Using a small, sharp knife, split the body in half. Remove the transparent, bony section. Wash the halves thoroughly under cold running water and then pull off and discard the skin. Cut the tentacles from the head, cutting just above the eye. (You may also have to remove the polyp, or beak, from the base of the ring of tentacles.) If you are using frozen squid, make sure it is properly thawed before cooking it.

Cut the squid meat into 1½ in (3.5 cm) strips. Blot them dry with paper towels. In a bowl, combine the rice and potato flours with the salt and pepper.

Heat a wok or large pan over high heat. Add the oil, and when it is moderately hot, quickly dredge the squid pieces in the flour mixture, shaking off any excess. Deep-fry immediately in batches. When the squid hits the hot oil it will splatter, so be careful. Remove with a slotted spoon as soon as the squid turns golden brown and drain well on paper towels. Keep warm on a platter until all the squid is fried, then serve immediately with the aïoli.

POACHED OYSTERS WITH CHAMPAGNE AND LEMON GRASS BUTTER SAUCE ≈

SERVES 4

2 lb (1 kg) oysters, shelled
(about 24)

4 lemon grass stalks
(page 18)
6 tablespoons finely
chopped shallots
1 tablespoon finely chopped
fresh ginger (page 17)
1 ¼ cups (300 ml)
champagne
1 ¼ cups (300 ml)
homemade Fish (page 34)
or Chicken (page 32)
Stock
6 tablespoons (75 g) cold
unsalted butter, cut in small
pieces
Salt and freshly ground white
pepper
Tomato-flavored Olive Oil
(page 40)
1 tablespoon finely chopped
fresh chives

OYSTERS ARE, RIGHTLY, ASSOCIATED WITH ELEGANCE AND STYLE. THEY ARE DELICATE AND I LOVE THEIR BRINY SEA FLAVORS. HERE I HAVE COMBINED THEM WITH THE REFRESHING BITE OF LEMON GRASS IN A CHAMPAGNE BUTTER SAUCE. THESE OYSTERS ARE LOVELY SERVED WITH STEAMED RICE (PAGE 35). THIS DISH ALSO MAKES AN EXQUISITE APPETIZER FOR ANY DINNER PARTY. DRIZZLE WITH TOMATO-FLAVORED OLIVE OIL FOR COLOR AND TASTE.

Drain the oysters in a colander, saving the liquid. Rinse the oysters.

Peel the lemon grass stalks to the tender, whitish centers and finely chop them. Combine the chopped lemon grass with the shallots, ginger, champagne, stock, and any oyster liquid in a pan and simmer for 15 minutes. Strain the liquid through a fine sieve.

Return the strained liquid to the pan, and over a high heat, reduce the liquid by half.

Turn the heat down to low, add the oysters, and cook for 2 minutes. Remove the oysters with a slotted spoon to a warm dish. Quickly whisk the butter into the liquid; add salt and pepper to taste. Pour the sauce over the oysters and drizzle with tomato-flavored olive oil. Sprinkle the chives, and serve immediately.

CURED SALMON WITH SICHUAN PEPPERCORNS ≈

This recipe was inspired by the executive chef at the Oriental Hotel, Bangkok. Norbert Kostner is Italian and has lived and worked in Thailand for over 30 years. Talented and inspired, he incorporates Asian spices and ingredients into his western-style cookery. I was most impressed by his cured salmon, which was as delicious as it was exciting. Instead of seasoning the salmon with dill, the traditional herb, he used whole roasted, crushed Sichuan peppercorns and orange slices, which permeate the rich fish, giving the salmon a wonderful, delicate aroma. The salmon is served raw but has been 'cooked' or cured by the salt and spices first. Although it takes a whole day to make, the process is fairly straightforward and simple. You will see it is well worth the effort, because it makes a perfect and grand party dish. The salmon will keep for at least one week in the refrigerator and any left-overs make wonderful sandwiches.

SERVES 15–20 AS A PARTY DISH

7–8 lb (3–3.5 kg) whole fresh salmon
2 oranges
3 oz (75 g) coarse sea salt
1 tablespoon sugar
3 tablespoons Sichuan peppercorns (page 21), roasted and crushed
Lemon wedges, to garnish

Have your salmon filleted and the head as well as any small bones removed at the fish market. You should have two large fillets weighing about 2–2½ lb (1–1.25 kg) each with the skin on. Make three shallow cuts in the skin of each fillet to allow the spices to penetrate. Keeping the skin on will help hold the shape of the fish during curing and when serving.

Cut the oranges into the thinnest possible slices and set aside.

Combine the salt, sugar, and Sichuan peppercorns. Rub both sides of the fillets with the salt–sugar–peppercorn mixture.

Cut out a sheet of plastic wrap on which a salmon fillet can fit comfortably. Lay one of the fillets on the plastic wrap skin-side down and then place a layer of oranges over the top of the fillet so that it is entirely covered with orange slices. Place the other fillet on top skin-side up and cover well with plastic wrap. Place on a tray and refrigerate for 24 hours.

After 24 hours, remove the plastic wrap, slice thinly and arrange on a platter with lemon wedges.

ASIAN-FLAVORED SALMON FISHCAKES ≈

SERVES 4
(MAKES 6–8 FISHCAKES)

½ lb (225 g) boneless
   salmon fillets
2 tablespoons fresh ginger
   juice, squeezed from fresh
   ginger (page 17)
2 tablespoons mirin
   (Japanese sweet rice wine)
   (page 18)
2 teaspoons coarse sea salt
1 teaspoon freshly ground
   five-pepper mixture (page
   21) or black pepper
1 ¼ cups (300 ml) oil,
   preferably peanut

For the Fishcakes:

3 tablespoons chopped
   fresh ginger (page 17)
4 tablespoons finely
   chopped scallions
3 tablespoons finely
   chopped shallots
2 teaspoons salt
1 teaspoon freshly ground
   five-pepper mixture (page
   21) or black pepper
3 tablespoons finely
   chopped cilantro
2 tablespoons finely
   chopped garlic
3 tablespoons extra virgin
   olive oil
3 tablespoons Dijon mustard
3 cups (175 g) dried
   breadcrumbs
All-purpose flour, for coating
2 eggs, beaten

THE CHINESE PREFER TO PURÉE THEIR FISH FOR FISHCAKES WITH EGG WHITE AND SEASONING AND THEN EITHER POACH OR FRY THEM. THE RESULT IS A BOUNCY AND ALMOST RUBBERY TEXTURE. I HAVE ALWAYS LIKED THE ENGLISH IDEA OF FISHCAKES IN WHICH THE TEXTURE IS RATHER MOIST AND FLAKY. I HAVE ADDED MY OWN ASIAN TOUCHES OF FLAVOR: GINGER (WHICH IS IDEAL FOR FISH) AND VARIOUS HERBS, SUCH AS CILANTRO, AND SCALLIONS. HERE, I USE RICH SALMON INSTEAD OF THE USUAL FIRM, WHITE FISH; I KNOW YOU WILL FIND THIS A LIGHT, DELECTABLE DISH. SERVE WITH A SALAD, DRIZZLED WITH LEMON-FLAVORED OIL (PAGE 38).

Rub the salmon fillets with the ginger juice and mirin. Combine the salt and pepper and sprinkle evenly on both sides of the salmon. Marinate at room temperature for at least 30 minutes.

Next, set up a steamer or put a rack into a wok or deep pan and pour in 2 in (5 cm) of water. Bring the water to a boil over high heat. Put the salmon onto a heatproof plate and then carefully lower it into the steamer or onto the rack. Turn the heat to low and cover the wok or pan tightly. Steam the salmon gently for 5 minutes. Alternatively, you can microwave it at full power for 3 minutes, covered. Let the salmon cool.

Flake the cooked salmon in a large bowl, removing any bones. Then add the ginger, scallions, shallots, salt, pepper, coriander and garlic. Drizzle in the olive oil, add the mustard and 2 cups (100 g) of the breadcrumbs and mix well.

Divide the salmon mixture into 6–8 pieces. On a floured surface, shape the pieces into round, flat patties with a butter knife. Dredge the cakes first in the flour, then the egg, and finally the remaining breadcrumbs.

Heat a wok or large frying-pan over a high heat. Add the oil, and when it is very hot and slightly smoking, turn the heat to low and add the salmon cakes. Fry for 3 minutes, then turn over and brown the other sides. Remove and drain on paper towels. Serve immediately.

EAST–WEST SALMON SANDWICH ≈

Serves 2 as a snack

2 x 1/4 lb (100 g)
   boneless, skinless salmon
   fillets
2 tablespoons fresh ginger
   juice, squeezed from fresh
   ginger root (page 17)
4 tablespoons mirin
   (Japanese sweet rice wine)
   (page 18)
2 teaspoons salt
2 teaspoons freshly ground
   five-pepper mixture
   (page 21)

For the *Persillade*:

2 tablespoons finely
   chopped fresh ginger
   (page 17)
4 tablespoons finely
   chopped scallions
½ teaspoon salt
Freshly ground black pepper
3 tablespoons extra virgin
   olive oil
3 tablespoons finely
   chopped cilantro
3 tablespoons finely chopped
   fresh curly parsley
3 tablespoons finely
   chopped fresh flatleaf
   parsley
2 teaspoons finely chopped
   garlic

For the Sandwich:

1 fresh, crisp baguette
6 fresh spinach leaves
10 basil leaves

In 1992 Mary Gostelow, a well-known restaurant- and hotel-industry consultant and writer, asked me to contribute to a special event for the 200th anniversary of the death of Lord Sandwich. I was thrilled to be in the company of some of the world's best chefs. Unfortunately, I was unable to attend the event, but Mary tells me that my sandwich was a big hit. I think you will also like it.

This recipe is for two but can easily be increased for more if you wish.

Rub the salmon fillets with the ginger juice and mirin. Combine the salt and pepper and sprinkle evenly on both sides of the salmon. Marinate at room temperature for at least 30 minutes.

Prepare the *persillade*. Combine the ginger, scallions, salt, and pepper in a small, heatproof dish. Heat the olive oil until it is quite hot, but not smoking. Pour this hot oil over the ginger, scallion, salt and pepper mixture. Scrape this mixture into a blender with the cilantro, the two parsleys, and the garlic and process until finely chopped and very well mixed. Add more olive oil, if necessary, as the mixture should be moist. Set the *persillade* aside.

Next, set up a steamer or put a rack into a wok or deep pan and pour in 2 in (5 cm) of water. Bring the water to a boil over a high heat. Put the salmon onto a heatproof plate and then carefully lower it into the steamer or onto the rack. Turn the heat to low and cover the wok or pan tightly. Steam gently for 5 minutes. Alternatively, you can microwave the salmon at full power for 3 minutes, covered. Let the salmon cool.

Pre-heat the oven to 350°F/180°C and warm the bread for 5 minutes. Divide the loaf in two, then split each half lengthwize and scrape out the insides. Spread the *persillade* on the inside of the bread, and top with the salmon fillet, spinach leaves, basil leaves, and tomato. Serve immediately.

Blanquette of Gingered Salmon and Shrimp ≈

Blanquette is a French classical culinary term for a ragoût of white meat (usually veal or poultry), or of fish or vegetables, cooked in white stock or water with aromatic flavorings. A sauce is then made from a roux of butter and flour and finished with cream and egg yolks. Blanquette became a classic of French bourgeois cooking. The sauce's rich, creamy, velvety texture also has great appeal to my palate. I have used the same idea here but have incorporated seasoning from my Chinese heritage, which adds tang. Ginger has a great affinity to fish and shellfish in the same way that lemon is used in European cooking. This simple, but very elegant, dish, drizzled perhaps with chive-flavored olive oil, goes extremely well with plain Steamed Rice (page 35).

Peel the shrimp and discard the shells. Using a small, sharp knife, remove the fine digestive cords. Wash the shrimp in a bowl of cold water to which you've added a tablespoon of salt. Drain and repeat. Rinse well and pat dry with paper towels. Cut the salmon into 1 in (2.5 cm) cubes. Sprinkle the salmon and shrimp evenly with the rest of the salt plus the five-pepper mixture and cayenne pepper.

If you are using fresh tomatoes, cut them into 1 in (2.5 cm) cubes. If you are using canned tomatoes, chop them into small chunks.

Peel and roll-cut the carrots by cutting a 1 in (2.5 cm) diagonal slice at one end and then rolling the carrot halfway before making the next diagonal slice. Blanch the carrots in salted, boiling water for 3 minutes. Remove and drain well.

Heat a wok or pan until it is hot, add the butter and quickly stir-fry the shrimp and salmon cubes for 3 minutes. Remove and set aside.

Return the wok or pan to the heat, add the ginger and shallots and stir-fry over a high heat for 1 minute. Then add the stock and continue to cook over a high heat, stirring, until the stock has reduced by half. Now add the crème fraîche, season to taste, add the peas and carrots, and cook for 2 minutes. Finally add the shrimp, salmon, and tomatoes and heat for 1 minute. Pour the mixture onto a warm platter, drizzle with chive-flavored olive oil, if using, sprinkle with chives, and serve immediately.

Serves 4–6

- 1 lb (450 g) raw shrimp
- 2 tablespoons plus 1 teaspoon salt
- 1 lb (450 g) salmon fillet, skinned
- ½ teaspoon freshly ground five-pepper mixture (page 21) or white pepper
- ½ teaspoon cayenne pepper
- 1 lb (450 g) tomatoes, peeled and seeded if fresh, drained if canned
- ¾ lb (350 g) carrots
- 3 tablespoons (35 g) butter
- 1½ tablespoons finely chopped fresh ginger (page 17)
- 3 tablespoons finely chopped shallots
- 1 cup (250 ml) homemade Fish (page 34) or Chicken (page 32) Stock
- ¾ cup (175 ml) crème fraîche
- Salt and freshly ground five-pepper mixture (page 21) or black pepper
- 8 oz (225 g) frozen petits pois
- Chive-flavored Olive Oil (page 37), to serve (optional)
- 2 tablespoons finely chopped fresh chives, to garnish

BROILED ASIAN CRÉPINETTES ≈

SERVES 4
(MAKES 20 CRÉPINETTES)

½ lb (225 g) caul fat
(crépine) (page 25)

1 lb (450 g) raw shrimp

2 tablespoons plus
1 teaspoon salt

½ lb (225 g) boneless,
skinless firm white fish,
such as halibut or cod,
coarsely chopped

4 tablespoons finely
chopped fresh basil

3 tablespoons finely
chopped cilantro

1 tablespoon finely chopped
fresh ginger (page 17)

2 teaspoons finely chopped
garlic

2 teaspoons roasted and
ground Sichuan
peppercorns (page 21)

2 teaspoons seeded and
coarsely chopped fresh red
chilies (page 16)

1 tablespoon light soy sauce
(page 23)

1 tablespoon dark soy sauce
(page 23)

2 tablespoons Shaoxing rice
wine (page 22) or dry
sherry

1 tablespoon extra virgin
olive oil

Both the French and Chinese use CRÉPINE, or caul fat from the pig, quite extensively. It can be bought at specialty butcher shops. Wrapping food in a light net of fat keeps the filling moist and flavorful while infusing it with the rich taste of the caul fat. This is an adaptation of the Chinese idea of wrapping fish, which is usually pounded into a paste. In this recipe I coarsely chop the seafood instead; then, after wrapping it in the caul fat, I broil it, which gives it a wonderful, smoky aroma. The CRÉPINETTES are delicious when served with french fries.

Soak the caul fat in a bowl of cold water for 20 minutes. This will allow it to unravel easily.

Peel the shrimp and discard the shells. Using a small, sharp knife, remove the fine digestive cords. Wash the shrimp in cold water with a tablespoon of salt. Drain and repeat. Rinse well and pat dry with paper towels. Coarsely chop the shrimp.

In a medium-sized bowl, mix the shrimp, fish, and all the other ingredients. Mix well.

Remove the caul fat from the water and pat dry with a dish towel. Cut the caul fat into twenty 5 in (13 cm) squares. Lay out a square of caul fat and place 3 tablespoons of shrimp–fish mixture in the middle. Fold in each side in turn to make a package. Repeat with the other squares until you have used up the entire mixture. Up to this point, the crépinettes can be made at least 3 hours ahead of time, refrigerated and wrapped with plastic wrap until you are ready to cook them.

Pre-heat the oven broiler to high or make a charcoal fire in the barbecue. When the broiler is very hot or the charcoal is ash-white, broil the crépinettes on each side for 3 minutes, until golden brown and crisp. Serve immediately.

Simple Broiled Fusion Fish ≈

Serves 4

4 x 5 oz (150 g) boneless, skinless halibut or sea bass fillets, or 1 whole fish, weighing 2¼ lb (1 kg)

For the Marinade:

6 tablespoons lime juice
3 tablespoons finely chopped fresh ginger (page 17)
6 tablespoons finely chopped scallions
2 tablespoons fish sauce (page 23) or light soy sauce (page 23)
2 tablespoon mirin (Japanese sweet rice wine) (page 18)
1 tablespoon sesame oil
1 teaspoon salt
½ teaspoon freshly ground five-pepper mixture (page 21) or black pepper

To Garnish:

1½ tablespoons finely chopped cilantro
Orange-flavored Oil (page 38), to serve
Lemon-flavored Oil (page 38), to serve

GRILLING ON A BARBECUE IS A FAVORITE TECHNIQUE OF MANY FUSION CHEFS AS WELL AS BEING QUICK AND EASY, IT IS A WAY OF ADDING NEW TEXTURES AND FLAVORS TO FOODS, ESPECIALLY MEATS AND SEAFOOD. THE INTENSE HEAT FROM THE HOT COALS GIVES A NICELY SEASONED CRUST WHILE IMPARTING A LOVELY, SMOKY FLAVOR. AT THE SAME TIME, THE FLESH BELOW THE CRUST REMAINS MOIST. THIS STYLE OF COOKING WORKS ESPECIALLY WELL WITH FRESH, FIRM WHITE FISH. MARINATING IT BEFORE GRILLING INTRODUCES EVEN MORE SUBTLE BLENDS OF FLAVOR. THIS RECIPE IS PERFECT FOR WARM-WEATHER AL FRESCO DINING, BUT THE FISH CAN ALSO BE COOKED UNDER THE BROILER. SERVE WITH VEGETABLES TO MAKE A COMPLETE, SATISFYING MEAL.

Blot the fish dry with paper towels. If you are using whole fish, make three slashes on each side of the fish.

Combine the marinade ingredients in a bowl. Add the fish and mix thoroughly. Marinate for 1 hour at room temperature, turning the fish from time to time.

Pre-heat the oven broiler to high or make a charcoal fire in the barbecue. When the broiler is very hot or the charcoal is ash-white, broil the fish fillets for 5–8 minutes (depending on their thickness) on each side, or the whole fish for 10–12 minutes on each side.

Garnish with chopped cilantro and serve immediately, drizzled with either or both orange- and lemon-flavored oils.

STEAMED FISH IN HERB BUTTER SAUCE ≈

FUSION COOKING ENTAILS THE ADOPTION OF NEW TECHNIQUES AS WELL AS THE ACCEPTANCE OF NEW INGREDIENTS AND FOOD COMBINATIONS. I AM VERY HAPPY TO SEE THAT EUROPEAN CHEFS ARE DISCOVERING THE ADVANTAGES OF THE STEAMING TECHNIQUE, ESPECIALLY WHEN APPLIED TO FISH. MY SOUTHERN-CHINESE COOKING HERITAGE PRESCRIBES THIS METHOD AS THE BEST WAY TO PREPARE FRESH FISH. COOKED SO GENTLY, THE FISH RETAINS ITS SUCCULENCE, TENDERNESS, AND FRESH TASTE.

HERE, I COMBINE FRESH FISH WITH DELICATE EUROPEAN AND ASIAN HERBS IN A LIGHT BUTTER SAUCE; TOGETHER, THEY HIGHLIGHT THE SUBTLE FLAVOR OF THE FISH. STEAMED RICE (PAGE 35) COMPLEMENTS THE DISH PERFECTLY.

ALWAYS ASK AT YOUR FISH MARKET FOR THE FRESHEST FISH POSSIBLE.

Pat the fish fillets dry with paper towels. Rub with the salt and pepper on both sides and set aside for 30 minutes at room temperature.

Next, set up a steamer or put a rack into a wok or deep pan and pour in 2 in (5 cm) of water. Bring the water to a boil over a high heat. Put the fish on a heatproof plate. Put the plate of fish into the steamer or onto the rack. Cover the pan tightly and gently steam the fish until it is just cooked. Flat fish such as sole or turbot will take about 5 minutes to cook. Thicker fish, such as sea bass and cod, will take 12–14 minutes.

While the fish is steaming, heat a small pan and add the shallots. Cook in the dry pan for 2 minutes, until fairly dried but not browned. Add the rice wine or sherry and cook until all the liquid has evaporated; then add the stock and cook over a high heat until it has been reduced by half. Slowly whisk in the butter, a piece at a time.

Remove the plate of cooked fish and arrange on a warm platter. Add the fresh herbs to the sauce, pour this over the fish, and serve immediately.

SERVES 4

1 lb (450 g) firm white fish fillets, such as cod, sole or turbot
1 teaspoon salt
½ teaspoon freshly ground five-pepper mixture (page 21) or black pepper

For the Herb Butter Sauce:

3 tablespoons finely chopped shallots
3 tablespoons Shaoxing rice wine (page 22) or dry sherry
2/3 cup (150 ml) homemade Fish (page 34) or Chicken (page 32) Stock
5 tablespoons (65 g) cold unsalted butter, cut in small pieces
1½ tablespoons finely chopped fresh chives
1 tablespoon finely chopped cilantro
1 tablespoon finely chopped fresh parsley
2 teaspoons finely chopped fresh chervil

WOK-ROASTED TUNA WITH SPICES ≈

SERVES 4

4 x 4 oz (100 g) thickly cut
tuna fillets
3 tablespoons olive oil

For the Marinade:

2 tablespoons light soy
sauce (page 23)
2 tablespoons mirin
(Japanese sweet rice wine)
(page 18) or dry sherry
1 tablespoon sesame oil
½ teaspoon salt
¼ teaspoon freshly ground
five-pepper mixture
(page 21) or black pepper

For the Spice Mixture:

1 teaspoon roasted, ground
Sichuan peppercorns
(page 21)
1 teaspoon ground cumin
1 teaspoon freshly ground
five-pepper mixture
(page 21) or black pepper
1 teaspoon salt
½ teaspoon five-spice
powder (page 17)
1 teaspoon sugar

To Garnish:

1 tablespoon finely chopped
cilantro
2 tablespoons finely
chopped scallions

JAPANESE FOOD, ESPECIALLY *SUSHI* AND *SASHIMI MADE WITH* FRESH AND HIGH-QUALITY TUNA, HAS BECOME EXTREMELY POPULAR. FUSION COOKS HAVE USED THE IDEA OF RAW TUNA BUT WITH A VARIATION: TUNA IS SEARED QUICKLY ON THE OUTSIDE, WITH THE INTERIOR REMAINING RARE. IT MAKES SENSE BECAUSE TUNA CAN OVERCOOK QUICKLY AND DRY OUT. HOWEVER, THE TUNA NEEDS A MARINADE AND SPICES TO COMPENSATE FOR THE SHORT COOKING TIME. ASIAN SPICES ARE IDEAL FOR ADDING ZEST TO AN OTHERWISE BLAND DISH. AGAIN, IT IS IMPORTANT TO GET THE BEST QUALITY TUNA YOU CAN AFFORD. STEAMED RICE (PAGE 35) GOES WELL WITH THIS DISH.

Lay the tuna fillets on a platter. In a small bowl, combine the marinade ingredients and drizzle the mixture evenly over the tuna. Allow to sit for 1 hour at room temperature.

In a bowl, combine the Sichuan peppercorns, cumin, pepper, salt, five-spice powder, and sugar and mix well.

Remove the tuna from the marinade with a slotted spoon and dry with paper towels. Set the marinade aside; it will be used later. Sprinkle the spice mixture evenly on both sides of the tuna fillets.

Heat a frying-pan over a high heat and when it is hot, add the oil. When the oil is slightly smoking, add the tuna fillets and sear them on one side for 2 minutes; turn over and sear the other side for another 2 minutes. Remove them to a warm platter. The tuna should remain rare. Quickly pour off the excess oil, pour in the reserved marinade, and deglaze the pan for 30 seconds. Pour this liquid over the tuna, garnish with cilantro and scallions, and serve immediately.

WOK-SMOKED FISH ≈

SERVES 4

2 teaspoons sugar

1 teaspoon plus ½ teaspoon salt

1 cup (250 ml) water

1 lb (450 g) fresh firm white fish fillets, such as sea bass or cod

1 teaspoon five-spice powder (page 17)

1 teaspoon dried thyme

¼ teaspoon ground five-pepper mixture (page 21) or black pepper

Vegetable oil, for greasing

For the Smoking Mixture:

½ cup (50 g) long-grain white rice

3 tablespoons brown sugar

1 oz (25 g) black tea leaves (page 24)

SMOKED FOODS HAVE A SUBTLE, HAUNTING AROMA AND TASTE. SMOKING IS A POPULAR TECHNIQUE USED BY FUSION COOKS BECAUSE IT IS EASY TO COMBINE ANY INGREDIENT AND TASTE.

MOST RESTAURANTS HAVE LARGE SMOKING OVENS; THE HOME COOK, HOWEVER, CAN EASILY REPLICATE THE METHOD BY USING A WOK OR A LARGE CASSEROLE. THE FISH IS BRIEFLY SOAKED AND THEN RUBBED WITH A COMBINATION OF EASTERN AND WESTERN SPICES AND SMOKED. SIMPLE AND QUICK, SMOKED FISH CAN BE MADE IN ADVANCE FOR CONVENIENCE. SERVE IT WITH VEGETABLES AS A MAIN COURSE OR WITH A SALAD AS A APPETIZER.

Mix the sugar, 1 teaspoon of salt, and the water together and pour into a deep dish. Then add the fish, cover, and put in the refrigerator for 30 minutes.

Combine the five-spice powder, thyme, the rest of the salt, and the pepper in a small bowl. Remove the fish and blot dry with paper towels. Sprinkle the spice mixture evenly on both sides of the fish.

Line the inside of a wok with foil. Add the rice, sugar, and tea leaves. Rub a rack with vegetable oil and place it over the smoking ingredients. Slowly heat the wok, and when the smoking mixture begins to smoke, put the fish on the rack and cover the wok tightly with foil. Turn the heat to moderate and smoke for 8–10 minutes, depending on the thickness of the fish. Remove from the heat and allow the fish to cool, covered, for another 2 minutes. When the fish is cool enough to handle, cut it into slices. Discard the smoking mixture and the foil, and serve the fish.

STEAMED FISH WITH LETTUCE AND CHILIES ≈

STEAMING IS A HEALTHY AND EASY TECHNIQUE FOR COOKING PERFECT FISH. THE HOT STEAM KEEPS THE FISH MOIST AND ALL THE NATURAL FLAVORS ARE PRESERVED. IT IS A COMMON AND POPULAR METHOD, WIDELY USED IN ASIA AND NOW IN EUROPE TOO. IN THIS RECIPE, THE FISH IS STEAMED AND SERVED WITH BRAISED LETTUCE AND CHILIES – AN UNUSUAL AND DELICIOUS ACCOMPANIMENT. DRIZZLE WITH ORANGE-FLAVORED OIL.

Sprinkle the fish fillets evenly with salt, pepper, and paprika. Put the fillets on a deep, heatproof plate and evenly scatter with the garlic and ginger.

Next, set up a steamer or put a rack into a wok or deep pan and pour in 2 in (5 cm) of water. Bring the water to a boil over a high heat. Carefully lower the fish and plate into the steamer or onto the rack. Turn the heat to low and cover the wok or pan tightly. Steam gently for 8–10 minutes, depending on the thickness of the fillets. Top up with boiling water from time to time.

While the fish is steaming, separate the lettuce leaves, trimming the tops. Then melt the butter in a large pan, add the chilies, water, salt, pepper, sugar, and lettuce. Bring to a simmer, cover, and simmer for 15 minutes.

When the fish is cooked, remove the plate from the steamer or wok. Drain the lettuce, reserving the liquid. Place the lettuce on a warm platter, arranging the fish on top. Reduce the liquid by half, stir in the crème fraîche, then pour this over the fish. Drizzle with the orange-flavored oil and serve immediately.

SERVES 4

1 lb (450 g) fish fillets, such as cod or sea bass, divided into 4 equal parts
1 teaspoon salt
½ teaspoon freshly ground five-pepper mixture (page 21) or white pepper
1 teaspoon paprika
1 tablespoon coarsely chopped garlic
2 teaspoons finely chopped fresh ginger (page 17)
2 tablespoons crème fraîche
Orange-flavored Oil (page 38), to serve

For the Lettuce:

1 lb (450 g) cos lettuce
2 tablespoons (25 g) unsalted butter
2 fresh red or green chilies (page 16), seeded and finely shredded
4 tablespoons water
1 teaspoon salt
½ teaspoon freshly ground five-pepper mixture (page 21) or black pepper
1 teaspoon sugar

Steamed Fish in Chinese Leaves ≈

Serves 4

1 lb (450 g) fresh, firm white
fish fillets, such as cod or
sea bass
1 head of Chinese leaves
(page 14)
1 teaspoon sea salt
1 teaspoon roasted and
ground Sichuan peppercorns
(page 21)

For the Sauce:
3 tablespoons chopped shallots
1 tablespoon finely chopped
fresh ginger (page 17)
3 tablespoons Shaoxing rice
wine (page 22) or dry sherry
6 tablespoons homemade Fish
(page 34) or Chicken
(page 32) Stock
2 teaspoons fine lemon zest
1 teaspoon fine orange zest
2 tablespoons (25 g) cold
unsalted butter, cut in small
pieces
Salt and freshly ground white
pepper
2 teaspoons finely chopped
cilantro
2 teaspoons finely chopped
fresh chives
1 teaspoon finely chopped
scallion
1 tablespoon finely chopped
red pepper
Basil-flavored (page 36) and
Tomato-flavored (page 40)
Olive Oil, to serve (optional)

Having grown up in a Chinese household, I always knew that steaming is the best way to cook the freshest fish. Delicate, hot vapors keep the fish moist and succulent, without compromising its briny flavor. Here, I have wrapped the fish in Chinese leaves (also known as Chinese cabbage) for a spectacular presentation which also keeps the fish even moister. Then I serve it with a fusion sauce, which makes the best of East and West. This is a perfect dish for a special dinner party, especially when drizzled with flavored olive oils. Serve it with vegetables or rice.

Divide the fillets into four equal portions. Remove four of the largest leaves from the Chinese leaves and blanch them in boiling water for 1 minute. Drain and allow to cool. Place each fillet on one end of a leaf. Sprinkle with sea salt and Sichuan peppercorns. Roll up each leaf, folding in the sides as you go.

Next, set up a steamer or put a rack into a wok or deep pan and pour in 2 in (5 cm) of water. Bring the water to the boil over a high heat. Put the wrapped fish onto a heatproof plate and then carefully lower it into the steamer or onto the rack. Turn the heat to low and cover the wok or pan tightly. Steam gently for 8 minutes, or until the fish is cooked. Remove the fish from the steamer, pour off any liquid on the plate into a small bowl, and reserve.

While the fish is steaming, combine the shallots and ginger in a pan and cook for 1 minute until dry; then add the rice wine or sherry and cook over a high heat until all the wine has evaporated. Now add the stock and any reserved steaming liquid and reduce by half. Add the lemon and orange zest. Then slowly whisk in the butter and salt and pepper to taste. Toss in the cilantro, chives, scallion, and pepper. Cook for 30 seconds. Pour the sauces over each leaf-wrapped fish. Drizzle with basil-flavored and tomato-flavored olive oils, if using, and serve.

MEAT

肉

Fast-broiled Steak with Five Spices ≈

SERVES 4

4 (sirloin) or rump steaks,
  weighing about 6–1/2 lb
  (175–225 g) each
1 tablespoon olive oil

For the Spice Mixture:

2 teaspoons salt
½ teaspoon freshly ground
  five-pepper mixture
  (page 21) or black pepper
1 teaspoon five-spice
  powder (page 17)
½ teaspoon roasted and
  ground Sichuan
  peppercorns (page 21)
2 teaspoons paprika
1 teaspoon Madras curry
  powder (page 17)

SPICES FROM ASIAN CUISINES ARE FREQUENTLY USED TO INCORPORATE EXOTIC TASTES AND FLAVORS INTO FOOD. THEY ARE ABSORBED QUICKLY, MAKING THEM IDEAL FOR BROILED FOODS. IN THIS RECIPE, I HAVE RELIED ON TRADITIONAL CHINESE FIVE-SPICE POWDER, COMBINED WITH OTHER SPICES TO INFUSE AN ORDINARY STEAK WITH SPECIAL AROMAS. SERVE THIS WITH SIMPLE BOILED OR SAUTÉD POTATOES.

Lay the steaks on a broiler pan and rub with the olive oil.

In a small bowl, combine the spice mixture ingredients and mix well. Sprinkle the mixture evenly over the steaks on both sides and leave in a cool place for 1 hour.

Pre-heat the oven broiler to high or make a charcoal fire in the barbecue. When the oven broiler is very hot or the charcoal is ash-white, broil the steaks on each side for about 5–6 minutes (if you like them rare) or longer if you want them well done.

Transfer to a warm platter and allow to rest for 10 minutes before serving.

Barbecued East–West Pork Satay ≈

A truly East-meets-West city is Singapore, where several different cultures merge harmoniously in a thriving, modern metropolis. I love eating in Singapore and always make a point of visiting the street food stalls that sell so many different styles of cooking, from Chinese regional cuisine and indigenous Malay foods to authentic Indian treats. The best of western food is offered, as well, in restaurants and hotels. A personal favorite is satay: marinated meats, skewered, and simply broiled. Here, I offer a version that combines the spices of two worlds. You can easily double the recipe for a larger crowd.

Cut the pork into 1 in (2.5 cm) cubes, trimming off any excess fat.

In a large bowl, combine the pork cubes with the marinade ingredients, mix well, and marinate the meat for 2 hours in a cool place, turning it from time to time.

Meanwhile, soak bamboo skewers in water for 30 minutes or so. Skewer the pork and set aside.

Pre-heat the oven broiler to high or make a charcoal fire in the barbecue. When the broiler is very hot or the charcoal is ash-white, cook the satay for 2 minutes on each side, until golden brown. Serve immediately, drizzled with sesame and chili oil, if you wish.

Serves 4

1 lb (450 g) tender, thick, boneless pork chops

For the Marinade:
1 tablespoon light soy sauce (page 23)
1 tablespoon pineapple juice
½ teaspoon salt
¼ teaspoon freshly ground five-pepper mixture (page 21) or black pepper
1 tablespoon mirin (Japanese sweet rice wine) (page 18) or dry sherry
½ teaspoon dried thyme
¼ teaspoon ground coriander
1 teaspoon sugar
1 tablespoon olive oil
2 teaspoons finely chopped lemon zest
Sesame and Chili Oil (page 39), to serve (optional)

BROILED PORK CHOPS WITH CHINESE SPICES ≈

Serves 4

4 x 4 oz (100 g) boneless
  pork chops

For the Seasoning Mixture:

1 teaspoon five-spice
  powder (page 17)
1½ teaspoons salt
½ teaspoon freshly ground
  five-pepper mixture
  (page 21) or black pepper
½ teaspoon roasted and
  ground Sichuan
  peppercorns (page 21)
½ teaspoon Madras curry
  powder (page 17)
1 teaspoon dried thyme
½ teaspoon cumin powder
Orange-flavored Oil
  (page 38), to serve

BROILING PORK CHOPS IS AN EASY METHOD FOR PUTTING TOGETHER AN APPETIZING MEAL WITH LITTLE EFFORT. THE SMOKE FROM THE BROILER CONTRIBUTES RICH FLAVORS OF ITS OWN. THIS RECIPE IS ESPECIALLY EASY, USING CHINESE SEASONING COMBINED WITH A WESTERN TOUCH. SERVE THE CHOPS WITH VEGETABLES OR WITH CORN CRÊPES (PAGE 194) AND A SALAD.

Place the pork chops on a large platter or tray. Combine the seasoning mixture in a small bowl, mixing well. Sprinkle half the seasoning mixture evenly over the pork chops, turn them over and sprinkle the remaining seasoning on the other side. Leave the chops in a cool place for an hour.

Pre-heat the oven broiler to high or make a charcoal fire in the barbecue. When the broiler is very hot or the charcoal is ash-white, broil the pork chops on each side for about 8 minutes. Remove to a platter and leave for another 8 minutes before serving.

Serve with orange-flavored oil drizzled on the side.

BROILED PORK CRÉPINETTES ≈

SERVES 4
(MAKES 14–15
CRÉPINETTES)

½ lb (225 g) caul fat
(crépine) (page 25)
1 lb (450 g) ground fatty
pork
2 egg whites
1 teaspoon salt
½ teaspoon freshly ground
five-pepper mixture
(page 21) or black pepper
½ teaspoon roasted and
ground Sichuan
peppercorns (page 21)
2 teaspoons paprika
2 teaspoons cognac
3 tablespoons finely
chopped scallions
2 tablespoons finely
chopped fresh chives
2 tablespoons finely
chopped cilantro
2 tablespoons finely
chopped fresh parsley
3 tablespoons finely
chopped fresh basil
2 tablespoons finely
chopped garlic
2 teaspoons finely chopped
fresh ginger (page 17)
All-purpose flour, for dredging
2 eggs, beaten
½ cup (25 g) dried
breadcrumbs

CRÉPINETTE IS THE FRENCH TERM FOR A SMALL, FLAT SAUSAGE, GENERALLY MADE OF GROUND MEAT WITH CHOPPED PARSLEY AND WRAPPED IN LACY CAUL FAT (CRÉPINE). CAUL CAN BE OBTAINED FROM SPECIALTY MEAT MARKETS. THE LACY WRAPPING KEEPS THE MEAT MOIST AND JUICY. YOU CAN MAKE LITERALLY ANY MEAT AND SEASONING COMBINATION – AN IDEAL VEHICLE FOR FUSION CHEFS. IN THIS RECIPE, I HAVE CREATED A MARRIAGE OF EASTERN AND WESTERN SPICES AND HERBS FOR AN EASY AND SUCCULENT DISH. IT GOES ESPECIALLY WELL WITH MASHED POTATO AND CUCUMBER (PAGE 186).

Soak the caul fat in a bowl of cold water for 20 minutes. This will allow it to unravel easily.

In a large bowl, combine the pork with the egg whites, salt, pepper, Sichuan pepper, paprika, cognac, scallions, all the herbs, the garlic, and ginger and mix well.

Remove the caul fat from the water and pat dry with a dish towel. Cut the caul fat into twenty 5 in (13 cm) squares. Lay out a square of caul fat and place 3 tablespoons of pork mixture. Fold in each side in turn to make a package. Repeat until you have used up the entire mixture. Up to this point, the crépinettes can be made at least 3 hours ahead of time, wrapped with plastic wrap, and refrigerated until ready to cook.

When you are ready to cook the crépinettes, dust them with flour, shaking off any excess, dip them in the beaten egg, and, finally, roll them in the breadcrumbs.

Pre-heat the oven broiler to high or make a charcoal fire in the barbecue. When the oven broiler is very hot or the charcoal is ash-white, broil the crépinettes on each side for 3 minutes, until golden brown and crisp. Serve immediately.

Braised East–West Oxtail Stew ≈

Here we have a delectable fusion of East and West flavors – soy sauce and rice wine from the East and tomatoes and orange zest from the West. Such flavors are assertive enough to stand up against the robust deliciousness of the oxtail. This is a hearty and satisfying autumn or winter dish that can easily be reheated. In fact, I think it tastes even better the next day. Serve with Steamed Rice (page 35) or pasta.

In a large pan, cook the oxtail pieces in boiling water for 20 minutes. Remove and drain well.

Heat a wok or large frying-pan until it is hot. Add the peanut oil and slowly brown the oxtail on all sides. Remove the oxtail with a slotted spoon and pour off and discard the excess fat. Now add the olive oil, onions, shallots and garlic and stir-fry the mixture for about 3 minutes. Then add the tomatoes, stock, the two rice wines or sherry, orange zest, hoisin sauce, soy sauce, salt, and pepper. Bring the mixture to a boil, reduce the heat to a simmer, cover tightly and cook for 3 hours, or until the oxtail pieces are tender.

Skim off any surface fat, garnish with cilantro sprigs, and serve immediately.

Serves 4–6

- 3 lb (1.5 kg) oxtail, jointed
- 2 tablespoons peanut oil
- 2 tablespoons extra virgin olive oil
- 2 small onions, coarsely chopped
- 3 tablespoons finely sliced shallots
- 3 tablespoons coarsely chopped garlic
- 1½ lb (750 g) tinned tomatoes
- 1 cup (250 ml) Homemade Chicken Stock (page 32)
- 3 tablespoons Shaoxing rice wine (page 22) or dry sherry
- 2 tablespoons mirin (Japanese sweet rice wine) (page 18) or dry sherry
- 2 tablespoons finely chopped orange zest
- 3 tablespoons hoisin sauce (page 22)
- 2 tablespoons light soy sauce (page 23)
- 2 teaspoons salt
- 1 teaspoon freshly ground five-pepper mixture (page 21) or black pepper
- Sprigs of cilantro, to garnish

KOREAN-STYLE BROILED BEEF ≈

SERVES 4

1 lb (450 g) chuck steak,
preferably on the fatty side

2 tablespoons light or
Japanese soy sauce
(page 23)

3 tablespoons pineapple juice

2 tablespoons mirin (Japanese
sweet rice wine) (page 18)
or dry sherry

1 tablespoon Shaoxing rice
wine (page 22) or dry sherry

2 tablespoons finely chopped
garlic

3 tablespoons finely chopped
scallions

1 tablespoon sesame oil

1 tablespoon sesame seeds,
toasted (page 23)

1 teaspoon salt

1 teaspoon freshly ground five-
pepper mixture (page 21)
or black pepper

Gordon's Cranberry-ginger
Relish (page 199), to serve

ONE OF THE TASTIEST BEEF DISHES I HAVE EVER EATEN WAS THIS DELECTABLE ONE FROM KOREA, POPULARLY KNOWN AS *KALBY*. IT RELIES ON A SIMPLE MARINADE AND QUICK BROILING, WHICH GIVES THE BEEF A SMOKY FRAGRANCE. AND THERE'S A BONUS: YOU DON'T NEED AN EXPENSIVE CUT; ON THE CONTRARY, THE FAT FROM A CHEAPER CUT CONTRIBUTES ADDITIONAL FLAVOR. THE PINEAPPLE JUICE IN THE RECIPE BREAKS DOWN THE FIBERS OF THE BEEF AND MAKES IT QUITE TENDER. RICE OR POTATOES GO WELL WITH THIS DISH.

Cut the chuck steak into 4 x ¼ in (10 cm x 5 mm) pieces. Combine the soy sauce, pineapple juice, mirin, and rice wine or sherry, garlic, scallions, sesame oil, sesame seeds, and salt and pepper. Let the beef marinate for 1 hour at room temperature.

Pre-heat the oven broiler to high or make a charcoal fire in the barbecue.

Meanwhile, soak long bamboo skewers in cold water. Remove from the water after 30 minutes.

Skewer the beef on the bamboo sticks and set aside. When the broiler is very hot or the charcoal is ash-white, broil the beef for a few minutes on each side. Serve immediately with Gordon's cranberry-ginger relish.

Fast-barbecued Ribs ≈

Serves 4–6

3½ lb (1.5 kg) pork
   spare ribs
2 teaspoons salt
1 teaspoon freshly ground
   five-pepper mixture
   (page 21) or black pepper

For the Sauce:
5 tablespoons hoisin sauce
   (page 22)
3 tablespoons sesame oil
2 tablespoons light soy
   sauce (page 23)
2 tablespoons dark soy
   sauce (page 23)
2 tablespoons mirin
   (Japanese sweet rice wine)
   (page 18) or Shaoxing
   rice wine (page 22) or dry
   sherry
3 tablespoons coarsely
   chopped garlic
2 teaspoons finely chopped
   fresh ginger (page 17)
2 tablespoons chili-bean
   sauce (page 22)
2 teaspoons sugar
3 tablespoons dried thyme
1 tablespoon Dijon mustard

THERE ARE VERY FEW FOODS WHICH ARE AS MUCH FUN TO EAT AS PORK SPARE RIBS. JUICY AND BURSTING WITH FLAVORS – THEY ARE FAIRLY EASY TO PREPARE IF YOU TRY MY METHOD. I COOK THE SPARE RIBS FIRST IN A LOW OVEN FOR 1 HOUR TO RENDER SOME OF THE FAT AND TO TENDERIZE THEM AT THE SAME TIME. THIS CAN BE DONE HOURS IN ADVANCE. THEN I MAKE A SIMPLE SAUCE USING CHINESE AND EUROPEAN INGREDIENTS. SINCE THE SPARE RIBS ARE ALREADY COOKED, IT TAKES BUT 20 MINUTES TO FINISH THEM OFF. THIS IS A WONDERFUL SUMMERTIME TREAT WHEN COOKED ON A CHARCOAL GRILL BUT CAN BE JUST AS EASILY COOKED UNDER THE OVEN BROILER. THESE RIBS GO EXTREMELY WELL WITH COLD KOREAN-STYLE NOODLES (PAGE 216).

Pre-heat the oven to 300°F/150°C.

Put the spare ribs in a baking dish and sprinkle both sides evenly with salt and pepper. Put into the oven and cook for 1 hour. Remove from the oven. The spare ribs can be done at least four hours in advance up to this point.

Combine the sauce ingredients in a blender and mix well.

Pre-heat the oven broiler to high or make a charcoal fire in the barbecue. When the oven broiler is very hot or the charcoal is ash-white, baste the ribs on both sides with the sauce ingredients and broil for 10 minutes on each side. Serve immediately.

NEIL PERRY'S RED-COOKED PORK BELLY WITH CHINESE MUSHROOMS ≈

NEIL PERRY IS A TALENTED CHEF, WITH A PERSONAL STYLE THAT TYPIFIES FUSION COOKERY. HE USES HIS FINELY HONED SKILLS TO CREATE CONTEMPORARY AUSTRALIAN CUISINE, DRAWING FROM EUROPE AND ASIA. I ESPECIALLY LOVE THIS RECIPE FROM HIS FLAGSHIP RESTAURANT, ROCKPOOL. NEIL'S LOVE OF ASIAN FOOD WAS SUCH THAT HE LATER OPENED ANOTHER POPULAR RESTAURANT, WOKPOOL, WHICH MADE ONLY FOODS FROM ASIA. FORTUNATELY, THIS CLASSIC DISH REMAINS ON THE MENU AND IS STILL ONE OF MY FAVORITES FROM HIS REPERTOIRE. NEIL USES PORK HOCK, WHICH I HAVE CHANGED TO PORK BELLY. THE LONG BRAISING INFUSES THE PORK WITH THE TYPES OF FLAVORS WHICH FUSION CHEFS ARE USING THROUGHOUT THE WORLD. SERVE THIS WITH GREEN RICE (PAGE 203).

Cut the unpeeled ginger into six fine slices. Put the ginger with the water and rice wine or sherry into a large pan or casserole. Bring the liquid to a simmer and then add the pork belly. Simmer slowly for 45 minutes, skimming all the while.

Then add the soy sauces, sugar, star anise, cinnamon, chilies, garlic, scallions and salt. Cover the pan tightly and continue to simmer for 1½–2 hours or until the pork is very tender.

While the pork is simmering, soak the mushrooms in warm water for 20 minutes. Then drain them and squeeze out the excess liquid. Remove and discard the stems, leaving the mushrooms whole.

When the pork is cooked, add the mushrooms and simmer for an additional 15 minutes. Remove the pork from the pan and let it cool slightly. (The braising liquid can now be cooled and frozen for re-use. Remove any surface fat before transferring it to the freezer.) Slice the meat thinly and arrange on a warm platter with the mushrooms and sauce. Serve immediately.

SERVES 6–8

3 lb (1.5 kg) boneless pork belly, with rind
2 oz (50g) dried Chinese black mushrooms (page 18)

For the Braising Liquid:

1 in (2.5 cm) fresh ginger (page 17)
5 cups (1.2 liters) water
2 ½ cups (600 ml) Shaoxing rice wine (page 22) or dry sherry
⅔ cup (150 ml) light soy sauce (page 23)
2 oz (50 ml) dark soy sauce (page 23)
⅔ cup (150 g) Chinese rock sugar (page 24) or all-purpose sugar
4 star anise (page 23)
3 cinnamon sticks
3 dried red chilies (page 15)
6 garlic cloves, crushed
6 scallions, whole
2 teaspoons salt

ROAST LAMB WITH ASIAN FLAVORS ≈

SERVES 4–6

2 x 12 oz–1 lb (350–
   450 g) lamb cutlets

½ teaspoon salt

½ teaspoon freshly ground
   five-pepper mixture
   (page 21) or black pepper

1 tablespoon peanut oil

3 tablespoons finely
   chopped shallots,
   squeezed dry

2 tablespoons finely
   chopped cilantro

2 tablespoons finely chopped
   fresh flatleaf parsley

2 teaspoons finely chopped
   garlic

2 teaspoons finely chopped
   fresh ginger (page 17)

25 g (1 oz) fresh
   breadcrumbs

1 tablespoon sesame oil

3 tablespoons (35 g) melted
   butter

THERE ARE FEW DISHES AS EXQUISITE AS ROAST LAMB CUTLETS. THOUGH EXPENSIVE, THEY ARE WORTH EVERY PENNY, PARTICULARLY FOR A SPECIAL OCCASION. THE FRENCH METHOD OF ROASTING LAMB WITH A SEASONED BREADCRUMB MIXTURE IS A POPULAR AND EASY PREPARATION WHICH I LOVE. HOWEVER, I CANNOT RESIST ALTERING THE RECIPE TO ADD MY OWN FUSION TOUCHES. SERVE WITH EITHER GINGER-LEEK PURÉE (PAGE 191) OR GORDON'S CRANBERRY-GINGER RELISH (PAGE 199).

Ask your butcher to trim the silvery-blue skin off the lamb and to dress the bones by removing the meat and fat between the bones. Season the lamb all over with salt and pepper.

Pre-heat the oven to 475°F/240°C.

Heat the oil in a large frying-pan, and when it is hot and slightly smoking, brown the lamb until it is golden brown. Remove and arrange inside a roasting pan.

In a bowl, combine the shallots, cilantro, parsley, garlic, ginger, breadcrumbs, sesame oil, and butter, mixing with chopsticks. Cover the lamb on all sides with this mixture, pressing down with your hands so the mixture adheres to the meat.

Roast in the oven with the meaty side up for 15 minutes. Remove and keep warm for 15 minutes before serving. Carve and serve immediately.

Asian Roast Beef with East–West Yorkshire Pudding ≈

Serves 6–8

6 lb (2.75 kg) prime-cut beef
with the bone

For the Seasoning:

1 teaspoon salt

1 teaspoon five-spice
powder (page 17)

2 teaspoons freshly ground
five-pepper mixture (page
21) or black pepper

1 teaspoon ground cumin

2 teaspoons roasted and
ground Sichuan
peppercorns (page 21)

2 tablespoons dried thyme

1 tablespoon dried oregano

2 teaspoons paprika

1 teaspoon chili powder

For the East–West
Yorkshire Pudding:

5 eggs, beaten

1 ¼ cups (150 g) all-purpose
flour

2 cups (475 ml) milk

1½ teaspoons salt

½ teaspoon freshly ground
five-pepper mixture
(page 21) or black pepper

3 tablespoons finely
chopped scallions

2 tablespoons finely
chopped fresh chives

2 teaspoons finely chopped
fresh ginger (page 17)

1 tablespoon finely chopped
cilantro

⅔ cup (150 ml) reserved fat
from the roasting pan

Although I rarely eat beef, when I do I always try to get the best that I can afford. I look for organic beef, where possible, with fat marbled throughout; the fat melts during cooking and gives the meat an intense flavor. Here, I have taken the English traditional roast beef and added a dash of Asian-inspired spices together with dried European herbs. I wholeheartedly agree with Delia Smith's advice to buy a cut *with the bone*. A good bit of advice is to have your butcher remove the beef from the bone and then retie it along with the bone. The bone acts as a good conductor of heat and helps the beef to cook evenly and to retain its juiciness.

I like my roast beef rare throughout, and the secret is to let the beef rest for an hour in a turned-off oven. It will continue to cook slowly, with all the juices intact. Of course, if you prefer beef well done, simply increase the cooking time by 15–30 minutes. Serve with your favorite vegetables.

Pre-heat the oven to 425°F/220°C.

Combine all the ingredients for the seasoning in a small bowl. Rub this mixture all over the top and sides of the meat. Place it, bone-down, in a large roasting pan.

Put the the roast in the oven for 25 minutes. Then reduce the heat to 375°F/190°C and cook for 1 hour.

Now, turn off the heat and let the beef rest in the oven for 1 hour.

Remove the beef and pour off the fat, which can be saved for your favorite Yorkshire pudding recipe (see the East–West recipe below); the juices can also be saved and served with the carved beef. Let the roast rest at room temperature for 20 minutes before carving.

Turn the oven back up to 425°F/220°C to cook the pudding. Combine the eggs and flour in a large bowl or food processor and beat until smooth. Then add the milk, salt, pepper, and the herbs.

Put the reserved fat in a large roasting pan and place on the burner. Heat until the fat is very hot and sizzling. Pour the batter mixture into the roasting pan and put it immediately in the oven. Cook for 30 minutes or until the pudding is golden and crisp. Serve immediately, with the roast.

ROAST MUSTARD-SOY SAUCE LEG OF LAMB ≈

ROAST LEG OF LAMB IS A DISCOVERY I MADE WHILE LIVING IN FRANCE DURING MY UNIVERSITY DAYS IN PROVENCE. MY ADOPTIVE FRENCH MOTHER WOULD ROAST LAMB, USING SIMPLY GARLIC AND FRESH ROSEMARY. I COULD NOT RESIST ADDING MY ASIAN CULINARY HERITAGE TO THIS CLASSIC RECIPE – SOY SAUCE. I OBSERVED THAT IT WORKED WONDERS ON LAMB. THIS EAST–WEST ADAPTATION ADDS A SAVORY TWIST TO THIS DELICIOUS DISH. IT GOES ESPECIALLY WELL WITH GORDON'S CRANBERRY-GINGER RELISH (PAGE 199); SERVE WITH POTATOES AND OTHER VEGETABLES.

Pre-heat the oven to 180°C/350°F.

Slice the garlic into small slivers. With a small, sharp knife, make small slits throughout the leg of lamb and insert the slivers of garlic.

Mix the mustard, soy sauces, salt, pepper, sesame oil, rosemary, and ginger in a blender. Rub this mixture all over the lamb.

Place the lamb in a roasting pan and cook for 1½ hours. If you like it well done, give it another 30 minutes. Remove the meat to a warm serving dish in a warm place and let it rest for at least 30 minutes before you begin to carve. Serve immediately.

SERVES 4–6

5 garlic cloves
1 leg of lamb,
   about 4 lb (1.75 kg)
5 tablespoons Dijon mustard
3 tablespoons dark soy
   sauce (page 23)
2 tablespoons light soy
   sauce (page 23)
2 teaspoons salt
1 teaspoon freshly ground
   five-pepper mixture
   (page 21) or black pepper
2 tablespoons sesame oil
3 tablespoons crushed fresh
   rosemary leaves
2 teaspoons finely chopped
   fresh ginger (page 17)

Broiled Lamb with Sesame Sauce ≈

Serves 4

4 x 6 oz (175 g) lean
    lamb chops

For the Marinade:

1½ tablespoons sesame oil
2 teaspoons light soy sauce
    (page 23)
1 teaspoon salt
1 teaspoon roasted and
    ground Sichuan
    peppercorns (page 21)
½ teaspoon freshly ground
    five-pepper mixture
    (page 21) or black pepper
1 tablespoon dried thyme
2 teaspoons whole dried
    rosemary leaves

For the Sesame Sauce:

3 tablespoons highest quality
    Japanese sesame paste
    (page 23) or creamy
    peanut butter
2 tablespoons mirin
    (Japanese sweet rice wine)
    (page 18) or dry sherry
1 tablespoon Japanese white
    rice vinegar (page 24)
1 teaspoon salt
½ teaspoon freshly ground
    black pepper
6 tablespoons homemade
    Chicken Stock (page 32)
2 tablespoons finely
    chopped scallions

Lamb was not a meat I had known in my Chinese childhood. The first time I had lamb was in France; I was surprised by its assertive, but delectable, flavor. I quickly learned that lamb marries well with Asian spices. In this recipe, I serve the lamb with a Japanese-inspired sauce. Use the most expensive Japanese sesame paste you can afford; the higher the price, the better the quality. Serve this delicious lamb with potatoes.

Mix the marinade ingredients together in a small bowl. Rub the lamb chops evenly with this mixture. Allow the meat to marinate for 1 hour at room temperature.

Pre-heat the oven broiler to high or make a charcoal fire in the barbecue. When the broiler is very hot or the charcoal is ash-white, broil the lamb chops for about 8 minutes on each side, until medium rare. Remove from the broiler, reserving any cooking juices, and let the chops sit on a warm platter for at least 20 minutes.

In a pan, combine the sesame paste, mirin or sherry, vinegar, salt, pepper, and stock. Mix vigorously. Bring to a boil and reduce slightly. Meanwhile, pour the reserved lamb juices and any that may have accumulated on the platter, into the sauce with the scallions. Pour the sauce over the lamb chops and serve immediately.

BRAISED SHOULDER OF LAMB WITH CHINESE FLAVORS ≈

SERVES 4–6

3½–4 lb (1.5 kg–1.75 kg)
shoulder of lamb

2 teaspoons salt

1 teaspoon freshly ground
five-pepper mixture
(page 21) or black pepper

3 tablespoons peanut oil

20 garlic cloves, unpeeled

1 tablespoon finely chopped
fresh ginger (page 17)

3 tablespoons finely sliced
shallots

3 tablespoons Shaoxing
rice wine (page 22)
or dry sherry

2 tablespoons light soy
sauce (page 23)

1 tablespoon chili-bean
sauce (page 22)

2 cups (475 ml) homemade
Chicken Stock
(page 32)

4 small fresh sprigs of
rosemary

3 fresh sprigs of thyme

2 tablespoons finely
chopped cilantro

2 tablespoons finely
chopped fresh chives

SHOULDER OF LAMB IS NOT ONLY ECONOMICAL BUT DELICIOUSLY SWEET, ESPECIALLY WHEN ROLLED AND BRAISED. ALTHOUGH IT IS NOT A FOOD THAT I GREW UP WITH, I LEARNED TO APPRECIATE IT WHILE LIVING IN FRANCE. I THINK IT GOES ESPECIALLY WELL WITH A HINT OF CHINESE SEASONING COMBINED WITH A TOUCH OF EUROPEAN. YOU WILL ALSO FIND THIS AN EXCELLENT DINNER-PARTY DISH, ESPECIALLY WHEN SERVED WITH FRAGRANT FRIED GINGER AND SCALLION RICE (PAGE 202). THE BONUS IS THAT IT ALSO REHEATS WELL.

Ask your butcher to bone the shoulder of lamb. Be sure to ask for the bone.

Pre-heat the oven to 375°F/190°C.

Sprinkle the salt and pepper evenly over the lamb. Heat a wok or large frying-pan over a high heat until it is hot. Add the oil, and when it is very hot and slightly smoking, turn the heat to low. Add the lamb and slowly brown on all sides for about 15 minutes. Transfer the lamb to a large, heavy casserole.

Drain off all excess fat from the wok or frying-pan, leaving just enough for stir-frying, then add the garlic, ginger, and shallots and stir-fry for 2 minutes. Transfer this mixture to the casserole; add the rice wine or sherry, soy sauce, chili-bean sauce, and chicken stock. Bring the mixture to a simmer and add the rosemary and thyme. Cover tightly and cook in the oven for 1½ hours, or until the meat is very tender. Let the meat rest at room temperature for 20 minutes before carving.

Slice the lamb and place the slices on a warm platter; remove the garlic with a slotted spoon and arrange the cloves around the lamb. Remove all surface fat from the liquid and reduce by one-third. Pour this over the lamb, sprinkle with cilantro and chives and serve immediately.

Spicy Broiled Satay Lamb ≈

One of the joys of visiting Singapore is to roam its famous food centers where you can literally eat your way through an array of open food stalls. The variety is amazing – ranging from noodles to seafood, or my favorite - satay. Thin strips of lamb, beef, pork or chicken are broiled on skewers and served with a peanut sauce. Here, I have used that inspiration to make my version of lamb satay. The marinade is briefly simmered and makes a nice dipping sauce. Serve these lamb satays drizzled with Curry-flavored Oil (page 38) for a savory appetizer or with rice as a main course.

Soak bamboo skewers in water for 30 minutes or so, to prevent them from burning.

Cut the lamb into slices 3 in (7.5 cm) long x 1½ in (4 cm) wide x ⅛ in (3 mm) thick. Thread the slices on the bamboo skewers and place on a long platter.

Combine the marinade ingredients in a medium-sized bowl. Pour this over the lamb and marinate for 1 hour at room temperature. Turn the lamb skewers once or twice. Remove them from the marinade. Put the marinade in a pan and simmer for 3 minutes to thicken it slightly. Set aside.

Pre-heat the oven broiler to high or make a charcoal fire in the barbecue. When the broiler is very hot or the charcoal is ash-white, broil the lamb satays on each side for 1 minute. Place on a warm platter and let them rest for 5 minutes before serving with the reserved marinade.

Serves 4–6

1½ lb (750 g) loin of lamb

For the Marinade:
1 cup (250 ml) pineapple juice
2 tablespoons best quality Japanese sesame paste (page 23) or peanut butter
2 tablespoons light soy sauce (page 23)
2 teaspoons chili-bean sauce (page 22)
1 teaspoon freshly ground five-pepper mixture (page 21) or black pepper
2 tablespoons chopped scallions
1 tablespoon finely chopped garlic
2 tablespoons crushed dried sage

Stir-fried Beef with Five Peppercorns ≈

Serves 4

1 lb (450 g) lean beef steak

1 tablespoon light soy sauce (page 23)

1 tablespoon Shaoxing rice wine (page 22) or dry sherry

2 teaspoons cornstarch

2 teaspoons sesame oil

3 tablespoons oil, preferably peanut

2 tablespoons cognac

4 oz (100 g) shallots, finely chopped

2 tablespoons five-pepper mixture (page 21), crushed

½ teaspoon salt

1 cup (250 ml) homemade Chicken Stock (page 32)

2 tablespoons (25 g) butter, cut in small pieces

Steak *au poivre* is a popular French bistro dish that has fallen out of fashion; however, it is a savory dish that I have always enjoyed. In my version I like the mixture of five peppercorns, which is much more fragrant than using just one type. The Chinese often find large pieces of beef intimidating, preferring to cut meat into slices and stir-frying it quickly, as in this recipe. The result is a fast dish that combines fusion elements of East and West for a unique slant on a classic. Serve with noodles, as illustrated opposite.

Cut the beef into thick slices 2 x ¼ in (5 cm x 5 mm), cutting across the grain. Put the beef in a bowl with the soy sauce, rice wine or sherry, cornstarch, and sesame oil. Mix well and then let the mixture marinate for about 20 minutes.

Heat a wok or large frying-pan over a high heat. Add the oil, and when it is very hot and slightly smoking, remove the beef from the marinade with a slotted spoon. Add it to the pan and stir-fry it for 2 minutes, until it is barely cooked. Remove and let it drain in a colander or sieve. Pour out all the oil, reheat the wok or pan over a high heat, then add the cognac to deglaze. Quickly add the shallots, peppercorns, salt, and stock and reduce by half over a high heat. Finally, add the butter, piece by piece. Then return the beef to the wok or pan and stir-fry for 30 seconds to warm it through. Serve immediately.

Fusion Steamed Meatloaf ≈

Serves 4

½ cup (50 g) fresh
  breadcrumbs
1 lb (450 g) ground beef
½ lb (225 g) ground pork
1 small onion, finely
  chopped
1 egg, beaten
1 tablespoon finely chopped
  fresh ginger (page 17)
2 tablespoons finely
  chopped scallions
1 tablespoon finely chopped
  cilantro
2 teaspoons finely chopped
  fresh thyme or 1 teaspoon
  dried thyme
2 teaspoons finely chopped
  fresh marjoram or
  1 teaspoon dried
  marjoram
1 tablespoon finely chopped
  fresh chives
2 tablespoons light soy
  sauce (page 23)
1 teaspoon salt
½ teaspoon freshly ground
  five-pepper mixture
  (page 21) or black pepper
¾ cup (175 ml) milk

Meatloaf is a baked mixture of ground meat, usually beef, pork, lamb, or any combination thereof, with breadcrumbs, seasonings, and egg. This hearty main dish was quite popular in 1950s' America. Using breadcrumbs was an acceptable method for stretching what was then expensive meat. Meatloaf fell out of fashion in the 1970s. However, since the late 1980s, it has made a dramatic comeback in many up-scale American bistro restaurants. This humble dish can be made quite delectable by varying its usual flavorings. Here I use some traditional Chinese seasonings mixed with distinctive western herbs. Rather than baking it, I steam it – a favorite Asian method of keeping food moist and juicy. The firm texture of the filling keeps the loaf intact. Make this dish ahead of time: it reheats well and also makes lovely sandwiches. It goes extremely well with Mashed Potato with Cucumber (page 186) as illustrated opposite.

Combine all the ingredients in a large bowl and mix well.

Lightly brush a 2 ½ cup (1.2 liter) heatproof dish or non-stick loaf pan with a film of oil and spoon the mixture into it.

Next, set up a steamer or put a rack into a wok or deep pan and pour in 2 in (5 cm) of water. Bring the water to a boil over a high heat, then carefully lower the dish or pan into the steamer or onto the rack. Turn the heat to low and cover the wok or pan tightly. Steam gently for 1 hour, or until the meat is cooked. Check the water level from time to time, adding more if necessary. Pour off any fat which may have accumulated.

Invert onto a warm platter and serve immediately.

ASIAN-FLAVORED BROILED STEAK ≈

SERVES 4

4 entrecôte (sirloin) or rump
steaks, about 6–8 oz
(175–225 g) each

For the Marinade:
1 tablespoon dark soy sauce
(page 23)
3 tablespoons light soy
sauce (page 23)
2 tablespoons oyster sauce
(page 23)
1 tablespoon sugar
3 tablespoons mirin
(Japanese sweet rice wine)
(page 18)
2 tablespoons sesame oil

THIS IS ONE OF THE EASIEST AND TASTIEST METHODS OF COOKING STEAKS.
SOY SAUCE IS AN ANCIENT CHINESE SEASONING THAT WORKS
WONDERFULLY ON MEATS. THE BROILED STEAK GOES PERFECTLY WITH
POTATOES AND SALAD.

Lay the steaks on a tray.

In a medium-sized bowl, mix all the marinade ingredients together
and spread the mixture evenly over each side of the steaks. Allow the
steaks to marinate at room temperature for at least 1 hour.

Pre-heat the oven broiler to high or make a charcoal fire in the
barbecue. When the oven broiler is very hot or the charcoal is ash-
white, broil the steaks on each side for about 5–6 minutes (if you like
them rare) or more if you want them well cooked.

Transfer to a warm platter and allow to rest for 10 minutes
before serving.

WOLFGANG PUCK'S SICHUAN-STYLE BEEF ≈

Wolfgang Puck is undoubtedly one of the most successful chefs in America today. An Austrian, he trained in France and honed his art in Los Angeles. His well-deserved success comes from his ability to blend the best of America into a cuisine of his own. In fact, he is among the world's pioneers in the art of fusion cooking. This recipe is an adaptation of Puck's version of Sichuan beef: instead of the traditional stir-frying, he relies on the broiler to cook the beef. Sliced and paired with a light salad, this dish is perfect for warm-weather entertaining.

For those who have a spicier palate, drizzle Sesame and Chili Oil on the cooked dish.

Serve with Spring Salad with Sesame Oil and Shallot Dressing (page 54) or a simple green salad.

Place the steaks on a tray, rub them with sesame oil, and sprinkle the Sichuan peppercorns evenly over both sides. Let the steaks marinate in the refrigerator overnight or for at least several hours.

In a small pan, bring the rice wine and shallots to a boil and continue to cook until reduced by two-thirds. Then add the stock, garlic, ginger, and chili flakes and continue to boil until the liquid is again reduced by two-thirds. It should be slightly thick by now. Slowly whisk in the butter, a piece at a time. Finally, add the soy sauce and cilantro. Remove from the heat and set aside.

Pre-heat the oven broiler to high or make a charcoal fire in the barbecue. When the oven broiler is very hot or the charcoal is ash-white, broil the steaks on each side for about 5–6 minutes (if you like them rare) or more if you want them well cooked.

Transfer the steaks to a warm platter and let them rest for 10 minutes. Reheat the sauce. Cut the steak into thin slices, pour the sauce over them, then drizzle over the sesame and chili oil, if using, and serve immediately.

Serves 4

4 sirloin or rump steaks, about 6 - 8 oz (175–225 g) each
2 tablespoons sesame oil
1 tablespoon roasted ground Sichuan peppercorns (page 21)
Sesame and Chili Oil (page 39), to serve (optional)

For the Sauce:
½ cup (120 ml) mirin (Japanese sweet rice wine) (page 18)
3 tablespoons finely chopped shallots
1 cup (250 ml) homemade Chicken Stock (page 32)
2 tablespoons coarsely chopped garlic
2 teaspoons finely chopped fresh ginger (page 17)
1 teaspoon dried chili flakes
3 tablespoons (35 g) cold unsalted butter, cut in small pieces
1 tablespoon dark soy sauce (page 23)
2 tablespoons finely chopped cilantro

Neil Perry's Braised Oxtail in Coconut Milk Paste ≈

Serves 4–6

3 lb (1.5 kg) oxtail, jointed
10 cups (2.25 liters)
    homemade Chicken Stock
    (page 32)

For the Coconut Milk Paste:

8 garlic cloves
½ lb (225 g) shallots,
    coarsely chopped and
    squeezed dry
15 white peppercorns
3 tablespoons peanut or
    vegetable oil
2 oz (50 ml) fish sauce
    (page 22) or light soy
    sauce (page 23)
⅓ cup (75 g) palm, rock or
    ordinary sugar (page 24)
2 teaspoons salt
1 teaspoon freshly ground
    five-pepper mixture
    (page 21) or black pepper
4 cups (900 ml) canned
    coconut milk (page 16)

To Garnish:

2 teaspoons peanut or
    vegetable oil for
    microwaving or 1 ¼ cups
    (300 ml) vegetable oil
    for frying
½ lb (225 g) shallots, thinly
    sliced
A large handful of fresh basil
    leaves
A large handful of fresh mint
    leaves

Neil Perry, one of the best chefs in Sydney, has ingeniously combined the flavors of Asia in his ground-breaking cuisine. This dish is typical of his mouthwatering cooking — oxtail is braised and then stir-fried in a flavorful coconut milk paste. Much of the work can be done ahead of time and the bonus is that the dish reheats well. Add the fresh herbs at the last moment, in any case. Steamed Rice (page 35) is ideal for this juicy dish.

Cook the oxtail pieces in boiling water for 15 minutes. Remove and drain well. Bring the stock to a simmer in a very large pan, add the blanched oxtails, cover, and simmer for 3 hours or until the oxtail is very tender. Skim the surface from time to time, removing any impurities. Remove the oxtail pieces with a slotted spoon and set aside. The liquid stock can then be skimmed of fat and impurities, strained through a fine sieve, and used for soup (see Oxtail Wonton Soup, page 70). The stock freezes well.

To make the coconut milk paste, first finely chop the garlic, shallots and peppercorns in a food processor. Then heat a wok or large pan until it is hot, add the oil and the garlic mixture and stir-fry for 1 minute or until it turns golden. Now add the fish sauce or light soy sauce, sugar, salt, pepper, and coconut milk. Add the cooked oxtail and cook until most of the coconut milk has evaporated. Turn the heat down to low and keep warm.

For the garnish, mix the shallots with the oil. Then scatter the sliced shallots so that they are in one layer on two plates. Microwave one plate of shallots on full power for 8–9 minutes (microwave oven temperatures vary). Check from time to time, making sure the shallots do not burn. They should be dry and slightly crisp. Do the same to the second batch. This can be done hours ahead of time. If you don't have a microwave, fry the shallots in 1 ¼ cups (300 ml) oil until slightly crisp.

Stir the basil and mint leaves into the oxtail and turn the mixture onto a warm platter. Garnish with the crisp sliced shallots and serve immediately.

BRAISED FUSION PORK STEW ≈

SERVE THIS LOVELY DISH WITH HERBAL VEGETARIAN FRIED RICE (PAGE 206).

SERVES 4

½ lb (225 g) carrots
½ lb (225 g) potatoes
4 thick spare rib chops,
    about 750 g (1½ lb)
3 teaspoons salt
1½ teaspoons freshly ground
    five-pepper mixture
    (page 21) or black pepper
2 tablespoons all-purpose
    flour
2 tablespoons peanut oil
1 small onion, sliced
8 garlic cloves
2 tablespoons finely
    chopped lemon zest
3 tablespoons finely
    chopped sun-dried
    tomatoes
3 tablespoons mirin
    (Japanese sweet rice wine)
    (page 18) or Shaoxing
    rice wine (page 22) or dry
    sherry
2 tablespoons light soy
    sauce (page 23)
1 tablespoon dark soy sauce
    (page 23)
1 tablespoon hoisin sauce
    (page 22)
3 star anise (page 24)
2 tablespoons rock sugar
    (page 24), crushed, or
    granulated sugar
2 cups (475 ml)
    homemade Chicken Stock
    (page 32)
½ lb (225 g) button
    mushrooms

THIS IS A HEARTY, COLD-WEATHER DISH THAT IS MOUTHWATERING AND SATISFYING. LONG, SLOW COOKING INFUSES FLAVORS FROM EAST AND WEST. I LIKE TO USE MEATY SPARE RIB CHOPS BECAUSE THEY ARE RICH, MAKING THEM PERFECT FOR SIMMERED DISHES LIKE THIS ONE. AN ADDITIONAL BONUS IS THAT THE STEW REHEATS WELL.

Peel the carrots and cut at a slight diagonal in 5 cm (2 in) pieces. Peel the potatoes and cut into chunks.

Blot the chops dry with paper towels. Combine 2 teaspoons of the salt, 1 teaspoon of the pepper, and the flour. Sprinkle this mixture evenly on both sides of the chops, shaking off any excess flour.

Heat a wok or frying-pan until it is hot, add the oil and when it is very hot, turn the heat to low and brown the chops on each side. Remove and set aside.

Add the onion and garlic and stir-fry for 3 minutes or until they are slightly soft. Then add the lemon zest, sun-dried tomatoes, rice wine or sherry, soy sauces, hoisin sauce, star anise, the rest of the salt and pepper, and the sugar. Pour the mixture into a heavy casserole and add the chicken stock. Bring the mixture to a simmer, add the mushrooms and chops to the casserole. Cover tightly and simmer gently for 45 minutes. Then add the carrots and potatoes and continue to cook for another 20 minutes, or until the meat and vegetables are tender. Skim off any surface fat and serve immediately.

POULTRY

雞鴨

Stir-fried Chicken with Chinese and Button Mushrooms ≈

SERVES 4

1 lb (450 g) boneless,
skinless chicken thighs or
buy 2 lb (900 g) chicken
thighs and remove the
bones

For the Marinade:
2 teaspoons light soy sauce
(page 23)
2 teaspoons Shaoxing rice
wine (page 22) or dry
sherry
1 teaspoon sesame oil
2 teaspoons cornstarch

For the Stir-fry:
1 oz (25 g) dried Chinese
mushrooms (page 18)
12 oz (350 g) button
mushrooms
1½ tablespoons peanut oil
1 onion, thinly sliced
2 tablespoons coarsely
chopped garlic
2 teaspoons salt
½ teaspoon freshly ground
five-pepper mixture
(page 21) or black pepper
2 teaspoons finely chopped
orange zest
2 tablespoons Shaoxing rice
wine (page 22) or dry
sherry
3 tablespoons oyster sauce
(page 22)
2 teaspoons sugar
A large handful of fresh basil
leaves

CHICKEN STIR-FRY IS SUCH AN EASY AND APPETIZING DISH TO SERVE. HERE, I HAVE COMBINED IT WITH TWO KINDS OF MUSHROOMS, THE DRIED BLACK ONES SO POPULAR IN CHINESE COOKING AND PLAIN BUTTON MUSHROOMS. THE TEXTURES OF THE MUSHROOMS ARE WONDERFULLY CHEWY, ADDING RICHNESS TO THIS UNUSUALLY TASTY DISH. FOR A SIMPLE MEAL, SERVE WITH VEGETABLE SALAD WITH CURRY-SOY VINAIGRETTE (PAGE 195).

If using unboned chicken thighs, remove the skin and bones or have your butcher do it for you. Cut the chicken into 1 in (2.5 cm) chunks and combine them in a bowl with the soy sauce, rice wine or sherry, sesame oil, and cornstarch. Allow to marinate for 20 minutes at room temperature.

Meanwhile, soak the Chinese mushrooms in warm water for 20 minutes. Then drain them, squeeze out the excess liquid, and discard all the water. Remove and discard the stems and cut the caps into thick strips. Slice the button mushrooms.

Heat a wok or large frying-pan until it is very hot; add the oil and then the chicken. Stir-fry the chicken until it is brown, about 5 minutes. Remove the chicken and drain off most of the oil, leaving just 2 teaspoons. Reheat the wok or pan until it is hot, quickly add the onion and garlic, and stir-fry for 2 minutes. Then add the salt, pepper, the Chinese mushrooms, and the button mushrooms and stir-fry for 1 minute. Now, return the chicken, add the orange zest and rice wine or sherry, and continue to stir-fry until the liquid has been absorbed by the mushrooms or has evaporated, about 4 minutes. Finally, add the oyster sauce, sugar, and basil leaves; stir the mixture and cook for another minute. Serve immediately.

Marinated Chicken with Herb-Rice Stuffing ≈

Serves 4–6

1 teaspoon salt

½ teaspoon freshly ground five-pepper mixture (page 21) or black pepper

3–3½ lb (1.5 kg) free-range chicken

1 tablespoon sesame oil

2 tablespoons lemon juice

Chicken is such a versatile food and is so adaptable to any flavoring that it is easy to see why fusion cooks love using it. In this recipe, the chicken is first marinated overnight with sesame oil and lemon juice and then stuffed with glutenous rice and an explosion of fresh herbs. The glutenous rice, also known as sweet or sticky rice, can be found in Asian supermarkets; it must be soaked first and then stir-fried with seasonings. Short, round, and pearl-like it has a higher gluten content than other rices. This special rice does not disintegrate with long cooking, making it ideal for stuffings. It absorbs flavors like a sponge and is well worth the search. Much of the work can be done the day before, making it ideal for a dinner party or a special evening. The result is an elegant dish that is a profusion of tastes, especially if served with Stir-fried Cauliflower with Cilantro (page 193). Any left-over chicken makes a delicious light lunch or terrific sandwiches.

Combine the salt and pepper. Sprinkle this mixture evenly over the skin and the interior cavity of the chicken. Now rub the chicken, inside and out, with the sesame oil and lemon juice. Cover with plasticwrap and refrigerate overnight.

Cover the glutenous rice for the stuffing with water and leave it overnight at room temperature.

The next day, drain the glutenous rice. Heat a wok or large frying-pan over a high heat until it is hot. Add the oil, garlic, and shallots and stir-fry for 20 seconds. Then add the pork and continue to stir-fry for 3 minutes. Now add the drained rice, soy sauce, rice wine or sherry, salt, pepper, and chicken stock. Turn the heat to low, cover, and cook for 20 minutes or until the rice has absorbed all the liquid. Remove from the heat and stir in the scallions and all the fresh herbs. Let the mixture cool thoroughly.

Pre-heat the oven to 475°F/240°C.

Fill the chicken with the rice stuffing; any extra can be served separately. Close the body cavity with a bamboo skewer.

Place the chicken on a roasting rack in a roasting pan, breast-side up. Now put the chicken inside the oven and roast it for 15 minutes. Then turn the heat down to 350°F/180°C and continue to roast for 40 minutes. Turn the chicken over and continue to roast for 10 minutes.

Remove the chicken from the oven and leave it for at least 15 minutes before you carve it. Carefully remove the skewer and drain any liquid that may have accumulated. Using a sharp knife, cut the chicken into serving portions, arrange them on a warm serving platter, and serve immediately.

For the Rice Stuffing:

7 oz (200 g) sweet glutenous rice

1½ tablespoons extra virgin olive oil

1 tablespoon coarsely chopped garlic

3 tablespoons finely chopped shallots

4 oz (100 g) ground pork

1 tablespoon light soy sauce (page 23)

1 tablespoon Shaoxing rice wine (page 22) or dry sherry

1 teaspoon salt

½ teaspoon freshly ground five-pepper mixture (page 21) or black pepper

2 cups (475 ml) Homemade Chicken Stock (page 32)

2 tablespoons finely chopped scallions

1 tablespoon finely chopped cilantro

1 tablespoon finely chopped fresh chives

1 tablespoon finely chopped fresh chervil

1 tablespoon finely chopped fresh thyme or 2 teaspoons dried thyme

1 tablespoon finely chopped fresh tarragon

Honey-soy-glazed Poussins ≈

Serves 4

4 x 12 oz (350 g) poussins
or use 12 oz squabs

For the Marinade:

2 teaspoons salt
1½ teaspoons freshly ground
    five-pepper mixture
    (page 21) or black pepper
2 tablespoons light soy
    sauce (page 23)
2 tablespoons mirin
    (Japanese sweet rice wine)
    (page 18) or dry sherry
2 tablespoons Dijon mustard
3 tablespoons honey

Sometimes available at gourmet meat markets, poussins (baby chickens) are perfect for today's busy lifestyle. They are not only tasty but cook quickly. Squabs can be used as an alternative. Here, I offer a simple marinade that fuses French and Asian flavors and results in the sweet and savory glaze that makes the birds so appealing. They can also be cooked on the broil or broiler. Serve them with Light Rice Noodles with Fresh Herbs (page 207).

Using a sharp knife, cut through the backbone of the bird, lengthwize. Cut off the backbone and tail. Crack the breast bone, so that the bird lies flat. Now make two small holes through the skin *below* and on either side of the breast. Tuck the legs through these holes. This will help hold the shape of the small hen or poussin during cooking. Repeat the procedure with the other three.

In a small bowl, mix the marinade ingredients very well. Rub the mixture both inside and outside each bird. Place them, skin-side up, in a heavy roasting pan. Let them marinate in the refrigerator for 1 hour.

Pre-heat the oven to 475°F/240°C and roast the birds for about 10–15 minutes, or until they are brown. Reduce the temperature to 350°F/180°C, and continue to roast for another 20 minutes. Remove the birds from the oven and let them wait for at least 15 minutes before serving.

Barbecued Spicy Chicken Wings ≈

3 lb (1.5 kg) chicken wings

For the Marinade:

3 tablespoons dark soy
  sauce (page 23)
1 tablespoon light soy sauce
  (page 23)
3 tablespoons mirin
  (Japanese sweet rice wine)
  (page 18) or dry sherry
2 tablespoons sugar
2 tablespoons chili-bean
  sauce (page 22)
1 tablespoon finely chopped
  orange zest
1½ tablespoons Madras
  curry powder (page 17)
1 teaspoon chili oil
  (page 15)

Chicken wings seem to me to be the most unappreciated food in European cooking. In my Chinese household, we frequently enjoyed chicken wings because they were inexpensive and we regarded them as tasty morsels. In this recipe, I combine spicy eastern flavors with western tastes for a quick, easy marinade that is so savory when barbecued. The recipe can be easily doubled or tripled for a larger crowd. Serve the wings with rice or even cold for a picnic treat.

Pierce the skins of the chicken wings with a fork; this will allow the marinade to penetrate. In a small bowl, mix the marinade ingredients. Pour the mixture over the chicken wings and mix well. Let them marinate in the refrigerator for 1 hour.

Pre-heat the oven broiler to high or make a charcoal fire in the barbecue.

When the broiler is very hot or the charcoal is ash-white, broil the chicken wings for about 10 minutes, turning from time to time to avoid burning.

Serve immediately or allow to cool and serve at room temperature.

Broiled Soy Sauce-Mustard Chicken Thighs ≈

Soy sauce and mustard are two ingredients that fuse beautifully, even though they are from two completely different food cultures. Chicken thighs can withstand the strong flavors of this easy-to-make sauce. Serve it with a salad for a light meal.

Remove the skin and bone from unboned chicken thighs. Lay the chicken thighs on a baking tray.

In a blender or food processor, mix the soy sauce, mustard, pepper, garlic, ginger, orange zest, cilantro, parsley, sesame oil and olive oil until smooth. With a spatula, smear each side of the thighs evenly with this mixture.

Pre-heat the oven broiler to high or make a charcoal fire in the barbecue.

When the broiler is very hot or the charcoal is ash-white, broil the chicken thighs on each side for 10–15 minutes, until they are brown and slightly firm to the touch. Remove the thighs from the heat and set aside to rest in a warm place for 10–15 minutes before serving.

Serves 4

- 1 lb (450 g) boneless, skinless chicken thighs or 2 lb (900 g) chicken thighs on the bone
- 3 tablespoons light soy sauce (page 23)
- 2 tablespoons Dijon mustard
- 1 teaspoon freshly ground five-pepper mixture (page 21) or black pepper
- 1½ tablespoons finely chopped garlic
- 2 teaspoons finely chopped fresh ginger (page 17)
- 1 tablespoon finely chopped orange zest
- 1 tablespoon finely chopped cilantro
- 1 tablespoon chopped fresh flatleaf parsley
- 1 tablespoon sesame oil
- 1 tablespoon extra virgin olive oil

Stir-fried Chicken with Broiled Peppers ≈

Serves 4

4 peppers, red, yellow and green

2 tablespoons extra virgin olive oil

1 lb (450 g) boneless chicken breast halves, skinned and cut into 1 in (2.5 cm) cubes

1 egg white

1 teaspoon salt

2 teaspoons cornstarch plus 1 teaspoon cornstarch blended with 1 tablespoon water

1 ¼ cups (300 ml) peanut oil or water, plus 1 tablespoon peanut oil

2 tablespoons finely sliced garlic

⅔ cup (150 ml) homemade Chicken Stock (page 32)

2 teaspoons chili-bean sauce (page 22)

2 teaspoons sugar

1½ tablespoons Shaoxing rice wine (page 22) or dry sherry

1 tablespoon light soy sauce (page 23)

As a student living in southern France, I discovered the taste of broiled or roasted peppers. Cooked over an open flame or under a broiler, the peppers acquire a sweet, smoky flavor that is simply exquisite. In this recipe, I have combined this very western cooking technique with the Chinese method of stir-frying. The result, I think you will agree, is fusion bliss. Serve it simply with rice.

Using tongs, hold each pepper directly over the flames of a gas burner and broil all over until the skin has blackened. Alternately, put them under a hot broiler, turning occasionally. After the peppers have blackened, place them in a paper bag and close it tightly. When the peppers have cooled, remove them from the bag and peel off the charred skin. Discard the seeds, cut into long strips, and drizzle them with the olive oil.

Mix the chicken with the egg white, salt and 2 teaspoons of cornstarch in a small bowl; refrigerate for about 20 minutes.

If using oil, heat a wok or large frying-pan over a high heat; then add the oil. When the oil is very hot, remove the wok or pan from the heat and immediately add the chicken pieces, stirring vigorously to keep them from sticking. When they turn white, about 2 minutes, quickly drain the chicken in a stainless steel colander set over a bowl. Discard the oil.

If you choose to use water instead of oil, bring it to a boil in a pan. Remove the pan from the heat and immediately add the chicken pieces, stirring vigorously to keep them from sticking. When the chicken pieces turn white, about 2 minutes, quickly drain them in a colander set over a bowl. Discard the water.

Wipe the wok or pan clean and reheat until it is very hot. Then add the tablespoon of oil. When very hot, add the garlic slices and stir-fry them for 2 minutes or until golden brown. Then add the stock, chili-bean sauce, sugar, rice wine or sherry, and soy sauce. Cook for another 2 minutes. Add the cornstarch and water mixture and cook for 20 seconds; add the chicken and pepper strips and stir-fry for another 2 minutes, coating the chicken thoroughly with the sauce. Serve immediately.

Roast Ginger Chicken ≈

Chinese home cooks tend either to steam, braise or fry a whole chicken. It is rarely roasted because most Chinese homes lack ovens. Roast chicken is, therefore, a great discovery for the Chinese who emigrate to European countries.

A simple procedure results here in a delicious dish with very little work. A mixture of East–West flavorings is sprinkled on the inside of the chicken to enhance it further. Serve this dish with Potato and Cucumber Puree (page 186) for a complete hearty meal.

Combine the five-spice powder, Sichuan peppercorns, pepper and salt. Sprinkle this mixture evenly throughout the interior cavity of the chicken. Now mix the sage, marjoram, ginger, and garlic in another bowl. Put the mixture loosely inside the cavity of the chicken. Close the body cavity with a bamboo skewer.

Pre-heat the oven to 475°F/240°C.

Meanwhile, place the chicken on a roasting rack in a roasting pan, breast-side up. Now put the chicken inside the oven and roast it for 15 minutes. Then turn the heat down to 350°F/180°C and continue to roast for 40 minutes. Turn the chicken over and continue to roast for 10 minutes.

Remove the chicken from the oven; turn it the right way up and let it rest for at least 15 minutes before you carve it. Carefully remove the skewer and drain any liquid that may have accumulated. Using a sharp knife, cut the chicken into serving portions, arrange them on a warm serving platter and serve immediately.

Serves 4–6

- 2 teaspoons five-spice powder (page 17)
- 2 teaspoons roasted and ground Sichuan peppercorns (page 21)
- 1 teaspoon freshly ground five-pepper mixture (page 21) or black pepper
- 2 teaspoons salt
- 3–3½ lb (1.5 kg) corn-fed or free-range chicken
- 3 sprigs of fresh sage or 2 teaspoons dried sage
- 2 sprigs of fresh marjoram or 1 teaspoon dried marjoram
- 20 slices of unpeeled fresh ginger (page 17) (size unimportant)
- 10 unpeeled garlic cloves, lightly crushed

Vietnamese-style Barbecued Five-spice Chicken ≈

Serves 4

2 lb (900 g) chicken thighs
  on the bone

For the Marinade:
3 tablespoons coarsely
  chopped shallots
3 tablespoons coarsely
  chopped garlic
2 tablespoons dark or
  ordinary sugar
2 teaspoons five-spice
  powder (page 17)
2 tablespoons mirin
  (Japanese sweet rice wine)
  (page 18) or dry sherry
1 tablespoon Shaoxing rice
  wine (page 22) or dry
  sherry
2 tablespoons fish sauce
  (page 22) or light soy
  sauce (page 23)
1 teaspoon sesame oil
½ teaspoon freshly ground
  five-pepper mixture
  (page 21) or black pepper

I GREW UP IN A CHINESE HOUSEHOLD TOTALLY OBLIVIOUS TO OTHER ASIAN CUISINES. ONLY WHEN I LIVED IN CALIFORNIA DID I DISCOVER THE RICHNESS OF VIETNAMESE, AS WELL AS THAI, CUISINE. YOUNG AUSTRALIAN CHEFS HAVE MADE THE SAME DISCOVERY WITH THE INFLUX OF THE VIETNAMESE TO SYDNEY. THE RESULT IS AN ADAPTATION OF SPICES TO MODERN AUSTRALIAN COOKING.

A PARTICULAR DISH WHICH CAPTURED MY CULINARY FANCY IN MY STUDENT DAYS WAS THIS FIVE-SPICE CHICKEN. THE SECRET, I LEARNED, WAS THAT THE CHICKEN SHOULD BE MARINATED OVERNIGHT TO CAPTURE THE ESSENTIAL DEEP FLAVORS. THEN IT IS SIMPLY BROILED, A PERFECT PARTY DISH THAT IS DELICIOUS, ESPECIALLY WHEN IT IS SERVED WITH MALAYSIAN CURRY MEE (PAGE 218).

Blot the chicken thighs dry with paper towels.

In a food processor, combine the marinade ingredients and purée them. In a large bowl, combine the chicken with the marinade and mix well. Cover with plastic wrap and refrigerate overnight.

When you are ready to barbecue the chicken, remove the chicken from the refrigerator and leave at room temperature for 40 minutes.

Pre-heat the oven broiler to high or make a charcoal fire in the barbecue. When the broiler is very hot or the charcoal is ash-white, broil the chicken thighs for 10 minutes on each side or until they are cooked.

Place on a warm platter and serve immediately.

Wok-smoked Chicken ≈

Chicken is a wonderfully versatile food and a favorite with fusion cooks and chefs around the world. An economical meat, the breast cooks quickly, perfect for today's busy restaurant or home kitchen. In this recipe, chicken breasts are rubbed with a combination of eastern and western spices and smoked in a wok or a deep casserole. You can serve them with a salad as an appetizer or light lunch. They also make delectable sandwiches.

Combine the sugar, salt, Sichuan peppercorns, pepper and thyme in a small bowl. Sprinkle this mixture on all sides of the chicken breasts. Place the chicken on a plate, cover with plastic wrap and put in the refrigerator overnight.

The next day, line the inside of a wok and its lid with foil. Place the rice, sugar, and tea leaves in the bottom of the wok. Rub a rack with vegetable oil and place it over the smoking ingredients. Slowly heat the wok and, when the mixture begins to smoke, put the chicken breasts on the rack, covering tightly. Turn the heat to very low and slowly smoke for 30 minutes. Remove from the heat and leave the chicken in the wok, covered, for another 5 minutes. When the chicken breasts are cool enough to handle, cut them into slices. Discard the smoking mixture and the foil. Serve at room temperature or cold.

Serves 4

2 teaspoons brown sugar

1½ teaspoons salt

1 teaspoon roasted and ground Sichuan peppercorns (page 21)

½ teaspoon freshly ground five-pepper mixture (page 21) or black pepper

2 teaspoons dried thyme

4 x 4 oz (100 g) skinless, boneless chicken breast halves

Vegetable oil, for greasing rack

For the Smoking Mixture:

⅓ cup (50 g) long-grain white rice

3 tablespoons brown sugar

2 oz (50 g) black tea leaves (page 24)

FUSION CHICKEN STEW ≈

SERVES 4–6

3-3½ lb (1.5 kg) corn-fed or
free-range chicken

2 teaspoons salt plus salt
and freshly ground five-
pepper mixture (page 21)
or black pepper to taste

6 slices unpeeled fresh
ginger (page 17)
(size unimportant)

9 scallions

2 tablespoons whole Sichuan
peppercorns roasted
(page 21)

1 tablespoon whole five-
peppercorn mixture
(page 21) or black
peppercorns

4 sprigs of fresh thyme or
2 teaspoons dried thyme

4 unpeeled garlic cloves,
crushed

8 oz (225 g) carrots

8 oz (225 g) asparagus

8 oz (225 g) red or yellow
peppers (1 large or about
2 small)

8 oz (225 g) snow peas

3 tablespoons crème fraîche

To Garnish:

1 tablespoon finely chopped
cilantro

1 tablespoon finely chopped
fresh chives

2 tablespoons finely
chopped scallions

THE CHINESE ARE MASTERS OF COOKING FOOD EFFICIENTLY AT LOW HEAT. BECAUSE OF THE COST AND SCARCITY OF FUEL, THEY DEVISED STEWING AND BRAISING TECHNIQUES THAT ALLOWED THEM TO PRODUCE DELICIOUS FOODS DONE TO PERFECTION. THIS IS PARTICULARLY TRUE WHEN IT COMES TO CHICKEN. OFTEN CHICKEN THAT IS IMPROPERLY STEWED IS STRINGY AND TASTELESS. THE CHINESE TECHNIQUE OF STEEPING PRODUCES MOIST CHICKEN WITH A SILKY, VELVETY TEXTURE. IN THIS QUICK RECIPE, THE STEEPING STOCK IS REDUCED, SEASONED, AND ENRICHED WITH A TOUCH OF CRÈME FRAÎCHE. THE STEW MAKES A COMPLETE MEAL SERVED WITH STEAMED RICE (PAGE 35).

Rub the chicken evenly with 2 teaspoons of salt. Place the chicken in a large pan, cover with water, and bring to a boil. Skim off any impurities; then add the ginger, 6 scallions, Sichuan peppercorns, five-peppercorn mixture or black peppercorns, thyme and garlic. Reduce the heat to a simmer, cover tightly and cook for 20 minutes. Turn off the heat and leave tightly covered for 1 hour.

Meanwhile, prepare the vegetables. Peel the carrots and cut diagonally into ¼ in (5 mm) dice. Cut the asparagus diagonally into 2 in (5 cm) pieces, discarding any tough ends. Cut the peppers into 1 in (2.5 cm) pieces. Cut the rest of the scallions diagonally into 2 in (5 cm) pieces. Trim the snow peas.

When the chicken has been steeped for 1 hour, drain and allow it to cool enough to handle. Cut the chicken into serving pieces.

Strain the steeping liquid through a fine sieve and skim off all surface fat. It is now a light broth. Return the broth to the pan and reduce by half over a high heat. Add the carrots to the broth for 2 minutes; then add the asparagus and peppers and cook for another minute. Finally, add the scallions and snow peas and cook for another minute. Remove the vegetables with a slotted spoon, and continue to reduce the liquid until you have about 1 ¼ cup (300 ml) left. Stir in the crème fraîche and salt and pepper to taste. Return the chicken and vegetables to the pan and reheat for 2 minutes, or until throughly warm.

Arrange the chicken and vegetables on a warm platter, pour the sauce over, sprinkle coriander, chives, and scallions on top and serve.

FIVE-SPICE ROAST POUSSINS WITH RICE WINE-BUTTER SAUCE ≈

SERVES 4

4 x 12 oz (350 g) poussins
   or 4 x 1 to 1 ½ lb Rock
   Cornish hens or 1
   tablespoon sesame oil

For the Marinade:
1 tablespoon five-spice
   powder (page 17)
2 teaspoons salt
1 teaspoon freshly ground
   five-pepper mixture
   (page 21) or black pepper
2 tablespoons finely
   chopped orange zest

For the Sauce:
3 tablespoons finely
   chopped shallots
5 fl oz (150 ml) Shaoxing
   rice wine (page 22)
   or dry sherry
5 fl oz (150 ml) homemade
   Chicken Stock (page 32)
2 tablespoons (25 g) cold
   unsalted butter, cut in small
   pieces
2 tablespoons finely
   chopped scallions

IN THIS RECIPE, I LIKE TO USE POUSSINS, WHICH ARE BABY CHICKENS, MAKING AN ELEGANT DINNER-PARTY DISH THAT IS EASY ENOUGH FOR TODAY'S BUSY COOK. ROCK CORNISH HENS ARE MORE READILY AVAILABLE AND CAN BE USED INSTEAD OF THE POUSSINS. THEY TAKE LITTLE TIME TO COOK AND LOOK SPECTACULAR. SERVE THIS WITH CURRY COUSCOUS WITH FRESH CHIVES AND APPLE (PAGE 198), FOR A COMPLETE MEAL.

Using a sharp knife, cut through the backbone of a poussin, lengthways. Cut off the backbone and tail. Crack the breast bone so that the hens lies flat. Now make two small holes through the skin *below* and on each side of the breast. Tuck the legs through these holes. This will help hold the shape of the hen during cooking. Rub sesame oil on both sides of the hen. Repeat the procedure with the other three hens.

In a small bowl, mix the marinade ingredients very well. Rub the mixture inside and outside each hen. Place them, skin-side up, in a heavy roasting pan. Let them marinate at room temperature for 1 hour.

Pre-heat the oven to 475°F/240°C and roast the hens for about 10–15 minutes or until they are brown. Reduce the temperature to 350°F/180°C and continue to roast for another 20 minutes. Remove the hens from the oven, place them on a platter, and hold them at room temperature for at least 15 minutes before serving.

While the hens are resting, place the roasting pan on a burner, add the shallots and cook for a minute; then add the rice wine or sherry and continue to cook, over a high heat, until the wine has evaporated. Now add the stock and bring to a boil, scraping the bottom of the pan as you stir. Remove the pan from the heat and whisk in the butter, a piece at a time. Once the butter is thoroughly incorporated into the sauce, sprinkle in the scallions. Spoon a few tablespoons of sauce on individual plates, place the hens on top, and serve immediately.

Broiled Coconut Chicken Curry ≈

Here is fusion cooking with an enticing combination: coconut, curry and lemon grass, blended to make a delicious marinade. The familiar broiled chicken is enhanced by these exotic touches. The secret is to allow enough time for the marinade to permeate the chicken. Then the marinade itself is briefly cooked and used for a sauce. Broiling the chicken adds a smoky deliciousness that transforms this ordinary dish into something special indeed. Serve with Ginger-leek Purée (page 191) and Steamed Rice (page 35).

Sprinkle the chicken thighs with the salt and pepper. Peel the lemon grass stalk to reveal the tender, whitish center and finely chop the center. Mix the lemon grass with the other marinade ingredients in a large bowl. Add the chicken thighs and mix well. Leave in the refrigerator overnight, covered with plastic wrap.

Remove the chicken thighs from the refrigerator about 1 hour before you are ready to cook them. With a slotted spoon, remove the chicken thighs from the marinade and reserve the marinade. Pre-heat the oven broiler to high or make a charcoal fire in the barbecue. When a broiler is very hot or the charcoal is ash-white, broil the chicken thighs for about 15 minutes on each side. They are cooked when they are slightly firm to the touch or can be easily pierced in the thickest part with a wooden skewer and the juices run clear. Remove the thighs from the broil and set aside for 5 minutes before serving.

While the chicken is broiling, put the reserved marinade in a small pan and bring to the boil. Turn down the heat and simmer for 5 minutes. Then strain the sauce through a fine sieve and put in a bowl. Serve with the broiled chicken thighs.

Serves 4

2 lb (900 g) chicken thighs
   on the bone
2 teaspoons salt
1 teaspoon freshly ground
   five-pepper mixture
   (page 21) or black pepper

For the Marinade:

1 lemon grass stalk
   (page 18)
14 oz (400 ml) can of
   coconut milk (page 16)
2 tablespoons fish sauce
   (page 22) or light soy
   sauce (page 23)
3 tablespoons lime juice
2 teaspoons lime zest
3 tablespoons Madras curry
   powder (page 17)

Stir-fried Thai Green Curry Chicken with Eggplant ≈

Serves 4

1 lb (450 g) skinless, boneless chicken thighs or 2 lb (900 g) chicken thighs on the bone

2 lb (1 kg) Chinese or ordinary eggplant (page 13)

2 teaspoons light soy sauce (page 23)

2 teaspoons Shaoxing rice wine (page 22) or dry sherry

1 teaspoon sesame oil

2 teaspoons cornstarch

1½ tablespoons oil, preferably peanut

3 tablespoons chopped garlic

1 tablespoon finely chopped fresh ginger (page 17)

3 tablespoons finely chopped scallions

2–3 tablespoons Thai green curry paste (page 23)

1 tablespoon fish sauce (page 22) or light soy sauce (page 23)

2 teaspoons sugar

A large handful of fresh basil leaves

Thai dishes have become very popular in the West, especially with many chefs who are practicing fusion cuisine. No wonder; Thai cooking is full of many fragrant aromas that are so enticing. Thai curry pastes are time-consuming and laborious to make but, fortunately, there are now high-quality Thai pastes available that can be bought at the supermarket. I find them perfectly acceptable and many have the authentic Thai flavors.

To cut down the fat, I first roast the eggplant in the oven, instead of frying them the traditional Thai way. In this manner, they don't absorb any oil. This step can be done hours ahead, and the rest is a quick and easy stir-fry. Serve this with plain Steamed Rice (page 35).

Remove the skin and bones from unboned chicken thighs or have your butcher do it for you.

Pre-heat the oven to 400°F/200°C. If you are using Chinese eggplant, roast them for 20 minutes; if you are using large eggplant, roast them for about 30–40 minutes or until they are soft and cooked through. Allow the eggplant to cool and then peel them. Put them in a colander and let them drain for 30 minutes or more. Chop the eggplant flesh. This procedure can be done hours in advance.

Cut the chicken into 1 in (2.5 cm) chunks and combine them in a bowl with the soy sauce, rice wine or sherry, sesame oil, and cornstarch.

Heat a wok or large frying-pan until it is very hot; then add the oil, then the chicken. Stir-fry for 5 minutes, then remove the chicken and drain off most of the fat and oil, leaving 2 teaspoons. Return the drained chicken to the wok or pan and add the garlic, ginger, and scallions and stir-fry for 5 minutes. Then add the chopped eggplant flesh and all the remaining ingredients except the basil leaves. Continue to cook for another 3 minutes, stirring from time to time. When the chicken is cooked, add the basil leaves and give the mixture a good stir. Transfer to a platter and serve immediately.

Soy-braised Duck ≈

Serves 4–6

3½–4 lb (1.6–1.8 kg) fresh or
   frozen duck (preferably a
   white Peking duck)
1 lb (450 g) Chinese leaves
   (page 14), cut in
   2 in (5 cm) pieces
Sprigs of cilantro (optional), to
   garnish

For the Sauce:

7 ½ cups (1.7 liters)
   homemade Chicken Stock
   (page 32) or water
2 ½ cups (600 ml) dark soy
   sauce (page 23)
1 ¼ cups (300 ml) light soy
   sauce (page 23)
1 ¾ cups (400 ml) Shaoxing
   rice wine (page 22) or dry
   sherry, or ¾ cup (200 ml (7
   fl oz) dry sherry mixed with ¾
   cup (200 ml) homemade
   Chicken Stock (page 32)
½ cup (100 g) rock sugar
   (page 24) or granulated
   sugar
5 star anise (page 23)
3 pieces of Chinese
   cinnamon bark (page 16) or
   3 cinnamon sticks
6 scallions
3 slices of fresh ginger
   (page 17)
5 garlic cloves, crushed
3 tablespoons coarsely
   chopped sun-dried tomatoes
2 tablespoons dried thyme

The rich flavor and easy availability of soy sauce has inspired fusion chefs and home cooks everywhere. Here is a fine example of a soy-braised duck which I sampled at the Mandarin Duck Bistro in Adelaide, Australia. At one time, this excellent restaurant, alas, no longer in business, was widely known as a pioneer in East–West fusion cooking. This dish can be made ahead of time and reheats well. Serve it with Green Rice (page 203). Left-overs make great sandwiches or you can use them in salads. The sauce can be frozen and re-used to braise duck or chicken.

Blanch the duck in a large pan of boiling water for 20 minutes. Remove and drain well.

Rinse the pan well, combine all the sauce ingredients in it and bring the mixture to a boil. Add the duck and turn the heat down to a simmer. Cover the pot and slowly braise the duck for 1 hour or until it is tender. Skim the surface fat from time to time; this procedure will prevent the duck from becoming greasy. Remove the duck. Skim off any remaining fat from the sauce. Then add the Chinese leaves and cook for 20 minutes.

Remove the Chinese leaves and place on a warm platter. Carve the duck into four or six serving pieces. Lay the duck on top of the leaves, add a ladle or two of sauce, garnish with cilantro, if using, and serve immediately.

Alternatively, you can let the duck cool thoroughly and serve it at room temperature. Once the sauce has cooled, remove any remaining surface fat.

Neil Perry's Wok-smoked Quail ≈

Another palate-enticing recipe from one of Australia's top chefs, Neil Perry. Smoking is one of his favorite techniques and provides a taste he loves. This delicate bird makes a smashing appetizer for a meal. The jasmine tea gives the quails a haunting aroma. Neil serves them with an eggplant salad; I highly recommend Asian-flavored Eggplant Crostini (page 60), which I think go very well with this delicious dish.

Set up a steamer or put a rack into a wok or deep pan and pour in 2 in (5 cm) of water. Bring the water to a boil over a high heat. Put the quail onto a heatproof plate and then carefully lower it into the steamer or onto the rack. Turn the heat to low and cover the wok or pan tightly. Steam gently for 8 minutes. Remove the quail and allow to cool. Then rub the sesame oil all over them.

Next, line the inside of a wok and a wok lid with foil. Place the rice, sugar, and tea leaves in the bottom of the wok. Rub a rack with vegetable oil and place it over the smoking ingredients. Slowly heat the wok and, when the mixture begins to smoke, put the quail on the rack, covering tightly. Turn the heat to very low and slowly smoke for 5 minutes. Remove from the heat and allow the quail to rest, covered, for another 5 minutes. When the quail are cool enough to handle, place on a platter and serve. Discard the smoking mixture and the foil.

Serve with the salt and pepper mixture and lemon wedges.

Serves 4

4 oz (4 x 100 g) quail
1 tablespoon sesame oil
1 tablespoon roasted and ground Sichuan peppercorns (page 21), mixed with 1½ tablespoons salt, to serve
Lemon wedges, to serve

For the Smoking Mixture:

2 oz (50 g) long-grain white rice
3 tablespoons brown sugar
2 oz (50 g) jasmine tea leaves

Peking Lemon Duck ≈

4–4½ lb (1.75–2 kg) duck,
   fresh or frozen, preferably
   Cherry Valley
1 teaspoon coarsely ground
   five-pepper mixture
   (page 21) or black pepper
2 teaspoons salt
2 teaspoons five-spice
   powder (page 17)
2 lemons, quartered
6 slices of unpeeled fresh
   ginger (page 17) (size
   unimportant)

I HAVE NEVER CONSIDERED MYSELF CHAUVINISTIC BUT I FIRMLY BELIEVE THAT NO ONE COOKS DUCK AS WELL AS THE CHINESE. WHAT CAN BE MORE WONDROUS THAN TO BITE INTO THE CRACKLING, MAHOGANY-COLORED SKIN OF A TEMPTING, MOIST, RICH DUCK! THE SECRET IS TWO-FOLD: FIRST, THE SKIN IS SEPARATED FROM THE FAT WHEN AIR IS FORCED INTO IT THROUGH THE NECK BY BLOWING THROUGH A STRAW OR EVEN USING A BICYCLE PUMP. LATER, WHEN THE DUCK IS ROASTING, THE FAT MELTS AWAY WHILE THE SKIN CRISPS SEPARATELY.

THE DUCK IS GIVEN A BATH OF VERY HOT WATER MIXED WITH VINEGAR AND ALLOWED TO AIR-DRY FOR A FEW HOURS. LATER, IT IS BATH OF HONEY AND DARK SOY SAUCE IS POURED OVER IT, GIVING THE SKIN A LOVELY GLAZED, LACQUERED LOOK. IN FACT, THE FRENCH CALL CHINESE ROAST DUCK 'LACQUERED DUCK,' WHICH I THINK DESCRIBES IT RATHER APTLY.

IN THIS RECIPE, I HAVE AGAIN MINED MY CHINESE CULINARY HERITAGE, WHICH I MERGE WITH MY INTEREST IN WESTERN TASTES AND FLAVORS TO PRODUCE A DUCK DISH THAT TAKES THE BEST FROM BOTH WORLDS.

DON'T WORRY IF YOU ARE UNABLE TO PUMP AIR INTO THE DUCK TO SEPARATE THE SKIN FROM THE FAT; IT IS A STEP THAT CAN BE SKIPPED. YOU CAN USUALLY FIND WHOLE DUCKS WITH NECKS, ETC. IN ASIAN MARKETS. HOWEVER, WHAT IS MORE IMPORTANT IS THE DRYING OF THE DUCK, WHICH HELPS TO PRODUCE THE CRISP SKIN THAT IS THE HALLMARK OF THIS DISH. IN ORDER TO SAVE TIME, I HAVE ALSO SKIPPED THE HOT WATER AND VINEGAR STAGE IN THIS RECIPE.

I FLAVOR THE DUCK WITH A MIXTURE OF FIVE-SPICE POWDER, AS WELL AS FIVE-PEPPER MIXTURE AND LEMONS. THE RESULT IS AN UNCOMMONLY ELEGANT DISH THAT WILL BRING COMPLIMENTS FROM YOUR FAMILY AND FRIENDS. SERVE THE DUCK WITH POTATOES AND VEGETABLES. IF THE DUCK IS FROZEN, THAW IT THOROUGHLY. RINSE THE DUCK WELL AND BLOT IT COMPLETELY DRY WITH PAPER TOWELS.

If the duck is frozen, thaw it thoroughly. Rinse the duck well and blot it completely dry with paper towels.

If you have a whole duck with the neck on and want to try the optional the forced air technique, hold the cavity shut with a dish towel and, using a clean bicycle pump, force air in to separate the skin from the fat. Pull out any excess fat from the cavity.

In a small bowl, combine the pepper, salt, and five-spice powder and mix well. Sprinkle inside the cavity of the duck with this mixture. Then stuff the cavity with the lemon quarters and ginger slices. Seal the flap of the cavity with a bamboo or metal skewer and secure the cavity with string.

Insert a meat hook near the neck.

Using a sharp knife, cut the lemons for the syrup mixture into ¼ in (5 mm) slices, leaving the rinds on. Combine the lemon slices with the rest of the syrup ingredients in a large pan and bring the mixture to a boil. Turn the heat to low and simmer for about 20 minutes.

Holding the hook, place the duck over the pan and then, using a large ladle or spoon, pour the syrup mixture over the duck several times, as if to bathe it, until all the skin of the duck is completely coated with the mixture. Hang the duck in a cool, well-ventilated place to dry; or, alternatively, hang it in front of a cold fan for about 4–5 hours, longer if possible. (Be sure to put a baking sheet underneath to catch any drips.) Once the duck has dried, the surface of the skin will feel like parchment.

Pre-heat the oven to 325°F/160°C. Meanwhile, place the duck on a roasting rack in a roasting pan, breast-side up. Put ⅔ cup (150 ml) of water into the roasting pan. (This will prevent the fat from splattering.) Now put the duck into the oven and roast it for 1¼ hours. Then turn the heat up to 450°F/220°C and continue to roast for 15 minutes, or until the skin is a rich, dark brown and very crisp.

Remove the duck from the oven and let it rest for at least 20 minutes before you carve it. Using a cleaver or a sharp knife, cut the duck into pieces and arrange them on a warm platter. Serve immediately.

For the Honey and Lemon Syrup Mixture:
2 lemons
5 cups (1.2 liters) water
3 tablespoons honey
3 tablespoons dark soy sauce (page 23)

CHICKEN SCALLOPS WITH FRIED GINGER ≈

SERVES 4

1 cup (250 ml) plus
   2 tablespoons peanut oil
3 tablespoons finely
   shredded fresh ginger
   (page 17)
4 x 4 oz (100 g) boneless,
   skinless, chicken breast
   halves
1½ teaspoons salt
½ teaspoon freshly ground
   five-pepper mixture
   (page 21) or black pepper
All-purpose flour, for dusting
2 eggs, beaten
1 cup (25 g (2) dried
   breadcrumbs
2 tablespoons (25 g)
   unsalted butter
Lemon wedges, to garnish

THIS RECIPE IS INSPIRED BY MY LOVE FOR THE FAMOUS MILANESE-STYLE BREADED VEAL. I SUBSTITUTE MORE READILY AVAILABLE CHICKEN FOR THE VEAL. THIS EFFORTLESS DISH IS THEN PAIRED WITH CRISPY-FRIED GINGER FOR AN UNCOMMONLY ELEGANT PRESENTATION THAT IS QUITE DELECTABLE. SERVE IT WITH FIRECRACKER CORN (PAGE 182).

Heat a wok or large frying-pan over a high heat until it is hot. Add the 1 cup (250 ml) of oil, and when it is very hot and slightly smoking, turn the heat to low and deep-fry the ginger until it is crisp and slightly browned. Remove with a slotted spoon and drain well on paper towels. The oil, now flavored with ginger, can be saved and used for stir-frying after it has cooled.

Place each chicken breast between two pieces of plastic wrap. With a large wooden mallet or empty bottle, pound the breasts until they are flat and about ¼ in (5 mm) thick. Sprinkle them evenly with the salt and pepper then dust with the flour, shaking off any excess. Now dip the chicken breasts in the beaten egg and, finally, in the breadcrumbs.

Heat a large frying-pan with the butter and the rest of the oil. Turn the heat to moderate and slowly pan-fry the breasts for 5 minutes on each side, until they are golden brown. Remove to a warm platter, scatter with the fried ginger, garnish with the lemon wedges, and serve immediately.

Japanese-style Marinated Broiled Quail ≈

Quail is a wonderful delicacy that is becoming more and more available. This small bird is quite delicious and easy to prepare. I especially like the Japanese method, which is a marinade that seeps into the quail meat, making it a savory treat. Once marinated, they cook quickly on a smoky broiler. This dish is perfect with a salad in summer and also makes an ideal appetizer.

Dry the quail inside and out with paper towels.

In a medium-sized bowl, mix all the marinade ingredients together and pour into a large, thick plastic bag. Put the quail inside, seal and let marinate at room temperature for at least 1 hour. Remove the quail from the plastic bag and keep the marinade.

Pre-heat the oven broiler to high or make a charcoal fire in the barbecue. When the charcoal is ash-white or the oven broiler is very hot, broil the quail, turning them frequently, for about 6 minutes so that they are cooked but slightly pink inside. Baste the quail with the remaining marinade.

Transfer to a warm platter and allow to rest for 10 minutes before serving.

Serves 6

6 x 4 oz (100 g) quail

For the Marinade:
1 tablespoon dark soy sauce (page 23)
1½ tablespoons light soy sauce (page 23)
2 teaspoons sugar
3 tablespoons mirin (Japanese sweet rice wine) (page 18)
1 tablespoon extra virgin oil

ASIAN DUCK CONFIT ≈

SERVES 6

6 fresh or frozen and thawed
    duck thighs and legs,
    about 3 lb (1.5 kg) in total
4 oz (100 g) coarse sea salt
6 x 12 oz (350 g) cans of
    duck or goose fat
8 unpeeled garlic cloves,
    lightly crushed
8 fresh ginger slices
    (page 17)
6 star anise (page 23)
3 cinnamon sticks (page 16)
2 tablespoons Sichuan
    peppercorns, roasted
    (page 21)

I SPEND A FEW MONTHS EACH YEAR IN SOUTH-WEST FRANCE, A REGION OF EXCELLENT BUT RELATIVELY UNKNOWN CUISINE. I HAVE GAINED A DEEP APPRECIATION FOR THE UNIQUELY DELICIOUS FOOD OF THAT AREA. MY GOOD FRIENDS, MONIQUE AND JACQUES PÉBEYRE, TAUGHT ME HOW TO MAKE SOME OF THEIR WONDERFUL REGIONAL SPECIALITIES.

ONE OF MY FAVORITES IS DUCK CONFIT, THAT IS, DUCK COOKED IN ITS OWN FAT AND STORED IN A JAR, COVERED IN THE SAME FAT TO PRESERVE IT. IT IS ONE OF THE OLDEST FORMS OF PRESERVING FOOD. CONFIT IS SURPRISINGLY EASY TO MAKE AND, SINCE IT KEEPS SO WELL, I THINK IT WORTHWHILE TO MAKE A LARGE BATCH. IN THIS RECIPE, I HAVE INCLUDED ASIAN SPICES TO GIVE THE CONFIT AN EVEN MORE AROMATIC TASTE AND FLAVOR. THE CONFIT GOES BEAUTIFULLY WITH LENTILS OR OTHER LEGUMES, OR POTATOES.

Place the duck pieces on a baking sheet and sprinkle evenly with the salt on both sides. Cover the duck with a dish towel and store in a the refrigerator overnight.

The next day, wipe off the salt, heat the duck or goose fat in a large pan and add the garlic, ginger, star anise, cinnamon, and peppercorns. Now add the duck pieces and cook slowly over a low heat for 1 hour. The duck should be cooked and tender.

Let the duck pieces cool in the fat, then transfer to an airtight container with the fat covering them until ready to use. The confit will keep for months if stored in this way in the refrigerator.

When you are ready to cook the duck confit, pre-heat the oven to 350°F/180°C.

Remove the duck pieces from the fat and cook in a shallow roasting pan for 40 minutes, or until they are crisp. Remove them from the hot fat which will have collected in the pan and drain on paper towels. Strain the hot fat and keep for future use. (You can use it to sauté potatoes.) Serve the duck immediately.

Brined Duck with Chinese Leaves ≈

Serves 4

3 tablespoons roasted and
  crushed Sichuan
  peppercorns (page 21)
¼ cup (50 g) coarse sea salt
3½– 4 lb (1.6 –1.8 kg) fresh
  or frozen duck (preferably
  a white Peking duck)

For the Stock:
2 tablespoons cumin seeds
5 cups (1.2 liters) water
1/2 cup (100 g) sugar
6 star anise (page 23)
3 cinnamon sticks (page 16)
2 tablespoons Sichuan
  peppercorns, roasted
  (page 21)
8 unpeeled garlic cloves,
  lightly crushed
8 slices of unpeeled fresh
  ginger (page 17)
  (size unimportant)
Peel from 1 fresh orange
2 scallions

Adelaide, Australia, has been a center of fusion-style cooking for years now. I have been invited there a number of times to cook my interpretation of fusion food. It was there that I met the extremely talented Urs Inauen. He is a European chef, grounded in the classics, but he is nevertheless open to Asian influences and ideas. Together, we made a number of special dinners for Australian wineries.

I was impressed by Urs's culinary skill, which is particularly apparent in this delicious duck recipe of Chinese inspiration. It is beautifully presented on a bed of braised Chinese leaves and tastes absolutely delicious.

This is not a fast-food dish and the necessary preparations must be done beforehand, but much of the work is easy, including the salting and the cooking. The result is a very impressive main course that is well worth the effort.

Heat a wok or large frying-pan over high heat. Add the cumin seeds and dry-roast for 2 minutes. Set aside. Add the Sichuan peppercorns and salt and stir-fry for 1 minute. Lay the duck on a tray and rub the warm salt and pepper mixture over the duck. Cover the duck with a dish towel and keep in a cool place or the refrigerator overnight.

The next day, soak the duck in cold water for 1 hour. Then blanch the duck in a large pan of boiling water for 5 minutes. Rinse in cold water and set aside.

Heat the water for the stock in a pan that is just large enough to hold the duck. Add the sugar, star anise, cinnamon, peppercorns, cumin, garlic, ginger, orange peel, and scallions. Simmer the stock for 45 minutes. Strain the stock, discarding the spices, and return the stock to the pan. Add the duck, then cover and simmer for 45 minutes. Turn off the heat and when the liquid is cool, refrigerate. Allow the duck to steep in the liquid overnight.

The next day, remove the duck and all traces of fat from the liquid. Bring the duck liquid to a simmer in a heavy casserole.

Cut the Chinese leaves into 2 in (5 cm) thick strips. Add these to the simmering duck liquid. Whisk in the butter, a piece at a time. Season with the salt and pepper and cook for 10 minutes or until the leaves are very tender. These braised leaves can be made ahead of time and reheated.

Remove the duck skin and cut it into thick strips. Heat the oil in a small pan and deep-fry the strips; turn the heat to low and fry until the strips are crisp. Drain well on paper towels.

Warm the duck meat briefly in the liquid in which the leaves were braised. Carve the duck into slices. To present the duck, place a portion of Chinese leaves on each plate. Then put the duck meat on top, pour on some of the braising liquid to moisten the duck, garnish with the crisp skin strips, and serve immediately.

To Finish:
1½ lb (750 g) Chinese leaves (page 14)
2 tablespoons (25 g) cold unsalted butter, cut in pieces
1 teaspoon salt
1 teaspoon freshly ground five-pepper mixture (page 21) or black pepper
⅔ cup (150 ml) peanut oil

WOLFGANG PUCK'S STIR-FRIED CHICKEN WITH GARLIC AND CILANTRO ≈

ONE OF THE BEST PRACTITIONERS OF FUSION COOKING IS UNDOUBTEDLY WOLFGANG PUCK, WHO MADE HIS REPUTATION AS CHEF TO THE STARS OF HOLLYWOOD. WOLFGANG, A TALENTED CLASSICAL EUROPEAN-TRAINED CHEF WORKING IN LOS ANGELES, WAS THE FIRST TO MIX ASIAN INFLUENCES IN HIS WESTERN COOKING. HIS LANDMARK RESTAURANT, CHINOIS, BROKE NEW GROUND BY SERVING FOOD THAT WAS A TRUE MIXTURE OF EAST AND WEST. HIS SUBSEQUENT SUCCESS PROVED THAT THE PUBLIC LOVED THE COMBINATION, ESPECIALLY WHEN COOKED BY THE SKILFUL HANDS OF WOLFGANG PUCK. A DISH THAT I PARTICULARLY ENJOY, AND THAT HAS INSPIRED ME, IS THIS CHICKEN DISH EATEN WITH LETTUCE LEAVES. IT IS FUN TO SERVE AND VERY DELICIOUS.

SERVES 4–6

1 lb (450 g) boneless, skinless chicken thighs
1 tablespoon Shaoxing rice wine (page 22) or dry sherry
1 tablespoon light soy sauce (page 23)
1 teaspoon freshly ground five-pepper mixture (page 21) or black pepper
2 teaspoons sesame oil
2 teaspoons cornstarch

For the Vinaigrette:
3 tablespoons white rice vinegar (page 24) or cider vinegar
2 tablespoons light soy sauce (page 23)
2 tablespoons peanut oil
1 tablespoon sesame oil
1 tablespoon lemon juice
½ teaspoon salt
¼ teaspoon freshly ground black pepper

For the Stir-fry:
8 oz (225 g) red or green peppers
2½ tablespoons peanut oil
3 tablespoons thinly sliced garlic
6 tablespoons finely shredded scallions
3 tablespoons mirin (Japanese sweet rice wine) (page 18) or dry sherry
2 teaspoons sesame oil
3 tablespoons finely chopped cilantro
8 oz (225 g) iceberg lettuce

Cut the chicken into 1 in (2.5 cm) chunks and combine them in a bowl with the rice wine or sherry, soy sauce, pepper, sesame oil, and cornstarch. Let it marinate for 20 minutes.

Make the vinaigrette by combining the vinegar, soy sauce, peanut and sesame oils, lemon juice, salt, and pepper in a small bowl. Mix well and set aside.

Meanwhile, cut the peppers into small dice.

Heat a wok or large frying-pan. Add 1½ tablespoons of the oil, and when it is very hot and slightly smoking, stir-fry the chicken for about 5 minutes. Remove the chicken, drain in a cilantro, and put into a bowl. Wipe the wok or pan clean. Reheat the wok or pan over a high heat and, when it is hot, add the remaining tablespoon of peanut oil. When it is smoking slightly, add the garlic and stir-fry for 30 seconds. Add the peppers and scallions and stir-fry for another minute. Now add the rice wine or sherry and sesame oil and stir-fry for 1 minute; return the chicken to the mixture and continue to stir-fry for 1 minute, mixing well. Add the cilantro and mix well. Turn onto a platter. Gently separate the lettuce leaves and arrange around the platter. Pour the vinaigrette into a small bowl and serve immediately.

Each diner puts some chicken mixture on lettuce leaves, adds the vinaigrette and eats with his or her hands.

MULTI-SPICED BROILED SQUABS ≈

SERVES 4

4 x 12 oz–1 lb (350–450
    g) squabs, quail, or other
    small game birds
2 tablespoons extra virgin
    olive oil

For the Marinade:

1 tablespoon salt
1 teaspoon cayenne pepper
1 teaspoon paprika
2 teaspoons five-spice
    powder (page 17)
1 teaspoon roasted and
    ground Sichuan
    peppercorns (page 21)
1 teaspoon freshly ground
    five-pepper mixture (page
    21) or black pepper
½ teaspoon ground cumin
    powder
1 teaspoon Madras curry
    powder (page 17)

AS A CHILD GROWING UP IN A CHINESE COMMUNITY, I ATTENDED MANY BANQUETS CELEBRATING WEDDINGS AND BIRTHDAYS. A POPULAR DISH WHICH EVERYONE LOOKED FORWARD TO WAS THE CRISPY FRIED PIGEON. SINCE THEN, I HAVE HAD AN ABIDING PASSION FOR PIGEON. I LOVE ITS RICH AND SLIGHTLY GAMEY FLAVOR AND TASTE. ITS ASSERTIVE NATURE MAKES AN IDEAL MARRIAGE WITH EAST–WEST SPICES. THIS EASY-TO-MAKE BUT NEVERTHELESS IMPRESSIVE RECIPE IS PERFECT FOR ANY SPECIAL DINNER PARTY. SOME GOURMET BUTCHER SHOPS CAN SUPPLY SQUABS WHICH ARE YOUNG AND TENDER. YOU CAN, HOWEVER, SUBSTITUTE QUAIL OR OTHER SMALL GAME BIRDS. SERVE WITH PENANG RICE NOODLES (PAGE 217).

First butterfly the birds by slitting them open through the back. Cut out the backbone and flatten them with the palm of your hand. With a small, sharp knife, make a small hole beneath either side of the breast bone and tuck the legs through each of the holes. This will help hold the shape of the birds while they broil.

In a small bowl, mix the marinade ingredients together and rub this mixture evenly on each side of the birds. Allow to marinate for 1 hour.

Pre-heat the oven broiler to high or make a charcoal fire in the barbecue. When the oven broiler is very hot or the charcoal is ash-white, drizzle the olive oil over the squabs and broil them for 8 minutes on each side or until they are cooked. Serve immediately.

STEAMED *FOIE GRAS* IN CHINESE LEAVES ≈

I DISCOVERED THE JOYS OF *FOIE GRAS*, OR FATTENED DUCK LIVERS, IN FRANCE. IT WAS THERE THAT I HAD AN OPPORTUNITY TO COOK THIS HIGHLY PRIZED DELICACY FOR FRENCH FRIENDS. I COULD NOT RESIST APPLYING FLAVORS FROM MY CULINARY HERITAGE. HERE, THEN, IS A GOOD EXAMPLE OF HOW ANCIENT SPICES CAN ADD A NEW TWIST TO A TRADITIONAL EUROPEAN FOOD. STEAMING PRESERVES THE DELICATE AND SUBTLE FLAVORS OF THE *FOIE GRAS*. THIS IS WORTH MAKING, PARTICULARLY FOR A SPECIAL OCCASION, AS A SPECTACULAR APPETIZER.

SERVES 4

- 1 head of Chinese leaves (page 14) or spinach
- 4 pieces of raw *foie gras*, about 3 oz (75 g) each
- 1 teaspoon sea salt
- 1 teaspoon roasted and ground Sichuan peppercorns (page 21)
- 1 tablespoon finely chopped fresh ginger (page 17)
- 2 tablespoons Shaoxing rice wine (page 22) or dry sherry
- 3 tablespoons homemade Chicken Stock (page 32)
- 2 tablespoons (25 g/1 oz) cold unsalted butter, cut in small pieces
- Salt and freshly ground five-pepper mixture (page 21) or white pepper
- 2 teaspoons finely chopped cilantro

Remove four of the largest leaves from the Chinese leaves or spinach and blanch them in boiling water for 1 minute. Drain and allow to cool. Place a slice of *foie gras* on one end of a cabbage or spinach leaf. Sprinkle with sea salt and Sichuan peppercorns. Roll up the leaf, folding in the sides as you go. Repeat until you have four rolls.

Next, set up a steamer or put a rack into a wok or deep pan containing 2 in (5 cm) of water. Bring the water to a boil over high heat. Put the wrapped *foie gras* onto a heatproof plate and then carefully lower it into the steamer or onto the rack. Turn the heat to low and cover the wok or pan tightly. Steam gently for 5 minutes. Remove the *foie gras* from the steamer and discard any liquid on the plate.

While the *foie gras* is steaming, put the ginger in a pan and cook for 1 minute until it is dry; then add the rice wine or sherry and cook over a high heat until all the wine has evaporated. Now add the chicken stock and slowly whisk in the butter, a piece at a time, with salt and pepper to taste. Toss in the cilantro, stir and serve over each wrapped *foie gras*.

FAST, FUSION BARBECUED CHICKEN ≈

3 lb (1.5 kg) chicken thighs
   on the bone
2 teaspoons salt
1 teaspoon freshly ground
   five-pepper mixture
   (page 21) or black pepper

For the Barbecue Sauce:
3 tablespoons hoisin sauce
   (page 22)
1 tablespoon light soy sauce
   (page 23)
2 tablespoons oyster sauce
   (page 22)
2 tablespoons dark soy
   sauce (page 23)
2 tablespoons Shaoxing rice
   wine (page 22) or dry
   sherry
2 tablespoons mirin
   (Japanese sweet rice wine)
   (page 18) or dry sherry
2 teaspoons white rice
   vinegar (page 24)
1½ tablespoons dried thyme
1 tablespoon chili-bean
   sauce (page 22)

BROILING CONTINUES TO BE A POPULAR COOKING TECHNIQUE FOR FUSION CHEFS. NO WONDER: IT IS FAST, EASY AND IT HELPS TO RETAIN FLAVORS. HERE IS A QUICK RECIPE THAT USES THE BEST OF EAST–WEST SEASONINGS TO CREATE A TASTY DISH. IT GOES EXTREMELY WELL WITH THAI-STYLE VEGETARIAN CURRY RICE (PAGE 201).

Place the chicken thighs on a baking pan and evenly sprinkle on the salt and pepper.

In a bowl, mix the sauce ingredients.

Pre-heat the oven broiler to high or make a charcoal fire in the barbecue. When the broiler is very hot or the charcoal is ash-white, broil the chicken thighs on each side for 10 minutes; then baste the thighs on both sides with the sauce and continue to broil for 10 minutes on each side or until they are cooked through. Serve immediately.

VEGETABLES

蔬菜

ⓋTofu with Fragrant Lemon Grass ≈

Serves **4** as a main
course

4 lemon grass stalks
  (page 18)
2 lb (900 g) firm, fresh tofu
  (page 13)
3 tablespoons oil, preferably
  peanut
6 tablespoons finely
  chopped scallions
3 tablespoons finely
  chopped fresh ginger
  (page 17)
2 tablespoons coarsely
  chopped garlic
4 teaspoons Madras curry
  powder (page 17)
2 teaspoons chili powder or
  flakes (page 15)
3 tablespoons Shaoxing
  rice wine (page 22)
  or dry sherry
4 tablespoons dark soy
  sauce (page 23)
½ teaspoon freshly ground
  black pepper
2 teaspoons sugar
4 teaspoons sesame oil
4 tablespoons roasted
  peanuts, coarsely chopped

I first tasted this delightful dish at Le Cheval, a popular Vietnamese restaurant in Oakland, California. Lemon grass is an herb most identified with Thai and Vietnamese cooking, but the Chinese, like me, are eager to adopt whatever new foods and ingredients will enhance their own cuisine; it is a matter of East meeting East.

Lemon grass has a mild but distinctive flavor which goes very nicely with the congenial tofu, imparting a refreshing taste to this vegetarian main-course dish. And, fortunately, lemon grass has become more and more easily available. Serve this dish with rice.

Peel the lemon grass stalks to the tender, whitish centers and crush them with the flat of a knife. Cut them into 3 in (7.5 cm) pieces.

Cut the tofu into 1 in (2.5 cm) cubes. Drain on paper towels for 20 minutes.

Heat a wok or large frying-pan over a high heat until it is hot. Add the oil, and when it is very hot and slightly smoking, add the lemon grass, scallions, ginger, and garlic and stir-fry for 20 seconds. Push the aromatics to the side of the wok, turn the temperature down, add the tofu cubes, and brown slowly on all sides. When the cubes are golden brown, sprinkle with the curry and chili powders, mixing well. Now add the rice wine or sherry, soy sauce, pepper, and sugar. Stir-fry this mixture for 1 minute. Add the sesame oil and turn the mixture gently several times to mix well. Top with the peanuts and serve at once, or allow to cool and reheat when ready to serve.

ⓥTofu in Aromatic Coconut Milk ≈

Soft tofu is like custard, very tender and silky. It thus makes for a light, refreshing style of vegetarian dish. (In most supermarkets, this kind is labeled 'Japanese tofu'.) Braised in coconut milk, it absorbs all the rich flavors of that exotic fruit.

In this recipe, again generously provided by master chefs at the Vietnamese restaurant, Le Cheval, in Oakland, California, the tofu and coconut milk are combined with aromatic spices in a delectable ensemble for a meat-free main course. Rice complements this dish well.

Gently cut the tofu into 1 in (2.5 cm) cubes. Drain on paper towels for at least 30 minutes.

In a medium-sized pan, combine the coconut milk, curry paste, scallions, ginger, rice wine or sherry, soy sauce, salt, pepper, and sugar. Bring the mixture to a simmer. Gently add the tofu and simmer for 15 minutes.

Turn the mixture onto a platter, garnish with cilantro, and serve at once.

Serves 4 as a main course

2 lb (900 g) fresh silky Japanese tofu (page 24)
2 x 14 fl oz (400 ml) cans of coconut milk (page 16)
4 tablespoons red Thai curry paste (page 23)
6 tablespoons finely shredded scallions
3 tablespoons finely shredded fresh ginger (page 17)
3 tablespoons Shaoxing rice wine (page 22) or dry sherry
2 tablespoons light soy sauce (page 23)
2 teaspoons salt
1 teaspoon freshly ground black pepper
2 teaspoons sugar
Sprigs of fresh cilantro, to garnish

Ⓥ CRACKLING RICE-PAPER ASPARAGUS ROLLS ≈

SERVES 4 AS A MAIN
COURSE (MAKES
ABOUT 15 ROLLS)

For the Filling:
1 lb (450 g) asparagus
1 teaspoon salt
½ teaspoon freshly ground
    five-pepper mixture
    (page 21) or black pepper
1½ tablespoons extra virgin
    olive oil
3 tablespoons finely chopped
    fresh chives
2 tablespoons finely chopped
    scallions
1 tablespoon finely chopped
    fresh cilantro
3 tablespoons drained and
    finely chopped sun-dried
    tomatoes in oil

For the Sealing Mixture:
3 tablespoons unbleached
    flour
3 tablespoons water

For the Rolls:
One packet dried rice paper
    rounds (page 22) in 8½in
    (22 cm) rounds
⅔ cup (150 ml) olive oil

ASPARAGUS, NATIVE TO THE MEDITERRANEAN, HAS BEEN CULTIVATED IN THE WEST SINCE ANTIQUITY. NOW WIDELY GROWN THROUGHOUT THE WORLD, IT IS A POPULAR VEGETABLE, PRIZED FOR ITS DELICATE FLAVOR. IN THIS RECIPE, I USE RICE PAPER, WHICH IS MADE FROM RICE FLOUR, WATER, AND SALT. I LOVE ITS ABILITY TO ENVELOP FOOD WITH A CRISP, CRACKLING SKIN WHILE KEEPING THE FOOD MOIST. THE ROLLS ALSO MAKE EXCELLENT APPETIZERS.

Trim the asparagus forming 4 in (10 cm) spears and discard the tough ends.

Blanch the asparagus spears in a large pan of boiling, salted water for 3 minutes. Drain immediately and plunge into cold water to stop the asparagus from cooking. Drain well.

Combine the asparagus with the salt, pepper, olive oil, chives, scallions, cilantro, and sun-dried tomatoes.

Make the flour paste by mixing the flour and water together.

When you are ready to make the rolls, fill a large bowl with warm water. Dip a round of rice paper in the water and let it soften for a few seconds. Remove and drain on a dish towel.

Place three asparagus spears and a little of the tomato–herb mixture in the middle of the rice paper and roll the top and the bottom edges over the asparagus at once. Fold up one side of the rice paper, and continue to roll to the end. Seal the end with a little of the flour-paste mixture. The roll should be compact and tight, rather like a short, thick cigar, about 4 in (10 cm) long. Set the roll on a clean plate and continue the process until you have used up all the asparagus. (The rolls can be made ahead to this point; cover loosely with a clean, dry dish towel and refrigerate for up to 4 hours.)

Heat a wok or large frying-pan over a high heat. Add the oil, and when it is hot and smoking, turn the heat down to medium and pan-fry the rolls, a few at a time, until they are golden brown. If they stick together, do not attempt to break them apart until they have been removed from the oil. Continue frying until you have cooked all the rolls. Drain them on paper towels, slice them in half if you wish, and serve immediately.

Ⓥ FRITTO MISTO OF ASIAN VEGETABLES ≈

SERVES 4–6

8 oz (225 g) lotus root
    (page 18)
8 oz (225 g) taro root
    (page 24)
8 oz (225 g) potatoes
5 cups (1.2 liters) peanut oil
A handful of fresh Italian
    flatleaf parsley
A handful of fresh basil
    leaves
Salt and freshly ground black
    pepper

THE RISE OF FUSION COOKING AROUND THE WORLD HAS LED TO A SURGE IN THE AVAILABILITY OF ASIAN VEGETABLES IN SUPERMARKETS. HERE, I OFFER A CRISP VEGETARIAN SIDE DISH THAT IS ADDICTIVE. *FRITTO MISTO* IS AN ITALIAN CULINARY TERM THAT LITERALLY MEANS 'FRIED MIXTURE' OF ANY FOODS. I COMBINE LOTUS ROOT, A LACY AQUATIC PLANT THAT HAS A CRISP, FIBROUS TEXTURE AND A MILD, DISTINCTIVE FLAVOR SOMEWHAT RELATED TO ARTICHOKES, WITH TARO ROOT, A STARCH THAT WAS USED IN CHINA AND SOUTHEAST ASIA LONG BEFORE RICE AND POTATOES. TARO ROOT TUBERS VARY IN SHAPE, BUT THEY ARE ROUGHLY SPHERICAL, VARYING FROM TENNIS-BALL SIZE TO ABOUT 9 IN (23 CM) DIAMETER, AND OFTEN COVERED WITH A ROUGH SKIN AND BROWNISH HAIRS. THEY ARE STARCHY, WITH A SWEET FLAVOR, DOUGHY TEXTURE AND A WHITISH FLESH, OFTEN WITH PURPLE STREAKS. BOTH LOTUS AND TARO ROOTS CAN BE FOUND AT CHINESE SUPERMARKETS OR GROCERS. THIS IS A PERFECT VEGETARIAN DISH.

Peel the lotus root and cut it crosswize into ⅛ in (3 mm) slices. Do the same with the taro root and potatoes.

Heat a wok or deep frying-pan over a high heat. Add the oil and when it is very hot and slightly smoking, lower the temperature to moderate. Fry half of the vegetables for 5–6 minutes or until they are crisp. Remove them with a slotted spoon and drain on paper towels. Prepare the second batch in the same way.

Quickly fry the parsley and basil leaves; drain on paper towels. Transfer the fried vegetables and herbs to a warm platter, toss with salt and pepper to taste and serve immediately.

⒱ Stir-fried Curried Celery ≈

CELERY IS AN UNDERVALUED VEGETABLE AND DESERVES MORE RESPECT. IT IS
DELICIOUS IN ITS OWN CRUNCHY, MILD, AND UNASSUMING WAY, AND ITS
DISTINCTIVE TASTE MAKES IT AN IDEAL FOIL FOR SPICY FLAVORS.

HERE, IT IS COMBINED WITH CURRY IN A SIMPLE, EASY-TO-MAKE DISH.
YOU WILL SEE THAT THIS HUMBLE VEGETABLE HAS A REAL ROLE TO PLAY.

Trim the base of the celery and all the top leaves. Separate the sticks.
With a small, sharp knife, string any tough sticks. Chop the sticks into
1 in (2.5 cm) sections.

Heat a wok or large frying-pan over a high heat. Add the oil, and
when it is very hot and slightly smoking, add the garlic and ginger
and stir-fry for 10 seconds. Then add the celery and continue to stir-fry
for 1 minute. Add the rice wine or sherry, curry powder, soy sauce,
sugar, and salt and continue to stir-fry for another minute. Then add
the water and continue to cook over a high heat for 3–4 minutes, until
the celery is just tender. Sprinkle the mixture with the scallions and
cilantro, mix well, transfer to a warm platter, and serve immediately.

SERVES 4 AS AN
ACCOMPANIMENT

1 lb (450 g) celery
1 tablespoon peanut oil
2 tablespoons coarsely
chopped garlic
2 teaspoons finely chopped
fresh ginger (page 17)
1 tablespoon Shaoxing rice
wine (page 22) or dry
sherry
2 teaspoons Madras curry
powder (page 17)
1 teaspoon light soy sauce
(page 23)
2 teaspoons sugar
½ teaspoon salt
3 tablespoons water

To Garnish:
2 tablespoons finely
chopped scallions
1 tablespoon finely chopped
cilantro

ⓥTofu Satays ≈

SERVES 2–4 AS A MAIN
COURSE

1 lb (450 g) firm, fresh tofu
(page 13)

For the Marinade:

3 tablespoons light soy sauce
(page 23)
1 tablespoon Shaoxing rice
wine (page 22) or dry sherry
1 tablespoon mirin (Japanese
sweet rice wine) (page 18)
or dry sherry
2 teaspoons sesame oil

For the Peanut Sauce:

3 tablespoons smooth peanut
butter or sesame paste
(page 22)
1 tablespoon chili-bean sauce
(page 22)
1 tablespoon chopped garlic
2 teaspoons chili oil (page 15)
2 tablespoons Chinese white
rice vinegar (page 24) or
cider vinegar
2 tablespoons light soy sauce
(page 23)
½ teaspoon salt
¼ teaspoon freshly ground five-
pepper mixture (page 21)
or black pepper
2 teaspoons sugar
2 tablespoons hot water

To Garnish:

4 oz (100 g) onions, sliced
8 oz (225 g) cucumbers, thinly
sliced

IN THIS RECIPE, FIRM TOFU CUBES ARE MARINATED AND BROILED, THEN SERVED WITH A SAVORY PEANUT SAUCE AND A GARNISH OF RAW ONION SLICES AND CUCUMBER. ROLL THOSE FLAVORS OVER YOUR TONGUE FOR A MOMENT: THEY SOUND DELICIOUS AND THEY ARE.

THIS PARTICULAR RECIPE IS REALLY AN EAST–WEST COMBINATION, INSPIRED BY A WONDERFUL VEGETARIAN RESTAURANT CALLED GREENS IN SAN FRANCISCO. WHEN PREPARED BY MASTER CHEFS, TOFU NICELY ILLUSTRATES ITS VERSATILITY AND ITS ABILITY TO ABSORB FLAVORS, BECOMING TRANSFORMED FROM BLAND MEEKNESS INTO AN ASSERTIVE, FLAVORFUL FOOD. TOFU READILY ACCEPTS THE CHARACTER OF A MARINADE AND STANDS UP BEAUTIFULLY TO THE BROILING PROCESS. EXPERIMENT WITH MARINADES OF YOUR OWN.

ALWAYS BUY THE FRESHEST TOFU; FOR THIS RECIPE YOU WILL NEED THE FIRM VARIETY BECAUSE SOFT TOFU IS NOT SUITABLE FOR SKEWERING. YOU CAN ADD OTHER VEGETABLES, SUCH AS SMALL TOMATOES, PEPPERS, AND ONIONS TO MAKE 'SHISH KEBABS'. AS WELL AS A MAIN COURSE, THIS CAN BE USED AS AN EXCELLENT SIDE DISH OR AN APPETIZER, .

Place the tofu between several layers of paper towels with a weight such as a heavy plate on top. Leave for 1 hour.

Mix all the marinade ingredients in a small bowl. Cut the tofu into 2 in (5 cm) cubes and add to the marinade. Let the cubes soak for 45 minutes.

Put all the ingredients for the peanut sauce in a blender and mix well. Transfer to a serving bowl.

Meanwhile, soak some wooden skewers in water for 30 minutes.

Pre-heat the oven broiler or prepare the barbecue. Thread the tofu cubes on the skewers, being careful not to put more than three or four on each. When the broiler is very hot or the charcoal is ash-white, cook the tofu cubes, basting once with the marinade. When one side is brown, turn them over, baste again, and cook until they are hot all through and quite firm.

Arrange the tofu skewers on a platter. Garnish with onion and cucumber slices and serve tofu with the peanut sauce.

ⓥAsparagus and Coconut Quiche ≈

SERVES 4–6 AS A MAIN
COURSE

For the Pastry:

1 ¼ cups (150 g) all-purpose
  flour
4 tablespoons (50 g) butter
½ teaspoon salt
2 tablespoons cold water
2 tablespoons light cream

For the Filling:

1 ½ cups (350 ml) light
  cream
6 tablespoons canned
  coconut milk (page 16)
1 tablespoon finely chopped
  fresh ginger (page 17)
6 oz (250 g) fresh
  asparagus, trimmed
3 eggs, beaten
1 teaspoon salt
¼ teaspoon freshly ground
  five-pepper mixture
  (page 21) or black pepper
A pinch of sugar
2 tablespoons finely
  chopped scallions
2 tablespoons finely
  chopped fresh chives
3 tablespoons grateded
  coconut

THIS VEGETARIAN QUICHE, A WESTERN DISH, IS ENHANCED WITH EASTERN SEASONING AND SPICES. A LIGHT TASTY DISH, IT MAKES A PERFECT LUNCHEON MAIN COURSE, SERVED WITH A SALAD, OR IT CAN EASILY BE A LOVELY APPETIZER FOR AN ELEGANT MEAL.

Combine all the pastry ingredients in a mixing bowl or a food processor in the usual way. Roll the dough into a ball on a lightly floured board. Cover with plastic wrap and refrigerate for 30 minutes.

Pre-heat the oven to 350°F/180°C.

Roll out the pastry to ⅛ in (3 mm) thick and press the pastry into a greased 8 in (20 cm) tart pan. Place a sheet of foil over the surface of the pastry and put about 12 oz (350 g) of dried beans on the foil to weigh it down. Bake the pastry for 12 minutes. Remove the beans and foil. Lightly pierce the pastry surface with a fork. Return the pastry to the oven and bake for 10 minutes. Remove and allow to cool thoroughly.

Pour the cream and coconut milk into a small pan, add the ginger, and simmer for about 15 minutes over a very low heat. Strain through a fine sieve; discard the ginger and allow the infused cream and coconut milk to cool.

Cut the asparagus at a slight diagonal into 3 in (7.5 cm) pieces.

Heat the oven to 400°F/200°C.

Arrange the asparagus evenly on the cooked pastry. Combine the infused cream and coconut milk with the eggs, salt, pepper, sugar, scallions, chives, and grated coconut. Pour this mixture on top of the asparagus in the pastry shell.

Bake the quiche for 25 minutes or until the egg has set. Serve warm or at room temperature.

ⓥ Stir-fried Rainbow Vegetables ≈

Whoever said vegetarian food has to be dreary and boring was manifesting a lack of imagination and a deficiency in the art of cooking. For example, here is a delicious vegetarian treat, appealing to the eye as well as the palate.

The various colorful vegetables constitute the 'rainbow,' and they are stir-fried and served with crisp lettuce and hoisin sauce to create an unusual combination of tastes and textures. I use ready-made pressed, seasoned tofu as a tasty meat substitute.

This dish makes a light snack or a good finger-food appetizer for a dinner party or any festive occasion. The rainbow vegetable mixture and lettuce leaves are served on individual platters and the hoisin sauce in a small bowl. Each guest puts a helping of each ingredient into a hollow lettuce leaf, rather like stuffing a pancake or a taco, and eats the filled leaf with the fingers. As an optional extra, you can deep-fry bean thread noodles and to serve on top of the rainbow vegetables.

Soak the dried mushrooms in warm water for 20 minutes; drain them and squeeze out any excess liquid. Trim off the stems and shred the caps into 2 in (5 cm) long strips. Peel the carrots and cut into 2 in (5 cm) fine shreds. Cut the bamboo shoots, zucchini, and pepper into 2 in (5 cm) fine shreds also. Finely shred the celery heart and pressed tofu. Separate and wash the lettuce leaves, spin them dry in a salad-spinner, and set aside in the refrigerator.

Heat a wok or large frying-pan over a high heat. Add the oil, and when it is very hot and slightly smoking, add the garlic, shallots, and scallions and stir-fry for 20 seconds. Then add the carrots and stir-fry for another minute. Now add the remaining vegetables (except the lettuce), the soy sauce, rice wine or sherry, oyster sauce, salt, and pepper and stir-fry the mixture for 3 minutes.

Turn onto a platter. Arrange the lettuce leaves on a separate platter, the hoisin sauce into a small bowl, and the bean thread noodles, if using, in another bowl and serve immediately.

SERVES 4–6 AS A SNACK OR APPETIZER

½ oz (15 g) dried Chinese black mushrooms (page 18)
4 oz (100 g) carrots
4 oz (100 g) canned bamboo shoots
4 oz (100 g) zucchini
4 oz (100 g) red or green pepper (about 1)
4 oz (100 g) celery hearts
4 oz (100 g) pressed, seasoned tofu (page 13)
8 oz (225 g) iceberg lettuce
1½ tablespoons oil, preferably peanut
1 tablespoon chopped garlic
3 tablespoons finely chopped shallots
3 tablespoons finely chopped scallions
2 teaspoons light soy sauce (page 23)
2 teaspoons Shaoxing rice wine (page 22) or dry sherry
3 tablespoons vegetarian oyster-flavored sauce (page 22) or dark soy sauce (page 23)
½ teaspoon salt
¼ teaspoon freshly ground five-pepper mixture (page 21) or black pepper
4 tablespoons hoisin sauce (page 23), to serve
1 oz (25 g) bean thread (transparent) noodles (page 19), deep-fried, to serve (optional)

ⓋBROILED VEGETARIAN SANDWICH ≈

4 oz (100 g) cauliflower

4 oz (100 g) zucchini

4 oz (100 g) carrots

4 oz (100 g) eggplant

2 oz (50 g) French beans or small green beans

1 large onion

4 oz (100 g) small button mushrooms

Extra virgin olive oil or Tomato-flavored Olive Oil (page 40), to serve

4 French bread rolls or chunks of baguette, slit open, to serve

For the Marinade:

1 teaspoon salt

½ teaspoon freshly ground five-pepper mixture (page 21) or black pepper

2 tablespoons light soy sauce (page 23)

2 teaspoons sesame oil

1 tablespoon extra virgin olive oil

1 tablespoon sugar

1 teaspoon chili powder (page 15)

THIS UNUSUAL TREAT — A PLEASANT SURPRISE TO THE PALATE FOR THOSE WHO THINK A SANDWICH *MUST* CONTAIN MEAT — WAS INSPIRED BY A SANDWICH I ENJOYED AT HONG KONG'S JOYCE CAFÉ. IT IS A TRENDY CAFÉ FAMOUS FOR ITS GOOD FOOD, WITH MANY OF THE MENU ITEMS BEING VEGETARIAN. THIS IS AMONG THE MOST POPULAR CHOICES.

THE STYLE IS A MIXTURE OF EASTERN AND WESTERN IDEAS, INCORPORATING CHINESE FLAVORS INTO WESTERN COOKING TECHNIQUES. HAVE THIS SANDWICH WITH SOUP FOR A COMPLETE AND SATISFYING LUNCH.

Cut the cauliflower into small florets about 1½ in (3.5 cm) wide. Cut the zucchini, carrots, and eggplant diagonally into thin 4 in (10 cm) slices. Cut the beans into 4 in (10 cm) pieces and slice the onion.

Blanch the cauliflower, carrots, and beans in a large pan of salted water for 3 minutes. Remove with a slotted spoon, plunge into cold water, and drain thoroughly.

Combine the marinade ingredients in a bowl; add the blanched vegetables with the rest of the vegetables and mix well. Marinate for 30 minutes.

Soak some bamboo skewers in cold water for 30 minutes. Preheat the oven broiler to high or make a charcoal fire in the barbecue. Thread the vegetables on the skewers, alternating the different sorts. When the broiler is very hot or the charcoal is ash-white, cook the vegetables until they are tender and cooked through.

Drizzle olive oil or tomato-flavored olive oil on the bread, top with the broiled vegetables and serve.

STIR-FRIED CUCUMBERS AND ZUCCHINI ≈

I OFTEN SPEND MY SUMMERS IN CATUS, FRANCE. WHILE I'M THERE, I MAKE SURE I VISIT MY FRIEND, ALAIN GASTAL. HIS MOTHER HAS A MAGNIFICENT GARDEN AND SHE USUALLY OFFERS ME SOME OF HER SUMMER HARVEST OF CUCUMBERS AND ZUCCHINI. ON ONE EVENING, I HAD INVITED FRIENDS FOR DINNER, AND WHEN MME GASTAL'S BOUNTY ARRIVED, I QUICKLY PUT TOGETHER THIS SIMPLE STIR-FRIED DISH, COMBINING THE TWO VEGETABLES IN AN UNUSUALLY DELECTABLE WAY. SALTING BOTH VEGETABLES BEFORE COOKING DRAWS OUT EXCESS LIQUID AND GIVES THEM A FIRM, SLIGHTLY CRUNCHY TEXTURE THAT GOES WELL WITH THE SPICES I HAVE USED HERE.

Peel the cucumbers, slice them in half lengthwize, and using a teaspoon, remove the seeds. Then cut the cucumber halves and zucchini into 1 in (2.5 cm) cubes. Sprinkle them with 2 teaspoons of salt and mix well. Put the mixture into a colander and let it sit for 20 minutes, to drain.

When the cucumber and zucchini cubes have drained, rinse them in water and then blot them dry with paper towels.

Heat a wok or large frying-pan over a high heat. Add the oil, and when it is very hot and slightly smoking, add the garlic, ginger, the remaining salt, and the pepper and stir-fry for about 20 seconds. Then add the cucumbers and zucchini and continue to stir-fry over a high heat for 5 minutes or until the vegetables are cooked. Stir in the chili-bean sauce, oyster or soy sauce, and sugar and continue to cook for 2 minutes. Then add the sesame oil and serve immediately.

SERVES 4 AS AN ACCOMPANIMENT

- 1½ lb (750 g) cucumbers (about 1½)
- 1 lb (450 g) zucchini
- 3 teaspoons salt
- 1½ tablespoons oil, preferably peanut
- 3 tablespoons coarsely chopped garlic
- 1 tablespoon finely chopped fresh ginger (page 17)
- ½ teaspoon freshly ground five-pepper mixture (page 21) or black pepper
- 2 teaspoons chili-bean sauce (page 22)
- 2 tablespoons vegetarian oyster-flavored sauce (page 23) or dark soy sauce (page 23)
- 2 teaspoons sugar
- 2 teaspoons sesame oil

ⓥFIRECRACKER CORN ≈

10 oz (275 g) fresh corn
  kernels (cut from about 2
  cobs), or frozen corn
  kernels
1 tablespoon oil, preferably
  peanut
2 small, mild fresh red chilies
  (page 16), seeded and
  finely chopped
½ teaspoon salt
¼ teaspoon freshly ground
  five-pepper mixture (page
  21) or black pepper
1 teaspoon sugar
2 teaspoons Shaoxing rice
  wine (page 22) or dry
  sherry
1 teaspoon sesame oil

ONE OF THE TRENDIEST RESTAURANTS IN SAN FRANCISCO IS BETELNUT, AN ASIAN BEER-HOUSE RESTAURANT WITH A VERY TEMPTING AND SATISFYING MENU. A PARTICULAR VEGETARIAN SIDE DISH I VERY MUCH ENJOYED AT BETELNUT IS THIS ONE. IT USES FRESH CORN, WHICH RELATIVELY NEW TO CHINESE CUISINE HAVING BEEN INTRODUCED ABOUT 300 YEARS AGO. THE DISH IS SIMILAR TO, BUT NOT AS EXPLOSIVE AS, A STIR-FRIED CORN DISH I HAD YEARS AGO IN SICHUAN, CHINA. EASY TO MAKE, IT NEEDS THE FRESHEST, SWEETEST CORN.

Cut the kernels off fresh corn cob. Blanch frozen corn for 10 seconds in boiling water and drain.

Heat a wok or large frying-pan over a high heat until it is hot. Add the oil, and when it is very hot and slightly smoking, add the corn, chilies, salt, and pepper and stir-fry for 1 minute. Then add the sugar and rice wine or sherry and continue to stir-fry for 2 minutes. Finally, stir in the sesame oil, mix well, and serve immediately.

ⓥSPICY ORANGE-FLAVORED TOFU ≈

Le Cheval is a deservedly popular Vietnamese speciality restaurant in Oakland, California, but, as its name suggests, it also reflects a French *esprit de finesse* along with its native culinary inventiveness. It offers a wide variety of luscious and satisfying tofu dishes.

This spicy, orange-flavored tofu is among the most delectable on the menu, with an East–West fusion touch. The tofu is lightly pan-fried in a little oil and then finished off with aromatic fresh orange zest, onions, and rice wine, with dried chilies adding their own pleasant bite.

Cut the tofu into 1 in (2.5 cm) cubes. Drain on paper towels for 20 minutes.

Heat a wok or large frying-pan over a high heat. Add the oil, and when it is very hot and slightly smoking, add the dried chilies and stir-fry for 20 seconds. Push the chilies to the side of the wok or pan, turn the temperature down, add the tofu cubes, and brown them slowly on all sides. When the cubes are golden brown, remove the tofu and chilies and drain on paper towels. Add the onions, orange zest, and garlic to the wok or pan and stir-fry for 3 minutes, until the onions are wilted. Now add the rice wine or sherry, soy sauce, pepper, and sugar. Return the browned tofu cubes to the wok or pan and stir-fry for 3 minutes. Add the sesame oil and turn the mixture gently several times to mix well. Serve immediately or allow to cool and reheat when ready to serve.

Serves 4 as a main course

- 2 lb (900 g) firm, fresh tofu (page 13)
- 3 tablespoons oil, preferably peanut
- 10 dried red chilies (page 15), halved
- 1 lb (450 g) onions, coarsely sliced
- 4 tablespoons grated orange zest
- 2 tablespoons coarsely chopped garlic
- 4 tablespoons Shaoxing rice wine (page 22) or dry sherry
- 4 tablespoons dark soy sauce (page 23)
- ½ teaspoon freshly ground five-pepper mixture (page 21) or black pepper
- 2 teaspoons sugar
- 4 teaspoons sesame oil

ⓥ Braised Fusion Mushrooms with Herbs ≈

SERVES 2–4 AS A MAIN
COURSE

2 oz (50 g) dried Chinese
black mushrooms (page 18)

2 oz (50 g) dried morel
mushrooms

2 lb (900 g) button mushrooms

3 tablespoons extra virgin
olive oil

4 tablespoons coarsely
chopped garlic

2 teaspoons salt

1 teaspoon freshly ground five-
pepper mixture (page 21)
or black pepper

4 tablespoons Shaoxing rice
wine (page 22) or dry sherry

4 teaspoons light soy sauce
(page 23)

2 teaspoons sugar

3 tablespoons (50 ml) heavy
cream

To Garnish:

2 tablespoons finely chopped
fresh chives

2 tablespoons finely chopped
scallions

MUSHROOMS CAN TURN A SIMPLE VEGETARIAN DISH INTO A LOVELY,
SATISFYING MAIN COURSE. IN THIS EASY RECIPE, I COMBINE DRIED CHINESE
MUSHROOMS, WHICH HAVE A RICH, SMOKY FLAVOR, WITH BUTTON
MUSHROOMS AND DRIED MOREL MUSHROOMS IN A MUSHROOM STEW.

Soak the dried Chinese and morel mushrooms in two separate bowls
of warm water for 20 minutes. Then drain the Chinese mushrooms
and squeeze out the excess liquid. Strain this mushroom liquid and
reserve. Remove and discard the mushroom stems and cut the caps in
half. Rinse the morel mushrooms, to remove any sand. Slice the button
mushrooms.

Heat a wok or large frying-pan over a high heat until it is
moderately hot. Add the olive oil and immediately add the garlic and
stir-fry for 15 seconds. Then add the salt and pepper and all the
mushrooms with the mushroom liquid and stir-fry them for 2 minutes.
Add the rice wine or sherry, soy sauce, and sugar and continue stir-
frying for 5 minutes or until the mushroom liquid has been reabsorbed
by the mushrooms or evaporated. Finally, add the cream and cook for
2 minutes. Give the mushrooms a few stirs, turn onto a warm platter,
sprinkle with chives and scallions and serve immediately.

ⓥMASHED POTATOES WITH CUCUMBER ≈

SERVES 4–6 AS AN
ACCOMPANIMENT

3 lb (1.5 kg) cucumbers
2 tablespoons salt
2 lb (900 g) potatoes
1 cup (250 ml) heavy cream
10 tablespoons (150 g)
    softened butter
1 tablespoon finely chopped
    fresh cilantro
Freshly ground five-pepper
    mixture (page 21) and salt

THIS AMBROSIAL VARIATION ON HUMBLE MASHED POTATOES IS EASY TO MAKE
AND WILL SURELY SURPRISE YOUR DINNER GUESTS AND FAMILY. THE
CUCUMBERS LIGHTEN THE POTATOES, AS WELL AS GIVING THE DISH AN
UNUSUAL TEXTURE.

Peel the cucumbers, slice them in half lengthwize, and using a
teaspoon, remove the seeds. Then cut the cucumber halves into slices.
Sprinkle them with the salt and mix well. Put the mixture in a colander
and leave for 45 minutes to drain. This rids the cucumber slices of any
excess liquid.

When the cucumber slices have drained, rinse them in water to
remove the salt and drain well. Purée in a blender or food processor.
Then squeeze any excess moisture from the puréed cucumbers with a
clean dish towel. Set aside.

Cook the potatoes, unpeeled, in salted water for 20 minutes, or
until tender.

When the potatoes are cool enough, peel them and pass them
through a ricer or food mill. Reheat them in a large, heavy pan. Bring
the cream to a simmer in a saucepan and whisk it into the potatoes.
Incorporate the butter and cilantro, mixing well. Add salt and pepper
to taste and set aside.

Just before serving, reheat the mashed potatoes, fold the cucumber
purée into it, and serve immediately.

BROILED CORN WITH SCALLIONS AND GINGER BUTTER ≈

CORN IS PERHAPS ONE OF NORTH AMERICA'S GREATEST CONTRIBUTIONS TO THE WORLD OF FOOD. IT IS ESPECIALLY GOOD WHEN QUICKLY BROILED AND SERVED WITH BUTTER. IN THIS RECIPE, I OFFER AN ALTERNATIVE TO PLAIN BUTTER, SPICING IT WITH ASIAN FLAVORS FOR AN EASY, VEGETARIAN DISH.

In a bowl, mix the butter, scallions, ginger, salt, and Sichuan peppercorns together using a wooden spoon. Put the mixture in the refrigerator.

Pre-heat the oven broiler to high or make a charcoal fire in the barbecue. Leaving the husks on, soak the ears of corn for 10 minutes in cold water: the corn cobs will steam in their husks while under the broiler. When the broiler is very hot or the charcoal is ash-white, broil the cobs for 15 minutes. Remove, and when they are cool enough to handle, pull off the husks and spread the cobs with the butter. Serve immediately.

SERVES 4 AS AN ACCOMPANIMENT

6 tablespoons (75 g) unsalted butter, softened at room temperature
5 tablespoons finely chopped scallions
1 tablespoon finely chopped fresh ginger (page 17)
2 teaspoons salt
1 teaspoon roasted and ground Sichuan peppercorns (page 21)
3 lb (1.5 kg) fresh corn cobs, husks left on

ⓥ Malaysian-inspired Vegetable Pancakes ≈

SERVES 2 AS A MAIN
COURSE (MAKES 5–6
PANCAKES)

4 oz (100 g) button
   mushrooms, thinly sliced
6 oz (175 g) spinach,
   washed, stems removed
2 tablespoons chopped fresh
   cilantro
3 tablespoons chopped fresh
   basil
6 oz (175 g) onions, thinly
   sliced
6 oz (175 g) zucchini, thinly
   sliced
1 tablespoon finely chopped
   fresh ginger (page 17)
3–4 tablespoons peanut oil,
   for frying
Salt, to serve

For the Batter:
2 ¾ cups (300 g) all-purpose
   flour
1 teaspoon baking powder
2 teaspoons salt
1 teaspoon paprika
½ teaspoon freshly ground
   five-pepper mixture
   (page 21) or black pepper
3 cups (750 ml) ice-cold
   water
2 egg yolks

THIS RECIPE WAS INSPIRED BY THE WELL-KNOWN OYSTER OMELETTE FROM SINGAPORE AND MALAYSIA, WHICH IS MADE WITH SWEET POTATO FLOUR. HOWEVER, INSTEAD OF USING OYSTERS, I USE FRESH VEGETABLES WHICH ARE PAN-FRIED AND HAVE A SLIGHTLY CHEWY TEXTURE THAT IS A TREAT. THIS DISH MAKES A WONDERFUL ACCOMPANIMENT TO ANY MEAT OR CAN BE A SUBSTANTIAL VEGETARIAN MAIN COURSE.

To make the batter, combine the flour, baking powder, salt, paprika, and pepper and add the water. Stir, without mixing thoroughly. Then add the egg yolks and stir gently, again without mixing thoroughly. The batter will be slightly lumpy. Add the vegetables and ginger and stir to mix.

Heat a non-stick wok or large non-stick frying-pan. Add a tablespoon of oil, and when it is hot, add some of the batter-vegetable mixture, tilting the pan so that the pancake becomes very thin. Cook for 1–2 minutes until it is brown and crisp. Turn the pancake over and cook the other side. Remove to a warm platter. Cook the remaining mixture in the same manner.

Sprinkle with salt to taste and serve immediately.

ⓋStir-fried Spicy Lemon Grass Vegetables ≈

SERVES 4 AS A MAIN
COURSE

1 lb (450 g) fresh broccoli

8 oz (225 g) carrots

8 oz (225 g) celery

2 lemon grass stalks (page 18)

1½ tablespoons peanut oil

4 oz (100 g) shallots, finely sliced

2 tablespoons coarsely chopped garlic

1 teaspoon salt

½ teaspoon freshly ground black pepper

2 tablespoons Shaoxing rice wine (page 22) or dry sherry

1 tablespoon chili-bean sauce (page 22)

1 teaspoon sugar

4–5 tablespoons water

2 tablespoons lime juice

2 teaspoons light soy sauce (page 23)

⅔ cup (150 ml) canned coconut milk (page 16)

THIS IS A THAI-INSPIRED VEGETARIAN DISH THAT IS A PERFECT ACCOMPANIMENT TO ANY MEAL OR THAT CAN SERVE AS A SATISFYING MAIN COURSE ON ITS OWN. IT IS AN EASY-TO-MAKE DISH THAT IS DELICIOUSLY AROMATIC.

Separate the broccoli heads into small florets and peel and slice the stems. Blanch the broccoli pieces in a large pan of salted, boiling water for several minutes; remove them with a slotted spoon and immerse them in cold water. Drain thoroughly. Peel and diagonally slice the carrots into 2 in (5 cm) pieces; blanch them in the same salted water as the broccoli and drain well. Cut the celery at a slight diagonal into 2 in (5 cm) pieces.

Peel the lemon grass stalks to the tender, whitish centers and slice the centers thinly into round pieces.

Heat a wok or large frying-pan over a high heat. Add the oil, and when it is very hot and slightly smoking, add the lemon grass, shallots, garlic, salt, and pepper and stir-fry for 1 minute. Then add the broccoli, carrots, and celery and continue to stir-fry for 2 minutes. Add the rice wine or sherry, chili-bean sauce, and sugar. Stir-fry for a few seconds and then add the water, lime juice, soy sauce, and coconut milk. Stir-fry at a moderate to high heat for 4 minutes, until the vegetables are tender and cooked. The vegetables are now ready to be served.

Ginger-leek Purée ≈

Growing up in a Chinese household, I only knew vegetables that were stir-fried or braised whole. Not until I lived in France did I discover the joys of puréed vegetables. I became particularly fond of leek purée; in this recipe, I enhance it with a touch of fresh ginger. Easy to make, it goes extremely well as a side dish with roast or broiled fish, poultry, or meat.

Trim the leeks and discard any yellow parts. Cut the leeks at the point where they begin to turn green and discard the green parts. Then split the white parts in half and cut them at a slight diagonal into 2½ in (6 cm) segments. Wash them well in cold water until there is no trace of dirt.

In a large pan, combine the leeks with the stock, ginger, salt, and pepper and simmer for 15 minutes or until they are very tender. Allow the mixture to cool slightly, and when it is cool enough, purée in a blender or food processor.

Return the purée to the clean pan, add the butter, and simmer for 3 minutes; then add the cream. Bring the mixture to a simmer again; it is now ready to be served.

2¼ lb (1 kg) leeks
2 cups (475 ml) Homemade Vegetable (page 33) or Chicken (page 32) Stock
2 tablespoons finely chopped fresh ginger (page 17)
2 teaspoons salt
1 teaspoon freshly ground five-pepper mixture (page 21) or black pepper
2 tablespoons (25 g) butter
3 tablespoons heavy cream

ⓥ Braised Eggplant with Mushrooms in Ginger Tomato Sauce ≈

SERVES 2–4 AS AN
ACCOMPANIMENT

½ oz (15 g) dried Chinese
black mushrooms (page 18)

For the Sauce:
8 oz (225 g) tomatoes,
peeled and seeded if
fresh, drained if canned
2 tablespoons extra virgin
olive oil
1½ tablespoons finely
chopped fresh ginger
(page 17)
1 teaspoon salt
Freshly ground five-pepper
mixture (page 21) or black
pepper
2 teaspoons sugar

For the Eggplant:
1 lb (450 g) Chinese or
ordinary eggplant
(page 13)
6 tablespoons (75 ml) extra
virgin olive oil
5 garlic cloves, crushed
1 teaspoon five-spice
powder (page 17)
2 teaspoons salt
½ teaspoon freshly ground
black pepper
⅔ cup (150 ml) water

THIS APPEALING RECIPE IS THE INSPIRATION OF CHEF TAM AT THE CHINA HOUSE AT THE ORIENTAL HOTEL IN BANGKOK; EVERY YEAR HIS WONDERFUL RESTAURANT OFFERS THE THAIS A TWO-WEEK CELEBRATION OF VEGETARIAN MENUS. HE CREATED THIS SAVORY TREAT BY COMBINING EGGPLANT WITH MEATY MUSHROOMS; THESE ARE THEN COOKED IN A SPICY GINGER TOMATO SAUCE – A FUSION DISH, IF EVER I SAW ONE. IT REHEATS WELL, MAKING IT IDEAL FOR PREPARING WELL IN ADVANCE.

I HAVE NOTED IN OTHER RECIPES THAT THE SMALLER, LONG, THIN CHINESE EGGPLANT ARE PREFERABLE TO THE THICKER EUROPEAN VARIETY BECAUSE OF THEIR SLIGHTLY SWEETER, MILDER TASTE. HOWEVER, YOU CAN USE THE STANDARD TYPE, IF NECESSARY. LEAVE THE PEELING ON THE EGGPLANT. SOME PEOPLE MAY FIND THE GOING A BIT CHEWY BUT THE SKIN IS NECESSARY TO ENHANCE THE TEXTURE OF THE DISH.

Soak the mushrooms in warm water for 20 minutes. Then drain them and squeeze out the excess liquid. Remove and discard the stems and finely shred the caps into thin strips.

If you are using fresh tomatoes, cut them into 1 in (2.5 cm) chunks. If you are using canned tomatoes, chop them into small chunks. Heat a clean wok or large frying-pan over a moderate heat, and when it is hot, add the olive oil, ginger, salt, and pepper and cook the ginger for 1 minute or until it is lightly browned. Add the tomatoes and sugar, reduce the heat, and simmer for 15 minutes. Remove from the heat and set the tomato sauce aside.

Cut the eggplants into 2 in x ½ in (5 cm x 1 cm) diagonal slices.

Heat a wok or large frying-pan over a high heat. Add the oil, and when it is moderately hot, add the garlic and stir-fry for 30 seconds. Then add the eggplant slices, five-spice powder, salt, and pepper and continue to stir-fry for 2 minutes.

Add the tomato sauce, mushrooms, and water to the eggplant and continue to cook for 5 minutes. Turn the heat to low, cover, and cook slowly for 15 minutes, until the eggplant is quite tender.

Serve immediately, or allow to cool and serve at room temperature.

℣ STIR-FRIED CAULIFLOWER WITH CILANTRO ≈

CAULIFLOWER, THAT SATISFYING VEGETABLE, IS NOT ONLY EASY TO PREPARE BUT IS ADAPTABLE TO ALMOST ANY SEASONING. HERE, I SIMPLY STIR-FRY IT WITH OLIVE OIL AND FINISH IT WITH A SHOWER OF FRESH CILANTRO.

Cut the cauliflower into small florets about 1½ in (4 cm) wide.

Heat a wok or large frying-pan over a high heat. Add the olive oil, and when it is hot and smoking, add the garlic and stir-fry for about 20 seconds to flavor the oil. Quickly add the cauliflower florets and stir-fry them for a few seconds. Next, add the ground coriander, salt, pepper, lemon zest, and stock or water. Turn the heat down and simmer for 10 minutes or until the cauliflower is tender.

Stir in the fresh cilantro, turn onto a warm serving platter, and serve immediately, drizzled with curry-flavored oil, if you wish.

SERVES 4 AS AN ACCOMPANIMENT

1½ lb (750 g) cauliflower
2 tablespoons extra virgin olive oil
4 garlic cloves, thinly sliced
1 teaspoon ground coriander
1 teaspoon salt
½ teaspoon freshly ground five-pepper mixture (page 21) or black pepper
2 teaspoons finely chopped lemon zest
⅔ cup (150 ml) Home-made Vegetable (page 33) or Chicken (page 32) Stock or water
3 tablespoons finely chopped fresh cilantro
Curry-flavored Oil (page 38), to serve (optional)

Ⓥ Corn Crêpes ≈

Serves 4–6 as an
accompaniment
(makes 10–12 crêpes)

2 lb (900 g) ears of fresh
corn or 1¼ lb (550 g)
frozen corn kernels
2 eggs, beaten
2 tablespoons rice flour
1 tablespoon finely chopped
fresh cilantro
1 tablespoon finely chopped
fresh chives
1 tablespoon finely chopped
scallion
1 teaspoon sugar
2 teaspoons finely chopped
fresh ginger (page 17)
1 teaspoon salt
¼ teaspoon freshly ground
five-pepper mixture
(page 21) or black pepper
2 tablespoons olive oil

Corn, one of the numerous vegetables introduced relatively recently into Asia, is now an extremely popular ingredient of the area's cuisine. Fusion chefs use it extensively and no wonder, it is a delicious food. This recipe makes makes an excellent appetizer but is just as good served as a side dish with any broiled food.

Cut the kernels from the ears of corn with a sharp knife or cleaver, if using fresh corn. You should end up with about 1¼ lb (550 g). If you are using frozen corn, thaw thoroughly. Set aside half the corn in a separate bowl. Combine the rest of the corn with the eggs, rice flour, cilantro, chives, scallion, sugar, ginger, salt, and pepper. Purée the mixture in a blender or food processor, then fold in the reserved corn.

Heat a frying-pan, preferably non-stick; add the olive oil, and when it is hot, spoon in 2 tablespoons of the mixture to make a crêpe, tilting the pan in the usual way. Cook the crêpe over a medium heat for 2–3 minutes or until golden brown on one side. Using a knife or spatula, turn the crêpe over and cook the other side until crisp and golden. Put on a warm platter and keep warm in a very low oven. Continue until you have used up all the mixture. Serve the crêpes as soon as possible.

VEGETABLES

Vegetable Salad with Curry-soy Vinaigrette ≈

This is a warm, delightful vegetarian salad with a bold dressing. Although the idea is French-inspired, the flavors are exotically Asian and very enticing.

Make the curry-soy vinaigrette by combining the mustard, curry powder, soy sauce, salt, pepper, and olive oil. Mix well and set aside.

Bring a pan of salted water to a boil. Drop in the tomatoes for 5 seconds, then remove, peel, and seed them. Cut the tomatoes into 1½ in (4 cm) pieces and set aside. Now add the broccoli, French beans, and cauliflower to the pan and cook for 3 minutes; then add the peas and cook for 1 minute. Drain the vegetables well, turn into a warm bowl and then add the water chestnuts and tomatoes. Drizzle in the curry-soy vinaigrette and add the shallots and chives. Mix well and serve immediately.

Serves 4 as an accompaniment

For the Curry-soy Vinaigrette:
2 teaspoons Dijon mustard
2 teaspoons Madras curry powder (page 17)
2 tablespoons light soy sauce (page 23)
2 teaspoons salt
1 teaspoon freshly ground five-pepper mixture (page 21) or black pepper
4 tablespoons extra virgin olive oil

For the Salad:
8 oz (225 g) fresh tomatoes
4 oz (100 g) broccoli, cut in small florets
4 oz (100 g) French beans
4 oz (100 g) cauliflower, cut in small florets
4 oz (100 g) podded fresh peas or frozen peas
2 oz (50 g) fresh water chestnuts (page 24), peeled and sliced
3 tablespoons finely chopped shallots, squeezed dry
3 tablespoons finely chopped fresh chives

ⓥ Ginger Vegetable Stew with a Herb Glaze ≈

Vegetables are as delicious as meat, especially when they are cooked with savory ginger. In this dish, I use all the available spring vegetables and combine them in a stew finished with fresh, earthy herbs. The resulting fusion of flavors makes this tasty recipe a meal in itself. The tomatoes must be fresh and ripe.

Serves 4 as a main course

4 oz (100 g) red pepper

4 scallions

2 tablespoons extra virgin olive oil

3 tablespoons finely chopped fresh ginger (page 17)

3 tablespoons finely chopped shallots

2 tablespoons chopped garlic

2 teaspoons salt

½ teaspoon freshly ground five-pepper mixture (page 21) or black pepper

1 cup (250 ml) Home-made Vegetable Stock (page 33)

3 sprigs of fresh thyme

6 oz (175 g) baby carrots

4 oz (100 g) baby corn cobs

6 oz (175 g) baby zucchini

8 oz (225 g) French beans or small green beans

For the Glaze:

8 oz (225 g) tomatoes

1 tablespoon sugar

2 tablespoons (25 g) unsalted butter

2 tablespoons finely chopped fresh chives

1 tablespoon finely chopped fresh cilantro

3 tablespoons finely chopped fresh basil

Salt and freshly ground five-pepper mixture (page 21) or black pepper

Bring a large pan of water to a boil; quickly drop in the tomatoes, blanch for 5 seconds and remove them with a slotted spoon. Peel them and cut them in half crosswize. Seed them by running your fingers round the center. Strain them through a fine sieve and save any juices. Discard all the seeds. Chop the tomatoes into ½ in (1 cm) cubes. Sprinkle the chopped tomatoes with the sugar and let them drain in a stainless steel or plastic colander for 30 minutes, saving any juices.

Seed the red pepper and cut it into 2 in (5 cm) strips. Slice the scallions diagonally into 2 in (5 cm) pieces.

In a wok or large frying-pan, heat the olive oil and add the ginger, shallots, garlic, salt, and pepper and cook gently for 3 minutes. Add the stock, sprigs of thyme, carrots, and corn. Cover tightly with a lid and cook over a high heat for 3 minutes until the carrots are partially cooked. Then add the zucchini; cover again and cook for another 2 minutes. Add the red pepper, French beans, and scallions. Cover again and cook for 4 minutes. Test the vegetables with a sharp knife to see if they are cooked.

In a separate pan, reduce all the tomato juices over high heat until only 1 tablespoon of glaze is left.

When the vegetables are cooked, remove them with a slotted spoon to a warm platter. To make the glaze, reduce the juices in the wok or pan by half, add the tomato glaze, the chopped tomatoes, butter, chives, cilantro, basil, and salt and pepper to taste. Cook for 1 minute and pour this over the vegetables. Serve immediately.

ⓋCURRY COUSCOUS WITH FRESH CHIVES AND APPLE ≈

SERVES 4–6 AS AN
ACCOMPANIMENT

2 tablespoons extra virgin
olive oil

8 oz (250 g) onions, finely
chopped

10 oz (275 g) couscous

2 cups (475 ml) Homemade
Vegetable (page 33) or
Chicken (page 32) Stock

1 tablespoon light soy sauce
(page 23)

1 tablespoon (15 g) unsalted
butter

2 tablespoons Madras curry
powder (page 17)

1 teaspoon sugar

2 teaspoons salt

½ teaspoon freshly ground
five-pepper mixture
(page 21) or black pepper

3 tablespoons finely
chopped fresh chives

4 oz (100 g) peeled apples,
finely chopped

ON MY FIRST TRIP TO MOROCCO, IN 1973, I FIRST ENCOUNTERED COUSCOUS, A CRUSHED WHEAT PRODUCT OF NORTH AFRICAN ORIGIN, WHICH CAN BE USED IN THE SAME WAY AS RICE AND PASTA. I ENJOYED THE TEXTURAL QUALITY OF THE GRAIN AND DISCOVERED HOW VERSATILE AND ADAPTABLE IT WAS. COUSCOUS HAS BECOME QUITE TRENDY AND IS A PERFECT FOIL FOR FUSION COOKING BECAUSE IT IS SO ACCOMMODATING TO DIFFERENT FLAVORS AND SPICES. THIS RECIPE TRANSFORMS IT BY COOKING IT IN VEGETABLE STOCK. IT MAKES A DELIGHTFUL ACCOMPANIMENT TO ANY POULTRY OR MEAT DISH.

Heat the olive oil in a medium-sized casserole, add the onions, and cook them gently over a low heat for about 5 minutes, without browning. Add the couscous, mix well, and continue to cook over a low heat for another 2 minutes. Now add the stock, soy sauce, butter, curry powder, sugar, salt, and pepper and bring the mixture to a boil. Mix well and remove from the heat. Cover tightly and leave for about 20 minutes. Remove the lid, stir in the chives and apples, and serve immediately.

GORDON'S CRANBERRY-GINGER RELISH ≈

This recipe comes from my chef-associate friend Gordon Wing, who is Chinese-American. An accomplished Chinese as well as an American chef, he mixes cuisines, giving his food an exotic, personal touch. This relish is a delicious accompaniment to any meat or poultry recipes in this book. It can be made well ahead and keeps in the refrigerator for up to three weeks. Try it with Korean-style Broiled Beef (page 114).

Combine all the ingredients in a large pan and bring to a boil. Simmer the mixture for 15 minutes over a low heat. When the berries pop open, the relish is done. Let the relish cool to room temperature and then serve.

Makes 1 lb (450 g)

12 oz (350 g) fresh or
  frozen cranberries
2 tablespoons finely
  chopped orange zest
¾ cup (175 ml) fresh orange
  juice
8 tablespoons maple syrup
  or honey
2 tablespoons finely
  chopped fresh ginger
  (page 17)

RICE, NOODLES, AND PASTA

Thai-style Vegetarian Curry Rice ≈

This is my vegetarian interpretation of a delicious and glorious Thai rice dish which uses spices and aromatics to transform the prosaic but congenial grain into a tasty and mouth-watering treat. Once the rice is made, the rest is quickly prepared. I find it reheats well in the microwave, making it a convenient dish that's just as delectable served cold or hot.

Cook the rice at least 2 hours before it is needed, or even the night before, according to the method for Steamed Rice on page 35. Allow it to cool thoroughly and put it in the refrigerator.

Heat a wok or large frying-pan over high heat. Add the peanut oil, sesame oil, and ½ teaspoon, salt and when very hot and slightly smoking, add the garlic, onion, ginger, the remaining 2 teaspoons salt, and the pepper. Stir-fry for 2 minutes. Add the rice and continue to stir-fry for 3 minutes; add the curry powder and mix well. Finally, add the peppers, corn, peas, and chili oil and continue to stir-fry for 3 minutes. Sprinkle in the scallions and cilantro, mix well, and continue to stir-fry for another minute.

Turn onto a warmed platter and serve hot, or cold as a rice salad.

2 cups (400 ml) long-grain white rice
2 ½ cups (600 ml) water
2 tablespoons oil, preferably peanut
2 teaspoons sesame oil
2½ teaspoons salt
2 tablespoons coarsely chopped garlic
1 onion, finely chopped
1 tablespoon finely chopped fresh ginger (page 17)
½ teaspoon freshly ground five-pepper mixture (page 21) or black pepper
1 tablespoon Madras curry powder (page 17)
6 oz (175 g) seeded and chopped red peppers
1 cup (100 g) fresh or frozen corn kernels
1 cup (100 g) frozen peas
1 teaspoon chili oil (page 15)
3 tablespoons finely chopped scallions
2 tablespoons finely chopped fresh cilantro

ⓥ Fragrant Fried Ginger and Scallion Rice ≈

Serves 4 as an accompaniment

2 cups (400 ml) long-grain
white rice

2 ½ cups (600 ml) water

2 tablespoons oil, preferably
peanut

3 tablespoons finely
chopped fresh ginger
(page 17)

4 oz (100 g) scallions, finely
chopped

2 teaspoons salt

½ teaspoon freshly ground
five-pepper mixture
(page 21) or black pepper

2 tablespoons finely
chopped fresh cilantro

Ginger root has been a major part of my culinary life — I may say, forever, inasmuch as it always graced my mother's kitchen. Along with soy sauce, scallions, and garlic, ginger is the fourth basic flavoring of south Chinese cuisine. And for good reason: its zesty bite can transform even the most mundane and bland food, such as rice, into something special.

Here is a simple rice dish which I often make to accompany other foods. The ginger is slowly stir-fried so that it caramelizes slightly and thus gives off a toasty fragrance.

Cook the rice at least 2 hours before it is needed, or even the night before, according to the method for Steamed Rice on page 35. Allow it to cool thoroughly and put it in the refrigerator.

Heat a wok or large frying-pan over a high heat until it is hot. Add the oil, and when it is hot, add the ginger, turn down the heat and slowly stir-fry until the ginger has browned. Then add the scallions, salt, and pepper. Stir-fry for 2 minutes. Add the rice and continue to stir-fry for 5 minutes or until the rice is thoroughly heated through. Finally, add the cilantro. Give the mixture several good stirs.

Turn onto a warmed platter and serve immediately.

 GREEN RICE ≈

RICE IS A MARVELLOUS FOOD THAT IMPARTS SUBSTANCE AND MILD CONGENIALITY TO ANY DISH. IT IS NOT NATURALLY A COLORFUL INGREDIENT BUT IT DOES ABSORB THE COLOR SPECTRUM AS WELL AS IT ABSORBS SPICES, SAUCES, AND SEASONINGS.

I FIRST ENJOYED THIS COLORFUL RICE DISH AT THE JOYCE CAFÉ IN HONG KONG. IT IS AN INTEGRAL PART OF THEIR POPULAR FUSION COOKING.

Cook the rice at least 2 hours before it is needed, or even the night before, following the method on page 35. Allow it to cool thoroughly and put it in the refrigerator.

Heat a wok or large frying-pan over a high heat until it is hot. Add the oil , and when it is very hot and slightly smoking, add the onions, garlic, shallots, scallions, chilies, sugar, salt, and pepper. Stir-fry for 3 minutes. Then add the rice and continue to stir-fry for 5 minutes until thoroughly heated through. Finally, add the cilantro and mix well.

Turn onto a warmed platter and serve hot, or cold as a rice salad, with broiled foods.

SERVES 2–4 AS AN ACCOMPANIMENT

2 cups (400 ml) long-grain white rice
2 ½ cups (600 ml) water
2 tablespoons oil, preferably peanut
½ lb (225 g) onions, finely chopped
2 tablespoons coarsely chopped garlic
3 tablespoons finely chopped shallots
6 tablespoons finely chopped scallions
2 green chilies (page 16), seeded and finely chopped
2 teaspoons sugar
2 teaspoons salt
½ teaspoon freshly ground five-pepper mixture (page 21) or black pepper
4 tablespoons finely chopped fresh cilantro

⒱ Chinese Mushroom Risotto ≈

Serves 4–6 as a main course

2 oz (50 g) dried Chinese
   black mushrooms (page 18)

2 tablespoons (25 g)
   unsalted butter

3 tablespoons extra virgin
   olive oil

1 small onion, finely
   chopped

3 tablespoons finely
   chopped shallots

2 teaspoons finely chopped
   fresh ginger (page 17)

1 ¾ cups (300 g) Italian
   arborio rice

5 cups (1.2 liters) hot
   homemade Vegetable
   Stock (page 33)

Salt and freshly ground
   five-pepper mixture
   (page 21) or black pepper

Freshly grated Parmesan
   cheese, to serve

Risotto is rice that has been slowly cooked to a smooth, creamy consistency, something that is quite unlike Asian steamed rice. As its name indicates, it is an Italian dish. The slow cooking ensures the rice absorbs the various flavors, seasonings, and spices. Rice lends itself to different flavors, and many ingredients may be blended into the ensemble. I have experimented with a variety of ingredients and found that Chinese mushrooms, with their smoky flavor and pleasing texture, are a delicious complement. Perhaps Marco Polo hit upon the idea first. Chicken stock is usually used in risottos but, if you are making a vegetarian menu, vegetable stock works well too.

Soak the mushrooms in warm water for 20 minutes. Then drain them and squeeze out the excess liquid. Remove and discard the stems and cut the caps into thick strips.

    Heat a wok or pan until it is hot and add the butter and olive oil. Then add the onion, shallots, and ginger and stir-fry on a medium heat for 2 minutes, until the onions are translucent but not browned. Now add the rice and mushrooms and continue to stir-fry for 2 minutes until the rice is well coated. Turn the heat to low, add some of the stock, and continue to stir until the rice has absorbed most of the stock. Continue to add stock, allowing it to slowly evaporate and become absorbed by the rice. Continue until you have used up most of the stock. This will take about 25–30 minutes. When the rice is cooked, add salt and pepper to taste and serve it on a warm platter with the Parmesan cheese.

ⓥHerbal Vegetarian Fried Rice ≈

SERVES 4–6 AS AN
ACCOMPANIMENT

2 cups (400 ml) long-grain
  white rice
2 ½ cups (600 ml) water
3 tablespoons extra virgin
  olive oil
3 tablespoons coarsely
  chopped garlic
2 teaspoons finely chopped
  fresh ginger (page 17)
2 tablespoons seeded and
  finely chopped fresh red
  chilies (page 16)
2 teaspoons salt
1 teaspoon freshly ground
  five-pepper mixture
  (page 21) or black pepper
4 tablespoons sun-dried
  tomatoes in oil, drained
  and coarsely chopped
3 tablespoons finely
  chopped scallions
3 tablespoons finely
  chopped fresh chives
3 tablespoons finely
  chopped fresh cilantro
3 tablespoons finely
  chopped fresh flatleaf
  parsley
3 tablespoons chopped fresh
  basil

THIS IS A FUSION RICE DISH I DEVELOPED FOR MY VEGETARIAN FOOD PROMOTIONS AT THE ORIENTAL HOTEL IN BANGKOK, THAILAND. IT IS A TASTY AND AROMATIC DISH BECAUSE I USE INDIAN BASMATI RICE. THE HERBS GIVE THE RICE A TANGY BITE. IT MAKES A NICE COLD RICE SALAD.

Cook the rice according to the method for Steamed Rice on page 35, at least 2 hours before it is needed, or even the night before. Allow it to cool thoroughly and then put it in the refrigerator.

Heat a wok or large frying-pan until it is hot; then add the oil. Add the garlic, ginger, and chilies and stir-fry for 15 seconds. Then add the rice, salt, and pepper and stir-fry for 2 minutes over a high heat. Mix well, pressing on the cold rice to break up any lumps. When the rice is thoroughly heated through, add the sun-dried tomatoes, scallions, chives, cilantro, parsley, and basil and stir-fry for another 3 minutes.

Spoon onto a warmed serving platter and serve hot or at room temperature.

Ⓥ LIGHT RICE NOODLES WITH FRESH HERBS ≈

IN THIS RECIPE, I USE FLAT RICE NOODLES, WHICH LOOK LIKE FETTUCCINE EGG PASTA. BECAUSE THEY ARE DRIED AND NEED LITTLE COOKING, THEY ARE VERY QUICK AND EASY TO USE. THEIR NEUTRAL AND LIGHT TASTE LENDS ITSELF TO A MORE ASSERTIVE FUSION FLAVOR, IN THIS CASE A MIXTURE OF CHOPPED HERBS. THIS IS AN IDEAL RECIPE FOR SPRING OR SUMMER. IT CAN ACCOMPANY A MEAT DISH OR IS A PERFECT LIGHT PASTA DISH BY ITSELF.

Soak the noodles in warm water for 15 minutes, then drain thoroughly.

Heat a wok or large frying-pan over a high heat. Add the oil, and when it is very hot and slightly smoking, add the scallions, garlic, sun-dried tomatoes, shallots, salt and pepper. Stir-fry for 30 seconds then add the noodles and stir-fry for 2 minutes, letting the noodles brown slightly. Add more oil, if necessary.

Finally, add all the herbs and lemon juice. Mix thoroughly and serve immediately.

SERVES 4 AS AN ACCOMPANIMENT

- ½ lb (225 g) dried flat rice noodles
- 3 tablespoons extra virgin olive oil
- 3 tablespoons finely chopped scallions
- 3 tablespoons coarsely chopped garlic
- 3 tablespoons finely chopped sun-dried tomatoes
- 3 tablespoons finely chopped shallots
- 2 teaspoons salt
- 1 teaspoon freshly ground five-pepper mixture (page 21) or black pepper
- 4 tablespoons coarsely chopped fresh basil
- 3 tablespoons finely chopped fresh chives
- 3 tablespoons finely chopped fresh cilantro
- 2 tablespoons finely chopped fresh tarragon
- 1 tablespoon lemon juice

ⓥVEGETARIAN NONYA LAKSA ≈

SERVES 2 AS A MAIN
COURSE OR 4 AS AN
ACCOMPANIMENT

1½ tablespoons oil, preferably
peanut oil

2 tablespoons coarsely
chopped garlic

1 tablespoon finely chopped
fresh ginger (page 17)

2 fresh red chilies
(page 16), halved, seeded
and finely shredded

½ lb (225 g) onions,
finely sliced

1 teaspoon ground cilantro

½ teaspoon ground turmeric

5 cups (1.2 liters) homemade
Vegetable (page 33) or
Chicken (page 32) Stock

½ lb (225 g) rice noodles
(page 19) or rice sticks

1 ¾ cups (400 ml) canned
coconut milk (page 16)

2 teaspoons Madras curry
powder (page 17)

2 teaspoons chili-bean sauce
(page 22)

1 teaspoon sugar

2 teaspoons salt

½ teaspoon freshly ground five-
pepper mixture (page 21)
or black pepper

To Garnish:

3 tablespoons finely sliced
scallions

2 eggs, hard-boiled and
halved

Sprigs of fresh cilantro

NONYA COOKING IS A MIXTURE OF CHINESE AND MALAY CUISINES, ALSO KNOWN AS 'STRAITS CHINESE' IN MALAYSIA AND SINGAPORE. THE WORD *LAKSA* DESCRIBES A ONE-DISH MEAL OF RICE NOODLES, TRADITIONALLY PREPARED WITH EITHER SEAFOOD OR CHICKEN. CLEARLY, THIS IS A VERSATILE DISH, AND IT CERTAINLY ADAPTS WELL TO THE VEGETARIAN MODE. ITS MANY AROMATIC INGREDIENTS AND SPICY FLAVORS ENSURE THAT IT IS AS TASTY AS THE ORIGINAL, NON-VEGETARIAN VERSIONS, BUT LIGHTER.

Heat a wok or large frying-pan over a high heat. Add the oil, and when it is very hot and slightly smoking, reduce the heat and add the garlic, ginger, chilies, and onions and stir-fry for 5 minutes. Add the cilantro, turmeric, and stock. Turn the heat to low, cover and simmer for 20 minutes.

Meanwhile, soak the rice noodles or rice sticks in a bowl of warm water for 20 minutes. Drain them in a colander or sieve.

Add the coconut milk and rice noodles to the simmering liquid. Season with the curry powder, chili-bean sauce, sugar, salt, and pepper and continue to cook for 15 minutes. Ladle the mixture into a large soup tureen and serve immediately with the garnishes on the side or on top.

Neil Perry's Stir-fried Hokkien Noodles with Ham ≈

Serves 2 as a main course or 4 as an accompaniment

½ lb (225 g) broad, flat, dried rice noodles (page 19)

2 tablespoons oil, preferably peanut

2 tablespoons coarsely chopped garlic

1 tablespoon finely chopped fresh ginger (page 17)

2 tablespoons coarsely chopped black beans (page 14)

2 oz (50 g) pickled mustard greens (page 19), thinly sliced

4 scallions, shredded

2 tablespoons Shaoxing rice wine (page 22) or dry sherry

2 tablespoons light soy sauce (page 23)

3 tablespoons oyster sauce (page 23)

¼ teaspoon freshly ground black pepper

1 tablespoon sugar

½ cup (100 ml) homemade Chicken Stock (page 32)

4 oz (100 g) smoked ham, finely shredded

1 ½ cups (175 g) fresh bean sprouts (page 13)

A small handful of fresh cilantro

Australians have taken to fusion cooking like ducks to water. They have adapted Asian dishes and infused them with European touches to create a unique cuisine that is unrivalled in the world. One of the best chefs is Neil Perry, a talented man with a true love of good food. This is one of his delicious recipes from Wokpool, one of his many popular restaurants, which I have shamelessly adapted. Hokkien is a dialect language group from southern China whose members are among the many Chinese who have emigrated to the Malaysian peninsula and from there to Australia. Hokkien noodles are a style of Singapore noodles popular in Australia.

Soak the rice noodles in a bowl of warm water for 25 minutes. Drain them in a colander or sieve.

Heat a wok or large frying-pan over a high heat. Add the oil, and when it is very hot and slightly smoking, add the garlic, ginger, and black beans and stir-fry for 30 seconds. Then add the noodles, mustard greens, and scallions and stir-fry for 2 minutes. Now add the rice wine or sherry, soy sauce, oyster sauce, pepper, sugar, and stock and continue to stir-fry for 3 minutes. Finally, add the ham, bean sprouts, and cilantro and continue to cook for 2 minutes. Serve immediately.

THE ORIENTAL HOTEL'S STIR-FRIED NOODLES WITH DEEP-FRIED TOFU ≈

THE ORIENTAL HOTEL IN BANGKOK IS JUSTIFIABLY RENOWNED AS ONE OF THE BEST HOTELS IN THE WORLD. PART OF THAT REPUTATION COMES FROM THE OFFERINGS OF ITS WONDERFUL KITCHEN, SUPERVISED BY CHEF NORBERT KOSTNER. HIS ABIDING INTEREST IN MAKING VEGETABLE DISHES TASTE AS GOOD AS ANY MEAT-BASED OFFERINGS MAKES HIM A PIONEER IN THE CULINARY WORLD. HERE IS HIS VEGETARIAN VERSION OF THE TRADITIONAL THAI RICE-NOODLE DISH.

SERVES 2 AS A MAIN COURSE OR 4 AS AN ACCOMPANIMENT

½ lb (225 g) broad, flat, dried rice noodles (page 19)
½ lb (225 g) firm, fresh tofu (page 24)
2 cups (175 g) Chinese or ordinary broccoli florets
1 cup (175 g) snowpeas
1 cup (175 g) French beans
4 oz (100 g) shallots
4 scallions
3 fresh red or green chilies (page 16)
2 cups (450 ml) plus 2 tablespoons oil, preferably peanut
2 tablespoons coarsely chopped garlic
2 tablespoons fish sauce (page 22) or light soy sauce (page 23)
1½ tablespoons lime juice
1 teaspoon salt
¼ teaspoon freshly ground black pepper
2 teaspoons sugar
3 tablespoons vegetarian oyster-flavored sauce (page 22) or dark soy sauce (page 23)
3 tablespoons finely chopped fresh cilantro
3 tablespoons coarsely chopped roasted peanuts, to garnish

Soak the rice noodles in a bowl of warm water for 25 minutes. Then drain them in a colander or sieve.

Drain the tofu, place it on paper towels and continue to drain it for 15 minutes. Gently cut the tofu into 1 in (2.5 cm) cubes.

Separate the broccoli into small florets, then peel and slice the stems. Blanch the broccoli pieces in a large pan of boiling, salted water for 3 minutes and then immerse them in cold water. Drain thoroughly.

Finely shred the snowpeas. If the French beans are large, slice them in half at a slight diagonal. If they are small, leave them whole.

Peel and thinly slice the shallots. Thinly slice the scallions at a slight diagonal into 1 in (2.5 cm) pieces. Seed and finely chop the chilies.

Heat 2 cups (450 ml) of oil in a wok or deep frying-pan until it is hot and deep-fry the tofu cubes in two batches. When each batch is lightly browned, remove and drain it well on paper towels. Drain off and discard the oil. Wipe the wok or pan clean.

Reheat the wok or pan , and when it is hot, add the rest of the oil; when it is very hot and slightly smoking, add the shallots, scallions, garlic and chilies and stir-fry for 1 minute. Then add the rice noodles, broccoli, snowpeas, and French beans and stir-fry for 2 minutes. Now add the fish or soy sauce, lime juice, salt, pepper and sugar and continue to stir-fry for 2 minutes, mixing well. Finally, add the oyster-flavored sauce or soy sauce and continue to cook for 4 minutes. Stir in the chopped cilantro and tofu cubes and cook for 30 seconds. Give the mixture a good stir and turn onto a warmed platter. Sprinkle with the peanuts and serve immediately.

⒱ Jade Noodle Bowl ≈

Serves 2 as a main course

1 oz (25 g) dried Chinese
   black mushrooms (page 18)
¾ lb (350 g) fresh or
   ¼ lb (100 g) dried spinach
   noodles or pasta
2 teaspoons sesame oil
5 cups (1.2 liters) homemade
   Vegetable (page 33) or
   Chicken (page 32) Stock
½ teaspoon salt
1 tablespoon light soy sauce
   (page 23)
2 fresh red chilies (page 16),
   seeded and shredded
¼ lb (100 g) firm tofu, (page
   24), shredded
1 ½ cups (175 g) fresh bean
   sprouts (page 13)

To Garnish:
3 tablespoons finely chopped
   scallions
Sprigs of fresh cilantro

This comforting, simple noodle treat found its inspiration in the Joyce Café in Hong Kong. It is a satisfying mixture of spinach ('jade') noodles with chili, seasoned tofu, mushrooms, and bean sprouts in a hearty broth. Once the broth is made, jade noodle bowl is easy to prepare for a perfect lunch or light supper.

Soak the mushrooms in warm water for 20 minutes. Then drain them and squeeze out the excess liquid. Remove and discard the stems and finely shred the caps into thin strips.

If you are using fresh noodles, blanch them first for 3–5 minutes in boiling water. If you are using dried noodles, cook them in boiling water for 4–5 minutes. Plunge the prepared noodles in cold water, drain them thoroughly, toss them in the sesame oil, and put them aside until you are ready to use them. They can be kept in this state if tightly covered with plastic wrap for up to 2 hours in the refrigerator.

Bring the stock to a simmer in a large pan. Add the salt, soy sauce, chilies, and tofu and simmer for 5 minutes. Then add the cooked noodles and simmer for 2 minutes. Now add the bean sprouts and cook for another minute.

Turn the contents of the pan into a soup tureen. Sprinkle with the scallions and cilantro and serve immediately.

ⓥLILLIAN'S TASTY NOODLES ≈

SERVES **4** AS A MAIN
COURSE

¾ lb (350 g) fresh wheat or
  egg noodles (page 19)
2 teaspoons plus
  1 tablespoon sesame oil
1 lb (450 g) green
  cabbage, shredded
1½ tablespoons plus
  2 teaspoons salt
2 tablespoons peanut oil
3 tablespoons coarsely
  chopped garlic
½ teaspoon freshly ground
  five-pepper mixture
  (page 21) or black pepper
2 tablespoons light soy
  sauce (page 23)
1 tablespoon dark soy sauce
  (page 23)
2 tablespoons Shaoxing rice
  wine (page 22) or dry
  sherry

I ALWAYS LOOK FORWARD TO SUNDAY DINNERS AT LILLIAN ROBYN'S HOME IN
EL CERRITO, CALIFORNIA. SOMETIMES SHE INVITES OTHER CHINESE FRIENDS
AND EACH OF THEM BRINGS A HOMEMADE DISH FOR THE OTHERS TO ENJOY.
'POT LUCK' SOUNDS SO CHINESE ANYWAY. IN ANY CASE, WE ALL
EXPERIENCE A DELICIOUS HOME-COOKED CHINESE BANQUET.

I RECALL WITH DELIGHT THIS VERY TASTY NOODLE DISH, WHICH LILLIAN
PUT TOGETHER ONE EVENING IN A MATTER OF MINUTES. IMAGINATIVE AND
YET EASY TO MAKE, IT IS A GOOD ALTERNATIVE TO THE USUAL RICE.

Cook the noodles for 3–5 minutes in a pan of boiling, salted water.
Drain and plunge them into cold water. Drain thoroughly and toss
them in 2 teaspoons of sesame oil. (They can be kept in this state, if
tightly covered with plastic wrap, for up to 2 hours in the refrigerator.)

Meanwhile, soak the cabbage in cold water and 1½ tablespoons
of salt for 1 hour. Drain the cabbage.

Heat a wok or large frying-pan over a high heat until it is hot.
Add the oil, and when it is very hot and slightly smoking, add the
garlic, the rest of the salt, and the pepper and stir-fry for 10 seconds;
then add the cabbage and continue to stir-fry for 2 minutes. Now
pour in the soy sauces and the rice wine or sherry. Cook over a high
heat for 10 minutes or until the cabbage is completely cooked. Add
the cooked noodles and continue to cook for 4 minutes or until the
noodles are heated through. Drizzle in the rest of the sesame oil and
give the mixture several turns. Serve immediately.

ⓋFragrant Coconut Noodle Soup ≈

A great discovery for me, as well as for many fusion chefs and cooks in the past decade, has been Thai cuisine. We love the sharpness, assertiveness, tanginess, spiciness, and richness which, for me, characterize this cuisine. These seemingly contradictory flavors work well when combined in soup and braised dishes. Despite the rich flavors, the resulting dish is light, especially for soups. Here I have combined lessons learned from this great cuisine into a lovely, hearty soup. Serve it at room temperature during warm weather; it works wonders. If you use vegetable stock and soy sauce instead of fish sauce, you can easily turn this into a dish suitable for vegetarians.

Soak the rice noodles in a bowl of warm water for 25 minutes. Drain them in a colander or sieve. Peel the lemon grass stalks to the tender, whitish centers and crush with the flat of a knife; then cut into 3 in (7.5 cm) pieces.

Heat a large, heavy pan over a high heat. Add the oil, and when it is very hot and slightly smoking, add the onion, garlic, and lemon grass and stir-fry for about 3 minutes. Stir in the stock, coconut milk and orange juice, turn the heat to low, cover and simmer for 10 minutes. Then add the tomatoes, chilies, orange zest, fish or soy sauce, sugar, curry powder, salt, and pepper and stir well. Now add the drained noodles. Cover and continue to cook for another 10 minutes.

Remove the lemon grass with a slotted spoon, stir in the lime juice, then pour the noodles and soup into a large tureen and serve immediately.

Serves 4

- ¼ lb (100 g) dried thin rice noodles (page 19)
- 2 lemon grass stalks (page 18)
- 1 tablespoon peanut oil
- 1 small onion, finely chopped
- 2 tablespoons coarsely chopped garlic
- 5 cups (1.2 liters) homemade Vegetable (page 33) or Chicken (page 32) Stock
- 2 x 15 oz (400 ml) cans of coconut milk (page 16)
- ⅔ cup (150 ml) fresh orange juice, strained
- 8 oz (225 g) canned tomatoes, chopped
- 2 fresh red or green chilies (page 16), seeded and finely shredded
- 2 tablespoons finely chopped orange zest
- 1 tablespoon fish sauce (page 22) or soy sauce (page 23)
- 1 tablespoon sugar
- 1 tablespoon Madras curry powder (page 17)
- 2 teaspoons salt
- ½ teaspoon freshly ground five-pepper mixture (page 21) or black pepper
- 1 tablespoon lime juice

Ⓥ Cold Korean-style Noodles ≈

Serves 2–4 as an
accompaniment

½ lb (225 g) somyun noodles
(page 20) or thin Chinese
wheat noodles (page 18)

2 teaspoons sesame oil

½ oz (15 g) dried Chinese
black mushrooms
(page 18)

2 tablespoons sesame seeds,
toasted (page 23), to
garnish

For the Sauce:

2 tablespoons finely
chopped garlic

1 tablespoon oil, preferably
peanut

2 teaspoons sesame oil

2 tablespoons light soy
sauce (page 23)

2 teaspoons sugar

2 tablespoons white rice
vinegar (page 24)

1 teaspoon salt

½ teaspoon freshly ground
five-pepper mixture
(page 21) or black pepper

1½ tablespoons seeded and
finely chopped fresh red
chili (page 16)

3 tablespoons finely
chopped scallions

While I was working at the Hotel Shilla Parkview in Seoul, Korea, I was delighted when the kitchen staff put together this delicious cold noodle dish. Upon asking them for the recipe, I discovered that it included a special type of noodle, somyun, made from a mixture of rice flour and wheat flour. When cooked, the noodles acquire a pleasant, textured character. This refreshing noodle dish makes an ideal summer lunch treat, or it could be served with any barbecue dish. If you cook the noodles in advance, don't toss them with the sauce until you are ready to serve.

Bring a large pan of salted water to a boil and cook the noodles for 3 minutes. Drain the noodles, plunge them into cold water, and drain them well. Toss in the sesame oil and then chill in the refrigerator.

Soak the mushrooms in warm water for 20 minutes. Then drain them and squeeze out the excess liquid. Remove and discard the stems and finely shred the caps into thin strips.

When you are ready to serve the noodles, combine the sauce ingredients in a small bowl. In a large bowl, mix the noodles and mushrooms together; then toss the noodles with the sauce, mixing well. Sprinkle the sesame seeds on top and serve immediately.

ⓥ Penang Rice Noodles ≈

Penang is a Malaysian city strongly influenced by Chinese history and culture. The Chinese culinary influence is particularly robust. I must admit that my partiality for Malaysian food stems from its clear affinity with southern Chinese traditions.

I particularly like the Malaysian rice noodle dishes, and here is a savory version which is easy to make and quite delicious.

Soak the rice noodles in a bowl of warm water for 25 minutes. Then drain them in a colander or sieve.

Heat a wok or large frying-pan over a high heat. Add the oil, and when it is very hot and slightly smoking, add the onion, scallions, garlic, Chinese greens, and Chinese chives and stir-fry for 4 minutes. Then add the noodles, rice wine or sherry, light soy sauce, oyster sauce or dark soy sauce, salt, and pepper and continue to stir-fry for 2 minutes. Add the bean sprouts and continue to cook for 2 minutes. Finally, drizzle in the sesame oil and give the mixture a good stir. Serve immediately.

½ lb (225 g) broad, flat, dried rice noodles (page 19)

2 tablespoons oil, preferably peanut

1 large onion, thinly sliced

4 scallions, cut diagonally into 1 in (2.5 cm) pieces

2 tablespoons coarsely chopped garlic

½ lb (225 g) Chinese greens such as bok choy (page 15), cut into 2.5 cm (1 in) pieces

6 oz (175 g) fresh Chinese yellow or green chives, or fresh chives, cut into 1 in (2.5 cm) pieces

1 tablespoon Shaoxing rice wine (page 22) or dry sherry

2 tablespoons light soy sauce (page 23)

2 tablespoons vegetarian oyster-flavored sauce (page 22) or dark soy sauce (page 23)

1 teaspoon salt

¼ teaspoon freshly ground black pepper

6 oz (175 g) bean sprouts (page 24)

2 teaspoons sesame oil

ⓥ MALAYSIAN CURRY MEE ≈

SERVES 2 AS A MAIN
COURSE OR 4 AS AN
ACCOMPANIMENT

1 lb (450 g) firm, fresh tofu
(page 24)
½ lb (225 g) dried or fresh
Chinese egg noodles
(page 19)
1½ tablespoons oil,
preferably peanut
2 dried red chilies
(page 15), halved
2 tablespoons coarsely
chopped garlic
1 medium (100 g) onion,
finely chopped
1¾ cups (400 ml) canned
coconut milk (page 16)
½ teaspoon ground turmeric
2 tablespoons Madras curry
powder (page 17)
1 teaspoon salt
1 teaspoon sugar
2 tablespoons light soy
sauce (page 23)
½ lb (225 g) fresh bean
sprouts (page 13),
trimmed
A handful of fresh parsley
leaves, to garnish

MALAYSIA IS AN INTERNATIONAL COMMERCIAL POWERHOUSE SITUATED AT A GEOGRAPHICAL CROSSROADS. UNDERSTANDABLY, THEREFORE, IT IS ALSO A CULINARY CROSSROADS OF CUISINES, SPICES, AND INGREDIENTS, WITH CHINESE AND INDIAN FLAVORS, ESPECIALLY, MERGING INTO A DISTINCTLY NATIONAL STYLE OF COOKING – ONE THAT HAS BEEN INFLUENTIAL IN THE COOKING OF AUSTRALIA, WHICH HAS MANY MALAYSIAN IMMIGRANTS AND IS A POPULAR HOLIDAY DESTINATION.

A GOOD EXAMPLE OF A POPULAR MALAYSIAN DISH IN AUSTRALIA IS THIS SIMPLE BUT DELECTABLE EGG NOODLE DISH (*MEE* IS THE MALAYSIAN WORD FOR 'NOODLES'). IT COMBINES BEAN SPROUTS AND TOFU, STANDARD INGREDIENTS USED BY CHINESE COOKS, WITH A LIGHT CURRY SAUCE THAT MANIFESTS THE INDIAN INFLUENCE.

Cut the tofu into 1 in (2.5 cm) cubes. Drain on paper towels for 30 minutes.

If you are using dried noodles, cook them according to the instructions on the package or boil them for 4–5 minutes. Then cool them in cold water until you are ready to use them. If you are using fresh noodles, boil them for 3–5 minutes and then immerse them in cold water.

Heat a wok or large frying-pan over a high heat. Add the oil, and when it is very hot and slightly smoking, add the dried chilies and stir-fry for 20 seconds. Push the chilies to the side of the wok or pan, turn the temperature down, and add the tofu cubes, browning slowly on all sides. When the cubes are golden brown on all sides, add the garlic and onions and stir-fry for 3 minutes, until the onions are wilted. Now add the coconut milk, turmeric, curry powder, salt, sugar, and soy sauce and simmer for 4 minutes. Add the noodles and bean sprouts and cook for 2 minutes, mixing well. Garnish with the parsley leaves and serve immediately.

ⓋShanghai-style Wontons ≈

This Shanghai-style wonton dish was inspired by a light, flavorful soup I had at the trendy Joyce Café in Hong Kong. The menu features a mixture of eastern and western influences and includes many vegetarian offerings. I found this one particularly delightful to the eye as well as the palate. The wontons are filled with chopped fresh Chinese leaves mixed with spicy preserved vegetables, and they are served floating in a fragrant soup.

Wonton skins can be obtained from Chinese grocers, as well as supermarkets. They are yellowish squares packed in small stacks and they can be bought fresh or frozen. Be sure to thaw them thoroughly if they are frozen.

Blanch the Chinese leaves for 1 minute in boiling salted water, remove with a slotted spoon, and plunge immediately into cold water. Drain and squeeze all excess liquid out. Tip into a bowl, add all the other filling ingredients and mix well.

When you are ready to stuff the wontons, put a tablespoon of the filling in the center of the first wonton skin. Dampen the edges with a little water and bring up the sides of the skin around the filling. Pinch the edges together at the top so that the wonton is sealed; it should look like a small drawstring bag. Repeat the procedure until all the filling has been used.

When the wontons are ready, bring the stock, soy sauce, and sesame oil to a simmer in a large pan.

In another large pan, bring salted water to a boil and poach the wontons for 1 minute or until they float to the top (you may need to do this in batches). Remove them immediately and transfer them to the pan of stock. (This procedure will result in a cleaner-tasting broth.) Continue to simmer them in the broth for 2 minutes. Transfer to either a large soup tureen or to individual bowls. Garnish with scallions and serve immediately.

Serves 4–6 (makes about 20 wontons)

½ lb (225 g) wonton skins (page 25)
3 tablespoons finely chopped scallions, to garnish

For the Filling:

¾ lb (350 g) bok choy (page 14), coarsely chopped
2 oz (50 g) Sichuan preserved vegetables (page 23), rinsed and finely chopped
½ teaspoon salt
½ teaspoon freshly ground five-pepper mixture (page 21) or white pepper
1 teaspoon light soy sauce (page 23)
2 tablespoons finely chopped scallions
1 tablespoon Shaoxing rice wine (page 22) or dry sherry
1 teaspoon sugar
2 teaspoons sesame oil

For the Broth:

5 cups (1.2 liters) homemade Vegetable (page 33) or Chicken (page 32) Stock
1 tablespoon light soy sauce (page 23)
1 teaspoon sesame oil

ⓥ Fusion Pasta with Chinese Greens ≈

SERVES 2 AS A MAIN
COURSE OR 4 AS AN
ACCOMPANIMENT

¾ lb (350 g) dried Italian
pasta, such as fusilli or
farfalle

1 lb (450 g) Chinese greens,
such as Chinese flowering
cabbage or bok choy
(page 14)

3 tablespoons extra virgin olive
oil

3 tablespoons finely sliced garlic

1 teaspoon salt

½ teaspoon freshly ground five-
pepper mixture (page 21)
or black pepper

2 tablespoons light soy sauce
(page 23)

1 tablespoon lemon juice

2 tablespoons finely chopped
fresh chives

2 tablespoons finely chopped
fresh cilantro

Freshly grated Parmesan
cheese, to serve

CHINESE GREENS ARE A SOURCE OF INSPIRATION FOR FUSION CHEFS. THESE
TASTY, SLIGHTLY BITTER GREENS WITH A RICH CABBAGE FLAVOR ARE THE
PERFECT FOIL FOR PASTA. HERE IS A DELECTABLE VEGETABLE PASTA DISH THAT IS
QUICK TO PREPARE AND DELICIOUS TO EAT.

Cook the pasta in a large pan of salted, boiling water, according to
the instructions on the package. Drain well and set aside.

Cut the Chinese greens into 3 in (7.5 cm) pieces.

Heat a wok or large frying-pan over a high heat. Add the oil ,
and when it is hot, add the garlic and stir-fry for 30 seconds until the
garlic has browned. Then quickly add the Chinese greens and stir-fry
for 3 minutes or until the greens have wilted a little. Now add the salt,
pepper, soy sauce, and lemon juice and continue to stir-fry for 1
minute. Return the cooked pasta to the wok and heat through, mixing
well with the greens. Add the chives and cilantro and give the mixture
a good stir. Turn onto a warmed platter and serve immediately, with
Parmesan cheese.

♥Pasta in Chili Tomato Sauce ≈

2 lb (900 g) tomatoes, peeled and seeded if fresh, drained if canned

⅔ cup (150 ml) extra virgin olive oil

1 medium (100 g) onion, finely chopped

2 tablespoons finely chopped fresh ginger (page 17)

3 tablespoons coarsely chopped garlic

2 medium-sized (100 g) carrots, finely chopped

1 large stalk (100 g) celery, finely chopped

3 tablespoons finely chopped scallions

2 tablespoons seeded and finely chopped fresh red chilies (page 16)

2 teaspoons sugar

2 teaspoons salt

1 teaspoon freshly ground five-pepper mixture (page 21) or black pepper

1 tablespoon Sesame and Chili Oil (page 39) or chili oil (page 15)

1 lb (450 g) dried Italian pasta, such as spaghetti

Freshly grated Parmesan cheese, to serve

There is nothing simpler to prepare than pasta with tomato sauce and there is hardly anything more delicious: comfort food at its most satisfying. To add a spicy twist to this classic Italian dish, I have chosen a few Asian flavors that make it even more satisfying. This quick and easy dish is perfect for vegetarians and serves as a light lunch or as a main course for an informal dinner party.

If you are using fresh tomatoes, cut them into 1 in (2.5 cm) cubes. If you are using canned tomatoes, chop them into small chunks.

Heat a large pan and add the oil, then add the onions, ginger, garlic, carrots, celery, scallions, and chilies and stir-fry for 2 minutes. Then add the sugar, salt, pepper, and sesame and chili oil or chili oil and continue to cook for 1 minute. Then add the tomatoes, turn the heat to low and simmer over a low heat for 30 minutes. The sauce can be made a day ahead to this point.

Cook the pasta in a large pan of salted, boiling water, according to the instructions on the packet. Drain well and put the pasta on a large, warmed platter.

Pour the sauce over the pasta and serve with Parmesan cheese.

DESSERTS

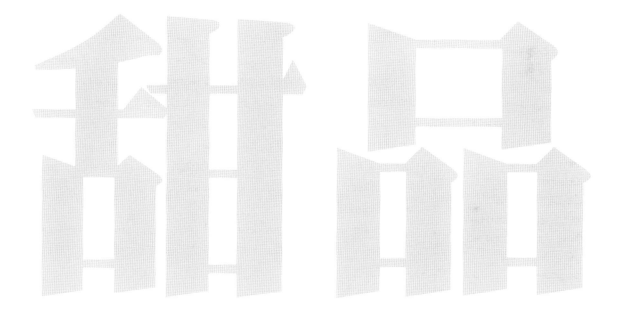

WARM MANGO COMPOTE WITH BASIL AND VANILLA ICE CREAM ≈

THIS IS A SIMPLE DESSERT THAT I HAVE OFTEN MADE FOR MY FOOD PROMOTIONS AT THE ORIENTAL HOTEL IN BANGKOK. MANGOES ARE POPULAR AND ABUNDANT IN THAILAND. THEIR RICH, FLESHY, AND SATIN-LIKE TEXTURE TRANSFORMS THIS RECIPE INTO AN EXQUISITE FINALE. VANILLA ICE CREAM FOUND IN SUPERMARKETS IS OF HIGH QUALITY AND A GREAT CONVENIENCE. THE COMBINATION OF THE COLD ICE CREAM AND WARM FRUIT IS UNBEATABLE.

Scrape the seeds of the vanilla pod into the sugar and mix well. Using a non-stick wok or pan, bring the sugar and water to a boil, add the vanilla pod, and simmer for 10 minutes. Remove the vanilla pod, dry it thoroughly, and save for future use by storing it in sugar. Peel the mangoes and cut the fruit into ¼ in (5 mm) thick slices.

Add the mango slices and a tiny pinch of salt to the syrup and simmer for 2 minutes, just enough to warm the fruit and not to cook it through. Remove from the heat and gently stir in the butter and the basil. Serve immediately, with scoops of vanilla ice cream.

SERVES 4

1 vanilla pod, split open
½ cup (100 g) granulated sugar
⅔ cup (150 ml) water
1½ lb (750 g) mangoes (2 medium)
2 tablespoons (25g) unsalted butter
6 fresh basil leaves, coarsely chopped
Salt
Vanilla ice cream, to serve

Orange Almond Cake ≈

Serves 4–6

¾ cup (175 ml) fresh orange
   juice, strained

3 tablespoons finely
   chopped orange zest

1 tablespoon orange-flower
   water

2 cups (120 g) dried
   breadcrumbs

¾ cup (90 g) whole
   blanched almonds, ground

2 egg yolks

⅔ cup (150 g) superfine
   sugar

½ teaspoon salt

4 egg whites

Confectioners' sugar, sifted,
   for dusting

THE CHINESE TRADITIONALLY LIKE TO SERVE SLICES OF FRESH ORANGE AFTER A MEAL AND THIS IS A REFRESHING EAST–WEST VARIATION ON THAT THEME. THE CAKE IS EASY TO MAKE AND QUITE DELICIOUS WITH VANILLA ICE CREAM, PLAIN YOGURT, OR CRÈME FRAÎCHE.

Pre-heat the oven to 350°F/180°C.

    In a large bowl, combine the orange juice, orange zest, orange-flower water, 1 ¾ cups (100 g) of the breadcrumbs and the almonds. In a separate bowl, beat the egg yolks with half the sugar and the salt and gently fold into the orange juice mixture. In another bowl, beat the egg whites until they become stiff; then beat in the remaining sugar and continue to beat until the whites form stiff peaks. Fold the beaten egg whites into the orange juice mixture.

    Lightly butter a 8 in (20 cm) square, non-stick baking tin and dust it with the remaining breadcrumbs. Pour in the cake batter and bake for 45 minutes or until done (a fine skewer should come out clean). Set aside to cool in the pan on a rack. Invert the cake onto a platter and dust with confectioners' sugar to serve.

Coconut Fruit Crumble ≈

Serves 6–8

2½ lb (1.25 kg) very ripe
   fruit, such as peaches,
   mangoes, cherries,
   raspberries and/or
   blueberries
1 ¾ cups (200 g) all-purpose
   flour
1 cup (200 g) sugar
1 ¼ cups (100 g) desiccated
   coconut
9–10 tablespoons
   (135 g) cold unsalted
   butter, cut in small pieces

Desserts are not a strong point of Asian cooking in general. Fresh fruit or gelatin-like puddings are what you will find in many parts of Asia. However, I do find the English-inspired crumble quite appealing; using fresh fruit, with a touch of exotic eastern coconut, it is a perfect fusion dessert. The basic recipe is from Monique Pébeyre, who is a French Anglophile. She serves it often in the summer, when fruit is abundant and in season. It is an easy, quick, and simple dessert to make. Although you can make it ahead of time, it tastes best served warm. You will find it quite delicious with vanilla ice cream.

Pre-heat the oven to 350°F/180°C.

If you are using peaches, pit them and cut into thick slices. If you are using mangoes, peel them, remove the large seed and cut the flesh in thick slices. If you are using cherries, pit them and leave them whole.

In a large bowl, mix the flour, sugar, coconut, and butter with your fingers until they are coarsely blended. Arrange the fruit in an ovenproof dish in one layer. Place the crumble mixture on top of the fruit and bake for 45 minutes or until the top is golden and bubbly. Allow to cool and serve warm or at room temperature.

CHOCOLATE CAKE WITH CANDIED GINGER ≈

CHOCOLATE IS RARELY FOUND ON ASIAN MENUS OR IN HOMES. HOWEVER, NOW THAT ASIANS HAVE TASTED THIS VERY WESTERN FLAVOR, IT HAS BECOME EXTREMELY POPULAR. IN THIS CLASSIC CHOCOLATE CAKE, I HAVE COMBINED CHOCOLATE WITH CANDIED GINGER TO GIVE AN EASTERN ZEST TO THIS WESTERN DESSERT. SERVE IT WITH LEMON GRASS CRÈME ANGLAISE (PAGE 237). IT IS ALSO DELICIOUS WITH LIGHTLY WHIPPED HEAVY CREAM.

(PAGE 237)

Pre-heat the oven to 350°F/180°C.

Combine the chocolate, butter, sugar, and candied ginger in a heatproof bowl; place this over a large pan of boiling water. Over a moderate heat, melt the mixture, stirring continuously, until the ingredients are thoroughly blended.

Allow the mixture to cool. Whisk in the egg yolks and then the flour. Mix thoroughly.

Whisk the egg whites until they form firm peaks.

Add one-third of the egg whites to the chocolate batter and mix vigorously. Then gently fold in the remaining egg whites.

Butter a 8–9 in (20–23 cm) cake pan. Pour in the cake mixture and bake until the cake is firm, about 35–40 minutes.

Allow the cake to cool thoroughly. Turn the cake onto a platter, dust with confectioners' sugar and serve.

SERVES 6–8

¾ lb (350 g) finest quality semisweet chocolate, broken in pieces
10 tablespoons (150 g) unsalted butter
½ cup (135 g) granulated sugar
2 oz (50 g) candied ginger, finely chopped
4 egg yolks
⅓ cup (40 g) all-purpose flour, sifted
6 egg whites
Confectioners' sugar, sifted, for dusting

Ginger Crème Brûlée ≈

Serves 8

1 vanilla pod

4 tablespoons superfine
sugar

2 cups (500 ml) heavy
cream

6 tablespoons finely
chopped fresh ginger
(page 17)

4 egg yolks

1 egg, beaten

2 tablespoons dark brown
sugar

CRÈME BRÛLÉE IS UNDOUBTEDLY OF FRENCH ORIGIN, BUT ENGLISH CHEFS
ADDED CERTAIN FLAVORINGS SUCH AS VANILLA, RUM, AND ORANGE LIQUEUR
TO CUSTARD SAUCE AND FROM THERE CAME UP WITH THE NOTION OF
SIMILARLY SPICING UP THE TRADITIONAL CRÈME BRÛLÉE. THIS DESSERT MAY
NOW BE FOUND ON ALMOST EVERY FUSION CHEF'S MENU ON EVERY
CONTINENT. I SUPPOSE IT SHOULD BE CALLED CRÈME BRÛLÉE ANGLAISE. IT IS
NOT SURPRISING THAT THIS RICH, SEDUCTIVE DESSERT SHOULD BE SO POPULAR.
I THINK IT IS PERFECT FOR ENTERTAINING SINCE MUCH OF THE WORK CAN BE
DONE AHEAD OF TIME – UP TO A DAY. IT IS ADAPTABLE TO MANY FLAVORS
AND HERE I USE MY FAVORITE – FRESH GINGER.

Pre-heat the oven to 350°F/180°C.

Slit the vanilla pod, lengthwize, scrape out the sticky seeds and
combine them with a tablespoon of the superfine sugar. Set aside.

In a small pan, combine half the cream with the ginger and
vanilla pod, bring to a boil, remove from the heat, and allow to cool
thoroughly, about 10 minutes. Strain the cream through a fine sieve,
discarding the ginger. Save the vanilla pod, dry it thoroughly, and put
into your sugar jar. Mix the vanilla and superfine sugar mixture into the
ginger cream.

In a large bowl, combine the egg yolks, beaten egg, and
remaining superfine sugar with the remaining cream; mix well. Finally,
add the ginger cream mixture and mix thoroughly.

Arrange eight 2½ in (6 cm) ramekins in a large baking pan and
pour in 1 in (2.5 cm) of hot water. Divide the mixture between the
ramekins. Bake for 30 minutes or until the custard is set.

Allow to cool thoroughly and refrigerate. This recipe can be made
one day ahead up to this point.

Just before serving, pre-heat the broiler to hot. Sprinkle the brown
sugar over each ramekin and broil until it has caramelized. Watch
carefully, so that the sugar does not burn. Allow to cool for a few
minutes so that the caramel can harden and then serve.

Rosemary and Thyme Shortbread Cookies ≈

Makes 18–20 Cookies

6 tablespoons (75 g) unsalted butter, at room temperature

4 tablespoons sugar

1 ½ cups (160 g) all-purpose flour

2 teaspoons fresh thyme leaves, finely chopped

1 teaspoon fresh rosemary, finely chopped

1 teaspoon edible flower petals, such as flowering sage or rose, finely chopped

These cookies were inspired by Daryle Ryo Nagata, executive chef of the Waterfront Center Hotel in Vancouver. He is a true mixture of East and West, with a Scottish mother and a Japanese father. These cookies make good use of herbs from the hotel's herb garden and fresh herbs are essential for the best flavor.

Preheat the oven to 325°F/160°C. In a large bowl, beat the soft butter, and sugar together until smooth. With a spatula, slowly incorporate the flour, herbs, and flower petals. Mix until you are able to gather the dough easily in one piece and then roll into a ball. Roll this out with a rolling pin to ¼ in (5 mm) thick, then cut into 18–20 cookies. Place them on a baking tray and bake in the oven for about 20 minutes or until they are slightly browned. Allow to cool and serve.

Granité of Japanese Plum Wine ≈

Serves 4–6

2 ½ cups (600 ml) Japanese plum wine

1 cup (100 g) granulated sugar

Inspired by an Italian sorbet, popularized in Paris in the nineteenth century, this dessert is half-frozen with a granular texture.

Japanese plum wine is usually made at home from unripe green fruit sweetened with sugar and then fermented with rice wine. Fortunately, it can be purchased, ready-bottled, from many Asian markets.

You can make this dessert without an expensive ice cream machine. Although the scientific basis is unclear, all who try *granite* agree that it aids the digestion.

Combine the plum wine and sugar in a pan and boil the mixture for 1 minute. Remove and allow it to cool thoroughly.

Pour the cool mixture into ice trays and freeze for 4 hours, without stirring. When you are ready to serve, break up the *granité* with a large fork. It should have a granular texture.

FIVE-MINUTE ORANGE CREAM ≈

A FRUIT DISH IS THE PREFERRED FINALE TO MOST OF MY DINNER PARTIES; IT IS REFRESHING, EASY TO MAKE, AND SEEMS TO BE JUST WHAT EVERYONE CRAVES AFTER A TASTY MEAL. THIS IS AN ORANGE DESSERT THAT I HAVE ADAPTED FROM MY EXPERIENCES OF EATING IN HONG KONG RESTAURANTS AND WHICH I HAVE MODIFIED TO MY TASTE BY REDUCING THE AMOUNT OF GELATIN. THE RESULT IS A SILKY, CUSTARD-LIKE DESSERT, ONLY SLIGHTLY FIRM BUT TEXTURED ENOUGH FOR ME AND, I HOPE, FOR YOU. A BONUS IS THAT IT TAKES ABOUT 5 MINUTES TO MAKE; IT'S PERFECT FOR ENTERTAINING BECAUSE YOU CAN EASILY DOUBLE THE RECIPE AND MAKE IT IN ADVANCE, IF YOU LIKE.

SERVES 4–6

- 2 ½ cups (600 ml) fresh orange juice
- 1 packet of gelatin
- ½ cup (120 ml) light cream
- 8 tablespoons granulated sugar
- 2 teaspoons finely chopped orange zest
- 2 eggs
- 1 cup (250 ml) heavy cream

Strain the orange juice, sprinkle the gelatin over the cold juice, and leave for 2 minutes. Then bring the mixture to a simmer in a pan. Slowly stir and let the gelatin dissolve thoroughly. Place the hot juice in a blender, add the light cream, and blend until smooth.

Add the sugar, orange zest, and eggs and blend for 10 seconds. Finally, add the heavy cream and continue to blend for another 20 seconds.

Spoon into individual serving dishes or into a large gratin dish, cover with plastic wrap, and chill for at least 3 hours before serving. This recipe can be made one or even two days ahead. Be sure to cover tightly with plastic wrap before storing in the refrigerator.

Apple and Lemon Grass Frangipane Tart ≈

Serves 6–8

For the Pastry:

2 ⅞ cups (300 g) all-purpose flour

12 tablespoons (175 g) cold unsalted butter, cut in small pieces

A pinch of salt

1 teaspoon granulated sugar

4 tablespoons heavy cream

For the Lemon Grass and Almond Mixture:

3 lemon grass stalks (page 17)

1 cup (100 g) blanched almonds

½ cup (120 g) sugar

1 egg

1 tablespoon (15 g) unsalted butter, melted

For the Apples:

1 lb (450 g) apples

3 tablespoons granulated sugar

2 tablespoons (25 g) unsalted butter, cut in small pieces

As a child in Chicago's Chinatown, I knew very little of European or American desserts. The one exception I remember very well is apple pie. For reasons that, even today, are unclear to me, the Chinese in my neighborhood enjoyed apple pie and coffee. Not that apple pie is anything but an excellent dessert; it is just not Chinese.

In my youth and while living in France, I discovered the joy of apple tarts, which are lighter, flakier, and more buttery than traditional apple pies. And when I helped out in my friend's kitchen, I learned so much as I watched the family make the delicious almond paste that adds something really special to the prosaic apple. The Marquis Frangipane, who is credited with creating the original recipe in the sixteenth century, could not have been more pleased at the enjoyment his treat brought to our table.

In this fusion version, a touch of lemon grass adds a zesty, subtle Asian touch to this French classic. It is a delicious dessert when served right from oven, and you can make it even more delightful by topping it with vanilla ice cream.

Blend all the pastry ingredients in a mixing bowl or in a food processor for a few minutes. Roll the dough into a ball on a lightly floured board. Cover with plastic wrap and refrigerate for 30 minutes.

Pre-heat the oven to 400°F/200°C. Peel the lemon grass stalks to the tender, whitish centers and finely chop. Grind the chopped lemon grass and almonds together in a blender; then add the sugar, egg, and melted butter and mix until it is a smooth paste.

Roll out the pastry to ¼ in (5 mm) thick and press it into a 8 in (20 cm) greased tart pan. Spread the surface of the pastry with the lemon grass and almond mixture. Place in the refrigerator.

Peel the apples and cut them into ¼ in (5 mm) slices. Remove the pastry from the refrigerator and arrange the slices, overlapping, in circles on the top of the tart. Sprinkle with the sugar and evenly distribute the butter pieces over the top. Bake in the oven for 1¼ hours or until the pastry is cooked and the apples are tender. Remove and allow to cool slightly. Serve immediately.

DESSERTS

Star Anise Crème Caramel ≈

SERVES 8

For the Caramel:
⅔ cup (150 g) granulated
   sugar
3 tablespoons water

For the Custard:
4 cups (750 ml) fresh milk
12 star anise (page 23),
   lightly crushed
1 vanilla pod
⅞ cup (185 g) granulated
   sugar
12 egg yolks
1 egg, beaten

Chinese cuisine, indeed oriental cooking in general, has never featured sugar-sweetened desserts, and because I grew up in a Chinese household, I was not familiar with desserts. During my school days, I used to succumb to the temptations of cake, candy, and ice cream, but it was only when I lived in France that I discovered the wonders of true western desserts. I especially remember how charmed I was when I experienced my first crème caramel. The silky texture of the custard and the contrasting caramel made a lasting impression on me. Here I offer a fusion version, one flavored with star anise, a Chinese pod with a robust, licorice-like taste. It imparts a lovely aroma to this classic dessert. For best results, make it the night before a dinner party.

Have ready a 5 cups (1.2 liter) soufflé dish or non-stick loaf pan. First, make the caramel by putting the sugar and water in a heavy pan and heating them. Stir the liquid and cook until it turns an amber brown, then remove it from the heat and pour it immediately into the dish or pan. Quickly tip it around to coat the entire bottom.

Pre-heat the oven to 350°F/180°C.

Pour the milk into a pan, add the star anise, and simmer for 10 minutes. Meanwhile, slit the vanilla pod, spoon out the sticky seeds, and combine the seeds with the sugar. The vanilla pod can be saved and put into your sugar jar.

Now whisk the egg yolks, whole egg, and vanilla sugar together in a large bowl. Remove the star anise from the milk and discard. Pour the milk in a steady stream, while it is hot, into the egg and sugar mixture, whisking until thoroughly blended. Then pour the liquid into the soufflé dish or loaf pan. Place the dish or pan in a large roasting pan. Pour in enough hot water to surround it up to two-thirds in depth and carefully transfer to the oven. Bake for 1 hour 25 minutes or until a toothpick or fine skewer inserted in the custard comes out clean.

Remove from the oven and allow to cool. Refrigerate overnight.

Just before you are about to serve the crème caramel, gently free it by running a knife around the edges. Invert the dessert onto a serving platter.

Lemon Grass Crème Anglaise ≈

There is nothing more satisfying than a velvety crème Anglaise or custard cream. In this recipe, the flavoring is the citrus fragrance of lemon grass. It is not difficult to make but you must be careful to keep stirring at a low temperature to keep the mixture from curdling. Once you have made this several times, you will find that it is a quick and easy dessert sauce that can enhance fresh fruit – or you can serve it with Chocolate Cake with Candied Ginger (page 229).

Peel the lemon grass stalks to the tender, whitish centers and crush them with the flat of a knife. Then finely chop them. Combine the chopped lemon grass with the milk in a pan and simmer for 15 minutes over a low heat. Remove the pan from the heat and steep for 20 minutes.

Strain the milk through a fine sieve and discard the chopped lemon grass.

Whisk the egg yolks and sugar together until the mixture is a pale yellow color. Then pour in the milk and mix well. Pour this mixture into a clean pan and simmer over a low heat, stirring all the while. When the sauce is thick enough to coat a spoon, it is done. Never let it boil. Strain the custard; it can be used immediately or cooled for use later.

Serves 4

2 lemon grass stalks (page 18)
2 ¼ cups (600 ml) milk
5 egg yolks
⅜ cup (75 g) granulated sugar

Index